DATE DUE

JAMES

the Brother of

JESUS

JAMES

the Brother of

JESUS

■

*The Key to Unlocking
the Secrets of Early Christianity
and the Dead Sea Scrolls*

■

ROBERT EISENMAN

VIKING

NG
Penguin Group
⁐., 375 Hudson Street,
ɔrk 10014, U.S.A.
, 27 Wrights Lane,
TZ, England
Ringwood,Victoria, Australia
Ltd, 10 Alcorn Avenue,
Toronto, Ontario, Canada M4V 3B2
Penguin Books (N.Z.) Ltd, 182–190 Wairau Road,
Auckland 10, New Zealand

Penguin Books Ltd, Registered Offices:
Harmondsworth, Middlesex, England

First American edition
Published in 1997 by Viking Penguin,
a division of Penguin Books USA Inc.

1 3 5 7 9 10 8 6 4 2

LIBRARY OF CONGRESS CATALOGING IN PUBLICATION DATA
Eisenman, Robert H.
James the brother of Jesus :
the key to unlocking the secrets of early Christianity
and the Dead Sea Scrolls / Robert Eisenman.
p. cm.
Includes bibliographical references and index.
ISBN 0-670-86932-5
1. James, Brother of the Lord, Saint. 2. Christianity—Origins.
3. Paul, Apostle, Saint. 4. Dead Sea scrolls—
Criticism, interpretation, etc.
I. Title.
BS2454.J3E37   1996
225.9'2—DC20   96-9635

This book is printed on acid-free paper.
∞

Printed in the United States of America
Set in Sabon

For:

Monobazus and Kenedaeos, the two grandsons of the 'Ethiopian Queen',
Freedom Fighters and Converts, who gave their lives
at the Pass at Beit Horon

and

Jesus son of Sapphias, the Leader of the 'Galilean' Boatmen
and 'the Party of the Poor', who 'poured out' their blood
until 'the whole Sea of Galilee ran red'

Contents

Illustrations and Maps

15 Pinnacle of the Temple, from which James is said to have been 'cast down'. (*Ordinance Survey of Jerusalem. C. W. Wilson. London 1865*)

16 Tomb believed in Christian pilgrimage tradition to belong to James, in the Kedron Valley beneath the Pinnacle of the Temple. (*Ordinance Survey of Jerusalem. C. W. Wilson. London 1865*)

17 Interior of 'James' Tomb' in the Kedron Valley. (Robert Eisenman)

18 Presumed bust of the Jewish historian Josephus. (NY Carlsberg Glyptothek Copenhagen)

19 Portrait bust of Nero's wife Poppea, whom Josephus visited in Rome and whom Nero kicked to death shortly before the Jewish Uprising of 66 CE. (Mansell Collection)

20 Wall painting from early Christian catacombs in Rome, with Balaam pointing at the star – by implication, evoking 'the Star Prophecy'. (Istituto Suore Benedittine di Priscilla)

21 Statue of Titus, the destroyer of Jerusalem and the Temple. (Mansell Collection)

22 Statue of Josephus' publisher Epaphroditus, who helped Nero commit suicide and was, seemingly, Paul's colleague by the same name in Phil. 2:25 and 4:18. (*The Messiah Jesus and John the Baptist*. The Dial Press 1931)

23 Trajan (98–117 CE), who was reportedly responsible for the deaths of Jesus' 'cousin' Simeon bar Cleophas and those of the descendants of Jesus' third brother, Judas. (Vatican Museum/C. M. Dixon)

24 The Emperor Hadrian (117–138) – like Trajan from Italica in Spain – who crushed the last Messianic Uprising, the Bar Kochba Revolt. (The Israel Museum, Jerusalem. AKG/Erich Lessing)

25 View of the Qumran cliffs from across the Wadi, showing Cave Four, where the bulk of the Scrolls were found – with the Dead Sea in the background. (Robert Eisenman)

26 View of Qumran graves showing North–South orientation. The Dead Sea is in the distance. (Robert Eisenman)

27 Ceremonial stairs leading to the Tomb of Queen Helen of Adiabene and her sons. Author and wife descending the steps. (Robert Eisenman)

28 Interior of the tomb of Helen's kinsmen, converts from Northern Syria and revolutionary heroes, mentioned variously in Josephus and Eusebius. (Robert Eisenman)

29 Balaam with the Messianic star from the catacombs in Rome, showing the Virgin with her 'only begotten' child. Josephus also refers to Helen's favourite son, Izates, as 'only begotten'. (Istituto Suore Benedittine di Priscilla)

30 View of the 'Land of Damascus' in the Syrian wilderness. (Robert Eisenman)

31 The Saleb of Syria, Beduin wanderers and tinkers, possibly descendants of the Judeo-Christian Rechabites. (*The Messiah Jesus and John the Baptist*. The Dial Press 1931)

32 'The Pool of Abraham' at Edessa ('Antioch-by-Callirhoe') in Northern Syria, the 'Land of the Osrhoeans'. (*Edessa, Beloved City*. J. B. Segal. Reprinted by permission of Oxford University Press)

33 Ruins at Pella in the Decapolis across the Jordan, to which 'the Pella Flight' of the Jamesian Jerusalem Community allegedly occurred. (Robert Eisenman)

34 Arabian Petra, where Paul may have gone after 'Damascus' – although he may have gone further afield in 'Arabia'. (Robert Eisenman)

35 Ruins at Hellenistic Jerash across the Jordan in the Decapolis. (Robert Eisenman)

36 The Mandaeans, a Sabaean baptizing group in Southern Iraq, laying on of hands. (*The Mandaeans of Iraq and Iran*. E. S. Drower. Reprinted by permission of Oxford University Press)

37 Legendary tomb of the Prophet 'Zechariah' next to the Tomb of James – probably connected to a Rich collaborator of that name whose body was 'cast down' without burial from the Temple Pinnacle into the Kedron Valley below by the Revolutionaries. (Robert Eisenman)

38 Columns 11–12 of the Habakkuk *Pesher* from Qumran, referring to 'the Cup of the Wrath of God' and 'the Day of Judgement'. (John Trever)

39 The Last Column of the Damascus Document at Qumran, referring to the reunion of the wilderness 'camps' at Pentecost, to curse all transgressing the Law.

40 Greek warning block in the Temple, forbidding Gentiles to enter the Sacred Precincts or Inner Court on pain of death. (Archaeological Museum, Istanbul. AKG/Erich Lessing)

41 Medallion supposedly depicting Paul and Peter. (*The Messiah Jesus and John the Baptist*. The Dial Press 1931)

42 Jewish coin from the Revolt against Rome, showing 'the Cup', reading 'Year Three of the Redemption of Zion'. Others read 'Freedom of Zion'. (Sonia Halliday Photographs)

MAPS

Acknowledgements

For their help in this volume I most particularly wish to thank Michael Baigent and my wife, Heather, for long hours of work labouring over difficult passages and proofs. I would like to thank Jane Baigent for her patience as well.

I also wish to thank Julian Loose at Faber and Faber for his constant encouragement, understanding, and deft hand. Ron Dubay, my student at California State University Long Beach, was a great help in reading parts of the manuscript, preparing charts, and working on the index. Thanks are also due to Luke Vinten.

I would also like to thank the President and Provost of California State University Long Beach, and, in particular, James Brett and the University Research Committee for their unstinting support. I would also like to thank Peter Mayer and Robert Dreesen at Viking/Penguin, who went a long way to help making this work possible.

Professor Robert Morgan of Oxford University read over some sections of the manuscript. His tolerant encouragement has always meant much to me. Neil Asher Silberman also gave me every encouragement, both in person and in writing, as did the innumerable others who have written me and whose letters, because of lack of facilities on my part and the work of this manuscript (deemed more important than personal responses), have gone unanswered. It is hoped that they will consider this book an adequate response.

Once Perfection comes, all imperfect things will disappear.
When I was a child, I spoke as a child, I thought as a child,
I reasoned as a child. But when I became a man,
I put aside childish things. For the moment we see as
through a glass darkly, but in time, face to face.

1 Corinthians 13:11–12

Our Lord and Prophet, who has sent us, declared to us that the Evil One,
having disputed with him forty days, but failing to prevail against him,
promised He would send Apostles from among his subjects to deceive
them. Therefore, above all, remember to shun any Apostle, teacher, or
prophet who does not accurately compare his teaching with [that of]
James . . . the brother of my Lord . . . and this, even if he comes to you
with recommendations.

Pseudoclementine *Homilies* 11.35 (Peter preaching at Tripoli)

Introduction

James the brother of Jesus, usually known as James the Just because of his surpassing Righteousness and Piety, is a character familiar to those with some knowledge of Christian origins. He is not so well known to the public at large, an inevitable if peculiar result of the processes being described in this book.

James is not only the key to unlocking a whole series of obfuscations in the history of the early Church, he is also the missing link between the Judaism of his day, however this is defined, and Christianity. In so far as the 'Righteous Teacher' in the Dead Sea Scrolls occupies a similar position, the parallels between the two and the respective communities they led narrow considerably, even to the point of convergence.

In the introduction to an earlier book on this subject in 1983, *Maccabees, Zadokites, Christians and Qumran,* I wrote with specific reference to James as follows:

> In providing an alternative historical and textual framework in which to fit the most important Dead Sea Scrolls, it is to be hoped that most of the preconceptions that have dominated Scrolls research for so long will simply fade away and new ideas will be brought into play and previously unused sources given their proper scope. When this is done, individual beings, the facts of whose lives tradition has distorted beyond recognition or who have been otherwise consigned to historical oblivion, will spring immediately to life and a whole series of associated historical fabrications and accusations evaporate.[1]

It is to the task of rescuing James, consigned either on purpose or through benign neglect to the scrapheap of history, that this book is dedicated.

Mentioned in various contexts in the New Testament, James the Just has been systematically downplayed or written out of the tradition. When he suddenly emerges as a principal personality and leader of 'the Jerusalem Church' or 'Community' in Acts 12:17, there is no introduction as to who he is or how he has arrived at the position he is occupying.

Acts' subsequent silence about his fate, which can be pieced together only from extra-biblical sources and to some extent seems to have been absorbed into the accounts both about the character we now call 'Stephen' and even Jesus himself, obscures the situation still further.

Once the New Testament reached its final form, the process of James' marginalization became more unconscious and inadvertent but, in all events, it was one of the most successful rewrite – or overwrite – enterprises ever accomplished. James ended up ignored, an ephemeral figure on the margins of Christianity, known only to aficionados. But in the Jerusalem of his day in the 40s to 60s CE, he was the most important and central figure of all – 'the Bishop' or 'Overseer' of the Jerusalem Church.

Designated as 'the brother' of Jesus, James the Just or the Just One is often confused or juxtaposed, and this probably purposefully, with another James, designated by Scripture as 'James the brother of John', the so-called 'son of Zebedee', thus increasing his marginalization. This multiplication of like-named individuals in Scripture was often the result of the same rewrite or overwrite processes just remarked.

There is a collateral aspect to this welter of like-named characters in the New Testament – even going so far as to include 'Mary the sister of' her own sister Mary (John 19:25). These instances are all connected with downplaying the family of Jesus and writing it out of Scripture. This was necessary because of the developing doctrine of the supernatural Christ and the stories about his miraculous birth.

James

The leader of the 'early Church' or 'Jerusalem Assembly' in Palestine from the 40s to the 60s, James met his death at the hands of a hostile Establishment before the events that culminated in the Uprising against Rome and the destruction of the Temple (66–70 CE). To have been 'Head' or 'Bishop' of 'the Jerusalem Church' (*Ecclēsia*) or 'Community' was to have been the head of the whole of Christianity, whatever this might be considered to have been in this period. Not only was the centre at Jerusalem the principal one before the destruction of the Temple and the reputed flight of the Jamesian community to a city beyond the Jordan called Pella,[2] but there were hardly any others of any importance.

For instance, the famous centre at Antioch in Syria, which may have been confused with the one at Edessa some two hundred miles further east, was only just being formed in the 40s and 50s, all others, in so far as they existed at all, being in a nascent state only. According to Acts, Antioch was where Christians 'were first called Christians' (11:26). It was the former capital of the Hellenized Seleucid kingdom, one of the off-shoots of the empire of Alexander the Great, and the Church there consisted mainly of Paul and several associates, including, it would appear, one person associated with the Herodian family in Palestine (13:1).

Because of James' pre-eminent stature, the sources for him turn out to be quite extensive, more than for any other comparable character, even for those as familiar to us as John the Baptist and Peter. In fact, extra-biblical sources contain more reliable information about James than about Jesus.

There are also strong parallels between the Community led by James and the one reflected in the Dead Sea Scrolls. This is particularly true when one considers the relationship of James to the person known in the Scrolls as 'the Teacher of Righteousness' or 'Righteous Teacher'. This book will build on the present debate concerning the Dead Sea Scrolls, presenting an alternative manner of viewing these documents. So many doctrines, allusions, and turns of phrase emerge from the material in the Scrolls common to both traditions that the parallels become impossible to ignore.

The research I am presenting here was originally completed under a National Endowment for the Humanities Fellowship at the Albright Institute in Jerusalem in 1985–6, the well-known 'American School', where the Scrolls were first photographed in 1947. It was during the tenure of this award that the insights became clear to me that led to the struggle for open access to the Scrolls, and the final collapse of the scholarly élite controlling their publication and, even more importantly, their interpretation.

But the subject of the person and teaching of James in the Jerusalem of his day is not only more important simply than his relationship to the interpretation of the Scrolls, it is quite independent of it. Even without insisting on any parallel or identification of James with the Righteous Teacher of the Scrolls, the Movement led by James – and it does seem to have been a 'Movement' – will be shown to have been something quite different from the Christianity we are now familiar with. James' relationship to the Scrolls is only collateral not intrinsic to this.

One of the central theses of this book will be the identification of James as the centre of the 'opposition alliance' in Jerusalem, involved in and precipitating the Uprising against Rome in 66–70 CE. The Dead Sea Scrolls, like other recent manuscript discoveries – as for instance those from Nag Hammadi in Upper Egypt, which came to light at about the same time as the Scrolls – while important, only further substantiate conclusions such as this, providing additional insight into it.

In the course of this book, it will become clear that James was the true heir and successor of his more famous brother Jesus and the leader at the time of whatever the movement was we now call 'Christianity', not the more Hellenized character we know through his Greek cognomen Peter, the 'Rock' of, in any event, the Roman Church.

Though Peter's name has now become proverbial, he may not be as historical as we think he is, and the role we attribute to him may possibly be an amalgam of that of several individuals by the same name, one a martyred 'cousin' of both Jesus and James and their reputed successor in Palestine, Simeon bar Cleophas. Nor does a normative adherence to Judaism and Christianity appear tenable after pursuing a study of this kind and grasping the real significance of James in the Jerusalem of his time.

Roman Power and its Effects

In historical writing, it is an oft-stated truism that the victors write the history. This is true for the period before us. Paul, for instance, would have been very comfortable with this proposition, as he makes clear in 1 Corinthians, where he announces his *modus operandi* of making himself 'all things to all men' and his philosophy of 'winning' and 'not beating the air' (9:24–27). So would his younger contemporary, the Jewish historian Josephus (c. 37–96 CE), who in the introductions to his several works also shows himself to be well aware of the implications of this proposition without being able to avoid its inevitable consequences.

There is in this period one central immovable fact, that of Roman power. This was as elemental as a state of nature, and all movements and individual behaviour must be seen in relation to it. But the unsuspecting reader is often quite unaware of it, when inspecting documents that emanate from this time or trying to come to grips with what was actually a highly charged and extremely revolutionary situation in Palestine.

This is the problem we have to face in this period, not only where individuals are concerned, but also in the documents that have come down to us. For example, in the Gospels, probably products of the end of this period, one would have difficulty recognizing that this highly charged, revolutionary situation existed in the Galilee in which Jesus wanders peacefully about, curing the sick, chasing out demons, raising the dead, and performing other 'mighty works and wonders'.

But in the parallel vocabulary of the War of the Sons of Light against the Sons of Darkness – a key document from the Dead Sea Scrolls treating the final apocalyptic war against all Evil on the earth, led by the Messiah and the Heavenly Host – these same Messianic 'mighty works and wonders' are the battles God fights on behalf of His people and the marvellous victories He wins. In this Scroll, known among aficionados as the *War Scroll*, we are in the throes of an apocalyptic picture of Holy War, with which the partisans of Oliver Cromwell's militant Puritanism in seventeenth-century England would have felt comfortable.

On the other hand, where the Gospels are concerned, we are in a peaceful, Hellenized countryside, where Galilean fishermen cast their nets or mend their boats. Would it were true. The scenes in the New Testament depicting Roman officials and military officers sometimes as near saints or the members of the Herodian family – their appointed custodians and tax collectors in Palestine – as bumbling but well-meaning dupes also have to be understood in the light of this submissiveness to Roman power.

The same can be said for the scenes picturing the vindictiveness of the Jewish mob. These are obviously included to please not a Jewish audience but a Roman or a Hellenistic one. This is also true of the presentation of the Jewish Messiah – call him 'Jesus' – as a politically disinterested, other-worldly (in Roman terms, *ergo*, harmless), even sometimes pro-Roman itinerant, at odds with his own people and family, preaching a variety of Plato's representation of the Apology of Socrates or the *Pax Romana*.

Josephus, whose own works suffer from many of these same distortions, was himself a defector to the Roman cause. Much like Paul, he owed his survival, as well as that of his works, to this fact. Both, it seems, either had or were to achieve Roman citizenship, Josephus in the highest manner possible – adoption into the Roman imperial family. His works were encouraged by persons, previously high up in the Roman Emperor Nero's chancellery (54–68) and equally favoured later under Domitian (81–96), with whom Paul also seems to have been in close touch.

Josephus sums up this obsequiousness to Roman power perhaps better than anyone in his preface to his eye-witness account of this period, the *Jewish War*, a work based at least in part on his interrogations, as a defector and willing collaborator, of prisoners. In criticizing other historians treating the same events, Josephus notes that all historical works from this period suffer from two main defects, 'flattery of the Romans and vilification of the Jews, adulation and abuse being substituted for real historical record'.[3] Having said this, he then goes on to indulge in the same conduct himself.

That historical portions of the New Testament suffer from the same defects should be obvious to anyone with even a passing familiarity with them. But the Dead Sea Scrolls do not, for the simple reason that they did not go through the editorial processes of the Roman Empire. The opposite; they were probably deposited in caves expressly to avoid it. The fact of Roman power, too, was probably the principal reason why no one ever returned to retrieve them. No one could have, because no one survived. It was that simple.

This power is also the key determinant behind the political and ideological orientation of several of the religious groups or parties in this period, including early Christians and Pharisaic Jews, not to mention the group responsible for the composition of the Scrolls themselves, who were in all likelihood destroyed by it.

The Jesus of History

The quest for the historical Jesus has held a fascination for sophisticated Western man for over two centuries now, but the quest for the historical James has never been pursued. Rather than be disconsolate that the material regarding James is so fragmentary and often presented from the point of view of persons like Paul who disagreed with him, it is the task of the historian to revive him, to rescue him from the oblivion in which he was cast, either purposefully or via benign neglect, and to revivify him.

This is not so difficult as it might seem, because the materials about James exist – quite a lot of them. It remains only to place them in a proper perspective and analyse them. This would be much more difficult to achieve for James' brother Jesus. But is Jesus as well known as most people think? Experts, lay persons, artists, writers, political figures from all ages and every time and place constantly assert the fact of Jesus' existence and speak of him in the most familiar way, as if they personally had certain knowledge of him. Unfortunately, the facts themselves are shrouded in mystery and overwhelmed by a veneer of retrospective theology and polemics that frustrates any attempt to get at the real events underlying them. Most who read the documents concerning him are simply unaware of this.

Questions not only emerge concerning Jesus' existence itself, at least as far as the character so confidently portrayed in Scripture, but also regarding the appropriateness of the teaching attributed to him there to his time and place. Where the man 'Jesus' is concerned – as opposed to the redeemer figure 'Christ' or 'Christ Jesus' Paul so confidently proclaims and with whom, via some personalized visionary experience, he claims to be in constant contact – we have mainly the remains of Hellenistic romance and mythologizing to go on, often with a clear polemicizing or dissembling intent. In fact, Paul, portrayed as appearing on the scene only a few years after Jesus' death, either knows nothing or is willing to tell us nothing about him.

Only two historical points about Jesus emerge from Paul's letters: firstly, that he was crucified at some point – date unspecified (1 Tim. 6:13, which is not considered authentic, adds by Pontius Pilate),[4] and, secondly, that he had several brothers, one of whom was one called James (Gal. 1:19). In fact, taking the brother relationship seriously may turn out to be one of the only confirmations that there ever was a historical Jesus.

Jesus in the Gospels

Where the Gospels are concerned, whatever can be said with any certainty about Jesus is largely presented in the framework of supernatural story-telling. Hellenistic mystery cults were familiar over a large portion of the Graeco-Roman world where Paul was active. They would certainly have provided fertile gound for the propagation of competing models among a population already well versed in their fundamentals.

One attitude, particularly important in determining the historicity of Gospel materials, is the strong current of anti-Semitism one encounters lying just below the surface. This anti-Semitism was already rife in Hellenistic cities such as Alexandria in Egypt and Caesarea in Palestine, and ultimately led to the destruction of the Jewish populations there.[5]

One can assert with a fair degree of confidence that while Messianic agitation in Palestine could be sectarian, it would not be anti-Jewish or opposed to the people of Palestine. This would be a contradiction in terms. Of course, there was internecine party strife, often vitriolic and quite unforgiving, but for a popular Messianic leader to be against his own people would be prima facie impossible and, one can confidently assert, none ever was – except retrospectively or through the miracle of art. The reader may take this as a rule of thumb. For corroboration, where native Palestinian literature is concerned, one need only inspect the Dead Sea Scrolls, which, while often vitriolic and uncompromising towards their opponents in Palestine and the world at large, are never anti-Semitic. The opposite.

Nor can we say that in the Gospels we do not have a composite re-creation of facts and episodes relating to a series of Messianic pretenders in Palestine in the first century, familiar from the works of Josephus, interlaced or spliced into a narrative of a distinctly Hellenistic or non-Palestinian, pro-Pauline cast. This includes some light-hearted – even malevolent – satire where events in Palestine are concerned. Josephus displays a parallel, but inverted, malevolence, calling examples of the charismatic Messianic type of leader 'religious frauds' or 'impostors more dangerous than the bandits and murderers', and 'deceivers claiming divine inspiration leading their followers out into the wilderness there to show them the signs of their impending Deliverance'.[6]

The Gospel of Matthew, even more than the other Gospels, has long been recognized as a collection of Messianic and other scriptural proof-texts taken out of context and woven into a gripping narrative of what purports to be the life of Jesus. In describing an early flight by Jesus' father 'Joseph' to Egypt to escape Herod – *à la* Joseph in Egypt and Moses' escape from Pharaoh in the Bible – not paralleled in the other Gospels, Matthew utilizes the passage, 'I have called my son out of Egypt' (3:15). Whether this passage applies to Jesus is debatable.

In its original Old Testament context (Hos. 11:1), it obviously refers to the people Israel as a whole. However, it does have very real relevance to a character in the mid-50s, whom Josephus – followed it would appear by the Book of Acts – actually calls 'the Egyptian', but declines to identify further. This Messianic pretender, according to the picture in Josephus, first leads the people 'out into the wilderness' and then utilizes the Mount of Olives as a staging point to lead a Joshua-style assault on the walls of Jerusalem.[7] But the Mount of Olives was a favourite haunt, according to Gospel narrative, of Jesus and his companions. We will note many such suspicious overlaps in the data available to us.

For his part, Josephus, predictably obsequious, applauds the extermination of the followers of this Egyptian by the Roman Governor Felix (52–60 CE). The Book of Acts, too, is quick to show its familiarity with this episode, including Josephus' tell-tale reticence in supplying his name.

Rather it somewhat charmingly portrays the commander of the Roman garrison in the Temple as mistaking Paul for him (21:38).

Other examples of this kind are the so-called 'Little Apocalypses' in the Gospels (Matt. 24:4–31 and pars.). In Luke's version of these, anyhow, Jesus is depicted as predicting the encirclement of Jerusalem by armies, followed by its fall. All versions are introduced by reference to the destruction of the Temple and generally refer to famine, wars, and sectarian strife, along with other signs and catastrophes. These probably have very real relevance to a section in the *Antiquities of the Jews*, in which Josephus describes in gory detail the woes brought upon the people by the movement founded by someone he calls 'Judas the Galilean' around the time of the Census of Cyrenius in 6–7 CE.

This is contemporaneous with Jesus' birth according to the time frame of the Gospel of Luke too and is also referred to in Acts (5:37). Josephus calls this movement the 'Fourth Philosophy', but most now refer to it as 'Zealot'. Here, as in the Little Apocalypses above, Josephus portrays this movement – the appearance of which, again, is contemporaneous with the birth of Christ in the Gospels – as bringing about wars, famine, and terrible suffering for the people, culminating in the destruction of the Temple.

These 'woes' also have relevance to another Messianic character, depicted in Josephus and a namesake of Jesus, whom Josephus calls 'Jesus ben Ananias'. This man, whom Josephus portrays as an oracle or quasi-prophet of some kind, went around Jerusalem directly following the death of James in 62 CE for seven straight years, proclaiming its coming destruction, until he was finally hit on the head by a Roman projectile during the siege of Jerusalem and killed just prior to the fulfilment of his prophecy.

The applicability of this story to the Historical Jesus (and in a very real way the Historical James), the facts of whose existence and its relevance to mankind's everyday existence have been so confidently asserted for the last nineteen centuries or more, should be obvious. In fact 'Jesus ben Ananias' was set free at the end of Josephus' *Jewish War* after having originally been arrested. The release of such a Messianic double for Jesus is also echoed in the Scripture as it has come down to us in the release of another 'double'. One Gospel anyhow calls this double 'Jesus Barabbas' – the meaning of this name in Aramaic superficially would appear to be 'the Son of the Father' – a political 'bandit' who 'committed murder at the time of the Uprising' and is released by Pontius Pilate (Matt. 27:26 and pars.).

It is reflected too in another curious episode in a narrative concerning which many profess scepticism but few have explained, called the Slavonic Josephus, because it came down through the Old Russian. An epitome of Josephus' *Jewish War*, like much in this period it is probably a forgery. However, in expanding the notices about Jesus from Josephus' later *Antiquities*, it portrays him as a revolutionary who is released only to be re-arrested before the final crucifixion scenario familiar to us.

Variant manuscripts of the works of Josephus, reported by Church fathers like Origen, Eusebius, and Jerome, all of whom at one time or another spent time in Palestine, contain materials associating the fall of Jerusalem with the death of *James* – not with the death of Jesus. Their shrill protests, particularly Origen's and Eusebius', have probably not a little to do with the disappearance of this passage from all manuscripts of the *Jewish War* that have come down to us. As will also become clear, other aspects from the biography of James have been retrospectively absorbed into the biography of Jesus and other characters in the Book of Acts in sometimes astonishing ways.

In fact, in what suggests that the Gospels and some Dead Sea Scrolls are virtually contemporary documents – and that the authors of the former knew the latter – it will be shown that fundamental allusions from the Scrolls have been absorbed into Gospel presentations of Jesus' relations with his Apostles. This subject is treated in the section focusing on Jesus' brothers as Apostles and Jesus' post-resurrection appearance to James. There, it will be shown that the presentation of the Apostles as peaceful fishermen on the Sea of Galilee incorporates a play on key ideological usages found in the Dead Sea Scrolls. This is the language of *casting down nets* implicit in episodes relative to appearances by Jesus to his Apostles along the Sea of Galilee both before and after his resurrection and in parallel notices in the Dead Sea Scrolls and Revelation. This language of *casting* or *throwing down* will also be shown to be integral to presentations of the death of James in virtually all traditions we are heirs to.

The 'Galilean' language, also part and parcel of the presentations of Jesus and his Apostles in these and like episodes, likewise can be thought of as playing on the name of the Movement developing out of the activities of Judas *the Galilean*, the founder of the Zealot Movement mentioned above, which Josephus and the book of Acts will also call the '*Sicarii*' or 'Assassins'.

Changing terms with ideological connotations into geographical place names tends to trivialize them. This is certainly the case with confusions relating to whether Jesus came from a place in Galilee called 'Nazareth' (never mentioned in either the works of Josephus or the Old Testament) or whether, like James, he followed a 'Nazirite' life-style or was a 'Nazrene' or 'Nazoraean', which have totally different connotations in the literature as it has come down to us.

These are complex matters and will doubtlessly be perplexing at first, but it is necessary to elucidate them to describe the true situation behind some of these highly prized scriptural re-presentations. It is hoped that the reader will soon get used to the kind of word play and evasions at work. The evidence, which might at first appear circumstantial, will mount up, allowing the reader to appreciate the validity of the explanations provided. This is not to say that the Jesus of history did not exist, only that the evidence is skewed and that the problem is more complex than many think.

The Study of James

The situation with regard to James is quite different and clearer, probably because except for the Gospels and the first eleven chapters of the Book of Acts it has not been so overwritten. Here, too, materials do exist outside the tradition of Scripture. Even scriptural materials regarding James, where not theologically refurbished, are very helpful. Where rewritten or overwritten, they can by comparison with external materials be brought into focus and sometimes even restored.

But one can go further. It is through the figure of James that one can get a realistic sense of what the Jesus of history might have been like. In fact, it is through the figure of James, and by extension the figure of Paul, with whom James is always in a kind of contrapuntal relationship, that the question of the Historical Jesus may be finally resolved.

The name 'James' should not cause too much of a stumbling block for readers, as this is a corruption of the Greek *Jacobus* moving into the Latin *Jacimus*. Except for *Jaime* in Spanish (which also knows *Iago*), in most European languages a version of the Graeco-Hebrew original *Jacobus* or *Jacob* is preserved. In this book 'James' will be used, despite consequent difficulties in visualizing what the name really was in Palestine.

The same is true with regard to 'the brother of Jesus'. In the original accounts – the Gospels as they have come down to us, Paul's letters, and Josephus – no embarrassment whatsoever is evinced about this relationship with Jesus, and James is designated straightforwardly and without qualification as Jesus' brother. There are no questions of the kind that crop up later in the wake of the developing doctrine of the supernatural

'Christ' and stories about his supernatural birth, attempting to depreciate or diminish this relationship. These stories about the birth of 'Christ' are, in any event, not referred to by Paul and appear first in the Gospels of Matthew and Luke, thus leading in the second century to embarrassment not just over Jesus' brothers, but the fact of Jesus' family generally, including sisters, fathers, uncles, and mothers.

Embarrassment of this kind was exacerbated by the fact that Jesus' brothers ('cousins', as Jerome would later come to see them at the end of the fourth century) were the principal personages in Palestine and Jesus' successors there, important in Eastern tradition generally. What exacerbated the problem of their relationship to Jesus even further in the second century was the theological assertion of Mary's 'perpetual virginity' and with it the utter impossibility – nay, inconceivability – that she should have had other children. This even led Jerome's younger contemporary, Augustine, in the fifth century, to the assertion reproduced in Muhammad's Koran in the seventh, that Jesus didn't have any father at all, only a mother![8]

To the ideologue, it was simply impossible that Jesus should have had a father or brothers, Gospel notices and references in Paul notwithstanding. Nor could Joseph have had *any* children by Mary. These had to have been by another wife. All such theological considerations will be set aside and all family designations treated naturally. If a person was said to have had a brother, then he was a natural brother, conceived by natural generation, not a half-brother, stepbrother, 'cousin', or 'milk brother'.

The wealth of extra-biblical sources relating to James has already been noted. If we include with these those in the Book of Acts, where not adulterated or retrospectively overwritten with more orthodox historical or theological materials, and notices in the letters of Paul, then there is a considerable amount of material relating to James. James is also mentioned in the Gospels, but here the material is marred by doctrinal attempts either to defame the family and brothers of Jesus or to disqualify them in some manner.

Though a parallel process is at work in the early chapters of the Book of Acts, as one moves into chapter 12 where James is introduced and beyond, the character of the material changes and quickens. For some reason Acts assumes that we already know who James is, in contradistinction to another James it calls 'the brother of John' – elsewhere 'the son of Zebedee' – whom it also conveniently disposes of at the beginning of chapter 12 preparatory to introducing the real James. It is possible to read through this material in Acts to the real history underlying it and the real events it transmogrifies.

The same can be said for Paul's letters, which provide additional straightforward witness to 'James the brother of the Lord' and *know no other James*. The Historical James can also be reconstructed from the underlying circumstances to which remarks in these letters are directed. These, plus a myriad of extra-biblical materials, such as Josephus, apocryphal gospels, non-canonical acts including the 'Pseudo-' or 'False Clementines', the Gnostic manuscripts from Nag Hammadi in Upper Egypt, and the mass of early Church literature all constitute sources about James. The documentation is that impressive.

If we include in this mix of materials the Righteous Teacher found in the Dead Sea Scrolls, where the commonality of language, themes, and historical setting provide additional correspondences, then we are truly in a position of some strength with regard to James.

The Historical Jesus and the Historical James

It is through documentation of this kind that we can resurrect the person of Jesus as well. The proposition would run something like this: let us assume that a Messianic leader known as 'Jesus' did exist in the early part of the first century in Palestine. Furthermore, let us assume that he had brothers, one of whom was called James.

Who would have known the character Jesus better? His closest living relatives, who according to tradition were his legitimate successors in Palestine, and those companions accompanying him in all his activities? Or someone who admits that he never saw Jesus in his lifetime, as Paul does, and that, on the contrary, he was an *Enemy* of and persecuted the early Christian community, and came to know him only through visionary experiences that allowed him to be in touch with a figure he designates as 'Christ Jesus' in Heaven?

The answer of any reasonable observer to this question should be obvious: James and Jesus' Palestinian companions. But the answer of all orthodox Church circles has always been that Paul's understanding of Jesus was superior and that he knew him better than any of Jesus' other Apostles or companions. Furthermore, it is claimed that the doctrines represented by James and the members of Jesus' family generally were defective in their understanding of Paul's Christ Jesus and inferior to boot. Given the fact that the Christianity we are heirs to is largely the legacy of Paul and like-minded persons, this is just what one would have expected and it should surprise no one.

Moreover, it has been retrospectively confirmed by the picture of Jesus that has come down to us in the Gospels as well. This is particularly evident in the picture of the Apostles in the Gospels as 'weak' (Matt. 14:31 and pars.), a term Paul repeatedly uses in his letters, almost always with derogatory intent, when describing the leaders of the community, particularly in Jerusalem, and their directives (Rom. 14:1–2 and 1 Cor. 8:7–9:22). Occasionally he parodies this, applying the term to himself to gain sympathy, but generally he uses it to attack the leadership, in particular those keeping dietary regulations or relying on Mosaic Law – even those whom, as he puts it, 'only eat vegetables', like James.

In the Gospels, reflecting Paul, when an Apostle as important as Peter 'sinks' into the Sea of Galilee for lack of 'Faith' or denies Jesus three times on his death night, the implications are quite clear. They are 'weak' in their adherence to the Pauline concept of 'Faith', as opposed to the more Jamesian one of salvation by 'works'. In addition, they have a defective understanding of Jesus' teaching, particularly of that most important of all Pauline doctrines, the *Christ*. This is the situation that has retrospectively been confirmed by eighteen hundred years of subsequent Church history too – however unreasonable or in defiance of real history it might appear.

Here, two aphorisms suggest themselves: 'Poetry is truer than history' and 'It is so, if you think so'. The first has a clear connection to the development of the documents that have come down to us. If the Gospels represent the 'poetry', and truly they are perhaps the most successful literary creations ever created both in terms of their artistry and the extent of their influence, then their authors were the poets. It was Plato, who, comprehending the nature of the ancient world better than many others, wished to banish the poets from his 'Republic' or ideal state – not without cause, because, in his view, it was the poets who created the myths and religious mysteries, by which the less critically minded lived. For Plato, this was a world of almost total darkness.

Where the second is concerned and early 'Christian' history in Palestine, one can say with some justice that it does not matter what really happened, only what people *think* happened. In essence, this is the theological approach of our own time and in the court of public opinion the decision has long ago been rendered, not only for Christians themselves, but also for the world at large, including Jews and Muslims – even, for instance, for modern-day Japanese, Hindus, or Latin American Indians – because for all these people the Jesus of Scripture is real too.

This is why the study of James is so important, because the situation is for the most part just the opposite of what most people think it is or consider to be true. The reader will, undoubtedly, find this proposition preposterous. How could so many people, including some of the greatest minds of our history – some even considering themselves secular – from so many different cultures and in so many different places, have been wrong? The answer to this question has to do with the *beauty* of the concepts being disseminated, however uncharacteristic of the Palestine of the period they might be, ideas epitomizing the highest ideals of *Hellenistic* Civilization.

Like Plato's picture of his teacher Socrates, Jesus refused to answer his interlocutors or avoid his fate. At least as far as his chroniclers are concerned, he met an end more terrible even than Socrates' – but then Socrates was not dealing with the might of Imperial Rome, only of Athens. Of course, the very terribleness of this end is what makes the drama and its symbols so attractive.

It is, it will be remembered, Plato's pupil Aristotle who informed us how the most successful tragedy inspires terror and pity. Indeed, much of the legacy of Plato and Socrates is incorporated into the materials about Jesus, including the notions of non-resistance to Evil and a Justice that does not consist of helping your friends and harming your enemies – all doctrines absolutely alien to a Palestinian milieu, such as that, for instance, represented in native Palestinian documents like the Dead Sea Scrolls.

Beauty and artistry are two reasons for the abiding appeal of the historical presentation of these documents, but so too, for instance, is the attractiveness of a doctrine such as Grace, not something anyone would have any need or desire to resist. Along with these, however, goes the lack of any real historical understanding of this period – which is complex and difficult to grasp – to the extent that oversimplifications, artifice and disinformation are preferred. In turn, these have operated on the level of general culture worldwide in an almost hypnotic fashion. It is this phenomenon that has been generalized to describe religion as 'the opiate of the people'. This is not true for all religions. Some operate in exactly the opposite manner.

The End Result

It will transpire that the person of James is almost diametrically opposed to the Jesus of Scripture and our ordinary understanding of him. Whereas the Jesus of Scripture is anti-nationalist, cosmopolitan, antinomian – that is, against the direct application of Jewish Law – and accepting of foreigners and other persons of perceived impurities, the Historical James will turn out to be zealous for the Law, xenophobic, rejecting of foreigners and polluted persons generally, and apocalyptic.

Strong parallels emerge between these kinds of attitudes and those of the Righteous Teacher in the Dead Sea Scrolls. For instance, attitudes in the Gospels towards many classes of persons – tax collectors, harlots, Sinners, and the like – are diametrically opposed to those delineated in the Dead Sea Scrolls, but in agreement with anti-Semitic diatribes of the time in Graeco-Hellenistic environments such as Caesarea and Alexandria.

At the centre of the agitation in the Temple in the mid-50s, hostile to Herodians, Romans, and their fellow travellers, James will emerge as the pivotal figure among the more nationalist-inclining crowd. In his incarnation of 'the Perfect Righteous' or 'Just One', he will be at the centre of the Opposition Alliance of sects and revolutionary groups opposed to the Pharisaic/Sadducean Establishment, pictured in Josephus and the New Testament.

The election of James as leader of the early Church, missing from Scripture in the form we have it, will be shown to be the real event behind the election of the Twelfth Apostle to succeed Judas *Iscariot* in his 'Office' (*Episcopate*), as pictured in the more orthodox presentation of the Book of Acts. James' death too, in 62 CE, will be shown to be connected in the popular imagination with the fall of Jerusalem in 70 CE in a way that Jesus' some four decades before could not have been.

Two attacks on James also emerge in our sources – both physical – one paralleling the attack pictured in Acts on the archetypal Gentile believer Stephen in the 40s, and the other in the 60s, described by Josephus and in early Church sources, ending in his death. The attack on Stephen in Acts, like the election of Judas *Iscariot*'s replacement that precedes it, will turn out to be totally imaginary – or rather dissembling – yet written over very real materials central to the life of James.

The *modus operandi* of New Testament accounts such as those in Acts, some merely retrospective refurbishment of known events in sources relating to the life of James, will be illumined. Once the aim and method of these substitutions are analysed and correctly appreciated, it will be comparatively easy to understand that the highly Hellenized Movement that developed overseas, which we now call 'Christianity', was, in fact, the mirror reversal of what actually took place in Palestine under James. It will be possible to show that what was actually transpiring in Palestine was directly connected with the literature represented by the Dead Sea Scrolls, which in its last stages was either equivalent to or all but indistinguishable from that circulating about and normally associated with James.

Paul, on the other hand, will emerge as a highly compromised individual, deeply involved with Roman officials and Herodian kings – a proposition given added weight by the intriguing allusions to a parallel character in the Dead Sea Scrolls called 'the Lying Spouter' or 'Scoffer' – even to the extent of actually being a member of the family of King Herod.

His contacts will go very high indeed, even into the Emperor Nero's personal household itself (Phil. 4:22). Appreciating this context will help rescue Jesus' closest relatives and his religious and political heirs in Palestine from the oblivion into which they have been cast either intentionally or via benign neglect. Coming at this juncture in the debate over the relationship of the Dead Sea Scrolls to Christianity, these kinds of insights should prove enlightening.

This book is written for both the specialist and the non-specialist, particularly for the latter, where interest, as in the case of the Dead Sea Scrolls, is often the most keen. Therefore, all the quotations and explanations necessary to pursue this subject will be provided in the book, which is meant to be complete in itself and treat James in a comprehensive and exhaustive manner. A first volume will treat all aspects of James' relationships to the New Testament, early Church sources, and the problem of the brothers of Jesus generally. A second volume will explore the Pella Flight and James' relationship to Eastern conversions and communities generally, as well as providing a more detailed, in-depth, and point-for-point analysis of his link-up with the Dead Sea Scrolls and an identification of the document now popularly known as 'MMT' as a letter (or letters) to 'the Great King of the Peoples beyond the Euphrates' Agbarus or Abgarus or the character we shall encounter as Queen Helen of Adiabene's favourite son, King Izates.

Readers are encouraged to make judgements for themselves and, where possible, to go to the primary sources directly and not rely on secondhand presentations. Because of this, secondary sources will not prove particularly useful, except in so far as they supply new, previously overlooked, data, because writings or materials later than 500 CE are for the most part derivative. Later writers too – even modern researchers – sometimes forget the motives of their predecessors, adopting the position and point of view of the tradition or theology they are heirs to. In the recent controversy regarding the Dead Sea Scrolls, a struggle developed with just such an academic and religious élite, not only over the publication of all the documents but even more importantly – and this conflict continues at the time of writing – over their interpretation.

All too often, a docile public has been easily dominated by a religious or scholarly hierarchy claiming to know or to have seen more. In religious matters, given the place of scholarly élites in upholding religious ones, this has been the case more often than not. Therefore, almost everything in this book, from the restoration of James to his rightful place as successor to his brother Jesus and heir to Christian tradition in Palestine, to the elucidation of the Dead Sea Scrolls in a manner at odds with dominant scholarly consenses, will occur outside the traditional or received order. Only a knowledgeable and enlightened public can change this state of affairs.

I have done my best to make the Dead Sea Scrolls, which have come along as if miraculously to redress the balance or haunt those who would adopt an ahistorical approach, available across the board to a wider populace. It is now time to move to the next level and a wider subject matter. The matters before us are not for those who docilely accept biblical writ or scholarly consenses as the final word. The criticism we are doing is historical and literary criticism, looking at the way a given author actually put his materials together and to what end. It is the weight of the gradual accumulation of detail and textual analyses of this kind that ultimately renders the presentation credible.

To follow the arguments, as well as to make sure the materials are being correctly presented from the sources, the reader is urged to have a copy of the New Testament, the works of Josephus and a translation of principal Dead Sea Scrolls at his or her disposal. Nothing more is really required. Even though all necessary quotations from these sources are provided verbatim in the book, it is still very useful to see them in their original context and to follow the sequencing and order surrounding a specific historical or legal point.

Where the New Testament is concerned, it should be realized that, aside from the Greek original, most translations are only that. But even a knowledge of Greek, while helpful, does not always guarantee clear understanding. Common sense is the better tool, for even those with the most accurate knowledge of languages often miss the underlying relationships or crucial meanings lying just beneath the surface of the text. Therefore, when it comes to key passages and allusions, I have tried to follow the original languages as closely as possible. These, I hope, will at least be consistent where key Palestinian usages are concerned. This is important, because often the sense of a translation one encounters is wrong.

With regard to the Dead Sea Scrolls, the best translation in English is that of G. Vermes in the Penguin edition, though this also should be used with caution where key formulations are concerned. Michael Wise and I recently published translations in the *Dead Sea Scrolls Uncovered* (Penguin, 1992) of what we considered the best Qumran fragments from the previously unpublished corpus. While helpful in emphasizing the 'Jamesian' aspects of a given document or its uncompromising 'Zealot' bent, it was not meant to be exhaustive or include the principal Qumran documents, which had already been published, though it does signal important sections from these last.

When using Vermes, it should be remembered that translations are simply one person's view of the sense of a given passage as opposed to another's. What is crucial is a firm historical grasp and literary-critical insight. His translations sometimes fall short in key passages, for instance, in the all-important interpretation of 'the Righteous shall live by his Faith' in the Habakkuk *Pesher* and other obscure materials related to this, describing the destruction of the Righteous Teacher and/or the Wicked Priest.

Often translations of pivotal terminologies such as *the Messiah, doing, works* (both based on the same Hebrew root), *justify*, the *Holy Spirit*, *Judgement* ('the Last Judgement'), *Belial*, and *Satan*, are inconsistent and sometimes even misleading. Occasionally, a critical phrase is omitted or singulars inexplicably changed to plurals. The more recent *Dead Sea Scrolls Translated*, by F. García Martínez, done in the Netherlands (Leiden, 1994), while more complete, is even more inconsistent and inaccurate, being rendered into English from the Spanish! Therefore, as far as possible, I have endeavoured to provide my own translations. The reader will be able to find my complete translations of the Habakkuk

Pesher, the Damascus Document, and the Community Rule – the three most important previously published Qumran documents, in *The Dead Sea Scrolls and the First Christians* (Rockport, 1996). These will be included in an appendix to Volume II.

Where Josephus is concerned, any translation will do, as fine distinctions such as these in a historical work are not so crucial. Josephus' works are packed with data and, as far as showing the scope and flow of events in this period, invaluable. Translations of the relevant passages are provided here too, along with the analysis necessary to understand them.

The same applies for Eusebius' *Ecclesiastical History* and the other early Church Fathers and their works. Eusebius, for instance, was Constantine's Archbishop and actually participated in many of the events resulting in Christianity's takeover of the Roman Empire. His works, though tendentious and often vindictive, present either epitomes or long quotations from Josephus and early Church historians such as Hegesippus, Papias, Clement of Alexandria, and Julius Africanus – now lost.

Wherever an important quotation is taken from a text, for instance from Josephus or the New Testament, an effort is made to give the reader some idea of its context or surroundings in the original. Too often in this field and religious matters in general, readers have been treated to words or quotations taken out of context. This is not only unfair to the original text, but misleading as well, allowing the person using the quotation to mystify or otherwise take advantage of the ignorance of the person for whom it is intended. Paul does this often. So do the Gospels.

It is important to look into the original contexts of passages used in scriptural and scholarly debate, because the ambience of such materials is important in determining the frame of mind and intent of the original, not its derivative application. References are confined as far as possible to primary sources, the trends implicit in secondary ones often ebbing and flowing with the times and one generation's consensus being overturned by the next's.

For this reason, readers are advised to go directly to the ancient sources themselves. It is in the ancient sources that the data is to be found and this is where the battle must be joined. What is required is a critical faculty, sensitivity to language, and simple common sense. These, one hopes, are shared by everyone.

Fountain Valley, California
May 1996

PART I

PALESTINIAN BACKGROUNDS

James

The Downplaying of James in Christian Tradition

Of all the characters of the period of Palestinian history ending with the destruction of the Second Temple by the Romans, one of the most under-esteemed and certainly under-estimated is James the brother of Jesus. James has been systematically ignored by both Christian and Jewish scholars alike, the latter hardly even having heard of him – his very existence being a source of embarrassment to them both.

Muslims, too, have never heard of him, since their traditions were bequeathed to them by Christians and Jews. This is certainly very curious, because the key ideology of *Faith and works together*, associated with James in New Testament Scripture, fairly shines through the Koran – 'believe and do good works' as Muhammad repeatedly puts it with an emphasis on doing. But in addition, Muslim dietary law is also based on James' directives to overseas communities as delineated in the Book of Acts (15:20–29),[1] the Arabs presumably comprising one such emerging overseas community.

This silence surrounding James, though latterly breached by the finds at Nag Hammadi in Upper Egypt and the author's theories about the Dead Sea Scrolls, was not accidental. The early Church theologian and historian Eusebius (260–340) finalized the process of the downplaying of James. He was the Bishop of Caesarea in Palestine and participated in Constantine's reorganization of his empire following his conversion. Though Eusebius acknowledged the New Testament Letter of James, like Jude, to be in general pastoral use, he nevertheless questioned its authenticity, presumably because its content and theological approach were so alien to him.[2]

Augustine (354–430), writing to his older contemporary Jerome (348–420), expressed his concern about problems between Peter and Paul signalled in Paul's Letter to the Galatians. Clearly, these were directly con-nected to James' leadership in the early Church and his directives. But, curiously, neither Augustine nor Jerome mentions James in this exchange at all. Martin Luther a thousand years later felt that the Letter of James should not have been included in the New Testament at all.[3]

It is not surprising that these arbiters of Christian opinion in their day should have felt the way they did, because it is hard to consider the Letter of James as 'Christian' at all, if we take as our yardstick the Gospels in their present form or Paul's letters. If we widen this interpretation somewhat to include the Eastern sectarian tendency, referred to in early Church literature as 'Ebionite' and deriving from an original Hebrew root meaning 'the Poor', and other parallel currents producing additional variations related to it, like the Essenes, Nazoraeans, Elchasaites, Manichaeans, and even Islam, we discover a different story. For its part, the Letter of James in its essence resembles nothing so much as the Dead Sea Scrolls, which is why, prior to their discovery, it may have been difficult to appreciate this.

Origen (185–254), who had also spent time in Caesarea on the Palestine coast, railed against traditions he knew giving James more prominence than he was prepared to accord him, namely those connecting James' death to the fall of Jerusalem. The normal scriptural view and popular theology to this day connects Jesus' death not James' to the destruction of the Temple. This is not only associated with the Little Apocalypses, but echoed in the famous Gospel assertion attributed to Jesus, 'I shall raise it up in three days' (John 2:19 and pars.).

Jesus is ostensibly presented as referring to the Temple, but John is most anxious to clarify this, adding, 'he was speaking about the Temple of his body'. Though Origen was later accused of heresy, his view of the tradition connecting the fall of Jerusalem to the death of James, which he credited to Josephus, is probably not a little connected with its disappearance from these materials as they have come down to us.

Eusebius contemptuously alluded to the poverty-stricken spirituality of the Ebionites, holding James' name in such high esteem. He did so in the form of a pun on the Hebrew meaning of their name, 'the Poor', thereby showing himself very knowledgeable about the meaning and implications of biblical references involving this usage, so basic for a consideration of James' person.[4] The euphemism 'the Poor' was already in common use as an honourable form of self-designation in the community responsible for the Dead Sea Scrolls – commonly called 'the Qumran Community', because of the location of the caves along the Dead Sea where the Scrolls were found, called in Arabic *Wadi* or *Khirbat* Qumran – as it was among those in contact with James' Jerusalem Community, most notably Paul.[5] The usage also figures prominently in both the Sermon on the Mount in the Gospel of Matthew and in the Letter attributed to James itself.[6]

The group or movement associated with James' name and teachings in Jerusalem is usually referred to as 'the Jerusalem Church' or 'Community', an English approximation for the Greek word *Ecclēsia*, which literally means 'Assembly'. It is also possible to refer to it as *Palestinian Christianity*, which would indeed be appropriate. But an even more popular notation one finds in the literature is *Jewish Christianity*.

Jewish and Christian Sectarianism

Sects such as these were at a very early time pronounced anathema by the Rabbis – the heirs of the Pharisees pictured in the New Testament – who took over Judaism by default seven and a half years after James' judicial murder. After the destruction of the Temple theirs was the only Jewish tradition the Romans were willing to tolerate in Palestine. The legal tradition they inherited has come to be known as *Halachah*, the sum total of religious law according to the traditions of the Pharisees. It is preserved in the literature of the Rabbis known as the *Talmud*. This includes what is also known as 'the Oral Law' and consists mainly of a document compiled in the third century called the Mishnah, a number of commentaries on it, and further traditional compilations, together known as either the 'Babylonian' or 'Jerusalem *Talmud*', depending on whether they originated in Iraq or Palestine.

The Movement headed by James from the 40s to the 60s CE in Jerusalem was the principal one of a number of groups categorized in the *Talmud* by the pejorative terminology *min* or *minim* (plural). This has now come to mean in Jewish tradition 'sectarian'. With the gradual production of this rabbinical literature – at the time of Jesus there were sectarian leaders who went under the title 'Rabbi' as well – a new form of Judaism was formulated no longer predicated on the Temple. This became dominant in Palestine only after the Romans imposed it by brute force.

Because of its palpably more accommodating attitude towards foreign rule and, at least while the Temple was still standing, to High Priests appointed by foreigners or foreign-controlled rulers, it was really the only form of Jewish religious expression the Romans were willing to live with. The same was to hold true for the form of Christianity we can refer to as 'Pauline', which was equally submissive or accommodating to Roman power. For his part, Paul proudly proclaimed his Pharisaic roots (Phil. 3:5).

This form of Judaism must be distinguished from the more variegated tapestry that characterized Jewish religious expression in Jesus' and James' lifetimes. This consisted of quite a number of groups before the fall of the Temple, some of which were quite militant and aggressive, even apocalyptic, that is, having a concern for a highly emotive style of expression regarding 'the End Time'. Most of these apocalyptic groups focused in one way or another on the Temple. They were written out of Judaism in the same manner that James and Jesus' other brothers were written out of Christianity.

'Christianity', as we know it, developed in the West in contradistinction to the more variegated landscape that continued to characterize the East. It would be more proper to refer to Western Christianity at this point as 'Pauline' or 'Gentile Christian'. It came to be seen as orthodox largely as a result of the efforts of Eusebius and like-minded persons, who put the reorganization programme ascribed to Constantine into effect. It can also be usefully referred to as 'Overseas' or 'Hellenistic Christianity' as opposed to 'Palestinian Christianity'.

Its documents and credos were collected and imposed on what is now known as the Christian world at the Council of Nicea in 325 CE and others that followed in the fourth century and beyond. These formally asserted the divinity of Jesus and made it orthodox. Eusebius, who came from Caesarea in Palestine, was Constantine's bishop and personal confidant. He had a major role in the organization and guidance of the Council of Nicea. The development of this genre of Overseas Christianity was actually concurrent and parallel to the development of Rabbinic Judaism – if something of its mirror image. Both were not only willing to live with Roman power, they owed their continued existence to its sponsorship.

To put this proposition differently: the fact of the power and brutality of Rome was operating in both to drive out and to declare heretical what is now called Jewish Christianity – 'Essenism' or 'Ebionitism' would perhaps be a better description of it in Palestine. In Judaism, what was left was a legalistic shadow of former glories, bereft of apocalyptic and Messianic tendencies; in Christianity, a largely Hellenized, other-worldly mystery cult, the real religious legacy of three hundred years of Roman religious genius and assimilation. This surgery was necessary if Christianity in the form we know it was to survive, since certain doctrines

6

represented by James, and probably dating back to his Messianic predecessor 'Jesus', were distinctly opposed to those ultimately considered to be *Christian*.

James the Real Successor to Jesus, not Peter

In the literature James' place as successor to and inheritor of the mantle of his brother was largely taken over by the more or less mythological presentation of the claims of an individual known, in the West, as 'Peter' or the 'Rock'. This was a logical end of the legitimization of certain claims advanced by the now Hellenized and largely non-Jewish, Gentile Church at Rome following the destruction of the Jerusalem centre in the wake of the Uprising against Rome. It is an interesting coincidence that 'the Jerusalem Community' of James the Just and the Community at Qumran disappeared at about the same time – though perhaps this is not so coincidental as it may seem.

This 'Rock' terminology reflected in Peter's name and the imagery related to it were actually in use contemporaneously in Palestine in both the literature at Qumran and in what were probably the documents of the Jerusalem Church.[7] In the latter, a version of it was applied to James, as well probably as to his successor, a man identified in the tradition as Jesus' – and therefore James' – first 'cousin', Simeon bar Cleophas. Simeon's father, Cleophas – depending on the degree of confusion – is usually seen as the brother or brother-in-law of Joseph.

This name resonates in interesting ways with the version of Simon Peter's name 'Cephas' encountered in Galatians, 1 Corinthians, and the Gospel of John. Acts 15:14, at the famous 'Jerusalem Council' actually refers to Peter as 'Simeon' – at a time when Peter had already supposedly fled Palestine on pain of death. We shall see that Simeon bar Cleophas is very likely *the second brother of Jesus*, Simon, as presented in Gospel Apostle lists, Christianity in Palestine developing in something of the manner of an Islamic Caliphate (and a Shi'ite one at that), that is, one centred on the *family* of Jesus.

James is not only the key to a re-evaluation and reconstruction of Jewish Christian history and the Jewish–Christian relationship, he is also the key to the Historical Jesus. The solution to this problem has evaded observers for so long primarily because they have attempted to approach it through the eyes and religious legacy of James' arch rival and sometime religious 'Enemy', Paul.[8] It is through James, Jesus' spiritual heir and actual physical successor in Palestine, that we are on the safest ground in approaching a historically accurate semblance of what Jesus himself, in so far as he actually existed, might have been like.

Of all the characters in the early stages of Christianity, Paul alone is known to us through reliable, first-hand autobiographical documents, that is, the letters attributed to him in the New Testament. They reveal his life, character and thought in the most personal manner possible. All others, even Jesus and most of those generally called 'Apostles', we know only by second- or third-hand accounts, if we know them at all. We have Gospels or letters purportedly written about them or in their names, but these must be handled with the utmost care.

It is also not generally comprehended that this is the sequence in which we should take the New Testament. Paul's letters and a few other materials – possibly including the Letter of James – come first and are primary. The rest come later and are secondary. The Gospels themselves are probably even tertiary. Biblical scholars have not come to a consensus on which aspects of this legacy can properly be considered historical. Nor have they succeeded in giving us, despite the bulk of their output, a very real picture of what might have occurred at this formative moment in human history or of the events surrounding and succeeding the life of the individual called, in the Hellenistic world, 'the Christ'.

When it comes to the person of Jesus' brother James, however, we are on much firmer ground, not least because he has been so marginalized and ignored. We have a number of facts concerning James' life attested to by a variety of independent observations within and without Christian tradition. It should not be surprising that the existence of an actual brother of Jesus in the flesh was a problem for the theologian committed to an a priori doctrine of divine sonship or the supernatural birth of Jesus Christ. In Roman Catholic doctrine it has been the received teaching since the end of the fourth century that James was the brother of Jesus, not only by a different father, an obvious necessity in view of the doctrine of divine sonship, but also by a *different* mother – the answer to the conundrum presented by the perpetual virginity of Mary. That is, James was a 'cousin' of Jesus.

This problem was already anticipated in the Gospels by the confusing proliferation of Marys, in turn related to confusions between Jesus' father Joseph and his 'uncle' Cleophas and the confusions between all the Simons, Judases, Jameses, and so on – to the extent that, as absurd as it may seem, we finally end up with Mary 'the sister of' her own sister Mary (John 19:25 – called there 'the wife of Clopas' as well).

We shall not dignify with a response attempts by Church writers, early or late, to prove James and Jesus had different mothers or, depending on their theological position, different fathers. We shall take these for what they are, embarrassment over the existence of Jesus' brothers and bids to protect the emerging doctrine of the supernatural Christ. These, developing out of a contemplation of Christ's deified nature, started gaining currency in the second and third centuries, but are totally absent from contemporary documents relating to the family of Jesus that survived the redaction processes of the New Testament.

There is also sufficient evidence to show James as a normative Jew of his time, even one referred to by the most extreme terminology 'Zealot' or '*Sicarii*', this in spite of his being the most important of the Central Triad of early Church leaders, whom Paul denotes as 'Pillars'.9 What a normative Jew might have been in these circumstances before the fall of the Temple will require further elucidation. For the purposes of discussion we are on safe ground, however, if we say that such a concept at least encompassed an attachment to the Law, whether from the perspective of the *Halachah* of the Pharisees or a more pseudepigraphic or apocalyptic perspective belonging to one of the other opposition groups. It also consisted of a feeling for Temple and Temple worship – at least before its fall – regardless of attitude towards the Herodian, pro-Roman Priesthood overseeing it.

At some point in the mid-40s, Cephas and John, two of those Paul designates as 'Pillars' in Galatians 2:9,10 along with another James, 'the *brother* of John' as distinct from James the subject of this book, disappear from the scene, probably in the context of conflict with Herodian kings such as Agrippa I (37–44 CE) or his brother Herod of Chalcis (44–49 CE). Thus, James was left to occupy the 'Christian' leadership stage in Palestine alone for the next two decades. At least this is what can be gleaned from the materials in Acts, however imprecise or mythologized they may be.

The Direct Appointment or Election of James

Whether James succeeded to this leadership by direct appointment of Jesus, or he was accorded it by the Apostles or 'elected', is disputed in the sources. However he emerged, such a succession seems to have been connected with the sequence of the post-resurrection appearances of Jesus to his Disciples, as depicted in the literature, or, as Eusebius puts it, following Clement of Alexandra, the order in which 'the tradition of Knowledge' was accorded individual leaders.11

9

There are lost resurrection traditions that accorded precedence even in this to James, despite attempts to obliterate them. One of these, found in the first post-resurrection appearance episode in the Gospel of Luke, depicts Jesus as appearing to 'Clopas' – that is, Simeon bar Cleophas or his father – together with another unnamed companion, possibly James, on the Emmaus road outside Jerusalem. A second is certainly to be found in 1 Corinthians 15:7, where Paul confirms an appearance to James and 'last of all' himself.[12]

In the former at least, if not in the latter, we have unassailable evidence of a tradition according precedence in the matter of the first appearance to a member or members of Jesus' family – 'Clopas', according to extant tradition, being, at the very least, *Jesus' uncle*. Interestingly enough, this appearance takes place in the environs of Jerusalem, not in Galilee as most other such Gospel renditions.

In addition, other early traditions, reflected to a certain extent in the Gospel of Thomas found at Nag Hammadi and in the Pseudoclementines – Hellenistic romances paralleling Acts, but from a Judeo-Christian point of view – actually speak in terms of a *direct* appointment of James by Jesus.[13] As opposed to this, early Church traditions via Clement of Alexandria (150–215), reported by Eusebius, not insignificantly, speak of an *election* of James or an election *by* the Apostles. Whatever the conclusion, there can be no doubt that James was the actual successor in Palestine, if not elsewhere.

Finally, there is the Letter ascribed to James in the New Testament, which Eusebius considers spurious. Despite its Jewish apocalyptic character and in spite of its purportedly late appearance on the scene, it was evidently imbued with such prestige that it could not be excluded from the canon. It can be shown to be a direct riposte to points Paul makes in his Letters to the Romans, Corinthians, and Galatians. Even if this is not sufficient to consider it authentic, its doctrines are enough like those of the Historical James, reconstructable from other sources, to contend that, at the very least, it represents authentic Palestinian tradition.

Despite its relatively polished Greek style, the antiquity of its materials can also now be confirmed by reference to its many parallels to doctrines in the Dead Sea Scrolls, not available previously. It also lacks the Gnostic tendencies so prevalent in later documents featuring the person of James. In it, too, the Temple would seem to be still standing and the catastrophe that was soon to overwhelm Jewish life in Palestine has seemingly not yet occurred. At present, opinions concerning it show a greater flexibility in their willingness to come to grips with at least the possibility of its authenticity.

Given its manifest parallels with the documents from Qumran, with which it makes an almost perfect fit, and doctrines attributable to the person of James from other sources, it has to be considered a fairly good reflection at least of the 'Jamesian' point of view. In fact, apart from the Pauline corpus and the 'We Document', on which – as we shall see – the second part of Acts is based, and a few worrisome phrases such as 'the Perfect Law of Freedom' (Jas. 1:25 and 2:12), it is one of the most homogeneous, authentic, and possibly even earliest pieces in the New Testament corpus. At this point, one should also note that the Letter of Jude, whose author refers to himself as 'the brother of James', is probably of the same order of authenticity and its tone echoes the Letter of James.

A parallel individual appears in Gospel Apostle lists, 'Judas of James', and he and Jude are probably identical with another Apostle known in apocryphal tradition as 'Judas Thomas' or 'Judas the Twin'. He is also probably referred to in a somewhat distorted, and therefore probably tendentious, manner in the Gospel of John as '*Didymus* Thomas' – literally 'Twin Twin'.[14]

In our discussion of Jesus' brothers as Apostles all these overlapping materials will be amalgamated to show that the same multiplication of names encountered *vis-à-vis* other members of Jesus' family is now being encountered with regard to this Jude as well. Since he will also prove to be equivalent to several other characters having the same or similar names in the sources, the cast of characters will therefore narrow considerably.

There are also two Apocalypses attributed to James in the Nag Hammadi corpus, as well as an additional riposte from James to Peter in the prelude to the version of the Pseudoclementines known as the *Homilies*. In this last there are also letters, reputedly from Clement to James and Peter to James. There is also a Gospel attributed to James, usually referred to as the 'Infancy Gospel' or the Protevangelium of James, averring, of all things, the perpetual virginity of Mary! As will be seen, its author might more appropriately have applied this doctrine to James' life-style. Who else to give a better testimony to 'facts' relating to the infant Jesus than the person represented as being his *older* brother? But it is most certainly spurious.

Finally there is a work, which the writer Epiphanius (367–404), a contemporary of Jerome and Augustine, claims to have seen, called the *Anabathmoi Jacobou* or the *Ascents of James* after the lectures James is pictured as delivering to the Jerusalem masses from the Temple steps. Epiphanius even gives quotations from this work, which further concretize James' role at the centre of agitation in the Temple opposing the Herodian Priesthood and decrying its pollution. This interesting text too no longer exists.

It was around this *Perfectly Holy* and *Righteous* 'Just One' in the Temple that in our view all parties opposing the Herodian/Roman Establishment, from the more violent and extreme to the less so, ranged. In this role as Bishop, James was also High Priest of the Opposition Alliance – thus, in effect, the *Opposition High Priest*. This is the role accorded him in early Church tradition as well and, as such, it is more or less equivalent to the individual dubbed, in Qumran usage, 'the *Mebakker*' or 'Overseer' and/or 'the High Priest Commanding the Many'.[15] This role is accorded the Teacher of Righteousness at Qumran as well.

Ultimately we shall place James at the centre of the Opposition Alliance of all the groups and parties opposing foreign rule in Palestine and its concomitant, foreign gifts and sacrifices on behalf of foreigners in the Temple. The opposition of this Alliance to Herodian Kings and the Herodian Priesthood led directly to the Uprising against Rome.

This forms the mirror image of the way Christian tradition portrays the Messianic individuals it approves of, who are pictured as sympathetic – or at least not antipathetic – to Rome. This kind of inversion will be shown to be a consistent aspect of the portraiture and polemics of this period. To rescue James from the obscurity into which he was cast, we should now turn to the history of Palestine preceding him, which set the stage for his life, as well as to a description of those sources on which our information about him is based.

2

The Second Temple and the Rise
of the Maccabees

The Return from the Babylonian Captivity under Ezra

According to biblical tradition, the First Temple was begun under David and completed under his son Solomon around the year 1000 BC. Surviving one serious threat from 735 to 701 BC by the Assyrians, which resulted in the destruction of the Northern Kingdom of Israel, it lasted until the Babylonian King Nebuchadnezzar destroyed it in 586 BC. Thus was ushered in the Second Temple Period, the end of which produced the characters so integral to the matters before us.

After the destruction of the First Temple, tradition describes an interregnum of some forty-five years – the Babylonian Captivity – when members of the upper classes were under enforced sojourn in Babylon. The building of the new Second Temple, which followed their return, proceeded in stages, taking approximately another hundred years to complete.

Primitive rebuilding efforts, as commanded by the Persian King Cyrus in 540 BC (Isaiah 44:28), began almost immediately under a scion of the previous royal line, Zerubbabel – that is, 'shoot' of David or Jesse out of Babylon (*Babel* meaning 'Babylon'). He was accompanied by a priestly individual, Jesus ben Yehozedek, presumably the son of the previous reigning High Priest, Yehozedek. Both names have important ramifications for our period, the second meaning 'God justifies' or 'God's Righteousness'. A leadership conjunction of priestly and royal individuals such as this is important for the Qumran Scrolls, as it is for the New Testament Letter to the Hebrews.[1]

What became of the organizational and building efforts of this first royal and High Priestly pair is unclear. At some point the Davidic part of the constellation seems to have dropped out, leaving only priests in the Persian manner in a kind of local autonomy. Some even think that the famous 'Suffering Servant' passages in the second part of Isaiah – called by scholars 'Deutero' or 'Second Isaiah' – have to do with the kingly part of this ruling dichotomy having come to a bad end. This would not be surprising in view of the political turmoil of the time.

Except for a genealogical list in 1 Chronicles 3:24, which ends a little before the beginning of the Maccabean period, nothing further is heard of Zerubbabel or his descendants, representing the Davidic or kingly part of this duality, that is, until the rise of various movements in the first century under the Messianic leaders of that time, leading to the destruction of Jerusalem and the Second Temple. It is interesting that the last descendant of Zerubbabel in 1 Chronicles above is someone called 'Anani' – in Hebrew meaning 'Cloudy One' – an allusion with overtones, when considering the all-important Messianic citation about the 'Son of Man coming on the clouds of Heaven' from Daniel 7:13.

Zerubbabel crops up as well in New Testament genealogies of Jesus, but neither Matthew nor Luke, who present differing versions of these genealogies, agrees with his genealogy in Chronicles.[2] Julius Africanus (170–245 CE), an early Church father, also dealt with the issue of these genealogies, claiming that so jealous was Herod of the genealogies of others that he burned all genealogical records in his own time so no one could possess one superior to his own.[3]

He further claimed that the genealogies of Jesus then circulating in early Christian communities were the work of members of the family of Jesus and his brothers who had withdrawn to two towns across the Jordan in the region of 'Damascus' – we must always watch this allusion in our study – he calls in Hebrew 'Nazara' and 'Cochaba', that is 'Branch' and 'Star', Messianic significations we shall encounter further. 'Cochaba' might also have been the place of origin of another Messianic contender of the second century, Shim'on bar Kochba or 'Son of the Star', the leader of the Second Jewish Revolt against Rome in 132–6 CE.

Temple-building efforts, seemingly begun under Zerubbabel and Jesus ben Yehozedek, were completed in the fifth century BC under the tutelage of two later returnees in the next century, Ezra and Nehemiah. By this time there is no longer any kingship to be seen, only a priesthood descended from Jesus ben Yehozedek. Chronicles takes his genealogy back to the First High Priest of the First Temple in David's and Solomon's time, Zadok.[4]

The mention of Zadok and Yehozedek is important, because the root on which this noun cluster is based, the three Hebrew letters Z–D–K, bears the meaning of 'Righteousness'. This is not only the basis for James' cognomen, 'the Righteous' or 'Just One', according to all early Church sources, but it is connected to the name of one of the sects in Jesus' time, which transliterates into Greek, Sadducee or *Zadduki/Zaddoki*. In Hebrew, *ee* or *i* is a suffix referring to a person who is or does a thing, in this case, a 'Zadok' or a '*Zaddik*', the latter meaning in English 'Righteous One'.[5]

Ezra and Nehemiah accomplished in the 400s BC what the previous generation could not, and a temple of sorts was finally completed, including, it would seem, a wall surrounding the city. How far these two individuals can be distinguished from each other is a matter of conjecture, as the accounts concerning them overlap. Nehemiah is certainly a real historical figure, but whether Ezra is merely a priestly gloss over the more secular and profane character represented by Nehemiah is an open question.[6]

What role he plays in his activities on the Temple Mount, if he is something other than a High Priest, is not clear at all. Though he is presented as a kind of second Moses re-establishing and reading the Law to the assembled returnees, they seem never to have heard it before (Ezra 9:10 and Neh. 9:3). Nehemiah's activities are clearer. For instance, he behaves like a powerful vicegerent from the Persian King, ejecting the previous High Priestly family – presumably the descendants of Jesus ben Yehozedek and as such 'Zadokite' – from its quarters on the Temple Mount.

Biblical accounts leave off here, and we go into something of a dark tunnel. The only thing that is clear is that we have, in a kind of local autonomy, a High Priest and with him, in the Persian manner, a reigning priest class in control. For this reason, this government is often referred to as a theocracy. This priesthood eventually becomes known as the line of Zadok, after the Zadok who officiated in David's and Solomon's times, the First High Priest in the First Temple.

The Sadducee Terminology and the Dead Sea Scrolls

When this *Zadduki* or *Sadducee* terminology actually emerges is not clear, but by the first century CE, Josephus is referring to priests in his own time as trying to claim descent from David's High Priest Zadok. Some of these claims even he does not entertain.[7] Jewish Talmudic literature (dating from the third to the seventh century CE) presents a similar picture, but extends the term *Sadducee* using it as a pejorative inclusive of all sectarians.

In the Dead Sea Scrolls, the usage has a slightly different signification, designating not simply genealogy, but something else. Whatever else this something is, it certainly includes the concept of Righteousness, which, as noted above, is the basis of the root cluster in Hebrew underlying the word *Sadducee* in Greek. This is how the term is used in the Pseudoclementine *Recognitions*, so important to a consideration of James. Here, the Sadducees are described as a group – like so-called 'Zealots' above – taking their rise in the time of John the Baptist and considering themselves 'more Righteous than the others', 'separating themselves from the Assembly of the People'.[8]

This definition of Sadducees is actually the way the term is defined by so-called Jewish 'Karaites' in the Middle Ages, who considered themselves latterday heirs to the Sadducees and actually called themselves the 'Righteous Ones'.[9] For both Josephus and the New Testament, this sense ends up by being rather expressed in terms of being 'harsher in Judgement'.[10] It should be appreciated that, whatever else the Qumran sectaries were, they were certainly very harsh and uncompromising where matters of 'Judgement' were concerned, and this aspect of their behaviour should become clear as we proceed.

To distinguish the usage 'Sons of Zadok' as it occurs in the Qumran texts from 'Sadducee', scholars often use the terminology 'Zadokite'. The use of the phrase 'Sons of Zadok' would probably actually coincide with the emergence of the Sadducee Party as a distinct group somewhere in the third to second centuries BC. It is not without interest, however, that when the Pseudoclementine *Recognitions* speaks of the 'Sadducees' as 'taking their emergence with the coming of John the Baptist', this is the picture we would support, at least in the Herodian period, of *two* groups of Sadducees, one Establishment and the other Purist or Opposition. These last look very much like what in other vocabularies might be called 'Messianic' or 'Zealot' and the basis of the split would appear to revolve about seeking accommodation with foreign power and the perceived Righteousness or Unrighteousness of the High Priests.

This picture also finds support from Talmudic texts, when read with care, as well as Jewish Karaite texts later on, both of which delineate such a split between *two* groups of Sadducees, one following someone called 'Zadok' and another group associated with 'Boethus'.[11] Josephus describes just such a split connected to someone he also calls 'Boethus', a priest Herod imported from Egypt after he murdered all the previous High Priests, the Maccabees. Herod married the daughter of this 'Boethus' after disposing of his previous wife, a scion of this previous Maccabean line of High Priests. Both these wives turn out to be named

'Mariamme' – the Hebrew analogue of the name 'Mary' in the New Testament.

But the split between this Zadok and Boethus also occurs at the time Josephus describes the birth of another movement, a movement he calls the 'Fourth Philosophy' – more popularly known as 'Zealots' – upon which, as we saw, he lays all the woes that descended on the people in the first century. Not only does Josephus begin his discussion of the various Jewish sects in both his major works with the rise of this movement, but in the second of these, the *Antiquities*, he ascribes the birth of this movement to not *one*, as in the *War*, but *two* individuals, Judas the Galilean, and a second, probably more priestly, individual he designates only as '*Saddok*', a term linguistically related both to the word '*Sadducee*' in Greek and the '*Zaddik*' in Hebrew, as we have seen.[12]

This again brings us back to the picture in the Pseudoclementine *Recognitions* of the Sadducees, 'separating themselves and taking their rise around the time of John the Baptist' and another famous notice in the Gospels, attributed to Jesus, that 'since the days of John the Baptist until now the Men of Violence have not ceased taking the Kingdom of Heaven by storm' (Matt. 11:12 and Luke 16:16). This reference to 'the Men of Violence', also found in the Damascus Document and Habakkuk *Pesher* at Qumran, is normally interpreted to mean what in other contexts goes by the name of 'Zealots' or '*Sicarii*'.[13]

Where Josephus' Judas and '*Saddok*' are concerned, the founders of the *Sicarii* or Zealot Movement, the figure they argue with and oppose, the representative of the reigning priestly Establishment willing to accommodate itself to Roman rule and Herodian kingship, is Joezer ben Boethus. He succeeded his father as High Priest under the Herodians at the beginning of the first century. This, too, is the time of the birth of 'Jesus' according to New Testament sources. Joezer ben Boethus is presumably the brother of Herod's second wife, named Mariamme. She is the mother of that Herod – mistakenly called 'Philip' in the Gospels – who will figure prominently in the stories about the death of John the Baptist.

The issue between this 'Boethus and *Saddok*', which Josephus delineates very clearly, is support of or opposition to the payment of the Roman tax. But this, of course, is the issue underlying the prominence given the Roman census – the Census of Cyrenius in 6–7 CE – at the time of the birth of Jesus in the mythologized portrait of this event in the Gospel of Luke (2:2). It is also a burning issue in the Gospel portraits of Jesus generally, where Jesus is presented as favouring the tax – though at one point Luke denies this, presenting one of the charges levelled against Jesus as teaching the people *not* to pay the tax to Caesar (Luke 23:2)![14] This is the context in which the notices about the *two* groups of Sadducees in Talmudic and Karaite sources – one supporting the priestly Establishment and the other opposing it – and collaboration with Rome generally should be placed.

The Maccabean Priesthood

The circumstance that stands out in the period prior to the rise of the Maccabees and the Jewish independence movement associated with them in the second century BC is the continuation of priestly control. With the coming of Alexander the Great in 333 BC, two successor states under Hellenistic kings descended from his generals arose in Asia: the Seleucids in Syria and the Ptolemies in Egypt at Alexandria. Judea or Palestine – consisting of primarily the region around Jerusalem proper – swung back and forth under the control first of the former, then of the latter. As a rule, relations with the Greek Ptolemies in Egypt were more cordial than those with the Seleucids at Antioch, the Ptolemies being more tolerant. This is important because the Independence War, which broke out in 167 BC, was pointedly waged against Seleucid Hellenization and intolerance.

The war against the Seleucids was led by Judas Maccabee and his real or imagined father, Mattathias.[15] Judas, like Jesus, had four brothers, most, like John, Eleazar (Lazarus), Simon, and Judas himself, with names familiar in New Testament usage. This war is celebrated in Jewish ritual by *Hanukkah* festivities to this day, which in the Jewish mind compete with Christmas. *Hanukkah* literally means 'Rededication', that is, the rededication of the Temple, which was considered polluted by Hellenistic Greeks as represented by the Seleucids. The struggles surrounding this war went on for some thirty more years until the rise of Simon's son John Hyrcanus (134–104 BC) to power.

With the attainment of independence, problems associated with being independent – if only for a hundred years – developed, and the groups and parties that came into prominence and form the substance of Gospel accounts come into focus. In this period, too, the Romans are extending their influence into the eastern Mediterranean after their victories over the Carthaginians, a Semitic people along the coast of North Africa and Spain. 1 Maccabees, which seems to have drawn on official chancellery records, makes much of Judas' friendly correspondence with the Romans. This correspondence is probably authentic, as is another with the Spartans, which proudly proclaims that the Jews and the Spartans are related and therefore 'brothers'![16]

At first the Maccabees seem to have affected only the title of 'High Priest'. At some point in the first or third generations, however, the Greco-Roman title 'King' was added to their nomenclature. Though the Maccabees were from a priestly family, the question has been raised, in the debate relating to the Dead Sea Scrolls, whether they 'usurped' the High Priesthood.[17] There is no indication whatsoever of such a usurpation, and the Maccabees seem to have occupied what appears to have been a very popular priesthood indeed. Josephus, for instance, at the end of the first century in Rome, evinces no embarrassment at the Maccabean blood he claims flows in his veins. On the contrary, he would appear to be most proud of it.[18]

The Book of Daniel and Apocalyptic

The appearance of the Romans in the eastern Mediterranean would appear to be referred to at an important juncture of the Book of Daniel, where their victory over the Syrian fleet in the eastern Mediterranean is mentioned (11:30–35 – 190 BC). This seems, in fact, to trigger the predatory activities upon the Temple by the Seleucid King Antiochus Epiphanes, the villain of both Daniel and the Maccabee books. Here too the Book of Daniel uses the key terminology the *Kittim*, which the Dead Sea Scrolls use to refer to foreign armies invading the country, to refer to the *Romans* (11:30).[19] This is important for sorting out chronological problems at Qumran.

Along with Ezekiel and Isaiah, Daniel is perhaps the most important scriptural inspiration for much of the apocalyptic ideology and symbolism of the Dead Sea Scrolls, as well as for the literature of Christianity. Daniel is also, chronologically speaking, one of the latest books in the scriptural canon, except perhaps for Esther. Esther, which came down to us through a more Eastern-oriented, extra-territorial transmission process, seems to be a more accommodating answer to Daniel's uncompromising Messianic and apocalyptic nationalism.

Daniel's clear association with the Maccabean Uprising in Palestine was doubtlessly one of the reasons why the Rabbis, following the uprisings against Rome, downgraded it from its position among the 'Prophets', placing it among the lesser 'Writings'. No doubt, the Rabbis saw Daniel as a representative of a new, more vivid, style of prophetic expression, which we now call apocalyptic. This style, which they downplayed because of its association with the movement that produced both the Maccabean Uprising and the Uprising against Rome, is very much admired in the documents from Qumran, as it is by New Testament writers. In it, prophetical and eschatological motifs – concerned with the 'Last Times' or the 'Last Things' – are combined amid the most awe-inspiring and blood-curdling imagery.

For instance, Daniel is the first document to refer to what might be described as a 'Kingdom of God'. God is not only described as 'enduring for ever', 'working signs and wonders in Heaven and on earth', and 'saving Daniel from the power of the lions' (that is, death), but as having a 'sovereignty which will never be destroyed' and a 'kingship that will never end' (6:26–28). Daniel also evokes the 'Son of Man coming on the clouds of Heaven', one of the basic scriptural underpinnings for the Messiahship of Jesus and a title always applied to him. This passage will also loom large below in the materials relating to James' activities in the Temple and the proclamation he makes there.

For Daniel, 'the Holy Ones' (*Kedoshim*) or 'the Saints of the Most High God' make war on an evil adversary or foreign invader who has violated the Temple and pillaged it for spoils. All these terms will be important for subsequent generations. This foreigner, who has 'abolished the perpetual sacrifice', is clearly described as Antiochus Epiphanes (7:13–8:12), the villain of Jewish *Hanukkah* festivities ever since. But Daniel also uses additional terms that became popular, particularly at Qumran, but also in the New Testament and the Koran, namely 'the Last Days', 'the Wrath', 'the End' or 'the Time of the End' and, of course, the resurrection of the dead (12:2–13). The way Daniel refers to the resurrection of the dead is particularly significant:

> Of those who lie sleeping in the dust of the earth, many will awake, some to everlasting life . . . cleansed, made white, and purged . . . [they] will rise for [their] share at the End of Time.

Aside from ambiguous allusions in Psalms and a similar reference in 2 Maccabees, in the context of Judas Maccabee's military activities (12:43–44), this is the only overt reference to this doctrine of resurrection in the entire Old Testament. It is noteworthy too that such references are normally associated with a kind of apocalyptic Holy War also outlined in

Daniel. The reference in 2 Maccabees is presented in the context of the Maccabean Uprising against Hellenization and foreign rule in Palestine. Parallel descriptions in 1 Maccabees raise the banner of 'zeal for the Law' (meaning the *Torah* or the Law of Moses) or taking one's 'stand on the Covenant' (2:27). We shall have occasion to refer to allusions like these with regard to James, as well as to the 'Zealot' Movement taking its inspiration from them. Josephus describes this movement, as already remarked, as beginning around the time the New Testament associates with the birth of Christ (4 BC –7 CE), and continuing on to the fall of the Temple in 70 CE and possibly even beyond.

It was apocalyptic literature of this kind that was seen by the Rabbis as the impetus behind the unrest that led to the disaster represented by the First Jewish Uprising against Rome (66–70 CE) and the destruction of the Temple and the State, not to mention the Second Uprising (132–6 CE). This literature was seen as fanning opposition to foreign rule. It encouraged an extreme *zeal for the Law*, that zealotry associated with Holy War, and a willingness to undergo martyrdom rather than to submit to foreign kingship, as well as an associated impetus towards Messianism.

Since these ideas were all seen as stemming from the party or parties opposed to what the Pharisee predecessors of the Rabbis had represented – that is, seeking accommodation with Rome and foreign powers generally at all costs – they were considered reprehensible. It is therefore understandable that in the version of Jewish history that the Rabbis transmitted and in the collection of documents they finally declared to be Holy Writ at the beginning of the second century CE, books like the Maccabees were set aside and Daniel given the lowest priority.

The Jewish Historian Josephus

The contemporary Jewish historian Josephus is important for a consideration of this whole period (37–96 CE). Without him, we would be almost completely ignorant of events. With him, we have a marvellous insight into and almost encyclopaedic reportage of what transpired. Josephus was born in the year 37 CE, that is, not long after the time he claims John the Baptist was executed and around the time that Paul either claims to have been converted or was on a mission of some kind to Damascus, where he ran foul of a representative of the Arabian King Aretas (2 Cor. 11:32).

The capital of this 'King Aretas', the fabulous Petra, was actually further south in today's Jordan. Aretas was also integrally involved in the events surrounding the death of John the Baptist on the other side of the Jordan. It was to Aretas' Kingdom, too, that Herod the Great, certainly through his mother and probably his father as well, had some connection, and, therefore, aside from being an Idumaean – Greek for Edomite – he (Herod) also must be considered an 'Arab', though a Hellenized one at that.

It was at approximately this time, too, that Gaius Caligula (37–41 CE), known in Palestine for having wished to erect a statue of himself like a god in the Temple in Jerusalem, became emperor. This very interesting episode is described both in Josephus and by the famous Alexandrian Jewish philosopher Philo, whose brother Alexander was 'the Alabarch' or the Ruler of the Jews of Alexandria.[20]

One can then state that certainly from the period 62 CE onwards, the year of James' death as recorded in the *Antiquities*, Josephus was a mature observer relying on his own experience and eye-witness reporting. For events in his works prior to around 55 CE, he is reliant either on what he hears from others – hearsay – or other written sources. Several of these sources, including Nicolaus of Damascus, who was an intimate of Herod, and Strabo of Cappadocia, he often mentions. His personal experiences are, in fact, incorporated in great detail into the book called the *Jewish War*, which he wrote directly after the events of 66–73 and which ends, significantly enough, with a description of the triumphal parade in Rome of Titus, the son of the new Roman Emperor Vespasian (69–79). Josephus, as a member of the latter's staff, personally witnessed this event. The commemorative Arch of Titus still stands in the ruins of the Roman Forum today, a chilling reminder of these age-old cataclysms.

But Josephus was also a turncoat, a traitor to his people. When reading him, this should always be kept in mind. It was on the basis of this betrayal that he was allowed to live and was not put to death like others who played a role in the events he describes. For Josephus *did* play a role in these events. Originally, by his own testimony, he was military commandant of Galilee – 'Commissar' might be more accurate – responsible for its organization and fortification in the early days of the Revolt. Given his role as a Pharisee priest, which he later used to extremely good effect, one wonders what his qualifications for such a command position might have been.

Josephus was an interrogator of prisoners and his popularity among his fellow countrymen can be deduced from the following episode, which he describes in the *Jewish War*. Deputized by the Romans, presumably because he spoke Hebrew, to call up to the defenders on the walls of Jerusalem during its siege and ask for their surrender, he was hit on the head by a projectile thrown by someone on the battlements. When he fell, a spontaneous cheer erupted among those watching from the walls. Their enemy Josephus had been wounded.[21]

And this was the great Jewish historian! With military commanders or commissars like Josephus, the Jews had no need of enemies, and the military catastrophe that overtook them was inevitable. Later he uses the prestige his priestly status allowed him in the eyes of the Romans to appeal to their credulity and the exaggerated awe they felt for such augurs or foreign oracles.[22]

It was to his role as a fortune-telling Jewish priest, supposedly held in high esteem by his own people, that his survival can be credited. He and several companions had taken refuge in a cave after the collapse of the military defence of Galilee, for which he was ostensibly responsible. The Romans were taking this time-honoured route on their way to lay siege to Jerusalem, and Josephus betrayed the suicide pact that he and a few companions had made – the normal 'Zealot' approach in such extreme circumstances. Instead, he and another colleague, after dispatching their comrades, surrendered to the Romans, an episode he relates quite shamelessly.

Ushered into the Roman commander Vespasian's presence, Josephus proceeded to apply the Messianic 'Star Prophecy' to him, prophesying that Vespasian was the one foretold in Jewish Scripture, who was going to come out of Palestine and rule the world. This was the prophecy that was of such importance to all resistance groups in this period, including those responsible for the documents at Qumran and the revolutionaries who triggered the war against Rome, not to mention the early Christians.[23] The following year Vespasian was to replace Nero (54–68 CE) as Emperor.

Of course, Josephus was not the only turncoat to whom sources attribute reversing the sense of the Messianic Prophecy, applying it to the destroyer of Jerusalem instead of to its liberator. Josephus, whether candid or not, considered himself a 'Pharisee', which is quite appropriate to this posture. Paul also proudly proclaims his own Pharisee origins in Philippians 3:5. The Book of Acts even has Paul claiming to have studied with Gamaliel, the grandson of one of the most important Pharisee fathers, Hillel, whose name is still proverbial in Judaism today (Acts 5:3 and 22:3). Hillel, together with another colleague named Shammai, also proverbial, was probably the head of the Herodian Sanhedrin, reconstituted after Herod seized power in 37 BC, and destroyed the remaining Maccabees and their seemingly 'Sadducean' supporters.

Acts pictures Paul as being very proud of his Roman citizenship. In Romans 13:1–7 he almost makes a religion out of loyalty to Rome, placing the *Pax Romana* and Roman Law, which he even calls 'God's Law', over Jewish Law or the law of his alleged countrymen (Rom. 13:4). His allegiance to this last – theological posturing or poetic allegorizing notwithstanding – was suspect at the best of times. For his part, Josephus obtained Roman citizenship after his obsequious humiliation before Vespasian and consonant adoption into the latter's family, the Flavians, whose name he came to bear.

The Rabbis, who became the Roman tax collectors in Palestine after the fall of the Temple, claim the same behaviour for the progenitor of the form of Judaism they followed, Rabbinic Judaism-to-be, Rabbi Yohanan ben Zacchai. Rabbi Yohanan seems also to have been involved in the process of fixing the Jewish Canon at the end of the first century. Like Hillel and Shammai before him with Herod, Rabbi Yohanan's behaviour with the Romans has become paradigmatic. He is described in rabbinic sources as applying the same 'Star Prophecy', the most precious prophecy of the Jewish people at that time, to the conqueror of Jerusalem, Vespasian, who was elevated to supreme ruler of the known civilized world after his military exploits in Palestine.

As the rabbinic presentation of this story goes, Rabbi Yohanan, after having himself smuggled out of Jerusalem in a coffin – quite appropriately, as it turns out; besides, it was the only exit possible at the time – had an arrow shot into Vespasian's camp, attached to which was a note claiming that 'Rabbi Yohanan is one of the Emperor's friends'.[24] Doubtless this was true, but the camp had to have been Titus', because Vespasian, the founder of the new Flavian line of emperors, had already gone to Rome at this point to assume his crown, leaving Titus behind to wind things up in Palestine. Rabbi Yohanan, as Talmudic materials present him, then had himself ushered into Vespasian's presence to proclaim the very same thing Josephus recounts *he* did, that Vespasian was the Ruler prophesied to come out of Palestine and rule the world.

Whether Josephus was a cynical opportunist or not, his account is the more credible, though both may be true. If so, Vespasian must have become very impatient of all these Jewish turncoats obsequiously fawning on him and proclaiming him the Ruler foreseen in Jewish Scripture, who was to come out of Palestine to rule the world (or maybe he didn't). For his part, the Romans accorded R. Yohanan the academy at Yavneh, where the foundations of what was to become Rabbinic Judaism were laid; whereas Josephus was adopted for services rendered – writing the *Jewish War* being one of them – into the Roman imperial family itself.

In Josephus' case, the contacts for his treachery had already been laid some time before. As he recounts it, he knew someone in the Roman camp, someone he had met on a previous mission to Rome on behalf of some obscure priests who, he contends, were being held on a 'trifling' charge of some kind.[25] These priests, like Paul according to Acts, had appealed to Caesar, that is Nero – 'Augustus' as Acts sometimes calls him (25:21–25) – and were probably connected in some manner to the 'Temple Wall' Affair. In this affair, which in our view led directly to the death of James, a wall had been built – presumably by 'Zealot' priests – to block the Herodian King Herod Agrippa II (49–93 CE) from viewing the Temple sacrifice while reposing and eating on the balcony of his palace.[26]

In his autobiographical excursus, called the *Vita* appended to the *Antiquities*, Josephus describes how, as a young priest in his mid-twenties, he went to Rome on a mission to rescue those who had gone there and been detained as a result, presumably, of the 'Temple Wall' Affair. Somehow he had gained access through a well-connected Jewish actor to Nero's wife, Poppea, whom he elsewhere describes as being interested in religious causes, Jewish or otherwise. It will be remembered that Nero, too, enjoyed the company of people of the theatre. So pleased was Poppea with the young Josephus that he apparently attained all he wished of her – and perhaps more – for he proudly brags that she sent him away laden with gifts. One wonders what else the artful young priest managed to achieve during his stay, apart from the contacts he made in Roman intelligence circles that served him so well when Roman armies finally did appear in Galilee three years later.

It was also as a result of the 'Temple Wall' Affair that the 'conspiracy' was hatched between Agrippa II and the then High Priest Ananus ben Ananus to remove James.[27] Indeed, it was at approximately this time that the ever mercurial and doubtlessly deranged Nero proceeded to kick Poppea, who was now pregnant, to death. After this, Nero too seems to have pursued his persecutions of the Jews more determinedly than ever, seemingly purposefully goading them into revolt.

Josephus was obviously, then, very well placed to produce his accounts of the history of Palestine and matters such as the rise of the Flavians and their qualifications either for Jewish Messiahship or divine honours, as the case may be, for which he was duly rewarded. In writing the *Jewish War*, for instance, he was putting the Flavians on the same level as the forerunner of the previous dynasty, the divine Julius. The only difference was that, whereas Julius Caesar wrote his own histories, Josephus, an adoptee and a captive, wrote theirs.

Historical Writing: Josephus versus the Gospels

Notwithstanding, Josephus was a very good historian indeed, not least because he had a prodigious memory. Like all foreigners trying to ape an alien style, he sometimes outdoes his mentors. Regardless of whether he understands all the currents of the history he is relating, or wants his reader to, he presents such a plethora of details that one can only marvel at his mind's retentiveness. He obviously wrote it all down from memory and his own experience immediately after amassing the information he presents, much no doubt from his interrogations of Jewish prisoners.

He is simply putting it all down, or at least *almost* all of it, which is the reason one must be careful when handling Josephus – this in addition to several errors, possibly made by a copyist, and occasional interpolations that have accrued over the centuries. For Josephus' writings were not, as one might expect, preserved by Jews or Jewish copyists. They were preserved by Christians, usually monks either of the Greek Orthodox or the Latin tradition. This was because they thought he mentioned several characters from early Christian history, particularly Jesus.

He does, but not necessarily in the manner many people would expect or even recognize. For this reason, many such testimonies, including the ones to Peter and Simon *Magus* we shall inspect below, escaped the copyists' deletions. On the other hand, these were also sufficient to ensure that his works were properly preserved. So thoroughly convinced were some in the Greek Orthodox tradition, for instance, that Josephus had mentioned Jesus that his works were appended to the New Testament as sacred writ. Eusebius also views Josephus somewhat in this light and thinks he is providing reinforcement for the Christian theological position, particularly regarding the terrible retribution visited upon the Jews.

Still, Josephus' works do not resemble the Gospels and the Book of Acts at all except in spirit. Characterized by mythologization, story-telling and appeals to Roman credulity, these last have more the nature of Hellenistic romance than of history books. As in the case of the other group of Hellenistic novels, called the Pseudoclementines after one of

Peter's travelling companions Clement, the Gospels, even though there are four of them, have, for instance, little of the historical detail that makes Josephus so valuable. For its part, the Book of Acts as history is often impossible to follow and, in due course, we shall be able to work out its historical method – if method it is.

Neither do the Gospels or Acts give any hint of the background situation of terrifying political strife, disaffection and day-to-day cruelties that resulted in thousands of crucifixions (not just *one*), which Josephus for puerile interests of his own lovingly dwells on. But the welter of historical data one finds in Josephus, however unpalatable, is subordinated in them to the deification of Christ and the conciliation of his message, so that one would not even know there was such internecine political strife and an intensity of hatred abroad that only the martyrdom of beloved leaders could produce.

To add to all this, one has the retrospective confirmation of the Pauline Gentile Mission and the allied presentation of Jesus as alienated from his own people and the members of his family, his successors in Palestine, recognizing Roman Authority, and in turn being recognized, at least obliquely, by its representatives.

Josephus, of course, is without the charm, allure, and grace of these accounts, but his defects – his historical ones, not his spiritual ones – do not particularly have to do with theological attitude. Rather, as we have noted, he is intent on praising the exploits of his Roman benefactors. In fact, having seen the power of Rome at a very young age, Josephus, like a number of others in Palestine of his time – the Herodians, for instance, or Paul, or even the High Priest Ananus, James' destroyer – had a keen appreciation of the futility of struggling against it, whatever the justice of the cause.

But Josephus vividly sets forth his own defects in the preface to the *Jewish War*, which, along with his thanks to his benefactors in the *Antiquities*, reads almost like a modern introduction. He describes 'the war which the Jews made against the Romans' as – hyperbole notwithstanding – 'the greatest of all time' and 'perhaps greater than any recorded struggle between cities fighting against cities or nations against nations'. He goes on to describe how 'in the early stages of the war [he] fought against the Romans', but was later an 'unwilling witness', a term he uses to characterize some of Titus' actions as well.

Finally he condemns

those with no first-hand knowledge of the affair, collecting vain and inconsistent stories *on the basis of hearsay* and writing garbled accounts of it,
while *eye-witness accounts* have been *falsified either to flatter the Romans
or to vilify the Jews*.[28]

Nothing could better enunciate the method and historical style of this
period, particularly of works that survived such as the Gospels and the
Book of Acts.

Despite his further protestations against misleading those 'ignorant of
these matters with *flattering and fictitious narratives*' and his own goal of
writing 'for *those who love truth*, not for those who please themselves', so
all-pervasive was the urge to survive and the need to ingratiate oneself
with one's conquerors that he cannot avoid the same conduct himself.
For example, he repeatedly refers to the revolutionaries as 'bandits',
'thugs' or 'murderers'. The religious leaders or 'prophets' who encouraged
them he dubs 'frauds', 'deceivers' and 'false prophets' – oblivious to his
own activities in this regard.

By contrast, he also repeatedly praises the magnanimity of his patron
Titus (79–81). Insisting on Titus' bravery, wisdom and gallantry, he
describes how he 'delayed the capture of a city in order first to allow the
people to surrender' or 'took pity on the common people who were help-
less against the revolutionaries'. Of course, after such a deadline passed,
the Romans regularly slaughtered the populace mercilessly, including
women and children.

The Habakkuk *Pesher*, which, unlike Josephus, almost did not survive
and did so only because it was deposited in the caves at Qumran, gives a
totally *opposite picture* of the behaviour of these rampaging foreign
armies who 'sacrifice to their standards and worship their weapons of
war' and 'took no pity even on the fruit of the womb'.[29] But Josephus
regularly praises 'the good order of the Romans', 'their clemency towards
the people' and 'their indulgence in sparing foreigners' (like himself), as
opposed to what he characterizes as '*the brutality of the revolutionaries
against the people*'![30]

Perhaps even more meaningfully, when one remembers the picture of
Roman behaviour generally in the Gospels, he presents the Romans as 'unwillingly attacking' the Jews, insisting that the Romans 'were invited into
Jerusalem by the Jews' own leaders', which is, as we shall see, true from a
certain perpective but not precisely in the manner Josephus is presenting it.

Finally, and most chillingly of all, Josephus asserts that the 'calamities' and 'misfortunes and sufferings' that overtook the Jews were inflicted on them because of their own behaviour – in this instance, because 'they were afflicted by sedition'. In the literature of the early Church fathers, particularly Eusebius, this observation is transformed into the accusation that 'the Jews suffered the calamities and misfortunes' they did 'because of their crimes against our Saviour'.[31]

This kind of displacement is particularly apparent in Josephus' presentation of the destruction of the Temple. For him, this was occasioned by the Jews' own 'tyrants', by whom he means, of course, the 'bandits and religious frauds' just mentioned. These now become the tyrants, not the Herodians or Romans, and it is they who 'draw upon the Holy Temple the unwilling hands of the Romans and the conflagration'. Not satisfied with this self-flagellation, he finally goes so far as to represent the Jews as even *burning down their own Temple* and then *jumping into the flames*.[32]

Compounding this parallel with Gospel method and presentation – though forced to admit what had to be obvious to anyone, that Titus 'destroyed Jerusalem' – for Josephus, 'the Temple was burned *against* the consent of Caesar'. In the same manner, the Gospels portray Jesus as being destroyed *against* the wishes of the Roman governor. Parallels of this kind are of the utmost importance, particularly when one realizes that in the Gospels Jesus is the 'Temple' (John 2:19), a presentation developed further and with a good deal of poetic artistry in the Pauline corpus.[33]

Finally, in describing 'the signs and wonders that went before' the destruction of the Temple, including 'what signs' happened to Vespasian 'relating to his taking over the Government', Josephus closes this catalogue of adulation and abuse with the most terrible lament of all: besides 'the misfortunes of my country . . . which under Roman rule had reached the highest level of prosperity only to fall to the lowest level of misery', the 'misfortunes of all other nations in recorded history seem small . . . and [for our misfortunes] we have *only ourselves to blame*'. This cry of *mea culpa* is so familiar, because one has already encountered it in the famous cry of the Jewish crowd in the Gospel of Matthew, 'his blood be upon us and upon our children' (27:25).

Josephus is, therefore, inaccurate when it comes to matters having a direct bearing on his own survival; in particular, his questionable relations with revolutionaries, apocalyptic groups, and sedition, as well as his attempts to ingratiate himself with his new masters. These can be corrected by compensating for them, as they can to a certain extent in the New Testament. But his meticulous reproduction of the minutiae of day-to-day events is unparalleled. He tells us everything he can remember within the parameters of his own necessary well-being and personal survival. For this reason, we have an encyclopaedic presentation of events and persons in Palestine in this period without equal in almost any time or place up to the era of modern record-keeping and reportage.

3

Romans, Herodians, and Jewish Sects

The Sects in the Second Temple Period

Josephus describes the Jewish sects of this period in a somewhat tendentious manner. The New Testament attempts a parallel presentation, but objective observers regard this picture as being largely based on Josephus. The *Talmud*, based on Pharisaic tradition, presents an equally tendentious picture of '*us*', that is, Rabbinical Judaism versus all other groups, lumped together simply as *minim* – 'sects'. Sometimes these last are even called 'Sadducees' without further elucidation as to whether they are the Sadducees of the New Testament period or another, more 'Zealot' group earlier or contemporaneous with them.

This *Sadducee* notation is also reflected in the important allusion, mentioned above, found in Qumran documents, 'the Sons of Zadok', which plays on the evocation of the term in the vision at the end of the Prophet Ezekiel (chapters 40–48) of the reconstructed Temple or the Temple of the Last Days. Related to it, in both Qumran texts and the New Testament, is the *Righteousness* and *Justification* ideology also expressed in terms of the letters *Z–D–K*, which is, as we have seen, the Hebrew root of the Greek 'Sadducee'. For the moment, it is sufficient to understand that the Sadducees depicted in the Qumran materials, if we can call them this, have almost nothing in common with those pictured in the New Testament or Josephus.

Where these more or less opposing groups of Sadducees – Herodian (Establishment) or separatist (Purist) – are concerned, there are, to be sure, common approaches to legal minutiae that so obsess the authors of Talmudic tradition and, one might add, their contemporary heirs. However, in the broad lines of hostility towards the Establishment and, for instance, its fornication – including divorce, marriage, and incest – there is almost nothing in common between them. Nor is there anything in common between them regarding *antagonism to foreign rule*, including foreign-appointed kings, foreign-appointed High Priests, and foreign gifts and sacrifices in the Temple, which so obsess the sectaries at Qumran.

These issues are also fundamental to those known in this period as 'Zealots', those who follow the demands of the *zeal*-oriented Covenant of Phineas (Num. 25:6–13), if 'Zealots' can be distinguished in any real way from these kinds of Purist Sadducees or Palestinian Christians. Where the relationship of Qumran to so-called 'Zealots' – later we shall also speak of '*Sicarii*' – is concerned, it is interesting to point out that Phineas, portrayed in Numbers as functioning in the wilderness at the time of Moses, is accorded the High Priestly Covenant in perpetuity, because of the 'zeal' he displayed in killing backsliders who were marrying foreigners, thereby deflecting *pollution* from the camp of Israel.

1 Maccabees 2:26 raises this Covenant on behalf of Judas Maccabee's father, Mattathias, and presumably all of his descendants succeeding to him. But this Phineas, who was Aaron's grandson, was also the High Priestly ancestor of the Zadok of David's time, an important connection between the *Zealot* and *Zadokite* ideologies. This idea of 'pollution' in the camp of Israel in the wilderness as relating to the issue of *mixing* with foreigners has important ramifications in the Qumran documents and is the focus of the 'Zealot' ethos.[1]

Sadducees, Essenes, and Zealots

The group Josephus and others following him call 'Essenes' also have much in common with Qumran *Sadducees* – not to mention with the so-called Zealots and Palestinian Christians following James – but, as with Opposition or Purist Sadducees, nothing with Establishment *Sadducees* of the Herodian period as pictured in Josephus and the New Testament.

There is an even better description of these Essenes, which includes several important points linking them closely with James' followers in Palestine, in a work called the *Refutation of All Heresies*, attributed to Hippolytus, an early third-century Church writer in Rome (160–235). This description is clearly a more detailed and possibly an even earlier version of Josephus' description of the Essenes in the *Jewish War*. In it, 'Zealots' and their more extreme counterparts, the '*Sicarii*' ('Assassins' – so styled because of the Arab-style dagger they concealed under their cloaks) are seen only as *Essenes* less prepared to compromise.[2] This is important and clarifies the sectarian situation in Palestine considerably.

There are other interesting and unique traditions in this work attributed to Hippolytus. One, for instance, identifies Jesus' second brother Simon with the Simon called 'the Zealot' in the Apostle lists of Luke and Acts. This cognomen, 'Zealot', is garbled somewhat or purposefully misconstrued in Mark and Matthew into the 'Cananaean' or 'Canaanite'. It is impossible to know where Hippolytus obtained these traditions, but that 'Simon the Zealot' was Jesus' second brother we would have been able to deduce even without recourse to Hippolytus, though this is useful in verifying such an analysis. It will also have a bearing on the problem of Simeon bar Cleophas, Jesus' and James' purported 'first cousin'.

Eventually we will be able to make sense of all these confusions relating to Jesus' mother, father, uncle and close cousins but, for the moment, suffice it to say that, with the destruction of the Jerusalem centre and its traditions in the wake of the Uprising against Rome in 70 CE, the resultant vacuum was inevitably filled by Gentile Christianity overseas. This resulted in the downplaying of Jesus' brothers and close family members, including so-called 'uncles' and 'cousins', until they were finally all but eliminated from the tradition.

At the end of the fourth century, Epiphanius, whose work was called in Greek the *Panarion* (*Medicine Box – Against Heresies* in Latin), has the greatest difficulty distinguishing Essenes from a group he calls 'the Jessaeans', followers, according to him, of David's father Jesse or of Jesus himself, or even 'Ossaeans', whatever it might mean.[3] This is not surprising, because even modern confusions relating to the term 'Essene' are legion. For this Josephus is partly responsible.

Philo of Alexandria, the first-century Jewish philosopher referred to above, describes a similar group in Egypt he calls '*Theraputae*', because of their expertise in health or medicinal matters, including presumably curings.[4] For its part, the New Testament does not refer to Essenes at all, nor does the *Talmud*, not at least *qua* Essenes.

This may be explained by the fact that all groups of this kind are simply being referred to retrospectively, as we have noted, as *minim* ('sects') or *Saddukim* ('Sadducees') after the Pharisees cum Rabbis took control of Jewish life in the wake of the failure of the Uprising against Rome. In using these notations, no attempt was made to draw fine distinctions, if in fact these were even appreciated by the time the Talmudic materials were finally redacted in the 'Oral Law' or Mishnah in the second and third centuries CE.

The *Talmud* does refer to 'Zealots' as *Kanna'im* ('those jealous of' or 'zealous for'), but not really as a group – rather simply as avenging priests in the Temple. This will have relevance to the way James' death is portrayed in early Church sources.⁵ This avenging zeal is not surprising in view of how the ethos of this group is explained in terms of 'the zeal of Phineas'.

1 Maccabees 2:28, as noted, evokes this slogan in describing how the progenitor of the Maccabean family, Mattathias, acted against backsliders, namely those who would abrogate the traditions of the Forefathers and collaborate with foreign rule. He slays them on the altar at Modein, the family place of origin, though precisely what altar this could have been defies explanation. The episode in the *Talmud* also explains the confusion in the Gospels between *Simon the Zealot* and the sobriquet *Cananaean*, the Hebrew '*Kanna'im*' going straight into the Greek transliteration 'Cananaean' or 'Canaanite' in English.⁶

The surprising absence of references to 'Essenes' *per se* in the New Testament is even more easily explained. The New Testament refers to Pharisees, Sadducees (sometimes 'Scribes'), Herodians, and even to a certain extent Zealots – these, as in the case of Simon the Zealot, within Jesus' following, not outside it. The same goes for the term *Sicarii*, probably reprised by names like Judas *Iscariot* and his father, Simon *Iscariot* (*thus* – John 6:71) and straightforwardly transliterated into Greek in Acts 21:38. The reason Josephus' Essenes are missing from this list is that this is the group that the New Testament is itself. That said, the New Testament is developing additional terminology to describe itself, that of 'Nazoraeans'/'Nazirites'/'Nazrenes' or, as some like Hippolytus would have it, 'Naassenes', a seeming combination of Nazrenes and Essenes.⁷ Though this complicates the situation, for Hippolytus these last are basically synonymous both with Essenes and another group always mentioned as connected to James, 'the *Ebionites*' or 'the Poor'.

The New Testament is aware of 'the Poor' allusions, and other related terms such as 'the Meek' or 'these Little Ones'; as is Qumran, which knows an additional variation, 'the Simple of Judah doing *Torah*', and a further one related to these and the manner in which the Gospels describe John the Baptist's activities in the wilderness, 'the Way'.⁸ This allusion, which is in omnipresent use at Qumran where it is applied to 'wilderness' activities too, is also in use in the New Testament as an alternative name for Christianity in Palestine.⁹ But all of these names are, obviously, by the middle of the first century, denoting Jewish Christians of one kind or another.

One of the problems with Josephus' picture of the sects is that, since he is covering a chronological time frame of some two hundred and fifty years, one does not really know to which period his points apply. His accounts are usually derivative and accurate only for the period in which he lives. Even here, as observed, he often dissembles, because of his own embarrassing relations with sectarian groups and his pre-Flavian, revolutionary past. As one can see in his *War* or his *Vita*, he was under tremendous pressure to explain his past and justify actions that enabled him, among the very few who participated in these cataclysmic events, to survive, and he constantly defends himself against attacks on his behaviour and his loyalty to Rome. Though Josephus was an important prophetical and biographical underwriter of the rise of Vespasian and Titus to power, Titus, who was involved with the Herodian princess Bernice – someone Josephus also knew – seems to have died or been removed under mysterious circumstances in 81 CE just two years after his father.

It is quite likely that Josephus also fell foul of Titus' younger brother and successor, Domitian (81–96), who was considered to be as mad, unpredictable, and sadistically violent as Nero had been. Indeed, the mercurial Domitian seems to have executed his secretary, Josephus' publisher Epaphroditus, who had also been Nero's secretary previously and someone with whom Paul appears to have been extremely intimate.[10] In addition, this Epaphroditus, as is clear from Josephus' introductions, encouraged Josephus in all his works, particularly his *Antiquities*, which was published in 94 CE just a little before both disappeared from the scene. Like Epaphroditus, Josephus just drops from sight around this time and may or may not have been executed in the course of Domitian's often brutal or sadistic approach to political affairs. Trajan (98–117), whose father had been commander of the Tenth Legion in Palestine under Vespasian and Titus, then proceeded to have his difficulties with Messianic agitation and unrest, particularly in the eastern portions of his empire.

For instance, his Sadducees bear no relation to the Qumran Sadducees (or 'Essenes') whatsoever. As he tells us quite straightforwardly, the former were dominated in all things by the Pharisees, except, it would appear, in the matter of resurrection of the dead, a distinction the New Testament is also quick to seize on.[11] His Sadducees are simply upper-class priests of the Herodian period, but how these Sadducees relate to the Maccabeans, who had been the High Priests for a century or more previously, is impossible to say.

The Maccabees, by and large, must be considered Sadducees, but they bear almost no relationship to the Sadducees Josephus and the New Testament are describing in the first century. In fact, as I have been at pains to point out, they bear more relationship to Qumran and to those later called 'Zealots' than anything else. I have in previous works referred to the Qumran or 'Purist Sadducees' as 'Messianic Sadducees', taking into account their Messianic tendencies. Others might wish to call them 'Essenes' or 'Zealots', as they do indeed display characteristics of both as described in Josephus. But they also display characteristics of what in other quarters are being called Nazoraeans/Nazrenes/Jewish Christians or *Ebionites*.

The point is that these sects or terminologies tend to slide around a good deal, depending on who is doing the observing, what vocabulary he is employing, and what his own misunderstandings or prejudices might be. Josephus is no exception. For instance, in his *Vita* he suddenly tells us about a 'wilderness' sojourn he made during a trial he says he was conducting of all the sects. There he meets a teacher he calls '*Banus*' – not a name, but a title or cognomen of some kind, probably having something to do with *bathing* – without telling us that this teacher is almost indistinguishable from Jewish Christians or Essenes, the group heading the list of Jewish sects he provides. His description of the activities of '*Banus*' will also have a bearing on how we are to understand James in relation to Josephus' testimonies.

There is indeed a bewildering plethora of these groups. This diminishes only when one appreciates the verbal acrobatics involved where subversive or threatening sects or a given writer's own embarrassing relations with them are concerned. In order to sort these various groups out, it is better simply to group them according to whether they supported the Pharisee Roman/Herodian Establishment or opposed it. Likewise, it is often more edifying to look at groups in terms of who their common enemies were. Then, as in the case of all the apparent Jameses, Simons, Judases, and Marys relating to Jesus' family, much duplication simply disappears.

Seen in this way, Jewish or Palestinian Christians (whatever might be meant by such designations), James' Jerusalem Church or Jerusalem Community, succeeded by Ebionites, Essenes, Zealots, and the group responsible for the documents found at Qumran – all can be thought of as opposed to the reigning Herodian Establishment and looked on as the various constituents of the Opposition Alliance.

The Qumran documents, for example, are not simply a random collection of disparate sectarian writings, but extremely homogeneous ones, betokening a movement. The same ideology, nomenclature, and dramatis personae move from document to document regardless of style or authorship. For instance, one never encounters a document approving of the contemporary Establishment – which in the writer's view must be seen as the Herodian one – never a document that is accommodating and not militant, zealous or apocalyptic.

For this reason, it is proper to refer to the authors of these documents as comprising a Movement of some kind which is always, at its core, anti-Establishment. Its precise name for the moment must be left indeterminate, but 'the Way', 'the Sons of Zadok', 'the Poor', 'the Simple', 'the Meek', 'the Perfect', 'the Sons of Light', 'the Holy Ones' or combinations such as 'the Zealots for the Day of Vengeance', 'the Poor Ones of Piety', 'the Zealots for Righteousness' and 'Perfect of the Way' are all terms cropping up in their repertoire as self-designations.

To add to all these groups, one has the bewildering assortment referred to by Church heresiologists of the third to the fifth centuries, like Naassenes, Nazoraeans, Sampsaeans ('Sabaeans' as we shall see) and Elchasaites, most located on the other side of the Jordan extending on up to Syria and Northern Iraq and significantly holding James' name in particular reverence – some, like the Ebionites, in absolute awe. Where the relationship of these groups to the Qumran documents, or for that matter to the New Testament, is concerned, their location across the Jordan in that 'Damascus' region so important to both is particularly significant. All of these groups too can be considered as allied or related in some way, all being anti-Establishment and having common enemies.

Where the first century CE is concerned, it is also useful to consider the opposition groups in terms of their various degrees of 'zeal', extending from the more pacifist to the more violent. This is how Hippolytus discusses his 'Essenes', who range by degrees to the most extreme *Sicarii*, namely those Josephus describes as committing suicide on Masada along the Dead Sea south of Qumran in the last instalment of the War against Rome. If one keeps one's eyes firmly fixed on support of or opposition to the Herodian Establishment, supplanting the Maccabean from the 60s to the 30s BC, one will never go far astray. Those supporting this Establishment can, echoing language found in the Dead Sea Scrolls, be described as 'seeking accommodation with foreigners', which the Greco-Idumaean Herodians and their Roman overlords were most certainly considered to be.

These are the kinds of distinctions that will prove useful in considering the most well-known Establishment Party, 'the Pharisees', who in their current embodiment of Rabbinic Judaism still constitute the Establishment among Jews today. This is a vivid reminder of just how enduring these traditions can be. Whether in their present-day Orthodox, Conservative, Liberal, or Reform embodiments, all not only claim to be heirs to the Pharisaic legacy but in addition – and, as we shall see, even more astonishing – that the Pharisees were *the popular party of the first century* CE.

For this reason, many Jews, even secular ones, are unable to grasp the true import of their own *Hanukkah* festivities, which are basically a celebration of Maccabean, anti-foreign, non-accommodationist, priestly zeal. This is because this tradition, too, which is diametrically opposed to the inherited one, has been downplayed, trivialized and virtually written out of Talmudic literature, where most references to the Maccabees are negative for the same reason that they are in Christianity.

It is no wonder that many scholars, Christian and Jewish alike, thought that the Maccabeans could have been candidates for 'the Wicked Priest', so important in the nomenclature of the Dead Sea Scrolls when these documents first appeared. Thus, the view was widely disseminated that the Maccabees had 'usurped' the High Priesthood from a previously more legitimate one.[12] This was not only to misunderstand the essence of the Maccabean Uprising, but the Qumran position with regard to such matters.

Anti-Nationalist Pharisees and Zealots

But the Pharisees were not the popular party of their time and place, despite Josephus' attempts – and those of Rabbinic Judaism thereafter – to prove otherwise. To clarify and highlight this, I have in my work generally redefined Pharisees as those 'seeking accommodation with foreigners'. This plays on phraseology in use at Qumran to characterize its opponents or enemies, 'the Seekers after Smooth Things' – even 'Smoothies'. Clearly this is a hostile designation. It is also possible to apply this appellation to Pauline or Overseas Christians, who, in terms of political attitudes anyhow, are not very different from Pharisees. This puts the proposition in the broad brushstrokes that have meaning for the period before us, dispensing with the kind of legal hair-splitting one usually hears about.

The Establishment groups, quite simply put, were the Pharisees, Sadducees and Herodians, the last being those members of the Herodian power structure and their associates not encompassed under the preceding two designations. One might as well add to these Pauline or Overseas Gentile Christians as the only Christian group of any consequence that really survived in the West after the obliteration of the Jerusalem centre and the Temple. If there is any question about this, one has only to look at Romans 13:1–7 noted above and the attitudes towards Roman law and authority displayed there.

Where, for instance, Roman citizenship is concerned, as Acts portrays events, Paul, unlike the other Apostles and, to be sure Jesus himself, is never loath to evoke this when he thinks it will do him some good or save him. In this sense, Paul is the arch accommodationist. So, too, is Rabbi Yohanan ben Zacchai, who, as we saw, applies what the Qumran documents and Josephus attest to be the most precious prophecy of the Jewish people of the time – 'the Star Prophecy' – to the destroyer of Jerusalem, the Emperor Vespasian. This would have been an impossibility for those responsible for the writings found at Qumran, whose tongues would have stuck to the proverbial 'roofs of their mouths' before indulging in such obsequious flattery.

But as I have been at pains to assert, Pauline Christianity and Rabbinic Judaism are two sides of the same coin. Both develop in conjunction with each other and both follow an accommodationist policy towards Rome, which is why no doubt both survived. In this context, the main difference is that one is pro-Law and the other against it. But the points of accommodation here are not the minor ones belaboured in Rabbinic tradition, such as those connected with dietary regulations, sexual purification or Sabbath observation, though these played a part. Rather, they are the broad lines of accommodation with foreigners in a political sense, seen by Qumran and 'Zealot'-style groups generally as 'breaking the Law'.[13]

These included, in addition to opposition to foreign kings, which the Herodians most certainly were considered to be by opposition groups, and opposition to the foreign appointment of High Priests – a consequence of the destruction of the Maccabean family by Herod, to which so-called 'Zealots' were so opposed, and most likely Jamesian Christians as well, opposition to the receipt of gifts or sacrifices in the Temple from or on behalf of foreigners, seen at Qumran and probably by Jewish Christians as well as 'pollution of the Temple'. This, as will be seen below, triggered the Uprising against Rome. Finally there were the sexual and marital practices to which the Pharisees and Sadducees turned a blind eye but which were opposed in the most extreme manner by all groups like those at Qumran and early Christians of the 'Jamesian' persuasion.

So far as Qumran was concerned, these practices included polygamy, divorce and, most importantly for making secure identifications in this period, *marriage with nieces* or *close family cousins*. This last was simply considered an extension of the ban on incest at Qumran.[14] Like the complaints of John the Baptist against the Establishment, such criticisms were obviously aimed at members of the Herodian family and their supporters. All are included under the broad phraseology of 'fornication' at Qumran, the specific condemnation of which is also prominent in all reports and traditions associated with James' teachings and directives.[15]

That the Pharisees are the popular party in this period, which the New Testament too in the interests of its anti-Jewish polemic is anxious to promote, is repeatedly and definitively gainsaid by Josephus, despite his attempts, pro-Roman and Pharisee fellow traveller that he is, to promote it. Over and over again, Josephus presents, often unwittingly, the people as opposing the *anti-nationalist* policies of the Pharisees. Predictably, *the people*, as in most times and places, are predominantly nationalist. They may have been forced to go along with the Pharisees and the Rabbinic Party that succeeded them after the fall of the Temple and the elimination of all serious opposition groups, but before this they most often opposed them.

For instance, it is clear that the Maccabean Uprising was not Pharisaic, yet this was most certainly *popular*. In fact, the Pharisees may have got their name, which means 'those who separated from' or 'splitters away', from a group in the second century BC described in 1 Maccabees as deserting the cause of the Maccabeans in favour of a foreign-appointed High Priestly claimant (7:13–18). 2 Maccabees 14:2 describes this person, whose only claim to the High Priesthood seems to have been genealogical, as having 'incurred pollution at the time of the Uprising'.[16] He obviously made no claims to the kind of higher 'Righteousness' and/or 'Piety' the *Zealot* heirs to the Maccabees appear to be demanding from the outbreak of this Movement between 4 BC and 7 CE (the time of Jesus' birth in the Gospel of Luke) to the War against Rome seventy years later, a demand also echoed in the New Testament Letter to the Hebrews (7:26).

Two generations later, Alexander Jannaeus (103–76 BC), Judas Maccabee's grand-nephew, is having similiar problems with Greco-Seleucid intervention before the Romans put an end to their regime in Syria in the next generation. Because of Alexander's cruelty, the people at first appear to favour intervention by the Seleucid King Demetrius. This event also appears to be described in the Dead Sea Scrolls, albeit retrospectively.

The Commentary on Nahum, as part of its lead-in to patently similar problems at the time of its composition after the coming of the Romans – whom it refers to as 'the *Kittim*' – is trying to delineate the atrociousness of the anti-nationalist policies of its opponents, denoted derogatorily as 'the Seekers after Smooth Things'. These last the Commentary depicts as supporting the incursion of Demetrius ('. . . trius' in the *Pesher*) and even 'inviting' him into the country.[17] It is at this moment, too, that Josephus first applies the notation 'Pharisees' to describe such groups.

Right from the start, Alexander appears to be having problems with them and must, therefore, be considered a Sadducee. Finally, when Alexander takes to the 'wilderness' around Jerusalem in the style of his great-uncle Judas Maccabee, as well as the sectaries at Qumran and John the Baptist, the people have a change of heart and support him, defeating the Syrians.[18] Alexander then turns on the Pharisees, who collaborated with the foreign invaders and betrayed him, crucifying some eight hundred of them or, as Josephus depicts it, hanging them up alive. It would appear that this event is also being described somewhat disapprovingly – presumably because of the 'hanging' or 'crucifixion' involved – in the Nahum Commentary, which is not otherwise hostile to Alexander. On the contrary, it is sympathetic to him.[19] However this may be, it is clear that *the people*, after some initial hesitation, *support* Alexander Jannaeus.

In the next generation, that of the Roman conquest (63 BC), there is another split between nationalists and anti-nationalists, this time between Alexander's obviously Sadducean younger son Aristobulus II (67–49 BC) and his more accommodating older brother Hyrcanus II (76–31 BC), the only Maccabean supporting the Pharisees. Once again, *the people support Aristobulus*, who in Josephus' own words 'turned sick of servility' and refused to abase himself before the Roman commander Pompey, who is coming in via Syria and Transjordan at precisely this moment.[20]

It is in the course of these events that the father of Herod – on his father's side, a Hellenized Idumaean; on his mother's, an Arab – ingratiates himself with the Romans, in the process promoting the more manageable and docile older brother, Hyrcanus, the High Priest enjoying Pharisee support. As a result, Herod's father – who was called Antipater – makes himself the first Roman Procurator in Palestine. Eventually he was able to secure for his son not only the kingship in Palestine, but also a Roman citizenship for himself and his heirs for services rendered in the interests of Rome in perpetuity.

During the course of these troubles, Josephus specifically identifies as

41

'Pharisees' those who take vengeance on the priestly supporters of the 'Zealot' younger brother Aristobulus – in this instance, equivalent to nationalist or 'Purist' Sadducees – who take refuge, significantly, in the Temple. These Pharisees *co-operate with* Herod's father Antipater and join the Romans in storming the Temple *against the will of the people*. As Josephus bears witness, they engage in the wholesale slaughter that ensues even more enthusiastically than the Romans. Josephus rather pictures the Romans as watching in bemused astonishment as these prototypically 'Zealot' priestly supporters of Aristobulus are cut down as they dutifully perform the obligatory Temple sacrifices even as the Roman soldiers and their Pharisee allies overwhelm them.[21]

At this point in his more detailed account in the *Antiquities*, Josephus introduces two characters missing from the *Jewish War*, two principal Pharisees he calls 'Pollio and Sameas'.[22] Since they are obviously meant to be representations of *famous* Pharisees, these are more than likely the legendary heroes of the *Talmud*, the Rabbinic pair Hillel and Shammai, though they could be the one preceding those two, who have similar names.

Josephus notes Pollio's and Sameas' soothsaying powers in predicting how Herod would eventually become king. This kind of soothsaying is also emulated with equally salutary effect in a later generation by another self-professed Pharisee, Josephus himself, not to mention the so-called 'prophets and teachers' involved in the founding of Paul's Antioch community, where 'Christians' were first called Christians according to Acts 11:26. Even more to the point, Josephus notes their recommendation to the people, 'to open the gates to Herod' and the Roman army, a recommendation that should be seen as paradigmatic of the Pharisee Party.[23]

The date is 37 BC. Herod and his Roman sponsors had been worsted with Persian help by a scion of the Maccabean family, the son of the Aristobulus mentioned above, Antigonus. Herod, who had fled to Rome, returned with a Roman army provided him by Mark Anthony. It is at this point that Pollio/Hillel and Sameas/Shammai give their prototypical advice to 'open the gates to Herod', which *the people*, as usual, promptly reject in favour of resistance. It is in the course of these events that Herod, by astute political manoeuvring and simple bloody-mindedness, is able to obtain the title of King, that is, 'King of the Jews',[24] even though he was not himself Jewish or of Jewish blood.

Rather he had 'spies posted everywhere' and 'never left off taking vengeance on those who had opposed him', which included the previously pro-Maccabean, presumably Sadducean, Sanhedrin. This he completely decimated, 'while those who supported him, he showered with benefits of all kinds' and promoted;[25] chief among whom were the two Pharisee leaders, Pollio and Sameas, the only ones from the previous Maccabean-dominated and nationalist Sanhedrin to survive. It is at this point, in 37 BC, that one can really begin to speak of a *Pharisee-dominated* Sanhedrin, the one pictured in the New Testament.

From this point on, particularly after the death of Herod in 4 BC, we get an endless succession of revolts until the final Uprising in 66–70 CE. This last certainly has to be considered 'popular', as all groups except the Pharisees, the Herodians and the High Priests, even the so-called 'Essenes' and, one must assume, the 'Jewish Christians' participated in it. With the demise of the Maccabean family too, this turmoil is exacerbated by a new principle of leadership authority, which probably should be called 'Messianic'. The High Priests created by the Herods are completely decimated by the 'Zealots' – and now these really are *Zealots*.

The Messianic Roots of the Uprising

It is a curious coincidence that Josephus launches into both his descriptions of the Jewish sects in the *War* and the *Antiquities* at just the point he comes to describe the Movement founded by the Judas *the Galilean*. This he calls a new 'philosophy which our people were before unacquainted with'.[26] In the *Antiquities*, as we saw, he adds another individual to his description of its beginnings. Someone he neglected to mention in the *War*, he refers to him mysteriously simply as '*Saddok*', that is to say, '*Zadok*' or 'the *Zaddik*'.

We shall have occasion variously below to describe this Fourth Philosophy or Movement, which Josephus declines to identify further, except to say that 'they had an inviolable attachment to liberty and will not call any *man* Lord'.[27] At present, it is sufficient to point out that this group or movement arises at just the moment one would expect it to, when the previous leadership has been eliminated and new leadership principles, including the *Messianic*, emerge.

Eleven years after the death of Herod the Romans annexed the country and, in anticipation of direct taxation by governors or procurators, imposed a census. This is the 6–7 CE Census of Quirinius (Cyrenius), Roman Governor in Syria, the Census by which the Gospel of Luke dates the birth of Jesus (2:1). The Gospel of Matthew by contrast has Jesus being born some time before the death of Herod in 4 BC, so that Herod can attempt to chase him down and kill all the Jewish children, as did Pharaoh at the time of *the birth of Moses*. The two accounts are, of course, irreconcilable.

This is the Census, and the taxation consonant upon it, referred to above, which 'the Zealots' or '*Sicarii*' oppose and against which Judas the Galilean and '*Saddok*' preach. It is supported by the Pharisees and, of course, *Herodian* Sadducees. This issue is also a burning one for Gospel narratives, and Jesus' riposte concerning it to 'the Pharisees and the Herodians' (Matt. 22:21; rather termed 'spies' in Luke 20:20), 'render unto Caesar what is Caesar's and God what is God's', has now become proverbial – strange because the Gospels have Jesus adopting *the Pharisee policy* on this.[28]

There is, in fact, a plethora of revolutionary outbursts even at the time of the death of Herod, with which the unrest begins, by groups Josephus pictures as being *zealous for the Law* – Mosaic not Roman – and as having 'an inviolable attachment to liberty'. One of these, led by someone he calls Judas Sepphoraeus – probably identical with Judas the Galilean – broke into the arsenal at Sepphoris in 4 BC, the principal town at that time in Galilee.[29] There is no doubt about the popularity of the Movement, because Josephus, in his lengthy description of it and the woes the people suffered in consequence of their support for it in the *Antiquities*, admits not only that 'our young men were zealous for it' but that 'the nation was infected by it to an incredible degree'.[30]

In addition to Jesus' birth being presented as coincident with its inception and the fact that its appearance triggers Josephus' discussion of the sects of his time, there is another interesting aspect to this Movement. At the end of the *Jewish War*, when describing the signs and wonders that presaged the fall of the Temple, of which people as superstitious as the Romans were so enamoured, Josephus finally reveals something that he neglected for some reason to tell us earlier. He claims that

> the thing that most moved the people to revolt against Rome was an ambiguous prophecy from their Scripture [ambiguous presumably because it was capable of so many interpretations] that one from their country *should rule the entire world*.

As with his picture of 'the Zealot woes', for Josephus they had only themselves to blame for what ensued, because they interpreted this oracle 'to suit themselves and went so mad because of it'.[31]

But this is precisely the Prophecy he has just finished applying to Vespasian, thus saving his own skin – as, one might add, did R. Yohanan and his Pharisees along with him. He does so again in this passage. This is the prophecy we have been calling 'the World Ruler' or 'Messianic Prophecy', 'the *Star Prophecy*'. At Qumran, where it occurs three times even in the extant corpus, it receives a wholly other, completely uncompromising, nationalistic and Messianic interpretation. In addition to remarking earlier how 'zealous' the young men were for this approach, Josephus notes that

> The Jews thought this prediction applied only to themselves, and therefore, many of their most learned men had deceived themselves in this determination.

But this is precisely the Qumran interpretation as well, the representatives of which would never have stooped to the cynical opportunism of applying it to the destroyer of Jerusalem Vespasian, whatever the short-term benefits. In revealing this, Josephus, of course, also reveals that Zealots and other parties displaying the 'zeal of Phineas' were not simply political, but religious and *Messianic* as well.

This is proof that the Uprising against Rome, aside from being popular – which it was most definitely – was also *Messianic*. What is more, that since the Uprising was Messianic – and ethically and historically this is of the utmost importance – the Jews lost everything not because they *opposed the Messiah*, as early Church Fathers or the New Testament in their tendentious presentation of Christ's death and its meaning would have us believe, but, on the contrary, because they *were so uncompromisingly Messianic*. This is no mean proposition and constitutes an important reversal or inversion of historical invective as it has come down to us.

Not only was the Uprising aimed at burning the palaces of the High Priests and the Herodian Kings but the debt records as well, in order, as Josephus makes clear, 'to turn the Poor against the Rich'.[32] Once again, this is the same genre of language evinced in the Letter of James and the Dead Sea Scrolls in their condemnation of 'the Rich'. It is also the language applied to the Movement led by James, by Paul (Gal. 2:10) and to the later Ebionites, so named because of it, as well as the nomenclature used by the Movement represented by the Scrolls to describe its own rank and file – called there as well 'the *Ebionim*' or 'the Poor'.[33]

Before leaving this subject of the outbreak of the Uprising in 66 CE, it is important to note that in a final moment of unparalleled candour

45

Josephus tells us that it was 'the principal Pharisees, the Chief Priests, the men of power [by which he means Herodians], and all those desirous for peace' who invited the Roman army into Jerusalem 'to put down the Uprising'. This is what Josephus meant in the Introduction to the *War* about how the Romans were invited into the city by 'the Jews' own leaders'.[34]

Here one comes to an even more startling detail provided by Josephus, if what he seems to be saying can be tied to characters we know in early Christian history. The intermediary in this process of inviting the Roman army into the city was a member of the Herodian family called 'Saulus' or 'Saul'. He is the one who delivered the message of call it 'the Peace Coalition' to the Roman army camped outside Jerusalem to enter, and a final report even *to Nero's headquarters*, then in Corinth in Greece, a favourite haunt too of the religious activities of 'Paul'. There will be more to say about this 'Saul' presently; he seems also to have been in Agrippa II's palace or the Citadel when the Roman garrison surrendered and were all butchered except for the captain of the guard who agreed to be *circumcised*.[35]

The anti-national, pro-Roman policy of the Pharisees should by now be clear. This is also the stance of the Pauline Gentile Christians, following the teaching of the person above, who even describes himself as having been trained as a Pharisee and, according to the picture in Acts anyhow, vaunts a Roman citizenship, something not easily acquired in these turbulent times. Nor can the Pharisees in this period by any twist of the imagination be considered 'the popular party'. If anything, the Zealot and/or Messianic were the popular parties (as nationalist parties predictably are) at least until the fall of the Temple and the re-education policy undertaken by the heirs of the Pharisees under Roman suzerainty thereafter.

The Coming of the Romans and the Herodians

Then what is the key to events, as described in the above analysis? It is the rise of the Herodians and the coming of the Romans. This is the reason for the widespread disaffection being expressed in this period and most of the unrest. This is also the crucial factor for making chronological determinations where the Dead Sea Scrolls are concerned, if one attempts to date them by the internal parameters of what is being said and expressed in them, rather than by external ones such as archaeology, palaeography, or carbon testing, all inconclusive. This was the pivotal mistake in early research relating to them, encouraged by the cartel that previously governed Scroll publication – and the interpretation it disseminated. This error led to the widespread perception that 'the Wicked Priest' mentioned in the Scrolls – particularly in the commentaries or *pesharim* – and the Establishment he represented, against which the Scrolls so fulminate, were Maccabean.

After the fall of the Maccabeans, Roman rule was imposed, sometimes through Herodian kings or sometimes more directly through Roman procurators. On occasion the two co-existed, as in the period just after the death of Herod's grandson Agrippa I in 44 CE. After the fall of the Temple the situation is unclear, because we have no Josephus to report it, and therefore we are without the tremendous detail he provides. It is against the backdrop of the fall of the Maccabeans and the rise of the Herodians in the first century BC, that the rise of various sects or movements, particularly nationalistic or Messianic ones, must be gauged. Again, if one keeps this and the fact of Roman power firmly before one's eyes, then almost all else follows comparatively easily.

We have already seen how these events transpired. First there was the Maccabean Revolution in 167 BC against the imposition of Syrian decrees and Hellenistic customs. These included hiding one's circumcision, which of course so infuriated incipient Zealots, naked athletic events in a newly constructed gymnasium, and the introduction of idols on the Temple Mount, most particularly the Olympian Zeus, which via a distorted transliteration into the Hebrew turned into what now is called 'the Abomination of the Desolation'.[36] This struggle over Hellenization continued for the next two hundred and fifty years. It is neither accidental nor unimportant that Christianity in the form we know it *represents its final triumph*.

This is moved along considerably by the imposition of Herodian rule and the Herodian or Pauline behaviour of being a Jew to the Jew, a Greek to the Greeks, 'a Law-Breaker to the Law-Breakers, a Law-Keeper to the Law-Keepers', that is, to do whatever was required, as Paul puts it in 1 Corinthians 9:24, to 'win . . . not beat the air'. Here Paul uses the imagery of stadium athletics, deliberately calculated to send his interlocutors, like James' Jerusalem Church 'Zealots' into paroxysms of rage. Herod, his putative forebear, as will be shown, believed most definitely in *winning not beating the air*.

The Dead Sea Scrolls provide the counterpoint, as does James – that is, not 'win at any costs' but martyrdom. Certainly these movements are 'old-fashioned', with commitment to absolute purity, unbending

Righteousness and uncompromising integrity, but this is perhaps their charm. In times where so much is so relative, there is something attractive about such above-board, totally honest and absolutely unyielding Piety and purity. There were no shades or reservations, no ifs, buts or temporizing. Everything is in the absolutely stark shades of Light or Dark, *engagé*, or, as Qumran eloquently puts it in numerous documents, 'straight', 'not straying to the right or to the left'.[37] If nothing else, their elegance, steadfastness and total commitment to absolute Righteousness cannot fail to impress the modern world as it rediscovers them.

For his part, Paul pretends not to understand this ethos, or calls it 'weak' (Rom. 14:1ff. and 1 Cor. 14:7ff.). Yet, complaining about attachment to circumcision, when Maccabean and Zealot martyrs for over two hundred and fifty years had laid down their lives rather than abjure it, is totally to close one's eyes to the driving forces in Palestine throughout this period. These are admirably summed up in the Maccabee Books, missing, not surprisingly, from the Jewish canon as it ultimately came down to us. Josephus, too, depicts ample examples of this ethos and the countless martyrs it produced long before martyrdom became prototypical of the ethos that Christianity claimed for itself.

Along with Herodian rule came the Romans. The first appearance of the Romans in the Eastern Mediterranean came just prior to this period in the late stages of the Punic War. They actually made their presence felt in the 60s BC, when they turned Syria into a Roman province, eliminating the last vestiges of Seleucid rule. Just as Caesar was making his inroads into Transalpine Gaul, the Rhine, Britain, and Spain in the West, Pompey was undertaking the siege of Jerusalem in 63 BC. He was abetted in this by internal dissensions within the Maccabean family itself, but also by a half-Arab, Hellenized intermediary by the name of Antipater, the father of Herod.

Not only does Antipater successfully ingratiate himself with Pompey and his adjutants – the most well known of whom was Mark Anthony – but he ends up as the first Roman Procurator in Palestine and the ultimate arbiter of political events there. After the assassination of Julius Caesar twenty years later, Mark Anthony, who distinguished himself in Palestinian campaigning, ultimately abets Antipater's son Herod in obtaining the Jewish Crown. Herod finishes the job of obliterating the Maccabean family. Those he doesn't execute he marries. But even these he eventually butchers, including his favourite wife Mariamme, the last Maccabean princess, whom he charged with unfaithfulness with his brother Joseph – the first 'Joseph and Mary' story – while he is away in Rome getting Octavius to reconfirm the crown Anthony had conferred on him (29 BC).

Mariamme was the granddaughter of both of Alexander Jannaeus' sons, Aristobulus and Hyrcanus, whose squabbling had brought the Herodians and the Romans into the country in the first place. In the end, Herod even had his two sons by her – who had been brought up in Rome – put to death, presumably because he was jealous of their Maccabean blood and because the crowd preferred them to him. Here Herod really did *kill all the Jewish children* who sought to replace him, as Matthew 2:17 would have it, but these were rather his own children with Maccabean blood! This behaviour even shocked his Roman sponsors, particularly Augustus, who upheld family values and was by all reports very displeased with it.[38]

But Herod survived all, got away with everything, including the absolute obliteration of the Maccabean family and grafting his own family on whatever remained of it, in the manner spoken of by Paul in Romans.[39] This mostly Idumaean, Greco-Arab line continued for three more generations until Titus, the man responsible for burning Jerusalem, made off with Bernice, a descendant of this line, as Caesar and Anthony had made off with Cleopatra – one of the last descendants of Alexander's ruling élite – before him. Nor does this give any more pleasure to the people of Rome – who do not appear to have wished to see a Herodian princess as their empress, than Caesar's and Anthony's actions had done. Bernice's fate is uncertain, but Titus seems to have put her away at some point prior to succeeding his father in 79 CE. Nor did Titus himself survive very long after his father.

Herod also had the last Maccabean High Priest, Mariamme's younger brother, Jonathan, put to death in 36 BC, when he reached the age of majority. Herod's marriage with the last Maccabean princess, Mariamme, would appear to have been contracted by her mother, Hyrcanus II's daughter, on the basis that Jonathan would become the High Priest on reaching majority.

Josephus pathetically records how, when the boy at thirteen years of age donned the High Priestly vestments, the Jewish crowd wept when he appeared in the Temple.[40] For those who would still cling to the contention that the people considered the Maccabean family usurpers, this should provide vivid testimony to the contrary. Wild with jealousy, Herod then had the boy taken down to his winter palace in Jericho and drowned while frolicking in the swimming pool with some of his attendants. He was *the last Maccabean High Priest.*

After this, Herod is careful to maintain personal contol over the High Priestly garments and appoints men, as Josephus himself observes, 'who were not of eminent families, some hardly priests at all'.[41] Once instituted, this was the policy followed by procurators such as Pontius Pilate after him (26–37)[42] and kings such as Agrippa I, his brother Herod of Chalcis, and his son, Bernice's brother Herod Agrippa II, until the Uprising against Rome. At this time 'the Zealots' elected their own High Priest, a lowly stone-cutter of the humblest origins whom Josephus calls 'Phannius', that is, *Phineas.* Such were the bloody origins of the Herodian High Priest class, tendentiously portrayed in the New Testament as the legitimate 'Chief Priests' and Sadducee party of the Jews!

This is the kind of detail Josephus provides, the pathos and the tragedy, and, unlike the detail one encounters in other texts that purport to be contemporary eye-witness accounts, this detail is patently *true.* At Herod's death, after he had indulged in all the cruelty and brutalities enumerated above and the total destruction of the national independence of the Jews and their previous royal priest line, revolutionary unrest began in earnest and continued for the next seventy years. This was possibly understood by exegetes like those at Qumran as the seventy-year period of 'Wrath' mentioned in Daniel 9:2. It continued until the outbreak of the War against Rome.

Actually, it continued for the next hundred and forty years until Hadrian crushed the Second Jewish Revolt in 132–6 CE and renamed Jerusalem Aelia Capitolina after his forename Aelius. He forbade Jews to enter Jerusalem or even to come within eyesight of it, except once a year to mourn its past glories. During this period, too, descendants of the family of Jesus and his brothers were involved in ongoing Messianic agitation and were martyred in their turn. This was the end of the earthbound Messianic hopes among the Jews, hopes that gradually turned more other-worldly, ethereal, or 'Gnostic'. This is what the imposition of Roman control really meant – destruction.

4

First-Century Sources Mentioning James

The New Testament and the *We Document* in Acts

The two most authentic testimonies to James' approach and role in the Jerusalem Church of his day are to be found in Paul's letters and in the second half of the Book of Acts, primarily, but not exclusively, in the document scholars refer to as 'the We Document'. The We Document in Acts is in the first person plural – therefore its designation. It intrudes variously after line 16:10. Seemingly it is a diary or travel document of some kind. For some, it is the only authentic material in Acts, though it is neither without problems nor continuous. It is even possible to contend that it is the real or authentic historical core of Acts and the basis of the whole presentation.

Had we to rely simply on Acts' presentation without Paul's definitive identifications, we would be in grave doubt as to just who this very powerful and popular James, described so reticently by Luke – the putative author of Acts – really was. Acts never tells us in any straightforward manner. James just appears out of nowhere in chapter 12, the same chapter that the more widely known other James, 'James *the brother of* John', 'the son of Zebedee', is conveniently disposed of and purportedly executed either by Agrippa I (37–44) or his brother Herod of Chalcis (44–9). Later we shall see how this execution relates to a parallel and more convincing one Josephus mentions at this time, the beheading of someone he calls 'Theudas'.[1]

James' identity and ideology are as solid as Paul's, because it is Paul who incontrovertibly confirms them. Therefore, Paul and James are inextricably entwined. What is more, Paul *never* mentions any *other* James. But Paul knows next to nothing about the person, ideology, and life of Jesus, except as an individual he feels he is in direct touch with in Heaven via a mechanism he and Acts refer to as the 'Holy Spirit'. This being, whom Paul calls 'Christ Jesus', often appears to be a carbon copy of Paul himself. So dubious did his claims regarding him appear to his opponents – and this *within the Church*, not outside it – that Paul was even mocked in his own lifetime as either a man of dreams or a 'Liar'.[2] It is useful to add that, aside from James, the only identifiable apostle who emerges in any substantial manner from Paul's letters is 'Peter', or, as the case may be, 'Cephas'. The portrait that emerges in these letters, not surprisingly, does not mesh with the one in Acts, to say nothing of the one in the Gospels.

Though there is continuing discussion among scholars about aspects of the Pauline corpus – the New Testament letters attributed to Paul – there is general agreement on the authenticity of the main, particularly those letters of principal concern to us in this book like Galatians, 1 and 2 Corinthians, Romans, and Philippians. These give us insight of the most intimate kind into the mind of Paul and historical insight into this period, which no defender of the integrity of the early Church and its doctrines would have had the slightest interest in forging or, for that matter, even preserving.

Here, it is perhaps edifying to cite a general rule: one should treat very cautiously any material reflecting the known or dominant theological position of the final redactors of a given document. Where authenticity is concerned, one is often on safer ground settling on traditions that seem surprising or incongruous in some manner, either historically, theologically or sociologically, or on traditions that would have a damaging effect on the theological consistency of that document. This is precisely the kind of material one would have expected to have been edited out or refurbished if it could have been, that is, had not the tradition behind its authenticity been widely disseminated, persistent, or very strong.

This is the case with the Letter of James. It is also the case with some of the very severe character deficiencies that emerge where Paul is concerned, not only in his own letters, but also in the Book of Acts, accurate or not. These include his insubordination, jealousy, incessant bragging and vindictiveness. As an example of a tradition surprising in its content, one could cite Paul's attestation that Jesus not only had brothers, but that they travelled with women (1 Cor. 9:5).

In the Gospels, to cite an obvious example, there is the presentation of Jesus' Apostles as being *armed* at the time of his arrest (Matt. 26:54). There are many more examples. Jarring anecdotes such as these are just the kind of material that would have been remembered in contradistinction to lengthy speeches or parables. The treatment of Jesus' close family, including his mother and his brothers in the early parts of the Gospels –

not to mention Jewish Apostles like Peter – despite their being noted in Paul's own testimony as among his closest followers, verges on the slanderous.

The material relating to James in Acts is of this kind as well. Were it not authentic and strongly supported, it is probable someone would have wished to delete it at some point. The downplaying of James in Christian tradition is important, not only where doctrine is concerned, but also because it is clear that James, as head of the Jerusalem Church and all that could be considered Christianity at the time, was superior to both Peter and Paul.

Paul, of course, repeatedly points out his personal disagreement with the rulings James makes and the instructions he receives from him. He even denigrates the authority of those he calls 'leaders', 'Pillars', 'Archapostles', 'who consider themselves important', or 'write their own references', and often displays his unwillingness to follow their views.[3] He never, however, contests James' legitimate right to exercise the position he occupies, nor the fact of his authority. In Galatians he makes it clear, too, that the character he calls either Peter or Cephas was subservient to James and not only obliged, but willing, to defer to James' leadership (Gal. 2:11–12).

Luke's reticence with regard to James in Acts contrasts markedly with the attitude of other groups relegated to sectarian status after the rise of Overseas Gentile Christianity to dominance. For these groups, James is the undisputed successor to Jesus and certainly 'the Bishop of Bishops' or 'Archbishop' and principal leader of all early Christianity. A particularly impressive example of this is to be found in the Gospel of Thomas. Here, in answer to the question by the Disciples, 'After you have gone who will be great over us?', Jesus is pictured as replying, 'In the place where you are to go, go to James the Just for whose sake Heaven and Earth came into existence.'[4]

This statement is pregnant with implications where the pre-existent 'Just One' or 'Zaddik', so important in Jewish mystical tradition or Kabbalah, is concerned.[5] It is also at odds with the orthodox tradition of the succession of Peter. It represents nothing less than the lost tradition of the direct appointment of James as successor to his brother. It is upheld by everything we know about groups that were expelled from orthodox Christianity in the years prior to and following Constantine's adoption of it as the official religion of the Roman Empire in the fourth century. Many of these groups dispersed into a variety of sectarian groupings in the

Syrian and Iraqui deserts, leading to a plethora of theological movements in the areas of Northern Mesopotamia and Syria. Some disappeared into Arabia only to re-emerge as Islam, in particular, as time went on, in its Shi'ite embodiment.

Pauline Christianity versus Jamesian: Anti-Semitism in the Gospels

In using the letters of Paul as our primary source material, we are on the firmest ground conceivable, for these are indisputably the earliest reliable documents of Christianity and can be dated with a high degree of certainty. They are patently earlier than the Gospels or the Book of Acts, which precede them in the present arrangement of the New Testament and which are themselves in large part doctrinally dependent upon Paul. Acts to some extent is dependent on Paul's letters for historical information as well.

This might strike the reader as a strange statement, because the New Testament is usually taken by readers at face value: Gospels first, Acts second, Letters third, and there is the natural imputation of some chrono-logical order to this. But this is a matter of convention only and was an order that emerged in the early centuries of the Church, to be consecrated as the fourth century progressed. In actuality, modern scholarship has been in agreement for some time that the Gospels are on the whole later creations than the letters of Paul, though based perhaps partly on early traditions and certainly, as I shall argue, at least doctrinally on these letters themselves.

What still must be decided and will undoubtedly go on being debated is when and where each Gospel was actually penned. Estimates vary from the late 50s or early 60s CE all the way to the mid-second century. Some estimates are even later, at least where final versions are concerned. We will not be able to resolve the matter here. Some even claim to have found Gospel fragments among the Qumran materials, but this, too, will prob-ably not ultimately be verified and it would be surprising indeed to find Hellenistic-style Gospels among such clear 'Zealot'-like material. The same is true of a more recent claim of finding an early manuscript version of one of the Gospels in a library in England![6]

In fact, the interrelationships between the four Gospels, particularly the three synoptics (so called because of their use of a common source or sources), are probably far more complex than most conceive. Take, for example, the Synoptic most people consider to be the most Jewish, the Gospel of Matthew. It is considered the most 'Jewish' because of the amount of Law-oriented material it contains, particularly in the Sermon on the Mount (5:1–7:29), and because of its extensive evocation of biblical proof texts. Yet Matthew also contains a stratum of anti-Semitic materials sometimes even more extreme than that found in the other Gospels – for example, the cry of the assembled Jewish masses, when Pilate hesitates to condemn Jesus, 'his blood be on us and our children' (27:25). This has echoed down the ages, the famous – or infamous – 'blood libel' in Christian history. In fact, Paul made the original blood-libel accusation in 1 Thessalonians 2:15 – if the text is authentic and not interpolated – when he called the Jews the 'people who put the Lord Jesus to death' and 'the Enemies of the whole human race'.[7]

Who could conceive of a crowd *en masse* uttering such an absurd statement, yet its presence at this point in Matthew is fraught with theological and historical significance. The answer is simple. No crowd ever did; it is based on a retrospective presentation of subsequent theology that certainly became concretized in the wake of the perspective exhibited by Paul and which by the time of Eusebius had grown to rich fruition, as the latter demonstrates over and over again in the viciousness of his invective.[8]

How can a document be both philo-Semitic and anti-Semitic at the same time? This is the kind of question that is asked in literary or historical criticism of the Bible. The answer, of course, is it cannot be. This is a contradiction in terms and relates to the different strata or overlays of contradictory source material it contains. Some think the earliest stratum in the Gospel of Matthew is the philo-Semitic one. This makes sense historiographically speaking. But Matthew also contains Jesus' post-resurrection validation of the Pauline Gentile Mission (the last two lines of the Gospel, 28:19–20), another bit of theological sleight of hand, which cannot be historical.

There are many examples of this kind in the Gospels, the relationships between which are so complex that no one will probably ever be able to sort them out to everyone's satisfaction. From internal textual considerations alone, however, it is possible to show that all the Gospels probably made their appearance after the fall of Jerusalem and the destruction of the Temple in 70 CE. This date, as has been explained, turns out to be a watershed for almost all the literary developments and movements that need to be discussed. It is certainly a critical juncture for the discussion of James.

In reality, a far-reaching consensus has emerged among scholars on this issue – we are speaking here of the date of the actual documents themselves, not the various traditions many contend underlie them – at least where the Gospels of Matthew, Luke and John are concerned. This is no mean circumstance, for it explains many things about them, not the least of which being the paucity of sound historical material and in some cases the outright historical dissimulation and disinformation they contain.

The only serious remaining debate on this issue centres around the Gospel of Mark. From the same internal textual considerations already noted, it is possible to show that Mark, too, was written after the fall of the Temple in 70 CE. The whole nature of its anti-Jewish polemic and opposition to the family and brothers of Jesus on the one hand and its pro-Peter orientation on the other distinguish it as having appeared *after the destruction of the Jerusalem centre* – in particular, after the attempt by the *Roman* Community to represent itself as the legitimate heir to Jesus and the Messianic Movement he represented, however absurd, historically speaking, this might have seemed to any objective observer at the time.

What could be more suitable, heralded as it was by the massive triumphal procession through the streets of Rome to mark the glorious triumphs of Vespasian and his son Titus, commemorated and consecrated in the works of Josephus and the Arch of Titus that still stands in the Roman Forum today? Here, the surrender of the Jews to the *Imperium Romanum* was taken, as it were, in perpetuity.

There are, in fact, several veiled references to events of this kind in the Gospel of Mark, for instance, in the introduction to the Little Apocalypse, where Jesus is made to predict the utter destruction of the Temple (13:1–2) and in the Apocalypse itself, when the Pauline Mission is anticipated (13:9–10) – but, even more importantly, in the depiction of the rending of the Temple veil at his death (Mark 15:38 and pars.). This veil was more than likely damaged in the final Roman assault on the Temple or in the various altercations and the turmoil preceding this. Josephus specifically refers to it, along with its replacement materials, as having been delivered over to the Romans after the assault on the Temple. It was doubtless on display in Rome, damaged or otherwise, along with the rest of the booty Josephus describes as having been paraded in Titus' Triumph.[9]

For his part, Jesus' meanderings about the peaceful Galilean countryside – at a time when Galilee was a hotbed of revolutionary fervour and internecine strife – doing miraculous exorcisms, cures, raisings and the like, while Scribes, Pharisees and synagogue officials murmur against him, resemble nothing so much as the incipient Paul travelling around the

Hellenistic Mediterranean. In fact, Galilee, as referred to in the Gospel of Matthew, is a leitmotif for Gentiles – 'Galilee of the Nations'/'Galilee of the Gentiles' (4:15). It was also the seedbed of the rise of the Zealot Movement whose adherents were called by some, 'Galileans'. These kinds of material, in particular, point to Mark as having been written, like the other Gospels, after the fall of the Temple and the destruction of Jerusalem.

However the resolution of the matter of the priority of the Gospels – and their interrelationships are probably far more complex than most would be willing to admit – it should suffice for the moment to say that when dealing with the larger part of the Pauline corpus, that is, with those letters that can with certainty be ascribed to Paul, we are dealing with the oldest and most reliable documents of Christianity, which have not failed to make their influence felt in the rest of the New Testament, despite the accident of their placement.

But a scholarly consensus of sorts has emerged even concerning the Gospels, which concedes that later religious history has made its influence felt, the only question being to what extent. Despite the last-ditch efforts by conservative scholars and fundamentalists to defend their historicity, based in part on a prior belief in the authority of Scripture, much material in the Gospels, even allowing for hyperbole, patently borders on the fantastic.

Even conceding the fact that the Gospel titles were not added until the second century, they are still representative of a genre of literature characteristic of the Second Temple Period and the Hellenistic world generally, called pseudepigrapha – meaning books written under a false pen-name – and do not represent the genuine reports of a man called Matthew, a man called Mark and a man called Luke – John aside – whoever these men might have been. For his part, Luke admits from the start he is working from sources (1:1–4), but here there still are questions about whether it is Luke or someone else doing the final redacting. These questions are too complex to be explored here, but they do not affect the nature of the conclusions we shall arrive at in this book.

Where the Book of Acts is concerned, the authorship by Luke is again taken as a given. Where Acts switches to the first-person-plural narrative of the 'We Document', it may be conceded that it is probably based on the genuine travel notebooks or diary of a travelling companion of Paul named Luke.[10] Here, as implied, we probably do have a genuine historical core, and fantastic raconteuring really does recede in favour of more matter-of-fact reportage and straightforward narrative. But what are we to make of much of what comes before in the first sixteen chapters of Acts, romantic legend and fantastic story-telling of the clearest sort?

The same considerations no doubt hold true, though in nothing like as clear a manner, for the records redacted under the names of Matthew, Mark and John as well. In fact, we will be able to show the kernels of real historical events beneath the surface of what can only, on occasion, be described as mythologization. Much information in the Gospels has been assimilated from other sources, including information, as we shall argue, about James, but also material from Josephus, Old Testament stories about heroes and prophets, and even episodes from the life of Paul.

It has even been suggested that if the Gospels did not present Jesus as the marvellous character they do, they would not be authentic, that is, it is just these fantastic aspects of the narrative that mark them as the authentic *Hellenistic* documents they are, though perhaps not authentic for the modern reader. Occasionally, one may come upon the authentic remains of historical truth, but, in general, where Gospel traditions are concerned, it is rather like the saying of Jesus reported in Pseudoclementine tradition, 'be like good money-changers, able to tell false coin from true'.[11]

Luke, of course, is a Greek, an admitted foreigner, but something that cannot help but strike the modern observer is the general flavour of Hellenistic anti-Semitism in the Gospels, in particular, when associated with the name of ostensibly *Jewish* witnesses such as Matthew, Mark and John. It is perhaps this attitude more than any other single characteristic that *marks them as having been composed by non-Jews* or makes it highly unlikely that in their present form they could have been redacted in a Jewish framework or been written by originally Jewish authors. They definitely reflect a Greco-Roman or Gentile background and mentality, despite the attempts by some to argue otherwise.

But what might strike the reader as more surprising still, the anti-Semitism of Gentile or Pauline Christianity is directed as much or even more towards the Jewish Apostles or the Jerusalem Church, particularly James, as it is towards Jews outside it. Paul is not so much concerned with Jews outside the Church, who are for him largely an irrelevant nuisance. Because Acts is largely retrospective and Paulinized, it has a different point of view, fobbing off or smoothing over these acrimonious exchanges within the Church. Actually, Paul's teacher, reputed to have been the Pharisee rabbi Gamaliel, who was descended from the Hillel mentioned earlier, is spoken of quite congenially in Acts. It is against his Jewish opponents within the Church that Paul directs his bitterest attacks, most notably against those he calls 'some from James' or James' Jerusalem Church colleagues (Gal. 2:12).

It should be categorically stated, as noted in the Introduction, that a Jewish document can be sectarian, that is, anti-Pharisee or even anti-Sadducee, as the Dead Sea Scrolls most certainly are and the Gospels at their most authentic sometimes are, but it cannot be anti-Semitic. This would be a contradiction in terms. It is possible to oppose persons of a different party or sectarian persuasion, nationalist or anti-nationalist, cosmopolitan or xenophobic, as Josephus does; but one cannot be against one's self – except abnormally. Paul sometimes exhibits this baffling characteristic, but, as we shall show, Paul is perhaps not really Jewish in the manner he thinks or advertises himself to be.

In Gospel criticism, therefore, we must set aside all such materials as incorporating a retrospective view of history and the anti-Semitism of Pauline or Overseas Christianity. These will include a large portion of the most familiar and beloved passages in the Bible, as, for instance, most of the parables, which, despite their parabolic thrust, are rarely very hard to decipher in this regard.[12] They would also include the most oft-quoted and highly prized sayings of Jesus, many now commonplaces of Western historical parlance.

All of these are almost always directed against the people of Palestine, and are, therefore, anti-Jewish and pro the Pauline Gentile Mission – for instance: 'the First shall be last and the Last shall be first',[13] 'a Prophet is never accepted in his own land and in his own house',[14] 'who are my brothers and mother to me?',[15] 'Woe unto you Choraizin and Bethseida, had the miracles that were done here been done in Tyre and Sidon, they would have converted long ago and put on sackcloth and ashes',[16] sayings on behalf of 'publicans' (tax collectors), 'prostitutes', 'Sinners' (often a leitmotif for Gentiles),[17] 'wine-bibbers', 'the good Samaritan', 'these Little Ones', 'the one lost sheep',[18] 'gluttons' (people who do not keep dietary regulations), 'the Phoenician woman', etc. – all more or less connected to the priority of the Gentile Mission, the admission of Gentiles into the early Church, and related matters.

At this point, perhaps, another favourite shibboleth of latterday scholarship will have to be jettisoned, that of the 'Judaization' of early Christianity, which is the point of view propagated by Acts too (15:5). In line with its polemic, for Acts and modern scholarship thereafter, the original doctrines of Jesus and the Apostles, who supported Gentiles and the Gentile Mission, have been undermined by the 'Jamesian' Jerusalem Church. This is an absurdity, and it must be stated categorically: there never was a 'Judaization' of early Christianity, only a progressively more rapid *Gentilization*.

This gathered momentum with the elimination of the Jerusalem centre by the hand of Roman power after the Uprising of 66–70 CE. Only when principles of this kind are properly grasped and many favourite platitudes and historical clichés jettisoned, will it be possible to make any progress towards a resolution of the quest for the Historical Jesus.

To make an honest attempt to get at the truth of this period, therefore, one must be willing to part with the popular idea of the Gospels, for instance, as 'eye-witness' accounts. The only 'eye-witness' we have in this sorry spectacle – apart from the Dead Sea Scrolls – is Josephus himself, and we have already covered his flaws. This is not to say, however, that one must part with one's faith. The Gospel portrait is sacred history, and as such recommends itself, in particular, to one's faith, if not necessarily to one's sense of historical accuracy.

There is a difference between sacred history and historical truth, whatever the cultural heritage. It is the same for the Old Testament as for the New, and for other religious legacies as well – Greek mythology, Hinduism, aboriginal religion. One is dealing in sacred history with what a given church or religious persuasion thinks happened to itself, not what necessarily or actually *did* happen. In this kind of history, events are often represented retrospectively and entwined with the dominant religious point of view of the time or the theology of the party that sets them into writing. One must be able to divorce one's faith, on the one hand, from one's critical faculties and historical judgement on the other – this is true for all religious groups, Jews as well as Christians. Otherwise, one will be unable to make any real progress on the road to discovering the historical reality behind the period before us.

Josephus' Testimonies to James and Other Early Christian Leaders

It is through the person of James, who is mentioned in a straightforward manner by his younger contemporary Josephus, that we have the most compelling testimony to the existence of his brother Jesus, whether one takes the name 'Jesus' symbolically or literally.[19] Some consider even the reference to James found in the Twentieth Book of Josephus' *Antiquities* interpolated; but, aside from the fact that little could be gained by such an insertion, the reference is convincing enough and fits in with what we know about James ideologically and historically from other sources.

In addition, it provides previously unknown and seemingly reliable data about the circumstances of James' arrest and execution. It is consistent, too, with the pattern of other such notices in Josephus' *Antiquities* about persons not mentioned in the *Jewish War*. Though it is always possible that the notice is not complete in the form we have it – Origen, Eusebius, and Jerome all report that they saw more – James does appear to have been mentioned in some manner at this point by Josephus.

Josephus also mentions a number of other extremely interesting individuals in the *Antiquities* – including Jesus – who for some reason are missing from the *Jewish War*. The *War* was written some twenty years before the *Antiquities* at a time when Josephus was still immersed in controversies relating to the Uprising against Rome. Obviously there were materials and individuals that he felt freer to mention in the 90s than he had in the 70s.

The list of these omissions from the *Jewish War* is interesting. Aside from Jesus and James, perhaps the most interesting is John the Baptist. There are, as will become clear, a number of others, perhaps not recognizable in their present form, but who will, in our view, have their clearly discernible counterparts in the New Testament. These will include Peter, Simon *Magus*, Theudas (that is, Thaddaeus) and Ananias, pictured in Acts as being commanded by God to go to 'Judas' house in Straight Street' in Damascus to meet Paul (9:10–11). Other individuals connected to Paul and mentioned also in the *War* are Stephen, Philip, Silas, Niger and, in our view, Paul himself.

One early Church source even claims Theudas was a friend of Paul.[20] Aside from being mentioned overtly in Acts, he will have his counterparts in the individual known as 'Judas of James' in Luke's Apostle lists ('Thaddaeus' and 'Lebbaeus' in Mark and Matthew) and in Syriac traditions about the conversion of King Abgar or Agbar.

Persons not specifically connected to Christian origins in Palestine, but for some reason also omitted from the *War*, would include Honi the Circle Drawer/Onias the Righteous, Pollio/Hillel, and Sameas/Shammai in the first century BC and *Saddok*, the associate of Judas the Galilean, in the first century CE, not to mention Judas the Galilean's two sons, James and Simon, themselves – significantly mostly persons who had something to do with subversive developments in Palestine or their opponents. Judas the Galilean, like Theudas, is overtly mentioned in Acts 5:36–37, and the deletion of the mention of the crucifixion of his two sons – 'James and Simon' in Josephus – will account for the anachronism that develops in that narrative as it presently stands regarding Judas and Theudas.

Josephus' reference to John the Baptist is perhaps the most complete and provides valuable new data that helps place John in a real historical framework, as opposed to the quasi-mythological one encountered in the Gospels. One of the things the notice clears up is the year of John's death, approximately 35–36 CE, which is, of course, totally at odds with how this is presented in the Gospels.[21]

Other aspects of John's career, which are clarified, are the nature of his doctrine of baptism and the twin doctrines of Righteousness and Piety (in Hebrew *Zedek* and *Hesed*), as the essence of his teaching. As Josephus explains it, these are 'Righteousness towards one's fellow man and Piety towards God' – what we shall henceforth refer to as 'the Righteousness/ Piety dichotomy'. For him, John's baptism was in the Jewish manner an immersion for purification of the body only, efficacious only in so far as the soul had already been purified beforehand by the practice of Righteousness. This is a very important distinction, which will be totally in accord with how these matters are presented in Qumran documents.

Josephus also clarifies the reason for John's execution, as opposed to the more mythologized one encountered in the Gospels. Mark 6:20 even has Herod taking John for a 'Righteous Man' (that is, 'a *Zaddik*')! Herod, that is, Herod Antipas (4 BC–39 CE), as distinct from his father Herod the 'Great' (Herod *the Terrible* would be more appropriate), feared the influence John had over the Jewish mob, which, according to Josephus, was prepared to do anything John might suggest, a further indication of the *popularity* of these opposition leaders. Herod, consequently, feared that John would lead *an uprising* and decided to have him executed, lest later he would have cause to regret not having done so. This execution, as in the case of Jesus, James and quite a few of these Messianic or 'opposi-tion' leaders – for instance James and Simon, the two sons of Judas the Galilean – was a preventative one.

This is the demythologized John. The story of John we are more famil-iar with is, of course, the more romanticized one: the henpecked Herod deferring at his birthday celebration to the tantalizing dance of Herodias' daughter Salome (she is not named in the Gospels; we need Josephus for this), John's head on a plate, Herod being loath to execute John – all these the artistic embellishments of literary enhancement or creative writing, not to mention a certain amount of dissimulation.

What is the reason for all these omissions in the *Jewish War* and their emendation in the *Antiquities*? It probably has to do with Josephus' own greater sense of personal security, if not some greater knowledge on his part. Of course, something may have happened to him in the 90s to interrupt this, as we have no way of knowing whether he suddenly went silent due to natural causes or for some other reason. Our other sources for this period, including the Roman historians Tacitus and Suetonius in the next generation, themselves sometimes dependent on Josephus, provide no information about his demise.

In the years following the Uprising, Josephus had to be concerned with people who wished to impugn his role in recent events, and he evinces just such a fear of powerful external critics in his autobiographical sketch the *Vita*, appended to the *Antiquities*. Here, for the first time, he answers the accusations of another historian who survived the war, Justus of Tiberius, impugning his loyalty to Rome. His highly suspect role in the events of the preceding years, particularly in Galilee, would have left him open to such charges, if not those of outright insurrection or subversion. His reticence about what to reveal and what not in the years following the Uprising, therefore, is not surprising. In particular he seems to have been careful about a good many characters with subversive or religious tendencies important for sectarian history in Palestine like James.

By the 90s and the writing of the *Antiquities* Josephus felt increasingly secure, and accordingly all these new characters pepper his narrative. So secure did he feel that in the *Vita* he even gives details of his personal and family life. But why shouldn't he? He had been adopted into the Roman imperial family itself. He had been an aide to Vespasian's son Titus, whom Vespasian had left behind to prosecute the war when he went to Rome to assume the emperorship. Josephus was not only an intelligence officer and an interrogator of prisoners, a position he exploited to good advantage, but he occupied a very intimate role among Titus' inner circle of advisers, which included not a few other turncoat Jews.

One, Tiberius Alexander, also mentioned in Acts 4:6 and Procurator in Palestine from 46 to 48 CE, was the son of the Alabarch of Alexandria and the nephew of the Hellenistic Jewish philosopher Philo. The Alabarch of Alexandria was the officially designated Roman leader of the Jewish community there. Tiberius Alexander, who can be considered the consummate imperial Roman bureaucrat and politician, had graduated through several government roles. When Vespasian went to Rome, Tiberius was left behind as Titus' commanding general for the siege of Jerusalem and perhaps to make sure Titus didn't make too much of a mess of things. Josephus, who knew him, refers to him in the *Antiquities*, somewhat uncharacteristically, as a backslider and convert to Roman paganism.[22]

Another was the Herodian princess Bernice, who, before her marriage to her uncle Herod of Chalcis (44–49), had been Tiberius Alexander's sister-in-law. Now she was Titus Caesar's Cleopatra-style mistress. She also appears in the Book of Acts conversing congenially with Paul, who obviously knew her too (24:23–25:32). Josephus certainly knew her as well. Not only does he tell us that she was the Richest woman in Palestine – possibly one of the reasons Titus was so keen on her – and of her rumoured incest with her brother Agrippa II, who also appears in the portrait in Acts, but how she later intervened with her brother to save Josephus' critic, Justus of Tiberius.²³ This was the circle of people around Titus, of which Josephus inevitably became a part. In fact, he remarks in the *Vita* that in the writing of the *Antiquities* he had access to Agrippa II's private files. This in itself can explain some of the new additions.

In the Introduction to the *War*, Josephus claims that the version generally available to the modern reader, the Greek version, was based on an earlier one he wrote either in Hebrew or in Aramaic for circulation in the East among his co-religionists there, to explain what really happened in Palestine – presumably to discourage them from becoming involved in similar enterprises. By 'East' at this time should be understood Northern Syria, Edessa or the area around Haran – Abraham's homeland – the area overlapping all of these and loosely referred to as Arabia and, most importantly, the Kingdom of Adiabene between Northern Mesopotamia and Persia, the royal family of which not only supported the Uprising against Rome, but participated in it on the Jewish side.²⁴

Josephus is so obsequious where the Roman imperial family and the exploits of his patron Titus are concerned, that it is difficult to take anything he says with regard to them with certainty. This in itself was something of the service he rendered these imperial patrons, but there was more. There have been claims that something of what Josephus said in his original version of the *Jewish War* survived in the manuscript now known as the Slavonic Josephus.²⁵ It is not possible to verify this one way or the other. There were also manuscripts of Josephus that survived into Arabic. Origen, the third-century Church theologian, and Eusebius, his successor in Caesarea in the next century, both claim to have seen a copy of Josephus different from the one we presently possess. This copy included a passage ascribing the fall of Jerusalem to the death of James *not to the death of Jesus* – a significant addition.

This passage does not exist in the notice about James in the *Antiquities* available to us at the present time and there really is no place it could reasonably have been inserted in that document, except for the 62 CE notice of the circumstances surrounding James' death. But Eusebius, after alluding to the additional material, goes on to give verbatim the version of the death of James in the *Antiquities* as we presently have it, so for him obviously there were two separate notices relating to the death of James in the works of Josephus that he was familiar with.

This leaves the version of the *Jewish War* which Origen, Eusebius and possibly Jerome must have seen in the library at Caesarea. Origen was outraged by what he saw and hastened to correct Josephus' version of the facts, insisting that he should have said Jerusalem fell on account of the death of Jesus. This in itself would probably explain the ultimate disappearance of this passage from all extant versions of Josephus' works – even the Arabic *Yusufus*.

If the passage connecting James' death to the fall of Jerusalem did appear in the version of the *War* available in the East, it is more or less possible to identify just where it might have occurred. It would have had to come either where Josephus discusses the death of the man responsible along with Agrippa II for the death of James, the High Priest Ananus, or at the end of the *War* with the portents connected with the destruction of the Temple, including the Star Prophecy and Jesus ben Ananias' mournful dirge.[26]

In any event, the material about James along with the material about John the Baptist are good examples of the kinds of additions one finds in the *Antiquities* that do not appear in the *War*. This clear and probably unenhanced reference to James is, as we have seen, also perhaps the clearest evidence we have of the existence of a Jesus. The equation is simple: if James existed – which he undeniably did – then Jesus existed as well.

The Testimony to Jesus

Everything in Josephus' life and works points to the fact that he was well acquainted with the movement that, for lack of a better terminology, the world now calls 'Christian'. In Palestine, we are probably on safer ground if we refer to it as the 'Messianic' one.[27] Nor is it possible that there were two competing Messianisms in Palestine, but rather probably only one, the one reflected in the literature we now call the Dead Sea Scrolls.

It is also hard to escape the impression from the manner in which Josephus describes James in the extant notice as 'the brother of Jesus who was called the Christ' that he had referred to Jesus previously. There is such a passage about Jesus in the *Antiquities*. However, it is so orthodox that many have rejected it as an interpolation. For instance, aside from attesting to his 'wonderful works', Josephus is made to assert that 'he appeared to them alive again after three days' and 'he was the Christ', which on the surface would make Josephus a believing Christian. This is not to say that at this point Josephus did not mention Jesus, only that the extant notice was not what he originally wrote.[28]

But the context of the present reference is peculiar indeed. From the time of the Census under Cyrenius in 6–7 CE to Pontius Pilate's Procuratorship – date uncertain, but Josephus gives it as 26 CE – Josephus' data thins considerably, probably because he did not have sources to cover this period. Directly following the notice in the *Antiquities* about Jesus, however, Josephus goes into a long excursus about Temple prostitution and someone who seduces an aristocratic lady by impersonating a god – the 'Mundus and Paulina' story. Before returning to the ostensible subject of his narrative at this point, *Pontius Pilate's administration in Palestine*, he goes on to tell another equally scurrilous, but related, story about how a Jewish teacher, whom he declines to name, together with three others – one should note the emphasis on the *three* here – converts another woman from the Roman aristocracy, Fulvia, to Judaism.[29]

This teacher had been exiled from Palestine on a charge of 'breaking the Law'. On the pretext of getting money to send as gifts to the Temple in Jerusalem, this teacher and his three companions defraud Fulvia. The overtones of this story for events in Palestine relating to Pauline fund-raising and other parallel activities cannot be missed. Fulvia's husband turns out to be a friend of the Emperor Tiberius (14–37 CE), who, upon hearing the story, exiles all the Jews from Rome.

But Tacitus, who agrees that Tiberius expelled the Jews from Rome because of these kinds of pernicious superstitions, places these events precisely in 19 CE – the year of Jesus' purported crucifixion according to the allegedly spurious *Acti Pilati*, which Eusebius fulminates against so effusively in his *Ecclesiastical History*.[30] These 'acts', which of course have now been lost, seem to have appeared in the fourth century and claimed to be based on the newly opened Roman chancellery records regarding the administration of Pontius Pilate. They have since been replaced by more orthodox writings in Pilate's name. Eusebius, of course, considers them forgeries, but, if authentic, they not only suggest an earlier date for the crucifixion of Jesus, but also that Pontius Pilate perhaps came to Palestine a decade earlier than is normally reckoned.

These incongrous episodes in Josephus about the seduction and defrauding of Roman aristocratic women occur at just the place he is supposed to be discussing Pontius Pilate's administration in Palestine and where he should be telling us more about Jesus, if he did mention him. As we just saw, Tacitus places this in *19 CE*. The 'Mundus and Paulina' episode ends with a *banishment* from Rome – in this case, Mundus'. The latter, whoever he was, imitates the Egyptian god Anubis in order to seduce Paulina, a married lady, in the Temple of Isis, thereby scandalizing all of Rome.

For some this could represent a subtle, if malevolent, burlesque of Christian infancy narratives. The Fulvia episode has to do with fund-raising activities overseas on the part of a teacher, 'condemned for Law-breaking' in Palestine, and 'three' of his associates. That Josephus does not mention Jesus again, except when speaking about James, does not mean that there was not more to his original reference than we presently have. There probably was, but given Josephus' character and his obsequiousness to Rome, this material would have disappeared in favour of this more comedic version.

Not only does the date of the 'Mundus and Paulina' episode in Tacitus, like the date of the death of John the Baptist in Josephus, cause problems where New Testament chronologies are concerned,[31] it overlaps later information in Suetonius about how during the reign of Claudius (41–54 CE) the Jews were banished from Rome for making propaganda on behalf of one 'Chrestus'.[32] Not only is this interesting where the matter of these several overlapping banishments is concerned, it is interesting because, firstly, 'Chrestus' is obviously supposed to be an approximation of 'Christ' and, secondly, for political purposes, at least in the period before the fall of the Temple, it shows that the Romans did not distinguish in any way between what we presently call Christians and Jews. For the Romans they were the same, particularly those carrying the incendiary bacillus of Jewish Messianic and apocalyptic propaganda.[33]

The 'Star Prophecy'

Overtly anyhow, Josephus considers himself a Pharisee and, where Roman power was at issue, the behaviour of two other, self-professed Pharisees in this period, Paul the founder of Pauline Christianity and R. Yohanan ben Zacchai, the founder of Rabbinic Judaism, parallel his. Nor do the constraints under which he operated differ very much from theirs, especially when he tells those stories about popular Messianic leaders who had been crucified by Roman administrators. Crucifixion was the exemplary Roman punishment for revolutionary or subversive behaviour. One of the first references to it comes in the wake of the Spartacus Uprising in the first half of the first century BC. These slave-class revolutionaries were crucified along the road from Naples to Rome in such numbers that there was little room for all the crosses.

Josephus' general view of the 'religious frauds' or 'magicians' he refers to in this period was that their influence over the people was more pernicious even than that of the 'robbers and assassins', and more dangerous. This was primarily because, as he puts it, they were scheming to bring about *both* religious reform *and* change in government, that is, they had a dual religious and political programme.[34] Therefore, by necessity if not inclination – in Josephus the two are often identical – the presentation of such 'impostors' or 'deceivers' was fashioned in an extremely negative manner, at least in versions of his work prepared for Roman circulation. As the censorship powers of the Church became absolute after Constantine, negative presentations of early Christian leaders, where recognizable – not as, for instance, in the *Mundus and Paulina* episode – undoubtedly would have been replaced by more sympathetic testimonies or deleted altogether.

A similar conundrum bedevils Josephus' presentation of responsibility for the fall of the Temple. There can be little doubt that the Temple in Jerusalem was destroyed – as was a lesser facsimile of it in Egypt afterwards – by an express Roman political decision, yet Josephus portrays the Jews as burning their own Temple down around themselves. The Romans, no doubt, perceived the Temple as being the seat of the pestilent Messianic Movement, which, Christian refurbishments notwithstanding, it was.

The description of these events would have come in the famous, lost Fifth Book of Tacitus' *Histories*, or possibly the missing portions of the *Annals*, but Sulpicius Severus in the fifth century provides an account that was probably based on it.[35] He portrays the Roman war council on the eve of the final assault on the Temple, where the definitive decision was taken by Titus' staff to destroy it, no doubt with the enthusiastic support of individuals such as Bernice, Philo's nephew Tiberius Alexander, and Josephus himself. Another Roman historian, Dio Cassius, notes the Roman amazement at the Jews who in despair threw themselves into the flames.[36]

For his part, Josephus is anxious to portray the Jews as burning down their own Temple and Titus as doing everything he can to quench the flames. In this manner he rescues Titus from the charge of impiety or Temple desecration, so important to a people as superstitious as the Romans. It is easy to recognize in Josephus' presentation of Titus the presentation of the behaviour of Pontius Pilate and Herod towards Messianic leaders such as Jesus and John the Baptist in the Gospels – not surprisingly, since all these documents were produced by similar mindsets under similar constraints.

Though on the basis of the corpus in its extant form, since he testifies that Jesus 'was the Christ', Josephus must be considered a Christian; elsewhere, as we have seen, Josephus informs us in no uncertain terms that he considers Vespasian to have been the one called from Palestine at this time to rule the world. Josephus' perversion of the 'World Ruler' Prophecy is comparable in its cynicism to the Hellenistic reformulation of it in the Gospels. Rabbinic literature is equally cynical in its presentation of R. Yohanan ben Zacchai, the founder of Rabbinic Judaism, as making the same opportunistic interpretation of this prophecy and applying it to Vespasian, presumably to save his skin.

This is the kind of chicanery and sleight of hand typical of this period. Josephus might have been a secret Christian, depending on one's definition of 'Christian' in Palestine – if one wants him, one is welcome to him – but not on the basis of his description of Jesus. On this basis, so was Pontius Pilate and, indeed, apocryphal Gospels asserting this duly appeared in early Christian centuries. These absurdities have gone so far that there were even Josephinist cults in the Middle Ages and, as noted, the Josephus corpus accompanied the Greek Orthodox canon.

In England his first translators, like William Whiston in Isaac Newton's time – whose works are still pirated today – were convinced they were dealing with a Christian. History can attest to few more cynical people who have portrayed themselves so frankly. Indeed, besides the wealth of historical data he presents us, if he has a virtue, this is it. He is honest to a fault concerning his own shortcomings and flaws. In fact, he does not even seem to recognize them as flaws at all.

5

Early Church Sources and the Dead Sea Scrolls

Extra-biblical Sources Relating to James

The existence of James the brother of Jesus is not only confirmed in the Pauline Corpus, the Book of Acts, and by Josephus, it is also echoed in the Gospels, though downplayed. It is further enlarged upon in the literature of the early Church. The principal sources are Eusebius of Caesarea at the beginning of the fourth century (c. 260–340) and Epiphanius of Salamis at the end of it (367–404), both from Palestine. Their testimonies about James overlap, but with interesting differences and emendations.

There is also a further, though much shorter, notice in Jerome's *Praise of Illustrious Men*. Jerome (347–420), whose principal work was also conducted in Palestine, most notably Bethlehem, was famous for his biblical scholarship, the basis of the Latin Vulgate Bible of today. His testimony again overlaps with both Eusebius and Epiphanius, the latter his less long-lived contemporary and, it seems, a Jewish convert to Christianity. While Eusebius and Epiphanius are more extensive, Jerome focuses on several aspects of the tradition that are extremely important for our understanding of James.

Actually, the greater part of these sources and testimonies is based on two earlier writers from the second century, both now lost. The first, Hegesippus (c. 90–180) was a second-century churchman, also from Palestine; the second, Clement of Alexandria (c. 150–215) was Origen's predecessor and teacher in Egypt. Their testimony, while not always in agreement, overlaps substantially, though Hegesippus' is more extensive. Eusebius is straightforward about his dependence on both and presents large sections from them, particularly Hegesippus, which he clearly denotes as their work. Without his verbatim quotations, we would be without these two all-important testimonies.

Hegesippus is by far the more substantial. He flourished within a century of James and, if not an actual convert, seems to have been a 'Jewish Christian', whatever may be meant by this term in this time. As a young man he would have known persons whose memory spanned the time frame involved or who would have known people with personal knowledge of the events and individuals in question. His testimony, therefore, is to be highly prized, but it is regrettable that none of his works has survived, except these excerpts in Eusebius.

Regardless of the effect of Eusebius' extensive appropriations on the survival of Hegesippus in the original, the modern reader must be grateful that his quotations are as meticulous as they are. It is, however, a most curious phenomenon that so many of the individuals Eusebius quotes with regard to information crucial for our understanding of early Christianity in Palestine have not come down to us in the original. One can only hope that Eusebius has excerpted the most significant passages.

Though some works of Clement of Alexandria have survived, the materials about James used by Eusebius and Epiphanius did not. Nor have any materials about James from Clement, additional to those quoted in Eusebius, survived. The reader should keep in mind that there are two Clements in early Church history. The first one in Rome, in whose name the Pseudoclementines have been redacted, was one of the earliest Popes at the end of the first century (c. 30–97). He seems to have been a member of the Roman patrician class and, like Mark, a travelling companion of Peter, at least this is what the various apocryphal stories redacted under his name suggest.[1]

It should be appreciated that the reason Mark's name came to be appended to the second Gospel is because he was considered to have been Peter's secretary, regardless of whether we can speak in any firm way of the historical Peter or even Mark.[2] Clement, Peter's Roman successor, may have played a similar role. In any event, not only is he designated as the first or second 'Pope' in Rome after Peter, a lively travel literature developed in his name, associated with the process of his conversion, known latterly as the Pseudoclementines, though it is no more 'pseudo' than any other literature we have to do with in this period of similar genre.[3]

What is important is that we are speaking here of literature, in this case, Hellenistic romance of a familiar genre, that of 'Recognitions' – therefore the name of one third–fourth century version of this Hellenistic novel that has come down to us, the *Recognitions of Clement*. Because this is a novel or Hellenistic romance does not mean that it is entirely devoid of historical fact. The second manuscript cluster that has come down to us is called the *Homilies of Clement*. This in large measure overlaps the first.

The 'Jewish Christian' or Ebionite tendencies of both clusters, now generally called the 'Pseudoclementines', have often been remarked. The only real difference between them is that the attack on James by Paul in the First Book of the *Recognitions* and the surrounding historical material there at some point seem to have been deleted from the *Homilies*, presenting a more sanitized version. Therefore, the *Recognitions*, in particular, provides important new information for our consideration of James, not so much doctrinally, but historically (the doctrines found in the Pseudoclementines are thought to represent those of a slightly later period and may or may not contain residues of the original James, but the historical events do).

The Clement on whose work some of the statements about James found in Eusebius and Epiphanius are based, however, is not this Clement, but a second-century Alexandrian theologian by the same name. Though he was a younger contemporary of Hegesippus, the testimony he provides is neither as extensive nor as useful as Hegesippus' impressive legacy. From what has survived, it can be concluded that he had information about James' role as successor to Jesus and the circumstances of his death.

But garbling of materials, either purposefully or otherwise, and mythologization have already begun to take place, even more than in Hegesippus' case, though he is only a little more than a century away from the events in question. Conflation – that is, combining or compressing one or more separate traditions into a single, often inaccurate, composite rendition – has also begun to occur. Still, Clement of Alexandria is a useful link in the process of transmission and another firm testimony to James' importance in first-century Palestine and other areas in the East heir to traditions relating to him. Nor does Clement evince any embarrassment over James' 'brother' relationship with Jesus.

As to Hegesippus, who he was and what the extent of his writings were, are shrouded in mystery. Were it not again for Eusebius, who like him came from Palestine, we would probably know nothing about his work, nor heard of him. Another curious work called 'Egesippus', supposedly attributed to Hegesippus, has come down to us through Latin, but this does not appear to be the work of Hegesippus at all, but rather a further epitome of Josephus and perhaps part of another lost work – this time by the Platonist Jewish philosopher, Philo of Alexandria.

An older contemporary of James, Philo (*c*. 30 BC–45 CE) was an extremely important personality in the first century and does exhibit tendencies later amalgamated into Christianity – particularly of the Pauline genre. Both he and Josephus made trips to Rome to make appeals concerning events in Palestine and what were perceived as miscarriages of justice there. Paul is also on record in Acts (not always the most reliable witness) as making a similar journey, though his mission from Acts' perspective is rather to report a miscarriage of justice with regard to himself. Paul and Josephus made missions, ostensibly to Nero, between 59 and 64 CE. Philo made one to Nero's predecessor Caligula earlier around 40–41.

Like the Fifth Book of Tacitus' *Histories*, the second part of Philo's *Mission to Gaius* is missing. Just as some notes from Tacitus may have been preserved by Sulpicius Severus, some of Philo may have come down through the '*Egesippus*'. What is missing in the second part of Philo's *Mission to Gaius* presumably would have given us more intimate material about Gaius Caligula's dealings with the anti-Jewish party in Alexandria, who also sent a legation to Gaius to counter Philo and presumably to support Pontius Pilate's activities in Palestine. It would very likely have told us a good deal more about Pontius Pilate as well, not least of which being the events surrounding the crucifixion of Jesus.

Even from the part of Philo's work that has survived a picture emerges of Pontius Pilate completely at odds with that in the Gospels. Philo went to Rome to attempt to dissuade Caligula from his design to have a statue of himself erected in the Temple in Jerusalem, a design, it would seem, encouraged by the Alexandrian anti-Jewish party. In the process, he also provided additional testimony to Pontius Pilate's bloodthirsty repressions and harsh penalties in Palestine more or less in line with the gist of Josephus' accounts, such as they are.

There are also lacunae in Josephus' materials about Pontius Pilate as we have seen. One thing is certain, Pontius Pilate was not the gentle individual later generations took for a Christian or even of Gospel portrait.[4] Rather he was cruelly repressive, not hesitating to shed innocent blood at the slightest provocation. In fact, it appears to have been largely as a result of the protests of individuals as influential as Philo that he was removed from Palestine and returned to Rome in disgrace.

There are also important materials that can be used in a study of James from two other early Church writers from the second century, Papias (*c.*60–135) and Justin Martyr (*c.*100–165). Justin Martyr does not mention James specifically, but the data he records are extremely helpful as regards the substance of what early notions of Christianity might have been, particularly the Righteousness/Piety dichotomy, which he considers the essence of Christianity.[5] He also provides interesting materials about what might have constituted Scripture in those days. Certainly he was not in possession of the various, differentiated Gospels we have today.[6] Where Paul is concerned, though both come from Asia Minor, Justin doesn't mention him at all, but seems rather studiously to avoid him. If this is an indication of some second-century doctrinal rift, it is interesting information indeed.

Even more interesting for our purposes is Papias, whose works have survived only in fragments. Eusebius knows of Papias' works and once again here and there gives excerpts from these. However, there are some fragments purporting to come from Papias which came to light in the last century.[7] If authentic, these are of the utmost importance for studying the family of Jesus, particularly the relationship of Jesus' uncle Cleophas to Mary, and by extension, the relationship of Simeon, Cleophas' son, to Jesus and James. Even if only a later epitome, the information they provide is very penetrating. As these relationships are clarified, so too can the existence of a fourth, rather ephemeral brother of Jesus, which tradition insists on calling Joseph again or 'Joses'.

Apocryphal Gospels, Apocalypses, Acts, and Anti-Acts

In these kinds of documents, too, we have important sources for the life, teaching, and person of James. In the Gospels – primarily the Synoptics – we have the testimony to and the enumeration of the brothers of Jesus, however downplayed these may be.[8] No embarrassment is evinced about the fact of these brothers. Nor is there any indication that they may be half-brothers, brothers by a different mother, or any other such designation aimed at reducing their importance and minimizing their relationship to Jesus.

In these reports Jesus' mother and brothers come to him to talk to or question him. They are four in number, James, Simon, Jude, and Joses. One or more sisters are also mentioned – one specifically named Salome (Mark 15:40). Other than some sayings that imply a disparaging attitude towards those close to Jesus and his immediate family and additional material in Apostle lists, there is little else in the Gospels relating to them. This attitude of disparagement directed against what can only be called 'the Jewish Apostles' – in effect comprising the nucleus of what is called 'the Jerusalem Church' – is a retrospective one and part of the anti-family and anti-Jewish polemic of Pauline or Overseas Christianity, not a historical one.

The fact of these brothers – particularly James, but others as well – also emerges in what are referred to as Apocryphal Gospels, those works in the gospel genre which for one reason or another did not get into the canon that finally emerged in Christianity after Constantine. Principal among these are gospels that are known only through secondhand accounts from Church Fathers, notably Origen, Eusebius, Epiphanius, and Jerome. These include, in particular, the Gospel of the Hebrews, the Gospel of the Nazoraeans, and the Gospel of the Ebionites. None of these gospels, which were all said to have been based on the Gospel of Matthew, has survived, nor is it clear that they were ever really separate gospels at all and not simply variations of each other. They do, however, exist in an independent manner in reports about them, and there are actually quotations from them extant from those claiming to have seen them. In several of these notices, James plays a significant role, particularly in post-resurrection appearances of Jesus.

In addition, James plays an important and prominent role in the Gnostic Gospel of Thomas, recently discovered at Nag Hammadi. Unlike most other gospels, the Gospel of Thomas abjures narrative in favour simply of presenting a list of sayings, all ascribed to Jesus. There are also other materials from Nag Hammadi, which further reinforce the importance James was accorded in the early centuries of Christianity, particularly in the East. There can be no doubt that this is the James of this book and that he was viewed in the manner almost of a Supernatural Redeemer figure superseded in importance only by Jesus himself. This is both curious and interesting, and once again confirms that James' role in the East was one of over-arching importance. It will be the view of this book that this status was only a little exaggerated beyond his true role in the Palestine of his day. Among these documents from Nag Hammadi presenting James as being of such commanding stature are the two apocalypses ascribed to or written in his name, now known as the First and Second Apocalypses of James.

Additionally, among known Apocryphal Gospels that feature the name of James, is the largely fictional Protevangelium of James, which claims to be an account of the infancy of Jesus, told from the point of view of James his closest living relative. Regardless of the credibility of this gospel, and in it we have the doctrine of the Perpetual Virginity of Mary, the importance of James is again highlighted – this time in his role of unimpeachable witness.

Where Books of Acts are concerned, there are other lost materials like the documents referred to by scholars as the '*Kerygamata Petrou*', the 'Teaching of Peter', or another lost work, the 'Travels of Peter'. These are difficult to reconstruct with any certainty, but are thought to have been incorporated in some manner into the cluster of documents known as the Pseudoclementines. It is difficult to overestimate the importance of these documents for a consideration of the person of James. Apart from doctrinal considerations, which are important for later second–third-century groups known in the field as 'Jewish Christians' or 'Ebionites', there are materials, particularly in the First Book of the *Recognitions*, that are important as a kind of anti-Acts. They present a picture of the early days of the Church in Jerusalem from the point of view not of a Luke or a Paul, but of a writer sympathetic to the views and person of James – and with him, the whole of the 'Jerusalem Church' Establishment, including the Jewish Apostles.

It can be objected that the Pseudoclementines are not history but fiction – hence the epithet 'pseudo'. But this is what we are dealing with in regard to most documents from this period, except those with outright historical intent like Josephus. On this basis, the Pseudoclementines do not differ appreciably from more familiar documents like the Gospels or the Book of Acts. Particularly, the first ten or fifteen chapters of Acts are so imaginary as to contain almost no overtly historical material that one can entertain with any degree of certitude. The Pseudoclementines are no more counterfeit than these. But that is just the point – all such documents must be treated equally, according to the same parameters. So difficult to credit are these early chapters of Acts in their present form that many specialists simply jettison them altogether. This is not the position of the present writer.

In fact, using the Pseudoclementine *Recognitions* for control, it is possible to make some sense out of these early and highly mythologized chapters of the Book of Acts. Nor are the Pseudoclementines to be regarded simply as pure fiction. Though they are framed in the guise of Hellenistic romance, so is Acts. That they are much longer than Acts should not present too much of an obstacle. The point is that there is occasionally reliable material in these accounts, particularly in the First Book of the *Recognitions*.

Here one might wish to apply the doctrine of incongruity, that is, when a fact is considered poorly documented for some reason or flies in the face of obviously orthodox materials, this is sometimes good grounds, not for dismissing it, but for taking it more seriously than one might otherwise have done. The actual physical attack by Paul on James, described in the *Recognitions,* is just such a piece of astonishing material. It will overlay lacunae and clearly counterfeit materials in the Book of Acts – for instance, about someone called 'Stephen' – so well that it will be all but impossible to discard.

The Pseudoclementines give a picture of the early Church in Palestine at odds with the one presented in Acts, yet meshing with it at key points. Though they have come down in several recensions, a case can be made for their being based on the same source as Acts – that is, the Pseudoclementines and Acts connect in a series of recognizable common joins, but the material is being treated differently in one narrative than in the other. Though the Pseudoclementines are more voluminous, it can be shown that the same source underlies both.

It matters not that the Pseudoclementines are considered by some to be third- or fourth-century documents, nor that our perspective is not the standard one. It is not the documents comprising the Pseudoclementines in their present form that matter. What matters is the *source* underlying them. At least where the beginning of the *Recognitions* is concerned, this can be shown to be the same as the one underlying the more fantastic and less historical first half of the Book of Acts before the 'We Document' intrudes in the second. In fact, both Acts and the Pseudoclementines are *We Documents*. Moreover, the Pseudoclementines are more faithful to the sense of this source and a more faithful representation of it than Acts.

Nor is it important that Acts in the form we have it is a second-century document. There is no final proof of this proposition, and even if there were, it would not matter. The Book of Acts, at least in the early chapters before the intrusion of the 'We Document', has been extensively reworked. Some might contend, so have the First and Second Books of the Pseudoclementine *Recognitions*, though this proposition is not proven. The point is that both are using sources. For the most part the Pseudoclementines are concerned with confrontations between Peter and Simon *Magus* in Caesarea, where both Origen and Eusebius saw the copy of the works of Josephus ascribing the fall of Jerusalem to the death of James and not Jesus. Acts is also concerned with this confrontation, but whereas it passes over it in a few sentences, the Pseudoclementines linger over its various metamorphoses *ad nauseam*.

However these things may be, the basic treatment of the confrontation between Simon Peter and Simon *Magus* in Caesarea, where the Pseudoclementines correctly locate it, can be shown to be more historical than the patently more fantastic presentation of it in the Book of Acts. The *Recognitions* also clear up Acts' lack of precision about Simon *Magus'* place of origin, which is identified as Gitta in Samaria. This is also confirmed in Eusebius.[9] This is just one example of the superiority of the novelizing of the Pseudoclementines over the novelizing of the Book of Acts, and that all references to 'pseudo' in these matters are relative.

Because of its confusion over this, Acts places Peter's confrontation with Simon *Magus in Samaria* instead of, as in the Pseudoclementines, *Caesarea*, where it properly belongs. When this confrontation is joined with Josephus' picture of the Simon 'the Head of an Assembly' (*Ecclēsia*) of his own or 'Church' in Jerusalem in the *Antiquities*, who also comes to Caesarea to inspect the living arrangements in Agrippa I's palace there around 44 CE, then we shall be able to make some final sense about all these overlapping and sometimes contradictory notices.[10]

Prefaced to the second cluster of Pseudoclementine materials, the *Homilies*, are two letters like those one finds in the New Testament. However these are not primarily from Paul as in the latter, but rather letters purporting to be from Peter to James and Clement to James. Putting aside the question of their authenticity for the moment and the fact that they parallel letters in the New Testament, that they are pointedly addressed to James as 'Bishop of Bishops' or 'Archbishop' shows that their authors had little doubt that James was the leader of the whole of Christianity in his time and that Apostles like Peter and Paul were subordinate to him.

In addition, these letters contain several points of importance for our consideration, for instance, that all overseas teachers required letters of introduction or certification from James and were required to send him back periodic reports of their activities – an assertion that makes sense. This is the thrust, too, of the 'we' aspect of these narratives and that of Acts, which makes more sense because of these letters. The 'We Document' is one of these reports. We would have had little trouble deducing this in any case from reading between the lines of Paul's shrill protests concerning his lack of such certification in the more familiar documents that have come down to us. But the fact of this requirement actually being present in these apocryphal letters introducing a narrative that has all the earmarks of an 'anti-Acts' is impressive. It is like finding a missing link. Had it not been present, we would have had to deduce it.

To sum up: it is our position that Acts and the Pseudoclementines are neither independent of nor dependent on each other; but parallel accounts going back to the same source: that is, the First and Second Books of the Pseudoclementine *Recognitions* do not go back to Acts, but to a common source both were using. That the Acts we have may have appeared at some indeterminant amount of time before the appearance of the *Recognitions* (if it did) does not alter this. But one can go even further than this. One can insist, however startling this may at first appear, that the *Recognitions* are more faithful to this underlying source – where points common to both are concerned – than Acts. The points of contact between the two are clearly discernible as, for instance, the persistent note of confrontations on the Temple Mount culminating in an attack led by Paul on someone, but so is the fact that Acts is changing the source on which both are based in a consistent and clearly discernible manner. At times this borders on what, in the jargon of today, might be called 'disinformation'.

These confrontations on the Temple Mount would also appear to be the subject matter of another lost work about James, from which Epiphanius quotes several passages. Epiphanius calls this work, which we have mentioned above, the *Anabathmoi Jacobou* – the *Ascents of Jacob*, a title that sets up interesting resonances with the Jewish underground mystical tradition known as *Kabbalah*. This work, which appears to relate to the discourses James gave in the Temple while standing on the Temple steps – hence the title – also relates to the picture in the early part of Acts of the Apostles going every day to the Temple as a group, and there either talking to the Jewish crowd or arguing with the Temple Authorities. This picture is also re-presented in the *Recognitions of Clement*, and some have theorized that materials from the *Anabathmoi* have ended up in the Pseudoclementines.

The materials that Epiphanius does excerpt are interesting in themselves and fill in some missing points about Paul's biography, as seen through the eyes of his opponents not his supporters, and place James at the centre of agitation in the Temple in the years leading up to the Uprising. Not only will this last assertion be shown to bear on how Temple service was being carried out by Herodian High Priests, but also to the rejection of gifts and sacrifices from Gentiles in the Temple by those Josephus calls either '*Sicarii*' or '*Zealots*' three and a half years after the death of James, triggering the Revolt against Rome. Both will also be seen reflected in the Dead Sea Scrolls.

The Dead Sea Scrolls

The most controversial and debatable identifications we will have to make in this study will concern the Dead Sea Scrolls. It will be asked, what have these documents to do with a study of and the person of James? The answer is simple. In the first place, they are parallel and, in some cases, contemporary cultural materials. Some may object that the Dead Sea Scrolls are earlier documents. Even if this proposition were proven for all the Scrolls found at Qumran, which it is not, the ideas represented in much of the corpus have a familiar ring, particularly when one gets to know those ideas and conceptualities associated with James' person or takes an in-depth look at the letter associated with his name in the New Testament. So, initially, it is certainly permissible to say that the ideas found at Qumran flow in a fairly consistent manner into the ideas associated with the Community led by James, regardless of the dating of the Scrolls.

But one can go further. Let us look at the dating. This is not secure at all. In the first place, it was based on imprecise palaeographic assumptions and conclusions.[11] Palaeography is not an exact science for any period or place – certainly not the period we have before us, where we have few (in fact, almost no) contemporary exemplars of manuscripts for comparison or control purposes to allow us to make secure, final determinations.

No one doubts that there are older documents among the deposit collectively now known as the Dead Sea Scrolls, documents like Ben Sira or Ecclesiasticus from what is called Apocrypha, numerous biblical manuscripts, versions of some of the Testaments of the Twelve Patriarchs, Enoch, Jubilees, and the like from what are also commonly called Pseudepigrapha – 'False Writings'. But no one can contest the fact that there are also newer ones, the only question being how new? It is these that must be seen as contemporary and in many instances containing ideas and allusions that are all but indistinguishable from those represented by the Community led by James. Documents of this kind are sometimes referred to as 'sectarian', meaning, in terms of our above discussions, non-Pharisaic or non-Rabbinic. These at the very least must be seen as including all the *pesharim* at Qumran (Hebrew plural for *pesher*).

But what is a *pesher*? A *pesher* is a commentary – at Qumran, a commentary on a well-known biblical passage, usually from the Prophets, but also from Psalms and sometimes even other biblical books like Genesis, Leviticus, or Deuteronomy. The important thing is that the underlying biblical passage being interpreted should be seen as fraught with significance in relation to the ideology or history of the Scroll Community. Often this takes the form of citing a biblical passage or quotation out of context or even sometimes slightly altered, followed by the words, *'peshero'* or *'pesher ha-davar'*, meaning 'its interpretation' or 'the interpretation of the passage is'. The text then proceeds to give an idiosyncratic interpretation having to do with the history or ideology of the group, with particular reference to contemporary events. The process is a familiar one to those conversant with the New Testament, particularly the Gospel of Matthew.

At Qumran these commentaries or *peshers* have been found in single exemplars only and none so far in multiple copies, which is not the case for other documents found there, biblical or sectarian. By sectarian, we mean new, non-biblical documents, many never seen or heard of before. The number of these new or sectarian documents reaches well into the hundreds. This is why the documents at Qumran are so astonishing. They are not just a random sampling or cross-section of the literature from this period, as some have theorized to lessen the import of such a homogeneous collection, but very uniform and consistent in content. Of course there are variations having to do with the style or personality of individual authors or period of origin, but the same doctrines move from document to document, the same terms, the same dramatis personae.

The point is that the literature represented by Qumran – and it is a literature – is a wildly creative one, and different authors are expressing themselves, sometimes in a most creative or poetic manner. However, one will never, for instance, find a document advocating compromise at Qumran. Nor one recommending accommodation with the powers-that-be or foreigners or those the writers designate in their sometimes infuriatingly obscure code, 'Seekers after Smooth Things', an epithet as pejorative today as it was then. One will never find a text denigrating the Law, nor advocating, for instance, 'niece marriage', 'polygamy', or 'divorce', all of which this group considered 'breaking the Law'.

The same imagery, too, moves from document to document, the imagery of 'Righteousness', 'Perfection', 'zeal', 'the Poor', straightening 'the Way', the Community as Temple, 'Holy Spirit' baptism, the 'Perfection of Holiness', and the same personalities: 'the Righteous Teacher', 'the Wicked Priest', 'the Spouter of Lies', 'the Comedian', or 'the Traitors'. There are multiple copies of some sectarian or non-biblical documents like the famous War Scroll, the Community Rule, the

Damascus Document – sometimes called because of the imagery it uses 'the Zadokite Document' – the Qumran Hymns, '*MMT*' or 'the Letters relating to Works Righteousness',[12] and others. The Damascus Document, for instance, was first found in the Cairo *Genizah* in Egypt at the end of the last century, which is why the location Cairo (CD) is always affixed to the designation for it.

The precise date of these documents is still a matter of some conjecture and much controversy. It is not that these documents do not come from the Second Temple Period. They do. The problem is trying to date them with more precision than that. Documents like the War Scroll and Hymns are no doubt 'late', that is, late in the life of the Sect or Community, the only issue being how late. From internal parameters, not to mention handwriting, I think one can date them in the first century CE. The discussion of the Damascus Document, the Community Rule, the Temple Scroll, and documents of this kind is more complex and will probably never be resolved.

Given the state of the archaeological and palaeographic data having to do with the Community responsible for these writings, I have said that one must make one's determinations on the basis of internal data – internal allusions and perspective of the document itself. Take, for example, the Community Rule, which many Qumran specialists have attempted to date in the second century BC – even earlier – on the basis of what they call handwriting, that is 'older' as opposed to 'newer' fragments.[13] A recent AMS Carbon-14 test on one exemplar of this document put it in the second or even the third century CE. These are the kinds of contradictions one encounters.

However in it we have the 'Way in the wilderness' text from Isaiah 40:3, applied in the New Testament to the mission of John the Baptist, referred to twice, and an exposition of the passage consistent with the internal mindset of Qumran, applying it to the Community's own 'separation' and activities in the wilderness.[14] In addition, there is a plethora of other allusions like 'the Holy Spirit', baptism, the Community as Temple, and 'spiritualized sacrifice' imagery so familiar in the Pauline corpus.[15] Given the parallels with what we know to be first-century ideas, *this document is late* – meaning first century CE – regardless of palaeography or any other kinds of external parameters that might be used to suggest otherwise.

The same can be said for the Damascus Document. This document was first found in 1896 at the Cairo *Genizah* – a manuscript cache from a synagogue in old Cairo from the Middle Ages – by Solomon Schechter,

Reader of Rabbinics at Cambridge and the founder of Conservative Judaism in America. At the time of its discovery, many people considered the document as 'Jewish Christian'.[16] With the Qumran finds a half-century later, parallels to this document were discovered, although just how many could not be determined until the final struggle for access to the totality of the corpus was concluded in the last few years. It was our request for access to these withheld parallels that triggered the controversy ending with the final release of the Scrolls – though, unfortunately, not reducing any of the acrimony endemic to this field.[17]

Again, on the basis of internal data in this document, the exegesis of 'the Star Prophecy' and other Messianic allusions – the first-century currency of which is indisputable – together with references to 'the Liar' and 'the Righteous One' or 'Righteous Teacher', paralleling similar notices in the *Pesharim*, the ideology of 'Justification', the Commandment to 'love your neighbour,' which the Letter of James calls 'the Royal Law according to the Scripture' and which Josephus designates as one of the fundamental parts of John the Baptist's 'Righteousness'/'Piety' dichotomy, and the 'Damascus' imagery one also finds in the Book of Acts – there are many more[18] – this document must be seen as having a first-century ambience as well, regardless of arguments to the contrary based on external data.

Recently a process of AMS carbon testing was initiated with regard to the Dead Sea Scrolls, largely as a result of the present writer's initiative and suggestions.[19] These tests produced skewed or mixed results and the final evaluation of them has to be seen as inconclusive. Sometimes these results were far too early and some far too late.[20] Nor were they carried out with the normal safeguards necessary for such evidence, namely, the use of double or triple blinds, objective selection and conveyance of materials by persons not party to the debate, and the like.

Neither were the tests that were done extensive or precise enough to provide the kind of results those conducting them claim. Nor were the concerns of 'opposition' scholars, who originally called for the tests, taken into consideration or met. Rather, given the nature of the parties conducting them, they were idiosyncratic and without any internal logic or consistency. Afterwards, the claims made for their precision were and still are far in excess of anything one can ordinarily expect from carbon testing.

Carbon testing is by nature imprecise, its parameters too uncertain to make determinations within a fifty- or even a hundred-year margin of error. The whole process of carbon dating must be independently calibrated either on the basis of known documents or on the basis of dendrochronology – tree-ring calibration. Where the former are concerned, hardly any exist except the finds from the Bar Kochba Period at Nahal Hever and Wadi Murabba‘at perhaps a century or so later, which is the reason why we called some time ago for the establishment of a data bank of documents of both unknown, as well as known, dating provenance, to establish such parameters.[21]

Nor can the accuracy claimed for such tests be anywhere near the accuracy that can be said properly to apply, carbon testing notoriously tending to archaize, meaning it makes documents seem older than they actually are. Plus, the tests only measure when a given plant or animal was supposed to have grown or died, not when a given manuscript was actually written on the finished product.[22] Carbon testing can be a useful tool, particularly where relative, not absolute, dating is concerned, that is to say in comparing ‘early’ or ‘late’ dating in the same test run, which is what the present writer was initially interested in seeing, to test the claims for ‘relative dating’ where palaeography was concerned.

Regardless of the claims, the results are only as good as the interpretation given them, which bears on another problem – laboratory predisposition or the tendency of a given lab to arrive at the results those using its services or sponsoring the tests desire. This is particularly the case with the two labs that were used, both of which overtly framed their reports to attack the opponents of and defend those sponsoring the tests conducted. Nor is it clear that either of these labs have been subjected to proper, blind external proficiency tests. The documents of known dating provenance that were supplied do not count in this regard, since, as just noted, there are no known documents from this period from any century other than the second.

Where results were arrived at that were at odds with what the laboratories were led to expect, they were simply dismissed. This problem is inherent even in the final reports written up in both series of tests that were done, which go out of their way overtly to support hitherto majority theories or archaeology and palaeography, vividly evincing the original predisposition of the lab involved.[23] The conceptualities engendered by these last two external indicators contradict the clear internal thrust of the documents themselves, rendering any attempt to make sense of them stillborn.

This has been the case from the beginning of Qumran research and still is. Therefore, since the earliest days of Qumran research little or no clear understanding of the Qumran documents has emerged, and this is once again the case today, since the Establishment consensus has re-formed itself. This is what is meant by going according to the internal data and the vocabulary, allusions, and internal ethos of the texts themselves as opposed to archaeological, palaeographic, or C-14 evidence.

Where we presently stand with regard to the results so far is that one is more or less in the same situation as one is with regard to palaeography. While a useful tool, carbon testing is only that and we are finally thrown back on the results of internal analysis to make final determinations of the date of the documents at Qumran. These depend as much on the interpretation of the data by the given lab conducting them as anything else and, therefore – in this field – are not secure enough to rule out an otherwise convincing explanation based on the clear thrust of the documents themselves, which in the case of the Scrolls is compelling indeed.

On this basis, all *pesharim* from Qumran must be seen as 'late'. This is not only because of allusion to formuli like 'the Last Priests of Jerusalem' and Habakkuk 2:4, 'the Righteous shall live by his Faith', which we know was being subjected to exegesis in the first century CE; but also the searing description of the foreign armies invading the country, who 'sacrifice to their standards and worship their weapons of war' – Roman Imperial practice of the first century CE – and Roman 'tax-farming' and final 'booty-taking' in the Temple, which did not occur after any assault except that of 70 CE.[24]

Since they have been found in single copies only, they would appear to represent the latest literature of the Community, the literature that did not have time to go into wide circulation or be reproduced in multiple copies. In addition, they are extremely personalized or idosyncratic, filled with the ethos of events transpiring in the cataclysmic 'End Time' or 'Last Days' spoken of in Daniel and the New Testament.

It is also primarily in these *pesharim* that one comes upon all the dramatis personae of the Community and its history so familiar to those acquainted with the literature at Qumran. For instance, in addition to the terms cited above, 'the Simple of Judah doing *Torah*', 'the Simple of Ephraim', 'the Violent Ones of the Gentiles', 'the Kittim', 'the Peoples', 'the Additional Ones of the Peoples', 'the city of blood' or 'the city built upon blood', 'the *Ebionim*' or 'Poor', 'the Meek', and so on. These allusions are tied in an apocalyptic manner to prized biblical texts, the reason for whose choice becomes extremely clear once one examines the vocabulary involved.

The author or authors of these commentaries definitely felt they were living in some cataclysmic 'End Time' and all the imagery, everything about their ethos, particularly in the sectarian texts, including the repetitive vocabulary they employ, points to the Roman Period – in fact, to be precise, to the Period of Imperial Rome.[25]

We shall be able to link these allusions – particularly from the *Pesharim*, but also from the Damascus Document, Community Rule, and War Scroll – in a clearly definable pattern to events of James' life. Not only this, but an additional effect will develop. When the events of James' life are superimposed on the materials from Qumran, particularly those having to do with the destruction of the Righteous Teacher by the Wicked Priest, additional data can be elicited from them that one would not otherwise have known or suspected. Seeming *non sequiturs* or obscure readings are cleared up, and additional data thus elicited from the texts.

No other character from any time or place during the two or three centuries of Palestinian history we are studying produces anything like the same match one gets when one views James in relation to the Scroll documents. Reigning theories of Qumran origins generally evade this issue and often do not even attempt to develop the internal evidence involved. This is the safer way, but in these materials we have to do with a *major movement* within Judaism and dramatis personae of no slight importance. It is impossible that these people should have failed to make an impression on their time and place, nor appear in the wealth of sources we have available to us for this period.

There are other considerations, too, that need to be analysed. Here we have two communities: 'the Jerusalem Community' led by a teacher called, in tradition, James 'the Just' – or, to follow the sense of the original Hebrew, James 'the Righteous One' – and the Community at Qumran led by an unknown teacher called 'the Righteous Teacher' or 'the Teacher of Righteousness'. Like James, he too appears to come to an unhappy end.

Whenever the details relating to the Qumran Teacher's life, teaching, and demise, are being developed in a *pesher*, the allusion played on in the underlying biblical text to produce the exegesis is in Hebrew invariably 'the *Zaddik*' or 'Righteous One'. This is so common that almost every available '*Zaddik*' text from the Bible is subjected to exegesis in some manner in the extant materials from Qumran.[26] This amounts almost to a rule of thumb. Significantly, one will find the same or similar texts being applied to James' demise in early Christian writings. This basic parallel regarding these two more or less contemporary Communities and their leaders cannot be overlooked, even if one is only used as a paradigm for the other.

It has been contended that the Scroll Community is at Qumran while the Jerusalem Community is in Jerusalem – thus they are different, however parallel their teachings. This might appear on the surface a fair statement, except that a careful analysis of the Qumran texts often places the Righteous Teacher and his followers in Jerusalem. On the other hand, materials in the Jamesian corpus definitively place James and all his Community in the region of Jericho near the location of Qumran.[27]

With regard to the actual physical site at Qumran and the fortress-like settlement located there, references to the wilderness 'camps' in the Qumran documents are invariably in the plural. On the basis of internal data there is no indication whatsoever where these 'camps' might have been located, except for two references in the War Scroll to, firstly, 'the wilderness of the Peoples' and, secondly, 'the wilderness of Judea'. The former is probably synonymous with what goes by the name of 'the Land of Damascus' or just plain 'Damascus' in the Document deriving its name from that designation. And in this document, the figure known as 'the *Mebakker*' or 'Overseer' or 'Bishop', who is either synonymous with or parallels another known as 'the High Priest Commanding the Camps', bears an uncanny resemblance to James and his role in the early Church.[28]

How Late are the Scrolls?

It remains only to determine what is meant by a 'late' document. Partially because of the pressure to attack the position taken by the present writer, some are now claiming in Qumran studies that no documents are later than the mid-first century BC. This absurdity was never posited in the early days of Qumran research, since everyone presumably realized how incapable of proof such a proposition would be.

Nevertheless, such an argument changes little regarding the position being developed in this book. All the doctrines, ideas, and orientations, all the exegeses that would then have been current among 'opposition' groups of the first century BC, can then be shown to have flowed full-blown and almost without alteration into the main 'opposition' orientation of the first century CE. Thus the argument of this book remains unaffected. Only the direct textual link to James or some other first-century 'Righteous One' or '*Zaddik*' would be broken, but, given the amount of evidence that we shall see in the second volume of this work that can be marshalled to show such a link with James, such a new approach has the appearance more of desperation than scholarship.

However the tenuousness of maintaining such an early position with regard to *all* manuscript production at Qumran should be clear to almost any fair-minded observer, except those who for theological, ideological, or psychological reasons of their own are propounding it. It is generally acknowledged that the Qumran Community was destroyed somewhere in the course of the First Uprising against Rome between 66 and 73 CE. This conclusion is based on the archaeology of the site and the coins found there, not the texts, which are inconclusive on this point. Establishment scholarship gives 68 CE for the date of the fall of the settlement at Qumran because of the numerous coins found there from the Second Year of the Revolt against Rome.

But finding a coin at a given locale is, firstly, no proof of who dropped it and, secondly, no proof of the year it was dropped. In the jargon of the discipline, it only provides a *terminus a quo* not a *terminus ad quem*, an earliest possible date, not a last possible. To add to this, the archaeology done on the site in the early 50s is incomplete and very controversial, showing many deficiencies of methodology. While much was found; much also seems to have been 'created'.

Many coins found there are now simply missing and some considered too oxidized to read.[29] This means that, if it is thought the texts in fact do relate to the site and were not brought there from somewhere else, and that the site fell during the First Uprising against Rome, then the only thing one can say with certainty is that it fell *some time before 73 CE*. This latter represents the date of the mass suicide at Masada some 50 kilometres south of Qumran, which completed the Roman takeover of the area. The assumption here is that the Scrolls were deposited in the various caves simultaneously with the fall of the settlement or the destruction of its buildings. But, once again, there are no certainties – the two events might not have been simultaneous.

In fact, there are coins from the Messianic Bar Kochba Uprising of 132–6 at Qumran as well. Since it makes no sense to think that Roman troops dropped Jewish Revolutionary coins at Qumran – an isolated one perhaps, but not in quantity – these have to be considered as having been dropped there by Jewish partisans. The careful observer will recognize a proposition here. The final *terminus ad quem* for Jewish presence at Qumran is, therefore – if such a presence is connected with the deposit of the manuscripts in the various caves in the neighbourhood of the site – the end of the Uprising 136 CE. Nothing less will do.

It may be that the manuscripts were deposited earlier. But how much earlier and at what precise date cannot be determined on the basis of the archaeological evidence available to us. This is the only properly scientific conclusion to draw based on the archaeological evidence from Qumran, such as it is. Here, one is thrown back once again, as ever, on the *internal data* or evidence of the documents themselves.

Recently, some new shards were found, seemingly by accident, among the debris of previous archaeological digging. Some of these contained writing and appear to be the records or receipts for supplies and services received from '*Jericho*'. At least one bore the dating formula, 'Year 2', that is, 'Year 2 of the Freedom' or 'Redemption of Zion' – or the Revolt against Rome of the coins mentioned above. Not only are these some of the first real day-to-day written evidence showing habitation well into the year 68 CE, they demonstrate the Community was not an isolated one. Nor was it divorced from circumstances, material, and events at Jericho (cf. Pseudoclementine *Recognitions* 1.70–71). In addition, they show that the Community at Qumran was sympathetic to and participating in the general resistance effort against Rome and certainly employing its calendar – which, of course, has been our argument all along.[30]

One final point, when considering the archaeological evidence for site abandonment at Qumran: habitation continued in the region of Qumran into the 80s and beyond.[31] Ein Feshka is a fresh-water oasis about two kilometres south of Qumran, where underground springs emerge from beneath the limestone cliffs along the shores of the Dead Sea. There are building remains here too and coin evidence going well beyond the supposed fall of Qumran in 68 CE. Nor does Ein Feshka seem to have been destroyed in the same manner as Qumran.

But Ein Feshka cannot be divorced from Qumran. If nothing else, the agriculture that sustained the population at Qumran was carried out there, since there is insufficient water at Qumran to support an agricultural enterprise. In twenty-five years of visiting the site I have seen the water flow down the waterfall at the top of the *Wadi* Qumran only once – this in an extremely wet year on the Bethlehem Plain in the hills above. The climate is not so different today from what it was in ancient times. The evidence from Ein Feshka indicates that Jewish habitation continued in the area beyond the *terminus* date designated by scholars for the deposit of the manuscripts at Qumran. In this case, then, nothing at all of certainty can be said about the deposit of the Scrolls in the various caves associated with Qumran. Only that it happened some time before the end of the Bar Kochba Uprising in 136 CE, when habitation in the region really does seem to have come to an end.

This brings us to a conundrum. What was the Qumran Community doing throughout two hundred of the most eventful years of Palestinian history, if, as the reigning hypothesis now seems bent on contending, all the documents date from a period before the coming of the Herodians and the Romans around 50 BC? For the purposes of argument, suppose a date of 68 CE or even 70 CE is recognized for the deposit of the Scrolls in the caves, regardless of the difficulties either date may present. This would mean the sectaries at Qumran had completely lost their creative energies; that their creative impulses had long before been sapped, and they were, rather, ignoring a hundred years of the most meaningful and eventful Palestinian history – which the rise and falls in the coin data show whoever was inhabiting the site at Qumran were quite sensitive to.

No, this new assertion is not convincing. Particularly since the references in the Scrolls themselves abound with allusions that have a fairly definitive first-century CE provenance. We have already noted some of these; there are many more. Additionally, the internal historical data of many of the documents seem to point to Roman Imperial Armies being the invaders – and this is in line with the all-pervasiveness of their power and the unfeeling brutality of their methods. The Scrolls also directly allude to the coming destruction of the Temple and its Priesthood, who are even referred to in the all-important *Pesher* on the Prophet Habakkuk as 'the Last Priests of Jerusalem'.[32] One is on much safer ground to avoid all interpretations dictated by ideological or theological preconceptions and admit the first-century CE provenance of many of the *later* Qumran documents. Indeed, they fairly cry out for such an interpretation.

PART II

THE HISTORICAL JAMES

6

The First Appearance of James in Acts

The Book of Acts as History

Historically speaking James first appears in a really tangible way in the Book of Acts. But the presentation is not a straightforward one. There are, as usual, puzzling lacunae. Materials known from other sources are left out and things that should logically have been covered are missing. To the perspicacious observer, however, the traces of these other data are still there, to be filled in by inference from what is said elsewhere or the underlying implications of the text itself or its sources. To the neophyte, this can be unsettling, but once he or she has grasped what is really occurring, it can be uplifting, approaching the joy of a discovery or enlightenment.

First, the reader should realize that the Book of Acts cannot be considered a historical presentation. There is too much mythologizing, too much that is out-and-out fiction, too much fantasizing. Important materials are left out, yet, underlying the presentation, the broad lines of a certain kind of history can be discerned.

For instance, how was the succession to Jesus managed? We hear about an 'election' of sorts, but then this turns out not to have been the election of Jesus' successor, which would have been the logical expectation at this point in a narrative purporting to cover the beginnings of the early Church, but rather clearly obscurantist material about the election of a Twelfth Apostle to succeed not Jesus but, of all people, 'Judas' his alleged 'betrayer'. This is the first bit of sleight of hand in Acts, and this election, as we shall see, will dovetail nicely with notices in early Church literature about a first election of James as *Bishop* or *Bishop of Bishops* of the early Church.

Questions like why there had to be 'Twelve Apostles' in the first place, or who – aside from the election of this inconsequential successor to Judas named Matthias – succeeded Jesus are passed by in silence. Then there are the questions about the identity of the majority of the Apostles or what a 'Bishop' or an 'Archbishop' actually was, not to mention how James came to be found in this position in the first place. Acts is normally thought of as being 'the acts' of the Apostles in general, that is, 'the Twelve',[1] who are variously listed according to which account one is following, and yet the author or authors of the narrative clearly know almost nothing about the majority of these Apostles.

At a very early stage the narrative moves over to the story of Paul – who is not really even an 'Apostle' at all – at least not one of the original ones (7:58) and, except as he comes in contact with one or another of these, the narrative completely loses interest in them. For instance, we know next to nothing about Peter after he conveniently leaves Palestine just in time to make way for the introduction of James in chapter 12. We are told nothing about his travels or experiences, not even what happens to him in Rome – if he ever gets there – and nothing about his death. We are not told about any of the other significant members of 'the Twelve' either, except James, and yet James is not supposed to be a member of 'the Twelve' or an Apostle. As we shall see, he was, if such a reckoning can in any sense be considered historical.

Clearly the narrator would have told us about things as important as these if he knew them. Either he did not know them or his interest lay in other things, or he *did*, and still his interest lay in other things. What things? As we shall see, almost exclusively Paul. For instance, when Paul comes to Rome in the last chapter of Acts, it would have been convenient to pick up Peter's story again if our narrator knew anything about it. He does not. Why not? Why don't we hear anything about Peter overseas? Even Galatians gives us more accurate material of this kind than Acts. What became of Peter? Our text, in time advertised as 'the Acts of the Apostles', is curiously silent on these things.

But even when it focuses on Paul, the text either from embarrassment or something else tells us nothing about his early career. Again, we can learn more by looking at the first chapter of Galatians. It does not tell us anything about Peter's demise either. We would have expected to have been informed of these things. Why weren't we? All the text does is bring us to Rome with Paul. Then it leaves us. We do not know what happened to Paul in the end any more than we do Peter – or James for that matter. We are left only with the information that Paul comes to Rome, and no one seems aware of what he is doing or why he is there – in fact, no one seems to care about or have heard of him at all. Paul is virtually free or, at most, under a kind of light house arrest.

It does no good to assert the narrator would have thought we knew

about Paul's end or Peter's. If the narrator had had this information –
dramatic as other sources seem to conceive of it – he would or should
have supplied it.[2] Why doesn't he? We do not know even if Paul went on
to Spain, as he was supposed to have done (Rom. 15:24–28), whether he
was re-arrested a second time or under what circumstances, or whether
perhaps he returned to Palestine, as some evidence seems to suggest.[3] We
shall supply evidence to support this suspicion later, but for the moment
suffice it to say that none of these questions is answered. Acts is not history.
It is not even particularly good narrative, romance, or fiction.

Nor does the text tell us about the dramatic events centring about
James' death, which, following even Acts' somewhat questionable time
format, also occurred at exactly the point Acts ends about two years after
Paul's arrival in Rome.[4] A lacuna of this magnitude is inexplicable, until
one realizes Acts tells us about few, if any, of 'the other Apostles' except
Paul. Of these presumed 'Twelve Apostles', Acts mentions John, but in
little or no detail, and has one small more or less fictional episode about
a 'Philip'. Peter is mentioned only in passing, to be discarded almost
completely after Paul makes his appearance. The first James – 'James *the
brother of John*' – is eliminated from the scene at this point as well, just in
time for the sudden eruption of the second James (James *the brother of
Jesus*) into the narrative.

In fact, just about all the other Apostles that Acts so carefully lists at
the beginning of its narrative are simply shadowy figures to flesh out the
twelve-man Apostle scheme it and the Gospels are so intent on presenting.
They are really only paper figures and the author of Acts really knows
next to nothing about them or, if he does, he is not very willing to be
forthcoming concerning them.

Indeed, it would be more accurate to say that Acts is really a narrative
about the 'acts' of the Holy Spirit, not the early Church or Apostles at all.
It traces the acts of the Holy Spirit in their various manifestations, and
true history goes by the board almost from the beginning. But then the
Holy Spirit is a doctrine most of all characterizing the Gentile Mission of
Paul. Why does one say this? Well, aside from receiving various visions
and instruction via the mechanism of the Holy Spirit, it is the Holy Spirit
that Paul claims as the final confirmation and verification, not only of his
doctrinal ideas, but his very Mission itself.

When Paul argues with the Jerusalem Leadership of the Church – which
he does – it is the Holy Spirit that in his view gives him equal status, even
superior 'Knowledge' to them (Gal. 2:2). It is the Holy Spirit that not only

certifies his credentials as an Apostle, but also his Mission generally. Not unmindful of this fact, the religio-historical narrative of Acts is careful to present the accoutrements of the descent of the Holy Spirit, as *speaking in tongues* and *miracles*, such as raisings, curings, and the like (2:4). The former allows the Gentile Mission to be taken out to all the peoples of the world, while the latter confirm this.

James the *Brother of Jesus* and James the *Brother of John*

The first reference to James in Acts comes in a request by Peter to the servants at 'Mary the mother of John Mark's house' – whoever this Mary may have been or this new John – after his escape from prison and before his departure to points unknown, presumably abroad or overseas. It reads: 'Report these things to James and *the brothers*' (12:17).

Before proceeding to the problems presented by it, we must first distinguish this James from several other Jameses, particularly the more familiar Great James or 'James the brother of John the son of Zebedee'. James the so-called 'Great' or 'James the brother of John' (Acts 12:2 – 'Zebedee' mercifully omitted here), as opposed presumably to 'James the Less' (Mark 15:40 – our *James*) and another 'Justus' who appears in Acts 1:23, is the James who occasionally appears along with James the Just, the brother of Jesus in the Gospels.[5]

He is the familiar James among the Apostles and the James most people think they are talking about when they speak of James. Few, if any, realize there was a second one even greater, and that the first is, in all probability, if not merely a minor character, simply an overlay or gloss.[6] The authors of Acts know nothing substantial about him and conveniently remove him at the beginning of chapter 12 just before the James we are speaking of appears. For his part, Paul never mentions a 'James *the brother of John*' and none of the Church Fathers knows anything else about him except apocryphally.

Yet his existence is confidently asserted by almost all who talk with knowledge about Scripture. Such is the power of the written word. What they are confidently asserting is that they have read about this James or know who he is or is supposed to have been, not that they know that he *was*. The same is true for his purported father 'Zebedee', another character again hardly more than simple fiction. For the present writer characters of this kind are simply meant as dissimulation to confuse the unsuspecting reader. When we stated in the Introduction that *poetry was truer than history*, this aphorism could not better apply than to this plethora of characters the whole world confidently assumes existed.

It is the 'brother' theme, however, that will allow us to place in clear focus who this second James may have been, once we have dismissed the nomenclature 'Zebedee' as poorly disguised, overseas fiction. We will encounter several others of this kind, so by the end of the book the *modus operandi* behind such overwrites should become plain – a case in point, the 'Agabus' who will catch hold of Paul's girdle in Acts 20:10–11 in order to stop him from going to Jerusalem. There will be no 'prophet called Agabus' as Acts would have it, though there will be a prophet of sorts mentioned in Josephus at this point and there will be an 'Agabus' or, rather, an 'Abgarus' or 'Agbarus'.[7] Another favourite New Testament character who probably does not exist will be Judas *Iscariot* – probably a play on Jesus' and James' *third* brother 'Judas the brother of James'.[8]

James – the real James – is never introduced or identified in Acts. He just appears. Actually he does not really appear here; this appearance is saved for chapter 15. He is alluded to parenthetically in Peter's request, 'tell these things [that is, Peter's miraculous escape and departure] to James and the brothers' after the alleged *other* 'James' has already disappeared from the narrative; but from what is said there, it is implied that our James – James the Just – was either mentioned earlier or we should know who he is. But how should we know who he is if in the present version of the document he was not mentioned previously or he was never introduced to us? Even this oblique mention of James, after the only other James we have ever heard of has been decapitated, does not tell us who he is.

Either one is willing to accept that a character as important as James could be just introduced into the text of Acts at this point in such an off-hand manner, or something is missing or has been discarded. He is obviously already the leader of 'the Jerusalem Church' – note the mention in Greek of the term for Church, '*Ecclēsia*' or 'Assembly', in the notice at the beginning of the chapter about how Herod the King 'put James the son of Zebedee to death' – and continues in this role for the rest of the book. Again, either James was of such importance to everyone at the time that we should know who he is or there is something missing from the text.

The actual episode occurs just after Peter, who has been having visions via the mechanism of the Holy Spirit and experiencing voices crying out to him from Heaven on the rooftop in Jaffa, goes to visit the household of a Roman Centurion named 'Cornelius' (Acts 9–11). All these episodes have as their root the admission of Gentiles or those who do not follow Jewish religious Law – 'the Law of Moses' – into the Church. Peter escapes from prison after having been arrested for some unexplained reason by 'Herod' (Acts 12:6). All these points need exposition. We are in the thick of the Jewish historical world in Jerusalem and along the sea coast of Palestine of the late 30s and early 40s CE.

The Herods

Setting aside for the moment the actual historicity of this curious Peter or Simon, involved in these kinds of activities along the Palestinian coast, and who he might have been – Josephus will tell us about a parallel 'Simon', the head of an 'Assembly' or 'Church' (also *Ecclēsia*) of his own in Jerusalem in the same period, whom 'Herod' would have very good cause to arrest or execute – it would be important to grasp who all these characters designated in the New Testament as 'Herod the King' actually were. Acts has this particular Herod beheading James the brother of John at the beginning of the chapter and dying 'eaten by worms' at the end of the chapter (12:23).

Curiously, the next chapter, 13, in swinging back to Paul and describing the nature and composition of his Antioch 'Church' or 'Assembly' (*Ecclēsia* again), begins with a reference to another 'Herod' – 'Herod the Tetrarch'. Here we can assume a certain amount of precision in the material before us ascribed to Luke, who is thought to be dependent on Josephus for historical notices of this type in any event.

This notice is referring to the 'prophets and teachers of the Church in Antioch', and what is striking as well is that in the very next line it includes the commandment, now ascribed to the Holy Spirit, 'to separate' themselves – in this case Barnabas and Saul – a central concept where the Dead Sea Scrolls are concerned, not to mention the mission of John the Baptist in the wilderness.[9] Aside from Barnabas and Saul, these include someone called 'Simeon' (Simon Peter again?) – here surnamed 'Niger'[10] – 'Lucius the Cyrenian' (probably Luke himself), and someone referred to as 'Manaen, the foster brother of Herod the Tetrarch'.

To complicate things, this is not the same 'Herod' as in chapter 12. Whatever one might wish to say about him, the fact of a 'Herodian' member of the founding Community for Gentile Christianity in Antioch[11] is in itself embarrassing enough. Ultimately, it will probably turn out that if one drops what is probably another nonsense name or overwrite, 'Manaen' (Ananias?), and transfers the descriptive phrase 'the foster brother of Herod the Tetrarch' to Saul or Paul, one might have a more accurate description of the truth of the matter.[12] When speaking about this 'Herod the Tetrarch', though, there can be little doubt that Acts means *Herod Antipas* (7–39 CE).

Antipas was one of the several Herods, sons of the original Herod, the latter usually referred to as Herod the Great to distinguish him from all the others. By this time the family was referring to all its members, much like all the 'Caesars' (by whom it was no doubt influenced and whom it was aping in more ways then one), as 'Herods'. This Herod, along with Herod Archelaus (4 BC–7 CE) whom we have already mentioned above in connection with the 4 BC disturbances and the Census Uprising following the original Herod's death, was the son of Herod's Samaritan wife. He is the Herod responsible for John the Baptist's death and the one King Aretas in Transjordan went to war with because he had divorced his (Aretas') daughter to marry his (Antipas') niece Herodias. He also appears in Luke as the 'Herod' who has an intervening interview with Jesus. For Luke,

> Herod greatly rejoiced, because he had been wishing to see him [that is, Jesus] for a long time . . . hoping to see him perform some miracle (23:8 – *thus*).

Herod the Great died sometime before 4 BC. We know this by the co-ordination of his reign with that of his patron the great Augustus – here the modifying adjective is appropriate – whom he obviously emulated as much as possible. However, unlike Augustus, who was a puritan and had no sons, Herod had numerous sons by some nine or ten different wives, only a few of whom could by any yardstick be reckoned as 'Jewish'. This will be an important problem for our period, not only as far as the Dead Sea Scrolls are concerned, but also for the Jerusalem Church, that is, who will be Jewish and what effect this perception has on the Jewish mass. If we take the Rabbinic delineation of this problem, the matrilinear yardstick – if your mother was Jewish, then you were Jewish – Herod did have at least two *Jewish* wives, both daughters of High Priests and both called Mariamme ('Miriam' or 'Mary' as we have seen).

The first Mariamme carried within her veins the last of the Maccabean Priest line. On both sides of her family she was of the blood of the heroic Maccabees, the Jewish High Priest line defunct after Herod. This in itself is a tragic enough story. Herod married her in 37 BC when he was besieging the Temple, seemingly by force. Ultimately he had her executed on the charge that she had been unfaithful with his brother Joseph (the original 'Joseph and Mary' story?), while he had left her to go to Rome and secure his kingship by transferring his allegiance from Mark Anthony to Augustus following their civil wars resulting from Caesar's assassination. In time, Herod also executed his two sons by her, who had been educated in Rome, because he feared the Jewish crowd would put them on the throne in his place, presumably because of the Maccabean blood that flowed in their veins (though not before they had reached majority and produced offspring of their own).

In a similar manner, years before, he also had her brother, a youth named Jonathan (Aristobulus in Greek, that is, Aristobulus III – the Maccabees often combined Greek with Hebrew names), killed for the same reason when he came of age and was able to don the High Priestly robes. It was the assumption of the High Priesthood by this Jonathan that probably explains Mariamme's willingness to marry Herod in the first place. In one of the most tragic moments in Jewish history, Herod, like some modern Joseph Stalin or Saddam Hussein, had Jonathan drowned while frolicking in a pool at his winter palace outside Jericho – this after the Jewish crowd wept when the boy donned the High Priestly vestments of his ancestors. The time was 36 BC after Herod had assumed full power in Palestine under Roman sponsorship as a semi-independent King, the preferred manner of Roman government in that part of their recently acquired Empire in the East or 'Asia' as it was called.

Herod, not being of Jewish blood or origins, might have been able to secure his kingship from the Romans in replacing the Maccabees as Jewish kings, but he was unable to secure their High Priesthood as well, however he might have wanted it. In Christian lore, Jesus achieves this, combining both kingly and priestly functions in his person in presumable succession to the Maccabees.[13] There can be little doubt that in arranging the marriage with Herod, theoretically forbidden under Jewish law (certainly as advocated by 'the Zealots'), those left in the Maccabean family aspired to rescue whatever remained of the fortunes of their family after thirty years of civil strife and war with Rome had so destroyed it.

Grateful to a fault, Herod proceeded to decimate the remainder of the Maccabean family, even that part of it that survived by subordinating itself to him and accommodating itself to Rome: first Jonathan, because the Jewish crowd, betraying its nationalist, pro-Maccabean sentiments, wept when Herod had permitted him to don the High Priestly garments when he turned thirteen; then Mariamme/Mary herself – though Josephus portrays Herod, soap-opera style, as being both in love with and hating her at the same time; then Hyrcanus II, Jonathan's grandfather from the generation of the 60s when the fraternal strife that resulted in foreign occupation began.

This Hyrcanus had been Judas Maccabee's great-grandnephew and had first introduced Herod's father Antipater to a position of power as his chief minister and go-between with the Romans and Arab/Idumaean power across the Jordan and in Petra. It was he who probably arranged Herod's marriage with Mariamme in the first place. As noted above, Herod then executed his own two sons by her – again probably for the same reasons – because the crowd, being nationalistic and Maccabean in sentiment, preferred them to him. Finally he executed Mariamme's mother and Hyrcanus' daughter, the wily old dowager Salome, who was the last to go besides these.[14] When Herod was done, there were no Maccabeans left, except third-generation claimants in his own family, whose blood had been severely cut by his own over three generations of cleverly crafted marriages.

The Children of the Flesh versus the Children of the Promise

It is interesting that Paul, in delineating his 'Mission to the Gentiles' and outlining a community where 'Jews and Greeks' could live in harmony (Rom. 1:16 and 10:12), speaks about the new 'Christians' of his cultivation and husbandry as being 'grafted upon the tree' (Rom. 11:23). Here, too, he also parodies and extensively exploits the 'Root' and 'Branch' imagery so widespread in Qumran documents, but with exactly opposite signification.[15] He says, for instance:

> Do not boast against the Branches, but if you do boast, [remember] you do not bear the root, but the root bears you. You will say, 'The Branches were broken that I might be grafted in'. (Rom. 11:18)

Paul also uses 'olive tree' symbolism here, by which he means Israel, identifying it with 'the branches broken off' (Rom. 11:19). Qumran, where 'the root' and 'the Branch' are applied directly to the Messiah, would have been shocked to see such imagery applied to new Gentile converts.[16]

It is in this section, too, that Paul first begins to use another related imagery, 'the seed of Abraham'. This, as Muhammad later, too, correctly appreciated, could be used to apply to Idumaean Arabs as well. Tied to this, Paul also first begins to stress another related theme, 'the Children of the flesh' as opposed to 'the Children of the Promise' or 'the Children of God' (Rom. 9:8). This allusion, which is also followed up in Galatians, is clearly being used in relation to his new Gentile Christian Community. In an inversion as mischievous as it is canny, Paul describes the latter as the *true Children of Sarah*, while the Jews he describes, somewhat scurrilously for his evidently unlettered audience, as the *Children of Hagar*, Sarah's Egyptian bondservant.[17] His play on the usage 'bondage' is important here, as it is throughout the corpus of his letters, since he always means by this, *bondage to the Law* or *the Torah of Moses*.

The reader will recall that in the first biblical book Genesis, the story of Abraham, Hagar, Sarah, and Ishmael is told in various forms. Ishmael is the illegitimate son of Abraham through Hagar the bondservant. He is really the firstborn. Sarah out of jealousy and wounded pride has Abraham banish them both into the wilderness to make way for her son Isaac, who is legitimate but comes later and to whom all Jews to this day trace their inheritance. It is a not incurious coincidence that Muhammad in his development of these materials six centuries later claims descent from this line of Ishmael via Hagar as one of the principal *Gentile* Peoples descended from Abraham – the Arabs, and one still hears this formula today.[18]

Paul has succeeded in making one of the most diabolical inversions of biblical warrant conceivable, reversing the Jews' own genealogical claims against themselves in developing his concept of his new 'Christian' Communities as the true 'Children of Abraham' or, as he also puts it, 'Children of God'. Muhammad is not far behind him. These new 'grafts upon the tree', according to Paul's new and ever more spiritualized Messianic 'root' and 'Branch' symbolism, resemble nothing so much as the family policy of the Herodians preceding him, a process in our view not unrelated to Paul's own family origins. This now becomes the new, more spiritualized form of Jewish Messianism that today we call 'Christianity' – according to this presentation, a quasi-Herodian, Hellenistic arboreal graft.

These 'Jewish', part Maccabean Herodians included in John the Baptist's generation the famous Herodias, who was a daughter of one of Herod's two sons by Mariamme (Mary) later executed by Herod. It also includes that personage referred to above in Acts 12:1 as 'Herod the King'. This individual, usually taken to be Agrippa I (37–44 CE), was named after one of the Emperor Augustus' favourite generals, Marcus

Agrippa. Agrippa I is another grandson of that Mariamme/'Mary' Herod also executed above and a *brother of Herodias.*

Most texts, including Josephus, refer to this Agrippa as 'Herod', though he had yet another brother actually named 'Herod', who succeeded him – Herod of Chalcis (44–49 CE), and the appellation 'King Herod' could with even more justice refer to him. Probably what we have pictured in Acts, in so far as it is reliable, is a conflation of both these Herods or the two compressed into one. Agrippa I did die in something of the weird fashion described in Acts 12:23 – he was probably poisoned even though he was an intimate of Claudius, because of Roman suspicions concerning his loyalty[19] – but the Herod in Acts 'who killed James the brother of John with the sword' and arrested Simon Peter, if the notices are reliable, was probably Herod of Chalcis his brother.

He is called Herod of Chalcis after the Kingdom he ruled somewhat north-west of Damascus in Syria – the Romans now parcelling out many of these Eastern Kingdoms as fiefdoms in return for services rendered to one or another of these Herodians, who were viewed as exceedingly trustworthy. It is not uninteresting that his son bears the typical Greco-Maccabean name of Aristobulus. This Aristobulus, in line with the Herodian family policy of marrying close family relatives, became the second husband of Herodias' infamous daughter Salome, whom tradition credits with the famous 'Dance of the Seven Veils' that ended with the mythological picture of John's head being delivered upon a platter.

The reasons for all this antagonism and all of these stories and subterfuges will become clear as we progress. In fact, a portrait of Aristobulus and Salome exists on the coinage issued in their names from Asia Minor. They were accorded another kingdom, which the Romans called Lesser Armenia, located in what today would be Eastern Turkey and Northern Syria, contiguous with Cilicia, from where Paul came and in which the Herodians were making inroads, and with two other kingdoms further south and east, Edessa or 'the Land of the Osrhoeans' (Assyrians) and Adiabene.

From the portrait on these coins there is nothing particularly seductive about Salome as far as one can see. However this is true as well of coins issued in the name of Cleopatra in Egypt, which rather portray a middle-aged, owlish-looking woman. On the back, there is the logo 'Great Lovers of Caesar'. Nothing could be more to the point than this. The same logo appears on coins of Herod of Chalcis and Agrippa I, their uncle, who might very well have been the lover of one or another of these Caesars.[20]

This 'Aristobulus' possibly also makes an appearance in Paul's greetings to various kinsmen at the end of Romans, one of whom he refers to most definitely as 'my kinsman Herodion' or 'my kinsman the littlest Herod'. The passage just preceding this refers to 'all those in the household of Aristobulus' and the year would be, like Galatians, sometime in the late 50s in Rome (Rom. 16:10–11).

The Marriage Policy of Herodians

These Herodians, as we shall often have occasion to refer to them, in this third generation descended from Herod and the last Maccabean Princess Mariamme, were one-quarter Jewish. The other blood line that flowed into them was carefully crafted and, as we shall see, Idumaean/Arab. Herod himself was primarily what today we would call 'Arab' in origin. In fact his behaviour, particularly where sexual mores and marital practices are concerned, is still very much that of what might be called a typical Middle Eastern chieftain or potentate.

Herod pursued the policy for his descendants of *niece marriage* or marriage to *close family relatives*, usually cousins. This marital policy, roundly condemned in the Dead Sea Scrolls, is probably the key datum of the kind we called 'internal' – as opposed to 'external' – for dating Qumran documents. So obsessed are the Qumran documents with this kind of sexual and marital behaviour – termed there along with 'divorce' and 'polygamy' as 'fornication' – all behaviour patterns not only characterizing Herod personally, but also Herodian family policy in the several generations succeeding him; that we have used this to insist that key documents making such complaints must be referring to a *Herodian Establishment*. There is no indication that Maccabeans previously, that is, before they were 'grafted' to Herodians, indulged in this kind of behaviour to any extent if at all. For Herodians from 60 BC onwards, this kind of behaviour – considered 'incest' at Qumran – was not only a matter of actual family policy preserving their mastery in Palestine and elsewhere in Asia, it was endemic.

It is this kind of sexual behaviour that will provoke the ire of leaders – now considered 'Christian' – such as John the Baptist against Herodians. Their disapproval of it is paralleled in documents, such as the Dead Sea Scrolls. Leaders like John the Baptist will lose their lives because of it. The popular picture of a Salome dancing at Herod's *Birthday Party* is just scriptural tomfoolery, although as always in these instances, not without a seed of historical reality – in this case, the seed is the problem of Herodian family morals and their sexual practices that were objected to by all these Messianic leaders like John the Baptist and after him, presumably Jesus, whoever he was.

The picture, therefore, that we have in the Gospels of a Jesus eating with 'tax collectors and Sinners' or speaking favourably about 'harlots' or 'prostitutes' is again just part of this casuistry.[21] Herodian Princesses, as we shall see, will be seen by the Jewish nationalistic mass as nothing better than 'harlots' or 'prostitutes' – Herodias is a case in point, but there will be others – and this issue, 'zanut' or 'fornication', inordinately dominates the mindset of those responsible for the Dead Sea Scrolls, as it does early New Testament documents like the Letter of James – so much so as to appear like an obsession. We will also be able show that other nationalist leaders like the Simon, mentioned in Josephus above, 'the Head of an Assembly' or 'Church' of his own in Jerusalem, will confront the Herodians in the Hellenistic centre of Caesarea – which they built as a sea port on the Palestinian coast and named in honour of Caesar – on this same issue, the marital practices of Herodians, in particular Herodian Princesses.

In this next generation, the fourth after the original Herod in the 40s–60s CE and the period James held sway in Jerusalem, the principal representatives of this line – now one-eighth Maccabean or Jewish – are three Herodian Princesses, two of whom make an appearance in chapters 24–26 of the Book of Acts, Bernice (ultimately the mistress of Josephus' patron Titus, the destroyer of Jerusalem and the Temple) and Drusilla. Both of these princesses have been divorced. Both ultimately took up with foreigners and deserted Judaism altogether. Bernice was not only divorced, she married her uncle as well – in this instance, the Herod of Chalcis above, her father Agrippa I's brother. Agrippa II, her brother who becomes king in the 50s and 60s just preceding the Uprising, also appears in Acts on her arm chatting amicably with Paul in prison (25:13). This is perhaps the original for the intervening interview in the Gospels between Jesus and Herod the Tetrarch (Luke 23:7–12), who really would have had no business in Jerusalem, his Tetrarchy – literally his 'fourth' of the Kingdom – being in Galilee and across the Jordan in Perea where John the Baptist was executed.

Here it is possible to lay another sexual-mores charge at the feet of these Herodian Kings and Princesses, 'incest', the basis in any event of the 'niece-marriage' charge so striking in the Scrolls. 'Niece marriage', on the other hand, has never been an infraction for Talmudic Judaism, nor is it in Judaism succeeding to it to this day. The Scrolls also pointedly condemn marriage with close family cousins on the basis of a generalization of the Deuteronomic Law of incest, and Josephus tells us that it was reputed that Bernice actually had an incestuous relationship with her brother Agrippa II.[22] The picture in Acts does not gainsay this. In fact, to some extent it reinforces it. This incest may have been contagious from Roman Imperial practices, like those of Caligula, who was a good friend of their father Agrippa I in Rome. Caligula was reputed to have had an incestuous relationship with his sister Julia before he was killed in 44 CE – the same year Agrippa I was removed from the scene.

On the other hand, 'niece marriage' may have been catching in the other direction – Herodians to Julio/Claudians – as Claudius, who succeeded Gaius Caligula in 44 CE by outlasting all his cleverer and more able family members, married his niece. The practice is strongly condemned in Roman sources as an innovation. To a certain extent it proved to be Claudius' undoing, as this niece, who was legended to have competed with the prostitutes of Rome in her harlotry, connived at his destruction as well. Ultimately, she was successful at putting her son by a previous marriage on the throne – the infamous Nero – and was repaid for her machinations by being brutally dispatched, in turn, by him.[23]

Both Claudius and Caligula were reputed to be great friends of Agrippa I, who had been brought up with them in Augustus' Imperial household in Rome after his father had been dispatched by his own father Herod. They restored the throne to this line. This had been denied Herod's descendants in the aftermath of the uprisings from 4 BC to 7 CE, the period in which the Gospels date the birth of Jesus. Therefore, the various tetrarchs, ethnarchs, and governors in the period till Agrippa I's re-emergence in 37 CE. This was the line, of course, with the original Maccabean royal blood which, however diluted, was significant to the Romans.

Agrippa I was restored to the throne of Palestine following the death of Tiberius, who had put him in prison for his too friendly relations with Caligula and Claudius. This also followed the removal of Pontius Pilate from Palestine after complaints like those of Philo's in his *Mission to Gaius* (Caligula), in particular, about his extreme venality and brutality. This was the year 37 CE, not long after the death of John the Baptist according to the time frame of Josephus' *Antiquities*. How such a chronology would gibe with a given year for the death of Jesus like 30 CE or 33 CE is not possible to determine, but none of the facts of Jesus' life as they are normally represented fit readily into the history of this period. If Jesus died after John the Baptist, as Scripture seems to think, then by Josephus' chronology it must be around 37 CE or just a little time before. If Jesus died before John the Baptist, then what are we to make of these scriptural accounts at all? Problems of this kind and others bedevil chronology and historiography when using quasi-historical documents like the Gospels. Using Acts is a little easier, because Acts often evinces knowledge – however overwritten – of parallel events in Josephus.

In the previous generation, Herodias had first been married to one non-Maccabean uncle – supposedly named 'Philip' in the New Testament, but actually named 'Herod'. After divorcing him, illegally according to Qumran legal parameters, she married another Herodian uncle, descended from a non-Maccabean, Samaritan blood-line. This one, as we saw, Herod Antipas (7–39 CE), was the Herod known as 'Herod the Tetrarch' in the New Testament (Luke 3:19 and Acts 13:1) and the individual both Josephus and the Gospels blame for the death of John the Baptist.

For his part, John is pictured in the Gospels as objecting to Herodias' divorce and remarriage on the basis of an obscure point in Mosaic law – violating the law of levirite marriage, a point that might have appealed to someone taking his view of the Jews in Palestine from books (Mark 6:17 and pars.). It was permitted to marry one's brother's or half-brother's wife, if that individual was childless and one were, so to speak, 'raising up seed unto your brother' which would be counted for your brother's inheritance or posterity.[24] For the New Testament, this was not the case, but there is nowhere any external proof of this.

In fact, the New Testament has the situation totally wrong here. The Philip it is calling 'Philip' is rather only called 'Herod' in Josephus.[25] Actually, he had at least one daughter by Herodias, this Salome. The Philip in Josephus is the Tetrarch of Trachonitis in Syria a little south of Damascus. He is *not Salome's father*, but rather *her husband*. It is he, Josephus specifically remarks, who dies childless, making way for Salome's next marriage to *her mother's brother's* son Aristobulus. But the Gospels, as we presently have them, have conflated all these things, producing what we presently perceive as truth. So ingrained has this picture become that it is now automatic to speak of two *Philips* and this *Herod*, who was the son of a second wife of Herod also named Mariamme – the daughter of an Egyptian Priest Herod had imported to replace the Maccabeans – as 'Herod Philip'.

Actually, however, to the non-Roman, non-Hellenistic native eye, there were all these other sexual and marital infractions sufficient to explain

John's objections to Herodias, in particular, her relations with *not one uncle, but two*, and her *self-divorce*, which even Josephus admits 'violated the Laws of our country'. This is the kind of 'divorce' the Dead Sea Scrolls so protest against and, no doubt, John the Baptist as well.[26]

It would be legitimate to query at this point, why among all these Herodian progeny – and the Herodian family was beginning to resemble a vast network like some royal families in the Middle East in our own time – was Herodias so desirable that two uncles were intent on having her, even to the extent of shedding John's blood and fighting a war with the Arabian King Aretas of Petra because of her? Attention to Herodian marital relationships would explain this.

The answer is twofold. The first is that of all the various Herodian lines this Maccabean one was the 'Richest', a factor further highlighted by the wealth that came to her brother Agrippa after his appointment as an actual king by his boon companion Caligula. Josephus specifically calls Agrippa I's daughter Bernice one of the 'Richest' women in Palestine and Herodias probably was not far behind her.

This is another important theme in our texts, 'the polluted Evil Riches' of the Establishment, a theme along with 'fornication' which is again paramount in both the Scrolls and the Letter of James. It is also prominent in the Gospels and in Josephus, all purporting to be first-century texts. This is certainly the principal reason behind Herodias' attractiveness to less fortunate, collateral Herodian lines, such as those of Herod (in the Gospels, 'Philip'), the son of Herod's second wife by the name of Mariamme, and Antipas, only the son of his Samaritan wife. It was also no doubt an important reason for the involvement of the future Roman Emperor Titus with Bernice Herodias' niece, as it no doubt was a century before for the various parvenu paramours of Cleopatra.

But there is a second reason as well, royal blood – in Cleopatra's case, stemming from those connected to Alexander the Great; in Herodias', the original blood of the Maccabees flowing in her veins. Apart from her 'Riches', this is sufficient to explain all this interest in developing a progeny-bearing relationship with her. But John the Baptist certainly would have had quite a few other objections besides 'Riches' that would have met the Qumran criteria for condemnation as 'unlawful' (Matt. 14:4). Where *fornication* was concerned, 'divorce', 'polygamy', 'niece marriage', and 'incest' – including the marriage of close cousins – and the Herodian family could certainly be accused of practising most or all of these.

When the Letter of James and other materials associated with him voice their objections to 'fornication' or contain imagery connected with this, for instance, when condemning 'the Tongue' in 4:4, all of these aspects of what was considered 'fornication' in this period by documents like the Dead Sea Scrolls should be uppermost in the reader's mind. Where, of course, those with royal blood are concerned, the Temple Scroll, drawing on the Deuteronomic King Law, adds another – marriage to a foreigner, insisting that the King should marry once and only once in the lifetime of his wife and this only to a Jewish woman.[27]

It is interesting that for Matthew 21:32,

> John came to you in *the Way of Righteousness*, and *you did not believe him* [note the Pauline thrust here] but *the tax collectors and the harlots believed him.*

'The Way of Righteousness' is, of course, a favourite Qumranism, but the true situation as far as John is concerned is rather *the opposite*. Aside from the joke of having 'the harlots believing' John (not to mention the travesty), if one understands that at this point the Roman tax collectors in Palestine were the Herodians, who acted the part of tax farmers, then the farcical thrust of this saying ascribed to Jesus in this supposedly *most Jewish* of all the Gospels is actually quite amusing. Those who inserted it into the Jewish *Messiah*'s mouth, no doubt, had a most macabre sense of humour. Once again, here, the saying of Jesus from the Pseudo-clementines, above, about being able 'to detect false coin from true', begins to develop the force of a hammer-like blow.

James the Brother of John and Theudas

Either Agrippa I, then, Herodias' brother and the father of this Bernice, or Herod of Chalcis, his brother, Bernice's second of some three or four 'husbands', would appear to be the 'Herod the King' in Acts, leading up to James' sudden appearance in the text, portrayed as 'stretching forth his hands to ill-treat some of those of the Assembly' or 'the Church' (12:1). Acts' use of '*Ecclēsia*' here is the same word Josephus uses when describing the individual he calls 'Simon' who wants to bar Agrippa I from the Temple as a foreigner and goes down to inspect his household in Caesarea to see what was being done there 'contrary to Law'. In the very next sentence in Acts, this 'Herod the King' puts 'James *the brother of John* to death with the sword'.

The phrase 'with the sword' is usually taken as meaning beheading. If it does, which is likely because it is an execution, then it would be useful to catalogue these various beheadings. This one parallels one mentioned in Josephus already alluded to somewhat obliquely in Acts 5:36, the execution of someone both Josephus and Acts refer to as 'Theudas'. We can say with some certainty that Theudas certainly was executed at around this time in the course of the suppression of these various seditious and charismatic leaders and Messianic pretenders that Josephus considers to be so dangerous. In fact, Acts 5:36 uses the same Greek word for 'put to death' in referring to him as Acts 12:2 uses in referring to the *beheading* of 'James the brother of John'. For his part, Josephus, as we saw, uses the designation 'Impostor' or 'Magician' to refer to him.

If one looks at the Talmudic enumerations of the various Jewish kinds of execution of this period found in Tractate *Sanhedrin* of the *Mishnah*, one will find that beheading was applied in Jewish religious Law to cases of subversion, treachery, insurrectionary activities, or the like. Some of the other kinds of execution described in *Sanhedrin* are quite gruesome, including pouring rocks down on someone or forcing burning pitch down his throat, but however tendentious Talmudic materials can sometimes be, crucifixion was not one of them. In fact, crucifixion or its Jewish equivalent, 'hanging upon a tree', was quite specifically forbidden under Jewish Law.[28]

The New Testament, particularly Paul in chapter 3 of his Letter to the Galatians, is quite aware of this, as is the Book of Acts following him (5:30 and 10:39). Paul, however, slightly alters the idea that it was 'a curse to hang a man upon a tree', to make it seem that it was the man hung upon the tree that was 'cursed', not necessarily the punishment. Thus, Paul develops his ideology of Jesus being 'cursed according to the Law' – as he seems to have thought he himself was – and from this that Jesus' death was a kind of expiatory activity by which Paul – and, for that matter, all mankind as well – was rescued either from this curse (Gal. 3:10 and 13) or, as he elsewhere puts it, its sin, that is, original sin (Rom. 5:12–15).

Though the passage relevant to this in Deuteronomy 21:23 does on the face of it carry something of this sense, it is clear from looking at the Scrolls that by this period this passage was not thought of as applying so much to the 'hanged' persons as such, but rather *the act of hanging*.[29] Still, the idea that there was something unclean about a man in a crucified state was no doubt widespread – not surprisingly in view of the gruesomeness and cruelty of this punishment – just as the idea that to cut off body parts or desecrate bodily parts after death probably had an impact upon the perception of the Holiness of that corpse, or lack of it.

As in many cultures, polluting the unburied body or dismembering it in some manner undoubtedly had a deleterious effect upon its redeemability. For those who believed in *resurrection of the body* – we are not speaking here about immortality of the soul, which is a more Platonic or Hellenistic concept – it undoubtedly did have a damaging effect, probably because the resurrection would be seen as being incomplete or somehow inhibited by the impure or incomplete state of the corpse. There is, however, a deliberate confusion of subjective and objective thrust in the way Paul approaches the issue in those important passages in Galatians, which also deal with 'Justification by Faith'.

Still, whatever 'the curse of the Law' involved, by the Second Temple Period this starts to be related to the act itself and its perpetrator, not so much the victim. In any event, for such a mindset, beheading was probably as much of a curse or objectively negative as crucifixion, no doubt the point of applying it to persons considered particularly blame-worthy in a political sense.

For his part, Josephus mentions at least four important beheadings in this period from the time of the Maccabees to the fall of the Temple. The first two are Maccabeans trying to regain their Kingdom following Herod's takeover in 37 BC, both sons of Aristobulus II.[30] The other two are Herod the Tetrarch's beheading of John the Baptist and the beheading of Theudas in the period of Herod of Chalcis and the Roman Governor Fadus (*c.*45 CE).

Apart from the impersonal, general mass of crucifixions by the Romans up to the fall of the Temple, Josephus mentions two that stand out: Jesus' if not an interpolation and that of James and Simon the two sons of Judas the Galilean, the founder of 'the Zealot Movement', who were executed a year or two after Theudas.

Of stonings, Josephus really only mentions those of Honi or Onias the Righteous, just before the Romans first assaulted the Temple in 63 BC presaging Aristobulus II's downfall; James in 62 CE; and another son or grandson of Judas the Galilean, one Menachem, in the events surrounding the outbreak of the Uprising in 66 CE. Puerile as these authors in the Roman Period often were, had there been others, Josephus probably could not have resisted telling us about them.

In the first place, there is the undoubted chronological proximity of the execution of 'James the brother of John' in Acts by either Herod Agrippa or his brother Herod of Chalcis and that of 'Theudas' in Josephus' *Antiquities*. Both are executed around the same time by either the same

individual or set of individuals and, regardless of Acts' political and theological agenda, one would assume for by and large the same reasons. As
we saw, Acts 5:36 uses the very same Greek allusion 'put to death' in
referring to Theudas' execution as Acts 12:2 does in referring to 'James
the brother of John'.

Theudas is an otherwise unknown individual. The reference to his execution in a speech put in the mouth of Paul's Pharisee teacher Gamaliel, the
grandson of the famous Hillel mentioned above, gives rise to the well-
known anachronism in Acts 5 at this point. This, in turn, is tied to another
deletion or oversight, the crucifixion of Judas the Galilean's two sons,
James and Simon, which follows almost directly thereafter in Josephus'
Antiquities. In Gamaliel's speech, supposedly in defence of early Christians
like Peter – in the Pseudoclementines, Gamaliel is supposed to be a secret
believer – Theudas is represented as somehow being related to the activities
of Judas the Galilean, but arriving on the scene before him.

As we also saw, Judas the Galilean is another Jewish revolutionary
leader and charismatic made much of in Josephus' works. Josephus calls
him 'the Galilean' in the *War*, but twenty years later in the *Antiquities* he
rather refers to him as 'the Gaulonite', meaning that he came from
Gamala – so called because of its resemblance to a camel's hump – in
Gaulonitis or today's Golan Heights on the other side of the Sea of Galilee
in Syria. There was another Jewish mass suicide there in the early days of
the Uprising against Rome, after Josephus was supposed to have fortified
it in his role as military commandant or commissar of Galilee, but failed
effectively to do so.

Galilee and Gaulon may be the same – certainly they are contiguous –
but Josephus probably means by this epithet 'Galilean' the sphere of Judas'
revolutionary activities, not his birthplace. For Eusebius, dependent on
other sources (namely Julius Africanus – 170–245 CE), 'Galilean' is the
name of one of the Jewish sects, namely those Revolutionaries known to
others as '*Zealots*', presumably because Josephus credits Judas and the
individual we have noted above, *Saddok*, with having founded this
Movement. Eusebius may be right in this contention. If he is, then there
are, of course, further pregnant implications when it comes to the
references to Jesus' *Galilean* activities and references to his adherents as
'Galileans' (Luke 22:59–23:6 and pars.). As with Jesus' purported origins
in 'Nazareth', there may again be these nagging confusions between
geographical place names and cognomens.

Judas the Galilean seems to have flourished from around the time of

Herod's death in 4 BC to 7 CE, the time of the Tax Uprising that brought Herod's son Archelaus' crisis-ridden reign to an end. Herod Archelaus was the brother of Herod Antipas and another son of Herod's Samaritan wife, Malthace. He was banished to Vienne in Southern France. Later, Herod Antipas and his wife Herodias were banished to Spain, when Caligula transferred his territories to her brother Agrippa I in 40 CE. Interestingly, in the next century another rabidly anti-Semitic, early Church Father, Irenaeus, flourished not far from these areas in Southern France as well (130–200).

With the banishment of Archelaus, the Romans imposed direct rule, via governors who were obedient – and answerable – to the Emperor and Senate, until the time of Agrippa I's emergence in 37 CE. The period in between not only turns out to be a period when we have a paucity of historical data compared to the ones just preceding and following it, but also the time identified by most as precisely that of Jesus' lifetime.

As the author of the Book of Acts has Gamaliel euphemistically describe Judas the Galilean's death:

> After this one [Theudas], Judas the Galilean arose in the Days of the Census and *led many people astray*. He perished and all of them scattered (5:37) –

but neither he nor Josephus ever directly tells us how or under what circumstances. Rather Josephus again turns to the subject of Judas the Galilean later in his narrative when discussing the preventive execution of '*James and Simon*, the sons of Judas the Galilean . . . who caused the people to revolt when Cyrenius came to take an accounting of the estates of the Jews' in the *Antiquities*. This would make 'James and Simon' quite old, since, as he describes it, their crucifixion appears to take place coincident with the event Josephus labels as 'the Famine' in 46–8 CE above.[31]

The Census of Cyrenius and the Sects of the Jews

The Census of Cyrenius, which was imposed after a series of uprisings led by Judas and other 'Messianic' leaders, which Herod Archelaus (4 BC–7 CE) was unable to control, is the event seized on as well by the author of Luke – the author also credited with Acts – to fix the date of Jesus' birth. This, of course, makes the birth of Jesus in the Gospels coincident with the birth of sectarian strife generally – in particular, what Josephus is calling the birth of the 'Zealot'/'*Sicarii*' Movement and what we would call the 'Messianic Movement'. Though the point of Luke's approach is to get

Jesus to Bethlehem to be born, so much does it fly in the face of the parallel one in Matthew that, as noted above, nothing of certainty can be said with regard to Jesus' birth at all, neither the place, the date, nor the political and social circumstances.

For Luke, if not Matthew, Jesus' parents are already living in Galilee. But since David came from Bethlehem, in his view Jesus, who is making Davidic-style claims to the Monarchy, should be born there as well. Scriptural warrant is assumed for some reason or other either to suggest or support this. Perhaps this was the popular religion, but there is no known prophecy specifically delineating such a requirement. In fact, further information regarding this requirement in John 7:42 has the crowd doubting Jesus' Bethlehem birth and therefore specifically denying that he comes from there. However this may be, the Lukan author uses the patently clumsy and obviously artificial strategem of a Roman-imposed census to get Jesus' family back to Bethlehem from Galilee and to develop his very popular 'no room at the inn' scenario. As a result, the Christ-child, like the Oriental mystery-religion god Mithra before him, is born in a manger, a favourite biblical folk tale without any historical substance whatsoever.

In any event, it is totally contradicted by the scenario in the Gospel of Matthew, which has Jesus' family living in Bethlehem all along. Here Herod – Herod 'the Great', *d.* 4 BC or before – having heard about 'the Star' ('the Star Prophecy') from the three wise men (the three Angels, one of whom turns out to be God, who announce Isaac's birth to Abraham in Genesis 18:10), decides Pharaoh-like to kill all the Jewish children.

All this, of course, is preposterous too, except (1) as a comparison of Jesus' birth to Moses' and (2) to reflect the perceived cruelty of Herod. Herod, of course, does end up killing 'the Jewish children' who would supplant him, his *own* Jewish children by his Jewish priestly wife Mariamme/Mary, and also kills her in the bargain. He also wants to kill quite a few others, as the story Josephus relates about his death illustrates. Here Herod arrests a goodly number of Jewish notables and places them in a stadium to be executed when he dies, so that there will be much weeping and crying at his death, a story much in line with the macabre masochism of his personality.[32]

But the Census of Cyrenius, referred to by Luke both in his Gospel and Acts, does have substance. Cyrenius was Governor of Syria, to whom the task fell to take an evaluation of the property and substance of Palestine for taxation purposes in advance of the imposition of direct Roman rule following the removal of the inept Archelaus. Josephus refers to this on three occasions in his works, the last, as we saw, when discussing the execution of James and Simon, the two sons of Judas the Galilean, in the *Antiquities*. It is this execution in the year 48 CE that explains the anachronism in the speech attributed to 'Gamaliel' in Acts – better still would be to 'Josephus', once one realizes that Acts' author(s), like many a Roman historian thereafter, was dependent on the latter (not to mention a few other sources).

The sequence in Acts 5:36–37 of Theudas, his revolt, Judas the Galilean, and the Census would follow that of Josephus in the *Antiquities* precisely, if we simply assume that Luke has for some reason left out the mention of the execution of Judas the Galilean's two sons, James and Simon. This would restore the proper chronological sequencing to the text and give us the mention of Theudas, followed by the mention of the execution of Judas the Galilean's *two sons,* followed by the explanation of who Judas was, namely, that he perished in the Census Uprising. As far as Jesus' birth is concerned, it is totally irrelevant to the Census (except perhaps symbolically); and Luke's story connecting the two, fictional in any event. Even Acts' order as it presently stands follows Josephus exactly, the only thing lacking being a few minor details that have dropped out or been deleted in the process of transmission or rewriting. Why, of course, the author left out the mention of the crucifixion of Judas the Galilean's two sons in the first place, we shall, most likely, never know.

What is interesting, though, is that Josephus uses the Uprising led by Judas the Galilean as the springboard to describe the Jewish sects in the first century in both the *War* and the *Antiquities*. It is edifying to compare the two descriptions of these sects found in them. In the earlier one – triggered by the appearance of Judas the Galilean and the mention of the imposition of direct Roman rule through a governor who 'had the power to impose the death sentence' – Josephus describes the normal three sects: 'Pharisees', 'Sadducees', and 'Essenes', and lingers in loving detail over the last, a group he was evidently very well acquainted with.[33]

Twenty years later in the *Vita* he informs us that as a youth – when he exhibited some of the same precociousness of lecturing the elders in the Temple Luke ascribes to Jesus – he decided to investigate the various Jewish sects.[34] He describes these something in the manner of Greek schools of philosophy (no doubt in line with the cultural tastes of his Greek-speaking audience – the Greek being the only complete version of his works that survived) and relates how he lived for three years as a kind of novice 'in the wilderness' with a teacher he denotes by the puzzling name of *'Banus'*. We will have more to say about *'Banus''* relation to James in due course, however for the moment suffice it to say that though Josephus ultimately describes himself as a Pharisee – this no doubt in the light of the political considerations delineated above – this would have been the period Josephus came by his extensive knowledge of 'Essenes' and other like-minded groups.

He also describes a *fourth group* owing its origins to the activities of Judas the Galilean and the other teacher he later identifies only by the equally puzzling sobriquet *'Saddok'*. Obviously it is in order to describe this group – 'the Fourth Philosophy' of Judas the Galilean – that he launches into his discussion of the sects at this point in the *Jewish War*. But though he promises to tell us about this group, he does not. Rather, as already noted above, he lingers over the *Essenes* in seemingly loving detail.

His descriptions of both Sadducees and Pharisees are cursory in the extreme and not very edifying, though they too have been picked up in the New Testament and used to characterize these groups. In the *Antiquities*, however, he makes good the omission, describing the ills associated with the Movement led by Judas and *Saddok* in great detail. This Movement, according to him, 'led our people to destruction', because 'our young people were zealous for it'.[35] As we have suggested, there can be little doubt that what he is describing is *the Messianic Movement* in Palestine. Others might call it 'the Zealot Movement', but Josephus never uses this terminology until after the Uprising and the killing of all the High Priests, particularly James' destroyer Ananus, as we have seen, in 68 CE. In fact, he never names it at all, except tantalizingly as 'the Fourth Philosophy'.

What he does do, however, is sharply curtail his description of 'the Essenes' in the *War* and take part of it and add it to his description of the Movement initiated by Judas and *Saddok* in the *Antiquities*. This is the moment Luke chooses to date the birth of *Christ*. In line with his Establishment sensibilities and pro-Roman sympathies, Josephus rails against the leaders of movements such as this, as we saw too, as 'impostors and Deceivers', worse 'even than the bandits and murderers' that so infested the country in this period – worse, according to him, because not only did they deceive the people, but they strove to bring about religious innovation and revolutionary change. Most often these disturbances took place at Passover time – probably because this could be looked upon as the Jewish National Liberation Festival when Moses led the ragtag group of former Jewish slaves out into the wilderness and, not only gave them freedom and the Law, but produced a nation.

Judas *the Brother of James* and Theudas

It is precisely in this manner that Josephus describes – disapprovingly of course – the 'Theudas' whose death so parallels that of 'James the brother of John' at the beginning of Acts 12. Calling him an 'impostor', in the sense of being a 'false prophet' or 'Deceiver', Josephus insists that he actually claimed to be 'a Prophet' and miracle-worker, and on this basis persuaded 'Many' (always an important usage in the Dead Sea Scrolls)[36] to follow him out into the wilderness, where he said he would part the Jordan River. In the Book of Joshua, Joshua is described as Moses-like, parting the Jordan River – in Exodus Moses parted the Red Sea – when he led the people of Israel into the Promised Land 'dryshod' (Josh. 3:13).

Evidently meant to be a Joshua *redivivus*, a Joshua brought-back-to-life or a Joshua incarnated, Theudas is reversing this and leading the people back out into the wilderness into trans-Jordan or further afield. When one appreciates that the name 'Jesus' is a Hellenized version of the name Joshua ('he who saves')[37] then one can appreciate that Theudas is a *Jesus redivivus* as well. Jesus goes out into the wilderness to confront the Devil or multiply loaves; Theudas, to part the Jordan River in reverse. For his troubles, his followers were decimated by Roman soldiers and he was *beheaded*.

The name, 'Theudas', has never been deciphered by any scholar and remains a mystery to this day. Certainly in the Greek – which is the only form in which we have it – it resembles the name 'Judas'. In our view, it is also a parallel to that character who in two Apostle lists anyhow is called 'Thaddaeus'.[38] This character, in turn, will turn out sometimes to be called 'Judas of James' or 'Judas the brother of James' and, as we shall further develop below, we would identify him as the *third brother of Jesus*, probably identical to the person other sources, such as the Gospel of Thomas, call 'Judas Thomas'. The claim implicit in the name, 'Judas Thomas', is that he is a 'twin' of some kind, *'thoma'* in Aramaic meaning 'twin'. The implication usually is that he is a twin of Jesus and, in addition, that he is Jesus' *third brother*, 'Jude' or 'Judas'. We would go further, considering the circumlocution 'Theudas' to be either a garbled form or conflation/contraction of the two names 'Judas' and 'Thomas'.

For the purposes of the argument or discussion, let us assume this to be the case. One can now see the importance of the 'brother' theme in the

Book of Acts, only this time we are not dealing with a 'brother of John' or even another 'James' but, rather, the *third* brother of Jesus – that is, *Judas the brother of James* – seen here by the text as a Joshua or Jesus *redivivus*. Again, the theme of beheading and the chronology are approximately right. We are somewhere in the period of Agrippa I or Herod of Chalcis succeeding him, that is, around 44–45 CE.

Let us, also, for the purposes of argument assume that 'James', the so-called 'son of Zebedee', is, also, an editorial gloss. Not only does Acts necessarily have to remove him at this point in order to make way for the appearance of James the Just the brother of Jesus, *the real James*, but what we have here in Acts are the faint traces, however indistinct, of the real event just beneath the surface of the fictional one.

To put this in another way – first of all, there *was* another brother of Jesus called 'Jude' or 'Judas'. In some texts this brother is alluded to as 'Judas Thomas', either evoking an actual twinship or the Joshua/Jesus *redivivus* theme of Josephus' narrative. Finally, there *really* was a 'brother' eliminated at this time, but this 'brother' was not the facile and more popularly known 'James the brother of John', but rather the lesser-known, but probably more real, 'Judas of James' – 'Jude the brother of James' referred to in the letter by that name. We shall have much more to say about this 'brother' in the section more or less devoted to him at the end of this volume, but that such a brother really did exist and produced offspring continuing down into the period of Vespasian, Domitian, and Trajan is also confirmed for us in Eusebius.

Here Eusebius, once again using sources lost to us – in this case, the Hegesippus we have noted above who lived closest to the time in question in Palestine (*c.* 90–180 CE) – confirms the existence of this third brother of Jesus and that he *had offspring*. The stories he vouchsafes us are quite charming. In two places, quoting Hegesippus verbatim, he refers to the offspring of one 'Judas called the brother of our Lord according to the flesh', one in the time of Domitian and one right before he describes the martyrdom of Simeon bar Cleophas – 'the cousin of our Lord' – in Trajan's time, who Hegesippus thinks lived to be a hundred and twenty, a slight exaggeration.[39] Interestingly, too, at this point Eusebius acknowledges that Simeon's mother was Mary and his father Cleophas, quoting Scripture. Still he cannot yet bring himself to admit that Simeon was a brother too, that is, Jesus' *second brother Simon*, but rather only 'of the family' or 'the relatives' of Jesus.

By the 90s these descendants of Jesus' third brother Judas are only simple farmers. Eusebius reports that Domitian (81–96), like his father Vespasian before him, attempted to round up all those people considered to be of the genealogy of David. Among these were the grandchildren of Jesus' third brother, Judas. When questioned about the nature of 'Christ and his Kingdom', they replied it was not an earthly one, but celestial and Angelic – but that at the end of the world, he (the Messiah) would appear 'to give to everyone according to his *works*'. One should note the Jamesian emphasis here on 'works' rather than simply Pauline 'Faith'. Thereupon Domitian purportedly dismissed them as simpletons. They were reported to have continued living until the time of Trajan (98–117).

We will be considering further the fate of this third brother, 'Judas of James', referred to in Apostle lists and tied in other Christian sources (mainly Syriac) with the individual called 'Thaddaeus', the reference to a 'James the brother of John' in this chapter of the Book of Acts being nothing but early Church obfuscation of these very interesting links.

There is one more link in this whole improbable, but very real, chain, and that comes in the documents generally considered to be Gnostic from Nag Hammadi and never seen before the last few decades of the present century. Here in two previously unknown Apocalypses attributed to the person of James – that is, James *Jesus' brother* not the other James – an individual named 'Addai', again obviously linked etymologically to the name of 'Thaddaeus', is referred to, as well as another, 'Theuda', paralleling him and referred to as 'the father' or 'brother of the Just One', that is, Jesus or even possibly James.

We could have arrived at this conclusion by following a variety of threads in the materials before us, and we have. But we believe this also to be the clear implication – given his working method – of the author of the Book of Acts. Once one begins to appreciate this working method and its clearly evasive and/or misleading thrust, much else, as already suggested previously, becomes clear in the early history of Christianity.

The First Appearance of James

As usual, for these kinds of seditious or subversive incidents, Acts portrays the events it is discussing, leading up to the first appearance of James in 12:17, as occurring during 'the Days of the Unleavened Bread', that is, Passover time. The 'Herod', who at this point beheads 'James the brother of John', is also pictured as going on to imprison Peter, because the beheading of this other James 'so pleased the Jews' (*thus*), meaning to put him on trial at the end of the Passover week (Acts 12:3). This is the kind of tendentious aside that so characterizes Acts and in fact all of the Gospels, and we shall have occasion to discuss more parallel events to these in Josephus' *Antiquities*, like the one involving the Simon the Head of 'a Church'/'*Ecclēsia*' of his own in Jerusalem, presently.

In any event, Acts now goes on to describe a miraculous escape by Peter from prison with the help of an Angel (12:5–10). This escape has interesting parallels with one later offered Paul (Acts 16:25–34). In this later episode, calculated to show the moral superiority of the Apostle to the Gentiles over this archetypally Jewish Apostle, Paul unlike Peter *refuses to escape* out of concern for the welfare of the guards (*thus*), mindful of the fact that earlier those designated to guard Peter were executed after he escaped (12:19). However this may be, Peter's escape is used to explain why Peter no longer either functions in Palestine or as head of the Church in Jerusalem. He is forced to flee the country, but not before James is, at last, introduced in 12:17 and Peter goes to a house in Jerusalem to inform him of his departure. This, at least, might bear some semblance of the truth.

The chapter ends with the death of this Herod, whoever he may have been, which, given the theatricality of its context, is normally taken to be the death of Agrippa I in the year 44 CE (12:20–23). The indications are that because of Agrippa I's growing imperial ambitions in the East, which were unacceptable, his Roman overlords arranged to have him poisoned. In any event, Josephus portrays Agrippa I, much like his patron Caligula, as collapsing in a seizure while dressed in gold leaf – presumably like Apollo or the sun – and giving a theatrical performance of some kind.[40] For its part, as we have seen, Acts portrays the Herod it is calling a 'king' as being struck down by an Angel because he looked so magnificent that people mistook him for a god. Like to some extent Judas *Iscariot* earlier (1:18), he was supposedly 'eaten away with worms and died' (12:23).

The house in Jerusalem where Peter is portrayed as going 'to leave a message for James and the brothers' is, of course, interesting. This house is pictured as having a servant with the Greek-sounding name of 'Rhoda' (12:13) and as being that of 'Mary mother of' – we would have expected the text to say at this point 'Jesus' or at least 'James'; but once again we are in for a surprise and it does not. Rather, it says, as we saw, 'John Mark'. John Mark is mentioned again in Acts as the man who deserted the mission of Barnabas and Paul in Pamphylia (15:37–39).[41]

In Acts 13:13 he is simply called 'John', and there is no hint of the bitterness evinced by Paul towards him in 15:39. Elsewhere, he would appear to be identified with the Gospel of Mark and Eusebius knows him as Peter's travelling companion.⁴² We were not aware that he had a mother called 'Mary'. Nor that he had a 'house' in Jerusalem in which *Mary lived*. Plus, it would seem not a little strange to go to a house where 'Mary mother of John Mark' lived to leave a message *for James the brother of Jesus* and the *other brothers*. It is simpler just to think that the text originally said 'the house of Mary *the mother of Jesus*' or 'Mary *the mother of James the Just*' or 'Mary *the wife of Cleophas*', and that this somewhat enigmatic substitution has taken place – and so it has remained to be enshrined in seventeen–eighteen centuries of pious history.

But it will not stand up to investigation. One can simply dismiss it as either pious fiction or look at it more deeply and attempt to make out the main lines of the original. We prefer the latter, and we do so on the basis of what seems the simplest and most reasonable under the circumstances. Acts is not *simply* pure fiction. There is real truth lying behind its substitutions or overwrites and the key often is *the family of Jesus*, in particular James, and how they are treated. Here, it is useful to observe that after the attack on James by Paul in the Pseudoclementine *Recognitions*, James is actually carried to his 'house' in Jerusalem. In the same vein in the Gospel of John, Jesus instructs 'the Disciple he loved' – always unidentified – *from the Cross* no less, to take Mary 'into his own home' (obviously in Jerusalem) and be her '*son*' (19:26–27). This is just following the passage in which Mary is identified as 'the sister of his mother Mary (wife) of Clopas' (19:25). This is precisely how this phrase appears in the Greek.

The reference in Acts 12:17 to 'brothers' is interesting as well. One can take these 'brothers' as brothers in the generic sense, that is, communal brothers, or the like, which is how it is usually taken. Or, since we are following the traces of 'the brothers' in this work, it is possible to take them as 'brothers' in the specific sense, meaning James and the other brothers of Jesus. The first is more likely, but one should always keep in mind the possibility of the second, since Peter has gone to 'Mary the mother of' someone's house to leave a message 'for James and the brothers' – otherwise unexplained.

These persecutions, too, we can take as authentic, that is, individuals like Theudas or Judas – Jesus' brother – really were beheaded and really did lose their lives, the only difference being the reason for these persecutions and repressions. In Acts' portrayal, these become rather distorted. For instance, in Acts the Jewish crowd is pleased by the beheading of James – that is, *Theudas* – and in the picture of 'Herod' there, being encouraged to take the further step of imprisoning Peter, once again we have the slight lateral movement in the portrayal of these things already signalled in Josephus' critique of the historians of this period.

The reason, of course, is that the later theology of the Gentile Church is now being retrospectively read back into the history of Palestine as the cause of all the repressions these early members of the Messianic Movement or the 'Jerusalem Community' in Palestine are undergoing. This vituperative theology is fully developed in Eusebius' works by the fourth century, but it is already highly developed in the second and third. But the real reason for these trials has to do with this constant revolutionary and religious strife, which, as Josephus documents so well, made its appearance with the Movement begun by Judas and *Saddok* at the time of the Census Uprising. These charismatic and religious leaders that punctuate the history of the next 135 years are all in one way or another connected with this Movement for political and religious freedom.

Take, for example, the appearance of another individual a decade or so after the beheading of Theudas, whom Josephus also designates as 'a prophet' and who so resembles Jesus in Scripture. Josephus describes this type of impostor or deceiver with amazing perspecuity. As a lead-in to introducing this *prophet*, he says that these

> *impostors and Deceivers* called upon the people to follow them into *the wilderness*, there to show them umistakable wonders and signs, that would be performed in accordance with the providence of God.[43]

In the Slavonic Josephus, so depreciated by most, these signs are called the 'signs of their *impending freedom*'.

The individual in this episode, for whom, following his last confrontation with James, Paul is mistaken in Acts by a Roman Centurion – is designated by no epithet other than 'the Egyptian'. Again he wants to do another 'Joshua'- or 'Jesus'-like miracle, this time not parting the Jordan River in reverse as Theudas, but demolishing Jerusalem's walls. The locale this time is not Jericho, but rather one familiar in Gospel narrative, the Mount of Olives. From there, what he intends to do is not take over the Temple and turn over the money-changers' tables like Jesus, but rather command the walls of Jerusalem to fall down and allow his followers to enter the city and presumably liberate it.

This *Egyptian* escapes only to be mistaken for Paul in Acts 21:38, but 400 of his followers are butchered by the Roman Governor Felix (52–60 CE). For Acts the number grows to 4000 and his followers are specifically called 'Sicarii'. The latter will be extremely important terminology, not only where Jesus' supposed betrayer, Judas Iscariot, is concerned, but also for a complex of related problems.

In Acts' version of the strife in Jerusalem, repression of theological dissidents of the Pauline kind is substituted for repression of subversive and religious malcontents and revolutionaries in Josephus, and the consonant pro-Roman and anti-Palestinian theology we know developed. As noted above, Acts' author at this point frames the reference to James as if he had already introduced him previously and consequently, therefore, we should know who he is. Of course, in Acts in its present form, he did not, but this is not to say that in the source underlying Acts or the original source he didn't. I think we will eventually be able to show that he did.

He must have. It is not possible, as we have stressed, that James suddenly erupts into the text in the same chapter in which the other James, confused for or written over him, is removed and the notice as it presently exists assumes that we know who he is. The text as we have it does not say that Peter went to the house of Mary and Rhoda to leave a message for James the Just, Mary's son, called the brother of Jesus. Nor does it, then, go on to delineate who this James was, which would have been normal if he had not previously been mentioned. No, it treats James as *known* – and he *was known*. We will be able to show, when analysing early Church sources and the Pseudoclementine *Recognitions*, that James was indeed mentioned earlier – probably on several occasions – but the traces have been overwritten with more obscurantist story-telling or mythologizing.

One of the places James would have been mentioned earlier would have been in the various comings and goings on the Temple Mount, described in Acts, where Peter and John are mentioned, but no James (3:1–11). This is surprising. These lacunae are made good in the Pseudoclementine *Recognitions*, where in the parallel material having to do with these early comings and goings on the Temple Mount, the *real James* – our James – is mentioned extensively.

In addition, James would have been mentioned in the first chapter of the Book of Acts, where the most important matter facing the incipient Church would have been regulated – that is, choosing the *successor* to the departed Messiah. Here the choosing of James as Leader of the Jerusalem Community and Bishop of the Jerusalem Church, so conspicuously missing from Acts in its present form, would have been described and this lacuna made up. Instead, a more novelizing and folkloric history takes its place in Acts, which purports to tell the story of what became of the individual who *betrayed Jesus* named 'Judas' – also the name of *the third brother of Jesus*. It is, rather, Judas' end that is depicted in Acts in the most lurid detail – this and how the matter of *succession to him* was regulated.

Then, too, James was probably mentioned a little prior to this material in chapter 12 of Acts about Peter and James, which is paralleled by an episode in the Pseudoclementine *Recognitions*, after James is attacked by Paul in the Temple, describing how James sends off Peter from the Jericho area to confront Simon *Magus* in Caesarea. According to Acts' chronology, this would be following the mention of Theudas and Judas the Galilean in chapter 5 and the story of the stoning of Stephen that follows in chapters 6–7 – itself probably replacing this attack on James.

Of course, there is no good reason *to stone* someone purportedly called 'Stephen' in Jerusalem and we will show that this episode actually replaces a different one, also preserved in the Pseudoclementine *Recognitions* about Paul's activities prior to his famous vision on the road to Damascus and conversion to Christianity. This episode will have to do with an actual physical assault by Paul on the Leader of the Community, James. This attack ended in grave injury to James but not death and his flight, together with most of the members of his Community, to somewhere in the Jericho area – that is, somewhere in the *neighbourhood of Qumran*. The substitution here will follow the same *modus operandi* as some of the other substitutions and overwrites we are noting here, but the main lines of the original materials are still discernible underneath.

Finally, there is the matter of the crucifixion of the two sons of Judas the Galilean, James and Simon, in the period around 48 CE during the procuratorship of Tiberius Alexander (46–48 CE). He, too, is mentioned in these early chapters of Acts as 'Alexander', the renegade nephew of Philo of Alexandria, although again the chronology is defective or distorted (Acts 4:6). This crucifixion, which is a curious one, is also important. In Josephus, it follows the mention of the Famine, the Theudas episode, and the description of the appointment of Tiberius Alexander as procurator.

The reason for the resumption of these procurators again is that, with the death of Agrippa I, his son Agrippa II was neither considered old enough nor sufficiently trustworthy to rule by himself. So the Romans started sending out governors again to rule in tandem with Herodian kings. Agrippa I's brother, Herod of Chalcis, rules for a time in his place, and he certainly did not have the 'grace' (*chrēstos*), as Josephus denotes it, of his brother Agrippa I. Herod's son Aristobulus – Salome's husband after *her previous husband Philip* had 'died childless' – is given the Kingdom of Lesser Armenia, obviously in compensation for not succeeding to his father in Palestine.

In a preventive execution aimed at heading off future troubles, resembling both Jesus' and that of John the Baptist, Tiberius Alexander ordered that these two sons of Judas the Galilean be crucified. Here, as we have seen, Josephus mentions Judas the Galilean, who caused the people to revolt at the time of the Census taken by Cyrenius or Quirinius, which forms the basis of the parallel notice in Acts. But why Alexander had these two crucified and what they had done to deserve such punishment, Josephus never explains. In addition, the parallels between the Messianic-style families of Judas the Galilean and that family purportedly stemming from either 'Joseph and Mary' or Cleophas and Mary remain striking. What are the connections between these two clusters of Messianic individuals and in what manner do they overlap? Short of an undoctored presentation of this period we shall undoubtedly never know.

7

The Picture of James in Paul's Letters

James as Leader of the Early Church in Galatians

Paul gives us the most vivid and accurate first-hand account of the pre-eminence of James in the early Church in Galatians. This account is not doctored, nor does it suffer – except peripherally – from the defects of retrospective history or theology. The opposite is true. Paul's antagonism to those in the early Church ('the Assembly') in Jerusalem, whom he feels are misguided and persecuting him, is patent. As an admittedly lesser being in a hierarchical organization, he exhibits a certain amount of formal deference to these leaders: 'those reckoned to be something' (Gal. 2:6) or 'recommending themselves, measuring themselves by themselves' (2 Cor. 10:12), among whom he would include James. In fact, as Paul's tirades in these letters develop, it becomes very clear that, not only is James principal among them, but Paul's respect for what we should term 'the Jerusalem Leadership' is only superficial and quite formal – nothing more.

Actually, he refers to this leadership in the most biting terms. In describing his flight from Judea to Syria and Cilicia at the end of the first chapter in Galatians – locales always important when considering the extent of Herodian family influence in the East – he insists that he will

> not give in or be subjected to those *false brothers* who spy on the freedom
> we enjoy in Christ Jesus, *so that they might enslave us.* (Gal. 2:4–5)

The 'freedom' he is talking about is *freedom from the Law*; the 'slavery', both enslavement to it and the Jerusalem Leadership – the 'we' referring here to his communities. The 'spying' has to do not only with this freedom, but also probably, quite literally, their nakedness (or, as Qumran would have it, 'looking on their privy parts'), that is, to see if they were circumcised or not.[1] The mention of 'pseudo' or 'counterfeit brothers' in this context is, of course, important.

It is in these passages, which end in an insistence that he 'does not lie' – again important for parallel Qumran aspersions on a person known there as 'the Liar' – that he describes how he first 'made Peter's acquaintance' and 'saw none of the *other Apostles except James the brother of the Lord*' (Gal. 1:18–20). In doing so, Paul states categorically that he did not 'go up again to Jerusalem for fourteen years' (2:1), which completely contradicts both chronological and factual claims in Acts. The actual words he uses here, 'to go up', further lend to the flavour of authenticity, as to this day this is the way Jews still refer to returning or travelling to Jerusalem.

The date then that Paul gives here for his next visit to Jerusalem – sometime in the early 50s – not to mention his contentions about not having seen 'any of the other Apostles except James the brother of the Lord' and being 'unknown by sight to the Assemblies [*Ecclēsiais*] in Christ in Judea' (Gal. 1:19–22), of course, completely gainsay the interim narrative in chapters 9–12 of Acts about his early career. This describes Paul returning to Jerusalem because of a famine that Acts describes as 'having come over the whole civilized world . . . in the time of Claudius' as part of famine-relief activities (11:28–30). This is the one in 46–8 CE that we have just highlighted with regard to the anachronism involving Judas the Galilean's two sons.

These activities mesh with parallel ones on the part of another new convert to Judaism, or perhaps Christianity, from these Eastern regions, the legendary Queen Helen of Adiabene. For the moment, the reader can take it as a rule of thumb that where there is a conflict between Galatians – or any other of Paul's letters for that matter – and Acts, these letters are to be preferred. Not only is Galatians autobiographical, and undoctored, it has on the whole the ring of *authentic history*.

Paul's Relations with the Jerusalem Leadership

Paul explains this second visit to Jerusalem extremely defensively as being a result of a private 'revelation' he had, establishing as well that, as he sees it, he had not *been summoned* to give an account of himself, as it might appear to less sympathetic eyes. As he puts it:

> I went up because of [a] revelation [*apocalypsin*] and privately laid before those reckoned to be important the Gospel which I proclaim among the Gentiles, lest somehow I might be running or had run in vain. (Gal. 2:2)[2]

Here, Paul gives play to the idea of a *private* 'revelation', by which he means that he is directly in touch with some other revelatory body, presumably 'the Holy Spirit'. Through it, he would appear to think that he is in direct communication with 'Christ Jesus', as he elsewhere terms the Supernatural Being or presence he claims to be communicating with.

He states this in another way in the very first line of the letter, if it is authentic:

> Paul, Apostle, not from *men*, nor through [any] *man*, but rather through Jesus Christ and by God [the] Father, who raised him from [the] dead. (Gal. 1:1)

The point Paul is trying to make here is that he was neither appointed by any 'man', nor the earthly Jesus, whom he never met, nor any body of 'men', such as, for instance, the Elders of the Jerusalem Church. Nor does he, as we shall presently see, carry any letters of appointment from such men (2 Cor. 3:1), but is beyond temporal authority, and not beholden to it.

In particular, he is not beholden to James or the Jerusalem Church Leadership. He is prepared to discuss things with them, and, where profitable, interact, but not to defer to them. He makes this attitude towards them clear when he says that he was not called to account by them, but went up 'privately' and not publicly, on his own recognizance as it were, to lay before those he speaks of as being 'of repute' (Gal. 2:2) or, sarcastically, as 'considered to be something' (2:6), the Gospel as he proclaimed it 'among the Gentiles',[3] for fear that the course he 'was running or had already run' would be 'in vain'.

The language of 'vain' teaching will reappear in the Dead Sea Scrolls, where the 'mission' or 'service' of *the Liar* is at issue.[4] In addition to this, Paul also enjoys employing the language of athletics, particularly that of 'running in the stadium', and he will use this 'running' imagery again in a particularly crucial section of 1 Corinthians when describing both his own freedom from the Law and his missionary activities. This he expresses as follows:

> All the runners at the stadium run, but one receives the prize. Therefore run in order to win . . . This is how I run, not uncertainly. This is how I fight, not beating the air. (1 Cor. 9:24–26)

In this section he also calls those who make problems over the Law or about eating forbidden things 'weak' (8:7–12 and 9:22). In Galatians, it is clear that what he means is that he is fearful that the leaders in Jerusalem might disavow the Gospel as he has already started teaching it – obviously without their permission – among the non-Jewish or Gentile 'Peoples'.

At this point he begins to grow extremely agitated about this interview with the Jerusalem Leadership even when recalling it in writing and starts to defend his doctrine that Greeks coming into the new Movement – whatever one wants to make of it at this point – need not be circumcised. This was evidently part of 'the Gospel' as he taught it among 'the Peoples' or 'Nations'. Introducing someone who accompanied him to this interview along with Barnabas – now often referred to as 'the Jerusalem Council' or 'Conference' – as Titus 'a Greek', Paul insists that on this account Titus was not 'required to be circumcised' (2:2–3).

Since much of the rest of the letter has to do with Paul's antagonism to the group he calls 'of the circumcision', even perhaps, 'the circumcisers', a party of people he actually identifies with James (2:12) and an issue he identifies with 'slavery versus freedom' – in this sense, 'slavery to the Law', the sign of which was circumcision, and, conjointly, a slavish adherence to the instructions of the Jerusalem or 'Jerusalem Church' Leadership.

In due course he concludes at the beginning of chapter 5:

> Therefore, *stand fast in the freedom with which Christ made us free*, and do not [submit] again to *the yoke of slavery* . . . Everyone who accepts circumcision is obliged *to do the whole Law* [note the emphasis on *doing* here]. Whosoever is justified by the Law *are set aside from the Christ*. You fell from Grace. (Gal. 5:1–4)

Here, one has a clear play on the kind of 'setting oneself apart' or 'separation' emphasized in the Dead Sea Scrolls or the 'Naziritism', based on the Hebrew root, *N–Z–R*/'to keep apart from', we shall encounter on the part of those like James. This *N–Z–R* root is widespread in the Qumran Damascus Document and there it is used to express – as in James' instructions to overseas comunities as pictured in Acts – what one should 'stay away' or 'abstain from', as for instance, 'fornication', 'polluted Evil Riches', and 'unclean' or 'polluted things' generally.[5]

> For in Christ Jesus, neither circumcision nor uncircumcision is [any longer] in force, but rather Faith working by love. You were *running* well. Who stopped you, that you did not obey the Truth? (Gal. 5:6–7)

One should compare this with the passage in the Letter of James:

> For whoever shall keep the the whole Law, but stumbles on one [small point], shall be guilty [of breaking] it all (Jas. 2:10),

which like Paul in these passages and in Romans cites Abraham in speaking about 'Faith working with works' (Jas.2:22). Not only does James use all the words Paul is using, like 'love', 'doing', and 'Truth', it is the clear riposte.

For his part, so incensed does Paul become at this point in Galatians that he concludes by making a pun on the act of circumcision itself:

> I even wish that those who are throwing you into confusion would themselves [meaning their own privy parts] *cut off.* (5:12)

As we shall show, he is also playing on yet another passage in the Damascus Document at Qumran, which cites the 'consumption of blood' as the reason the Israelites were 'cut off' in the wilderness.[6]

But Paul utters this crudity, not only in the midst of again evoking 'being called to freedom', but directly following this, the Love Commandment, that is, 'love your neighbour as yourself', which he now describes as being 'the whole Law' (5:12–14). But this is precisely the Commandment cited in the famous passage from James on 'the Royal Law according to the Scripture', also evoking 'doing', but this time in the sense of 'doing' or 'keeping the whole Law', not breaking it (2:8–10).

This Commandment is also evoked at a crucial juncture in these passages in the Damascus Document above as well. It is interesting that Paul's use of the language of 'biting' and 'swallowing' in the context of allusions to 'being consumed' or 'destroyed', which directly follow this (Gal. 5:15), are all paralleled by extremely important usages of this genre having to do with the destruction of the Righteous Teacher and Establishment perfidy generally in the Habakkuk *Pesher* from Qumran.[7]

Later Acts speaks of a travelling companion of Paul called 'Timothy', whose 'father was a Greek' and who was evidently not circumcised, but whom Paul had 'circumcised on account of 'the Jews' in the neighbourhood' (16:3). It is not always possible to distinguish this Timothy from the Titus in Galatians and other letters – Titus is not mentioned in Acts – just as it is not always possible to distinguish the individual Paul is calling Silvanus in his letters from the Silas in Acts.[8] Often the one is a Greek name; the other, simply the Latin. As with many other reckonings already encountered, these may not be all separate individuals. However, at least in Galatians, the point being made about Titus not needing to be circumcised *is very* clear.

Paul is having problems with the Jerusalem leadership at this juncture over circumcision, because as he attests in his own words, 'some *false brothers* stole in secretly to spy on the freedom which we enjoy in Christ

Jesus (Paul's name for his Supernatural Saviour) so that they might reduce us to slavery' or 'bondage'. The play on the *brothers/pseudo-brothers* parallel may be identical to the play on the 'false' or 'pseudo-Apostles' in 2 Cor. 11:13, also in the context of using the language of 'bondage' and 'swallowing' and reiterating that he 'does not lie' (2 Cor. 11:20 and 31). Once again, despite the emotion he displays, Paul's meaning in these passages is unmistakable. Whenever he is speaking about the Law or James – often the two are interchangeable – he uses the language of 'bondage' or 'slavery' and 'pseudo'/'falseness'. This applies, too, to the leadership exercised by individuals like James.

Something has happened here that puts Paul into bad repute with this leadership. That something clearly has to do with 'circumcision' and the fact that some of those accompanying him – whom Paul calls 'Greeks' and therefore 'not obliged to be circumcised' – were not circumcised. For Acts, Paul has such persons circumcised anyhow out of deference to the Church Leadership and in order to continue his missionary activities. We cannot necessarily depend on Acts here, but its gist is the same as Galatians on the issue of whether people like Titus or Timothy need to be circumcised. Galatians appears to be claiming Titus was not. Acts avers Timothy was. It is of little importance – the issue is the same.

Rather what is important is that at this point in Galatians Paul launches into an attack on the Jerusalem Leadership, in which he testifies to the undeniable fact that James was the principal leader and all, even Peter, were subordinate to him and had to defer to him. At the same time, he avows his intention to safeguard 'the Truth of the Gospel' as he teaches it among the Gentiles. As he puts it,

> not even for an hour did we yield in subjection, so that the Truth of the Gospel might continue with you (2:5),

this addressed to those for whom the letter was first intended, his co-religionists in Galatia in Asia Minor, whose situation he claims to be defending.

The people he is referring to here, those to whom he 'will not yield in subjection', designated by the pronouns 'some', 'whom', or 'they' in Gal. 2:6 and 2:12, turn out to be none other than the Leadership of the Jerusalem Church, or as Paul puts it in his own inimitable manner:

> those considered to be something, not that whatever they were [or 'their importance'] makes any difference to me, since God does not accept the person of men.[9]

Paul now repeats this 'those of repute' or 'those reckoned to be important' for emphasis:

> Those of repute had nothing to add to me. On the contrary, they recognized that I had been entrusted to teach the Gospel of the Uncircumcision just as Peter [was] of the Circumcision. (Gal. 2:7)

It is in the midst of these startling revelations and controversies that Paul reveals that James is not only *one* of the leaders and principal men, but *the* Leader.

But before he does so, he makes the equally astonishing claim that:

> He who worked [or 'wrought'] in Peter the Apostleship of the Circumcision also worked in me [the Apostleship] to the Gentiles [*Ethnē*]. (2:8)

It is impossible to know how to take this statement. Does Paul mean God or the Father, who worked through Peter to create his Apostleship, also worked through him (Paul) to create his? Or does he mean Jesus or the being he calls *Christ Jesus in Heaven* did this? If he means the earthly Jesus, then it is an impossibility, since Paul presumably never saw 'Jesus' in his lifetime. If he means the Supernatural Jesus, then we have only his testimony to this, and it is not surprising that many made light of and belittled it, even perhaps going so far as to call him a 'Liar'.[10]

Paul then moves on to introduce his version of the Central Leadership Trio of the early Church in Jerusalem, and with it, another conundrum, for he does not refer – at least in most versions of this material as it has come down to us – to Peter *per se*, but rather at this point to 'Cephas'. Normally 'Cephas' is taken as identical with Peter, even though Paul resumes the normative reference to 'Peter' two lines later in 2:11. In doing so, he introduces James for the second time and it is crystal clear *this* James is not 'the brother of John' as in the Gospels.

> So James, Cephas, and John, those reckoned to be Pillars, being aware of the Grace which was given to me, shook hands with Barnabas and me in fellowship, that we [should go] to the Gentiles, while they [go] to the circumcision. (2:9)

Here, then, we are not only apprised that James is someone 'reckoned to be something', but one of those in the front rank of the leadership, as it were a 'Pillar' or leader, in fact, as we shall see, *the all-encompassing Leader*. Paul has already belittled these in his Galatians 2:6 aspersion above, 'whatever they were makes no difference to me' and 'those reckoned important conferred nothing to me'. In 2 Corinthians 11, Paul will call such persons 'Hebrews' (11:22) and 'the Highest Apostles' – literally 'Apostles of the Highest Degree' or, if one prefers, 'Archapostles' (11:5, repeated in 12:11).

Paul introduces this 'Pillar' terminology here, something we had not heard previously, in confirmation of their importance or status. It is similar to the 'Foundation', 'Rock' and 'Cornerstone' imagery one encounters in the Gospels and Letters with regard to Peter or Jesus himself. These terms can be found in the Dead Sea Scrolls, particularly in the Community Rule and Hymns, including additional ones like 'a firm Foundation which will not shake', 'Wall', and 'Tower' or 'Fortress'.[11] This last, in particular, is equivalent to two epithets we shall see were applied to James: 'the Bulwark' and another puzzling circumlocution '*Oblias*', defined as 'Protection' in early Church texts and meaning, most likely, something akin to 'Fortress'. Where the idea of 'Pillar' is concerned, it is also in use in relation to the person of 'the *Zaddik*' in that tradition known as *Kabbalah*.

The '*Zaddik* the Pillar of the World' in *Kabbalah* and the Gospel of Thomas

'*Kabbalah*' means that which is received, the received tradition. It is the Jewish mystical tradition. One of its better known tenets is the idea of 'the *Zaddik*' or 'the Righteous One'. James is known in almost all early Christian texts as 'the Just' or 'Just One', and this eponym is, in fact, equivalent to that of 'the *Zaddik*' in Jewish *Kabbalah*.

One of the most popular and impressive of Jewish mystical texts is that known in the Middle Ages and thereafter as the *Zohar* or *Book of Splendour*, '*Zohar*' being translated into English as 'Splendour'. The term refers, among other things, to the 'splendour' on Moses' face after he came out either from the cloud on Mount Sinai or the Tent of Meeting in the wilderness, described in Exodus 24:39 and Numbers 6:25 in the Old Testament.

Paul seems to be aware of something resembling the Jewish mystical tradition even at this comparatively early date. In fact, he derides this same 'splendour on Moses' face' in the 2 Corinthians letter we have just referred to above in a section extolling 'the New Covenant of the Spirit' (2 Cor. 3:7). In this passage he likens the 'letters of recommendation', also just mentioned (which he lacks), to *the dead letters of the Law on the Tablets from Mount Sinai,* commenting that 'the letter kills, but the Spirit brings life' (2 Cor. 3:1–6).

133

For the ancient Hebrews, Moses' face glowed so brilliantly after being in the presence of God that he was obliged to cover it with a veil when he emerged from the Tent of Meeting so the people would not be irradiated. It is this 'veil' that Paul heaps abuse upon and with it the most sacred traditions of the Jewish People – in the process implying that Moses was a charlatan. One fairly reels before the lengths he was willing to go to in some of these polemics and verbal acrobatics.

This aspersion, that Moses put a veil over his face so the Israelites would not know 'the light of the Law had been extinguished', is not unlike the claim in Galatians 4:24 that the Jews were the descendants not of Sarah, but of Abraham's Egyptian bondservant Hagar, as was their Covenant – the allusion to the word 'bondage' being the operative point here – not Sarah, already remarked above. Both employ the kind of allegorical elucidation of Scripture pioneered by Paul's older contemporary, the famous Philo of Alexandria, the uncle of Tiberius Alexander (one of those who made the decision to destroy the Temple).

We have already noted his dextrous use of 'the hanged man being a curse' in Galatians 3:13 and the clear insult he intended pursuant to this by referring to the Jewish months, times, and festivals – called at Qumran 'the monthly flags' and 'festivals of Glory', but in regard to which Paul also uses his 'slavery' metaphor – as 'weak and beggarly elements'.[12] Not only is Paul playing in aspersions of this kind on the 'weakness' and 'Poor' vocabulary he often uses when discussing leaders like James, but such disrespect was calculated to enrage his interlocutors.

Even if his more Hellenized audiences did not, Paul knew how precious such traditions were to the pious Jews against whom his polemics were directed. But Paul, also, gives further evidence of being acquainted with this mystical tradition and its literature, which goes by the name of 'Hechalot Mysticism', that is, the mysticism of Heavenly Ascents or journeys to Heaven. In 2 Corinthians 12:1–4, again, just after his aspersions on the Hebrew 'counterfeit Apostles' and 'Archapostles' and referring to his own 'visions', 'incomparable revelations', and that he 'does not lie'; he claims to have known people involved in just such mystical journeying. Coincidentally, or otherwise, as in Galatians 2:1 above, this is 'fourteen years before' again. As Paul describes it, the unidentified 'man' he is referring to (James?) was 'caught up to Paradise',[13] where he 'heard unutterable sayings'.

There is additional literature which gives evidence to associate James with this mystical tradition of 'Ascents' as well, particularly the lost work

Epiphanius describes as the *Anabathmoi Jacobou* – 'the Ascents of James'. The two Apocalypses associated with James' name at Nag Hammadi are also full of the language of mystic enlightenment, including the portrayal of the mystic 'kiss' of Gnostic wisdom James either gives or receives from Jesus.[14]

But the 'Pillar' language Paul uses here in Galatians to describe the Central Three of 'James, Cephas, and John' would be sufficient to associate James with the '*Zaddik*' tradition, enshrined in all Jewish Kabbalistic and later *Zohar* tradition, even if we did not know James was known by 'the Just' or 'Just One' in all early Church tradition. This epithet was also presumably applied to 'the Righteous Teacher' or 'Teacher of Righteousness' in the Dead Sea Scrolls. Not only does it bear a relationship to the linguistically parallel 'Sons of Zadok' ideology at Qumran, but also to expressions like 'Sons of Righteousness' and 'Sons of the *Zaddik*', sometimes considered to be errors, but which in this context are probably not.[15] In addition to the 'Cornerstone', 'Foundation', 'Wall', 'Tower', and 'Fortress' imagery found there, there are other allusions like 'the Fountains of Living Water', 'the Mystery of Being', and 'the Throne' that later became the staples of Jewish mystic enlightenment.[16]

The allusion 'Pillar', as we have it, certainly was originally used in Proverbs, another text very much absorbed in the tradition of '*Zaddik*' theorizing, which specifically asserts that 'the *Zaddik* is the Pillar of the World' (Prov. 10:25). In turn, this idea is expounded in *Zohar* tradition, where it is associated with Noah, the first '*Zaddik*' mentioned in the Book of Genesis and, in fact, the first archetypal Saviour. The exposition is as follows:

> *Noah was a Righteous One.* Assuredly so after the Heavenly pattern, for it is written: '*The Righteous One is the Foundation of the world*' and the Earth is established thereon. For, this is *the Pillar that upholds the world.* So Noah was called *Righteous in this world* . . . and acted so as to be a Perfect copy of the Heavenly ideal . . . an embodiment of the world's *Covenant of Peace.* (*Zohar* 1.59b on *Noah*)

There is much more in the *Zohar* on 'the *Zaddik*', including both an allusion to 'protecting the People', an idea just encountered above having to do with James' 'Bulwark' sobriquet and Noah's expiatory suffering.[17] The connection of James with Noah, the first 'Righteous One', is another element that shines through the traditions about James. These include James' vegetarianism, his rainmaking, and his Noahic-like directives to overseas communities as recorded in Acts, to the extent that one can conceive of a *redivivus* tradition associated with the first '*Zaddik*' Noah, not unlike that associated with Elijah and John the Baptist in the New Testament.[18]

In this passage from the *Zohar*, the pre-existence or supernatural nature of 'the *Zaddik*' is stressed, an idea encountered as well in the Prologue of the Gospel of John in terms of '*Logos*' and '*Light*' imagery, in the description there of Jesus' entrance into the world. But there is another allusion in the recently rediscovered Nag Hammadi Gospel of Thomas – 'the Twin' or 'Judas Thomas' – the putative third brother of Jesus after James and Simon. This bears on the ideal of this pre-existent *Righteous One* or Heavenly *Zaddik* – in more mundane terms, James in his role as *Perfect Righteous One*. In turn this also bears on the appointment of James as Leader of the Jerusalem Church and therefore of all Christianity everywhere as successor to Jesus. It reads as follows:

> The Disciples said to Jesus: 'We know that you will depart from us. Who is it that shall be great over us [meaning after he is gone]?' Jesus replied to them: 'In the place where you are to go [presumably Jerusalem], go to James the Just, *for whose sake Heaven and Earth came into existence.*' (Logion 12)

Aside from being a tradition incorporating the long-lost direct appointment of James by Jesus as Leader of the early Church, it also bears on the idea of 'the *Zaddik*'. Yet it is a thousand years earlier than the above description in the *Zohar*, which was purportedly written in Spain in the 1200s–1300s. Thomas' description of James as 'for whose sake Heaven and Earth came into existence' is related to the one in the *Zohar* above about the *Zaddik* being 'the Pillar that upholds the world . . . a Perfect copy of the Heavenly ideal'. Not only is it a statement about the pre-existence of the *Zaddik*, it bears on Paul's allusion to 'those reputed to be Pillars' in Galatians 2:9 and later allusions in early Church tradition like the mysterious '*Oblias*' or '*Bulwark*' applied to James. That 'James the Righteous One' is someone for whose sake 'Heaven and Earth came into existence' means that not only are Heaven and Earth predicated on his existence but, as 'the *Zaddik*', he precedes them or is pre-existent.

The reader will recognize in this something equivalent to what goes by the name of 'the *Logos*' or 'the Word' in the Gospel of John above. There is also something very akin to it in what goes by the name in Shi'ite Islam of 'the *Imam*' doctrine. All these terms have common aspects and are more or less equivalent. The main connecting links between them have to do with a kind of incarnationism and pre-existence. In the Shi'ite doctrine, there is even a 'Hidden' aspect, not unrelated to the 'Standing One' ideology, as we shall encounter it in Jewish Christianity or Ebionitism below.[19] All are basically variations on 'the Primal' or 'Secret Adam' tradition – the bedrock of 'Jewish Christian' or 'Ebionite' ideology – which when translated into Greek became identified with the new terminology of 'the Christ'.

Noah the First *Zaddik* and Abraham's *Ten Just Men*

There is another tradition associated with the pre-existent *Zaddik* or 'Standing One' in Jewish *Kabbalah*, that is, the legend of 'the Ten Just Men', augmented in later tradition to thirty-six.[20] The tradition is, in fact, a *Noahic*-style one, similar to the one about James as 'Pillar' in this pivotal discussion by Paul in Galatians and in the allusion to James' place and role in the Nag Hammadi Gospel of Thomas. Its implications are that the world is supported upon the existence of 'Ten Just Men' – *the Ten primordial Righteous Ones* – and, just as in the *Zohar* tradition about the first *Zaddik* Noah, it is their existence that *upholds the world*.

Actually, in Genesis, there are two 'escape' and 'Salvation' episodes of this kind related to Righteous Ones. The first is the Noah episode, just signalled, where Noah is designated as 'Righteous and Perfect in his generation' (Gen. 6:9). This allusion is also the basis of the 'Perfection' ideal so important, for instance, in the Sermon on the Mount (Matt. 5:48) and for Dead Sea Scroll ideology.[21] It is, no doubt, related to the perception of James' *Perfect Righteousness* and *Piety* as well. Because Noah is so *Perfect* and a *Righteous One*, God is portrayed as saving him and, through this Salvation, allowing him to save the world through his progeny – 'the world below' as the *Zohar* would have it.

The second 'escape' and 'Salvation' episode in Genesis is that of Lot. This is a famous episode, which everyone knows. But not everyone realizes it is an episode having to do with the role and nature of 'the *Zaddik*' again. After having encountered three Angels – the 'three wise men' of Gospel portraiture – who announce (for the second or third time) that he and Sarah are going to have a son, Abraham remains with one of these Angels (who later turns out to be God – Gen. 18:22). The other two go down to see how Abraham's nephew Lot is doing in the plain below in Sodom and Gomorrah.

Finding these cities to be full of fornication and illicit sexual behaviour – the sexual emphasis in relation to a story about *Zaddikim* (Hebrew plural for *Zaddik*) is important – God determines to destroy these cities. At this point there transpires a bargaining scene between Abraham and God. Abraham asks God to withhold destruction from the city, that is, he intercedes with God on behalf of mankind. God agrees, but only on the basis that there should be found there fifty Just Men, that is, fifty *Righteous Ones*. Abraham asks for forty. God agrees. The bargaining goes on. Finally, it is determined that for the sake of 'Ten Just Men' God will withhold destruction from the city (Gen. 18:32).

This number becomes proverbial. In time it also becomes the minimum number required for Jewish communal prayer, the two, no doubt, being seen as connected, that is, the prayer of *Ten Righteous Men* can in some manner provide sustaining power to the world, a proposition repeated in James 5:16 in relation to the prayer of Elijah – another of these incarnated forerunners – for rain, or as it is put there, 'the working prayer of the Just One much prevails' (Jas. 5:16).

Somehow the number here is augmented in Jewish mystical tradition to thirty-six (the numerical value in Judaism of the word *life*), the reason for which cannot be determined. Its bearing, however, on the situation of James and, later, his relationship to the city of Jerusalem, will become clear. Tradition will also credit this kind of 'rainmaking' to James, and, as we shall see below, there is an eschatological or salvationary dimension to this.[22] To the new biblical exegete James in his role as 'Pillar', 'Wall', or 'Bulwark'/'Shield' will provide the sustaining 'Protection' required to guarantee *Jerusalem*'s continued existence – Jerusalem being substituted for Sodom.

The concomitant to this is, of course, that once 'the *Zaddik*' – in this case James – was removed, existence of the city could no longer, like Sodom and Gomorrah in mythological tradition, be sustained and its destruction was assured. This whole process related to the application of these '*Zaddik*', 'Pillar', and 'Protection' epithets to James' person. Even in the circumscribed materials that have come down to us, the destruction of the Temple and Jerusalem some seven and a half years later by Roman armies was tied by exegetes to his death. In the context of '*Zaddik*' theorizing, the sense of this is not punishment, as per later *Christian* reformulation, but once the requisite 'Shield' or 'Protection', James, had been removed, Jerusalem could no longer remain in existence.

Paul's Picture of the Central Three, James, Cephas, and John

Paul, in concretizing this role of James as 'Pillar' in Galatians 2:9, had already confirmed in line 19 of the previous chapter, that it was *this James* he met and not some other. There really is no other James, since by Paul's own testimony we are well into the 50s as it is and Acts has the other James – credible or not – removed from the scene by the mid-40s coincident with the *beheading of Theudas*. Therefore, even if we credit Acts' presentation, erroneous as it may be, the other James *was already dead at this point*.

But in this passage from Galatians Paul makes it unmistakably clear which James we are dealing with. In one of the most meaningful statements in Christian religious history, Paul unequivocally describes a stay he made in Arabia and his later return to Damascus – whatever might be meant by these geographical notations at this point – and identifies James as follows:

> But when it pleased God, who *chose me from my mother's womb* and called me by His Grace to *reveal His son in me*, that I should announce him as the Gospel among the Nations, I did not immediately confer with *any human being*, nor did I go up to Jerusalem to those [who were] Apostles before me. Rather *I went away into Arabia* and again *returned to Damascus*. Then after three years I went up to Jerusalem to make the acquaintance of Peter [we can assume this to be in the late 30s or thereabouts] and I remained with him *fifteen days*. Nor did I see any of *the other Apostles except James the brother of the Lord*. Now the things I write you are *true, for before God, I do not lie* [this last has the character of an oath]. (Gal. 1:15–20)

We have in these sentences some of the most important historical data of early Christianity. First of all, in counter-indicating Acts' parallel presentation of events, they reveal that document to be defective on these points and a not very artfully concealed rewrite. Secondly, they introduce *the really important James* in no uncertain terms, not only placing him, as someone Paul knows, on a level with Peter, but also *among* the Apostles – questions about the sense of this terminology for the moment aside – another fact that Scripture (in this instance, the Gospels and the Book of Acts) is most anxious to disguise. As we proceed, we shall also be able to show that Jesus' brothers were, indeed, *reckoned as Apostles* and are to be found in Apostle lists even as presently constituted. But let us take these points one at a time.

In the first place, we can say from Paul's testimony that the James he is talking about here – whom he calls 'the brother of the Lord', whether this brothership is to be taken as real or symbolical – is on the same level as the Peter whose acquaintance he appears to be making *for the first time*. Again, it is not clear whom he means by this 'Peter' as in the next chapter, as we have seen, he also speaks about someone he calls 'Cephas' (Gal. 2:19 – 'Cephas' is an Aramaic appellation, usually taken as meaning 'Rock', just as Peter means 'Rock' in Greek).

Recently a burial urn was uncovered in the neighbourhood of Jerusalem with just such a name – '*Kepha''* in Aramaic, that is, our 'Cephas' here – inscribed on it.[23] Eventually we shall look at the relationship of this configuration of letters to other appellations like *Cleophas*, *Alphaeus*, and *Clopas* – even 'Caiaphas' – all either variants of or linguistically related to it. However, by speaking of 'the other Apostles', it is quite clear that Paul means that *both* James and Peter are to be reckoned among the Apostles, whatever may be meant by the term at this point. This is surprising, as most would not reckon James or the brothers of Jesus generally among the Apostles. Nor, at this point, is Paul speaking of 'Twelve' Apostles as part of a fixed scheme.

As we shall see below, this idea of 'the Twelve' or 'Twelve Apostles', as the Gospels and the Book of Acts would have it, is somewhat formal and even rather childish. As we shall also see, in 1 Corinthians, too, it is pretty clear that not only was James among the original Apostles, this *Twelve Apostle* scheme was one that aided the historiographical and doctrinal approach of books like the Gospels and Acts. Stemming from the ideas of those either unsophisticated in Palestinian history or purposefully trying to archaize or dissemble, it is not at all certain that such a scheme was ever really operative in the Palestine of the time.

In its favour – apart from the rather tendentious Apostle lists in the Gospels and Acts – is the reference in a key document among the Dead Sea Scrolls (the cluster of materials going by the name of the Community Rule) to a central Council made up of 'Twelve Israelites'. This, too, probably archaizes to a certain extent, being based on a no longer extant biblical framework of *twelve* actual Israelite Tribes. In this reference in the Community Rule, which is also using 'spiritualized Temple' imagery, there is allusion as well to 'Three'. But here, too, there are difficulties and it is not possible to tell from the allusion in the text whether we have Twelve plus Three or whether 'the Three' are meant to be included in 'the Twelve', this being the presentation of the Gospels, though not necessarily Galatians. The probability is in favour of the former.[24]

'The Three' being spoken about in the Dead Sea Scrolls are specifically referred to as 'Priests' – 'three Priests' – either added to a central Council of twelve, that is, twelve Israelites, or part of it. But the imagery being used here with regard either to 'the Twelve' and 'the Three' is similar to that in the New Testament. In fact, the former are referred to in the Community Rule – presumably in view of their Israelite blood – as 'a House of Holiness for Israel', that is, the Twelve Tribes; the latter, 'a Holy of Holies for Aaron', that is, the Central Priestly Triad.

There can be no doubt that what we have here is what – following Paul's vocabulary in 1 Corinthians 2:13 – should be called 'spiritualized Temple' imagery, both a *spiritualized Temple* and *spiritualized Holy of Holies* within the Temple.[25] In the Community Rule at Qumran, this imagery is accompanied by *spiritualized sacrifice* and *spiritualized atonement* imagery as well, that is, this Council – which is the governing body of the Community – is referred to not only as 'making atonement for the land' and 'atoning for sin by *doing Righteousness*' (note the emphasis on 'doing'), but 'a sweet fragrance', 'a well-tested Wall, that Precious Cornerstone, whose Foundations shall neither rock nor sway in their place'.[26] This is also the case in the Christianity of the Gospels and this Letter by Paul to the Galatians when treating 'the Central Three', a triad seemingly at once part of and above 'the Apostles' – or to use the language of the Qumran Community Rule, 'the Council of the Twelve'.

But again, it is when treating these 'Three' that we run into difficulties in the New Testament, because the enumeration of them is not the same in the Gospels as it is in the Letter to the Galatians.[27] We have already heard in Galatians that *the Central Three*, that is, 'those of repute' or 'reputed to be something' (whose importance 'made no difference' or 'nothing conferred' to Paul), or 'reputed to be Pillars', are James, Cephas, and John. James and John, here, are not specified as being brothers, as they are in the Gospels, or even related, and, indeed, whoever this John is – also never mentioned by Paul again – the 'James' reputed to be 'his brother' (that is, John's brother) in Acts and the Gospels had long since disappeared from the scene. However, in the Gospels it is quite clear that the Central Three are supposed to be Peter, James, and *John his brother*, meaning Peter, James, and John 'the two sons of Zebedee' (Matt. 10:2, 17:1, 26:37 and pars.).

It should be immediately apparent that all of these are slightly different enumerations. In the Gospels, Jesus is pictured as transfiguring himself before the latter Three 'on a high mountain', but, as we have remarked, all such recitals in the Gospels must be taken with a degree of scepticism. In any event, the rule of thumb we suggested above should apply here. Where there is a conflict between data in these and reliable passages from the letters attributed to Paul, the latter are in all cases to be preferred. Not only this, but it is the 'brother' theme, when inspected carefully, which will be seen to be causing the difficulties – whether, for instance, with regard to 'Andrew *his brother*' (in this case Peter's 'brother' – Mark 1:18 and pars.), 'John his brother' (Mark 1:19 and pars.), 'James the brother of John' (Acts 12:2), or Jesus' brother, so much so that the movement of this phrase, 'his brother', has all the earmarks of a shell game.

This is also the case with names like 'Judas of James' in Luke's Apostle lists (Luke 6:16 and Acts 1:13), overwriting 'Thaddaeus' in Matthew and Mark. No such list is even present in John. Nor is John aware of 'James and John his brother' or vice versa, though he does speak of 'the sons of Zebedee'. In fact, John never mentions *a single James at all* and the only 'John' he mentions explicitly – aside from the circumlocution 'the Disciple Jesus loved'[28] – is John the Baptist.

However, the Gospel of John is explicit in identifying 'Cephas' with 'Peter' and makes a special point of having Jesus himself make this identification when he introduces him in the first chapter (1:42). But we can take this Gospel as rather late and it is not at all sure its author understood these distinctions, though he may have. For instance, note how he is already calling the individual, known as 'Judas Thomas' in other sources ('Judas the Twin'), 'Thomas called *Didymus*' ('Twin Twin' – John 11:16 and 21:2).

The Post-Resurrection Appearances of Jesus to the Apostles in the Gospels

The reference to Cephas as one of the 'Pillars' in Galatians 2:9 is interesting. In chapter 1, Paul preceded this by referring to someone he calls Peter whose acquaintance he made along with James fourteen years before in Jerusalem (1:18). He follows with his description of the confrontation, when he and Peter meet once again in Antioch and are forced to respond to 'some from James' over the issue of 'table fellowship with Gentiles' (2:11–12). It is not at all certain, as we have suggested, that we are dealing with the same individual in these three separate notices and the problem has been worried over by scholars with little result.

The point is that there may be another individual with this name *Cephas*. Paul uses this appellation to refer to him in 1 Corinthians on several occasions, particularly regarding disputes in Asia Minor with someone called Apollos (1 Cor. 1:12 and 3:22) – who, according to Acts, 'knew only John's baptism' (Acts 18:25)[29] – or regarding the fact that 'Jesus' brothers travel with women too' (1 Cor. 9:15). But the main reference he makes to 'Cephas' in 1 Corinthians – never Peter – is in the list of post-resurrection appearances by Jesus in chapter 15, where Cephas is listed as the first person to whom Jesus appeared after his death (15:5).

In the way the reference presently stands, Jesus 'appeared to Cephas, then to the Twelve', Cephas does not appear to be one of the Apostles.[30] All this is very puzzling. The answer again may relate to problems surrounding Jesus' brothers in Scripture. It is possible that the *Cephas* being referred to in between the references to 'Peter' in Paul's letters is another 'Simon' or 'Simeon' – the Simeon *bar Cleophas* mentioned above as Jesus' *first cousin*. Just as Simon Peter in Scripture is represented as being the successor to Jesus, this Simon or Simeon is represented by early Church tradition as being the successor to James. He is also of the family of Jesus, Cleophas being specifically denoted as the uncle of Jesus.

As we proceed, it will probably transpire that this Cleophas is not the uncle of Jesus, but rather his father, and there are traditions that to some degree represent him as such. In John 19:25, for instance, he is represented as the husband of Mary and this is probably true. For Origen, who was exiled to Palestine from Egypt for a time in the third century, when discussing the passage from the Josephus he knew ascribing the fall of Jerusalem to the death of James not Jesus, this Cleophas was actually *the father* of James, Simon, Jude, and Joses – those brothers represented as being the brothers of Jesus in Scripture – but these now by a previous mother, not Mary.[31] Again, the reasons for all these transmutations and circumlocutions should be growing clearer. They are twofold: one, to protect the divine sonship of Jesus; and, two, the emerging doctrine of the perpetual virginity of Mary.

These post-resurrection appearances by or sighting traditions about Jesus have long been recognized by scholars as being associated in some manner in early Church enumerations with one's place in the hierarchy of the early Church, that is, the earlier he appeared to you, the higher up in the hierarchy you were. Paul sets the stage for this by referring to this appearance to Cephas and others in 1 Corinthians above. Unfortunately there is no first appearance to *Peter* recorded in *any* of the Gospels, or anywhere else for that matter.[32] In fact, John 20:6–7 records that when Peter went into the tomb it was empty and there were only the burial clothes of Jesus neatly piled to one side. For Matthew and Mark, Peter does not even enter the tomb; rather the *two* Marys do – one specifically called 'Mary the mother of James' (Mark 16:1; cf. Luke 24:10) – where they encounter 'the Angelic being(s)'. It is he, now wearing the 'dazzling clothing', 'white as snow',[33] who tells them of Jesus' resurrection and his departure for Galilee. Luke has two Angels, not one, and, of course, nothing about a departure for Galilee, but rather Jesus predicting his coming crucifixion and resurrection 'on the third day' while 'yet in Galilee' earlier (24:6–7). For Luke, the two Marys now 'told these things to the Apostles', and it is only after this that Peter rushes to the tomb, where, seeing only 'the linen clothes' again, he departs 'wondering at what had happened' (24:10–12).

Matthew also has the two Marys rushing to tell 'the Disciples' what they had seen. But curiously, at this juncture it is they who actually encounter Jesus, seeing him along the way. For his part, Jesus is presented as uttering words similar to those reported of Peter to the servant at 'the house of Mary the mother of John Mark' in Jerusalem in the crucial introduction of James in Acts 12:17, to wit, 'Go, tell my brothers to go into Galilee and there they will see me' (Matt. 28:10). For most of the Gospels, further appearances then proceed to take place in Galilee, all except the Gospel of Luke.

The Gospel of Luke does record a post-resurrection appearance in the neighbourhood of Jerusalem – this, the famous sighting on the Road to Emmaus. Mark 16:12 also refers to this, noting how 'after these things, he [Jesus] appeared in another form to two of them as they walked on their way into the country', but this ending from Mark is considered a later addition.

Where this 'Emmaus' was supposed to be is also a question. Presentday reckonings have it more or less due west of Jerusalem at the foothills of the road from the coast mounting to Jerusalem – a location now called Latrun after the name of a Crusader 'tower' there (where the Arabs and Israelis fought a key battle for control of the Jerusalem road in 1948). Luke specified that Emmaus was 'sixty furlongs from Jerusalem' – about seven and a half miles – whereas Latrun is about twenty-five miles and therein lies the conundrum.[34]

For Luke, Jesus appeared to someone called '*Cleopas*', obviously identical to the Cleophas considered Jesus' 'uncle' we have been following, and *another unnamed person* (24:13–18). The nature of this episode is similar to the 'doubting Thomas' one in John 20:26–29 and an episode in the apocryphal Gospel of the Hebrews, conserved in the writings of Jerome, about *a first appearance to James*. In these, Jesus actually sits down, breaks bread, and apparently eats with the individual(s) involved, to prove the fact of his corporeal resurrection and, therefore, his *bodily* needs.[35] In Luke, however, when report comes to 'the Eleven and those with them' of this appearance on the Road to Emmaus outside Jerusalem to Cleopas and another, they are represented as crying out in unison, 'the Lord is risen indeed and appeared unto *Simon*' (24:33–34).

But, unfortunately, no appearance to a 'Simon' has taken place anywhere – certainly not in this first appearance 'along the way' to Cleopas, unless we are dealing with the traces of an early appearance to *members of Jesus' family*.[36] This would concretize their place in the post-resurrection appearance sequence, given by Paul in 1 Corinthians 15:7, that is, an appearance rather to *James and Simeon bar Cleophas*, the latter, we shall show, all but indistinguishable from 'Simon the Zealot', already being called in writings attributed to Hippolytus and in Syriac sources in the third century, *the second brother of Jesus*.

Paul's *Lying*

Paul's insistence in Galatians 1:16 that he did not discuss the version of the Gospel he taught or the fact of the revelation of, as he puts it, God's 'son in him' with any *other human being* – literally 'with flesh and blood' – is interesting. As well, it accords, as we have seen, with the way he introduces himself and his Apostleship generally in Galatians 1:1:

> Paul, Apostle, *not from men nor through man*, but through Jesus Christ and God the Father, who raised him from among the dead.

That is, he did not receive his teaching commission from *any man*, as, for instance, a leader or 'Pillar' of the Jerusalem Church with the stature or authority of a James, but rather *direct from Jesus himself*, whom, of course, by this time Paul is referring to as 'Christ', to signal his *supernatural* as opposed to his natural persona.

This also recalls the sense one gets from reading 2 Corinthians, confirmed, as we have seen, in the Pseudoclementines, that the Apostles required *letters of recommendation from James*. In line with his contempt for such things, which he compares sarcastically in 2 Corinthians 3:7 to 'the service of death' and the dead letters written on the stone of the Ten Commandments, Paul insists his appointment is *direct from Jesus Christ* –

meaning *the Supernatural Christ*, to whom in Heaven, he has, as it were, a direct line via 'the Holy Spirit'. This is the only certification he needs, which accords with his reasons for not discussing with anyone else the Gospel about *Christ Jesus*, as he taught it among the Gentiles. He didn't need to. He only had to discuss it with the Heavenly Jesus through the medium of the Holy Spirit.

He did not recognize earthly authority, not the Jerusalem Church leaders, nor the decisions of the so-called 'Jerusalem Council' as we shall see – only the visions he was receiving. This was all very well and good for Paul, but one can imagine the kind of problems it might have caused him among his contemporaries. We can get an inkling of these by reading between the lines in his letters and comprehending the doctrines about him in the Pseudoclementines and materials of similar orientation.

Paul was obviously being mocked by some – within the Church not outside it – as 'the Man of Dreams', 'Lies', or 'Lying', or what was also characterized in a parallel parlance as 'the Enemy'.[37] This is confirmed tangentially by Paul's defensiveness with regard to such epithets, as evidenced at the end of his testimony in Galatians to his all-important meeting with Peter and James in Jerusalem (Gal. 1:20 and 4:16). It is neither accidental nor incurious that exactly where he comes to speak of 'James the brother of the Lord' and in 2 Corinthians, the Hebrew 'Archapostles', that Paul feels obliged to add: 'Now before God, (in) what I write to you, I do not lie' or, again, 'I do not lie.'

This will not be the only time that Paul will via refraction refer in his defensiveness to 'the Liar' epithet evidently being applied to him by some *within* the Movement not outside it. It is, as just noted, connected to the all-important 'Enemy' terminology, known to have been applied to him in later Jewish Christianity or Ebionitism. In the context of referring to Jewish observances and festivals as 'weak and beggarly elements' (Gal. 4:9), his opponents – again *within* the Movement – as 'wishing zealously to exclude' him and his communities (4:18), and the Covenant on Mount Sinai as 'born according to the flesh' of the *Arab bondservant Hagar* and, therefore, 'bringing forth to bondage' (4:24), Paul worries over his *'becoming your Enemy by telling you the Truth'* (4:16). This remark should be viewed over and against one in James 4:4 insisting that 'whoever makes himself into a Friend of the world turns himself into an Enemy of God', which plays, as we shall see, on the original biblical characterization of Abraham as 'the Friend of God'.

There are some eight other indications of this 'Lying' epithet in the

Pauline corpus alone.[38] That Paul alludes to it here in the midst of this pivotal testimony to the existence of James, while at the same time explaining why he (Paul) was unknown by sight to anyone else in the Movement in Palestine, is extraordinary. It is as if Paul associated the idea of 'Lying' with something to do with his relationship with James, whose acquaintance he made during his first visit to Jerusalem after his 'revelation' of Christ as the 'son in' him, and that he knew some of James' followers were applying this kind of language to him and his activities. Why would Paul feel constrained to adjure – and this in the form almost of an oath – that he 'does not lie' with regard to the claims he is putting forth concerning this revelation and his first meeting with James?

Paul uses this 'Lying' terminology at several other crucial junctures in his letters, particularly in Romans 3:4–8 and 9:1, where he speaks about wrongful accusations concerning himself, circumcision, the Law, and how by 'telling the Truth' he has made himself 'a curse from Christ' to his opponents. He also uses it in 2 Corinthians 11:31 above, to attack his 'Hebrew Archapostle' interlocutors and boast about the escape he made from Aretas' representative in Damascus in a basket. 1 Timothy, the authorship of which is disputed, also pictures Paul as averring he is 'an Apostle' and insisting he 'speaks the Truth of Christ and does not lie' (2:7).

The riposte to these things is, of course, found in the Letter of James at a likewise crucial juncture, following the rebuke of the 'Empty Man' (2:20) and evocation of the Lying 'Tongue', which 'cannot be tamed', 'boasts great things', and is 'a world of Unrighteousness all in itself' (3:1–8). It is succinctly put:

> If you have bitter jealousy and contentiousness *in your heart*, do not boast or *lie against the Truth*. This is not the Wisdom that comes down from above, but *earthly, man-made, devilish* [note the reversal of Paul's 'flesh and blood' aspersions and the allusion to the idea of 'devilishness']. (3:14–15)

The application of all these epithets to the situation of Paul will become clearer as we progress.

The same context is apparent in the Dead Sea Scrolls: 'Truth' is always juxtaposed with 'Lying', 'Righteousness' with 'Evil', 'Light' with 'Darkness', a fornicating, rebellious, jealous, and spouting 'Tongue' with obedience and good conscience. These kinds of allusions are widespread at Qumran. Not only is the vocabulary almost interchangeable with these crucial parts of the Pauline or Jamesian corpus, but the same kind of imagery is in use. When one appreciates that James occupies a position in early Christianity equivalent to the one occupied by the Righteous Teacher at Qumran and the same kinds of allusions are being applied to them in both and to their enemies, then the points of contact between the two draw ever closer.

But there is 'Lying' going on here. Someone is not telling 'the Truth', whether purposefully or simply out of ignorance – either Paul or the authors of the Book of Acts. In the first place, no vision on the road to Damascus takes place in Galatians. It is true that twice, just after mentioning 'Damascus' in Galatians 1:17 and before doing so in 2 Corinthians 11:32, Paul vigorously protests he 'does not lie', but he does not mention a vision on the way to Damascus.

What he does mention, leading up to this 'Damascus' allusion in Galatians, is that God had set him aside and called him from his 'mother's womb' (1:15), which would appear to be an exactly parallel claim to the one in early Church literature regarding the person of James. According to Hegesippus, James was considered 'consecrated from his mother's womb' or what in biblical Judaism would go by the notation of *life-long Naziritism*. In the Bible a 'Nazirite' was someone like Samuel or John the Baptist, both dedicated to God from their mother's womb. The description of James will conform to these parameters. So will parallel ones in the Dead Sea Scrolls.

Paul's claim, especially since it is leading up to his introduction of James, must be seen as a rival one to this Naziritism of James, with whom he was always in such competition, a Naziritism that must be seen as common knowledge in the Jerusalem of the time. In addition to it Paul, also, claims that God called him

> by His Grace to reveal [*apocalypsai*] His son in me that I might preach the Gospel about Him to the Gentiles. (Gal. 1:16)

Contradictions between Acts and Paul about Damascus and Arabia

Acts' disagreements with Galatians and 2 Corinthians are worrisome, too, where Paul's activities in this 'Damascus' are concerned. Acts presents Paul as going to the house of someone called 'Judas' on a street called 'Straight' (9:11). The allusion connects with characterizations of the mission of John the Baptist in the Gospels and the way the Dead Sea Scrolls characterize their Community's activities 'in the wilderness'.[39] This reference to a 'Judas' will link up with another 'Judas' or 'Thaddaeus' in notices connected to the evangelization of Edessa and, as we have already noted, in Matthew and Mark, this 'Thaddaeus' takes the place of 'Judas of James' in Luke.

In this 'house' in Damascus Paul meets 'Ananias', a name that will crop up in conversion stories also related to both King Agbarus or Abgarus of Edessa, 'the Great King of the Peoples beyond the Euphrates', and Queen Helen of Adiabene and her son Izates further East. As Acts 9:17 portrays it, Paul receives his commission to teach to the Gentiles from Ananias and not directly from God via revelation or visionary experience. Nor does Acts mention at this point anything about an intervening trip or flight to 'Arabia' as Paul refers to it in Galatians 1:17.

The meaning usually given to 'Arabia' is that area around Petra. 'Petra', like 'Peter', is a Greek word meaning 'Rock' or 'Stone', because the city – fabled in modern story as 'rose-red' and 'half as old as time' – was cut out of stone in the Transjordanian wilderness, overlapping to some extent the area called 'Idumaea', the classical home of the Edomites in Jewish Scripture. Once again, it is also an important usage for focusing on evangelical activities in Northern Syria and Mesopotamia having to do with both King Agbarus and Queen Helen/King Izates.

Another reason it is important is because of Paul's own Arab and/or Edomite ('Idumaean') connections or roots. According to Galatians, when Paul gets his revelation about the 'son in him' and the Gospel of Jesus Christ he was to teach to the Gentiles, he did not go to Damascus, but directly 'into Arabia'. Petra grew up on the other side of the Jordan as the centre of the Arabian Kingdom, which flourished there because of its trading connections to Southern Arabia and the Mediterranean. This Kingdom is referred to by scholars as 'Nabataean' after Ishmael's first-born son Nabaioth in the Bible – also Esau's wife's brother.[40] But it is easier simply to understand it as 'Arab', a term by which it was known then and still is today.

This Kingdom, which in any event was Hellenistic in culture, was taken over by the Romans around the time they took Damascus in the period of their conquest of Palestine from the 60s to the 30s BC. Its kings served under Roman tutelage. While Herod's father, Antipater, was reputed to be either from 'Greek' or 'Idumaean' background, his mother was an Arab from Petra probably of noble birth, if not actually related to the King. Though, according to some, perhaps to some extent Judaized, Herod and his father retained these Arab and Idumaean connections so important to their rise to power, so much so that those descended from them were often called 'Idumaeans'.

Some actually were, completely. For instance, Herod's sister Salome – the namesake of the Salome in the John the Baptist story – was married to an Idumaean named Costobarus. Whenever Josephus mentions the Herodian family member he calls 'Saulus' or 'Saul', he invariably associates him with this name Costobarus and another apparent relative Antipas.[41] We have already suggested on the basis of the reference in Acts 13:1 that Herod the Tetrarch, another of these Antipases, was in some manner related to Paul.

The wealth of the family of Antipater (the first Antipas), and thereafter Herod's, was based on these Transjordanian connections and involvement in the Arabian trade that came through Petra and then across the Dead Sea to Jerusalem or directly to the Mediterranean Coast. This consisted of aromatic resins from Southern Arabia and seemingly spices and silks from India. It is depicted in the infancy story from Matthew and the picture of the three wise men coming from the East with their 'frankincense and myrrh' (2:11).

That Paul, after his vision, would proceed to the Idumaean/Arab centre of this trade on the Transjordanian side of the Dead Sea – if he did – is important. In view of his possible Herodian origins, this would not be surprising, given the connections of Herod to this city. For instance, Herod's father had assisted Pompey's adjutant Aemilius Scaurus – mentioned pejoratively in the commemorative 'Priestly Courses' texts from the Dead Sea Scrolls – in his relations with Petra.[42]

Paul's possible Herodian connections also loom large in the power he was able to wield at a comparatively young age in Jerusalem and in 'Damascus' – as they do, the Roman citizenship he purportedly carried and 'was born to'. This last, according to Acts, is to save him more than once (16:38 and 22:28). In turn, the status he commanded also played its part in his struggle for power *vis-à-vis* James in the Jerusalem Church.

Paul refers to the Arab King Aretas in the same breath that he mentions 'Damascus' and 'not lying' in 2 Corinthians 11:32. Josephus connects this Aretas and the campaign he waged against Herod Antipas around 37–8 CE to events surrounding the death of John the Baptist – also on 'the other side of the Jordan'. Josephus claims that the Jewish crowd took Antipas' defeat by Aretas as retribution for what Antipas had done to John. We have already suggested that Paul was somehow involved in this conflict – obviously on Antipas' side – as by his own testimony he is a fugitive from the representatives of this same Aretas.

This, as we have seen, forms the backdrop to his escape down the walls of Damascus in a basket, unless Paul escaped *twice* in a basket down the walls of Damascus – a doubtful proposition. This is transformed in Acts into an escape because '*the Jews* were plotting to kill' Paul (9:24). But Paul's activities in 'Arabia' probably extended much further afield than Damascus or even Petra. The pivotal reference to 'the New Covenant at Damascus' in the Dead Sea Scrolls, too, probably will have even more interesting inferences, when it comes to discussing 'the Cup of the New Covenant in' the blood of Christ in Paul's 1 Corinthians and Gospel versions of 'the Last Supper'.

For Acts, as we have seen, there is no flight to Arabia at all, unless 'Damascus' is identical to 'Arabia'. For Acts Paul, rather, fearlessly proclaims his doctrine that 'Christ was the son of God in the *synagogues*' at Damascus (9:20). To begin with, it is hard to believe that there were plural 'synagogues' in the city we now refer to as Damascus. Since it was not known to be a particularly Jewish city at this time, there may not have been any at all.

But, of course, there is another possibility already implied above – that the 'Damascus' mentioned in Acts is not *the city of Damascus* at all, but rather that region which the Dead Sea Scrolls – in particular, the document known as the 'Damascus Document' because it repeatedly refers to it – call 'Damascus'. For the Damascus Document, 'Damascus' is the name – perhaps even a code – for *the whole region* where those rededicating themselves to 'the New Covenant' were 'settled' or had retreated.[43]

'The New Covenant' is also a name used in early Christianity for the Movement we associate with Christianity. Latterly, of course, it has become the name of the biblical presentation of what we take to be this Movement – 'the New Testament'. The terms 'New Testament' and 'New Covenant' are identical in Greek. Of course for the Dead Sea Scrolls, 'the New Covenant in the Land of Damascus' is really only rededication to the Old Covenant or a renewal. Whereas for Paul, and the Letter to the Hebrews following him, it is a 'New Covenant in the blood' of Christ, encompassing all of what Paul was implying by the 'Gospel of Christ Jesus' he taught.

As Acts would have it, 'Paul confounded the Jews who dwelt in Damascus' both in the way he proclaimed Jesus as 'the son of God' and 'proved he was the Christ' (9:22).[44] The Jews there, hearing of Paul's career 'in Jerusalem destroying those who *called on this Name*' and that he had come with letters from the Chief Priests, now 'plotted to kill him' (9:21–23).

There follows the episode of Paul being 'let down the walls of Damascus in a basket' (9:25). This is the episode paralleled by 2 Corinthians 11:32, the only difference being that it is not 'the Jews' who wish to arrest Paul, but rather 'the Ethnarch' of the *Arabian* King Aretas. Nor is it 'the Jews' he eludes, but rather this representative of Aretas. But this is typical of the working method of Acts, as we have been delineating it, *to invert* accusations made against Roman or Herodian officials. The same is done in the Gospels, not only with the execution of John the Baptist, connected to events involving this King Aretas, but also that of Jesus.

Acts now proceeds to present Paul as returning to Jerusalem and Barnabas as introducing him 'to the Apostles'. There Barnabas tells them of how Paul saw 'the Lord in the Way and that he spoke to him' and that he had 'spoken out boldly in *the Name of Jesus in Damascus*' (9:27). This use of 'in the Way' here, of course, parallels the report in Luke by Cleopas and the unnamed other to the Eleven of how Jesus appeared to two of them 'in the Way' on the Road to Emmaus.[45]

Acts now basically repeats this same happenstance, describing how Paul 'was with them coming and going in Jerusalem speaking out boldly in the Name of the Lord Jesus' (9:28). Of course, none of this accords with the picture in Galatians, where Paul rather says:

> Then, after three years, I went up to Jerusalem to make Peter's acquaintance, and I remained there fifteen days, but *I did not see any of the other Apostles* except James the brother of the Lord. Now what I write you, behold, before God, *I do not lie*. (1:18–20)

What is the point of all of these obfuscations and reversals? The reader will draw his or her own conclusions.

Paul now finishes up his description of his early career in Galatians with the words: 'Then I came into the regions of Syria and Cilicia' (1:21). These are the areas of Southern Asia Minor and Northern Mesopotamia we shall be looking at later. Herodians had been making inroads in these places for some time.[46] Paul also explains at this point why no one knew him by sight in Palestine:

> But I was not known by face to the Communities [*Ecclēsiais*/'Assemblies' again] of Judea which [are] in Christ, which had only heard that he who once had persecuted them, was now proclaiming the Gospel, [that of] the Faith he once ravaged and they were glorifying God in me. (1:22–24)

For Acts, on the contrary, it is now the same 'Hellenists' who were involved in Stephen's death who now wish to 'get hold of' Paul and 'put him to death'. Who these mysterious 'Hellenists' were will present another conundrum, which we shall attempt to unravel when we discuss this episode about the stoning of Stephen below.

> Becoming informed of this, the brothers brought him down to Caesarea and sent him away to Tarsus. The Assemblies throughout the whole of Judea, Galilee, and Samaria now enjoyed peace. (9:30–31)

All this is very mysterious and makes almost no sense at all, except that the picture in Acts has huge discrepancies when compared with the one in Galatians and doesn't mesh at all. Acts now turns to more mythologizing and story-telling with regard to Peter's 'tablecloth' vision on a rooftop in Jaffa and how a Roman Centurion – also from Caesarea – comes to visit him there, leading up to Peter's flight overseas and the introduction of James.

8

James' Succession and the Election to Fill
Judas *Iscariot*'s *Office*

The Succession of James in Paul and Acts

As presented by Paul, James is the Leader of the early Church *par excellence*. Terms like 'Bishop of the Jerusalem Church' or 'the Leader of the Jerusalem Community' are of little actual moment at this point, because from the period of the 40s to the 60s CE, when James held sway in Jerusalem, there really were no other centres of any importance. Overseas, the Pauline Mission was just getting started in the 40s and 50s, and even the centre in Rome can hardly be thought of as functioning to any extent. All deferred, in any case, to the Jerusalem Centre until it was destroyed.

Paul gives more information about the pre-eminence of James in the confrontation in Antioch that follows his discussion of what transpired in Jerusalem in regard to 'the Gospel as he proclaimed it among the Gentiles'. This discussion of the parameters of the Pauline 'Gentile Mission' in Galatians 2:1–10 is known in some quarters as 'the Jerusalem Council', and a parallel presentation of sorts – including important rulings directly attributed to James – forms the subject matter of chapter 15 of Acts. Of course, Acts 15's presentation of this 'Council' is quite different from Paul's picture of the Jerusalem meeting in Galatians 2:1–10, and its chronology totally so, to the extent that there is even a question as to whether the events depicted in the two narratives can be considered the same.

Despite problems of this kind, in both accounts James clearly emerges as the Supreme Ruler of the early Church, to whose rulings all must defer or bend. Acts even records James' directives to overseas communities on the matter of what was to be required of Gentile believers – pictured as the upshot of the 'Conference' in Acts – in three slightly varying versions.[1] Something not too dissimilar from what Acts reports must have emanated from whatever occurred in Jerusalem, though Paul does not report it in Galatians, because several of these directives turn up in his discussions in

1 Corinthians (5–11). There his response is one of angry aggressiveness, whereas in Galatians he blandly remarks that 'those reputed to be Pillars' or 'reckoned as important' had 'nothing to add' to the version of the Gospel that he proclaimed 'among the Gentiles' (Gal. 2:6).

That James was the leader in his own time is consolidated for us later in Acts too, particularly in the more reliable 'We Document'. This intrudes into the text in Acts 16:10, following James' mysterious appearances in chapters 12 and 15 and directly after Paul circumcises 'Timothy' (16:1–3) – in anticipation of crossing over from 'Asia' to do missionary work on mainland Greece and in 'Europe'.[2] Paul makes it unmistakably clear in Galatians as well that James is the leader of the Jerusalem Community ('Assembly') and of the Church as a whole.

James is the Head of Christianity of his day, whatever this may have been said to be. The so-called 'Bishop of Jerusalem' is not simply one among equals, the somewhat retrospective picture of later Church documents downplaying James, but rather 'the Bishop of Bishops' or overarching leader, the picture in the Pseudoclementines, and the 'Archbishop' or leader of the whole Movement everywhere.[3] Whether there was a prior or intervening leadership of 'Peter' can be argued and we shall probably never be able to arrive at a satisfactory conclusion on this point.

In reporting that the Jerusalem Leadership – the only leadership of the time – *agreed* that he should go 'to the Gentiles and they [James, Cephas, and John] to the circumcision' (Gal. 2:9), Paul focuses attention on the issue of 'circumcision'. By his own chronology, this must have been sometime in the early 50s, perhaps 50–51 CE. Those 'circumcised' or 'of the circumcision' must, as Paul understands, be called Jews. They could, however, also include Gentiles who had circumcised themselves – thereby for all intents and purposes becoming Jews – as Timothy would have been, if Acts 16:3's testimony regarding him can be taken at face value and not simply as a riposte to Galatians.

The problem regarding circumcision occupies much of Paul's attention throughout Galatians. This was the issue between Paul and the Jerusalem leadership regarding Titus (identical with Timothy?), whom Paul felt, 'being a Greek, was not compelled to be circumcised' (2:3). It is exemplified by Paul's complaints that 'pseudo-brothers crept in to spy on the freedom we enjoy in Christ Jesus, so they might reduce us to bondage' (2:4), that is, *bondage to circumcision, bondage to the Law*, and, by implication, *bondage to their leadership*. This would include, as we have already observed, actual physical 'spying' on body parts.

Rather, as Paul states in Galatians 2:10, the 'only' condition that the Pillars, James, Cephas, and John, put on his activities was:

that we should remember *the Poor*, which was also the very thing I was most diligent [in wishing] *to do*.

Not only should one note the emphasis on 'doing' -- always an important emphasis in these discussions – but the allusion to 'the Poor' at this juncture is another very important usage integrally related to James' Jerusalem Community. Though it is possible to take it simply in its adjectival sense of being Poor and nothing more, there can be little doubt that 'the Poor' was the name for James' Community in Jerusalem or that Community descended from it in the East in the next two–three centuries, *the Ebionites*.

These 'Ebionites' derive their name from this notation: '*Ebion*' (plural *Ebionim*) in Hebrew meaning 'the Poor'. The term is also used repeatedly at the beginning of the all-important second chapter of the Letter of James, leading up to the citation of 'the Royal Law according to the Scripture' – the Righteousness Commandment, 'you shall love your neighbour as yourself' (2:8). Here James terms 'the Poor' chosen by God as 'the heirs to the Kingdom', to whom the Piety Commandment of 'loving God' is applied (2:2–6).[4]

It is the Community of these Ebionites, particularly in the East, that held the name of James in such reverence, claiming descent from his Movement, whether direct or indirect, in first-century Palestine. For Eusebius in the 300s, this Movement is *too Jewish*, for it insists on circumcision for all converts or participants and, therefore, adherence to Jewish Law.[5] Circumcision is the outward sign of adherence to the Covenant in Judaism, and carries with it, as Paul understands (Gal. 5:3), the implied corollary of observance of the Law.

Eusebius, coming from Palestine, understands the Hebrew import of the term 'Ebionite' better than most. For him, these Ebionites have a more primitive understanding of Paul's 'Christ', conceiving of him as 'a plain and ordinary man only', generated by natural not supernatural means and advanced above other men only in his 'practice of virtue' – that is, his 'Righteousness'. In other words, their Christology is 'poverty-stricken' and Eusebius shows that this is his opinion by making a pun on their name, that is, that they harboured 'poor and mean' notions about Christ, primarily, that *he was only a man*.

Peter and Paul Subordinate to James in Antioch

After having made it clear from his perspective what the rulings of the Jerusalem Conference were, Paul now proceeds to give his version of the events that followed these rulings in Antioch. Antioch was the capital of the former Seleucid Empire in Syria, that Empire in the East that descended from one of Alexander's generals, Seulucus, after Alexander's death in 323 BC. There were other 'Antioch's around the Middle East, most notably a city about two hundred miles further east in Syria or Assyria, called Edessa, which was originally *also called Antioch at this time* – Antioch Orrhoe.[6]

But for the moment, let us assume that Paul means by Antioch, the capital of the Seleucids in Syria. This is what this passage is normally taken to mean, though aside from these notices in Acts and Galatians, there is no indication that this Antioch ever really functioned as an important early missionary centre. For Acts 11:26 and 13:1 previously, Antioch, too, was the centre of Paul's nascent Gentile Christian Community, and many of its founding members are enumerated in Acts, mostly with Greek names. One, as we have already noted, was 'the foster brother of Herod the Tetrarch' or Herod Antipas.

In his picture in Galatians of his subsequent confrontation with Peter over *table fellowship with Gentiles* that ensues after 'some from James' or James' messengers come down to 'Antioch', Paul makes it clear that whoever we may think 'Peter' was, he was not *the Head of Christianity in the days of Paul*. His picture of a Movement headed by James is also borne out by Acts' presentation of James' rulings at 'the Jerusalem Council' and at the time of James' final confrontation with Paul (15:19–29[7] and 22:20). In Paul's account, Peter emerges as someone overseas in competition to some extent with himself, but not with James. Peter is clearly *under James* and subservient to his rulings, because he must defer to him and follow his instructions when his representatives or the ubiquitous 'some' arrive from Jerusalem (Gal. 2:12).

To show that it is not simply the modern reader who might have difficulty with these passages, one has only to look at the extant correspondence between Jerome and Augustine, mentioned earlier, in the early 400s CE. Augustine, who is a younger teacher, queries the older and respected scholar Jerome, who has spent much of his adult life inspecting and collecting biblical manuscripts in Bethlehem in Palestine. He asks him about this very set of events in Galatians and the fact that Peter emerges from the episode as something of a 'hypocrite', at least this is the way Paul portrays it and this is the way we have seen it ever since.[8]

At first Augustine could get no satisfactory response from the older scholar. Finally Jerome, long-sufferingly, does answer him, asking him 'not to challenge an old man . . . who asks only to remain silent', and basically counselling him not to trouble himself over problems that were divisive and could not be solved in any event. For his part, Augustine appears to have taken the counsel to heart, because we never hear from him about these points again. He seems to have been able to quiet his own intelligence or suspicions, whatever these may have been – he twice accuses Paul of *lying* about Peter – but the modern reader need not do this.

For Paul – depending on whether Peter and the 'Cephas' he is picturing are actually the same person – Peter is a figure of respect and authority, but not *too much respect* nor *too much authority*. He is subject to the instructions of James, which makes James' position as the Leader or Bishop of the Jerusalem Church the over-arching one. Peter seems to be functioning – if we can read between the lines – as something of an inspector of overseas communities, a travelling representative of Jerusalem. For these purposes, the Letters from Peter to James and Clement to James, which introduce the Pseudoclementine *Homilies* and are framed in the nature of first-person reports, are edifying.

It is perhaps because of this position that Peter looms so large overseas and that, particularly in Rome, notions of the transmission of the central role or successorship become focused on him ('on this Rock I shall build my Church') and by extension Rome itself. But certainly the overall centre at this point is Jerusalem. It is only with the disappearance of the Jerusalem centre, an event certainly connected with the 66–70 CE War against Rome (as all our traditions in any case aver),[9] that there was scope for Rome to rise to ascendancy.

For Paul,

> But when Peter came to Antioch, I opposed him to his face, because he was to be condemned, for before *some came from James*, he used to *eat with the Gentiles* [*Ethnōn*/Peoples]. (2:11–12)

This is the 'table fellowship' controversy, that is, *table fellowship with Gentiles*. There is no doubt this James must be the 'James the brother of the Lord' just mentioned twice previously by Paul as if by way of introducing this confrontation. The problem is simple and has to do with Jewish dietary regulations and the Law, which in turn have to do with circumcision, the outward sign of the Covenant, and therefore, as Paul puts it in Galatians 5:3, being 'a debtor' or one 'obliged *to do the whole Law*'.[10]

Jewish Law encompassed a full set of dietary regulations, which most people are familiar with to some extent. In turn, these made it impossible for Jews observing these regulations to keep normal commerce with non-Jews, who were seen as being in a state of uncleanness, not the least because of the foods they ate and the manner in which they prepared them. Not just Gentiles, but Jews not keeping these dietary regulations as well – fractiousness that still looms large among modern Jews.

This is what the question of *table fellowship with Gentiles* is all about – 'keeping' or 'not keeping the Law'. As Paul sees it, the emissaries or representatives of James – these 'some from James', whom he also describes as being allied to 'those of circumcision' (that is, *those insisting on circumcision* or *the party advocating circumcision*) – arrived in Antioch, either in Syria or further afield in Edessa in 'the Land of the Osrhoeans' or 'Assyrians',

> But when they came, he [Peter] stopped doing this and *separated himself* being afraid of those of [the] circumcision. And the rest of the Jews joined him in this hypocritical behaviour. (Gal. 2:12–13)

The issues here are much greater than Paul is willing to admit. Clearly all the *Jews* are shunning Paul. James' directives would appear to be all-embracing and everyone must obey him. The only parallel that one can think of is in the Dead Sea Scrolls, particularly the Community Rule but also in the Damascus Document, where someone who 'overtly or covertly breaks *one word of the Torah of Moses on any point whatsoever* shall be expelled from the the Council of the Community', and no one 'shall co-operate with him in work or purse in any way whatsoever', nor shall he 'approach the pure food of the Assembly'.[11]

The parameters of this aforesaid ostracization resemble the rebuke in the Letter of James about the person 'keeping the whole Law, but stumbling over one small point being guilty of breaking it all', which follows the stress on '*doing* the Royal Law according to the Scripture' – the all-Righteousness Commandment (2:8–10). They also reflect the angry break between Barnabas and Paul, immediately following 'the Jerusalem Council' and right before Timothy's circumcision, because John Mark 'had withdrawn from them in Pamphylia and would not co-operate with them in work' (Acts 15:38).

By 'the rest of the Jews' or 'those of the circumcision' in Paul's version of things in Galatians – which also includes a break with Barnabas – Paul clearly means *the Jewish Apostles* and others caring about such things and following James' leadership. So, therefore, *all* the Jewish members of the early Church 'behaved hypocritically' and appear to have followed James' leadership in the matter of 'eating with the Gentiles' (Gal. 2:13).

Paul puts the issue in terms of circumcision and, throughout much of the rest of the letter, goes on to rail against both the practice of circumcision and Jews generally, so incensed was he at the events he recounts – and so frightened, as he explains at the beginning of the letter, that the Community he planted in Galatia will be likewise seduced by similar claims (Gal. 1:6–12). From his presentation, it is not only clear that James is the overarching leader of the early Church, to whom all must defer including Peter, but also that Paul's report of the Jerusalem Council and what those in Jerusalem thought they had agreed to is not precisely either what Paul says it was or what the author of Acts presents it as being.

It is also clear that in some sense circumcision and observing the Law were considered a *sine qua non* for all full-fledged or bona-fide members of the early Movement or Community – whatever name one chooses to give it. This absolutely accords with the literature we have from Qumran, which in so many ways parallels these materials, that is, first one had to *convert to Judaism*; then one could make some claim to being *heir to* its traditions. Put in another way, before one could claim to be an 'heir to' the promises of the Law (Gal. 3:29) – including the Prophets – one had to take the Law upon oneself. One could not, for instance, participate in the Messianism of the Messianic Movement without first taking upon oneself the traditions of the religion that brought this Messianism into being.

Whether one agrees with this proposition or not, it was, doubtlessly, how the majority of 'those' in Jerusalem saw the situation. Certainly all Jews in 'Antioch' (wherever this was) saw the situation like this, at least when they were directed so to behave by those 'from James', who had arrived from Jerusalem and obviously represented his position. So bitter was Paul at this unsettling state of affairs, that he accuses both Peter and Barnabas of hypocrisy, saying, 'and even Barnabas was carried away by their hypocrisy', that is, 'separated and drew back for fear of the party insisting on circumcision' (Gal. 2:12-13).

These are the matters that so upset Augustine in his queries to Jerome, to which he was told only that such passages were 'exceedingly difficult of interpretation'.

Being *Separate unto God* or a Nazirite

The use of the word 'separate' or 'separation' with regard to Peter's actions, after being called to account by the representatives of James, is used, as noted earlier, in crucial contexts in the two organizational documents from Qumran known as the Community Rule and the Damascus Document. The first uses the term in relation to the interpretation of the 'Way in the wilderness' Prophecy associated in Christian tradition with the mission of John the Baptist in the wilderness; the second, in interpretation of Ezekiel 44:15, the scriptural basis of the promises about 'the Sons of Zadok' or 'the Zadokite Priesthood', and the evocation of what are called 'the Three Nets of Belial'.[12]

While the second 'net' or 'snare' described there has to do with 'Riches', a theme forming the bedrock of the Letter of James' allusions to 'the Poor' and 'the Rich', the first and third 'nets' have to do with 'fornication' and 'pollution of the Temple'. The truly Righteous in the Community – 'God's Community' or those of 'Perfect Holiness' or 'the Perfect of the Way' – the *true* 'Sons of Zadok', are instructed to 'separate from the Sons of the Pit' and 'go out from the Land of Judah and live in the Land of Damascus'; in the Community Rule, 'to separate from the settlement of Unrighteous men and go out in the wilderness and prepare the Way of God'.[13]

In fact in the Damascus Document, it is this improper 'separation' in the Temple that creates the 'pollution' problem – the improper 'separation of clean and unclean', in particular, *improper separation* from people who 'lie with a woman in her period' or as a matter of course or normative family practice *marry their nieces or close family cousins*. The Damascus Document adds, 'anyone who approaches them shall not be free of their pollution'.[14]

I have identified the 'fornication' and 'pollution' allusions tied to these practices as relating to Herodians. 'Riches' does too. This issue of 'separation' is also of fundamental importance to the 'Two Letters on Works Reckoned as Righteousness' or '*MMT*', which also pay particular attention to the subject of gifts and sacrifices from Gentiles in the Temple and carry some of the points of James' directives to overseas communities as enunciated in Acts.[15] The former, like the theme of 'lying with women in their periods' in the Damascus Document, of course, violates the rules of proper 'separation of clean from unclean, Holy from profane', being raised here.[16]

In these crucial passages in the Letter to the Galatians, Peter and the other Jews within the Movement are portrayed as being somewhat lax regarding matters such as these overseas or, as present-day Jews would call it, in the *Diaspora*. They are being called to account by the evidently more 'zealous' or 'Zealot' Jerusalem Community – this is how James and his followers will be described later in Acts 21:20 in any event, that is, as 'Zealots for the Law' (*Zēlōtai*) – which insists on a more strict legal adherence to these matters.

Therefore, James and his representatives are calling those to account in 'Antioch', whether the one in Syria or Edessa in the Kingdom of the Osrhoeans. Like anyone spending most of his time in *the Diaspora* – except the most rigid or zealous – Peter is presented here as being more easy-going, but still deferential when called to account to James' Leadership. The same is true of Barnabas – whoever he was.

We have just noted the parallel materials in Acts, where Barnabas sails off with the 'John Mark' – the same 'John Mark' remarked earlier with regard to 'the house' of *James' mother* – from which it is clear that Barnabas and John Mark will not co-operate any longer with Paul in their travels, that is, they shun him. 'John Mark', it seems, had returned to Jerusalem (13:13 – this two chapters before Acts' picture of the 'Jerusalem Conference') to report on Paul and presumably the freer nature of the Gospel he was proclaiming among the Gentiles.

This kind of 'shunning' or 'excommunication' would also appear to be the gist of these passages here having to do with the representatives of James coming down to Antioch to see that his directives – whatever they were – were being properly carried out. This is the treatment, as we have also just seen, recommended in the Scrolls for someone who either 'overtly or covertly' breaks any small point of the Law, that is, not to keep 'table fellowship' with him nor co-operate with him 'in work' (in the sense of *service* or *mission*) and 'Riches' or common purse. Though, strictly speaking, these strictures in the Community Rule would appear to apply to communities in Palestine or further afield in 'the Land of Damascus', there is nothing to stop one from extrapolating them to a situation such as the one being described here in 'Antioch' as well.

Paul now attacks Peter and *the other Jews* copying him in his behaviour – including Barnabas – in the following manner (the accusation Augustine objected to):

But when I saw that they did not *walk uprightly* according to the Truth of the Gospel,[17] I said to Peter before everyone: 'If you, being a Jew, live in the

Gentile not a Jewish manner, why do you compel Gentiles to Judaize [in this context obviously meaning, to live like the Jews, take on the Law, and to circumcise]?' (Gal. 2:14)

Paul does not tell us Peter's response. Rather, he uses this episode to launch into a long diatribe for the benefit of his church in Galatia on 'Justification, not by works of the Law, but rather through Faith in Christ Jesus' (Gal. 2:16 and 3:11). This goes on for several chapters and ends up in some of the most important and celebrated formulations of Christian theology, in particular, on circumcision (the issue with which the whole exercise began), the saving death of Christ, and how Christ took the curse of the Law upon himself.

These passages will have particular relevance to the kind of curses in both the Community Rule and Damascus Document above, most notably in the newly published last column of the latter and the presentation there of the rededication to 'the New Covenant in the Land of Damascus' at Pentecost.[18] Paul closes his attack on Peter in chapter 2 of Galatians with the complaint, 'if Righteousness is through the Law, then Christ died for nothing' (2:21). Throughout he mixes symbolic language with rational theology in a way that would confuse even the most hard-headed observer. Paul admits this himself, where he refers to 'allegorizing' and evokes 'the two Covenants', the one of Hagar from 'Mount Sinai in Arabia' (the Jewish one) and the new one 'of the Promise' of Sarah, 'the free woman . . . born according to the Spirit' (4:24–29).

Paul's description here in Galatians, therefore – from which he launches into his discussion of Christianity, Christ's death, the value of Grace over the Law – introduces the person of James and his representatives as his interlocutors. As Paul reveals himself – through these verses and by inference – James materializes as well, but in the opposite position. Peter and the other Jewish Apostles become swing figures in this archetypical confrontation between Paul and James; but James is not only identified, the main lines of his positions fleshed out, but also his position in the early Church straightforwardly acknowledged.

The Successor to Jesus and the True Prophet Ideology

James' position is also developed in various ways in early Church literature, most notably by Clement of Alexandria and Hegesippus as conserved in Eusebius. It is also treated, as we have seen, in the Pseudoclementines and to a certain extent in the Gospel of Thomas. By contrast, it is missing from Acts in its present form. In the course of this discussion, how James emerged as the Leader of the early Church will be seen to be present in Acts as well, at least *in the source* the authors of Acts used to reconstruct the material they present.

The first question that should be addressed is how does one choose a leader to head the early Church and Christianity of the time? There are really only two methods. The first is by *direct appointment*, that is, that Jesus personally regulated the situation of succession to him in his life-time and this carried on into the early Church. In their own way in fact, this is how the Gospels present the matter too, but so does the Gospel of Thomas. The second is via an *election* or some kind of *consensus*, either the consensus of the Community as a whole or the consensus of its principal leaders – and this is the procedure presented by the authors of Acts where *the succession to Judas Iscariot* is concerned.

This situation is perhaps best understood by looking at the analogous one in a more recent 'Community', considering itself heir to the promise of Abraham, that of Islam. There, too, the succession to the Prophet Muhammad was seen as a matter of some urgency. Early Islam, which unfolded to some degree within the light of written history, represents this as occurring in two ways. The one, supported in what came to be known as Shi'ite Islam, represents this as being *a family Caliphate*, that is a succession within the family of the Prophet – the word 'Caliphate' in Arabic actually meaning 'succession'. This is, of course, analogous to the claims of those supporting James in early Christianity.

The second, bearing on the more 'orthodox' or familiar form of Islam known as 'Sunni', supports the position that the Successor to the Prophet was chosen in an election by the Community as a whole, or, at least by those most qualified in it – what it calls 'the Companions of the Prophet'. These last are, of course, analogous to what goes in Christianity under the title 'Apostles' (who are, in effect, little more than 'Companions') and represents a somewhat less emotional way of looking at the situation.

That Muhammad is called 'the Prophet', too, turns out not to be without resonance in early Christianity. That is because for 'Jewish Christianity' – what we have been calling 'Ebionitism' above – the 'True Prophet' ideology was a significant one. In fact, both Jesus and Muhammad were, in the view of the writer, thought of by their partisans to some extent in this manner, the claims of one, in the writer's view, resonating with and being invigorated by the claims of the other.[19]

The 'True Prophet' ideology is also to be found in the Dead Sea Scrolls or at least the prophecy on which it is based. This prophecy from Deuteronomy 18:15ff. is among the Messianic proof-texts found at Qumran, and is the basis of the idea that a Prophet would succeed the heritage defined by Moses in the Old Testament.[20] For those of an Ebionite frame of mind, and some Christians succeeding to it, *Jesus is that Prophet*. For Islam, succeeding to this, Muhammad is not only 'the True Prophet', he is *the Seal of the Prophets* as well.[21] He is also, following Paul's ideology, another 'Apostle to the Gentiles', the Arabs being another one of such 'Peoples'.

This doctrine appears to have come down through Jewish Christianity and the Ebionites, to the teacher or 'prophet' at the end of the first century or the beginning of the second known as 'Elchasai', and the 'Elchasaites' following him, described in all early Christian heresiologies.[22] Through them and other Ebionite-style, daily baptizing groups in Northern Syria, the doctrine came through Mani and the Manichaeans in the third and fourth centuries – particularly in the marshes of Southern Iraq where we shall see the group known as 'the Sabaeans of the marshes' were known to have existed – down to 'the Prophet' Muhammad and Islam in the seventh.

In a very real sense, for their respective followers, both Jesus and Muhammad are 'True Prophets'. In Islam, the succession to 'the Prophet' developed in the two manners we have just described. In early Christianity prefiguring this, the process seems to have been similar. Both streams can be identified in extant reports about *James' succession to his brother* – the one of direct succession or appointment and the other, election. In Christianity, because of traditions about the resurrection and the time it is claimed Christ spent on earth before his 'Ascension', one might add that of a third, the various post-resurrection manifestations many are familiar with. As we shall see, all of these procedures in one form or another involved James.

The Picture of James' Succession in Early Church Texts

Eusebius himself is the best repository of these traditions attesting both to *the direct succession of James* and also his *election* – this to the Office of 'Bishop'. Eusebius puts this proposition in the first chapter of the Second Book of his *Ecclesiastical History* as follows:

> James, who was surnamed the Just by the Forefathers on account of his superlative virtue, was the first to have been *elected to the Office of Bishop of the Jerusalem Church*.[23]

The sequencing Eusebius follows here is important. At the end of Book One, this notice is preceded by an allusion to the execution of John the Baptist, mention of Cephas, Thaddaeus, and James in that order, and the story of the conversion of the King of the Edessenes, 'Thaddaeus' and '(Judas) Thomas' participating.

The references to 'Cephas', 'Thaddaeus', and 'James' occur because he is discussing 'the Seventy' – 'no list of whom is anywhere extant' – as distinct from 'the Apostles'.[24] Eusebius reckons James, not to mention Cephas and Thaddaeus, among these 'Seventy' – clearly the number of 'the Jerusalem Church' or 'Assembly' – and, citing Paul's attestation of Jesus' post-resurrection appearance to him in 1 Corinthians 15:7, for the first time identifies James as 'one of the so-called brothers of the Saviour'. Because Cephas is also mentioned in this same context in 1 Corinthians, he puzzles over the fact that Clement of Alexandria in the second century considered Cephas 'one of the Seventy Disciples who had the same name as the Apostle Peter', though did not consider him the same person.

The mention, too, of 'Thaddaeus' at this point, whom Eusebius also reckons – unlike Matthew's and Mark's Apostle lists – as 'one of the Seventy', leads him directly into the story of the correspondence with 'King Agbarus, the celebrated King of the Peoples [*Ethnōn*] beyond the Euphrates', with which he closes Book One and which he places around 29 CE.[25] It is directly following these events that he moves into his presentation of the traditions about *the election of James as Bishop of the Jerusalem Church* at the beginning of Book Two – in exactly the place it should have been dealt with – 'at the same time', as he puts it, as the 'election by lot' to replace 'the Traitor Judas'.

His sequencing in the first chapter of Book Two is also important. His reference to choosing the replacement for 'Judas the Traitor', Matthias (Acts 1:26), whom he calls 'one of the Disciples of the Lord' (again presumably one of these 'Seventy'), leads him to mention the appointment of 'the Seven to administer the common fund' by 'the laying on of hands by the Apostles', a procedure specifically applied in the Pseudoclementines to James' appointment of overseas messengers. This, in turn, leads to allusion to Stephen ('one of them') and his martyrdom by stoning '*by the murderers of the Lord*, as if ordained specifically for this purpose'.[26]

Curiously, but not unrelatedly, *the election to replace Judas* and *the stoning of Stephen*, like *the laying on of hands*, will also turn out to have their direct counterparts in the biography of James and be stand-ins for or reworkings of critical episodes in it. After detailing the various traditions from Clement of Alexandria about James' election and appointment to the Episcopate of Jerusalem, the very next event he describes is the dispatch of Thaddaeus by Thomas to Edessa and King Agbarus, 'the Great King of the Peoples beyond the Euphrates'. Nor does he mention the beheading of the 'the Apostle James' for another eight chapters (almost a decade later) – and this in a fairly doctrinaire manner right out of the Book of Acts. For him this leads directly into the *beheading of Theudas* and the Famine.[27]

As should be clear, often Eusebius is more aware of what is going on behind the events he is presenting than at first meets the eye. For instance, he first describes the election to replace 'the Traitor Judas' in chapter 12 of Book One as follows:

> Tradition also relates that Matthias, who was reckoned with the Apostles in the place of Judas, and he who had been honoured with him at the time of the casting of lots is also said to have been called among the Seventy.

The defeated candidate, whom Eusebius neglects to mention, is someone Acts 1:23 calls 'Joseph, called Barsabas, who was surnamed Justus'. Later in Acts 15:22, as 'Judas surnamed Barsabas', he conveys, together with Silas, Paul, and Barnabas, James' directives to overseas communities in the form of an *epistle* from Jerusalem down to Antioch. We shall be able to identify this first 'Barsabas surnamed Justus', as an overwrite for James; the second, 'Judas surnamed Barsabas', being an overwrite for Jesus' third brother, 'Jude' or 'Judas of James'.

Even the given name of the first Barsabas, 'Joseph', will recur in Eusebius' introduction of James, whom he says 'was called the brother of the Lord, because he was called *the son of Joseph*'. Though willing to acknowledge as much for James, Eusebius protests, where Jesus is concerned, rather citing Matthew 1:18, that 'the Virgin' was 'already found with child by the Holy Spirit before they came together' (*thus*)![28] The language of *casting lots*, both Acts and Eusebius use in describing this election, will reappear in Gospel stories of the Roman soldiers 'casting lots' for Jesus' 'clothes' (John 19:24 and pars.),[29] and the 'Office' (*Episcopē*), that Acts 1:20 claims was filled here, really will be that of 'Bishop' or 'Overseer' of the early Church in Palestine.

Election or Casting Lots

Before proceeding to what Eusebius relates of James' appointment to this Office 'with' or 'by the Apostles', the matter of election and/or 'casting lots' needs to be addressed. One first encounters a procedure of this kind in this period in the history of the Maccabean family. It is directly related to the office of the High Priesthood and who should occupy it. From thence, it moves into the procedures of what some refer to as 'the Zealot Movement'. When the Jewish religious hero Judas Maccabee purified the Temple after its liberation in the second century BC, he did so in conjunction with its rededication. This has always been celebrated thereafter by Jews as the Festival of the Rededication or *Hanukkah*.

Judas presided over these activities like some powerful Vicegerent, but Josephus actually represents Judas as being 'elected High Priest'. He repeats this claim three times,[30] though it is nowhere presented in the several Maccabee Books purporting to tell the story of Judas Maccabee, his father Mattathias, and his brothers John, Simon, and Jonathan – popular names that have transferred themselves into the early history of Christianity not without reason.

The Maccabee Books do present an election of sorts, when Judas' second brother Simon is acclaimed High Priest by the priests and people (1 Macc. 14:41). This may be simply pro-Maccabean propaganda, but it was *an election of sorts* and certainly an acclamation, a procedure also recognized in the Gospels on behalf of Jesus.[31] For 1 Maccabees, Simon accepts this acclamation in perpetuity, until such time 'that a trustworthy Prophet should come' and regulate the situation definitively. Here, no doubt, is yet another trace of the 'True Prophet' ideology weaving itself through the history of this period. From the perspective of the Christian tradition and the High Priesthood of Jesus outlined in the Letter to the Hebrews, that 'Prophet' must, no doubt, be considered to be John the Baptist.

But in 'the Zealot Movement' this notion of 'an election' becomes extremely important. Repeatedly, in one uprising after another from 4 BC to 66–70 CE and beyond, Josephus presents the Revolutionaries as demanding *the election by the people* of a High Priest of *greater purity* and 'Piety' than the Herodian High Priesthood that had been imposed on them. Sometimes this is an outright election; at other times it is represented as 'choosing by lot'.[32] For instance, in his presentation of the revolutionary events of 4 BC–7 CE after Herod's death, Josephus presents the Revolution-aries – this should mean both religious and political – as demanding *the election of a High Priest*. The demand he describes would seem to have much in common with the procedure called 'choosing by lot'.

Josephus describes a similar process of 'choosing by lot' or 'drawing straws', when he and his associates were hiding up in a cave in Galilee after one of the numerous defeats he suffered there as military commissar of Galilean defence strategy in the early days of the Uprising. Josephus and a colleague, he confides somewhat conspiratorially, *drew the short straws*. They then proceed to dispatch all the others in the typical pre-arranged suicide pact characterizing these 'Fourth Philosophy' resistance strategies and, in one of the most brazen betrayals ever boasted of in literature, personally surrendered to the Roman Emperor-to-be Vespasian then commanding the Roman troops in Palestine.[33]

When describing 'the last days' – that is, the last days of the Temple in the 66–70 CE events – but particularly as these accelerated after 68 and the elimination of all the Herodian-appointed High Priests, Josephus describes the election by 'the Innovators' of a last High Priest before the Romans invest the city – one 'Phannius' or 'Phineas', a simple *Stone-Cutter*.[34] Josephus constantly refers to 'the Innovators' in this period – the political and religious reformers and/or Revolutionaries who have all been lumped, somewhat imprecisely, under the general heading of 'Zealots', even though it is not clear what the currency of this term actually was or whether it was being used in any consistent way to describe them. Nor does the choice of someone by the name of 'Phannius' seem accidental in view of its symbolic importance to Zealotry in general, making one wonder just how fortuitous or random such a process 'of lots' could have been even in theory.

Phineas, as we have seen, was the proverbial grandson of Aaron through his son Eleazar – in the Gospels 'Lazarus' – a favourite name in this period and a direct ancestor of the 'Zadok' of David's time. Considered the prototype for all 'Zealot' priestly behaviour, there was actually a *redivivus* tradition associated with him not very different from the one the Gospels evoke to describe the links of John the Baptist to another priestly forerunner displaying 'zeal' in 'the wilderness of Damascus', Elijah.[35] There was also a concomitant 'rainmaking' tradition associated with Phineas' name, which has links not only to similar traditions about Elijah, and through him, James, but also to another interesting character who is part of this whole complex of rainmaking *Zaddiks*, Honi the Circle-

Drawer – so-called because of *the circles he reportedly drew to bring the rain.*[36]

The archetypical episode in the life of Phineas, evoked in support of Maccabean claims to the High Priesthood, as we saw, was when Phineas, Aaron's descendant, out of 'zeal for God' deflected pollution from the camp of the Israelites *in the wilderness* by killing backsliders marrying Gentiles. As a result, he won 'the Covenant of an Everlasting Priesthood' and the right 'to make atonement on behalf of the Sons of Israel' for himself and 'his seed' in perpetuity (Num. 25:13). This Covenant is evoked in 1 Maccabees 2:27 on behalf of Judas Maccabee's father, Mattathias or Matthias, the reputed progenitor of the whole family. This is also the name – perhaps not coincidentally – of the winning candidate in Acts' rather fictionalized presentation of the 'election by lot' to fill *Judas Iscariot*'s now vacant 'Office'.

Therefore, when Paul, in characterizing his community as 'Abraham's seed', claims they are all now 'Sons of God through faith in Christ Jesus', in whom 'there is neither Jew nor Greek, neither bondman nor free, neither male nor female, but all one in Christ Jesus' (Gal. 3:28–29), it is the direct opposite of the events described above. This more cosmopolitan Pauline Mission 'to the Gentiles' is the mirror reversal, as it were, and the negation of some two hundred and fifty years of Palestinian history spent fighting foreigners, Hellenization, and – rightly or wrongly – perceived pollution incurred by mixing with overseas peoples. That Paul is misunderstood by contemporaries such as these should not be surprising.

That they should wish to kill him, as the 'We Document' in Acts describes (23:12), should also not be surprising. It all depends on one's point of view, and from the Palestinian point of view, Paul was a cosmopolitanizing 'Traitor', giving victory to the forces they and their ancestors had fought against incessantly, ever since Matthias had raised the banner of revolt, assuming the purified High Priesthood some two centuries before. Matthias did so, according to 1 Maccabees, reiterated in Josephus, by evoking 'the zeal for the Law' and 'Covenant' claimed on behalf of Phineas in Numbers. Whereas Matthias kills backsliders on the altar at Modein, as we have seen, Phineas deflected pollution from the camp – and God's Wrath consonant upon it – by killing Jews who had *mixed with Gentiles.*

Nothing could illustrate the conflict of these times more vividly, nor the mentality enshrined in the documents from Qumran. This *is the ethos* of the Qumran documents. In the writer's view, it will also be the ethos of the Movement led by James, the better part of whose followers are distinctly called – even in Acts – both 'Priests' (6:7) and 'Zealots for the Law' (21:20).

Paul also uses the term 'zeal' consistently in his letters but, once again, it is clear that he is aware of the use of this term by those opposing him. In every case he reverses their use of the term denoting 'the zeal of the Ancestors', 'zeal for their customs', 'zeal for the traditions and the Law', to indicate rather, *zeal in his mission* or *zeal for his new-found Faith in Christ Jesus*, by whose 'Grace' Paul had been deputized to preach to the Gentiles. He has also been deputized to found a community based not on the Law, but 'Faith in Christ Jesus', where there are, as, for instance, Ephesians 2:19 would put it, 'no more aliens or foreign visitors'.[37]

Phineas, rather, wins the High Priesthood, according to the account in Numbers, for his descendants in perpetuity, because of the *zealous* behaviour he displayed in *killing backsliders* and *warding off pollution from the camp of Israel*. For those of this 'Zealot' persuasion, killing backsliders – including Paul – was no sin at all. It was a virtue. Priests of the Phineas stripe condoned killing as long as this killing was in the interests of Righteousness and purification or, if one prefers, warding off pollution. This is the ethos of 'the Zealot'/'Messianic Movement' – one is not recommending it, simply illustrating it – and this ethos was totally at odds with the Pauline Mission. They are on a collision course. It only remains to insert James into the picture to understand what was taking place from the 40s to the 60s CE, both in Jerusalem and around the Mediterranean in the world at large among those interested in such matters.

When 'the Zealots' or '*Sicarii*' choose as the last High Priest before the destruction of the Temple one Phannius, a simple Stone-Cutter, Josephus represents this as being 'by lot', which, he says, they claimed to be 'an ancient practice'.[38] Snob that he is and temperamentally not so different from Paul, Josephus rails against this choice in terms of the utmost outrage, claiming he (Phannius) was of too humble origins and hardly a priest at all. Perhaps he does protest too much. Perhaps, too, Phannius was too 'Poor'.

There is more behind this 'election' than meets the eye. It is not always clear just how this 'choosing by lot' differs from outright election. The '*Sicarii*' here are clearly representing it as the ancient procedure of choosing High Priests. As we have seen, for Acts and Eusebius following it, Matthias, Judas' successor (note the playful reversal of the names from the original Maccabee story even here) is chosen 'by lot' (1:26). There is something almost mystical or magical about the procedure, as if God's will were involved. In the choosing of Phannius in these 'last times' right before the butchering of the Establishment High Priests by those Josephus now calls 'Zealots' (in particular, that Ananus, responsible for the death of James, whom we shall propose as 'the Wicked Priest' of Dead Sea Scroll allusion) there is clearly more than just ordinary symbolism.[39]

Josephus also portrays the last desperate act of the partisans of Masada, whom he over and over again identifies as '*Sicarii*', as conducting several rounds of just such a 'casting of lots' before their mass suicide to choose those to be responsible for putting their comrades and their families to death.[40] As we have seen, 'the *Sicarii*' or 'Assassins' were the extreme wing of the Zealot Movement, so designated for the curved, Arab-style daggers or '*sicae*' they carried under their garments.

In fact, archaeological excavations on Masada have unearthed a shard that may have been used in just such an 'election', that of Eleazar Ben Jair – named, of course, for Aaron's son, the father of Phineas. As with 'James and Simon' at the time of the Famine some twenty-five years before, Josephus identifies him as 'a descendant of that Judas who persuaded the greater part of the Jews . . . not to submit to the taxation census when Cyrenius was sent to Judea to make one'. He was the leader of the final nine hundred or so hold-outs on the Fortress of Masada, whose mass suicide is pictured by Josephus in vivid detail.

It is interesting that in delineating the so-called misdeeds of these extremists – 'for which God brought upon them their deserved punishment' – Josephus turns against them the very 'Righteousness'/'Piety' dichotomy of 'loving your neighbour' and 'loving God', which these groups seem to have prized so much. Not only does he say that they 'strove with one another' in 'Evil works' as to 'who should run the greatest lengths in *Impiety towards God* and in *Unjust acts towards their neighbours*', but he describes them as 'plundering those Richer than themselves'.[41]

He also re-creates Eleazar's last speech, which is fraught with the themes basic to this period and the detail one finds in Thucydides' parallel picture of Pericles' funeral oration. Since Josephus had been an interrogator of prisoners for the Romans, this could account for the vividness of his detail. As we saw, he himself was supposed to have committed suicide in this manner. However, it would have been absurd to have someone as duplicitous as Josephus involved in 'drawing lots'.

This idea of betrayal and treachery is widespread in the literature of this period, not simply in the well-known manner in which it is used in the

Gospels or Acts with regard to someone the authors refer to as *Judas* 'the Traitor' (Luke 6:16), but also in the Dead Sea Scrolls. There, the 'Traitor'/ 'Traitors' language is widespread – this in relationship to those who 'betray' the Righteous Teacher or the Community in some manner and who are even called 'Traitors to the New Covenant'[42] – but this 'betrayal' has, once again, almost exactly opposite signification to the one that has been made so popular in the scriptural presentation before us.

The elections before us in this period, then, as in the case of Acts 1:26's presentation of the election 'by lot' to replace Judas *Iscariot* – echoed in Eusebius' *Ecclesiastical History* above – are probably all elections in the normal sense of that word, miraculous or supernatural overtones notwithstanding. As in the instance of the Masada 'casting of lots', not only do both seemingly involve '*Sicarii*', they are preceded or followed by *a suicide* – Judas' or Judas the Galilean's *Sicarii* heirs'.[43] The problem, though, with this election to succeed Judas *Iscariot* in Acts is that it is probably not only to the wrong 'Office', but also concerns the wrong person. What we would have expected at this point in a narrative like Acts is the 'election' for the Leadership of the whole Community *in succession to Jesus*. Eusebius, of course, refers to it in this way, indeed using it to introduce how *James was chosen leader*.

Peter's Citation of Psalms 69 and 109 in Acts

The author of the Book of Acts at this point represents this election of Judas' successor as being of such importance that two scriptural passages from Psalms 69 and 109 are applied to it, that is, we are to think the events have either been presaged in Scripture – which is normally the case with these epoch-making or primordial occurrences – or explained by it. As Acts puts it in a speech attributed to Peter:

> The Scripture had to be fulfilled in which the Holy Spirit spoke before by the mouth of David concerning Judas, who became a guide to those who took Jesus (1:16).[44]

The passages from these Psalms are, as is usual, taken completely out of context. Neither really fits the situation of Judas in this episode, nor his successor, at all.

This is not surprising, as this is normal for New Testament scriptural exegesis, but it may surprise the newcomer unfamiliar with these matters. In this instance, what has clearly been done was to search Scripture and just so long as a word or phrase fitted or was close to the plotline or event being described, this was seen as sufficient. A similar method is followed in the Dead Sea Scrolls, particularly in those documents we have already described as *pesher*s – but in the latter not quite so blatantly, as the ethos of the interpretation generally remains the same as that of the underlying passages.

The similarity is important here, as it makes one think that these kinds of materials may have been taken from what might have been extant *pesher*s of the Qumran type. At Qumran, what usually but not always happens is that a given Scripture is quoted more or less in its entirety, for instance, chapters 1–2 of Habakkuk or Psalm 37. Both of these are originally '*Zaddik*' texts, that is, among other things, they deal with the activities and fate of 'the *Zaddik*' or 'Righteous One' – James' cognomen. As with the Gospels or here in Acts, the Qumran exegete probably searched Scripture for these meaningful texts that could be related to the recent or past life of the sect or Community and important events or teachings connected with it. In this sense, the teaching or fate of the Community and some of its most important leaders or enemies were to be found by searching Scripture.

In early Church literature, James was looked upon in precisely the same manner. Eusebius, quoting Hegesippus, will insist that important cognomens of James, like 'the Just One' or '*Oblias*' ('Protection of the People') could be found just as at Qumran by searching Scripture, most notably, Prophets and Psalms. Quoting his second-century source Hegesippus, Eusebius even goes so far as to apply a passage from Scripture to James' fate – this from the Prophets, however, not Psalms – exactly as Acts does the above passages to events connected to its story of Judas' fate. In fact, as we shall see below, quoting this source, he develops the circumstances of James' death – just as the Gospels do Jesus' – on the basis of another '*Zaddik*' text, Isaiah 3:10.

The New Testament normally operates somewhat differently. Though it handles Scripture in the same manner as the Qumran *pesharim* or here regarding either James or Judas *Iscariot*, usually the texts are strung together and arranged in the form of a story. Rather than follow a given biblical text to its conclusion in terms of events, historical references, and the like, as the *pesharim* from Qumran often do, the Gospels generally take one or another passage from Scripture in an attempt to reconstruct a life story – in this case, Jesus'. Quotations, mainly from the Prophets and Psalms, are strung out in a fairly disembodied manner, just so long as they can be said to relate in some way to the story or move its plot forward. For example, one of the main scriptural texts being used to develop and represented as underlying the story of Jesus is Isaiah 53, popularly known as one of the 'Suffering Servant' texts. Not surprisingly, it is a *'Zaddik'* text as the Isaiah 3:10 text applied to James above. It is the same, whatever Gospel one is using. All attempt to tell either the same or a parallel story.

The passages, quoted in Acts in relation to the *casting of lots* or *the election of the Twelfth Apostle*, as already signalled, come from Psalms 69 and 109. For the Gospels, these are also favourite sources for the biography of Jesus. The quotation from Psalm 69, as given in Acts 1:20, 'let his encampment become desolate and let no one be dwelling in it', in the biblical Hebrew is rather recorded in the *plural* (that is, 'their camp'/'their tents') in what is actually an *extremely Zionistic* psalm, so much so that it even ends on the hope of 'rebuilding the cities of Judah' and 'dwelling in them' (69:36).

The original reads with additional import, where Qumran wilderness 'camps' are concerned, as well as those 'Rechabites' we shall show to be integrally related both to James and Matthew 27's description of Judas *Iscariot*'s dealings, 'let *their* camp be deserted and *their* tents be not lived in' (69:25).[45] Psalm 69 is also a *'Zaddik'* text containing references to 'the Poor' and 'the Meek', not to mention the famous passage also found in the Gospels about 'being given vinegar to drink', those bearing on 'being a foreigner to my brothers, a stranger to my mother's sons', and finally the one in the Gospel of John, attributed to Jesus referring to the Temple, 'zeal for My father's house consumes me'; but nothing that could be construed as applying in any sense to *Judas Iscariot* – quite the opposite.[46]

It actually contains an allusion to being 'swallowed' into 'the deep', an allusion important for Qumran presentation of the destruction of the Righteous Teacher. This is presented in the context of 'not *sinking* in the depths of the sea', but rather 'being *saved* from the mire', all important when it comes both to the Qumran imagery of 'being saved' and allied Gospel portrayals of the Apostles *casting their nets* into the sea, or Peter 'casting himself down' or 'sinking into the Sea' (John 21:6–11 and Matt. 14:30 – including allusion to 'save me').[47]

Its commonality with Psalm 109, another 'Suffering Servant'-type recital similar to Isaiah 53, would appear to be the mutual references to 'the Poor' and 'the Meek' (109:16–22), full of meaning, of course, with regard to the Community of James, not to mention the Qumran Scrolls. Not only does it use favourite Qumranisms like 'Deceitfulness' and 'a Lying Tongue', but it also has something of the character of an execration text or 'cursing' more in line with parallel materials one finds in Qumran texts.[48] In fact, its atmosphere is most un-Christian, vengeful, full of wrath, and completely uncharitable – again more like that of Qumran.

The reference to 'let someone else take his Office' (109:8), the second of the two passages applied by Peter to the election to replace Judas in Acts 1:20, is quoted like most scriptural allusions in the Gospels completely out of context. Like Psalm 69, its atmosphere is once more one of being encompassed by adversaries, and the sentiment is being expressed that, just as he ('the Poor One') is being judged by such an *Evil* accuser, that adversary, too, should 'be judged' mercilessly (109:7–20). It really has nothing whatever to do with the situation of *Judas Iscariot's replacement*, though since it does refer to an official capacity of some kind – in this case 'judgeship' – on the face of it, it has more to do with *James' capacity* as 'Bishop' or 'Overseer of the Jerusalem Church' than anything involving Judas. In fact, this is *exactly the sense of the term* Luke uses to translate the usage in Acts 1:20 into Greek: '*Episcopēn*', that is, *Episcopate* or *the Office of the Bishop*!

In the underlying Hebrew of Psalm 109:7 this allusion to 'Office' (*Pekuddah* – *Episcopate* in Acts) has to do with the Hebrew letters *P–K–D* – meaning 'to command' or 'give orders'. This usage is an extremely widespread one at Qumran, particularly in the Damascus Document, where it is used to apply both to an individual called 'the *Mebakker*' or 'Overseer' and another one, paralleling him, called 'the Priest *Muphkad*' or 'the High Priest Commanding the Camps'. The 'Overseer' or '*Mebakker*' is by and large indistinguishable from this 'Commander of the Camps', an office even expressed in terms of an 'Assembly of the camps', and he has the final say in matters of 'Judgement'. He also is described as having mastery over 'all the secrets of men and their innumerable Tongues' and is charged with 'sustaining the Poor [*Ebion*] and the Meek ['*Ani*]'.[49] This *P–K–D* root is also connected at Qumran to the idea of a 'Visitation' – God 'visiting' the earth in order *to command it.*[50]

Psalm 109 also repeatedly refers to 'clothing', another usage of import in notices about both James' and Jesus' death – for instance, in Matthew 27:35 and Mark 15:24 it is now the Roman soldiers who 'cast lots' for Jesus' 'clothing' directly following the allusion to 'giving him vinegar to drink' from Psalm 69:21 above.[51] It ends with an allusion to *the soul of* 'the Poor One' (*Ebion* again). This is not only the basis of the word 'Ebionite' in early Christian tradition, but is the scriptural underpinning for many parallel allusions in the Qumran Hymns to 'the soul of the Poor One' (*Ebion*), a composition incorporating much of the imagery of these and parallel psalms.[52]

The tradition about Judas' suicide also accompanies this allusion to Matthias assuming Judas' 'Episcopate' in Acts. This is related in an obscure and extremely enigmatic manner to a field it calls '*Akeldama*' – 'Field of Blood' (1:19). We shall see the importance of these 'blood' allusions ('*dam*' in Hebrew), when it comes to discussing 'the Cup of the New Covenant' in Jesus' blood and 'the New Covenant in the Land of Damascus'. But the scenario in Acts here does not agree with the Gospel of Matthew at all. In Matthew, after much wrestling with 'blood' and 'blood money' (and thereafter Pontius Pilate's 'the blood of this Just One' – 27:24), Judas '*withdrew* and . . . hung himself' (27:5).[53]

For Acts 1:18–19, Judas rather takes a 'headlong' and gory fall in the '*Akeldama*' or 'Field of Blood', a plunge described in terms of his 'being broken open in the middle and all his guts gushing out'. This it pronounces his 'reward of Unrighteousness' (*Adikias* – note the play in Greek here on the Hebrew '*Akeldema*') and brings us back to Josephus' description of the '*Sicarii*' suicide on Masada at the close of the *Jewish War*. In complaining about their 'Unrighteousness [again *Adikias*] towards their neighbours' as opposed to their Righteousness, Josephus expressed the hope that they would receive their just 'reward'. The verbal dependence between the accounts of these two stories about '*Sicarii*' suicide should be clear.

The Suicide of Judas *Iscariot* and the Succession to his 'Office'

For Acts, the 'casting of lots' now follows after these two quotations from Psalms and the person chosen to fill Judas' 'Office' or 'Episcopate' would then 'become a witness (with the other Apostles) of his Resurrection' (1:22) – a point we shall encounter in *all traditions about James*. In our view, at this point Acts is overwriting another account it knows that is introducing James at this point and detailing who he was. This would include the two very nationalist, Jewish psalms just outlined above, which Acts now applies to the election of *Judas Iscariot*'s successor.

For Acts 1:23 this successor is to be chosen by lot in an election between two candidates. One of whom, with the tell-tale name of *Joseph*

Barsabas, 'surnamed Justus', is never heard from in Scripture again. Another 'Barsabas', as we saw, does ultimately reappear in Acts 15:22 as 'Judas surnamed Barsabas'. We are circling around the names of Jesus' brothers again. This dispatch of 'Judas Barsabas' by James to 'Antioch' will look suspiciously like the Syriac legend of Thomas ('Judas Thomas') dispatching 'Thaddaeus' to King Agbarus in Edessa.[54]

Since Judas Barsabas' is one of two messengers sent by the Jerusalem Church, carrying an epistle with James' rulings following Acts' description of the Jerusalem Council, he must be seen at the very least as paralleling those Paul in Galatians 2:12 identifies as 'some from James', the appearance of whom at *Antioch*, coupled with their insistence on *abstaining from table fellowship with Gentiles,* provokes Paul's bitter outbursts against 'those of the circumcision' and 'circumcision' generally. In our view he (Judas Barsabas) is to be identified with 'Thaddaeus' or 'Judas Thomas' in the Agbarus legend or 'Judas the Zealot' in Syriac sources connected to it.

All such 'Barsabas', 'Barnabas', and 'Barabbas' surnames are important and often connected to the names of Jesus' family members. 'Barabbas', for instance, in the Gospels is something of a stand-in for Jesus himself. He is the man who had been arrested 'in the Uprising' for 'committing treason and murder' (Mark 15:7 and pars.) For John 18:40, this makes him 'a Bandit' (*Lēstēs*), the word Josephus always employs when talking about Revolutionaries[55] and the person the crowd is depicted as preferring to Jesus. In some texts he is even called 'Jesus Barabbas', thereby correctly recognizing *Barabbas* as an Aramaic cognomen with the meaning 'Son of the Father'.

Barsabas has no such ready equivalent in Aramaic, except the '*Saba*'/ '*Sabaean*' terminology we shall encounter having to do with daily bathing. Barnabas, if it is a real name and not another circumlocution, would mean something like 'son of the Prophet'. The point is that such names often overlap the members of Jesus' family or Jesus himself. For example, Barnabas is often associated with 'Joseph', the name of either Jesus' father or brother. 'Joseph called Barsabas, who was surnamed Justus', the losing candidate in the 'election' to fill Judas' 'Bishopric', as we saw, is an obvious write-in *for James the Just himself.* In this regard, the addition of the cognomen 'Justus' to his name and the use of the word '*Episcopē*' to describe the 'Office' he is to fill are determinant.

In other words, we have in these passages at the beginning of Acts an election by lot for some leadership position within the early Church, represented here as being because of the treachery and suicide of someone called Judas or 'the *Iscariot*', and the defeated candidate turns out to be someone called *Justus* – here, curiously, this Latin version of James' cognomen is actually transliterated into the Greek. The victorious candidate, too, like Judas *Iscariot* himself, bears the peculiarly Maccabean name of 'Matthias', even though there already is one 'Matthew' listed among the Apostles. Even Matthew is alternatively called 'Levi the son of Alphaeus' in Mark 2:14, 'Alphaeus' being another of those names, such as Lebbaeus, Cleophas, and '*Oblias*', associated with Jesus' family members. Like the Joseph 'called Barsabas surnamed Justus', this Matthias is never heard from in Scripture again except to fill in this somewhat artificial Twelve-man Apostolic scheme.

The *Sicarii* and the *Christians*

All this may be sheer coincidence, but if not, then it is extremely curious. In fact the cognomen or surname '*Iscariot*' given to this Judas, the election for whose replacement Acts is picturing here, is itself very peculiar. Some have represented it as being a place name, but no one has ever found what place it can without doubt be said to relate to. Others have seen a hidden meaning to it, for instance, '*Ish she hischir auto*' – 'the man who hired him out' – which, while ingenious and very convenient, is nevertheless also far-fetched.

The most popular delineation for the meaning of this cognomen is '*Sicarios*' – the name that Josephus, as we have seen, gives to this most extreme segment of the *Fourth Philosophy* 'Innovators' or 'Zealot Movement' – that is, in garbled Greek, 'Judas the *Sicarios*'. Most of the consonants and vowels tally – in Josephus, *Sicarioi/Sicariōn*; in the New Testament, *Iscariot*. All that has happened is that the first '*i*' and '*s*' have been reversed, and the last '*i*' has been replaced by a '*t*'. This does not differ in kind to the reversals one encounters in names like 'Cleophas', 'Alphaeus', 'Lebbaeus' above and the epithet '*Oblias*', which we shall see applied to James.

Named, as we have seen, for the curved Arab-style dagger they carried under their garments – Josephus calls it 'Persian', which, he says, resembled the short Roman '*sica*', except it was smaller – in these last chapters of Book Seven of the *War*, the *Sicarii* suddenly become, as it were, the dominant revolutionary party after the fall of the Temple in 70 CE, *particularly abroad* – that is, like so-called '*Christians*' they were involved in *missionary* work![56] Not only does Josephus specifically denote them as the Party involved in the Masada suicide, at the same time he definitively links them to the refusal 'to submit to the taxation census when Cyrenius was sent to Judea to make one'. This is an extremely important conjunction, which we had never heard put in quite the same way before.

It is *an admission*, if we can call it this, ranking in importance alongside the one at the end of Book Six in the wake of the fall of the Temple, that the thing that most moved the Jews to revolt against Rome was 'the Star Prophecy'. It is also the same conjunction made in the Gospel of Luke relating to the birth of Christ (*Christos* – Luke 2:2–11). As Josephus describes it:

> At that time [the Census of Quirinius] the *Sicarii* banded together *against all those willing to submit to the Romans, treating them in all respects as enemies, plundering their Riches* . . . *contending that such persons were no different than foreigners* by so cowardly *betraying that freedom the Jews* defended to the final degree, admitting *they preferred slavery to the Romans*.[57]

Not only does he put the situation in Palestine in a nutshell, branding all collaborators – including himself – as 'Enemies' – he is now using the term '*Sicarioi*' in place of 'the Fourth Philosopy' or 'Zealots'. No less important is his use of the language of 'freedom' and 'slavery', so reversed and allegorized in Paul's approach to them. For Josephus, again playing off the 'Poor' terminology and parodying usages like 'plundering Riches', which have the exact opposite signification at Qumran, these people simply wished to 'plunder the Riches' of the classes who sought accommodation with Rome.

After the Masada suicide in 73 CE, he follows others to Egypt and Cyrene (Libya), locales also figuring to some extent in Acts. Here he says:

> Some of the faction of the *Sicarii* [here *Sicariōn*] . . . not content with having saved themselves, again embarked on new revolutionary scheming, persuading those that received them there *to assert their freedom*, to esteem the Romans as no better than themselves and to look upon *God as their only Lord and Master*.

This then is clearly the dual *political* and *religious programme* he described as being more dangerous even than 'the Bandits'. It is also now clear that he means us to understand by the term '*Sicarii*', the *Fourth Jewish Philosophy* in the *Antiquities*, which he never really gave a specific name to previously – the one founded by *Judas and Saddok*, whom, he claims, 'had *an inviolable passion for freedom*, saying God was *their only Lord and Master* . . . nor indeed, do they heed the deaths of their relatives and friends, nor can any such fear make them call any *man* Lord'.

The 'freedom' Josephus repeatedly alludes to here is political, not that 'freedom from the Law' or 'freedom' he enjoys in Christ Jesus that Paul so extols. Josephus picks up this idea of 'not *calling any man Lord*' again in his description of the *Sicarii* in Egypt, where, calling them 'desirous of' or 'attempting Innovation', by which he often, but not always, means sedition or revolution, he says:

> They could not get any one of them to confess or to come to the verge of confession *that Caesar was their Lord* . . . meeting the tortures and the fire with . . . a soul that wellnigh rejoiced in them . . . But what was most astonishing was the courage of the children, not one of whom could be brought by these torments as to *name Caesar for their Lord*.

A more perfect picture of 'Christian' martyrdom could hardly be imagined.

In Cyrene, likening the 'madness of the *Sicarii*' to 'a disease',[58] Josephus outlines how such *Sicarii* continued to cause disturbances among 'no small number of *the Poor*'. This again involved 'leading them out into the wilderness, there to show them the signs and apparitions' – this even in Cyrene in North Africa, Luke's probable place of origin. Drawing now upon his own personal experience, Josephus begins to link the language of 'plot' and 'treachery', so important in Gospel accounts of 'Judas', with these '*Sicarii*'. The principal leader in Cyrene, a charismatic revolutionary called Jonathan, turns out to have been 'an enemy of Josephus', making accusations falsely implicating him, as well as 'teaching the *Sicarii* to accuse men falsely'.[59]

It is important to remark that the term '*Sicarios*' is a quasi-anagram and a possible pejorative in Greek for the term 'Christian'. Not only is this in the author's view the essence of things, Josephus would even appear here to be using it generically, that is, all individuals of the genre of those *making false accusations* or *betraying people*, begin to be called '*Sicarii*'. Jonathan 'made a plot' with the Roman Governor Catullus of Cyrene 'to falsely accuse the Rich among the Jews', thus, 'causing all the Rich Jews to be slain'. Again, we have the inversion of the true situation as reflected in documents like the Dead Sea Scrolls.

'One of those against whom this treacherous accusation was laid was Josephus, the writer of these books.' But because of 'the intercession' of his patron Titus, this 'plot' did not succeed, and Jonathan received 'the punishment that he deserved. He was first scourged and then burned alive'! As for Catullus,

> Continually seeing the ghosts of those he had slain standing at his side . . . his distemper grew ever worse, so that *his very guts rotted and fell out of his body* . . . as great an example of how God in his providence inflicts punishment on the Wicked.[60]

A greater resemblance to how Acts describes the end of the character it is calling 'Judas *Iscariot*' and how 'all his bowels gushed out' cannot be imagined. It is on this note, too, that Josephus brings the *Jewish War* to a close.

The *Sicarii* first appear in the *War* in the time of Felix (53–60 CE), when James is very much 'in command' in Jerusalem. Though for all intents and purposes the same as 'Zealots', the first overt act Josephus ascribes to them is *the assassination of the High Priest Jonathan*, the son of that Ananus pictured in the Gospels, together with his son-in-law Caiaphas, partially responsible for the crucifixion of Jesus. Even more importantly, he is the brother of the Ananus the son of Ananus responsible seven years later for the death of James.

The father, 'Annas' – the second '*a*' having been transposed in the transliteration – is mentioned in Luke 3:2, John 18, and Acts 4:6. He is the progenitor of a very important line of Herodian High Priests. Succeeding Joezer b. Boethus (the High Priest opposed by Judas and *Saddok* on the issue of paying taxes to Rome) as High Priest from 7 to 15 CE, this Ananus was appointed High Priest by Cyrenius in the wake of the Census Uprising at the same time that, Josephus specifically notes, 'Antipas and Philip took over their respective Tetrarchies' in Perea and Galilee.[61] Some four or five of his sons served as High Priests, leading up to the fall of the Temple in 70 CE.

Jonathan is the one assassinated by the *Sicarii* in 55 CE. This, together with the 'Temple Wall Affair', mentioned earlier, leads inexorably to the death of James. In fact, Josephus gives his explanation of the name '*Sicarii*' in the *Antiquities* right before he describes Agrippa II's discomfiture in the Temple Wall Affair in 62 CE. Neither is it incurious, nor in the writer's view coincidental, that these so-called '*Sicarii*' first officially appear on the scene to take vengeance upon or remove someone from Annas'/Ananus' family, itself allegedly involved in the destruction of Jesus. It will be the next son of this Ananus who seven years later will be responsible (along with Agrippa II) for the destruction of James – 'the *Zaddik* of the Opposition Alliance'.

There is a certain sequentiality in these events: the assassination of Jonathan, the Temple Wall Affair, the judicial murder of James, the stopping of sacrifice in the Temple on behalf of Romans and other foreigners by the 'Zealot' lower priesthood, the War against Rome, etc. – even the fire in Rome that preceded this outbreak after the death of James, which was blamed on Christians.[62] This cycle of violence and counter-violence, though wholly un-'Christian' in the normal sense of the term is, in our view, thoroughly characteristic of all *true documents* emanating from this 'Opposition' orientation or 'Messianic' tradition – including the Dead Sea Scrolls.

It is also characteristic of these passages remarked above, from Psalms 69 and 109 supposedly being applied by Peter in Acts to the process of replacing the 'suicide Judas'. Once again, it is 'the *Sicarii*', the true heirs of the Movement founded by 'Judas *the Galilean*', who commit suicide on Masada after the fall of the Temple in 73 CE. Again, the coincidences are many – too many – and the name 'Christian' begins to look like an anti-nomian, overseas refurbishment of the '*Sicarii*' terminology elsewhere – or a kind of transparent code for it.

In the same manner, the 'Zealots', for instance, being nationalistic, xenophobic, Law-oriented, etc., are the mirror image of Paul's cosmo-politan, pro-Roman, and anti-nationalist orientation. The linkage of Judas *Iscariot* with Matthias also evokes the name of Judas *Maccabee* and his father, Phineas-oriented forerunners, whose uncompromising, anti-foreign behaviour is celebrated in the First Maccabees Book. One wonders if the Judas 'the Traitor', who commits suicide in the New Testament, in addition to being a parody of the name of the founder of this *Sicarii/Zealot* Movement, is not also a parody of 'Jews' and 'Judaism' – terms derived from this name as well. This sense has not been missed down through the ages, the epithet 'Judas' even carrying something of this con-notation. All of these points are worth pondering when attempting to come to grips with Gospel stories and these overwrites at the beginning of the Book of Acts.[63]

One final point should be addressed. We have already seen how Hippolytus in his description of 'Essenes' – constituting, in our view, a more complete version of Josephus' contradictory notices in the *War* and the *Antiquities* – identifies a more extreme group of what he calls 'Zealot' or '*Sicarii* Essenes'. Aside from 'being unwilling to call any man Lord' and being willing to undergo any sort of torture rather than 'eat things sacrificed to idols' (in Josephus' *War* this is rather, 'eat forbidden things', but here Hippolytus' version appears *more precise*), these threaten to kill anyone they hear 'discussing God or his Laws' who 'refuses to be circumcised'.

Origen (in the same section that he tells us about the missing passage in Josephus' *War* ascribing the fall of Jerusalem to James' death not Jesus') defines '*Sicarii*' as those attempting to *forcibly circumcise others* – this, in violation of the Roman '*Lex Cornelia de Sicarius*'.[64] In other words, '*Sicarii*' not only implies 'Assassins', but those forcibly circumcising others. Dio Cassius tells us that this ban, which Origen claims the judges in his time were zealously enforcing, came into effect in Nerva's time (96–98 CE).[65] For his part Jerome, in claiming that Origen had 'castrated himself with a knife', quotes Paul's own critique of 'Zealots' (Rom. 10:2), to ridicule Origen, saying he (Origen) did this out of 'zeal for God, but not *according to Knowledge*'.[66]

However this may be, what is not open to question is that the election of '*Judas Iscariot*''s successor occurs at just the point in the story of early Christianity when we would have expected to hear about James' election as Bishop of the Jerusalem Church. The 'Office' or 'Episcopate' filled here, for which '*Justus*' is the defeated candidate, *should have been* that of the Leader of the early Christian Movement, not just an insubstantial replacement in the 'Twelve Apostle' scheme never heard from in Christian history again. In our view, the authors of Acts are very well aware of this and everything we have here, including the material found in the two psalms Peter evokes, is an overwrite for this known election of James. In fact, Acts does know the true history, but is intent on neutralizing and deflecting it.

When Acts does come to remark the presence of this James – 'the Just' or '*Justus*' in all subsequent tradition – eleven chapters later, following the convenient removal of his insubstantial stand-in or double 'James the brother of John', it does so, as we have seen, as if it had already introduced him previously. Any good narrative would have required this. In fact, it *did* introduce him, right from the start – or at least the documents underlying it did – when it came to the amusing little divertimento about 'the filling of Judas *Iscariot*'s Office' (*Episcopēn*) – the 'Office' James occupies in all early Christian tradition. Certainly this was not 'the Office' occupied by the ephemeral Judas or either of his equally inconsequential and ephemeral successors. For early Christian tradition, too, as reported by Eusebius and others, *this was the Episcopate that was filled*.

9

The Election of James
in Early Church Tradition

Eusebius' Account of the Election of James

Eusebius gives the notices regarding James's election, as we saw, immediately following the references to 'Judas the Traitor', the casting of lots to elect Matthias, and the stoning of Stephen,

> by *the murderers of the Lord*, and so he was the first to carry off the Crown implied by his name [Stephen in Greek meaning 'Crown'] gained by the victorious martyrs of Christ.

Like the election of Matthias, the stoning of Stephen also replicates important events in the biography of James and we shall deal with this transposition of Judeo-Christian history in Palestine and the 'Gentilization' of its martyrs it represents as we proceed. For a start, however, one should note in Eusebius' extolling of these 'victorious martyrs of Christ' the same basic elements of Josephus' descriptions of 'Zealot'/'*Sicarii*' martyrs in Egypt and Cyrene.

Eusebius then launches into his first mention of James, coincident with these events, starting with the clause:

> At the same time also James, called the brother of our Lord, because he is also called the son of Joseph.[1]

Immediately aware that he has a problem, he interrupts his narrative to explain:

> For Joseph was esteemed the father of Christ because the Virgin was betrothed to him when, before they came together, she was found with child by the Holy Spirit, as the sacred writing of the Gospels teaches.

While taken as history by some, information of this kind is obviously of a different genre.

Eusebius' approach here is similar to Origen's a century before, who seems to have first theorized that perhaps James was called 'the brother of

185

the Lord' because he was the son of Joseph by a *different wife*. In other words, both Eusebius and Origen are willing to stretch credulity by suggesting, on the one hand, that James was *Joseph's son* by a different mother; while, on the other, rejecting Joseph's paternity of Jesus, the remaining basis for James' 'brother' relationship to Jesus. James is not 'the brother of Jesus', he is not even his 'cousin'! This is to say nothing about the credulity involved in accepting stories about the Holy Spirit fathering anything.

The reader will recognize this as all very tortuous and evasive and, indeed, it cannot be gainsaid that Gospel narratives, while popular for almost two millennia, are often quite fantastic – if fantasy is the appropriate appellation. In addition, Eusebius prefaces his description of Stephen, as we saw, with the following words:

> He was the first, also, after our Lord, who at the time of his ordination, as if ordained to this very purpose, was *stoned to death by the murderers of the Lord*.[2]

He means, of course, *Jews* again.

If, for a moment, we break loose from the historical fetters of this presentation and recognize the improbability of the Historical Stephen, a *Greek* being stoned to death in Palestine at the instigation of the group Acts 6:1 calls 'the Hellenists', we will also recognize that the stoning of Stephen fits the known parameters of James' fate as discussed both in Josephus and by Eusebius in what follows these initial references. Again, as in the case of Josephus' descriptions of the 'inviolable passion for liberty' of '*Sicarii*' in both *Egypt* and *Cyrene*, 'the Synagogue' of these Hellenists in Acts 6:9, whatever this is supposed to mean in Jerusalem, is 'called the one of *Liberty*' and 'of *the Cyrenians* and of *the Alexandrians*.' Once again, more is going on just beneath the surface of Acts than is at first apparent!

Eusebius continues:

> This same James, therefore, whom the ancients on account of the excellence of his virtue surnamed 'the Just', was stated to have been the first to be elected to the Episcopate [*Episcopēs*] of the Church at Jerusalem.

Here Eusebius uses the exact same word in Greek, *Episcopē* ('Bishopric' or 'Episcopate'), that the narrative of Acts has just used to describe 'the Office' *the successor to Judas Iscariot was elected to* (Acts 1:20).

The hypothesis identifying the tradition about James' election with the election to replace Judas in Acts is virtually proved. Not only is the over-lap in vocabulary striking, but Eusebius also uses the word '*Ecclēsia*' or 'Assembly' to describe this 'Church' which elects James (again the very same word Josephus uses to describe the 'Assembly' headed by the 'Simon' he knows in the early 40s who wishes to bar Herodians from the Temple as foreigners). Eusebius makes no bones about these things, though for the time being he does not tell us who the direct source of his tradition is – Clement of Alexandria or Hegesippus.

Nor is he in any doubt about the contemporaneity of this event with Acts 1–7's picture of the defeat of 'Justus' and the election of Matthias and the martydom by stoning of Stephen. He, also, has no doubt that James' cognomen was this same, 'the Just' or 'the Just One', and this obviously on account of his *superabundant Righteousness*. Nor does he make any bones about the fact that *an election occurred*. An election *did* occur. Whether this was the same as some of the other 'Zealot'/'*Sicarii*' elections described above or similar to this rather fantastic one to elect the unknown Matthias, which starts the narrative of Acts, is hardly relevant. We have this important missing link in Christian history and tradition, along with a number of other details attested to by Eusebius, just at the place and chronological point we would expect it to be.

Eusebius now goes on to describe the election of James more fully, as it is evidently of the utmost importance to his sources. In doing so, he changes the substance somewhat of what he has just said. The source he is quoting is Clement of Alexandria (*c.* 150–215) about a century and a half removed from the events in question.

> The Sixth Book of his *Hypotyposes* [*Institutions*] represents the following: 'Peter, James, and John after the Ascension of the Saviour, did not contend for the Glory, even though they had previously been honoured by the Saviour, *but chose James the Just as Bishop of Jerusalem.*

Though enough time has elapsed for an orthodoxy to emerge, Clement now concurs that there was an election of sorts, but not by the whole Church or Assembly, but rather simply by *the Principal Three*. These he designates, following the presentation of 'the Inner Three' in the Gospels, as Peter, James, and John – at this point clearly meaning the 'James the Apostle' or the other James. This section of Clement's works has not survived.

But immediately, Eusebius supplies another tradition, this time from the next or Seventh Book of Clement's *Hypotyposes*, but now following

Paul's presentation of the Central Three in Galatians and 1 Corinthians, where no *other James* is mentioned. This focuses on the post-resurrection appearances of Christ and what Clement calls 'the gift of Knowledge':

> After the Resurrection, the Lord imparted the gift of Knowledge to *James the Just and John and Peter*. These gave it to the other Apostles and the other Apostles gave it to the Seventy, of whom Barnabas was one.

Now the Central Triad has changed. It is no longer Peter, James, and John of Jesus' transfiguration on the mountain in the Synoptics, but rather James the Just (now occupying the premier position as per Paul in Galatians 2:9), John, and Peter. Not only does Clement add James' cognomen 'the Just One', missing in Galatians, but he takes the liberty of changing Paul's 'Cephas' back to the more traditional 'Peter', even though one book earlier, as we already saw, he admitted there were 'two by this name', one – Cephas – being 'one of the Seventy' or a 'Disciple'.

Aware that between his Sixth and Seventh Books, Clement has been sowing not a little confusion, Eusebius now quotes his clarification of this:

> Now there were *two* Jameses, one called *the Righteous One, who was cast down* [*blētheis*] *from the Pinnacle* [or *Wing*] *of the Temple* and beaten to death with a laundryman's club, and the other, who was *beheaded*.

This is a very interesting testimony indeed, because, firstly, it shows that Clement is already concerned about the confusion between the two Jameses, and, secondly, it is the first testimony we have had about two central elements in the descriptions of James' death, *being cast down from the Pinnacle of the Temple* and *being beaten to death with a fuller's* or *laundryman's club*. Both will loom large as we proceed.

For the moment, it should be remarked that Clement mentions them as separate, if consecutive, events. In doing so, he unwittingly unravels a mystery concerning them that has bedevilled scholarship and puzzled commentators ever since. Josephus presents James as having been stoned to death in 62 CE. However, the relationship between such a stoning and his brains being beaten out with a laundryman's club is unclear. One should remark here, too, the quasi-parallel to the 'headlong fall' Judas *Iscariot* takes, 'bursting in the middle and his bowels gushing out' in Acts 1:18.

As we shall see, both events – the *stoning* and the *headlong fall* – can be shown to have occurred, albeit separately, in James' life. Unfortunately, by the beginning of the third century, Clement no longer knows this and is conflating the two, *originally separate*, events, and turning them into a single happenstance. Nevertheless, Eusebius is already showing Clement to be much concerned about these overlaps, as presumably Eusebius was himself.

Eusebius' presentation of Clement's transmission tradition in the early Church is also interesting. Clement presents the tradition of transmission 'after the Resurrection' as being 'to James the Just and John and Peter' in that order. By presenting *James the Just* as first, he presumably means us to understand that either the first appearance was to him or he was the most important, or both – probably both. In addition, by insisting that 'these gave it to *the other Apostles*, and *the other Apostles* to the Seventy, of whom Barnabas was one', he implies that James, like John and Peter, was *an Apostle*. Not only this, but the number of Apostles for him at this point appears to be indeterminate.[3] Nor does he mention Stephen at all.

Before departing this subject and going on to a discussion of Thomas (that is, Judas Thomas) and Thaddaeus – two other Apostles (or 'of the Seventy Disciples' depending on who is doing the reckoning), connected to the 'brother' problem – Eusebius appends one more citation about the centrality of James. He states:

> Paul also mentions this same Just One when he writes: 'But of the other Apostles I saw none, except James the brother of the Lord.'

We have, of course, already discussed this, the most famous reference to the historicity and existence of James in Paul's letters. Not only do we have here, because of the word 'other' again, clear indication that James is to be reckoned, as in Clement, *among the Apostles*; but, in referring to this allusion to James in Paul's Galatians 1:19, Eusebius simply uses James' cognomen, 'the Righteous One' or 'Justus'. Presumably this is because, by the fourth century, so identified has it become with James in Eusebius' mind that the two names are identical. However, as we shall see, Hegesippus in the second century is already using James' cognomen in this manner, so the identity is an ancient one.

Thaddaeus, Judas Thomas, and the Conversion of the Osrhoeans

As already pointed out, Eusebius follows his first mention of Jesus' post-resurrection appearance to James in his *Ecclesiastical History* with the episode describing the conversion of the Edessenes by Judas Thomas and Thaddaeus. This episode, which he claims to have personally 'taken from the public archives of the city of Edessa' and translated from the Syriac himself,[4] is part historical, part marvellous, and also interesting. It is usually referred to as the conversion of King Agbar ('Acbar' in some Latin texts) or Abgar and associated with a Kingdom Eusebius refers to as 'the Osrhoeans' – meaning 'the Assyrians'.

This episode, while missing from Acts – although, as we shall see, it is not – is also documented by other Syriac accounts and, no doubt, represents an attempt to account for the growth of 'Christianity' in Northern Syria and Mesopotamia.[5] For Acts 11:26, leading up to the beheading of 'James the brother of John', the introduction of the real James, and 'the coming down from Jerusalem to Antioch' of a prophet called 'Agabus' to predict the Famine, 'the Disciples are first called Christians' in the Community there. For Eusebius, 'Agbarus reigned over the Peoples beyond the Euphrates with great glory' – note the important usage of the word '*Ethnē*' for 'Peoples'/'Gentiles' here, which, of course, is the term Paul uses to designate the recipients of *his missionary activities*.

The story has probably even moved on to become associated with the *evangelization of India*, still associated in myth and story with 'Thomas'' name, though it is doubtful any real-life Thomas ever went that far – whoever this mysterious 'Thomas' was. It is also probably associated with another conversion in the East, that of Queen Helen of Adiabene. It is difficult to sort out the various borders and kingdoms in this area and a group of petty kings referred to in Roman jurisprudence as 'the Kings of the Peoples'. This term in Hebrew is also used at a critical juncture of the Damascus Document where 'the Liar' and his 'spouting', 'the Princes of Judah', and 'the venom of their ways' are elucidated. Here, 'the vipers' in 'their wine is the venom of vipers' from Deuteronomy 32:33 are directly identified with '*the Kings of the Peoples*'.[6]

The story of the conversion of Queen Helen is told by Josephus just prior to the Theudas episode and the notice about the Famine. It is repeated by Eusebius, sometimes under the title of 'the Queen of the Osrhoeans'. The extent of this Adiabene – probably equivalent to today's Kurdistan along the Tigris in Northern Iraq – and how far it either encroached upon or overlapped Edessa and 'the Land of the Edessenes' is not something that can readily be determined from our sources.

In Syriac sources, Queen Helen is presented as *Abgarus' wife*.[7] The name *Agbar* or *Abgar* is somewhat generic, associated with kings from this area, much the same as 'Herod' was in Palestine and 'Aretas' in Petra and Transjordan. In the same manner, the name – or title – 'Monobazus' will run through the male members of Helen's family. It should be appreciated that 'Abgar' had *many* wives and marital alliances and that Josephus, also, considers Helen's husband Monobazus, whom he says was 'surnamed Bazeus', to be her brother.[8]

Whatever the truth of these assertions, the two conversions – Agbar's and Helen's – are amazingly similar and contemporaneous, just as these two buffer areas in Northern Syria and Mesopotamia between Rome and the Parthians in Persia are contiguous. The only difference is that, for Josephus, Helen's conversion is to what he thinks is *Judaism*, not Christianity. The question really is whether at this point there was any perceivable difference.

As Josephus tells the story, two men get in among the women in the harem of a king allied to Queen Helen's husband. One, 'Ananias', bears the name of the individual with whom Paul becomes involved in 'Damascus', also in Syria, in the conversion scene in Acts 9:17. He is also the intermediary in the Agbar correspondence in Eusebius' story of the conversion of the Edessenes. The second individual is not named, but both appear to teach a doctrine that does not require circumcision for Salvation, because Helen had a horror of circumcision. As Josephus puts the doctrine they are preaching: 'worship of God . . . counted more than circumcision.'[9] Does this sound familiar? Once again the issue turns on the need or lack of need for it.

These details in Josephus are, of course, much more precise than in the legend of King Agbar as it has come down to us through Eusebius and Syriac sources. That it is a very old legend is clear from Eusebius' personal interest in it and he says he got it from 'the ancients'. In any event, it is earlier than his time. We will show that traces of it and the Queen Helen story – which very definitely *is* old – will be discernible in the Book of Acts. Therefore, a version of it that could be parodied in Acts' own inimitable manner was already circulating at the time of Acts' composition. As for Eusebius, he proudly retells it 'verbatim' just as he found it in the Edessa archives. In doing so, he correctly identifies Thomas as 'Judas', which he did not do previously and which not even the Gospels do, except by implication, thus providing – if such were needed – additional testimony to the accuracy and antiquity of his source.

As to the story itself, where 'Thaddaeus' is concerned, it adroitly combines 'Apostle' language with that of 'the Seventy' – no mean feat. As Eusebius recounts the story, 'Judas, who is also Thomas, sent out Thaddaeus to [Agbar], as an Apostle being one of the Seventy'. In the

Apostle lists of Matthew and Mark, 'Thaddaeus' comes directly after 'James the son of Alphaeus' and right before 'Simon the Cananaean' ('Simon the Zealot' in Luke). In some manuscripts of Matthew he is 'Lebbaeus surnamed Thaddaeus'. But in the Gospel of Luke, 'Thaddaeus' suddenly metamorphoses into 'Judas [the brother] *of James*'![10] The time frame of the Agbarus affair is 'after the Ascension', and the story itself gives the events it is recounting as 29–30 CE according to the Syriac reckoning, which would then put Jesus' crucifixion somewhat before that, an interesting piece of data.

For his part, Josephus tells his Queen Helen story just prior to his story about 'Theudas' and relates it to 'the great Famine that then took hold of Judea', which he dates some time before the crucifixion of the two sons of Judas the Galilean in 48 CE and for which he says both Helen and her son sent up Famine relief.[11] Eusebius does likewise, using the Theudas story from Josephus to trigger his own about Helen and the Famine and the detail of her family's marvellous funerary monuments in Jerusalem.[12]

All these matters are very complicated, but suffice to say that Acts 11:29–30, in its introduction to the beheading of 'James', claims that Paul returned to Jerusalem the first time with Barnabas in order to bring the collection that had been done in Antioch *because of the Famine*. Eusebius thinks the two stories about Famine relief are related, and no doubt they are, but he also thinks the Famine is related to the beheading of 'James the brother of John' (read 'Judas the brother of James'). Finally, Acts introduces in relation to the Famine, a purported 'prophet' it calls 'Agabus'. Like 'Thaddaeus', 'Judas Barsabas', and other presumable messengers 'from James', he 'came down from Jerusalem to Antioch', in this instance, *to predict the Famine* 'via the Spirit' (11:28).

This 'prophet' will conveniently reappear again in Acts just before Paul's final trip to Jerusalem to see James. Here, too, he 'comes down from Judea', this time to Caesarea, where he is portrayed as warning Paul against going to Jerusalem and predicting Paul will be sent to Rome in chains (21:10–13). Despite the factual obfuscation going on here and the disinformation, I think we can say that the 'Agbarus' and Queen Helen legends, however distorted, are making an appearance here in Acts. In the process, we should be able to see that this 'Agabus' who predicts the Famine in Acts is but a thinly disguised version of the name of Queen Helen's husband in Syriac sources, 'Agbarus' or 'Abgarus'.

Though innocuous enough on the surface, this insight dramatizes the cavalier manner in which Acts treats historical information. As we will discover, Helen too *will actually appear in Acts*, but this in a form so surprising it would not have been recognized previously. The clue will be the Famine and the financial agents she sends out in connection with her Famine-relief activities. All these insights will also argue for *the antiquity of* the Agbarus legend, even as Eusebius claims, not a late invention of his rarely very fertile mind. We are in these notices being treated to a bird's-eye view of Acts' working method, such as it is, and the manner in which it treats facts known from other sources.

The second prophecy Acts associates with this 'prophet named Agabus' we shall be able to parallel in Jewish Christian legend as well and additionally in Josephus, but it will not have to do with Paul's adventures in Caesarea, nor the fact of his being sent to Rome in chains as Acts would have it (21:10–14). On the contrary, the 'prophecy' will have its parallels in *two very mysterious oracles* having to do with James in Jerusalem: one the mysterious oracle, from Jewish Christian sources following the death of James, occasioning the flight of the Jewish Christians across Jordan to Pella; the second in Josephus – the mournful prophecy of *Jesus ben Ananias*, who went around Jerusalem for seven and a half years following the death of James predicting its fall before he was finally hit on the head and killed by a Roman projectile.

Be these things as they may, there are some conclusions we can draw from all these overlaps and interplays. Let us assume that the 'Thomas' terminology refers, in addition to 'twinning', to a *brother of Jesus*. Let us also assume that 'Judas Thomas', 'Thaddaeus', and 'Theudas' are identical. From other sources like the Pseudoclementine *Homilies* and *Recognitions*, we shall be able to show how James in his role of leader of the Jerusalem Church certainly does send out Apostles and others with instructions on overseas missions. Paul inadvertently confirms this when he discusses the 'some from James' that are sent down to check into affairs in Antioch in Galatians 2:12, but also when he fulminates about his opponents having written recommendations in 2 Corinthians 3:1–8.

This is not to mention his parallel reference to 'Cephas and the brothers of the Lord', who travel with women as he does himself in 1 Corinthians 9:5. These 'brothers of the Lord' cannot include James, since James does not appear to do any travelling, but as far as can be determined remains the whole time in Jerusalem. The question of which 'Antioch' one is referring to also must be kept in mind. For his part, Josephus even refers to a *third* 'Antioch' – Charax Spasini at the top of the Persian Gulf – in his discussion of the conversion of Queen Helen and her sons.[13]

Finally, let us also assume our sources are for the most part garbled, usually the case in oral transmission, and also anxious to cover over the leadership of James as far as possible, obliterating the traces of his existence. Then we can picture a scenario in which it is rather *James who sends out Judas*, that is, 'Judas of James' or 'Jude the brother of James' (even 'Judas Barsabas' in Acts) *to Edessa*, which ends among other things in the conversion of the Edessenes, an occurrence reverberating across the length and breadth of our literature, including Acts. We shall also be able to envision a scenario, where the contents of this mysterious correspondence are reflected in the letter (or letters) known in Dead Sea Scrolls studies as '*MMT*' – also addressed to a very important and pious king – a relationship we shall treat in more detail later.[14]

Two other facts lend credence to this scenario and further clinch the presentation: the overlap between 'Theuda, the [brother or father] of the Just One' and 'Addai' in the two Apocalypses to James, and the identification of the individual who 'preached the Truth to the Edessenes' in several Syriac sources as 'Judas the Zealot'.[15] This 'Zealot' notation, now linked to this 'Judas''s name, will account for a good deal of the embarrassment, confusion, and overwriting we are encountering in all these sources. The 'Zealot' terminology will also account for confusions or obfuscations regarding another individual, the *second* or *third brother* of Jesus named 'Simeon' or 'Simon'.

This individual will be called, among other things, 'Simon the Zealot', both in Luke's Apostle lists and the work attributed to another Church father, Hippolytus of Rome (*c.* 160–235).[16] Simon the Zealot is also very likely the individual who appears in the doubling of 'Judas *Iscariot*' with his father or brother 'Simon *Iscariot*' in John 6:71, 12:4, etc., above. In the Apostle list in the Gospel of Luke, for instance, the two individuals known as 'Judas [the brother] of James and Judas *Iscariot*, who also became the Traitor', follow each other in that order – this, directly following the reference to 'Simon the Zealot' (6:15–16). Here, once again, it is concern over the 'Zealot', '*Sicarii*', and 'brother' themes that is causing all the problems.

The 'Zealot' terminology will also be applied to James, or at least the majority of his 'Jerusalem Church' followers in Acts 21:20. In fact, if one looks hard enough, one will also find it in Josephus' description of the conversion of Queen Helen of Adiabene.[17] For his part, Eusebius mentions Helen a second time in Book Two in the context of discussing the Famine-relief mission of Barnabas and Paul (chapter 12), having originally mentioned their mission in conjunction with the beheading of 'James the brother of John' in chapter 8 earlier. Not only does this directly follow allusion to the beheading of Theudas and the Famine under Claudius in chapter 11, Eusebius specifically ties their mission and Helen's.

He then follows this up in chapter 13 with the curious story about *another* Helen, this one the travelling companion and consort of Simon *Magus*. Painting Simon *Magus* as a kind of incipient Rasputin and quoting Justin Martyr and Irenaeaus, he describes how he and this Helen were both adored as gods by Simon's Roman followers, though, as far as Justin is concerned, she 'formerly lived in a brothel in Tyre of the Phoenicia'.[18] This is the kind of scurrilous invective we shall ultimately find in Acts with regard to Queen Helen. Rabbinic sources, too, hint at severe purity concerns regarding Queen Helen.[19] To add to this, in the Pseudoclementines, which – like Eusebius at this point – also deal extensively with the interrelations of Peter and Simon *Magus*, Simon *Magus* claimed to be the 'Great' or 'Hidden Power' above God, equivalent to 'the Christ' or 'the Standing One'. It is he who fills a vacancy among the Disciples of one 'Dositheus' (probably 'Doetus' in Josephus – 'Dorcas' in Acts) himself a follower of John the Baptist.[20]

Occasionally Simon *Magus* takes on or is given *the personality of Paul*. Given the sketchy nature of these sources, it is impossible to go further. Still, there is the possibility of a closer relationship between these two 'Helen's than might otherwise be apparent.

Other Testimonies to James' Election or Direct Appointment as Successor

Eusebius also refers to the direct succession of James in several other contexts in his *Ecclesiastical History*, in the process supplying us with valuable information about his character and person. In chapter 23 of his Second Book, introducing the lengthy testimony that will form the backbone of his long discussion of James, Eusebius returns to the matter of James' succession to the position of leadership of the early Church. In his previous discussion, with which Book Two began, it will be recalled that he had put this proposition – in his own words – as follows:

> This same James, to whom men had accorded the surname of the Just One . . .
> was recorded to be the First elected to the Throne of the Bishopric of the
> Church in Jerusalem.

This testimony is interesting, not only because of his use of the word

'*Ecclēsias*' or 'Assembly' for Church and '*Episcopē*' for Bishopric, already noted, but also for his use of the words 'the First' to apply to James and his insistence that all this 'was recorded'.

Now, again in his own words, he puts this:

> James the brother of the Lord . . . was *allotted the Episcopate* in Jerusalem *by the Apostles.*

Here his use of the term 'Apostles' is, once again, plural and not limited to the Central Three.

This latest phrasing may be a rephrasing or conflation of what he said on this subject at the beginning of Book Two, either quoting Clement to the effect that the Central Triad – the *Peter, James, and John* of the Gospels – 'chose James the Just as the Leader of the Church in Jerusalem' or, preceding this, the above note that James the Just 'was elected' to the Episcopate of the Jerusalem Church – the implication being *by the whole Assembly.*

This would have, of course, consisted of 'the Seventy', 'Assemblies' in Judaism being typically composed of seventy persons. This number originally represented the number of people who went down with Jacob to Egypt and, following this, up with Moses on Mount Sinai to receive the Law (Exod. 1:5 and 24:1). These 'Seventy', reduced perhaps or transmogrified in Acts to the 'Seven' of the Stephen episode, are often even called 'Elders' in the Old Testament, as they are, for instance, in Acts in referring to Paul and Barnabas bringing Famine-relief aid 'to the Elders' in Jerusalem (11:30) or, in parallel, Paul going up to see 'the Apostles and the Elders' in chapter 15's picture of the 'Jerusalem Council'. It is a particularly vivid aspect of the 'We Document''s scene in 21:18 of Paul going before James and 'the Assembled Elders' (*Presbyteroi* – Presbyters) in their last confrontation.

The number 'Seventy', so much a part of these scenarios, also represented the Rabbinical understanding of the number of 'Peoples' or languages on the earth. This sense has not been lost in the episode immediately following the election to replace Judas in chapter 2 of Acts about the descent of the Holy Spirit on the whole Assembly, together with its principal accoutrement of the 'speaking in Tongues' – the 'Tongues' necessary to take the Gentile Christian message out to the rest of the world![21] The parallel, here too, to Moses giving the Law to the Assembled Elders, should not be missed.

In the second version of Clement's testimony about James' succession, which Eusebius provided in the first chapter of Book Two, the implication was that James received his office *directly from Jesus,* and this *after the Resurrection,* that is, 'After the Resurrection, the Lord conferred the Gift of Knowledge on James the Just, John, and Peter', etc. This idea is re-inforced towards the end of his *History,* in Book Seven, when Eusebius comes to discuss 'the Throne of James' in Jerusalem.²² There he varies this position just slightly, saying:

> James, who as the Sacred Scriptures show, was generally called *the brother of Christ,* was *the First to receive the Episcopate of Jerusalem from our Saviour himself.*

There is no mention here of 'after the Resurrection', though some texts add 'and [from] the Apostles'. This is the first time we encounter the usage 'the brother of Christ' and not the usual 'brother of the Lord'. It is also the first we have heard of this *Throne of James,* not Jesus. It was obviously a relic of some kind still extant in Jerusalem in Eusebius' time, for he also notes both that it 'has been preserved to this day' and that

> The Christians there look after it with such loving care, making clear to all the veneration in which saintly men high in the favour of God were regarded in time past and are regarded to this day.

This testimony would appear to reflect what is to be found in the Apostolic Constitutions, a work probably of Syriac origin from the second or third centuries, in which is found the reference about 'Judas the Zealot' taking the Truth to the Edessenes in Northern Syria, *not* Thaddaeus or Judas Thomas.

This work has much in common with some of the Qumran organiza-tional texts, particularly the Damascus Document. In the Apostolic Constitutions, the Office of Bishop is much laboured over and there is a notice about the *direct appointment* of James almost exactly like the one at the end of Eusebius above. This is given at the beginning of a long speech attributed to James with instructions for future bishops, and reads, with James speaking in the first person:

> I, James, *the brother of Christ according to the flesh,* but his Servant regarding the Only Begotten God and one *appointed Bishop of Jerusalem by the Lord himself* and the Apostles, do ordain . . . ²³

Here, of course, we have both the references to 'the brother of Christ' in Eusebius above – and this *in the flesh* – and the appointment 'by the Lord himself', the addition of the words 'and the Apostles' seeming, once again, as an addendum to Eusebius, to be an afterthought in deference to traditional sensibilities. It would also, as we shall see, appear to be the source of a similar rendition from Epiphanius below, a half-century after Eusebius.

Here we have two further contradictions in the testimonies from Eusebius to the idea of James being appointed by the Inner Three: the one claiming James to have been 'elected' or 'chosen by the Apostles'; and the other, that he received the Office *directly from Jesus*. Admittedly, all this is confusing, but it reflects some of the confusion in the early Church regarding this succession. What is not in question is that James *did succeed* and *did receive the Office*, the only question being, as far as Eusebius or his sources are concerned, *how he received it* and *at what point*.

In addition to these testimonies, Eusebius refers to the succession of James one more time. In the lengthy materials that follow his reference to James 'being allotted the Episcopate in Jerusalem by the Apostles' in the beginning of chapter 23 of Book Two, Eusebius also quotes Hegesippus, 'who flourished closest to the days of the Apostles' (c. 90–180 CE), to similar effect. In the Fifth Book of his *Commentaries*, he says:

> But James, the brother of the Lord, who, *as there were many of this name, was surnamed the Just by all from the days of our Lord until now*, received the Government of the Church with [or 'from'] the Apostles.[24]

Not only does Eusebius aver that Hegesippus 'gives the most accurate account concerning him', which is certainly true, but there is no question here either that James *received* the Government or 'Episcopate' of the Church. The only question is whether it was 'with' or 'from the Apostles'. If 'from', this, once again, implies an election of some kind, depending on what one means by 'Apostles'. As in Paul's Famine-relief mission to 'the Elders' after 'Agabus' predicted the Famine in Acts 11:30 or to 'the Apostles and the Elders' at 'the Jerusalem Council' in Acts 15:2 – this might simply be the *whole Assembly*, which is the writer's view.

Jerome (348–420), another scholar who like Origen spent a good deal of his life in Palestine, writing in the century after Eusebius, also picks up material from Hegesippus, whose works he evidently read as well. For him however, James, 'who is called the brother of the Lord and surnamed the Just', was not 'the son of Joseph by another wife, as some think'. Rather, taking a cue from the Gospel of John, he accepts an even more preposterous solution, that James is 'the son of Mary *sister of the mother of the Lord'*.[25] In the Gospel of John, of course, she is not only the sister of Jesus' mother, but 'Mary the wife of Clopas' (19:25).

In other words, Mary has a sister called 'Mary', who is the wife of this omnipresent 'Clopas', elsewhere regarded as Joseph's brother and the uncle of James and Jesus and the brothers – all very convenient. For the moment, however, suffice it to remark the lengths to which all commentators will go to rescue the divine sonship and supernatural nature of Jesus Christ even as early as the second century.

Like Eusebius, Jerome gives two versions of James' election or appointment as Bishop of the Jerusalem Church, his own understanding of what he has read and a direct quotation from Hegesippus, both of which more or less parallel Eusebius. According to his understanding, James was either 'ordained' or 'elected by the Apostles as Bishop of Jerusalem' *immediately after Jesus' Passion.*

What is significant in this is the time frame, that 'after our Lord's Passion' James was *'immediately elected by the Apostles* Bishop of Jerusalem'.[26] In our view, this is the missing *appointment episode* that should have occurred at the beginning of Acts, but which did not and was rather replaced by the incongruous and incomprehensible material regarding the succession to Judas *Iscariot* presently found there. This would also have explained James' mysterious emergence in Acts' narrative eleven chapters later, as if we should know who he is. Thus far Jerome and ourselves are in agreement.

The next version which he gives, as he says, is a quotation from:

> Hegesippus, who lived nearest the time of the Apostles, in the Fifth Book of his Commentaries writing of James, says [this may be from Eusebius], 'After the Apostles, James the brother of the Lord, surnamed the Just, was made Head of the Church at Jerusalem. Many indeed were called James . . .

The only real difference from the version of this testimony quoted in Eusebius is the use of the preposition 'after', which may just as easily be 'with' or 'from'. For Jerome, James received the control of the Church 'after the Apostles', meaning presumably *after their appointment*. For Eusebius it is 'with' or 'from' them. There is no real way to resolve these small inconsistencies, but simply to keep them in mind for further analysis.

Another older contemporary of Jerome, Epiphanius, Bishop of Salamis, who lived at the end of the fourth century (367–404), admits to having read Eusebius but, like Jerome, it is not clear either whether he knows Hegesippus first hand or via refraction through Eusebius. He also claims to know Clement, and an unknown work, as we have noted, unmentioned by any other theologian – the *Ascents of Jacob* – purportedly discourses by James on the steps of the Temple.

This theme of the 'steps of the Temple' will be important,[27] but there is also a greater significance to this word 'ascents', for instance, 'the Psalms of Ascents' in the Bible. There is the 'Ascents' tradition in *Kabbalah*, that is, the 'Ascents' through various degrees of Neoplatonic Enlightenment or '*Gnosis*' – Ascents to the Higher Heavens or '*Hechalot*', as the literature of this tradition is called. Regardless of whether this lost book about James is a work of Jewish Mysticism or not, there may be traditions about James which do accord with this kind of mystical tradition and the idea of ascending via the Holy Spirit to the higher spheres.[28]

Like Eusebius, who reproduces Hegesippus, Epiphanius, too, gives James' various cognomens or epithets, including 'the Just One' and '*Oblias*', which he translates as 'Wall'. Eusebius translated this as 'Protection' or 'Bulwark'. In doing so, Epiphanius presents exactly what we have already heard from Eusebius about James' succession, that 'he was the First to receive the Office of Bishop' – 'Episcopate' again.[29] Epiphanius' emphasis is on James being 'the First', or his priority, not on who chose him – terminology also encountered in Paul and the Gospels, not to mention, as we shall see, the Dead Sea Scrolls. Again, there is no doubt that James is the *first* Bishop or Overseer.

For Epiphanius, this Office is not just relegated to Jerusalem, but a general title – a more accurate reflection, in our view, of what the situation really was. Epiphanius is obviously not willing to concede necessarily that James was 'chosen by the Apostles', nor the Inner Three, nor even a general election by 'the Jerusalem Assembly', which is more or less the picture in Acts of the election to succeed the suicide Judas. Rather the implication again is that James received this Office *directly from Jesus*.

The Direct Succession of James

This is confirmed in the next bit of information Epiphanius attaches to his testimony not present in any of the other materials we have so far examined, that is, that he was

The First to whom the Lord entrusted his Throne upon earth.[30]

This is doubtless an extremely interesting piece of information. Nor is there any clue as to where Epiphanius, like so many of the other interesting details he provides, got this material, though it does echo what we heard from Eusebius above, which would probably mean it came from Hegesippus. On the other hand, it is also possible it is from the *Ascents of Jacob*, which Epiphanius culls for much interesting detail of this kind. Wherever it came from, once more it shows the tremendous prestige James enjoyed across the whole Eastern Mediterranean up to the 400s, when Epiphanius and Jerome both lived.

Once again, it provides testimony that it was Jesus himself who entrusted 'his Throne upon earth' to his brother James, though it is not clear whether he did this *while on earth* or in some other manner. However this may be, the 'Throne' imagery is a central element of it. It also recalls the appointment episode in the Gospel of Thomas:

> In the place where you are to go [presumably Jerusalem], *go to James the Just for whose sake Heaven and Earth came into existence.*

Not only is this a direct appointment scenario in Jesus' lifetime – interestingly enough, attributed to someone probably connected in some manner to his third brother, 'Jude' or 'Judas' – it too contains, as we have seen, echoes and inferences of Kabbalistic thought about 'the Righteous One' or '*Zaddik*', that is, his pre-existence or the fact that he 'supports the earth'. This is also the implication of Eusebius' assertion – again based on Hegesippus – that the continued presence of James in Jerusalem 'provided a strong Bulwark' or 'Protection to the place'.[31]

'Throne' imagery, whether it relates to the idea of 'the Bishop's Throne' or one in *Kabbalah*, upon which the whole idea of the mystical Knowledge of 'the Heavenly Throne' is based – called in Judaism *Merkabah Mysticism* – is always important. Even Muhammad in the Koran has inherited the use of some of this 'Throne' imagery, and gives evidence on more than one occasion – as does Islamic tradition thereafter – that he has been involved in some of the 'Mysticism of Heavenly Ascents' Paul also testifies to.[32]

There are two more *direct-appointment*, as opposed to *election*, scenarios we have not yet treated in any detail. The first is to be found in the key Book One of the Pseudoclementine *Recognitions* (1.43). Though perhaps not always the most exact recounting and sometimes suffering like Acts from a surfeit of novelizing, still the presentation of the succession of James found there is the most sensible and convincing.

In it, too, James is not only repeatedly referred to as 'Bishop', but also, as we have seen, 'Bishop of Bishops' or 'Archbishop'. There, right before a long excursis by Peter on the identity of the Ebionite 'True Prophet' ideo-logy with that of the New Testament 'Christ', the leadership of James is referred to in a most matter-of-fact and straightforward manner:

> The Church of the Lord which was constituted in Jerusalem multiplied most plentifully and grew, being governed with the most Righteous ordinances by James, *who was ordained Bishop in it by the Lord.*

Not only is this clearly a 'direct appointment' scenario, but, paralleling the sense of the Gospel of Thomas above and Epiphanius' reference to Jesus entrusting his 'Throne on earth' to James, it seems to have occurred in Jesus' *own lifetime.* Its language of 'most plentifully multiplied and grew' parallels several similar notices that punctuate the Book of Acts, where they operate as transitions, tying together separate episodes.[33] The differ-ence is that the 'most Righteous governing' and 'ordination' are missing from Acts, though perhaps not completely.

This emphasis, too, on 'Righteousness' and his 'governance' is borne out in almost all the other sources. It is also borne out with regard to the role of 'the *Mebakker*' or 'Overseer' in the Dead Sea Scrolls, in particular, the Damascus Document, which, interestingly enough, specifically speaks of 'ordinances' or 'Judgments' where 'the *Mebakker*''s responsibilities or governance are concerned.[34]

Sleight of Hand in Acts

We are now in a position to return to Acts' treatment of this all-important, but missing election or appointment of James as successor. As we have discussed, Acts does not present the election of a successor to Jesus as leader of the Messianic Community in Palestine – by whatever name one calls it, *Christian, Zealot, Essene, Jerusalem Assembly*, or some other – but rather a successor to *Judas'* position.

After the introduction addressed, as in the Gospel of Luke, to Theophilus ('Lover of God' – in Hebrew, possibly even 'John') and with its typical evocation of the Pauline 'Holy Spirit', 'the Disciples' are pictured as conducting this election (presumably 'with the Apostles'). In line 1:15, these are numbered at 'about 120', but this must be seen as a pro-forma approximation only, meant, we must assume, to represent the number of 'the Jerusalem Assembly'. Elsewhere, the number of these 'Disciples', as we have seen, is put at 'Seventy'.

The Apostles, whom we are told Jesus 'chose', are 'given authority' or 'command through the Holy Spirit' before 'he was taken up' – that is, he is pictured as giving them 'authority' or 'command' in his resurrected state on earth before the Ascension (1:2). This parallels the notice in Hegesippus and its various reflections about 'the command of the Church being given to James together with the Apostles', not to mention the use of the word 'command' relative to the duties of 'the *Mebakker*' at Qumran.

The Lukan author of Acts also pictures the Apostles as being instructed 'not to leave Jerusalem', because at some point before too long they were going 'to receive Power via the descent of the Holy Spirit upon' them (1:4–8). (Note the use of the word 'Power' here, which will become more and more pronounced as these notices about James proceed.) This will occur at Pentecost with the descent of the Holy Spirit upon the whole Community. The first part of these instructions, *to go to* or *not to leave* Jerusalem, parallels the notice in the Gospel of Thomas above about the Disciples asking Jesus, who would be great over them, and being instructed, 'in the place where you are to go [meaning presumably Jerusalem], go to James the Just'.

After forty days – seemingly spent on the Mount of Olives – and Jesus' assumption to Heaven, 'they [meaning the Apostles again] return to Jerusalem' (Acts 1:12–14). At this point Luke names them again, and the names are the familiar ones, including Matthew and Thomas, but Judas *Iscariot* or the son 'of Simon *Iscariot*' is missing. The last three, 'James [the son] of Alphaeus [Cleophas?], Simon the Zealot, and Judas [the brother] of James', are of particular interest, as we saw, because they coincide with the names of three of Jesus' brothers. We shall return to them again when discussing 'Jesus' Brothers as Apostles', but for the moment it is sufficient to remark that we probably have a garbled reference to Jesus' *brothers as Apostles* right here.

We have already encountered several notices in Paul implying that James was to be reckoned among the Apostles, though Paul gives no definitive number of these – at least not in Galatians. He does in 1 Corinthians 15:5, where he speaks of Jesus appearing after his resurrection to 'the Twelve', but this is probably an interpolation, since there were only suppposed to be *Eleven* at the time.

Acts 1:14 also notes a house with an 'upper chamber' in connection with the Apostles' return to Jerusalem – presumably the same one as in Gospel portrayals of the Last Supper – where they go or appear to be staying 'together with the women and *Mary the mother of Jesus* and *with his brothers'*. Here Mary is not called 'Mary the mother of John Mark', as she was when we encountered a similar Mary with a 'house' in Jerusalem – also linked to a reference to 'the brothers' – in the introduction of James in 12:17. We shall hear about this 'house' again, not only in the Gospel of John, but also in the Pseudoclementine *Recognitions*.[35]

In Matthew a parallel Mary is called Mary 'the mother of James and Joses' (27:56); in Mark, 'Mary the mother of James the Less, Joses, and Salome' (15:40); and in Luke, 'Mary the mother of James' (24:10). Elsewhere, Mark 15:47 simply calls her 'Mary the mother of Joses' (read Jesus?) and Matthew, totally perplexed, finally ends up calling her simply *'the other Mary'* (27:61). Thus, even in Acts' run-up to its *election by lot* to fill Judas' 'Episcopate' or 'Bishopric', we have *at least* one and probably *two* additional references to the brothers and family of Jesus.

Pentecost and *Tongue* Imagery

We can now proceed to the events surrounding this election. Peter is presented as 'standing up in the midst of the Disciples' – 'the Assembly' once again – and proposing that an election be held (Acts 1:15–22). I think that we can safely say that this would correspond to what we heard in Hegesippus, Clement, and Eusebius that Peter and the other Apostles did not contend for the Episcopate or Overseership, but rather stood aside and 'chose' or 'elected' James the Just the brother of Jesus.

Peter now refers to the *other* Judas, not 'Judas [the brother of] James' just referred to in the list of the Apostles present in Mary's house; but rather – evoking him with the scriptural exegesis from Psalms we reviewed above – here, he is called 'Judas who became the guide of those who took Jesus', and his death, associated with something called 'the Field of Blood', is described in, as we saw, gory if fantastic detail – including two references to the 'fall' Judas supposedly takes (1:16–25). This, of course, is presented in terms of his 'Unrighteousness', as opposed presumably to James' 'Righteousness'. We have already shown some of the parallels between these kinds of details and the suppressed details of James' life and demise.

In Acts, the time frame is presented as being somewhere after forty days, but prior to the coming of Pentecost, that is, $7 \times 7 + 1$ or fifty days after Passover or Easter – Jews referring to this festival as *Shavu'ot* or the Feast of Weeks. In connection with it, Acts recounts even more fantastic events and happenings – none properly speaking historical, but all associated with the descent of the Holy Spirit (so integral to Paul's claims) on the whole Community. Later it pictures Paul as hurrying on his last trip to Jerusalem (before being sent to Rome as a prisoner) to be in time for the celebration of this Pentecost, which seems to have been the occasion of an annual reunion of some kind for the Community (Acts 20:16).

For the all-important Damascus Document at Qumran, this celebration seems also to have been the time of an annual *convocation of the Community* and a key festival. For the Damascus Document – except for the 'cursing' which is also a strong part of Acts' portrayal of the death of Judas *Iscariot* and the Jews' responsibility for the crucifixion of Christ – it is the exact opposite of Acts' Gentilized refurbishment of it. For the last column of the Damascus Document, it is a day of rededication to the Covenant of Moses and 'cursing' those who would 'reject' or 'stray either to the right or left of the Law',[36] allusions harking back to the traditional idea of *Shavu'ot* as commemorating the giving of the *Torah* to Moses on Mount Sinai fifty days after the Exodus from Egypt.

In Acts' revised portrait of it, Pentecost rather confirms the *descent of the Holy Spirit on the whole Community* and, in the process, the *new mission to all the Nations*. This is accompanied by the imagery of 'a rushing, violent wind', 'forked Tongues as of fire', and 'the speaking in other Tongues as the Holy Spirit gave it unto them' (Acts 2:1–4). This kind of imagery is also to be found in the 'Tongue' imagery in the Letter of James. There it is applied to an opponent who cannot control his 'Tongue', described as uncontrollable and 'full of death-giving poison', and accompanied by the imagery of 'violent winds' and allusion to 'boasting', 'cursing', and 'a world of Unrighteousness' (Jas. 3:1–10).

The references to 'violent winds' and 'a world of Unrighteousness' are particularly crucial for showing the relationship of these lines in the Letter of James to parallel usages in these first two chapters of Acts.[37] Also, the image of 'death-giving poison' is repeated in parallel passages in the Damascus Document, mentioned above, having to do with 'the Lying Spouter's' or 'Windbag's' 'spouting' or 'walking in the Spirit' or 'spilling' or 'pouring out wind' – 'wind' and 'Spirit' being, in fact, the same word or homonyms in Hebrew.[38] The imagery of 'death-giving poison' is important in Paul, also amid allusion to 'cursing', where the Law is pictured as bringing death – even the death of Christ – not life.[39]

In fact, the 'Tongue' imagery in the Letter of James is generically parallel to 'Lying' and 'spouting' imagery, used to describe the ideological adversary of the Righteous Teacher at Qumran.[40] In Hebrew, the word for 'language' is 'Tongue' and, as already remarked, this is the way the expression is used in describing the mastery of the *Mebakker* or Overseer 'of all the Secrets of men and all their numerous *Tongues*'.⁴¹ It is his 'Judgements' regarding the excommunication of Law-Breakers that are being evoked in the context of the Pentecost reunion of the inhabitants of the wilderness camps in the last column of the Damascus Document.

'Wind' imagery has particular relevance, as should be clear, to the imagery in both Acts and the Letter of James relative to the 'Tongue' or 'Tongues' just described. So does another allusion used to describe the activities of the Liar both at the beginning and the end of the Damascus Document, 'pouring out on Israel the waters of Lying'.⁴² The first column of the Cairo Damascus Document describes how this Spouter or Scoffer

> removed the boundary markers which the First – 'the Ancestors' – had laid down, abolishing *the pathways of Righteousness* [n.b. the issue of 'un-righteousness' again],

and therefore 'causing them to wander astray in a trackless wilderness', calling down upon them 'the curses of His Covenant'. This is the same imagery played upon in this Last Column of the Damascus Document above – again in connection with this same Pentecost convocation of the wilderness 'camps' – about 'cursing', 'expelling', and 'no longer keeping company' with those who 'caused them to wander astray in a trackless waste without a Way' and 'transgress the boundary markers laid down for' them.

Here, in Acts, in another of his Qumran-style exegeses, Peter is also represented as specifically evoking this kind of 'pouring out' imagery. (So is Jesus in Last Supper scenarios, where he evokes, the Cup of the New Covenant in his blood, 'which was *poured out for the Many*'.) But instead of the 'waters of Lying being poured out on Israel' in the Damascus Document above, it is now *the Holy Spirit being poured out on the Jerusalem Community* (2:17–18 and 2:33). The same allusion is repeated when Acts extends this to Gentiles in 10:45. Peter even quotes 'the Prophet Joel' at some length to the effect that

> I will pour out My spirit on all flesh, and your sons and daughters shall prophesy . . . see visions. (Acts 2:17; Joel 3:1–5)

Notice that this prophecy of Joel, which is as usual unremittingly Zionistic and irredentist, is full of the imagery of being 'given wine to drink' and 'drunkenness', even 'carrying gold and silver into the temples', 'casting of lots', and 'cleansing their blood'.⁴³ It is precisely at these two junctures in the Damascus Document about 'spouting to them' or 'pouring down on Israel the waters of Lying', too, that other biblical passages are invoked to condemn 'those seeing Lying visions' or 'prophecies', in particular, as in column 8, amid the evocation of 'wine', 'poison', 'venom', 'vipers', and 'Gentiles'/'Peoples', 'walking in windiness' or the 'Spirit and the Spouter of Lying spouting to them'.[44]

In his long exegetical discourse defending against the charges mocking this 'speaking in Tongues' at Pentecost as 'new wine' and 'drunkenness', Peter now quotes several psalms. In the same breath, he calls David 'a prophet', presumably because David was considered to have written the Psalms. The first, Psalm 16:9, has a tell-tale reference to 'Tongue' again, now *David's Tongue* (singular).[45]

Peter is also pictured as quoting a short passage from Psalm 132, another extremely Zionistic psalm about David with an additional tell-tale reference to the '*Ebionim*' or 'Poor'. It contains an allusion to the 'Throne' again, this time David's Throne – now to be 'Christ''s and presumably in succession to him, James' (Acts 2:30). Continuing this imagery associated with 'the Throne', Peter goes on to quote Psalm 110 – which contains the famous 'being a Priest for ever after the order of Melchizedek' allusion – on 'making your Enemies a footstool', imagery occurring at Qumran and attributed to Jesus in the Gospels as well.[46]

In doing so, Peter is pictured as making the same accusation against the Jews as Paul does in 1 Thessalonians 2:15, accusing them of crucifying Jesus and 'putting him to death' (2:23). He repeats this in Acts 2:36, where in informing 'the House of Israel that God had made him both Lord and Christ', he now is pictured as charging, 'this the same Jesus *whom you crucified*'. In two similar, later attacks in 4:10 and 5:30, Peter is also pictured as making the same charges before the Chief Priests and Sanhedrin (in 4:8, it was 'the Rulers of the People and Elders of Israel').

The second includes the charge of 'hanging on a tree', which Paul makes in Galatians 3:13 and out of which he develops his key theological construction about Jesus 'redeeming us from *the curse of the Law*'. In making these interpretations of biblical materials, the sense or significa-tion of the underlying text is almost always reversed or inverted. The same kind of reversing one's opponents' arguments is almost always happening in the polemics reflected in the Qumran texts, Acts, and the Letter of James – a particularly good case in point being this allusion to 'pouring on Israel the waters of Lying' in the first column of the Cairo Damascus Document, and its multiple variations.[47]

However all this may be, the winner in this all-important election to fill Judas' 'Office' or 'Episcopate' is Matthias. One is tempted to invert the name of the defeated candidate, 'Joseph Barsabas surnamed Justus' – this even in Greek, though 'Justus' is Latin – to read 'Justus Barsabas son of Joseph'. Even without doing this, however, the whole must be completely reversed. Neither this Matthias – a name first appearing in this period in connection with *Judas Maccabee's father* – nor 'Joseph Barsabas' is ever really heard from again (though '*Judas* Barsabas' is).

In fact, in the Pseudoclementines, Matthias will even become identified with *Barnabas*.[48] Whatever one makes of all these Judases and Matthiases, so much a part of the Zealot/*Sicarii* Movement of both Judas the Galilean and the Maccabees, the election – so obliterated here – is doubtlessly that of James the Just as Bishop of 'the Jerusalem Church' or 'Assembly', an office paralleled in the more native Palestinian framework of the Damascus Document at Qumran by that of 'the *Mebakker*' – amid evocation of 'the New Covenant in the Land of Damascus', 'the Star Prophecy', and other Messianic designations.

The Book of Acts versus the Pseudoclementines

Chapter 2 of Acts concludes with the following description:

> Every day, steadfastly they went as a body to the Temple and breaking bread in the houses, they partook of food ['the pure food' of Qumran?] with gladness and simplicity of heart, praising God and finding favour *with the whole of the people* [a clear confirmation of the popularity of this Movement], and the Lord daily added to the Assembly of those being saved. (2:47)

This is just the picture one gets in the Pseudoclementine *Recognitions*, as well, of visits to the Temple on a regular basis by James and his Community and their debates or discourses with the Chief Priests either in the Temple or on its steps. As the *Recognitions* puts it (paralleling Acts, Peter narrating) in its run-up to the final debate *on the Temple steps* before Paul's *physical assault on James*:

> The Priests . . . often sent to us, asking us to discourse to them concerning Jesus, whether He was the Prophet whom Moses foretold [that is, 'the True Prophet' or 'the Eternal Christ'; for John 12:34, 'the Prophet out of the Law who lives for ever']. But while they often made such requests to us, and we sought for a fitting opportunity, the Church in Jerusalem, was most

plentifully multiplied and grew [this is followed by the notice about *being governed with the most Righteous ordinances by James, who was ordained Bishop in it by the Lord*]. (1.43)

This accords with the various notices which punctuate Acts' narrative of the early days of the Community in Jerusalem and connect each of the separate, if often mythological or fantastic, events together. In Acts 5:12–13, leading to the assault on 'Stephen', the phrasing is:

They all used to meet by common consent in the Portico of Solomon [that is, *in the Temple*]. No one else ever dared to join them, but *the people were loud in their praise*, and *the multitudes of men and women who believed in the Lord increased steadily*.[49]

Here the parallel with the Pseudoclementines is almost precise. Only the equally drumbeat picture of James' leadership in the Pseudoclementines is missing in Acts' narrative.

It is not uninteresting, too, that many of the themes at this point in Acts are taken up in the Pseudoclementine *Recognitions* – as for instance the common purse (Acts 4:34–5:10) and the speech by Gamaliel (5:34–40), represented here as a secret supporter of the Community. As in some manuscripts of the Gospel of Matthew, 'Lebbaeus' is the name of the Apostle called 'Judas of James' in Luke instead of 'Thaddaeus'. After he speaks, 'Simon the Canaanite' takes his turn *on the Temple steps* and then 'Barnabas who was also surnamed Matthias' and 'substituted in place of Judas as an Apostle' (*thus*), and finally Gamaliel.[50]

In the Syriac rendition of this, 'Barnabas' is now called 'Barabbas who became an Apostle instead of Judas the Traitor'. Even these overlaps and confusions have a certain peculiar logic, and one can perhaps assume that the author of the *Recognitions* was transforming his version of the source underlying Acts in his own likewise tendentious and inimitable fashion.

Following Gamaliel's speech and the anachronism there in the chronological transposition of Theudas with Judas the Galilean, Acts 5:42 now picks up the theme again of the Apostles being constantly in the Temple:

They preached every day both in the Temple and in private houses, and their proclamation of the Gospel of Jesus the Christ was never interrupted.

For its part 6:1, leading into the attack on or the stoning of Stephen and the murmuring of the Hellenists against the Hebrews, picks up the 'multiplication' theme again: 'And in those days, the Disciples were multiplying.' The language here is almost word for word that of the *Recognitions*, the only thing missing being *the election of James* again. The words the Pseudoclementines give us here concerning the requests by the Chief Priests to 'the Archbishop James' for debates with the early Christian Community in the Temple or on its steps are also directly paralleled in chapters 3–5 of the Book of Acts. In turn, these harmonize very well with the requests by the Chief Priests in the long narrative from Hegesippus about James' final days in Eusebius. In this account – to a certain extent also recapitulated in Epiphanius and Jerome – the Chief Priests are shown as coming to James and asking him *to stand* on 'a wing' or 'the Pinnacle of the Temple' and quiet the people.

As Eusebius puts it, quoting Hegesippus verbatim:

> From which some believed that *Jesus was the Christ* [this note about Jesus 'being the Christ' is also the point of James' speech at this point in the *Recognitions*]. But the aforesaid heresies did not believe either in the Resurrection or that *He was coming to give to every one according to his works* [note here, the 'Jamesian' emphasis on 'works' and compare with James 2:15–26 and 5:7–8], but as many as did believe, did so *on account of James* [thus far, this more or less parallels the Pseudoclementines] . . . There arose a riot among the Jews and Scribes and Pharisees, saying that the whole people was in danger of looking for Jesus as the Christ. So they assembled, and said to James, 'We beseech you to restrain the people, who are going astray after Jesus as though he were the Christ. We beseech you to persuade all who are coming to the feast of the Passover rightly concerning Jesus; for all obey you. For we and all the people testify that you are Righteous [or 'the Righteous One'] and *do not respect persons*. Therefore, persuade the people not to be led astray after Jesus, for all the people and ourselves have confidence in [or obey] you. Therefore stand upon a wing [or 'the Pinnacle'] of the Temple that you may be clearly visible from above and your words readily heard by all the people.[51]

There follows the account, again following Hegesippus, of the attack on James and his fall from, not 'the steps' this time, but the wing or Pinnacle of the Temple. This is the sequencing followed in the Pseudo-clementines too, though there James only falls from the steps of the Temple and the nature of the attack differs somewhat. Nor does James die because of it. It is our position that this attack, as pictured in the Pseudoclementines, is *a more accurate representation* of the events as they really occurred than those in early Church literature, which are all more or less dependent on each other and will be seen as clearly attempting to cover up *embarrassing* aspects of this attack.

This presentation in Eusebius/Hegesippus is very similar to what we see in the Pseudoclementines and even in Acts. It is also very strong testimony to the authenticity of the Pseudoclementine account at this point anyhow – or at least its underlying source. In this sense, the Pseudoclementine tradition is a *more primitive version* of the episode, which, by the second century and Hegesippus, is already beginning to undergo its various transformations.

The language of 'being led astray', twice alluded to in this account credited to Hegesippus, is very important and widespread in the Dead Sea Scrolls. One should also pay careful attention to all allusions to 'standing' – as, for instance, James standing on the wing or steps of the Temple – as they will often bear on a Jewish Christian or Ebionite doctrine of 'the Standing One', also found in these Pseudoclementines and mentioned with regard to Simon *Magus* above.[52]

It is important as well to remark the great respect the Jerusalem Community leaders enjoy among the crowd. There is really no point to lie in favour of this presentation; on the contrary. James is presented as so popular that the Herodian Establishment feel the people will do whatever he 'commands' them to do. It is even stated that 'all obey you', that is, he is the popular Leader among the people, and they will do whatever he says. This is exactly the presentation in Josephus of the events surrounding the death of John the Baptist as well. There, Josephus says that Herod Antipas feared that the people would be prepared to do whatever John said and he fears that John will lead an uprising. This is also the approach of the Gospel presentation of Jesus, which constantly emphasizes his wide popularity and the strategems the High Priests, therefore, must undertake to incarcerate him. There can be little doubt that this is, in fact, *the truth* of the situation.

When discussing James' '*Zaddik*' nature and the 'Righteous One' ideology generally, it is possible to make some sense out of these testimonies. The same where the Righteous Teacher at Qumran is concerned, and his '*Zaddik*' nature, which so parallels James'. In our understanding, James was 'the *Zaddik*' of the Opposition Alliance, meaning that all the people – including the Rulers – were obliged to pay him homage, and as such, *obey him*.

Additional Parallels Between Acts and the Pseudoclementines

It should be noted that the presentation at the end of Book One of the Pseudoclementine *Recognitions* of James' debate with the Priests in the Temple comes before the attack in which he is 'thrown down the steps of the Temple' and 'breaks his leg'. It comes after the speeches of the other Apostles on the Temple steps and Gamaliel. This is the order in Acts as well. There Gamaliel's speech at the end of these verbal confrontations on the Temple Mount precedes that of Stephen, which, in turn, precedes the latter's *stoning*, in connection with which Saul or Paul is introduced (Acts 5:34–8:1).

In the Pseudoclementines James 'speaks from a height, so that [he] can be seen by all the people'. This speech has much in common with the one pictured here in Eusebius/Hegesippus, before *he is stoned* as well. This is particularly true of James' answer to the question, 'what is the Gate to Jesus':

> He is sitting in Heaven *on the right hand of the Great Power* and he is about to come on the clouds of Heaven.[53]

The language here of 'being seated on the right hand of the Great Power' is exactly that accompanying the 'footstool' imagery from Psalm 110:1–3, which Peter uses in the parallel narrative in Acts – also in the general ambience of verbal confrontations on the Temple Mount – to accuse the *Jewish crowd* (not the High Priests) of murdering Jesus (2:30–35).

This imagery, which is based on Daniel 7:13 and contains the 'Great Power' language so important to later sectarian understanding of 'the Christ', is clearly that of the Redeemer Jesus *coming in Power on the clouds of Heaven with the Heavenly Host*. It is paralleled to some degree in James' speech on the Temple steps in the Pseudoclementine *Recognitions* at this point as well. Here James is pictured as giving the scriptural warrants for *two comings*, the first, more humble, having already transpired. But the second 'in Glory' would be more supernatural and mighty – that is, the Messiah coming on the clouds of Heaven with the Heavenly Host – in which he would reign over *'those who believe* in him and *do everything* that He commanded'. Note in this last the tell-tale 'Jamesian' combination of *belief* and *doing* good works, or as James 2:22 would have it, Faith working with works – a combination that even proceeds into the Koran at a later date.[54]

James' proclamation of the Messiah 'coming with Power on the clouds of Heaven with the Heavenly Host' at Passover in the Temple is the crucial one for Jerome as well. It also forms the high point of the presentation of the War Scroll at Qumran and is the reason why – despite the seeming alienness and peculiarity of its vocabulary – this probably should be considered a *Jamesian* work.[55] The same vision will be attributed to Jesus in what will turn out to be the retrospective presentation of his responses to Sanhedrin trial for 'blasphemy' in 'the High Priest's House' the night of his execution in the Gospels (Matt. 26:64 and Mark 14:62). But, even more importantly and most tellingly, it is also the vision Acts 7:56 vouchsafes to Stephen immediately preceding its picture of *his stoning* and Paul's appearance on the scene.[56]

It is the author's view that all of these presentations are, in fact, prefigured in the two versions of James' speech in the Temple prior to the attack on him or his stoning in the Pseudoclementine *Recognitions* and the early Church accounts above, which we shall proceed to review presently below.

PART III

JAMES' ROLE IN THE JERUSALEM OF HIS DAY

IO

James' Rechabitism and Naziritism

The Privy for the High Priests, the Prostitute's Hire,
and Judas *Iscariot*'s *Price of Blood*

Having delineated James' election or appointment – 'ordination' for
Jerome – to the leadership of the Jerusalem Church/Assembly, we are now
in a better position to consider his person and role in the Jerusalem of his
day after his sudden eruption into Acts in chapter 12. To do so, it is best
to work backwards and begin with the later testimonies in early Church
literature and close with the more contemporary literature at Qumran.
There are also several references that bear on James' person and the
events of his life in Talmudic literature.

One echoes Matthew's story about Judas *Iscariot casting* his ill-gotten
'pieces of silver into the Temple' Treasury, which the High Priests then
use 'to buy a Potter's Field [the portentous 'Field of Blood' here and
in Acts] for a cemetery for foreigners' (Matt. 27:7). The reference to
'foreigners' here is a particularly important one and parallels references to
'the Gentiles' or 'the Peoples' in the Pauline corpus and also at Qumran.

The Talmudic references centre on a character called Jacob of Sihnin or
Kfar Sechania, a town supposedly in *Galilee*. One should keep in mind the
mix-ups, previously discussed, regarding the terms '*Sicarii*' and '*Galilean*'
in relation to these locations and that James' name in both Hebrew and
Greek was Jacob. This is not to mention the homophonic character of
Sicarii and *Sihnin*.

In one of these, Jacob comes to cure a famous Talmudic rabbi of snakebite,[1] echoing the story at the end of Acts about Paul on his way to Rome
curing himself of snakebite on the island of Malta (even though there are
no poisonous snakes on the island of Malta – 28:3–6). It also reverberates
with another story Eusebius attributes to Papias (*c.*60–135 CE) about
'Justus surnamed Barsabas' (no Joseph or Judas affixed).[2] Instead of
snakebite, this 'Justus Barsabas' – obviously to be equated with the
individual Acts is calling 'Judas surnamed Barsabas', who takes James'

epistle to 'Antioch' – 'drank poison, but by the Lord's grace suffered no harm'.

The most famous of these stories about Jacob of Kfar Sechania in the *Talmud* echoes the debate over the lawfulness of putting Judas *Iscariot*'s 'price of blood' into the Temple in Matthew 27:6. The famous Rabbi, Eliezer ben Hyrcanus, also was supposed to have had heretical tendencies and was actually *excommunicated* at one point by his fellow rabbis on the suspicion of being *a secret Christian*. Jacob tells him a story about 'Jesus the Nazoraean', this time relating to, not a 'Traitor's hire', but a 'harlot's hire'.

In support of this, he quotes two scriptural passages: one from Deuteronomy 23:18 about 'bringing a prostitute's hire into the House of God' and the other Micah 1:7: 'from the earnings of a prostitute she [the Temple] gathered them, and to the hire of a prostitute [the High Priesthood] they should return.' All stories about 'prostitutes' or 'harlots' in this period are very important, as they usually have something to do with both condemnations of *fornication* and attacks on the Establishment and their sexual mores. Jacob's story, which is rather bawdy and actually quite amusing, has to do with how Jesus the Nazoraean saw the issue of contributions to the Temple from *prostitutes* – one particular class of unclean persons at Qumran.

In fact, it gainsays parallel ones in the Gospels – as they have come down to us – about Jesus keeping 'table fellowship' and actually *eating with* 'Sinners' and, not insignificantly, 'tax collectors' and saying to 'the Chief Priests and Elders of the People' things like: 'the tax collectors and the prostitutes *go into the Kingdom of God before you*' or 'the tax collectors and the prostitutes *believed*' John the Baptist, which on the face of them are preposterous (Matt. 21:31–32). In the Talmudic story, not only do Jacob and Jesus exhibit the characteristic hostility towards the High Priests and the Establishment we have come to expect from 'opposition' leaders of this kind, but Jesus is presented as being unsympathetic to prostitutes or harlots too, quite different from how the Gospels portray him.

We have already suggested that in the Gospels such stories actually evoke the Herodians, who were not only the principal Roman tax collectors in Palestine – in fact, really tax farmers – but whose most famous female representatives (e.g., Herodias, Drusilla, Bernice, and Salome, who all appear in the New Testament) were viewed by 'opposition' groups of the kind we have been describing as *no better than prostitutes*. At

Qumran they are viewed simply as *fornicators*, that is, they divorce, marry more than one husband, and marry their uncles.³

So this Talmudic story has on another level, also, to do with the Herodian aristocracy contributing to the Temple, as, of course, it would have done regularly and extravagantly. In it, Jacob actually evinces quite a funny sense of humour. He provocatively starts the discussion by quoting Deuteronomy 23:18 about 'a prostitute's hire in the House of God' and, taking advantage of Eliezer's momentary astonishment, rhetorically asks whether or not it would be 'lawful to use such hire to construct an *outhouse for the High Priest*'.

It should be remarked that in Deuteronomy 23, this matter about the earnings of sacred prostitutes (17–18) is directly preceded by curses on 'Balaam the son of Be'or' and the proscription on admitting Edomites (a term often designating 'Herodians') into 'the Lord's Congregation' unto the third generation (23:1–9). This is followed by allusion to 'going out to the camps to face the enemy' (an allusion found in the War Scroll at Qumran), 'God walking with them in the camps' (also found in the War Scroll), and the 'the camps being Holy' (23:19–24). This is the context in which the issue of latrines is then discussed and their placement outside the camps in a manner completely in tune with Josephus' and Hippolytus' descriptions of 'Essenes' and the literature at Qumran. From these things, Deuteronomy 23 then moves directly into the issue of the 'prostitute's hire'.⁴

Picking up this issue of toilets, Jacob now immediately answers his own question by citing a quotation he attributes to 'Jesus the Nazoraean' to the effect that 'since it originated in filth, it can be applied to filth', meaning that it would be a good thing 'to build a privy' or 'outhouse for the High Priest' with such earnings. Not only is the audacity of this question astonishing in its contemptuous sarcasm, but it parallels a saying of Jesus in orthodox Scripture, basically used to widen the permissions regarding forbidden things or, as Mark puts it, to declare 'all things pure'. The whole discussion, which begins with Jesus addressing the question of 'eating with unwashed hands', ends with the now proverbial 'not that which enters the mouth defiles a man'. This 'is cast into the toilet bowl' or 'privy', but rather 'that which goes forth out of the mouth defiles a man' (Matt. 15:17–18 and Mark 7:15–20).⁵

Here the points to watch are the blanket permissions Jesus draws about purity and the 'toilet bowl' imagery. In Matthew's version, Jesus also employs the characteristic imagery of 'casting out' or 'casting down', which so permeates the Gospels and which we shall show to be so crucial to early Church traditions about the death of James as it relates to that of the Righteous Teacher at Qumran. In Matthew, Jesus immediately follows up his discussion about 'casting' (*ekballetai*) unclean food down the toilet bowl or privy and 'declaring all things clean', with the episode about the 'Canaanite woman' ('Greek Syrophoenician' in Mark), in which he hesitates to 'cast down [*balein*] the children's bread to the little dogs' (15:26).

Interestingly, the Deuteronomy 23:18 passage about 'a prostitute's wages', Jesus the Nazoraean considers 'filth' in the Jacob of Kfar Sechania tradition above, is also coupled with the evocation of something called 'the hire of a dog' – this generally thought to carry the sense (clear from the context) of male prostitution.

Mark goes further. He too begins this discussion of 'purifying all food' and 'declaring all things clean' with allusion to 'coming from the market place' and not having to wash your hands like 'the Pharisees and *all the Jews* do' (7:2–5). Paul, too, answering James' directives to overseas communities on 'food sacrificed to idols' in 1 Corinthians 10:23–25, evokes this *market-place* imagery in making a parallel point:

> all things are Lawful for me . . . Eat everything that is sold in the market place. There is no need to raise questions of conscience.

We shall see the relevance of this statement by Paul momentarily.

Though Mark does not specifically apply here the 'casting out' language, Matthew uses, to unclean things going out the belly and down the latrine (7:19), he does employ it in the very next episode – his version of Jesus 'casting the unclean spirit out' (*ekballē*) of the Syrophoenecian woman's daughter (7:24–26). Mark applies it to this situation; whereas Matthew just applied it to the toilet bowl. However this may be, the 'casting out' (*ekballō*) of demons or unclean spirits is the characteristic power Jesus gives the Apostles to deal with clean and unclean things generally.[6]

Like Matthew, however, Mark then does proceed to use the 'casting-down' language in the second half of this episode, the part about 'taking the children's bread and casting [*balein*] [it] to the dogs' (7:27–29).[7] This kind of language and these themes will again reappear in John 21's version of Jesus' post-resurrection appearances along the Sea of Galilee and 'the Disciples' – called by Jesus 'little children' – 'casting down' their nets there. In Matthew, Mark, and Luke, as we shall see, these scenes occur earlier, with Jesus choosing his principal Apostles along the Sea of

Galilee or giving the Twelve the authority 'to cast out [*ekballein*] demons' (Mark 3:15 and pars.).

Throughout all of these matters, we will have in the Gospels the typical reversal of themes in favour of the Pauline 'Gentile Mission'. This is also clear in the stricture Matthew pictures Jesus applying – in response to '*the Pharisees*' – to the issue of 'things entering the mouth not defiling a man', but 'being cast down the toilet bowl' (Matt. 15:11–17), to wit, 'Every plant which my Heavenly Father has not planted shall be uprooted' (15:13). The Jewish legal prescriptions having to do with the prohibition of unclean things, including 'washing the hands' and the 'washings of cups and pots and brazen vessels' in Mark 7:4, are just these kinds of 'plants'.

In turn, this position is completely gainsaid in the series of parables – also in Matthew – having to do with 'the Tares of the Field' and 'the Enemy who sowed' the Evil seed (13:24–41). These are just about the only anti-Pauline parables in the Gospels and end with the characteristic condemnation of 'those *doing*' or '*practising* Lawlessness', who 'shall be cast into a furnace of Fire' (*balousin* – 13:41–43). We shall see how this imagery, particularly that of 'the Enemy', 'doing' or 'Doers', 'the Righteous' – who here 'shall shine forth in the Kingdom of their Father' (note the plural reference to *Divine Sonship*) – and the 'Fire', will recur in both the Letter of James and the Habakkuk *Pesher* from Qumran.

Matthew follows this up with another parable comparing the Kingdom of Heaven 'to a net being cast into the sea', which like John 21 makes repeated mentions of 'casting down' (*blētheisē* – 13:47–50). The unifying allusion in this parable, having to do with 'fish' again – *rotten fish* – with 'the Field of Tares', is 'casting them [*balousin*] into the furnace of Fire' and there being 'the wailing and the gnashing of teeth' (13:50). Here, the reference is rather to 'separating the Wicked [the rotten fish] from the midst of the Righteous' rather than the Scrolls' *separating the Righteous from the midst of the Wicked*.[8]

Even more startling than any of these reversals is the amazing reversal of themes and imagery one finds in Matthew's version of Judas *Iscariot*'s suicide. That this, like the matter of the prostitute's wages to build an out-house for the High Priest in Jacob of Kfar Sechania's tradition about Jesus the Nazoraean, also has to do with 'the High Priests' and the Temple 'Treasury' is made clear even in the version of Judas *Iscariot*'s suicide as Matthew provides it:

And the High Priests took the pieces of silver and said: 'It is not Lawful to put them in the Treasury, since it is *the price of blood*.' (27:6)

Not only does this incorporate a play on the banning of 'blood' in *both* Jewish dietary *and* sexual prohibitions, but also on Paul's contention in 1 Corinthians 10:23 (first enunciated in 1 Corinthians 6:12) about 'all things being Lawful for me'. This is the position Matthew basically pictures Jesus as adopting in the 'unwashed hands' episode above that nothing 'entering the mouth defiles a man'. Rather these 'go through the belly *to be cast out into the toilet bowl*'. As Paul puts this in 1 Corinthians 6:13, immediately following his first quotation of his 'all things Lawful' permission and also grouping dietary prohibitions systematically with sexual ones:

Food is for the belly and the belly for foods, but God will bring both to nothing. However the body is not for fornication, but for the Lord. (1 Cor. 6:13)

The subject of 'blood', central to both of these, will also be integral to 'the Cup of the New Covenant in his blood' ideology, with which Paul will follow up these permissions from 1 Corinthians 10:16–11:25. In Luke's version of 'the Last Supper' (varied slightly in Matthew, Mark, and John), in which 'Judas *Iscariot*' will also be repeatedly evoked, this will be expressed, as we saw, in terms of 'the Cup of the New Covenant in my blood which is poured out for you' (Luke 22:20). This will represent, as we shall show, yet another esoteric reformulation into Greek from the Hebrew 'New Covenant in the Land of Damascus', found in both the Damascus Document and the Commentary on Habbakuk from Qumran – '*Dam*', the Hebrew word for 'blood', being equivalent to the first syllable of the word 'Damascus' as written in Greek; '*Chos*', the Hebrew word for 'Cup', the last.[9]

This proscription on 'blood', which is part and parcel of the basic 'First Covenant' with Moses on Mount Sinai ('in Arabia' in Paul) and the legendary 'Noahic' one preceding it,[10] will also constitute the first and most fundamental element in James' prohibitions to overseas communities, to which Paul seems to be responding in 1 Corinthians 6–11. Two others are 'fornication' (with reference to which Paul follows up the first enunciation of his 'all things are Lawful for me' permission) and 'food sacrificed to idols', which he contemptuously deconstructs after the second (1 Cor. 10:28).

The proscription on blood also relates to James' extreme Naziritism and vegetarianism, not to mention his 'life-long virginity', called by Epiphanius 'his virgin life-style' (the root perhaps of later Christian 'Virgin Mary' renovations – more reversals).[11] In turn, all of these will have to do with a new group embodying many of such 'Nazirite' traits, the biblical 'Rechabites', known, for instance, too, for their *proscription on wine*, another trait early Church sources will ascribe to James.

In Hebrew, the word 'Nazirite', meaning 'consecrated' or 'separated', is based on a root meaning *set aside* or *keep away from*. One should remark the play on this word represented by the designation 'Nazoraean', applied in Jacob of Kfar Sechania's story to Jesus and, it would appear, to James' followers generally. In Hebrew 'Nazoraean' (sometimes 'Nazarean' in Scripture) has a slightly different root, meaning 'keeping' or 'Keeper'. In Scripture, too, this sometimes – but not always – gets rephrased, particularly in translation, as 'of' or 'from Nazareth'![12]

Not only is this 'Nazirite' ideology sometimes expressed as 'Nazoraean', but one should note the play on it represented by the Hebrew term '*Nezer*', 'the Crown' or 'diadem' worn by High Priests, which bore a plate inscribed with the words, 'Holy to God'. Both 'the diadem' and these words will have special import for notices recorded in early Church tradition about James. In Hebrew, '*Nezer*' also has the secondary meaning of *the unshorn locks of the Nazirite* – his 'Crown', so to speak – which tradition also says was *worn by James*. The symbolism inherent in this will have particular relevance for Acts' substitution of the stoning of Stephen, a name also bearing the meaning of 'Crown' in Greek, for the attack on or stoning of James.[13]

These references to 'blood' (or 'wine') not only circulate somewhere around Judas *Iscariot*'s attendance at the Last Supper, but Matthew also goes on to describe, as we have seen, how the High Priests consulted together and 'bought the Potter's Field for a cemetery for foreigners' with the money or 'price of blood' that Judas 'cast into' the Temple Treasury (Matt. 27:5–6). This episode is transformed in Mark and Luke into the parable ascribed to Jesus – missing from Matthew – about the 'Poor' widow 'casting' her one or two mites 'into the Temple Treasury'.[14]

It is also echoed somewhat in the saying attributed to Jesus relating to the unclean things of the belly 'being cast into the toilet bowl'. In our view, the parallel presentation of Jesus in Rabbinic tradition, basically supporting extreme purity and cleanliness, is a truer version of what the *Historical Jesus* actually said than any of these others, obviously retrospectively assimilating Paul's theology on the subject.

One should also note the partial play, in Matthew's reference to 'the Potter's Field' or 'Field of Blood', on his earlier parable about 'the Tares of the Field' (13:36).[15] Even more germane is the *Potter* part of this *Field* allusion. This will allow us to unravel the whole tangle of these interlocking materials and connect them to the 'Rechabites', who will ultimately probably be identifiable – along with Ebionites, Nazoraeans, and 'Essenes' – as another of these synonymous terminologies for James' 'Jerusalem Church' Community.

The Rechabites, their Abstention from Wine, and the Cup of Blood at the Last Supper

In identifying this 'Potter's Field' with 'the Field of Blood' (27:7–8), Matthew says he is going to quote a passage from the Prophet Jeremiah, the prophet who first extensively delineated whom these 'Rechabites' were, but he does not. Instead, he quotes a passage from *the Prophet Zechariah*, which he paraphrases as follows:

> Then that which was spoken by *Jeremias the Prophet* [*thus*] was fulfilled – that is, when the High Priests took the pieces of silver that Judas *Iscariot* had cast into the Treasury and bought with them the Potter's Field, 'called the Field of Blood to this day' – 'And I took the thirty pieces of silver, the price of him who was priced, on whom they of the sons of Israel set a price, and gave them for the Potter's Field, as *the Lord had commanded me.*' (27:9)

To understand Matthew's seeming confusion about the source of this quotation, one must start with the allusion in the last clause, 'the Potter's Field, as the Lord had commanded me', to 'command' or 'being commanded'. This phraseology nowhere appears in the biblical Zechariah, but, as will become plain, it is the central focus of *Jeremiah*'s presentation of *Jonadab son of Rechab*'s 'commands' to his descendants not to drink wine, plant no 'field', nor build any permanent abode in Jeremiah 35:1–19. Likewise, the term 'the Potter's Field' does not appear in the original Zechariah 11:12–13, but only in Matthew's paraphrase of it above.

Acts 1:18–19 provides a totally different picture, not based on Zechariah 11:12–13, nor mentioning any 'Potters' at all. In it, it will be recalled, Judas *Iscariot* does not 'hang himself', rather he 'falls face downwards, his entrails gushing out'. Rather too he buys his *own* 'Field' out of his 'Reward for Unrighteousness', the 'Akeldama, which is, in their own language, Field of Blood'. Nor is there any question of Judas *Iscariot* 'casting' thirty pieces of silver into the Temple Treasury or the High Priests buying anything 'with them'. In our view, the latter element comes from the Talmudic story from Jacob of Sihnin above, where *the Priests* buy a *toilet* not a Field of Blood – the 'price of blood' or 'bloody' fornication (Deuteronomy's 23:18's 'prostitute's hire') being the key connection.

What *does* appear in Zechariah 11:13 is the phrase 'cast them to the Potter in the House of God', and Matthew obviously knows this, because he uses it to develop the phraseology he uses. The original biblical version of this passage from Zechariah reads as follows:

> And the Lord said to me, '*Cast it to the Potter*' [the reason for the 'casting' language regarding Judas' *casting down the pieces of silver in the Temple* in Matthew 27:5 above], a goodly price, that I was valued at by them.' And I took *the thirty pieces of silver and cast them to the Potter in the House of the Lord*. (11:12–13)

This allusion to 'casting to the Potter' is normally taken as a euphemism for the Temple Treasury. This is clearly how Matthew understands it too, since he now uses it to develop his version of how *Judas Iscariot cast the pieces of silver into the Temple* – not to mention its variation in Mark and Luke's picture of the *Poor* widow casting her one or two mites *into the Temple Treasury*. It is also how it is understood in the Greek Septuagint, significantly also employing the all-important 'casting' language, '*enebalon*' missing from Matthew in its present form.[16]

For Matthew 27:6, the High Priests now

> take the silver and say, 'It is *not Lawful to put them into the Treasury*, because it is *the price of blood*.'

The emphasis on 'Lawfulness' here brings us right back to Jacob's anecdote about Jesus' view of the 'Lawfulness' of 'bringing a prostitute's hire into the House of the Lord your God' (in Zechariah 11:13, 'the House of the Lord'). It also circles back to the contrapositive of this represented by Paul's blanket permission, 'all things are Lawful for me', in 1 Corinthians 6:12 and 1 Corinthians 10:23, and the variation of Matthew's food in 'the belly being cast down the toilet bowl' that follows. As will be recalled, this read: 'Food is for the belly and the belly for foods, but God will bring both to nothing' (1 Cor. 6:13). As we saw, not only was the 10:23 permission followed by a caustic reference to a principal element of James' directives to overseas communities, food or 'things sacrificed to idols' (10:28), but 6:12 was followed by evocation of a second of these directives, 'fornication'.

Bearing on the point about 'a prostitute's hire in the House of the Lord' from Deuteronomy 23:18 Jacob makes above, this reads: 'the body is not for fornication, but for the Lord' (1 Cor. 6:13) and 'he who commits fornication sins against his own body' (6:18). The caution against 'fornication' then culminates in the injunction against 'sharing the members of Christ with a prostitute's members' or 'being joined to a prostitute', not 'joined in one Spirit to the Lord' (6:16–17).[17] As in Matthew's High Priests buying a Field of Blood above, we are simply in a variation of the more profane Rabbinic tradition in Jesus' name, *condemning a prostitute's hire in the Temple* and recommending *building a privy for the High Priest* instead. Paul has simply allegorized or spiritualized these things once again.

One should also notice how Paul's statement preceding this in 1 Corinthians 6:11, about 'being washed, made Holy (and) Righteous in the name of the Lord Jesus', simply reverses and spiritualizes the one about not 'washing one's hands before eating' in Matthew 15:2–15:20 (amid the tell-tale evocation of 'fornications' and 'adulteries' in Matthew 15:19). This 'not-washing' theme will reappear when we consider James' bathing habits in early Church texts and Josephus' characterization of 'the Essenes' as preferring 'being unwashed'.[18] It is also played upon and reversed in the scene of Pilate's 'washing his hands' of 'the blood of this Righteous One' that follows the report of Judas' suicide in the Gospel of Matthew above (27:24).

The theme of 'joining', connected to both 'a prostitute's members' and 'the House of the Lord' in Paul's 1 Corinthians 6:16–17 statement, is also important in the Qumran documents and will reappear in the Nahum *Pesher* and Damascus Document in the context of *strangers* or *foreigners* 'attaching themselves to' or 'joining' the Community.[19] Even more significantly, it is preceded by the citation of the Three Nets of Belial prohibitions on 'fornication', 'polluting the Temple', and the charge against the Establishment of 'sleeping with women in their menstrual flow'. In the Damascus Document, this last becomes the bridge between the 'fornication' and 'pollution of the Temple' charges and, in it, all are inextricably connected, whether taken actually or allegorically.[20]

Not only does it directly involve the all-important theme of 'blood', it brings us back to Judas' saying, 'I have sinned, delivering up guiltless blood' and the High Priests' refusing to put 'the price of blood' into the Treasury in Matthew 27:4–6,[21] not to mention Pilate 'being guiltless of the blood of this Righteous One' that follows in 27:24. In evoking this refusal on the part of the High Priests to put Judas' silver pieces in the Treasury, rather 'buying the burial ground for foreigners *with them*' (in the Jacob of Kfar Sechania anecdote, constructing the High Priest's toilet *'with them'*), Matthew now uses the 'Potter' allusion in the passage from Zechariah that he quoted in support of this (in the Jacob episode, Deuteronomy was quoted) to develop his crucial 'Potter's Field' designation (Matt. 27:7–9).

Again, none of these elements has survived in Acts, except the allusion to '*Akeldama*' or 'Field of Blood', which appears to be connected as much to *the bloody fall* Judas *Iscariot* allegedly takes as to 'the price of blood' ('prostitute's hire' in the Rabbinic tradition about Jesus *ha-Nozri/*'the Nazoraean' or 'Keeper' above) it is supposedly bought with.

To bring us full circle – in Rabbinic tradition, too, the 'Potters' in this allusion to 'the Potter's Field' in Matthew are, in fact, *also Rechabites*. These 'Rechabites', whom we mentioned above with regard to James' Naziritism and *abstention from wine* – not to mention sexual activity generally – are defined in Rabbinic tradition and here in Jeremiah as 'keeping the oath' of their father Jonadab the son of Rechab to 'drink no wine, plant no field, nor build any permanent abode', and, also, are thought to have been 'Potters'. The root used in the Rabbinic tradition anyhow to express this 'keeping the oath' is *'linzor'*, the root in Hebrew of *Nozrim* – 'Christians' in the *Talmud* – and *Nazoraeans/*'Keepers' above.[22] Interestingly, Matthew 26:71 now applies this 'Nazoraean' terminology, also alluded to in the Rabbinic tradition about the High Priest's privy, to Jesus – this right after 'the Last Supper' and before his description of 'the Potter's Field' and Pilate 'washing his hands'.

It is this 'Potter' and 'Field' imagery – not to mention the allusion to 'Jeremiah the Prophet' – that Matthew so deftly capitalizes on to build his version of Zechariah. Now the reason for this incongruous mention of the Prophet Jeremiah should be clear. It is in Jeremiah that 'Jonadab son of Rechab', the proverbial eighth-century BC 'father of the Rechabites' and his 'house' are delineated. These are called *Rechabites* because they '*kept the Commandments* their Father *gave them* and *did all he commanded them*' (35:18 – note the 'doing' emphasis here), including 'dwelling in tents' (35:10) and '*living on the ground like Strangers*' (35:7). This is where the allusion to *command* or *commanded* that now appears in Matthew 27:9–10's version of Zechariah – which like 'the Potter's Field' nowhere appears in the original – comes from.

Not only does this lie behind the sentence, *'gave them* for the Potter's Field *as the Lord commanded me'*, in Matthew 27:10, it is also the root of 'the Potter's Field for the *burying ground of Strangers'* in Matthew 27:7. In our view, this is what appeared in the original source about Jesus and James which Matthew and Luke were using. That is, we have in this the underlying text or scriptural warrant, as it originally was, material that Matthew then revises, leaving behind the tell-tale traces of this citation *from Jeremiah on the sons of Jonadab son of Rechab* as it appeared in his original source.

Though at one point Rabbinic tradition used the term *'linzor'* or 'keeping', so important for our purposes, to express this, Jeremiah rather employs the more widely used synonym *'shomer'* or *'shomerto'* (35:18), also carrying the sense of 'keeping'. This term is, in turn, at the root of the definition of 'the Sons of Zadok' in the Community Rule at Qumran as the *'Shomrei ha-Brit'* or 'Keepers of the Covenant',[23] a parallel group of *wilderness-camp* and *tent*-dwellers. We shall identify these Covenant-Keepers at Qumran with these 'Nazirites' or 'Keepers of the Command of their Father' at the root of this 'Nazoraean' terminology, basically rendering all these parallel terminologies as simply variations on a theme.

One should note the repeated emphasis in these descriptions of the faithfulness of the Rechabites to *the Commandments of their father* on both 'keeping' and 'doing'. Both will emerge as intrinsic to the Jamesian and Qumran traditions. This is also the case regarding the allusions to 'father' or 'their father', which also will become so wrapped up with traditions about Jesus and the 'Commandments' of his 'Father' (John 10:18 and 14:31). It is this repeated use of the word 'Commandments' or 'command' in Jeremiah's testimony about *Rechabites* that now ends up in the addition of the word 'command' – not to mention 'the Potter's Field' – to Matthew 27:10's version of these lines from Zechariah, neither of which is present in the original.

The Rechabites are commanded to 'drink no wine', nor 'build houses in which to live and not to possess any vineyard, field, or seed' that 'you may *live on the ground you live upon as Strangers'* (Jer. 35:6–9). These allusions, plus the fact that the Rechabites were considered to be 'Potters', are the root of the High Priests' buying 'a Potter's Field as a burial-ground for Strangers' in Matthew 27:7, for which Matthew purports to be evoking Jeremiah, but rather gives a conflated version of Zechariah 11:12–13 – note the carry-over here of words like 'Field', 'ground', and 'Strangers'. This is the 'Field' both Matthew and Luke now go on to designate as 'the Field of

Blood'. These allusions to 'living' or 'dwelling on the ground' or 'land' will also find an echo in the allusions to 'living' or 'dwelling in the Land of Damascus' to be encountered in the Damascus Document at Qumran.[24]

If more verification of these overlaps were needed, Matthew adds the words 'to this day' to his description of 'the Field being called the Field of Blood to this day' in 27:8, while in Jeremiah 35:6 the phrase *ad-'olam* – 'to eternity' or 'for ever' – is added to Jonadab son of Rechab's, 'our Father's', Commands *to drink no wine*. Further along, these words 'to this day' are actually used in Jeremiah to describe how Jonadab's sons 'obeyed the Commandments of their Father' (35:14).

One should also note the reference to 'pots' and 'cups' used regarding efforts to tempt the Rechabites to drink wine (35:5). The allusion to 'pots' needs no further clarification; that to 'cups' (*chosot*) will have extraordinary significance for our period, particularly where the various inverted symbolisms growing out of the Commandment 'to drink no wine' are concerned. It will go through various adumbrations, including that of the imagery of the 'Vengeance of the Wine Cup of the Lord', in key documents in both the Dead Sea Scrolls and Revelation.[25]

In our view, these are the passages that originally appeared in the source underlying our present accounts – which also included the introduction of James, missing from Acts in its present form. This source was using part of or the whole of Jeremiah 35:1–19 about the Rechabites, just like early Church sources thereafter, to explain the peculiar characteristics of James' – as well as Jesus' – being, which probably did not differ very greatly. Matthew also took material from sources like those behind the Rabbinic story from Jacob about the High Priest's privy and overwrote them; Acts, sources behind the early Church accounts of the death of James, to develop the story about the suicide or 'fall' of the character both call 'Judas *Iscariot*'.

'The Cup of the New Covenant in His Blood' and 'Drinking No Wine'

We shall see below how Rabbinic tradition also connects these 'Rechabites' – whom we would identify as 'proto-Essenes' – with the High Priest or High Priest class, noting how the 'daughters of the Rechabites married the sons of the High Priests' or vice versa. Not only will this refusal on the part of the House of Rechab to 'drink wine' be exactly the behaviour early Church sources predicate of James, it is played on and again reversed in the picture in the Synoptic Gospels (Matthew, Mark, and Luke), preceding Judas' betrayal of Jesus' *new* Commandment 'to drink' *the wine at the Last Supper* – the wine in this case being symbolical of *his* blood (Matt. 26:27 and pars.).[26]

Once again, Matthew's repeated emphasis on 'blood' is critical. We have already hinted at its relationship to the terminology 'Damascus' and 'the New Covenant erected in the Land of Damascus' in the Dead Sea Scrolls above – again in the Damascus Document. In fact, Matthew's account of Judas' actions begins with his evocation of parallel notations at the Last Supper – note the emphasis in this scenario on 'food' or 'eating' again, which Paul duly picks up in 1 Corinthians 6:13 and 10:16.[27] At this moment Jesus takes the bread, blesses it, and bids all eat. Then he takes the cup, and bids all drink – again, words completely paralleled in 1 Corinthians 10:16 by Paul. Now the 'blood' is 'the blood of the New Covenant'.

In referring to it, Matthew even employs the 'pouring' imagery encountered in the Damascus Document as well but, in it, varied somewhat and applied to the ideological adversary of its position, 'the Man of Lying' or 'the Lying Spouter'. This is also further refined in Acts' picture of the descent of the Holy Spirit, being *'poured out* upon all flesh' – that is, the Apostles and the Assembly at Pentecost (2:17–18). Now Matthew applies it, not to 'Spouting' or 'Pouring out Lying', as in the Damascus Document and at Qumran, but to 'the blood of the New Covenant being *poured out* for the Many for remission of sins' (26:28). Even the term 'the Many' used here is, as we saw, the Qumran terminology for the rank and file of the Community.[28]

Of course, we are now in a world of almost pure allegorization, thematic variation, and repeated wordplay. Judas is now the one 'delivering up guiltless blood' (27:4). Not only do we have wordplay here relating to the theme of *consuming blood while eating*, conceived of by Paul as 'guiltless' or, at least, legally speaking not reprehensible; but we shall see how this 'delivering up' is used in an almost diametrically opposed manner, also in the Damascus Document at Qumran – at one point, too, in relation to 'consuming blood'.[29] Judas receives 'the price of Blood', the same 'hire' the High Priests refuse to put in the Temple Treasury, but, with which, they buy the Potter's Field (in the Jesus the Nazoraean story, the High Priest's privy) – now considered synonymous with 'the Field of Blood' – instead.

All this ends up in Matthew, as we saw, with Pilate averring that he is 'guiltless of the blood of *this Righteous One*' and releasing Barabbas instead, while the Jewish crowd rather cries out, 'Let *his blood* be on us and our children' (Matt 27:23–25). Note here how the '*Zaddik*' language and that of 'guiltlessness' and 'blood' is now put in the mouth of a *Roman Governor* on record as having been perhaps the most brutal ever sent to Palestine.

In the picture before us here in Matthew, Jesus 'takes the cup' and commands 'all to drink' the wine 'of the New Covenant in [his] blood' (26:28 – 'the Cup [of] the New Covenant in [his] blood' in Luke 22:20). We shall see how this 'wine', 'cup', and 'blood' imagery is played upon in the 'blood' and 'Cup' language we already showed to be embodied in the word 'Damascus' above, not to mention in 'the Cup of the Lord' and 'the Cup of the Wrath of God' in scenarios relating to James and the death of the Righteous Teacher at Qumran.[30]

However, in the very next line in Matthew and Mark, Jesus suddenly and inexplicably reverses himself, saying,

> But I say unto you, that I will *not henceforth drink of this fruit of the vine at all* until the day when I drink it with you new *in the Kingdom of my Father.*
> (Matt 26:29 and Mark 14:25)

There can be very little doubt that this basically repeats the 'Commandment' the sons of the Rechabites receive from 'Jonadab their Father' in Jeremiah 35:6, 8, and 14, to 'drink no wine'. Even the words 'wine', 'vineyard', 'Father', and 'to the day' are to be found in the above passages from Jeremiah. In particular, one should note how:

> Jonadab the son of Rechab, who commanded his sons not to drink wine . . . and they did not drink to this day, but rather obeyed the Commandments of their Father. (35:14)

We have seen how this 'obeying the command of their Father' reappears in Matthew 27:10's citation of Zechariah 11:13 as 'the Lord commanded me'.

This is even more in evidence in the sections of 1 Corinthians 10–13 evoking 'the Cup of . . . Communion with the blood of Christ' and 'drinking this Cup' – the Cup, according to the Gospel of Luke, of 'the New Covenant of my blood' – which 'proclaims the death of the Lord'.[31] Here it is stated:

> So that whoever should eat this bread [that is, of his 'body'] or should *drink the Cup of the Lord unworthily* shall *be guilty* of the body and blood of the Lord . . . for he who eats and drinks unworthily, eats and drinks *Judgement to himself* . . . (1 Cor. 11:27–29)

Personal pique on Paul's part aside, this is nothing but the 'vengeance' imagery we shall find associated with the imagery of this 'Cup' in the Habakkuk *Pesher* – but, importantly, also in Revelation. It is also simply Pontius Pilate's disclaimer at the end of this whole string of references to 'the Cup' and the 'blood' in Matthew – including the point about Pilate now 'washing his hands' (not 'the Jews' as in the Gospels and Paul) – of 'not being guilty of the blood of this Righteous One' and the Jewish crowd, like the descendants of Jonadab the son of Rechab above, taking the 'blood' on themselves and their 'children' (Matt. 27:24–25). We shall encounter all of this language in the Habakkuk *Pesher*'s picture of the death or destruction of the Righteous Teacher at Qumran – paralleling the death 'of the Lord' above – including *cup/Cup of the Lord* wordplays, allusion to 'the body', the specific command to 'drink', and 'being eaten' or 'swallowed', in this instance by 'the Cup of the Wrath of God'.

This 'drinking the Cup of the Lord' symbolism, which we will see referred to in Jesus' post-resurrection appearance to James in the Gospel of the Hebrews, is now combined by Paul in 1 Corinthians 10–11 with repeated evocation of 'eating everything sold in the market place' or 'eating all set before you and not raising questions of conscience' (10:25–27 – 'conscience' is a euphemism for 'the Law' in Paul), finally even including what James specifically bans in his directives to overseas communities in Acts, 'things sacrificed to idols' (10:28). But, one should also note, James in these categories is specifically portrayed as also banning 'blood', and, of course, this must be taken *both* symbolically and profanely.[32]

All this is another classic case of New Testament reversal – though on a much vaster scale – an absolutely astonishing reversal of the sense of the Prophet Jeremiah's description of the Rechabites, who *keep the command of their Father to drink no wine, own no field*, and *live only in tents*, so that they 'may live many days on the face of the land on which [they] live'. Just as this bowdlerized or somewhat refurbished description introduces the election to fill the Office of the Overseer or *Mebakker* ('Bishop') in this first chapter of Acts, so too it will serve as a good introduction to James' Naziritism – Naziritism being a basically analogous term to or variation of this Rechabitism – this, not to mention the 'priestly' connotations we shall see go along with both.

It also relates to the more distant parallel in the Damascus Document's 'New Covenant in the Land of Damascus', in regard to which the *Mebakker*'s mastery of 'all the Tongues of men' is evoked, and where presumably there was some *living in tents in the wilderness camps*. We shall now encounter all of these traits which Jeremiah ascribes to his 'Rechabites' again in early Church descriptions of James, not to mention a tradition in Eusebius, attributed to Hegesippus and recapitulated by Epiphanius, that identifies the witness to the stoning and death of James – his so-called first 'cousin' (or brother) Simeon bar Cleophas – as *'one of the Priests of the Sons of Rechab, one of the Rechabites'*![33]

James as *Zaddik* – His Righteousness

In addition to the material in Galatians, Corinthians, and Acts, which mention James, we have, as we have seen, approximately three extant testimonies to James' role in the Jerusalem of his day from the 40s to the 60s CE – Eusebius, Epiphanius, and Jerome – all overlapping and probably based on Hegesippus, Clement, or both. While Eusebius, being slightly earlier, is not surprisingly more extensive – and he tells us he is quoting Hegesippus verbatim – Epiphanius' and Jerome's accounts are at times more precise, especially where James' High Priestly activities on the Temple Mount are concerned.

Despite these occasional imprecisions, we shall reproduce Eusebius' famous testimony from his *Ecclesiastical History* in detail – as to some extent we already have – augmenting it and correcting it, when necessary, with the sometimes more precise materials from Epiphanius and Jerome. We shall, also, be able to enlarge on it with materials from Origen, the Pseudoclementines, and to some extent the two Apocalypses of James from Nag Hammadi. Origen's source, by his own testimony, is Josephus, a Josephus attested to as well by Eusebius and Jerome, which all may have seen in Caesarea, or at least Origen and Eusebius did – a version that sadly no longer exists. Jerome may be dependent on the previous two whom, interestingly enough, he seems to view as *heretics*.[34] The source for the Pseudoclementines, particularly the sequence of events in the *Recognitions* – deleted from the *Homilies* – regarding James and the early history of the Church in Jerusalem, is unknown.

The first thing to observe in relation to all these accounts is the coupling of the attribute of pre-eminent virtue or Righteousness (*Zedek* in Hebrew; *Dikaios* in Greek) with the person of James and, therefore, the sobriquet 'the Righteous' or 'Just One' attached permanently to his name – sometimes used in place of his name itself. To avoid problems in Greek, Latin, or English, it is often useful to employ the Hebrew original, 'the *Zaddik*', which, as we have seen, underlies this sobriquet. This is particularly useful for the purposes of evaluating parallel usages in the Dead Sea Scrolls, as, for instance, 'the Teacher of Righteousness' or 'Righteous Teacher', 'the Sons of the Righteous One', or even 'the Sons of Righteousness'.[35]

This attribute is to be encountered even in the testimony to James, which Origen, Eusebius, and Jerome claim to have seen in the copy of Josephus available to them. Though nowhere to be found in the extant Josephus, it is painstakingly quoted by Eusebius – who implies it is from the *War* – in the following manner:

> And these things happened to the Jews to avenge James the Just, who was the brother of Jesus, the so-called Christ, for the Jews put him to death, notwithstanding his pre-eminent Righteousness.[36]

Here it is not immediately clear if 'the Jews' put James to death, notwithstanding his pre-eminent Righteousness, or Jesus, so close is this last to traditional notions of the import of Jesus' death. But on closer analysis, it is clear Eusebius or the Josephus he saw means James.

Origen reproduces something of the same idea, though he claims Josephus referred to it in the *Antiquities*. Since Josephus' *Antiquities* does not encompass a discussion of the fall of the Temple *per se* as the *War* does, it is more likely that Eusebius is more correct in this matter. Origen gives the tradition as follows:

> So great a reputation among the people for Righteousness did this James enjoy, that Flavius Josephus, who wrote the *Antiquities of the Jews* in Twenty Books, when wishing to show the cause what the people suffered so great misfortunes that even the Temple was razed to the ground, said, that these things happened to them in accordance with *the Wrath of God* in consequence of *the things which they had dared to do against James the brother of Jesus who is called the Christ*.

Then he adds:

> The wonderful thing is, that though he did not accept Jesus as Christ, he yet gave testimony that *the Righteousness of James was so great*; and he says that the people thought that they had suffered these things *because of [what had been done to] James*.[37]

This is extremely interesting testimony and hardly something either Origen or Eusebius would or could have dreamed up entirely by themselves, because it contradicts authoritative Church doctrine as they understood it, which rather ascribed the fall of Jerusalem, as Origen himself contends, to Jesus' death not James'.

There can be no doubt that both *actually saw* this testimony in copies of the Josephus they knew. Testimony to James does exist in the extant *Antiquities*, as noted, but it does not include this point. In the *Antiquities* Josephus does make a similar statement about John's 'Righteousness', and the emphasis on *Righteousness* is the common thread running through all these traditions. There he says that the people attributed the defeat Herod Antipas (that is, 'Herod the Tetrarch') suffered at the hands of King Aretas to John's death.

Jerome, too, gives us a version of this tradition about James:

This same Josephus records the tradition that this James was of *such great Holiness and repute* among the people that the downfall of Jerusalem was believed to be on account of his death.[38]

It is not clear from this, however, whether he has actually seen Josephus for himself or is simply repeating these words of his two predecessors.

Eusebius has also reproduced various early Church traditions relating to the death of James. Two features of these descriptions, as he presents them, should be noted. These argue strongly for the authenticity of Hegesippus' very detailed description of James and the existence of a much longer exegetical work on the death of James in the manner of the *pesharim* at Qumran, upon which this was based. The first is the allusion to a key scriptural passage, Isaiah 3:10–11. Not only is this passage exactly parallel to ones like those in the Habakkuk and Psalm 37 *Pesher*s applied to the death of the Righteous Teacher at Qumran, but, as we shall see, its vocabulary was actually absorbed into the former of these.[39]

Like these, it is a *Zaddik* passage, which is the starting point around which the commentary or *pesher* turns. So is Isaiah 53:1–12, the famous passage about 'the Suffering Servant' applied to Jesus' death in early Christian tradition. This, along with Habbakuk 2:4, 'the Righteous shall live by his Faith', and Genesis 15:6 on how Abraham was 'Justified ['made Righteous'] by Faith', became the bases for subsequent Christian theological understanding of Jesus' death. Where Isaiah 3:10–11, however, is concerned – apart from the Righteous Teacher at Qumran – there is no evidence that it was ever applied *to anyone other than James*.

The second feature contributing to the impression of the tradition's authenticity – which relates to the first – involves the application to James of this important conceptuality of 'the *Zaddik*'. This is also applied to Jesus in the New Testament and Gospel accounts, which – as we have seen – even go so far as to put this precious Palestinian ideology into the mouths of both Pontius Pilate and his wife (Matt. 27:14 and 19)! The same conceptuality was clearly, also, being applied in Qumran exegetical texts to the Righteous Teacher or *Moreh ha-Zedek*, the pre-eminent leader of that Community.

Leaving the Teacher of Righteousness at Qumran aside, one might properly say that the ideology applies even more pointedly to James' person than to Jesus' and a certain confusion or retrospective appropriation of traditions may have occurred where its application to the highly mythologized figure of the latter is concerned. Certainly the tradition ascribing the fall of Jerusalem to *the death of James*, applies more logically where chronology or ideology are concerned, to 'James the Righteous One' than Jesus.

Eusebius begins his crucial testimony by describing James as having been:

> universally esteemed to be the most Just of men, on account of the elevated Philosophy and Piety [literally 'Devotedness to God'] he exhibited during his life.

He no doubt means by these last what we have been calling the Righteousness and Piety dichotomy, consisting of the two virtues that will become very much associated with James' person, as they are in Josephus' presentation of John the Baptist and Jesus, as Scripture presents him. These two attributes are also very much associated by Josephus with Essenes in his descriptions of them and very much in evidence in the documents at Qumran.[40]

In his famous description of Essenes in the *War*, as well as that of John the Baptist in the *Antiquities*, Josephus makes it very clear what was implied by this dichotomy. Righteousness is 'Righteousness towards men', that is, the sum total of one's social obligations in this world towards one's fellow man. This is very often summed up in a single commandment, known from the Ten Commandments and often presented as the essence of Jesus' teaching in Scripture, 'love your neighbour as yourself'.[41] This, therefore, can best be termed the *Righteousness Commandment*.

As will also become clear from its use at Qumran and in the New Testament, this included an economic dimension as well. One could not *love one's neighbour as oneself* if one made economic distinctions between oneself and one's neighbour or, to put it simply, if one were *Richer than one's neighbour* – therefore, not only the extreme antagonism towards 'the Rich', but the pivotal emphasis on 'the Poor' in all traditions associated with James – not to mention Jesus – as well as those associated with the Righteous Teacher in all the texts at Qumran.[42] This, of course, moves into 'the Poor' or 'Ebionite' terminology and its variations.

The second of these virtues, 'Piety' or 'Piety towards God', summed up the totality of one's specifically religious obligations *towards God*. This was also expressed in terms of 'love', and still is – that is, 'you should love the Lord your God with all your heart and with all your might' – 'loving God', the second of the two 'Love' Commandments. It too is part and parcel of Josephus' descriptions of both Essenes and John the Baptist. Where the former are concerned, it is under this category that Josephus lists all the 'Essene' specifically ceremonial or sacramental obligations, such as bathing, not anointing oneself with oil, and wearing only linen. It is also presented as one of the two fundamental underpinnings of Jesus' teaching in the Gospels.[43]

Justin Martyr (*c.* 100–165 CE), a Palestinian native as well and a contemporary of Hegesippus, writing in Asia Minor in the mid-second century, also designated these two Commandments as the essence of Jesus' teaching.[44] As we saw, they are the basis of all theorizing of those opposing Roman/Herodian hegemony in this period. Both permeate all traditions associated with James and the Letter under his name in the New Testament.[45] They also permeate the documents at Qumran, most notably the Damascus Document, which could be characterized as something of an Opposition 'Acts'. Their use here in Eusebius – at least by implication – is further testimony of the authenticity of these descriptions emanating from the period of such concern to us in the first century, which Eusebius is recapitulating.

This testimony is echoed in the passage from the Fifth Book of Hegesippus' *Commentaries* quoted verbatim by Eusebius: 'He was called *the Just by all men* from the Lord's time to ours', a period of perhaps a hundred years. Here the attestation 'by all men' is further proof of James' popularity. Hegesippus repeats this attestation to James' pre-eminent Righteousness two more times even as conserved in Eusebius. There can be little doubt that James' renown in the Palestine milieu familiar to Hegesippus was widespread or acknowledged 'by all', and very robust, and this even one hundred years after the events Hegesippus claims to be recording.

This 'Righteousness', and the ideology associated with it, is not only the basis of the cognomen to this effect always attached to his name, it would appear to be a basic element of all traditions associated with James, even more than for his reputed brother Jesus. Though the Book of

Acts on three separate occasions applies 'the Righteous One' ideology to Jesus, it is more the 'Saviour' idea implied by the name 'Jesus' itself, or the 'Son of God' or '*Christos*' idea in some manner associated with it, not to mention 'the Nazoraean' or '*Nozri*', that was thought of as characterizing Jesus.[46]

This 'Righteousness' ideology is also the basic one where 'the Teacher of Righteousness' – the central character in the Qumran documents – is concerned. If James is not identical with him, then he is certainly a parallel character or one of a long series of individuals bearing this title, because James certainly taught a *doctrine of Righteousness*. This doctrine was epitomized – as both the Letter attached to James' name and parallel portions of the Damascus Document attest – by the Commandment to 'love your neighbour as yourself'.[47] It is epitomized, too, in the notion of 'the Poor', one of the principal forms of self-designation at Qumran, and the name either of James' group *per se* in Jerusalem or the group in early Church accounts after this, which took him as its progenitor.

James as 'Holy from his Mother's Womb' and a Nazirite

By Eusebius' testimony – and also Jerome's – Hegesippus goes on to distinguish James from others by that name, 'since there were many', by saying, 'He was Holy from his mother's womb.'[48] The word 'Holy' (*Hagios* in Greek) being used here is different from his two other attributes 'Pious' and 'Righteous'. It corresponds to a third Hebrew word, '*Kedosh*', and will bear on the claims we shall encounter below for James as High Priest as well. In the plural, it is equivalent to what goes in English by the name 'Saints' – Hebrew, *Kedoshim*.

Singular or plural, it is a widespread usage in Hebrew prayer and at Qumran. When used in the plural, it is often used to denote 'the Holy Ones' or the Heavenly beings 'coming on the clouds', including 'the Angels and spirits' – whatever could have been understood as a 'spirit' in those days (the Arabic word, *jinn*, from which the word in English *genie* is derived, is one well-known equivalent). This is the way the term is used in the War Scroll at Qumran, most notably in the all-important passage in Columns 11–12 (repeated in 21–22), following up the exegesis of the Star Prophecy. This will parallel the proclamation Hegesippus attributes to James, of 'the Son of Man sitting in Heaven on the right hand of the Great Power and coming on the clouds of Heaven', in the Temple on Passover, 62 CE, another of those declarations constantly attributed *to Jesus* in the Gospels.[49]

Jerome also repeats another tradition about James' 'Holiness' not present in any other source:

> this same James, who was the first Bishop of Jerusalem and known as Justus, was considered to be so Holy by the People that they earnestly [or 'zealously'] sought to touch the hem of his clothing.[50]

The importance of this tradition, relative to James' Holiness, cannot be overestimated. It, too, is retrospectively attributed to Jesus in Scripture, and this repeatedly, including the themes of both 'touching' and 'the hem' or 'fringe of his garment'!

The reader should appreciate that the sanctity of the fringes of garments was always a uniquely Jewish concern that would have mystified foreigners. In one important, particularly exaggerated, example of this, a woman, who has had her *menstrual flow for twelve years*, touches 'the hem of his [Jesus'] garment' (Luke 8:44–47 repeats the word 'touch' *five* times in four lines; Mark 5:27–31, *four*). Here Jesus perceives 'the Power' – just alluded to in James' proclamation in the Temple at Passover of the Son of Man seated 'on the right hand of the Great Power' – going out of him. In other such examples Jesus cures the sick around the Sea of Galilee (here called 'Gennesaret'), who 'earnestly seek to touch the hem of his clothing', so they can 'be made whole' (Matt. 14:36 and Mark 6:54).[51]

The incident about the woman with the exaggerated menstrual flow, also repeated in Matthew 9:20, very much resembles the one about Jesus 'casting out demons from'/'casting down crumbs for' the Syro-phoenecian/ Cananite woman or her daughter following his evocation of 'the toilet bowl' saying above. In both of these there is just the slightest hint of a caricature of Helen of Adiabene, who in Rabbinic sources was said to have undergone three consecutive, Nazirite-oath periods of seven years each or twenty-one years in all for uncleanness. We shall encounter an additional, somewhat racialist slur on her in Acts – this, too, involving genitalia.[52]

In Matthew, this story is preceded by Jesus' tell-tale talk of 'putting new wine in old wineskins' and the new 'wine being poured out' (Matt. 9:16–17 and pars.), not without relationship to Rechabite attitudes towards wine above and the total complex of this kind of subject matter. There is also not a little play on the theme connected to these things of prohibiting relations with 'women in their menstrual flow' in the key passages about Temple 'pollution' and 'fornication' in the Damascus Document.

In the context of the way Eusebius and Jerome use the term 'Holy' as descriptive of James, it has a slightly different connotation. Here, one might also use the equivalent 'consecrated' just as in the matter of *Naziritism* above, that is, 'consecrated' or 'set aside from his mother's womb', to describe what they are talking about. In fact, if one really wants to be precise about this, classically the High Priest wore a linen mitre or head-dress, upon which was attached a gold plate with the inscription 'Holy to God' (Exod. 28:36–38) in the sense of being consecrated to God – '*Kedosh*' carrying the sense of *both* 'Holy' and 'consecrated'. This head-dress with the gold plate, as we saw, was also designated as 'the Holy Crown,' the '*Nezer ha-Kodesh*' (Exod. 29:6 and Lev. 8:9),[53] as in the case of the unshorn hair or 'Crown' of the Nazirites also mentioned above.

Once again, the use of the word '*Nezer*', combined with evocation of the 'Holiness' or 'Consecratedness' of the High Priest, will be of significance. Parallel-wise, the notion of 'being consecrated' or 'separated' ('set aside') is the basis of what generally goes by the term 'Nazirite', which is based on the same root as '*Nezer*'. In fact, this is the way Epiphanius understands the term as he applies it to James. He even calls James 'a Nazirite', by which he specifically means *consecrated*, thereby correctly signalling the Hebrew sense of the underlying root.[54]

In this sense, the word can be seen as a kind of synonym for 'Holy' and this is what both Hegesippus and Jerome are obviously referring to when they apply the word '*Hagios*' in Greek to James. 'Holy to God', therefore, can be seen as having both 'priestly' and 'Nazirite' connotations, and the combination of these will have additional significance when both Epiphanius and Jerome come to insist that James wore 'the mitre' of High Priest – '*Nezer ha-Kodesh*' in Hebrew – and actually *entered* the Holy of Holies in the Temple.

Interestingly, when speaking of James as 'a Nazirite', Epiphanius gives John the Baptist as another example 'of these persons consecrated to God'. In doing so, he cites Luke 1:15, which pictures the Angel predicting that John 'will drink neither wine nor strong drink', so pregnant with meaning regarding so-called 'Rechabites' above and which all sources also predicate of James. Epiphanius does not, however, cite Luke 7:33 further to this about John – in contrast to Jesus (*thus*) – 'neither eating bread nor drinking wine'. The issue of Jesus aside, these points are never mentioned in other descriptions of John, not even by Josephus. If we substitute 'meat' for 'bread' – overlapping terms in Hebrew – then, of course, the resultant meaning is that John (unlike Jesus) was both a 'Rechabite' or 'Nazirite' and vegetarian, and virtual convergence with known information about James is achieved.

If we also keep in mind the Rabbinic notices above that 'the sons' or 'daughters of the Rechabites' married those of the High Priests and did service at the altar, then again we move closer to the High Priesthood being ascribed to James in early Church sources, even if only esoterically. Luke 1:15 also predicts of John that 'He shall be filled with *the Holy Spirit even from his mother's womb.*' This too simply rephrases what we just heard in Hegesippus about James being 'Holy from his mother's womb' above. Once again, additional convergence develops about what the Gospels say or imply either about Jesus or John with known facts about James' life.

Holy from his Mother's Womb and Jesus the *Nazoraean*

Not only is this note 'from his mother's womb' salient in Luke's testimony about John, bringing us back to Hegesippus' original about James 'being Holy from his mother's womb' in both Eusebius and Jerome, but Luke reprises the usage 'Holy' in the new variant so important to Paul's Gentile Mission, 'the Holy Spirit' (*Pneuma Hagion* – paralleling the word 'Holy' again even in the Greek). Competitively, Paul, combining the sense of 'being set aside' and 'mother's womb', refers to himself in Galatians 1:15 as being 'set aside' or 'chosen from my mother's womb', adding the additional contention that God 'revealed His Son in me' in 1:16.

The combination of both of the elements of 'womb' and 'the Holy Spirit', now moves on to become the basis of Luke's account – not to mention Matthew's – of the birth of Jesus from 1:26–42. These will also include another element from the biography of James, lifelong 'virginity', which Epiphanius, drawing on Palestinian tradition, considers intrinsic to his delineations of James' *extreme Naziritism.*[55] This too is now injected and combined with these other two elements in the narratives of Jesus' miraculous birth – all encapsulated as well in the second-century Protevangelium of James, setting forth the doctrine of Mary's 'perpetual virginity' and supposedly ascribed to *James.*

For Matthew, Mary is the 'virgin' *not James*, and 'found to be with child of the Holy Spirit' (*thus* – 1:18–23). As Luke enlarges on this, Jesus is 'a Holy Thing' (*Hagion*), which Mary, 'who was a virgin', 'conceived in [her] womb', when 'the Holy Spirit came [down] upon' her (1:27–35). Here again we have the *womb* and *Holy Spirit* elements, the plausibility of all this aside.

Then, applying 'what has been written in the Law of Moses' to his 'being brought to Jerusalem and presented to the Lord', Luke quotes Exodus

13:2: 'Every male opening a womb shall be called *Holy to the Lord*' (2:22–23 – the variant of the phrase 'Holy to God' on the High Priest's mitre or '*Nezer*' in Exodus and Leviticus above).[56] Once more, terms known to tradition as specifically applying to the life and person of James are being applied to somewhat different effect to persons and situations more in keeping with the New Testament or Pauline ethos.

Epiphanius takes the point one step further, tying the whole complex of usages *not to Nazirite, but to Nazareth,* asserting, 'Jesus had been conceived in the womb in Nazareth'.[57] Now we have moved from 'Nazirite' to 'Nazareth', and, as it will transpire, 'Nazarean' or 'Nazoraean'. These last, as we saw, were based on a slightly different root in Hebrew, *N–TZ–R* instead of *N–Z–R*. We encountered this related Hebrew root, *linzor* – meaning 'to keep' or 'observe' – with regard to the Rechabites above and how, for instance, the sons of the Rechabites '*kept* the Commandments of their Father' Jonadab son of Rechab.

It is this idea which actually underlies the title Luke now applies to Jesus – whom he calls 'a Man, a Prophet' – 'the Nazoraean' (*Nazoraios*) in 24:19, and again, in Peter's mouth, in Acts 2:22. There he calls him 'a Man by God, set forth to you by works of Power', amid references to 'Galileans', 'speaking with other Tongues' (the word for *languages* in Hebrew), 'new wine', the Holy Spirit 'being poured out on all flesh', and the Jews crucifying Christ. Not only do we have in these references hints at the Ebionite and Elchasaite 'Primal Adam' ('First Man') and 'True Prophet' ideologies, but it should be appreciated that the title '*Elchasai*' in the last-named tradition is based on the meaning in Aramaic and Syriac, 'Hidden Power'.[58]

Matthew 26:70 picks up this title 'the Nazoraean' (*Nazoraios*) right after Jesus' evocation of 'the Son of Man sitting on the right hand of Power and coming on the clouds of Heaven' in 26:64 – the exact words of James' 62 CE proclamation in the Temple on Passover in early Church accounts – and the reference to Jesus as 'Jesus the Galilean' (*Galilaios*) in 26:69, an allusion that also accompanies Acts reference to this title (2:8 – *Galilaios*). After evoking this title, Matthew then goes on to tell us about Judas and 'the Field of Blood'. Mark, probably incorrectly, rather replaces Matthew's reference to 'Jesus the Galilean' – preceding the one to 'Jesus the *Nazoraean*' – with 'Jesus the *Nazarean*' (*Nazarēnos* – 14:67 and 16:6).[59] This often gets translated, following Mark – but not, as we have just seen, either Matthew or Luke – as 'Jesus the *Nazrene*' or 'the Sect of the *Nazrenes*'.

It was Matthew who first spread the misconception that the title 'Jesus the *Nazoraean*' should in some manner relate to 'Nazareth', by quoting the prophecy: 'He shall be called a Nazoraean' (*Nazoraios*) which, closing his narrative of Jesus' early years, he associates with 'withdrawing to parts of Galilee [*Galilaias*] and going to live in a city called Nazareth [*Nazaret*]' (2:22–23). This cannot be the derivation of the term, as even in the Greek, the spelling 'Nazareth' and 'Nazoraean' differ substantially.[60]

These scriptural passages also form the basis of Epiphanius' tortuous discussion trying to link the 'Nazoraean' terminology to the town of 'Nazareth', for which he now cites Matthew's story about Jesus growing up in Nazareth. As he tells it, now combining Matthew and Luke, this includes the tell-tale allusion to Jesus being '*conceived in the womb in Nazareth*'. Not only is this simply a variation of the traditions we have been encountering above about 'being consecrated' or 'a Nazirite from the womb', it actually includes the edifying note:

> All Christians were once called Nazoraeans. For a short time they were also given the name Jessaeans [that is, 'Essenes'], before the Disciples in Antioch began to be called Christians.[61]

The problem is that there is no scriptural passage, 'he shall be called a Nazoraean' in the Old Testament, and the passage on which this was, according to Matthew, supposed to be based is unclear. One can, however, assume that one or another of the Old Testament references to the idea of being 'a Nazirite' was probably intended. Though Matthew says the reference comes from 'the Prophets', examples of individuals of this kind in Old Testament narrative are Samuel and Samson. Again Matthew is probably mistaken. The Bible twice avers about Samson that 'the child shall be a Nazirite unto God' (Judg. 13:5–7) and once – speaking in the first person – that 'I have been a Nazirite unto God *from my mother's womb*' (16:7). Given the tell-tale references to both 'Nazirite' and 'womb', this last was probably the original behind the refurbishment in Matthew, not to mention these references to 'mother's womb' in early Christian texts about Paul and James. This reference to 'mother's womb' is also to be found in the Qumran Hymns.[62]

Of course, Samson's behaviour is *the exact opposite* of what a good Nazirite was conceived of as being, but some of the qualities of a proper Nazirite or a 'Consecrated' or 'Separated One', that is, a razor never coming near his head and not drinking wine, are recapitulated in this parody.[63]

The problem is, as well, that in these two word clusters in Hebrew –

Nazirite and Nazoraean/Nazareth – we have two separate consonants, a '*z*' and a '*tz*', which transliterate only into a single consonant '*z*' in Greek (though Epiphanius does mention another group in this connection, 'the Nasaraeans', based on a different consonant, *sigma* – 'Naassenes' in Hippolytus above, in Greek, probably a variation on 'Essenes').[64]

In Hebrew these two parallel words, when spelled one way, that is, with a '*tz*' as in *Nazoraean*, simply mean 'Keeper' as we have seen; spelled another – 'Nazirite' with a '*z*' – *consecrated* or *to be separated*. In turn, in Christian thought, this often gets confused with what is called by the term 'Nazarene', even though, as Matthew puts it, this really does read 'and he shall be called a Nazoraean'. This is probably due more to Mark's use of 'Nazarene' (1:24, etc.) and confusion of these terms than anything else, but Mark uses 'Nazoraean' in 10:34 as well.[65] All these can be applied to what in Hebrew is meant by the usage 'Nazirite' – a 'Consecrated' or 'Separated One'. They really cannot mean 'from Nazareth', as the notation occurs elsewhere in the Gospels, though all such plays on words were probably purposeful.

In Christian tradition, as it has come down to us through the narrative in Acts, this 'Nazirite' ideology really does seem to have been in vogue, because when Paul encounters James for the famous final showdown during his last trip to Jerusalem, James describes to him how there are quite a few penitents in the Temple who have 'taken an oath upon themselves', meaning not a life-long but a temporary Nazirite oath (Acts 21:18–23). The procedures for these are described in both the Book of Numbers and, in extended fashion, in the *Talmud*.[66]

If this episode is any measure, it would seem James' early Christian Community in Jerusalem really *did* value the Nazirite-oath procedures. This would also seem to be true for those *Sicarii*-like assassins, who take an oath or 'with a curse, curse themselves, *not to eat or drink till they have killed Paul*' (Acts 23:12).[67] Since in one form of the notation, the notion of *being separated* or *separation* is closely associated with it, this idea too would have played an important role in the early Community's thinking and religious behaviour, as it does Qumran's, which, as the Gospels do John the Baptist, characterized itself as 'separating from the habitation of the Men of Unrighteousness to go out into the wilderness to prepare the Way of the Lord'.[68]

In another episode in Acts, which might, in fact, comprise an echo of or be a confusion with the one just remarked, 'Paul had his head shaved' before or after a sea voyage from Cenchrea in Corinth 'to Syria' because of a *vow he took* (18:18).[69] 'Shaving the head' is a very important aspect of temporary Nazirite-oath procedures, just as letting 'no razor come near one's head' is of life-long Naziritism predicated of James and other 'Rechabite' types.

By contrast, in temporary Naziritism of the kind portrayed in the episode in Acts where James puts a penance on Paul to show that he himself still 'walks orderly *keeping the Law* [note the tell-tale theme of 'keeping' here] and there is no truth to the rumours circulating' about him (21:24), shaving the head occurs upon completion of the oath or vow period, usually seven days. But, of course, there *is* truth to these rumours concerning Paul's regular observance of the Law – which in Galatians 3:10–13 he describes as 'a curse' – and in these concerns about what he teaches others, in regard to which Acts again pictures James as delivering his directives to overseas communities (21:25).

Be this as it may, Paul pays for the expenses of 'the four who had taken *a vow* upon themselves'. According to James' express instructions, this should have included 'shaving their heads', but it is not clear whether Paul actually does this as these procedures are interrupted by a riot precipitated by Jews from Asia, who see him in the Temple (21:26–27). According to Acts, Paul did actually do this earlier at Cenchrea above, the sea port on the Aegean side of the Isthmus of Corinth (18:18). In the author's view, 'shaving his head because of a vow' has no relevance in the context of the sea port at Cenchrea, and what is occurring at this point in Acts is proba-bly a garbling of events taking place later in Jerusalem in the Temple, where 'cutting one's hair' or 'shaving one's head' was part of the purifications associated with the observances of temporary Naziritism as accurately described by James in Acts 21:24.

A similar procedure seems to have crept into Islam, where James' instructions to overseas communities are also honoured.[70] In the *Hajj* or Islamic Pilgrimage, 'the *Hajji*' or pilgrim has his head shaved at the end of the proceedings – much like James' followers here in Jerusalem – to show that he has been to the sacred precincts of Mecca and taken part in them. We can now see that temporary 'Nazirite' activity of this kind clearly also had significance for James' Jerusalem Community or Assembly, at least as portrayed in Acts, and the name often accorded them, 'Nazoraeans', playing on this and no doubt other characteristics, was probably not simply an accidental one.

The notion of 'being consecrated' or 'separated' implicit in this Naziritism – temporary or life-long – is highly prized, also, both in the traditions associated with James and the literature of the Dead Sea Scrolls. In the latter, as we have seen, the idea of 'being separated' is the basis of the scriptural exegesis of the passage from 40:3 applied in the Gospels to John the Baptist's teaching, 'make a Straight Way in the wilderness'. In the Community Rule at Qumran, this passage is evoked twice and the time for this 'preparation of the Way in the wilderness', 'to separate from all those who have not turned aside from Unrighteousness' and 'to do' all that was 'commanded' (note the parallel with both Jamesian and 'Rechabite' ideology here) would appear to be the present.[71] Also, as we have seen, in Hymns the idea of being 'Holy from the womb' is directly referred to.

At Qumran, not only is the Community called 'the Community of Holiness', and its members, 'the Men of Holiness', 'the Men of Perfect Holiness', and 'the Perfect of the Way'; but another name for those following this Movement is 'the Sons of Zadok', the Hebrew root, as we have seen, of the Greek transcription 'Sadducees'.[72] In the Community Rule at Qumran, 'the Sons of Zadok' are defined either as 'the Priests *who keep* the Covenant' or more generally, as 'the Keepers of the Covenant' *par excellence* – the 'Rechabite' overtones of both of which should be clear. In the Damascus Document, 'the Sons of Zadok' are those who will be saved and save others by the practice of Justification ('making Righteous') or, turning eschatological, they are those 'who *will stand* in the Last Days'.[73] In it, the idea of 'separation' is basic, not only 'going out from the Land of Judah *to dwell* in the Land of Damascus' (note the 'Rechabite' emphasis again on 'dwelling on the land'), but, also, improper 'separation' of clean from unclean – 'Holy from profane' – in the Temple.

It will be recalled that this is the basis of the 'pollution of the Temple' charge preceding these materials in the Damascus Document and comprising the last of the 'Three Nets of Belial' – 'pollution of the Temple', itself being not unrelated to James' directives to overseas communities even as represented in Acts, in particular, his prohibition reported there on 'the pollutions of the idols' (15:20). This 'pollution of the Temple' charge in the Damascus Document, in turn, is tied to both 'fornication' and the 'blood' implied in the charge of 'sleeping with women in their periods' the document connects to both and the original one of *improper separation* both in the body and in the Temple – imagery Paul also revels in.[74] That is, they do not observe proper 'separation' of clean and unclean things, not only in the Temple, but elsewhere. This is why the Temple *is polluted*.

We have already found parallel allusions used by Paul in 2 Corinthians

6:15–16, which raises the question, 'what agreement does Christ have with Beliar [note, the corruption of the Damascus Document's 'Belial'] . . . *a Temple of God with idols?*' Not only does this pick up the *idolatry* theme in James' ban on 'things sacrificed to idols', but it even echoes the Damascus Document's, Rechabite-style Commandment to 'go out from the Land of Judah and dwell in the Land of Damascus':

> so come out from among them and *be separated* . . . and do not touch [any-thing] unclean . . . *be cleansed from every pollution* . . . *Perfecting Holiness* in the fear of the Lord. (2 Cor. 6:17–7:1)[75]

As we have remarked, the language parallels here are almost precise and almost every word or usage here in 2 Corinthians is also found in the *Damascus Document from Qumran.*

This is particularly true of the allusion to 'Perfection of Holiness', which in the Damascus Document is actually given as an alternative name for the Community.[76] Not only should one remark here the Nazirite/Jamesian emphasis on being 'Holy' or 'Perfect Holiness' – also the language on the High Priest's *Nezer* or mitre – but also the the imagery Paul uses in this context of adoptionist *sonship* – 'and I shall be a Father to you and you shall be to me sons and daughters, saith the Lord' (2 Cor. 6:18), which is replicated almost word for word in the Qumran Hymns in the context there of being 'Holy from the womb'.[77]

Even more importantly, one should remark the contrast represented by these kinds of ideas with the words attributed to Peter in Acts in the famous episode about the descent of the Heavenly tablecloth: 'But God taught me *not to call any man profane or unclean*' (Acts 10:28). Words such as these are the very opposite of those found in other documents at Qumran, like the ones I have called 'Two Letters on Works Reckoned as Righteousness' (referred to by some by the rather arcane '*MMT*'), which I have associated with a *Jamesian* point of view. In these letters, as in the Damascus Document above, the problem is just the opposite – the *pollution of the Temple* by unclean gifts or sacrifices, most notably, on the part of *Gentiles*. Not only do these directly reprise two other 'Jamesian' categories, fornication and things sacrificed to idols; but they end in direct evocation of the famous passage from Genesis 15:6 about how 'Abraham *was justified*' – in this case by 'works' not Faith.[78]

In Acts, Peter receives the very opposite 'command' than these vegetarian-style 'Rechabites': 'kill and eat' (10:13), which is vouchsafed to him in a context of Jesus being described as 'from Nazareth' (not a

Nazoraean – 10:28), 'those of the cicumcision' being 'amazed that the Holy Spirit had been *poured out* upon Gentiles' (10:45), and 'the Jews' accused of putting Jesus 'to death by hanging him on a tree' (10:39). Here we come back to the issue of 'table fellowship' with Gentiles, so bedevilling the early Community and Paul's conflict with James in the Letter to the Galatians, the basic issue behind the Gentile Mission dispute.

Nazirite, Nazareth, and Nazoraeans

In Christianity, the issue of being a 'Nazrene', as Mark and Luke would have it, is based on the attempts via Greek transliteration to associate this title with the town 'Nazareth' in Galilee, whose very existence in this period cannot be confirmed. This, then, becomes identified as the place of residence of the Messiah-to-be. Therefore, in Matthew, as we saw, 'He shall be called a Nazoraean' becomes, in popular parlance, 'He shall be called a Nazrene', and both are presented as applying to the fact that Jesus' family moves or emigrates to the town of Nazareth 'in Galilee' – notice again the parallel to Qumran emigrations out of 'the Land of Judah to dwell in the Land of Damascus'.

Epiphanius, above, manfully wrestles with how the 'Nazoraean sect', as he calls it, to which he attaches both James and Simeon Bar Cleophas after him, is connected to 'Nazareth'. Acts 24:5 replicates this language, as we have seen, in picturing 'a certain Tertullus' as describing Paul, after his confrontation with James and arrest by the Roman Authorities, as 'a *disease* carrier, *encouraging rebellion* among all the Jews of the habitable earth and a leader of the *Nazoraean sect* [literally 'heresy']'.[79]

The only real sense that emerges from Epiphanius' discussion is the information that 'the Nazoraean sect' was still flourishing in his own time (fourth century) on the other side of the Jordan in Perea (where, of course, John the Baptist had been active and finally executed), further north in the Pella region of the Decapolis ('the Ten Cities', of which Damascus also was one – where he claims the Disciples fled after the death of James 'since Christ told them to leave Jerusalem'), the Damascus region itself (which for some reason he refers to as '*Cochaba*', meaning in Hebrew 'Star'), and north as far as Aleppo (Beroea).[80] This, of course, is more in agreement with the Dead Sea Scrolls' idea of a 'New Covenant in the Land of Damascus' than anything like the *emigration to Galilee* that the Gospel of Matthew assumes the 'Nazrene' or 'Nazoraean' terminology is depicting.

There are other problems, too, with the simplistic transferral of a sectarian title to a geographical place name. The first is that, though the scriptural reference clearly aims at evoking *Nazirite* ('Nazoraean' or 'Nazrene' nowhere appearing *per se* in any Old Testament formulation), 'Nazareth', as we have seen, is actually based on the uniquely Hebrew '*tz*' rather than the more familiar '*z*' (which sometimes transliterates into Greek as '*s*') – the root usage that underlies it being the idea of 'keeping' or 'observing', usually used in terms of 'keeping the Law' or 'Covenant' or *observing the customs of the Ancestors*, though there is also sometimes the notion of 'keeping things secret' as well.[81] There is also another Hebrew word based on this spelling, which compounds the confusion, that is, the '*Nezer*' or 'Branch', a very important usage where Messianic prophecy is concerned.[82]

In Christianity, this idea of 'Nazrene' has become associated with the very name of the religion itself. Jesus is called 'the Nazrene' without anyone knowing precisely why or what it is supposed to mean. The form cannot mean 'Nazareth', as we noted, at least not grammatically. Jesus is said to come 'from Nazareth'. On that basis, his followers are said to be 'Nazrenes' or 'Nazareans', and that is the end of it. The word in its alternative – and probably original – sense of 'Nazoraean' has been used in the East in Semitic languages to speak of 'Christians' to this day. Since the words, 'Christ' and 'Christianity' deriving from it, are decidedly Greek, 'Nazoraean' is the way this movement is described in Hebrew, Arabic, Syriac, and the like. Epiphanius and Jerome (Hippolytus speaks of 'Naassenes' as we saw), for instance – not to mention Acts – certainly understand this as an alternate name for Christianity in Palestine, where the Greek word 'Christian' would have no meaning. There is even a non-canonical Gospel entitled in this manner, 'the Gospel of the Nazoraeans', '*z*' here, of course, representing the letter '*tz*' in Hebrew.

But the basis of this root, the allusion to 'keeping' or 'observing' – that is, 'the Keepers of the Covenant', the definition of the 'Sons of Zadok' in the Community Rule, or observing the Law – implies the exact opposite of Pauline Christianity as we have come to know it or the 'Christianity' that has finally come down to us. For Paul, keeping such things, even having oneself circumcised, the sign of the Covenant, would be considered a curse. As he puts it, 'the Law cannot bring life', only death (Gal. 3:21). (He may be right, depending on one's point of view, but this is not the issue. Right or wrong is not what we are attempting to determine – only what happened.) For Paul, only the figure he calls 'Christ Jesus' can 'bring life'.[83]

In Hebrew, too, as a result of this terminology, Christians are called 'Nozrim' to this day, either based on those who follow 'the Branch' or those who are 'Keepers'. The term probably cannot derive from the word 'Nazareth', though Nazareth could derive from it – that is, there could be a city in Galilee which derived its name from the expression *Nazoraean* in Hebrew, but not the other way around as the Gospels seem to prefer. In Arabic too, again succeeding to this usage, Christians are to this day called *Nasrani* (note here how the 's' has taken the place of the 'z').

There is also another sectarian designation in Arabic and that is the *Nusayri*, who reside in Northern Syria to this day. Another name for this sect is 'the '*Alawi'*. This in some sense derives from the name of Muhammad's successor – at least from the Shi'ite perspective – and close family relative 'Ali. That is, they derive their name from their allegiance to 'Ali as the successor to the 'True Prophet' of Islam.[84] These *Nusayris/ 'Alawi*s are a secretive Imamist sect in Syria with Christian overtones. This '*Imam*' idea, in turn, has connections with the Jewish Christian 'Secret' or 'Primal Adam' ideology, which permeates the Pseudo-clementines literature. All this is obscure, but the 'Nazirite'/'Nazoraean' conceptualities appear to have had a long association with the ideal of 'the Christ', which at first glance would appear to be an attempt to translate 'the Primal Adam' notation from more Semitic language-milieus into Greek.[85]

Where the city 'Nazareth' is concerned, we have already noted that Josephus never mentions it in any of his works, which are, as we have seen, *very* detailed. Josephus was military commandant, or at least commissar of Galilee, responsible – according to his own self-advertisement – for the fortification of the area in the course of Roman attempts to reconquer it after the 66–67 disturbances. He lists all the towns he had something to do with or fortified. Nazareth is nowhere among them. Nor is it listed in any biblical setting previously. The principal city of Galilee for these purposes is rather 'Sepphoris', a city not far from present-day 'Nazareth'.

Sepphoris, however, is very much involved in the story of Judas *the Galilean*, the founder of Josephus' 'Zealot'/*Sicarii* Movement'.[86] In the *Antiquities*, Josephus makes it clear that Judas *did not come from Galilee*, but rather from that area presently called 'Golan'. Called 'Gaulonitis' in this period, it is the area leading towards Syria above the Sea of Galilee presently under dispute between Syrians and Israelis. Actually, Judas came from one of the cities Josephus fortified there, Gamala, so named because the spur of land on which it was situated resembled the hump of a *camel* ('*gamal*' in Hebrew and Arabic).

The fate of this city in the course of the Roman reconquest of Galilee was tragic. Josephus describes the mass suicide that took place there after the collapse of his defective defence strategy. It is a pitiful description and this kind of mass suicide, as at Masada thereafter, seems to have been characteristic of the fall of cities in the area. Perhaps this, too, is one of the significations of the 'Galilean' terminology – certainly it is reflected in the picture of 'Judas *Iscariot*''s suicide. For Eusebius, following Hegesippus, 'Galilean', as we saw, appears to have been another name for either the 'Zealot' or 'Christian' orientation.[87] Certainly 'Galilean' cannot describe where Judas the Galilean came from any more than 'Nazoraean' can Jesus.

We have seen how these two titles were juxtaposed in Matthew 26:69–71 – paralleled to some extent in Mark 14:67 – above. Judas came from the Gaulon. In Jesus' case, *Nazoraean* and *Galilean* would both appear to be esotericisms referring to the 'Messianic' or 'Zealot Movement'. 'Nazareth', if it existed at all, may have been a little village not far from Sepphoris. On the other hand, 'Nazareth' may have sprung into life to meet a later need.[88]

Where Judas 'the Galilean' is concerned, Sepphoris also has special significance, because Josephus describes how his followers broke into the armoury there to arm themselves. Note the parallel here to Jesus arming his followers in Luke 22:36–38, following its picture of Jesus' pronouncement about 'the Cup of the New Covenant in [his] blood' and 'Judas [the son] of Simon *Iscariot*' – as John 13:26 would have it – going out supposedly 'to deliver him up' or 'betray him'. Prior to Judas the Galilean's arming *his* followers from the armoury at Sepphoris, Josephus describes the end of a rabbi or teacher (the term he actually uses is 'sophist'), whom he characterizes as 'expert in the Laws of their country' – someone he calls 'Judas the son of Sepphoraeus'.[89] This clearly relates to the place name 'Sepphoris' in the same way that 'Nazareth' is supposed to relate to Jesus.

There does, indeed, appear to be much overlap and confusion regarding these place names, areas of origin, and the name of a given movement or sect stemming from these kinds of leaders. This 'sophist' or 'rabbi' Josephus calls 'Judas Sepphoraeus' harangues the young people to pull down a Roman eagle that Herod had erected over the entrance to the Temple 'contrary to the Law' and thereby strike a blow for freedom, winning for themselves 'the reward which the Law confers on *works of Piety*' – this is 'works Righteousness' with a vengeance – since 'they would have died keeping and observing the Law of their fathers'. Note the tell-tale emphases on 'keeping' and 'observing' again.

This rabbi is hardly to be distinguished from Judas the Galilean subsequently, even though for Josephus Judas Sepphoraeus, together with another 'rabbi' he calls Matthias (again note the Maccabean names), are burned alive ('being guilty of sacrilege under their pretence of *zeal for the Law*'), while Judas the Galilean goes on functioning and Josephus never does delineate his fate. Josephus (or his sources – this is forty years before Josephus was born), may have been mistaken about this detail, as later in the *Antiquities* he says only Matthias was burned. Here, Josephus portrays the people as preferring the burning of the rabbis and their followers rather than having 'a greater number prosecuted', a point of view echoed in John 11:50's picture of Caiaphas' famous explanation to his fellow Chief Priests about Jesus: 'It profits us more that one man die for the people, rather than the whole nation perish.'

Nazara and Cochaba: the 'Branch' and the 'Star' Prophecies

Likewise, Christians of all ages have generally thought Jesus 'the Nazrene' denoted a geographical notation, misunderstanding the ideological implications of the terminology. Actually, Julius Africanus (170–245 CE) also refers to two villages associated with the members of Jesus' family – the group known as 'the *Desposyni*' in early Christian tradition.[90] These he locates in Judea and calls 'Nazara and Cochaba'. He says the relatives and descendants of Jesus and his brothers inhabited these cities and came from there. But no such cities can be identified in Judea of this period. Epiphanius, as we have seen, places Cochaba in Syria in the region of Damascus. Julius Africanus, however, may have in mind what Matthew 19:1/Mark 10:1 call 'the coasts of Judea on the other side of the Jordan', which dovetails nicely with all these notices about activity across Jordan and in the so-called 'Damascus' region.[91]

Both names have Messianic overtones. '*Nazara*' relates to either 'the Branch' or the 'Nazirite' terminology above – it is not possible to tell which from Greek transliteration, as we have seen. This imagery is common in Messianic ideology in this period and the language associated with the name of Christianity in the East and Jesus' cognomen 'the Nazoraean'. '*Cochaba*' is obviously based on the Hebrew word for constellation or star, from which another Messianic Revolutionary in the second century,

'Bar Kochba', derives his name, even though he seems to have come from another town in these areas, 'Chozeba'.⁹²

We have already had much to say about the 'Star' symbolism inherent in this name, particularly when talking about texts at Qumran, where 'the Star Prophecy' is quoted three times in very important contexts in the Damascus Document, the War Scroll, and in the collection of Messianic proof-texts known as the Messianic *Testimonia*, mentioned above.⁹³ This 'Star' denotes a very important Messianic ideology and symbolism. It is based on Numbers 24:17 that 'a Star would rise from Jacob, a Sceptre to rule the world'. For this reason, together with 'the *Shiloh* Prophecy' about 'the Sceptre', to whom 'the Peoples would gather', and 'the Staff' (Gen. 49:10), it was called the 'World Ruler Prophecy'.⁹⁴

If any prophecy shows the power of oracles or fortune-telling in human history and on the human mind, it is the Star Prophecy. It is interesting because, in the Old Testament, it is not even associated with a Jewish prophet, but rather a Gentile one, 'Balaam'. Allusions to 'Balaam', seen as one of the archetypal 'Enemies' in the *Talmud*, will occur repeatedly in our subject matter, as will wordplay related to the archetypal adversary 'Belial' – in Paul the defective 'Beliar' above – and its underlying meaning in Hebrew, *balla'-'Am*, 'swallowing' or 'consuming the People'.⁹⁵

We have already encountered plays on the signification of this name in the Pauline corpus in 'eating' or 'swallowing with the mouth' allusions in important contexts there. But the *B–L–'* circle of language will be of even more pivotal importance at Qumran, especially when speaking of the destruction of the Righteous Teacher and his adversaries, ideological and temporal; just as the 'Righteousness' circle of language, playing off the Hebrew letters *Z–D–K*, is important in talking about supporters of the Righteous Teacher and his behaviour. We shall denote this *ba–la–'a* or 'swallowing' language as applying to Herodians and their hirelings (here, the fact that both 'Balaam' and 'Bela'' related to it – the name of the first *Edomite* king in the Bible – are both called sons of Be'or will be determinant), including, in particular, their characteristic activity, 'consuming the People'.

2 Peter 2:15, a letter steeped in Qumran-type imagery, speaks of Balaam – like Judas *Iscariot* in Acts above – as 'loving the Reward of Unrighteousness'; likewise Jude 1:11 speaks of his 'error' in terms of his same 'reward'. In Revelation 2:14, Balaam is characterized as 'teaching'. Moreover, the picture of him 'casting a net before Israel to eat *things sacrificed to idols* and commit *fornication*', has the strongest parallels

with pivotal Qumran imagery about the 'Three Nets of Belial' in the Damascus Document, connecting it to James' instructions to overseas communities above. All show some understanding of the implications of the terminology. In Talmudic literature, there is also some indication that this 'Balaam' terminology was applied to Paul.[96]

Whether or not the imagery did apply to Paul, the *Star Prophecy* is highly prized at Qumran. In the War Scroll it is directly applied to a Messianic 'no mere Adam'.[97] In the Damascus Document, 'the Star' is tied to 'the Sceptre' and 'the Staff' (*Mehokkek*) and defined as 'the Interpreter of the *Torah* who came to Damascus'. But, playing on its underlying Hebrew root meaning of 'decree' or 'Law-giver', so is 'the Staff' or '*Mehokkek*'. He, too, is defined as 'the Interpreter of the *Torah*' who 'decreed' how they 'should walk during the Age of Unrighteousness' when they went out 'to sojourn in the Land of Damascus' 'until the *Standing up* of he who pours down' or 'teaches Righteousness at the End of Days'.[98]

Not only is this exposition immediately preceded by allusion to those

who remove the boundary and lead Israel astray [cf. 2 Peter 2:15 above] . . . speaking *rebellion against the Commandments of God* given by the hand of Moses . . . *prophesying Lying* to turn Israel away from following God;

but this material is specifically played on in Christian Scripture relating to an opposite kind of teacher who came to Damascus, 'confounding the Jews who dwelled in Damascus' by the manner in which he proved Jesus 'was *the Christ*' (Acts 9:22). The imagery of 'leading astray' is strong in the Little Apocalypses attributed to Jesus in the Synoptic Gospels, where 'many false prophets will arise and lead Many astray' (Matt. 24:5 and 11). In the Habakkuk *Pesher*, in particular – as well as here in the Damascus Document – it is the characteristic activity of 'the Liar' who 'leads Many astray'.[99]

Josephus understands that the Star Prophecy was the moving force behind the Uprising against Rome in 66–70. As the writer has emphasized, this prophecy was pivotal in showing that the Uprising against Rome was not simply a political or anti-colonial one – the manner in which it is normally portrayed – but rather *Messianic* and/or religious. Josephus subverted the revolutionary thrust of this prophecy by applying it to the Roman Emperor-to-be Vespasian. So successful was he in this regard – as was his patron Titus – that this whole process has been widely mis-understood. For services rendered Josephus was adopted into the Roman Imperial family itself.

The service that Josephus rendered these patrons was to deflect the force of this prophecy from unknown, charismatic insurgent leaders to the events culminating in the rise of the Roman Emperor Vespasian, the progenitor of 'the House of the Flavians'. Rabbinic Judaism, true to its Pharisaic roots, indulges in the same interpretation as Josephus, applying the Prophecy – through the person of its founder Rabbi Yohanan ben Zacchai – also to the Roman Emperor-to-be Vespasian. Paul, of course, applies it to the Supernatural Redeemer figure, he calls 'the Christ' or 'Christ Jesus', an individual he never met except through the visionary experiences he claims as his private 'revelations' (*apocalypseis* – 2 Cor. 12:1 and 7).

It is certainly also true that we must see this Prophecy not only at the root of events culminating in the Uprising(s) against Rome, but also in the rise of Christianity. Echoes of it are to be encountered not only in 'the Star' over Bethlehem of the Gospel of Matthew (2:2–10) – where 'seeing the Star, they rejoiced with overwhelming joy' – but also in the name of the Jewish revolutionary hero of the next century, 'Simon *Bar Kochba*'. Correspondence from this legendary hero has been found in caves in the Judean Desert not far from those of Qumran. Here, his name is not Bar Kochba, 'the Son of the Star', but rather Bar Kosiba, demonstrating definitively that the title 'Kochba' was deliberately adopted and was not a family name.

Talmudic writings, playing on the resonance of 'Choziba' with the Hebrew word for 'Lying'/'*Chazav*', mock his claims to Messiah-hood, insisting rather that 'a Liar has gone forth out of Israel'.[100] Not only does this last, once again, vividly confirm the anti-Messianic orientation of the Rabbis, it comprises a pointed parallel to the way Qumran is applying this same 'Liar' terminology to the Adversary of the Righteous Teacher, who has so many similarities to Paul.

For Suetonius, Tacitus, and Roman historians thereafter, basing themselves on Josephus, this 'World Ruler' Prophecy is the foundation of the Uprising against Rome, that is, the Jews were led astray by an 'ambiguous oracle' from their ancient literature, capable of manifold interpretation, that 'a World Ruler would come out of Palestine'.[101] They were mistaken in this, as Josephus, like these other historians, is anxious to point out.

This is also the position of Rabbinic Judaism following the Pharisaic point of view, which both Paul and Josephus also claim as their legacy. Of course, the position of Qumran is *directly* the opposite. There is no mistaking this, which is why, presumably, these documents ended up in caves along the Dead Sea. No one lived to come back and retrieve them. This was the price paid for an alternative interpretation of this prophecy, the apocalyptic one of the War Scroll, recapitulated too in James' proclamation of 'the Son of Man sitting on the right hand of the Great Power and about to come on the clouds of Heaven' in the Temple on Passover, 62 CE.

The Damascus Document also signals the 'Lying' interpretation of prophecies of this kind by 'the Liar', who 'walks in the Spirit' or 'pours out windiness' and sees 'Lying visions' or 'prophesies Lying'.[102] For Rabbinic Judaism, Bar Kochba – alias *'Bar Choziba'* – is dubbed 'the Liar', because he was no Messiah as evidenced by his spectacular failure and the resulting disaster that overtook his people. Paul, who also protests so exaggeratedly that he does 'not lie', takes the safe side of things applying the 'World Ruler' Prophecy to the other-worldly Redeemer figure he calls 'the Christ'. He was not in too much jeopardy with such an interpretation, and, not surprisingly, his is the interpretation that has survived – or at least enjoyed the greatest vogue – for the last nineteen hundred years.

James' Naziritism versus Paul's

This is how important these matters are. Plus, they are intertwined with other complexities. For Eusebius, Epiphanius, and Jerome, James is a life-long Nazirite. He was also a vegetarian. As Eusebius puts it quoting Hegesippus:

> He drank no wine or strong drink, nor did he eat meat. No razor came near his head, nor did he anoint himself with oil, and he did not go to the baths.

Whatever one makes of this testimony, it certainly is that of 'a Nazirite', one either 'separated' or 'consecrated', 'Holy from his mother's womb'. In fact, it is more. The elements of 'not anointing himself with oil', 'not going to the baths', and 'not eating meat', that is, being a vegetarian, are additional to what was normally understood as Naziritism, or even for that matter, Rechabitism. Epiphanius will add the note of *abstention from sexual activity* – 'life-long virginity' as he puts it. All of these writers will add the element of 'not wearing wool, but only linen', which will have much to do with James' role in the Jerusalem of his day and his functioning as a *priest*, or the 'Opposition High Priest'.

All of these traits would appear to have to do in these descriptions with how James was 'consecrated' or 'Holy from his mother's womb' or his 'very great Holiness'. It is a not incurious parallel that Paul, in airing his differences with James in Galatians 2 – or at least 'those' messengers or representatives 'from James' – also insists, as we have seen, that God 'separated' or 'chose' him (Paul) from his 'mother's womb'. The 'some from James' materialize at various junctures in Acts or Paul's letters, where they come down to 'trouble' Paul's communities, most notably, by 'insisting on circumcision' and keeping the regime of extreme purity that would make 'table fellowship' or 'eating with Gentiles' – and thus the whole Gentile Mission – impossible.

We have already dealt with the parallels between this kind of 'separation' described by Paul and the 'separation' or regime of 'Perfect Holiness' and 'Perfection of the Way' demanded by communities such as Qumran. Not only are these phrases actually used at Qumran, they are implicit in all descriptions of James. Paul speaks about this kind of 'Nazirite from the womb' or 'consecration' in the context of speaking about how God 'chose' him in the same manner and 'revealed His son in [him]', how the Gospel, as he taught it 'among the Gentiles' or 'Peoples', was the result of a direct 'revelation of Jesus Christ' (*apocalypsin* – Gal. 1:15–16), and how if anyone preached a Gospel contrary to the one he has preached – 'even an Angel in Heaven' – 'he is to be accursed', this in the same breath as affirming his 'zealousness for the Traditions of (his) Fathers' or his 'Zealotry' (*Zēlōtēs* – 1:6–14).

Paul makes this astonishing claim, as well as others about 'not Lying' or 'seeking to please men' amid reference to 'Damascus' and 'Arabia'. Given this context, one can only assume that Paul knows well the parallel claims circulating around the person of James and chooses to emphasize his own importance by making such claims for himself. Obviously, these were made with much less justification, at least where his 'Nazirite' life-style was concerned. However, where 'brazen speaking' is concerned, as Paul himself triumphantly avers, he is nothing loath.[103]

James' Vegetarianism, Abstention from Blood, and Consuming No Wine

'Loving God', 'Things Sacrificed to Idols', and James' Vegetarianism

James' Naziritism or 'Holiness from his mother's womb' is not the only claim about James that is reversed in Paul's discussions. Whereas James clearly is said to abstain from eating meat, Paul emphasizes its consumption, or, as we have seen, in 1 Corinthians:

> Eat everything that is sold in the market place. There is no need to raise questions of conscience. (10:25)

Paul expresses this position in chapters 6–10 of 1 Corinthians, where he is patently discussing one of the categories of James' directives to overseas communities, the prohibition on 'things sacrificed to idols' (1 Cor. 8:1, 8:10, and 10:28).[1]

Not only does he preface this discussion with reference to a second of these categories, 'fornication', he uses the same 'net' language that we have already seen Balaam taught Balak 'to cast [*balein*] before the sons of Israel, to eat *things sacrificed to idols* and *commit fornication*' in Revelation and the parallel 'three nets', which Belial set up as 'three kinds of Righteousness' to ensnare Israel in the Damascus Document. In the Revelation 2:14 phraseology, this 'snare' or 'net' is literally expressed as 'scandal' or 'stumbling block'.

As Paul expresses this in 1 Corinthians 7:35:

> I say this for your own profit, not to *cast a snare* before you [*epibalō*] . . . that you might *wait upon the Lord* without distraction.

He means, as should be clear, that he is not trying to divert anyone from the Jamesian prohibition on fornication, or as he puts it 'one's virginity' (7:36–37). Here he is actually using this language with regard to another of the traits we shall see Epiphanius predicates of James, 'his virginity', that is, James life-long *virginity* (in our view, retrospectively absorbed into accounts of Mary).

It is with regard to this Paul denies trying to 'ensnare' or 'net' anyone, meaning – he is speaking equally here about both men and women – if one cannot keep the command of 'virginity' (James' life-style and possibly Jesus'), it would be better perhaps to marry. Even the language 'profit' he uses here will appear in his later discussion of 'things sacrificed to idols' in 10:28–33 and the 'waiting upon the Lord' we shall encounter in the Habakkuk *Pesher* and the Gospel of John. That, in this context, Paul knows some might have been applying the 'casting a net' aspersion to him – as elsewhere he knows they are doing the 'Lying' and the 'Enemy' epithets – is devastating.[2]

As we have seen, in the Damascus Document, the prohibition of 'fornication' is pivotal, as is 'pollution of the Temple' or, as James puts it, 'the pollutions of the idols' (Acts 15:20) related to it. This is also reflected in Paul's discussion of the 'building we have from God, a House not made with (human) hands, but Eternal in the Heavens' (2 Cor. 5:1).

In the next chapter, the command 'wherefore come out from among them', 'be separated', and not to 'touch any unclean [thing]', ends in the famous query, 'what Communion does Christ have with Beliar . . . the Temple of God with idols?' (6:15–17). Not only is this query connected to 'Righteousness and Lawlessness', pertinent to the Damascus Document's presentation of Belial's 'nets' as 'three kinds of Righteousness', it is related to the issue of unclean foods either in the Temple or in the body, both being parallel subjects in Paul's allegorizing dialectic.

For Paul, all of these subjects are interrelated and the basic answer he gives to *all* James' directives is, 'all things are Lawful for me' (1 Cor. 6:12 and 10:23). Even though, 'not all things profit' or, as he puts it in 1 Corinthians 8:1, 'build up', Paul is basically stating his position on 'freedom' and 'bondage' once again, that is, freedom from the Law or slavery to it.

The 'building' language, which he uses throughout 1 Corinthians, is fundamental to Paul's view of himself as the 'architect' or 'builder' of a Community (3:9–14). It fixes the context of the contrary kind of aspersion, as for instance, in the Habakkuk *Pesher* on the Adversary of the Righteous Teacher it calls 'the Spouter of Lying, who *led Many astray* by *building a worthless city on blood* and *erecting an Assembly on Lying*'.[3]

The reader must realize that in Paul we are dealing with one of the most able rhetoricians Western culture ever produced. Greek philosophers like Plato before him might rather have applied the epithet 'sophist' to him, from which our modern word 'sophisticated' springs, and, indeed, his method is sophistry, but it is able sophistry and extremely creative. Paul is extremely 'sophisticated' compared, for example, to some of his less able and more simplistic adversaries.

So incensed does Paul become with these adversaries, after terming persons who worry over 'reclining in an idol Temple' or 'eating things sacrificed to idols', 'weak' in 1 Corinthians 8:10, that he blurts out:

> So if meat causes offence to a brother, I shall never eat flesh again forever, so as not to offend [literally 'scandalize'] my brother. (8:13)

This is the same theme he was addressing in 1 Cor. 6:11–13, amid reference to 'being washed', 'justified', and 'made Holy', before he turned to 'fornication' and 'being *joined* to a prostitute's body' in 6:16. It culminated in the allusion to 'meats are for the belly and the belly for meats' and his oblique reference to 'the toilet drain'.

Now, following a discussion of 'loving God' (Piety), 'love building up' and his adversaries' 'weak consciences being polluted' (in 8:10, it becomes, 'weak consciences' needing 'building up'), he concludes:

> Food [literally, 'meat']4 does not commend us to God; neither if we eat, do we have any profit, nor if we do not eat, do we fall short. (8:8)

Here Paul also introduces the language of 'causing to stumble' or 'stumbling block' – 'causing offence' or 'scandalizing' in 8:13 – the same language the Letter of James used to refer to those 'who keep the whole Law, but stumble over one point, being guilty of [breaking] it all' (2:10). Now it is directed against those objecting to 'reclining in an idol Temple' and synonymous with causing 'the weak brother's fall' or even more pointedly, 'wounding their weak consciences' (8:9–12).

But who, as in the case of Balaam 'casting a net' or 'offence' (*scandalon*) in Revelation above, is Paul's strength a 'stumbling block' to or 'scandalizing' here? Who are these 'weak brothers' with 'their weak consciences' (always a euphemism for those observing the Law), who make issues over table fellowship and consuming unclean foods when these things do not matter – who worry over 'things sacrificed to idols', when they, too, do not matter?

> Then, concerning the eating of things sacrificed to idols, we know that an idol corresponds to nothing in the world and that there is no other God except One5 . . . but some with *conscience of the idol*, even now eat as of a *thing sacrificed to an idol*, and *their conscience, being weak, is polluted*. (8:4–7)

A more ingenuous discussion of the subject of 'things sacrificed to an idol' could not be imagined. This has to be seen not only as a discussion of James' directives to overseas communities, enumerated in Acts and refracted here, but also as a *direct attack* on James, even though it is delivered in the most evasive manner conceivable.

Paul discusses this theme under the aegis of the two references, to 'love' and 'building' at the beginning of the chapter in 1 Corinthians 8:1–3. As he puts it, 'Knowledge' (Greek: *Gnōsis*; at Qumran, *Da'at*), 'concerning things sacrificed to idols', 'puffs one up, but rather love builds up' (8:1). Note the sarcastic play on 'those considered important' here. We shall see a similar attack using the same language of being 'puffed up' from Habakkuk 2:4, leading up to the all-important exegesis of 'the Righteous shall live by his Faith', in the Habakkuk *Pesher*. There, as here, the language will be reversed, but used to intone: 'they shall multiply upon themselves their sins and they will not be pleased with their Judgement' – meaning *eschatological* Judgement.[6]

In particular, Paul equates the 'Knowledge' or 'knowing' such persons are showing with 'loving God' (8:3), the second of the two Love Commandments making up the Righteousness/Piety dichotomy above. Where Josephus' Essenes and John the Baptist are concerned, 'loving God', it will be recalled, is the sum total of one's obligations to God. In James 1:12 such persons are promised 'the Crown of life'; in James 2:5 it is 'the Poor' that God chose as 'heirs to the Kingdom he promised those who love him'.

A clearer attack on such a 'puffed-up' individual with 'Knowledge' – these same 'those reputed to be something' or 'Pillars' in Galatians 2:2–9, among whom Paul places James – could not be imagined. The reference to 'Knowledge' or '*Gnosis*', which Paul is clearly parodying here, also finds its counterpart in the exhortation addressed to 'all the Knowers of Righteousness' at the beginning of the Damascus Document.

Paul's Attack on James' Naziritism and Vegetarianism in Romans

Paul reinforces this 'love' theme and connects it to the 'eating' one in his Letter to the Romans, again turning both against James. Here, after referring to 'the Branches' and 'Root' in chapter 11, the 'body' and the 'members' in his version of the Sermon on the Mount in chapter 12, and his view of the 'tax' issue in 13, Paul again raises the issue of 'love'. Nothing could be more bizarre than to refer to 'good works', 'Judgement', 'loving one another', and 'conscience' in the context of allusion to *paying taxes to Rome* (Rom. 13:2–8). Paul actually quotes this second of the two Love Commandments in 13:9, 'you shall love your neighbour as yourself'. James, on the contrary, discusses it in the context of being 'a *Doer*', not 'a *Breaker*', '*keeping the whole Law*', 'Judgement without mercy' for those who don't, and condemnation of 'making oneself a Friend of the world', not a 'Friend of God'.

The Damascus Document, too, evokes this commandment, called in James 'the Royal Law according to the Scripture' and the second part of the Righteousness/Piety dichotomy. There the context is 'the New Covenant in the Land of Damascus', 'separating polluted from clean', 'setting up the Holy Things according to the precise teaching about them' (here actually employing the *consecrated to God (N–Z–R)/Holy to God* language used in reports about James' Naziritism above), 'separating from all polluted things', 'not defiling one's Holy Spirit', and 'walking in all these things in Perfect Holiness'.[7] The sense here, of course, is the exact opposite of Paul in 2 Corinthians 6:14–7:1 above on 'Christ' and '*Beliar*', also evoking 'separation' and ending with allusion to 'Perfecting Holiness in fear of God'.[8]

For Paul, however, in another tortured, yet clear riposte to James, one should:

> owe nothing to anyone, except to *love one another*, for he who *loves the other has fulfilled the Law* . . . Love does not work any ill to one's neighbour, therefore love is the fulfilment of the Law. (Rom. 13:8–10)

This too has become part and parcel of Jesus' teaching in Scripture. Continuing in this vein, Paul again raises the issues of eating and foods, turning them around, as per his wont, from the Jamesian position:

> Do not let the one who eats despise the one who does not eat . . . do not *put a stumbling block, a cause of offence*, before your brother . . . I know and am persuaded in the Lord Jesus that *nothing is unclean in and of itself – except to him who judges things to be unclean*. To him it is unclean. But if, on account of meat, your brother is aggrieved, you are no longer walking according to love. Do not with your meat destroy him . . . do not destroy *the work of God for the sake of meat*. (Rom. 14:3–20)

Almost all the themes we have been following can be found in these words. Not only does Paul combine the 'stumbling' language with that of 'scandalizing'/'giving offence', he also evokes that 'judging' so important in the Letter of James, and descriptive of 'the *Mebakker*' at Qumran. Also the 'walking' language, so fundamental to Qumran, is reversed (compare this to James speaking to Paul in Acts 21:25's 'We Document', 'that all may know . . . you yourself also walk regularly keeping the Law'), as is the language of 'works', the Damascus Document itself being addressed to these same 'Knowers of Righteousness, who understand the works of God'.[9]

That Paul is discussing in this context the issue of 'consuming meat' is irrefutable. In so doing, he inadvertently expresses the opinion, clearly his own basic one:

> One believes he may eat all things; another, *being weak, eats* [*only*] *vegetables.* (13:2)

That this is an attack on James seems also almost irrefutable. That its author is cloaking the issue in an attempt to appear accommodating should also be clear. But the basic position here does, once again, redound to the situation of James' vegetarianism. For Paul, again being about as insulting as he can be, this is just *weakness*. His basic position is that such things do not matter, that *all* the food, as he has told us, in the market place *is clean*.

So, once again, we may see that these traditions about James, preserved via Hegesippus in Eusebius, Jerome, and others, do, in fact, have substance behind them. It is clear, as well, that these had to do with the manner in which James was seen as 'Holy' or 'consecrated from his mother's womb', or a certain concept of being a life-long Nazirite or Naziritism that seems to have been important to the Jerusalem Assembly and even early Christianity as a whole.

This ideology is also reflected to a certain extent in the background to Paul's last conflict with James and his 'Jerusalem Assembly' in the climax of Acts in chapters 21–23, when Paul is mobbed on the Temple Mount and unceremoniously ejected from its precincts. It is patent that this ejection has to do with the accusation of introducing Gentiles or their sacrifices into the Temple precincts, a burning issue both in the 'Zealot' claims against the collaborating High Priesthood and similar complaints in the Dead Sea Scrolls.

That Paul makes the same claim as James – being 'separated' from his mother's womb – for himself, while all the time adopting the very opposite position to him on the issue of 'separation of clean from unclean', makes all these allusions all the more interesting, and his position regarding them all the more disingenuous.

Not only then do we have, in this passage in Paul's Letter to the Romans, collateral verification of James' vegetarianism – insisted on in all the ancient sources – but also something of the reason for it. This, undoubtedly, had to do with following a regime of extreme purity or, as both Paul and the Damascus Document from Qumran put it, of 'Perfect Holiness' or 'Perfection of the Way', and this, in turn, was related to – however obliquely – the issue of accepting or rejecting *polluted gifts and sacrifices in the Temple*.

Pollution in the Wilderness Camps

Similar concerns are in evidence at Qumran, at least where the issue of *gifts* and *sacrifices in the Temple* is concerned. John the Baptist, even in the fragmented and garbled accounts that have come down to us, would seem to have had tendencies in this direction, and we have seen this in the notices from Luke about 'drinking no wine and eating no bread [meat]' above. The problem in John the Baptist's case is the idea, propounded in the other Synoptics – not surprisingly completely missing from Luke – that he ate 'locusts' (Matt. 3:4 and Mark 1:6). If he did, he probably would not have survived very long in the area around the Jordan River and the east side of the Dead Sea he is pictured as having inhabited.

There is little testimony to this from other sources about John, and it has been suggested that the word 'locusts' is based on a garbling from either the Hebrew or Aramaic into the Greek.[10] A similar problem is encountered in Acts' picture of another of James' directives to overseas communities, 'to abstain from strangled things', also seemingly a garbled translation of some kind. One suggestion is that John ate 'carobs'; there have been others. Epiphanius, in preserving what he calls 'the Ebionite Gospel', rails against the passage there claiming John ate 'wild honey' and 'manna-like vegetarian cakes dipped in oil'.[11]

Regardless of translation problems and mistransliteration from one language to another, it is pretty sure that John would have been one of these wilderness-dwelling, vegetable-eating persons Josephus regards as either impostors, magicians, or Deceivers, fomenting revolt under the guise of religious 'Innovation'. Josephus says as much in his description of John in the *Antiquities* – though his treatment of John is much gentler than is his normal wont. This is also the inference to be drawn from Luke's testimony, including even the note about his being Holy 'from his mother's womb' (1:15).[12]

As it turns out, one of the first of these vegetarian, insurgent or subversive leaders was Judas Maccabee himself. 2 Maccabees 5:27, in its picture of the founding moment of Judas Maccabee's revolutionary activities – also in the wilderness – in 167 BC, has this to say:

> Judas, called Maccabaeus, however, with about nine others, *withdrew into the wilderness* and lived like wild animals in the hills with his companions, *eating nothing but wild plants to avoid contracting defilement.*

If one is prepared to take it at face value, this statement just about says everything where these wilderness-dwelling 'Zealots' were concerned, and one has in this notice much of what was behind such behaviour in this period, the issue once again being 'contracting defilement' or 'pollution' from unclean persons.

Judas Maccabee, as we have seen, was the primary leader behind the great Jewish National Liberation struggle of the second century BC, commemorated by the festivities Jews refer to as *Hanukkah* – meaning *dedication* or *rededication of the Temple*. 1 Maccabees presents Judas dividing the responsibility for these events with other members of his family, the progenitor of which and the purveyor of the archetypal 'Covenant of Phineas' being his father, Mattathias or Matthias – the namesake of the 'Matthias' in the Acts' picture of the election to *replace Judas* we connected with James' succession to *his* brother above.

1 Maccabees is what might be called family history, but this episode about Judas' *vegetarian* diet and his *wilderness* life-style is missing from it. 2 Maccabees, though considered inferior by some because of its patent miracle tales, presents the events solely from the point of view of Judas himself. It is not particularly interested in other family members and does not mention the patronymic ancestor 'Matthias' at all.

For 2 Maccabees, Judas is the legitimate successor to the previous High Priestly line, which was destroyed because of local intervention by a *foreign power*, in this instance, the Seleucid heirs of Alexander the Great, whose capital not surprisingly was *Antioch*. Judas is a kind of Messianic Priest–King of the kind Jesus is presented as being in later literature. This probably explains Judas' vegetarianism, as it does John the Baptist's, if we see John in succession to Judas as an insurgent, Prophet-like leader demanding a Priesthood of greater purity devoid of pollution by foreigners.

For Judas, *the Temple has been polluted* – a charge we shall encounter over and over again in Qumran literature, and to a certain extent echoed, as we have seen, in this early Christian literature. The sacrifice in the

Temple has been polluted, then halted. In the time of John the Baptist, 'the Zealots', James, and Qumran, this will be seen as being because of the acceptance of gifts and sacrifices on behalf of or by Gentiles in the Temple.

Something of this picture even emerges in the account of Paul's unceremonious ejection from the Temple after James imposes the *Nazirite*-style penance upon him in Acts 21:23–24. This episode actually connects the problem of *Temple pollution* to the *admission of Gentiles in the Temple*: 'He has brought Greeks into the Temple and polluted this Holy Place' (21:28) – a matter very much argued over in this period, as the erection of inscribed stone warning-markers in the Temple barring foreigners from the Temple on pain of death verifies. Two of these have since been found.[13]

Whether by accident or design, Acts 21:30 actually employs a variation of the words the Damascus Document uses to deal with the allied issue of 'separating from the Sons of the Pit and keeping away from [*lehinnazer*] polluted, Evil Riches . . . and from the Temple Treasury'.[14] The words used in the latter – quoting Malachi 1:10 – are 'bar the door'; in the former, they 'shut the doors' behind Paul. In fact, in Acts 24:6, when the charges relative to this episode are brought before the Roman Governor Felix, in addition to being 'a ringleader of the sect of Nazoraeans fomenting rebellion among all the Jews in the inhabited world', Paul is accused – this time by 'Tertullus' – of 'attempting to pollute the Temple', the very words used in the Damascus Document's Three Nets of Belial charges to attack the Establishment. Only now the Establishment is directing them against Paul.

In the picture of events surrounding Judas Maccabee's 'wilderness' sojourn, 'the Abomination of the Desolation', referred to in Daniel and so much a part of New Testament predictions ascribed to Jesus, has been set up in the Temple by the invading Seleucid King, Antiochus Epiphanes, thereby desecrating it. Antiochus is generally acknowledged to be 'the Eleventh Horn' with evil 'eyes and a mouth full of boasts' in Daniel's apocalyptic presentation of these momentous events (7:20). He is referred to in similar manner in both 1 and 2 Maccabees.[15]

In this 'Abomination of the Desolation', we probably have a Hebrew play on a Greek name, in this case characterizing the statue of the Olympian Zeus that we know Antiochus erected in the Temple – or what was left of it. So not only is the Temple in ruins and abandoned, but *polluting idols have been erected in it*. This is the background to Judas' 'wilderness vegetarianism'. Again the point revolves around extreme purity regulations. Judas should be seen as not simply a warrior, but a 'Priestly Zealot' of sorts – one probably observing as well the extreme purity regulations of the Nazirite regimen or at least the one connected to Holy War. The two are not very different in any case.

For elucidation of this, the War Scroll at Qumran is probably one of our best guides. Here the picture is very simple, *extreme purity regulations are in effect in the wilderness camps* – new texts in recently released Qumran documents show these camps undeniably to have been real – because the Heavenly 'Holy Ones', the Angelic Host of Daniel and other prophetic visionaries, were seen to 'be with' the Holy warriors in these camps. As the War Scroll vividly puts it:

> No boy or woman shall enter their camps from the time of their leaving Jerusalem to go to war until their return. And no one who is lame, blind, crippled, or a man who has a lasting bodily sore in his flesh or is afflicted with pollution in his body – all of these shall not go with them to war, but rather, all of them shall be men *voluntarily enlisted for war* and *Perfect in Spirit and body* [here our 'Perfection' ideology again]. And no man who is *sexually impure* on the day of war shall go down with them, *because the Holy Angels are together with their hosts.*[16]

This is the picture of the 'wilderness camps' described in the literature found at Qumran. The categories of persons barred from these Holy 'camps': blind, lame, the crippled, or sexually impure, are just the categories of persons Jesus is pictured as having repeated intercourse with in the Gospels.

'The High Priest commanding' these 'camps' – a kind of High Priestly battle priest – rules in conjunction with 'the *Mebakker*', whom we have already identified as a kind of *Overseer* or *Bishop*.[17] Extreme purity regulations, associated with such regimens of temporary or life-long Naziritism, wilderness sojourns, or the kind of wilderness-camp regime described at Qumran, are, doubtlessly, also connected with what is implied under the notion of 'the *Zaddik*' or 'Righteous One' in this period. It also helps to understand the ideology behind this vegetarianism, the conception behind which is comparatively simple and straightforward.

The First *Zaddik* Noah and Being 'Called by Name'

Both vegetarianism and the '*Zaddik*' ideal go back to the Noah story in Genesis, the first *Zaddik* in the Bible. In this episode, Noah is described as 'Righteous and Perfect in his generation', and because of this – and for Jewish mystical ideology ever after – the first soteriological redeemer figure for mankind ('soteriological' in this context meaning one 'who saves'). Not only is Noah the first '*Zaddik*', but the scriptural warrant for a second ideology, so dear to the Second Temple theorist and basic to Qumran vocabulary, presents itself – 'Perfection'. This is very often missing from Rabbinic ideology, but it is a concept Jesus is pictured as teaching in the Sermon on the Mount in the Gospel of Matthew: 'Therefore, you should be Perfect as your Father in Heaven is Perfect' (5:48).

Earlier Jesus put this: 'Unless your Righteousness *exceeds* that of the Scribes and Pharisees, you shall in no wise enter the Kingdom of Heaven.' Coupled with this last is the anti-Pauline and James-like condemnation on 'Whoever shall break the least one of these Commandments and teach men to do so shall be called *least in the Kingdom of the Heavens*' (5:19–20). Noah saves mankind because of his 'Righteousness' and 'Perfection', and all mankind is descended from his descendants – at least this is the mythological structure of Genesis the bibliophiles of the Second Temple Period seem to have been so enamoured of.

The Book of Ecclesiasticus – also called *Ben Sira* after the name of its author, Jesus Ben Sira – in its famous enumeration of 'the Pious Men' (*Anshei-Hesed*) presents Noah as 'the *Zaddik*' (44:17 – again the Righteousness/Piety dichotomy). This praise includes Phineas and his 'zeal for the Lord', and ends, at least in the Hebrew version, with an evocation of 'the Sons of Zadok'.[18] This book was originally known only through a Greek recension. Then a Hebrew version was found in the Cairo *Genizah*, the repository in old Cairo where Solomon Schechter first found the copies of the Damascus Document so interesting to us today. Since that time, Hebrew fragments of it have also been found, of all places, among the few documents found at Masada and, of course, at Qumran.

In Rabbinic literature Noah is so highly thought of that, in order to explain what was meant by the allusion to 'Perfect' with regard to him, it was contended that Noah was 'born circumcised'![19] Not only does this show the high regard in which he was held and primitive attempts to wrestle with the 'Perfection' ideology, but not even Christianity went so far as to make such claims for Jesus, a successor among these primordial Righteous Ones who are presented in the literature as Supernatural Redeemer figures.[20]

Noah, of course, is also a very important figure in the Qumran literature, as he is all apocalyptic literature, apocryphal or sectarian. The Damascus Document, in introducing its view of pre-existence, foreknowledge, and predestination, puts the proposition as follows:

> He [God] knew their works before they were created and he hated their generations . . . And He knew the years of their *Standing* and the number and the meaning of their Eras for all Eternal being and existences, until that which would come in their Eras for all the years of Eternity. And in all of them He raised for Himself *men called by Name* that a remnant might survive in the Land and fill the face of the earth with their seed. And *He made known to them His Holy Spirit by the hand of His Messiah*, and He [it] is Truth, and *in the correct exposition of His Name, their names [are to be found]*, and those whom He hates, *He leads astray.*
>
> And now, my sons, listen to me and I will uncover your eyes that [you may] see and understand *the works of God* ['he that has eyes let him see' in Gospel formulation] in order to choose that which pleases [Him] and reject that which He hates, in order *to walk Perfectly in all His ways* . . . They were caught in them [the 'nets' or sins], because they did not keep the Commandments of God . . . All flesh on dry land perished; they were as though they had never been because they *did their own will* and did not *keep the Commandments of their Maker.*[21]

There is so much in these lines that is relevant to a discussion of the differences between Paul and James, but for the purposes of economy, one should note the allusion to the 'Holy Spirit', which is being revealed 'by the hand of His Messiah' (the usage here is singular)[22] and the strong emphasis on both 'keeping' and 'doing the Commandments', also found in the commandments of Jonadab son of Rechab to *his* descendants.

This same dichotomy is also strong in the Letter of James, as it is in Qumran literature generally when it comes to defining what is meant by a true 'Son of Zadok'. The actual definition of this term – aside from the more eschatological one that follows in the Damascus Document – provided by the Community Rule is, as we have seen, 'the Keepers of the Covenant' (*Shomrei ha-Brit*). This is the synonym, of course, for the terminology 'Nozrei ha-Brit' – again 'the Keepers' or 'Observers of the Covenant'. In both contexts, 'the *Nozrim*' or the 'Nazoraeans' are 'Keepers of the

Covenant', the exact oppposite of what we now after two millennia of Pauline dogma consider 'Nazrenes' or followers of Jesus *the Nazarean* to be.

All of this, of course, is very esoteric, but what the Damascus Document is doing in these introductory columns – among other things – is describing just what a true 'Son of Zadok' is and what he is conceived of as *doing*. Therefore the document is often referred to as the 'Zadokite Document', which, were it not for another of its esotericisms – 'the New Covenant in the Land of Damascus' – might be a better name for it. Either will do, because the 'Damascus' issue is also germane to any discussion of early Christianity in Palestine.

Noah, therefore, is one of these primordial or true 'Sons of Zadok', in fact, with the possible exception of Adam, the first of these. He is also the first *Zaddik*, 'keeping Faith in' and 'making atonement for the land'.[23] We see in this something of the 'Pillar' ideology, applied in Galatians by Paul to James, and its variation, the 'Bulwark' or 'Protection' metaphor, associated in early Church accounts with his being.

The Damascus Document also speaks in terms of being 'called by Name' when discussing these primordial Righteous Ones of the stature or importance of Noah.[24] In the Book of Genesis this power of 'naming' is attributed to Adam (2:20). As Muhammad puts this in his own inimitable way in the Koran, 'And God taught Adam all the names.'[25] Acts, too, is very interested in 'naming', the power of which it associates with Jesus – who for Paul in 1 Corinthians 15:45–47 is 'the Second Man' or 'Last Adam'. Acts, as well as the Pseudoclementines, is very interested in the saving Power of 'the Name Jesus' (4:12),[26] and it uses this vocabulary right from the start where the activities of the Jerusalem 'Pillar' Apostles are being described, among whom we should include James (2:21, 3:16, etc.).

Some would call such 'Power' magic, which is, of course, one of the accusations Josephus levels against many of these subversive leaders and impostors, who he claims are disturbing the well-being of the nation, that is, they are magicians. However one chooses to comprehend all of these things, Noah clearly had an extraordinary significance where one is coming to grips with the '*Zaddik*' ideal and the person of James who will come to embody it.

In the *Zohar*, where the passage from Proverbs about 'the *Zaddik* the Pillar of the World' is being analysed, Noah acted, as we saw, as to be a true copy of the Heavenly ideal, 'an embodiment of the world's Covenant of Peace'. Ben Sira also vouchsafes this Noahic 'Covenant of Peace' to the archetypal embodiment of the 'Zealot' High Priest, Phineas, as well as his descendants, including the later 'Sons of Zadok'.[27] Whatever one might think of the historical roots of the *Zohar* in thirteenth-century Spain, statements of this kind certainly are instructive, especially when one looks at the Dead Sea Scrolls.

The significance of this is amplified in the section called 'Phineas' towards the end of the *Zohar*, where its author, as we have seen, shows familiarity with the 'suffering *Zaddik*' ideology. As the *Zohar* puts it:

> When God desires to send healing to the Earth, He smites one Righteous One . . . with suffering . . . to make atonement . . . and sometimes all his days are passed in suffering to *Protect the People*.[28]

Despite its appearance over a thousand years after the early Church accounts about James' pre-eminent 'Righteousness', statements like this have a peculiar prescience. For instance, the very term used here, 'Protection of the People', will appear when James' '*Zaddik*' nature is delineated in these passages Eusebius is citing from Hegesippus.

1 Peter, for instance, another letter replete with Qumran imagery and vocabulary, is very much concerned with the idea of 'suffering for Righteousness' sake' (2:19–3:14). In speaking of this, it too evokes Noah and the Flood, which it identifies with 'being saved by water', imagery it will then use to propound the new Christian ideal of baptism (3:20–21). But this letter, which is addressed to 'the Elect Sojourners in the *Diaspora* . . . of Asia' – note the 'Rechabite' language of 'sojourning' again – also knows the language of 'being foreknown before the Foundation of the world, but manifested at the Last Times' (1:20), 'the Precious Cornerstone' (2:7), 'the Name of Christ' (4:19), 'making Perfect' (5:10), and

> the living stones being *built up into a spiritual House,* a Holy Priesthood to offer *spiritual sacrifices pleasing to God.* (1 Pet. 2:5)[29]

Like the 'suffering *Zaddik*' idea in the *Zohar* above, this is paralleled almost word for word in the language of spiritualized 'atonement' and 'Temple' applied to the members of the Council of the Community in the Community Rule at Qumran. One should also take note of the repeated emphasis on the Commandment 'to be Holy' and 'being Holy in all your works' throughout 1 Peter (1:15–16), which we shall ultimately see evolve into a Priesthood for James.

Finally, 1 Peter 5:8 talks about 'the Enemy' (which it identifies with the

Greek *'Diabolos'* notation) in terms of his 'swallowing up' – language and imagery we shall see to be absolutely fundamental at Qumran and the destruction of the Righteous Teacher delineated there. It also speaks of the beauty of 'the Hidden Man of the heart' (3:4). Not only does this language about the *'Zaddik'* ideal and *'Noah'* being an embodiment of 'the world's Covenant of Peace' link up with the parallel imagery of 'the Primal Adam' or 'Secret Man' ideology in Eastern tradition – referred to by Paul in 1 Corinthians 15:45–47 above – but as these move west they become fixed in the Hellenistic notion of 'the Christ'.

Abstention from Blood

In addition to explaining Noah's 'Perfection' – as is so often the case, *in physical terms not spiritual ones* – Rabbinic Judaism also sets forth a general Covenant in his name, 'the Noahic Covenant'. The ideology behind this Covenant is presented in various places in the *Talmud*, but its main thrust has to do with what is expected by God of all mankind, irrespective of national grouping; since, because of the Flood, Noah not Adam becomes the new father of mankind. Noah is presented in this literature, therefore, as setting forth the basic laws that all men are obliged to follow *qua* men, even if they do not come under the Mosaic Covenant.[30]

However, according to the logic of this presentation, the Mosaic Covenant or the Laws supposedly given Moses *applied to Jews only*, that is, *people born under this Covenant*. This is a very important distinction. Paul in his letters is very interested in the ramifications of such thinking, since he has turned to groups theoretically coming under the terms of what the Rabbis would refer to as 'the Noahic Covenant'. Paul is anxious to emphasize that his communities should *not* come under the Mosaic Covenant, that, contrary to what seems to have been the position of the Jerusalem Leadership, they should not allow themselves *to be circumcised*; for then they would come under the terms of the Mosaic Covenant, in particular the Law – circumcision being the sign of the Covenant (Gal. 5:1–9). All this, no doubt, strikes the modern reader as somewhat arcane, but these were *real* issues and the real, burning and bitter arguments that were going on at the time.

In the Old Testament presentation, Noah and his family obviously could not have eaten meat, because if they had, there would have been *no* animals left to populate the earth. Again, it should be emphasized, these points may seem silly, but for those people – ancient and modern – who habitually confuse literature or story-telling with reality, these become the terms of the debate. There is also the problem in the Old Testament narrative as it has come down to us of whether Noah had seven kinds of the clean animals and only a pair of all unclean or a pair of all. This discrepancy is generally acknowledged to be based on the two text lines that are thought to compose the Noah story and the fact that a bright redactor realized at some point that, if Noah sacrificed some of these animals at the end of the Flood when he finally regained dry land, as one line avers, then there would have been none left of that species to repopulate the world. This is true and, if nothing else, illustrates the problem of taking archetype and story literally or confusing them *with fact*.

Whatever the conclusion here, Noah is certainly pictured as making a sacrifice and concluding a compact of sorts with God. In this, God promises not to destroy the earth again – or as He puts it, 'not to curse the earth again on account of man' (Gen. 8:21). By the end of the second narrative of these events, this has been magnified into a 'Covenant'. This is the 'Covenant' that Rabbis and others at the end of the Second Temple Period are so intent on explaining and giving substance to.

In the course of these matters, Noah, as we have seen, is pictured as, firstly, making a sacrifice from the clean animals and birds which propitiates God and, secondly, being given leave *to consume flesh* or *meat*. The only caveat that God is pictured as making is that mankind was 'not to eat *the blood of flesh with life in it*' (Gen. 9:4). Of course, Jews to this day have taken this as the scriptural warrant for a whole complex of legislation involving the killing, preparation, and eating of animal life, and, in particular, the abstention from *consuming blood* – the life of the slaughtered animal being considered to be in the blood and therefore not consumable. In Islam, the situation is more or less the same. In Christianity, following the dialectic of Paul in Romans and 1 Corinthians above, this concern has gone by the boards.

But this was *not* the case for early Christianity in Palestine. It was quite the opposite. All of these matters contributed to the issues discussed above under the rubric of 'table fellowship with Gentiles'. The same is true in the Dead Sea Scrolls – in particular, the Damascus Document. In the discourse beginning with the above material requiring 'walking in Perfection in all His ways', 'keeping the Commandments of God', and the revelation of 'the Holy Spirit by the hand of His Messiah', the reason given for why the children of Israel were 'cut off' after the Mosaic period was that 'they ate *blood* . . . in the wilderness' – 'each man *doing* what was right in his own eyes'.[31]

Whereas Paul will utilize this language of 'cutting off' to make an obscene pun about cutting off one's sexual parts in circumcision (Gal. 5:12), for the Damascus Document at this point, Abraham and the other 'Keepers of the Covenant' are designated 'Friends' or 'Beloved of God'. This is exactly the language the Letter of James uses, when arguing with its interlocutor or spiritual adversary – the man teaching that Abraham was rather 'justified by his Faith' not works (Gal. 3:6–29). Speaking to this Adversary, the Letter of James points out:

> Don't you realize you Empty Man that *Faith without works* is useless. You surely know that Abraham our father *was justified by works* . . . You see that *Faith was working with works* and that *by works Faith was Perfected*. And the Scripture was fulfilled which says, 'Now Abraham believed God and it was reckoned to him as Righteousness, and he was called *Friend of God*'. (Jas. 2:20–23)

This scriptural warrant from Genesis 15:6 is also a cornerstone of Paul's famous discussions in Galatians 3:6 and Romans 4:3, but of course with exactly opposite intent.

This notion of 'blood' and consuming it, is, therefore, one that exercises those responsible for the literature at Qumran to no small degree. In other documents Qumran refers to how 'the Spouter of Lying led Many astray to build a Worthless City upon blood' and 'a City of Blood' quite derogatorily.[32] We shall have occasion to connect allusions such as these with Paul's innovative doctrine, 'Communion with the Blood of Christ' and his reinterpretation of 'the New Covenant' in 1 Corinthians 10–11. Luke adds, as we saw, the slightly differing twist, 'this is the New Covenant in my blood, which was poured out for you' (22:20).

Certainly 'pouring out' the blood was a fixture of all Jewish ritual practice, as it has become to some extent for Muslims. Even in stories about Abraham's sacrifice of Isaac, which James 2:21 evokes to support its position on Abraham 'being justified by works' (in Islam this becomes the sacrifice of Ishmael), there is no intimation that the consumption of his blood was permitted even symbolically. In this Noah episode in Genesis, as we saw, it is expressly forbidden:

> You shall not eat the blood of flesh with life in it. I will demand an account of your lifeblood. I will demand an account from every beast and from man. I will demand an account of every man's life from his fellow man. (9:4–5)

When the Damascus Document ascribes the 'cutting off' of the Children of Israel 'in the wilderness' to the 'consumption of blood', the reference is to Numbers 11:31–32 and how the Children of Israel ate quail there. While neither the authors of Exodus 16:30 or Psalm 105:40 – which also refer to this episode – regard eating this quail in a negative manner, but rather an illustration of God's solicitude for Israel, Numbers does. For its part, the Damascus Document is so incensed about 'consuming blood' that it deliberately highlights this episode, adding the words they 'were led astray in these things' and 'complained against *the Commandments of God*'.[33]

In the Genesis narrative, in some sense the permission to eat meat would appear to have been tied up with the sacrifice Noah made after the Flood, that is, it was only after this sacrifice that, for the Second Temple mind anyhow, it was permissible to eat meat again. Once again, to repeat, Noah and those with him clearly did not consume meat during the period of the Flood and their incarceration in the ark. With Noah's atoning sacrifice, they were free to eat meat once again with the caveat that they *abstain from blood*.

'Pleasing Men' or 'Friendship to the World' in Paul and James

Two conclusions emerge from this. The first has to do with James' instructions to overseas communities; the second, Paul's *modus operandi*. James' directives to overseas communities are presented in three different versions in Acts.[34] They are presented there as a result of what is usually called 'the Jerusalem Council'. This episode begins in Acts 15:1 with the laconic note that:

> Some, having come down from Judea, were teaching the brothers: 'Unless you are circumcised according to the custom of Moses, you cannot be saved.' A commotion, thereupon, ensued and much discussion . . . and Paul and Barnabus and certain others were appointed to go up to . . . Jerusalem [and inquire] about this question.

One should note the ubiquitous 'some' again and the focus on 'being saved' or 'Salvation'.

As usual, Acts portrays the reception Paul and Barnabas receive in Jerusalem as a joyous one. All of this is, of course, totally counter-indicated in Paul's account in Galatians – if we can take the two accounts as parallel – where Paul, as we have seen, claims that he went up to Jerusalem on his own initiative or as a result of a private 'revelation'. It was only *after* these rulings or an agreement of some kind that Paul informs us that these ubiquitous 'some' are 'from James' and reveals that they were 'of [the party of] the circumcision' (Gal. 2:12). Acts has completely reversed the series of events, portraying the effects as the cause; nor is it clear that Paul's reception in Jerusalem, after the fourteen-year absence described in Galatians, was all that joyful.

Be these things as they may, the upshot of the conference, as portrayed from Acts' point of view, begins with the Damascus Document-style introduction: 'God has known his works from all eternity', but, whereas in the Damascus Document the allusion is to being 'called by Name' (this applied to 'the Elect of Israel'), for Acts it is now rather 'the Gentiles upon whom My Name has been called' (15:16–17). James is clearly presented as making the kind of 'Judgements' predicated of 'the *Mebakker*' in the Damascus Document above. He 'rules':

> Therefore I judge, we should not trouble those Gentiles turning to God, but write to them to abstain from the *pollutions of idols* [cf. 2 Corinthians 6:16 above], from *fornication*, and from what is strangled and from *blood*. (15:19–20)

In the 'epistle' that Acts pictures James as sending to Antioch via 'Judas Barsabas', this is slightly rephrased as 'abstain from things sacrificed to idols and from blood, and from what is strangled and fornication' (15:29). Six chapters later, Acts 21:25 repeats the phraseology of this second version in its picture of James' final confrontation with Paul and the culmination of the speech James makes to Paul, reiterating what Gentile believers are 'to observe' and 'keep away from' (note the Rechabite/Nazirite thrust of these two usages).

At this point, James sends Paul into the Temple to have himself 'purified' and his 'head shaved', along with the four others evidently under a Nazirite oath of some kind as we have seen. In this connection, Paul was to pay all their expenses, he obviously being deemed to have quite a good deal more money than they had. For Acts 21:24, the reason James gives for this penance, as we saw too, is simple, but extremely significant in view of all the themes we have been discussing in this context: so that 'all may know that the things they have been told about you are not so, but that you yourself also walk regularly keeping the Law'.

We have already encountered the use of the phrase 'walking in the Way'. It is, of course, a widespread mode of expression at Qumran –

'keeping the Law' being the basis of the definition of 'the Sons of Zadok' in the Community Rule at Qumran, and we have also just encountered it in the definition of the 'Friends of God' in the Damascus Document above, an expression we should also, therefore, now group among these several parallel allusions.

It is, of course, a key usage in the Letter of James introducing the attack on the 'Empty Man' and the basis of the attack on the 'Breakers of the Law' there (2:8–2:14). But of course, as we know, Paul does no such thing. He does not 'keep the Law' – or, if he does, he does so only as a convenience or to further his mission. Paul's view of the Law is succinctly given in Galatians. It is 'a curse' (3:10–13).

The Letter of James follows up this attack on 'breaking the Law' by playing, as we saw, on both the theme of Abraham as a 'Friend of God' (a leitmotif too in Islam – in succession to non-orthodox Christianity) and Paul's use of 'Abraham's Faith being reckoned as Righteousness'. As will be recalled, Paul uses this passage from Genesis 15:6 to underscore his 'Justification by Faith' ideology and his total break with Jewish or Mosaic Law preceding him.[35] But Islam goes further. Picking up Paul's 'Faith' ideology, it has transformed his use of the Abraham model into an attack not only on the Mosaic tradition, but on Christianity too. Just as Paul uses Abraham in Romans and Galatians to develop the position that, though Abraham *came before* Moses and the Law, he was nevertheless 'saved' in some manner; for Muhammad, 'Abraham's Religion' *came before both* Judaism and Christianity, and Islam is just a return to Abraham's original monotheism.

For Paul, 'Abraham was justified' or 'saved by his Faith', and the 'Faith in Christ Jesus' he is preaching and that of his new converts is 'Abraham's Faith'. Because of this, they are all 'Sons of', or 'Children of Abraham'; whereas for Muhammad (a 'True Prophet' to the Gentiles or Peoples), his people, the Arabs, need not evoke being *spiritualized* heirs of Abraham, as Paul's Hellenistic converts must – 'grafts upon the tree' as Paul so deftly puts it in Romans – but rather, taking his cue from Ishmael's genealogy in Genesis, they are *actual* physical descendants or 'heirs'.

The difference, however, is that in true *Jamesian* style, Muhammad has combined this with an extreme 'works–Righteousness' approach. As the Koran repeatedly commands in its capsule descriptions of Islam, 'believe and do good works', including even a James-like emphasis on 'doing' also typical of Qumran. Nothing could better epitomize the

Jamesian insistence – in rebuking the 'Empty Man' – on Abraham's 'Faith and works working together' than this (Jas. 2:20–23).

As the Letter of James, also, goes on to put it after attacking 'the Tongue' as a 'world of Unrighteousness' and 'little member, which boasts great things' – note the play on Paul's idea of being 'one member' of 'the members of one body' in 1 Corinthians 12:14–27:

> But if you have bitter jealousy and *contentiousness in your heart*, do not boast and *lie against the Truth*. This is not the wisdom that comes down from above, but earthly, beastly, demonic . . . He who speaks against his brother and who judges his brother speaks *against the Law* and *judges the Law*. But if you judge the Law, you are not a *Doer of [the] Law*, but a judge (Jas. 3:5–4:11).

In the course of this rebuke, James insists, in one of its most telling formulations: 'Don't you know that *making the world your Friend* makes God your Enemy. Whosoever chooses the world for his Friend turns himself into an *Enemy of God*' (4:4). So telling is this attack, all based on the 'Friend' theme and playing on Paul's evocation of Abraham as 'the Friend' or 'Beloved of God',[36] that it is one of the most instructive and insightful allusions in the history of this period.

The use of this expression 'Enemy of God' is characteristic of the Ebionite terminology as applied to Paul. The best example of this is in the attack on James in the Temple by 'the Enemy' Paul in the *Recognitions* above.[37] Paul himself shows awareness that some were applying the epithet of 'the Enemy' to him in early Christian history, when he asks in Galatians 4:16, 'Have I your Enemy become, by speaking Truth to you?' In this, he also shows cognizance of the 'Lying' epithet – an epithet also reflected in this 'Tongue' imagery here in James – being applied to 'the Liar' in Dead Sea Scrolls, as he did earlier when speaking of 'James the brother of the Lord' in Galatians 1:19–20.

In Galatians 4:17–25 this leads directly into an attack on 'those who are zealous' – 'to exclude' others – and the Mosaic Covenant on 'Mount Sinai in Arabia', 'bringing forth slavery'.[38] It is interesting that here too he uses the 'casting out' language (*ekballō*), that Josephus' 'Essenes' apply to their miscreants and the Gospels apply to the 'authority' Jesus gives his principal Apostles: 'cast out the slave woman and her son', not the free one born according to the Promise and the Spirit, 'which things are all allegorized'. Here, too, Paul is talking about Abraham's two wives 'Agar' and Sarah and their two sons, Isaac and Ishmael.

The 'making oneself a Friend to the world' – the very opposite activity of 'making oneself a Friend of God' as a real son of Abraham should – and the accusations in James against the Tongue as 'boasting', of course, relate to much in Paul's letters, particularly when Paul himself is describing his achievements.[39]

In 1 Corinthians, the letter in which Paul announces himself as the 'architect' or 'builder' and wrestles with James' directives to overseas communities leading up to enunciation of the doctrine of Communion with the blood of Christ, Paul presents the philosophy of his working method such as it is. Some might call it cynical or self-serving. Those to whom it recommends itself would merely call it pragmatic, but, as we shall see, there can be very little pragmatism in dealing with the Jerusalem Church Leadership or individuals at Qumran like 'the *Mebakker*' or 'High Priest Commanding the Many' and those inhabiting the wilderness camps. They saw things in black and white.

Paul states in 1 Corinthians 9:4, clearly in response to these and other kinds of charges, after having just dealt with the twin issues of 'things sacrificed to idols' and vegetarianism: 'My defence to those who examine me is this: "Have we not [the] authority to eat and drink?"' – this directly preceding a reference to 'the brothers of the Lord and Cephas' (9:5). Here it should, once again, be appreciated that the role of 'the *Mebakker*' at Qumran was to 'examine' people and make 'Judgements'.

Then Paul turns again to the issues of boasting, authority, and freedom:

> Not that I boast of preaching the Gospel, since it is a duty which has been laid on me . . . for being *free from all*, I made myself *the slave of all* so as to *win the most*. And to the Jews, I became as a Jew *to win the Jews*. To those under the Law, I who am *not a subject of the Law*, made myself a subject to the Law, to win those who are subjects of the Law. To those without the Law, I was free of the Law myself – though not free from God's Law being under the Law of Christ – to win those without the Law. For the weak I made myself weak. To all these, I made myself all things to all men that by all means some I might save. (1 Cor. 9:16–22)

No clearer philosophy of 'making oneself a Friend to the world' has ever been so baldly or unabashedly put on record. In fact, in announcing this philosophy of 'winning', Paul has perhaps identified himself as *the first modern man*. It only remains for his interlocutor in the Letter of James to turn it around, reversing it into the calumny, 'the Enemy of God'. Not only do we have in this again an allusion to Paul's 'slavery'/'freedom' dichotomy, but again the references to 'weakness' or those with 'weak consciences' – both euphemisms for not 'eating things sacrificed to an idol' or 'eating only vegetables'.

The Issue of Blood and the Ban on Gentile Gifts and Sacrifices in the Temple

But Paul goes further, using the imagery of Greco-Roman stadium sports so abhorrent to those in the Palestine of his day. The followers of Judas Maccabee, with whose 'wilderness' sojourn to escape just such involvement with the ways of men we began this discussion, are pictured as being particularly horrified by the erection of a Greek gymnasium in Jerusalem and the conducting of Greek athletic sports there by naked men, so that persons of turncoat propensities sought to hide their circumcisions or even somehow reverse them (1 Macc. 1:15-16). Judas' response was to have all *forcibly circumcised*.

Paul continues, stating:

> All the runners at the stadium are trying to win, but only one of them receives the prize. You must run in the same way – meaning to win. All the fighters at the games go into strict training; they do this just to win a crown that will wither away; but we do it for a crown [*stephanon*] that will never wither. That is how I run, intent on winning; that is how I fight not beating the air. (9:24-26)

There is no clearer statement of winning at all costs on record and, as it turns out, Paul did win. One can only imagine the impression the announcement of such a philosophy made on the Jerusalem Church Leadership. One thing is sure, to have had such an individual among one's foot soldiers – if we can use the term – would have been a difficult proposition indeed for any leadership, even putting aside Paul's precious Roman citizenship and contacts with the Jerusalem Establishment.

These 'rulings' or 'Judgements' that James is pictured as making as Bishop of the Jerusalem Church come down heavily on the issue of 'blood', which has ramifications both for Qumran and the Noahic Covenant as we have seen. They also come down on two other themes associated with James, 'fornication' and 'things sacrificed to idols' – itself bearing on the two issues of 'table fellowship with Gentiles' and 'idolatry'. One may assume that the proscription on the consumption of blood would – particularly if held with the same vehemence as that enunciated at Qumran – also extend to the mystery-religion phenomenon of *Communion with the Cup of the blood of the Christ*, which Paul proceeds to introduce into his understanding of Messianism and the death of the Messianic Leader from 1 Corinthians 10:14–11:30. The Synoptic Gospels, of course, represent this as being introduced by Jesus himself at the Last Supper (presumably a Passover supper, where, of course, the 'blood' on the doorposts of the Israelite's houses was a prominent feature).

Therefore James' proscription on 'blood' in the directives to overseas communities, as depicted in Acts, would seemingly also extend to the *consumption of the blood of the crucified Messiah*, even if taken in its most extreme sense – this apart from obvious Noahic bans on human sacrifice and consuming human blood generally. This, of course, brings us full circle and back to James' strange evocation of Abraham's willingness *to sacrifice his son Isaac* as evidence of Abraham's 'Faith working with his works' (2:21–22). Not only is this somewhat tortured, it is also echoed in the Gentile Mission claim that God chose 'to sacrifice His only-begotten' son in the world, a comparison expressly drawn in Hebrews 11:17. It may also have relevance to the willingness of the partisans on Masada – whom Josephus calls '*Sicarii*' – *to sacrifice their children*, who may also have thought they were following the example, James cites, of Abraham.

The issue of 'things sacrificed to idols' also bears in Paul's letters on the table-fellowship theme, forbidden foods, and by extension Paul's slur on James' vegetarianism. These, in turn, bear on the proscription on 'idolatry', an issue also dealt with in the Temple Scroll at Qumran. There, another variation of this theme, 'skins sacrificed to idols', is evoked in the context of dealing with Temple *pollution*. This follows the discussion of persons *disbarred from the Temple*, like lepers, the blind, the lame, people with a running discharge, and others, the groups Jesus is pictured as interacting and keeping table fellowship with in the Gospels. The implication is that persons bringing gifts in such 'skins' into the Temple are to be treated as similarly unclean.

That the theme of such 'skins' or idolatrous gifts in the Temple Scroll has something to do with barring Gentiles from the Temple should also be clear. This is reinforced by looking at parallel injunctions and disbarments in the recently published '*MMT*', which I called 'Two Letters on Works Reckoned as Righteousness'. Not only is this last significant in terms of our discussion, but is based on allusions in both to the 'works' that will 'be reckoned to you as Righteousness' and 'doing' the 'works of the Torah'.[40] The connection of these to the themes we have been treating here should also be clear. As we have already remarked above, these letter(s) too are primarily interested in Gentile gifts in the Temple, and not only ban such Gentile 'skins' in the Temple, but also specifically raise the Jamesian issue of 'things sacrificed to idols'.

Paul, once again, shows his awareness that all these things belong together in the section of 2 Corinthians 6:14–7:1 evoking 'Beliar' and 'idols in the Temple of God'. Admonishing the 'Beloved' ('Friends') to cleanse themselves 'of every pollution of flesh and Spirit, Perfecting Holiness', Paul states:

> Do not be adversely yoked with unbelievers. For what has Righteousness in common with Lawlessness, and what Communion Light with Darkness, and what accord does Christ have with Beliar, and what does a believer share with an unbeliever, and what agreement does *the Temple of God have with idols*? And that is what we are, *the living Temple of God* . . . 'Therefore come out from the midst of them and be separated,' says the Lord, 'and the unclean touch not [Isa. 52:11], and I will receive you, and I shall be to you a father, and you shall be to me sons and daughters.'[41]

Not only do we have here the 'Light' and 'Dark' imagery, as we saw, but also the *plural* divine sonship of the Qumran Hymns. Paul knows all the correct motifs to evoke, only he is reversing them or employing them tendentiously if Qumran is any guide.[42]

The reference here to Isaiah 52:11, leading up to Isaiah 53 – so important to the Christian theological picture of Jesus – would make an extremely telling *'pesher'* of the Qumran style. As both the Temple Scroll and *MMT*, Isaiah 52:11 also refers to the cleanliness of 'the vessels of the Lord', and such a *pesher* could culminate in the presentation of the 'Justification' activity of 'the suffering *Zaddik*' of Isaiah 53:11. This same kind of allusion to the 'justifying' activity of the Sons of Zadok, 'those called by Name to stand in the Last Days', precedes the evocation of the 'Three Nets of Belial' metaphor in the Damascus Document.

Indeed, as Paul alludes to these themes here, they do bear on the 'pollution of the Temple' theme in the 'Three Nets of Belial' section of the Damascus Document, which include, as well, the condemnation of 'fornication' and on 'Riches', also prominent in all the literature about James. But the theme of 'pollution of the Temple' can be linked with another prominent theme of this period, *stopping sacrifice and refusing gifts on behalf of Gentiles in the Temple*. There can be no doubt that Paul is responding, at least in part, to this situation and is familiar with it.

Josephus tells us in the *War* that the sudden change with regard to this custom by 'the Revolutionaries' – also translatable as 'Innovators' – was 'an innovation'. He claims that the 'Ancestors had always accepted the gifts of Gentiles' and 'never taken the *blasphemous* step of forbidding anyone to sacrifice'.[43] These are his very words.

Not only is his use of the word 'blasphemous' important for the trial and stoning of James the Just at this time, it is this theme of *stopping sacrifice on behalf of Gentiles in the Temple* and *refusing their gifts* that punctuates Josephus' description of disputes in the Temple in the run-up to the Uprising against Rome in the 50s and the 60s. This is the period in which James held sway in the Temple and, as early Church accounts repeatedly insist, *among the people*. It is the stopping of these sacrifices and the refusal to accept such gifts – seen by some as 'pollution of the Temple' – by the lower priesthood or the priests responsible for the day-to-day operations in the Temple

> which laid the foundation of the War with the Romans, for the sacrifices offered on behalf of that nation and the Emperor were in consequence rejected.[44]

The Final Triumph of Hellenization

But this is not the whole story. There is another theme, related to it, the admission of Gentiles into the Temple, or, if one prefers its reverse, the barring of Gentiles from the Temple. This also punctuates this period from the 40s to the 60s leading up to the Uprising against Rome in 66–70 CE. It is also intrinsic to Paul's activities, both in his own presentation of how God chose him 'from the womb to reveal His Son in' him to 'announce the Gospel among the Gentiles' and how Acts presents the scene in the Temple, in which Paul is mobbed after having been sent in by James to go through the procedures of a temporary Nazirite oath and pay the expenses of four others so involved. The cry raised there, aside from 'teaching against the people, the Law, and this place', is that '*he has brought Greeks into the Temple and polluted this Holy Place*' (21:28 and 24:6).

That this theme was of concern in this period is verified by Josephus' discussion of the stones that were put up in the Temple to warn foreigners on pain of death of inadvertently intruding into the Sacred Precincts. This is the situation that is reflected in Acts' picture of this riot surrounding Paul in the Temple. As noted, two of these warning stones, inscribed in both Greek and Hebrew, have since been discovered, and the point made in them about foreigners, that their death would be 'their own responsibility', is exactly the point made in the Gospel of Matthew, where Pilate is depicted as *washing his hands* 'of the blood of' Jesus, but reversed (note the additional typical inversion here of the Jews 'washing their hands before eating' and 'blood'). The crowd, there, is rather pictured as crying out gleefully, 'let his *blood* be upon us and on our children' – a most terrible cry that, it is worth repeating, has haunted the Jews through the ages (27:24).

But the point Paul makes in 2 Corinthians 6:14–7:1 above is that his Community *is* the Living Temple. Elsewhere, as we saw, he identifies this Community with 'the members' of the single body of Christ (1 Cor. 12:12–27). There is much intertwining imagery of this kind in Paul, which is often difficult, but useful to separate out. Throughout he emphasizes the Community as 'the building', both as spiritualized Temple and body of Christ.

While Paul is an imagist or symbolist, his interlocutors are literalists, and this creates an often insurmountable chasm. As Paul over and over again reiterates, he is 'building' a Community where both Greeks and Jews can live in harmony (Gal. 3:28).[45] As Ephesians puts it – a letter some consider to be in the Pauline genre – there are no 'foreigners or sojourners'. Using the language of the Community Rule at Qumran and Paul elsewhere in 1 Corinthians, Ephesians 2:19–22 insists that Jesus Christ is the Precious 'Cornerstone'; the Prophets and Apostles, 'the Foundation'; and the members 'the building', all growing into 'the Holy Temple in the Lord'.

Rather all are equal or free in Christ Jesus or, as Galatians 2:4 puts it, 'the freedom we have in Christ Jesus'. This is the direct riposte to these scenes in the Temple we are describing and these problems. Those who wish to bar Paul from the Temple are reflecting their awareness that he *wishes to bring foreigners into it* – whether actually or spiritually. There is no doubt he does spiritually. As he puts it in 1 Corinthians 2:10–15, he teaches 'spiritual things spiritually'.

All these matters were comprehensible to the Hellenistic spirit and mind. *The consumption of blood* was part and parcel of the ceremonies of a welter of Hellenistic mystery cults that had as their goal the conquest of death – the same goal Paul announces in his letters (1 Cor. 15:54–57), the end being, as he puts it, to enter the tomb with Jesus or 'being crucified with Christ' (Gal. 2:20).[46] They are certainly *not* understandable in a Palestinian Jewish milieu.

One should correct this slightly – at Qumran, there was the imagery of spiritualized Community, spiritualized Temple, spiritualized sacrifice, and spiritualized atonement, as in the Community Rule where we have the imagery of the Community Council as the Temple. But Paul's imagery is a little more circuitous: the Community *is* Jesus, Jesus is the Temple, therefore, the Community *is* the Temple. The end is the same. There is even the imagery in the Community Rule of the 'three Priests' of the Community Council as the 'Holy of Holies' or 'Inner Sanctum of the Temple'. But further than this, those of a Palestinian perspective were generally unable to go. Nor did anyone see the Law as metaphor, except someone like Philo in Alexandria – but his arguments were already highly Hellenized and, in any event, not in Palestine, which is an important difference.

For those *in* Palestine, Paul was, indeed, trying to introduce Gentiles into the Temple, spiritualized or real. Therefore there were plots to kill Paul – again seemingly among some who had taken a kind of *Nazirite* oath as described in Acts 23:12. But it is doubtful whether Jesus could have held a doctrine, such as *introducing foreigners into the Temple or consuming blood*, even if only symbolically, and still have been the popular leader he is presented as being. Such an anomaly could only have existed in the always rather mischievous imagination of those responsible for the dissimulation in the Gospels and the Book of Acts. This was certainly aimed at pulling the teeth of the Messianic Movement in Palestine and turning it against itself and into its mirror opposite.

Seen from this vantage point, Paul represented the final triumph of that Hellenization the Jews began struggling against in the generation of Judas Maccabee, two centuries before, and had been combating ever since. So too was the religion we now call 'Christianity'. From Paul's point of view, it was normal to reconcile the claims of Judaism with those of Hellenism, and profitable to do so. From the Jewish perspective in Palestine, particularly the 'Zealot' one, it was anathema to do so. Therefore, the clash – the very real 'plots' against Paul become transmogrified in these accounts into *Jewish plots* against Jesus or the Messiah.

There were also very real plots against James, but these were on the part of the Herodian quasi-Jewish Establishment, *not the Jewish mass*. All accounts are quite specific about this. The majority of James' Jerusalem Church followers are described, by no less an authority than Acts itself in the same episode we have been discussing – the ejection of Paul from the Temple, as 'Zealots for the Law' (21:20). These are the actual words used. They are, also, the horns of the dilemma. Nor is there any escaping from them. The only escape from this dilemma is to the Dead Sea Scrolls, which lead us in the proper direction where Jewish life and thought in Palestine from the first century BC–CE is concerned.

The Simon who Wishes to Bar Herodians from the Temple as Foreigners

Initially, then, we have these 'Zealot' or '*Sicarii*'-like groups that wish to kill Paul for introducing Gentiles into the Temple. If he did not introduce them except spiritually or allegorically, he certainly wished to introduce them as 'heirs according to the Promise' – as he puts it in Galatians 3:29. But there are also Zealots, those 'Fourth Philosophy' subversives seeking *innovation* who wish to bar Herodians from the Temple.

Josephus will introduce us to one such Zealot leader, whom he calls 'Simon'. This Simon was able to call an 'Assembly' of his own in Jerusalem.[47] The time is the early 40s. The very word '*Ecclēsias*' Josephus uses here in the Greek is the same word used throughout Acts and these early Church sources for discussing the 'Church' or 'Assembly' in Jerusalem. That is, this Simon, whom Josephus refers to as a 'somebody' again and 'very scrupulous in the Knowledge of the Law', is the head of his own 'Church' in Jerusalem, contemporaneous with Simon Peter depicted in Acts.

And what does this Simon wish to do? He does not wish to *admit Gentiles into the Community*, as Acts pictures Peter being instructed to do after receiving his vision of the Heavenly tablecloth on the rooftop in Jaffa (10:1–11:18). Here Peter learns 'not to call any man profane or unclean' just before receiving the Roman Centurion Cornelius' messengers (10:28). Rather the Simon in Josephus wishes to *bar Herodians from the Temple* ('which belonged only to native Jews') as non-Jews and 'unclean'. Of course, they were – in particular, Agrippa I, the brother of that Herodias responsible for the death of John the Baptist and the father of the three princesses, Bernice, Mariamme, and Drusilla we have mentioned so often above, who in native Messianic eyes would have been no better than 'harlots'.

That is, this Simon in Josephus wishes to do the *very opposite* of the Simon in Acts, who is also pictured as being the head of an 'Assembly' of his own in Jerusalem. Whereas Simon Peter learns, in the words of Paul's travelling companion Luke, that he should no longer 'call any man unclean' or make any distinctions between Jews and Gentiles and that now he can eat forbidden foods – 'what God has made clean, let no man declare unclean' – Simon in Josephus wishes, not only to *make* distinctions between Jews and Gentiles, but to go on making them and take these up to the highest level and *bar pseudo-Jews* like the Herodians from the Temple.

It is the position of this book that the Simon in Josephus is *the demythologized Simon* in the New Testament, just as Josephus' John the Baptist is *the demythologized John*. Furthermore, in the next generation, not only do these same 'Zealots' wish to bar Agrippa I's son Agrippa II from the Temple, but his sister Bernice too. Bernice, as remarked, ultimately becomes the mistress of Vespasian's son Titus, the destroyer of Jerusalem and the Temple – a fact Josephus is at great pains to obscure. Josephus did not earn his adoption into the Roman Imperial family of the Flavians for minor services only.

But he does note, true to his penchant for sexual innuendo, that Bernice was rumoured to have had an incestuous relationship with Agrippa II her brother.[48] This is very much the picture that emerges too in the 'We Document' in Acts, where Bernice appears together with Agrippa II – seemingly as his consort – in amiable interviews with Paul (25:13–26:30). So does her sister Drusilla, whom Acts 24:24 has the temerity to identify only as 'a Jewess', even though by this time, after a number of sexual indiscretions, she had *deserted the Jewish religion altogether* – this Josephus specifically notes – and married Nero's freedman, the infamous Governor Felix (52–60 CE).

Of course, all this will bear on the second theme in the 'Three Nets of Belial' in the Damascus Document and the Letter of James, 'fornication', which Paul, too, is anxious to paper over, despite his pro forma protestations to the contrary, since he himself has relations with clear fornicators – most notably these same Bernice, Agrippa II, Drusilla, and Felix. One could hardly imagine John the Baptist, who had but two decades before lost his head because of such confrontations, conversing so congenially with such persons, or James for that matter, from what we know of his uncompromisingly continent life-style. As it is, Paul converses with them – there is no reason to contradict Acts' picture at this point – with his usual congeniality or deference, even obsequiousness.

It is here Acts 24:6 acknowledges for the second time that the *actual charge* of 'pollution of the Temple' was being directed against Paul, then calling Drusilla 'a Jewess' without further explanation. But what kind of a Jewess could Drusilla have been? It was only her father's grandmother Mariamme who was 'native-born', as Josephus puts it in the episode about Simon wishing to bar her father Agrippa I from the Temple, the rest of her ancestors being either Idumaean Arab or Greek. Acts does not explain how she merits the appellation, nor, what is even more important, that she was *an Herodian*.

As Luke presents it in Acts: after *often* conversing with Felix about 'Righteousness' and the coming 'Judgement' – curious subjects to be discussing with the blood-thirsty Felix (24:22–26) – Paul is pictured as obsequiously asking Agrippa II and Bernice of all people, 'King Agrippa, do you believe the Prophets? I know that you believe' (26:27) and discoursing with them in detail about his vision on the road to Damascus and the Gentile Mission. Then Agrippa II responds:

> 'In a little while you would persuade me to become a Christian.' And Paul: 'Not only in a little, but I would wish to God you and all those hearing me this day would very much become as I also am except for these bonds.' (26:28–29)

At this point according to Acts, Agrippa II and his consort Bernice – the future mistress of Titus the destroyer of the Temple – turn aside to Festus (60–62 CE) and say more or less what Pontius Pilate and other Roman Governors are depicted as saying in the literature: 'This man has done nothing deserving of death or chains' (26:31).

Festus was Felix's successor and it is upon his death that King Agrippa II and his High Priest Ananus get together *to destroy James*. As if to emphasize the parallel with what happened to Jesus – the only difference being that Paul is upper-class and holds a Roman citizenship and Jesus does not – Acts has Agrippa add, 'This man might have been let go if he had not appealed to Caesar' (26:32). The scenario here of an intervening interview with high Herodians, combined with hearings before the Roman Governor, is exactly the same as the Gospel of Luke, who *also authored Acts*.

As Acts develops the story, it is a good thing Paul was not let go, as *'the Jews . . . were preparing an ambush to put him to death'* (25:2–3). Earlier, similar partisans or *'Sicarii'/'Zealots'* are pictured as having

> made a plot, putting themselves *under a curse* and *vowing neither to eat or drink until they killed Paul.* (23:12)[49]

At this time Paul's 'sister's son', a person of some influence – though Acts interestingly declines to name either *him* or *his mother* – intervenes and informs the Roman Captain commanding the Citadel of these things.[50]

The latter, thereupon, provides Paul with a huge escort: 200 soldiers, 200 auxiliaries, and 70 cavalry, and conducts him to Caesarea on the coast (23:23). The gist of this Captain's letter to Felix, quoted verbatim in Acts, is revealing:

> This man had been seized by the Jews and would have been put to death by them, but having come upon the scene with troops and learned that he was a Roman citizen, I rescued him. (23:27–28)

This theme of the 'Jews' wishing to put to Paul to death, when he has done nothing deserving of death, has apparently been absorbed into Gospel accounts of 'Jesus'' death. The only problem is that while in Paul's case it makes sense, provided 'Zealots'/'*Sicarii*' are substituted for 'Jews'; in Jesus' case, it does not (unless we mean by 'Jews', *Herodians* and their accomplices).

In the run-up to the Uprising against Rome following the death of James in the 60s, King Agrippa II – who appears in these passages in Acts and is responsible, in our view, along with the High Priest Ananus, for the death of James – is finally barred with his sister Bernice from the Temple and for that matter *all* Jerusalem, even though his great-grandfather Herod and father King Agrippa I had been involved in building the Temple in its present form. In fact, this building had just been completed in time for its destruction by the Romans in 70 CE.[51] Just prior to James' death at the beginning of the decade, the same species of 'Zealots' responsible for this had already *erected a wall to block Agrippa II's view of the sacrifices* in the Inner Court of the Temple. It had been his habit to eat while reclining with his guests on a veranda of his palace with a fine perspective of the sacrifices in the Temple.[52] It would have been interesting to know what kind of food he was eating and who his guests were on these occasions.

These were the things, not to mention that 'Zealot' groups like the one led by Simon (the head of an 'Assembly' of his own in Jerusalem) would not even have considered him Jewish in the first place and the rumour of his incest with his sister Bernice, that led to their both being banned from Jerusalem by 'the Innovators' or Revolutionaries and the burning of their palaces.

Belial, Balaam, and Polluting the Temple

The extreme purity demanded by such Temple 'Zealots' throughout the century is vividly presented, as we have already remarked, in the Temple Scroll from Qumran. Some call this document a Second Law, because it deals with much more than just the Temple and and was delivered in the first person, as if God were speaking – presumably to Moses and the whole people. In the column about the exclusion of certain classes of unclean persons from the Temple (just preceding that about the inadmissibility of bringing 'skins sacrificed to idols' into the Temple), a barrier of the kind ultimately erected against Agrippa II and his dining companions when Festus came to Palestine around 61 CE is called for to protect the Temple from even being 'seen' by someone referred to in connection with evocation of the terminology *'Bela''* or *'balla''/to swallow*.

This terminology, of course, relates to the 'Belial' terminology at Qumran and the *B–L–'* circle of language. This circle of language, centring around the root meaning in Hebrew of 'swallowing', more or less functions in opposition to a parallel circle of language relating to *Z–D–K* or 'Righteousness'. As we have seen, 1 Peter 5:9 shows clear knowledge of this language, when it uses the 'Enemy' terminology in speaking of the *'Diabolos'* ('Belial' at Qumran), then connecting it with an allusion to 'being swallowed up' – the letters *B–L–'* in Hebrew always having the root meaning of *to swallow* or *consume*. Paul too uses this language in Galatians 5:11–15 after referring to 'the scandal of the cross', wishing his circumcising opponents 'would themselves cut off', and citing the all Righteousness Commandment, 'love your neighbour as yourself'.

It is also connected to related allusions in the New Testament like 'Balaam'. Not only is 'Balaam the son of Be'or' referred to in 2 Peter 2:15 – a letter replete with Qumran imagery, which calls Noah the 'Preacher of Righteousness' (2:5) – and Jude 1:11; but Revelation 2:14, in the context of referring not to 'Belial' but 'the Diabolos' (2:10) and 'Satan' (2:13), describes, as we have already seen, how 'Balaam taught Balak to cast [*balein*] a net before the sons of Israel to eat things sacrificed to idols and commit fornication'.[53]

Here, of course is the 'Three Nets of Belial' language of the Damascus Document at Qumran. For the Damascus Document, 'Belial . . . ensnares Israel by setting them up as three kinds of Righteousness'.[54] We have now come full circle. The only thing missing is reference to the third net,

'Riches', but even this is made good obliquely in this section of Revelation, in the Letter of James, and elsewhere, not to mention in these stories about Bernice, Agrippa I, and Agrippa II. Not only are all parallel presentations, but what is being called 'pollution of the Temple' in the Damascus Document is equivalent to the formulation 'things sacrificed to idols' in *MMT* ('skins sacrificed to idols' above), 1 Corinthians, and Acts; and the original suggestion we made, that Paul is operating within the same ideological context as the Scrolls at Qumran, which we derived from considering his use of terms like 'things sacrificed to idols' and 'Beliar' in 1–2 Corinthians, is correct.[55]

When the 'Zealots' or '*Sicarii*' finally did seize control of the Temple Mount in the aftermath of all these demands as the Uprising turned more extremist and moved into its 'Jacobin' phase, the first thing they did – in Josephus' own words – was to burn the debt records 'to cause a rising of the Poor against the Rich'.[56] As remarked, they also burned the Herodian palaces, including both Bernice's and that of her brother Agrippa II, presumably the one in which he had reclined and viewed the Temple sacrifices while eating. Later, they also burned all the palaces of the High Priests appointed by Herodians, all of whom appear finally to have been slaughtered, including James' nemesis Ananus.

In fact, the issue we have been discussing here was the crux of the issue chosen by the lower priests when they stopped sacrifice on behalf of foreigners, including the Emperor, and rejected their gifts in the Temple. Not only do these gifts relate to Paul's Gentile Mission and the way it inverted these things, but this rejection was also contrary to the practice and point of view of the reigning Herodian High Priests responsible for the death of people like James. The rejection of these gifts and sacrifices was the issue on which the lower priests (called by some 'Levites') chose to take their stand *three and a half years after the death of James*.

The carnage that ensued, including the butchering of most or almost all of the High Priests and the burning of their palaces and those of the Herodians, culminated in the election, as we have mentioned, of the simple 'Stone-cutter' Phineas. As opposed to this, the highly Paulinized 1 Peter, however retrospectively, presents the following recommendation:

> For the sake of the Lord, accept the authority of every social institution: the Emperor as the Supreme Authority and the Governors as commissioned by him to punish criminals, and praise good behaviour. God wants you to behave well, so . . . *fear God* and *honour the Emperor*. (2:13; cf. Paul in

Romans 13:1–8, which uses the 'all Righteousness' Commandment to the same effect)

One should remark in these contexts the reversal of the 'God-fearing' language at Qumran, which not only appears in this episode about erecting the barrier against unclean persons in the Temple in the Temple Scroll, but also at the end of the Damascus Document.[57] At this time, too, right before the Uprising, the lower priests or Levites won the right – according to Josephus – to wear *the white linen of the High Priests*.[58] This is one of the last complaints Josephus makes before giving his list of High Priests from Solomon's time to the present at the end the *Antiquities*.

Acts, too, is very interested in 'the number of priests' who are joining the new Movement. As it avers in the preamble to the stoning of Stephen:

> And the word of God increased. And the number of the Disciples in Jerusalem multiplied exceedingly, and *a great multitude of the Priests* were obedient to the Faith. (6:7)[59]

In the same vein, later on, Acts 21:20 characterizes the majority of James' followers as 'Zealots for the Law', a priestly notation, as we have seen, going back both to Maccabean High Priestly claims and the zeal of Phineas by virtue of which they were said to have won their High Priestly office in perpetuity. To put this into a proper context, these same early Church descriptions of James, that we are considering here, not only insist that he wore the mitre of the High Priest, but also that he wore *white linen*. It is difficult to escape the impression that all these matters are connected in some manner, and that the Qumran documents, however one chooses to date them, are the key to unlocking these connections.

Noah's and James' Vegetarianism Re-evaluated

We now have the wherewithal to explain both the vegetarianism ascribed to Judas Maccabee in 2 Maccabees and to James in these various early Church accounts and its sophisticated reversal in Paul. Judas goes out *into the wilderness* with nine other men and eats nothing but 'wild plants to avoid contracting defilement', that is, Judas eats only vegetable fare. John the Baptist – also designated 'a Righteous One' in both Josephus and the Gospels – does as well.[60] James, too, because he was 'Holy' or 'consecrated from his mother's womb' – and also presumably because he was 'a *Zaddik*', is pictured as abstaining from wine, strong drink, and animal *food*. We shall also hear presently that he did *not anoint himself with oil, nor wear wool but only linen, nor involve himself in sexual activity*.

Where the matter of abstaining from meat and eating only vegetable fare is concerned, one can conceive of a scenario based, as we have suggested, on this Noahic ideology, where because the sacrifice in the Temple was interrupted or performed improperly by impure men having no claim to Righteousness and, as a consequence, 'polluted', the 'Noahic' permission to eat meat was considered to be withdrawn or no longer in effect by these desert sojourners mindful of the *extreme purity demands of Perfect Righteousness*. This goes back to the salvationary experience of the first *Zaddik*, Noah. Noah, as we saw, was not permitted to eat meat all the days of the Flood, until he gained dry land and made a *proper* sacrifice. But he was to pour away the blood and not eat the flesh with blood in it, because 'the life' of the animal was considered to be in the blood. Only then was he permitted to resume eating animal life. To some, however, this permission might only have appeared dependent on a proper sacrifice made by *Righteous High Priests in the Temple.*

Even if this were not the case, it was perhaps deemed better for those observing the commands of 'all Righteousness' (Matt. 3:15) and the extreme purity regulations of 'Perfect Holiness' or 'Perfection of the Way' to avoid consuming animal fare. This is certainly the case regarding Judas Maccabee. Judas was probably not a vegetarian while the Temple was properly functioning, but became one when it was considered defiled for some reason or the sacrifice was interrupted and, in the words of the Little Apocalypse attributed to Jesus in the Gospels, 'the Abomination of the Desolation was standing where it ought not to stand'.

This also appears to be the case for those Paul euphemistically describes as 'weak' or having 'weak consciences'. Though Paul disagrees with such people and feels 'there are no forbidden things', still so as not to be the cause of a brother's 'stumbling' (1 Cor. 8:9), it is better, as he puts it, to refrain from *forbidden things*, especially when such persons or their representatives were present. As for himself, he grandiosely announces, 'since meat causes my brother to stumble [literally 'scandalizes'], I will never eat meat again' (1 Cor. 8:13). But, of course, as he makes very clear in Romans 4:2, he is not serious here only posturing.

Often James' vegetarianism and the peculiar dietary habits of many of these charismatic Revolutionaries or 'Innovators' is taken for some kind of asceticism. From what we are seeing here, this is not the case. It has to do with the demands of all Righteousness and Perfect Holiness. Just as those following the regime of 'Righteousness towards one's fellow man' and 'Perfecting the Way' developed an extreme poverty regime, because to make economic distinctions between oneself and one's neighbour would not be *Righteous*; so too, those following the extreme purity commandments – particularly when Temple sacrifice was interrupted or being performed by individuals of questionable purity who were not *true Sons of Zadok* – had some question about whether or not it was permissible to consume meat.

The permission for this had been granted Noah only after a proper sacrifice and commitment to the Covenant. The caveat had always been 'not to consume the life', that is, *blood*. Those following these extreme purity regulations in wilderness camps, in preparation for 'the Last Days' so vividly outlined in the Qumran literature, would have been concerned about this. James was obviously one of these. For his part, true to the epithets applied to the Opponent in James 3:8 of 'not controlling' his Tongue, Paul heaps abuse on precisely such persons, who 'being weak in Faith . . . eat only vegetables' (Rom. 14:2), while all the time recommending to his communities a kind of oblique tolerance of them based on a mixture of contempt and pity. There is no respect for or awe of their stature in the face of what was reckoned as their overwhelming 'Piety' and 'Righteousness' – what he derogatorily characterizes as 'their weak consciences'.

The last category of James' directives to overseas communities, as pictured in the Book of Acts, is 'abstain from strangled things' ('abstain from' being the same 'Nazirite-type' language one finds in the Damascus Document). This allusion in Greek, 'strangled things', which is a translation or transliteration of some kind, is very peculiar. Again, this would appear to be a garbling of something as it moved from one language or cultural milieu to another or an idiomatic usage of some kind that is no longer clearly understood. As it stands in the Greek, it makes very little sense and Paul does not respond to it *per se* in his 1 Corinthians response.

But there is sense that can be made of it and this sense cuts in two directions. It can be thought of as being related to the original prohibitions given to Noah – again the putative Noahic Covenant – about *blood* or *the lifeblood* in Genesis 9:4–5. Here God is portrayed, it will be recalled, as saying to Noah, 'You must not eat flesh with life in it, that is, its blood . . . I will demand an account from every beast and from man.' It is not incurious that God includes the animal's blood in this reckoning, that is, beasts *that have shed other beasts' blood* – presumably they, too, have consumed 'the lifeblood'.

So, it is possible to see in this a reflection of the prohibition on *the consumption of blood* James himself has already enunciated in these directives, as well as the general 'Noahic' prohibition on manslaughter, to which, in any event, it is connected even in the Bible. Genesis 9:6 itself goes on to raise the issue of blood vengeance or 'pouring out' or 'shedding blood', at least where mankind or 'Adam' is concerned.

The second way of looking at it, however, and perhaps the more convincing one, is to realize that strangulation was the means most carnivores employed to destroy their prey. Certainly this is true of great cats and other pack-hunters. Certainly, too, in the case of poultry it is the normal means humans employ in slaughter, not to mention the time-honoured custom of 'hanging' such slaughtered things. There is a third possibility related to this, that the respondents in question were simply not using the Jewish ritual custom of slaughtering things with the knife.

However these things may be, this prohibition of James probably had to do with what in English goes by the name of 'carrion', again probably based on the Noahic Covenant above. Therefore it would have been seen in a more general way as applicable to all Noah's human descendants and, no doubt, as in Jewish Law generally, probably also would have included some sense of beasts or fowl that died of themselves or dead as a result of disease, not by just ritual slaughter or the action of beasts of prey. The problem was, as with John the Baptist's 'locusts' above, transliteration into Greek – or better still transmogrification – from a so far undetermined *Semitic original*.

In fact, this interpetation is basically confirmed, if one goes to the Koran again, the heir, as we have been pointing out, to many of these traditions and formulations relevant to Jewish Christianity and, in particular, those called 'Ebionites'/'the Poor'. Not only do we have in the Koran the repeated reiteration of the Jamesian position: 'Believe in Allah, the Last Day, and do good works' (this uttered by Muhammad when speaking of one Qumran-style Jewish group he is both familiar with and approves of, who keep Qumran-style, *all-night vigils in caves*); but also a kind of stark works/Righteousness throughout, that is, you are saved not by intercession or variations of Pauline conceptualities of 'Grace', but only by 'the works you have sent before you'.[61] Here, of course, is 'the works' in the works/Righteousness equation with a vengeance.

In the Koran, too, one has a variation of Paul's claim to be an 'Apostle to the Gentiles' – now one of the titles of 'the Prophet' (that is, the Ebionite 'True Prophet' ideology, developed in the Pseudoclementines) of Islam. For Muhammad, 'Islam' itself – just as Paul on his brand of Christianity in Romans – is 'Abraham's Religion' or 'the Faith of Abraham'.[62] In the Koran, too, we also have, perhaps even more impressively, actual evocation of James' directives to overseas communities as presented in the Book of Acts reproduced almost verbatim. In fact, these become in effect – unlike in Christianity in the West – *the basis of all Islamic dietary Law* thereafter. As Muhammad succinctly puts it:

> Abstain from swineflesh, blood, things immolated to an idol, and carrion. (2:172, 5:3, 16:115, etc.)

The 'swineflesh' prohibition, of course, is normative in Jewish dietary law. It was, no doubt, understood in James' instructions to overseas communities and probably so self-evident that it was not even thought worthy of mention. But the interesting things in Muhammad's presentation are that which is 'immolated to an idol', 'blood', and 'carrion'. 'Things immolated to an idol' is clearly simply the terminology of James' first prohibition to overseas communities – 'things sacrificed to idols' – so disingenuously laboured over in 1 Corinthians by Paul and evoked too in '*MMT*' (which we shall later identify as a 'Jamesian' letter(s) to an ostensibly Judaized 'Arab' monarch in Northern Syria – Abraham's putative homeland as well). 'Blood', too, is the *second* category of James' directives to overseas communities as reported in Acts, and we have already discussed it sufficiently.

But the third, 'carrion' in Arabic, is the key. It, no doubt, is a better translation of whatever was originally intended in the original Semitic form of these directives than the version of it that has survived in the Greek, which seems to have preserved only one sense of what was intended, that is, *strangulation* or things killed by action on the windpipe. 'Carrion' is no doubt what was originally intended and carrion is what has survived into the Arabic. It certainly makes more sense. It is an overpowering fact that many of these traditions from *Jamesian* Christianity have survived into Islam, its unwitting, but in fact, clearly, similarly apocalyptic and uncompromising heir.

In support of this, Pseudoclementine *Homilies* 7.8 not only presents Peter as a daily bather and vegetarian (like James), but teaching 'to abstain from the table of demons [cf. Paul in 1 Cor. 10:21], that is, food sacrificed to idols, dead carcasses from animals *which have been strangled or caught by beasts*, and from blood' – and the transmission into Islam is confirmed.[63]

The Noahic Covenant, the 'Balaam' Circumlocution, and the 'Joiners' at Qumran

All the themes of these directives, therefore, are connected in some way, as we have suggested, with the Noahic Covenant. This Covenant, pre-served in Rabbinic literature, is usually presented as comprising a variety of moral and behavioural qualities, chief among which are the three commandments against: (1) idolatry, (2) fornication, and (3) man-slaughter or murder. All of these are implied in one way or another, too, in the directives given by James to overseas communities, even in the admittedly tendentious picture Acts provides.

We have been insisting all along that the one on 'food' or 'things sacrificed to idols' is just an offshoot or variation of the one on idolatry generally. This is verified for us in Paul's correspondence, tendentious as it may be as well. This is also certainly the thrust of the 'Three Nets of Belial' allusion in the Damascus Document, backed up in its own way in the presentation in Revelation of what 'Balaam taught Balak' by way of 'deceiving Israel'. That these so-called 'prophets' are Gentiles from areas on the other side of the Jordan in Syria, Perea (Moab), and Idumaea is also interesting when it comes to considering Paul's claims, as reported in Acts, of being a 'teacher or prophet' of some kind (13:1).

In fact, Paul's claim to be of 'the Tribe of Benjamin' is also interesting on this account, 'Benjamin' sometimes functioning as a variation of the 'Belial'/'Balaam' terminology. Bela‘ in Old Testament genealogies – reliable or otherwise – is not only an Edomite King, as we have seen, but 'the son of Be‘or', the *same* parentage ascribed to *Balaam*. He is also presented as *Benjamin's firstborn son* (Gen. 46:21 and 1 Chron. 7:6)! Not only have we already noted a word or name identical to it in the Temple Scroll connected with classes of persons *debarred from the Temple*, on at least four different occasions the epithet 'Sons of Belial' is applied in the Old Testament specifically to *Benjaminites* (Judg. 19:22, 20:13, etc.).

It is for reasons such as these that we believe the Belial/Balaam/Bela‘ circle of language was being applied in some manner to Paul by those hostile to him, as it was to all Herodians. Of course, because of their Edomite or Idumaean origins or connections, the 'Herodians' may already have been making such claims themselves to consolidate the dubious proposition of their Judaic or Hebraic origins – both Edom's progenitor, Esau, and Ishmael being *descendants of Abraham*. Paul is also making this a claim on behalf of himself in the context of reference to Abraham in Romans 11:1 and Philippians 3:5 above. He never calls himself 'a Jew', simply an 'Israelite' or 'Hebrew' – in Philippians 3:5 'a Hebrew of the Hebrews' – which of course his 'Benjaminite' origins, real or symbolical, would have entitled him.[64]

In Romans 11:1, he adds, not insignificantly nor unlike Muhammad thereafter, 'of the seed of Abraham'. At this time there were no longer any real tribal affiliations among Jews of the kind Paul is signalling, except where Priests and Levites were concerned. Significantly no such claims really ever occur at Qumran, where the term 'Jew' is already in use, these having largely disappeared some *700 years earlier*. There also is some indication in Rabbinic literature and certainly in the War Scroll at Qumran that 'Benjamin' was a terminology applied to all *overseas persons* or *Diaspora* Jews. That Paul was of 'the Tribe of Benjamin' would in these contexts appear to be more obfuscation and reverse polemics, converting what may have been his opponents' pejoratives to positive effect.

In addition, where the Arab connections of Herodians are concerned, Herod's mother was *an Arab from Petra* and his sister was originally married to Costobarus the Idumaean, whose progeny were systematically mixed into the Herodian line.[65] In respect to their 'Arabness', Herodians too take on the appearance of precursors of Muhammad. Where Paul – originally 'Saul' – is concerned, there is another reason Benjamin specifically is evoked in this literature directed at relatively naïve overseas ears. Conveniently, the archetypical Saul, David's predecessor as king, was of the Tribe of Benjamin (Acts 13:21) – *ipso facto*, so too was his latterday namesake Paul.

The applicability of James' ban on 'fornication', like that of Qumran, to this state of affairs is also self-evident, and we have been at pains to explain its significance. It goes far beyond the rather pro-forma and superficial references to it in Paul's letters, though there is this more or less straightforward overt sense too. For instance, as we saw, when Jesus is presented in highly prized portions of the Gospels as 'sitting with tax collectors and Sinners' or speaking positively about 'prostitutes', this is meant to counter-indicate just the kinds of injunctions one gets in James' directives and at Qumran – to show that Jesus, the loving and forgiving Messiah, did not judge persons of this genre, but even kept 'table fellowship' and *ate with them*, always an important theme.

This is the upshot, too, of the tablecloth vision vouchsafed to Peter in Acts, in which he learns not to make distinctions between 'Holy and profane' just in time to inspect the household of the Roman Centurion Cornelius from Caesarea. Here, Cornelius is described as

> a *Righteous One* and a *God-Fearer*, one *borne witness to by the whole nation of the Jews* (Acts 10:22; cf. 1 Pet. 2:13 above),

much as Felix, the brother of Nero's favourite freedman Pallas and merciless butcher of innumerable resistance leaders, is described later in Acts as 'having very accurate knowledge about the things of *the Way*' (24:22). Both assertions are, quite simply, preposterous.

The visit Peter makes to Cornelius' household in Caesarea, where he again explains, as we saw, 'God has taught me not to call any man profane or unclean', while the 'pious' Roman Centurion is 'fasting and praying' (Acts 10:30), will be equivalent to the one his namesake, Simon in Josephus, the Head of an Assembly of his own in Jerusalem, pays to the household of Agrippa I, again in Caesarea. In Acts' version of these occurrences, not only does Peter assert 'that it is unlawful for a *Jewish* man to keep company with or come near one of another race', but he concludes that 'in every Nation, he who *fears Him* [our 'God-Fearing' language again, now applied to a *Roman Centurion*] or *works Righteousness* is acceptable to Him' (10:28 and 35).[66]

Acts even attributes to Peter a parody of the quality all accounts predicate of James, that he 'was not a respecter of persons' – played on too in the charge levelled against Paul of 'seeking to please men' (Gal. 1:10 and James 2:4). For Peter in this speech, it is rather God who 'is not a respecter of persons' (Acts 10:34). Unlike Peter, the Roman Centurion; the Simon in Josephus *who inspects the household* of Agrippa I in Caesarea, wants to *bar Herodians from the Temple* as unclean, not accept them. Agrippa – whose beneficence and reputation among the Jews Josephus, as we have already remarked, extols – showered this Simon with gifts and then dismissed him. For his part, the Simon in Acts learns to make no distinctions between men, nor 'call any man unclean'!

But these 'table fellowship' scenes in the Gospels are such favourites for precisely the same reason that more obsessive, purity-minded Jews have never comprehended how much foreigners in general instinctively wished to see them discomfited. The man-on-the-street in the world at large – if not in Palestine – wishes for the most part to feel that 'prostitutes', 'tax collectors', and 'Sinners' like himself are acceptable and rub the faces of the Holier-than-thou, more piously pretentious types into the mud of everyday existence. The presumably Hellenistic authors of these Gospel scenes seem to have understood this very well and played on it – as Paul obviously did. What fun it must have been to portray 'the Messiah' in Palestine as *keeping company* with such persons, knowing full well the opposite was true and how much types like those at Qumran abhorred them. This is not to mention the latterday satisfaction they would have derived from having people *actually believe it for nearly two thousand years* had they but been around to enjoy it.

But these scenes have a political edge as well. The Herodians in this period were, as we have seen, the Roman tax collectors in Palestine. As basically tax farmers, their usefulness to Rome in part rested on their effective collection and transmission of revenues. If some spilled off into their own pockets, so much the better. But of course the Herodian Princesses we have thus far encountered were also 'harlots', none more so than Bernice, Titus' mistress-to-be, whose 'Riches' even Josephus admits were prodigious. There is little doubt that her sister Drusilla – Felix's 'Jewish' wife in these scenes in Acts – was Rich too. Otherwise, apart from her royalty, what would Felix's interest in her have been?

When Jesus is portrayed as eating with such classes of persons:

> the Son of Man came *eating and drinking* . . . a glutton and a wine-bibber, *a friend of tax collectors and Sinners* (Matt. 11:19 and Luke 7:34) –

this right after John the Baptist is portrayed as 'neither eating bread, nor drinking wine' – Scripture is saying that Jesus, unlike his putative brother James, *approved* of such persons. Nor did Jesus make a fuss over purity regulations regarding food, nor make distinctions between people or nations regarding table fellowship on such a basis – meaning Jesus was a 'Paulinist' or Paul *knew Jesus better* than his closest associates!

In fact, as we have remarked, one can almost make a rule of thumb regarding such polemics. Where there is a statement in Paul – who according to his own testimony never met Jesus and had no first-hand knowledge of his teaching – that is echoed in the Gospels, one can assume the progression is rather from Paul, then into Gospel redaction, and not vice versa. The unschooled person, innocent of such strategems and the power of literary re-creation, normally reverses this. It is not for naught that Jesus is portrayed as valuing 'these Little Ones' or 'Simple Ones' – meaning those who have no knowledge nor any pretence to any – over all others (Matt. 18:14 and pars.).[67]

We have already seen one important such speech above, where Jesus is portrayed as saying:

> Not that which enters the mouth makes a man polluted; but that which goes forth out of the mouth, this pollutes a man. (Matt. 15:11; Mark 7:15)

In response to questioning, Jesus becomes so agitated on this score that he lists most of the Noahic prohibitions, that is, Evil inclination, murder, adultery, fornication, theft, Lying, blasphemy, covetousness, etc. (Matt. 15:19 and Mark 7:22), adding how 'that which goes into the mouth, goes into the belly, and is *cast out* the toilet bowl'.

The New Testament redactor, however, grows so effusive on this score that he ends up having Jesus conclude: 'These are the things which *pollute a man*, but eating with unwashed hands *does not make a man unclean*' (Matt. 15:20 and pars.). Because of an ancient artificer's antinomian bias, poor Jesus is pictured as gainsaying what has become for modern hygiene a fundamental rule. Setting aside for the moment the issue of whether the Law is relevant or not, to consider material of this kind either 'the Word of God' or 'a revelation of the Holy Spirit' is, once again, simply absurd. Rather, it is more edifying to regard it as the mischievous and malevolent polemics it really is.

Since the meaning of the Greek term 'strangled things' can also be looked upon as having to do with homicide and since the priestly author of this aspect of the Noah narrative does consider the taking of animal life to be a form of homicide, then we have in James' directives to overseas Communities, even as refracted in Acts, a reflection of three of the principal Noahic proscriptions: idolatry, manslaughter, and fornication. But this is not surprising. If the episode as Acts records it, or something somewhat approximating it, is true, then it should not be surprising that 'the *Zaddik*' and 'Perfect One' James applied what were seen as the terms of the Covenant attributed to his archetypal predecessor Noah to the salvationary status of persons and communities who had not yet come into the Mosaic Covenant and/or under the Law.

Often such persons are referred to, as we have seen in Acts' picture of the Roman Centurion Cornelius – an extreme case – as 'God-Fearers'. A 'God-Fearer' would appear to be someone who has attached himself to the Jewish Community or 'Synagogue' (as Acts often expresses it – 13:15, etc.), but has not yet come in completely or taken the whole of the Mosaic Law upon himself.

At Qumran, we can also detect such a status in the usage '*ger-nilveh*', resident alien, or the allied terminology, '*Nilvim*' or 'Joiners', evoked in the Damascus Document's eschatological (involving 'the Last Days') exposition of the 'Zadokite Covenant' from Ezekiel. Not only have we already seen how important this usage is in Paul's allusion to 'being joined' either to 'a prostitute's body' or 'God' after his 'food for the belly' analysis in 1 Cor. 6:13–20; but in the Book of Esther, the term 'Joiner' specifically denotes non-Jews 'attaching themselves to' the Jewish Community in some kind of associated status (9:27).

It is important also to note that in important contexts of the Damascus Document, for instance, the one referring to 'seeing *Yesha'*/'Salvation', and the Temple Scroll on barring classes of unclean persons from the Temple noted above, there is conspicuous reference to this idea of 'fearing God' as well.[68] That in these directives, depicted in Acts, James would apply the categories of the Noahic Covenant to the salvationary state of such God-Fearers, '*ger-nilveh*'s or '*Nilvim*' is not only not surprising, but eminently reasonable.

The Rechabites as *Keepers*, *Doers* and Potters Once Again

This wilderness life-style based on 'separation from the Sons of the Pit' so as not to *incur their pollution* or *mix with* them or those having contact with them,[69] either parallels or to some extent is actually based on, as we have seen, the *Rechabite* life-style. It is difficult to know whether there were any actual 'Rechabites' as such left in the Second Temple Period, but, as we shall see, Eusebius' source Hegesippus is certainly using this expression in the second century to apply to successors or supporters of James.

The expression is curious, one shrouded in mystery. The fullest presentation of Rechabites comes in Jeremiah 35, as we also saw above, where Jonadab the son of Rechab is pictured as giving instructions to his descendants that they would neither 'drink wine . . . plant vineyards, build houses, sow seed, nor own property', but rather live only in tents 'so that you enjoy long life on the land which you sojourn upon'. This takes us back to the 800s BC, when Jonadab is pictured as an associate of the Israelite King Jehu, a king chosen by the Prophet Elisha.

We have already seen how Jeremiah emphasized in his panegyric to Jonadab's descendants both the themes 'keeping' and 'doing', that is, they '*kept* the Commandment their ancestor gave them' or 'observed all his rules and *did* all that he commanded'. The 'Rechabites', therefore, are one of the first groups of so-called 'Keepers', the basis of the definition of 'the Sons of Zadok' in the Community Rule at Qumran. The behaviour of these Rechabites – to whom the Prophet Jeremiah himself seems to have been connected – is contrasted sharply with the other Israelites in Jeremiah's own time (*c.* 605 BC), who are about to be destroyed by God for just the opposite kind of behaviour, 'lack of Faithfulness'.

In 2 Kings 10, Jonadab is presented as a colleague of Jehu. His 'heart' and Jehu's are 'True' to each other. Together they destroy the family of Ahab and Jezebel and wipe out the remnants of 'Baal' worship or idolatry. Importantly, aside from the episode in Numbers about Phineas' 'zeal' and Elijah's 'burning zeal' in 2 Kings, this is the only other episode in the Old Testament where 'zeal for the Lord' (Jehu's and Jonadab's) is specifically evoked (2 Kings 10:16). Therefore Jonadab son of Rechab is also 'zealous for God' or a prototypical 'Zealot'. In addition, like James and other Nazirites, he does not drink wine or strong drink. Whether or not Rechabites as such still existed some 700–800 years later can be debated, but the connection of this picture with the life-style attributed to James should be patent.

The life-style of the Rechabites, as we have implied, also has something in common with that of 'Nazirites', the classical account of whom occurs in Numbers 6:1–21. There the two characteristics that are emphasized are:

> separation from wine and strong drink, and neither drinking the juice of grapes, nor eating grapes, fresh or dried . . . no razor shall touch his head until the time of his consecration [or 'separation'] to the Lord is complete. (6:3–6:5)

Obviously both of these themes bear on the description of James via Hegesippus in all early Church sources:

> He was Holy from his mother's womb; he drank no wine or strong drink, nor did he eat meat; no razor touched his head, nor did he anoint himself with oil . . .[70]

Epiphanius adds, he 'died a virgin at the age of ninety-six', which relates to the Rechabite 'long life on the land' in Jeremiah above.

But the strong emphasis on 'abstention from wine' or 'strong drink' and neither 'drinking the juice of nor eating grapes fresh or dried' in Numbers' description of the Nazirites, also, bears on the life-style of Jonadab's descendants, who seem to have made this a fetish and the very basis of their unsettled or sojourning life-style embodying non-attachment to material or settled produce.

Where James is concerned, both the theme of abstention from wine and strong drink reappears, as does 'the razor not touching his head' in connection with the idea of either being 'consecrated' or 'separated'. This is also a *priestly* theme, as we have seen, and it is even evoked in Ezekiel's 'Zadokite Statement' (44:20–21). For the Rechabites the 'abstention from wine' theme, if not the 'long hair' one, is central – though as we have already noted, the themes of 'the unpruned vine' and 'unshorn hair' (not to mention 'the *Nezer*' or 'Crown' of the High Priests) are related in Hebrew.[71]

As we have seen, Eusebius is quite aware of the connection of the 'Rechabite' theme to something having to do both with James and/or the members of his immediate family. In the account of the death of James, which follows the account of James' life-style and epithets in Hegesippus, the 'Rechabite' ideal very prominently comes into play. As reported by Eusebius, Hegesippus also knows that these are the 'Rechabites spoken of by Jeremiah the Prophet' (and unlike Matthew above on Judas *Iscariot*, he *gets his prophet right*). In this account, 'one of the Priests of the sons of Rechab', that is, a 'Rechabite Priest', calls out to those who are stoning James, to cease what they are doing, saying 'Justus' ('*Zadok*' in Hebrew) or 'the Just One is praying for you'. James, too, is pictured as repeating 'on his knees' the cry attributed to Jesus in Luke 23:34: 'Father, forgive them, for they know not what they do.'

In Epiphanius' parallel account, where he actually says that James 'was a Nazirite and therefore connected to the Priesthood', this 'Rechabite Priest' is named and now becomes Simeon bar Cleophas.[72] That is, however historical these confusing notices may be, in Epiphanius' view, Simeon bar Cleophas, the 'cousin of' and successor to James as Head of the Jerusalem Community, and no doubt early Christianity in the East as well, was 'a Rechabite Priest', whatever one might wish to make of this circumlocution.

In the writer's view, much can be made of it, particularly when one reviews the evidence and data from Qumran in conjunction with these early Church accounts of the Jewish Christians or so-called 'Ebionites'. If we take full note of the contexts in which the term emerges, which ancient exegetes also did, then both 'keeping' and 'zeal' are associated in some manner with either the Rechabites or their progenitor.[73]

In the letter ascribed to James, too, the 'keeping' terminology is prominent throughout, not to mention the *doing*. It is also, as we have seen, the essence of the definition of 'the Sons of Zadok' at Qumran, that is, 'the Keepers of the Covenant'. In the first adumbration of this in the

Community Rule, 'the Priests' are associated with this as well, not to mention the command '*to separate* from all the men of Unrighteousness, who walk in the Way of Evil'.[74] Therefore, one can conceive of all of these terminologies, 'Nazoraeans', 'Sons of Zadok', 'Rechabites', and the like, as being in a sense parallel or variations on a theme.

For the Letter of James and Qumran, there is an additional one, that is, 'doing' or 'Doers'. This finds repeated use in James, and it and variations of it are found throughout the literature at Qumran – as it is in all literature from the works–Righteousness perspective – as, for instance, the Koran. 'Doers of the *Torah*' is a key terminology in the Habakkuk *Pesher*. This is particularly the case in exegesis of Habakkuk 2:3, the scriptural warrant at Qumran for what goes by the name of 'the Delay of the *Parousia*' in Christianity – the delay of the Last Days and the coming of Christ in Glory. It is also a precondition to the exegesis in this *Pesher* of Habakkuk 2:4, 'the Righteous shall live by his Faith' – the basis of Paul's theological approach in Galatians and Romans – making it clear that we have to do with an approach opposite to him on these things.[75]

We are in the rarefied air of high theological debate here, one side marshalling its scriptural passages against the other, one side turning the scriptural passages evoked by the other back against it. For the Letter of James, these 'Doers' ('of the word' or 'of the work' – 1:23–1:25) '*keeping the Royal Law according to the Scripture*', are ranged against 'the Breakers of the Law' in exactly parallel fashion as at Qumran (2:8–9).[76]

As noted, this term, '*Osei ha-Torah* (*Torah*-Doers), has been identified as one of the possible bases of the nomenclature 'Essenes'.[77] The latter notation puzzled scholars, since it does not appear in either the New Testament or the *Talmud*. Rather, it is found in both Josephus and his Jewish contemporary, Philo of Alexandria, the author of the *Mission to Gaius* mentioned above. His nephew, Tiberius Alexander, mentioned in Acts 4:6, was also Titus' chief of staff when he destroyed the Temple. Bernice, too, was originally married to a relative of his (probably his brother) and another seems to have been married to her sister, the third Herodian princess Mariamme, who divorced her previous husband, the son of the *Herodian Temple Treasurer,* to marry someone apparently even *Richer*.

One possible derivation of 'Essenes' is via the Aramaic for 'Pious Ones' (*Hassidim* in Hebrew), but this derivation, while appropriate, cannot be proved. Epiphanius thinks that the word actually denotes 'Jesus' or his father 'Jesse', that is, 'Jesusians' or 'Jessaeans'.[78] But this, too, while perhaps the reality, is laboured. "*Osei ha-Torah*' or ' '*Osaeans*' (in Epiphanius, 'Ossaeans' or 'Ossenes') works best, and has the additional benefit of not only being Hebrew, but an actual term used in the Qumran documents. If this is true and the basis of 'Essenes' is the word 'Doers' in Hebrew, then we have another additional parallel here not only to Nazirites, but Nazoraeans, Rechabites, and Sons of Zadok as well.

Another notice about Rechabites in 1 Chronicles 2:55 identifies them as 'Kenites'. Their genealogy is traced back to Caleb the son of Hur from Ephratah (2:50). This last has significance regarding the location of Jesus' birth, 'Ephratah' in Scripture being designated as equivalent to Bethlehem.[79] Now 'the Kenites' were considered to be Jethro's people from Sinai, with whom Moses resided, a daughter of whom he married – that is, Moses' descendants were to some degree to be identified with 'Kenites'. Subsequently, tradition pictures them as living among the Tribe of Judah.[80] Though these relationships are somewhat abstruse, what is most important in all this is that these 'Kenites' were considered to be metal-workers or smiths, that is, 'Potters' – the words are interchangeable in Hebrew, '*Yozrim*', a term moving directly into the usage '*Nozrim*' for Christians, itself underlying the 'Nazoraean'/'Nazarean' terminology.

This brings us full circle. If we now return to the Rabbinic tradition about 'Potters being Rechabites who kept the oath of their father', a gloss on 1 Chronicles 4:23, we can see that these 'Tinkers' or 'Potters' are considered to be descendants of the Tribe of Judah as well. Not only is the tradition somewhat obscure, but in it they are described as 'sojourning in plantations and enclosures' and employed 'in the workshop of the King', with whom they are said to have 'dwelled' as well. This brings us back to the workshop of 'the Potter in the House of the Lord' in Zechariah 11:13, alluded to in connection with Judas *Iscariot*'s suicide in Matthew 27:9 above.

It also follows a garbled note in 1 Chronicles 4:22 about a previous involvement of some kind with Moab across the Jordan – the 'Perea' of John the Baptist's area of activity – and perhaps 'Bethlehem'. The Catholic Vulgate has them, like David's ancestor, taking wives from 'Moab before returning to Bethlehem long ago'. These accounts also associate them with an area or town in this region known as 'Chozeba' (4:22). This may have been the original behind Bar Kochba's name, the Jewish Messianic leader and revolutionary of the next generation.

Whatever the significance of these aspects of the *Rechabite/Potter* problem, those called 'Rechabites' had no fixed abode, lived in tents, and, in particular, were not attached to material things. Not only did 'their father Jonadab son of Rechab' give them commandments and ordinances, which 'they kept' (*linzor*), he was also a 'Zealot for the Lord' involved in Jehu's final destruction of idolatry. The reason, clearly, that his descendants were pictured as 'living in no fixed abode nor cultivating the grape' was to emphasize their non-attachment to material things and, therefore, their 'zeal for God'. The 'making oneself a Friend of the world' or 'Friend' or 'Enemy of God' derogations can be thought of as related to these. *Per contra*, Jesus, on the other hand, is portrayed in the Gospels as a 'wine-bibbing' '*Friend of tax collectors and Sinners*' (Matt. 17:19; Luke 7:34).

Whether they still existed in James' time is beside the point. James too, is pictured by Eusebius, Epiphanius, and Jerome as 'abstaining from wine and strong drink, no razor ever touching his head', and 'a Nazirite', in his case – since 'he was consecrated from his mother's womb' – a *life-long Nazirite*. Further, as the term 'Holy' or 'consecrated' sometimes implies, a 'Priest', in his case, according to our sources, a *High Priest*. If we combine the accounts of Eusebius and Epiphanius, both obviously based on Hegesippus before them, then James also had a brother – this will be our argument – one of the *Desposyni* or family of Jesus in Palestine (one should recall Julius Africanus' claim that these came from two towns in Judea or Transjordan called 'Nazara and Cochaba') who was a 'Rechabite' priest.

What does this mean? All three, Eusebius, Epiphanius, and Jerome, will now go on to proclaim not only James' claims to priestliness, but, also, the even more astonishing claim that he actually wore the mitre of a *High Priest*. Of course, the reader will have noted that in all that has been stated above we are moving towards making *High Priestly* claims on behalf of James. This will be associated with another claim we shall encounter in all these texts, that James 'wore no woollen garments and only wore linen', that is, the linen the priests in the Temple wore.[81]

The Sons or Daughters of the Rechabites as High Priests

In the Qumran literature there are the 'Sons of Zadok' claims associated with 'the Priests who were the Keepers of the Covenant' or just simply 'keeping the Covenant', there is the priestly behaviour of the 'Essenes', there is the note in Acts about a 'multitude' of Priests ('the Many' at Qumran?) joining the Movement connected to James' leadership in Jerusalem, there is 'the Zealot Movement' itself and its allied claim of 'the zeal of Phineas' first raised by Maccabeans to legitimatize their new priesthood and reflected in the single historical notice we have about Jonadab son of Rechab. Finally, there are the High Priestly claims made on behalf of Jesus in the Letter to the Hebrews, that he was a 'Priest after the order of Melchizedek' (5.6, etc., together with repeated claims about his 'Perfection'), which even the unschooled will be able to recognize as a variation, when taken esoterically not literally, of 'the Sons of Zadok' claim.

There is also an earlier notice about a Rechab – the first one we have – that may or may not have something to do with our subject, namely, that 'Rechab' in the period of David and Saul was a Benjaminite, connected in some manner to 'Be'orite's (2 Sam. 4:2). Though this is a negative notice, again we are cutting into familiar themes here. There is a hint in this notice, too, of being 'sojourners' or 'resident aliens' (4:3). This theme of 'resident aliens' is important vis-à-vis the 'God-Fearer' ideology we have been encountering and the language of 'joining' or 'Joiners' connected to it in Esther and elsewhere – also denoting Gentiles associating themselves in some fashion with the Jewish Community, but not necessarily taking the Law upon themselves in a permanent or thoroughgoing manner.

This theme of 'resident alien' (ger-nilveh), as we have seen, is very strong in another Qumran Document, the Nahum Pesher. This is an extremely important Qumran document, almost rivalling in significance the Pesher on the Prophet Habakkuk. As usual, it is a 'Zaddik' text, that is, in the underlying biblical text, there is a reference as in the Habakkuk text, to the Hebrew word 'Zaddik' or 'Righteous One', James' cognomen. In this Pesher the resident aliens (ger-nilvim) are associated with two further esoteric usages. Firstly, the 'City of Blood', which we have already suggested connects in some manner to Paul's 'erecting a Community' – even if only symbolically – based 'on blood', that is to say, drinking 'the Cup of the blood of Christ'. Symbolic or real, it would not matter to the purist at Qumran or 'the Zealot'.

The second is a usage which plays off another found in the Habakkuk Pesher, 'the Simple of Judah doing Torah'. This allusion to 'Simple' not only is the parallel of 'these Little Ones' in the Gospels, but another term in these texts and at Qumran generally, 'the Ebionim'/'the Poor' or 'the Meek'.

The last notice about Rechabites we have in the Old Testament is that one of their descendants, Malchijah son of Rechab, returned with the émigrés in the time of Ezra and Nehemiah (Neh. 3:14 – c. 450 BC). To him was given the responsibility of repairing one of the Jerusalem gates known as 'the Dung Gate', also not without significance, as the Dung Gate, as its name implies, was the 'Poorest' gate of all. It also appears to have been known as or hardly distinguishable from 'the Gate of the Essenes'. Malchijah is one of the twenty-four priestly courses listed in 1 Chronicles 24:9. If this is the same group as that of 'Malchijah the son of Rechab', then we have another notice of a further genealogical link of the Rechabites to the Priesthood functioning in Jesus' and James' day.

But in this idea of their ability 'to repair gates', one also has a hint of their craftsman-like skills, and we are back to our Potters, smiths, or tinkers again. This is not to mention the note of 'carpentry' associated with either Jesus in Mark 6:3 or his father in Matthew 13:55.[82] In Nehemiah 3:31, this Malchijah is actually also called 'the metalsmith's son'!

This brings us back to Rabbinic literature once again and not only reinforces these notices about the *Rechabite* life-style, but once again connects them, however tenuously, to the High Priesthood and *doing service at the altar*. Let us assume that these wilderness 'sojourners' or 'Potters' – people, who with an eye towards extreme purity regulations and avoiding human entanglements, purposefully pursued a life-style with no permanent abode and abstained from wine or even cultivating vineyards – did somehow become involved in a genealogical manner with the High Priesthood, as these Rabbinic notices attest. Then these notices give the impression not only that this did occur, but how it happened.

In these Talmudic notices we hear in a *midrash* – a folkloric expansion – on this same Jeremiah 35 passage about Rechabites, that 'the sons of Rechab were married to the daughters of the High Priests' and 'did service in the Temple' at least in the period just preceding the compilation of the materials in question. Another Talmudic tradition reverses this claiming 'the daughters of the Rechabites married *the sons of the High Priests*'. This last brings us very close to the picture in the Gospel of Luke of John the Baptist's origins, who 'drank no wine' and wore a kind of clothing typical of the wilderness-dwelling descendants of these 'Potters'.[83] However these things may be, we have in these Rabbinic notices extremely important testimony to the fact of wilderness-dwelling types like such 'Rechabites' – whom in other descriptions might be called 'life-long Nazirites', or even possibly 'Nazoraeans' – *doing service in the Temple*.

In fact, around 1165 CE, the Spanish traveller, Benjamin of Tudela, claims to have encountered large numbers of such Jewish 'Rechabites' in Arabia north of Yemen, who (James-like) also, 'ate no meat, abstained from wine', 'lived in caves', and continually fasted, being 'mourners for Jerusalem' and 'Zion'.[84]

12

James' Bathing and Clothing Habits

James Wearing Only Linen and His *Yom Kippur* Atonement

The next point in all these early Church testimonies, that James wore only linen and was in the habit of entering 'the Sanctuary' or 'Temple' *alone*, now becomes more important than ever and is connected with Temple service and priestliness. The actual text, again from Hegesippus, is given most completely by Eusebius and reads as follows:

> He did not *anoint himself with oil*, nor did he *go to the baths*. He alone was allowed to *enter into the Place of Holiness*, for he did not wear wool, but linen, and he *used to enter the Temple alone*, and was often found upon his bended knees, interceding for the forgiveness of the people, so that *his knees became as callused as a camel's*, because of the constant importuning he did and kneeling before God and asking forgiveness for the people.[1]

The handling of this pivotal notice by our three principal sources is both illustrative of how their minds were working and what they originally saw in the source or sources before them. Jerome, obviously working from the same source as Eusebius – perhaps even Eusebius himself, though this is doubtful – echoes Eusebius' version of Hegesippus in connecting James' 'wearing only linen and not wool' with the fact of his 'entering the Temple'. What is different, however, is that, whereas Eusebius speaks of James entering 'the Sanctuary' or 'Holy Place', Jerome actually calls this 'the Holy of Holies', meaning the Inner Sanctum of the Temple.

Given the fact that the two usages, 'Temple' and 'Holy Place', which occur separately in Eusebius' quotation, are different in Greek, I think we can be persuaded that Jerome, who knew Hebrew, is more accurate on this point, especially as rendered into English. In addition, it is equally clear, when taking into consideration Jerome's rendering, that what is being spoken of here is the atonement that the High Priest was permitted to make once a year in the Holy of Holies, supplicating God for forgiveness on behalf of the sins of the whole people.

The sins can be thought of either as communal or of omission, that is, sins that you were not conscious of or had no power over in their commission. Sins that you were aware of or had power over obviously could be expiated in the normal manner.

This is the basis of the Jewish Day of Atonement or Festival of *Yom Kippur* to this day. That is, it is quite clear that what is being pictured here in these somewhat garbled accounts is a *Yom Kippur* atonement of some kind which James was reported to have made. This was made in the Holy of Holies by the High Priest once a year (Exod. 30:10 and Lev. 16:34 – this last followed in Leviticus 17:10–11 by the absolute proscription on 'eating any blood' both for all of the House of Israel and the sojourning stranger [*ger*]).

The purity arrangements regarding this atonement were stricter than normal and definitely involved 'bathing' (Lev. 16:4). Normally the High Priest wore eight garments of fine linen and wool. But on the Day of Atonement, he wore only four: linen coat, linen breeches, linen girdle, and linen head-dress or mitre. These were to be white and of coarse, not refined linen, in pursuance of Leviticus 16:4's prescription that these also be 'Holy'. The emphasis on 'Holiness' is very important where James is concerned and these are clearly the clothes James is pictured as wearing on an ordinary basis in consequence of his extreme Holiness.

The Day of Atonement was commemorated on the Tenth Day of the Seventh Month (Exod. 12:3 and Lev. 27:32), the people already having been prepared for it by festivities at the beginning of this the Jewish holy month. These rose to a climax in the pilgrimage festivities at Tabernacles or the Feast of Booths in the Temple, thought to commemorate not only 'wilderness' sojourning again, but also in some manner dedication to or receiving the *Torah* or the Law.

As Jerome puts it:

> He alone had the *privilege of entering the Holy of Holies*, since indeed *he did not wear woollen garments only linen*, and *he went alone into the Temple* and prayed on behalf of the people, so much so that *his knees were reputed to have acquired the hardness of camels' knees*.

Here Jerome reproduces all Eusebius' points, but in a more convincing rendition, since he makes plain what was meant by 'Holy Place'.

Epiphanius reproduces these things somewhat differently again and, fanciful or not, he does have the merit of understanding their significance *vis-à-vis* the matter of a *Yom Kippur atonement*. As he puts it, having just noted that James was 'a Nazirite' and, therefore, 'consecrated' – once again Epiphanius, aside from his numerous *faux-pas*, shows himself adept at grasping the true thrust of many of these matters:

> But we find further that he also exercised *the Priesthood according to the Ancient Priesthood*. For this reason he was permitted to enter the Holy of Holies once a year, as Scripture says the Law ordered the High Priests.

He rephrases this in his second version of these things as follows:

> To James alone it was permitted to enter the Holy of Holies once a year, *because he was a Nazirite and connected to the priesthood* . . . James was a distinguished member of the priesthood . . . James also wore a diadem [the '*Nezer*' or sacerdotal plate] on his head.[2]

In the first version, he reiterates this, saying:

> Many before me have reported this of him – Eusebius, Clement and others. He was, also, allowed to wear the mitre on his head as the aforementioned trustworthy persons have testified in the same historical writings.

Epiphanius has substituted 'mitre' for 'linen' here, and we must make a decision as to which to consider more reliable, Eusebius/Jerome or Epiphanius. There may be reasons for supporting either side, but 'linen' is a little more conservative. Still, in all Old Testament accounts 'the mitre' or High Priestly head-dress was made of linen anyhow (Exod. 28:39 and pars.). Since both Jerome and Epiphanius associate it with his entering the *Inner Sanctum* of the Temple, I think we can assume that James did wear linen, always keeping in mind that the claim of wearing the mitre of the High Priest – with the words 'Holy to God' emblazoned on its plate – was always possible as well.

In any event, Epiphanius adds to his testimony, saying 'he only wore a linen cloak', associating this with the 'linen cloth' the young man left behind in the curious episode related to Jesus' arrest in Mark 14:51. In addition, as just noted, Epiphanius understands that, however one construes these matters, they are related to at least one *Yom Kippur* atonement of some kind that James made. We say 'one', because this is what seems to have been involved, again always reserving the possibility that the practice may have been habitual or there may have been many. In any event our sources all tell us of *at least one*.

Epiphanius now goes on in his extensive analysis of these things to tell us of the High Priesthood of Jesus, the one denoted in Hebrews as the

Priesthood 'after the order of Melchizedek' (5:6 and 7:15–22). Hebrews goes on to describe this further as bringing the

> perpetual intercession . . . of a High Priest, who is *holy*, unblemished, *unpolluted, separated from Sinners*, and *higher*. (7:25–26)

The phrase 'a Priest forever after the order of Melchizedek' ('the King of Righteousness') is from Psalm 110:4. Leaving aside whether we should regard its meaning there as esoteric or real, the psalm also uses the imagery of 'making your enemies a footstool' (110:1), found in both Acts and at Qumran, and incorporates the phrase 'Holy from the womb' we have already seen predicative of James as descriptive of such a priest (110:3).

Epiphanius sums this up in the orthodox manner as follows:

> And he sits on the Throne of David and has transferred David's crown and granted it, with the High Priesthood, to his own servants, the High Priests of the Catholic Church.

We have encountered this 'Throne' allusion with regard to James before, but for Epiphanius, this Priesthood would appear to have been different from that exercised by James, which was simply 'the Priesthood according to the Priestly Order of old', though the two reckonings may be thought of as overlapping.[3]

So persistent is this note of James' 'asking forgiveness on his knees on behalf of the whole people' that it is picked up in all accounts of James' death – accounts in which Epiphanius substitutes the name of Simeon bar Cleophas ('Clopas') for 'one of the Priests of the sons of Rechab, a son of Rechabites' found in Eusebius. We shall see below how both the themes of James' 'knees' and his 'linen clothes' figure in further adumbrations of these matters in accounts relating to Christ's death.[4] Though it is possible Epiphanius confused 'linen' and 'headplate', both characteristic of what High Priests wore, it is difficult to believe that he made up 'Simeon bar Cleophas' as the witness to James' death all by himself. For this reason and others, Epiphanius would appear to be operating from sources additional to Eusebius where matters such as these are concerned.[5]

The fact, too, that all accounts connect James' 'praying on behalf of the people' with both his atonement in the Temple and his subsequent stoning will have interesting additional consequences when it comes to connecting his stoning with the atonement in the *Inner Sanctum*. In Epiphanius Simeon bar Cleophas cries out with regard to James' stoning, 'Stop, he is uttering the most marvellous prayers for you'; in Eusebius simply, 'the

Just One is praying for you' – 'the Just One', as we have seen, used in place of James' very name itself.

James' 'knees growing as hard as the nodules' of the knees of a camel, because of all the 'supplicating God' or the 'praying' in the Holy of Holies or in the Temple he did, is so original that it is difficult to imagine that Hegesippus simply made it up. It is eye-catching bits or snippets of information like this that often add to the credibility of the whole testimony.

Whether James' 'hardened kneecaps', which resembled the calluses of a camel, should be associated with one *Yom Kippur* atonement, several, or the habitual praying he did in the Temple will be for the reader to determine. However, it is very easy to imagine that at one point James did go into the *Inner Sanctum* of the Temple, the Holy of Holies, to make atonement on behalf of the whole people and that he was so 'Holy' and 'Pious' that he stayed there 'on his knees' the whole day in supplication to God. In other words, this was the Righteous prayer of a Priest/*Zaddik*.

This is one way of looking at it. There may be others. Much scorn has been heaped upon this testimony, particularly in Christian scholarship, but this was before the discovery of the Dead Sea Scrolls. Since that time, not only do we have the ideology to support such a picture of an 'Opposition' Righteous (or 'Zadokite') High Priesthood, but in the Habakkuk *Pesher*, there is a tantalizingly obscure notice about seemingly mortal difficulties between the followers of the Righteous Teacher (referred to as 'the Poor'/'*Ebionim*') and the Wicked Priest.[6]

But the details of this scenario, in fact, do recommend themselves as a prelude to the events of James' execution. So clear and compelling, where credibility is the issue, do these become that they even supplant those relating to Jesus' death in the Gospels. For instance, it is in a context such as this, either in the Holy of Holies before his stoning or in the course of his stoning afterwards, that one can truly imagine the phrase ascribed to Jesus and Stephen in Scripture and James outside it: 'Father, forgive them, for they know not what they do' being uttered (Luke 23:34 and Acts 7:59–60).

In the latter Paul becomes the witness and there is the puzzling issue of 'the witnesses' *clothes*' (7:58). We shall be able to bring this picture of *the stoning of Stephen*, together with Stephen having 'bent to the knees' as 'he prayed', into greater proximity with *the stoning of James* and 'the prayer' he uttered according to our sources – these now accompanied by the note of 'a laundryman's club to beat out *clothes*'.

The Background to James' Atonement in the Temple

The issue of James' 'wearing only linen' also bears on the notice in Josephus about the lower priesthood winning the right to wear 'linen' in the run-up to the destruction of the Temple in the 60s, at the end of the period James held sway in Jerusalem. Josephus does not date this event precisely, but he obviously considers it an 'innovation' and one more nail in the Temple's coffin, for, as he puts it, 'all this was contrary to ancestral Laws, and such Law-breaking was bound to make us liable for punishment'.[7] He means, of course, Divine retribution and Divine punishment and the coming destruction of the Temple.

He uses the same language to describe another 'innovation', as we saw, that of the stopping of sacrifice by these same lower priests on behalf of Romans and other foreigners in the Temple in this same period, which started the Uprising against Rome. As he describes the run-up to this in the 50s, the time of Felix's original coming to Palestine, he refers to the 'bands of brigands and impostors who deceived the masses. Not a day passed, however, but that Felix captured and put to death many of these Deceivers and Brigands.'[8] For Josephus, it will be recalled,

> Those who would deceive the people and the religious frauds, under the pretence of Divine inspiration *fostering innovation* and *change in Government*, persuaded the masses to act like madmen and *led them out into the desert* promising them that there God would give them *the tokens of freedom*.[9]

Paul uses the same language when he alludes to 'those who would spy on the *freedom* we enjoy in Christ Jesus' in Galatians. One can say that Paul, whose view of 'freedom' and 'slavery' is obviously not political, is simply transforming into the spiritual sphere what such 'Deceivers' or 'Innovators' are demanding on the physical one. Philo is doing the same thing in his allegorization of Old Testament material. But Paul, his contemporary, by his own admission is 'teaching by the Holy Spirit spiritual things spiritually' (1 Cor. 2:13) and 'allegorizing' (Gal. 4:24).

Having just described the attack, 'the Egyptian' on the Mount of Olives – whom Acts portrays as mistaken for Paul – launches on the Temple, Josephus sums up the situation as follows:

> The Deceivers and the Brigands, banding together, incited *Many* to revolt, exhorting them to assert *their freedom* and and threatening to kill any who

submitted to Roman Dominion and forcibly to put down any who voluntarily accepted *slavery*.

In the process, Josephus notes that these people went through Judea 'plundering the houses of the Rich and murdering their owners'.[10] When the Revolt finally broke out, those Josephus describes as 'Innovators' or 'desirous for social or revolutionary change' burned the debt records in an attempt 'to turn the Poor against the Rich'.

Later, as we saw, they not only burn the palaces of the Herodians and High Priests – the Herodians by this time had already departed into the Roman camp outside the city – but kill most of them. The reader must simply pay careful attention to the vocabulary of this period and all overlaps in the sources, no matter the context, while at the same time being careful to part the mist of purposeful obfuscation.

In the *Antiquities*, when describing the '*pollution* with which *the works* of the *Brigands infected the city*', Josephus describes the situation that developed under Felix, during whose Procuratorship similar problems broke out in Caesarea between Greeks, who had the support of the legionnaires, and the Jews.[11] Caesarea, it will be recalled, was the scene in Acts of Paul's cordial interviews with Felix and his Herodian in-laws and Paul's incarceration too in 'Herod's palace'. After the assassination of Ananus' brother Jonathan by the most extreme group of Revolutionaries he calls '*Sicarii*', Josephus notes how:

> They committed these murders not only in other parts of the city but even in some cases in the Temple; for . . . they did not regard even this as a *desecration*. This is the reason why, in my opinion, even God himself, *loathing their Impiety*, turned away from our city, and because, He *deemed the Temple to no longer be a clean dwelling place for Him*, brought the Romans upon us and *purification by fire upon the city*, while He inflicted *slavery upon us* together with our wives and children; for He wished to *chasten us by these calamities*.

Not only is the charge of 'blasphemy' we shall see levelled against James and in the Gospels against Jesus now turned against the extremists; but the woes of the Jews are the fault of the *Sicarii*.

This is the way, with hindsight, that Josephus describes the events in the 50s, events in which Paul and James played key roles. He is, of course, turning the language of those who pursued such 'innovations' in upon themselves. One should remark how self-serving or facile his view of history is paralleling, too, so closely the way the Gospels portray the death of Christ. We shall see the same language used in the Damascus Document, but there applied to 'the Seekers after Smooth Things' and other collaborators who attacked 'the Righteous One' and 'all the Walkers in Perfection with the sword'. As a result of this, too, it is remarked that 'the Wrath of God was kindled against their Congregation, devastating all their multitude, for *their works were* as unclean before Him' and 'He delivered them up to the avenging sword of vengeance of the Covenant' – a favourite theme throughout the Damascus Document.[12]

Josephus speaks the same way when the Roman garrison in the Citadel – the same garrison that rescued Paul from the bellicose mob in the Temple seven years earlier – is slaughtered in the early days of the Uprising, all save one, its captain, who agreed to have himself circumcised:

> And the city polluted by such a stain of guilt as could not but arouse a dread of some *Visitation from Heaven*, if not of vengeance from Rome.[13]

Josephus is, of course, writing with the advantage of hindsight. So is Christianity in its similar portrayal of the downfall of the Jews as a result of the death of Jesus Christ. As Eusebius, Constantine's confidant and a principal founder of High Church Christianity as we know it, puts it over and over again:

> The Divine Justice for their crimes against Christ and his Apostles finally overtook them, *totally destroying the whole generation of these evildoers from the earth*. But the number of calamities which then overwhelmed the whole nation . . . the vast numbers of men, women and children that fell by the sword and famine, and innumerable other forms of death . . . and the final destruction by fire, all this I say, any one that wishes may see accurately stated *in the History written by Josephus* . . . Such then was *the vengeance* that followed *the guilt* and *Impiety of the Jews against the Christ of God*.[14]

Eusebius has no pity here, not even for the suffering of women and children, nor the starvation of thousands upon thousands; in fact, so intoxicated is he by theology that he revels in it.

But the real truth of the time undoubtedly lies embedded in these descriptions in Josephus and their obvious reversal of the real philosophy of 'the Innovators'. This last, as repeatedly signalled in this book, can now be said to be manifestly revealed in the documents known as the Dead Sea Scrolls and a *real* understanding of the Community led by James the Just. Writing of the end of the governorship of Felix – the individual who probably arranged Paul's appeal to Rome – Josephus states:

> There was now enkindled *mutual enmity and class warfare* between *the High Priests on the one hand and the Priests and Leaders of the masses of Jerusalem on the other.* Each of the factions formed and collected for itself a band of the most reckless Innovators, who acted as their leaders. And when they clashed, they used abusive language and *pelted each other with stones.* And there was *not even one person to rebuke them.*[15]

Here we have a moment of candour rare in Josephus.

Seen in a different light, one can see in this description the debates in the Temple between the two factions, pictured in both the Pseudo-clementines and Acts, however tendentiously – including even the rioting – and events like the stoning of James. Even the note of there being 'no one to rebuke them' is reversed in the picture in early Church sources of the words of James' successor Simeon bar Cleophas, the 'Rechabite Priest', who *rebukes* those stoning James the Just.

Not only do we have in this picture both the themes of the High Priests being opposed by the lower priests – who, in turn, were 'the leaders of the masses' and 'stoning' – but Josephus follows up this description with his picture of how the High Priests shamelessly sent their servants to the threshing floors '*to steal the tithes of the Poorer*' Priests, who consequently 'starved to death. *Thus did the violence of the contending factions over-whelm all Justice.*'[16] One can picture this description being applied to and even seen in terms of the death of James 'the Just One', who was the Leader of the faction calling itself – both at Qumran and in early Christianity – 'the Poor'.

Josephus portrays the fact of the lower priests winning the right to wear linen in the context of these events and this kind of rioting. Though these facts all need further evaluation and elucidation, for the moment it should suffice to state that James' role as a priest among the masses in the midst of all this revolutionary strife is emerging. Nowhere is it better explained than in the literature at Qumran, the literature of that group we can now see as part of those seeking just these kinds of 'Innovations'. We certainly do have there the theme of the Rich High Priests 'stealing' the tithes of the Poor Ones.[17] Moreover its authors saw the Temple as 'polluted', but not for the reasons Josephus attempts to disseminate or, from a slightly different perspective, Paul and early Christian theologians following his lead do.

The Temple is polluted because of *the acceptance of polluted gifts in the Treasury*, because of the acceptance of fornicators in the Temple, because of improper 'separation of Holy Things', and relations with foreigners and those to whom Paul's very mission is addressed – Gentiles.

In such a context, one can see Paul's final entry into the Temple to show that 'there is no truth to the rumours' that he does not 'regularly follow the Law' as something of a stalking horse for Herodian family interests in the Temple. The charge raised among the mob in the riot Acts pictures as ensuing there is that Paul is *introducing foreigners in the Temple*. One way or another he is. The same cry is no doubt on the lips of these extreme 'Zealots' or '*Sicarii*', who are behind the troubles in Jerusalem being described by Josephus. As Acts would have it, James' followers are a mixture of 'priests' – obviously lower priests – and others who are '*zealous for the Law*' (21:20). This is the same picture Josephus has just given us regarding confrontations and stone-throwing on the Temple Mount in the early 60s.

James and *Banus*

But this reference to James 'wearing only linen' also has interesting over-tones with someone Josephus calls only '*Banus*', clearly another of these individuals dwelling in the wilderness showing the signs of 'impending freedom' or 'Deliverance'. John the Baptist and others are of the same mould. This individual is someone Josephus describes with affection, as he ostensibly does John and James. Never explaining what he means by *Banus*' name, Josephus describes him as 'living in the wilderness' and 'eating nothing than what grew of its own accord', meaning, he was *a vegetarian*. His picture of him has much in common with the one of James that has come down in early Church sources.[18]

Even *Banus*' name, like James' title, '*Zaddik*' or '*Zadok*', is probably not a name but really a title. Never definitively deciphered by scholars, it is probably a loan word via Latin having something to do with his most characteristic activity 'bathing'. If not, then like James' other title, '*Oblias*' or 'Protection of the People', it is probably a code.

Even more than being a vegetarian, there is a 'Rechabite' aspect to Josephus' description of *Banus*, since he does not *cultivate*. Like Judas Maccabee earlier he eats *only wild plants*. Once again, many of the themes we have been pursuing come together. *Banus* has to have been functioning 'in the wilderness' in the mid-50s, the period Josephus – who was born in 37 CE – states he spent three years with him. If Josephus did spend three years with him, it would account for his sympathetic treatment, even though he is normally opposed to such religious 'impostors and Deceivers' who lead the people out 'into the wilderness'. Josephus would seem to have an equal affection for John the Baptist and James, but there is more to link the two than this.

Three years, too, is the time frame Paul describes in Galatians of his having been 'to Arabia and then returned to Damascus' (1:17–18). It is, also, the approximate novitiate period for the Movement described in Qumran documents, another of these Communities 'in the wilderness' or 'at Damascus'.[19] However one takes this allusion by Paul to 'Arabia', 'wilderness' areas of this kind in Judea and Transjordan were not highly populated. Certainly Josephus' knowledge of the 'Essenes', must have come from this period, as in the *Vita* he describes having made a trial of the three sects: Pharisees, Sadducees, and Essenes, undergoing great hardship in the process.

Josephus also describes *Banus* as a daily bather and utterly chaste. This is exactly the same language Epiphanius uses to *describe James* leading up to his stoning and Simeon bar Cleophas' rebuke of those who stoned him, that 'he died a virgin at the age of ninety-six', repeatedly focusing on James' 'virginity'. Again, this links up with notices in both Josephus and Hippolytus about how incredibly 'long-lived' those they call 'Essenes' were because of their continent life-style:

> They are long-lived – most over a century – in consequence of the simplicity of their diet and the regularity of the mode of life they observe.[20]

We can forgive exaggerations over the age of these 'elderly and honourable' men, who, Epiphanius claims, followed the 'Nazirite' life-style. In a similar vein, following Hegesippus, Eusebius contends '*Simon* son of *Clopas* (*thus*) was crucified under Trajan at the age of a hundred and twenty'. This would have been in approximately the year 106–7.[21] These exaggerations and imperfect transmissions of data should not be too disconcerting, especially in view of the overlaps in traditions having to do with 'Simon'/ 'Simeon bar Cleophas' and 'Peter' already signalled. Epiphanius, quoting a book he calls 'The Travels of Peter' – meaning the Pseudoclementines – says that the Ebionites thought Peter was *celibate* too – in addition claiming that he was a *daily baptizer* and *vegetarian*. The reason, he says, the Ebionites give for this last is important – *because animal fare was 'the product of sexual intercourse'* too.[22]

For Epiphanius – and he does not give his source for this, but since it is detailed, most likely it is Hegesippus – all '*Joseph*'s sons [in due course we shall identify 'Joseph' and 'Cleophas'] *revered virginity* and the *Nazirite life-style*.²³ In associating the 'virginity' of these life-long Nazirites with the doctrine of 'the Holy Virgin', Epiphanius once again points the way towards comprehending another reversal we have been emphasizing. But what makes sense with regard to James and individuals like '*Banus*' following the regime of extreme purity in the wilderness makes little, if any, sense when it comes to 'honouring the vessel in which the Salvation of the human race dwelt' – words Epiphanius uses in explaining why the 'Holy Virgin' was also revered, words more aptly descriptive of *James*.

As Epiphanius, again so incisively, expresses this: 'She would not have sexual relations *with a man*.'²⁴ But, of course, this claim, except theologically speaking, is absurd, and James' *chasteness* has simply been transferred in tradition to Mary and the 'Virgin birth'. It is almost certain, despite facile attempts to disclaim it, that whoever Mary was, she had at least *four sons* and *two daughters*. Rather, it is James, who had *no sexual relations with women*, another example of retrospective theological inversion of, in our view, *real* detail from the life of James.²⁵

James' and *Banus*' 'chaste' life-style was, no doubt, connected to the extreme purity regime and that abhorrence of 'fornication' we have already seen integrally associated with James' name, not to mention the ethos of Qumran. But there is an additional element, too, where all these wilderness-dwelling 'Zealots' were concerned. As the Community Rule from Qumran – which also incorporates the theme of ritual immersion or bathing in streams, rivers, and pools, including a note of 'being cleansed by the Holy Spirit' – puts it in exposition of 'the Way in the wilderness' Prophecy of Isaiah 40:3:

> [*The Way*] is the study of the *Torah*, which He commanded by the hand of Moses . . . and [he] shall be as a man *zealous for the Law*, whose Time is *the Day of Vengeance*.²⁶

In the War Scroll from Qumran, this is set forth in a slightly different format, but the thrust is the same. This document describes how God 'shall accomplish Mighty Works by *the Holy Ones of His people*' ('the Consecrated Ones' also referred to in the Community Rule). As we saw, there shall be no woman, boy, blind, or cripple, or person 'smitten with pollution in his body' with them when they go out to the wilderness camps '*to war*', 'no one impure because of a bodily emission' (this was the same rule for the High Priest in the Holy of Holies at *Yom Kippur*).

And there shall be a space of about 2000 metres between all their camps and the place serving as a latrine, and no indecent nakedness shall be seen around any of their camps.

'All will be men, volunteering for war, *Perfect in spirit and body* [here, our Pauline 'spirit'/'body' vocabulary again] and prepared for *the Day of Vengeance* . . . for the Holy Angels are together with their hosts.'[27]

It then goes on in exposition of the Star Prophecy to picture the coming of the Heavenly Host together with a Messiah-like individual, in the manner of Daniel 7:13, 'on the clouds', 'shedding of Judgement on all that grows on earth like rain'. The terms of this proclamation not only mirror Jesus in the Sermon on the Mount (including 'Perfection' imagery – Matthew 5:45–48), in the Little Apocalypses, and at 'the House of the High Priest'; but even more so, James in the Temple in the events that culminate either in the attack on him by Paul or his being thrown down from a wing of the Temple and stoned and clubbed.

The Letter of James also climaxes in the imagery of rain, comparing the 'coming of the Lord' and 'Judgement' to the coming of rain (5:4–8), concluding with the evocation of Elijah's miraculous prayer for rain (5:16–18).[28] We shall hear about another '*Zaddik*' – Honi or Onias – preceding James, possibly related to his family or at least John the Baptist's, who, like Josephus' description of Essene sabbath observation, drew circles to bring the rain. Epiphanius will also evoke James' own rain-making capability in the course of his second notice about James wearing the mitre of the High Priest but never woollen clothes and describing how once, 'during a drought, he lifted his hands to Heaven and prayed, and at once Heaven sent rain'.[29]

Banus' eating things growing only of themselves is best explained by the notice about Judas Maccabee, who, when the sacrifice in the Temple was interrupted, retreated into the wilderness, lived in caves – another favourite motif connected with wilderness experiences – and ate nothing but 'wild plants to avoid contracting defilement'. Here, too, we have the extension of the 'vegetarian' theme to the Rechabite life-style of individuals, who, to avoid earthly attachments and corruptions – and no doubt 'Riches' – would cultivate nothing and would not even construct a permanent dwelling. Doubtlessly they, too, lived in caves, tents, or lean-tos of the kind probably preferred in the wilderness 'camp' ideology of Qumran. All these matters are connected and, depending on the observer and his particular point of reference, a given nomenclature is employed to describe them – thus, the plethora of titles we see associated with them.

No doubt, all these various groups were not inhabiting the wilderness at the same time. Wilderness habitation is a tenuous thing. Plus, anyone out 'in the wilderness' would more or less be known to everyone else. That is the way of wilderness sojourning, whether anchorites or recluses. Since settled life is so rare, all these groups not only would have known of each other's existence, but what each other represented. The same is true today for anyone living around or near the Dead Sea or, for example, solitary miners in any out-of-the-way locale. Every settlement, every person doing anything out of the ordinary is *known* by everyone else. This is true where bedouin are concerned as well.

In any event, all these nomenclatures are not all separate reckonings. Where the descriptions overlap, however tenuously, they must be seen as the same or allied movements. The same for these various groups. They are connected with the Maccabean ideal of eating non-cultivated plants. They are connected with living in caves. They are connected with the extreme purity regime. They are connected with attempts to bring on 'the Last Days'. They are connected with the description of the wilderness 'camps' in the Qumran literature. They are connected with Josephus' numerous and fulsome condemnations of such groups – meant, of course, to impress his Roman overlords – even though as a young man he spent time among them. Paul too, no doubt, did the same. Hence his in-depth knowledge of them also.

A final note about *Banus*' clothing, which now connects with our 'linen' theme where James is concerned, as it does the general one of non-cultivation about Rechabites and that of not wearing *woollen* garments reported of James. The number of these overlaps between *Banus* and James, given the paucity of materials about them overall, grows ever more curious. When speaking of *Banus*' clothing, Josephus tells us he wore nothing but *'clothing that grew on trees'*. There can be little doubt what he means by this despite the clumsiness of the Greek he uses to express it. He means 'plant'- or 'vegetable'-based not *woollen* clothes, that is, that *'Banus'* and other 'Priests' would only wear clothing of natural fibre or *linen*.

Not only are *'Banus'* and James obvious contemporaries, but the connections between them grow stronger, as do Josephus' connections to and reticence about them both. We have already seen that by the time of writing the *Antiquities* in the 90s, Josephus felt more secure than he had directly after the Uprising. He could afford to be less circumspect regarding individuals connected to his own activities in relation to such charismatic 'wilderness'-dwelling types. In light of the execution of his patron – Paul's possible associate and Nero's secretary – Epaphroditus, and one or two other reputed Christians in the then-Emperor Domitian's household, including Flavius Clemens (possibly the Clement of our literary fame) and possibly his wife, Flavia Domitilla, and new accusations surfacing against Josephus himself, this sense of security might have been ill-founded.[30]

Daily Bathers in Transjordan, Syria, and Iraq

In the case of 'Banus' – the meaning of his name notwithstanding – there is also the note about his repeated *bathing*, to wit, he 'bathed himself *in cold water* frequently both night and day'. Josephus presents this – particularly with his overseas audience in mind – as having to do principally with preserving his chastity. This may or may not have been how *Banus* saw it.

In this period, we have repeated references to 'Daily Bathers' – 'Hemerobaptists' as Eusebius calls them – when discussing how 'James the Just suffered martyrdom like the Lord and for the same reason' and the election of Simeon by universal consent as 'Bishop' of 'the Church' (*Ecclēsia* – the restriction to 'Jerusalem' this time dropped). Eusebius lists seven 'sects that once existed among the Jews'. As we saw, these included – in addition to the normal Pharisees, Sadducees, Essenes, and Samaritans – 'Galileans, Hemerobaptists, and Masbuthaeans'.[31] Putting aside for the moment the meaning of 'Masbuthaeans', 'Galileans' could as well relate to followers of Judas the *Galilean* – so-called Fourth Philosophy 'Zealots' and 'Sicarii' – as it can to those Acts says were first called 'Christians', not in Palestine but Antioch. 'Hemerobaptists' were daily bathers.

Often in our texts, the Flood brought on by the first *Zaddik* Noah's salvationary *Righteousness* and *Perfection* is connected with baptismal imagery. Baptism itself is simply another word for what goes in Judaism by the phraseology *ritual immersion*. The Dead Sea Scrolls, themselves, are full of direct or esoteric reference to baptism and ritual immersion. If the settlement at Qumran has anything to do with the practices of the Community pictured in the literature found near it, then the abnormally high number of ritual-immersion pools – which fit Rabbinic specifications for such installations – further evidence this, particularly in a wilderness locale where water was if nothing else scarce and does not even appear to have flowed perennially.

One recently published text, Professor Wise and I entitled a 'Baptismal Hymn', even describes such a ritual immersion and 'being cleansed by purifying waters'.[32] Both Hellenistic and Arab texts describe ritual bathers of this kind in Northern Syria, who face the rising sun and appear to worship it. Mandaeans in Iraq, claiming descent from followers of John the Baptist, portray themselves in their literature in a similar manner.[33] In Iraq, they were originally called 'Sabaeans' from the Syriac root *Sabu'a* meaning 'washed ones', from which, of course, the signification '*masbuta*'/'bathing' or 'immersion' is derived, the basis of Eusebius' mysterious 'Masbuthaeans'.

By Epiphanius' time – and, it should be remembered, Epiphanius came originally from Palestine – these sects of daily bathers were already strongly developed. Most he places across the Jordan and further north in Syria, and from thence on into Northern and Southern Iraq, where the Mandaeans – who call their priests '*Nasuraiya*' (that is, *Nazoraeans*) – are still to be found today. For Epiphanius, the 'Ebionites', whom, together with another group called the 'Sampsaeans', he places in this region on the other side of the Jordan as well, used water lavishly 'thinking they can purify themselves through baptisms'.[34] These 'Sampsaeans', as he describes them (that is, 'Sabaeans'), whom he also identifies with another group he refers to as 'Elchasaites', came out of the 'Ossaeans' on the other side of the Dead Sea in Perea (or Moab) where John the Baptist had previously been active, as were the various groups of 'Nazoraeans'.

Here, Epiphanius links up with the obviously earlier Apostolic Constitutions, an anonymous third-century Syriac work, probably contemporary with the Pseudoclementines and sometimes also attributed to Clement. This has the 'Essenes', like our *Nazirite* Rechabites above, '*separating themselves and observing the laws of their Fathers*'; and, like Eusebius, includes both Hemerobaptists and Masbuthaeans side-by-side in its group of *Jewish* heresies. For it, 'the Ebionites', also a Jewish sect, spring from these last. Interestingly, in the kind of phonetic reversal that should be becoming familiar in all these transpositions from one language to another, the Apostolic Constitutions refers to '*Masbuthaeans*' ('bathers') as '*Basmothaeans*'.[35]

Ultimately, these Northern Syrian daily-bathing and vegetarian groups, called by some 'Elchasaites' and by others 'Sabaeans', move into groups like the Manichaeans and Mandaeans in Southern Iraq, the latter known in later Arabic texts as 'the *Subba*' or 'the Sabaeans of the marshes' – the marshes being at the mouth of the Tigris and Euphrates Rivers.[36]

In fact, it is to Arabic texts and Islam we must turn to get a proper picture of these 'Sabaeans'. In the Koran and Islamic legal theory, while traditionally mistaken for a 'Southern Arabian' people, the 'Sabaeans' are one of the three groups of earlier 'Monotheists' Muhammad has encountered. With Christians and Jews, they are reckoned as 'People of the Book'.37 For Epiphanius, two centuries earlier, the group he is calling 'Sampsaeans' – identical to the 'Elchasaites' of Northern Syria and Iraq – are already 'intermediate' between Jews and Christians, and all these groups are vegetarian bathers.38 Clearly both must be seen as equivalent to what are being reckoned as 'Sabaeans' in Islam – 'Masbuthaeans' in Syriac.

Even Pliny in the early 70s is already locating a group he calls the 'Nazerini' in Northern Syria.39 Lucian of Samosata, a second century, Hellenistic traveller and writer, who contemptuously dismissed Jesus as 'a magician' and 'revolutionary', gives us a marvellous contemporary picture of Daily Bathers on the Euphrates in Northern Syria in his own time. These prayed to the rising sun, baptizing themselves at dawn. They ate nothing but wild fruit, milk, and honey – probably the food John the Baptist also ate.40 Like these and *Banus* – probably James too – Josephus' Essenes 'girded their loins with linen cloths, bathing their bodies in nothing but cold water, for purification'.41 Here, once again, one should note the emphasis on 'clothing', this time the linen girdle or 'bathing clothing'.

Hippolytus (*c.*160–235 CE), a century later, tells how a book by the individual he calls 'Elchasai', was brought to Rome, and he describes the followers of this *Elchasai* as having an incarnationist doctrine of many 'Christs', Jesus 'continually being infused into many bodies, manifested at many [different] times'.42 This, of course, is nothing but the '*Imam*' doctrine of *Shi'ite* Islam, which we have already compared to the 'Primal Adam' in the Ebionite Pseudoclementines. Calling *Elchasai* 'a Righteous Man', Hippolytus also attributes to him the doctrine of 'the Standing One' – already encountered in the Pseudoclementines above and one of the variations of 'the Primal Adam' – which he says *Elchasai transmitted to the Sobiai*. We are back to the daily bathing or Hemerobaptist 'Sabaeans' again.

Epiphanius also identifies the 'Standing One' doctrine as *Elchasai*'s, saying the Ebionites got it from him. As he puts this, they 'think that Christ is some Adam-like figure invisible to the naked eye, ninety-six miles high' ('ninety-six' now being applied to *Christ*'s height instead of *James*' age), having earlier noted, 'they say that Christ is Adam, the First Man created'. Earlier too he expressed this in terms of Christ being 'a Power', some 'ninety-six miles' high – once again, the 'Power' language of the Gospels. He 'comes into Adam' – in the Gospels this is in the form of 'a dove' – and 'clothes himself with the body of Adam', 'taking Adam off and then putting him on again as he wishes'.[43]

One should also note that Hippolytus' 'Naassenes' – whom he seems to think are an earlier group of 'Priests', *following the teachings of James*, have more or less this same doctrine of 'the Perfect Man'. They call him either 'Man' or 'Adam' – the 'Primal Adam' ideology delineated in the Pseudoclementines again – even sometimes, 'the Son of Man'.[44] For the Pseudoclementines, which appear to think that Simon *Magus* – together with another Samaritan named Dositheus – learned this doctrine from John the Baptist, 'the Standing One is the Exalted Power which is above the Creator god and can be thought of as being the Christ' or 'the Great Power of the High God ['that is, in other words, the Christ'] superior to the creator of the world'.[45]

Not only do these doctrines peer through the Gospels even in their present form, for instance, in the references to 'the Great Power' and the repeated allusions to 'standing', but their antiquity is attested to by Paul himself, who knows that Adam is 'the First Man' (that is, 'the Primal Adam') and that Jesus, 'the Son of Man' or 'the Lord out of Heaven', is 'the Second Man' and 'Heavenly' or 'a Heavenly One' – what he also refers to as 'the Last Adam' (1 Cor. 15:45–49). This, in turn, means that the knowledge of these doctrines and their identification with 'the Christ' comes before the Gospels in their present form and, true enough, reflections of the 'Primal Adam' ideology and the 'standing' vocabulary are to be found in the Dead Sea Scrolls.[46]

Not only are all these groups bathers, but so, too, is the group Hippolytus is calling, after Josephus and others, 'Essenes'. In Hippolytus' long description of this group, which, as we saw, contains additional information not present in Josephus, not only do the Essenes (as in Josephus and like *James*) abjure 'anointing themselves with oil', they wear 'linen girdles to conceal their privy parts' – perhaps the real point behind these ubiquitous 'clothing' allusions – and, like *Banus* and James, *'wash themselves in cold water'*. Detailing the extremity of all the ablutions these 'Essenes' do in 'cold water' both for the purposes of purifying themselves *and* sexual continence, Hippolytus concludes, echoing Josephus again but divulging more: 'Despising death, they rejoice when they can finish *their course in good conscience*' (see Paul in 1 Corinthians 9:24 and Galatians 5:7 above on 'finishing his course' and 'running the race to win').

If, however, anyone would even attempt to torture persons like this, either to induce one of them to speak Evil against the Law or *eat what is sacrificed to an idol*, he will not succeed, for such a one *submits to death* and *endures torture* rather than *violate his conscience*.[47]

Here, as we saw as well, we have so-called 'Essenes', because of their 'conscience', willing to undergo torture and martyrdom over a point echoed in James' directives to overseas communities and, as it turns out, *MMT* – 'abstaining from eating food sacrificed to idols', a point Paul so contemptuously refers to as 'weak'. As Paul puts this, evoking, as previously described, 'loving God' (that is, 'Piety') and scornfully referring to 'wounding' his opponents' 'weak consciences' (8:1–13):

> Some with conscience . . . eat of *things sacrificed to idols* and *their conscience, being weak, is defiled.* (8:7)

Not only do the ubiquitous James-like 'some' turn up, once again, in these aspersions by Paul, but nothing could better illlustrate the identity of these Essenes, Jewish Christians, Qumran sectarians, and Paul's Jerusalem Church interlocutors. This is how important Hippolytus' version of Josephus' testimony about 'Essenes' really is.

Sabaeans, Elchasaites, and Manichaeans

But it is to the Muslim geographer, al-Biruni (973–1048), we must turn to clarify further some of these confusions and overlaps. Al-Biruni's predecessor, the Encyclopaedist Muslims call 'The *Fihrist*' (c. 995), saw Sabaeans as the remnants of Babylonian '*star*' worshippers' in Iraq. Unlike him, al-Biruni identifies *two* groups of Sabaeans in Northern Syria in and around Haran, Abraham's city, from where the Elchasaites also came – described in the *Fihrist* as stemming from 'the remnant of the Jewish tribes who remained in Babylon'.[48]

One should note that this is exactly the region around Edessa Orrhoe – Antioch-by-Callirhoe – which was the scene of the conversion of Eusebius' Agbarus, 'the King of the Peoples beyond the Euphrates', who seems also to have considered himself in some manner a descendant of Abraham. Likewise, Queen Helen and her sons around Haran and further east in Adiabene.

It is worth remarking to show the importance of all these traditions that, even in the third century, Hippolytus places the locale, in which the ark of Noah settled on the mountains, in 'the land of the Adiabeni'. For al-Biruni, these 'Sabaeans' claimed to be descended from 'another son of Methusalah besides Lamech called 'Sabi'' – patronymic for *Sabaean* – who gave them 'a Divine Covenant' (the 'Noahic Covenant' again, now presumably also including *bathing*) and also traced their genealogy to Enosh son of Seth. '*Enosh*', it should be appeciated, meaning in Aramaic 'Man' (note the 'First Man'/'Primal Adam' overtones), was another name accorded *John the Baptist* among these Eastern daily-bathing groups.⁴⁹

Like the Manichaeans, another of these *vegetarian* Elchasaite groups in the third century, but who rather abjured 'bathing', al-Biruni reports that the Sabaeans turned 'towards the North Pole in prayer' or, as he rephrases it, both groups prayed 'towards the middle of the dome of Heaven at its highest place'.⁵⁰ But this is exactly the North–South orientation of the graves at Qumran, which has so puzzled scholars ever since the discovery of manuscripts in the nearby caves.⁵¹ What seems to be emerging is a general network of *bathing* communities, all with links to Nazirite-style or Nazoraean groups on both sides of the Dead Sea and in Northern Syria in the region of Haran and Edessa. If this is the reason for the North–South orientation of the graves at Qumran, then one can see the Qumran Community too as simply another of these Sabaean/Masbuthaean/Sampsaean/Nazoraean/Rechabite/Ebionite/Essene-type communities.

In Southern Iraq – which, later in this work, we shall show to be connected to members of the family of Helen of Adiabene and her husband (in Syriac tradition Agbarus above) – these traditions pass to the Mandaeans and Manichaeans, and from thence into Islam. In fact, Muhammad might have visited this region in his commercial activities where he would have encountered 'Sabaeans' and we shall definitively be able to show that he knows the traditions of Northern Syria and Edessa about Judas Thomas, James, and Addai – all of whom he will call 'Arabian' prophets.

Mani (216–277 CE), who was born in the region of Basrah (also called 'Mesene') at the mouth of the Tigris/Euphrates, really provides the missing link between these kinds of Sabaean/Elchasaite groups and later Islam. Basrah or Mesene, which was also called 'Antiochia' in Seleucid times, is the location Josephus calls 'Charax Spasini' in his story about the conversion of Queen Helen's favourite son, the 'only begotten' Izates.

Mani was said to have been born to an 'Elchasaite' (*Sabaean* Bather) family there.⁵² Anticipating Muhammad's titles later in Islam, he was known to his followers as both 'Messenger of God' and 'the Seal of the Prophets' – the 'True Prophet' ideology rampant among all Elchasaite/

Ebionite-type groups. The most elevated followers of Mani were known as the '*Siddiks*', that is, in Hebrew, '*Zaddiks*' or 'Righteous Ones'. These Mani taught in the *Jamesian* manner:

> to prefer *being Poor to Riches*, to *suppress fornication and sexual desire*, and to *separate from the world*, to be *abstinent* [presumably from strong drink – *lehinnazer* at Qumran], to fast continually and to give alms as much as possible.

He also 'forbade them to acquire any property except food enough for one day and dress for one year. He further forbade them [the *Saddiks*] *sexual intercourse* and ordered them to continually wander about the world preaching his doctrines and *guiding people in the Right Path*'.[53]

In the themes of sexual continence, being Poor, antagonism to Riches and fornication, and abstinence from strong drink, we recognize the attitudes attributed by early Church texts to James, and, of course, forbidding the *Siddiks* to acquire any property is nothing but a variation on the life-style of the *Rechabites*, whose regimen has also made itself felt among the Mandaeans. But, whereas Mani, while retaining vegetarianism, dispensed with bathing, the Mandaeans – the names are perhaps not unrelated – retained it with a vengeance. They still practise it, including the *Essene* custom of wearing special 'linen clothing' while bathing, to the present day. With regard to these names, 'Mani' and 'Mandaeans', one should also just remark in passing the curious prefiguration represented by the name 'Manaen the foster brother of Herod the Tetrarch' in the list of Paul's associates at 'Antioch' in Acts 13:1 above.

Not only are these 'Mandaeans' mostly craftsmen, particularly metalworkers and *carpenters* – and especially builders of boats, which they used in these southern marshes – they also observe the Rechabite *prohibition on wine* (which has also gone into Islam), despite the fact that the vine figures prominently in much of their literature.[54] Likewise, their 'Priests' are consecrated, Rechabite-style, in temporary reed huts or lean-tos. Still referring to themselves even today as '*Nazuraiya*'/'Nazoraeans', the tenth century CE *Fihrist* makes it clear that 'Elchasai' – in Arabic '*al-Hasih*' – was also *their* founder.[55] Not surprisingly, therefore, they go to extreme lengths in baptismal lustrations and have a highly developed doctrine of the 'Hidden' or 'Secret Adam', whom they identify with Adam's third descendant '*Enosh*' (in Aramaic, 'Man') – in the Bible, the first 'to invoke the name of the Lord' (Gen. 4:26).

But this, of course, is nothing but our original Elchasaite ideology of

Christ being infused into many bodies and 'the Perfect Man' or 'Adam' doctrine of Epiphanius' 'Naassenes'. In the Ebionite terminology of the Pseudoclementines, this is 'the Primal Adam' or 'Standing One' and in later Shi'ite ideology in Islam, succeeding to all these, 'the *Imam*' or 'the One who stands before'.

The Mandaeans, not surprisingly, also honour John. He is called by them 'Yahya as-Sabi', (like Noah's uncle 'Sabi' above) and his father is '*Abba Saba Zachariah*'. They also claim John was taught by '*Enosh*' or 'Man' (Hebrew, '*Adam*').[56] This is probably something of what the Synoptic Gospels are trying to imply in portraying John as *Elijah redivivus*.

Epiphanius, while also naming Daniel's father '*Sabaa*', presents Elijah as being a descendant through David's High Priest, Zadok, of Phineas and of the same priestly course as the Maccabees. Not only will Elijah be a recipient of the 'Phineas *redivivus*' tradition, but the 'rainmaking' one – specifically evoked too at the end of the Letter of James and bestowed by Epiphanius on James as well.[57] Like his slightly later contemporary, Jonadab the son of Rechab, Elijah too is described in Kings as 'exceedingly zealous for the Lord God of Hosts' (1 Kings 19:9 and 14), language not unlike that appearing in 'the fervent working prayer of the *Righteous One*' regarding Elijah in the Letter attributed to James (5:16).

Banus', John the Baptist's, and James' Bathing, Food, and Clothing

This 'bathing' ideology goes back, at least in Western Christian tradition, to John the Baptist – whatever meaning one chooses to ascribe retrospectively to the bathing procedures he and many of these allied groups derived their names from. John himself was executed at Machaeros, a Maccabean/ Herodian Fortress in Moab or Perea in Transjordan almost directly across the Dead Sea from the bathing installations situated also at Qumran.

The kind of clothing John wore and the food he ate are matters of intense interest as well in all extant descriptions of his activities. He is described in the famous passages in Matthew and Mark as wearing '*camel's hair clothing* and a leather girdle *about his loins*' and eating 'locusts and wild honey' (Matt. 3:4 and Mark 1:6). It is phrases like 'about his loins' and 'wild' that are the link to descriptions of our other *vegetarian* types and daily bathers, like James and/or the 'Essenes', Masbuthaeans, and other 'Bathers' of various kinds. The *clothing* part of this description goes back to that of Elijah above, as 'hairy and gird with a leather girdle about his loins' (1 Kings 1:8).

In the second part of this description of John, if not the first, one must, as we saw, make allowances for inaccuracies arising out of translations of little understood terms from Hebrew or Aramaic into Greek. In both Josephus' and Hippolytus' descriptions of the 'Essenes', we observed that the idea of wearing 'linen about their loins', *even when they bathed* because of their modesty and sexual chastity, is a persistent one. In turn, this moves through descriptions of the Masbuthaean Bathers in Northern Syria, like the 'Elchasaites', down to the Mandaeans in Southern Iraq, 'the *Subba* of the marshes' even to the present day.

Hippolytus in his extended presentation of 'the Essenes', when speaking of their 'ablutions *in cold water,*' actually uses the words 'linen girdles' to describe how they clothed themselves 'for the purpose of concealing their private parts'. For his part, Josephus speaks of 'the linen cloths' with which the Essenes 'girded their loins' before 'bathing their bodies in cold water'.[58] The only difference is that New Testament accounts, in the interests of portraying John as an Elijah *redivivus*, have substituted the 'leather girdle' from Elijah's story for 'linen girdles' in these. It is impossible to tell what the actual truth is here, but since what is at issue where John and the Essenes are concerned is 'bathing' – not an issue in the biblical accounts of Elijah's archetypical, 'exceeding great zeal' – in the writer's view this is what the New Testament accounts are really trying to say.

In any event, where John's food is concerned, as already remarked, it is doubtful if such fare could have sustained him in seasons when there were no locusts or wild honey, nor was insect fare of this kind really considered fit consumption for strict constructionists in Law, which these wilderness 'Keepers' normally were. Epiphanius' lost 'Gospel of the Ebionites', as we saw, maintained that John ate 'wild honey' and vegetarian 'cakes baked in oil', reflecting the picture of Lucian of Samosata's daily baptizers in Northern Syria at the headwaters of the Euphrates, who ate 'wild fruits and drank milk and honey' and slept out 'under the open sky'.[59] This description in the Gospel of the Ebionites, coupled with the 'eating nothing but wild plants' in 2 Maccabees' description of Judas' wilderness regime, certainly is a more convincing picture of the diet of these wilderness-dwellers than the highly improbable and even insulting 'locusts and wild honey'.

In fact, Josephus' description of '*Banus*'' food consumption and the type of dress he wore would probably be a more accurate reflection of what John would have eaten or worn in these circumstances than these more popular New Testament reconstructions. As will be recalled,

Josephus contends that '*Banus* lived in the wilderness and wore no other clothing but that which grew on trees [*linen*] and had no other food than that which grew of its own accord ['wild plants'/Rechabite fare], and bathed in cold water persistently, night and day, in order to preserve his chastity',[60] – the last paralleling Epiphanius on James' sexual continence.

Where the rest of the New Testament presentation of John is concerned, it must be treated with the same extreme caution. At every point, Josephus is superior. For instance, for him,

> John was a good man and exhorted the Jews to live virtuously, both as to *Righteousness towards one another* and *Piety towards God*. And so to come to baptism, for that *washing* would be acceptable to Him if they made use of it, not in order *to remit whatever sins they committed*, but for *the purification of the body* only, provided that the soul had been thoroughly cleansed beforehand by practising Righteousness.[61]

Not only do we have again here the 'Righteousness'/'Piety' dichotomy and the emphasis on 'doing', but this description of John's baptism is exactly *the reverse* of New Testament ones and undoubtedly *more reliable*. It, also, accords with that in the Community Rule at Qumran.[62]

Herod (that is, Herod Antipas) seeing 'the great influence John had over the masses' and the enthusiasm with which they received him, 'feared he would lead them to rise up' and revolt and, therefore, took him to Machaeros bordering his domain and the Arab King Aretas' in Petra. There he put him to death. No mention is made of Herodias, nor her daughter Salome's tantalizing dance, though references to these characters abound in the surrounding information in Josephus. Nor is there any mention either of the hallowed picture of John's *head upon a platter* being sent to Salome and Herodias, missing in any case from Luke and John.

In Josephus this note about 'sending someone's head' to someone is also part of the story of the execution of John. But there it is the *Roman Emperor Tiberius* who wants the head of the *Arab King Aretas of Petra* 'sent to him', for what he had *done to Herod Antipas* – that is, defeated him militarily after this Herod divorced his (Aretas') daughter to marry Herodias. This, Josephus says, 'the Jews considered vengeance on him for what he had done to John the Baptist' – another example of Gospel *lateral transference* and *inversion*.

It should be clear that Josephus' presentation is the *demythologized* John, although highly mythologized portraits in the New Testament

333

incorporating the kind of 'birthday parties' Romans loved so much (even today attractive to a wide popular audience) and flattering portrayals of the Herodian family certainly made better story-telling. The 'baptism' and/or 'ablution' pictured in Josephus' description of John was simply a water cleansing or immersion, and, no doubt – as in the accounts of *Banus* and 'the Essenes' – a *cold water one* at that, 'provided the soul had already been *purified* beforehand by *the practice of Righteousness*'. This is the Qumran view as well, just as it is the presentation we are developing of *the demythologized James.*

To show the tendentiousness of these various New Testament accounts, the Gospel of Mark, which has the fullest presentation of these materials, states that 'Herod feared John, *knowing him to be a Righteous One* and *Holy*' (6:20) – presumably '*Holy from his mother's womb*', echoed too in Luke 1:15 above about John and early Church accounts about James. In other words, Herod recognizes John as '*a Zaddik*' and 'Holy One', the same 'Holy' we have been following in early Church accounts of James' 'Naziritism' and 'priestliness'.

This does replicate parallel materials in Josephus noting that Herod '*feared John*', but *not* because he considered 'him a *Zaddik* and Holy'. For Josephus, rather, Herod 'fears John', because of his influence over the crowd, 'who were greatly inflamed by his words' and 'seemed as if they were of a mind to be guided by John in everything they did'. Therefore, the execution is with malice aforethought. As Josephus puts it,

> Herod thought it best, fearing an Uprising, *to strike first* and *put him to death*, lest he should *later repent* of his mistake when it was too late.

In other words, it is a preventative execution, and here we have the typical New Testament reversal of themes, particularly the one of political revolution. One should also note how this reference to 'repent' is reversed again in the New Testament accounts of John's philosophy of 'repentance', missing as such from Josephus, but arguably part of his message.

Not only this, but as we have seen, Salome does not dance before Herod at his birthday party, however much 'fun' such artistic rewriting may have been.[63] It is she who is married to this Herod's brother 'Philip', the Tetrarch of the territory of Trachonitis just south of Damascus, not her mother. No doubt John, who was active in these areas *on the other side of the Jordan, was involved* in protesting these things and executed accordingly. When this Philip predeceases Salome and 'dies childless', as Josephus puts it, she marries Aristobulus, Herod of Chalcis' son, Agrippa I's nephew.[64] All these things are turned around in the New Testament accounts as we have them.

Here Gospel accounts suffer from the two major flaws Josephus says all historians in this period suffer from in his Introduction to the *Jewish War*: 'flattery of the Romans and vilification of the Jews'. Josephus is quite right about this, but, as it turns out, his work is little better in these regards, but if the reader is careful to keep these flaws always before his or her eyes, he or she should have little difficulty separating 'false coin from true'.

Here we must address the matter of *Banus'* immersions, John's 'washing', and James' bathing habits. As we have seen, Josephus says of *Banus,* in approximately the year 53 CE, that he lived in the wilderness, wore clothing that was of vegetable not animal consistency, was a vegetarian eating only *wild*-growing vegetation, and *night and day bathed regularly*.

Not only do we have at Qumran (and in Islam), the theme of keeping all-night vigils,[65] but most of these things could have been said about John the Baptist as well. John's baptism most certainly was a water immersion or 'washing' of some kind. In fact, Josephus' account uses two separate words here, one implying 'baptism' and another, 'washing' or 'ablution'.[66] But John was already dead by the mid-50s and the time of this picture of *Banus* in Josephus. For its part, the New Testament portrays John's spirit being immediately reborn in Jesus, regardless of the fact that, given its chronology, Jesus was probably dead before the time of the above incidents in Josephus concerning John seemingly around 35-36 CE.

This leaves us with James. We have already signalled several possible overlaps in the tradition regarding Jesus and James, and this 'bathing' scenario may be an additional one. James was alive and, in fact, leading the Community in the mid-50s. The Pseudoclementines place him together with his whole community – reckoned at about 'five thousand' – in the Jericho area not far from the Jordan River and the Dead Sea.[67] Like '*Banus*', he very definitely did wear *only linen* – and not 'camel's hair' or 'leather' as John the Baptist is reported to have done in the Gospels. According to Epiphanius, James was also 'chaste', as were all 'the sons of Joseph' – or fellow members of the *Rechabite*-Priest tradition.

Of course, all traditions insist on James' unalterable opposition to 'fornication'. Where '*Banus*' is concerned, as noted, Josephus makes it clear that the 'bathing in cold water', which he shared with 'the *Essenes*', was connected to his sexual abstinence. As we have seen, too, Epiphanius even goes so far as to connect not wearing animal fibres like wool to animals

335

being the product of sexual intercourse, though in James' case this could relate to his vegetarianism and priestliness as well. For Josephus, too, and Hippolytus, most 'Essenes', whose *cold-water bathing* habits they describe in detail, abjure marriage 'adopting other men's children' and 'esteem sexual abstinence and the control of the passions as a special virtue'.[68]

In the tradition above based on Hegesippus, James 'did not anoint himself with oil, nor *go to the baths*'. In Epiphanius this reads 'he never washed *in a bath*', giving us inadvertently the clue to the seeming inconsistencies here.[69] In Josephus and Hippolytus, this custom of 'not anointing oneself with oil' is an 'Essene' one, oiling the body, as we saw, evidently being considered Greco-Hellenistic and, as they put it, 'polluting'. Both give it at the beginning of their descriptions of 'the Essenes' in the context of how they 'despise Riches . . . and share (goods) with each other [Hippolytus includes, 'sharing with the Poor' here], so that . . . no one will be *Richer* than another'. Therefore this abstention from oiling their bodies, as was the custom in Greco-Roman baths, clearly had to do with their poverty regimen and avoiding luxuries – meaning *luxurious* or *warm* baths conspicuously present in Herodian palaces, as at Jericho, Herodion, and Masada.

This peculiar shared antipathy of James and the 'Essenes' to 'anointing themselves with oil' – not noted with regard to any other individuals – would, in my view, be enough to identify James with this group, regardless of how one chooses to define the last. However, here Josephus adds another curious note to their considering 'oil a defilement', that the Essenes also 'preferred being *unwashed*' or, in some translations, 'preferred keeping *a dry skin*' (clearly implying that 'they did not anoint themselves *with oil*').

Again, this is confirmed by repeated notices in the rest of Josephus' or Hippolytus' descriptions of the 'Essenes', which over and over again repeat the theme about 'not anointing themselves with oil' and 'bathing in cold water'. This would in our view absolutely prove the case regarding James' bathing habits – meaning, he did *not* either *anoint himself with oil* or take *hot baths* in the Roman style; however, like '*Banus*', 'Essenes', and other 'Nazoraeans', he very definitely took *cold baths*.

Essenes, Zealots, and Nazoraeans

The context in which Josephus provides these details is interesting too. Josephus has two descriptions of the Essenes, one in the *War* and the other in the *Antiquities*. Both of these descriptions begin with the discussion of Judas the Galilean's activities at the time of the Census of Cyrenius – coincident in Luke's Gospel with 'Jesus'' birth moment. The one in the *War* is noteworthy for its implied promise to describe this sect ('heresy') or movement, but ends up, rather, dwelling, as we saw, on so-called 'Essenes', while making short shrift of Sadducees and Pharisees, and ignoring Judas' revolutionary 'sect' altogether.

In the later *Antiquities*, now calling this sect a 'Fourth Philosophy', Josephus drastically curtails his treatment of 'the Essenes'. In fact, he cuts a section from his discussion of 'the Essenes' in the *War* and adds it to his presentation of Judas the Galilean's 'Fourth Philosophy' in the *Antiquities*. This is the section about their willingness to undergo 'deaths of the most horrific torture', which, as we saw, Hippolytus connects to their refusal *'to eat things sacrificed to an idol'*. Josephus simply presents this last as 'to eat the things forbidden them'.⁷⁰

The one thing Josephus makes quite clear about Judas' sectarians is that 'they have an inviolable *attachment to freedom*, insisting that *God alone is their only Ruler and Lord*', and 'having had God for their Lord, refuse to pay taxes to the Romans and submit to any mortal masters'. For lack of a better term, many call these 'Fourth Philosophy' Innovators, 'Zealots', even though Josephus never, in effect, uses the term until the the Uprising against Rome, and this only after he has begun referring to the 'pollutions' of those he also designates as '*Sicarii*' in both city and Temple. When he does use the term, 'Zealots', he really applies it only to one of several contending subversive groups – specifically the one *opposing* the High Priest Ananus, James' executioner.

Ultimately these let the unruly 'Idumaeans' into the city, who proceed to slaughter all the High Priests, ending up in possession of the Temple.⁷¹ For Josephus, with these Idumaeans, 'the Zealots' are more blood-thirsty even than 'the *Sicarii*', who end up in the fortress on Masada.⁷² But, the common point between his first description of the 'Essenes' and his later description of Judas' Galilean 'Innovators' is that:

> They also think little of dying any kind of deaths, nor do they heed deaths of their relatives or friends, nor can any such fear make them *call any man Lord*.

But this is exactly what Hippolytus adds to his description of those 'Essenes', who 'will *not slander the Law* or *eat things sacrificed to an idol*'. Immediately one recognizes this last as the characteristic of James' followers in the New Testament at almost precisely this point in history.

In Hippolytus' version of Josephus, there are, it will be recalled, several groups of 'Essenes'. The more extreme – those who even kill persons 'refusing to undergo the rite of circumcision' – 'are called Zealots or *Sicarii*'.

> Some have declined to such an extent in discipline, that as far as those are concerned who follow *the ancient customs* [note the 'Rechabite' cast here], they refuse even *to touch them*, and if they come in contact with them by chance, they *immediately resort to washing*, as if they had touched some one belonging to an alien tribe.[73]

Like Josephus' 'Zealots' above, these, too, 'refuse to call *any man Lord*, except the Deity, even though someone tries to torture or even kill them'. Of course, the Christianity we know is the very reverse of this, at least as far as the point all these descriptions agree upon about 'not calling *any man* Lord' (the impetus behind the presentation of Jesus as more than 'a man' or supernatural?).

At one point Josephus described these 'Essenes' as recommending to the young Herod 'to love Righteousness and practise Piety towards God'. He repeats this in describing the novice's final initiation into 'the Pure Food' of the Community after a three-year probation: in addition to 'swearing not to reveal any of their secrets to others even if compelled under mortal torture to do so' and 'to expose Liars',

> he is made to take the most *tremendous oaths* that, in the first place, he will practise *Piety towards God* and then, that he will *observe Righteousness towards men*.[74]

This is, of course, exactly what he pictures John the Baptist as teaching in the *Antiquities* above.

The reader will immediately recognize these as the two Love Commandments, that is, to 'love God' and to 'love one's neighbour as oneself'. Aside from being the essence of John the Baptist's teaching, they are also pictured in the Gospels as the essence of Jesus' teaching – this, as in Paul in Romans 13 above, as a follow-up to his position on '*paying the tax to Caesar*'.[75] They are also central to the James' position and the letter transmitted in his name makes this abundantly clear, citing them both (Jas. 2:5–8).

We can now identify them as the basic ideology of the Opposition Alliance, 'Piety' being the sum total of all one's obligations towards God – one's *ceremonial obligations* – and 'Righteousness' being one's obligations to one's fellow man – one's *social obligations*. This is exactly how Josephus portrays them in his description of 'the Essenes' as well.

For those, like James and at Qumran, following the 'all Righteousness' Commandment and the ideal of 'Perfection of the Way', the second clearly also had an economic dimension. Therefore, their title 'the Poor' and their emphasis on 'not being Richer than one's neighbour', the implication being that one could not 'love' or 'practise Righteousness towards one's fellow man', if one made economic distinctions between oneself and him.

These oaths, as Josephus describes them, include the admonition: 'They will forever hate the Unrighteous and participate in the fight of the Righteous.' Not only are these kinds of imprecations similar to those about 'living Piously' and 'being accursed, living and dying, and punished with everlasting punishment' should one lie that James is pictured as giving to the Elders at the beginning of the Pseudoclementine *Homilies*; but one should note how Paul uses this kind of language in 1 Corinthians 9 above, when speaking of 'running the course to win . . . *not fighting* uncertainly or beating the air'. This kind of admonition also seals the identity of the position being enunciated here with the point of view of Qumran, where we hear about 'everlasting hatred for the Sons of the Pit' and that those 'who have set idols upon or walk in stubbornness of heart shall have no share in the House of the *Torah*'.[76]

Again, this is the very reverse of the sentiment put into Jesus' mouth in the Sermon on the Mount, also in the context of discussing the Love Commandment and as a rejoinder to those who 'love your neighbour, but hate your Enemy' (the self-evident Qumran, Zealot, and Essene position): 'Love your Enemies and bless those that curse you, do good to those that hate you' (Matt. 5:43).[77] All of this is pregnant with meaning for the case of 'the Enemy' Paul, who, despite protestations to the contrary, generally shows no more 'love for his enemies' than does Qumran.

Piety to God and Paul's Baptism

Not only, as we have seen, does Josephus contend that those he is calling 'Essenes' were 'despisers of Riches', but further overlaps between their approach and that of both Qumran and James are manifold. For instance, it will be recalled that Josephus contends:

> They are *long-lived, most of them over a century*, in consequence of the simplicity of their diet and the regularity of the mode of life they observe.

This, of course, links up, as we saw, with the notices in Eusebius and Epiphanius about the great age of early Church leaders in Palestine –

hyperbole aside – as a consequence of their '*Nazirite life-style*', James supposedly being ninety-six when he was martyred and Simeon bar Cleophas a hundred and twenty![78]

In addition, Josephus specifically groups the Essene love of 'washing' and 'bathing' under the heading of 'their Piety towards the Deity'. Here, not surprisingly, is another blatant contradiction of the picture of the Paulinized 'Jesus' recommending '*not* washing one's hands when eating' in the Gospels. After discussing how the Essenes – in the manner of Lucian's 'Daily Bathers' or 'Sabaeans' on the upper Euphrates and Elchasaites and Sabaeans there generally – *greet the sun in prayer* and work all morning, Josephus describes how 'they *clothe themselves in linen* and *bath in cold water*', purifying themselves before the common meal.

So scrupulous are these 'Essenes' in Josephus and Hippolytus that in addition to retiring to more isolated places and digging a trench in which to defecate, as we saw above, afterwards they 'wash themselves as if defiled'.[79] In the same vein, should a senior be touched by a junior, even inadvertently, 'they must bath themselves *as if they had been touched by a foreigner*'. Hippolytus includes additional points, namely, the necessity of washing 'after coming in contact with' someone *uncircumcised*. This, of course, links up with his additional point, noted above, about how the '*Sicarii*' 'Essenes' forcibly circumcise people on pain of death!

Here, it will be recalled, Acts 10:28 portrays Peter as specifically counter-manding this exact point. Learning not to call any food 'profane or unclean' in his tablecloth vision above, Peter rephrases this in the follow-up conversation he has on entering the *Roman* Centurion Cornelius' *house* in Caesarea: 'You know that it is not Lawful for a Jewish man to be *joined to* or *come near a foreigner* [*allophulō*], but God taught me to call no man *profane or unclean*.' These are almost the precise words, albeit now reversed, of Josephus and Hippolytus above, including the use of the precise word, '*allophulos*', that Josephus also uses in Greek to refer to 'foreigner' or 'Gentile'. Here too, once again, is the 'joining' vocabulary Qumran uses in terms of 'joining' the House of God or Jewry generally or 1 Corinthians 6 above uses to mean 'being joined to' either 'the body of a prostitute' or 'the Lord' (meaning 'the body of Christ').

In addition, these points are totally contradicted by the Pseudo-clementine *Homilies*, which, as we saw, not only shows Peter as completely observing the points of James' instructions to overseas communities, but also dietary regulations and being a Daily Bather, 'greeting the sun in prayer', and a vegetarian as well. What is more to the point, it even has

Peter straightforwardly stating, in a manner diametrically opposed to Acts, 'We do not take our food at the same table as Gentiles . . . because they live impurely.'

The Letter of James, too, as will be recalled, twice refers to this 'Piety' Commandment or 'loving God' in the context of repeated reference to 'the Poor', 'the Perfect', 'the Complete' as opposed to 'the Rich', expressing this in terms of 'the Crown of life' or 'Kingdom, which the Lord has promised those that love Him' (Jas. 1:12 and 2:5). The Damascus Document also evokes this directly following its allusion to 'separating from the Sons of the Pit', not defiling one's 'Holy Spirit', and 'walking in Perfect Holiness'. It does so by rephrasing Exodus 20:6 on the '*Hesed* ['Piety' – in this context meaning 'Lovingkindness' or 'Grace'] that God *does to those that love* and *keep Him – for a thousand generations*'.[80]

The Qumran Hymns actually refer to those 'separated' in this manner as 'chosen from their mother's womb', God, therefore, being 'a Father to all the Sons of [His] Truth'. In the context of referring to 'loving [God's] Name', 'being Justified', and 'purified by the Holy Spirit', they then proceed, once again, to pronounce this same '*Hesed*' or Grace as being bestowed on those who 'love' (God) and 'keep' His Commandments *to stand* in His 'presence for ever'.[81]

In the New Testament, the First Letter of John likewise is virtually a sermon on 'Perfection', 'love of God', which it evokes some six times in five chapters, and 'keeping His Commandments' (4:8–5:3).[82] Paul, too, plays on this 'loving God' theme throughout his writings, always with reverse signification to that of the Essenes or at Qumran. We have already seen how he begins his discussion of James' and Hippolytus' Essenes' prohibition on 'eating things sacrificed to idols' and the defilement of his opponents' 'weak consciences' with an allusion to 'love building up' and 'loving God', but not being 'puffed up' (8:1–3).

In one particularly significant section of Romans, in speaking about 'Justification by Faith', including 'being justified now *by blood*' (that is, Jesus' 'blood'), and presenting how Abraham's belief 'was counted for him as Righteousness', Paul expresses this in terms of 'the love of God being *poured out* in our hearts by the Holy Spirit, which was given unto us' (Rom. 3:13–5:5).

We have already spoken of a parallel use of such imagery at Qumran. This is expressed in the Community Rule in the context of allusion to purifying the body by ablution and 'making it *Holy* by cleansing waters':

And then God will refine by His Truth *all the works of Man* and *purify him from among the Sons of Man*, Perfecting all the Spirit of Unrighteousness within his flesh and *purifying it by means of the Holy Spirit of all Evil works*. He will *pour upon him the Spirit of Truth like baptismal waters* [*washing him*] *of all Abominations of Lying* and he shall be immersed in the Spirit of Purification that he may cause the Upright to grasp the Knowledge of the Most High and *the Wisdom of the Sons of Heaven in order to teach the Perfect of the Way, whom God has chosen as an Everlasting Covenant*. And *all the Glory of Adam* [this is the same 'Ebionite'/'Elchasaite' vocabulary one finds in the Damascus Document in the context of describing 'the House of Faith' God would build in Israel introducing the definition of 'the Sons of Zadok'] *will be theirs*. And there will be no more Unrighteousness and all the works of Deceitfulness will be put to flight.[83]

Not only is this the essence of cleansing the soul by the Holy Spirit in conjunction with water immersion, as Josephus describes it, associating it with John the Baptist's wilderness teaching; but it also incorporates this allusion to the Ebionite/Elchasaite 'Primal Adam' ideology, so central to all these baptizing groups here, in Northern Syria and Southern Iraq, and identified in Christianity, as we know it in Scripture, with 'the Christ' descending on Jesus (in the form of 'a dove').

We have already seen how the Gospel of Luke, perhaps the most Pauline of all the Gospels, applies the language of 'being filled with the Holy Spirit' to John the Baptist and his being (like James and the Righteous Teacher from Qumran) 'Holy from his mother's womb'. For Acts, also by Luke, Paul in Ephesus expounds his view of what the Gospels and Acts refer to as 'being baptized by the Holy Spirit' in relation to someone called Apollos, who, as we saw, before *departing for Corinth*, taught 'in the Way of the Lord' and 'knew only *the baptism of John*' (18:25).

Arriving in Ephesus after Apollos had departed, Paul clarifies this, saying 'John indeed baptized with the baptism of repentance' (19:4). Not only does this reverse the original sense of Josephus' picture of Herod Antipas' concern over 'repenting' for not having killed John the Baptist; but the words, 'baptism of repentance' make it clear that we have to do here with what the New Testament considers to be *John the Baptist*'s baptism, since this is how his baptism is described in Mark 1:4 and Luke 3:3.

Despite this being normally understood as the baptism of someone called 'the Apostle John' in Ephesus, in our view this is simply the water baptism of John the Baptist above that we have already found meticulously delineated in Josephus. For Acts, on the contrary, Paul, after 'baptizing to the Name of Christ Jesus', 'lays his hands upon them' and 'the Holy Spirit came upon them and they were *speaking in Tongues* and *prophesied*' – again the accoutrements of the Pauline Gentile Mission (Acts 19:5–6). This is the same baptism by the Holy Spirit that was 'poured out' on them at Pentecost in Jerusalem at the beginning of Acts (2:18) and upon new Gentile converts in Acts 10:45 after Peter's tablecloth vision in Caesarea – again with the same effects.

Paul also speaks about problems with an individual called Apollos at the beginning of 1 Corinthians, this time not in Ephesus as above, but *in Corinth* (1:12 and 3:5). It is in the course of this discussion that Paul also expounds, as we saw above, how by means of the Holy Spirit he 'teaches spiritual things spiritually' (2:13). He then goes on, using the imagery of 'planting God's field' and 'building God's building' to illustrate this, ending with the metaphor of how he 'planted' and 'Apollos watered' (3:16). Again it is confirmed that Apollos' baptism or 'John's baptism' primarily involved *water* or *washing the body*.

Paul is also pictured as using this language of 'washing' or 'bathing', when it is now he who is portrayed as being 'filled with the Holy Spirit', upon meeting Ananias in Damascus and being 'baptized' by him to 'wash away sins' (Acts 9:18 and 22:16). The Letter to Titus, considered in the Pauline 'school', again associates this 'regenerative washing' with 'the pouring out of the Holy Spirit' and, this time the Saviour's *'love of God'* – what it calls 'being saved, not by practising *works of Righteousness*, but according to Mercy' (or 'Grace' – in Hebrew, *Hesed* again – 3:5). This again is almost precisely the language of the Qumran Damascus Document above.

In 1 Corinthians 6:11, when speaking of 'being joined to the Lord in Spirit' and the issue of 'food being for the belly and the belly for food', Paul puts this as follows:

> *But you were washed*, but you were *made Holy*, but you *were justified* in the Name of the Lord Jesus and by the Spirit of our God [that is, 'Holy Spirit' baptism again],

then going on, as we saw, to speak about the 'body' and 'fornication'. In the same manner, Josephus, in his description of Essenes above, pictures their 'girding their loins with linen cloths and washing their bodies in cold water', practices he then goes on, in his later description of *Banus*' similar bathing habits, to associate with *Banus*' abstention from fornication or sexual continence.

James' Bathing and John's Clothing: Final Conclusions

These descriptions are not only the key to understanding *Banus'* relation to the Essenes, they are also the key to understanding Hegesippus' original testimony about James 'wearing only linen, never anointing his body with oil, and never entering the baths'. The problem, as we saw, was the *bathing*.

This testimony about James is immediately followed in all sources, drawing on Hegesippus, by information about how he entered the Temple, wearing the mitre of the High Priest, and 'prayed on his knees' in the Holy of Holies, so that 'his knees became callused as *a camel's* hide'. It is worth repeating Epiphanius' eloquent presentation of this (part of which we have already reproduced earlier) in its entirety:

> I find further that he also exercised the Priesthood according to the *Ancient Priesthood* [the 'Rechabite' or 'Nazirite' one – possibly even the one Hebrews is calling the 'Priesthood after the order of Melchizedek']. For this reason he was permitted to *enter the Holy of Holies once a year*, as the Bible lays down in the Law commanding the High Priests. He was also allowed to wear the High Priestly diadem [that is, the '*Nezer*' or '*Crown*'] on his head as the aforementioned trustworthy men – Eusebius, Clement, and others – have related in their accounts.[84]

But if James did go on the Temple Mount in a regular manner, as even the Book of Acts reports the Central Three or Paul's 'Pillars' did, then he certainly was involved in the kind of ritual immersion procedure required there. Anyone going on the Temple Mount and involved in sacred activities there would have been expected to undergo the pro-forma ritual purification or immersion – *even foreigners*. Certainly everyone entering the Inner Court of the Temple would have to go through the procedure of ritual immersion, and the Priests even had a large underground ritual bathing facility there.[85] For his part, the High Priest had two of them set aside for his own use, one for *Yom Kippur* on the *roof* of the Chamber where the *skins of sacrificed animals* were kept. Even this motif has a certain link-up with James and the whole issue of '*skins* sacrificed to idols' in *MMT* and the Temple Scroll at Qumran.

This requirement, *to bathe*, would have been all the more true if, as Epiphanius is insisting, what James was doing was a *Yom Kippur* atonement, that is, an atonement the High Priest was commanded to perform in the Holy of Holies once a year on behalf of the people. As we have seen, the purity regulations surrounding this were especially severe and Leviticus 16:4 'commanded' that the High Priest wear 'Holy' clothes of coarse not fine linen, and *definitely* enjoined bathing. In fact, during the normal service for the Day of Atonement on the Temple Mount, the High Priest immersed himself five times![86]

Most certainly, then, James did *bathe*, and this testimony about '*Banus*' and the Essenes washing 'in cold water' is the key to what is meant in these garbled, albeit still comprehensible, notices about James. Where '*Banus*' is concerned, as we saw, Josephus portrays this as connected to his sexual chastity. Even a second group of 'Essenes', portrayed in both his work and Hippolytus, who differ from the first in that they marry, only have sexual relations for the purpose of procreation. In any event, all these individuals are, doubtlessly, part of the same or similar movements, and James and *Banus* are, likely as not, descriptions of the *same* person. In other words, James is noteworthy because he *did* bathe, not because he *did not*.

That Josephus says the same things about 'Essenes' that early Church sources say about James is further proof of this proposition – particularly the point about 'being unwashed'. Josephus did not mean that Essenes were 'unwashed' any more than early Church sources – had they understood the materials before them – meant this about James. In fact, Essenes immersed themselves all the time as did all daily baptizers. It is the note about bathing in *cold water*, emphasized in all our sources, which is the key. Not surprisingly, this is linked to abjuring 'fornication' as well, integrally connected in all sources to James, as it is, the Righteous Teacher at Qumran.

Epiphanius, as we have seen, specifically makes this link, connecting James' bathing practices with his sexual continence and his wearing only linen, saying (to repeat): 'He [James] died a virgin at the age of ninety-six. No razor came upon his head. He did not go to the baths. He did not partake of animal flesh, and he wore no under tunic, using only a linen cloth.'

As we saw above too, Epiphanius links this with the young man in Mark 14:51–52, considered by some to be John's 'Disciple Jesus loved' – possibly James – who fled naked at Jesus' arrest, 'leaving behind only the linen cloth' which he wore 'about his naked body'. This resembles nothing so much as 'the linen girdle' Josephus' and Hippolytus' 'Essenes' wore about their loins while bathing.

As if for good measure, Epiphanius repeats this testimony a second time when talking about James' 'knees growing as hard as a camel's from all the continued kneeling before God he did out of *excessive Piety*':

> Thus, they no longer called him by his name, but rather they surnamed him 'the Righteous One' [possibly 'Zadok']. He never washed in a bath, nor partook of animal flesh.

To this, Epiphanius adds the curious detail: 'nor did he wear sandals'.[87]

It is unclear from what misunderstood or garbled source he may have derived this, though it should be observed that the Priests in the Temple – particularly after they had cleansed themselves – did not wear any footwear but went barefoot. For his part, Hippolytus, in talking about 'the Overseer' of the Essenes ('the *Mebakker*' at Qumran), who took care of upkeep and common property, makes it clear that Essenes did not own '*two* cloaks or a *double* set of sandals'. John in the wilderness, in *condemning* 'the crowds coming out to be baptized by him', also gives a variation of this commandment about 'having' or 'not having *two* cloaks' to his charges, then going on to speak about Jesus' 'sandals' generally (Luke 3:11, 9:3, and pars.). As Josephus puts this:

> They do not change their garments or sandals, until they are torn to shreds or worn threadbare with age.[88]

But it is the linking of James' 'never anointing himself with oil' and 'never going to a bath', as found in Eusebius and Jerome, which finally, as we saw, clinches the chain of data in this regard, for certainly, if James went into the Temple in the manner described, he bathed. Since at this point, as with Josephus' Essenes being 'unwashed', the material is linked with never anointing oneself with oil and wearing only linen (also reprised in Ezekiel's new requirements for 'the Sons of Zadok', which include James' Jerusalem Council prohibition of 'carrion' – Ezekiel 44:15–31); one can say, probably definitively, that what James did was *not take hot baths* in the Greco-Roman style. Likewise, he *did not anoint his body with oil* in this style. But as far as cold baths were concerned, he took them, and this regularly as a matter of course, as did '*Banus*' and 'the Essenes', and probably, too, over the slightest purity infraction. Since James was in the habit of going, according to our sources, *every day* into the Temple, he immersed himself in a ritual manner daily.

It is interesting too that, when discussing John the Baptist's dress, our New Testament sources probably play on or reverse details from James' biography as well. We have already seen how this has occurred in points about Jesus' biography. Over and over again we hear that James 'did not wear wool only linen', immediately followed in all sources by comparing the calluses on 'his knees' to the nodules of 'a *camel*' because of all the importuning of God he did in the Temple or Holy of Holies.

In reconstructing a parallel and little understood dress pattern for John about 'wearing *clothing* of the hair of a *camel*', Matthew and Mark appear, somewhat playfully, to have come up with the scenario that has now become 'the Gospel Truth'. First they pick up the point about Elijah 'wearing a leather girdle about his loins' from 2 Kings 1:8, even though the Gospel of John specifically denies John *was* Elijah and, like these other daily bathers, John probably wore only 'a linen girdle about his loins'. The Gospel of Luke, as we noted, picks up Hippolytus' Essenes' not having even 'two cloaks' and turns it into *John*'s command, a favourite in Gospel lore, 'He who has two cloaks, let him give to him who has none' (Luke 3:11 – in 9:3 above, Jesus actually gives the 'Essene' command).

All three Synoptics pick up the the 'sandals' theme, playing, no doubt, on the Messianic 'Staff' (*Mehokkek*) not departing from between 'the *Shiloh*'s' feet[89] and Psalm 110:1's 'making your enemies a footstool' – the same, intensely Zionistic Psalm, which then goes on to evoke 'a Priest for ever after the order of Melchizedek' and being 'Holy from the womb' as, in turn, descriptive of such a priest (110:3–4). These combined now become the proverbial words John utters – in the context also of referring to his 'baptizing with water' – about Jesus, 'the thong of whose sandals' he (John) is 'unworthy to loose' (Luke 3:17 and pars.).

One should note in relation to the '*Yom Kippur* atonement' and 'no sandals' themes as regarding James, pious Jews to this day, harking back to the same ancient scruples, wear no leather shoes on *Yom Kippur*; and in addition to the Priests, who went around barefoot, anyone entering the Temple at all, after purifying himself, appears to have removed his sandals, a custom, as ever, faithfully conserved in the Muslim practice of wearing no footwear in mosques. Even more to the point, the penances put upon one observing extreme atonement on *Yom Kippur* in Talmudic tradition are *exactly* those recited in these early Church traditions about James: neither *wearing shoes*, *bathing* (for pleasure), *lubricating the body with oil*, nor *cohabitation*.[90]

From this perspective, we are justified in averring more or less categorically that John *did not* wear wool or any other animal hair. Nor probably did he dress in Matthew's and Mark's 'camel's hair with a leather girdle about his loins'. What he did probably do was dress in the manner of all these individuals inhabiting the wilderness from James to 'the Essenes' to '*Banus*'.

We can now extend this to a final conclusion: this material incorporating the word 'camel' concerning John the Baptist's dress is simply a detail from these testimonies to *James' excessive Piety*. What it does is combine materials from James' 'not wearing wool and only linen' with the constant praying he did in the Temple, 'his knees becoming hard as *a camel's hide*'. These, of course, make perfect sense in this context about James, while in the sources about John, they do not. Nor should such a vivid simile about 'camel's hide' be lightly gainsaid. In any event, the coincidences and language overlaps certainly are curious. If it is true that the 'camel' in the one retrospectively assimilates the 'camel' in the other, not only do we have, then, additional testimony to the antiquity and veracity of these vivid traditions about James – at least as old as these Gospel narratives about John – but, once again, we have very *real* material and language from traditions about James being retrospectively assimilated into portraits in the New Testament of its heroes.

Where Josephus' '*Banus*' and the 'Essenes' are concerned, we can assume they followed the same customs, particularly in the practice of wearing only linen and taking cold baths. Where James is concerned, we can assume that he, too, followed these customs, that is wearing only linen and taking cold baths in a regular manner 'to preserve his chastity' as Epiphanius avers and which Josephus reports of *Banus*. One can assume that none of these individuals took *hot baths* of the kind found at Masada and Herodian palaces generally, which to some degree reflected the licentiousness of their sexual and family practices. Nor did any of these persons use oil in connection with the bathing they did, nor anoint themselves in the manner of anyone in a Greco-Roman bathhouse, evidently enjoying some vogue in Palestine in this period particularly in palaces built by Herod himself.[91]

The final word in all of this, once again perhaps, belongs to Epiphanius. In describing his version of Hegesippus' 'seven Jewish heresies', which substitutes 'Herodians' for the redundant 'Masbuthaeans' in Eusebius, he concludes:

> Only a few, rare Nazoraeans are still to be found, and these in Upper Egypt and beyond Arabia, but the remainder of the Ossaeans [Essenes], who used to dwell where their Ancestors did, *above the Dead Sea* and *on the other side with the Sampsaeans* [that is, the *Sabaeans*], no longer practise Jewish customs. *They have now become associated with the Ebionites.*[92]

Historical Interlude

Having delineated James' election or appointment to leadership of the Jerusalem Assembly, we are now better able to understand his sudden appearance in Acts 12. Peter is presented as having just escaped from prison after being incarcerated because of a persecution launched by 'Herod'. As we have noted, this is most probably *Herod* Agrippa, known as Agrippa I, because he was actually appointed 'king' by Caligula. It may be his brother, *Herod* of Chalcis, who was more strict with trouble-makers. Married to his niece Bernice, Agrippa I's daughter, Herod of Chalcis demanded and obtained from Claudius the right to control the High Priest's vestments, thereby controlling the appointment to the High Priesthood.[93]

It is his son, Aristobulus, that Salome, pictured in the New Testament as dancing for the head of John the Baptist, married after *her* husband 'Philip the Tetrarch died childless'. Later these two succeed to another Roman petty Kingdom further north, Lower or Little Armenia, either carved out of or contiguous with the Kingdom of Helen of Adiabene's husband. We shall discuss Paul's 'Herodian' connections further below. Paul is pictured as leading the attack on James in the Pseudoclementines and being involved in the one on Stephen in Acts – if the two can, indeed, be separated. Paul refers in Romans, as noted, to his cousin or kinsman 'the Littlest Herod' in the same breath as sending his regards to 'all those [in the household] of Aristobulus'. If this Aristobulus is equivalent to Herod of Chalcis' son Aristobulus, then the influence Paul wielded in Jerusalem while still a comparatively young man would no longer be surprising, nor would his intercourse with the chief priests, whom his putative kinsman Herod of Chalcis demanded and received control over. At the very least it reveals Paul to be an aristocrat linked to ruling Herodians.

In its account, Acts presents Paul, during his last visit to Jerusalem – presumably 60 CE, as James is still alive and the Roman Governor Felix is just on the point of returning to Rome – as having a sister and nephew in Jerusalem, a nephew with strong enough Roman connections to be able to apprise the Captain of the Guard in the Citadel of an impending plot, presumably on the part of '*Sicarii*' or *Nazirite* 'Zealots', to kill Paul. As a result of this, Paul is given a large Roman escort down to the Mediterranean sea-port town named by the first Herod after Augustus,

Caesarea – the thoroughly Hellenized centre of Roman administrative activity, where Roman Governors and Herodian Rulers preferred to reside away from the constant turmoil in Jerusalem.

Acts' reticence with respect to who Paul's nephew was, and for that matter his sister, is suspicious. Possibly this was Cypros (3), named after Herod's mother, Cypros (1) and his daughter Cypros (2)'s daughter. This Cypros (3) was married, not insignificantly, to the *Temple Treasurer*, Helcias – himself descended from another close collaborator of Herod by the same name.[94] We shall return to this subject presently, but suffice it to say that Paul's infiltration of 'the Messianic Movement' twenty some odd years previously – before going overseas for 'fourteen years' – would obviously be a very worrisome matter to his antagonists.

If our interpretation of the Qumran documents is correct, concern over this infiltration is in evidence in these too.[95] In the first place, we shall encounter in them the extreme hostility to 'niece marriage' and marriage with close family cousins – called 'incest' at Qumran – which we noted is so characteristic of Herodian practice, particularly of the line most often mentioned in this book, the line containing Herodias, Salome, Bernice, Drusilla, and Agrippa II, in which New Testament documents are most interested as well. We shall reserve comment at this point about Qumran's total fascination with 'the Liar' epithet, applied to the ideological adversary of the Leader of the Community, 'the Righteous Teacher'.

John the Baptist's interest in the theme of 'fornication' is, of course, patent. He loses his life, if our texts are to be credited, because of his objections to it. All involved in the destruction of John are also involved in the kinds of 'fornication' that so obsess the writers of the Qumran documents. This concern does not just appear in a single document; it moves across the whole of Qumran literature, finally becoming obsessive.

These are, also, the people involved in the destruction of the character both the New Testament and Josephus call 'Theudas', paralleled by the beheading of the person the New Testament calls 'James the brother of John'. They are also the people involved in the imprisonment of Peter, if Acts' narrative at this point leading up to the introduction (or reintroduction) of 'James the brother of Jesus' is to be credited – and there is no reason to doubt its general picture of these antagonisms.

It is also possible to demythologize 'Peter' somewhat as well. As we have seen, Epiphanius insists that, according to the Ebionites, Peter, too, was one of these 'daily bathers', bathing 'every day before eating even bread'. This is also the picture developed across the breadth of the

Pseudoclementine *Homilies*.[96] Let us look at these few things Acts either knows or is willing to tell us about 'Peter' before he drops from its narrative altogether. After the episode introducing James, Peter is never heard from in Acts again, except for the pro-forma and seemingly perfunctory appearance in 15:7–14, where he is also referred to as 'Simeon'. Peter is now portrayed as supporting Paul on the issue of 'circumcision' and opposing those whom Acts is now referring to pejoratively as 'Pharisees' – that is, Christians who are 'Pharisees' (15:5)!

Paul in Galatians calls them 'some from James'. This is the episode which is usually referred to as 'the Jerusalem Council', in which James, in following Peter's speech, is portrayed as making his 'rulings' *vis-à-vis* Gentiles we have been discussing above. These are sent down 'to Antioch and Syria and Cilicia' (here 'Antioch' appears to be outside of 'Syria') by two representatives, one Judas, now also called 'Barsabas', and another Silas (Acts 15:22–23). To add to the confusion, Barnabas and Paul are pictured as going along as well.

If the first reference to a 'Barsabas' in the 'election to fill Judas' Office' had to do with one brother of Jesus called 'James', we can probably take this second as having to do with another 'brother' – this time 'Judas'. This episode, including the motif of an 'epistle' – whose contents are actually set forth – begins to look very much like the stories coming out of 'Edessa Orrhoe' or 'Antioch by Callirhoe', about Judas Thomas and Thaddaeus – in Gospel Apostle lists also surnamed 'Lebbaeus' or 'Judas of James'.[97] To add to the rather fanciful version of these events found in Acts, 'Judas and Silas' are also called 'prophets' (15:32), but then Acts is prepared to use this kind of terminology very loosely.

The 'epistle' theme reinforces the feeling that there is some connection between the 'Judas' here and the 'Judas the Zealot' in the conversion of 'King Augarus' or 'King Agbarus' in Syriac sources like the Apostolic Constitutions, not to mention the 'Thomas' ('Judas Thomas') in the presentation in Eusebius.[98] We shall encounter this theme as well in the 'letter' (or two 'letters') known as '*MMT*', also treating the subject of 'things sacrificed to idols', 'Gentile sacrifices', and 'skins' ('skins sacrificed to idols'?) in the Temple and addressed seemingly to a King interested in *Abraham's* 'salvationary' state. Galatians does not name the representatives that James sends down to 'Antioch' at this point, only that they do not come with Paul and Barnabas and their arrival is actually the occasion of the rift between Paul and Peter and Barnabas over *table fellowship with Gentiles*. We have just seen the *real* Peter's view of such 'table fellowship' in the Pseudoclementine *Homilies* above.

This probable anachronism of Peter at 'the Jerusalem Conference' is the last mention of Peter in the Book of Acts, a book, at least ostensibly, treating all the Apostles. As already stated, not even Peter's days in Rome are mentioned, nor anything about his ultimate fate. With James' sudden appearance in Acts, Peter and the *other* James just disappear. It can be safely observed that Acts is anxious to paper over the differences between Paul and other 'Pillar' Apostles like Peter. It knows the true history, or at least has an inkling of it, and wishes somehow to harmonize it.

To do this, it plays on the one positive motif from its perspective in Paul's picture of his criticism of Peter in Galatians, Peter as a swing figure originally willing to eat with Gentiles or 'keep table fellowship' with them (as it is generally called). In Peter's last cameo in Acts – how he returned to Jerusalem after fleeing for his life being unexplained – Peter is presented as speaking in favour of Gentiles, and by extension, Paul's 'Gentile Mission' generally, and against those who would impose circumcision on them or conversion to Judaism prior to 'being Heirs to' the Covenant's promises. In the process, Peter is to some degree given credit for James' directives to overseas Communities, but we can certainly understand this as an anachronism or interpolation – or both.

In any event, as we just saw, the *real* Peter probably did not take his 'food at the same table as Gentiles' at all (and this 'because they lived impiously'), following the regulations of James' directives to overseas communities meticulously. This accords with the picture Paul gives in Galatians 2:10–14 precisely and may even account for the mix-up between 'Cephas' and 'Peter' in that letter. In fact, in these notices in the Pseudoclementine *Homilies*, we are provided with a picture of James' directives to overseas communities more precise and more complete even than in Acts, including the key, really, to what Paul is so exercised about in 1 Corinthians 10:21 comparing 'the table of the Lord' to 'the table of demons'. For the *Homilies*, 'the table of demons' *is* 'food sacrificed to idols'.[99]

James as Opposition High Priest and *Oblias*

James as *Oblias* or Protection-of-the-People

Both Eusebius and Epiphanius, basing themselves again on Hegesippus, tell us that James was known by two important cognomens. The first we are already familiar with, 'the Righteous' or 'Just One'. This they render from the Hebrew '*Zaddik*' into the Greek '*Dikaios*', and from thence on into the Latin '*Justus*'. The second is '*Oblias*'. Both are a consequence of James' 'Holiness from his mother's womb' (itself tied to his Nazirite/ Rechabite life-style by way of the first of the two 'Love' Commandments: James' 'Piety towards God') and his having entered the Holy of Holies on at least one occasion to make a *Yom Kippur*-style atonement on behalf of the whole people.

Neither writer is able properly to transliterate the second cognomen '*Oblias*', providing, therefore, only an approximate transliteration in the Greek. Nor has anyone ever discovered what this curious epithet really means, or exactly what the Hebrew it was originally based on was, though both Eusebius and Epiphanius give ample indication that they *think* they know what it meant. To be sure, there is always the possibility that the term was just another of these variations on the *B–L–'*/'*Belial*'/ '*Diabolos*' language circle in both Hebrew and Greek, possibly – like the parallel *Adikaios*/'Unrighteousness' – carrying a meaning of *against the Devil* or *against Belial*.

There is something of this root in the mysterious '*Lebbaeus*' name found in the Apostle list in some versions of the Gospel of Matthew and attached to the Apostle 'Thaddaeus', an individual we shall also show to be part of James' and Jesus' family circle. We shall also show that 'Lebbaeus' is related to 'Alphaeus', the *father* of 'James the Less' in Apostle lists, and a clear corruption of Jesus' 'uncle's' name 'Cleophas'. However these things may be, 'Oblias' and 'Lebbaeus' probably represent something of the same thing, their relationship having to do with the curious recurrences of the letters *B* and *L* making up their names whether in Hebrew or Greek.

'*Laos*' in Greek has something of the meaning of 'to the people'. Having said this, there is no term in Greek even remotely resembling the formulation '*Lias*'. We have already laboured over the similar rendering in Greek '*Banus*' above, concluding it incorporated something of the sense of what in Latin had to do with 'bathing' or 'bather' – even if not, implying that the individual in question actually did these things. Likewise, despite the admitted absurdity of mixing Hebrew with Greek word roots, the first syllable, '*Ob*', would seem to be based on some Hebrew description incorporating something of the sense of 'Protection', 'Bulwark', or 'Strength' (in Hebrew, "*Oz*' or '*Ma'oz*').

Both Eusebius and Epiphanius, though they are obviously in the dark as to its precise derivation, think '*Oblias*' means this. Immediately after describing how James was continually in the Sacristy 'on his knees praying for forgiveness for the People [in, as noted, a kind of *Yom Kippur* atonement] so that his knees were as callused as a camel's', Eusebius goes on to tell us:

> Because of his superlative Righteousness, he was called the Righteous One [*Dikaios*] and Oblias, which translates out in Greek, 'Protection-of-the-People' and 'Righteousness' [*Dikaiosunē*],

He then adds to his discussion, 'as the Prophets declare concerning him'.[1]

This is a very pregnant addition, for it means that James' two cognomens, '*Zaddik*' and '*Oblias*', were to be found by searching Hebrew Scripture, particularly the Prophets, but also Psalms, which, as at Qumran (and again *later in Islam*), were viewed as a prophetical composition in this period. We have been following '*Zaddik*' throughout this book. It is to be found over and over again in Scripture, particularly in the first two episodes in Genesis having to do with '*Zaddikim*' (plural for *Zaddik*), the Noah and Lot 'escape' and 'Salvation' episodes. There are numerous '*Zaddik*' references in Scripture, many of which are picked up, even, in the extant Qumran texts and interpreted in terms of events in the life of the Righteous Teacher.[2]

There are also notices about 'Justification', which derive from the word '*Zedek*'/'Righteousness' or '*Zaddik*'/'Righteous' or 'Righteous One', based on a verbal complex literally meaning in Hebrew 'to make Righteous'. The reader should pay particular attention to the roots of words in Hebrew, which like most Semitic languages – Aramaic, Syriac, and Arabic – is built on three-letter root patterns. The root should be obvious here, Z–D–K.

In the Qumran documents, where the Righteous Teacher (*Moreh* or

Yoreh ha-Zedek) is always presented in expositions of key scriptural passages evoking the usage '*Zaddik*', we shall have to do with other language clusters of this kind. Two, for instance, *R–Sh–'/*'Wicked' or 'Evil' and *B–L–'/*'swallow', are always identified with an Establishment High Priest apparently responsible for the destruction of the Righteous Teacher. The first not only reverses the *Righteousnessness* in his name, but also his characteristic 'Justifying' activity, in the sense of 'making' someone 'Evil' or 'condemning'. The second means 'to swallow' in the sense of *eating* or 'consume' in the sense of *destroying*.

Other important Scriptural passages having to do with '*Zaddik*' are picked up in the New Testament and applied to Jesus. Most important of these are Isaiah 53:11, which incorporates both the usages 'Righteous One' and 'justifying' in the sense of '*lehazdik*', meaning 'to make Righteous', together with Genesis 15:6 on how Abraham's 'Faith was reckoned to him as Righteousness'. These are the *actual* Hebrew words, which in Paul's reformulation in Greek, become 'Abraham was justified by Faith' (Rom. 3:24–4:2) – reformulated in James 2:21–24's Abraham 'was justified by *works*' (echoed in the Qumran '*MMT*'). But it should be clearly understood that this usage 'justified' in Greek, despite the sense (or mis-sense) in English of 'making excuses for oneself', has in its original Hebrew the meaning of 'making' or 'being made Righteous'.

Isaiah 53:11: 'My servant the Righteous One will justify Many', and Genesis 15:6 are two-thirds of the tripartite scriptural foundation of early Christian theology. The third is Habakkuk 2:4, 'the Righteous shall live by his Faith', another basic component of Pauline theological exposition, refracted to some extent in the Letter of James (2:23). Together with Genesis 15:6 above, Paul subjects this passage from Habakkuk to exegesis in Galatians 3:11, and Romans 1:17 and 4:2–5:5.

It is also quoted in the Habakkuk *Pesher*, where it forms the basis of its eschatological exposition of 'the Last Times' or 'the Last Generation'. This commentary on the first two chapters of Habakkuk gives the Qumran perspective of this passage, which, as might be expected, is *Jamesian* rather than *Pauline*. This perspective limits the applicability of Habakkuk 2:4 – and that of 2:3 preceding it, which has to do with what is called 'the Delay of the *Parousia*' in Christianity, 'the Delay of the Last Generation' at Qumran – to 'Doers of the *Torah* in the House of Judah', which has to mean, *all Jews*. That is, these two passages do *not* apply to 'non-Doers of the *Torah* inside the House of Judah', and most emphatically not to 'non-*Torah*-Doers' outside it – the ostensible beneficiaries of the Pauline *Gentile Mission*.

355

For Epiphanius, James, surnamed 'the Righteous', was the eldest of 'Joseph's' six children by a wife – not Mary – whose name he either doesn't know or declines to give. Not only was he 'a Nazirite' and 'consecrated from his mother's womb', but he was called '*Oblias*', which for him means either 'Fortress' or 'wall'.[3] It should be remarked that he leaves out the suffix 'of the People' (equivalent to the Greek '*Laos*'?), as in Eusebius' *Oblias* as 'Protection-of-the-People', but otherwise, as can be seen, he is in substantial agreement with Eusebius on this mysterious term's meaning.

In a later description of James, Eusebius provides a variation on the term – 'Bulwark', which still retains the general sense of 'Wall'/'Fortress'/ or 'Protection'. Whatever it means, it results from James' superabundant 'Righteousness' and his functioning in the Temple in some manner as a Priest or *Opposition* High Priest. Both Eusebius and Epiphanius present the epithet in this context.

It is interesting that Eusebius provides us with this second version of this epithet after describing how:

> After the ascension of our Saviour, the Jews had followed up their *crime* against him by devising *plot after plot* against his Disciples,

and going on to describe how:

> The members of the Jerusalem Church, by means of an oracle given by revelation to acceptable persons there, were ordered to leave the City before the War began [meaning the War against the Romans] and settled in a town in Perea called Pella.

Pella is a town across Jordan on the northern edge of Perea (or 'Moab') in an area in the period being called 'the Decapolis', meaning 'Ten' Hellenistic towns, of which Pella was one. The Fortress of Machaeros, for instance, further south – where John the Baptist was executed – is in Perea. Eusebius concludes:

> That, as if *Holy Men* had utterly abandoned the Royal Capital of the Jews and the whole Land of Judea, the Judgement of God at last overtook them for their *abominable crimes against the Christ* and His Apostles completely *blotting out* that Wicked Generation from among men – [4]

a very pleasant description, typical of Eusebius.

Going on to describe famine, the eating of children – this, '*the vengeance that followed the guilt of the Jews and their Impiety against the Christ of*

God' – and 1,100,000 people that perished from the sword, Eusebius now explains 'that for forty years after *their crimes against Christ*', the presence in Jerusalem of

> most of the Apostles and Disciples delayed its destruction. Primary among those still surviving, was James himself, known as the brother of the Lord, the first Bishop of the city. By remaining in Jerusalem, they afforded, as it were, the *strongest Bulwark* ['*Protection*'] to the place.[5]

At this point, Eusebius goes on to quote from Josephus' testimony at the end of the *Jewish War* about how the 'impostors and people telling Lies about God, perverted the miserable people', in particular, concerning 'a Star standing over the city *like a sword*'. In Matthew, this 'Star' becomes – pacified as ever – the *Star over Bethlehem* (2:2–10); and in 'the Star Prophecy', so widespread at Qumran, it is the Messiah again. Josephus, also, goes on to speak, in the section Eusebius is quoting from at the end of the *War*, about the Star Prophecy, to wit, that 'a world ruler would come out of Palestine', and applies it to Vespasian, a fact, Eusebius, too, now remarks.[6]

Josephus also mentions at this point about how one 'Jesus ben Ananias', a simple peasant, went around the city proclaiming its coming destruction, starting 'four years before the war' at Tabernacles, 62 CE. But this is precisely the moment when he pictures James as being stoned in the *Antiquities*! Like our 'Jesus' in the Gospels, this 'Jesus', too, is arrested by the Jewish Authorities, who

> felt some demon was responsible for the man's actions . . . brought him to the Roman Governor, where he was *scourged till his flesh hung in ribbons*, but he uttered no pleas, nor shed any tear [our 'Essene' behaviour again, if not that of the Gospels], but raising his voice with all his power, answered to every blow, 'Woe, woe to Jerusalem!'[7]

Not only is this prototypical for Jesus' behaviour before Pilate in the Synoptics, as we earlier remarked, it is also the the prototype for the Little Apocalypses attributed to Jesus in the Synoptics – but, of course, now being uttered in relation to James' *death*, not as a preliminary to Jesus'.

Two later manuscripts of Eusebius quote the rest of Josephus' testimony regarding Jesus ben Ananias. That this occurred under Albinus immediately following the stoning of James is made very clear.

> He never *cursed those who daily struck him* [Jesus' 'turn the other cheek' as reported in the Gospels], nor blessed those who gave him food, but rather

kept up the same melancholy wail, 'Woe, woe to Jerusalem' and 'Woe, woe to the people, to the city, and to the Temple'.

Josephus even gives the exact amount of time that this individual continued this mournful refrain, seven years and five months (that is, approximately Passover, 70 CE), until he was struck on the head with a projectile just prior to the fall of the city. Josephus even makes a joke about this too, claiming he then uttered, 'Woe, woe to me also', and died immediately.

In Josephus, this 'Jesus' is freed after having been severely scourged by the Roman Governor (and earlier, too, by the Jewish Authorities). Interestingly enough in the Gospels, Jesus' double, 'Jesus Barabbas', a man 'who in the insurrection had committed murder', is also freed by the Roman Governor (Matt. 27:16–26 and pars.); in the Slavonic Josephus, so too is Jesus.[8] Whatever one may make of these curious overlaps, their closeness to the pattern of events surrounding the arrest of Jesus in the Gospels is undeniable.

In due course, we shall have more to say about *Jesus ben Ananias'* relationship to the mysterious oracle which was given to the members of the Jerusalem Community, occasioning their 'flight' across the Jordan to Pella in Perea. Both Eusebius and Epiphanius mention this oracle, Eusebius, as we just saw, in connection with these same 'calamities' that surrounded the destruction of Jerusalem.[9] Both the oracle by Jesus ben Ananias *directly upon* the death of James and the one occasioning the flight of James' followers across the Jordan will have relevance to another oracle Acts pictures 'a certain Prophet called Agabus' giving Paul before his last visit to Jerusalem and final confrontation with James about 60 CE (21:10).[10]

Acts, it will be recalled, also pictures this 'Agabus' as giving an earlier oracle in 'Antioch' in the 40s 'about a great Famine that was going to come over the whole civilized world' (11:28). This precedes an earlier trip to Jerusalem Acts says Paul made, but not paralleled in Galatians. This 'Famine', in turn – again, it will be recalled – is connected to the beheading of Theudas (paralleling that of 'James the brother of John' in Acts 12:1), the preventative crucifixion of Judas the Galilean's two sons, and the conversion of Queen Helen of Adiabene, whose kinsmen, Monobazus and Kenedaeos, finally play such a prominent role in the opening engagement of the Uprising against Rome.

This is the context in which Eusebius makes his second testimony to

James' role as 'Bulwark' or 'Fortress' in Jerusalem. The reader should appreciate that there is much garbling of sources going on here, whether playful or otherwise. Interestingly enough, the two Greek words Eusebius uses here are both military in tone, referring to a 'fortified Stronghold' or 'strong Bulwark'. Paul, who also shows familiarity with such military language when attacking those who 'frighten you with letters' and 'those Super Apostles', who 'commend themselves', once again – as per his wont – spiritualizes it:

> For the weapons of our warfare are not bodily, but powerful [enough] through God to *overthrow Strongholds*. (2 Cor. 10:4–5)

But what is the meaning of this 'Wall' or 'Fortification' language so descriptive of James' second cognomen '*Oblias*'? How is it to 'be found in Scripture' as Eusebius reports and as James' other Hebrew cognomen, 'the *Righteous One*' or '*Zaddik*', was? This is an intriguing question.

There are several possibilities. First, it should be appreciated that this *Protection*, *Fortress*, or *Bulwark* language is of the same genre and sense as the *Pillar* language Paul has already applied to James, Cephas, and John – 'reputed to be something' – in Jerusalem (Gal. 2:9). But there are other words in Hebrew, also synonyms, which come close to the sense of this usage. These, found in Psalms and Prophets and reflected to some extent in the New Testament, are also, as we have seen, in use at Qumran in both the Community Rule and the Qumran Hymns.

Fortress, Rock, Bulwark, and *Cornerstone* Imagery at Qumran

In the Hymns Scroll found at Qumran, we find much of the imagery that we have already encountered in these passages describing James in early Church Literature. These should, perhaps, not be called 'Hymns', which is a little misleading. It implies a parallel with the Psalms in the Bible, but this document, found in Cave I – the first cave discovered at Qumran in 1947 – also tells something of a story. Written in the first person, it relates some of the experiences of its narrator, who appears to be a real person.

He, in turn, repeatedly refers to himself, as we saw, as 'the Poor One' or '*Ebion*' – familiar terminology where James' followers are in question – as well as what he repeatedly calls 'the soul of the Poor One', apparently meaning, as in the biblical Psalms, his quick or 'life'.[11] In a key allusion in the Damascus Document, for instance, we hear of an attack or 'pursuit with the sword', apparently led by the Liar, on 'the soul of the Righteous

One (*Zaddik*) and all the Walkers in Perfection', which parallels the sense of 'the Soul of the Poor One' here in Hymns.[12]

In addition, Hymns repeatedly refers to 'Righteous works', 'Perfection', 'the Way', 'Piety' – even, for instance, an interesting expression like 'the Poor Ones of Piety' (*Ebionei-Hesed*) together with allusion to 'the soul of the Meek One' – 'zeal for Righteousness', 'zeal' against 'the Seekers after Smooth Things', and 'zeal' against all 'Lying interpretations'.[13] There is also a distinct note of predetermination and foreknowledge not very different from Paul in Romans 8:28–9:11, also discussing 'loving God' (*Piety*), 'separating', and 'telling the Truth' and 'not Lying', or the famous prologue to the Gospel of John – not to mention the same intense interest in 'Light' one finds there.

For instance, John expresses these things as follows:

> In the beginning was the word and the word was made flesh, and the word was with God . . . All things were made by Him . . . and the life was the Light of men and the Light shines in the Darkness . . . and to as many as received Him, to them he gave the right to become Children of God. (1:1–12)

In the Qumran Hymns, we read:

> You have created the earth by Your Power, and the seas, and the deep . . . You have fashioned all their inhabitants by Your Wisdom . . . In the Wisdom of Your Knowledge, You established their End before ever they were . . . What can I say that is not foreknown and what can I utter that is not foretold . . . so You can make manifest Your Power through me? You have revealed Yourself to me in Your Power *as Perfect Light* [here, of course, our 'Power' vocabulary again].[14]

> And my Light shall shine forth in Your Glory, for as Light out of the Darkness, so You enlighten me . . . You have known me from the time of my father . . . For my father knew me not and my mother abandoned me to You, for *You are Father to all the Sons of Your Truth*.[15]

> For you [have poured] your Holy Spirit upon me . . . established [the spirit of man] before ever creating it . . . *You alone created the Righteous One, establishing him from the womb* . . . to *stand* [and the 'standing' vocabulary] before You in Everlasting abode, illumined with Perfect Light forever with no more Darkness in unending Eras of joy.[16]

Not only do we have in both the language of plural Divine Sonship, but in the second we repeatedly encounter the important phrase applied to

James in early Church literature above, that he 'was Holy from his mother's womb'. In the section where he speaks about God being 'a Father to all the Sons of [His] Truth', the narrator enlarges the proposition as follows:

> [You have] chosen me from the womb, from the belly of my mother You Perfected me, and from the breast of her who conceived me have Your mercies been [always] upon me.

Put in another way, as above, 'You alone created the Righteous One, establishing him from the womb'. Nothing could better give the sense of early Church testimonies to James being 'consecrated' or 'a Nazirite from his mother's womb' than these passages.

But in them, too, our text goes further, using the very *Oblias*-style language of 'Strength', 'Fortress', and 'Protection' we have been encountering above with regard to James and 'Peter' in orthodox Church scripture. We are even treated to 'Rock' imagery so familiar in Peter's very name, which is, indeed, parallel to the kinds of allusions we are encountering regarding James and now in these Hymns relating to whomever their author was – presumably the Righteous Teacher himself or a parallel figure.

As these Hymns from Qumran put it in two succeeding sections (and, in one way or another, throughout):

> But I will be as one who comes to a Fortified City and strengthened behind a Strong Wall until rescued, and . . . I will depend on You, my God, for You put [the] *Foundation on Rock* and . . . build *a Bulwark of Strength*, which shall not sway, and . . . its *Gates shall be Doors of Protection*, barring entrance with bars of Strength which cannot be broken.[17]

> For You have upheld me by Your Strength, You have *poured your Holy Spirit upon me* . . . and Strengthened me before the wars of Evil . . . You have made me like *a Fortress of Strength, like a Strong Wall*, and established *my Building upon Rock* and my Foundations are like Eternal Foundations . . . and all my Ramparts are like Fortified Walls, which do not sway on their Foundations.[18]

One immediately sees that this imagery is the same as that being applied to James in early Church sources. But in these Hymns, too, we have the essence of what lies behind the peculiar epithet '*Oblias*', preserved in all sources about James, which was seen to have carried something of the sense of 'Protection', 'Shield', or 'Strong Wall', at least this is the definition given in early Church sources.

All these metaphors are present in the above imagery of the Qumran Hymns as adjectives or images of self-designation used by their author. As we have seen '*lias*' means something like 'people' or – if it is a paraphrase of a Hebrew original – 'to the people' or, as Eusebius puts it via Hegesippus, 'of the people'. For Epiphanius, '*Oblias*' simply means 'Wall' or 'Fortress' (the Greek *Teixos*),[19] which exactly parallels these phrases in the Qumran Hymns Scroll. Then what is meant in Hebrew by the Greek '*Ob*'? The closest Hebrew, as we saw, is "*Oz*'/Strength or another variation, also used in Hymns, '*Ma'oz*' or 'Shield' or 'Protection' again. This word "*Oz*' is often coupled in the Psalms of the Bible in extremely interesting contexts with the phrase 'to the people'.

In Psalm 29, it is used on two occasions amid imagery important to Qumran. In the first instance, 'give unto the Lord . . . Strength' (29:1), it introduces allusion to the 'voice of the Lord breaking the cedars of Lebanon' (29:5) and 'the voice of the Lord shaking the wilderness' (29:8). Allusion to 'Lebanon' and 'the cedars of Lebanon' is extremely important in many Qumran *pesharim*,[20] while 'a reed shaking in the wilderness' is just the allusion the New Testament uses in describing John the Baptist (Matt. 11:7 and Luke 7:24). Finally the psalm concludes, after evoking 'the Lord sitting upon the waters' or 'Flood', with the assurance that the 'the Lord will give *Strength to His people*' (29:10–11).

In Psalm 61 the actual words from the Hymns Scroll are used, 'a Fortress of Strength', together with 'Rock' imagery (61:2–3), imagery that also fairly permeates the next Psalm 62. This next psalm not only includes three references to 'Salvation' – '*Yesha*'' or '*Yeshu'a*' (62:1–7) – but also allusion to 'Piety' (*Hesed*) and 'paying a man according to his works' (62:12). 'Strength' or "*Oz*' is also used repeatedly in Psalm 68, preceding the thoroughly Messianic Psalm 69, in which two allusions familiar from Gospel presentations of Jesus are used, 'zeal for [my Father's] House consumes me' (69:9) and 'for my thirst, they gave me vinegar to drink' (69:21), and over and over again the language of 'the Righteous', 'swallowing', 'the Poor', 'the Meek', and 'Salvation' occurs (69:15–33).

In Psalm 68, the phrases 'Strength', 'Strength to the people', and even 'His Strength is in the clouds' (68:28 and 34) – again together with references to 'Salvation' (68:19) and 'the Righteous Ones' (68:3) – are actually used, finally in terms of 'rain' imagery and evoking 'the coming of the Heavenly Host *in Power* upon the clouds' (68:35). This last allusion, again incorporating the imagery of 'Power' and applied to the imminent return of Jesus in Scripture, will not only be at the heart of James'

Messianic proclamation in the Temple – which all these early Church sources will integrally tie to his demise – but the like-minded proclamation in the Qumran War Scroll as well, where, incorporating the imagery of Daniel too, the 'Messiah' is presented as coming with the Heavenly Horsemen or Heavenly Host upon the clouds, that is, 'the clouds of Heaven', and bringing Judgement 'like rain'.[21]

There is also one other important occurrence of this genre of 'Fortress' imagery at Qumran, that of 'the Precious Cornerstone', meaning *the Cornerstone of the Temple*. This is found in a crucial passage in the Community Rule, where it is connected to spiritualized 'Temple' imagery generally as applied to the Community Council.

The last is also described, it will be recalled, as an 'Eternal Plantation', language Paul reproduces in discussing how Apollos does the watering and himself as the architect who lays the Foundations of 'God's building' (1 Cor. 3:6–12). This kind of 'Foundations' and 'Cornerstone' imagery is also present in Ephesians 2:19–22's characterization of the Community as 'the Holy Temple' and 'Household of God'. As Acts 4:11 puts this in Peter's mouth, referring to Jesus (echoed in 1 Peter 2:7): 'This is the Stone, which you the builders have set at naught, which has become the Head of the Corner' (Psalm 118:22).

Amid allusion to 'being set apart as Holy' – our 'Nazirite' language again – and spiritualized 'atonement' imagery, the members of this Council are described as 'a sweet fragrance', 'an odour of Righteousness', 'a House of Perfection and Truth for Israel', and finally again, 'a Fortified Wall, a Precious Cornerstone, whose Foundations will neither rock nor sway in their place'. All this is delivered within the context of the commandment, used in the New Testament to describe the Mission of John the Baptist:

> separate from the midst of the habitation of the Men of Unrighteousness and go into the wilderness, to prepare the Way of the Lord, as it is written, 'Prepare in the wilderness the Way of [the Lord], make straight in the desert a Pathway for our God.' (Isa. 40:3)[22]

How could one get closer to the imagery of the first 'Christians' than this?

Onias the Righteous and Honi the Circle-Drawer

It should be clear that this imagery in the Community Rule from Qumran parallels what is being applied in these early Church testimonies to James, not only regarding the mysterious *Oblias* cognomen connected in some manner with his '*Zaddik*' nature, but also the references to James providing 'Protection to the People' or being a 'Strong Bulwark' or 'Fortified Wall'.

There is, also, another possibility, which, while on the surface may be far-fetched, in any event contains an element of truth – that the title, '*Oblias*', which both Eusebius and Epiphanius saw in Hegesippus from the second century, either garbles or has something to do with the Greco-Hebrew name '*Onias*'. Even if this is not true, James still has a relationship to an individual by that name in the first century BC, referred to in Talmudic literature as 'Honi *the Circle-Drawer*', since another name for him, as we have seen – and the name Josephus uses if not the *Talmud* – is 'Onias *the Righteous*', that is, Onias the *Zaddik*.

This 'Righteous One' terminology in this period is interesting. The first person referred to in this manner is an individual called Simeon *the Righteous* around 200 BC or before. This individual turns out to be the hero, not only of Talmudic transmission scenarios, but an apocryphal biblical book, Ecclesiasticus – in Hebrew, Ben Sira, after the name of its putative author, Jesus ben Sira.

Ben Sira was previously known only in Greek and allied recensions, though it was always suspected that a Hebrew original had existed. Such an original finally came to light in the materials from the Cairo *Genizah*, a huge cache of medieval Hebrew manuscripts found in a synagogue in old Cairo in 1896. Documents found there do relate to those found fifty years later at Qumran, because two recensions of the all-important Damascus Document, still in use today, were first discovered there. Fragments of this Hebrew version of Ben Sira were found not only among the materials at Qumran, but among the fragments of the few documents later found in the debris at Masada, *where the Jewish 'Sicarii' committed suicide* in the year 73 CE rather than submit to Rome.

What the relationship of Ben Sira is to Qumran is difficult to say, but it very likely centres about the '*Zaddik*' cognomen attached to Simeon's person in his capacity of High Priest in the era just prior to the Hellenizing 'pollutions' that led to the Maccabean Uprising. Not only does this prefigure the similar title attached to James' name, but several other individuals, particularly someone in the next century, as we saw above, known as 'Honi the Circle-Drawer' after the circles he drew to *bring rain*.

Ben Sira is the only biblical work signed with a date. It was written, presumably in Egypt, in 132 BC by a grandson of the individual whose name it bears. Not only is the 'Simeon' or 'Simon', with whom the famous panegyric to 'Famous Men' concludes, surnamed 'the Righteous One' and described in the most exalted terms, he is pictured in his glorious High Priestly vestments, which 'shone like the sun shining on the Temple' (50:7), as making a *Yom Kippur* atonement again, presumably a *Righteous* one. The Hebrew version of this paean, which makes it clear we are dealing with *'Anshei-Hesed'*/'Men of Piety' or 'Hassidim' – practitioners again, therefore, of the first part of our Piety/Righteousness dichotomy – not the 'Famous Men' of Greek translation.

Found at Qumran, Masada, and the Cairo *Genizah*, it applies both the 'Sons of Zadok' terminology and 'the Covenant of Phineas' – that 'Zealot Covenant' applied as well to the archetypal progenitor of the Maccabean line Mattathias thereafter (1 Macc. 2:27 and 2:54) – co-equally to the High Priesthood of Simeon the *Zaddik* and his descendants in perpetuity.[23] This paean to 'the Men of Piety' of preceding generations not only includes the Noahic 'Covenant of Peace', but begins in the Hebrew version with a reference to Noah also as 'the Righteous', 'Perfect and Righteous in his generation', with whom 'Everlasting Covenants were made' (44:17–19). It ends with a quotation from Psalm 148:14, again on behalf of Simeon the *Zaddik*: 'He lifted up the horn for His people, the praise for all His Pious Ones' (*Hassidim* – 51:15).

Not surprisingly, considerable attention is paid to both Phineas and Elijah as priests. The latter is praised for his 'word', which in the manner of John the Baptist in Scripture is called 'a flaming torch', and his 'zeal'. Phineas, described as 'third in Glory' (after Aaron and Eleazar), is likewise praised for 'his zeal' and 'being steadfast when the people rebelled' – words reminiscent of the Damascus Document at Qumran.[24] He is also extolled for the atonement he made on behalf of Israel, as a result of which the Noahic 'Covenant of Peace' was sealed with him and his descendants securing for them 'the Command of both Temple and the people . . . and the High Priesthood in perpetuity' (45:23–24). We have just read about this 'Covenant of Peace' in the War Scroll from Qumran above.

Not only was Simeon the *Zaddik* descended from an Onias, but he was the father of an Onias, the names 'Simon' and 'Onias' seeming to alternate in his genealogical line.[25] Simeon's son Onias is an important character in the Second Book of the Maccabees, both in its introduction of Judas and its denouement, and he would appear to have been the High Priest just prior to the outbreak of the Maccabean Uprising. His 'Piety and Perfect observance of the Law' are specifically remarked and 2 Maccabees goes on to describe him as 'the Protector of his countrymen' and 'this Zealot for the Laws' (3:1 and 4:2). The parallel at this point with James could not be more precise.

Onias' martyrdom under Antiochus Epiphanes (175–163 BC), the Eleventh Horn 'with a mouth full of boasts' of Daniel 7:8 – not insignificantly, in Antioch (2 Macc. 4:34) – triggers the Uprising led by Judas. Together with the Prophet Jeremiah, this Onias makes a post-mortem return at the end of the narrative to give the Messianic sword of vengeance to Judas, presumably in confirmation of both his High Priestly and avenging activities (15:26). There is, therefore, in the view of 2 Maccabees, no interruption between the High Priesthood of Onias and that of Judas Maccabee. Nor does Judas' father, Mattathias, play any role as he does in 1 Maccabees – Judas is simply the *direct* heir to the saintly Onias. Not only does Onias appear to be surnamed, like his father, 'the *Zaddik*', but the description, 'Protector of his fellow countrymen', applied to him in connection with evocation of his 'zeal for the Law' – not to mention his martyrdom – prefigures the application of this '*Oblias*' terminology to James two centuries later in these early Church accounts, the resonance of this epithet with the name 'Onias' also being curious.

Another 'Onias the *Zaddik*' in the next century, 'Honi *the Circle-Drawer*', also prefigures James in at least two respects – one, in the direct application of the cognomen 'the Righteous One' to his name and, two, that he is described also as being able *to bring rain*. Thirdly, like James, he suffers martrydom and this by stoning.[26] Though possibly casual, these connections seem too real to be simple coincidence.

In Talmudic tradition, Honi is the father of another individual called 'Righteous' with a curious sobriquet, 'Hanan *the Hidden*'. Not only does he also appear to have been *a rainmaker*, but identical with John the Baptist, the name 'Hanan' in Hebrew coming from Johanan, 'God comforts', or 'John'. The *Talmud* calls Hanan (sometimes 'Hanin') the son of a daughter of Honi and, in its own picaresque style, says he was called 'Hidden because he liked to *hide himself in the toilet*', reminiscent of its 'toilet' traditions regarding 'Jesus the Nazoraean', James, and 'the Essenes' above.[27]

Actually this 'Hidden' tradition is probably to be associated with the 'Hidden' or 'Secret Adam' tradition, mentioned above, which ultimately goes into what Shi'ite Islam is calling to this day 'the Hidden *Imam*'. As such, it carries a *redivivus* aspect. In the *Zohar*, the first *Zaddik* Noah, who 'sought Righteousness', is twice referred to as '*hiding* himself' or '*being hidden* in the Ark on the Day of the Lord's Wrath to escape the

Enemy'.[28] The allusion to 'the Enemy' in this context, applied in Jewish Christian/Ebionite tradition to James' assailant, *Paul*, is always interesting.

In the *Talmud*, there is also a 'Rip van Winkle' tradition associated with this Honi, which again carries with it, of course, the implication of a *redivivus* tradition like the one associated with Elijah and John in the Synoptics. Honi is said to have fallen asleep under *a carob tree*, only to awake seventy years later, when his grandson was still alive and the tree bore fruit! We have already seen how in some traditions 'carobs' were said to have been the true composition of *John's* food.[29]

Finally, the *Talmud* knows another rainmaking grandson of Honi it calls 'Abba Hilkiah', contemporary with James. The rainmaking tradition adhering to all these priestly *Zaddiks* was obviously an important one, and we shall find more incidences of it when discussing Queen Helen of Adiabene's 'Naziritism' and her conversion. As we are developing it here, it is not unconnected with the '*Oblias*' or 'Bulwark' tradition adhering to James' person.

This 'rain', as in the War Scroll at Qumran, often carried with it the connotation of eschatological Judgement. In the War Scroll, this 'Judgement' is associated with the coming of the Messianic 'King of Glory' and Heavenly Host ('upon the clouds') and 'falls like rain on all that grows on earth', meaning, as in Matthew 5:45 in 'the Sermon on the Mount', 'sending rain on the Just and Unjust' alike. This is the sense too of the Flood associated with the *saving* actions of the first *Zaddik* Noah. This association of the 'coming of the Son of Man' ('Jesus', but also 'Man'/'Adam') with 'the days of Noah' and 'entering the ark' is expressly drawn as well later in Matthew's Little Apocalypse (24:37–39; also Luke 17:26–27); and, in Ben Sira's praise of former 'Men of Piety', even Ezekiel's 'vision of the Glory' of the Chariot is linked to 'torrential rain' and apocalyptic Judgement (Ben Sira 49:8–10, based on Ezekiel 13:11–13 – 'the Lying Spouter' section so important to Qumran – and 38:22).[30]

Phineas too, as we saw, the archetypal progenitor of *priestly zeal*, was considered in apocryphal literature one of these archetypal rainmakers. Since, like the one associated with Elijah and John, this was a *redivivus* tradition as well, it also seems to be a part of the 'Primal Adam' tradition, a conceptuality even hinted at in Ben Sira 49:19, introducing Simon the *Zaddik*, that 'above every living creature is Adam' and, presumably too, the reason the panegyric did not begin with Adam.

So was Phineas' putative descendant, Elijah, whose 'zeal' Ben Sira too specifically notes. Elijah's miraculous rainmaking, hinted at as well in Ben

Sira (48:3), is also signalled, as we have noted, in the last chapter of the Letter of James in the context of its evocation of apocalyptic Judgement, 'rain', and 'the coming of the Lord'/'the Lord of Hosts . . . with Power' (upon the clouds?), as is 'the prayer of a Righteous One' which brings the 'rain' (Jas. 5:4–18).

This evocation of Elijah's prayer and rainmaking, in fact, directly connects to the picture of James' rainmaking in the extant account of Epiphanius. Epiphanius makes this claim in the aftermath of his description of James' 'Naziritism' and how, it will be recalled, he never cut his hair, wore only linen, and was connected to the Priesthood, entering the Holy of Holies once a year to 'ask forgiveness before God out of his super-abundant *Piety*'. He then informs us:

> And once during a drought [45–48?], he lifted his hands to Heaven and prayed, and at once Heaven sent rain . . . Thus, they no longer called him by his name, but his name was, rather, 'the Just One'.[31]

This association of James' sobriquet, 'the Just One' or 'the *Zaddik*', with his 'rainmaking' is extremely important. For the Letter of James, so efficacious was this 'prayer of the Just One' that Elijah, who in 1 Kings 20:10–14 is not simply 'zealous', but '*exceedingly zealous* for the Lord', could both 'pray a prayer' for the rain to come, but also for it to cease (Jas. 5:18).

Honi, whom Josephus calls 'Onias the Just One', received his other sobriquet, 'the Circle-Drawer', on account of the *circles he drew to bring the rain*, out of which he would not step until it came. We hear about similar circles being drawn by Josephus' and Hippolytus' 'Essenes', who in their observation of the Sabbath would not step out of a certain radius even to relieve themselves – this, of course, the parody in the Rabbinic tradition about Hanan *the Hidden* 'hiding himself in the toilet'! Not only is Qumran concerned with such scrupulous purity, specifying the exact location of the latrines from 'the camp',[32] but we have also seen the caricature of such concerns in the somewhat ribald Rabbinic tradition about Jacob of Kfar Sechania (or Sihnin) and Jesus the Nazoraean's recommendation to the High Priests about their toilets and 'a prostitute's hire'.

But the connections go deeper than this. If Honi is the father of Hanan the Hidden, and Hanan equivalent to John the Baptist, then James is probably a descendant of Honi. Again, the Rabbinic notices about 'the sons' or 'daughters of the Rechabites' marrying 'the sons' or 'daughters of the High Priests' give us additional basis for understanding relationships such as these. In particular, the Gospel of Luke portrays Jesus as related to John the Baptist and, specifically, that their mothers, who were 'the daughters of Priests', were cousins (1:36). Setting aside theological concerns about the bona fides of James' relationship to Jesus – or, for that matter, the historicity of 'Jesus' himself – if we accept the materials before us at face value, this would place James the Righteous and Josephus' 'Onias the Righteous' (the *Talmud*'s 'Honi the Circle-Drawer') in a direct genealogical – to say nothing of an ideological – line.

Epiphanius, charming as ever, but also sometimes incisive, puts this proposition as follows. Following his points about 'no razor ever touching' James' head, etc., he insists that James

> wore *no second tunic*, but used only a linen cloak, as it says in the Gospel, 'The young man fled, leaving behind the linen cloth which he had around him' [Mark 14:51 – this the 'bathing' clothing of the 'Essenes']. For it was John and James and James, these three, who practised this Way of life: the two sons of Zebedee and James the son of Joseph and brother of the Lord [note how Epiphanius groups these two Jameses together here] . . . But to James alone, it was allowed to enter once a year into the Holy of Holies, *because he was a Nazirite* and *connected to the Priesthood*. Hence Mary was related in two ways to Elizabeth and James was a distinguished member of the Priesthood, because the two tribes alone were linked to one another, the royal tribe to the priestly and the priestly to the royal, just as earlier in the time of the Exodus, Nahshon, the scion from the tribe of Judah, took to wife a previous Elizabeth daughter of Aaron. (Exod. 6:23)[33]

Aside from the overlapping between the two Jameses and a certain amount of garbling, this is extremely incisive testimony and parallels the Talmudic traditions about 'the sons of the Rechabites marrying the daughters of the High Priests' or vice versa. Not only do we have a certain resonance of the name 'Nahshon' with Hippolytus' 'Naassenes' above, but Exodus has Elizabeth as *Aaron's wife* and *Nahshon's sister*, not *Nahshon's wife* and *Aaron's sister*, reflecting these reversals concerning 'sons' or 'daughters' of the High Priests in Talmudic traditions above about these Rechabites.

Elsewhere Epiphanius not only knows on the basis of the *Anabathmoi Jacobou* that Herod was *not* Jewish, but a *foreigner*, but sets forth the proposition that Alexander Jannaeus – the most powerful of the previous Maccabean Priest–Kings – prefigured the combination of priestly and royal lineages one finds in James and Jesus.[34] The same evocation of the combination of priestly and royal lineage in the Damascus Document at

Qumran has always puzzled commentators, but we see in these references about James' lineage in Epiphanius a parallel ideology in formation.

In the Damascus Document, and to some extent the Community Rule, where it is coupled with 'the Prophet' or 'True Prophet' terminology so important to Ebionite groups,[35] a Messianic 'Root of Planting', as we saw, is referred to as being 'from Israel and from Aaron', as well as a 'Messiah from Aaron and Israel'. The latter is referred to in the Damascus Document on three separate occasions as *singular*, and coupled with an allusion to 'standing up'.[36] As we have seen, 'standing' in Hebrew can simply mean 'arise'. But it can also mean more pregnantly, as per 'the bones' passage in Ezekiel 37:10, 'be resurrected' in the sense of 'arising from the dust'. If the latter signification, then of course what is being signalled in the Damascus Document is the hope for a Messianic return.

In the latter regard, too, one should remember the connection of 'the Standing One' ideology to that of 'the Primal Adam' and 'the Power' or 'Hidden Power' in Ebionite Christianity and among other daily bathing groups like so-called 'Elchasaites' – all usages we have now encountered both in early Christianity and in these documents from Qumran. These are the kinds of ideas that are at stake in these very interesting relationships.

The story of John's birth in Luke, and the consanguinity of Elizabeth and Jesus' mother Mary signalled there, also bears the seeds of this kind of dual royal and priestly genealogy. That the zealous Maccabean Priest–Kings, the forerunners of these kinds of heroes, incorporate the same combination of priestly and royal offices, points to the closeness of these kinds of conceptualities. From the early Christian perspective, the whole presentation of Jesus as 'a [High] Priest forever after the order of Melchizedek' – a concept also seemingly in vogue among the Maccabeans – is set forth in a letter addressed, interestingly enough, 'to the Hebrews' in Rome (Heb. 7:16–26).

Though the authorship of this letter is disputed, there can be no disputing the concept that Epiphanius is drawing on to arrive at his conclusions. The same ideology is to be found in the Qumran materials, even the ideological interest in Melchizedek.[37] This, in turn, supports the interpretation of the Qumran documents we have been attempting to delineate, that the Maccabean and early Christian approaches flow into each other, and the Qumran documents do not differ appreciably from either. Far from being anti-Maccabean, the normative view of the Qumran Scrolls propagated by the scholarly cartel controlling them for 'forty years', the Scrolls – being opposed to any hint of compromise or accommodation – have everything in common with the ethos of the Maccabeans and nothing whatsoever with those opposing them.

On the contrary, what the Scrolls are is *anti-Herodian*, Herod being perceived both as a 'foreigner' and 'Covenant-Breaker', whom the Romans appointed King. By extension, they are also opposed to that Priesthood, perceived of as 'polluted', owing its appointment to him, his heirs, or the Roman Governors *in collusion with all of them*. This is the Pharisee/Sadducean Establishment so familiar in Gospel portraits and to those who have read Josephus.

The Zadokite Covenant and the *Zaddik* Idea

This brings us back directly to Honi's death, his rainmaking, and the reason for the '*Zaddik*' appellation as applied to him. Consistent with the unbending orientation evinced in all Dead Sea Scrolls, aside from bringing rain, Honi would not tolerate *accommodation with foreigners* or *collaboration of any kind*. Deriving his other cognomen from the circles he drew to bring the rain – whether eschatological or material 'rain' is beside the point – he drew these circles, according to Talmudic sources, during one particularly severe drought. This is the backdrop, too, to Epiphanius' testimony to James' rainmaking, and here one has a good insight into newly emerging terminology of 'the *Zaddik*' or 'Righteous One' that we are encountering in this period. Because Honi was 'a Righteous One', he presumably – like Elijah – had influence in both the earthly and Heavenly spheres.

This conceptuality seems to have come to the fore for the first time in a serious manner in Ezekiel. Ezekiel, along with Isaiah, is an extremely important prophet to those responsible for the literature found at Qumran. Not only is Ezekiel responsible for 'the Zadokite Covenant' found in an addendum to his other ecstatic and apocalyptic prophecies – an addendum about the ideal or the new reconstructed Temple (Ezek. 40–48) – this is the material seized upon at Qumran to develop an ideology of a 'Priesthood', referred to, as we have seen, in terms of 'the Sons of Zadok'.

Some might consider 'the Sons of Zadok' to be simply genealogical descendants of the first Zadok in David's and Solomon's time, the first High Priest of the First Temple. This would appear to be the normative definition of those called 'Sadducees' in the Herodian Period, that is, those pictured in the famous delineations in the Gospels and presented in Josephus as being dominated by the Pharisees in all things, but disagreeing with them primarily on the matter of 'the Resurrection'.[38]

In Ezekiel, however, the Sons of Zadok are represented as *opposed to* a previously reigning Establishment in the Temple, which on a strictly genealogical basis might, also, be construed as being descendants of the original Zadok of David's time and therefore legitimate (44:6–15). However in Ezekiel, the new 'Sons of Zadok' have a qualitative component as well. They are 'the Holy' or 'consecrated ones' – note the variation of the 'Nazirite' terminology above – who '*kept* what they were *charged to keep*'. In other words, they were 'Keepers' or, more specifically, 'Keepers of the Covenant' (Ezek. 44:15 and 48:11). But in addition – and perhaps more importantly – they *object to Gentiles in the Temple*. Despite Josephus' rather disingenuous protestations to the contrary, Ezekiel is quite specific about this, repeating it, as we saw, twice:

> Say to those that have *rebelled against God* of the House of Israel . . . : 'May your hearts be full with *all your Abominations*, in that you have *admitted foreigners, uncircumcised in heart* and *uncircumcised in body into My Temple to pollute it* . . . *breaking My Covenant* and . . . *not keeping what you were charged to keep regarding My Holy Things* . . . No foreigner, *uncircumcised in heart* and *uncircumcised in body shall enter My Temple*, nor any foreigner among the Children of Israel [that is, 'resident alien']. (44:6–9)

Not only should one remark the note about 'rebelling against God' we just encountered with regard to the praise of Phineas in Ben Sira above, also a staple in the Dead Sea Scrolls, Ezekiel goes on to remark the idolatry of the previous Establishment (44:12) and how the new 'Keepers' or 'Sons of Zadok . . . are not to wear wool', but only

> linen diadems . . . linen girdles about their loins, so as not to *be moist* [meaning 'to perspire'] nor shave their heads . . . nor drink wine . . . but to teach My people [the difference] between *Holy and profane, polluted and clean* . . . (44:15–23)[39]

Ezekiel even includes in these instructions, as noted, the ban on carrion found in James' directives to overseas communities:

> The *priests* should not eat of any thing that is *dead of itself, nor torn*, whether it be fowl or beast. (44:31)[40]

This ban on 'admitting foreigners into the Temple to pollute it' is exactly the objection that Josephus ascribes to Simon, the Head of his own 'Assembly' or 'Church' (*Ecclēsia*) in Jerusalem. He is against *admitting Herodians* into the Temple. Two principal characteristics of Ezekiel's description are picked up, too, in Qumran representations of its *new* 'Sons of Zadok': firstly, as we have seen, they are defined as 'the Keepers of the Covenant' *par excellence*; and, secondly, it is quite clear that they disapprove of Gentile gifts and Gentile sacrifices in the Temple.

This last is, of course, the behaviour of so-called 'Zealots' or '*Sicarii*' among the lower priesthood in 66 CE, who stop sacrifice on behalf of Romans and other foreigners in the Temple, thereby triggering the War against Rome. Remembering that the prototypical ancestor of Zadok, Aaron's grandson Phineas, warded off pollution from the camp by killing backsliders – specifically designated as those marrying Gentiles – the Herodians, regardless of gender, would have been seen by persons such as these as being involved in approximately the same behaviour.

The Damascus Document adds an additional, 'eschatological' dimension to the qualitative ones being expressed here. In its delineation of 'the Zadokite Covenant' of Ezekiel 44:15, it describes 'the Sons of Zadok' as '*those who would stand*' or '*stand up at the End of Days*'. These would both '*justify the Righteous* and *condemn the Wicked*'. Not only do we have here the essence of 'Justification' theology as Paul is developing it, the emphasis on 'Last Times'/'Last Days' turns the whole exegesis eschatological. When linked to the notion of 'standing' or 'standing up' – so much a part of the 'Standing One' vocabulary described above – then one begins to have a statement close to what is being developed in New Testament Redeemer scenarios, that is, of Supernatural Redeemer figures, such as Jesus or even 'Peter', participating in 'the Last Judgement'.

For Qumran, there are two streams of people entering 'the Kingdom' or, if one prefers, the Heavenly Domain of the Righteous: firstly, the Righteous *living*, and, secondly, the Righteous *dead*. Where the first category is concerned, since in theory they go into the Kingdom living, presumably they would not have to *be resurrected*. Paul wrestles manfully with this issue, which he calls 'a Mystery', in 1 Corinthians 15:51–57 after, not surprisingly, evoking both the 'First' and 'Second Adam' and the 'Primal Adam' and 'Last Man' ideologies. It is for such persons that the notion of 'standing', in the sense of 'going on' functioning at 'the End of Time' in the Damascus Document, might be appropriate. The Righteous dead would have to be resurrected first. Though nowhere explicitly stated in the materials before us, this ideology is implied.

The 'Sons of Zadok', therefore, according to the Damascus Document exegesis of Ezekiel 44:15, would appear – when taken eschatologically – to refer to a supernatural class of quasi-Redeemer figures. At Nag Hammadi in Upper Egypt, something of this role and theme is certainly being accorded James in the Apocalypses ascribed to his name, which are full of many of the motifs we are analysing here.[41] We say 'supernatural', because anyone who has gone through a dying and a resurrection process, must to a certain extent be, as Paul implies in 1 Corinthians 15:52–54, taken as being beyond the natural. For Christianity, 'Jesus' is obviously such a figure, though, for the authors of the New Testament, he not only enjoys a supernatural resurrection and ascension, but a supernatural birth as well. This is beyond the ideology of Qumran, as we have it, which runs more towards the 'adoptionist sonship' schemes one finds among more 'Jewish Christian' groups.[42]

This brings us to the Hebrew etymological links of the words 'Zadok' and '*Zaddik*'. Even the uninitiated in the complexities of Semitic languages will be able to see that these two words are based on the same three-letter root, Z–D–K. 'Zadok' is a proper name; while '*Zaddik*' is a verbal noun based on a concept. The double '*D*' in the second does not appear in Hebrew orthography and is a matter of grammatical convention – and, to a certain extent, transliteration into Greek – only. Also, in Qumran Hebrew, the vowels '*o*' and '*i*', again matters of convention, are indistinguishable. So, in very real terms, '*Zadok*' and '*Zaddik*' are, at least, in written Hebrew of the period *the very same word*. This fact was, surely, not lost on our biblical exegetes of the time, who enjoyed both wordplay and stretching the conventions of the language before them, wherever it could serve an exegetical end.

This point is reflected in the transliteration into Greek of the familiar word 'Sadducees'. Even the beginner should be able to recognize immediately that this term is based on the Hebrew root Z–D–K, in this case, 'Zadok' or even 'Zadduk'. Once again, we are clearly in the realm of conventions or confusions relating to transliterations into a second tongue. 'Sadducee' can just as easily be based on the Hebrew word '*Zaddik*' as 'Zadok', the vowels *i*, *u*, and *o* being virtually indistinguishable where Qumran epigraphy is concerned.

In fact, in our interpretation of the 'Sadducee' problem – Qumran *Sadducees* following a Righteousness-oriented interpretation, as we have seen, of 'the Zadokite Covenant' of Ezekiel, and Establishment *Sadducees* of the Herodian Period and perhaps earlier, only insisting on a genealogical link with the 'Zadok' of ancient times – we come down very heavily on the point about one group following a more esoteric understanding of 'the Zadokite Covenant' and insisting on a qualitative dimension involving 'Righteousness', even going so far as to introduce an additional eschatological dimension to this. Even the Book of Acts, Josephus, and the Pseudoclementines insist that 'the Sadducees' were 'stricter in Judgement' than other groups, whatever might be meant by 'Judgement' in this context.[43] The 'Priesthood forever after the order of Melchizedek' as developed in the Letter to the Hebrews, again incorporating the *Z–D–K* root, is but a further eschatological adumbration of this ideology.

Josephus introduces the character he is calling '*Sadduk*' or '*Saddok*' at the beginning of the first century. Along with Judas the Galilean, he leads the agitation against Roman taxation in Palestine. This accompanies the Census of Quirinius/Cyrenius in 6–7 CE, that Luke, anyhow, identifies with the circumstances surrounding the birth of *Jesus Christ*. Though Luke's may or may not be a historical account, it does relate the circumstances of Jesus' birth to the Tax Revolt in Palestine coincident with the birth of the Movement associated with Judas and *Saddok*. Is this partner of Judas the Galilean in Josephus' account in the *Antiquities* of the founding of this Movement, opposing the taxation in Palestine, an individual with the actual name of 'Zadok' or a teacher with the title of 'the *Zaddik*' – much as the Righteous Teacher seems to be in Qumran tradition and, of course, James in early Church tradition? It is impossible to say, only that confusion over the derivation of the term 'Sadducee' is apparent in these materials as well.

This same confusion, also, exists in James' title 'the Just' or 'Just One', which Epiphanius tells us was so identified with his person as to replace his very name itself. This is the implication of Hegesippus' account as well. Are we dealing simply with the descriptive epithet 'the Just One' or does this imply the use of the Hebrew name 'Zadok' itself as applied to James, since the two are interchangeable? It is impossible to say, but, as explained, where the Latin version of this name is concerned, in the Roman Jewish catacombs 'Justus' in Latin is equivalent to 'Zadok' in Hebrew. Once again, we have come full circle.

Ezekiel's New Philosophy of the *Righteous Man*

This brings us to Ezekiel's key presentation of the 'Righteous Man' or 'Zaddik'. Ezekiel launches this discussion after evoking a new and 'Ever-lasting Covenant' God intends to make with Israel in place of the one which was broken (11:18–21 and 16:60–63).[44] He describes 'the Righteous Man' as someone who 'does', 'walks in', or 'keeps all My Laws' or 'Judgements' (18:9 and 21) – the definition of 'the Sons of Zadok' at Qumran, reflected too in 'the Doers of *Torah*' terminology introducing the exposition of 'the Righteous shall live by his Faith' in the Habakkuk *Pesher*.[45] One should also note that, among other things, this Righteous Man is not an idolator and 'does not sleep with a woman in her period' (18:6 and 15), the very charge also levelled against the Establishment in the 'Three Nets of Belial' section of the Damascus Document, immediately following its exegesis of the Zadokite Covenant.[46]

In this detailed definition of the 'Righteous Man', Ezekiel, also, specifically counter-indicates Mosaic Law as it has been previously understood. Unlike the Levitical and and Deuteronomic positions previously, the sins of the fathers are *not to be visited upon the sons*. Rather, what is being presented here is individual responsibility. The Righteous Man, as Ezekiel puts it, will not suffer for someone else's sin. He will not die. It is

the man who has sinned who is the one who must die. *A son is not to suffer for the sins of his father, nor a father for the sins of his son.* (18:17–21)

In this incredible presentation, not only do we have the emphasis on 'doing', which finds parallel expression in the Letter of James – or as Ezekiel puts it, 'in the future I mean to judge each of you by what *he does*' – but here too we have the notion of Justification, that the Righteous or Zaddik 'is made Righteous [or 'justified'] by what he *does*'. Ezekiel is discussing, by now, very familiar terrain to us.

Finally, in explaining how God means 'to judge everyone by what *he does*', the text introduces the idea of putting 'a *new heart* and a *new spirit*' into the House of Israel and repentance as being part and parcel of the process (18:30–32). As it presents the proposition:

Repent and turn away from all sins . . . therefore repent and live.

There can be little doubt that this section is intrinsic for the development of the idea of 'the Righteous Man' or '*Zaddik*' and, in particular, the theorizing surrounding the 'Righteousness' ideology which one finds in the Dead Sea Scrolls. It is also intrinsic to the *Jamesian* position in the development of early Christianity. The vocabulary here is totally in harmony with both the Letter of James and the Scrolls.

What is interesting, too, is the direct countermanding of Deuteronomic ideas of retribution represented by the development of the idea of 'the *Zaddik*'. Where Christian intellectual development is concerned, the notion that a whole people should be 'guilty' of some historical tragedy is also gainsaid, were there any truth to it in the first place. The idea, as portrayed in Matthew, that a whole people would cry out after Pilate 'washes his hands' (saying, 'I am innocent of the blood of *this Righteous One*'), 'his blood be upon us and upon our children', is, of course, completely counter-indicated by this material in Ezekiel. The reason is that the idea of blood liability has been countermanded in Ezekiel and, as the Damascus Document puts it, 'each man is to *stand on his own watch-tower*'.

There is another aspect to this new '*Zaddik*' ideology, first encountered in Ezekiel, that is worth noting. This has to do with Ebionites or 'the Poor Ones', holding on to the tradition of James' leadership and ostensibly stemming from his Jerusalem Community or Palestinian Christianity. Existing somewhere across the Dead Sea 'in Arabia' and the 'Damascus' region of what is today Jordan and Syria, they appear to have flourished in the second–third centuries, dropping out of sight in the fourth or fifth after a barrage of withering Church criticism was directed against them by a succession of High Church Fathers, including Irenaeus, Hippolytus, Origen, Eusebius, Epiphanius, and Jerome.

From this criticism and documents like the Pseudoclementines we can ascertain that not only did they revere James, but that they considered Jesus a mere man, naturally generated by Joseph and Mary and that they insisted on being circumcised, 'because Jesus was'. They followed 'the *Torah* of Moses' in a fairly assiduous manner and considered Paul to be a heretic, 'an apostate from the Law' and the 'Enemy' incarnate.[47] Aside from 'the Perfect Man' or 'Primal Adam' and 'the True Prophet' ideology, two other interesting ideas emerge, primarily in the Pseudoclementines. One is that of the '*Syzgeses*' or 'Opposites' – *Light* versus *Dark*, *Truth* versus *Lying*, *Righteousness* versus *Evil*, *the Poor* versus *the Rich*, *straightening the Way* versus *leading astray*, *the Friend* versus *the Enemy*, etc. – again completely reflected in the Qumran corpus.

The second is that of 'False Pericopes in Scripture', which is not quite so in evidence at Qumran, but which has gone full blown into Islam alongside the Qumran/Ebionite 'Lying' epithets. For the Ebionites – at least the later embodiment evinced in the second-century Pseudo-clementine literature – false passages had been introduced into Scripture, principally in the Law.[48] As one can see in Ezekiel's presentation of 'the *Zaddik*' or 'Righteous Man', such an idea may be seen as descending from his clear-cut countermanding of the Deuteronomic idea that 'the sins of the fathers were visited on the sons' or, as Qumran puts it in particularly pregnant allusions both introducing and following its exposition of Ezekiel's 'Zadokite' Covenant:

> And they dug a well rich in water, and he who rejects them ['the Commandments of God . . . *the Hidden Things, concerning which all Israel has gone astray . . .* which Man ['the Adam'] *must do that he might live through them*] . . . But God, in his marvellous Mysteries, atoned for their sins and forgave their iniquities, and He *built for them a House of Faith in Israel* [both the 'building' and the 'House' metaphors in Paul], the likes of which never stood from ancient times till now. Those who hold fast to it are destined to live victoriously [the 'steadfast' language Ben Sira uses to praise Phineas. For his part, Paul uses the 'victorious' allusion in 1 Corinthians 15:54 above to discuss the 'Mystery' of immortality, following evocation of the 'Primal Adam'/'First Man' ideology in 15:45–49] and *all the Glory of Adam* will be theirs.

> But with the completion of the Era of the number of these years, there shall be no more attaching oneself to the House of Judah, but rather a man will stand on his own watchtower [in the manner of Ezekiel's 'Righteous Man' and see Habakkuk 2:1 – note as well the 'standing' language again].[49]

Whether the Qumran sectaries, following the teachings of a teacher they called 'Righteous' or 'the Righteous One' – 'the Son of Zadok' or 'the *Zaddik*' *par excellence* – were aware of all the implications of the Prophet Ezekiel, they certainly seem to have valued the new emphasis he was placing on 'the Righteous One' and the doctrine of 'Righteousness' attached to it. Of course, for those at Qumran, Ezekiel's vision of the Temple and the idea of 'keeping the Covenant' attached to it, as well as his new 'Sons of Zadok', as they were interpreting the notation, were fundamental. The same is true for the 'Jerusalem' Community following James and those Irenaeus, Hippolytus, and Eusebius are calling 'Ebionites', succeeding to that Community.

The Stoning of Honi the Circle-Drawer

Honi, otherwise known as 'Onias the Righteous', was one such '*Zaddik*', as was, according to Rabbinic tradition, the most impressive High Priest of the previous line, Simeon the *Zaddik* (*c.* 200 BC). Evidently Honi's 'Righteousness' was so efficacious that the Heavens would, either, withhold or give rain in accordance with his prayer and/or the circles he drew. This is how it is put in the Letter of James, as we have seen, in introducing Elijah's equally archetypal rainmaking activities:

> The powerful prayer of the Righteous One much prevails. (Jas. 5:16)

For it, Elijah – 'a man of the same orientation as us' – has the same intercessionary power as James, for

> he prayed a prayer that it should not rain, and it did not rain upon the earth for *three years and six months* [1 Kings 18:1 has only three years. The numerology is rather that of Daniel 7:25, 'a time, two times and a half', which also, possibly, has relevance for the time between James' death in the autumn of 62 CE and the outbreak of the Uprising in 66], and he prayed again and the Heavens brought forth rain and the earth bore its fruits. (Jas. 5:17–18)

Not only does the Letter of James end on this note of the efficacious prayer of 'the Just One' bringing rain, it follows the picture of final eschatological Judgement and 'the coming of the Lord' leading up to it (Jas. 5:6–7). As we have seen, James is presented as one of these primordial Righteous Ones, rainmakers, and 'Pillars', whose very being is fundamental to the existence of the world. The Gospel of Thomas puts this proposition in its version of the direct appointment of James as successor as: 'In the place where you are to go [presumably Jerusalem], go to James the Just, for whose sake Heaven and Earth came into existence.'

Aside from Hanan the Hidden, considered by some to be equivalent to John the Baptist, as we have seen another grandson of Honi, Abba Hilkiah, also brought rain in the period in which James held sway in Jerusalem. This descendant of Honi was approached in the fields at the time of a drought by the representatives of the Jerusalem Establishment, whom he treated with contempt. The Rabbis tell the same story about Hanan the Hidden, to whom they also attach the above tradition about his 'hiding himself in the toilet'. Only when they sent little children to implore him did he ultimately bring the rain.

In our Jewish Christian and early Church sources about the life of James, this same kind of entreaty on the part of the Jerusalem Establishment characterizes both the account of the request to James for debates on the Temple stairs in the Pseudoclementines and the final request to James to come to the Temple to quiet the masses in Jerusalem, who were 'looking towards Jesus as the Christ' or, in these circumstances, for a Messianic return.[50]

Josephus recounts the episode of the stoning of Onias the Righteous, which prefigures the stoning of James, at a key juncture in the story of the loss of Jewish independence. It would perhaps, therefore, be well to summarize to some extent events leading up to this. After the Maccabean Uprising, from the 160s to the 140s BC, the mantle of successor in the Jewish independence movement fell to Judas' brother Simon's heirs – Judas himself seemingly having no children. The first of these was John Hyrcanus (134–104 BC), Judas' nephew, who, Josephus claims, wore three mantles: 'King, High Priest, and Prophet' – giving examples of each.[51]

The next was Alexander Jannaeus (103–76 BC) – also called 'Jonathan' – John's third son, who married his brother's wife, Salome Alexandra, after his brother was killed. Like John, he was having difficulties with the Parties, which seem to have been developing at this time, particularly the Pharisees. This is the first mention of 'Pharisees', who for the most part *opposed the Maccabees*. As we have seen above, despite their pretence of legal and religious scrupulousness, they always appeared to be willing to accommodate themselves to foreigners and accept foreign rule in Palestine, most notably High Priests receiving their appointment from foreigners just so long as these priests could come up with a satisfactory genealogy and the Pharisees were accorded the proper respect and kept their hands on true power. This is certainly the situation as it develops into the Herodian Period.

This Salome Alexandra and the elder of her two sons, Hyrcanus II (76–31 BC), who appear to be mentioned negatively in a newly published calendrical Scroll from Qumran,[52] were the sole Maccabeans that can safely be said to have been 'Pharisees'. Indeed her uncle, one Simeon ben Shetach, was one of the conservators of Pharisaic tradition and an heir, according to Rabbinic tradition, of Simeon the *Zaddik*, leading some decades thereafter to the famous Pharisee pair, Hillel and Shammai.[53]

Her younger son, Aristobulus II (67–49 BC), was more impulsive and of a different stripe altogether, resembling more his revolutionary great-uncle Judas, at least where the issues of national independence and

1 Coin of Antiochus Epiphanes, *c.* 167 BC, Daniel's 'Eleventh Horn' who provoked the
Maccabean Uprising.
2 The Roman general Pompey, whose troops stormed the temple in 63 BC.
3 A & B Maccabean Era tombs at Modein.

4 Columns 4–5 of the Community Rule from Qumran, describing ritual immersion and
'Holy Spirit' baptism.
5 One of the mysterious water storage facilities at Qumran, probably a ritual immersion pool.

6 Entrance to artificially hollowed-out water channel at Qumran channelling run-off down to pools.

7 Run-off of winter rains flooding down the cliffs of the Wadi Qumran, filling the cisterns.

8 View of the water storage area at Qumran at the bottom of the waterfall, with the Dead Sea in the distance.

9 Another of the many bathing pools at Qumran, this one still able to hold water today.
10 Ritual immersion among the Mandaeans, Disciples of John the Baptist in Southern Iraq.
11 Ruins of the Arabian city of Palmyra in the Syrian Desert, on the caravan route
to Northern Syria.

12 Fortress of Machaeros, where John the Baptist was executed, across the Dead Sea in Transjordan and Perea.

13 Aerial view of Caesarea, the centre of Roman administration in Palestine from the Herodian Period onwards.

14 Temple steps at the Southern Wall, where James perhaps debated with the Temple Authorities, and where Paul, aided by the Roman Chief Captain, addressed the crowd
15 Pinnacle of the Temple, from which James is said to have been 'cast down'.

16 Tomb believed in Christian pilgrimage tradition to belong to James, in the Kedron Valley
beneath the Pinnacle of the Temple.
17 Interior of 'James' Tomb' in the Kedron Valley.

18 Presumed bust of the Jewish historian Josephus.
19 Portrait bust of Nero's wife Poppea, whom Josephus visited in Rome and whom Nero kicked to death shortly before the Jewish Uprising of 66 CE.
20 Wall painting from early Christian catacombs in Rome, with Balaam pointing at the star – by implication, evoking 'the Star Prophecy'.

zeal were concerned. When the crisis arrived, the people ultimately show what side they are on. This crisis arrives in the midst of the events recorded about Onias the Righteous/Honi the Circle-Drawer, his rainmaking, and, finally, his stoning by the Pharisee partisans of Hyrcanus II – in Josephus the 'rainmaking' as such is really accorded to the partisans of Aristobulus II.[54]

For lack of a better term, we have termed Aristobulus' Party the Sadducee/proto-Zealot one – or 'Purist Sadducees' – as opposed to a more compromising Sadducean strain in the Herodian Period (and possibly also in the pre-Maccabean) familiar in Josephus and the New Testament. Like the Pharisees to whom they were allied, these 'Sadducees' made no claim to national independence or 'zeal' as a precondition for occupying the High Priesthood and were not interested in a 'Righteousness', 'Zealot', or eschatological interpretation of Ezekiel's 'Zadokite Covenant' of the kind one finds circulating at Qumran and also presumably among supporters of Judas Maccabee and his grand-nephew Alexander Jannaeus. Rather, they were satisfied with the pretence of genealogical purity – pretence, because Ezra and Nehemiah make it clear that many of the priestly clans returning from the Exile could not prove their genealogies and some were not priests at all.[55]

Thus, there are really *two* groups of 'Sadducees', one along with Pharisees and Herodians forming the Establishment in New Testament presentations. These are best termed, as we saw, 'Herodian Sadducees'. Like the Pharisees, by whom Josephus says they were dominated, they are accommodating in the extreme. However, unlike the Pharisees, when the Temple is destroyed in 70 CE, they cease to exist, having completely lost their *raison d'être*.

The other 'Sadducees' – epitomized by Judas Maccabee, his father Mattathias, Alexander Jannaeus, and this Aristobulus II – are consistently more resistance-minded, xenophobic, non-accommodating, and 'zealous for the Law'/'Zealot', no doubt following a more Phineas-minded approach to Ezekiel's 'Zadokite Covenant' (the 'Covenant of Peace', it should be recalled, Phineas won for himself and his descendants by killing backsliders intermixing with foreigners and introducing pollution in the camp of Israel). 'Purist' Sadducees in the Maccabean Period, they become the 'Messianic' Sadducees in the Herodian Period. They develop in the first century into so-called 'Zealots', 'Essenes', or '*Sicarii*' and 'Palestinian Christians' or the 'Jerusalem Church' followers of James the Just, and follow a more esoteric understanding of the Zadokite Covenant based on

'Righteousness' and/or 'zeal' – the two attributes we most often hear about in early 'Christian' reports about James.

Their orientation was consistent: they would never compromise with foreign power, would not accept foreign gifts or sacrifices in the Temple (considered a form of 'pollution' or 'idolatry' by James and at Qumran), and reckoned Herodians both foreigners and fornicators, whose authority in Palestine could never be acquiesced to. They could not allow Herodians entrance into the Temple, nor could the High Priests the Herodians or the Romans appointed be considered legitimate. With the destruction and almost total obliteration of the Maccabees by Herod and his father (what remained were absorbed into the Herodian family), a new principle of authority emerged and came to the fore – the Messianic one. This was based on Messianic or quasi-Messianic passages found in Scripture very much in evidence in the literature at Qumran. *Uncompromising* and *inflexible* in the extreme, this Movement also tended towards an apocalypticism of the 'Last Times'/'Last Days'.

These events are reflected in a Qumran document known as the Nahum *Pesher*, a commentary on Nahum 1–3. It is about as 'Zealot'-like, uncompromising, and apocalyptic as one can get. Alexander Jannaeus seems to have run into trouble with a Seleucid King named Demetrius (*c.*85 BC). Encouraged by anti-nationalist groups like the Pharisees, Demetrius tried to re-exercise Seleucid control in Palestine. Alexander fled into the fastness of *the wilderness* with, as Josephus reports, 'six thousand of his supporters'.[56] For their part, the *people* ultimately grew sick of intervention by foreigners – the policy advocated or acquiesced to by the Pharisees – and rallied to Alexander's support, thereby disproving the proposition that the Pharisees were the popular party in Palestine, which indeed anti-nationalist parties seldom if ever are – even in modern times.

The proposition of the popularity of the Pharisees has been a leitmotif of later historical writing, after the Pharisees finally did seize power with the Herodians and the help of Roman troops, and after the destruction of the Temple, too, when together with Pauline Christians they were the only Jews the Romans were willing to live with. In the guise of this later Rabbinic adumbration, they consistently followed a pro-Roman orientation even after Herodians themselves had long gone the way of all flesh.

This brings us next to the setting of Honi the Circle-Drawer's demise. Alexander Jannaeus by all appearances is 'the Furious Lion' in the Nahum *Pesher*, 'who takes vengeance on the Seekers after Smooth Things [the

Pharisees and their fellow-travellers], in the process hanging men up alive, a thing not done in Israel since ancient times'. The First Column of the *Pesher* – previously unavailable in most translations, but very important – had already called down violent apocalyptic Judgement in the form of hurricane, storm, and flood (Nahum 1:3–7) upon 'the Kittim', soliciting their utter destruction 'off the face of the earth'. It is clear, at this point, that the *Pesher* is retrospective in character since 'the Kittim' *come after* 'the Greeks'. The *Pesher* then takes the opportunity to condemn all 'hanging up alive' (for Romans, 'crucifixion'), an issue Paul is very anxious to capitalize on in Galatians 3:13 and Acts makes a set-piece of its condemnations of 'the Jews' by the Apostle it is calling 'Peter' (5:30 and 10:39).[57]

Alexander pre-deceased his wife in 76 BC and she ruled with her sons for another eleven years, overturning his *anti-Pharisee* policy. These Pharisees, whom she sponsored, in turn, mercilessly visited their wrath upon Alexander's supporters. This was the time of the Roman expansion into the Eastern Mediterranean, echoes of which are reflected in a number of Qumran documents.[58] Caesar's antagonist, Pompey, had been pursuing his campaigns in the East and put an end to what was left of the Seleucids in Syria. Then he made his way down into today's Transjordan, where he encountered the Arab King at Petra and the remnants of what used to be the Edomites in Southern Transjordan and Palestine, now called 'Idumaeans'. The date was approximately 65 BC.

As we have seen, Herod's father Antipater had connections to both 'Arabs' and 'Idumaeans'. Married to Cypros, a highborn 'Arab' woman probably related to the King of Petra, Antipater also had connections to the Greeks in towns like Gaza and Ashkelon along the Palestine coastline and obviously was involved in the spice, incense, and balsamic oil trade going on in these areas. Josephus calls him 'very Rich', the source obviously of his influence and an important motif to follow in this period where Qumran and the orientation of James are concerned.[59] As a consequence, he became *the first* Roman Procurator in Palestine and managed to obtain *Roman citizenship* for himself and his descendants (perhaps even more valuable in the circumstances than 'the Covenant of Phineas') on account of this and his conspicuous service to Rome. He is the first of the pro-Roman fortunehunters we encounter in this period.

Which brings us to the direct circumstances surrounding Honi's death. Alexander Jannaeus' son Aristobulus, impatient of his mother's Pharisee policies and involvement with foreigners like Antipater and Aretas in Petra, overthrew his Phariseeizing brother Hyrcanus II after her death.

Representing the same popular support and ideological perspective as his father, Alexander Jannaeus, he defeated his brother in battle *near Jericho*, forcing him to make over his kingly and High Priestly offices to him and ended the Pharisee depradations on their father's erstwhile supporters. Herod's father, Antipater, an extremely able operative with contacts both in 'Arabia' and along the Palestine coast, found sanctuary for Hyrcanus II with Aretas in Petra. Finally, he enlists Pompey, who is making his way down from war with the Persians in Armenia into Syria, and his adjutant Aemilius Scaurus – referred to at Qumran as a 'murderer' – to his cause.

In the meantime, Aristobulus, now King, and his proto-'Zealot', 'Purist Sadducee' supporters, who, as it turns out, seem to have been mostly priests, takes sanctuary, not insignificantly, *in the Temple*. First, Antipater returns with an army comprised of Aretas' Arab forces and the few supporters left to the collaborationist Hyrcanus, besieges Jerusalem, and prepares to assault the Temple. It is at this point that Josephus interrupts his narrative to tell us about the miracles of Honi or Onias, whom he now not only calls 'a Righteous Man', but 'the Beloved' or 'Friend of God', language we also know about from the Letter of James and the Damascus Document at Qumran.

For a change, Josephus' story more or less accords with what the *Talmud* has to say about Honi, which also applies the 'Righteous Man' appellation to Honi. But, it is Josephus' application of 'the Beloved' or 'Friend of God' description to Honi that *absolutely* accords with the way 'Zadokite' history is presented in the Damascus Document, as well as the description of Abraham as 'a Friend of God' in the Letter of James (2:23 and 4:2). Josephus describes Honi as follows:

> At the time of a certain drought, he [Onias *the Righteous*] had *prayed to God* to put an end to the searing heat, and God heard his prayers and sent them rain. This man had *hidden himself*, seeing that this sedition would last a long time.[60]

Not only do we have here 'the prayer of the *Zaddik* . . . bringing rain' of the Letter of James 5:16–18, but also the 'Hidden' ideology already noted with reference to Noah and the Flood above. The *Talmud*'s Honi was *hidden* for 'seventy years', because it took that long for the fruit of the carob (or possibly even a palm tree), under which he slept, to ripen. At the end of this period, he awoke and *ate its fruit*.

The 'Hidden' terminology is also applied to Honi's putative heir, John the Baptist, whose mother Elizabeth is described as 'hiding herself' in the infancy narrative of Luke 1:24, as it is in the *Talmud* to Honi's grandson 'Hanan the Hidden', who, it will be recalled, was supposedly accorded this name because 'he hid himself in the latrine'. The Protevangelium of James, an infancy narrative ascribed to James – which, as we have seen, first propounds the doctrine of Mary's *perpetual virginity* – rather, has Elizabeth '*hiding* John' from Herod 'in a mountain cave'. *Herod*, who wants to kill him – possibly the basis of the parallel motif in Matthew 2:13 about *Jesus?* – now asks *John*'s father, 'Where have you *hidden* your son?'[61]

The Koran follows up these things, in the process totally confusing John and Jesus. For it, *both* Elizabeth *and* Mary 'withdraw' themselves and now it is *Mary* who '*hides herself* in a far-off place' (19:22) – the 'mountain cave' of the Protevangelium of James above. It is now Mary who is '*consecrated*' *to God while still in her mother's 'womb'* and she now – like Noah in Jewish mystical tradition above – needs 'Protection' from 'Satan' or 'the Adversary' (3:36). This is the same kind of shift we encountered regarding James' 'life-long virginity' to Mary's in this same second-century Protevangelium of James.

For Muhammad, too, in a clear recapitulation of Naassene/Ebionite/Sabaean 'Perfect Man' ideology, the Spirit now 'assumes for Mary the form of a *Perfect Man*' (Koran 19:17 – here is our link between 'the Perfect Man' and 'Holy Spirit' conceptualities), and, when speaking about proclaiming the 'Hidden Things' and how John, like Mary, is always 'chaste' (that is, 'a virgin' – Koran 3:39–46 and 21:91), Muhammad describes this again, 'Lo, the likeness of Jesus is the *likeness of Adam*' (Koran 3:59). Muhammad specifically links John's father, John, Jesus, and Elijah together and, reflecting Dead Sea Scrolls terminology, calls them 'of the *Righteous*' (6:86) and John, 'a Prophet of *the Righteous*' (3:39).

Even more telling in this Koranic presentation, the *Talmud*'s 'carob tree', associated with Honi's seventy-year sleep above, now enters Muhammad's description of John's relationship to Jesus as well, only it is now *Mary* instead of Honi, who *sits down under the carob* tree and *eats the 'ripe fruit'* that falls from it.[62] Nothing could better demonstrate the interrelatedness of all these traditions than this. In some manner they are all part of an identifiable whole and the story of Honi and his progeny is somehow connected to these traditions about John, Jesus, and James. It should also be clear that all these motifs then move into the Islamic Shi'ite doctrine of the 'Hidden Imam' or 'Standing One' as well.

The Stopping of Sacrifice on Behalf of Romans and Other Foreigners in the Temple

To return to Aristobulus and his priestly partisans in the Temple and Hyrcanus' besieging them outside. For Josephus, Hyrcanus' supporters now trot out Honi. Here Josephus specifically notes that they are aware of and wish to make use of the intercessionary power he previously displayed in *praying for rain*, a matter also seemingly echoed in the First Column of the Nahum *Pesher* above. The *Talmud*, also, notes the efficacy of Honi's intercessionary powers, comparing them with *Elijah*'s! Hyrcanus' supporters rather want him to *curse* 'Aristobulus and those of his faction' in the Temple. When Honi refuses, they stone him.

This is an extremely paradigmatic episode and configuration of parties and forces. The time, as we saw, is Passover, 65 BC, two years before Pompey's Roman army – with *Pharisee* support – storms the Temple, putting an end to the nationalism of Maccabean rule and ushering in the *Herodian Period*. It is the *only* Sanhedrin-style stoning Josephus records before the stoning of Honi's putative descendant, James, another of these probably *Rechabite*-style 'Priests'. He really records only one other stoning of any significance in this 250-year period leading up to the fall of the Temple, the stoning of Menachem, another son or grandson of Judas the Galilean, on the Temple Mount some four years after James'. This occurred after Menachem's '*Sicarii*' supporters – or, as Josephus terms them elsewhere, 'Robbers' – had broken into the armoury and taken control of Masada and Menachem put on the 'Royal' purple; but was nowhere near as formal as James'.[63]

In Honi's case, the *Talmud* had already recorded the threat of excommunication levelled against Honi by Simeon ben Shetach – the archetypal progenitor of the Pharisees, as we saw, and brother of Alexander Jannaeus' wife and Aristobulus' and Hyrcanus' mother, Salome Alexandra. In the course of these confrontations, the *Talmud* compares Honi – not John as in the New Testament – to *Elijah*, observing, in words attributed to Simeon ben Shetach, that he alone possessed 'the keys to rain' and was allowed, therefore, to take 'the Name of Heaven' in vain.[64] From this emerges the conclusion that the stoning of Honi by Hyrcanus' Pharisee supporters was based on perceptions of 'blasphemy' related to possessing such 'powers' and such 'keys'.

For Josephus, the 'zealous' priests, making up the majority of

Aristobulus II's supporters, had been cheated by those outside the walls of the animals they had purchased for the purpose of making Passover sacrifices. Therefore, they took vengeance for this 'Impiety towards God' and, by implication, the stoning of Honi, by themselves, now, *praying for rain* – in this case, Divine 'rain' as eschatological vengeance, as, for instance, in Noah's Flood and that being called down upon the Romans in the First Column of the Nahum *Pesher* above.

In other words, Aristobulus' supporters, as pious priests, are also '*rain-making*' *intercessors*. At this point, according to Josephus, God sends down 'a terrible hurricane', which devastates the whole country – in his words, 'taking vengeance on them for the murder of Onias'.[65] All of these points, most particularly the Divine vengeance following Onias' stoning, prefigure events both before and after the stoning of James.

Herod's father now brings Pompey, the Roman Commander, into this configuration of forces, to finish what had been interrupted by Honi's stoning. As he describes it, both brothers, Hyrcanus the older and Aristobulus the younger, rushed to Pompey as he made his way down from Damascus into Transjordan preparatory to crossing into Palestine, attempting to conciliate him with gifts. However, Aristobulus soon 'turned sick of servility and could not bear to abase himself any further' to the Romans.[66]

This is a turning point of Jewish history and, once again, paradigmatic of the 'Purist Sadducee'/'Zealot' orientation. Antipater now transferred his allegiance and the cause of Hyrcanus, he represented, from the Arab King Aretas of Petra to Pompey and his adjutants, most notably, Aemilius Scaurus, Pompey's second-in-command (described in the text about the Priestly Courses in the Temple from Qumran, as we saw, as a 'murderer').[67] Herod's father is adept at exploiting the connections he developed with Pompey, his adjutants, and their successors, like Gabinius and his adjutant Mark Anthony, who develops a special fondness for *Herodians* (no doubt because of the lucrativeness of their bribes). Aristobulus is put under arrest and ultimately sent to Rome in chains, while his supporters, once more, take refuge *in the Temple* for a last stand.

The year is 63 BC. Pompey's forces now besiege the Temple, as described, and, as Josephus pictures the scene, Pompey is amazed at the steadfastness of those Jews who resisted and could not help but admire it. In the midst of the bombardment by catapult, Aristobulus' priestly supporters went about their religious duties in the Temple, as if there were no siege at all. They performed the daily sacrifices and purified themselves with the utmost scrupulousness, not interrupting these even when the Roman troops finally stormed the Temple:

> Even when they saw their enemies overwhelming them with swords in their hands, *the priests* [Aristobulus' supporters] with complete equanimity went on with their Divine worship and were butchered while they were offering their drink-offerings and burning their incense, preferring their duties in worship of God before self-preservation.[68]

These are obviously exceedingly zealous and Pious 'Zadokite' priests. Josephus adds, almost as an afterthought, but 'the greatest part of them were slain by their own countrymen of the opposing faction' – that is, the Pharisees supporting the turncoat Hyrcanus, who with the help of Herod's father Antipater, brought the Romans into the country in the first place.

The inevitability of the process is stunning. This pattern is consistent and will be re-enacted in the events of 37 BC, where Herod himself, now backed by Roman troops provided him by Mark Anthony, his father's friend, storms Jerusalem, thereby putting an end to insurgency and Maccabean rule. Once again, it is the Pharisees, Pollio and Sameas – probably the Rabbinic pair Hillel and Shammai – the only survivors of the previously Maccabean-dominated Sanhedrin, who counsel the people to 'open the gates to Herod' and the Romans. For this, they are duly rewarded and Herod, not surprisingly, 'prefers them above all others'.[69] Typically, the people, however, ignore this advice in favour of resistance, again showing that the Pharisee position on *accommodation to foreign power* was not the popular one.

The same is true in the period of the New Testament during the run-up to the War in 66 CE. It will be recalled that, in another crucial insight in his work, Josephus reveals that it is 'the Chief Priests [the *Herodian* Sadducees], the principal Pharisees, and the men of power [the *Herodians* themselves]', and, as he puts it, 'all those desirous of peace', who send for the Roman Commander, Cestius, outside the city to enter Jerusalem with his troops and put down the Uprising.

Likewise, as we saw, the Uprising was triggered by the same 'zealous' lower priesthood, who stopped sacrifice on behalf of Romans and other foreigners in the Temple – including the Emperor – and rejected their gifts. Not incuriously and again, as already remarked, the intermediary between this more accommodating 'Peace' coalition within the city and the Roman troops outside it was a mysterious Herodian ('a relative of

Agrippa'), whom Josephus identifies as 'Saul' or 'Saulus'. We have met this 'Saulus' before in his works, because in the *Antiquities*, after the stoning of James, Josephus pictures Saulus, his brother Costobarus, and another relative, Antipas, as leading a riot in Jerusalem, in which they 'used violence with the people . . . to plunder those weaker than themselves'.[70] It is difficult to avoid seeing some connection to Paul, originally known too in Acts as 'Saulus', and the unruly behaviour he displayed in Jerusalem after the stoning of 'Stephen' prior to his conversion.

This picture of a 'zealous' lower priesthood stopping sacrifice on behalf of Romans and other foreigners not long after the stoning of James replicates to some extent that following the stoning of Honi – 'Onias the Righteous', 'the Friend of God' – and Honi's refusal to condemn those of similar zeal in the Temple in the previous century. These priestly supporters of the more nationalist, last real Maccabean Priest–King, Aristobulus, go on with their 'Pious' sacrifices in honour of God, to the amazement of the Romans, as we saw, even while they are being cut down by those of the opposite faction in the Temple precincts.

They are the epitome of later 'Zealots', the same class of priests who supported Judas Maccabee's activities a century before and those pictured in the Book of Acts as joining the Movement led by another latterday 'Pious *Zaddik*' and 'Righteous' High Priest James (in this instance, directly *preceding the stoning of Stephen*), the greater part of whose supporters, even Acts call 'Zealots for the Law' (Acts 6:7 and 21:20). Not only are they responsible for the War against Rome, they are epitomized by the documents we find at Qumran, and the mindset they represent is that of an absolutely unbending insistence on purity and uncompromising militancy, best expressed in terms of the word 'zeal'.

By the time of the first century, it should therefore be clear that there is a Messianic strain to their mindset and ideology. This can be seen not only from the general tenor of most of the documents at Qumran and those sources underlying the New Testament approach – transformed to bring them in line with a more spiritualized Hellenized Messianism overseas; but also from the identification of the Messianic Prophecy by Josephus as the driving force behind the Uprising against Rome.

The moment we have before us here is a pivotal one. It is pivotal not only in illustrating this unbending, uncompromising attitude of priestly and apocalyptic 'zeal', but also in defining the situation that would characterize Jewish existence from that time forward. Josephus describes this very well. From the time of the stoning of Honi and the massacre of the

'Zealot' priests in the Temple following it, the fact of Roman power has to be reckoned with and how parties respond or adjust to it. All parties opposing it will ultimately be eliminated.

James as the *Friend of God* or *Oblias* and the Fall of Jerusalem

We now have a better foundation for understanding the early Church fathers' insistence that James was not only called *'Oblias'*, but that in some sense this meant 'Protection of the People' or 'Fortress' and that James acted like a *Fortified Wall* or *Strong Bulwark* to Jerusalem. There can be little doubt that this had to do with his *'Zaddik'* nature or, as all our sources put it, his 'superlative Righteousness' and, as such, functioning as 'the Friend' or 'Beloved of God'.

There is one other possible interpretation of the *'Oblias'* appelative, already alluded to above. This has to do with the *B–L–'* circle of language, used in Hebrew to characterize the enemies or opponents of 'Righteous Ones' or 'Righteous Teachers' of this kind. As we have seen, this also operates in parallel Greek contexts and in some sense does have to do with 'Enemies' *par excellence*, either *'Belial'*, 'Balaam', and even 'the *Diabolos'*/'Devil' in Greek. In the sense, therefore, that it is connected to his *'Zaddik'* nature and applied to James, we can think of him as being the opponent *par excellence* of such individuals or, if one prefers, the *'Adiabolos'* or *'Abelial'*.

It is interesting that the Letter of James, in citing Elijah's rainmaking miracle and, consequently, his intercession with God, not only makes much of the idea of 'the prayer of the Just One bringing rain', but focuses on the 'Friend of God' ideology in developing its stance opposing 'the Tongue' or 'the Enemy of God' (Jas. 3:5 and 4:4). In fact, in speaking about 'making oneself a Friend of the World and turning oneself into an Enemy of God', it actually recommends 'subjecting oneself to God and resisting the Devil' (*Diabolos* – Jas. 4:7). In 2 Corinthians 6:15, addressing himself to the 'Beloved Ones' separating themselves 'to perfect Holiness in the fear of God' and echoing the Qumran Hymns' view of God as the 'Father to all the Sons of Truth', so does Paul. We are clearly in the realm of the Jewish Christian/Ebionite *'Szygeses'* or 'Opposites' again.

In biblical terms, Abraham is the archetypical 'Friend' or 'Beloved of God'. In attacking the position of the individual whose 'Tongue' cannot be subdued and 'is an uncontrollable Evil, full of death-bringing poison'

(3:8),[71] the Letter of James sets forth its position that such a person – clearly intended to represent James' opposite number – made himself 'a Friend of the World' by following a doctrinal approach that was too facile or pragmatic.

This should be compared, as already explained, with Paul's insistence in Galatians 1:10–11 that he was 'not seeking to please men', nor 'teaching a Gospel according to Man'. In the process, this individual, who 'could not control his Tongue', not only seems to have taught that 'Abraham was justified by Faith', but showed himself incapable of observing proper communal discipline. By showing 'Friendship to the world', therefore, this 'Empty Man', 'turned himself into the Enemy of God' (Jas. 2:20–4:4).

The Damascus Document, too, as we saw, knows the 'Beloved' or 'Friend of God' terminology and uses it, in particular, when describing how, in the aftermath of the Flood, the Children of Noah 'did not keep the Commandments of their Maker' and 'went astray', applying it in the first instance to Abraham, but to Isaac and Jacob, 'the Heirs to the Covenant forever' as well. Those individuals, like Abraham, who 'kept the Commandments of God' – and, significantly, *did not eat blood* – are denoted 'Beloved Ones' or 'Friends of God'. It will be recalled that three columns after this, in the context of evocation of 'the New Covenant in the Land of Damascus' and 'separating oneself from the Sons of the Pit', the Damascus Document also goes on to evoke the Righteousness Commandment of 'loving your neighbour as yourself'.

Showing that this applied to not making economic distinctions between oneself and one's neighbour, the Damascus Document immediately follows this up with the prescription to 'strengthen the hand of the Meek and the Poor' (*Ebion*), concluding on the note of 'walking in these things in *Perfect Holiness*'. In connection with this, it then evokes Deuteronomy 7:9's 'loving God' – the Piety Commandment – and 'keeping His Covenant' or 'Commandments', which it interprets in terms of 'the Promise' or 'Faith' that they shall live 'for a thousand generations'. In like manner, the Letter of James speaks to 'the Beloved Brothers', evoking 'the Poor' four times in five lines. This it does in terms of 'keeping the Royal Law according to Scripture, *You shall love your neighbour as yourself*' (the Righteousness Commandment) and 'the Poor as Rich in Faith and Heirs to the Kingdom promised to those that love Him' (2:2–2:8).[72] The language correspondences between the two could not be closer.

In Islam, of course too, Abraham is the archetypical 'Friend of God'.

In the Koran, Muhammad uses the terminology 'Friend' in the same way that he is using the new terminology 'Islam' or 'surrendering to God' he is developing – just identifiable in James' allusion to 'submitting to God and resisting the *Diabolos*' (Jas. 4:7). In this sense, 'Friend', in the Letter of James and at Qumran, and 'Muslim' – the man who 'surrenders' or 'submits' himself to God's will – are basically parallel concepts. In James, Abraham is 'a Friend', because he *did submit* and, therefore, 'his Faith was reckoned to him as Righteousness' (2:21–23); for the Damascus Document, because 'he did not choose the will of his own spirit' and 'kept the Commandments of God'.73

For Muhammad – Abraham, Isaac, Ishmael, and Jacob all 'surrendered' and, therefore, are all to be considered 'Muslims' (2:133). As the Damascus Document puts it, Abraham 'became a Friend of God, because he kept the Commandments of God', but so did Isaac and Jacob. Therefore, they are all 'Keepers', all 'Beloved' or 'Friends of God and Heirs to the Covenant forever' too. For Josephus, in the torrential downpour or whirlwind mentioned with regard to Onias the Righteous' death, so is Honi. As such, at least as far as the Community Rule at Qumran is concerned, they are all 'Sons of Zadok' too – 'Sons of Zadok', therefore, simply being another one of these equivalents to 'Friends' or 'Beloved of God' as well.

As Eusebius puts it, as we have already seen above, after discussing God's vengeance on the Jews 'for their crimes against our Saviour', with regard to James' 'Protection' or 'Fortress' role (to repeat):

> Providence had deferred their destruction *for forty years after their crimes against Christ*, and all that time, most of the Apostles and Disciples, including James himself . . . were still alive, and by their presence in the city, furnished the place with *the Strongest Bulwark*.74

Regardless of the tendentiousness and/or historicity of this account, James' role as 'Strong Bulwark', 'Protection-of-the-People', or '*Oblias*' was more complex than simply that of a 'Shield'. It was connected as well to his '*Zaddik*' nature and the notion of 'the *Zaddik* the Pillar of the World' in the manner of the second episode about '*Zaddikim*' in Genesis above (the first involving Noah) – the 'Ten Just Men', also *involving Abraham*.

Paul, as we saw, makes this reference to James as being one of the 'Pillars' at a pivotal point in Galatians where he is discussing the legitimacy of his Mission to the Gentiles and his attitude to those who were Leaders or Apostles before him. Not only does Paul make it clear that their 'importance means nothing' to him, but, as he puts it, 'God has no favourites' or 'does not accept men's importance' (2:6–2:9). James too – it will be recalled – in the same breath that it refers to '*keeping* and *doing* the Royal Law of Scripture, you should love your neighbour as yourself', speaks about not 'respecting' or 'being partial to persons' (Jas. 2:9). For it, such persons convict themselves as 'Law-Breakers' – prominent vocabulary, too, in the Habakkuk *Pesher* from Qumran.[75]

In fact, as we saw above, Paul had already made it clear in Galatians that 'the Gospel' which he taught did not come 'from *men*', but rather a Heavenly 'Revelation of Jesus Christ' (1:11–12). In this context, he picks up the theme of 'Friendship to the world' in the Letter of James above, stating:

> Even if an Angel from Heaven should preach a different *Gospel* to you than that which we have preached to you, *let him be cursed*. As we have said before . . . if anyone preaches to you another Gospel *contrary to what you received from me, let him be cursed*. (1:8–9)

Pleased, seemingly, by his own intransigence here, he goes on to pose the question: 'So now, *whom am I trying to persuade*, men or God, or am I *seeking to please men at all*?' (1:10). In this, too, he appears to make clear his cognizance of the 'Friend of the world' accusations being levelled against him.

Having regard to these passages in Galatians, in which Paul proceeds to refer both to 'going away into Arabia' and 'returning again to Damascus' and James as 'the brother of the Lord', it should be clear that Paul knows the position exemplified by the Letter of James – or the accusation found there – concerning the individual, who has 'turned himself into an *Enemy of God*'. It is also made clear in Galatians 4:16 that he knows that this accusation of being an 'Enemy' – applied apparently, too, in 'Ebionite' tradition to Paul – is being applied to him.

We have also already observed in regard to these passages that this has to do with 'telling the Truth' and Paul's insistence that 'before God [he] does not Lie' (Gal. 1:20 and 4:16). But both of these fall within the Qumran parameters of aspersions on 'Lying', as well as those in the Letter of James about the Tongue 'being full of death-bringing poison' and how 'out of the same mouth issues forth blessing and cursing' (3:8–3:10). They also play, again seemingly quite consciously, on the intransigent 'cursing' of those 'straying to the right or left of the Law' in the Last Column of the Damascus Document and like-minded imprecations at Qumran.[76]

Not only does Paul in Galatians 1:8–9 above return the compliment – 'If anyone teaches a Gospel contrary to the one we have taught, let him be accursed' – in 3:10–13, as we have seen, he takes this 'cursing' a step further, making it the theological basis of his presentation of Christ. As he puts it, 'Christ', being 'hung upon a tree' (his euphemism for crucifixion), 'having become a curse for us, redeemed us from the curse of the Law'. Not insignificantly, he does so directly after evoking – like James 2:23 – how 'Abraham's Faith was reckoned to him as Righteousness' (Gen. 15:6) and in the very context of citing 'the Righteous shall live by Faith' (Gal. 3:10). This too will be the focus of the Habakkuk *Pesher* from Qumran and, in due course, we shall see just how important all these traditions about Abraham are to 'Jamesian' Communities further east.

Having cognizance of the tradition – based on Abraham's bargaining with God and, as in Ezekiel above, not judging 'the Righteous with the Sinner' – for the sake of Ten Just Men God would withhold destruction from a place or city (Gen. 18:23–29); one can now see that this is the way these original followers of James probably saw his relationship to Jerusalem. By his existence there, he provided the city with 'a firm Foundation' or 'Bulwark'. When he, 'the Righteous One' *par excellence*, was removed, Jerusalem could no longer remain in existence and was doomed. Therefore, in all versions of the tradition, the death or removal of James is immediately followed by the coming of Roman armies to destroy the city.

This is exactly the way Eusebius puts the proposition, when discussing the election of Simeon bar Cleophas to succeed James as 'Bishop of the Jerusalem Community' or 'Second Bishop' of the early Church. Since Jerusalem was by this time in ruins, it is difficult to see Simeon simply as *second Bishop of Jerusalem*. (Whether Simeon is the cousin germane of Jesus, as Eusebius puts it, or the second or third brother of Jesus – also 'Simon' or 'Simeon' – will be discussed later.) Eusebius put this proposition as follows:

> After the martydom of James and the capture of Jerusalem, *which followed immediately*, there is a firm tradition that those of the Apostles and Disciples of the Lord that were still alive, assembled from every place, together with those who were of the family of the Lord according to the flesh . . . to discuss whom they should choose as worthy to be the successor to James and voted unanimously for Simeon bar Cleophas.[77]

More or less the same sequence of events is followed in the Habakkuk

Pesher from Qumran. As part and parcel of its discussion of the destruction of the Righteous Teacher by the Wicked Priest, the text raises the matter of the destruction of Jerusalem and 'the Last Priests of Jerusalem' and how 'in the Last Days their Riches and plunder would be given over' to 'the Additional Ones of the Gentiles' (*Yeter ha-'Amim*). This it interprets to mean 'the Army of the Kittim', who come in fury and anger to destroy all things in their path, 'the fear and dread of whom is upon *all the Peoples*'. The similarity in sequencing here – the one *vis-à-vis* James and the other, the Righteous Teacher at Qumran – should not be ignored.[78]

Josephus' Testimony Connecting James' Death to the Fall of Jerusalem

There is one further point that must be considered with regard to the '*Oblias*' epithet, and it was already noted, as remarked at the beginning of this book, as early as the third century by the Alexandrian theologian Origen. In two works, *Contra* Celsus and his Commentary on Matthew, he claims to have found in his copy of the *Antiquities* of Josephus a passage attributing the fall of Jerusalem to the death of *James* not Jesus.[79] Eusebius seems to have seen a similar passage in his copy of Josephus' works – in his case, he claims it was in the *Jewish War*. The most likely place this would have occurred is in the cursory description of Festus' Governorship in the extant *Jewish War*. Jerome in the next century – like these other two, someone with access to Palestinian documents – claims to have seen the same passage, though it is not clear whether he actually saw it or heard about it through the works of these others. As he puts it:

> This same Josephus records the tradition that this James was of *such great Holiness* and enjoyed so great a reputation among the people [for Righteousness] that *the downfall of Jerusalem was believed to be on account of his death*.[80]

In normative Christian usage, Jesus is considered to have predicted both the downfall of Jerusalem and the destruction of the Temple, and Origen's outrage at having come upon these passages in the copy of Josephus available to him – presumably in the library at Caesarea on the Palestine coast, where Eusebius, too, had later been Bishop – and Eusebius' own concern over this discrepancy, might be not a little connected to its disappearance in all extant copies of Josephus' works. It should be recalled that in the Little Apocalypses of the Gospels, where Jesus is presented as both predicting Jerusalem's encirclement by armies and the destruction of the Temple, Jesus is normally considered to have predicted the destruction of Jerusalem as well.[81]

As Origen puts the proposition in *Contra Celsus*:

> But at that time there were no armies besieging Jerusalem . . . for the siege began in the reign of Nero and lasted till the government of Vespasian, whose son *Titus destroyed Jerusalem on account, as Josephus says, of James the Just*, the brother of Jesus, who was called Christ; but, in reality, as the truth makes clear, *on account of Jesus Christ the son of God*.[82]

Origen puts this proposition even more vehemently earlier in the same work, attacking his interlocutor Celsus as 'a Jew', who is willing to accept that 'John baptized in the wilderness', but not 'the descent of the Holy Spirit on Jesus in the form of a dove' – in itself extremely interesting testimony.

Directing Celsus, therefore, to Josephus' description of John's baptism in the *Antiquities* – which, of course, if he were not just posturing, would counter-indicate everything he was asserting concerning John and his baptism[83] – Origen now uses this reference to Josephus to raise the question of 'seeking the cause of the fall of Jerusalem and the destruction of the Temple'. He, then, contends that in the *Antiquities*, Josephus said

> that these disasters happened to the Jews as a *punishment for the death of James the Just*, who was the brother of Jesus called the Christ, the Jews having put him to death, although he was a man of pre-eminent Righteousness.

He grants that Josephus,

> though not a believer in Jesus as the Christ . . . in spite of himself, was not far from the truth . . . since he ought to have said that *the conspiracy against Jesus was the cause of these calamities befalling the people*, since they put to death Christ, who was *a Prophet* [the Ebionite 'True Prophet' ideology].[84]

But, not satisfied with this statement of what has virtually ever since become the official theology of Christ's death, Origen demonstrates how much the issue exercises him by repeating the position in a somewhat different form.

Starting with the point that Paul – '*a genuine disciple of Jesus*' – admitted that 'this James was the brother of the Lord', he adds a new caveat not found in Paul's writings or, for that matter, the Gospels, that this was 'not so much on account of their *blood relationship* or having been brought up together, as because of his *virtues and doctrine*'. This is a new understanding of the issue, that James and the other brothers were not *blood* brothers, but rather symbolic or adoptionist brothers. He now proceeds, once more, to interpret the statement about James in Josephus:

> If then, he [Josephus] says that it was on account of James that Jerusalem's destruction overtook the Jews, how much more in accordance with reason would it be to say that it happened on account of Jesus Christ, of whose divinity so many churches, converted from a flood of sins, bear witness, having *joined themselves* to the Creator.[85]

This is the 'joining' metaphor, again, of such importance for Qumran formulations. The Damascus Document, as we saw, as well as to some extent the Nahum *Pesher*, referred to a category of individuals who 'joined' themselves to the Community in the wilderness, the rank and file of which it called 'priests' – defined 'Rechabite'-style as 'the Penitents of Israel who went out from the Land of Judah to sojourn in the Land of Damascus'. Paul, also, it will be recalled, knows the language of 'joining' or being joined 'to the members of Christ' and not 'a prostitute' (1 Cor. 6:16–17).

Origen's expressions of outrage surely had much to do with this passage or passages being omitted from versions of Josephus' works thereafter. It is interesting how developed this theological approach had already become by Origen's and Eusebius' time. Regardless of one's opinion of the historicity of sections of the Gospels picturing Jesus' prediction of either the fall of Jerusalem and the destruction of the Temple, or both, these kinds of retributive statements have much in common with those in Josephus blaming the 'Fourth Philosophy' teaching of Judas and *Saddok* for the same catastrophes that overtook the people.

Even the reproach that, because of them, the people 'were led captive unto all the nations and Jerusalem trodden under by the Gentiles', so parallels these early Christian ones blaming the Jews for Jesus' death as to awake the gravest reservations. In Eusebius, as we have seen – and now Origen – this charge is only slightly transformed into the lateral one that their loss of Temple and commonweal was 'the vengeance that followed the guilt and Impiety of the Jews *against the Christ of God*'.[86]

Of course, one man's logic is another's unreason. It may seem to Origen reasonable to attribute such catastrophes to the death of Jesus Christ, which according to official Church documents occurred some forty years before. But Josephus, who lived through the events in question, said, according to Origen and Eusebius, that the majority of Jews attributed these catastrophes to another event – *the death of James*.

This would be a far *more* logical attribution, since the death of James occurred, if Josephus can be relied upon, in 62 CE, about seven and a half years before the appearance of the Roman armies before Jerusalem and the final destruction of the city in 70 CE. As in the case of God's vengeance for the death of a previous 'Righteous One', Honi, and the defeat Herod Antipas suffered in his war with a later Arab King Aretas of Petra – whom Paul refers to when discussing how he was let down the wall of Damascus in a basket (2 Cor. 11:32–33) and which Josephus says the people attributed to what Herod Antipas had done to John the Baptist – this is the kind of sequentiality that would make most sense to the general population. To have attributed the fall of Jerusalem and the destruction of the Temple to Jesus' death, except retrospectively, would be something like people today attributing the Second World War to the assassination of President McKinley or the election of Theodore Roosevelt to the assassination of Abraham Lincoln.

Furthermore, such an attribution has the additional factor in its favour of being surprising and running counter to received tradition or orthodoxy. It is, in fact, more in accord with the way the human psyche works, which is why all commentators make such a point of emphasizing that immediately after James' death the fall of Jerusalem occurred. Surprisingness of this kind, as we have pointed out, often adds credibility to a given tradition, simply because it has *survived* in the face of officially received opinion and flies in the face of what later generations consider orthodox doctrine or 'Gospel Truth'. In historical research, it is often traditions of this kind, bearing the most surprising content, that carry a kernel of actual historical truth.

In his more recently discovered Commentary on Matthew, Origen puts the proposition of Jerusalem being destroyed on account of the death of James with greater equanimity, also focusing on James in a sharper manner:

> And so great a reputation for Righteousness did this James have, that Flavius Josephus, who wrote the *Antiquities of the Jews* in twenty volumes, when wishing to exhibit the cause why the people suffered so great misfortunes that even the Temple was razed to the ground, said, that these things happened to them [the Jews], because of the Wrath of God in consequence of *the things which they had dared to do against James the brother of Jesus*, who is called the Christ.

This he repeats, for perhaps the fifth time:

> And the wonderful thing is that, though he did not accept Jesus as Christ, he yet gave testimony that the *Righteousness of James was so great*, saying

that, the *people* thought they had suffered these things on account of James.[87]

For his part, Eusebius puts the same proposition as follows. Whether he is dependent on Origen is not clear:

> So admirable a man, indeed, was James, and so celebrated among all for his Righteousness, that even the wiser part of the Jews were of the opinion that this was the cause of the immediate siege of Jerusalem, which happened to them for no other reason than the crimes against him. Josephus, also, has not hesitated to superadd this testimony [elsewhere] in his works: 'These things', he says, 'happened to the Jews to avenge James the Just, who was the brother of him that is called Christ, and whom *the Jews had slain, notwithstanding his pre-eminent Righteousness.*'[88]

Even in the 400s, though emphasizing James' 'Holiness' – that is, his Naziritism – rather than his Righteousness, Jerome, as we saw, puts the proposition much in the way Eusebius and Origen did, which makes it seem as if these various commentators were seeing something like these words somewhere in Josephus' works. Still, Eusebius does not hesitate throughout his *Ecclesiastical History* to reinterpret the words he himself reports seeing and castigate the Jews for what *they did to Jesus*, repeatedly asserting that the loss of their Temple and country was the result.

But the attribution of the destruction of the Temple and the fall of Jerusalem to the death of James, of course, makes more sense not only because of the proximity of these several events, but also the constant insistence on the theme of James' Righteousness and the '*Oblias*'/ 'Bulwark'/'Protection' imagery associated with it. In ending his quotation from Hegesippus' testimony to the circumstances and events surrounding the death of James, Eusebius collapses the time interval between these events even further, with the words: 'Immediately after this [that is, James being thrown down from the Pinnacle of the Temple and stoned] Vespasian invaded and took Judea.'

Overlaps in the Testimonies about James' Death and Jesus'

But before going on to review this ample testimony to the circumstances and causes of the events surrounding the death of James, it should again be emphasized that no such similar passages exist in extant copies of Josephus. Josephus does describe the death of James in the Twentieth and last Book of his extensive *Antiquities of the Jews*. But this Book does not really describe the outbreak of the war against Rome or the destruction of the Temple; rather it ends, somewhat abruptly, following these passages about the death of James and the situation in Jerusalem just prior to the Uprising. Meticulous as ever, Eusebius also provides a verbatim transcript of Josephus' testimony to the death of James in the *Antiquities*. Josephus puts the death of James in 62 CE, directly after the death of Festus, the Roman Procurator mentioned with regard to his relations with Paul at the end of Acts (24:27–26:32), and before Albinus, his successor (62–64), arrived in the country.

Though Josephus observes that 'those who seemed the most equitable of the citizens and such as were the most uneasy of the breach of the laws, disliked what was done', and complained to Albinus and Agrippa II, the nominal King, he neither mentions James' superabundant *Righteousness* nor, as he did with regard to John the Baptist's death and Antipas' discomfiture, that *the majority of the citizens attributed the fall of Jerusalem to what was done to him.*

This presents us with a conundrum. The book in which Josephus would, most likely, have mentioned such a happenstance would have been the *Jewish War*, since it deals with these years and their aftermath. But in the *Jewish War*, there is no mention of James whatsoever, nor any of these other characters from Scripture so interesting to us, like John the Baptist, Simon the head of his own Assembly in Jerusalem, Simon *Magus*, or 'the Egyptian', who led so many '*Sicarii*' out into the wilderness and for whom Paul is mistaken in Acts (21:38). Nor, for that matter, does it mention Honi, *Saddok*, James and Simon, the two sons of Judas the Galilean, or the two Pharisee fathers, probably meant as a representation of the famous Rabbinic 'Pair', Hillel and Shammai, who predict Herod's future 'greatness' and whose basic foreign-policy proposal seems to be to 'open the Gates [of Jerusalem] to the Romans'.

There is no explanation for these clear and consistent lacunae in the *Jewish War*, which are made up in the *Antiquities*, only that, as we have seen, Josephus did not feel as confident in the 70s after the just-completed cataclysmic events in Palestine as he did in the early 90s, when the *Antiquities* was published, and, therefore, he was not as forthcoming. Either this, or he had new material at his disposal, presumably the archives of Agrippa II in Rome, whom he mentions with suitable obsequiousness in the *Vita*.[89] There is always the more conspiratorial explanation that, having originally taken part in the Uprising against Rome and been responsible, according to his own braggadocio, for the military defence of Galilee – which even an amateur can recognize as catastrophic – he was at pains to cover up his embarrassing links to subversives like the mysterious '*Banus*', whom we have shown above to at least parallel James and the Righteous Teacher at Qumran, if not more.

Josephus also appears to have mentioned Jesus, as we saw, among this colourful, but otherwise confusing, cast of characters, which is apparently one of the reasons for the preservation of his works and their amazing persistence in Church circles, Catholic and Greek Orthodox. The reason this testimony, also in the *Antiquities*, is considered an interpolation by most observers is that Josephus suggests that Jesus may have been more than 'a Man' – our Ebionite/Elchasaite *Primal Adam* ideology again? – averring him to have 'been the Christ'. Additionally, he calls his followers 'Christians' and refers to his resurrection 'on the third day'.

Since this testimony is so orthodox where later Christian doctrine is concerned, it is doubtful that this was the kind of thing Josephus could or would have said at this point, given his attitude towards such 'Deceivers or impostors' leading the people 'out into the wilderness, there to show them the signs of their impending freedom'. The question is whether this quasi-orthodox interpolation is totally original, inserted into the text where the several 'calamities' occurring during Pilate's long administration are mentioned, or whether it is a re-formulation of a less orthodox original. In other words, Josephus may have said something about a character called 'Jesus' at this point, but given his normal attitude to such 'wonder-workers', it would have been different from this.

As we have also seen, at the very point that Josephus is presented as telling the story of this rather orthodox Jesus, he moves directly into the bizarre, but certainly revealing story, which may actually have been a ribald satire of early Christian infancy narratives – if they had developed by this time. Typically, he also refers to this event, which ended in the alleged banishment of the Jews during the reign of Tiberius (14–37), as 'a calamity' for the Jews. Actually, such a banishment is not referred to by Roman historians like Suetonius, who rather tells the story of a banishment of the Jews from Rome a decade or so later in the reign of Claudius (41–54), significantly enough, for *making propaganda on behalf of one 'Chrestus'*.⁹⁰

Instead of immediately telling about this banishment after his worrisome testimony to Jesus as 'the Christ', Josephus rather tells us the story of 'Mundus and Paulina', which is totally irrelevant to anything he is narrating. This story – it will be recalled – had to do with a woman called

'Paulina', who was rich, modest, and pious, and a young man, 'Mundus'. He bribes the priests in the Temple of Isis to convince this woman that the God Anubis had fallen in love with her, and she, having told her husband a god *wished to lie with her*, came to the Temple to spend the evening. At this point the rake Mundus, concealed in the Temple, leapt out and enjoyed her favours all night long. Tiberius, on hearing the story, crucified the priests (note the parallel with Jesus), demolished the Temple of Isis, and having her statue thrown in the river, *banished Mundus*.

Only at this point does Josephus tell the story of the banishment of the Jews from Rome in one paragraph. This has to do with another *rich* and *pious* woman Fulvia, who, as we have described above, had embraced Judaism in Rome, and a teacher, driven from Palestine on the tell-tale charge of 'breaking' Jewish Law. In Rome, with *three other men*, none of whom are named, he persuades Fulvia to send purple and gold (the royal colours) to the Temple in Jerusalem. Instead of transmitting it, however, the teacher and his three assistants spend it themselves. For this rather far-fetched story, 4000 Jews are banished to Sardinia and a greater number punished for being unwilling to join the army because of 'their keeping the Laws of their ancestors'.

There is something very peculiar about these stories, which are immediately followed up by descriptions of additional 'tumults' and Pilate's repression of what are obviously Messianic disturbances among the Samaritans.[91] It is impossible to say what is going on, but, at least in the Mundus and Fulvia stories, Josephus appears to substitute titillating trivia for more substantial turns of events. Additionally, the parody of Christian birth narratives about Jesus, represented by the Mundus and Paulina story, would be typical of Josephus and others of a similar frame of mind.

It is, also, possible that something quite different appeared in earlier versions of Josephus, but given the limitations in our sources, it is difficult to conclude anything further, except to inspect materials in other sources, like the Slavonic Josephus below, which might represent what originally may have been a much longer section about Jesus, for which these curious materials were substituted. When substitutions of this kind did occur, given the nature of the materials, it was often done by substituting a section of equal size so as not otherwise to interrupt the pagination.

As just noted, there is another testimony to Jesus in Josephus' works, and this is in that curious collection of citations that has come down under the title of the 'Slavonic Josephus'. Though generally held in low esteem by most scholars, all materials of this kind should be treated equally according to the same methodological approach. Talmudic materials are not usually on a much higher level, nor the Gospels themselves – nor, for that matter, the early part of the Book of Acts. In the study of Islam, for instance, it has turned out that traditions, considered for some reason to be defective in orthodox thought or of questionable authority, often turn out to represent the earliest strata, and that one should be chary of rejecting out of hand any traditions that appear for some reason defective on the surface or of questionable religious authority.

The materials in the Slavonic Josephus are materials such as these. As we have seen, an abbreviated version or epitome of Josephus' *Jewish War*, which came down through Eastern European traditions, particularly the old Russian or Slavonic, it contains much that makes it suspect. However, the references to both John the Baptist and Jesus are perplexing and should be studied. Here, John is presented, like other charismatics of the day, as wishing to lead an uprising – he leads the people out in the wilderness 'to claim their freedom' and show them 'the Way of the Law', and his diet was 'stems, roots, and fruits'.[92] Like James and other Nazirites/ Rechabites, he is presented as a *vegetarian* and as *abstaining from strong drink*.

Jesus is referred to only as 'the Miracle-Worker', and the presentation is surprising in the extreme, for it has the people yearning 'to throw off the Roman yoke' and requesting him 'to destroy the Roman army'. It also presents this unnamed 'Miracle-Worker' as first having been arrested by the Romans and after scourging and torture – much in the manner of the release of Jesus' alter ego or double, Jesus Barabbas, in the Gospels – released. Otherwise, the presentation of Jesus is quite pedestrian.

In Gospel presentations, for instance, Barabbas was arrested for 'making insurrection in the city and murder' (Luke 23:19 and Mark 15:7). There is, also, the Jesus ben Ananias mentioned above in the received Josephus, who in the period of the run-up to the War against Rome was first arrested by the authorities, because he daily predicted the imminent *destruction of Jerusalem*, this commencing just following the death of James. These allusions are so surprising as to give one pause, because if they are forgeries – which quite likely they are – it is difficult to conceive of who might have had an interest in such forgeries. Be this as it may, the fact that James' death occurs in such close proximity to the fall of Jerusalem and the destruction of the Temple, and that in some manner these events are considered integral to his death, again dovetails very nicely with the materials we are considering here.

It is interesting that in the testimony to the death of James the Just later in the *Antiquities*, Josephus calls him 'the brother of Jesus who was called the Christ', words missing from the earlier reference to Jesus in the *Antiquities* discussed above. In Eusebius' version of the missing testimony from Josephus about the siege of Jerusalem occurring 'for no other reason than their crimes against him', that is, *James* not Jesus – later assimilated into traditions about *Jesus* not James – it should be noted, that Eusebius calls James 'the brother of him that is called Christ, whom the Jews had slain, notwithstanding his pre-eminent Righteousness', Jesus' name missing from the citation.

In Origen's version, once more, we encounter the formulation 'James the brother of Jesus who was called the Christ', as in the citation about James in the *Antiquities* as it has come down to us. This will not be the only tradition circulating about the death of James assimilated into traditions about Jesus. As we shall see, at the time of the actual stoning itself, the words imputed to Jesus on the cross (not to mention to Stephen when he is stoned) are used to characterize James' last words – and this in all three primary commentators, Eusebius, Epiphanius, and Jerome – 'Forgive them, Lord, for they know not what they do.'

Ananus' Death and the Death of James

In the extant *Jewish War*, Josephus does relate someone's death to the fall of Jerusalem, but, interestingly enough, it is *not James*, but his opposite number and nemesis, the High Priest Ananus. Responsible along with Agrippa II for the death of James, this Ananus, as we saw, was the son of the Ananus mentioned in the Gospels as having a role in the trial and condemnation of Jesus. Since Josephus is such an uneven observer, in the *War* he is at his obsequious best where Ananus is concerned; but in his *Vita*, appended two decades later to his *Antiquities*, he castigates this Ananus so vehemently that it makes one wonder whether he could be talking about the same person. Since Josephus had business and other dealings with Ananus during his tenure as military commissar of Galilee, responsible – or so he claims – for its fortification, he had been in personal touch with the latter, who was then in control of affairs in Jerusalem – most notably, it would appear, perhaps profiteering or skimming the profits along with Josephus from the corn and olive-oil price-fixing schemes of another of Josephus' enemies, John of Gischala.[93]

Since Ananus does turn out to be the *bête noire* of our study, and the man primarily responsible for the 'conspiracy' to remove James, and since these discrepancies are so glaring, it might be worth subjecting them to a little more scrutiny. Because of the animus he has developed against Ananus, who was involved in attempts to remove him from command in Galilee, Josephus characterizes such attempts as basically being 'bribes' and Ananus, consequently, as 'corrupted by bribes'. He even implies that Ananus 'was conspiring' to have him killed, a theme bearing comparison to the characterization of the Establishment in its dealings with Pontius Pilate in the presentation of the execution of Jesus of the Gospels.

In the *War*, however, Josephus describes Ananus quite differently. He describes him as 'venerable and a very Just Man', the very words that all sources use to describe *James* and our '*Zaddik*' terminology again, now applied to James' nemesis Ananus. Nothing loath, Josephus goes on to extol him, saying:

> Besides the grandeur of that nobility and dignity, and honour, of which he possessed, he had been a *lover of equality, even with the Poorest of the people*, He was a great *lover of liberty* and an admirer of democracy in government, and did ever prefer the *public welfare before his own advantage*.[94]

But these, too, are almost exactly the kinds of things one hears in sources about James. Particularly the note about Ananus being 'a lover of equality' replicates the descriptions of James as 'not deferring to persons' we have already heard about and will hear about further in descriptions of James' death, not to mention their additional refurbishment in Paul above. Again, there would appear to be reversals going on, now regarding Ananus, James' executioner.

Ananus is in control of Jerusalem after the initial rebellion in the period from 66–68 CE with another of Josephus' very close 'friends' among the Chief Priests, Jesus ben Gamala. Josephus reproduces long speeches by both, demonstrating that they were 'friends' of Rome, attempting only to reign in the extremist lunacy of those who had got control of the Temple and whom for the first time he has started calling 'Zealots'. Though claiming, as he puts it, like the followers of James in Acts, to be 'Zealots for good works', in Josephus' view, they were rather 'Zealots for Evil and Zealots for Pollution' – note, here, how he has started using the language of the Qumran charges against the Establishment, but once again with reverse effect.

Throughout his whole description of the demise of the Chief Priests at the hands of those he is calling 'Zealots' at this point, it is interesting that he uses the language of 'pollution of the Temple', 'plundering', 'booty', and the like which permeates the Dead Sea Scrolls, particularly the Habakkuk *Pesher*, but also the Damascus Document – but always with inverted signification.[95]

As we have seen, this is the moment that those he is now overtly calling 'Zealots' depose the High Priests. Preferring a venerable procedure of their own, the 'casting of lots' also evoked in the election of James as 'Bishop' or the election to replace Judas 'called the *Iscariot*', they elect an individual of the meanest blood and circumstances, choosing one 'Phannius', that is, Phineas, a simple 'Stone-Cutter'. Though we remarked the 'Stone-Cutter' theme above, we did not connect it at that point to the 'Rechabites' being 'craftsmen' in all traditions, not to mention its latterday spin-off in the ideology of being 'Masons'.

These 'Zealots' now invite another group of unruly and extremely violent individuals – more violent in Josephus' view even than themselves – into the city, with whom, probably through their mutual Transjordanian connections, they appear to be allied. This terminology, 'the Violent Ones' or 'the Violent Ones of the Gentiles' is used in the Scrolls – particularly in the Psalm 37 *Pesher*, like the Habakkuk *Pesher*, another '*Zaddik*' text – to describe those who take vengeance on 'the Wicked Priest' for the death of 'the Righteous Teacher'.[96]

Josephus calls these unruly or 'violent Gentiles', 'Idumaeans', and they are at this point, most certainly, pro-revolutionary and anti-Roman. Later, when the revolutionary cause goes badly, Titus himself personally conciliates them.[97] Let into the city by 'the Zealots', they rush crazily through its narrow streets, relieving the siege of the Zealots *in the Temple* by the orthodox High Priests. They then proceed to slaughter all the High Priests, in particular Josephus' two friends, Ananus and Jesus ben Gamala. Upbraiding and desecrating their naked bodies – possibly even urinating on them or cutting off their sexual parts – they then 'cast' (*ballousin*) their corpses outside the walls of the city without burial 'to be devoured by dogs and gnawed on by wild beasts'.[98]

It is at this juncture that Josephus takes the opportunity to make his accusation against the whole of the Jewish people, now attributing the destruction of Jerusalem and the Temple to the 'impious' death of James' opponent Ananus, not James' (or even Jesus') as per the contentions in Christian sources. He opines that

I cannot but think it was because God had doomed this city to destruction as a *polluted city* and was resolved to *purge his Temple by fire,* that he cut off these *its greatest defenders and Protectors,* who had but a little time before worn the sacred vestments . . . and been esteemed venerable by those dwelling in the whole habitable earth . . .[99]

Not only do we have here again the Qumran language of 'pollutions', but also of 'Protection' applied to James in early Church sources, both, as usual, now reversed.

At this point, too, Josephus compares the 'Impiety' involved in the treatment of Ananus' corpse by the Zealots and Idumaeans to not taking down those crucified from the crosses before sundown or, as he puts it:

They proceeded to such a degree of Impiety, that they *cast out their corpses without burial,* even though the Jews would take so much care for the burial of men, that they even took down malefactors, condemned to crucifixion, and buried them before the setting of the sun.

It is difficult to escape the impression that this is the point being made in the parallel description in the Gospel of John about the crucifixion of Jesus (19:31–37), and, of course, the implied accusation of the Impiety involved in *his* crucifixion. Points from this description also emerge in descriptions of the death of James, in particular, the motif of 'breaking his legs', but with slightly varying connotation, and further ones like breaking his skull with a laundryman's club, and constant reiteration of the 'casting out'/'casting down' language.

This is certainly bizarre and there is something peculiar here, particularly in view of the fact that in his later *Vita,* Josephus denounces Ananus as 'corrupted by bribes'. That all these early Church fathers, Origen, Eusebius, Jerome, etc., feel that they saw a copy of Josephus attributing the fall of Jerusalem to James' death – not Jesus' and probably not Ananus' either – averring that the greater part of the Jewish people held this view as well, just compounds the conundrum.

Josephus completes this panegyric by insisting that Ananus too knew 'the Romans were not to be conquered' and, like Jesus in the Gospels, foresaw 'the Jews would be destroyed', then going on to attribute the destruction of Jerusalem and the purging of the Temple by fire to the impious things done to Ananus' corpse by 'the Zealots' and 'the Idumaeans'. Not only do these points dovetail perfectly with the descriptions in the Dead Sea Scrolls, relating the destruction of the Wicked Priest to 'the Violent Ones of the Gentiles' – paralleling 'the Idumaeans' – who took vengeance 'upon the flesh of his corpse' for what he had done to the

Teacher of Righteousness, they parallel almost perfectly the kinds of things being said about James the Just, including the attribution of the fall of the city to his death in all these sources or sources about other sources.

In his description of Ananus' trumped-up charges against James in the *Antiquities* and about 'those of the citizens who cared most for equity and who were most uneasy at the breach of the Law involved', we have already seen that Josephus calls Ananus 'rash in temperament and very insolent' and as a 'Sadducee' – meaning, an *Establishment* Sadducee – 'more savage than any of the other Jews in judging malefactors'. If we add to these reversals the parallel embodied by the care displayed by the Jews to take those crucified down before sundown in order to afford them a proper burial, a key component in the story of the crucifixion of Jesus in the Gospels, it should be clear that one is treading in these accounts on very delicate ground indeed.

The solution to these numerous contradictions and overlaps will never be accepted by everyone, but certainly in the version of Josephus' works that was circulating among Hebrew or Aramaic-speaking people in the East – most notably probably in Edessa and Adiabene – which Josephus says he wrote before the Greek which was produced for a more Roman-oriented audience in the West, one can imagine Josephus saying something of what he is recorded as saying about the High Priest responsible for James' murder about James himself. This is particularly true if the '*Banus*' referred to above, an individual Josephus seems to have viewed with more than ordinary affection, has any relationship to James. We have already expressed the view that he does.

PART IV

THE DEATH OF JAMES

14

The Stoning of James and
the Stoning of Stephen

The Traditions about the Death of James

We are, now, finally in a position to discuss the several versions of the death of James and relate these, not only to the religio-political circumstances of the Jerusalem of the day, but to the death of the High Priest Ananus, the death of the Righteous Teacher in the Dead Sea Scrolls, and, curiously as it may seem, the death of Stephen as described in Acts. The best place to begin for the death of James is, once again, early Church sources and Josephus. The most extensive of these sources, Eusebius, as usual, records almost all the verbatim extracts necessary – principally from Hegesippus, but also whatever he considered useful from Clement of Alexandria and Josephus.

There are complementary materials in Epiphanius and Jerome. There are also materials in the Pseudoclementine *Recognitions* about confrontations on the Temple Mount not only between James and the High Priests, but James and the anonymous figure dubbed 'the Enemy'. Reading, too, between the lines of Acts and the Pseudoclementines, other details will emerge that will enable us to derive a good picture of what actually went on. The Nag Hammadi codices from Upper Egypt, based as well on these accounts – but also seemingly on Sabaean or Manichaean sources – provide additional vivid material for this picture.

Since Eusebius' account is by far the most extensive, it is preferable to turn to his first, complementing it where necessary from the others. He gives us three separate notices about the death of James: the first from Clement, the second from Hegesippus, and the third from Josephus. All three are *extra-biblical* sources. The first two, though patently distorted, are less corrupted by the retrospective imposition of a later religio-historical consensus than parallel materials in the Book of Acts.

This raises the question of why the Book of Acts didn't include such a pivotal event as the destruction of James, 'the Bishop of Jerusalem', three decades after the death supposedly of his illustrious predecessor 'Jesus'.

Didn't it know what happened to James? In turn, this brings us back to the puzzling question, why Acts didn't include the equally important election or appointment of James as successor to his famous kinsman.

One might respond that this was not Acts' intent. Acts' intent was to show the 'acts' of the Holy Spirit as it devolved upon the early Community, culminating, in particular, with the appointment of Paul and his activities following this. Ending almost coincidentally with the time of James' death two years after Paul's arrival in Rome in 60 CE, it sketches in the briefest of terms his activities there under a kind of loose house arrest – if it can be called arrest at all – and ends with the insistence that Paul continued 'teaching the things concerning the Lord Jesus Christ with all freedom without hindrance' (28:31).

Still, this response rings hollow and we are left with the question, why are all these important events from the early history of the Church missing in the narrative of Acts? Another possible response is that James was not 'an Apostle', but this, too, is unsatisfying. As well, the traditional title of the book, the 'Acts of the Apostles', is clearly inappropriate to the materials contained, because the 'Acts' of most of the original 'Apostles' are ignored in favour of a rather questionable parvenu Paul, who, about a third of the way through the narrative, metamorphoses into its central focus and darling. But in any event, we shall be able to show in due course that James was 'an Apostle', whatever might be meant by this notation.

As we have seen above, a vast amount of extremely important material is missing from Acts, in line with its rather tendentious, historical focus – if it is appropriate to call it *historical* – to show the birth, triumph, and over-whelming importance of Gentile Christianity or, as Acts 28:28 puts it, 'to make known that the Salvation of God is sent to the Gentiles' – not to mention, of course, the metamorphosis of the paradigmatic 'Apostle to the Gentiles' himself, originally 'the Enemy' of the early 'Christians' in Palestine, that individual first introduced in 7:58 as 'Saulus', later trans-muted into 'Paul'.

Aside from the matter of the direct succession of James and his election as Leader of the Movement in Palestine – replaced by the rather meaning-less and probably bogus one to fill the shoes of the proverbial 'Twelfth Apostle' *Judas* – we hear nothing of Peter's travels overseas, nor how Peter got to Rome, what he did elsewhere, as, for instance, in Antioch – covered concretely and much more effectively in Galatians – nor how Peter met his death. We say 'meaningless' here, because neither Matthias nor *Joseph* Barsabas Justus (later called '*Judas* Barsabas' in Acts), the two candidates to replace 'Judas', is really ever heard from again. James, though, intrudes forcefully into its story-line in chapter 11 in a manner that implies he had either already been introduced previously or, in any event, that we should know who he is. Simultaneously, his double and namesake, the confusing 'James *the brother of John*', as we saw, is conveniently eliminated from the narrative.

Nor do we hear about the John alluded to here either, nothing about his activities, what he does in Asia Minor, if he did finally arrive there and not some other John, nor his death either. We don't hear anything about the other Apostles either – if we can agree who these were – only a smattering of information about Philip and his encounters with both Simon *Magus* and an 'Ethiopian' eunuch, about whom we shall have more to say later – largely mythologized in any event (8:4–40). All the other Apostles are simply names: Matthew, Bartholomew, Andrew, Thaddaeus – if he can be distinguished from 'Thomas' or, for that matter, 'Judas Thomas' or 'Judas the brother of James'. Their only function appears to be to flesh out the 'Twelve-Man' Apostle scheme, in any case mythological probably too. Even Matthias, whose election the narrative makes such a point of at the beginning, simply evaporates.

We do not even hear what Paul did after he arrived in Rome, except for a hint in Romans 15:24–28 that he might have gone to Spain. We hear nothing of his death either and are dependent on the early Church fathers for this, and, of course, nothing about the death of James, which, given what we know from other sources, should have been a central focus of any narrative about early Church history in Palestine. These defects in the narrative of Acts as history should be clear, but it is these that make the material from extra-biblical sources about James, as persistent and numerous as these are, so impressive. One does not usually get this sort of historical data about any other character in the New Testament from sources outside the New Testament.

For instance, even a character, as substantial as Paul obviously is within the framework of the New Testament, all but vanishes when one considers additional reliable sources *outside* the New Testament. Jesus' story, more highly mythologized and retrospectively fleshed out than Paul's within the framework of the New Testament, is, again, virtually non-existent when one considers extra-biblical sources. Though there *is* material about Peter and Thomas, Judas Thomas and Thaddaeus from extra-biblical sources, most – but not all – is patently mythological as well.

Aside from Josephus' picture of John the Baptist, only James emerges as a really tangible and historical character when one considers the length and breadth of these sources. Plus, the new data that emerges never fails to surprise and, to a certain extent, even delight. That is what makes these extra-biblical accounts of the death of James so impressive.

James' *Broken Legs* and Proclamation in the Temple at Passover

Eusebius presents the death of James in two places. The first account he gives of this is from Book Seven of Clement of Alexandria's *Hypotyposes* (*Institutions*), which is no longer extant in the original. This he gives right after Clement's description in Book Six of how Peter, James, and John, though they were preferred by Jesus, did not contend for the honour, but rather 'chose James the Just as Bishop of Jerusalem'. Here, Clement, aware of the difficulties inherent in both his account and that of the Book of Acts, adds:

> There were however, two Jameses, one called 'the Just One', who was thrown [*blētheis*] from the Pinnacle [or 'Wing'] of the Temple and beaten to death with a fuller's [laundryman's] club, and the other who was beheaded.[1]

Picking up this account again some chapters later in his discussion of the 'plots and crimes of *the Jews*' against Paul, and for that matter James, Eusebius states:

> Unable to endure any longer the testimony of the man, who on account of his elevated philosophy and religion was deemed *by all men to be the most Righteous*, they slew him, using anarchy as an opportunity for power, since at that time Festus [Procurator 60–62] had died in Judea, leaving the province without governor or procurator.

The lack of a governor following Festus' death in 62 CE is a detail from Josephus' account of the death of James. For its part, Acts had already mentioned this Festus' ongoing discussions with Paul (24:27–26:32).

> But as to the manner of James' death, it has already been stated in the words of Clement, that 'he was thrown [*beblēsthai*] from a wing of the Temple and beaten to death with a club'.[2]

Jerome avers that this is the bare bones of what existed in early Church testimony from the no longer extant accounts of Hegesippus and Clement, but he adds an important new element, not found in previous accounts. Combining the material, as he himself states, from the

Twentieth Book of Josephus' *Antiquities* with that of the Seventh Book of Clement's *Institutions*, he writes:

> *Cast down* from a Pinnacle of the Temple, *his legs broken*, but still half alive, raising his hands to Heaven, he said, 'Lord, forgive them for they know not what they do.' Then struck on the head by the club of a fuller, such a club as fullers are accustomed *to wring out wet garments with*, he died.[3]

The point about James' prayer is from Hegesippus, though it also appears in Acts' account about Stephen and may have appeared in Clement as well. But there are several new points: one, the more detailed description of the fuller's club and, most importantly two, *the absolutely new element about James' broken legs* (not *Jesus'* – in the Gospel of John, it will be recalled, the Roman soldiers refrain from *breaking Jesus' legs*). This is extremely important material and one does not know from where Jerome got it, but probably from Hegesippus.

In any event, this phrase will provide one of the final keys to unravelling what really happened in these times of such importance to the ethos and self-image of Western historical understanding. It will be possible, even without this notice, by using other elements in these overlapping traditions about the death of James – not to mention Jesus' – to determine what really took place, but, with it, we will be able to reach what amounts to confirmation, as it were, of the scenario we are proposing.

It should also be immediately recognizable that we are, once again, in the historical tangle regarding the death of James' nemesis, the High Priest Ananus, and the mix-up between what Josephus seems to have said about Ananus and what, according to other traditions, he said about James. For instance, as we saw, Jerome knows the tradition attributing the downfall of Jerusalem to James' death, saying,

> This same Josephus records the tradition that this James was of such great Holiness and reputation among the people that the fall of Jerusalem was attributed to his death;

yet, in Josephus' extant *Jewish War*, the same seemingly irrelevant note about the Jews' 'breaking the legs' of the victims of Roman crucifixion to ensure they received a proper burial before the sun went down, follows the description, as we just saw, about *what was done to Ananus' corpse*. Both precede Josephus' eulogization of *Ananus'* 'Righteousness and Piety' and claim that the removal of this 'benefactor of his countrymen' made

Jerusalem's destruction a certainty. This claim, as remarked, even included *Ananus' prediction of this destruction*. Once again, this tangle of themes exposes the overlap of materials we are encountering in these sometimes conflicting or diametrically opposed reports.

To return to the most detailed report about James, Eusebius notes, 'but Hegesippus, who belongs to the first generation after the Apostles, gives the most accurate account of him' – namely James. Now quoting verbatim from Hegesippus, Eusebius proceeds to give the long description from what he identifies as 'the Fifth Book of Hegesippus' *Commentaries*'. This was evidently the last book of Hegesippus' work, because Eusebius tells us later that it only 'consisted of five books',[4] so we can assume that these materials represent something of the climax to its presentation – as, indeed, they do to some extent *Josephus' Antiquities*.

Noting that James' cognomens, '*Zaddik*' and '*Oblias*', could be found by searching Scripture and that 'even the Prophets declare concerning him', Eusebius then reproduces Hegesippus' very detailed account of James' death with the words:

> Some of the seven sects, therefore, of the people, which have been men-
> tioned by me in my *Commentaries*, asked him [James], 'What is the Gate [or
> 'Way'] of Jesus?'

Showing how precise his quotation from this second-century Church historian is, Eusebius retains Hegesippus' internal references, even though at this point he does not enumerate what these sects were. He does in a later passage, where his note about the election of Simeon bar Cleophas to succeed James for some reason triggers a discussion of Hegesippus' life.

We have mentioned Hegesippus' enumeration of these sects above. Eusebius not only notes here that Hegesippus knew Hebrew, but that he was 'a convert from the Hebrews'. There can be little doubt, therefore, that Hegesippus knew the traditions of Palestine quite well, but came out of a group we should call for lack of a better term, 'Jewish Christian'.

Hegesippus describes these 'heresies' as denying 'the Resurrection' and that 'he was coming to give everyone according to his works' (obviously meaning the Messiah). For some reason, then, describing them as 'being against the Tribe of Judah and the Messiah', Hegesippus insists that 'as many as did believe, did so on account of James'.[5] Not only is this vivid testimony to the power of James' presence in the Jerusalem of his time and, by consequence, his status as 'the *Zaddik*', it is an unequivocal assertion of the clearest doctrine associated with James, *works Righteousness*, the denial of which Hegesippus sees as heretical.

Perhaps the clearest expression of this doctrine, besides the Letter of James itself, is to be found, as already remarked, in the Koran, which repeatedly reiterates the Jamesian *'believe* and *do* good works.'[6] Here, Muhammad, clearly the heir to some of these underground traditions, over and over again avers the doctrine of Salvation by 'works' and 'works' alone, that is, it is your works stored up in Heaven, or as he puts it, that 'you send before you' that will 'save' you on the Judgement Day. No intercession by another is acceptable nor, for instance, would it then be possible for someone else 'to die for *your* sins'.[7] This is a basic tenet of the Koran and it, quite clearly, emanates from one unequivocal source.

In addition, this idea of someone 'coming to give everyone according to his works', which Hegesippus here specifically identifies as an essential part of James' doctrine, is also part and parcel of his account that follows of James' apocalyptic proclamation in the Temple at Passover – presumably 62 CE, but possibly before too – of the imminent coming of the Messiah and the Heavenly Host with Power on the clouds of Heaven. The mention of 'Power' in this account also recalls, as it does in the Gospels, 'Ebionite'/'Elchasaite' notions of 'the Hidden' or 'Great Power'.[8]

This proclamation in the Hegesippus account is the crucial one, leading directly to James' death. The circumstances in which Hegesippus portrays James as making it in the Temple at Passover (the Jewish National Liberation Festival) are significant. It is these assembled crowds in Jerusalem, which James is asked by the Pharisaic/Sadducean Establishment to pacify. He then delivers his oration. It is equivalent to lighting an incendiary and crying 'fire' in a crowded room.

James' Popularity in Eusebius

James' oration directly links him to the perspective of the War Scroll from Qumran – the famous 'War of the Sons of Light against the Sons of Darkness' – which mounts to a climax in its interpretation of the key 'Star Prophecy' with the *same Messianic proclamation*, including even 'the coming of the Heavenly Host on the clouds of Heaven'. This is alluded to in a similar apocalyptic and eschatological manner in the last chapter of the Letter of James in the context of evoking 'the Saving prayer of the Just One' and how Elijah could command the Heavens both to rain and to withhold rain.

These constitute a very powerful configuration of materials. The identification of the proclamation of final Messianic Judgement that James makes – where the Messiah, Daniel-like, 'on the clouds of Heaven' leads the Heavenly Host – with the kind of apocalyptic 'Judgement' that in the War Scroll from Qumran 'is poured out like torrential rain on all that grows', would appear to be an *authentic* piece of data from the biography of James.

Eusebius via Hegesippus now proceeds to picture the consternation in the Pharisee/Sadducee Establishment, and uses the language of 'tumult', already encountered in Josephus' description of the reign of Pontius Pilate as Procurator of Judea and the rise of the Movement triggered by Judas and *Saddok*, to describe what transpires.[9] Josephus also applies this language in the *War* to Jesus' appearance, as well as Pontius Pilate's introduction of the Emperor's bust on the standards of his troops into Jerusalem, not to mention his positioning these troops among the crowds who come to Caesarea to implore him to remove these images from the Temple. At a pre-arranged signal, these soldiers pull concealed clubs from under their garments and beat many of the supplicants to death.[10]

Hegesippus' account of the 'tumult' related to James' proclamation in the Temple is marred somewhat by the retrospective introduction of Paul's 'Christ' ideology. This conceptuality, nowhere mentioned in any other materials associated with James, does not appear in his directives to overseas communities in Acts, nor his Letter, nor Paul's discussions of his difficulties with James or people of the 'Jamesian' point of view. Otherwise Hegesippus' account reads quite straightforwardly and appears realistic.

As Eusebius puts it, quoting Hegesippus, the Jewish Establishment is concerned that 'there was danger that the whole people would now expect Jesus as the Christ' (read 'Messiah', the 'Christ' concept in Greek probably having no currency in Palestine yet, except as a translation of the Naassene/Ebionite 'Perfect Man'/'Primal Adam' ideology). Therefore, they send to James and say,

> 'We beseech you, restrain the people, since they are being led astray regarding Jesus, as if he were the Christ.'

Here, again, we have vivid testimony to James' role as 'Protection' or 'Bulwark' among 'the people', flowing out of his '*Zaddik*' function in the Jerusalem of his day.

This request to James by the Scribes or Sadducees and Pharisees of Gospel portraiture is consistent in all sources. It also forms the backdrop of the Pseudoclementine *Recognitions* account of the debates on the Temple steps between the Apostles led by James and the Temple Establishment. It forms the backdrop, as well, of accounts of how James' putative forebear in the previous century, Honi the Circle-Drawer, is sent for by a similar configuration of parties either to make rain or to quiet the assembled crowds opposing foreign rule in Pompey's time, as it does the way another of Honi's putative descendants in James' time, one 'Abba Hilkiah', is sent for. The *Talmud* portrays the representatives of this same Establishment, because they are afraid of Abba Hilkiah, as sending 'two students' to him *while* he is working in the fields to ask him to make rain. (In a related incident, it sends 'little children to get hold of the hem of the clothes' of Hanan the Hidden – *Honi's daughter*'s son.)[11] It is useful to remark in this episode, which forms part of the accounts of rainmaking in Tractate *Ta'anith* in the *Talmud*, how gruffly Abba Hilkiah treats the Establishment Rabbis, further consolidating the picture of Opposition *Zaddiks* with power and influence among the people as opposing Establishment Pharisees and Herodians.

In Hegesippus' account, the Scribes and Pharisees are constrained not only to recognize James' following 'among the people' as a popular charismatic leader, but also to utilize it in damping down the rampant Messianic agitation and expectation. This picture of rampant, energized Messianism is borne out not only by Josephus' ascription of the final cause of the Uprising against Rome to the effect of the Messianic 'Star Prophecy' on the young men 'who were zealous for it', but also in the wide-ranging Messianism of the Qumran documents.[12] Regardless of the tenor of his Messianism – pacifistic and Romanizing, like the picture of Jesus in the Gospels and Paul; or more aggressive and eschatological, the sense in Josephus and the Scrolls – one cannot escape the impression that James' popularity as '*Zaddik*' of the 'Opposition Alliance' was of such magnitude that even the Establishment had to reckon with his pre-eminent standing among the people and defer to it, even while attempting to exploit it.

The same picture emerges in the *Anabathmoi Jacobou*, which, like the Psuedoclementines, again focuses on James' pre-eminent position in the Temple and Jerusalem twenty years earlier in the mid-40s. As in the *Recognitions*, to which it is, no doubt, related, James is pictured as a power-ful force among the masses. For its part, the scene in the *Recognitions* culminates in a debate on the Temple stairs. Even the Book of Acts, regardless of how overwritten, contains vestiges, as already remarked, of these debates in its picture of early Christian comings and goings on the

Temple Mount and the extreme interest generated by this among the people over the Messianic issues being discussed and disseminated.

These chapters from Acts 3–6 clearly provide a retrospective and highly Paulinized, anti-Semitic picture of these debates in the Temple or on its steps. Though these are framed in terms of arguments about the doctrine of the supernatural 'Christ' and Jews as 'Christ-killers', from which James as a central figure is entirely deleted in favour of a more sanitized Central Triad of Peter, James, and 'John his brother'; still, shining through the whole is a picture of the true situation of the time and the extreme Messianic agitation of the period from the 40s to the 60s CE.

For his part, Hegesippus puts the gist of this request by the Scribes and Pharisees as follows:

> We beseech you, persuade all the people who are coming for the Passover Festival concerning Jesus, for we all have confidence in you. For we and all the people testify to you that you are *the Just One* and *not a respecter of persons*. Therefore, persuade the people not *to be led astray* concerning Jesus, for *we and all the people must obey you.*

Again, this is extremely revealing testimony, for it shows James' influence and position among the general populace, which was just as clearly based on their perception of him as 'Perfectly Righteous' or 'the Righteous One' or 'Zadok' *par excellence*. However, yet again, it completely reverses what Josephus has just finished telling us about James' opposite number Ananus above, namely that Ananus 'delighted in treating the humblest persons as equals'. It is difficult at this point not to break out laughing at such blatant dissimulation by pro-Roman and Establishment writers of this kind.

For the Gospels also, Jesus 'does not defer to anyone nor regard the person of men' (Mark 12:14 and pars.). It is important to appreciate that the Synoptics allude to this trait to introduce Jesus' pro-Roman and obviously Paulinized stance on the *tax issue*, the implication being, in the light of all these reversals, that James taught just *the opposite*. For Matthew and Mark, Jesus delivers this in response to attempts by 'the Pharisees and *the Herodians* to ensnare him' or 'catch him up' (22:15 and 12:13); for Luke, in response to 'secret agents pretending to be *Righteous Ones*, so that they might *deliver him up* to the power of the Governor' (20:20).

In these variations, one should not only pay attention to the implied parallel with the language later applied to the archetypal traitor *Judas Iscariot* 'delivering him [Jesus] up', but the play on the language surrounding Belial with his 'nets' and Balaam and Balak, 'ensnaring Israel'. One should also note that this language of 'delivering up' is widespread in the Scrolls – particularly the Damascus Document – but there it is God 'visiting' the earth for destruction and the people being 'delivered up' because of Law-breaking, backsliding, and transgressing the Covenant.

Before considering James' actual proclamation, it is important to note several additional points in this series of questions the Gospels have the Establishment put to Jesus. In the Synoptics, these Pharisee and Herodian attempts to 'ensnare Jesus' are immediately followed by questions to him by 'the Sadducees' regarding 'the Resurrection', patently based on Josephus' description of Sadducees (Matt. 22:23–27 and pars.). But the example cited is a nonsense one, that is, if a woman, in turn, married seven brothers, whose wife would she be at the Resurrection? This is a patent parody – even a malevolent one – of the 'Zealot'-like 'Seven Brothers' story in the more extreme of the two Maccabee Books, 2 Maccabees. In this episode, which encourages martyrdom for the Law, each of the seven brothers undergoes indescribable torture in turn, but *encouraged by their mother*, 'despise their own existence for the sake of His Laws . . . to live again forever' (7:1–42).[13]

Aside from Daniel 12:2–3, this is the first overt enunciation of the doctrine of Resurrection in any biblical book, presented, significantly, in the context of announcing an ideology of Holy War, which, in the terminology we have been delineating here, would, therefore, originally have been a 'Purist Sadducee' doctrine. In the treatment of the resurrected state in the Gospels, it is simply being trivialized, scoffed at by what can now be referred to as 'Herodian Sadducees'. Luke has Jesus designating those enjoying the Resurrection as 'Sons of the Resurrection', and even 'Sons of God' (20:36), which, in the manner the Damascus Document at Qumran is using the terminology, would then be equivalent to the 'Sons of Zadok'.

Just as interesting, this interchange with the 'certain Sadducees' is now followed up in Matthew by Jesus answering the Pharisees (for Mark, 'one of the Scribes') by citing the two Love Commandments, of 'loving God' and 'loving your neighbour as yourself', we have become so familiar with and which so connect all these 'Opposition' groups in the Herodian period. All three Gospels now end this series of questions by the Establishment to Jesus by identifying 'the Christ' with 'the son of David' (Matt. 22:41–45 and pars.). In so doing, they cite the patently nationalistic 'making your enemies a footstool' from the all-important, Messianic Psalm 110 above, also cited twice in Hebrews (1:13 and 10:13).[14] Not only does this Psalm refer to its subject as 'a Priest forever after the Order of Melchizedek', 'sitting at the right hand' of God, and sending his 'Strength out of Zion'; this subject is also referred to by the tell-tale phraseology '*Holy from the womb*' (110:3–4).

To return to the relationship of these passages to James. Not only is James' opposition to the Herodian/Pharisee Establishment, and by implication the Roman Authorities, being trivialized and reversed in literary story-telling and mythologization revolving around 'Jesus'; again we see that traditions associated with James, such as 'not being a regarder of persons' or being 'Holy from his mother's womb' and, therefore, 'a Priest' or 'High Priest' – whether of 'the Sons of Rechab' or 'after the order of Melchizedek' is immaterial – are being retrospectively absorbed into crucial aspects of the presentation of Jesus. To be sure, one can think of these allusions as being applicable to *both* James and Jesus, but at least superficially they appear to apply more readily to James – whether to Jesus too is a matter of opinion.

The traditions Eusebius is preserving here, about James' popularity among the people and being a '*Zaddik* and not respecting persons' – most particularly (as his *alter ego*, Ananus, in Josephus or Jesus in the Gospels) where 'Riches' or 'Poverty' are concerned – do not aid Roman Church claims, for the pre-eminence and proper tradition line of Peter which Eusebius also presents. Rather, Eusebius reproduces these claims on behalf of James in spite of himself, *because they were in his sources*. When taken seriously, this testimony about James' popularity and his influence – and that of the '*Zaddik*' idea generally – over the mass is of the utmost importance for understanding the true state of affairs in Jerusalem in the run-up to the War, as it is for understanding some curious and thoroughly unexpected positions in the Scrolls.

If one allows for the retrospective understanding of second- and third-century Church theologians, who are already convinced about the antiquity of the 'Christ' terminology, one imagines that what James was called upon to discourse on in the Temple to quiet the Passover crowds hungering after the Messiah was the nature and understanding of the Messianic idea. This is the basic issue in the debates on the Temple steps, as recorded in the Pseudoclementine *Recognitions* leading to the attack on James by the 'Enemy' Paul. Epiphanius' *Anabathmoi Jacobou* adds the two issues of the legitimacy of the Herodian Priesthood and the rejection of the sacrifices. Whatever the conclusion about these things may be, these issues set the stage for the final destruction of James.

James' Proclamation in the Temple and Jesus' Temptation by the Devil

Eusebius, quoting from Hegesippus, now continues his description of these tumultuous events:

> 'Stand, therefore, upon the Pinnacle of the Temple that you may be clearly visible on high and your words readily heard by all the people, for because of the Passover all the tribes have gathered together and numbers of Gentiles too.' So the aforesaid Scribes and the Pharisees made James stand [note the 'standing' terminology here] on the Pinnacle of the Temple, and shouting to him, cried out, 'O Just One, whose word we all ought to obey, since the people are led astray after Jesus, who was crucified, tell us what is the Gate to Jesus?' And he answered shouting out loudly, '*Why do you ask me concerning the Son of Man? He is now sitting in Heaven at the right hand of the Great Power and is about to come on the clouds of Heaven.*'

The word 'Pinnacle' (*Pterugion*) here may also be translated 'wing' or 'parapet', and is twice repeated in the narrative. This links it indisputably with the famous story about Jesus' Temptation in the Wilderness after his baptism by John, where exactly the same phraseology is used: 'He [the Devil or 'the *Diabolos*'] set him upon the Pinnacle [*Pterugion*] of the Temple' (Matt 4:5 and Luke 4:8). In this episode, Jesus 'is led by the Holy Spirit out into the wilderness', where he is 'tempted by the Devil' for forty days (Matt. 4:1 and Luke 4:2). Rather than '*Diabolos*', Mark 1:13 uses '*Satan*' and portrays Jesus, not as 'led' out as in Matthew and Luke, but 'cast out' (*ekballei*).

This mixture of allusions both to the '*Diabolos*' and 'Satan' in one and the same document is, as we have seen, typical of Qumran, as it is Paul, Revelation and interestingly enough the Koran.[15] Mark also has – followed later by Matthew 4:11 – 'and the Angels ministered unto him', which is exactly what appears in the Second *Surah* of the Koran, there rather applied to 'Adam'. In this mysterious Koranic reference, it is '*the Angels prostrated themselves before Adam . . . all save Iblis*' (2:34). This is, of course, nothing but the 'Primal Adam' ideology of the Elchasaites, Ebionites, Simon *Magus* and Paul, now used as descriptive of Adam himself and his 'standing', not just of Jesus in the Gospels (2:34). But this '*Iblis*', here too, is nothing but the '*Belial*' in the Scrolls – '*Diabolos*' in the New Testament.

This Temptation episode, again in the Synoptics, is nothing but a negative parody of Josephus' 'Deceivers and false prophets, who lead the people out in the wilderness, there to show them the signs and wonders of their impending freedom'. In Matthew 4:3 and Luke 4:3, 'the Devil' even tells Jesus that, if he is 'the Son of God' (the new, more Western Christian, variation on 'the Primal' or 'Second Adam'/'Hidden Power' ideology), he should 'command these stones to become bread'. This is, of course, precisely the kind of miraculous 'signs or wonders' Josephus has just condemned above. In later Gospel episodes Jesus does do such miracles, even this very multiplication of loaves in the wilderness this 'Temptation by the Devil' episode denies he is willing to do (Matt. 15:33 and Mark 8:34)!

But to come to the point about 'the Pinnacle of the Temple', as the episode continues, the Devil now 'sets him [Jesus] upon the Pinnacle of the Temple' and challenges him to 'cast [himself] down' (*bale* followed by *katō* – in the episode recorded by Eusebius about James above, '*kataballō*'). This, of course, is precisely the scenario of this episode in the James story, including word for word almost the exact same language. The only difference is that in Clement and Hegesippus, as we shall see, James actually *is 'cast down' from the Pinnacle of the Temple* – in the Pseudo-clementines, as we shall see later, 'headlong' and *from its 'steps'*.

The implication in these Gospel scenarios – which in this sense must be *late* – is that what happened to James was *evil* or a 'temptation by the Devil'. Jesus wouldn't do such things! In the Gospel rewriting, Jesus is only *challenged* by the Devil, Simon *Magus*-like, to 'cast himself down'. Though the Devil ('*Diabolos*') is pictured, *inter alia*, as now offering him 'all the Kingdoms of the world and their Glory', Jesus refuses, answering in words now proverbial, 'Get thee behind me Satan' (Matt. 4:10 and Luke 4:8).

The allusion to Simon *Magus* is appropriate too. Not only, as we have seen, do the Pseudoclementines first attribute a variation of the 'Primal Adam'/'Standing One' ideology to Simon *Magus*, but there does appear to have been an episode regarding his confrontations with Peter in Rome, where Simon is pictured as 'throwing himself down' from a height to impress the multitudes with his miraculous 'Power'.[16] One also should note the parallel represented by the Damascus Document material about 'those who hold fast to' the 'House of Faith' which God 'built for them in Israel' being promised 'Eternal life' or 'life Victorious'. This, in turn, introduces the eschatological exposition of 'the Zadokite Covenant' from Ezekiel, where this same 'Glory' is expressed as 'and all *the Glory of Adam shall be theirs*', again reflecting 'Primal Adam' conceptualities.[17]

Interesting, too, at this juncture in the Gospel of John, which omits Jesus' Temptation by the Devil, John the Baptist admits that he 'only baptizes with water' (confirming Josephus) and he is 'not the Christ', meaning, not the embodiment of 'the Primal Adam', 'the Second Adam' or 'Lord out of Heaven' – as Paul would have it. He also contends that he is *not Elijah* (that is, he doesn't make rain), nor 'the Prophet' (he is not the Ebionite 'True Prophet'), while at the same time admonishing – it will be recalled – that 'there is [One] *standing* in your midst, whom you do not know' – the Ebionite/Elchasaite/Sabaean 'Standing One' ideology again – 'whose shoe latchet I am unworthy to loose', presumably because this 'Standing One' was so grand (John 1:25-26). Note too, how in Matthew's and Luke's versions of Jesus' refusal of 'the Glory' represented by 'all the Kingdoms of the World', Mark's 'Satan' vocabulary returns.

Since these Gospel Temptation narratives are at once so polemical and symbolic and so clearly directed against those going out into the wilderness to do miracles or, as Josephus explains, 'to show the people the signs of their *impending freedom* there' (again note the reverse play on this represented by Paul's 'freedom' from Mosaic Law dialectic); there can be little doubt, regardless of how astonishing this might at first appear, that the original tradition about 'being set upon the Pinnacle of the Temple', *first appeared in these traditions about James* being placed upon 'the Pinnacle of the Temple' to quiet the Passover crowds hungering for the Messiah, conserved by Hegesippus in the middle of the second century.

The Gospel refurbishments of these various materials are, once again, clearly directed against those looking to build earthly 'Kingdoms' and challenge, therefore, Caesar's Dominion in this world. But this is exactly the point about the polemic over the tax issue accompanying the description of Jesus (not James) as 'not deferring to anyone nor regarding the person of men' in the series of questions put to Jesus (again not James) by the Establishment Parties, which is directly followed in Matthew and Mark (Luke puts this elsewhere) by the citation of the Righteousness/Piety dichotomy, in particular, 'you should love your neighbour as yourself'. Once again, it should be appreciated, that this is exactly the order followed by Paul in the anti-'Zealot' Romans 13, citing the Righteousness Commandment, as we saw, as a reason for 'paying taxes' to Rome and 'giving all their due' (13:6–9).

In these Gospel renditions of Jesus' responses to the Establishment, Jesus is portrayed as recommending, at least on the surface, 'to give tribute unto *Caesar*', which, of course, all these 'Zadokite'-style Nazirite, Revolutionaries were quite unwilling to do. In fact, the 'Galilean' or '*Sicarii* Movement', founded by Judas and '*Saddok*', is pictured in Josephus as beginning on just the note of opposition to paying the tax to Rome. But, for Luke 23:2, 'misguiding the people, *forbidding [them] to pay tribute to Caesar*, claiming that he himself, "Christ", was a King', is just the charge levelled against Jesus.

In addition to all these polemical reversals, it should now be growing clear that the tradition about the Devil 'setting Jesus upon the Pinnacle of the Temple' and Jesus' refusal to 'be tempted' and 'cast himself down' (*kataballō*), a favourite detail of Gospel stories about Jesus as we have received them, was first probably an element in these traditions about James, to whom – like the related matter of *Jerusalem's fall* – they *more properly appertained*. In addition to this, it should be clear that the extent of the absorption of extra-biblical materials about James into the biblical narrative of Jesus is also increasing.

Also interesting in this citation from Hegesippus about James 'not deferring to persons' and '*standing* on the Pinnacle of the Temple' is the way the Pharisees and Scribes are portrayed as using the terminology 'the Just' or 'Righteous One' ('Zadok'?) – echoed in Luke 20:20 above about '*spies themselves* feigning to be *Righteous*' – in place of the very name, James, itself. Hegesippus' narrative, in fact, rarely employs the name James again, at least not in direct conversation, but rather only the 'Just One'. This can hardly be accidental and links up with the kind of word-play based on the *Z–D–K* three-letter roots, applied to '*the Righteous Teacher*' at Qumran.

We have already mentioned that the phrase about 'the Door' or 'Gate to Jesus' as a possible synonym for the 'Way of Jesus'. In fact, in John 10:9, Jesus calls himself 'the Door', by which he appears to mean 'the Gate of Salvation'. Similarly, at the end of the famous Sermon on the Mount, just before warning against 'false prophets coming in sheep's clothing, who inwardly are ravening wolves' – imagery that will basically reappear below in the anti-Pauline Parable of the Tares – 'the Gate', paralleling John above, is seen as 'the straightened Way that leads to life' (Matt. 7:13–15).[18]

This allusion caps a long train of polemics in 'the Sermon', itself following up Matthew's 'Temptation' narratives, in which most themes important to this book are evoked one way or the other. Principal in terms of the above issues is Jesus' polemic transmuting the Righteousness

Commandment of 'love your neighbour' into 'love your enemies', in connection with which, the 'tax collectors' are, once again, directly evoked (5:43–47). In addition, Jesus also employs, as we saw, the 'rain' imagery of the War Scroll (5:45), followed by evocation of the Qumran-style and Jewish Christian 'Perfect Adam' ideology, namely, 'be Perfect as your Father in Heaven is Perfect' (5:48). The whole finally ends up with reference to the Noahic-style 'rain falling and the flood and windstorm coming', but the 'House . . . founded upon Rock' not falling (7:24–25).

Hippolytus, in discussing the group he calls the 'Naassenes' ('Sebuaeans' in Epiphanius), also, ties the 'Gate' imagery to the 'Primal Adam' ideology. Saying that, like al-Biruni's 'Sabaeans' centuries later, the Naassenes pray towards 'the Dome of Heaven' (that is, the North), Hippolytus notes that, for the Naassenes, 'Adam is the Primal ['First'] Man' and Jesus, 'the True Gate', through whom the Perfect Man enters. As they appear to have believed, 'the Perfect Man is incapable of *being saved* unless he be born again'.[19] So in all these presentations, 'the Gate to Jesus' is generally connected in some manner to 'the Perfect Man'.

In Hegesippus' version of these matters, James ostensibly declines to answer the question about 'the Gate of Jesus' in favour of the more apocalyptic and biblical proclamation of 'the Son of Man', 'sitting in Heaven on the right hand of the Great Power about to come on the clouds of Heaven'. Not only do we have here the 'Great' or 'Hidden Power' ideology, but for him, anyhow, 'the Son of Man' is literally 'the Gate of Jesus' or 'Perfect Adam'. Before proceeding, however, it is important to grasp that in Hebrew 'Son of Man' literally is 'Son of Adam' (in Aramaic, 'Son of Enosh') and, therefore, what we have, the reference to the imminent 'coming of the Son of Man on the clouds of Heaven' – in the War Scroll, as we shall see, identified with 'the Heavenly Host' – is basically a more incendiary version of the 'Primal' or 'Perfect Adam' ideology. As Paul puts it in his own inimitable way, as we have seen, in 1 Corinthians 15:45–47:

> Also it is written, 'the First Man Adam became a living soul', so the Last Adam became a life-giving Spirit . . . The First Man is made of dust out of the earth. The Second Man is the Lord out of Heaven.

The quotation, attributed above by Hegesippus to James, which we compared to throwing a lighted match into an excited mix of pilgrims, in the Temple at Passover, is both immediate and intense. When one grasps its aggressively apocalyptic, Messianic character, it becomes the central proclamation of one of the most amazing episodes ever recorded in religious history. Particularly now, in the twentieth century, as the Dead Sea Scrolls – unknown for some nineteen centuries – come to light, not only are the words attributed to James by Hegesippus paralleled almost word for word in that famous War Scroll, they come precisely at the point where the Messianic 'Star Prophecy' is being elucidated.

Before leaving the subject of 'the Gate', we should note that Luke 13:24 knows the language of 'the narrow Gate' and combines it, as in Matthew 7:25 and the Damascus Document above on 'the Glory of Adam', with the imagery of 'the House' – and, following this, 'shutting the Door' (now reversed from how it was used in Acts 21:30 and, it will be recalled, against 'the Sons of the Pit' or 'of Belial' in the Damascus Document). Even more importantly, it goes on, then, to combine it with the '*ekballō*' language of 'being cast out' of 'the Kingdom of God', just encountered in Mark's version of Jesus being 'cast' or 'driven out into the wilderness' to be 'tempted by *Satan*'. Only now it is directed against *Jews* (Luke 13:28). This leads immediately into the famous 'the Last shall be First and the First shall be Last' in Luke 13:30 and 'everyone exalting himself being humbled' in 14:11 (repeated in 18:14) – which we have already identified as, among other things, a pro-Pauline attack on the Jerusalem Church 'Pillars' – and attacks on Jerusalem generally, 'that *kills the Prophets* and *stones those sent to her*' (13:34). Here, too, occurs an allusion to a bird protecting its children 'under its wings', which absolutely appears to recur in the Qumran 'Hymns of the Poor'.

This long section of the Gospel of Luke, unparalleled in its totality in Matthew and Mark, begins with 'dining' and 'not washing' problems (11:37) and allusions to 'the blood of Zachariah' (11:51) and that of 'the Galileans, Pilate mingled with the sacrifices' (13:1). Coming down forcefully on the side of excluded persons from the Temple, like 'the Poor, the maimed, the blind and the lame' (14:3 and 14:21) against father, mother, 'brothers, and kinsmen' (14:12 and 14:26) – even 'the ninety-nine Righteous Ones in the wilderness' in favour of eating with 'tax collectors and Sinners' (15:1–7) – it ends, as in Eusebius'/Hegesippus' presentation of James' last proclamation in the Temple above, in evocation of 'the coming days of the Son of Man' and/or 'when the Son of Man comes' (13:22–18:8), which it combines with evocation of the first two *Zaddik*-escape and Salvation episodes in Genesis (Noah and Lot), comparing the 'day of the coming of the Son of Man' to 'the days of Noah' and, 'entering the ark and the Flood', to 'Fire and brimstone raining down' (17:25–29).

James' Proclamation of the Son of Man Coming on the Clouds of Heaven and the Dead Sea Scrolls

The sequentiality in Church accounts of the destruction of the Righteous One, James, followed by the appearance of the foreign armies and their devastation and destruction of the country, is, for all intents and purposes, replicated in another famous apocalyptic and eschatological document from Qumran we have been referring to, the Habbakuk *Pesher*. The Habakkuk *Pesher*, as remarked, expounds the first two chapters of the Prophet Habakkuk in an eschatological and apocalyptical manner and includes, most importantly, Paul's key, 'the Righteous shall live by his Faith' quotation from Habakkuk 2:4, which it elucidates in terms of a final apocalyptic Judgement.

The subjects treated – though not perhaps exactly in order – are: the destruction of the Righteous Teacher by the Wicked Priest, for which the 'the Cup of the Lord's Vengeance would come around to him' (the Wicked Priest); the devastation of the country by foreign armies, called 'the *Kittim*' or 'the Additional Ones of the Peoples'; and how the booty and Riches 'of the Last Priests of Jerusalem, who gathered Riches and profiteered from the spoils of the Peoples', would 'in the Last Days be *delivered up* to the hand of the Army of the *Kittim*'.[20] In the last column, all of these will ultimately be eschatologically condemned and 'destroyed from off the earth', as would all backsliders and idolators generally – 'all Gentiles serving stone and wood', which, 'would not *save them* on the Day of Judgement'.[21]

It is important to watch the use of the word 'Peoples' at Qumran – which in Hebrew is not always the same word as 'Gentiles' – in particular, as we have noted, 'the Kings of the Peoples' (Greek '*Ethnē*') in the Damascus Document and Roman administrative terminology referring to such 'Peoples' and their 'Kings' – especially in the East. In my view, when used in a Palestinian framework, this refers to 'Herodians', here in the Habakkuk *Pesher*, most notably, emphasizing their exploitation and ill-gotten enrichment. When used to relate to outsiders further afield, as, for instance, 'the Additional Ones of the Peoples', this term is specifically identified with 'the Army of the *Kittim*', that is, 'the Romans'. Note, too, Paul's use of a parallel vocabulary, which we have been signalling and continue to signal throughout, the 'Apostle to the Gentiles' (*Ethnē*, the same word used for 'Peoples' above).[22]

Anyone conversant with Scripture will immediately recognize that

James' response to the Scribes and Pharisees, as pictured in this description from Hegesippus, is an allusion to the famous Messianic passage in Daniel 7:13:

> And I gazed into the visions of the night, and I saw, coming on the clouds of Heaven, one like a Son of Man [in Hebrew, 'Son of Adam' – in the original Aramaic, 'Son of Enosh'].

Those familiar, too, with the language of Christian theological discussion, will also immediately recognize this title, 'the Son of Man', as one of the most precious of those considered denotive of Jesus in Scripture. What is not normally, however, recognized is that the War Scroll from Qumran is operating in exactly the same ideological, and even scriptural framework.

In Column 11, where the Star Prophecy is finally expounded, first, the actual Prophecy, 'a Star will rise from Jacob, a Sceptre to rule the world' from Numbers, is quoted in its entirety. Then it is analysed in detail. But in the three columns preceding this, the situation in 'the camps', where 'the Holy Angels are with our Hosts' and those 'Perfect in Spirit and body prepared for the Day of Vengeance', is delineated and 'the Kingdom is to be the God of Israel's'.[23]

It is the latter, who 'strengthens' and 'fortifies all the mighty Warriors', 'making war through the Holy Ones of His People'. The last are most certainly equivalent to Daniel 7:21's *'Kedoshim'* or 'Saints' and would also, no doubt, have to include all those following 'Nazirite'-style 'Holiness from the womb', as James and John the Baptist. For this reason, not only is 'all indecent lewdness to be kept from the camps' ('since the Holy Angels are together with their Hosts'), but the battle raiment of the Priests, which is to be of 'linen' – including presumably the 'linen' mitre evoked in Epiphanius' version of Hegesippus' description of James – is described in great detail. This is not to be worn 'in the Temple' thereafter, nor are these Priests 'to profane themselves with the blood of the Nations of Vanity' (or 'Emptiness').[24]

Here, too, we begin to get reference to 'the form of Adam and the generations of his seed' and 'the Power' of God, as in 'the Son of Man sitting on the Right hand of the Great Power' in James' proclamation, is repeatedly evoked. So are God's 'mighty works and wonders'. Unlike the Gospels, however, where the same words are used to characterize Jesus' more peaceful and Hellenized 'mighty works' in Chorazin, Sidon, and Tyre (Matt. 11:20–23 and pars.), these 'works' are military victories like David's victory over Goliath or Pharaoh's chariots being overthrown into the Red Sea.

Over and over again it is reiterated that these military victories are accomplished by the earthly 'Holy Ones of the Covenant' with the help of 'the Holy Angels' and 'the Host of the Heavenly Holy Ones' *on the clouds*. This is expressed as follows:

> The Power is from You not us. Our Strength and the Power of our hands accomplish no *mighty works*, except by Your Power and the Power of Your mighty bravery.[25]

Aside from this tell-tale 'Power' vocabulary, one should also note the belligerence of this expression. It is important for fixing the ethos of the literature at Qumran. At this juncture, we even get a more aggressive variation of Pauline 'Grace' doctrines and God is praised as

> having *saved* [*them*] by [His] Mercies and not by [their] works, because [they] have transgressed and sinned iniquitously.[26]

Uttered as a kind of formulatory penitence, it does not undermine the basic 'works–Righteousness' ethos of the corpus generally. Still, it provides an excellent window on the Palestinian root Paul used to develop his more spiritualized, non-military notions of 'Grace'.

In the War Scroll, David's victory over Goliath sets the basic *Davidic* ambience of what follows, including the interpretation of 'the Star Prophecy'. This is a crucial moment for Qumran exegesis, and it is no overstatement to say for that matter, the world generally. Not only is this interpretation specifically framed in terms of the Messiah-like 'no mere Adam', showing, as nothing else can, that this 'Star Prophecy' *was interpreted Messianically* at Qumran;[27] but it will now develop into the language of Daniel's 'Son of Man coming on the clouds' with the Heavenly Host or, as the Gospel of Matthew puts it, echoing James above, 'the Son of Man coming with Power and great Glory' or 'sitting on the right hand of Power and coming on the clouds of Heaven' (24:30, 26:64 and pars.).[28]

It is important to note the context of both of these scriptural passages in the Gospels – the first in the Little Apocalypse, delivered by Jesus on the Mount of Olives before his arrest after commenting, on seeing the Temple, 'there shall not be left one stone here upon the other'; the second, his speech before 'the entire Sanhedrin', composed of 'Chief Priests and Elders' at 'the House' or 'the Court of the High Priest' in the night at Passover. The 'Chamber' on the Temple Mount, in which the Sanhedrin normally sat was called the Chamber of Hewn Stone, but, according to Talmudic sources, in the period in which James and Jesus were supposedly being tried, this 'House' or 'Court of the High Priest', moved to a location outside the Temple (note the reiteration of the 'Stone' and 'Passover' themes here).[29]

The second of these two proclamations, given almost verbatim in all three Synoptics, is word for word the one attributed to James, standing either on the steps of the Temple or its Pinnacle before the assembled crowds at Passover. Once again, critical materials from the life of James, clearly known to the authors of the Gospels, would appear to be retrospectively inserted into the pro-Roman, anti-Jewish biography of 'Jesus'. It is, of course, possible to turn this around and assert the opposite, but the inconceivability of a *midnight Sanhedrin* at 'the Home of the High Priest' on the *eve of Passover* would seem to counter-indicate this. The reader will be the judge.

Surprising too, quoting Isaiah 31:8's 'by the sword of *no Man*, the sword of *no mere Adam*', the War Scroll now specifically goes on to evoke the 'Primal Adam', thus tying all these themes – the Davidic, 'the Star', 'the Son of Man', 'the Perfect Adam', and the 'Messiah' – together in one extended proclamation, ultimately combining 'clouds' and 'rain' imagery and expressing this Judgement, as we have seen, in terms of 'coming on the clouds' and 'shedding of rain on all on earth'.

That all of these motifs come together here in exegesis of the 'Star Prophecy' in the War Scroll at Qumran is about as much proof as one could ask that the approach we have been following is correct. Nothing less would have prepared us for this and, without it, we could not have identified the presence here of the totality of these motifs. Directly preceded by an evocation of 'the form of Adam', this exegesis is directly followed by an extended description of the Heavenly Host coming on the clouds, richer than in any other source and repeated a second time at the end of the Scroll.

For it, the Messiah-like Leader 'joins the Poor' ('*Ebionim*' repeated twice – our Jamesian 'Ebionites' again) and 'those bent in the dust' to rise up 'against the *Kittim*' and justify God's 'True Judgement on all the sons of man'.[30] It reads:

By the hand of Your Messiah[s] . . . so that You may glorify Yourself in front of Your Enemies and overthrow Belial's Legions, the Seven Nations of Vanity, and by the hand of the Poor Ones of Your Redemption,[31] with the fullness of Your *Wondrous Power*, You have [opened] a *Gate of Hope* [the 'Gate' imagery again] to the cowering heart . . . for You will kindle the Downcast in Spirit [a synonym for 'the Poor in Spirit' in Matthew 5:13

above], who shall be as a flaming torch in the chaff to ceaselessly consume Evil until Wickedness is destroyed.

In the exegesis in the Damascus Document, this same 'Sceptre' is the Messianic 'Leader', also referred to in another Messianic fragment seemingly connected to these matters, 'The Messianic Leader [*Nasi*]'.³² In the Damascus Document he 'will utterly destroy the Sons of Seth', a clear synonym for 'the Seven Nations of Vanity' and mentioned here in Numbers 24:17 too. In addition to remarking the repetition of the word 'Power' in these passages, one should compare the 'torch in the chaff' simile to the words of John the Baptist, quoted in the Gospel of Matthew and applying to 'one coming more Powerful than' he – meaning Jesus – 'whose shoes', John supposedly 'was not fit to loose' or 'carry'.

> He shall baptize you with the Holy Spirit and Fire, whose winnowing fan is in His hand [words just encountered repeatedly in the War Scroll above] to purify His threshing floor, and He will gather His wheat into his storehouse, but He will burn up the chaff with unquenchable fire. (Matt. 3:11–12)

The references to 'harvesting wheat', 'burning', and 'Fire' will, to be sure, recur in the sequence of parables following the evocation of 'the Enemy' in the Parable of the Tares, the only real Jewish Christian parable in Scripture (Matt. 13:24–50). The allusions to 'burning' and 'Fire' are also very strong in eschatological contexts elsewhere at Qumran – as they will be later throughout the Koran – particularly in the evocation of 'the Last Judgement'.³³

At this point the passage from Isaiah 31:8, just mentioned above, is introduced into the exegesis, implying the Messiah to be 'more than a Man, more than a mere Adam', while at the same time linking him to vanquishing the *Kittim* – here clearly the Romans – with 'the sword'. It reads:

> And from that time, You announced the Power of Your hand over the Kittim, with the words, 'And Assyria shall fall by the sword of no Man, but by sword of no mere Adam You shall consume him [Hebrew: 'eat him'].'

The idea of 'consuming' or 'eating' here – already encountered in the description of the *Kittim* in the Habakkuk *Pesher* above, including their tax-collecting activities – takes off from the 'flaming torch consuming the chaff' descriptive of 'the Poor in Spirit' above, now applied directly to the situation of 'the Star'/'Messiah' and his constituency, 'the Poor' (*Ebionim*) and 'those Bent in the Dust'.

Because, by the hand of the Poor Ones and the hand of those Bent in the Dust ['the Poor in Spirit'] will the Enemies from all the lands and the Mighty Ones of the Peoples be humbled, so that they will be *paid the Reward on Evil Ones* . . . to justify the Judgement of Your Truth on all the sons of man in order to make for Yourself an Eternal Name among the People.34

One should also note the use of the word 'sword' in this quotation from Isaiah, which sets the tone of the whole exegesis and gives it its more warlike, Messianic cast. The note of eschatological Judgement, to which the exegesis mounts, is important too. In it, once again, is the allusion to 'Peoples'.

This idea of doing something for the 'Great Name' of God is most vividly encountered in Ezekiel 36:20–23 – also addressing 'the Son of Man' – the magnificent climax to Ezekiel's apocalyptic visions, including the same vehement and uncompromising nationalism we are encountering here and the famous 'standing up' of the bones as 'a vast and immense army'. Not only is this note of final eschatological Judgement, towards which the exegesis mounts, paralleled at the end of the Habakkuk *Pesher* in the repeated evocation there of 'the Day of Judgement'; the reference to 'justifying the Judgement' in the context of evoking 'the Reward on Evil Ones' is also interesting in terms of the parallel phraseology the same *Pesher* uses to describe how they inflicted 'the Judgements on Evil' on the Wicked Priest and 'took vengeance upon the flesh of his corpse'. Indeed, this 'Reward on Evil Ones' (including allusion to 'eating' in the sense of 'destruction') is also the language of the Isaiah 3:9–11 passage applied to James' death in all early Church literature and reflected here in the Habakkuk *Pesher* on the destruction of 'the Poor' as well.

As in Gospel evocations of 'the coming of the Son of Man' in the War Scroll, the Messiah will render Judgement with the help of 'the Poor' and 'those Bent in the Dust' on 'the Mighty Ones of the Peoples'. Not only do we have in these climactic portions of the War Scroll at Qumran, the Star Prophecy interpreted in terms of Daniel 7's 'Son of Man' – the basis as well of James' proclamation in the Temple on Passover, 62 CE – this is accompanied by inclusion of the scriptural warrant for someone 'more than Man' or 'the sword of a Higher Adam' to accomplish this victory over all foreign armies and bring the final eschatological Judgement. Again we have the coupling of nationalist and 'Zealot' Messianic warlikeness with what superficially, anyhow, would appear to be the more spiritual 'Primal Adam' ideology of daily-bathing 'Ebionite'/'Essene' groups. This is a crucial melding and defines the religio-historical situation in 62 CE almost perfectly.

For its part, the War Scroll moves directly into an extensive description of 'the coming of the Heavenly Host on the clouds of Heaven' of such ecstatic beauty and brilliant creativity as to be overwhelming.

> For You will fight with them from Heaven . . . because the majority of these Holy Ones are in Heaven, along with the Host of Your Angels in Your Holy Abode praising Your Name, together with *the Elect of the Holy People whom You have set aside for Yourself* . . . for whom You have recorded . . . the Covenant of Your Peace and over whom You will reign for all Eternal Ages.[35]

The terminology 'Holy Ones' is repeated so often here that it is clear that what is being envisioned is a Holy Army of some kind, composed of Nazirite-style 'consecrated' ones, 'set aside' to God, of the kind discussed with regard to James' 'Holiness' above. In addition, the Noahic-style 'Covenant of Peace' bestowed upon this 'Holy Elect' would appear to parallel that being bestowed upon 'the Sons of Zadok' in perpetuity in the Hebrew version of Ben Sira, found at both Qumran and Masada, and Phineas' heirs in Numbers above. Once again, it is clear that these 'Holy Ones', 'Nazirites', or 'Saints' and 'Sons of Zadok' are simply parallel terminologies.

The text then turns completely warlike, having the nature of an exhortative for battle or, as it now must be termed (using the language of Islam), 'Holy War':

> For You have commanded the Hosts of Your Elect [in the Damascus Document, 'the Sons of Zadok'] in their thousands and their Myriads, together with your Holy Ones and the Army of Your Angels, who are mighty in battle, together with the Elect of Heaven and Your blessings, to smite the Enemies of the land with the Greatness of Your Judgements.

Its imagery is now purely confrontational, militaristic, and eschatological, including the rationale for the Qumran 'camp'-style communities:

> because you are a Terrible God in the Glory of Your Kingdom and the Assembly of your Holy Ones is among us to give us Eternal aid. We shall despise kings and mock and scorn the Mighty, because our Lord is Holy and our Glorious King ['His Messiah'] is with us, together with the Holy Ones, the Mighty Host of Angels are under His command[36] and the Valiant

Warrior is among our Assembly [or 'Church'], and the Hosts of His Spirits [Islam: '*Jinn*'] are with our foot soldiers and our horsemen.

This finally gives way to a key simile comparing the coming of the Heavenly Host to clouds, making it clear we are completely in the realm of Daniel, the New Testament's 'Son of Man coming on the clouds of Heaven with Power and Great Glory', and the totality of 'rain' and 'Judgement' imagery we have been following:

> They are like clouds, clouds of dew [covering] the earth, as torrential rain, shedding Judgement on all that grows on earth.

Here, of course, is the 'rain' imagery, linked to that of coming eschatological Judgement, that we have been signalling in our presentation of 'the *Zaddik*' as rainmaker and one begins to appreciate that one is in a much more sophisticated universe of poetic imagery and symbolism than one might have suspected hitherto. Of course, Paul is working in the same poetic universe of allegory and metaphor, but to opposite effect. The allusion to 'shedding Judgement on all that grows on earth' parallels Matthew 5:45's God 'sending rain on the Righteous and the Unrighteous' alike, we have encountered above, as well as the allusion comparing the coming of the Son of Man to 'the Days of Noah' (Matt. 24:37–38, Mark 13:26-27, and Luke 21:27).

Just for good measure this 'rain' simile is repeated again, almost word for word, at the end of the War Scroll. Here, referring now to God 'keeping his Covenant with us and opening *the Gates of Salvation* [*Yeshu'ot*] for us numerous times', the text proclaims again:

> For Yours is the Might and in Your hands, the battle . . . for our Ruler is Holy and the Glorious King is with us. The H[ost of His Spirits is with our foot soldiers and horsemen. They are as clouds, clouds of de]w covering the earth and as torrential rain shedding Judgement on [all that grows there. Arise hero] . . . smite the nations, your enemies, and consume guilty flesh with your sword [this last clearly being a Messianic allusion].[37]

Not only do we have here the 'God our Ruler' ideology of Josephus' *Sicarii* or 'Zealots', there can be little doubt of the Messianic thrust of all this, not to mention its blood-curdling warlikeness – perhaps a necessity in the circumstances. The fresh and original imagery here once again recapitulates the Messianic 'sword' of the 'no mere Adam' passage from Isaiah 31:8 above, including even the allusion to 'consuming'/ 'eating'.

Judgement, which is to fall like 'rain on the Just and Unjust' alike, is also called throughout the War Scroll, and Qumran documents generally, 'the Day of Vengeance'. Those participating in this 'Judgement' are the Host of Heavenly Holy Ones and the Elect of Israel – 'Sons of Zadok' in the Damascus Document – or 'the Holy Ones' of the Community of 'the Elect', 'the Consecrated of God'.

The Imagery of the Heavenly Host and Coming Apocalyptic Judgement in James

This is almost precisely the picture one gets in these early Church accounts of James' proclamation in the Temple on Passover of the Son of Man coming on the clouds of Heaven, curtailed somewhat from the War Scroll in line with the shorter narrative style of these reports. That such a proclamation is attributed to James, to whom the 'rainmaking' tradition also adhered, at this pivotal moment in his activity is astonishing – but the parallels in materials relating to James go further than that.

The Letter of James is also steeped, as we have already seen, in the language of 'doing' and 'Doer', the same root as the word, 'works'/ 'ma'asim', so much a part of the vocabulary at Qumran. In it, 'Salvation' is not simply 'a free gift of Faith' as in Paul; rather there will be 'Judgement without mercy on those who do not *do mercy*' (2:13). In the last chapter, its author – James or another – launches into a thorough-going and completely uncompromising apocalyptic. This begins with condemnation of *the Rich*: 'And now you Rich, weep, start crying for the miseries that are coming to you' (5:1).

This condemnation of 'the Rich', as we have seen, is also a set piece of Qumran ideology, expressed most vividly perhaps in the 'Three Nets of Belial' section of the Damascus Document. But the condemnation of the Rich is also a principal theme associated with those holding the tradition associated with James' name most dear, 'the *Ebionim*' or 'the Poor'. The same was, no doubt, true for those following the Righteous Teacher of Qumran, where the terminology 'the Poor' and several of its parallels, as we saw, permeate the corpus.

The all-consuming tirade against 'the Rich' in the Letter of James, including the assertion, as we have seen, that the Rich 'put the Righteous One to death' (5:6),[38] rises to its climax also with the apocalyptic proclamation of 'the *coming of the Lord*' (5:8). That this comprises what generally goes under the phraseology 'the Lord of Hosts' is made clear as well four lines before (5:4). It is this same 'Lord of Hosts' who is implicit in the vivid imagery in the War Scroll, evoking the coming of the Lord or, possibly even, the Messianic 'King' with the Heavenly Host on the clouds of Heaven. This is also the implication of the episode from early Church literature about the proclamation by another of these 'Just Ones', James, of 'the Son of Man sitting on the right hand of the Great Power', not to mention its New Testament parallels.

As in these other contexts, in James we even have an allusion to the tell-tale Messianic 'Gate' or 'Door' usage once again: 'Behold, the Judge is standing before *the Door*' (5:9). This also incorporates the 'standing' imagery once again, amid that of the final apocalyptic Judgement, and even ends with the evocation of the coming of 'spring' and 'autumn rain', the implication being that this is the equivalent of eschatological Judgement. Its spirit is vengeful, uncompromising, and completely parallel to the spirit one finds in the War Scroll at Qumran.

It reads as follows:

> Your gold and silver are corroding away, and the same corrosion will be like a testimony against you, and shall eat your flesh like Fire. It was a burning Fire that you stored up as treasure in the Last Days. (5:2–3)

Not only do we have here the language, attributed to Jesus by Matthew in the Sermon on the Mount, of 'moth and rust' corroding stored-up earthly treasure (6:19–20), but also that of 'eating' or 'devouring flesh with a sword', used in the War Scroll and Isaiah 31:8's 'no mere Adam' Prophecy above.

Linguistic parallels such as these should not be dismissed lightly. One should also note the language here of 'the Last Days' and 'a burning Fire', which – as already remarked – fairly permeates the literature at Qumran, particularly the Habakkuk *Pesher* – as it does the Koran in Islam. These allusions pinpoint the Letter of James as being thoroughly apocalyptic and eschatological; and, as in the interpretation of Habakkuk 2:4 in the Habakkuk *Pesher* and the interpretation of 'the Zadokite Covenant' in the Damascus Document from Qumran, once again we are in the world of 'the Last Generation' or 'the End Time'.

It is here the letter ascribed to James evokes 'the Lord of Hosts':

> Look, the hire of the workers who mowed your fields, which you kept back, cries out, and the cries of the reapers have reached the ears of the Lord of Hosts. (5:4)

Interestingly, the Hebrew word for 'Hosts', '*Sabaoth*', is transliterated in this passage *directly into the Greek*. This cry for vengeance is mimicked in Matthew's story (introducing Jesus' proclamation of 'the Son of Man coming on the clouds of Heaven with Power and great Glory') of Jesus' attack (not John's) on the 'serpents' and 'offspring of vipers', trying to 'escape the Judgement of Hell' (Matt. 23:33–38 – reflected, too, in Luke 11:45–52).

Here it is recast into a cry of vengeance for 'the blood of Abel the Righteous', killed in the Genesis story by Cain (note the tell-tale 'Righteous' cognomen here), and 'Zachariah the son of Barachias', 'murdered between the Temple and the altar'. This last probably reflects, as we saw earlier, that 'Zachariah', killed by the Zealots in the Temple after they slaughtered many of the High Priests – in our view – in vengeance for James. It also turns into the blood-curdling condemnation of Jerusalem and Jews, as 'killing all the Prophets and stoning those who have been sent to her', which, except for the disputed events being discussed here, in classical times never really occurred. Prophets may have suffered, but few, if any, were ever really 'killed' or 'stoned'.

Not only does this directly evoke the James stoning (the 'stone upon stone' observation that directly follows perhaps, as we saw, reflecting the 'Stone Chamber' material about Sanhedrin 'blasphemy' trials, in particular, James'), but here, too, Jesus' speech in Matthew ends up predicting the destruction of the Temple – 'your House shall be left desolate to you' (23:38).[39] It is also possible to see the 'worker's hire' in this allusion to the 'coming of the Lord of Hosts' in James as a reverse parallel to the 'prostitute's hire' in the 'Jacob of Kfar Sechania' story disparaging High Priests.

James continues:

> It was you who condemned and put the Righteous One to death. He offered you no resistance. Therefore, be patient, brothers, until the coming of the Lord, just as the farmer waits for the precious fruit of the earth, having patience until it receives the rain [either] earlier or later, you also must *be patient, fortifying your hearts*, because *the coming of the Lord* has drawn near. Do not *grumble against each other*, so that you will not be condemned. *See, the Judge stands before the Door.* (Jas. 5:4–10)

Here, of course, we have the allusions to 'Gate', 'rain', and 'standing', just encountered in these early Church accounts and the War Scroll from Qumran, as noted above. There is also, though, the recommendation to 'be patient until *the coming of the Lord of Hosts*', who, by implication, will exact the relevant Vengeance and Judgement. This is the whole scheme of the climactic end of the Habakkuk *Pesher*, which also deals with eschatological Judgement and counsels patience, presenting the scriptural warrant for what goes in Christian eschatological theory as 'the Delay of the Parousia'. This exegesis is delivered in interpretation of Habakkuk 2:3, 'if it tarries, wait for it', preceding Habakkuk 2:4 and asserts that 'the Last Days' would be 'extended beyond anything the Prophets have foretold'.[40]

The allusion to 'fortifying your hearts', connected to this evocation of 'the coming of the Lord' and 'Judgement' in the Letter of James, is word for word that found above in the War Scroll and Damascus Document at Qumran and, once again, strongly parallels the 'strengthening' symbolism circulating about James' cognomens in the early Church accounts. The allusion, too, to 'murmuring' or 'grumbling against each other' is precisely that found in both the Community Rule, and seemingly the Damascus Document, at the point at which both overlap, the penance for which is thirty days.[41]

Earlier too, in the section evoking the Righteousness Commandment, 'loving one's neighbour', and the Piety Commandment, 'loving God', James asserts that it is the Rich who oppress the Poor by 'dragging them before tribunals' (2:6). Again in the Damascus Document at Qumran, the penalty for having people condemned to death in the Courts of the Gentiles – which has not a little relevance to the portrait of the death of Jesus in the Gospels – is death.[42]

This allusion, to the coming of the Lord of Hosts in eventual final Judgement and the consonant condemnation of the Rich 'for murdering the Just' or the 'Righteous One' in James, concludes with the efficaciousness of 'the working prayer of the Just One'. This cites, as we saw, Elijah as a man with the power to pray for it not to rain and, praying again, cause the 'Heaven to send forth rain' (5:16–18).

The Stoning of Stephen in Acts

To conclude, in our view, placed upon 'the Pinnacle' or 'steps of the Temple' by the Jerusalem leadership to quiet the Messianic expectation seemingly rampant among the people, James proclaimed the standing of the Messiah 'on the right hand of Power' and his imminent apocalyptic coming 'with the Heavenly Host on the clouds of Heaven'. There is one final point relating to this episode, which yet again helps point the way to

Acts' historical method. In particular, it helps unravel the mystery of the attack in the Temple by the Jewish mob upon someone Acts is calling 'Stephen'.

In a significant parallel to the attack on James, described in the first Book of the Pseudoclementine *Recognitions*, it is at this point in Acts that Paul is introduced. To draw the parallel closer, Stephen undergoes the same ultimate fate as James – stoning. In addition, just as the character in Acts, who is the witness to this stoning, afterwards emerges as *Paul*; in Eusebius' version of the stoning of James, the witness – it will be recalled – turns out to be 'one of the Priests of the Sons of Rechab, the *Rechabim*' (Eusebius actually preserves the Hebrew plural here, transliterated into the Greek). In Epiphanius, as we saw, it is Simeon bar Cleophas, James' close relative and direct successor in the Leadership of the Jerusalem Church.

In Acts' version, there is one additional reversal in line with its story line following the man who was originally the 'Enemy' of the early Christian Church in Palestine. Whereas both Epiphanius' Simeon and Eusebius' 'Rechabite Priest' disapprove of the stoning and call upon those perpetrating it to stop, Paul 'entirely approves'. As Acts puts this:

> And the witnesses laid their clothes at the feet of a young man called Saul . . . and Saul entirely approved of putting him to death. (7:58–8:1)

'Saul', of course, in Acts after the start of his missionary journeys metamorphoses into 'Paul'.

We shall have more to say about this episode below. There are a few points that should be made about it and Stephen's speech preceding it. As presented in Acts, this speech, seemingly lifted almost bodily from Joshua's farewell address to the assembled tribes at Shechem in the Old Testament (Josh. 24:2–24), makes a mistake in the location of Abraham's burial site traceable back to the speech attributed to Joshua (24:32). Like Joshua, Stephen is presented – however bizarre this may appear to be from the mouth of a seemingly Gentile convert – as telling the *Jews* (now his tormentors) their *own* history.

The speech ends with the identifiably Pauline-style attack on all Jews, including presumably the Jerusalem Church Leadership, as 'always resisting the Holy Spirit' (7:51). Then, alluding to the Prophecy of 'the coming of the Just One' (language we have already seen tied to attacks on the Rich in the Letter of James), Stephen, too, is pictured as making the accusation against the Jews of killing the Prophets and of being Christ-killers. As Stephen is depicted as saying:

Which one of the Prophets did your fathers not persecute, and they killed the ones who prophesied the coming of the Just One, of whom now, too, you have become betrayers and murderers. (7:52)

Not only have we just seen the same charges attributed to Jesus above in the matter of 'the blood of Abel the Righteous' in the context of condemning the Temple to destruction, similar charges against the Jewish mob are put into Peter's mouth earlier in Acts, to wit, 'You laid your lawless hands on him and crucifying him, put him to death' (Acts 2:23). But the original accusations of this kind were, chronologically speaking, probably first made by Paul in 1 Thessalonians – if authentic. For Paul, it is 'the Jews, who not only put the Lord Jesus to death, but also their own Prophets' (2:15). These are just slightly transposed from James 5:16 above, where it is the Rich who 'put the Righteous' or 'Just One to death'.

This charge against the Jews of both 'putting the Lord Jesus and their own Prophets to death' has reverberated down throughout history in the most terrifying – and unexamined – manner. For example, even the Koran, normally anti-Pauline in orientation, picks it up mindlessly and repeatedly describes the Jews as 'killing all the Prophets' – this, despite the fact that in the Old Testament anyhow, as we just saw, there is hardly a single prophet that the Jews can demonstrably be said to have killed, not even Moses. But where accusations go, history is no arbiter of truth.

Paul makes the 1 Thessalonians accusation – again, if authentic – in the context of the kinds of allusions we have been referring to above about trying 'to please' either 'men or God'. It will be recalled that the context above sometimes had to do with Abraham as 'a Friend of God' or 'making oneself a Friend to the world'. The context in 1 Thessalonians is interesting, because it involves 'being forbidden to teach to the Gentiles' (2:16). What Paul is doing once again is, in effect, responding to the kind of charge made in the Letter of James against the person who teaches 'Abraham was saved by Faith' and who, by attempting to be a Friend of men, 'turns himself – unlike Abraham, 'the Friend of God' – into the Enemy of God'.

Again Paul reverses this accusation turning it against those 'forbidding us to speak to the Peoples that they may *be saved*' (note the parallel to the 'some who came down from Judea teaching that unless you are circumcised you cannot *be saved*' that triggers 'the Jerusalem Council' in Acts 15:1). Those forbidding this, as in Galatians, would presumably be the Leadership of the Jerusalem Church, with whom Paul is at odds.

These are now lumped with Jews generally, again reversing James above. Now it is these who '*do not please God and are the Enemies of the whole human race*'(1 Thess. 2:15).

It is this which follows the accusation of 'both killing the Lord Jesus and their own Prophets'. This argument, which was basically one about the efficacy or non-efficacy of the Law, takes on the most terrifying ring about 'blood libel', but, once again, we are in the world of contraries and reversals. For James, it was 'the Rich', who 'put the Righteous One to death'. For Paul/Stephen, this becomes the Jewish people as a whole.

The importance of this passage from Acts, however, doesn't end here:

> Filled with the Holy Spirit and gazing intently up to Heaven, Stephen [James-like] saw *the Glory of God* and *Jesus standing at the right hand of God*, and cried out, '*Behold, I see the Heavens opened, and the Son of Man standing at the right hand of God.*' (7:55–56)

Here, of course, are almost the exact words and the same proclamation attributed to James at this critical juncture in early Church sources, including even the words, 'at the right hand of God' and 'the Son of Man', though missing from the War Scroll at Qumran, implied there as well – not to mention these two reiterations of the word 'standing' (or 'the Standing One' ideology again).

But the resemblance does not stop there. The next words are also simply variations of those we encounter in the story of James' death, including the note of being 'thrown' or 'cast' (*ballō*) down – here 'cast out' (*ekballō*) – and crying out virtually the exact words attributed to James in these early Church accounts and Jesus, too, in Gospel accounts of his last words on the cross.

The episode closes as follows:

> And crying out *with a loud voice*, they stopped their ears with their hands and rushed at him with one mind, and having *cast him* [*ekballō*] out of the city, they stoned ... Stephen *as he prayed* ... and *falling to his knees*, he cried out *in a loud voice*, 'Lord lay not this sin on them.' (Acts 7:57–60)

Again, these are almost precisely the words attributed to James in the Hegesippus account reproduced by Eusebius and, of course, those attributed to Jesus on the Cross in the Gospel variations. No one can miss the parallels and overlaps between these early Church accounts of the stoning of James and the Book of Acts account of the stoning of the elusive and quite puzzling character known as 'Stephen'.

Not only are the constant themes of James' 'praying' and his 'falling' reiterated here, but also James crying out with a very 'loud voice', twice repeated in very dramatic style in the account in Hegesippus, not to mention the ever-present motif of 'his knees'. 'Stephen', for instance, is also the name of Paul's *first convert* in Greece (1 Cor. 1:16 and 16:15). As we saw, not only does it mean 'Crown' in Greek, it parallels the word in Hebrew used to designate the mitre worn by the High Priest – also a colloquialism for the *hair of the Nazirites* – both themes again connected *with James*.

What is the reason for all these resemblances? What is behind these various overlaps and reversals? As in the instances of the election of 'Judas *Iscariot*' (not to mention the suspicious 'fall' he takes), 'James the brother of John', and quite a few others – including 'Agabus', the 'eunuch' of the Ethiopian Queen, 'Cornelius', and Peter – we are in the area of another substitution being made in the *official history* that directly bears on the downplaying or outright elimination of James from Scripture, this one taking the place of an extremely embarrassing, actual physical assault by Paul on James, which is now recorded only in the Pseudoclementine *Recognitions*.

We are now in a position to deconstruct the received narrative in favour of some of these other curious survivals in early Church history and thus reconstruct the actual history of Jewish Christianity or the Jerusalem Community of James the Just in Palestine. The issue will be between materials, that have somehow ended up in the novelizing history of the Pseudoclementine literature and elsewhere, and the equally novelized material in the first fifteen chapters of the Book of Acts.

The Wicked 'Encompassing' or 'Swallowing' the Righteous in both Eusebius and at Qumran

After James' proclamation of 'the Son of Man coming on the clouds of Heaven', the account preserved by Eusebius presents the masses as 'glorying' in this testimony and crying out – as in Gospel accounts of Jesus' entry into Jerusalem – 'Hosanna to the son of David', which in Hebrew translates out as 'Save us, son of David' (Matt. 21:9–15 and pars.). Regardless of one's view of the accuracy of this response, 'the same Scribes and Pharisees' are pictured as having thought better of their action in giving James such a prominent forum at such a Feast Day, and conspiring with one another:

They said to each other, 'We made a mistake in providing Jesus with such testimony, but let us go up and *cast him* [James] *down* [here *kataballō*], so they – the people – will be frightened and not believe in him.' And they *cried out*, saying 'Oh! Oh! Even the Just One has erred ['is deceived'].'

Not only do we have here the use of James' title 'the *Zaddik*' or 'Zadok' in place of his very name itself and the language of 'casting' Acts is applying to the attack on Stephen; but also the words, 'crying out' (used twice in Hegesippus), to describe the manner in which Scribes and Pharisees addressed James. Acts also uses *these very words*, 'they cried out with a loud voice', to describe the manner in which 'the Elders and the Scribes' of the Sanhedrin 'stopped their ears with their hands and rushed on Stephen with one mind, *casting him out* of the city' (7:57).[43]

Therefore, even in the few words Acts is using here to describe the Sanhedrin trial and stoning of the character it is calling at this point 'Stephen' – no real introduction, no explanation of where he came from or who he was – the link-ups between the main points in the two accounts are very strong, verging almost on identity. In fact, as we just saw, the correspondences are *precise*, since Acts repeats the words, 'cried out in a loud voice', again in its rendition of Stephen's last words – *having gone 'down on his knees, he cried out in a loud voice,* "Do not lay this sin on them"' (7:60). But in the Hegesippus account the words are applied to James, when he cries out 'in a loud voice, "Why do you ask me concerning the Son of Man? He is sitting in Heaven on the right hand of the Great Power."'

It is, also, not without significance that in the Letter of James we have the references to both 'the prayer of the Just One much prevailing' and the 'murder of the Just One' given in the context of allusion to the coming of the Lord of Hosts and final eschatological rain. In Acts, parallel references to the 'murder of the Just One' – in this instance made to apply to Jesus – and 'those who prophesied His coming' precede the actual accomplishment of Stephen's murder. In Eusebius' account, a verbatim transcript from Hegesippus, we now have the parallel and immediate averral that in perpetrating this event – the stoning of the Just One James –

they fulfilled the Prophecy written in Isaiah, 'Let us take away the Just One, for he is abhorrent to us, wherefore they shall eat the fruit of their doings.'[44]

This version of the passage in question, Isaiah 3:10, is not the same as that of the received version, 'Say to the Righteous, all is well, for they [the

445

Evil] shall eat the fruit of their doings.' Once again we are presented with a conundrum: different scriptural traditions retain different accounts of key materials, in this case, diametrically opposed. The passage, as it occurs in Eusebius, is rather to be found in the version that has come down to us in the Greek Septuagint. Either it or the received version has been changed, garbled, or reversed in favour of a given exposition.

This is often the case at Qumran, where a certain passage is varied ever so slightly to aid in a desired exegesis. Here it may be happening in early Church texts as well. But the important thing is that the vocabulary that so appealed to the sectaries at Qumran and early Christianity is present. In this case, as at Qumran generally, it is the contrast of the Wicked doing something Evil to the Righteous – even including the additional tell-tale play on 'eating', here implying punishment or vengeance. Similar passages are present in other documents from Qumran, for instance, at the beginning of the Habakkuk *Pesher*, where the words, 'the Wicked encompasses the Righteous', basically begin the exegesis (Hab. 1:4 – note also Habakkuk 1:13, where the usage 'swallowing' occurs as well).

Passages such as these at Qumran are usually interpreted in terms of something terrible happening to the Righteous Teacher. The same is true in this parallel early Church account relating to James. This is persuasive evidence that this kind of scriptural exegesis, involving the same vocabulary, was in use at Qumran regarding the Righteous Teacher, as in early Christianity regarding James. Hegesippus himself says as much in elucidating James' cognomens with the comment, 'as the Prophets declare concerning him'.

For the Habakkuk *Pesher*, 'the *Zaddik* is the *Moreh ha-Zedek*' (that is, the Righteous Teacher). In the *Pesher* on Psalm 37, another '*Zaddik*' text, passages like, 'the Wicked plots against the Righteous' (Ps. 37:12) or 'the Wicked watches out for the Righteous and tries to put him to death' (37:32), are subjected to this same kind of exegesis. Therefore, the usage '*Zaddik*' in any underlying text from Scripture is almost without exception interpreted in Qumran exegesis to mean 'the Righteous Teacher'. This is parallel to the way Isaiah 3:10 is being expounded in early Church accounts having to do with James – not to mention others being applied to Jesus in the New Testament. Again, this is what Hegesippus seems to have meant by asserting 'as the Prophets declare concerning him'.

However, if one looks at the other usages contained in these key passages about these deaths, one can go further than this. 'Righteous' and 'Evil' in any biblical text are almost always interpreted in Qumran usage

446

to mean 'the Righteous Teacher' and 'the Wicked Priest' respectively. Where the biography of James is concerned, these would be James and his nemesis, the High Priest Ananus. On one occasion, 'Evil' in the underlying text (Hab. 1:13) is applied to the second adversary of the Righteous Teacher, 'the Liar', and others of his persuasion, seemingly 'the Traitors', terminology also known to the New Testament. The former is described as 'rejecting the *Torah* in the midst of their whole Congregation'. In James' biography, such an individual would be equivalent to his ideological adversary, Paul.

The actual usage in Habakkuk 1:13 is, 'the Wicked swallows up one more Righteous than he' (*'balla'* – used in the sense of 'destroying' and paralleling our 'eating'/'consuming' allusions just signalled above).[45] As we have been remarking, these letters, *B–L–'*, also at the root of the Hebrew names 'Belial' and 'Balaam', strangely as it may seem, appear to go, too, into parallel accounts of the death of James in the Greek and the usage we have been highlighting with regard to these, *'ballō'*, 'casting' or 'throwing down' – not to mention the Greek parallel embodied in the peculiar nominative, 'the *Diabolos*' or 'Devil'. These parallel, if somewhat lateral usages, fairly permeate Gospel narratives and New Testament usage generally.

At Qumran, important usages like these are legion and seem to provide the *modus operandi* the sectaries used to choose the texts they wished to interpret. These include 'the Poor' (*Ebion*), 'the Meek' (*'Ani*, a synonym for 'the Poor' in Psalm 37:15), 'Lebanon' (Hab. 2:17), 'plotting', 'booty', 'Riches', 'Anger'/'Wrath', 'Perfection', etc. Psalm 37, for instance, contains allusions to: 'though he *falls*, he shall not *be cast down*' (24) and 'the Salvation of the Righteous Ones is from the Lord. He is their *Protection*' (39). The same phrase, 'Protection on the day of trouble', occurs in Nahum 1:7 in passages also subjected to exegesis at Qumran.[46]

Had the Qumran exegete gone on to chapter 3 of Habakkuk (he stops at the end of chapter 2), he would most certainly have been in familiar terrain; for there one finds allusions to 'Anger', 'devouring the Meek' (Hab. 3:14), God riding upon His 'chariots of Salvation' and going forth with His Messiah 'for Salvation' (*Yesha'* – Hab. 3:8 and 13). Where 'devouring the Meek' (*'Ani*) is concerned, the verb used is again the familiar 'eating' above. It is certainly not impossible that further *peshers* on passages such as these were originally part of the Qumran repertoire, and either were not written down or did not survive. The same can be said for a prophet like Isaiah, where, for example, there are already several *pesher*s at Qumran on a good many passages familiar to us from early Christian usage.

If one looks at the usages surrounding the Isaiah 3:10 passage, applied above in Hegesippus to the death of James, one finds similar vocabulary – for instance, 'Lebanon' imagery (Isa. 2:13) – another favourite at Qumran, particularly where the fall of the Temple and the Priesthood is concerned. In fact, almost every occurrence of 'Lebanon' in the Bible is subjected to exegesis at Qumran, even in the extant corpus. These occur mostly in Isaiah and Habakkuk above, but also in a particularly pregnant context of apocalyptic final 'Judgement', 'whirlwind', and 'Flood' from Nahum 1:4, remarked earlier. In Rabbinic literature, 'the fall of the cedars of Lebanon' is a metaphor for the fall of the Temple, specifically the one in 70 CE, the 'whiteness' inherent in the Hebrew, playing on the *white linen* the Priests wore in the Temple, not to mention the fact that the Temple had originally been constructed out of *cedar wood*.[47]

There is also reference to causing the people 'to go astray and swallowing the Way of Your Paths' (3:12), 'Tongue' imagery (3:8), 'grinding the face of the Poor' and 'robbing the spoils of the Poor' (3:14–15, both using the ''*Ani*' of Habakkuk 3:14 above and the second paralleled exactly in the Damascus Document and Habakkuk *Pesher*),[48] 'the Lord of Hosts taking away from Jerusalem and Judah the stay and the staff' (3:1), 'foreigners devouring' the country (1:7 – 'eating it', again the exact sense of the Habakkuk *Pesher* on Habakkuk 1:16–17 and Isaiah 31:8 in the War Scroll above), 'washing clean' (1:16 and 4:4), and 'idolatry' (2:18).

The context of this allusion to 'idolatry' is particularly interesting. Just as at the end of the Habakkuk *Pesher*, it is eschatological condemning idols. The apocalyptic material condemning 'the Rich' at the end of the Letter of James speaks in exactly the same way – 'your gold and silver are being eaten away . . . your flesh eaten like fire' (5:2–3). Isaiah 2:20 expresses this as 'casting your idols of silver and gold . . . to the moles and the bats', which, in turn, is contained in a general allusion to final, apocalyptic Judgement and 'going into the clefts of the rocks . . . when the Lord arises to violently shake the earth' (2:18–21), more or less paralleling the allusion to fiery earthquake and torrential Flood in Nahum 1:5–8 above, also subjected to exegesis in the Nahum *Pesher* at Qumran. All of these could easily be interpreted in terms of an oracle to flee from Jerusalem because of impending, violent and fiery catastrophe.[49]

There is even the tell-tale allusion to the favourite usage at Qumran, B–L–' or 'swallowing', in Isaiah 3:12 above. This occurs *directly following*

Isaiah 3:9–11, applied to James' death in Hegesippus, and following this, 'leading the people astray', an allusion also found at both the beginning of and in the Last Column of the Damascus Document, where the teaching of 'the Liar' is being described. Perhaps coincidentally, perhaps not, all of these allusions are then followed in Isaiah 3:13 with another to 'standing' again – in this instance, 'the Lord *standing up to judge the Peoples*'.

It is hard to believe that such a fortuitous conjunction of images would not have appealed to our sectaries. This crucial *B–L–'* language circle, as we have been implying, is pregnant with meaning when discussing the destruction of 'the Righteous Teacher' at Qumran, as it will be when discussing James. At Qumran, it will not only be applied to what the Wicked Priest did to the Righteous Teacher, but also the Vengeance God, in turn, would take on him for 'swallowing the Righteous Teacher'.

As the Habakkuk *Pesher* pointedly puts it, just as the Wicked Priest 'swallowed him' or 'swallowed them' (the followers of the Righteous Teacher, called 'the *Ebionim*', even though '*Ebionim*' nowhere appears as such in the underlying Habakkuk text at this point); so too 'would he be paid the reward which he paid the Poor', always combined with the reiteration of the idea of God's Vengeance – 'God would condemn him to destruction' – for what he had done to the Righteous Teacher.[50]

This is also expressed in terms of another genre of imagery, pregnant with meaning for the parallel contexts we are discussing here – 'Cup' imagery, symbolizing God's retribution and which we shall elucidate further as we proceed – or 'the Cup of the Wrath of God would come around to' or 'swallow him' as well. This is the imagery Paul will use to such momentous effect when developing his ideas about 'the Cup of the New Covenant in his – Christ's – blood'; Luke 2:20 adds notably, 'which is poured out for you'.

This notion of retribution is also the context of these lines applied by early Church exegetes to the death of James, 'Let us remove the Just One, for he is abhorrent to us.' Taken according to the received version, the line following this reads:

> Woe unto the Wicked. It shall be ill with him, for the Reward [*Gamul*] of his hands will be done to him. (3:11)

The very same word, '*Gamul*' or 'Reward', used in exactly the same way, is brought into the crucial description of the destruction of the Righteous Teacher in the Habakkuk *Pesher* and how the Wicked Priest, who 'plotted to destroy the Poor', 'swallowed him', meaning the Righteous

Teacher. As this is then put, 'the Reward which he paid the Poor would be paid to him'. Here the word *'Gamul'* ('Reward') again comes into play as in Isaiah 3:11 and as we saw it above in the War Scroll on 'the Poor'. That we are, in these lines surrounding Isaiah 3:10 applied in early Church literature to the death of James, in a similar exegetical framework to that of Qumran should be patent.

The conclusion is, therefore, simple. Since this material about the Wicked 'being paid the Reward he paid' others from Isaiah 3:10–11 nowhere appears in the materials from Habakkuk under consideration, it is clear that the writers at Qumran knew this material from Isaiah 3:10–11 and were incorporating it into their presentation of *the death of their 'Righteous Teacher'*. In other words, the Community of James in Jerusalem and the Community at Qumran were using the exact same passage in exactly the same way and applying it to the destruction respectively of two leaders, James the Just and the Righteous Teacher. One could not ask for more powerful proof of their identity than this.[51]

James' Death in the Account of Hegesippus

As the Eusebius extract from Hegesippus finishes the account of the stoning of James the Just:

> So they went up and *cast down the Just One* [*kataballō* – again James' cognomen used in the place of the name itself], saying to one another, 'Let us *stone* James the Just,' and they began to stone him, since *the fall* had not killed him.

In fact, this parallels almost completely the account in Acts of Stephen's stoning, including the very same repetitions of the words 'stoning' and 'casting', not to mention the tell-tale allusion to the 'fall' James took, which reappears in both Stephen's *'falling* to his knees' and the bloody 'fall' Judas *Iscariot* takes at the beginning of Acts.

It will be recalled that Acts' account is preceded by Stephen's verbal attack on the Jews as 'receiving the Law and not keeping it' (7:52–53) – this as part and parcel of his charge that they 'killed all the Prophets' and were 'Traitors' because they put 'the Just One' to death. In the Habakkuk *Pesher*, such 'Traitors' are 'Traitors to the New Covenant'. Amid allusions to 'Covenant-Breakers', their opposite number, 'the Keepers of His Commandments' – or our proverbial 'Sons of Zadok' again – actually seem to participate with God in 'executing of Judgement on the Peoples', while it is the Wicked Priest, not Jews generally, who is condemned and taken to *Gehenna* for admonishment. It is interesting, too, that just as Stephen hurls the charge of being 'uncircumcised in heart' against the Jews generally (7:51), in the Habakkuk *Pesher* this is hurled against the Wicked Priest.[52]

In looking at the description of Stephen's death again, it would be well to repeat the echo one finds there of James' words to the assembled Passover crowds about the Son of Man coming on the clouds of Heaven. The account of Stephen's last words in Acts reads (as we saw):

> Looking up to Heaven, he [Stephen] saw the Glory of God and Jesus stand-ing at the right hand of God. He *cried out*, 'Look, I see the Heavens open-ing and the Son of Man standing on the right hand of God ['standing' repeated twice for emphasis]. And *crying out in a loud voice*, they . . . rushed on him with one accord, and *casting him out* of the city, they *stoned him* . . . And they stoned Stephen *as he prayed* . . . and *falling down on his knees, he cried out in a loud voice*, 'Lord, do not account this sin to them.' (Acts 7:55–60)

For its part, Hegesippus' account of James' stoning continues as follows:

> But he turned and *fell to his knees*, saying, 'I beseech You, O Lord God and Father, *forgive them, for they know not what they do.'*

There are so many important overlaps in these brief descriptions of the two stonings that it is difficult to know which ones to stress more. As previously observed, the theme of 'falling to his knees' is common to both accounts. Surprisingly, too, it is an element in the account of James' 'knees becoming as hard as a camel's' in the original picture of James' praying in the Inner Sanctum of the Temple and a general fixture of these accounts. The note of 'crying out in a loud voice' we have already seen to be common to both, as James is pictured as 'crying out in a loud voice', and, of course, in all accounts he always *starts to pray* at this point. Finally the words attributed to James not only parallel Stephen's at this point in Acts, but are the precise words attributed to Jesus in Luke 23:34.

Where the 'casting down' or 'falling' goes, we shall have occasion to inspect such language further to determine whether at some point James 'was cast down' or 'fell', or both. In fact, this element probably first appears in the story of the attack by Paul on James in the Pseudoclementine *Recognitions*. This work first appeared in the West in Latin owing to the efforts of one Rufinus of Aquileia (*d.* 410 CE), a friend of Jerome's, who wrote a preface to both it and the *Homilies* at the end of the fourth century.

But the work itself undoubtedly goes back to much earlier materials, including some mentioned by Hegesippus, Origen, and Epiphanius' so-called '*Anabathmoi Jacobou*'. Jerome, himself, also clearly knew parts of it, either as the 'Travels of' or 'Teaching of Peter', but he and Rufinus eventually fell out doctrinally, perhaps even as a result of things like the latter's publishing this document. Though there is no extant Greek version of it, there is a Syriac one, which accords well with Eusebius' own finding of previously forgotten or overlooked materials in Syriac archives.

The attack on James by Paul that it presents – *in the 40s not the 60s* – takes the place of the attack on Stephen in the Book of Acts, after which, even in Acts, Paul is pictured as going berserk in a frenzy of riotous behaviour. As the *Recognitions* vividly pictures it, whether in Rufinus' Latin or the Syriac, this attack is a physical one too and results in the tell-tale 'fall' James takes, but this time *not his death*. The 'fall' in the allusion to James' and Stephen's death in both the Hegesippus/Eusebius version and in Acts really paves the way to connecting the two attacks and sorting out some of the conflicting elements.

The 'fall' James takes from a great height in the 40s does not result in his death, merely injury. Instead, he flees to Jericho (in the region of Qumran) and lives to fight again another day. It is this that becomes confused and for various linguistic reasons, which we shall come to understand, is played upon in all the early Church accounts of James' death as they have come down to us. Even, as we have them, these accounts appreciate that James was not killed in this 'fall' – it took a stoning to do this – and even Acts' replacement account seems already to be conserving some of the sense of these variations by having Stephen 'fall to his knees' (one will find similar motifs in the Second Apocalypse of James from Nag Hammadi). Whatever one finally makes of this, at least it preserves the curious motif of the matter of James' 'knees'.

As the *Recognitions* puts this attack on James by the Enemy Paul *in the 40s not the 60s*:

> Our James began to show . . . that the two advents of him [Jesus] are fore-told: one in humiliation, which he has accomplished; *the other in Glory* [Acts 7:55's Stephen 'filled with the Holy Spirit, looking into Heaven, and seeing *the Glory of God*'] . . . And when matters were at that point . . . *an Enemy* [a marginal note in one of the manuscripts identifies this 'Enemy' as Paul] *entered the Temple with a few others* and began to cry out [our 'crying

out' again] . . . to excite the people and raise a tumult . . . Therefore he
began to drive all into confusion with shouting . . . and like a madman,
excite everyone to murder. (cf. Acts 8:3)

Then ensued a tumult on either side of beating and the beaten. Much blood
was shed and there was a confused flight, in the midst of which *the Enemy
attacked James* and *threw him headlong from the top of the steps* [the
'Pinnacle of the Temple' motif in other accounts], and supposing him to be
dead [the Syriac adds, 'since he fell'], did not care to inflict further violence
upon him [the 'violence'/'Violent Ones' in the Scrolls]. But our friends lifted
him up, for they were more numerous . . . and we returned to the house of
James [the 'house' in Jerusalem, to which Peter goes to leave a message for
'James and the brothers' in Acts 12:20] and spent the night there in prayer.
Then before daylight we went down to Jericho to the number of five
thousand men.[53]

This is then followed by the information that 'the Enemy' received letters
from the Chief Priests to go to Damascus 'to arrest all who believed in
Jesus, and with the help of Unbelievers [language later typical of Islam]
throw the Faithful into confusion' (compare with Acts 9:22's account of
how Paul 'confounded the Jews who dwelt in Damascus'),[54] which makes
it unmistakable that it is Paul we have to do with in this account.

This is the attack that is replaced by the stoning of Stephen in the
orthodox story, as it finally emerged and came down to us in Acts. In the
writer's view, there is *no* 'Stephen', except a Stephen in Corinth, Paul's
first convert in Achaia or Peloponnesian Greece, or another in Josephus,
'the Emperor's servant Stephen', attacked in the neighbourhood of
Jerusalem by rampaging 'Zealots', who may in any event have been the
same individual as Paul's colleague in Corinth.[55]

The 'Stephen' in Acts is a fictitious stand-in, as are quite a few other
characters we have already called attention to in Acts (there will be
more) – this one for the attack by Paul on James in the early 40s, which
was evidently considered so embarrassing by early Church writers that it
was unmentionable – but not forgotten. This is basically the only difference, too, between the account called the Pseudoclementine *Recognitions*
and the Pseudoclementine *Homilies*. In the *Homilies*, as we saw, the
attack by Paul on James and its circumstances have also been deleted and
the narrative reformed accordingly.

As this somehow metamorphoses in Acts' final presentation, it is reconstituted with elements taken from *the stoning of James*, which early
Church tradition considers to have occurred in the 60s. We shall show

how the particulars of these two attacks can be harmonized below. This account in Acts, as to some extent the presentation of Jesus in the Gospels, was manufactured with an anti-Semitic patina, which over the millennia has not failed to have its effect. When Qumran referred to its adversary as 'the Liar' and the embodiment of all 'Lying' – insults later picked up somehow in Islamic tradition and turned against Judaism and Christianity generally[56] – presumably it knew whereof it spoke.

One should finish the description of James' stoning in the 60s as Eusebius has conserved it. This is found in one form or another in a variety of sources, including now Nag Hammadi and Manichaean. It concludes in the following manner:

> Thus they were stoning him, when one of the Priests of the sons of Rechab, the son of those Rechabites [Eusebius/Hegesippus, as noted, gives the Hebrew plural here, 'Rechabim', literally transliterated into the Greek – thus, bespeaking its antiquity], spoken of by *Jeremiah the Prophet* [it will be recalled, the same words mistakenly occur in Matthew 27:9 about Judas, when Zechariah is intended. In 27:5 it is Judas who 'throws down' the coins], cried out, saying, 'Stop what you are doing, the Just One is praying for you.' And one among them, who was a fuller [a laundryman], took the club with which he beat out clothes and struck the Just One on the head . . . Thus, he suffered martyrdom, and they buried him on the spot by the Temple, and *his monument is still there by the Temple* . . . And immediately Vespasian began to besiege them.

This then is the account of the martyrdom of James given by Eusebius, purportedly a word-for-word translation of Hegesippus. Except for mix-ups between the Temple and Holy of Holies and regarding James' bathing habits, this seems likely.

Eusebius adds the pious words, whether his own or Hegesippus': 'He became a true witness both to Jews and to Greeks that Jesus is the Christ', and then moves on, giving the relevant materials from Josephus, to connect the siege of Jerusalem and the destruction of the Temple to *James' death*.

James' Burial Marker, Judas *Iscariot*'s *Fall*, and *the Field of Blood* Again

The refererence Eusebius preserves to a grave-marker or monument to James at the place 'where he fell' is interesting and not without relevance. Eusebius or his source – it is impossible to tell which – certainly considers it was still there at the time of writing. This would mean either the second or the fourth century. Had Eusebius, who like Hegesippus came from Palestine, not seen it, one imagines he might have mentioned this. Jerome does in his seemingly more precise variation on the tradition:

> His tombstone with its inscription was well known until the siege of Titus and the end of Hadrian's reign [meaning Jerome did not see it].[57]

Regardless of chronology, there can be little doubt that *someone saw* James' grave-marker or monument outside the Temple in the Kedron Valley at some point. This is directly beneath the Temple-compound walls as one looks down from what is being called in these traditions 'the Pinnacle of the Temple'. Somehow the tradition developed that James was pushed down from here, a place too from which Jesus was supposedly tempted 'by the Devil' to jump in Gospel Temptation-narrative traditions.

Today there are still funerary monuments there from the Second Temple, one of which identified as 'the Tomb of St James'. The tradition, identifying James' tomb with this monument at the bottom of the Mount of Olives in the Kedron Valley beneath 'the Pinnacle of the Temple', is very old and Jerome seems to know something of it by his words, 'Some of our writers think he was buried on the Mount of Olives, but they are mistaken.' The significance of this monument or marker for the stories that developed about the circumstances and physical aspects of James' death is important. Even today, if one stands on the south-east corner of the Temple wall facing the Mount of Olives and the Kedron below, one readily sees the monument of this tomb.

From the still-legible Hebrew inscription carved on the stone within, it can be identified as the sepulchre of the Priestly Course of the Bnei-Hezir, one of the priestly clans returning with either Ezra or Nehemiah from the Babylonian Captivity (Neh. 10:20). This in no way invalidates it as related to James' family, since the relationship of James' maternal – if not paternal – priestly ancestors to one or another of the priestly clans is impossible to determine. Interestingly enough, the names listed in the dedicatory inscription appear to be from the family known as 'the Boethusians', the priestly clan Herod brought in from Egypt after he executed his Maccabean wife to marry their daughter – also called Mariamme.[58] In the next generation, one Joezer b. Boethus becomes the direct opponent of Josephus' Judas and *Saddok* in the matter of the non-payment of the newly imposed Roman tax at the time of the Census of Quirinius.

In fact, the takeover of this tomb, implied by its association with James' burial, might be the root of another highly prized, but almost certainly mythological, tradition about a 'Joseph of Arimathaea' donating his richly appointed tomb *for the burial of Jesus* (Matt. 27:57 and pars.). 'Joseph of Arimathaea' is another name with no historical substance whatsoever, and the place his sobriquet is supposed to represent has never been identified.59 As we shall see in Volume II, this may be another instance of traditions about James retrospectively being absorbed into traditions about Jesus.

However this may be, one can certainly envision a set of circumstances where someone conversant with the tradition about James' 'fall', looking down on the Kedron Valley Tomb from the walls of the compound of the Temple, might have imagined the tomb – so clearly visible below – implied that James took this fabulous 'fall' from 'the Pinnacle of the Temple', when in reality he only 'fell' from the Temple steps during the attack by 'the Enemy' Paul. The Pinnacle 'fall', of course, few could have survived, which is the thrust of its transmogrification into the story of Jesus' Temptation by the Devil in Matthew and Luke.

The element about James' 'headlong fall' also reappears, as already explained, in the story about the 'headlong fall' that Judas *Iscariot* – another largely mythological character with a curious surname – supposedly takes in the Book of Acts, accompanied by its own suitably bloodthirsty details. This, too, was connected with some kind of burial ground. Called the 'the Field of Blood' in Acts and Matthew, Matthew also identifies it as 'the Potter's Field', a field supposedly 'for the burial of strangers' or possibly even 'the Poor'. Interestingly enough, too, as we saw, it is connected to 'Rechabite' priestly traditions, and by extrapolation, 'Essenes'.

It will be recalled that the story was told at the beginning of Acts as part of the 'election' scenario to explain why it was necessary to fill the 'Episcopate' of Judas and the defeated candidate was called 'Justus' even in Greek (1:23). Having 'bought a field out of the reward for un-Righteousness, he fell headlong [this word 'headlong' is approximately the word used in the description of James' fall from *the Temple steps* in the Pseudoclementines, when attacked by the Enemy Paul] and *bursting open, all his bowels gushed out.*' The parallel with the fall James takes, where his head is burst open from the blow of the fuller's club in all early Church sources above, should also be clear.

We are again in the area of fictional refurbishment. Even though these are some of our most cherished cultural heirlooms, the overwritten original elements do, on careful inspection, gleam through. What originally was in the underlying material is impossible to say with precision, only something about the election of James as successor in the Leadership of the Community or 'Bishop', combined with intimations, as should be clear, of what was later to befall him. As already stressed, all materials having a bearing on the family of Jesus, the brothers, or namesakes of anyone connected family-wise to the Messianic Leader, must be treated with the utmost circumspection.

For instance, in this tradition, instead of the curious material about 'a fuller' with his club, we now have an interesting parallel allusion to 'Potters', even though 'the Potter's Field', as such, nowhere appears in the original Prophecy being cited in Matthew, whether from Jeremiah or Zechariah. Both this 'fuller' and this 'Field' are connected in some manner either to death or a burial place. This is not to mention the whole matter of 'the Rechabites', to whom both traditions in some sense also relate. Then there is the notice, also supposed to relate to this 'Prophecy', about coins both being 'thrown' into the Temple Treasury and rejected from it. The last is one of the principal themes of this period, and something we shall have occasion to identify with James' name as well, that is, *the rejection of gifts and sacrifices on behalf of foreigners in the Temple*, the issue that finally started the *War against Rome*.

In passing, one should also note the exposition of this 'Potter's Field' or 'Field of Blood' – either because of Jesus' 'blood', Judas' 'blood', or the 'blood money' Judas finally receives and *casts into the Temple Treasury*, as ultimately having to do with a burial place *for foreigners*. One appreciates how far-fetched many of these connections might superficially appear, but as in so much of the data connected to this subject, the evidence does mount up beyond the coincidental, becoming quite substantial. Their trivialization in episodes such as the one about Judas' 'bursting entrails', however silly or macabre, really does begin to appear quite malevolent. The reader will be the judge.

Interestingly enough, it is not 'the Chief Priests' of the Herodian Period, who reject moneys and gifts such as this, but rather the more 'Zealot' *lower priesthood* of the 40s to the 60s, the same individuals who want to ban Gentiles – including Herodians – from the Temple as polluting it. Not only does this become a principal theme leading up to the Uprising against Rome – one Josephus more and more rails against in his works as the period of the Uprising approaches – in fact, we have identified it as being at the root of one of the 'Three Nets of Belial' accusations in the Fifth Column of the Damascus Document following the eschatological exegesis of the 'Zadokite Covenant' in the Fourth. Even the specific charge of 'polluting the Temple Treasury' occurs in the exposition of this 'pollution of the Temple' charge in the Sixth Column of the Damascus Document. Parallels of this kind, if not finally decisive, are none the less extremely insightful.

Furthermore, if James can be identified as more than simply parallel to 'the Teacher of Righteousness' at Qumran – which he most certainly was – but *actually identical with him*, then the 'Three Nets' of 'Riches', 'fornication' – both paralleled in known materials about James – and 'pollution of the Temple' become prototypically his. In fact, his prohibition of 'things sacrificed to idols' or 'the pollutions of the idols' in Acts' formulation of the results of the 'Jerusalem Council' (15:20–29) – which we shall also show to be at the root of the '*MMT*' correspondence – can be seen as being but one important aspect of the more over-arching 'pollution of the Temple' charge.

It is also interesting that, in explaining this 'pollution of the Temple' charge, the Damascus Document invokes the issue of 'blood', in this instance, not 'the New Covenant in the Cup of His Blood' of Gospel portraiture, but *menstrual blood* and the consonant charge of *sleeping with women in their periods*.[60] It uses this not only to link the 'fornication' with the 'pollution of the Temple' charge, but in doing so, to imply that it is contact with Gentiles, in this case, their gifts and sacrifices in the Temple, that has occasioned the problem of 'pollution of the Temple' in the first place. As the Damascus Document so graphically expresses it in Columns Five and Eight, enlarging on the issues of 'fornication' and 'pollution of the Temple Treasury', 'whoever approaches them cannot be cleansed . . . unless he was forced' – in our view, in this case implying approaching Herodians and other foreigners.[61] But Matthew identifies his 'Field of Blood'/'Potter's Field' in some manner with 'Gentiles' or 'foreigners' too.

The common element in the Matthew and Luke accounts, even though all the rest is contradictory and probably dissembling, this 'Field of Blood' has interesting parallels in the literature of Qumran as well – that is, the 'City of Blood'/'Worthless City' or 'Assembly ['Church'] built upon Blood' allusions encountered in two separate, but parallel, contexts in the Nahum *Pesher* and the Habakkuk *Pesher*. Interesting too, in the former it is connected to evocation of sending emissaries or 'Apostles to the Peoples'; while in the latter, the 'City of Blood' is accompanied by 'building' imagery and interpreted, in turn, in terms of 'leading Many astray' and 'performing a Worthless Service' and 'raising a Congregation ['Church'] upon Lying' – identified with 'the Lying Spouter's' doctrine.[62]

In perhaps our boldest attempt at achieving a synthesis between the Community of James and the Community at Qumran, we have identified these kinds of allusions in the Habakkuk *Pesher* with Paul's 'building a Church' upon Communion, or the consumption of *the Blood of Christ*. As Luke puts it, in his version of the Last Supper in which 'Judas *Iscariot*' too plays a central role and is roundly condemned, 'This Cup is the New Covenant in my Blood, even that which is poured out for you' (22:20).

Not only is the idea of 'pouring out' integrally connected with the Pauline idea of 'the Holy Spirit' in the Book of Acts, but where connections involving plays on language and doctrines at Qumran are concerned, the 'New Covenant' is an all-important aspect of what is going on in the wilderness at 'Damascus' in the document by that name and, as we also saw, 'pouring out' is the root of the way Qumran is referring to 'the Spouter of Lying' – which quite literally means, the 'Pourer-out of Lying'. We shall take one final step more in this regard, when we show that even the word 'Damascus' in Greek (of 'the New Covenant in the Land of Damascus' at Qumran) is being utilized by Paul or these Gospel artificers in some esoteric manner to produce the new formulation, 'the Cup of the New Covenant in my Blood' – 'Blood' and 'Cup' being in Hebrew '*Dam*' and '*Chos*'.

It is in this same Letter to the Corinthians, it should be recalled, that Paul not only ranges himself against James' 'Jerusalem Council' directives prohibiting the consumption of 'blood' and 'things sacrificed to idols', but first develops this idea of 'Communion with the Blood of Christ', however repugnant such a notion might have seemed to such 'Zealot'-minded groups as those at Qumran, not to mention James, who, we have just seen, specifically *forbids it*. It is this doctrine that is retrospectively attributed to Jesus in these highly prized scriptural accounts of the 'Last Supper'. If anything proves the dictum, referred to in the Introduction, that 'Poetry is truer than History', this does.

Paul also develops this idea of 'Communion with the Blood of Christ' by using 'building' imagery as we have seen, at one point even calling himself 'the architect' (1 Cor. 3:10). In the Nahum *Pesher*, a variation of this 'City of Blood' notation is developed in terms of a 'City of Ephraim' and 'those Seeking Smooth Things at the End of Days, who walk in Lying and Unrighteousness'.[63] The imagery is complex, but none the less decipherable.

Therefore, once again, we have come full circle to 'the City of Blood'/ 'City built upon Blood' relating to Paul's understanding of the death of

Christ and the 'Fellowship' or 'Communion', which he stresses, engendered by *the Blood of Christ*. Here too, then, this 'Field of Blood' allusion has its overtones, not all completely straightforward and some esoteric, but none the less part and parcel of the overlaps, plays on words, and doctrinal reversals in the interests of the ongoing Gentile Christian and anti-Semitic (in the national not necessarily the ethnic sense) polemic.

The Trials of Jesus and James for Blasphemy or Political Conspiracy

In these kinds of parallels to the 'headlong fall' Judas *Iscariot* takes, or his suicide, one should once more remark the parody his suicide embodies of the suicide carried out by the '*Sicarii*' followers of 'Judas the Galilean' on Masada three years after the fall of Jerusalem and the implied condemnation of this earlier 'Judas'.[64] Contrariwise, in the Letter of James, Abraham's willingness to sacrifice his son Isaac, not unlike what these extreme '*Sicarii*' did on Masada and 'Zealot' practice generally, might have been seen as the ideological licence for such a 'suicide' or 'Sanctification of the Name' (*Kiddush ha-Shem*)/martyrdom. In James, of course (and following this, as usual, the Koran), it is taken as the supreme testing of the Faith of this archetypal 'Friend of God' and the epitome of the most elevated sort of 'works Righteousness' (2:21); while in Hebrews, *per contra*, it is taken as the most elevated example of his 'Faith' (11:17).

The conspiratorial note, also part and parcel of this account of Judas' 'Treachery' (not to mention the usage 'delivered up', which is over and over again used in the Dead Sea Scrolls – particularly the Damascus Document – with completely opposite signification), and that of 'blasphemy', repeatedly reiterated in the Gospels' scenario for Jesus' trial, are also present in the James scenario. In the case of James, the cast of characters is slightly different – the 'conspiracy' being between Ananus and the King Herod Agrippa II. This same sense of 'the Wicked Priest conspiring to destroy the Poor' is also present in the Habakkuk *Pesher*, that is, between the Herodian King and the High Priest appointed by him, not between 'the Chief Priests' and the largely mythological 'Judas *Iscariot*' – whose name has now become proverbial for 'Treachery' – of Gospel narration.

The Gospel of John even brings the Kedron Valley into this arrest scene (18:1), in which the tomb beneath the Pinnacle of the Temple assigned in Christian tradition to James is located, though, for Acts, the Mount of Olives is a 'Sabbath's distance' from Jerusalem (1:12), which was probably meant to show that Jesus did not go beyond 'the Sabbath limit'.

This inadvertently vividly illustrates the derivative nature of these narratives, the Mount of Olives being about fifteen minutes' walk from the east-facing Gate of the Temple or 'the Steps' leading up to the gate on the south side of the compound, showing knowledge of the dictum, known in both Rabbinic literature and at Qumran, that 'the Sabbath limit' was about half a mile.[65]

One should note that in the material prefacing Matthew's picture of Judas' suicide, now it is the High Priest who tries to identify 'the Christ' with 'the Son of God' (26:63 and pars.). It is at this point that Jesus, like James in the Hegesippus narrative, announces to him and the rest of the Sanhedrin that 'You shall see the Son of Man sitting at the right hand of *Power* and *coming on the clouds of Heaven*' (26:64). For Luke, the question is, 'are you then the Son of God' and in Jesus' reply, 'the Son of Man' is simply '*seated at the right hand of the Power of God*' (22:69–70).

It is at this point that the High Priest 'rends his clothes' and accuses Jesus of 'blasphemy'. Consulting the Chief Priests and the members of the Sanhedrin, pictured as assembled at 'his House' in the middle of the night, these together pronounce him 'worthy of death' (Matt. 26:65–66; Mark 14:64). But this is the same sequence of the scenario of James' proclamation in the Temple of 'the Son of Man standing on the right hand of the Great Power' and his condemnation for 'blasphemy' by the Sanhedrin, convened by the High Priest. On these points there would appear to be overlaps between the two narratives and elements of Jesus' narrative are being absorbed into that of James, or vice versa – probably vice versa.

But, if James really did go into the Holy of Holies of the Temple to pronounce the Holy Name of God in a kind of *Yom Kippur* atonement – the basis of the charge of 'blasphemy' in the *Talmud*[66] – such a charge more suits the circumstances of James' stoning, the punishment for blasphemy, than it does the crucifixion of Jesus. For Roman juridical practice, crucifixion, as remarked, is one of the punishments for insurrection and has little, if anything, to do with blasphemy. Typically, in the Synoptics anyhow, Jesus is pictured as remaining silent and refusing to answer – except for small, annoying responses – any and all questions about the basically parallel 'Son of Man', 'Christ', and 'Son of God' notations.

But the parallels do not end here, Matthew continues, that

They spat in his face [instead of breaking open his 'head' as in the accounts of James or the ban on 'spitting in their midst or to their right' in accounts of 'Essenes'], beat on him, and some struck him with the palm of the hand [instead of 'with the laundryman's club' – Matt. 26:67 and pars.].

This is immediately followed by materials about Jesus being 'a Galilean' and 'a Nazoraean' (Matt. 26:69–71 – in Mark 14:70/Luke 22:69, it is *Peter*, rather, who is *mistaken for* 'a Galilean'), Judas' suicide and the High Priests buying 'the Potter's Field', and the interview with Pilate.

Appropriately, in line with the punishment of crucifixion for 'sedition' not stoning for 'blasphemy', after the intervening episode of what to purchase with Judas *Iscariot*'s 'hire' in Matthew, the twin issues of Jesus' Kingship and whether it is Lawful to pay the tribute money to Caesar are raised. In Luke, who adds this second part of the charge sheet, this reads:

> We found this man perverting our nation, *forbidding* [*the nation*] *to give tribute to Caesar*, and *claiming himself to be Christ, a King*. (23:2)

This charge about 'forbidding to pay the tax to Caesar' – aside from the related one about 'claiming to be a King' – as previously remarked is utterly surprising, since the Gospels go to such lengths to portray Jesus as recommending just the opposite (Luke 20:22–25 and pars.).

The recommendation 'to pay the tribute', of course, as explained above, is the Pauline position delineated in Romans 13:6–7, presented in conjunction no less with or, as a consequence of, the Righteousness or Love Commandment, 'You shall love your neighbour as yourself' (13:9). The contrary of this position in the charge sheet as presented in Luke accords rather with Pilate's condemnation of Jesus for 'sedition' that follows (Luke 23:24 and pars.) – as it does the stance in the Scrolls, rejecting gifts and sacrifices in the Temple on behalf of foreigners, including the Roman Emperor that triggers *the War against Rome*. In our view, forbidding the people to pay the tax in this charge sheet in Luke was the *authentic* position of the Messianic Movement in Palestine and all its *bona-fide* representatives – there being no Messianism in Palestine that *recognized the Roman Emperor*.

Pilate is now pictured as asking whether Jesus was 'King of the Jews' (Matt. 27:11 and pars.), a question appropriate to the crucifixion penalty for 'sedition' that ensues. Crucifixion would not have been imposed for 'blasphemy', a charge more in accord with James pronouncing the forbidden Name of God in the Holy of Holies and ultimately the 'stoning' that ensues. If Jesus was or did claim to be 'a King', in particular without Roman authorization, the implication is that this was a treasonable offence.

For Luke, Herod even asks if Jesus is 'a Galilean' (23:6), clearly meaning, since we have just been talking about *the tax issue* and, not unconnectedly, Judas *Iscariot* ('the *Sicarios*'), someone of the stripe of Judas the *Galilean*. The identification of Peter as 'a Galilean' by 'one of the High Priest's maids' in all three Gospels (Mark 14:66–69 and pars.) is on the order of Acts' picture of Peter speaking to 'Rhoda the maid' at 'the house of Mary the mother of John Mark' to leave a message for James (Acts 12:13–17).

For his part, Pilate is pictured as tendentiously intepreting this, as throughout New Testament Scripture, to mean Jesus *comes from Galilee* – a point Luke now uses to move over to an intervening interview with 'Herod', missing from the other Gospels, because the administrative jurisdiction of this 'Herod' theoretically included Galilee! This intervening interview is more in accord with the probably true picture of Paul's conversations in Acts 25:23–26:32. After an interview in Caesarea with the Roman Governor Felix and his consort Drusilla 'the Jewess', *Paul* moves along to an interview with *Herod* (Agrippa II) and his consort, Bernice, the future mistress of Titus.

Theoretically, the 'Herod' who interviews Jesus is the same *Herod the Tetrarch* (Herod Antipas) who condemned John the Baptist in a similar scenario, because he too had administrative jursidiction across Jordan in Perea on the eastern side of the Dead Sea. There now follows the material in Matthew 27:19–24 about Pilate and Pilate's wife wishing 'nothing to do with' or being 'guiltless of the blood of this Righteous One' (repeated twice – clearly of the same order of historical merit as the irresistible dance Salome did at Herod's 'birthday party'), which, again, has more to do with the nomenclature of the James story than of the Jesus scenario before us. This episode culminates, as will be recalled, in that terrible cry in Matthew 27:25 that has haunted Western Civilization ever since: '*His blood* be upon us and on our children' – another of these variations on the 'blood' scenario.

But the ultimate reason behind all these feints and sleights of hand is simple. Josephus straightforwardly presents it when he states in his Preface to the *Jewish War* – to repeat:

> The war of the Jews against the Romans was the greatest of our time, greater too, perhaps than any recorded struggle whether between cities or nations. Yet persons with *no first-hand knowledge*, accepting baseless and inconsistent stories on hearsay, have written garbled accounts of it; while those of *eyewitnesses have been falsified either to flatter the Romans or to vilify the Jews*, eulogy or abuse being substituted for accurate historical record.

One could not wish for a more prescient comment historically speaking. This essentially sums up the situation with regard to historical writing in this period – this in a preface, in which, Josephus otherwise claims that:

> The Romans *unwillingly set fire to the Temple* . . . as Titus Caesar, *the Temple's destroyer* has testified. For throughout the war, he [Titus] *pitied the common people*, who were helpless against the Revolutionaries . . . *And for our misfortunes we have only ourselves to blame.*

One should note that Josephus' picture of the Romans 'unwillingly setting fire to the Temple' matches the Gospel picture of Roman Governors and their Herodian minions *unwillingly condemning Christian Leaders to death*. To make the parallel even more immediate, one has only to remember that in the Gospels, as per Paul's ideas above, Jesus is the Temple![67]

These are the kinds of insights that can emerge from looking at the parallels in a seemingly inconsequential story like that of the 'headlong fall' Judas *Iscariot* supposedly takes and how his stomach 'burst open', and comparing it with that of the story of the ' headlong fall' James takes in early Church sources, either from the Pinnacle of the Temple or its steps.

The reason we opt for the historicity of the James materials – with reservations – over the Gospels is that they are more consistent and *make more sense in the historical context*. It is that simple – historical sense can be made out of them, which is more than can be said for the story of 'Judas *Iscariot*'s stomach bursting open', or, for that matter, the story of Jesus being condemned by the High Priest for 'blasphemy' and taken for 'a Righteous One', first by Pontius Pilate's wife and then, Pilate himself.

This is the same Pilate whom Philo records as the most bloodthirsty among the Governors in Palestine. Nor did Pilate scruple to shed human 'blood' and he was removed on this account by – of all people – the equally bloodthirsty and insane Caligula. The testimony about the attack on James in the Temple and James' 'fall' is extremely important and makes sense, that is, elements from it can be fitted into the historical background of Palestine and what we know from other sources and they mesh. Before going on to resolve those elements which do not make sense and which are either overwrites, garbled tradition, or out-and-out fraud, it is important to remark that these stories about 'Judas *Iscariot*', 'Stephen', 'Mary the mother of John Mark', 'John the brother of James' – often even Jesus himself – make the material relating to James' death, his being buried on the spot where he 'fell' (connecting with 'the Potters Field'/'Field of Blood' story about 'Judas' above), very old indeed.

If we accept the basic core of historicity in them – and there is a lot to accept in Hegesippus' materials (paralleled by those in the Pseudo-clementine *Recognitions* and what remains of the lost *Anabathmoi Jacobou* in Epiphanius' excerpts, regardless of how these have been trans-mogrified or garbled in the accounts by Clement of Alexandria, Origen, Eusebius, Jerome, and the two Apocalypses of James from Nag Hammadi) – then we have to accept a central core of material about James, together with its tell-tale notices about a 'fall' of some kind, his proclamation of 'the Son of Man coming on the clouds of Heaven' in the Temple at Passover (attributed to Jesus in the Gospels), the charge of 'blasphemy', his 'stoning', and the various allusions to 'the Righteous One', 'his knees', the 'efficaciousness of his prayer', and his 'falling to his knees and praying', at least as old as the earliest redactions of Gospel accounts and the Book of Acts. These latter contain the same or parallel materials about their heroes or, sometimes, their enemies.

The traditions about James, therefore, were known and had already begun to be overwritten at least by the time of the *earliest appearance of parallel materials* now in the New Testament documents we are so familiar with and which have become cornerstones of Western culture. When was this? Dare we say probably before 100 CE? Justin Martyr, for instance, who was born in Samaria but afterwards lived in Asia Minor, by the 130s appears to know many Gospel traditions and stories, particularly those of Matthew and Luke – which he calls 'the Memoirs of the Apostles', but not exactly in the form we have them. However, he shows little, if any, knowledge of the Book of Acts. Nor does he mention Paul's name at all, though he does have a quasi-parallel theology. Justin, for instance, knows Isaiah 3:10 in the *Septuagint* version above, 'Let us bind the Just One, for he is abhorrent to us'; but, interestingly, he is already applying it to *Jesus'* death not *James'*.[68]

15

The Death of James in its Historical Setting

The Stoning of James in Other Early Church Sources

Eusebius now goes on to present the passages from Josephus that have relevance to James' trial and execution, as well as those – discussed above – which connect the fate of Jerusalem to what happened to him. These materials for the most part do exist in the Josephus we have and, if authentic – which they appear to be, really do give proof of the impact James was already having on the contemporary scene in the Jerusalem of his day and, it seems, thereafter, till the time of Josephus' writing at the beginning of the 90s.

Unfortunately we cannot say as much for Jesus, at least in the form we have him in Josephus, which, as noted, most would consider an interpolation, to say nothing of the Gospels.

Before going on to examine these additional materials which Eusebius provides, we should compare the parallels to the Hegesippus Eusebius conserves in Clement, Epiphanius, the two Apocalypses of James recently found at Nag Hammadi in Upper Egypt, and Jerome. Eusebius more or less sums up what Clement of Alexandria in the latter part of the second century knows about the traditions regarding James' death as follows:

> But as to the manner of James' death . . . in the words of Clement, 'He was thrown [beblēsthai] from the Pinnacle and beaten to death with a club.'

There is nothing different in this tradition from the one from Hegesippus some twenty or more years earlier.

Epiphanius does not add much more. He corrects Eusebius' version of James' activities in the Temple, making it clear he went into 'the Holy of Holies', as he puts it, 'once a year', where he prayed on his knees till they became 'hard as camel's hide from his continued kneeling before God out of his excessive Piety' – an obvious description of a 'Yom Kippur' atonement.

As we saw, Epiphanius is obsessed with James' age: 'he also died a virgin

466

at the age of ninety-six',[1] which, as in the case of the age of Simeon Bar Cleophas succeeding him – 'one hundred and twenty years' according to Hegesippus – can be viewed as simply recapitulating Josephus' contention about how 'long-lived' those he is calling 'Essenes' were. For Epiphanius, James reigned in Jerusalem for 'twenty-four years after the Assumption of Jesus', which, if Josephus' dating of James' death is correct, would place Jesus' death in 38 CE, the year, approximately, Josephus assigns to the execution of *John the Baptist*.

When it comes to James' death, Epiphanius basically repeats Eusebius' presentation, though the language is even more that of the attack on James by Paul in the 40s, as per the Pseudoclementine *Recognitions*:

> A certain fuller beat his head in with a club, *after he had been thrown head-long from the Pinnacle of the Temple* and *cast down*. But having done no wrong at all, *he fell to his knees* and *prayed for those who had thrown him down*, entreating God with the words, 'Forgive them, for they know not what they do.'

Not only do we have the 'casting down' language again here (repeated three times), but the reiteration of the 'being thrown headlong', seemingly from the Pseudoclementine *Recognitions*' account of Paul's attack on James on 'the steps of the Temple' in the 40s. The 'falling to his knees and praying' is, of course, part and parcel of Acts' presentation of Stephen and his prayer.

But Epiphanius adds new material:

> Thus, even Simeon bar Cleophas, his cousin, who was *standing* not far away, said, 'Stop, why are you stoning the Just One? Behold, he is praying the most wonderful prayers for you.'[2]

Aside from another of these tell-tale allusions to 'standing', again one has here the 'the Just One' epithet used in place of James' very name itself and the crucial emphasis on 'praying'. But now, in place of Eusebius' 'one of the Priests of the sons of Rechab', one has the startling reference, we have previously remarked, to James' 'cousin', Simeon bar Cleophas.

Should we credit this tradition? It is extremely original and there is nothing to counter-indicate it. Nor does it create a wrench in the historical processes as we have been documenting them. But where did such a tradition come from and why isn't it in Eusebius? There is no way of knowing, except that Epiphanius' information in general is richer and fuller than Eusebius', even though he is not quite so meticulous in quotation and/or citing of his sources.

Like his contemporary Jerome, who, not surprisingly, dislikes him personally, Epiphanius is prepared to conflate various sources. But he does give more accurate information than Eusebius about James *actually entering the Holy of Holies to make an atonement* and a wealth of additional material about James' 'Naziritism', vegetarianism, sexual abstinence, and the like, which has been so helpful in unravelling all these correspondences. He, also, has vastly superior material about the sectarian situation in Palestine generally and the 'Primal Adam' ideology in particular. For instance, under his description of the Ebionites, he says:

> For some of them say *Christ is Adam*, the First created . . . *a Spirit higher than the Angels and Lord of all* . . . He comes here when he chooses, as when he came in Adam . . . He came also in the Last Days, put on Adam's body, appeared to men, was crucified, resurrected, and ascended . . . but also, they say . . . *the Spirit which is Christ came into him* and put on the Man who is called 'Jesus'.[3]

This doctrine, the importance of which we have begun to suspect above, seems more and more accurately to describe the incarnationism of this period.

Suppose we were to say, as also concluded above, that by 'Rechabite' Eusebius was trying to say something similar to 'Essene', 'Nazirite', or 'Ebionite'; then out of this band of Essene or Ebionite 'Priests', one, James' 'cousin' and successor, Simeon bar Cleophas, emerged as the next 'Bishop of the Jerusalem Community' in Palestine (only, after the fall of the Temple and Jerusalem, there clearly was no 'Jerusalem Community' any longer to speak of).

Suppose, too, that instead of any of these vocabularies we were to use one more familiar to modern ears – especially since the discoveries of the Dead Sea Scrolls – the Qumran 'Priests' or 'Sons of Zadok'. For Epiphanius, James is a 'Nazirite' Priest with an obviously even greater concern for purity matters than usual. Now our sources begin to *mesh absolutely*. We shall have more to say about Simeon bar Cleophas when we treat the subject of 'Jesus' Brothers as Apostles' below, but for the time being it might be well to entertain the implications of both accounts, that the witness to this stoning was both 'a Rechabite Priest' and James' 'cousin', without attempting to determine where the material came from (probably Hegesippus).

Another point would also be interesting in this intermixing and overlapping of sources. If we now superimpose the story of the stoning of

Stephen from Acts upon the story of the stoning of James from Epiphanius and Eusebius, then Simeon Bar Cleophas or the Rechabite Priestly 'witness' becomes James' (and presumably Simeon's) ideological adversary *Paul*. As Luke/Acts puts it, after describing how 'having cast him out of the city, they stoned him'.

> And the witnesses put down *their clothes* at the feet of a young man Saul. And *they stoned Stephen as he was praying* [repeated a second time] . . . And Saul consented to putting him to death. (Acts 7:58–8:1)

We have already called attention to the repetition of the 'stoning' motif here as if something has been interjected or added. The 'clothes' theme is already an important one, as in the traditions about James we have the reiteration of the various types of 'clothes' he wears, but there is also the play on the special linen bath clothing the Essenes wore generally and the additional implied play now on the 'laundryman beating out clothes' theme *vis-à-vis* James' death. What are we to make of these curious usages and overlaps? How else can sense be made of such senseless survivals from earlier traditions? Why would the witnesses lay 'their clothes' anywhere?

However this aspect of this particular puzzle may be, once again, in line with the mirror reversals we find in this literature, Paul takes the place of his opposite number, James' successor in Palestine, Simeon bar Cleophas – the only difference being that while one approves the other disapproves of what was done. We shall have more to say about interesting juxtapositions such as this presently, but before attempting to resolve some of the contradictions and *non sequitur*s in this account, we should take a look at the two other sources that contain material related to it: firstly, the two Apocalypses of James from so-called 'Gnostic' texts at Nag Hammadi and, secondly, Jerome's account.

The Stoning of James at Nag Hammadi

The Nag Hammadi materials were found in Upper Egypt around the time the Dead Sea Scrolls were found in Palestine. Unlike the Scrolls, they were written in codex or book form, which seems to betoken a later practice, and clearly purposefully concealed. They emanate from Coptic Egypt some time in the third or fourth centuries and appear to be a somewhat later anti-orthodox strain than the materials at Qumran. They are known as 'Gnostic' because of the emphasis on this kind of 'Knowledge' or 'knowing' and a predilection for an other-worldly kind of *Gnosis*. There is at

Qumran a similar interest in what in Hebrew is called '*Da'at*' – 'Knowledge' in Greek – but the emphasis is not so intellectual, spiritualized, or deferred into a more other-worldly framework.

Rather, Qumran is still interested in the present, as is apparent from some of the Messianic proclamations there, and would appear to represent a phase when 'this-worldly' Messianic hopes had not yet been completely frustrated. Just as the Righteous Teacher plays a principal role in the Qumran documents, James – who joins Jesus as a kind of Super-natural Redeemer figure in the Nag Hammadi texts – plays a principal role in the codices which have become available from this often anti-Establishment and good-humoured corpus.

For instance, in the document of the sayings of Jesus called the Gospel of Thomas – presumably after the third brother of Jesus, 'Judas Thomas' or 'Judas the Twin' – there occurs the passage about the direct appointment of James mentioned earlier, which makes it clear, as both Epiphanius and the *Recognitions* above imply, that James was appointed Successor by his brother in his lifetime. The saying attributed to Jesus, it will be recalled, was, 'In the place where you are to go, go to James the Just, for whose sake Heaven and Earth came into existence'.

Scholars have been particularly interested in this Gospel, because they believe it represents an earlier stage of development, when materials about Jesus were simply preserved as 'sayings' – as they are in this Gospel – before the more familiar Gospel format of 'the story of Jesus', concluding with his crucifixion and resurrection. As a source for these later narrative-type Gospels, 'Q' (from the German word '*Quellen*' or 'Source'), was hypothesized to represent, for instance, some of the additional material – in particular, *sayings* – found in Luke or Matthew and not found in Mark. The Gospel of Thomas is thought to be this sort of collection.

In addition, this particular direct appointment of James, as we saw, incorporates some mystical-type materials found in Jewish *Kabbalah* (the Jewish underground mystic tradition), and relates to the role of 'the *Zaddik*' both as pre-existent, as in the Qumran Hymns or as it emerges in Paul's appellation for James in Galatians and medieval Jewish *Zohar* tradition, 'the *Zaddik* the Pillar-of-the-World'. The language of this episode in the Gospel of Thomas is also reflected, somewhat esoterically, in the language of the First Apocalypse of James at Nag Hammadi:

> To you again he will say: 'Where shall you go?' You are to answer him: 'To the place from which I have come, there shall I return.' (34.16–20)

Though not exactly that of the Gospel of Thomas above, it is an easily recognizable linguistic variation of it.

Though this Apocalypse is poorly preserved in places, most of the themes connected to the James story, as already encountered above, clearly emerge. The language of 'Perfection' and 'Salvation' is reiterated throughout and James is constantly referred to as 'my brother', though it is such a late stage in the tradition, that material brotherhood is denied in favour clearly of a symbolical one.[4] James' cognomen 'the Just One' is persistently evoked (32.2), as is the constant 'praying' he does, and the 'kiss' given Jesus by 'Judas' in Orthodox Scripture would now appear to be the more mystic one exchanged between James and Jesus (31.2–32.10), thus linking traditions about Judas to inverted ones about Jesus' family members themselves – again most notably James. All this occurs in the course of what is clearly a first post-resurrection appearance *to James*.

James' major disciple is referred to as 'Addai', an appellation we shall have more to say about presently; in the Second Apocalypse he will be transformed into 'Theuda', identified as a 'relative of the Just One'. We shall liken him to Theudas and, via this, the name 'Thaddaeus' and ultimately 'Judas Thomas'. This Second Apocalypse is said to have been dictated to Mareim, 'one of the Priests' (44.16). Again what kind of Priest is not mentioned, but this personality is already to be found with regard to James in what Hippolytus refers to as 'Naassene' tradition – either the Essenes, Nazoraeans, or both.

In discussing the doctrine of the 'Perfect Man' or 'Primal Adam' of the Naassenes, whom he also calls 'Priests', Hippolytus mentions, not Mareim, but 'Mariamme' – the Hebrew original for the name 'Mary' – namely that 'James the brother of the Lord delivered the tenets' about the doctrine of 'the Primal Adam'/'Perfect Man' and 'handed down numerous discourses to Mariamme'. Origen, his contemporary, also speaks of a group centring about the name 'Mariamme', but appears to know absolutely nothing about them.[5]

In extensive exposition of the doctrine of 'the Primal Adam and of that Spiritual One that is born again', which elsewhere he calls *the Gate* 'to the Perfect Man' and ascribes – prior to all others – to these 'Naassenes', Hippolytus also invokes the Gospel of Thomas and, in some manner, relates Adam to someone or something he calls 'Mariam'. Again this ideology is specifically referred to at the end of the First Apocalypse of James (41.26).

The 'Hidden' ideology or someone 'hiding' something is, also, specifically

referred to in both Apocalypses (36.14 and 47.17) – in the First, introducing another allusion to 'Addai' and the tradition, already encountered
in Hegesippus and Clement above, that James' death was followed
immediately by the War against Rome (36:17–18). Either his death or
Jesus' is referred to at the end of the First Apocalypse with the words, 'For
a Just One will perish through Unrighteousness' (43.21), which seems to
be an approximation of Isaiah 3:10 above. In any event, it approximates
the language we have been encountering, applied to the death of James in
early Church tradition and that of the Righteous Teacher in the tradition
represented by Qumran. The associated tradition – called in early
Christian language, the 'Pella Flight' Tradition – is also in evidence, to wit:

> You, too, will they seize ['they' being 'the tax collectors'], *but leave
> Jerusalem*, for she it is who always gives *the Cup of Bitterness* to all *the
> Sons of Light*.

Not only does it use the language of 'Strength' and 'Perfection of
Salvation' to introduce this oracle about leaving Jerusalem, but this 'Cup
of Bitterness' and 'Sons of Light' language is completely paralleled in the
documents at Qumran. The imagery of this 'Cup' will have the most
profound implications as we proceed, not only where the death of the
Righteous Teacher is concerned, but also as far as Paul's understanding of
'the New Covenant in the Land of Damascus' or 'the Cup of the New
Covenant in his Blood', as we have already seen.

The imagery at Qumran of this 'Cup' has been misconstrued by many
commentators, by whom it is often interpreted to mean 'the Wicked Priest'
was a drunkard! The imagery, as it is used in the Habakkuk *Pesher* and
elsewhere at Qumran, rather has to do with the 'Cup of the Wrath of
God', which 'Cup' the Wicked Priest also will be forced to drink as punishment for what he did to the Righteous Teacher.[6] This is also the way the
imagery is used in the Book of Revelation:

> He also shall drink of the wine of the Wrath [also 'venom' at Qumran] of
> God, which is *poured out undiluted in the Cup of His Wrath*. (14:10)[7]

This imagery is continued into Revelation, chapter 16, there in connection
with the language of 'blasphemy' and 'blood'.

The language of the 'Sons of Light', too, is used omnipresently at
Qumran as a term of self-designation for the members of the Community.[8]
The term also appears in the New Testament, as for instance in John
12:36, where it is used in conjunction with the 'Son of Man' and

'Christ' language and, as in the War Scroll, coming Eschatological Judgement.

It also occurs in Paul in 1 Thessalonians 5:5, where again it is used in conjunction with the 'coming of the Lord from Heaven', Eschatological Judgement (4:16), and another favourite Qumran usage, 'Sons of Day' ('Sons of Dawn' at Qumran). This language of the 'Day' and 'Dawn' must be seen in relation to the outlook of Essenes and/or Hemerobaptists like the Sabaeans generally, who supposedly prayed to the rising sun or worshipped the dawn.[9] In 1 Thessalonians, too, the language of 'Wrath' and 'Salvation' also occurs (5:8–9) and Paul ends the letter by sending 'a holy kiss', as he does in Romans and Corinthians, an image that will now be seen to permeate both Apocalypses and the mechanism of the relationship of Jesus to James.

Ephesians, whether actually written by Paul or simply of his school, also alludes to 'the Children of Light' in the context of 'Light' and 'Darkness' imagery generally (5:8). In addition, it presents Christ as 'an offering and a sacrifice to God, an odour of a sweet fragrance' (5:2). This is the exact language applied to the members of the Council of the Community – 'a House of Holiness for Israel and a Foundation of the Holy of Holies for Aaron' – in the Community Rule at Qumran as we saw. These are also described as 'a sweet fragrance' and 'pleasing odour atoning for the Land'.[10]

Not only do we also have in Ephesians the references to the James-like 'deceiving with Empty words' and 'the Wrath of God' of this section of the First Apocalypse of James, but almost word for word the language of the Community Rule regarding there being 'no lewdness, no foolish talking, or guffawing' in the Community of the Holy Ones (5:3–6).[11]

In the First Apocalypse of James at Nag Hammadi, this oracle, to 'leave Jerusalem', is attributed to Jesus, who throughout the text is referred to as 'Rabbi'/'my Master'. In early Christian usage, the oracle, called as we saw the 'Pella Flight' Tradition, is attributed to James or occurs either consonant with or as a consequence of his death.[12] Throughout this First Apocalypse, not only do we have repeated reference to the 'seizing' found in these early Church accounts of the death of James, but also the omnipresent use of the language of 'casting down' or 'casting out', which also occurs in the Second Apocalypse.[13]

The Second Apocalypse of James is more straightforward, containing many of the details of James' death, with which we have already become familiar in these early Church accounts. In its picture, James is standing not 'on the Pinnacle' but, as in the Pseudoclementines, 'on the steps of the Temple' – in this instance 'the fifth flight' (45:24). Whether to deliver his 'discourses' or the speech in Hegesippus/Eusebius or as part of 'Ascents' of some other kind is not completely clear.

As already suggested, these 'Ascents' have much in common with the degrees in Jewish Mysticism or *Kabbalah*, or what goes by the name in the latter of '*Hechalot* Mysticism', the 'Mysticism of *Heavenly Degrees*' or '*Ascents*'. Indeed, there is much in traditions relating to James and his possible forebears and/or predecessors, Honi the Circle-Drawer and Hanan the Hidden, which would appear to prefigure this tradition to the extent, at least, that all these individuals are proverbial '*Zaddiks*'.

In fact, the 'Hidden' tradition, which via the 'Primal Adam' ideology actually moves into the '*Imam*' tradition of Shi'ite Islam of Northern Syria and Iraq, is hinted at in both Apocalypses (e.g., 46:15). It is also hinted at in the tradition about 'the Sons of Light', which begins with the question, 'who is this Son of Man', in John 12:34–36 above. As we have seen as well, Paul too hints at it in 2 Corinthians 12:2, when he speaks of 'having known a Man in Christ fourteen years before' – the time span in Galatians between Paul's first meeting with James in Jerusalem, and his second – who 'was caught away' or 'ascended into the Third Heaven' (2 Cor. 12:2).

In both Apocalypses, much is made of the 'kiss' Jesus gives James, itself not unconnected with the tradition of 'Hidden' Knowledge (56.15). Though, of course, this has to do with both the direct appointment of James and the 'Beloved' or 'Friend' tradition, or James, like Abraham, being the 'Friend of God'; in line with more Gnosticizing tendencies of these Apocalypses, this becomes a more mystical kind of embrace of the sort that transfers '*Gnosis*' or 'Knowledge' from the teacher to the adept. Like the young man in the linen loincloth, whom Jesus is pictured as teaching at the end of the Gospel of Mark (14:51–52), James is also pictured as being 'stripped and going about naked' (46.15).

The theme of this 'Beloved', connected to such a kiss and the 'Friend of God' metaphor generally – so much a part of the language and presentation in the Gospel of John of 'the Disciple Jesus loved' – appears repeatedly here, only it is applied to James (56.15–57.17). Though the Second Apocalypse is fragmented to some extent as well, much is also made of James' cognomen, 'the Righteous' or 'Just One', but here the author makes a big point of James and Jesus having different mothers and being only 'milk' or 'stepbrothers', but having *different fathers* as well (50.11–51.25).[14]

By far the most interesting material in the Second Apocalypse comes: firstly, at the beginning, with the reference to 'Theuda' (Theudas) 'the relative of the Just One', who, as we saw, basically takes the place in the narrative of 'Addai' in the First Apocalypse and the only other name of any note – besides 'Mareim' – mentioned; and, secondly, at the end of the Apocalypse, with the narrative of the stoning of 'the Just One'. This contains many colourful, new details. Certainly these are not all reliable, but they show how vibrant and alive this tradition about James' stoning was in the East in the second and third centuries.

After a reference to the coming destruction of the Temple and to 'the judges taking counsel' (60:20–25), it reads as follows:

> On that day, the whole people and the crowd were getting stirred up, and appeared to be disagreeing with each other, and he arose, after speaking in this way and departed. But he entered again the same day and spoke for a few hours.

This appears to parallel the debates on the Temple steps and James' departing after his first speech, as recounted in the Pseudoclementine *Recognitions*, to return again the next day.

> And I was with the Priests, but I did not reveal our kinship.

It is difficult to understand who this narrator can be other than Simeon bar Cleophas, the witness to the stoning of James in Epiphanius' version of Hegesippus, either him or a reference of some kind to the 'kinship' of James and Jesus.

The mention of 'Priests', again here, is, of course, interesting in view of the reference to James' Disciple 'Mareim' at the beginning of the Apocalypse as being 'one of the Priests' and the whole issue of the relationship of 'Rechabite'/'Nazirite'/'Essene Priests' to those in the Temple generally. It also links up with the peculiar notice in the Book of Acts of a large number of 'Priests' having made their conversion that we noted above.

The 'kinship', then, is either between James and Jesus or Simeon bar Cleophas and James – it is difficult to decide which from the context.

> For all of them were crying out in unison, 'Come, let us stone the Just One.' And they arose, saying, 'Yes, let us put this man to death, that he will be taken from out of our midst, for he is abhorrent to us.'

But, of course, this is almost a word-for-word quotation from the account of Hegesippus, as preserved in Eusebius, including even the citation from Isaiah 3:10, 'let us remove the Just One for he is abhorrent to us', according to the Septuagint version, now moulded into the very narrative itself.

It is interesting that though this passage has exactly the reverse sense in the Judeo-Christian biblical tradition we are heirs to, in the first–second century Epistle of Barnabas – itself probably of Alexandrian origin and full of Qumranisms, such as 'the Way of Holiness', 'the Way of Light', the 'uncircumcised heart', etc. – again, the reference is as it appears in the Septuagint, 'Let us bind the Just One, for he is abhorrent to us.' What is more, as in Justin Martyr thereafter, it is applied to Jesus' death not James'.[15] In fact, even the version of this passage, which Justin quotes as part of his opponent Trypho's (Tarphon's?) Scripture, does not agree with the received version.[16] There is something very peculiar about all the variations in the reception of this pivotal scriptural proof text. It is almost as if someone involved in the normative scriptural tradition were trying to obscure how it was being interpreted in the first century.

> And when they came out, they found him standing on the Pinnacle of the Temple beside the *firm Cornerstone*.

The 'Cornerstone' allusion, attached to this episode about James' death, is a new element, but not a completely surprising one. The imagery of 'Stone' and 'Cornerstone' is part and parcel of that applied to the Disciples in early Christianity and omnipresent in the Dead Sea Scrolls, as we have seen. It is interesting, too, that, in the Epistle of Barnabas, the imagery of the 'firm Cornerstone' is linked to the quotation of this same Isaiah 3:10 passage above.[17] There can be little doubt that what we now have here in this Apocalypse is the picture of James standing on the Temple Pinnacle, or possibly the Temple balustrade common to all these early Church sources.

> And they were bent upon *throwing him down* from that height. And *they cast him down*.

As in Epiphanius' version of Hegesippus above and, in fact, Eusebius' as well, the 'casting down' language is, once again, repeated twice.

Unfortunately, there now follows a short lacuna in the text and, though one would like to know what is missing, the narrative then resumes with a completely new twist:

> And they . . . seized him [this clearly after his 'fall'] and [struck] him as they dragged him on the ground [this more or less the picture we get of Stephen in Acts – not to mention Jesus in the Gospels]. They stretched him apart and placed a *stone on his stomach*, which they all kicked with their feet, saying, 'You have gone astray.'

Not only do we have here the allusion to 'being misled' or 'erring' that one has in the normative Hegesippus account, but one assumes that what was meant here was the accusation of 'blasphemy' regarding James above, lost now in translation through various languages, though the sense of theological error is present.

Our writer now, of course, fairly runs away with himself in bloodthirsty enthusiasm:

> Again, they raised him up, since he was still alive. They made him dig a hole. Then they made him stand in it. After they covered him up to his stomach, they stoned him in this way [all this is truly original, but, except as it reproduces the various Rabbinic parameters for stoning, one can assume, utterly apocryphal]. But he stretched forth his hands, saying the following prayer, which he was accustomed to saying.

We are now in familiar terrain again, including the element of 'praying'. We shall treat this gruesome account of their making him dig a pit and placing a stone on James' stomach further below. Once again, these last have to do with refracted Talmudic accounts of such procedures.

The prayer that is given is not the 'Forgive them Father, for they know not what they do', but rather an entirely original, more Gnosticizing, one. One can imagine that this prayer was recited in the Community that produced this account in commemoration of what it thought James said when he died. It is a totally original 'discourse', and may be one of the 'discourses' James was said to have 'given Mareim' at the beginning of the Apocalypse or something from Epiphanius' *Anabathmoi Jacobou*. In kind, though not in subject, it is not so different from the discourse attributed to James in the debates on the Temple steps in the Pseudoclementine *Recognitions*, before he was 'cast down' by Paul.

Its main emphasis is on asking for 'Grace', 'Salvation', and 'resurrection'. Interestingly enough, it uses the language of 'Strength' so associated with James in the other accounts, and of 'Light', 'Power', and 'being saved' – the last phraseology prominent in the description of the destruction of the Righteous Teacher in the Habakkuk *Pesher* at Qumran.[18] Even more interestingly, there is the tell-tale reference to the 'Enemy', that appears in the Pseudoclementine account of the attack on James by Paul.[19]

The Importance of James in Jerome

The material about the stoning of James in Jerome, though derivative and clearly abbreviated, is equally interesting. This is not only because of the prominence Jerome accords both James *and* Jude, but because of the way Jerome combines sources and finally introduces new – and in fact crucial – material that will eventually show the way towards a synthesis of *all our sources*.

We have already seen how in his Commentary on Paul's famous testimony to James in Galatians, Jerome supplies the additional piece of information that 'so Holy was James that the People tried to touch the fringes of his garment' as he passed by. For Jerome, James is second in importance only to Simon Peter; and Jude, whom he identifies (as in the Letter attributed to his name) as 'the brother of James', he places fourth after Matthew – even before Paul, who is fifth. Jerome is writing about 'famous' or 'illustrious writers' in the history of the Church up to his time, among whom he includes, notably, the non-Christians Philo, Seneca, and Josephus as eleventh to thirteenth respectively. It is worth remarking that in this work, *Lives of Illustrious Men*, treating one hundred and thirty-five persons from Simon Peter onwards, the section on James is the 'longest' except for Origen, *longer even than that on either Peter or Paul*.

Beginning once again with James' eponym, 'the Just One', Jerome allows – unlike the Second Apocalypse of James from Nag Hammadi above – Joseph as his father. However, like his sometime acquaintance Epiphanius, he continues the theme of a *second mother*, only adding the preposterous Mary 'the sister of' her own sister Mary of the Gospel of John as his candidate.[20] He goes on to give most of the details regarding James' person and life we have already encountered in other sources, most notably his view, that James 'was *immediately* appointed Bishop of Jerusalem by the Apostles after our Lord's Passion'. 'Immediately' is the operative word here, which echoes the position of the Pseudoclementine *Recognitions* on this point, only for him James 'ruled the Church at Jerusalem for thirty years', while for Epiphanius above it was only 'twenty-four'.

He quotes Hegesippus on James' Naziritism, that is, he 'was Holy from his mother's womb', his abstention from strong drink, meat, anointment with oil, shaving, etc. He insists he wore only linen, not 'woollen clothes'. Here is the omnipresent theme of *clothing* again, as well as that of his being 'on his knees' and 'praying' – again, 'his knees were reputed to be of the hardness of camels' knees', because of all the praying he did. But in this he agrees with Epiphanius, whom he considered 'an old fool', not Eusebius – to the effect that:

> He alone enjoyed the privilege of entering the Holy of Holies . . . and *went into the Temple alone* and *prayed on behalf of the people*, to such a degree, that his knees were reputed to have acquired the calluses of a camel's knees.

To arrive at the picture of a perfect *Yom Kippur* atonement, one has only to substitute that he *went into the Holy of Holies alone*, not the Temple.

Jerome presents a version of the stoning and death of James, which is obviously derived from what he saw in both the no longer extant Sixth Book of Clement of Alexandria's *Institutions* and in the Fifth Book of Hegesippus' *Commentaries*, already discussed above. What is new in his account is that he combines this with the testimony from the Twentieth Book of Josephus' *Antiquities*, as Eusebius tries to do, which he claims was also present in the Seventh Book of Clement of Alexandria's *Institutions*. This is a new claim, the veracity of which it is impossible to judge, but to do so, it would be useful to quote at length what, in fact, Josephus actually said in his famous testimony to James with which he more or less brings the *Antiquities* to a close.

Before doing so, one should remark, as we have already done above, that Jerome claimed that

> This same Josephus records the tradition that this James was of so great Holiness and reputation among the people that the destruction of Jerusalem was believed to have occurred on account of his death –

this, in addition to his claim above, that 'so great a reputation did James have for Holiness' among the people of Jerusalem that – like the Rabbinic tradition about Honi's 'grandson' – they used to try to 'touch the fringes of his clothing' as he walked by.

It is interesting that Jerome repeats this claim about 'James the Apostle' in his note on Josephus as a writer. He phrases this as follows:

> In the Eight[eenth] Book of his *Antiquities*, he most openly acknowledges that Christ was put to death by the Pharisees on account of his great miracles, that John the Baptist was truly *a Prophet*, and that Jerusalem was destroyed *because of the murder of James the Apostle*.

We shall discuss the claim that James was reckoned among the Apostles below. However, data is piling up that makes it clear that the James who was Jesus' brother *was* reckoned among the Apostles, unless we choose to think that Jerome means here, 'James *the brother of John*', supposedly *beheaded* in the time of Herod Agrippa or his brother Herod of Chalcis – which Jerome clearly does not.

What is also interesting here is that Jerome finally makes it clear, in his view, just where this testimony about Jerusalem falling because of the death of James came from in Josephus' works – Book Eighteen of his *Antiquities*, two books earlier than the extant description of the death of James in Book Twenty. Of course, the testimonies about John and Jesus are still extant in Book Eighteen, but not in the precise words Jerome presents them. For instance, it is not specifically stated 'that Christ was slain by the Pharisees on account of his great miracles', nor that Josephus considered John 'a Prophet', at least not in the testimony to John as it presently stands.

But Jerome is too careful a scholar simply to claim something exists when he has not seen it or it does not. Therefore one must assume that he saw something of what he says. Perhaps the nonsense Paulina and Fulvia episodes that follow the suspicious-sounding account of the crucifixion of Christ in Book Eighteen replaced some more extensive commentary of the kind Jerome says he saw in Book Eighteen, which included the material about Jerusalem falling 'because of the death of James the Apostle' not Jesus.

In his long biographical note about James, Jerome also mentions Paul's testimony to seeing James in Jerusalem in Galatians 1:19, which, he claims, 'even the Acts of the Apostles bear witness to', without noting that the two testimonies are, as we already saw, in almost complete contradiction. He also presents material about James from a no longer extant apocryphal Gospel – not Thomas, but one he calls 'the Gospel according to the Hebrews'. Not only does Jerome claim that 'Origen, too, often made use' of this Gospel; but, like Eusebius in matters of import, he quotes the relevant passage relating to a first post-resurrection appearance by Jesus to James, which he personally claims to have 'translated into Greek and Latin', obviously, verbatim from the Hebrew.[21] This appearance relates very closely to Luke's Emmaus Road sighting of Jesus, which we shall treat more fully in the Part on 'Jesus' Brothers as Apostles', and both contain elements that normally go under the heading of the 'doubting Thomas' episode in normative Scripture.

Parallels with material relating to 'Thomas' are important because of the importance of Thomas in Nag Hammadi tradition and because of his name, that is, 'Twin' – '*Didymus* Thomas' or 'Twin Twin' in the Gospel of John – and the implication this carries of some relationship to the members of Jesus' family or the brothers of Jesus, not to mention the appellation 'Judas Thomas', actually used with '*Didymus*' in the dedication, as we saw, of the Gospel of Thomas, that is, 'Judas the Twin', probably identical with the Letter of Jude's and Jerome's 'Jude the brother of James', whom we shall treat more extensively below as well.

This tradition, which Jerome sees fit to quote from the Gospel of the Hebrews, also can be related to the missing tradition of a first appearance by Jesus after his resurrection to James the Just. In it, we now have Jesus 'giving his grave clothes to the Servant of the Priest' – in the Dead Sea Scrolls, this almost always means 'the High Priest'[22] – which makes altogether more sense than anything we have so far encountered about 'clothes' or 'the High Priest's Servant' in the Gospels or the Book of Acts, because it was the individual to be stoned who was to be naked, not 'the witnesses' or *those doing the stoning*.

In it, too, is also a reference to 'the Cup of the Lord', which James is supposed in some manner to have drunk – perhaps at 'the Last Supper', perhaps symbolically. We have already described how this imagery functions in the Gospels, Revelation, and the Dead Sea Scrolls with regard to both the Righteous Teacher and the Wicked Priest, but it has not previously been clear that this imagery could be related in the literature directly to James. This imagery of 'the Cup' is also related in Gospel tradition to 'the two sons of Zebedee' (the second of whom James so much parallels), that they would 'drink the Cup' Jesus was going to drink – meaning martyrdom (Matt. 20:20–28 and Mark 10:35–45), even though no martyrdom tradition has come down to us for 'John the brother of James'.

But heretofore we never had such 'Cup' imagery directly applied to James. The next step is a comparatively simple one and we shall take it in due course. In the Habakkuk *Pesher*, among the Dead Sea Scrolls, when it comes to presenting what the Wicked Priest – the Establishment High Priest – did to the Righteous Teacher, 'Cup' imagery is employed, that is to say, just as he tendered the 'Cup' to the Righteous Teacher/*Zaddik*, so too would 'the Cup of the Lord's Wrath' or 'the Cup of the Wrath of God' come around to him 'and he would drink his fill'. As previously remarked, this is generally interpreted in Dead Sea Scrolls research – often incapable of relating to literary metaphor – to mean that the Wicked Priest *was a drunkard*, meaning, 'he drank too much wine'!

Jerome also thinks, in contradistinction to Epiphanius, that James 'ruled the Church of Jerusalem for thirty years' until, as he presents it with his customary precision, 'the Seventh Year of Nero and was buried near the Temple, from which he had been *cast down*'. Here is the by now familiar theme of 'casting down', once again associated with James' death. Like Eusebius, as we saw, he notes that 'his tombstone with its inscription was well known until the siege of Titus and the end of Hadrian's reign' (*c.* 138 CE and the end of the Bar Kochba Revolt too).

James' Death in Josephus: Opposition and Establishment Sadducees

In order to see just how Jerome incorporates the testimony of Josephus in Book Twenty of the *Antiquities* into his account of the fall James takes from the Temple Pinnacle and his stoning, it would be well to present the testimony of Josephus about James' death in its entirety. If acceptable, it is not only the most accurate material we have relating to James' death, but also fixes the chronology of these events, which in turn lead up with some inexorable fatality to the outbreak of the War against Rome.

Eusebius also gives it in the finale of his account of the death of James after relating this death to the coming destruction of the Temple and the fall of Jerusalem. His version is for all intents and purposes consonant with the present text of Josephus and reads as follows:

> Upon learning of the death of Festus [Acts 25:1–26:32], Caesar [Nero] sent Albinus to Judea as Procurator, but the King [Agrippa II] removed Joseph from the High Priesthood and bestowed the dignity of that office on the son of Ananus, who was also himself called Ananus [Ananus ben Ananus]. It is said that this elder Ananus was extremely fortunate, for he had five sons, all of whom became High Priests of God – after he had himself enjoyed the office for a very long time previously – which had never happened to any of our other High Priests.[23]

The information about the High Priest Ananus' family – our candidate for the Wicked Priest at Qumran – is missing from Eusebius, but it is interesting, because: firstly, Josephus elsewhere, as we saw, says the same things about James' nemesis, Ananus ben Ananus, namely that the destruction of Jerusalem was the result of his grisly death, and, secondly, the elder Ananus, who was High Priest for a very long time either just prior to or in the period of Pontius Pilate, is pictured in the Gospels as having played a significant role in the death of Jesus (Luke 3:2/John 18:3).

Even as a young man, Agrippa II (49–93), by virtue of the dignity bestowed on his father Agrippa I (37–44) by Caligula and Claudius, enjoyed the privilege of appointing Jewish High Priests, a privilege that after Herod's death devolved upon the Roman Governors or Procurators. Previously, in the Maccabean Period, this privilege was not an issue, since the Maccabees functioned in the manner of hereditary High Priests as well as Kings.

Only with Herod's ascendancy and the destruction (or absorption) of the Maccabeans did this become an issue. Herod's father, the first Roman Procurator in Palestine, carved out a kingdom with the help of the Pharisees, and it was Herod who first insisted on controlling the vestments of the High Priest, a lever over the control of affairs in Palestine in this period. In fact, at the beginning of the all-important Book Twenty of the *Antiquities*, Josephus provides Claudius' 45 CE letter 'to the whole Nation of the Jews', granting to Agrippa II, whom he calls 'friend' and 'a man of the greatest Piety' (thus), and his uncle Herod of Chalcis and his son Aristobulus (the husband of that Salome involved in the death of John the Baptist) control over the High Priest's vestments.[24]

To continue with the testimony of Josephus as presented in Eusebius:

> The younger [Ananus], who, as we have said, obtained the High Priesthood [from Agrippa II], was rash in his temperament and very insolent. He was also of the sect of the Sadducees, who were the most uncompromising of all the Jews, as we have already observed, in execution of Judgement.

One sometimes wonders which 'Judgement' Josephus has in mind, human or eschatological. His manner of describing 'Sadducees' here is interesting, because elsewhere, as noted, he tells us that the Sadducees in the Herodian Period were dominated in all things by the Pharisees. This is, indeed, the impression that emerges in the New Testament too. The Pseudo-clementine *Recognitions*, cognizant of the derivation of 'the Sadducees' from the root 'Righteousness', rather has it that the Sadducees considered themselves 'more Righteous than the others, separating from the Assembly of the People'. For it, this division of 'the People into many Parties began in the days of John the Baptist'. As this is put in the Syriac version: the 'Sadducees arose in the days of John, and because they were Righteous Ones, separated from the people'.[25]

Obviously, these last are not the Sadducees as presented in Josephus or the New Testament – in all probability dependent on Josephus – which is one of the reasons, I have, linking such delineations with parallel significations found in the Dead Sea Scrolls, argued for *two* groups of Sadducees – the first, making no such claim to being 'more Righteous' than anyone else, but rather only a tenuous genealogical link to the 'Zadok' of David's time a thousand years before; the second, an Opposition group emphasizing 'Righteousness' as the key constituency of Salvation.[26] In their literature, as it is found at Qumran, they really do advocate 'separation from the People' – a signification found over and over again – and the basis of the 'pollution of the Temple' charge found, for instance, in the Damascus Document.

The latter document, as we have seen, criticizes all Establishment groups – Pharisees, Sadducees, and, if in the Herodian Period, those Herodians in league with them, over the issue of improper 'separation' of clean and unclean in the Temple, expressed graphically in terms of 'sleeping with women in their periods', or associating with people who did. This is also the sense of the critique one finds in the two 'Letters on Works Righteousness', known more widely as '*MMT*', ostensibly addressed to a King – if Maccabean, possibly Alexander Jannaeus; if Herodian, Agrippa I, the father of Agrippa II involved in the death of James.[27] As we shall see here and in Volume II, there is also a third – perhaps even more likely possibility – 'Abgarus' or 'Agbarus', the Great King of the Peoples 'beyond the Euphrates' or even Queen Helen's favourite son, 'Izates' – if the two can always be distinguished.

Josephus describes the Pharisees in perhaps his earliest reference to them in Book Thirteen of his *Antiquities* as 'not apt to be severe in punishments'. At the same time he describes the Sadducees, to whom he attaches Judas Maccabee's nephew John Hyrcanus, the father of Alexander Jannaeus, probably alluded to as 'the Angry Lion' in the Nahum *Pesher* above, as 'quite contrary' to the Pharisees.[28] But if the Maccabees were 'Sadducees', they cannot have been Sadducees of the Herodian stripe. Alexander Jannaeus' more popular and nationalistic son, Aristobulus, was poisoned by supporters of the Romans, Brutus and Cassius, and his two sons, Alexander and Antigonus, were both beheaded by Roman officials for insurrection. These are about the only beheadings recorded in Josephus aside from some revolutionary opponents of the Herodian regime earlier and that of John the Baptist and 'Theudas' in the next century, making a sequentiality here, should one choose to regard it.

As mentioned previously, after Herod stormed Jerusalem in 37 BC with troops Mark Anthony had given him, he had the previous Sanhedrin executed, except for Pollio and Sameas, the two *Pharisees* who predicted his rise to power and recommended to the people 'to open the gates' to him – these, the new-style 'prophets' of the Herodian Period that Paul and the Book of Acts seem so enamoured of.[29] As Josephus says, they were 'honoured by Herod above all the rest', but Herod 'never left off taking vengeance upon his enemies'.

These enemies must be seen as the previous Sadducean-dominated Sanhedrin and the supporters of Aristobulus II and his two sons. On the contrary, Herod 'had spies placed everywhere', even sometimes joining them surreptitiously himself, 'and many there were who were brought to the Citadel Hyrcania, both openly and in secret, and there put to death'. This is exactly the treatment meted out a generation or two later by Herod Antipas – 'Herod the Tetrarch' in the Gospels – to John the Baptist at the Fortress of Machaeros directly across the Dead Sea as the crow flies from Hyrcania.[30]

Though these 'Maccabean' or 'Purist Sadducees' might have been 'stricter in Judgement' than others and thoroughly uncompromising to boot, they certainly were never collaborators, nor did they have anything in common with the so-called 'Sadducees' in the Herodian Period except the name. The latter were rather a motley assortment of 'Rich' families vying with each other, often through bribes or contributions to Herodians or Roman officials, to occupy the High Priesthood, obviously making no insistence other than a genealogical one for the High Priesthood – and, according to Josephus, sometimes not even this. Certainly they made no claim for 'Piety' or 'higher purity', as so-called 'Galilean' Zealots or '*Sicarii*' did.

The Dead Sea Scrolls evince a similar uncompromising insistence on 'Righteousness' and absolute, unrelenting 'Judgement'. They do not compromise, nor is there any ethos of accommodation – particularly with foreigners – but always exhibit a thoroughgoing and unbending zeal that even considers the Temple polluted because of the accommodating behaviour of the Establishment High Priests there – it is hard to conceive of this as the Maccabean Period![31]

Our presentation of *two* groups of Sadducees, as we saw, is borne out in Rabbinic tradition as well. Here, *two* groups of 'Sadducees' are noted, those following Boethus and those following *Saddok*.[32] But this allusion to the name 'Boethus' makes it crystal clear, even in this Rabbinic tradition garbled as it may be, that we are in the Herodian Period and the rise of the '*Sicarii*'/'Zealot' Movement – the Movement founded by Judas the Galilean and his mysterious colleague '*Saddok*'. It was in this period that the Sadducees *split* into sycophant and resistance wings – the latter perhaps better understood as '*Messianic* Sadducees'. This was also the time consonant with 'the birth of Christ' in Christian tradition.

To crown his destruction (or co-option) of the Maccabean line, Herod brought a High Priest in from Egypt, Simeon b. Boethus, whose daughter, Mariamme II, he married after putting the last Maccabean Princess – his previous wife – Mariamme I, to death. It was this Priest's son, Joezer ben Boethus, whom Josephus portrays as opposing the founders of the '*Sicarii*'/'Zealot' Movement, Judas and *Saddok*, over the issue of *paying taxes to Rome*, that is, Roman rule in Palestine.

Where James, who is one of the heirs of the 'Opposition Sadducee' tradition, is concerned, Josephus' account now, perhaps more comprehensibly, continues:

> Ananus, therefore, being of this character, and supposing that he now had a favourable opportunity, Festus being dead and Albinus still on the road, called a Sanhedrin [Assembly] of the judges and brought before them the brother of Jesus, who was called 'the Christ', whose name was James, along with certain others, and when he had presented a charge against them of *breaking the Law, delivered them to be stoned.*

> But those citizens who seemed *the most equitable and the most careful in observation of the Law* were offended by this and sent to the King secretly asking him to send to Ananus requesting him to desist from doing such things, saying that he had not acted legally even before. Some of them also went out to meet Albinus, who was on the way from Alexandria, informing him that it was not lawful for Ananus to convene a Sanhedrin without his consent. Induced on account of what they had said, Albinus wrote to Ananus in a rage threatening to bring him to punishment because of what he had done. As a result, King Agrippa took the High Priesthood from him after he had ruled only three months and replaced him . . .

This is an extremely detailed testimony and it certainly has – except perhaps for the point about 'Jesus being called the Christ' – the straightforward ring of historical truth. It is matter of fact, down to earth, and unembellished. There is, in the manner of Josephus' often rather flat prosody, nothing fantastic in it – no exaggeration. In particular, the note about Albinus being on the way from Alexandria when he received the information about Ananus' illicit condemnation of James has the kind of detail and immediacy that carries the sense of historical authenticity.

Since Josephus immediately goes on to present Albinus as being no better than previous governors and corrupted by the gifts and bribes from these same 'Rich' Sadducean High Priests, he is no apologist for Albinus' behaviour and seems willing to give a fair appreciation of his flaws as well as his one seeming virtue – his objection to the flouting of his authority in the matter of the execution of James. Whereas before he arrived in the country, he seems to have resented the affront to his authority represented by Ananus' behaviour; afterwards, he gave a free hand to the Richest High Priests and made common cause with them against those Josephus has now started calling 'Sicarii'.

As Josephus describes it, these 'Rich' Sadducean High Priests, allying themselves with 'the boldest sort of men', went to the threshing floors and violently appropriated the tithes due to 'Priests of the Poorer sort'. As previously remarked, he repeats this notice twice, first under Felix around 59–60 CE – at the point where Acts has Paul first put under protective custody by Felix in Caesarea – and once under Albinus, 62–64 CE, directly after the illegal stoning of James.

In both instances, these predatory activities of the High Priests give way to violent clashes, stone-throwing, 'and class hatred between the High Priests on the one hand and the Leaders of the Multitudes of Jerusalem on the other'. These are exactly the sort of 'Leaders' the early Christians are portrayed as being in Jerusalem – especially in the Temple – in Acts. These last Josephus now calls 'Innovators' again, a term in Greek also meaning 'Revolutionaries'.[33] It is stone-throwing of this kind, too, albeit official, that is connected in all accounts to James' death.

The first description of this kind of behaviour in 59–60 CE is followed by the 'Temple Wall Affair', directed against Agrippa II's dining habits and his viewing of the Temple sacrifices while reclining on his balcony and eating. This is somewhere after 60 CE, around the time he and his sister, Bernice, appear in Acts (25:13–26:32) interviewing Paul. The second such description is followed by rioting led by one Saulus, his brother Costobarus, and their kinsman Antipas, whom Josephus describes as 'using violence with the People' following James' stoning, somewhere around the year 64 CE. In 64, Albinus, hearing the next Governor, Florus (64–66), was coming to replace him, emptied the prisons, arbitrarily putting many to death, but letting others go with 'the payment of bribes', so that Josephus ruefully observed, 'the country was filled with Robbers'.[34] This seems to be something of the backdrop the New Testament uses to portray Pontius Pilate's behaviour three decades before.

In fact, Josephus would have been in a good position to know about many of these things, because, as he tells us in his *Autobiography*, written around the year 93 CE, after the War, he struck up a very close friendship in Rome with this same King Agrippa, who wrote sixty-two letters to him and appears to have vouchsafed much information Josephus did not previously know. Two of these letters, addressed to 'my dear Josephus' – as we saw – Josephus appends to his book.[35]

The language of 'Law-keeping' and 'Law-breaking' one finds in this notice from Josephus about James' death is interesting and echoes that found as well in both the Letter of James and the Habakkuk *Pesher*.[36] The implication that there are *two* kinds of Law, one *Torah* and one Roman Administrative, is played upon by Paul in Romans 13:1–7 and 1 Corinthians 7:19, when he discusses the obedience one owes to the Authorities and what he calls 'God's Commandments', by which he often means *Roman Law*. In Paul and the New Testament generally, the words 'Lawful' or 'guilty' can often mean lawful according to Roman Law not biblical.

The theme, in Josephus' notice about James' death, of Ananus' 'ruling', agrees with the manner in which the Habakkuk *Pesher* presents 'the Wicked Priest', whom at one point is referred to as 'ruling Israel'. This comment has much disturbed commentators, making them think they had to do with Maccabean Priest-Kings not Herodian High Priests. As can be seen from this allusion to Ananus in Josephus, all High Priests can be said to have 'ruled Israel'. This is again emphasized at the end of the *Antiquities* when Josephus enumerates all the High Priests starting in David's time, saying:

> Some of these [the High Priests] *ruled during the reign of Herod* and his son Archelaus, although after their deaths, the Government became an aristocracy and the High Priests were entrusted with *ruling the Nation*.[37]

The idea that James was stoned with 'several colleagues' also agrees with the way the various attacks on the Righteous Teacher and his colleagues is delineated at Qumran. These last, too, are often presented in the plural.[38] In our view, James was the Leader of these 'Poorer sort of Priests'. This is supported, however tendentiously, in Acts 6:7's notice above of 'a great multitude of Priests being *obedient* to the Faith' – the word 'obedient' here linking up with the repeated allusions to 'obeying the Just One' just encountered in the Hegesippus account. These might be termed 'Nazirite' or 'Essene Priests'. In any event, they were, in the words of Acts 21:20, 'all Zealots for the Law'. As such, James was 'the *Zaddik*' of the Opposition Alliance, the centre about whom these disturbances or confrontations in the Temple turned, whose removal in 62 CE made the Messianic Uprising that followed inevitable.

The Conspiracy to Remove James

Josephus' account very definitely points to a 'conspiracy' between Ananus and Agrippa II to take advantage of the anarchy, consequent upon the interregnum in Roman Governors, to remove James. Their friendship was solidified in Rome in the early 50s during the course of previous distur-bances of this kind and appeals to Caesar, which resulted in Felix, the Emperor's freedman, being sent out to Palestine as Governor.[39] Felix's brother, Pallas, was Nero's lover, and Nero took power almost directly after this event, after having his kinsman Claudius assassinated, which may have contributed to the downward spiral of events in Palestine.

'Conspiracy' is definitely the language the Dead Sea Scrolls use, too, with regard to the destruction of the Righteous Teacher by the Wicked Priest – the word in Hebrew there is 'zemam'/'zammu', 'he conspired' and 'they conspired'.[40] This is also the language that permeates the Gospels, particularly as regards Judas *Iscariot* and the High Priests, albeit inverted or reversed once again, not to mention early Christian usage generally *vis-à-vis* 'the Jews' as a whole.

But why was this and what could this 'conspiracy' have been? Josephus refers to Agrippa II as 'the last King of the Jews' – paralleling the phrase, 'the Last [High] Priests of Jerusalem', in the Scrolls – with appropriate obsequiousness and congeniality in his *Autobiography*. In the same breath he also complains bitterly about Agrippa's role in saving his enemy, Justus of Tiberius, who, following recent Messianic disturbances in Libya or 'Cyrene', came forward with new accusations of sedition against Josephus, which may ultimately have led to Josephus' demise.[41]

This Agrippa had almost as much cause to seek James' removal as the High Priest Ananus did. If we place James at the centre of agitation in the Temple over whether to allow Herodian Kings into the Temple, to accept their gifts or appointment of High Priests, and the acceptance of gifts and sacrifices from foreigners generally – including on behalf of the Roman Emperor – then these individuals had ample reason to blame James for a good many things, not least of which, his continued attacks on their 'Riches'.

In fact, the way the James episode is interposed between several other important bits of information at the very end of the *Antiquities* – most of which are missing from the *War* – makes it clear that more emphasis should be placed on it than might otherwise be the case. As suggested, it is important to look at the sequentiality of the events covered in the all-important, last book of the *Antiquities* (Book Twenty).

Immediately following James' death, as remarked, Albinus co-operated with the High Priests in launching a campaign to rid the country of the *Sicarii* – whom Josephus also calls 'Robbers'.[42] In fact, Josephus uses the term '*Sicarii*' to designate those following the Fourth Philosophy even before he uses the term 'Zealots' at a later point in the *Jewish War*, and, in the *Antiquities*, the designation 'Zealot' doesn't even occur. Rather, Josephus first uses the term 'Zealots' to describe (in the *War*) those who slaughter the Establishment High Priests responsible for the death of James, burning all their palaces as the Uprising moves into its more virulent or 'Jacobite' phase. In our view, this is vengeance for what these Establishment 'Sadducees' did to James.

As for 'the *Sicarii*' – those allegedly carrying curved, Arab-style daggers under their 'garments' – they are first introduced, it will be recalled, in 55 CE, when they are responsible for the assassination of Ananus' brother Jonathan, the then High Priest.[43] No doubt they did not call themselves by this appellation, but Josephus makes it clear that, extreme 'Zealots' as they were, they were the heirs to the Movement founded by Judas the Galilean and *Saddok*. They finally end with their families at Masada where they commit mass suicide rather than surrender to the Romans even after the fall of the Temple. In this sequentiality, the judicial murder of James in the early 60s by Ananus is retribution for the murder of his brother in the 50s by 'the *Sicarii*'.

In discussing this assassination of Ananus' brother, Jonathan, by 'the *Sicarii*' in the 50s in the *Antiquities*, Josephus makes the same accusation against extremist groups he does in discussing the butchering of Ananus in the *War* in the 60s. In the latter, it will be recalled, he stated:

> I cannot but think it was because God had condemned this city [meaning Jerusalem] to destruction as a *polluted* city that He *cut off* [note the possible play here] these its greatest defenders and benefactors [meaning Ananus ben Ananus and Josephus' own friend, Jesus ben Gamala].[44]

In the former, he goes further, falling back on the *mea culpa* admission of guilt, which so punctuates his assessment of the lawlessness of the Zealots. This is certainly one of the prototypes for the more famous cry, 'his blood be upon us and our children', in Christian Scripture and theology thereafter. In both instances, these accusations have been enlarged from an accusation against a particular extremist group to one against *a whole people*.

Regarding Jonathan, this reads, as previously described, as follows:

> And this seems to me to have been the reason why God, out of his hatred for these men's Wickedness [the *Sicarii*'s], rejected our city. As for the Temple, He no longer considered it sufficiently pure for Him to inhabit therein, but brought the Romans upon us and threw fire upon the city to cleanse it, and brought upon us, our wives and children, slavery, that he might teach us wisdom.[45]

This is, of course, exactly the accusation in Christian Scripture and Christian theology, slightly transmuted and transferred, as it has come down to us. But Josephus is saying that it is because of terrorist murders of Establishment High Priests like Jonathan and Ananus, not because of the Jews' murder of Christ, that the Jews suffered. Still, the common thread of the motif of the '*Sicarii*' – if '*Iscariot*' and '*Sicarios*' are related usages – occurs in both. Of course, Josephus is displaying the grovelling sycophantism and subservience of the typical captive,[46] but even the theme of 'pollution of the Temple', so fundamental to the Qumran position – not to mention Paul's theme of 'slavery' – remarkably is present in the above extract and reversed. For Josephus, it is now the fanatical, purity-minded extremists who are *polluting the Temple*, not the *collaborating High Priests*.

One can, however, take a further step and state with some certainty that it was because the Jews *were so Messianic* that they lost everything, not vice versa as in the New Testament and Phariseeizing Rabbinic Orthodoxy too, the mirror reversal of Christian Orthodoxy. The last step in this is simple. One need only identify these 'lawless' bands of '*Sicarii*' and 'Zealots' as enthusiasts for 'the Star Prophecy' at Qumran and part and parcel, therefore, of the Messianic Movement. And Josephus does just this, as we have seen, in a much overlooked key section at the end of the *War* dealing with omens and oracles of the destruction of the Temple.

He concludes these by saying that 'what most encouraged' the Jews to revolt against Rome

> was an ambiguous oracle found in their Sacred Writings, that at that time, one from their country would become Ruler of the whole inhabited world –

'ambiguous', as we saw, because Josephus, as Rabbinic Judaism thereafter, then goes on to apply it to *Vespasian their conqueror*. In the parallel to the New Testament 'Little Apocalypse's above, he had observed in the *Antiquities* that the spread of the Movement he calls 'a disease', started by

'Judas and *Saddok*' ('which before we were unacquainted with') 'among our young men, *who were zealous for it*, brought our country to destruction'.47 In other words, it was *because the Jews were so 'zealous'* for the World-Ruler Prophecy, and that Messianism consequent upon it, that they lost everything – not the opposite way round.

The New Testament has by implication rather reversed this, making it seem as if – because of the accusation of *killing Christ* – the Jews as a whole were *anti-Messianic*. But this is patently untrue as we can see. The Establishment Classes were, including the Pharisee progenitors of Rabbinic Judaism today. But, by making it seem as if *the Jews as a whole* killed or collaborated with the Romans in the killing of Christ – the point of the Gospels and the Pauline corpus – they make it appear as if the mass of the Jews were not Messianic and opposed Messianism, when, in fact, just the opposite was true. It was because the mass of the Jews *were* so Messianic, as Josephus amply illustrates, not because they supported the Establishment and/or the '*Pax Romanum*' of the Roman Authorities, however one interprets this, as the Gospels would have us believe – that God brought these calamities and political disasters upon them. Thus Josephus.

In his description of the significance of the World-Ruler Prophecy at the end of the *Jewish War*, Josephus also describes the signs and portents connected to how God, disgusted with the Temple, departed from it – things that, no doubt, much impressed the superstitious Romans, as they would many today. These included the appearance of 'armed chariots and armies marching across the clouds at sunset', certainly a play on the coming of the Heavenly Host on the clouds in James' proclamation in the Temple and the War Scroll above. There is also 'a Star, which stood like a great dagger', not over the birthplace of Jesus in Bethlehem portending the Salvation of Mankind – as in the Gospel of Matthew, *but over Jerusalem portending its doom.*48

In these descriptions, Josephus over and over again reverses the charges of 'Impiety towards God' and 'pollution of the Temple' on the part of the present Authorities into 'Impiety towards God' and 'pollution of the Temple', because of the blood shed by these '*Sicarii*' and 'Zealot' bands. So intent is Josephus on these charges against 'the *Sicarii*' that he even follows them down into Egypt and Libya after the War is over with the same charges.49 In this regard, we have even speculated, as in the case of 'Judas *Iscariot*' above, whether there is not some play on the word 'Christian' – the two appellatives, 'Christian' and '*Sicarii*', being in Greek virtual acronyms – going on here or vice versa; or whether those Josephus is derogatorily calling 'Sicarii', particularly but not exclusively in Palestine, are not being called 'Christians' in other contexts, particularly overseas. This is certainly true of 'Judas'.

In the Damascus Document and to some extent in the document called 'MMT' at Qumran, the charge of 'pollution of the Temple' is directed against the Establishment Parties and probably included this matter of accepting gifts and sacrifices on behalf of foreigners. But, according to Josephus, it is 'the Chief Priests and principal Pharisees' – the same groups the New Testament blames for the condemnation of 'Jesus Christ' – who try to dissuade the people from rejecting such 'gifts and sacrifices', claiming it would lay the city open 'to the charge of Impiety'.

As Josephus pictures it, the last-named claim it is 'an innovation in their religion', since their forefathers had always accepted gifts from foreigners and forbidden no one from offering sacrifices, even adorning the Temple with them and raising dedicatory plaques to them.[50] But by saying this, Josephus neglects to mention the view of Ezekiel 44:1–15 above, so dear to the Qumran Damascus Document and the prophet perhaps held in highest repute by such extremist partisans and these 'zealous' Lower Priests who wish to reject such sacrifices.

This is the problem with Josephus, who rarely gives the entire picture where insurgent groups are at issue. His account shifts according to what his sources say and what seems most expedient. Like Paul, who follows a similar *modus operandi* regarding doctrinal matters, Josephus is an apologist, who is completely unaware of his own disingenuousness.

The Attack on James and Saulus' Riotous Behaviour

In this period, it is always useful to group parties together according to who their common enemies were. On this basis, the 'Christians' in Jerusalem (whatever one might wish to say about their ideology or whatever name to apply), the 'Zealots', 'Sicarii', and the 'Messianists' responsible for the literature at Qumran, can all be said to have the *same* enemies, namely the Pharisees, 'Establishment Sadducees' or the High Priests, and the Herodians. In addition to this, when one examines the sequence of events leading up to and following James' judicial murder in the last book of the *Antiquities*, one first encounters the disturbances of the late 40s and early 50s in Chapter Six, involving hostilities between Samaritans and Jews as well and their apparent respective Messianic expectations.

However distorted, this too receives an echo in Acts in the confrontation in Samaria between Peter and Simon *Magus* (8:18–25). It is as a result of these disturbances that Ananus (the son of the Ananus pictured in the Gospel of John as participating in the trial of Jesus – 18:3–24), is sent to Rome with another High Priest called Ananias, on one of these by now familiar 'appeals to Caesar'. There he cements his relationship with Agrippa II in the days just before Claudius' assassination (*c.* 53 CE). Ananus was only Captain of the Temple at this point, while Ananias – sometimes confused with Ananus – was the 'Richest' of the High Priests. It is clearly on account of his 'Riches' that Albinus, following James' stoning, co-operates with him in mopping up 'the *Sicarii*'.[51]

One should also note that, in this narrative in Acts, Peter follows up this visit to Samaria by 'going down to the Saints that lived in Lydda'. This is before his vision of the Heavenly tablecloth which will bear on his visit to the household of the Roman Centurion 'Cornelius' in Caesarea. In the above episode in Josephus, Lydda is the scene of the Messianic disturbances between Samaritans and Jews. Acts pictures Peter as curing a paralytic 'named Aeneas' and raising a sick widow 'called Tabitha', which Acts re-interprets as 'being called Dorcas', in Lydda (9:32–43).[52] All this without comment, as if it were perfectly normal.

We must compare this to Josephus' collateral account of *Messianic disturbances* and *rapine* between Samaritans and Jews *in Lydda*. Josephus calls the Jewish leader of the 'Innovators' or 'Revolutionaries' there, 'Dortus'! This individual, who he says was reported by 'a certain Samaritan' to have had *four assistants*, was executed – presumably by crucifixion.[53] What malevolent fun the authors of Acts would appear to be having, transmuting history into meaningless dross.

In the next chapter – Chapter Seven of Book Twenty – Josephus interrupts his narrative to discuss the intricate tangle of marriages and divorces and the personal and political consequences of these relating to the family of Agrippa II and his three sisters, Bernice, Drusilla, and Mariamme III, all relevant to the 'fornication' charge at Qumran and its seeming reflection in the Letter ascribed to James and James' own directives to overseas communities in Acts. This is followed in Chapter Eight by Josephus' picture of how 'the *Sicarii*'

> went up to the city [Jerusalem], as if they were going to worship God, while they had daggers under their garments, and by mingling in this manner among the crowds, they slew Jonathan.

Then commenting how 'the Robbers [*Lēstai*] infected the city with all sorts of pollution' and 'Impiety', terms he basically uses to designate all 'Messianists', 'Zealots', or '*Sicarii*', Josephus now reiterates the by now familiar:

The impostors and Deceivers persuaded the Multitudes to follow them out into the wilderness under the pretence that there they would perform marvellous wonders and signs made possible by God's Providence.

In the *War*, it will be recalled, he varies this slightly, saying: 'Wishing to foster revolutionary change, they exhort the masses to assert their liberty' and, feigning Divine inspiration, 'lead the people out into the wilderness in the belief that there God would show them the signs of their approaching freedom'. Adding, 'they also threaten to kill all those willing to submit to Roman Rule', he goes on to describe in both, how they rob and burn the houses of the Rich, killing their owners.[54]

At this point, too, in both books, Josephus describes Felix's brutality in dealing with one of these 'impostors' or 'Messianic Leaders', the unnamed Egyptian, for whom Paul is mistaken, again by a Roman Centurion, in Acts 21:38 – the chronology of both is the same, *c.* 59–60 CE. Not only does Josephus (it will be recalled as well) call this 'Egyptian', 'a Prophet', he describes the Joshua-like miracles he wishes to do, such as commanding *the walls of Jerusalem to fall down*. For the *War*, 'He wished to establish himself as a Tyrant there, with his companions as his bodyguard.'[55]

Some would identify this 'Egyptian', who in both accounts escapes in the subsequent confusion, with Simon *Magus*, who was also said to have come from 'Gitta' in Samaria.[56] The Redeemer figure of the Samaritans, called 'the *Taheb*', also seems to have been a Joshua-like figure or a 'Joshua *redivivus*' or a 'Joshua come-back-to-life'. Some twenty-five years before – again under Pontius Pilate and coinciding with our 'Jesus' episode in the Gospels – Josephus records another disturbance or uprising led by such a Messiah-like individual in Samaria. Looking suspiciously like the 'Jesus' episode in the Gospels, this Uprising was also brutally repressed by Pilate, including, it would appear, a number of crucifixions – only the locale was not the Mount of Olives, but Mount Gerizim, the *Samaritan Holy Place*.[57] In fact, early Church writers often mix up Samaritan sects, including ones supposedly originated by Simon *Magus* and a colleague of his, 'Dositheus' – probably our 'Dorcas' or 'Dortus' above – with ones circulating about Daily Bathers like John, James, and other 'Essenes'/'Ebionites'.[58]

Confusion between the activities of Paul and Simon *Magus* also bedevils Pseudoclementine literature. For whatever the reason, both Paul and Simon would seem to have been in the service of the Herodian family – Simon *Magus* conniving at the marriage between Felix and Agrippa II's sister Drusilla. This marriage is also mentioned in Chapter Seven by Josephus above, where characteristically Simon is called 'a Cypriot' – a mix-up probably having to do with Simon's place of origin, 'Gitta', or the general Jewish name for Samaritans, 'Cuthaeans' ('*Kittim*'?). Where Paul is concerned, we shall in due course suggest that he is probably an actual member of this family. Again, all of these episodes and issues would appear to bear a relationship – however remote – to James' position of authority over the masses in Jerusalem and on the reason for his ultimate removal.[59]

Arguments in the Temple and Increasing Violence

As Chapter Eight of Book Twenty continues, Josephus documents the warfare that broke out, following this violence between *Samaritans and Jews*, between the Jewish residents of Caesarea and the Greco-Syrian ones. The last he describes as 'being proud of the fact they supplied the greater part of the Roman soldiers there'! In Josephus, this strife in Caesarea is part of the background to the stoning of James. In Acts, similar strife is part of the background to the stoning of Stephen, which is occasioned by 'the murmuring' of so-called 'Hellenists' (that is, 'Greeks') against 'Hebrews' over 'the daily [food] distribution,' in which widows were somehow overlooked (*thus* – 6:1). In Josephus, it is the equal citizenship and privileges the Jews of Caesarea claimed with the 'Hellenists' or 'Greeks' there.[60]

In Josephus, this strife is so important that, again, 'it provided the basis for the misfortunes that subsequently befell our nation', something he has also said concerning various incidents surrounding the stoning of James. Not only will the Greek residents in Caesarea finally bribe Nero's Secretary for Greek Letters 'with a large sum of money' to write a letter 'annulling the grant of equal privileges *to the Jews*'[61] (notice how this theme of 'equal rights' is once again reversed in Acts' portrayal of problems within the early Christian Community between 'Hebrews and Hellenists' prefacing the stoning of Stephen), but Felix, the Roman Procurator, finally crushes these disorders by slaughtering a good many of the Jews. In doing so, 'he allows his soldiers to plunder many of their houses which were full of money', until 'the more responsible Jews (that is, the more accommodating ones) alarmed for themselves, begged for mercy' and 'to be allowed *to repent for what had been done*'.[62]

In pursuance of this theme of violence in Caesarea, Josephus will go on to describe the brutality of these same Caesarean Legionnaires in the next decade (the 60s), leading up to the War against Rome, as being the foremost cause goading the Jews to revolt. It is, almost incredibly, a Centurion from these same brutal Caesarean Legionnaires that Acts 10:2 portrays – following Peter's visit to Lydda and the 'mighty works' he did there – as 'Pious and God-fearing, doing many good works for the people, and [James-like] *supplicating God continually*'. In Acts 10:22, continuing this indecent parallel with James, it calls him 'a *Zaddik* ['Righteous Man'] and God-fearing, confirmed by the whole nation of the Jews' (*thus*)! 'Tabitha', also called 'Dorcas', was described as 'full of good works and doing charity' ('*Zedakah*' in Hebrew) as well (8:36).

It is worth remembering that this Centurion called Cornelius is said to come from the 'Italica Contingent', Italica being a town in Roman Spain near presentday Seville, from which both Trajan and Hadrian in the next century came (Acts 10:1). For his part, Trajan's father – also 'Trajan' – had been a decorated soldier in Palestine with Vespasian's and Titus' victorious legions.[63] It is interesting that in Josephus' *Antiquities*, one 'Cornelius' is a messenger from this same Caesarean milieu sent to Rome to request that the High Priestly vestments be given over to the control of the Herodians, Herod of Chalcis, Aristobulus his son and husband of the infamous Salome, and Agrippa II, still a minor. This is to say nothing of resonance with the '*Lex Cornelia de Sicarius*' above.[64]

According to Acts, it is in anticipation of visiting Cornelius, 'a Centurion of the Italica Regiment', that Peter receives his tablecloth vision on the rooftop in Jaffa, where he learns, firstly, there are no forbidden foods (see Paul's 'all things are Lawful for me' in 1 Corinthians 6:12 and 10:23 above); secondly, he was wrong previously to think he should not keep table fellowship with Gentiles, and, thirdly, 'wrong to make distinctions between clean and unclean', 'Holy and profane'. Since God '*is not a respecter of persons*', all being equal in Christ Jesus, the conclusion is that 'the repentance unto life having been given to Gentiles too' (Acts 10:1–11:18).

Not only do we have here the expression, 'not respecting of persons', found in descriptions of James, but the actual use of the word 'repentance' found in Josephus' narrative too above, but used there to characterize how the more 'accommodating' Jews in Caesarea begged forgiveness from Felix for their countrymen's behaviour.

In the *War*, Josephus characterizes

> the number of Robbers he [Felix] caused to be crucified, and the common people caught and punished with them were a multitude not to be enumerated.[65]

This is the same Felix, with whom Paul after his arrest converses so felicitously, along with Drusilla, Felix's wife, whom Acts somewhat disingenuously only identifies as 'a Jewess' (24:24). Actually, she is, as we saw, a Herodian Princess, the sister of King Agrippa II above. For Acts, Felix 'knew a lot about *the Way*', a designation it uses throughout when speaking about early Christianity in Palestine (24:22).[66] He should do, since he put to death a good many of its representatives, a point wholly lacking in Acts' portrayal.

Ultimately complaints made by the Jews of Caesarea against Felix reach as far as Rome and he is removed by Nero – though not otherwise punished because of the high connections he enjoys – and replaced as procurator by Festus (60–62). According to Acts, Paul converses rather congenially with Festus too – along with King Agrippa II and Bernice – over a variety of Jewish subjects and Messianic expectations. This, for some two chapters (25:1–26:32). Bernice, it will be recalled, is Agrippa II's sister too, about whom Josephus preserves a charge of illicit sexual connection with her brother. According to Josephus, extremely 'Rich', she is the future mistress of Titus the destroyer of the Temple and Jerusalem.

The High Priest – unnamed at this point and described only as 'the Ruler of the Jews', but earlier called 'Ananias' – is presented as preferring charges against Paul (25:2). Earlier, too, the Pharisees and the Sadducees, were presented as arguing with each other in a Sanhedrin setting over the issue of the Resurrection of the dead and Paul, as cleverly exploiting this to get the better of both of them (23:6–10). In Acts 24:15 he gives *Felix* a lecture on the same subject!

Nor is there any hint in Acts' presentation of Paul's arrest and transport under protective escort to Caesarea (where Acts 23:35 actually allows that he stayed in *King Agrippa II's palace*) of the strife between Hellenes and Jews at this time in Caesarea documented by Josephus. Rather the issue is presented as being complaints against Paul to Felix by the Jews, specifically including the High Priest Ananias above and someone with the Greco-Latin name of 'Tertullus' (24:1), and the strife is either between different parties of Jews arguing with each other or with Paul over issues like 'the Resurrection of the dead' (in 24:15, of 'the Just and Unjust alike').

In the earlier episode, Ananias is actually pictured as ordering Paul to be 'hit in the mouth' (23:2) – in the succeeding interview before Felix, he only calls Paul 'a leader of the *Nazoraean Heresy*' and 'a disease-bearer, moving insurrection among all the Jews in the habitable world' (24:5).[67] This is hardly Paul, though the accusation is certainly true of some others.

In any event, Ananias probably wasn't even High Priest at this time (60 CE) and the picture of him participating in complaints before the Governor probably has more to do with those, a decade before, when he did hold that office and the above Messianic disturbances broke out between Samaritans and Jews under the Procurator Cumanus (48–52 CE). This brought on the military intervention of Quadratus, the Governor of Syria, who thereupon sent all parties, including Cumanus, to plead their case before Claudius not Nero.

Transposition and confusion of chronology is fairly standard practice in New Testament narratives. As will be recalled, this is the first appearance of the Younger Ananus on the scene, who was then only Captain of the Temple, and it was as a result of these appeals to Caesar that he and Agrippa II became close friends in Rome – the time approximately 54 CE just before Claudius' death.[68] Still, for once Acts has the issue right, 'pollution of the Temple' (24:6), because Paul is perceived as having introduced Gentiles and, no doubt consequently, their gifts as well into the Temple – which he most certainly did, if not actually physically, then certainly spiritually. In fact, Caesarea is a favourite centre for Pauline activities, as will become clear in the run-up to Paul's last confrontation with James in Jerusalem, before the mêlée in the Temple, which occasions Paul's arrest in Acts and confinement in Agrippa II's palace in Caesarea.

But, in our view, the real cause of James' death and the real arguments between the Jews aside from the pro-forma squabbles over Resurrection of the dead highlighted in Acts (an issue anyone interested in this time could easily have discovered from reading Josephus) is documented in the very next episodes in Chapter Eight of Book Twenty of Josephus, leading directly into Chapter Nine's presentation of the stoning of James and its aftermath. None of those things is properly documented in Acts. Here,

> the High Priests and the principal men of the multitude of Jerusalem [paralleling the term 'the Many' for the rank and file at Qumran], each gathering about them a company of the boldest men and those that *loved Innovation* . . . and when they fought each other, they hurled reproachful words at each other, throwing stones as well.

This is, of course, the situation in Jerusalem showing serious argument and stone-throwing between two factions, the High Priests and those described as being of the People. It is also the prototype for the situation in the Temple, as described in early Church sources centring around the stoning of James. Not only would these disputes appear to be the immediate historical context of James' death, but the events that follow them lead directly to the outbreak of the War against Rome – itself provoked by the Caesarean Legionnaires under Fadus (64–66 CE) who succeeds Albinus (62–64) – and the destruction of the Temple. All that is left to do is to place James at the centre of the faction representing the People.

But there is more. It is at this point in the *Antiquities* that Josephus first gives us his description of:

> the impudence and boldness of the High Priests, who actually dared to send their assistants to the threshing floors, to take away those tithes that were due the Priests, with the result that 'the Poor' among the Priests starved to death.[69]

It will be recalled that Josephus repeats this description a second time directly after the stoning of James during Albinus' regime. Josephus ties this 'robbing sustenance' or 'robbing the Poor', which we shall also see reflected in descriptions of 'the Last Priests of Jerusalem' in the Habakkuk *Pesher*, not only to Ananias, but also the other priests, saying,

> they took away the tithes that belonged to the Priests [probably including our 'Nazirite' or 'Rechabite Priests', of whom James was the leader] and did not refrain from beating such as would not give these tithes to them, so that these Priests, whom of old were supported by these tithes, died for want of food.[70]

Josephus clearly has mixed emotions here. Sometimes he sympathizes with the Lower Priests dying for want of sustenance, whom he actually designates as 'the Poor'. He must have understood this situation very well, for this would be the class he came from – therefore his criticism of 'the Chief Priests'. But, at other times, he catches himself and continues his criticism of 'the Robbers' or '*Lēstai*', whom, he now says, caused the Uprising against Rome. Sometimes he treats Agrippa II – later his confidant – and Bernice, Agrippa II's sister, sympathetically, while at other times he is critical.

As a young Priest, Josephus studied with the '*Banus*' described above, that is, he followed the regime of daily bathing in the wilderness, telling us that 'Banus bathed both night and day *in cold water* to [like James] preserve his virginity', and that for three years he, Josephus, 'imitated him in this activity'. We have already suggested that these activities, centring about this chronological contemporary of and 'double' for James, comprised something of a training ground for young priests, at least 'Rechabite'-style ones. Josephus has, therefore, conflicting emotional allegiances, mixed with a strong desire to survive. Both are evident in the various contradictory statements he makes.

The next episode he describes, preceding 'the Temple Wall Affair' leading directly to the stoning of James, exhibits these personal conflicts as well. Here, too, Josephus notes how Festus (60–62 CE), like Felix before him and Albinus to follow (62–64 CE), was active in putting down such wilderness 'sojourners' or 'Deceivers'. Acts, too, talks about Festus' regime in Judea, in regard to the unjust imprisonment or protective custody of Paul, who himself was mistaken for such a 'Deceiver'.

Here, Josephus tells us that

> Festus, too, sent armed forces, horsemen and foot soldiers, to fall upon those seduced by a certain Impostor, who had promised them *Salvation* ['*Yeshu'a*' or '*Yesha*'' in Hebrew] and *freedom* from the troubles they suffered if they would follow him into the wilderness.[71]

Nor does Josephus name this new 'Impostor' either, simply stating that the forces Festus dispatched destroyed 'both the Deceiver himself and those following him', information even more scanty than that concerning 'the Egyptian' preceding it. There can be little doubt that this event is a repeat of the previous one, the only difference being that 'the Egyptian' escaped. As in the stone-throwing on the Temple Mount and the 'Rich' Priests plundering the Poorer ones, events framed in Josephus by the murder of James, there does seem to be some repetition or telescoping of events, perhaps due to faulty redaction or Josephus' own dissimulation.

But not a murmur about these sorts of difficulties is ever uttered in Acts' narrative of parallel chronological events, only that 'the Jews' – *all of them*, including what appear to be Nazirite-style 'Assassins' or '*Sicarii*' – are trying *to kill Paul*, because he has tried, even by Acts' own rather one-sided presentation of their complaints, to *introduce Gentiles into the Temple*. 'The Jews' also make an endless series of complaints against Paul both to Felix and Festus, and Paul himself is finally saved by the sympathetic intervention of these governors, not to mention that of

Agrippa II and his two wayward sisters. It is even possible that Felix with his intimate connections to Nero's household, actually paves the way for Paul's trip to Rome a year or two after his own return. In any event, the reader will now come to appreciate that Acts' account is quite obviously skewed or, at the very least, flawed.

The Temple Wall Affair in 62 CE

This brings us to a closer look at the Temple Wall Affair, which we have briefly passed over. It took place almost simultaneously with Paul's 'appeal to Caesar' in Acts – 'Augustus' as he is called in Acts 25:21–25. So important was this confrontation between Temple purists and those supporting the admission of Herodians into the Temple, that its upshot involved appeals to Caesar on the part of numerous individuals, two of no less importance than the High Priest appointed by Agrippa II and now specifically identified by Josephus as Ishmael b. Phiabi – not 'Ananias' as in Acts above – and one 'Helcias', the Keeper of the Temple Treasure! In fact, Paul and even Josephus himself may have been involved in the appeals surrounding this incident, which led inexorably to the death of James.

Helcias' father or grandfather – the genealogical lines are unclear here – had been a close associate of Herod. Herod had specifically chosen him to marry his sister Salome after forcing her to divorce an earlier husband, the Idumaean 'Costobarus', whom we shall hear more about below and whom Herod suspected of plotting against him; and ever after, the genealogies of all these lines are very closely intertwined.[72] That the Herodians generally kept a tight grip on money matters through this side of the family is clear. As we shall see, too, if it turns out that our contention that Paul was a 'Herodian' can be proved, it is this line going back to Costobarus and Herod's sister Salome to which he belonged.

The second or third 'Helcias' in this line, he was a close associate of Herod of Chalcis and, seemingly, personally responsible for the execution in prison of Agrippa I's friend, the elder Silas.[73] His son, Julius Archelaus, whom Josephus also knew in Rome and compliments in the dedication to his *Antiquities* as an avid reader of his works, was married for a time to the Herodian Princess Mariamme III, Agrippa II's third sister, before she divorced him in favour of, probably, the even 'Richer' Alabarch of Alexandria, Demetrius.

It will be recalled that Philo, the Alexandrian Jewish philosopher, and his nephew, Tiberius Alexander, the son of the previous Alabarch, Philo's brother Alexander, were members of this fabulously wealthy Egyptian Jewish family. Tiberius Alexander, Titus' military commander at the siege of Jerusalem, presided over the destruction of the Temple, while the family itself seems to have had control of commerce down the Red Sea as far as India and the Malabar coast. It is from this it derived its wealth – 'Riches' that, no doubt, played a role in some of the dynastic and political manoeuvring going on here.

Ten other unnamed participants in the Temple Wall Affair were sent to Caesar as well. Since their appeals occur at *exactly the same time* as Paul's in Acts, it is hard to conceive they are not connected in some manner. In fact, all do relate in one way or another to *barring Gentiles* or *their gifts from the Temple*, the issue that starts the War against Rome. Herodians had been perceived of as 'foreigners', ever since the visit of Simon, 'the Head of an Assembly [*Ecclēsia*] of his own', to Caesarea in the 40s. The Temple Wall Affair is of the same genre of episode as this, and relates to the wish on the part of this mysterious 'Simon' to bar Agrippa II's father from the Temple as a Gentile.

Here Josephus again shows why he is in such a quandary, for he is clearly on the side of the 'Zealot Priests' in the Temple, who build the wall to block Agrippa II's view of the sacrifices being conducted there. As he describes this affair, which according to his sequencing, *immediately* precedes the stoning of James, Agrippa II built himself a very large dining room in the royal palace at Jerusalem. This palace appears to have been first erected by the Maccabees, his ancestors via his grandmother Herod's wife Mariamme I, just overlooking the Western Portico of the Temple. Since it was situated on higher ground, it provided an excellent prospect of the sacrifices there.

As Josephus describes the scene:

> The King was enamoured of this view, and could observe, as he reclined and ate, everything that was done in the Temple. This very much displeased the Chief Men of Jerusalem [whoever these were], for it was contrary to tradition and Law that proceedings in the Temple, particularly the sacrifices, be observed. They, therefore, erected a high wall upon the uppermost portico which belonged to the Inner Court of the Temple towards the West [that is, directly over our presentday 'Wailing' or 'Western Wall'].[74]

But though his behaviour was certainly in poor taste, particularly if he was entertaining Gentiles and eating forbidden foods as he reclined and ate, which one imagines he was, it is not specifically against the Laws of the country, at least not as these are preserved in the Pharisee tradition, represented by the *Talmud*. *Mishnah Yoma* 2:8, for instance, notes how on the Day of Atonement the people stood in the Court of the Temple, from where they presumably viewed the sacrifices. There is only a prohibition of being in the Temple when the priestly functions *per se* were being performed.

But the problem here is more complicated than this and has to do with the attempt by the Simon, the Head of a 'Church' in Jerusalem of his own, to have Agrippa I barred from the Temple as a foreigner. By the time, too, that gifts and sacrifices from Gentiles are banned altogether by the 'Zealot' Lower Priesthood in 66 CE, Agrippa II himself, together with his sister, the arch-fornicator Bernice, will have been barred from Jerusalem altogether, not to mention that their palaces will be burned in the immediate euphoria of the early days of the Uprising.[75]

In fact, this is the position of one document from Qumran, the Temple Scroll, sometimes called the Second Law because of the many new and stricter legal points it details. This document, which like Deuteronomy has God speaking in the first person, not only devotes a whole section to this and related issues but, in doing so, uses the language of 'Bela'' or *'balla''/*'swallowing'. We have already discussed how this usage has something to do with Herodians, 'Bela'' in the Bible having been not only a 'Benjaminite', but also the first *Edomite King*.

In the Temple Scroll, it is explicitly set forth that a high wall or a wide escarpment of some kind be built around the Temple, so that what goes on inside would neither be interrupted nor, it would appear, even 'seen' by Gentiles and other classes of unclean persons, forbidden entrance to it. In using this language, one should always compare it to the classes of persons admitted in the New Testament to share the table or person of 'Christ Jesus'.[76]

This directive can be seen as directly relating to both the issue of Agrippa II's dining habits and the attempt to bar his father from the Temple as a foreigner.

The Belial and Balaam Circle of Language and Revelation

The language circle relating to the Hebrew letters *B–L–'* is a complex one, but suffice it to say that it is related to the words *Bela'*, *Balaam*, and *Belial*, all based on the same root in Hebrew, meaning, as we have seen, 'to swallow' or 'consume'. At Qumran this has the secondary meaning of 'to destroy'. We have been following this language particularly with regard to Paul's position on eating forbidden foods above.

For the Damascus Document, it is the 'Three Nets of Belial', as we saw, that seduce Israel away into committing 'fornication', 'Riches', and 'pollution of the Temple'. This same allusion, including these same 'nets', is used in Revelation, a document that both begins with the image of seeing the Messiah 'coming on the clouds' and ends with 'the bright and morning Star' (1:7 and 22:16).[77] We shall presently see how these 'nets' reappear, reversed again or at least trivialized, in the 'nets' Jesus' core 'Apostles' or 'Disciples' abandon to follow him. For Revelation, it will be recalled,

> Balaam taught Balak *to cast* [*balein*] a net before the Sons of Israel to eat *things sacrificed to idols* and *commit fornication*. (2:14)

Both 2 Peter, which is permeated by the imagery of Qumran, and Jude, which knows the imagery of 'the Lord coming with His Myriads of Holy Ones to execute Judgement upon all' (1:14–15), also know the imagery represented by the name 'Balaam', 'who loved Unrighteousness' and led people 'astray from the Straight Way' (2 Pet. 2:15 and Jude 1:11). So do the Rabbis, for whom Balaam is one of the four 'Enemies of God', and they interpret his name according to its Hebrew roots, *bala'-'Am*, to mean 'he who consumed the People'.[78]

But in this section of Revelation, too, we have the wherewithal to connect the essentials of James' instructions to overseas communities, as reported in Acts on three separate occasions – 'abstain from fornication, things sacrificed to idols, strangled things, and blood' – with the parallel Damascus Document condemnations having to do with how the Establishment has polluted the Temple by not observing proper 'separation' in it, that is, 'separation of pure from impure', and using the language of sexual impropriety and 'blood' to express this. This will also turn out to be true for the Letter or Letters – addressed to a 'King' and evoking the matter of how Abraham was 'justified' – known as '*MMT*'.

The key element, here, was the charge of 'pollution of the Temple', which Revelation now transforms into James' all-important proscription on 'things sacrificed to idols', or, as Acts also phrases James' directive on this issue combining the sense of both, 'the pollutions of the idols' (15:20). As we have seen, Paul struggles mightily against this proscription in 1 Corinthians – particularly in 8:3–13 under the heading of 'loving' or 'Piety towards God' and 10:14–33 on 'partaking of the Lord's table and the table of demons'.

Paul, also, knows the language of 'Beliar', referring to it, as we also saw, within the context of comparing 'Righteousness with lawlessness', 'the Temple of God with idols', 'being separated' and 'not touching any unclean thing, Perfecting Holiness in fear of God'. This comes in his famous 'what has Christ to do with Beliar' queries in 2 Corinthians 6:14–7:1, replete with allusions permeated by the vocabulary of Qumran. We are now at the point not only of breaking the various codes that were being used in this period, but of solving many of our other puzzles as well.

The Habakkuk *Pesher* uses the language of 'swallowing' or 'consuming' – again rooted in the Hebrew letters *B–L–'* – graphically to discuss how the Wicked Priest 'pursued after the Righteous Teacher to swallow' or 'to consume him', that is, to *bala'* him. That is to say, to do the things that the Herodians consistently did to the People, 'swallow', 'consume' or 'destroy them'. In return, as the Habakkuk *Pesher* pointedly puts it, he too would be 'swallowed' or 'destroyed', that is, God would 'consume him'.

Two columns further along, this is expressed as: just as 'he plotted to destroy the Poor', so, too, 'would God condemn him to destruction'.[79] The idea that God is involved in this process becomes very clear. Therefore, to express this, the Habakkuk *Pesher* evokes the imagery of 'drinking the Cup to his fill', that is, the Cup of the Wrath of God – meaning Divine Vengeance. As already noted above, this was misinterpreted in the early days of Qumran research to imply that the Wicked Priest was a drunkard, and that, therefore, he must have been killed at a banquet! It is not worth commenting further on this idea.

But Revelation also knows this imagery and applies it to he who 'worships the Beast':

> He shall drink of the wine of the Wrath of God, which is poured undiluted into the Cup of His anger (14:10).

This is expressed two chapters further on as

> For they poured out the blood of Saints and the Prophets, and you gave them blood to drink (16:6),

and again:

> And the cities of the Peoples [*Ethnoi* – in the New Testament, Paul's 'Gentiles'; in the Scrolls, as explained, Herodians] fell and Babylon the Great [more 'Balaam'/'Belial' imagery] was remembered before God to give her the Cup of the wine of the Wrath of His anger. (16:19)

Not only does this word 'Babylon' represent a further adumbration of the basic 'Balaam'/'Belial' imagery, but the imagery of the 'Beast' or 'Animal' is also present in the passages from Rabbinic literature above, where Balaam and the other 'Enemies of God' are treated. Here, playing on the imagery of *'be'or'/'be'ir'* ('beast' or 'animal' in Hebrew), it is connected to *Be'or the father of Balaam*.

Some of this imagery also appears to be present in the Letter of Jude, where an allusion to 'animals' does make an appearance of sorts, along with two other of these 'Enemies', Cain and Korah, who are described as making the same 'error of Balaam' (1:10–11).[80] Curiously enough, another of these 'Enemies', Gehazi – sometimes considered in these Rabbinic allusions to be a pseudonym for Paul – also makes an appearance in a crucial section of the Damascus Document referring, as we saw, to 'turning aside from the Fountain of Living Waters', 'rejecting the Commandments of God', and betraying 'the New Covenant in the Land of Damascus'.[81]

The 'pouring' imagery in Revelation here is a fundamental one to Qumran, especially, as we also saw, when it comes to mentioning the ideological Adversary of the Righteous Teacher, 'the Man of Lying'. He is described in the Damascus Document as 'removing the bound' and, Belial-like, 'pouring over Israel the waters of Lying'. In the Habakkuk *Pesher* he also has an alternative name, the *'Mattif ha-Chazav'*/'Spouter of Lying', which means in Hebrew literally, 'the Pourer out of Lying'.[82] It is, of course, a favourite metaphor in the Gospels and Acts, particularly when speaking at the Last Supper about 'the Cup' of Jesus' blood 'being poured out' or the descent of the Holy Spirit.

The imagery of 'the Cup of the Wrath of His anger', connected to this in Revelation above, is also exploited at Qumran. In fact, this precise phrase 'the Wrath of His anger' is used in the Habakkuk *Pesher* to express the manner in which the Wicked Priest 'swallows' or 'consumes' the Righteous Teacher. Not only are the 'Wrath' and 'Cup' – *'Cha'as'* and *'Chos'* in Hebrew – played upon in relationship to the death of the Righteous Teacher in the Habakkuk *Pesher*, but the allusions to 'wine', 'venom', and 'Wrath' are also juxtaposed in the Damascus Document to produce the same connotations as they have in Revelation above.[83] We have already suggested that this 'Cup' and 'Blood' imagery – *'Chos'* and *'Dam'* – are part and parcel of the usage 'Damascus'.

Of course, in Christianity as we know it, this 'Cup' imagery is spiritualized even further and moves over into 'the Cup of the New Covenant' in the Blood of Christ, 'which was poured out for you', or 'Holy

Communion', as it is developed in 1 Corinthians 10:16 and 11:27 by Paul and for the Gospels, by Jesus too at the Last Supper (Luke 22:20 and pars.).

Even so, a few residues of the more eschatological Qumran usage survive in these images of 'Wrath' and 'wine' in Revelation. Not only are they associated with Divine Vengeance as can readily be seen, but they are connected to 'giving them blood to drink' – this last, while playing on the Hebrew idea of 'not drinking blood', meant retributively as at Qumran, and certainly deprecatingly as in James' directives to overseas communities; not redemptively as in its inversion by Paul. Where the language of Paul's inversion is concerned, it will be recalled that, in the Damascus Document, the Children of Israel were 'cut off' in the wilderness for 'blaspheming the Commandments of God' and 'eating blood'.[84]

Even 'the Liar' at Qumran is sometimes associated with this 'Belial'/'Balaam' language cycle and 'swallowing' imagery.[85] But so too, it should be appreciated, is the language of 'Benjamin', Paul's purported heredity in Acts and Philippians 3:5. Not only are the 'Sons of Belial' and 'the Sons of Benjamin' equated in the Old Testament, but the principal 'son of Benjamin' is 'Be'or' – the same 'Be'or' normally associated in these scriptural allusions with 'Balaam the son of Be'or' (Num. 22:5 and Deut. 23:4). In fact to come full circle, 'Bela'', the first Edomite King in the Old Testament, is also reckoned as 'the son of Be'or' (Gen. 36:32 and 1 Chron. 1:43). One can be sure that none of the subtleties of these inter-relationships would have been missed by the exegetes of this period.

But this passage from Revelation about 'Balaam teaching Balak' – note the '*ba-la-'a*' symbolism in both names – 'to cast a net before the Sons of Israel to eat things sacrificed to idols and commit fornication', also provides us with an additional and perhaps the definitive key to link James' destruction in early Church sources to the destruction of the Righteous Teacher at Qumran. In this section of Chapter 2 from Revelation, paralleling similar combined usage in the Dead Sea Scrolls, the notations 'Satan' and 'the Devil' are mentioned together in the same context and surrounded by the language of 'patience', 'labouring', 'works', 'being Poor', 'Riches', 'those who claim to be Apostles', but are rather 'Liars', and 'the morning Star'.[86] By this time the reader should be able to recognize these common Qumran and/or Jamesian allusions.

In Revelation, Satan is simply '*Satan*', directly transliterating the original as it appears in Hebrew (Rev. 2:13). But 'the Devil' is '*Diabolos*', and used in conjunction with the allusion to 'casting' (*balein*) we have just seen above, used in connection with 'Balak' and 'Balaam' (2:10). It doesn't take much insight to see the relation of these expressions in Revelation to those at Qumran centring about the allusion to 'Belial' and 'swallowing'/ 'consuming' and, through these, to the English word 'Devil' as we now employ it.

In linguistic theory, two common consonants are considered sufficient to establish some sort of loan or linguistic connection, as, for instance, in the case of Paul's 'Beliar' for 'Belial' in 2 Corinthians 6:15 above, which is more obvious. So even this all-important and crucial reference to 'Belial', as it is found in the parallel material in the Damascus Document from Qumran about 'nets', is by implication present in Revelation as well.

Not only, then, does this passage from Revelation about 'Balaam and Balak' allow us to definitively associate James' prohibitions to overseas communities with the complaints in the Damascus Document relating to 'the Sons of Zadok' and the flaws of the Establishment that end up in 'pollution of the Temple'; we now have the wherewithal for understanding all the repetitious references to 'casting down' or 'casting out' that cling so persistently to the materials before us and which we have been remarking in all the early Church accounts of James' destruction without suspecting the real underlying relationship. In due course, we shall also have the wherewithal for connecting these things to the Letter or Letters known as 'MMT'.

In Greek, 'throwing', 'casting down', 'casting out', and so on, are all related to the verbal root 'ballō' – in the case of 'casting down', 'kataballō'; in the case of 'casting out', as in the 'Stephen' episode above in Acts or Josephus' 'Essenes' as regards backsliders, 'ekballō'. When we come to discuss Jesus' post-resurrection appearances to James and others, we will encounter additional adumbrations of this (albeit, in the writer's view, caricatured and inverted once again) in the 'casting down nets'/'casting out demons' we shall encounter having to do with the Apostles.

We have now come full circle. Incredible as it may seem, our exegetes are applying the same kind of symbolism both in Hebrew and Greek to the events relating to the destruction of the Righteous Teacher and James and using the same basic linguistic cluster to do so, even in different languages. This root has come into European language as 'the Diabolos' – the Devil, that is, 'the Adversary' or 'Slanderer', based on the Greek word, 'diaballō', to throw against, accuse, or charge (see Luke 16:1).

How using these parallel language circles in both Hebrew and Greek to characterize such an important event as the destruction of the Righteous

Teacher from Qumran and that of James by using the linguistic code or symbolism relating to 'the Devil' or 'Devilish' things must have pleased our scriptural exegetes. That the use of this terminology with regard to the death of James was purposeful will be sufficiently demonstrated by the fact that probably *no fall of the kind recorded in early Church accounts in Greek*, having to do with the death of James, ever really occurred – though, strictly speaking, one probably did some twenty years before in the attack on James by 'the Enemy' Paul, which is preserved in the Pseudoclementine *Recognitions* (though this did not result in his death).

That this 'Devil' or 'devilish' linguistic code was being applied specifically to Herodians and their hangers-on – of whom Paul was, as should be becoming increasingly clear, considered one – is true for two important reasons: firstly, they were seen as *foreigners*, either 'Arabs' or 'Idumaeans' (Edomites – to whom the code involving 'Bela'' originally applied) and, secondly, their strategems, by which they 'swallowed' or 'consumed the People', were considered 'Devilish'. In fact, as we have suggested, Herodians were probably making just such 'Benjaminite' or 'Edomite'/'Abrahamic' claims – 'Esau' being a descendant of both Abraham and Isaac). Furthermore, along with those being made, perhaps, by 'Idumaean Arabs' generally who participated on the 'Zealot' side in the War against Rome and the destruction of the High Priest class, these can be considered forerunners of Muhammad and Islam's later 'Ishmaelite' claims on behalf of *all* Arabs.[87]

When the Temple Scroll comes to the problem of classes of unclean or polluted persons intruding into or, as it would appear from the context, actually 'seeing' the Temple or the sacrifices there, the relevant passage, as we have seen, reads:

> And you shall make a great wall [or escarpment] measuring a hundred cubits wide in order to *separate* [here again, the typical language of 'separat-ing clean from the unclean'] the Holy Temple from the city, and [they?] shall not come [plural, but unspecified] Bela' [or balla'] and *pollute it*, but make My Temple Holy and fear My Temple [this can also be read as 'see', as in 'not seeing', a sense that follows four lines later, though the double entendre might be intentional].

Here, God, as usual where these new revelationary – not interpretive – documents are concerned, is speaking in the first person. That is to say, this is to be considered a *new* Book of Law on the level of any previous ones.

The meaning of *'Bela''/'balla''* (in written Hebrew the words are indistinguishable) is of course, as usual, disputed, and it is difficult to decipher what it means, but its use here is certainly very peculiar and the passage itself, very charged. Nor are the classes of forbidden persons enumerated, though at the end of the column the specific issue of the 'separation' of lepers, people with running sores, and bodily emissions is discussed. Still, the very presence of an allusion like 'Bela'' in such a charged context was clearly meant to signify *something* more than just the 'suddenly' it is usually taken as meaning. If today we can intuit something of what it might have meant having to do with the various occurrences of the 'Belial'/*B–L–'* language circle, one can be pretty sure the people of that period could as well – and probably did.

Interestingly enough, this allusion is directly followed by a discussion of the curious issue of the Temple latrines again, a matter we have already seen to be of such pregnant import when it came to the issue of Judas *Iscariot*'s 'hire' or contributions to the Temple above. The issue here is where to locate the Temple outhouses, in this case, a distance of 300 cubits north-west of the city is specified – and here the issue of 'seeing' is actually raised, as it is explained that the reason for this distance is to avoid 'it [the Temple] being *seen* from any distance'.[88]

The whole issue of 'not polluting [the] Temple' or 'the City of [the] Temple' is continued into the next column of the Temple Scroll (XLVII), which would appear now to pick up the 'Be'or' language code – in this case *'be'orot'/*'with skins' (plural). Admittedly, this is esotericism in the extreme, but the issue is here – 'polluting the Temple' or the city 'in which I dwell' with idolatrous things – if one chooses to remark it. This is expressed in terms of 'skins sacrificed to idols', unless this is just a coincidence, which is hard to imagine in two succeeding columns bearing on such sensitive issues.

The same issue is raised again in *'MMT'*, a letter which is dealing with Gentile gifts in the Temple, 'things sacrificed to idols', not bringing such 'skins' into the Temple, and which considers 'Jerusalem the Holy camp' and 'the foremost of the camps of Israel'.[89] Though ostensibly talking about 'the containers' or 'vessels' of things brought into the Temple and even its city ('wine', 'oil', 'and all their eatables' are specifically cited), the Temple Scroll also ties this allusion directly to the ban on 'things sacrificed to idols', part and parcel of James' directives to overseas communities as preserved in Acts and refracted in 1 Corinthians. To add to this, *'MMT'* even includes the Jamesian ban on 'fornication' (because they are all supposed to be 'the Sons of Holiness') and hints at the ban on carrion in banning 'dogs from the Holy camp' (that is, Jerusalem), because 'they eat the bones with the flesh still on them'.[90]

Again, it is hard to believe this is simply accidental, though it might be – 'skins' being but the special case of the more general 'things' found in the prohibitions ascribed to James – or 'eatables' in general, as Paul then goes on to discuss the issue in 1 Corinthians 8–11, ending with his enunciation of the doctrine of 'Communion with the Blood of Christ'. 'Skins', of course, cannot be 'sacrificed to idols', as one cannot really sacrifice a skin to anything, though one can donate it. At any rate, it is simply an aspect of the more general category, expressed in James' instructions above in terms of 'things sacrificed to idols' and, according to Revelation now as well, part and parcel of the illegal permissions 'Balaam' and 'Balak' extended to Israel.

Again, this places aspects of materials from the Temple Scroll, which also deals with the sexual mores of the King, into our 'Bela''/'Belial'/'Benjamin' language circle above, whether intentionally or by accident. Even if one thinks the Temple Scroll too early – a widely held view – one cannot deny the allusions are there and the language is present. Even with a date at the beginning of the Herodian Period – and additional limitations found in the Temple Scroll on the King 'marrying one and only one wife and not divorcing', that she must be a 'Jewish woman', and condemnations on 'niece marriage' make it pretty clear we are in the Herodian Period not before[91] – these condemnations do relate to Herod, if not his heirs, and the Scroll does envision barring unclean individuals, including foreigners like Herod, and their gifts – here referred to in terms of being 'sacrificed to idols' – from the Temple.

In fact, the wide escarpment or high wall evoked here, even if only by implication, also would bar such individuals – here connected directly to the usage 'Bela'', esoteric or otherwise – from even 'seeing the Temple' or what was going on inside. This brings us back to the Temple Wall Affair above, directed against Agrippa II and his *seeing* the sacrifices while reclining on his balcony dining.

It is now possible to see what the issue is, as laid out generally in both the Temple Scroll and the Damascus Document from Qumran and elsewhere. As already observed, a third document from Qumran, which some label '*MMT*', but which we have called 'Two Letters on Works Reckoned as Righteousness', also addresses this issue of impure things and foreign gifts in the Temple, as well as the related behaviour of the King. It certainly is not too early, but contemporary with the issues we are discussing here.[92] The issue is twofold. It has to do with improper 'separation' in the Temple between 'clean and unclean things', as in the Damascus Document, and the issue of foreigners in the Temple itself, of which the presence of Herodians there is simply a particular case.

Herodians in the Temple and Appeals to Caesar

All these matters are paralleled in the literature we have before us, such as Acts, the Pseudoclementine *Recognitions*, and that of the early Church, with notices of arguments in the Temple between the so-called 'Christian' Party following James and the High Priests, in which the people are depicted as supporting 'the Christians', or at least being on the verge of doing so. Later we shall see how the individual called Simon, the Head of 'an Assembly' (or 'Church') of his own in Jerusalem, wishes to bar Agrippa II's father from the Temple in the 40s and goes to inspect his residence in Caesarea, after which he is heard of no more – or so it would appear. We shall identify this individual with the *Historical Peter*, and his 'Assembly', that of the so-called 'Christians' in Jerusalem or 'the Jerusalem Church', the central issue behind these disputes being the barring of Herodians like Herod Agrippa I and his son Agrippa II, who was even more despised, from the Temple as foreigners.

Paul as usual, of course, inverts this issue, cosmopolitanizing it and the related issue of rejecting Gentile gifts and sacrifices in the Temple generally. His being mobbed in the Temple, where he acts as a kind of 'stalking horse' for the Herodian family on these issues, occurs at exactly the time of these other events and is but a special instance of the general unrest generated by these concerns.

Where Herod Agrippa II is concerned, despite Josephus' somewhat ambiguous attitude towards him, there is no hesitation on the part of the 'Zealot'/'Messianic' extremists as to what they think of him: he is charged with incest with his sister Bernice – seemingly the 'Richest' woman in Palestine and later the mistress of Titus the destroyer of the Temple – and he and she are barred, not only from the Temple, but all Jerusalem as well by these same Zealot 'Innovators' after the Temple Wall Affair in the run-up to the War, this in spite of the fact that his great grandfather, Herod, started the reconstruction of the Temple and it was finished owing to his own and his father's 'philanthropy'.[93]

It should be noted that 'incest', too, is specifically condemned in the

Damascus Document and both Agrippa's and his sister Bernice's palaces were, as we have seen, burned at the beginning of the Uprising, when, according to Josephus, 'Zealot' partisans attempted to 'turn the Poor against the Rich', even more importantly, burning the debt records as well. Two years later, as we also saw, when 'the Idumaeans' entered the struggle on the side of 'the Zealots', the palaces of the principal High Priests were burned as well – seemingly in vengeance for James – and many of these same High Priests were slaughtered.

It is this Temple Wall Affair that immediately preceded the stoning of James. Alongside the consolidation of relations between Agrippa II and Ananus in Rome and the attempt by one Simon 'the Head of a Church of his own in Jerusalem' to have Agrippa II's father, Agrippa I, barred from the Temple as a foreigner in the 40s, it provides something of the backdrop to the devastating and catastrophic events that are to follow. As Josephus describes it – leaving aside for the moment who was behind the riotous behaviour and stone-throwing on the Temple Mount that seem to have preceded this Affair and to have been the popular response to provocations like Agrippa II's 'reclining and eating' while viewing the sacrifices – those in control in the Temple erected a high wall on the uppermost portico of the Inner Court facing west. As already remarked, as well, Agrippa II's behaviour would have been all the more provocative, if he were entertaining foreign visitors or eating forbidden foods.

> When completed, [this wall] not only blocked the view from the palace dining room, but also from the Western Portico of the Outer Court of the Temple, where the Romans used to station guards at Festivals in order to control the Temple [the same guards that a year or two earlier intervened to save Paul in Acts]. At this King Agrippa became very angry and still more, Festus the Procurater, who ordered them to tear it down.

It is, clearly, from this Portico, when Paul is being mobbed in the Temple and unceremoniously ejected from it in Acts 21:30–33, that the Roman 'Chief Captain . . . with soldiers and centurions' rescue him from the Jewish mob. This mob, as is usual in Acts' retelling, is characterized as 'seeking to kill him' (that is, Paul). The time is directly after the Festival of Pentecost, 59–60 CE, a festival with unusual importance both in the New Testament and the Scrolls.[94] Festus and Agrippa are, of course, also the individuals with whom Paul converses so felicitously two–three chapters later in Acts.

It is interesting, too, that in Book Twenty of the *Antiquities*, just after he describes the beheading of Theudas, followed by the preventative crucifixion of Judas the Galilean's two sons James and Simon at the time of the Famine by the Jewish Alabarch of Alexandria's son Tiberius Alexander (46–48 CE) and just before he describes an attack just outside Jerusalem on someone he identifies as the Emperor's servant 'Stephen', followed by the Messianic disturbances between Jews and Samaritans in the environs of Lydda and leading to the appointment of Felix as Governor; Josephus describes how *at Passover*, one of the soldiers, guarding the Temple and standing on the top of this same Portico, 'lifted up his skirt and exposed his privy parts to the crowd'. In the *War*, he is described as turning around, lifting up his clothing, and *farting* at the assembled multitudes, which strikes one as being even more realistic. In either case, the soldier expressed his sentiments in an extremely graphic and unambiguous manner.[95]

Before proceeding, one should note, as always, the quasi-parallel sequence in Acts of reference to 'Judas the Galilean' in chapter 5, the stoning of Stephen (in 6–7), and Peter's problems with Simon *Magus* in *Samaria* and Peter's subsequent visit to *Lydda* (in 8–9). Tiberius Alexander, whom Josephus also describes as a backslider from 'the religion of his country', appears in Acts in the context of disturbances on the Temple Mount as well (4:6); and the circle of Jewish turncoats and Herodians he is involved with will grow in importance as events mount towards their climax.

In the matter of the soldier exposing his privy parts to the crowd, his lewd gesture provokes a huge stampede in which thousands (in the *War*, Josephus speaks of 'ten thousand'; in the *Antiquities*, 'twenty') are supposedly trampled, and this at Passover. Again Josephus explains that it was 'the customary practice of previous governors of Judea', fearing revolutionary activity – literally 'Innovation' – on the part of the crowds at Festivals, to station

> a company of soldiers at armed alert to stand guard on the Porticoes of the Temple to quell any attempts at Revolution that might occur.[96]

At this point, too, in its narrative of how Paul was mobbed at Pentecost, because the crowd thought he had introduced foreigners into the Temple, Acts also introduces the reference to 'the Egyptian'. For his part, Josephus places the affair of this 'Egyptian, claiming to be a Prophet' right after he described 'the Robbers', who concealed 'daggers under their cloaks' and assassinated Ananus' brother, the High Priest Jonathan, and right before his description of the bloody battles between Greeks and Jews in Caesarea – which would put us some time in the mid-50s.

In Acts' picture, it will be recalled, the 'Chief Captain', responding to Paul's question about whether he knew Greek, concludes Paul is

> not the Egyptian who before these days caused a disturbance leading some four thousand of the *Sicarii* out into the wilderness. (21:38)

The reference here in Greek to '*Sicarii*' again corresponds to Josephus' introduction of the term just prior to the Temple Wall Affair, itself followed in the *Antiquities* by the exodus of *a second*, unknown 'certain Impostor' into the wilderness under Festus (60–62 CE). In the *War*, it will be recalled, Josephus introduced the terminology '*Sicarii*' five years earlier at the time of the murder of Jonathan.[97]

Looking at this reference in Greek in Acts leaves little doubt of its relationship to the title '*Iscariot*', associated with the name of the mysterious 'Judas' in the Gospels (though, curiously enough, not in Acts), wherein the only difference in epigraphy is the inversion of the *iota* or 'i' with the *sigma* or 's', and we have already noted its general resemblance to 'Christian'.

At the conclusion to the construction of the Temple wall during Festus' procuratorship, Josephus, as we just saw, describes both Festus and King Agrippa as extremely angry. When Festus instructs the Jews to tear it down, they, in turn, send ten principal men together with Ishmael and Helcias the Temple Treasurer mentioned above – *twelve in all* – to Nero. In Rome, Nero's wife Poppea, whom Josephus describes as a 'Worshipper of God' (a term paralleling that of 'God-Fearer' usually applied to Gentiles attaching themselves to the Jewish Community in some manner, but not yet taking all the requirements of the Law upon themselves),[98] intercedes on behalf of *the builders of the wall*.

These she allows to go free – all except Ishmael the High Priest and Helcias, whom she, with Nero's seeming connivance, keeps back, obviously expecting to get some financial consideration from them, which, no doubt, they eventually provided. One can imagine that, in all such matters, there was some financial remuneration that went along with such decisions. Special attention should be paid to these contacts in the household or entourage of Nero. Later, in Domitian's time, there are actually said to be *Christians*, as we have seen, in the Imperial household, Flavius Clemens and Flavia Domitilla. The reader should note that, as in Josephus' case, the prenoms here associate them with the Flavian family. As will become clear, Paul, too, has his own high level contacts in the household of Nero.[99]

For his part Agrippa II, hearing the news of his discomfiture in the matter of the Temple Wall Affair, not surprisingly, changes the High Priest. This sets the stage for what he does shortly thereafter, when Festus – the Governor whom Acts portrays as also sending Paul to Rome on his appeal – dies suddenly (62 CE), that is, he immediately changes the High Priest, this time, seemingly, *to pave the way to dispose of James*. In such a scenario, one must conclude that Agrippa II sees James as the real focal point behind the various difficulties he is experiencing in the Temple and appoints a High Priest more willing to deal with this irritant.

It would also appear that by this time Nero is becoming quite fed up with all these various representations on the part of Jews – among which one should include Paul's – for his future behaviour towards them not only becomes more extreme, but the last Governor before the War, Florus (64–66), would appear to be purposefully attempting to goad the Jews to revolt.[100]

Where such appeals to Caesar go, we have had, it will be remembered, appeals to Caesar on the part of 'the High Priest' Ananias and Ananus in the previous decade over the matter of Messianic disturbances and problems between Jews and Samaritans at Lydda and on the part of Paul, but also Josephus himself records in his *Autobiography* that he made his first trip to Rome at the age of twenty-six – a year or so *after the stoning of James* – in relation to another such appeal. This one, as he tells us, was on behalf of 'certain Priests of [his] acquaintance', who were arrested

> on a small and trifling charge . . . put in bonds and sent to Rome to plead their case before Caesar when Felix was Procurator of Judea.[101]

This was around the time of Paul's original arrest in the Temple, protective custody in Agrippa II's palace, and discussions with the Roman Governor Felix and his wife Drusilla. It is on behalf of these unnamed 'Priests' that Josephus now goes directly in Rome to this same *Empress Poppea*, who in addition to taking an interest in religion, seems to have had a propensity for young men. In fact, it is not long after this that Nero, in 65 CE, in a fit of rage, kicked her to death in the stomach, presumably because she was pregnant.

Unfortunately, Josephus does not tell us what the 'trifling charge' was for which these 'certain Priests' were being held for so long – by his reckoning, some five years or more – but his silence perhaps speaks reams. However, he does tell us that, like James, they were 'very excellent men' and, on account of 'their Piety towards God' (the first element in our

'Piety'/'Righteousness' dichotomy), vegetarians, at least they practised vegetarianism while being held in Rome if not elsewhere.

It is under this heading of their 'Piety towards God', it will be recalled, that Josephus, in his lengthy description of the 'Essenes' in the *War*, tells how they 'rose before the sun' and 'prayed to the rising sun . . . bathing their bodies in cold water' and, like priests, wearing nothing but white linen when they bathed and ate. Under this heading, too, Josephus tells us 'the Essenes' ate nothing but specially prepared foods and that 'these men were skilled in the crafts at which they laboured assiduously' (that is, they were 'tinkers') at the same time as these other activities, which suggests 'Rechabite' orientation.

The 'Priests', therefore, on whose behalf Josephus undertook his journey to Rome, directly following the death of James and after his own earlier stays with 'Essenes' or followers of the so-called '*Banus*', must have been 'Essene'-type or 'Rechabite Priests' of the 'Jamesian' stripe, eating nothing but nuts and dates in their incarceration. This they did, it seems clear, both to preserve their purity, but also because, like James and *Banus*, they were observing the absolute purity regulations of extreme 'Naziritism' (or, if one prefers, 'Zealotism'). One can be sure, too, that they did not eat 'things sacrificed to idols' either in Palestine or Rome. For his part, it should be remarked, it was during this trip that Josephus laid the groundwork for his own eventual betrayal of the Jewish people.

Though, atypically, Josephus declines to reveal the reason why these Pious Priests, on whose behalf he first went to Rome, were detained, it is hard to believe it did not relate in some way either to the Temple Wall Affair, or, at least, the plundering of tithes of 'the Poor Priests' by the 'Rich' High Priests, and even James' death. We have already expressed the view that the Temple Wall Affair provides the actual backdrop for the removal of James. Read discerningly, it not only provides insight into what the issues really were and what was going on behind all these events, but the reason why Josephus was of such two minds about them, and this despite his later friendship with Agrippa, who died in 93 CE around the time he came to publish the *Antiquities* and *Autobiography*.[102]

This then becomes the backdrop for the removal of James after Festus dies and Albinus is on the way, at which point Agrippa appoints Ananus High Priest. But none of these matters are covered in the parallel account at the end of the Book of Acts. Rather, disturbances in the Temple – such as they are – are represented as being occasioned by reactions to *Paul's* person, teaching, and activities. Not only is the Roman Chief Captain pictured as allowing Paul to deliver a prosyletizing speech to the Jewish mob, 'wishing to kill him', but after discovering Paul to be a Roman citizen, he forces 'the Chief Priests' and the entire Jewish Sanhedrin to hear him. Here the High Priest, now called 'Ananias' – this is very definitely an anachronism – hits Paul in the mouth and Paul responds (presumably because of the white linen he wears) by calling him 'a white-washed wall' (23:3). Paul proclaims that he is a Pharisee and being judged because of his hope for 'the Resurrection of the dead' and the Jews now fall to fighting among themselves over this doctrine (23:6–10).

The same scenes are more or less re-enacted under Felix and Festus in Caesarea in the next few chapters over the next two years, where Paul is in, what appears to be, a kind of protective custody. But there is nothing about these other disturbances, nothing about warfare between Jews and Samaritans, nothing about debates, riots, and fights between the High Priests and the Jewish mob, between King Agrippa and the Jews in the Temple, between the people of Caesarea and the Jews – none of these things – only Paul's difficulties with the Jewish people, itself presented as a unified whole.

This situation is clearly not credible, especially in view of the fact that James apparently goes on functioning in Jerusalem during the next two years while Paul is supposedly imprisoned in Caesarea with little serious difficulty from these groups until Agrippa II – taking advantage of the interregnum in Roman governors caused by the death of Festus, after his discomfiture in the Temple Wall Affair – uses the occasion of his appointment of Ananus as High Priest to definitively remove that individual whom he has clearly identified as the source of his various problems, *James the Just*. Nor do James or the other members of the Jerusalem Community appear to visit Paul at all during his two-year incarceration, at least not by Acts' testimony, which is rather intent on calling attention to Paul's cordial relations with Roman Governors and Herodian Princesses and Kings – hardly the social companions of *James*.

If we place James at the centre of these various disturbances in the Temple and identify him as the popular *Zaddik* – the *Zaddik* of the Opposition Alliance – and Paul, rather than his confederate, as his opponent in this same Movement, we arrive at a more credible picture of the true situation in Jerusalem in these times. Then the removal of James becomes crucial and necessitated by his position representing the more 'Zealot' forces among the more purity-minded Lower Priest classes within the Temple. The Dead Sea Scrolls delineate just such a 'Zealot' priestly or purist strain within an 'Opposition' framework and the ideological and literary framework upon which it might be constructed – particularly their idea of an Opposition High Priesthood based on the 'Righteousness' ideology, that is, the 'Sons of Zadok' were not simply genealogical High Priests, but High Priests of 'the Last Times', basing their qualifications on Higher Righteousness and Perfect Holiness. In this way, the picture we are painting becomes even more credible. In this context, one might also wish to identify James as the author of '*MMT*', since it fits perfectly into the range of issues and circumstances we have been delineating here. This, in fact, would make '*MMT*', which is definitely framed in terms of a 'letter' – however alien it might superficially appear – the actual 'letter' sent down by James to 'Antioch' with 'Judas Barsabas' at the conclusion of the so-called 'Jerusalem Council' in Acts.

Adding selected materials from the Book of Acts just lends further credence to this picture. For instance, not surprisingly just prior to the *stoning of Stephen*, Acts describes a large number of 'Priests' coming over to so-called 'Christianity' in Palestine. Furthermore, it describes the larger part of James' Jerusalem Church followers, in the midst of James' final verbal confrontation with Paul and just prior to Paul's subsequent mobbing in the Temple, as 'zealous' or 'Zealots [*Zēlōtai*] for the Law' (21:20).

In Volume II, we shall treat the issue of Paul's final confrontation with James over

teaching all the Jews among the Gentiles to break away [literally, 'apostatize'] from Moses and *not to circumcise* their children, *nor walk* in the customs [of the Forefathers – typical Qumran language]. (21:21)

Suffice it to say that the Jewish mob then adds the charges of 'teaching everywhere against the People, against the Law, and against this Place', meaning the Temple, which it claims he (Paul) has 'polluted' by introducing foreigners into it – that is, 'Greeks' (*Hellēnas* – Acts 21:28).

The Attack by Paul on James
and the Attack on Stephen

The Violence in Jerusalem and the Riot Led by Saul in Josephus

Immediately following the stoning of James, as we saw, Josephus again describes how Ananias and the other High Priests, who 'joined themselves to the most brutal kind of people', sent their servants to the threshing floors to steal the tithes of 'the Priests of the Poorer sort', beating those who resisted, so that 'those of old' – possibly our purist Nazirite-style 'Priests' – who used to be maintained by tithes, died of want.

This reference to this brutality, it will also be recalled, is repeated twice in the *Antiquities* under two different governors approximately four years apart – once at the end of Felix's tenure just before the Temple Wall Affair and James' death that followed and once in Albinus' just after it. This is interspersed with notices about how the '*Sicarii*' ('Christians'?) now struggle daily with the 'Rich' High Priests (particularly Ananias), kidnapping each other's partisans and the attempts by the latter in conjunction with the new Roman Governor Albinus to suppress them. Though this same Ananias is pictured as making complaints against Paul in Acts, which may or may not have substance, it is impossible to think these matters are not somehow connected with the death of James.[1]

Josephus immediately goes on to describe how Agrippa II, involved, as we have seen, in the conspiracy to remove James, now beautifies two largely Gentile cities, Beirut (modern Lebanon's largest city), and one in today's Golan Heights in Syria on the way to Damascus, Caesarea Philippi, which he renames (temporarily one assumes) 'Neronias' to honour Nero! Making it clear that this included erecting pagan statues, as his ancestors Agrippa I and Herod had done before him, Josephus, in another of his turnarounds, now directly admits for the first time that:

> The hatred of his subjects for him increased accordingly, because he took their posterity to adorn a foreign city.

This is as we would expect, that these rulers were hated by the people, but now Josephus not only admits it, but provides one reason for it – their cosmopolitan involvement with foreign powers and interaction with foreigners generally, including beautifying their shrines and cities.[2]

Josephus not only describes these '*Sicarii*' as per usual as 'Robbers' (*Lēstai*) – the term is the same as the one used in the Gospels to describe the two men between whom Jesus is crucified (Matt. 27:38 and pars.) – but also how they try to force the Roman Governor Albinus through Ananias 'to release prisoners'! Here again we have the prominent theme connected with the presentation of Jesus' death in the Gospels, only now involving '*Sicarii*'. This is coupled with the reiteration of another omnipresent Gospel theme, bribery, so much so, that when Albinus finally leaves Jerusalem two years later,

> he brought out all those prisoners who seemed to him most plainly worthy of death and . . . took money from them and dismissed them. Thus, were the prisons emptied, but the countryside filled with Robbers [*Lēstai*].

This repetition of familiar and revered themes in connection with these Roman governors is so constant as to begin to make the Gospel presentation seem to some degree hollow.[3]

The level of violence, priest against priest, now increases:

> They got together bodies of the people and frequently went from throwing reproaches at each other to throwing stones.

Again, this atmosphere is familiar from the picture in early Church sources of confrontations and debates in the Temple centring around attacks on James and reports of riots that finally end up in his death – the only difference being the supposed subject matter behind these riots and debates.

In particular, Josephus follows this description of the death of James with an extremely interesting note about one 'Saulus' and an individual who is obviously his relative, Costobarus, whom in the *War* he identifies as Saulus' brother. In the *War*, too, he connects both to two other individuals, Antipas, another of their 'kinsmen' and later the Temple Treasurer, killed either by 'Zealots' or by '*Sicarii*', and Philip, the Captain of Agrippa II's guard.[4]

The namesake and ancestor of this Costobarus was, as we have seen, married to Herod's sister Salome I. He was the *real* Idumaean in these Herodian genealogies. Herod had him executed because he feared he was conspiring to supplant him. After this, as we also saw, this first Salome married Herod's intimate friend Helcias, the ancestor of several of these Temple Treasurers and himself probably the original holder of the office. The forebear too probably of Antipas just mentioned, he was also the grandfather or great grandfather of Julius Archelaus, whom Josephus was later to know fairly intimately *in Rome*. Julius himself was originally the husband of the Herodian Princess Mariamme III, before she divorced him for richer pickings in the family of the Alabarch of Alexandria – the family of the famous Jewish philosopher Philo of Alexandria and his nephew, Tiberius, the commander of the troops who destroyed the Temple.[5]

In Josephus' words, these two, Saulus and Costobarus, now 'collected a band of thugs', doubtlessly not unlike the violent bands of ruffians collected by the High Priests he had just been describing two sentences earlier. In this regard, one should bear in mind Acts' picture of the authorizations the young Paul obtains, also *from the High Priests*, to pursue 'Christians' to Damascus (9:2). As Josephus describes them:

> They were of the royal family and, because of their kinship to Agrippa, found favour, but they *used violence with the People* and were ready to *plunder anyone weaker than themselves.*

Josephus adds as usual, but significantly in view of the context:

> And from that moment, particularly, great suffering fell upon our city and all things grew steadily worse and worse.[6]

This theme of 'Violence' done to people or land is very strong in the Dead Sea Scrolls, where it is linked to the expression 'the Violent Ones'. This violence is described in great detail, including extended reference to 'the Poor' (*Ebionim*), the situation of how the High Priests in general – called 'the Last Priests of Jerusalem', an expression making it, I submit, fairly plain that we are in the Herodian Period – and the Wicked Priest (who 'profiteered from' the Violence of 'the Peoples' – in this context, 'Herodians'), 'gather Riches' and 'spoils' in the run-up to the destruction of the Temple and the fall of Jerusalem.

In the course of these presentations, we hear about 'the Violent Ones', not only in the Habakkuk *Pesher*, but also in the Psalm 37 *Pesher*, where they are called, significantly, 'the Violent Ones of the Gentiles'. In the Habakkuk *Pesher*, the expression occurs in particularly crucial sections relating to the destruction of the Righteous Teacher and a number of individuals with him, referred to as 'the Poor'. The text runs:

The Wicked Priest . . . became proud [literally, 'puffed up'] and he deserted God and betrayed the Laws because of Riches. He plundered and collected the Riches of the Men of Violence, themselves rebels against God, and took [in the sense of, 'profiteered from'] the Riches of the Peoples [in our view, Herodians, whom, it should be appreciated, were at this time Roman tax collectors, or, even more accurately, tax farmers in Palestine] multiplying upon himself sinful guilt.[7]

This is broken by the reference in the next column to 'the Last Priests of Jerusalem' – the plural usage, too, would seem to place this firmly in the Herodian Period. Our writers presumably knew whereof they spoke, when they further described these 'Last Priests' as

profiteering from the spoils of the Peoples. But in the Last Days their Riches together with their booty would be given over to the hand of the Army of the *Kittim*.

Moving back to the subject of the Wicked Priest, our text now goes into the passages we have treated above about the Vengeance God would visit on him 'because he conspired to destroy the Poor':

And as to what is written, 'Because of the blood of the township and the Violence of the land [here our 'blood' imagery again, but now coupled with the tell-tale imagery of 'Violence'], its interpretation is, 'the township' is Jerusalem, where the Wicked Priest committed his works of Abominations [to be contrasted with the Righteous Teacher's 'works of Righteousness'] polluting the Temple of God, and 'the Violence of the land', relates to the cities of Judah, where he plundered the sustenance ['Riches'] of the Poor [*Ebionim*].[8]

Josephus' Saulus and Paul's Herodian Connections

The notice in Josephus about Saulus 'using violence with the People' has a bearing not only on the attack on James by the Enemy Paul as described in the Pseudoclementines, but also the real events lying behind the 'Stephen' episode in Acts. As we saw, Paul himself writes in his Letter to the Romans, in a passage not generally disputed, that his 'kinsman' is someone he calls 'Herodion' or 'the littlest Herod' (16:11). In the same breath, he sends regards to those he refers to as 'of Aristobulus', that is, either 'relatives of' or from the 'household of Aristobulus' (16:10).

Agrippa I's brother and successor, Herod of Chalcis (44–49 CE), it will be recalled – also originally married to Agrippa I's daughter Bernice – had a son by the name of Aristobulus, who was married to the Salome connected in the Gospels to the death of John the Baptist. No doubt, they spent much of their time in Rome, but when Nero enlarged Agrippa II's Kingdom at the expense of Herod of Chalcis's domains, he compensated Aristobulus and Salome by giving them the Kingdom of Lower Armenia in Northern Syria and Asia Minor not far from Paul's own base of operations there.

But Paul, as Herodians generally, also held Roman Citizenship, a rarity in Palestine at this time. Acts makes much of this, for instance, in the jovial banter between Paul and the Roman Chief Captain on the Temple steps following Paul's ejection from the Temple by the crowd (Acts 22:26–29). Josephus, too, acquired Roman Citizenship, obviously going through much to obtain it, and was adopted into the Roman Imperial family itself. However Roman Citizenship had already been bestowed in the previous century upon all the offspring of Antipater and his son Herod for conspicuous service to the cause of Rome – in fact, the Roman takeover of Palestine itself was due in no small part to their efforts. Where Paul is concerned, his citizenship enabled him to wield inordinate importance in Jerusalem at a comparatively very young age as a servant to the High Priests and repeatedly saved him by Acts' own reckoning from imminent punishment and even death. It is hard to picture Jesus in similar circumstances pulling out a Roman Citizenship to escape punishment or death.

Be this as it may, one of the most curious and, as it turns out revealing, examples of such an escape comes when a nephew of Paul, whom, as we already remarked, Acts declines to name, but living in Jerusalem with an entrée into Roman official circles, discovers 'a conspiracy' on the part of the Jews 'to kill Paul' (23:16). This is on the part of those who have all the characteristics of '*Sicarii*', except they take a suspiciously familiar '*Nazirite*'-style oath, 'cursing themselves not to drink or eat till they had killed Paul'. This oath-taking is repeated three times in this episode, the language varying to

> with a curse, we have cursed ourselves to taste nothing until we have killed Paul. (Acts 23:14; in 23:21, this is 'not to eat or drink'.)

This is extremely intimate information, and it should be contrasted with the omnipresent 'cursing' language at Qumran, deftly exploited and turned against those employing it by Paul in Galatians 3:13 to produce, as we saw, his fundamental synthesis about Christ 'saving us from the curse of the Law'.

Paul's nephew then informs the Roman Chief Captain of the Temple Guard, who with 'seventy horsemen, two hundred soldiers, and two hundred spearmen', sends Paul to Felix in Caesarea to be 'kept in Herod's Palace'. One should note the apparently historical, precise detail at this point in Acts, which includes even the contents of the letter the Captain sent to Felix. This contrasts markedly with the general mythologizing of Acts in earlier chapters.

It would be interesting to know who was the mother – also unnamed but living in Jerusalem – of this young man, who had such cordial relations with the Romans that he can enter their fortresses and produce such an astonishing escort. Six years later, at the time of the outbreak of the War with Rome, the 'Saulus' in Josephus seems to enjoy a similar relationship with the Roman Chief Captain in either the Fortress called Antonia or the Citadel.[9] She is possibly to be identified with Cypros IV, the wife of Helcias, the Temple Treasurer, we have just highlighted above.[10] In Herodian genealogies, this would make her not only the sister of both Saulus and Costobarus, but also the mother of that Julius Archelaus just mentioned above, who like Josephus also ended up in Rome obviously living in some comfort and an avid reader of the latter's works.

If this is true – and the proof is not definitive – then Paul comes from a very important line indeed and it is not surprising that his nephew, whom we might tentatively identify as Julius Archelaus, had such ready access to the Temple Guard. As we saw, this line goes back through a daughter of Herod and his Maccabean wife, Mariamme I, to the Idumaean Costobarus, the husband of Herod's sister Salome I. The endogamy here, so roundly condemned at Qumran, is dizzying.

This is consistent with the picture of the Herodian Paul in the Pseudo-clementines leading the attack on James in the 40s. The only problem is the time frame, approximately twenty years' difference. The Saul in Josephus reappears, as we also saw, in the 66 CE events as the intermediary between 'the Peace Party' in Jerusalem and Herod Agrippa II's army and that of the Romans outside it. Again, this Saul has either just escaped from Agrippa II's palace or the Citadel, where the whole Guard has just been slaughtered in the first moments of the Uprising – all, that is, but the Captain, who, as we saw, was *forcibly circumcised*.[11]

This linking of Saulus with the names of Costobarus and Antipas is certainly genealogical. As we saw above, this younger Antipas was also for a time Temple Treasurer, but was killed by 'the Robbers' (the *Sicarii* – specifically, one '*John the son of Dorcas*') prior to the eruption into the city of 'the Zealots' with their 'Idumaean' partisans and the consonant slaughter of the High Priests, including James' murderer Ananus.[12] In the meantime Saulus fled with his brother and Philip to the Roman Commander Cestius' camp, and from there to Nero, who, as he often was, was residing *in Corinth*. There, Saulus reported on the situation in Palestine and blamed the then Governor Florus (64–66 CE), rather than Cestius, for the catastrophe that had occurred. It is at this point and location that the future Roman Emperor Vespasian is given his commission to repress the Jewish Uprising in Palestine. Since this also seems to have been part of Saulus' recommendation to Nero, Saulus may have accompanied him, but Josephus trails off here and we do not hear of his ultimate fate.

If Paul is related to the Costobarus in Herodian genealogies and in addition, Herod Antipas, that is, 'Herod the Tetrarch' – as the name 'Antipas' here also seems to imply – whose 'foster brother' was referred to in Acts 13:11 as one of the founders of Paul's curious Antioch Community where 'Christians were first called Christians'; it would also explain what Paul was doing on his mysterious visit to Damascus, when he ran afoul of the Arabian King Aretas (2 Cor. 11:32), who was then at war with Saulus' putative kinsman Herod Antipas who executed John the Baptist at about this same time. For Acts 9:22, it will be recalled, Paul rather ran afoul of '*the Jews, who dwelt in Damascus*'.

However these things may be, Acts' presentation of Paul's last days is fuzzy in the extreme. Acts appears to know nothing about Paul's death or, if it does, is unwilling to tell us about it because it was presumably too embarrassing. It is to early Church sources we must go for the information that Paul was beheaded, probably by Nero, and a somewhat preposterous version of Peter's death as well.[13] Acts ends in 62 CE, the year of James' death, with Paul under loose house arrest – if even this – in Rome (28:30–31).

In Romans, the same letter that includes these pointed greetings to Paul's 'kinsman, the Littlest Herod' – more than likely the son of Salome and Aristobulus, whose household in Rome has also possibly just been greeted in the preceding line (Rom. 16:10) – Paul also expressed his intention to visit Spain (15:24–28), from where Gallio and his brother Seneca came. Galba, no doubt with his own contacts in Nero's court, who succeeded Nero in 68 CE, had been Governor there too, and it was the place of origin of the future Emperors Trajan (98–117) and Hadrian (117–138) as we have already observed.

THE DEATH OF JAMES

Not only did Gallio, whose presence in Corinth in the early 50s as Governor has now been archaeologically verified, intervene to save Paul, even going so far as to have the Jewish leader of the synagogue there beaten in his presence, because, as Acts so charmingly puts it, 'none of these things mattered to Gallio' (that is, Jewish legal quibbles – 18:17); but a lively apocryphal correspondence has been preserved between Seneca, his brother, and Paul.[14] Here, Acts is involved in another of those stupefying reversals, mistaking Paul's acolyte Sosthenes in 1 Corinthians 1:1 for 'the ruler of the synagogue', whom Gallio drives from the Judgement Seat and the Corinthians beat.

Seneca was the young Nero's tutor and the real power behind Nero's Emperorship before Nero forced him to commit suicide in 65 CE. There is no reason to suppose this correspondence between Seneca and Paul to be totally groundless, but whether it was or not, Paul's contacts went, as we have had cause to observe, very high up in the Emperor Nero's household. At the very least these involved his own intimate associate Epaphroditus, by whom he sends greetings 'especially to those in Caesar's household' (Phil. 2:25 and 4:18).[15] It would be difficult to conceive that this 'Epaphroditus' could be anyone other than Nero's *own* secretary *by the same name*, who was later blamed by Domitian for killing or, at least, helping Nero to kill himself.

This same Epaphroditus also seems to have been Josephus' publisher and Josephus notes in a brief dedication to him how he had been involved in 'great events'. Eventually Domitian had Epaphroditus – who had been his secretary as well – executed in 95 CE, a year or two after the appearance of the *Antiquities* and about the time Domitian executed his own uncle, Flavius Clemens, for being a secret Christian as well. For his part, Josephus too may have himself run afoul of Domitian.

Whether or not everyone can agree with all these points, there is no reason to believe that Paul could *not* have returned to Palestine, after his 'appeal to Caesar' and his initial trip to Rome to see Nero around 60 CE. Of course, if he did so, this would have had to have been with and by Nero's accord, that is, he would have entered his employ. Perhaps this is why Acts is so silent as to Paul's ultimate fate. As noted, Paul is reputed to have planned or made at least one additional trip to Spain following his appeal to Caesar in Rome, and with the contacts he had in Corinth and Rome, this too would not have been surprising. If he did return to Palestine, he could have done so around the time that the 'Saulus' in Josephus led the riot in Jerusalem prior to the Uprising against Rome.

Early Church texts put Paul's death some time after the outbreak of the War against Rome around the years 68–69. Here we do begin to approach convergence with Josephus' Saulus, who disappears at approximately the same time from Josephus' narrative, but not before he provided Nero with a final intelligence report on events in Palestine and was involved in the actual appointment of Vespasian as commander. There are too many coincidences here for them simply to be ignored.

The Attack on James and the Attack on Stephen

These matters, true or otherwise, are not completely ungermane to the presentation in the Pseudoclementine *Recognitions* of Paul's attack on James in the Temple in the 40s, which itself bears on the tangle of data relating to the stoning of Stephen in the 40s and the stoning of James in the 60s. In Jerome's presentation of James' death, one or two interesting points emerge relating to how the *Recognitions* present the attack on James in the Temple by the Enemy Paul *in the 40s*, if not *the 60s*. The very statement of the possibility of such an attack by Paul on James sends shudders up the spines of orthodox theologians and believers and has done from the moment of the first appearance of the Pseudoclementines.

There is clearly something very peculiar about the sequencing of events relating to these two stonings as we have them in Acts and Josephus. Of course there is the twenty-year gap in the chronology between them, but we have this concerning the two riots too, the one in Acts led by Paul, after the attack on Stephen in the 40s and the other in Josephus led by Saulus after the attack on James in the 60s. It is almost as if these two documents are totally remaking each other's chronology. Then, too, though Acts places the riot led by Saulus in the 40s – where according to the Pseudoclementines it most likely occurred – it transposes the stoning of James in the 60s with that of Stephen in the 40s. Josephus does the same with the riot led by Paul in the 40s, seemingly transposing it to the 60s.

What is the explanation? There is none that will satisfy everyone. Not only does the riot led by Saulus in Josephus follow the stoning of James in the same manner that the riot led by Saulus in Acts follows the stoning of Stephen, we also have the various repetitions in Josephus of the theme of the 'Rich' Priests robbing those of the 'Poorer' kind, which ties these matters directly to the picture in the Habakkuk *Pesher* from Qumran of the death of the Righteous Teacher. This is not to mention the picture of the Rich High Priests and their bully boys arguing with the 'representatives of the People' in the Temple, which in these various documents always goes from harsh debate to riot and stoning, and the picture in both Josephus and the New Testament of the violence such 'Violent Ones' are willing to use with the People – terminology, too, actually appearing at Qumran.

Again the reader must always keep in mind that the Gospels and Acts have more the character of literature; while Josephus, history. Can we think that for some reason Josephus has transposed these two riots? It would be difficult to imagine why, and there is also the matter of the alleged crucifixion of Judas the Galilean's two sons, James and Simon, in the 40s in the *Antiquities* (all three of these being the names of Jesus' three brothers), missing from the *War*, but seemingly foreshadowing the crucifixion of the grandchildren of Jesus' brother Judas under Domitian or Trajan. On the other hand, the question about the authenticity of the picture in Acts is simpler – either one accepts Acts' presentation as it is, full of fantastic history, repetitions, and rewriting, or admits there are huge holes in it, mistaken historical information, bodily liftings from other sources, and oversimplification verging on dissimulation or outright fallaciousness.

Unfortunately, some of this last occurs in precisely the area having to do with final confrontations in Jerusalem between Paul and James, the arrest of Paul, his incarceration under protective custody in Caesarea, and his appeal to Caesar. This last includes the picture of the Chief Priests wanting, '*Sicarii*'-style, to kill Paul and making grandiose 'plots' against him – a totally unconvincing picture – when we know from Acts that they were originally in league *with him* and from Josephus, that they were at the time, in fact, rather involved in intense internecine strife with *the Leaders of the insurgent mob* in Jerusalem.

Then, too, there are Paul's various theological speeches – one like James' 'on the steps' of the Temple in front of a Jewish mob thirsting for his blood (Acts 21:40); another, before the Chief Priests and the Sanhedrin. There is also the charge against Paul by the High Priest Ananias, the so-called 'Elders' (*Presbyteros*), and someone called 'Tertullus' – hardly a Hebrew name – in Caesarea before Felix of 'being a ring-leader of the Nazoraean Heresy' and 'a trouble-maker, moving insurrection among all the Jews in the habitable world' (24:5) – a charge that, while certainly true for some others, hardly describes Paul.

There is also Paul's own obsequious remark to Felix, the butcher of so many Jewish Revolutionaries in Palestine and himself promoting or exacerbating the strife between Greeks and Jews in Caesarea:

> Knowing, as I do, that for many years you have been the Judge of this Nation, the more cheerfully do I make my defence as to things concerning myself. (Acts 24:10)

This sycophancy compares favourably with Tertullus', ostensibly speaking in condemnation of Paul:

> We are enjoying great peace through you [Felix] and by your forethought very worthy things are being done for this Nation. (24:1)

Perhaps Tertullus is speaking for the Greeks of Caesarea; he can hardly be speaking on behalf of the Jews. But if this is true, then why this alleged attack on Paul?

This is paralleled by the complete confusion Acts shows about Hellenists and Jews in the early Community in Jerusalem, in which Stephen, perhaps the archetypal *Gentile* convert, with a typically Greek name meaning, as we saw, 'Crown' (though interpreted in early Church literature to mean the martyr's 'Crown', not unrelated, as previously explained, to the 'Crown' of James' Nazirite hair), is presented as a 'Hebrew', while his antagonists within the Community are presented as 'Hellenists'. Not only is Paul's reference to the number of years Felix had been in the country a little exaggerated, but the obsequiousness Paul displays, if Acts is to be believed, fairly takes one's breath away. Of course, this is quite normal for Paul when dealing with powerful people he wanted something from – not, of course, with those he did not.

The note about finding Paul 'attempting to pollute the Temple' in Acts 24:6 and earlier in 21:28 does, however, ring true. At least, this charge was in the air in this period, both where the relevant documents from the Dead Sea Scrolls are concerned and Josephus' description of events leading up to the stopping of sacrifice on behalf of foreigners in the Temple in the *War*. We even hear of it by refraction in Paul's letters. But 'Tertullus'' accusation of being a 'Nazoraean' and 'fomenting world revolution', specifically denied by Paul in Romans 13, would be more appropriately directed against James and his mass of 'Priestly' followers, 'all Zealots for the Law' – and, in fact, probably was.

Then there is the picture of Felix and Drusilla – whom Acts 24:24 calls 'a Jewess' – listening to Paul declaim about Faith in Christ Jesus, 'Righteousness', and the Last 'Judgement', and Felix talking with Paul *often*, hoping, in Acts' words, 'Riches would be given him by Paul' (*thus*). This finally ends with Felix, in order 'to find favour with the Jews, leaving

Paul in bonds' for Festus the next Governor to deal with (Acts 24:26–27).

But Felix is not interested in finding favour with 'the Jews', as by Josephus' account it is 'the principal Jewish inhabitants of Caesarea who went to Rome to accuse Felix' before Nero and, of course, ultimately fail. In fact, the outcome of these complaints, as we have seen, is disastrous for the Jews and the equal privileges they previously enjoyed with the Greeks of Caesarea are annulled. This, not because of bribery *by the Jews*, but rather because, as we saw, the Hellenizing inhabitants of Caesarea *bribe* Nero's Secretary for Greek Correspondence! Josephus calls this individual 'Beryllus', but Epaphroditus too probably occupied a similar post. According to Josephus, this and the brutality of Caesarean Legionnaires generally – individuals such as 'Cornelius', the so-called 'Centurion of the Italica contingent' – is the direct cause of future Jewish misfortune, because the Jews of Caesarea became 'more unruly than ever' because of this, until War with Rome was kindled.

This chaos between Greeks and Jews in Caesarea, as already remarked, also finds an echo, however remote, in the background to the stoning of Stephen in Acts, just as that between Samaritans and Jews, following the beating of 'the Emperor's Servant Stephen' by 'Revolutionaries' does in the unlikely stories about confrontations between Philip, Peter, and Simon *Magus* in Samaria and, following this, in Lydda. So, too, the various appeals to Caesar relating to these matters find their echo in the various appeals to the Roman Governor in Caesarea in Acts, all of this supposedly *on account of Paul*, and, of course, Paul's own appeal to Nero Augustus Caesar in Rome.

Acts, also, throws Paul into this mix in Caesarea on several occasions without one word about the inflammable social and political situation there between Greeks and Jews. Rather, in its view, it is Paul's own 'Hellenist' or 'Greek' associates from Caesarea and further afield, some of whom accompany him on his last trip to Jerusalem to see James, that provoke the attack on him in Jerusalem because the crowd thinks that 'he has brought Greeks into the Temple' (21:28).

The Two Simons in Josephus and Acts and their Confrontations in Caesarea

The designation in Acts of Drusilla simply as 'a Jewess' is cynical in the extreme and clearly deceptive, because, as we have highlighted, whether Herodians like her were Jewish or not was the burning issue of the day.

The 'circumcision' issue, too, so much a part of Paul's assault on Judaism in his letters, looms large in Drusilla's marital difficulties as Josephus reports them. Agrippa I, her father, the one Herodian who made the greatest efforts to mollify his subjects in this regard, first demanded from Antiochus of Commagene (another Kingdom in Asia Minor bordering on Little Armenia and Paul's Cilicia) that he circumcise his son, Epiphanes (later leader of 'the Macedonian Legion' in the War against the Jews) before he could marry her. When he bridled at this, Drusilla – reportedly a great beauty – was given by her brother Agrippa II, after her father's death, to Azizus the King of Emesa (presentday Homs not far from Damascus in Syria) – who did 'consent to be circumcised'.

But at the conniving of one Simon 'a magician', whom Josephus calls 'a friend' of Felix in Caesarea, she was finally persuaded 'to forsake her current husband and *marry*' *Felix*.[16] Also conniving at this marriage was her sister Bernice, the future mistress of Titus, whose marital practices, as we have seen, were a catalogue of acts railed against in the 'Three Nets of Belial' section of the Damascus Document – not to mention the Letter of James. Drusilla's, and, of course, Bernice's behaviour is 'fornication' at its highest. Bernice is characterized along with Simon as helping 'to prevail upon her [Drusilla] to break the Laws of her Ancestors and marry Felix'.[17]

Though in some manuscripts he is called 'Atomus' – probably a garbled allusion to the 'Primal Adam' idea, attributed to Simon in all sources – this *Simon* can be none other than the proverbial 'Simon *Magus*' of Acts and early Church literature, and, should we say it, the *demythologized Simon*. Though Josephus also calls him 'a Cypriot', this would appear to be another of those confusions based on '*Kitta*' or '*Kittim*' in Hebrew, originally the islands Crete or Cyprus, but generalized in Daniel, 1 Maccabees, and the Scrolls to include Western nations generally, particularly those across the sea – this, not to mention that, even as late as the twelfth century, Jews like the Spanish traveller, Benjamin of Tudela, were still calling 'Samaritans', '*Cuthaeans*'. But the Pseudoclementines and other early Church works, including Eusebius who had access to Syriac sources, correctly identify Simon's place of origin, as we have seen, as 'Gitta' in Samaria.

Acts has quite a few of such 'Cypriots' involved with Paul and his teaching, including even Barnabas, whom it also calls 'Joses' (4:36). For it, Paul, as part of his first missionary journey with Barnabas, supposedly also *to Cyprus*, even has a Peter-like confrontation with one 'Elymus *Magus*' (13:8). Not only is this individual called 'a Jewish false prophet, whose name was Barjesus' and associated with the Roman Proconsul in

Cyprus, whose name was 'Sergius Paulus'; Paul's confrontation with him, as a 'Son of the Devil' (*Diabolos*) and the 'Enemy of all Righteousness', is clearly mythological and smacks of the confrontations between Peter and Simon *Magus* elsewhere. If it could be properly deciphered, it would no doubt provide the most interesting original material.[18]

Where these confrontations between Peter and Simon *Magus* in any event go, the Pseudoclementines are demonstrably more accurate than Acts, which confuses Simon's place of origin, Samaria, with the locale of these confrontations as reported in the Pseudoclementines and in Josephus, Caesarea. If we now identify Peter with the Simon in Josephus, 'the head of an Assembly of his own' in Jerusalem in the same period, who wants to *bar Drusilla's father Agrippa I from the Temple as a foreigner* and is invited to *come to Caesarea* to inspect the latter's household; then, of course, we get almost a *perfect match* – only we must, as usual, always remember to *reverse everything* (not to mention a good example of the kind of dissimulation going on).

According to Josephus, Agrippa I invited this 'Simon' from Jerusalem to inspect his household to see 'what was being done there contrary to Law', dismissing him afterwards with a trifling gift.[19] Of course, the reader will immediately recognize this to be the real basis of the visit of 'Peter' to the household of the Roman Centurion 'Cornelius' in *Caesarea*, when he learns not to make distinctions between Jews and foreigners and 'to call no man profane'. We are now in a position, too, to identify correctly the true nature of the confrontation between the two Simons – *in Caesarea*, not Samaria as in Acts – the confrontations in Samaria, as we saw, relating to other confrontations, first between 'Galileans' and 'Samaritans' and then between 'Jews' and 'Samaritans' in Samaria, in which someone called 'Doetus' or 'Dorcas' was ultimately crucified.

That Paul is seemingly sometimes confused in both Acts and the Pseudoclementines for Simon *Magus*, both of whom probably went to Rome in Felix's wake, is another interesting aspect to this puzzle. That Felix left Paul in bonds, because he worried about Jewish public opinion when he left for Rome, however, is also quite far-fetched (Acts 24:26 – the same words are used in 25:9 to describe Festus' concerns, with perhaps more substance). Rather, it is more likely that Felix, with his close contacts in Nero's own household in Rome, *paved the way for Paul's appeal to Caesar*. This would be particularly likely if, as we have suggested, Paul was a Herodian with links to Felix's wife Drusilla and if the numerous sessions they had – 'over two years' according to Acts – were more in the nature of strategy or intelligence sessions, which also on the face of it seems more likely.

Once in Rome, Paul is surprised to find himself relatively free. He

> stayed two whole years in a house he rented himself . . . proclaiming the Kingdom of God and teaching the things about the Lord Jesus Christ without hindrance and with all freedom. (28:31)

On this note Acts ends, with not a word about Paul's fate, how he was killed, if he was, or whether he returned to Jerusalem. Nothing is vouchsafed beyond the impression that his 'house arrest' did not seem to limit his activities.

The reason why it has been suggested that 'the Egyptian', for whom Paul is mistaken by the Roman Chief Captain in Acts, is a representation of Simon is that Simon was reputed to have learned his magical arts in Egypt. That Simon was also responsible – as one of the '*Taheb*'-style redeemer-figure impostors – together with another colleague of his, 'Dositheus', both, according to the Pseudoclementines, allegedly Disciples of John the Baptist, for many of the disturbances in Samaria, recorded in Josephus and refracted to some extent in the Book of Acts, just increases these points of contact. However these matters may be, one can still dimly perceive through all the dissimulation the real nature of the conflict between Simon and the Simon *Magus* in Josephus, again refracted as we have been suggesting in the Book of Acts. These confrontations between them *in Caesarea on the Palestine coast*, not further inland in Samaria as in Acts, form a main focus of the Pseudoclementine literature.

The real course of events in Caesarea, however, up to the time of Felix's marriage to Drusilla, despite all this fantasy and romance, as we have seen, shines through pretty clearly in Josephus and can be fairly reliably reconstructed. Acts' version of the protests against Paul in Caesarea to the Roman Governors, Felix and Festus, by the Jewish High Priests, are more like the protests these various groups – including these same High Priests – were making in Rome over how *Roman Governors*, such as Cumanus, Felix, and Festus, were behaving in Palestine, most notably relating to problems in Lydda, Samaria, Caesarea, and the Temple Wall Affair in Jerusalem.

Of course, there is no historical basis to Acts' 'tablecloth' vision to Peter 'on a rooftop' in Jaffa. Nor is there any *visit by Peter* to *the household of the Roman Centurion Cornelius* in Caesarea. What there is, is this visit of the Zealot 'Simon' ('Peter' in Acts), who wanted to bar Agrippa I from the

Temple, to the latter's household in Caesarea in the early 40s 'to see what was done there contrary to Law'. This becomes transformed in Acts into an episode where Peter learns that he can eat forbidden foods and discovers he should not discriminate against Gentiles. As we have been suggesting, nothing better illustrates Acts' historical method of reversal than this.

What becomes of this 'Simon' is unclear, as we never hear of him again in Josephus – nor do we, for all intents and purposes, 'Peter' in Acts. For Josephus, Agrippa I gives Simon a gift and dismisses him. As we have seen, the confrontations between Simon Peter and Simon *Magus* in Acts are presented as having something to do with 'the laying on of hands', 'the Holy Spirit', and Simon offering to buy this 'Power' with money (again we have our 'Power' vocabulary and possible mix-ups with how Paul was perceived – 8:9–20). These are presented as taking place in 'Samaria', following which everyone seems to make up and 'they preached the Gospel to many villages of the Samaritans' (8:25). For the Pseudo-clementines, these occur more accurately in Caesarea and have to do with debates over various subjects like 'the Primal Adam', 'the True Prophet', and the nature of the Christ.

But having regard for the anti-'fornication' theme in both the Letter of James and the materials at Qumran – not to mention the confrontations between John the Baptist and these same Herodians over the same issue in the previous decade – I think we can safely assert that the confrontations in Caesarea between the two Simons had principally to do with Simon *Magus* conniving at the divorce of the Herodian Princess, Acts identifies only as 'a Jewess', from an individual who had expressly *circumcised* himself in order to marry her and convincing her to marry Felix instead. In Suetonius, Felix is said to have married *three* princesses, so he must have had a penchant for this kind of thing. Interestingly, the son he eventually had by Drusilla, named Agrippa, clearly after her brother or father, 'perished in the eruption of the mountain of Vesuvius in the reign of Titus Caesar'.[20]

So this 'Simon *Magus*' again – perhaps not unlike Paul – was a hench-man of Felix, whereas Peter, in the manner of Qumran and like John the Baptist in the previous decade, who lost his head in the same kind of confrontation, *opposes* this kind of 'fornication' among Herodians. Even Josephus is forced to remark that divorce on the part of the woman was against the Laws of her country and that, by doing so, Drusilla had 'transgressed the Laws of her Forefathers'. Probably for the same reason someone it calls 'James the brother of John' was beheaded in the run-up to the introduction of James, Acts presents Simon Peter as being arrested by 'Herod the King'. This event probably did occur and, for a change, whether accidentally or by design, the New Testament has its 'Herods' right.

I think it is safe to say that the 'Simon' who agitated against allowing Agrippa I into the Temple, even though his ancestors built it, and who went so far as to inspect his household in Caesarea, would ultimately have been arrested, despite Josephus' silence on this point – if not by Agrippa I himself, then certainly by Herod of Chalcis (44–49), his less tolerant and magnanimous brother who succeeded him. The father of that Aristobulus, who ended up marrying Salome involved in the death of John the Baptist, did end up rounding up trouble-makers after Agrippa I's untimely death, including, interestingly enough, one 'Silas', who had previously been one of the latter's boon companions.[21]

All these coincidences in names, which recur as names of 'Christians' in the New Testament, are odd. Even 'Cornelius', as we have seen, appears in Josephus in this period in connection with this Herod of Chalcis. Cornelius, it will be recalled, is the bearer of a letter from Claudius the Emperor in Rome to Cumanus (48–52), the Governor preceding Felix who ruled in conjunction with Herod of Chalcis, on the subject of granting Herod and his nephew Agrippa II control of the High Priestly garments.

Tholomaeus – 'Bartholomew' in the Gospels – is a Jewish 'arch-Robber' in Perea across Jordan, where John the Baptist had just been executed the decade before, who 'made much mischief in Idumaea among the Arabians'.[22] 'Silas' above, seemingly succeeded by his son with the same name, is the general of Agrippa I's army – not probably a very frightening affair – as is 'Philip', 'Saulus'' colleague above, the army of King Agrippa II. Namesakes of all these individuals, most connected in one manner or another with Paul in Acts' version of history, are connected in Josephus in some manner with *Herodians*.

Even one 'Simeon called Niger' in Acts appears with Paul and 'the foster brother of Herod the Tetrarch' as one of the founding fathers of Barnabas' and Paul's 'Antioch' Community, where Christians were first called 'Christians' (13:1). In Josephus, as we saw – though the relationship might simpy be coincidental – 'Niger' is a leader across Jordan in Perea of 'the Idumaeans', who 'showed exceptional valour in their battles with the Romans'. Immediately following the rampage of these 'Idumaeans' with 'the Zealots' and their killing of Ananus and the other High Priests, Niger somehow ran afoul of these same 'Zealots' – possibly over the issue of circumcision. Josephus describes his execution – as we have already remarked – in terms that can only bring to mind Jesus' in the Gospels:

> Frequently crying out and pointing to the scars of his wounds, he was dragged through the centre of the city. When he was brought outside the gates . . . in his dying moments, Niger called upon them [the Jews] the vengeance of the Romans, famine and pestilence, to add to the horrors of war, and besides all that, internecine strife.

This last is, of course, nothing if not the Little Apocalypses in the Gospels. Josephus completes the picture – no doubt fleshed out from his own interrogations of prisoners – by adding:

> All of which curses upon these Impious men were ratified by God, and this most Righteously, because before long they tasted their own madness [note the play here on the *Righteousness*-oriented ideology of some 'Zealots' like those at Qumran].²³

Individuals of this kind, such as Niger, Philip, Silas, and Saulus, among whom we should also group the sons of Queen Helen of Adiabene in Upper Mesopotamia on the border of Armenia and Persia, are perhaps best referred to as Herodian 'Men-of-War' – some pro-Roman; others, revolutionary.²⁴ Josephus specifically comments in his *Autobiography* on the miraculous escape of Philip's 'two daughters' from the Roman slaughter at Gamala – Judas the Galilean's birthplace. In Acts, Paul, curiously, stops to stay with a 'Philip the Evangelist' in Caesarea before his final journey to Jerusalem to confront James. As already remarked, like the 'Philip the *Strategos*' of Agrippa II's army in Caesarea, he too has 'daughters' – now 'four virgin daughters who prophesy'. It is to this house that the 'prophet called Agabus' comes (Acts 21:8–10).

Where 'Philip the Evangelist' is concerned, there is clearly a problem because, whereas in the Gospels he is cited among the Apostles, in early Church literature he is only one of 'the Seven' or 'a Disciple'. Here, too, in Acts he is called one 'of the Seven'. As for the 'Silas' in Josephus, who may or may not bear a relationship to Paul's companion Silas, he really was arrested by 'King Herod' – Herod Agrippa I – and this at his 'birthday party' no less, because of his pretence of being Agrippa I's equal. After Agrippa died, Herod of Chalcis and Helcias – our Temple Treasurer again and, it would seem, a boon companion of Herod of Chalcis – executed him, making it seem as if by Agrippa's order, but Josephus may be mistaken here.²⁵

In the course of these matters too, Josephus comments on the brutality of the Caesarean Legionnaires – among whom we must no doubt include Acts' 'Cornelius' – in much the same words he used when discussing the letter by Nero's Secretary for Greek Correspondence, annulling the equal rights of the Jews, noting:

> These were the very men that became the source of very great calamities for the Jews later on and sowed the seeds of the War which began under Florus [64–66]. Therefore, when Vespasian conquered the country, he had them removed from the region.[26]

The Fornication of Herodian Women

For his part, Agrippa I died under mysterious circumstances in 44 CE. He had been brought up in Rome as a 'foster brother' of both future Emperors, Caligula and Claudius, and imprisoned by Tiberius for predicting – no doubt, joyfully – Tiberius' coming death (our 'fortune-telling' theme once again). When Tiberius died (37 CE), Caligula freed this Agrippa and gave him his grandfather Herod's Kingdom, and Claudius, who became Emperor after Caligula was murdered in 41 CE, confirmed him in this.

But Agrippa I appears to have harboured greater ambitions than this, and there is a suspicion of foul play associated with his death. As remarked, this would appear to be portrayed in Acts 12:23 – in Josephus he is at a theatre festival in Caesarea dressed like a god in 'a garment made wholly of silver'[27] – and Agrippa does seem to have wanted to get together a treasonable alliance of some kind on the Roman frontier with Persia of petty Kings in Northern Syria, Asia Minor, Armenia, and Iraq, even perhaps encompassing Persia, because of all the Jews residing there. Whatever his ambitions, they came to naught and he seems to have been poisoned. Out of regard for his father, Claudius gave his Kingdom to his son Agrippa II at the expense of Herod of Chalcis, whose family was compensated in ways already detailed.

Agrippa I's other daughter, Bernice, *divorced* her husband Polemo, the King of Cilicia – Paul's purported place of origin – even though he too, like Drusilla's first husband Azizus in Syria, had 'circumcised himself' expressly to marry her. It is she who appears in Acts on the arm of her brother, Agrippa II, to question Paul after Felix departed for Rome (25:23). In her case, Josephus not only specifically remarks how she had originally been *married to her uncle* Herod of Chalcis above, by whom she had a son Bernicianus, but how, again like her sister Drusilla, after *divorcing herself* from Polemo of Cilicia, 'she forsook the Jewish Religion' altogether, a euphemism for taking up with Titus, the future destroyer of Jerusalem – 'circumcision', as in the case too of Drusilla with Felix above, evidently no longer being a concern.

But it is precisely this kind of 'divorcing' – not specifically condemned in Rabbinic Judaism as we know it (except on the part of a woman) – which is roundly condemned at Qumran. For his part, Josephus actually remarks Bernice's 'licentiousness' – 'fornication' in the language of Qumran – and added that Polemo was persuaded to circumcise himself only 'because of her Riches'. As far as Drusilla is concerned, as in the Gospel picture of John being executed by Herod at his 'birthday party', Josephus avoids blaming her by making it out that she was under the spell of a 'magician', that is, *Simon Magus*, who convinces her to abandon her religion and divorce someone who had circumcised himself in good faith and to marry Felix, who quite evidently had not.[28] In this regard, one should not forget that Suetonius identifies Felix's brother Pallas in Rome as originally being Claudius' *Treasurer*.

All of these marital and sexual imperfections are specifically condemned at Qumran as 'fornication' – the first 'Net of Belial' – the second, it will be recalled, not surprisingly, being 'Riches'. The third, as we have seen, relates to allowing Herodians of this stripe into the Temple. John the Baptist, too, lost his head in confrontations over similar sexual infractions by Herodians. The tendentious picture in the Gospels of Herod's 'birthday' festivities and the consonant picture of Herod (in this case Antipas) not 'raising up seed unto his brother' – a somewhat simplistic attempt to come to grips with the 'fornication' of Herodians by using biblical parameters only – should be put aside.

It is not without relevance in this regard that Suetonius also tells us how enthusiastic Titus was in *celebrating birthdays*, and how he captured Jerusalem 'on the occasion of his daughter's birthday'. According to Suetonius, this so delighted and encouraged his soldiers 'that they thereupon hailed him as Emperor'.[29] Josephus, too, picks up this thread of his zeal for birthday celebrations:

> During his stay in Caesarea, Titus celebrated his brother Domitian's birthday with great lavishness, reserving for this occasion the punishment of many Jewish captives, the number of whom destroyed in contests with wild

beasts or with one another or in the flames exceeded 2,500. To the Romans however, the various forms in which these victims perished all seemed too light a penalty. After this Titus went on to Berytus [Beirut], a city in Phoenicia and a Roman colony, where he made a longer stay, displaying even greater magnificence on the occasion of his father Vespasian's birthday, both as to the lavishness of the spectacles and the costliness of the various other items of expenditure. Here, too, innumerable captives perished in the same manner as before.[30]

It is not without moment that this zeal for birthday celebrations has probably made itself felt in Gospel accounts of John the Baptist's demise. It can be observed that Herodias broke Qumran proscriptions on 'fornication' in two respects: firstly, by divorcing a husband. As we have seen, both divorce *and* polygamy were specifically forbidden in the 'Three Nets of Belial' section of the Damascus Document. Divorce on the part of a woman was, in any event as noted, frowned on by Jewish Law. But for the Temple Scroll at Qumran, as already remarked as well, divorce by the King was especially pernicious. He was to marry once – and this only to a *Jewish* woman – his whole life or during the lifetime of the woman.

Herod did none of these things, marrying multiple Gentile women – he had at least *ten wives* – by whom he had a host of offspring, and indulged in polygamy promiscuously, so that Jerusalem resembled something akin to the presentday Kingdom of Saudi Arabia, though one line, that of the two Agrippas, Herodias, Bernice, Drusilla, and Mariamme III, predominated, evidently because they were the only ones thought of as being even remotely Jewish – and/or Royal on account of their Maccabean grandmother, Mariamme I. Secondly, Herodias married not just *one* uncle, but *two*.

The Damascus Document starts its excursus on these matters by evoking the allusion in its favourite prophet, Ezekiel, to 'Lying visions' and 'worthless' prophets 'following their own Spirit without seeing'. One should note, too, how, in this chapter 13, Ezekiel uses the imagery of torrential rain and whirlwind to describe God's Fury and the Wrath with which He destroys 'the wall', upon which the false prophets are 'daubing' (13:11–13 – a wonderful metaphor, which continues several columns later in the document).

The Damascus Document also evokes the 'spouting' imagery of Micah 2:6 on 'Lying visions' and 'the Spouter who will surely spout', language recapitulated in the Habakkuk *Pesher*'s picture of the Lying Spouter's 'Worthless Service' and the 'Emptiness' of his works.[31] The context in

Micah of God's tender care for 'the House of Jacob' and 'the Enemy', 'who walks in the Spirit and Lying', 'robbing its children forever of [God's] Glory' (2:7–11), no doubt, would have appealed mightily to Paul's enemies. It definitively links the Jewish Christian 'Enemy' terminology in a scriptural context to the 'Spouter of Lying' vocabulary employed at Qumran. It is the combination of these two imageries that the Damascus Document invokes at this critical juncture:

> The builders of the wall behaved in this manner [that is, the manner of those caught in 'the Three Nets of Belial'], the manner of the Spouter, of whom it was said, 'He shall surely spout.' They shall be caught in fornication twice by taking a second wife while the first is still living, whereas the principle of creation is 'Male and female He created them' [Gen. 1:27] . . . And concerning the Prince it is written, 'He shall not multiply wives unto himself' [Deut. 17.17] . . . Additionally, they pollute the Temple, because they do not separate according to the *Torah*, but rather, they lie with a woman during the blood of her period. And each man marries the daughter of his brother and the daughter of his sister [the prohibition on niece marriage], whereas Moses said, 'You shall not approach your mother's sister. She is your mother's near kin.'

> But while the Laws against fornication are written for men, they should be extended to women. When, therefore, a brother's daughter uncovers the nakedness of her father's brother, she is as near kin. Furthermore, they pollute their Holy Spirit and they open their mouth with a Tongue full of insults [or 'a blaspheming Tongue'] against the Laws of the Covenant of God, saying, 'They are not sure.' They speak an Abomination [or 'blasphemy'] concerning them. They are all kindlers of the Fire and lighters of firebrands [Isa. 50:11]. Their nets are spiders' nets and their eggs are vipers' eggs [Isa. 59:5]. No man who approaches them can be cleansed, unless he was forced. Like a thing accursed shall his house be guilty.[32]

The harshness of these last phrases really does illuminate the ambience of this period. No one who knows the New Testament can fail to remark the resemblances too, including most importantly the allusion to 'vipers' eggs', which can just as easily be read as the 'vipers' offspring' or 'offspring of vipers' John the Baptist is quoted as using in attacking the Pharisees and Sadducees (Matt. 3:7 and pars.). In Matthew 12:34, it should be remembered, Jesus is pictured as hurling this same epithet at the Scribes and Pharisees and again in 23:33, calling down on them 'the Judgement of Hell'.

But the point here is that John condemns Herodias because of manifold infractions of these prohibitions and loses his head in the process. This is how 'fornication' really is understood at Qumran, where there are so many parallels to those doctrines attributed to John the Baptist in the Gospels and Josephus. We submit this is also the 'fornication' referred to in James' directives to overseas communities and the letter ascribed to his name. The Temple Scroll puts these issues a little more succinctly, forbidding niece marriage outright and calling it 'an Abomination'.[33]

It is our position therefore, that this same issue of 'fornication' is also at the root of the confrontation *at Caesarea*, recorded in the Pseudoclementine literature, between Simon *Magus* and Simon Peter, not in Samaria as a more dissimulating version of the same confrontation is portrayed in Acts. Nor is it about the nature of 'the Christ', as it is most often pictured in many of these accounts, though this might have played a part – but rather about the *marital practices* and *sexual mores* of these Herodian women, over which so many Messianic Leaders were undone and lost their lives.

In such a context, it would not be at all surprising if the Simon in Josephus' *Antiquities* – the 'Zealot' Simon, who wants to bar Herodians from the Temple as foreigners, not the New Testament one, who 'learns' not to make distinctions regarding Gentiles – was, in fact, imprisoned and ultimately forced to flee as in Acts, but not for the reasons specified, that is, arguments about the nature of Christ and the Resurrection. This is the mythologized Simon; the reality is probably something a little more mundane and fleshly.

One can also conclude that such a confrontation between Simon Peter and Simon *Magus really did occur* and that Simon *Magus*, as the 'Simon' or 'Atomus' in Josephus, really was in the employ of the Roman Governor and the Herodian family, for which reason like Paul he finally ends up going to Rome. Furthermore, one can infer that he taught the legality of divorce, including on the part of a woman – as Paul puts this twice in I Corinthians, 'for me all things are Lawful' – and, as in Paul, that circumcision was not required and, therefore presumably, that relationships like those with Felix and Titus were both permissible and desirable. In these regards, it should be recalled that Simon was supposed to have had as his 'Queen', one *Helen*, whom he is said, in early Church sources, to have picked up in the brothels of Tyre in Phoenicia![34]

For its part, the Pseudoclementine *Recognitions* makes it very clear that after the bloodshed in the Temple, because of the riot led by 'the Enemy' Paul and the flight of the whole Community to the Jericho area (the region of Qumran); as leader of the early Church, *James sent Peter* to Caesarea to confront Simon *Magus*. We infer that the issue must have been, as with John the Baptist previously, the marital practices of the Herodian family. Like the 'Zealot' Simon in Josephus, we would place Peter – the demythologized Peter – who is said in early Church sources to have forced Simon to flee to Rome, on the opposite side of the spectrum on issues such as this, more in tune with Qumran and other martyred Leaders in the Messianic Movement, such as John the Baptist.

That Peter confronted Simon over the issue of the 'fornication' of the Herodian family and the things Simon was either permitting or encouraging them to do, and 'circumcision' is, in our view, a simple truism. Peter *did not* – as per Acts' tendentious portrait – argue against 'those insisting on circumcision' (11:2–3 and 15:7–11).

Acts' Paulinization of Peter in Jaffa and Caesarea

The same can be said for the picture of Peter earlier in Acts visiting the household of the *Roman Centurion Cornelius* in Caesarea. Nothing could be further from the truth. In fact, this is an inversion of the truth and outright disinformation. In the first place, it should be clear that the visit of Simon Peter to the Caesarean Legionnaire is a double for the visit of the Simon in Josephus to inspect Agrippa I's household in Caesarea to see what was being done there contrary to Law.

Acts' portrayal of Peter's visit to Cornelius' household is just the opposite. Acts describes Cornelius, it will be recalled, as 'a Righteous One', 'Pious and God-Fearing', 'doing many Righteous ['charitable'] works to the people and praying to God continually', 'borne witness to by the whole Nation of the Jews' (10:2 and 10:22). Not only do we have here, as we saw, almost all the elements from early Church portraits of James, but the cynicism of applying these characteristics to a *Roman Legionnaire from Caesarea*, the description by Josephus of whose brutality and incessant goading the Jews to revolt against Rome we have just provided above, is extreme. Were it not that these matters were so serious and have been repeated as pious truisms for almost two millennia, it would be difficult to suppress one's incredulity.

In this episode Peter learns, as we have repeatedly made clear, 'not to make profane what God has made clean', nor 'to call any man profane or unclean' (Acts 10:15 and 28), that is, not to make problems over dietary regulations and make distinctions between men on the basis of race –

noble sentiments, but just the opposite of what the Simon in Josephus is envisioning as regards King Agrippa I and Peter's teachings in the *Homilies*.

Peter goes on to characterize God as 'not being a respecter of persons' (10:34), basically a variant of the words Paul uses in Galatians 2:6 to attack 'Pillar' Apostles like Peter and James, 'God does not accept the person of man.' We already saw as well how this too represented an inversion of the description of James as 'not respecting persons' in Hegesippus' account of James' proclamation in the Temple on Passover, reversed yet again in Josephus' fawning description of James' murderer and arch-nemesis the High Priest Ananus above, as 'treating even the humblest as equals'.³⁵ Again, it is difficult to suppress one's incredulity.

The attack on the Pillar Apostles in Paul's Letter to the Galatians then moves on to excoriate 'Cephas' and 'those of the circumcision' party generally on just the points about 'keeping dietary regulations' and 'withdrawing from Gentiles' we have in Acts' account of Peter's behaviour in the aftermath of his tablecloth vision, the only problem being that, according to Acts' chronology, this vision precedes these encounters in Antioch, so if Peter (or 'Cephas') had ever really been vouchsafed such a vision, why would Paul have to be attacking Peter on these issues in the first place – not to mention the fact that they are totally gainsaid in the Pseudoclementines.

However this may be, the upshot of this episode in Acts is that Peter is now represented in a speech to Cornelius' 'kinsmen and closest friends' as extending – in the Pauline manner – the applicability of James' 'Righteousness' based on 'works' to all Gentiles and, in the process to be sure, once again making the blood accusation against 'the Jews'. This reads:

> But in every Nation, he who *fears* [*God*] and *works Righteousness*, is acceptable to Him . . . Jesus, who was *from Nazareth* . . . went around *doing good* [*works*] and healing all those who were oppressed by the Devil [*Diabolou*] . . . in the country of the Jews and in Jerusalem, whom they *put to death by hanging on a tree* [this last patently echoing Paul in Galatians 3:13 above]. (Acts 10:35–39)

The issue of 'circumcision' crops up at this point in Galatians as well, as it does following this in Acts' picture of those supposedly accusing Peter when he went back 'up to Jerusalem' to report what had happened in Jaffa and Caesarea:

> *Those of the circumcision* [this, word for word again from Galatians 2:12] contended with him, 'You went in to men uncircumcised and ate with them.' (11:2–3)

The caricature of Peter's 'Jerusalem Church' interlocutors is an effective one. Of course, Acts' alleged 'Jewess' Drusilla and her sisters did much worse.

Not only does this episode anticipate Peter's behaviour as portrayed in Galatians, but the very words it uses more or less echo Paul's rebuke of Peter – a rebuke that so upset Augustine in his correspondence with Jerome above – itself turning on the matter of James' leadership:

> For before *some from James* came down, [Peter] used to eat with the Gentiles, but after they came, he *drew back and separated himself* being afraid of *those of [the] circumcision*. (Gal. 2:12, as Acts 11:2)

Here again we have the precise wording 'separation' again, so important to the charge sheet of 'the Three Nets of Belial' and the Qumran orientation generally, but also for the language of 'Jamesian Christianity'. The reference to 'circumcision', here, not only links it to the episode we are exploring at Caesarea and its aftermath in Jerusalem in Acts, but unequivocally identifies those following James with those 'insisting on circumcision' (the '*Sicarioi*'?).

Knowing the history of Caesarea in this period, which more or less paralleled that of another hotbed of Greek anti-Semitism, Alexandria, the authors of Acts must have been in a really playful mood when composing these scenes about Peter on the rooftop in Jaffa visiting the Roman Centurion in Caesarea – or rather recomposing them. Something approaching 1 million Jews were wiped out during the course of apparently Messianic disturbances in Alexandria and its environs in Trajan's reign (98–117 CE) – the numbers have never been accurately counted.[36] Trajan and Hadrian, it will be remembered, came from the same Roman town of Italica in Southern Spain mentioned here in Acts, whether accidentally or by design, as Cornelius' *place of origin*.

Whatever the conclusion regarding this allusion to 'Italica' in Acts 10:1, there can be little doubt that Acts' Cornelius episode, just as the Stephen episode to like effect preceding it, *never happened*. In fact, regardless of what Peter is depicted as learning or unlearning here, the episode in its present form definitively proves that Jesus did not regulate the twin issues of 'forbidden foods' or 'table fellowship with Gentiles' in his lifetime and *never taught anything* on these issues remotely resembling what has been attributed to him!

The over-zealous artificers in the Book of Acts have, at least, achieved this, though, patently, this was not their goal. The reason is quite simple. Had he done so, Peter, his purportedly closest living associate, *would have known of it* and, therefore, not needed this Paulinizing 'tablecloth' vision to conveniently regulate these issues on the eve of his visit to the Roman Centurion's household in Caesarea. But, on the contrary, since Peter is portrayed as not knowing such things, Jesus did not teach them – because, either Jesus *did not* teach these things, in which case Peter would need this vision, or Jesus *taught them*, in which case Peter would not. One or the other, but not both. Either this episode in Acts or the picture of Jesus teaching things like 'nothing which enters the mouth defiles a man, but that which goes forth out of the mouth defiles a man' in Matthew 15:6's 'toilet bowl' episode above or eating with classes of unclean persons, like 'tax collectors', 'Sinners' (a catchword for 'Gentiles' in Galatians 2:15), and 'being a glutton', preferring 'prostitutes', and the like, is false.

But, in any event, this episode in Acts is really included only to explain and, ultimately, counteract the episode pictured by Paul in Galatians, where Peter is portrayed as withdrawing from 'table fellowship' with Gentiles when the 'some from James' come down to Antioch. It *Paulinizes* Peter, putting the basic elements of the Pauline approach – 'food is for the belly and the belly for food' and 'circumcision is nothing and uncircumcision nothing' (1 Cor. 6:13 and 7:19), including 'Holy Spirit' baptism, into his mouth. It also proves – and this definitively – that Jesus *never taught any such things* in his lifetime, because, if he did, why would Peter, his reputed closest associate, need a Pauline vision to confirm them?

Of course, official history and orthodox doctrine, as presented in the Gospels and the Book of Acts, have a ready response to this. Peter, who denied the Master three times on his death night (Matt. 26:75 and pars.), simply *misunderstood* the teaching of the Master. In this episode in Acts, the Heavenly Voice that accompanies the descent of the Heavenly table-cloth with its forbidden foods – similar to the voice Paul is always hearing – cries out to him *three times* before Peter understands the gist of its teaching (Acts 10:16). In the Gospels, Peter sinks into the Sea of Galilee for *lack of Faith* – the quintessentially Pauline position – when trying to replicate Jesus' miracle of 'walking on the waters' (Matt. 14:31 and pars.).

In fact, the real Peter shines through, even in the tablecloth episode as it presently stands, in his insistence that 'I have never eaten anything profane or unclean' (Acts 10:15, repeated with slight rephrasing in 11:8). In effect, this visionary episode puts the overall issue very elegantly, when it has Peter explaining to Cornelius and entourage, 'You know, it is not Lawful for a Jewish man to have intercourse with or come near one of another race' (10:28) – thus directly relating it, whether by design or accidentally, to the impetus behind the visit of the 'Simon' in Josephus to Caesarea who wants to exclude Agrippa I from the Temple as a foreigner.

Confrontations over Circumcision and the End in Acts

'Circumcision' was also the issue complicating both Drusilla's and Bernice's marriages to several royal personages in Syria and Asia Minor and to Felix, whose brother Pallas stood at the hub of power in Rome. It is, as can be seen, also at the heart of Paul's confrontations in Galatians with those 'from James', who came down to press the 'table fellowship' issue in 'Antioch', and Peter's riposte to the same 'those of circumcision' following his 'table-cloth' vision in Acts, which permits him not only to eat with Gentiles, but even to visit the household of a Roman Centurion in Caesarea.

As a result of these interventions, clearly by James, those formerly keeping company with Paul, supposedly in 'Antioch', including Peter and Barnabas, 'drew back and separated' themselves 'for fear of those of the circumcision' – this within the Church not outside it. This kind of ban or excommunication by Paul's Jewish associates – shunning might be more to the point – is a typical Qumran procedure, familiar from the literature there.[37]

It should be noted that in the aftermath of this 'tablecloth' vision, too, Barnabas is pictured as being sent by 'the Assembly in Jerusalem' ('the Jerusalem Church') to 'Antioch', where Acts, as we saw, probably accurately, observes 'the Disciples were first called Christians' (Acts 11:26). A series of passages ensues with representatives repeatedly coming down *from Jerusalem to Antioch*, beginning with this one involving 'Paul and Barnabas' in 11:22, but also one immediately following in 11:27 having to do with 'prophets coming down from Jerusalem to Antioch', one of whom with the most peculiar and no doubt garbled name of 'Agabus' – about whom we shall hear more in due course.

The chapter ends with Paul and Barnabas returning again to Jerusalem supposedly on Famine-relief operations consonant upon the prophecy by this so-called 'Agabus' of the Famine (46–48 CE – 11:29). This is totally gainsaid by Paul's own testimony in Galatians, which has Paul, as we have seen, not returning to Jerusalem – after his initial flight – 'for another fourteen years', or approximately 51–52 CE. This is continued into Chapter 12 with the totally extraneous information about the elimination of the other 'James *the brother of John*', Peter's miraculous escape from prison and subsequent flight, the completely offhand introduction of the principal James, and how 'Herod' – no further identification given –

'being eaten by worms, expired' (Acts 12:23). But, as usual, nothing about what Barnabas and Paul did in Jerusalem is mentioned during the whole of the chapter – only the laconic observation at its end, that, 'having completed their mission', they returned to Antioch 'taking John Mark with them' (12:25).

Chapter 13 returns to the enumeration of these so-called 'prophets and teachers of the Assembly at Antioch', including Niger, Paul, and the curious individual called 'Herod the Tetrarch's foster brother'. Then ensues the confrontation with 'the Son of Devil' ('*Diabolos*', that is, 'Belial') and 'Enemy of all Righteousness', Elymus *Magus*, and the laconic aside about how 'John left them and returned to Jerusalem' (13:13). Finally, in chapter 15, 'And certain ones, having come down from Judea, were teaching the brothers that unless you are circumcised according to the Law of Moses, you cannot be saved' (15:1). This will be the exact point that will emerge in both Josephus' and Talmudic descriptions of the conversion of Queen Helen of Adiabene's son, somewhere in the region of Haran in Northern Syria or further east, by a teacher who finds him reading the Law of Moses.

In Acts' reckoning, it provokes the so-called 'Jerusalem Council', resulting in the directives James sends in the letter to overseas communities above. In the aftermath of this, two individuals, now identified as Judas Barsabas[38] and Silas – 'themselves also prophets' – are purportedly sent with Paul and Barnabas to convey James' letter to 'the Many' in 'Antioch' (15:30). These matters would appear to be the real reason behind the break between Paul and Barnabas, who are presented as parting company here because of a rift over John Mark, 'the man', in Paul's view, 'who withdrew from them in Pamphylia and would not share in their work' (15:38–39).[39]

At this point, in chapter 16, what we have referred to as the 'We Document' – a first-person plural travel account – more or less interjects itself into the narrative. Therefore just about everything from chapters 11 to 15 in Acts deals with the repetitious theme of *representatives coming down from Jerusalem to Antioch* – mostly spurious and retrospective – to cover over the rift that occurred in 'Antioch' after Paul's return from Jerusalem, as retold in Galatians. As is made clear in that letter, and intermittently in Acts, for the most part these come *directly* 'from James', dogging Paul's footsteps over circumcision, table fellowship with Gentiles, and dietary regulations generally.

Paul's easygoing view of circumcision, no doubt, would have been very convenient for Herodians wishing to marry local kings in Northern Syria and Asia Minor and also well in line with his, and what would appear to be Herodian, aims generally in the East: to build a community where Greeks and Jews could live in harmony (Gal. 3:28, 1 Cor. 3:24, etc.). But chapters 16–21 are really simply about one extended journey in Asia Minor and mainland Greece, at the end of which Paul hurries back to Jerusalem to be in time for the Festival of Pentecost – apparently the time of reunion of the Community, as it is in the wilderness 'camps' in the Dead Sea Scrolls – and runs into the well-known difficulties with James and the Jerusalem mob in the Temple we have been describing.

Where the rest of Acts is concerned, we would contest the picture of 'the Jews' from Jerusalem bringing 'many and weighty charges against Paul' and Paul's defence, that 'neither against the Law of the Jews, nor against the Temple, nor against Caesar, did I commit any infraction' (Acts 25:8). We would also contest Festus' desire, repeated twice, 'to acquire favour(s) with the Jews' (25:7–9). Before this, as already observed, Acts has Felix 'hoping Paul would give him Riches' (24:26). In fact, the situation was just the opposite, and a Jewish delegation went to Rome to complain about Festus as well and, because Festus was less well placed than Felix, they were more successful.[40]

Nor is the picture of Paul discoursing in detail about his career and other doctrinal concerns with Agrippa and his reported consort, the 'licentious' Bernice, his sister, and asking him obsequiously, 'King Agrippa, do you believe in the Prophets? I know you believe' (26:27), the least bit convincing. As will be recalled, Agrippa II replies, 'A little more, and you would persuade me to become a Christian', and, nothing loath, Paul responds, 'I wish to God in no small measure that both of you soon . . . should become such as I also am' (26:28–29). The scene, while no doubt essentially true, is a good example of how far New Testament authors were willing to go in refashioning the fundamentals of the Messianic Movement in Palestine and retouching the image of the ruling élite. At which point Bernice and Agrippa stand up, and speaking aside to one another, say, 'This man has done nothing deserving of death or chains', and then to Festus, 'If he had not appealed to Caesar, this man could have been set free' (26:31–32).

The picture of Paul trying to convert Agrippa II would, no doubt, have sent Messianists of the time into paroxysms of derision – just the attitude one finds in the *Pesharim* at Qumran concerning 'the Lying Spouter' or 'Man of Lies' there. Not only was Agrippa, along with the High Priest,

Ananus, he appointed, *responsible for the death of James*; his sister, Bernice, as we have already remarked several times, was the future mistress of Titus. Both were connected to people like Philo's nephew, Tiberius Alexander, the Roman Commander at the siege of Jerusalem. All, no doubt, were involved in the decision the Romans finally took *to destroy the Temple*. In fact, Agrippa II had already been involved in the decision to call Cestius' Roman troops into the city four years before to put down the Uprising. In the end, as we saw as well, Agrippa retires along with other 'Traitors' like Josephus to spend his last days comfortably in Rome.

Not only did the Zealot 'Innovators', in the aftermath of this revealing scene in Acts, ban both Agrippa and Bernice from Jerusalem altogether, but, to show their real attitude towards them – and that of 'Messianic Revolutionaries' generally – their palaces were burned in the first days of the Uprising, when these same Zealot 'Innovators' 'turned the Poor against the Rich'. No doubt Paul did confer with Agrippa II, Bernice, and Festus at some length, as he did Felix and Drusilla earlier, but it is doubtful if the picture in Acts is accurate as to the exact subjects discussed or precisely what was said. As we have already suggested, the numerous sessions Paul had with Felix over the 'two-year' period detailed in Acts (24:26–27) were doubtlessly more in the nature of intelligence debriefings than theological or religious discussions, as Acts, rather disingenuously, attempts to portray them. It was, very likely, during the course of these exchanges that James' pivotal role among the Jewish mass and at the centre of Messianic agitation in the Temple was made plain by Paul to his Roman and Herodian overlords.

If this is so, then Paul also has a hand in the 'plot' to destroy and bring about the death of James, which would not be surprising in view of Paul's manifold differences with him, the manner of his frequent discomfiture by James, and his admitted previous destruction of such Messianic Leaders (1 Cor. 15:9 and Gal. 1:13). Paul would, then, have identified James as the pivotal figure behind the unrest in Jerusalem – certainly among so-called 'Zealots' and probably *Sicarii* as well.[41] If James is a parallel figure to and has anything in common with the individual known as 'the Righteous Teacher' at Qumran, then this certainly would be the case. In our view, this is the ultimate reason behind James' demise and why, at one point in the Qumran Habakkuk *Pesher*, the same 'swallowing' imagery, that is finally applied to the Wicked Priest's 'conspiracy' to destroy the Righteous Teacher, is also applied to 'the Liar's' activities.[42]

Of course, Acts, as usual, reverses this into *a conspiracy* by the Zealots and the High Priests *to destroy Paul*!

One should also remark, when Festus is explaining to Bernice and Agrippa II Paul's appeal 'to be examined by Augustus', how he 'found him to have done nothing deserving of death, but because he had appealed to Augustus', he decided to send him to Rome (Acts 25:21–25:25).

There is surely more lurking beneath these events than appears on the surface. The fact of these sessions in Caesarea and the space Acts devotes to them in its apologetics is impressive – some six chapters, almost a quarter of the narrative. Certainly they took place, but more was probably discussed during the 'two years' of these sessions than this, and why is Acts so silent as to whether anyone from James' Jerusalem Community ever came down to visit Paul during his entire 'imprisonment'? Rather Acts only emphasizes these contacts with Roman Officials and their protégés. This is not the only thing Acts is silent about.

The Truth About the Death of James

The Blasphemy Charge Against James

It is to the fourth-century Church theologian Jerome we now must turn, who in a few allusions finally gives us the key to sort out all these overlaps, transpositions, and *non sequiturs* in the various stories about the attack on and death of James. Even though Jerome presents the data about James' death in just two or three sentences, several points emerge from his version which overlap the presentation of the attack on James in the Temple by 'the Enemy' Paul in the 40s not the 60s in the Pseudoclementine *Recognitions*. As we have already stated, the very possibility of such an attack sends chills up and down the spines of orthodox believers and theologians and has done for centuries. Can it be possible that Paul did this – can the Pseudoclementine *Recognitions* be true? Not only is it possible and it did probably happen, but there is more – much more.

Though we have already presented some of the material from Jerome in other contexts, it is now worth returning to him in more detail. When one reads Jerome carefully, one can see we have not made very much progress in theological debate or in historical research since his time. He already knows most of the things we know about biblical research. For instance, he is aware that not all the letters of Paul may have been written by Paul, that Hebrews might have been written by Barnabas, that Jude is the brother of James, and that there is a question about the authenticity of the Letter attributed to James because of its excellent Greek – all points still discussed by biblical scholars today. In short, he is a very modern man, which may simply be to say he tries to use his mind. Nevertheless one must approach his work with caution, for in it there is still an orthodox theological orientation, coupled with a desire to protect the Church at all costs which must be reckoned with.

When Jerome comes to present the death of James, he prefaces this with the usual – probably direct – quotation from Hegesippus, describing James' Naziritism, which, while already quoted, is worth repeating:

> He alone enjoyed the privilege of entering the Holy of Holies, since, indeed, he did not wear woollen, but only linen clothes, and went into the Temple alone and prayed on behalf of the People, so that his knees were reputed to have acquired the callusness of a camel's knees.

We already explained how this could be nothing other than an account of a *Yom Kippur* atonement.

Like Eusebius, Jerome also claims to be quoting Hegesippus directly, but makes no bones about the fact that it was the Holy of Holies into which James went. One should also remark the repetition of the important themes of 'knees' and 'kneeling' and 'clothes' and 'clothing', which have become ever more prominent as we proceed. For Jerome, this atonement in the Holy of Holies, as should be obvious, was a function of James' 'Priestly' activities and, therefore, his functioning as a kind of 'Opposition High Priest' – not so much of his 'bathing' ones or the other aspects of his 'Piety' or life-long Nazitism or 'Holiness', which were more in the manner of those Josephus is calling 'Essenes' or parallel 'Sabaean', 'Elchasaite', or 'Mandaean' practices of Northern Syria and Southern Iraq.

Then Jerome, combining what he claims to be the accounts of both Clement and Josephus, provides the following description:

> On the death of Festus who governed Judea, Albinus was sent by Nero as his successor. Before he had reached his province, Ananias the High Priest [*thus*], the youngest son of Ananus of the class of Priests, taking advantage of the state of anarchy, assembled a Sanhedrin and publicly tried to force James to recant that *Christ was the Son of God*.[1]

Here Jerome replaces the usual chronology of James' death, being immediately followed by the fall of Jerusalem of the other early Church accounts, with Josephus' chronology.

By 'Ananias', he clearly means 'the High Priest Ananus ben Ananus', but his confusion – whether his own or a copyist's error – is interesting, since the distinction between Ananias and Ananus is not always clear even in Acts, which knows no 'Ananus' – nor clearly drawn in Josephus. Both were extremely 'Rich' and we have already noted the pivotal role 'Ananias' played in collusion with Governors like Albinus in 'robbing the tithes of the Poorer Priests' in Josephus' accounts of the violence High Priests were willing to use with the People.

In combining Josephus and the early Church accounts, which Jerome generally credits as a single whole to Clement of Alexandria, the charge against James in the Sanhedrin trial that he extracts from Josephus becomes one of refusing to deny that Jesus was 'the Son of God'. This charge, along with *the Sanhedrin trial*, is missing from the accounts we have excerpted from Eusebius, Epiphanius, and Hegesippus, however, the charge brings us right back into the Gospel accounts of *the death of Jesus*.

Clement's account of these things has not been preserved, except in so far as it may or may not have been echoed here in Jerome and works like Eusebius'. Still, as in the Gospels, it is this insistence that in Jerome's account leads directly to the 'blasphemy' charge, for which stoning was the punishment in the classical Jewish sources. This point might simply have been a later emendation or Jerome's own invention. On the other hand, as Jerome himself implies, it may already have been in Clement's no longer extant account. The charge itself is certainly not in Josephus, though the trial, of course, is.

It will be recalled that in Eusebius, in response to the question, 'the Scribes and Pharisees' demanded of James when he 'stood on the Pinnacle of the Temple', 'What is the door to Jesus the Crucified One' (or 'Hanged One'), James simply moves on to his proclamation of how Jesus, specifically identified as 'the Son of Man is sitting on the right hand of the Great Power and will come on the clouds of Heaven' (presumably meaning, 'with the Heavenly Host'). This is a scenario of final apocalyptic Judgement, which, as we saw, has much in common with the extended exposition of 'the Star Prophecy' in the War Scroll from Qumran.

In most early Church accounts of the debates on the Temple steps, such as those in the Pseudoclementine *Recognitions* – refracted to some degree also in Acts – the writers are mainly intent on showing James to be demonstrating in what manner Jesus could be 'the Christ'. That is to say, a Supernatural Being, a Redeemer Figure seated 'on the right hand of Power', but with distinct Greco-Hellenistic overtones. As in the case of the 'Son of Man' notation, one might legitimately call this too a Greco-Hellenistic variation of the 'Primal Adam' ideology of the various Ebionite/Nazirite/Elchasaite groups dressed up in new attire.

It should also be remembered that in Hebrew, the notation 'Son of Man' is actually transcribed as 'Son of Adam' – '*Adam*' being one of the synonyms for the word '*Man*' in Hebrew – and even on the face of it, we are in the same ideological universe as Paul's 'Second Adam' or 'Second Man' ideology at the end of 1 Corinthians. It should also be appreciated that the use of the expression 'the Christ' in this context, as a Greek equivalent to what goes by the name of 'the Primal Adam' or 'First' or 'Second Man' ideologies in other milieus, also, more and more takes on the appearance of an overseas play on the homophonic 'Sicarios' or 'Iscariot' terminology in Palestine, or vice versa. Though this cannot be proved in any definitive way, it increasingly begins to recommend itself.

It is Paul, who, by his 'revelations via the Holy Spirit', is wedded to the idea of a Supernatural Figure, with whom he is in almost constant contact – at least he believes or claims that he is – and whom he calls 'Christ Jesus'. This may or may not be the same individual as Jerome is referring to in this single reference to 'the Son of God'. Obviously normative Christian theology would say it is. It is only a fine point, but it is important for determining just what early Church accounts thought the charge against James for 'blasphemy' really constituted.

Finally one must always keep in mind the confluence of all these terminologies in Paul's 'Second Adam' or the Ebionite 'Primal Adam' terminologies, which certainly have a Supernatural aspect or – put in another way – a component involving 'Divine Sonship'.

The Parallel Blasphemy Charge in Pictures of the Trial of Jesus

As we already alluded to, 'blasphemy' really is a specific charge in Judaism. It is outlined in some detail in the *Talmud*, which is claiming anyway to present materials going back to the period in question or even before. Whether it does or not or how accurately it might do so is a matter of opinion. In the *Talmud*, the punishment for 'blasphemy' is stoning, though this is less clear in the Old Testament.[2]

Jesus, for example therefore, does not die a blasphemer's death! We have treated this in some detail earlier, but we should look at this charge against Jesus in the Gospels in more depth. Jesus may have been condemned for 'blasphemy', which the New Testament appears sometimes to be claiming (Matt. 26:65 and pars.), but the charge sheet against him is unclear and varies from Gospel to Gospel. The Gospel of John, for instance, puts this charge into the mouths of the Jewish crowd, who purportedly cry out that 'he made himself the Son of God' (19:7). For Matthew 26:63 and Mark 14:61, it is the High Priest who identifies 'the Christ' with 'the Son of God', but both charges appear simply to be a retrospective emendation, the second, in any case, more properly relates to the James story as Jerome recounts it on the basis of Clement of Alexandria.

According to the Gospels, Pilate, quite properly, shows himself interested only in the charge of 'making himself a King' when examining Jesus. In the Gospel of John, which we did not discuss in this regard to any extent previously, Pilate, portrayed as prevaricating, is corrected by the Jewish mob, which, in a clearly tendentious account, once more tells him his job: 'Everyone that makes himself a King, speaks against Caesar' – whereupon Pilate condemns Jesus.

John even depicts the crowd as warning Pilate, if he releases Jesus, he is not 'a Friend of Caesar' (19:12) – terminology used on Herodian coins like those of Agrippa I, his brother, Herod of Chalcis, and the latter's son Aristobulus and his consort, the infamous Salome. The *Talmud* even portrays its hero, Rabbi Yohanan ben Zacchai, as using this 'Friend of Caesar' terminology, when, after having himself smuggled out of Jerusalem in a coffin (the appropriate vehicle, perhaps, under the circumstances), he humiliates himself before Vespasian and applies 'the World Ruler Prophecy' to him.[3]

For good measure, the Gospel of John even has 'the Chief Priests' assert at this point, 'We have no King but Caesar' (19:15). Spiritually this may have been true, but it is doubtful 'the Chief Priests' – Paul's supposed opponents before both Felix and Festus in Acts – would have asserted it so blatantly, except in cases of extreme duress to save themselves. Of course this certainly would have been the motto of Rabbi Yohanan ben Zacchai above, and, in fact, all his *Pharisee* followers after the fall of the Temple and even before, but hardly that of Messianic Revolutionaries, Qumran sectaries, and Jamesian Christians, among others – if there is any difference between any of these – before it.

Like the Chief Priests in this scene, Paul's preference – 'Pharisee' that he claims to be – for this kind of 'Judgement' is made clear in Acts above. When asked by Festus if he was 'willing to go up to Jerusalem to be judged', presumably by these same 'Chief Priests', Paul is portrayed as responding:

> I am standing before *the Judgement Seat of Caesar*, where I ought to be judged. (Acts 25:10)

The answer Jesus gives to Pilate's question, 'Are you the King of the Jews?': 'My Kingdom is not of this world' (John 18:33–38), identifies John, anyhow, as late – demonstrably later, for instance, than the early second century and the correspondence, noted above, between Pliny the Younger and Trajan. The latter (at least according to Eusebius), when instructed by Trajan as Governor of Bithynia in Asia Minor to investigate Christians (112 CE), 'found no fault in them' – a response equivalent to Pilate's in John, 'I find no fault in him' (19:4–6, paralleled in Luke 23:4–15).[4]

In any event, it is as late or later than similar inquiries, also described by Eusebius – this time following Hegesippus again – in Domitian's time (81–96 CE) of the sons (or grandsons) of Jesus' *third brother Judas*. Depicted as simple country menials, these respond to questions 'concerning the Christ and His Kingdom' almost exactly as Jesus is depicted as doing here in John:

> That it was not of this world, nor earthly, but Heavenly and Angelic, when *He would come in Glory to judge the quick and the dead and give every man according to his works*. At this, Domitian *found no fault with them*, but having contempt for them as simpletons, dismissed them.[5]

The reader will note the repetition here of James' proclamation of the Son of Man coming in Glory in the Temple at Passover, again precisely as depicted in Hegesippus – including the note about 'give every man according to his works'.

For Luke, the charge sheet to Pilate is, it will be recalled, quite specific:

> We found this man *leading the people astray* and *forbidding* [*them*] *to pay tribute to Caesar*, saying that *he himself, Christ, is a King*. (23:1)

Here Luke combines Jesus' 'being a King' – which Pilate alludes to in his 'Are you the King of the Jews' question – with the 'Christ' ideology. Going on to emphasize the issue of 'insurrection and murder' concerning Jesus' alter ego Barabbas (23:19), Luke also twice plays on the point concerning whether Jesus and his followers – Peter in this case – were 'Galileans'. In the process, he shows an understanding of the confusion between taking this terminology literally or in the more symbolical sectarian or subversive sense (22:59 and 23:6).

In his picture, the Jewish crowd is now doing the 'blaspheming' (22:65: 'they said many other blaspheming things to him'). When 'the Chief Priests and Scribes gather' in his Sanhedrin scene, the two questions, 'are you the Christ' and 'are you the Son of God', follow one after the other (22:67–71). These then lead into the only real answer Jesus makes as far as Luke is concerned:

> Henceforth shall the Son of Man be seated at the right hand of the Power of God –

which is again, of course, the proclamation attributed to James in the Temple on Passover by Eusebius and Hegesippus, as well as by Jerome – before all three move on to the stoning material.

But Luke is quite consistent in the manner in which he separates the thrust of these 'blasphemy' materials – which hardly concern Pilate at all, or for that matter the Romans – from social agitation or insurrectionary activities, for which in Roman Law (*not Jewish*) the punishment was *crucifixion*. Matthew and Mark, on the other hand rather, combine the two queries into a single question: 'Are you the Christ, the Son of God' (26:63 and 14:61), showing that they think the two expressions, 'the Christ' and 'the Son of God' are basically either two aspects of the same thing or identical.

Mark, however, like John above, is the only Synoptic to have Jesus actually answer in the affirmative – Jesus' words, 'I am', taking the place of 'henceforth you shall see, etc.' in Matthew and Luke. But this being said, just as in Luke above, Matthew and Mark also immediately go on to attach their version of the two notations combined into a single phraseology to *Jesus'* proclamation (not *James'*):

> Henceforth you shall see the Son of Man sitting at the right hand of Power and coming on the clouds of Heaven. (Matt. 26:64 and Mark 14:62)

It is at this point that Matthew and Mark depict the High Priest as 'rending his clothes', specifically giving the verdict, 'You have spoken *blasphemy*' and 'all of them condemning him to be worthy of death'.

But this is just what one would expect, because the claim of being either 'the Christ' or 'the Son of God', or both, is a theological one and the crux of issues between Christians and Jews even today. Since the claim is not on the surface, anyhow, a political one, *this is the claim* that gives rise, as in Jerome's presentation of the events leading to *James'* stoning above, to the 'blasphemy' charge. One should also note the 'clothes' theme again – in this instance, the 'clothes' the High Priest tears, not, for instance, those deposited at the feet of Paul in Acts.

For his part, not only does Luke avoid any overt mention of the 'blasphemy' charge against Jesus – picturing it rather as what the men taking Jesus to the 'High Priest's House' do to him (22:65: 'and they said many things to him, blaspheming him') – he also uses the issue of Jesus 'being a Galilean' to interrupt the more political scene with Pilate with an intervening interview with 'Herod' (namely Herod Antipas, Tetrarch of Galilee and Perea). This interview and this scene are unique to Luke's Gospel and are followed directly by the final climactic condemnation before Pilate.

However, in all three Synoptic Gospels, *the Sanhedrin trial of Jesus* for 'blasphemy' at 'the High Priest's House', that always precedes these, ends on the note of their – in Matthew and Mark, 'the High Priests, the Elders, and scribes'; in Luke, the men conveying Jesus to 'the High Priest's House' – 'spitting in his face and striking him with blows'. This is not only similar to how 'the High Priest Ananias' has people hit Paul 'in the mouth' in Acts 23:2, but, as we have already remarked, also the James martyrdom scene in all the various presentations. Matthew adds 'with the palms of their hands' (26:67). For Luke, the men conveying Jesus 'beat' him, 'striking his face' (22:63–64).

Mark and Luke even include the curious element of their 'covering' Jesus' face, which parallels a similar note in the bizarre picture in the Second Apocalypse of James from Nag Hammadi of James' stoning, where after having James dig a hole, they 'cover him' up to his abdomen before they stone him.[6] In fact, the sequence and scenario here in the Gospels is exactly the same as that of James' martyrdom scene in all sources above. Of course, this may have been common to all the puppet trials and executions of the period, but in the James scenario the 'blasphemy' charge with more sense does move directly on to a stoning, and this, without the patent attempts – in spite of the fact that crucifixion in this period was pre-eminently *the Roman punishment for insurrectionary* and *subversive activities* – to rescue Roman officials or their underlings from any taint of collusion or responsibility.

Jesus Before Herod and Paul Before Agrippa II and Bernice

Luke, as one would expect – if he truly was the travelling companion of Paul – takes these whitewashing attempts or the power of creative writing to even greater heights. As in the case of 'Jesus the Nazoraean' or 'Nazirite', supposedly coming from 'Nazareth' elsewhere in the Gospels, Luke either misunderstands or purposefully obscures the 'Galilean' accusation, making it appear as if it involves only geographical and not socio-revolutionary aspects (23:4–6). Using his patently superior knowledge of Josephus, as just noted, Luke exploits Pilate's question about whether Jesus was 'a Galilean' to intersperse a quick intervening interview with 'Herod' (that is, Herod Antipas), since this was his 'Jurisdiction' (23:7).

The Herod in question, 'Herod the Tetrarch', is the same 'Herod' who carried out the preventive execution of John the Baptist across the Jordan, also in 'his Jurisdiction'. It is his 'foster brother' supposedly – it should be recalled – who is a *founding member* of the Pauline 'Antioch'

Community. The picture of Jesus' execution even outdoes this in the way it dissimulates on the question of Roman and/or Herodian involvement. In the Gospel of Matthew, Pilate's wife sends him a message, warning him to 'have nothing to do with *that Righteous One*' (in other words, now *she* is using the '*Zaddik*' terminology), because just that day she had a dream, where she 'suffered many things because of him' (27:19). Once again, we are in the Roman world of superstitious fantasy and 'birthday parties'. Luke adds the colourful detail, that Herod and Pilate, supposedly 'previously at odds, both became friends with each other on *that very day*' (23:12)!

At a later period consonant with the stoning of James, Agrippa II and Ananus the High Priest do seem to have become friends in Rome, during the latter's 'appeal to Rome' following the beating of 'the Emperor's Servant Stephen' and the crucifixions at Lydda, as do the Roman Governor Albinus and the 'Rich' High Priest Ananias thereafter in Judea. Of course, Felix is such a friend of the Herods that he even married one of their daughters, the 'Jewess' Drusilla. In Luke, however, the note about this alliance between Romans and Herodians just serves to exculpate them both from any complicity in the murder of 'Christ', which is the real point of the episode. Therefore, at its conclusion, Pilate is made to say to the 'Chief Priests and the Rulers and the people':

> You brought this man to me as one who *perverts* ['misleads'] the people, but behold, having examined him before you, *I found no fault in this man touching on those things you charge him with. No, nor yet Herod . . . nothing deserving of death has been done by him.* I will, therefore, punish and release him. (Luke 23:13–16)

But, of course, this is just the conclusion we would have expected if Christianity were to circulate and survive in the Roman Empire at this time. If it had not been, we would have had to invent it – as it, no doubt, was in the first place. In any event, it agrees perfectly with the scenes in Acts between Agrippa II (who really was a 'King', unlike the Herod the Tetrarch who interviews Jesus and, in Mark 6:14 below, destroyed John the Baptist) and the Roman Governor Festus, who really do examine Paul and conclude with even more verisimilitude:

> *This man might have been released* if he had not appealed to Caesar. (Acts 26:32)

Of course, the intervening interview with 'Herod' in Luke is nothing but a refurbishment of this more substantial one in Acts. The dramatis personae, Agrippa II and Bernice are, therefore, correctly identified, because, although undergoing a certain amount of enhancement, the episode is not a *complete* historical rewrite or completely counterfeit. The real fate of people who incurred the displeasure of Herodian Rulers or Roman Governors is described in Acts' portrait of James and Peter – however mythologized – and John the Baptist in the unembellished presentation of Josephus. Likewise, in Josephus' presentation of 'Theudas' ('James the brother of John' in Acts), the followers of 'the Egyptian', whom Felix mercilessly butchers, or the two sons of Judas the Galilean, reportedly crucified during the Governorship of Tiberius Alexander, and others.

Folkloric presentations, as in the case of the Gospels on John the Baptist's being considered by 'King Herod' a 'Holy and Righteous Man' (Mark 6:14 and 20), or Pilate's wife considering Jesus a 'Righteous One', or here, 'Herod, rejoicing greatly when he saw Jesus because for a long time he had *desired to see him do some miracle*' (Luke 23:8. This is the same 'Herod' who is pictured as having just executed John. If this were not so invidious, it might perhaps be tolerable), are simply the stuff of bedtime stories – but here, even worse, as they have the additional prejudicial intent, as Josephus himself makes clear, of 'flattering the Romans and vilifying the Jews'. For Luke 23:47, to add insult to injury, it is another of these ubiquitous Roman Centurions, who, upon viewing Jesus' death on the cross, after which 'darkness came over the land' for three hours, concludes 'surely this was a *Righteous One*'!

Not only this – but time and time again, elements integral to the story of James, such as his being called '*by all* a Righteous One' or being brought before the Sanhedrin, as per Jerome above, on a charge of 'blasphemy', appear to be retrospectively assimilated into the details of Jesus' end. For instance, as we have seen, from the material in Josephus, we cannot even tell whether the beheading of John happened before or after the alleged date of Jesus' crucifixion. If we go by Josephus' dating, it appears to have happened afterwards.

'Herod the Tetrarch' is the Governor of the area of Perea across Jordan, which is why the beheading of John takes place at the Fortress Machaeros on the east side of the Dead Sea. However, it not clear how much time this 'Herod the King', as Mark puts it, actually spent in Jerusalem. Though he really was the half-brother of Herodias' first husband, as Matthew and Mark more or less would have it, there all semblance of historical reality ends. As we saw, Herodias' first husband was never called 'Philip', but rather 'Herod' taken as a prenom. It was her daughter Salome, who married 'Philip', the Tetrarch of Trachonitis, a Province east of Damascus in Syria, and he *did predecease her*. Luke's story about an intervening interview by 'Herod' with Jesus, like all the others, is simply preposterous fiction. Even worse, it is malevolent, aimed at whitewashing Herodians and focusing vilification on 'the Jews'.

The *Blasphemy* Charge and James' *Yom Kippur* Atonement

So one is left with the conundrum, what was the basis of the 'blasphemy' charge against James – for this is the only charge of the many above that can really be substantiated in the end, all the others, particularly where Jesus is concerned, simply being rewrites or retrospective absorptions of data concerning James. There are two principal death penalties in Jewish practice of this period, as reflected and sometimes even refracted in the *Talmud*. The first is for subversive or insurrectionary behaviour – beheading, and the list of the various beheadings in Josephus and the New Testament in this period, as we have suggested, is worth cataloguing.

Beheading was also known to the Romans, but their preferred means of exemplary punishment for low-caste malefactors was crucifixion, at least this was so since the Spartacus Uprising in the early first century BC, in the aftermath of which the road from Rome to Naples was filled with crosses.[7] This was not the case for patrician malefactors and other *citizens*, who were usually banished or offered the choice of committing suicide, for instance, taking poison.

Starting with Aristobulus II's two sons, Antigonus and Alexander, who were beheaded by the Romans in the 40s to the 30s BC with Herodian collusion, the beheadings in Josephus, often echoed in the Gospels and Acts, are few and quite specific. Nor was Josephus, lurid as he was, likely to miss any of these. These are, in the first century CE, John the Baptist, Theudas, and, in Acts, 'James the brother of John'.[8] All have in common that the objects were accused of *political* or *subversive* crimes, and their executioners – Herod Antipas, and Agrippa I or Herod of Chalcis – at least made a pretence of following Jewish practice.

Strictly speaking, it was the Roman Governor, Fadus (44–46 CE), sent out immediately following Agrippa's sudden death, who executed Theudas, but Herod of Chalcis was King at the time. For his part, 'James the brother of John', was, as we have seen, conveniently removed in time to make way for the *real* James and beheaded in Acts by someone called 'Herod the King' – either Agrippa I or Herod of Chalcis, who died in 49 CE around the time the Roman soldier exposed himself to the Jewish crowd at Passover, causing a murderous stampede, and the Emperor's servant Stephen was beaten on a road outside Jerusalem.

Both beheadings appear to relate to the Famine in 46–48 CE, the beheading of Theudas occurring just before Josephus mentions it; the beheading of 'James the brother of John' occurring just after it in Acts. Acts' chronology here is patently absurd and is, in any event, completely defective – a case in point, Agrippa I's death (44 CE), placed following all these events at the end of chapter 12 *after* 'the Famine', referred to at the end of chapter 11. Thus Acts makes it seem as if Agrippa I died *after* 46. Another, the anachronism caused in the first place by its reference to Theudas' death in Gamaliel's speech in chapter 5:36, as coming before 'Judas the Galilean arose' (he means, of course, *before* the crucifixion of the *two sons* of Judas the Galilean, as we have seen).

The second Jewish death penalty is stoning. The examples of these are also straightforward: Honi the Circle-Drawer (Onias the Just), Stephen, and James the Just. Though there are a few other, even more lurid, punishments described in *Talmud Sanhedrin* (one, for instance, paralleling the picture of dropping a stone on someone's heart in the Apocalypse of James' depiction of James' death),[9] 'blasphemy', for which stoning was clearly the prescribed punishment, is quite specifically related to taking the Lord's Name in vain, in particular, pronouncing the forbidden Name of God.[10]

This does not seem to have specifically included being or claiming to be 'the Son of God'. In any event, there is no evidence of it in any source, that is, outside the New Testament. In Jewish literature from this period, all 'the Righteous Ones' were considered to be 'the Sons of God', as several texts, including Wisdom and the Gospels, attest. This is the position, too, of that very important Dead Sea Scroll document known as the Hymns, where symbolic or 'adoptionist Sonship' is a basic ideology. This is also true of the recently published 'Son of God' text.[11]

That this idea was an issue, either in the execution of Jesus or the execution of James, is most likely a retrospective imposition of later differences between Christians and Jews. This is because the specific doctrine of Jesus' Divinity itself had probably not even developed by this time. In any event, 'Divine Sonship', at least in its esoteric sense, was not really an issue in this period. Of course, above, we have already noted the relationship of it and the 'Son of Man' ideology to the 'Son of Adam' or 'Primal Adam' one – and, therefore, 'the Christ'.

The other idea, mentioned as being of concern in these texts, that *Jesus was the Christ*, again seems to have been an ideology with more meaning overseas in the Hellenistic world than Jewish Palestine, since the term does not seem to have any currency in this period in Palestine as far as one can tell. Even the author of the Book of Acts, as we have seen, admits that 'Christians' were first so called in Antioch in Syria – if indeed it is this 'Antioch' Acts has in mind – some time around the 50s.

There is no evidence of such a concept in the Scrolls, though there is evidence of the 'Primal Adam' ideology, as we have seen, related in some manner to it. In addition, there is the idea of a Supernatural 'Messiah' in the War Scroll, related to notions of Divine Sonship, 'the Christ', and 'the Primal' or 'Second Adam' ideology, who comes on the clouds of Heaven with the Heavenly Host to 'shed Judgement like rain on all that grows on earth'. In it, too, the Archangel Michael is in some manner associated with this process, but this is about as 'supernatural' as the Dead Sea Scrolls and probably James ever get.

Nor do either of these two concepts form part of any 'blasphemy' proceedings against James or Jesus, despite New Testament and early Church claims to the contrary, though, as we have just seen, Jerome does include it as one of the charges against James. But, aside from assuming that one or another of these ideas did upset the Jerusalem Authorities in some undocumented way, one can make sense of the 'blasphemy' charge, where James is concerned, in a way one cannot with Jesus. James' stoning certainly implies such a 'blasphemy' charge was made against him, any-how, if not against Jesus. The solution, therefore, has to do with James' 'Nazirite' Priestly activities – in particular, his wearing the High Priestly diadem with the words 'Holy to God' emblazoned on it and entering the Holy of Holies either regularly or at least once. It involves all the supplicating before God for 'forgiveness for the People', presumably as part of an atonement he did there in the manner of an 'Opposition High Priest' of some kind, so that his 'knees became as callused as a camel's'.

These activities are *actually* documented on the part of James and render the 'blasphemy' charge sensible, where he is concerned, in a way that it is not regarding Jesus. True, the Gospels do show Jesus at one point taking over the Temple and interrupting commerce there – for the Synoptics anyhow, the immediate cause, seemingly, of his arrest – as well as exhibiting other intemperate forms of behaviour there,[12] but there is nothing in the picture of Jesus, as we have it, to suggest 'blasphemy'. Insurrection and subversion yes; 'blasphemy' no – unless, of course, he too *went into the Holy of Holies*. This, according to all sources, James did. All the sources are unanimous on this point, and, astonishing or otherwise, we must consider it sensible.

It was the practice of the Jewish High Priest to go into the Holy of Holies to seek forgiveness on behalf of the people for communal sins and/or sins of omission, if not commission, once a year on *Yom Kippur*, the Jewish Festival of Atonement. The point is that it was forbidden to pronounce the sacred Hebrew Name for God represented by the four letters *YHWH*, except in this way by the High Priest on *Yom Kippur*, God's Divine Name being considered so Holy it was not to be uttered. According to tradition, only Moses and a few Patriarchs before him had been taught it and uttered it.[13] This does not mean that Jews did not know how to pronounce it; they certainly did, though now it is mispronounced by many Christian groups as 'Jehovah' – this in the wake of mistranslations and attempts to approximate it.

Jews have indeed now, also, forgotten how to pronounce this Name and, in any event, always substitute the Hebrew word 'Lord' ('*Adon*'/ '*Adonai*' – 'my Lord') in its place in prayer or reading. It was upon this that the Christian mistranslations were based, the vowels for 'Lord' being mistakenly substituted for the vowels in 'Yahweh'. This too is why in translations of the Old Testament into English formerly, one always came upon the phrase, 'the Lord', for God wherever the four sacred letters occurred. But, in ancient times, the High Priest was expected to go into the *Inner Sanctum* of the Temple (the Holy of Holies) on *Yom Kippur* – at all other times it was forbidden, except for certain cleaning or repair operations – and there pronounce the forbidden Name of God, when presumably 'on his knees' he implored Him for *forgiveness on behalf of the whole people.*

This is why the details that these early Christian sources describe regarding James most certainly do seem like a *Yom Kippur* atonement. For, if James went into the Holy of Holies once a year alone, by himself, praying 'on his knees for forgiveness of the people', so that they grew 'callused like a camel's', and if he did wear the mitre and linen of the High Priest as they attest; then this was what he was doing.

However intriguing, it is useless to ask how or why he did this or had this right. This is what our sources are telling us, even perhaps without realizing it. For this reason, James has been described by more contemporary, hostile 'Christian' reactions as 'the Pope of Ebionite fantasy'.[14] This is a matter of opinion. Surely what he is pictured as doing here is less fantastic than some of the things we are asked to believe about Jesus in the Gospels and many of the Apostles in the Book of Acts, things these same critics hardly blanch to credit.

How James as Opposition High Priest Could Have Made Such an Atonement

But, regardless of such ideas, there do exist not one, but two ways of understanding this testimony. The first is from the 'Zealot' perspective. From the beginning of this Movement – actually as far back as the days of Judas Maccabee and his father Mattathias (portrayed in 1 Maccabees 2:24–27 as exhibiting the 'zeal of Phineas', when he slew backsliders on the altar at Modein and defended his country's national traditions) – the 'Zealots' did not fail to make the claim for a High Priest of greater purity and higher Piety.[15]

This finally plays out in the butchering of all the High Priests appointed by the Romans and Herodians and the burning of their palaces – for these do seem to have been very 'Rich' – by those Josephus in the end denotes as 'Zealots' as the Uprising became more extremist from 68 CE onwards. Agrippa II's palace had already been burned, as had that of his sister and sometime consort Bernice. In turn, she doubtlessly carried complaints about these acts to her next consort, Titus, which has to be considered a factor in the decision to burn Jerusalem and destroy the Temple.

Also participating in this destruction with Titus was, as noted, the Jewish backslider, Tiberius Alexander, the son of the Alabarch of Alexandria and named, obviously, after the Roman Emperor by that name, whom Vespasian had left in command of the forces besieging the Temple under Titus. These 'Zealots' or extreme '*Sicarii*' elect as High Priest in this final extreme phase of the Uprising, as will be recalled, a Poor 'Stone-Cutter' by the name of 'Phannius' (Phineas), against whom Josephus rails as if he was no priest at all (note again the 'Rechabite' theme of being *an artisan* here).

The second concerns the Dead Sea Scrolls. These postulate a new Priesthood, referred to by the mysterious terminology, 'the Sons of Zadok'. Though the latter may have a genealogical dimension, this is nowhere stated as such. Rather it has a qualitative or eschatological one, that is, these 'Priests' are primarily described as 'keeping the Covenant'. In addition, there is definitely an esoteric play in this terminology on the idea of

'Righteousness' ('*Zedek*' in Hebrew), as we have seen, and in the only other real definition we have of these in the Dead Sea Scrolls, 'the Sons of Zadok' are definitely spoken of in terms of 'Justifying the Righteous [that is, 'making the Righteous Righteous'] and condemning the Wicked'.[16]

It is also said that the period of their rule is preordained and they are 'the Elect of Israel who will *stand at the End of Days*'. Here one should also note the play both on the idea of Resurrection, that is, 'standing', and the Ebionite/Elchasaite 'Standing One' ideology, already detailed. None of these appositives is genealogical; all, on the other hand, are qualitative and, as we previously observed, even eschatological, meaning they have to do with the 'Last Things' or 'the Last Times', things like, 'the Day of Judgement', expressly evoked as well in the Habakkuk *Pesher*. In fact in the Habakkuk *Pesher*, 'the Elect of Israel' are described in just this manner, that is, like Jesus' favourite Apostles in the New Testament, they participate in the Last Judgement or, as it is expressed there, 'God's Judgement before many Peoples'.[17] Therefore, it is fair to say, there is even a 'Supernatural' component to these definitions of 'the Sons of Zadok' at Qumran.

In the 'Three Nets of Belial' section of the Damascus Document, these new 'Zadokite' Priests are clearly opposed to the reigning Establishment or priestly hierarchy of the day, and, therefore, we have described them as an 'Opposition High Priesthood'. In the Damascus Document, 'Priests' are matter-of-factly defined as 'the Penitents of Israel who departed from the Land of Judah to dwell' or 'sojourn in the Land of Damascus', and, aside from the numerous esoteric implications of this, the play on the 'Rechabite' ideal of 'sojourning' should definitely be noted once again.[18]

There is even an individual described in the literature at Qumran, as we saw, as 'the *Mebakker*' or 'Overseer' of the wilderness camps. He would definitely appear to be paralleled by someone called 'the High Priest commanding the camps', and he acts and his duties are in all things like those of a 'Bishop' in early Christianity.[19] In fact, the term '*Mebakker*', as we have seen, approximates that of 'Bishop' in early Christian texts, as does his 'Office'.

If we put James, whose followers in Acts are definitively identified as 'Zealots for the Law', into either of these scenarios – 'the Pope of Ebionite fantasy' notwithstanding – we are not far from achieving an almost perfect match. At the very least, we have the wherewithal for understanding not only how this presentation of James as a kind of 'Opposition High Priest' arose, but also how at certain times, or at least once, in or before

62 CE, he could have been allowed into the Holy of Holies of the Temple and stayed there all day 'on his knees' – 'the *Zaddik*' of his generation, the 'Bulwark'/'Protection of the People'/'*Oblias*',[20] importuning God to forgive them, themes that are constant in all the traditions relating to him.

The Habakkuk *Pesher* delineates the argument between 'the *Zaddik*' or 'Teacher of Righteousness' – also called 'the High Priest' there and in parallel materials in the Psalm 37 *Pesher* – and 'the Man of Lying'/'Spouter of Lying', who 'rejected the Law in the midst of their whole Assembly'. It, also, delineates an additional dispute with 'the Wicked Priest', clearly the Establishment High Priest eventually responsible for the death of or destruction of 'the Righteous Teacher'. It even tells us in its somewhat obscure manner of those events leading up to the destruction of the Teacher of Righteousness and difficulties on *Yom Kippur* between this 'Priest' and the 'Teacher''s followers, known as 'the Poor'.

The signification of these events is not easily clarified, because of the obscurity of some of the language being used, but we shall attempt to unravel it in a follow-up volume of this book. At the very least, these events involving the Teacher and a number of his followers, designated as 'the Poor' or 'the *Ebionim*', do tell us about difficulties concerning confrontations between them and the Establishment High Priest – 'the Wicked Priest' ('the Priest', positive or negative, always meaning 'the High Priest' in the jargon of these documents) – on *Yom Kippur*, which seems to have been celebrated on different days, because of calendrical differences between those depicted in the Qumran texts and the Establishment.

These bitter confrontations lead to tragic consequences also treated in the Psalm 37 *Pesher*, a commentary centring around the terminology, 'the *Zaddik*', too, which the reader will now immediately recognize as James' cognomen. In the course of these confrontations, the Hebrew word 'causing to stumble' or 'casting down', used both in the Letter of James and corresponding Pauline and early Christian usage, is also employed.[21]

If, as such an 'Opposition High Priest', James did go into the Holy of Holies on *Yom Kippur*, whether on the same day as that celebrated by the Establishment High Priests or on a different day as that attested to by the calendar used at Qumran, then whatever the circumstances of this atonement, he certainly would have pronounced the Divine Name of God in the course of it. Early Church accounts and attempts retrospectively to impose later theological consenses on the materials before us notwithstanding, this certainly could, and most probably did, lead to the

Sanhedrin proceedings being described and the consonant charge of 'blasphemy' (retrospectively absorbed into Gospel accounts of 'the trial of Jesus'), for which James would have been stoned. Those unidentified people, described in Josephus as 'the most equitable of the People,' that is, the 'most Just' among them, would, no doubt, have sent representations complaining to Albinus, who was then on the road, pointing out to him his prerogatives as Governor, just as Josephus describes they did.

Josephus at this point is following his pre-Uprising behaviour: that is, he is prepared to be sympathetic towards leaders like *'Banus'* and James, particularly if they were, as suggested, the same person and under whom he actually studied. It has even been suggested, as we saw, regardless of how sensational it sounds on the surface – and I am more and more predisposed to credit it – that Josephus' father, called 'Matthew', was the 'Levite' possessed of such consummate writing skills, known by that name in the Gospels (Luke 3:24).[22]

The picture of such complaints to the Roman Governor on the part of the Jewish mob is paralleled in our Gospel accounts of the death of Jesus, but again with inverted and, as it were, hostile effect. That is to say, however preposterous it may be, the High Priest, 'the whole Jewish Sanhedrin', and the crowd never tire of pointing out to Pilate, the Roman Governor, that he is obliged to put Revolutionaries and insurrectionists (like Jesus) to death. Otherwise, as they put it (as we saw), he 'is no Friend of Caesar' (John 19:12).[23]

This is hardly the sense of the representations of those Josephus calls 'the most equitable' of the Jews, who 'were most rigorous in observation of the Law and disliked what was done' to James. These, rather, explain to Albinus that the High Priest *had not the power to convene the Sanhedrin* and *impose the death penalty without the consent of the Roman Governor*[24] – totally different advice – and, therefore, even according to Roman administrative practice, he had acted illegally. Again, another of these multitudinous contradictions between the *real* facts of this period and how they are portrayed in historical portions of the New Testament.

In fact, during this period, the *Talmud* contends that the Jewish Sanhedrin did not apply the death penalty, because for 'forty years' prior to the fall of the Temple it 'was exiled' – these are its very words – from its previous location in 'the Stone Chamber' on the Temple Mount to a new place of sitting outside it called *'Hanut'*. This language is played on in this sensitive passage of the Habakkuk *Pesher* about how the Wicked Priest pursued after the Righteous Teacher to *swallow him with his venomous anger in his House of Exile*. And at the completion of the Festival of Rest of the Day of Atonements [*thus*], he appeared to them to *swallow them*, causing them to stumble [literally, '*cast them down*'] on *the Fast Day, the Sabbath of their Rest –*

'them' being 'the Poor' or 'the Simple of Judah doing *Torah*', upon whom the Wicked Priest committed 'Violence' and whose 'sustenance he stole'.[25] In Josephus' account, paralleling this, 'certain others' – in these accounts, always the ubiquitous followers of James – were also 'accused of being Law-Breakers and delivered over to be stoned'.

Since the three successive 'his'es or 'him's in this passage are indefinite in Hebrew, we will be able to show in due course how they have been misinterpreted by a majority of commentators and how the allusion to this mysterious, 'his House of Exile' or 'Exiled House', will actually reflect these Talmudic references about 'the Exile of the Sanhedrin' in the period of the stoning of James (not to mention Jesus' crucifixion) from its normal place of sitting on the Temple Mount. Not only this, but they will also reflect the peculiar reference to the 'Sanhedrin' trial of Jesus in 'the High Priest's House' in most Gospel accounts, not to mention the play, encompassed by the various allusions to 'anger' or '*cha'as*' one encounters here, on 'the Cup' or '*Chos*' of Divine Vengeance.[26]

Unlike the picture of the complaints by the Jews to Pilate of the opposite kind in the Gospels, the complaints to Albinus over this infraction were probably true – but to little avail. After an initial show of pique and some play-acting, Albinus soon followed the ways of previous governors and *made alliances with these same High Priests*, exerting himself with them to destroy 'the *Sicarii*' and leaving the country, in Josephus' words, through his '*release of prisoners*' – another theme integral to the presentation of the crucifixion of 'Jesus' in the Gospels – in worse condition than it was before. In fact, almost in a shambles.

The Crucial Elements in Jerome's Testimony about James' Fall

As Jerome's testimony, conflating Josephus with early Church sources, continues:

> When he [James] refused to deny that Christ is the Son of God, Ananius [*thus*] ordered him to be stoned.

Jerome now proceeds to portray this stoning exclusively on the basis of early Church sources – except for the information with which he concludes from his now lost version of Josephus, that Jerusalem fell because of the 'great Holiness and reputation of James among the People'. As we saw, this reads:

> *Cast down* from the Pinnacle of the Temple [we have just encountered this 'casting down' or 'causing to stumble' language in the Habakkuk *Pesher* above – not to mention that found in the Letter of James and by refraction in the Pauline corpus as well], *his legs broken*, but still half alive, and raising his hands to Heaven, he said, 'Lord, forgive them for they know not what they do.' Then struck on the head by the club of a laundryman, such a club as laundrymen are accustomed to beat out *clothes* with, he died.

After citing the tradition connecting James' death to the fall of Jerusalem from the now no longer extant version of Josephus available to him, Jerome goes on immediately to note Paul's famous testimony in Galatians to James: 'Of the other Apostles, I saw none except James the brother of the Lord' (1:10), claiming that 'the Acts of the Apostles [too] bears witness to the matter'. But Acts *does not*. In fact, it says just the *opposite* of what Paul claims here, that 'he was with them [that is, all the Apostles] in their coming and going in Jerusalem, where he spoke out boldly in the Name of the Lord Jesus' (9:28); whereas in this material in Galatians, Paul claims he 'saw none of the other Apostles' except Peter and James (note the implication here that James is to be included *among* 'the Apostles'), and this upon his oath, he 'does not lie' and that, furthermore, he

> was unknown by face to the Assemblies which were in Christ in Judea, who only heard that he who had once persecuted [them], now preached the Gospel of the Faith he once ravaged. (1:22–23)

The thrust of this testimony should be clear.

In the rest of his biographical description of James – whom he places second only to Peter in this list of a hundred and thirty-five 'Illustrious Men' – Jerome moves on to provide the new traditions he knows about James from a document he calls 'the Gospel of the Hebrews' which, he explains, he

> recently translated into Greek and Latin and which Origen, too, often made use of.

This, he vouchsafes, not only includes a note about how Jesus gave *his* '*grave clothes* to the Servant of the High Priest', but also the description of how James was *the first to see Jesus after the Resurrection*, which we shall treat further later. Here, the point about 'clothes' or 'grave clothes' is a little further clarified.

Jerome ends this biographical note about James with the tradition we have noted above of how James was:

> buried near the Temple from which he had *been cast down* [again *kata-ballō*].

Here of course, once again, we have the repetition of the B–L–' language circle, now expressed not in the Hebrew – where it relates to the idea of 'swallowing' and 'destruction' – but in Greek, where it is *always* associated with James' being 'cast down' from the Temple. As should be becoming clear, the repetition of this linguistic usage in all traditions in Greek relating to attacks on or the death of James is the exact parallel to its use in the traditions relating to the death of the Righteous Teacher at Qumran, there expressed in terms of the analagous Hebrew usage, neither of which are particularly edifying except for the identical or corresponding linguistic root.

We shall also find this linguistic usage reappearing in the various mythological descriptions of how Jesus' Apostles, as 'fishermen', 'cast down their nets', not to mention allusions connected to the '*Diabolos*' ('*Belial*' in Hebrew) being 'cast into a furnace of the Fire' (Matt. 13:42–50). There is even a possibility, as we saw, that the usage relates to the '*Oblias*' terminology, so significant where James' role of 'protecting the People' from precisely the kind of 'Devilishness' implied by this linguistic configuration is concerned. That is to say, James was 'the anti-Swallower' or 'anti-Adversary'. While this cannot be proven, it is part of the discernible cycle of linguistic inversions and re-inversions surrounding this term.

We shall also treat the '*B–L–*'' language circle, connected in Hebrew to the destruction of the Righteous Teacher at Qumran and the Divine Vengeance pursuant upon this, in more detail below. At the same time, we shall consider the post-resurrection sighting materials, specifically recorded in this Gospel preserved by Jerome, as bearing on a *first appearance by Jesus to James* as well.

Jerome ends this testimony with the note – it will be recalled – that

> His tombstone with its inscription was well known until the siege of Titus and the end of Hadrian's reign [that is, the period of the Bar Kochba

Uprising]. Some of our writers think he was buried on the Mount of Olives, but they are mistaken.

This presumably relates to a locale in the Kedron Valley below the Pinnacle of the Temple, where the presentday tomb ascribed by pilgrims over the centuries to James' name now stands. Again, tomb traditions, familiar from the story of Jesus, seem to be impeding into the details about James or vice versa.

There are other thematic repetitions in this testimony from Jerome, which, short as it is, is packed with data. Most important of these are the 'blows to the head' we have already encountered with regard to Jesus, Stephen, and, in Acts as well, even Paul. Where James is concerned, they are tied to an allusion to 'a fuller's' or 'laundryman's club', one used to 'beat out clothes'. The theme of this 'striking' again, joined to the motif of how James 'raised his *hands* to Heaven', is not unreminiscent, as we have suggested, of the phrase, 'some struck' Jesus 'with the hand' in the Gospel of Matthew 26:67.

As we have seen, this 'prayer' attributed to James, not to mention his praying in the *Yom Kippur* scenario above for forgiveness of the People in the Holy of Holies, is also recapitulated in the New Testament in both the last words ascribed to Jesus and Stephen's last prayer, also significantly 'on his knees'. The 'clothing' theme is this time associated with the double reference to the 'laundryman's club', not to mention the reference in Jerome's 'Gospel of the Hebrews' above to Jesus' 'grave clothes'. Here it is combined with the new one of James 'breaking his legs' in the fall – in Jerome, from 'the Pinnacle of the Temple', but in the *Recognitions* of Clement from 'the top of the Temple steps'. It also recurs in the Gospels in connection with Jesus' crucifixion and how the soldiers 'broke the legs' of those on the crosses who had not yet expired.

Before explaining the significance of these notices and their importance for unravelling the whole tangle of information and traditions we have before us, it would be well to look at the theme of the 'fuller's club', to which Jerome feels constrained to refer twice, adding a quick explanatory parenthesis even in this short biographical sketch. We shall presently encounter this same allusion to the 'laundryman's club' in the Gospel of Mark in crucial scenes about Jesus' 'Transfiguration' before his core Apostles, but here the idea of this 'club' or 'clubbing' definitely relates to the Rabbinic material, we noted above, from *Talmud Sanhedrin* about how stoning procedures were carried out. In Rabbinic tradition, this material will also relate to information about *falling from the Temple wall*. One note about such a 'fall' or 'push' is preserved and relates to an individual who, though obviously condemned by the Sanhedrin to death – in this case, by stoning – but because of *whose popularity* the punishment could not be effected, the priests were to gather around, jostling him, and cause him to fall off the Temple wall.[27]

In *Mishnah Sanhedrin*, the Talmudic Tractate that deals with things like trials for 'blasphemy', as well as these sorts of punishments before the Sanhedrin – therefore its name – it is specifically stated that

> If a priest [other versions add the words: 'even a High Priest'] served in a state of uncleanness . . . the young men among the priests were to take him outside the Temple and *split open his brain with clubs*.[28]

It should be noted that in Hebrew the word being used here for 'clubs' is actually *faggots*, the precise word that will reappear in the scene in the Pseudoclementines of Paul's attack on James in the Temple, which we shall further describe below, where 'the Enemy' picks up 'a faggot' or 'stake' from those by the Temple altar. It should be appreciated that it was the custom to stack such 'faggots' near the altar for firewood.[29]

When coupled with these Talmudic notices, the implication is that James was serving in a state of uncleanness or he had no right to be there in the first place. The reference here to 'splitting open his brain' as well is exactly parallel to all our accounts of James. It should be patent that aspects from both of these traditions have been absorbed into the James story as it has come down to us in early Church tradition, or vice versa.

Again, however, the important note here is that the priest was 'serving in a state of uncleanness', which turns around the charges being made at Qumran (echoed with inverted signification even in the Pauline corpus) of 'polluting the Temple'. That charges of this kind were being hurled back and forth in the Temple between opposing groups of 'priests' and their more violent-minded partisans – Josephus calls them 'men of the boldest sort' or 'thugs' – in the period leading up to the War against Rome, particularly in the time James held sway in Jerusalem, is particularly clear from Josephus' accounts above, again tendentiously refracted in the parallel narrative of Acts.

Here, once again then, is evidence relating to a priest, accidentally on purpose either being 'thrown down' from the Temple wall or taken outside the Temple and having his brains beaten out with a club on charges having something to do with improper Temple service or serving in a state of uncleanness. This links up very strongly with the idea that James *went into the Holy of Holies* and there rendered atonement on behalf of the people on the most sacred day of the Jewish year. For those of the opposing party, no doubt, he would not even have been considered a proper priest at all; for those of his own party, if not genealogical, he was 'consecrated to God' or 'Holy to God', and therefore the High Priest by virtue of the 'Perfection of his Holiness'. The calendrical differences – mentioned above too – of the kind signalled in the Qumran literature, and known to have existed between the Establishment Priest class and their Pharisee/ Herodian supporters and these opposition groups, would only have exacerbated these differences and the feeling that, at least from the Establishment perspective, these 'blasphemy' or 'uncleanness' charges were legitimate.

I think we can safely say that this is where the idea of people beating James' brains out with a club in early Church literature comes from – not to mention the whole scene of James being put into a hole in the Second Apocalypse of James, which echoes Talmudic parameters for such alternative stoning methods in Tractate *Sanhedrin* almost precisely – this, plus the very real likelihood that this was the final *coup de grâce* after being stoned for blasphemy, as the *Talmud* attests. That James, under such circumstances in the course of a *Yom Kippur* atonement, would have pronounced the forbidden Name of God – and this in the *Inner Sanctum* of the Temple – would only have increased the determination of his opponents to destroy him in this manner.

James *Broke His Legs* in a Fall

It is now possible to turn to the new data Jerome has provided us regarding James' 'being cast down' from the 'wall' or 'Pinnacle of the Temple' and, though 'still half alive' his legs 'being broken' in the fall. That Jerome combines this point with the picture from early Church sources about the final attack on James, the precise dating of the stoning of James from Josephus, 62 CE, when Albinus came to the country to take up his position following Festus' untimely death, and the convening of a full Sanhedrin to try James, has to do with Jerome's understanding or, perhaps, misunderstanding of the sources before him.

His point about the charge, 'that Christ is the Son of God', is based on both the theological tradition from early Christian writers previously and their picture of James' proclamation in the Temple of the Son of Man coming on the clouds of Heaven. Josephus nowhere mentions this particular charge in his description of the final Sanhedrin proceedings the High Priest Ananus 'pursued' against James. But in providing us with this note about James' 'legs being broken' *in the fall* he takes *prior to his stoning*, Jerome – no doubt unwittingly – supplies us with the key datum to sort out all these traditions and overlaps.

As already remarked, this theme has been absorbed in a most macabre manner and combined with similar material in Josephus in accounts of Jesus' crucifixion and death. The Gospel of John, for instance, seemingly aware of this matter in Josephus' description of the Impiety displayed by the Idumaeans in their treatment of Ananus' corpse, shows an intense interest in whether Jesus' 'legs were broken' or 'not broken', repeating the point three times in as many lines (19:31–33). For John, unlike in the *Talmud* and Josephus below, because 'bodies might not remain on the cross on the Sabbath, for the Festival Day [that is, the Passover – this almost word for word the notice about '*Yom ha-Kippurim*' in the Habakkuk *Pesher* above] was a Sabbath', the soldiers went and broke the legs of the 'two thieves' (*Lēstai* – the same word, as we saw, Josephus employs when speaking of '*Sicarii*' or 'Zealots'), with whom he was crucified, but Jesus' legs didn't need breaking because 'he had already expired' (19:32).

Curiously enough, this follows a note about Jesus' 'clothes' again. To focus momentarily on this 'clothes' issue: first, as picturesquely described in Scripture, the Roman soldiers 'divided' these among themselves and then 'cast lots for' his cloak (not, it will be noted, *to elect* Judas *Iscariot*'s replacement as in Acts or the 'Zealot' High Priest in Josephus or, as the priests generally did on the Temple Mount, to divide up which chores would be performed by which priest on a given occasion). For the Gospel of John, however, because Jesus' cloak was 'seamless, woven from the top throughout', they could not *divide it (*19:23)!

Not only was the division of these clothes and the casting of lots for his cloak for John 19:24 – paralleled seemingly in Matthew 27:35 – supposedly the fulfilment of a prophecy from Psalm 22:18: 'they divided my garments among them and cast lots for my clothes'; for John 19:28, too, so is the point that follows about Jesus crying out concerning his thirst – this based on Psalm 22:15 as well.[30]

But Psalm 22, which also begins with the famous words Matthew and Mark proceed to attribute to Jesus on the cross at this point as well, 'My God, my God, why have you forsaken me', actually contains the key passage we have been following throughout in both the Qumran Hymns about the adoptionist or Divine Sonship of the Righteous Ones and early Church texts about James' life-long Naziritism, namely,

> You drew me *out of the womb*, You entrusted me to my mother's breasts. Cast out upon Your lap from my birth, You have been *my God from my mother's womb*. (22:9–10)

Reproduced almost verbatim in the Hymns from Qumran, these lines specifically contain the allusion to his 'mother's womb', so descriptive of the 'Holiness' ascribed to James and others of his kind, such as John the Baptist in Luke. Clearly a wellspring of scriptural proof-texts, this psalm also focuses throughout on the terminology 'the Meek', synonymous at Qumran with 'the Poor', both so important in that form of Christianity called therefore 'Ebionitism' – not to mention that of his 'soul' related to it in Qumran documents like Hymns and the Damascus Document generally (22:20).

But John also uses this point about their 'breaking Jesus' legs', or rather their 'not breaking' them, to proceed to give some extremely grue-some, though familiar, details about Jesus' death, in order that, in his view, several additional scriptural passages should 'be fulfilled'. In the first of these, to fulfil Zechariah 12:10 referring to 'being pierced', the Roman soldiers are now pictured as piercing Jesus' side in the famous passage about 'blood and water coming out' (19:34). Next, both of these occur-rences – not pictured in any of the Synoptic Gospels – are presented as fulfilling another scriptural passage, 'not a bone of him shall be broken' (19:36), combining materials from Psalm 34:20 and Exodus 12:46.

Interestingly, the first-named is another of these psalms centring around the fate of 'the *Zaddik*', so appealing to the mindset both at Qumran and in early Christianity, to whom three references are made (34:15–21). Like Psalm 22 above, it also makes repeated reference to 'the Meek', as well as his 'soul' and 'the soul of His [the Lord's] Servants' generally (34:3 and 23), language permeating the Qumran Hymns. Even more importantly, in the all-important first column of the Cairo Damascus Document, where 'the Liar''s Law-breaking is condemned, he and his confederates are described as attacking 'the soul of the *Zaddik*' and some of his colleagues. For Psalm 34, 'the Angel of the Lord encamps round about' (the 'camping' allusion evokes the all-important Qumran ideology of the wilderness 'camps') these 'Meek' and 'Righteous', saving them and delivering the Righteous One, 'not one of whose bones, therefore, was to be broken'.

It is also interesting to note that in the Talmudic passages dealing with executions, such as stoning for blasphemy and the like, the rationale given for such alterations in the execution scheme – as, for instance, pushing a man off a precipice above – was the dictum that it was preferable that the outward appearance of the accused's body should look to all intents and purposes undamaged! It is interesting to remark, as well, the Talmudic insistence that an individual be stoned *naked* – having to do with the 'clothes' issue again, an issue that then looms large in subsequent discussion about what to do in the case of the stoning of a lewd woman, whose body the stoners might find attractive![31]

But John neglects to tell us that the context of the second of these two passages about 'no bones being broken', from Exodus 12:46, has to do with the barring of foreigners and those 'who are *not circumcised*' from taking part in *the Passover meal*! Not only does this passage, then, have to do with the eating of the Passover meal, but the implication of quoting it is that Jesus is the new Passover meal – that is, Paul's 'Communion' with the body and blood of Christ Jesus again.

Here in Exodus, it is laid down that the meat thereof 'shall not be carried out of the house, nor shall a bone of it be broken', which is about verbatim the quotation from John above, although here meaning *the Paschal lamb*. But the context in Exodus is, quite specifically, that *no 'foreigner* or hired servant shall eat thereof', only 'the sojourner' or 'resident alien' on the condition that he *be circumcised* (12:45–48). Exodus continues in this vein in the following manner:

> No *uncircumcised person* may take part. This same law applies to the native of the resident alien among you . . . *All the males of his household must be circumcised*. He may then be admitted to the celebration, because he becomes, as it were, a native-born. (12:48–49)

Nothing could be further from the spirit of Christianity, as we now know it, than this – in fact, it is the very opposite of it. Why, then, does John feel free to take it out of context from a passage with the exact opposite sense of the one he is giving it? No doubt, he considered himself to be following the same allegorical approach to Scripture that Paul announces in Romans and Galatians, where Paul finally has the Children of Israel as 'children of the bondservant' Hagar and the new Christians as 'children of the freeborn' Sarah, or Moses putting a veil over his head, not to protect the Children of Israel from the splendour of his receiving the Law, but so they would not know *its brilliance had gone out* – the allegorical approach made popular with regard to Old Testament by Philo of Alexandria, the uncle of that Tiberius Alexander who with Titus, Bernice, and others was reponsible for *destroying the Temple*.

Materials of this kind were undoubtedly part of a compilation of Messianic proof-texts of some kind. One of these is still known and today called 'Pseudo-Epiphanius'. Shorter such compilations have also been found at Qumran, whose exegetes would have revelled in the above materials. No doubt, so would the teacher Josephus describes, who got in 'among the males' of Queen Helen of Adiabene's household, and that of her son Izates, and taught them that unless they were circumcised they 'could not be saved'.[32] We shall see how important this episode is when dealing with Philip's conversion of 'the eunuch of the Ethiopian Queen' in Acts below. How different is this to the behaviour in this regard of backsliding Herodian Princesses above.

The same is true for those teachers Paul so fulminates against – in Galatians 2:12 'some from James'; in Acts 15:1 'some who came down from Judea' – who, in 2 Corinthians, 'write their own recommendations' (3:1 and 10:12) and who, in particular, are *teaching circumcision* to his communities (Gal. 5:11–12). But John is not particularly interested in the true import of the materials he is employing – and, typically, reversing – which in their original context have nothing whatever to do with the point he is making, only that they can be used to propel his narrative forward and make his choice of key words or turns of phrase seem either legitimate or portentous. The same is true for the other Gospel writers.

But nothing could, in effect, be more disingenuous than the manner in which they feel free to take material out of an original scriptural context that has just the *opposite* sense of what they now intend it to have, relying on the relative ignorance of their audience and that it, satisfied by their analyses, would not normally go or be able to go to the original. This is clear, for instance too, in the manner in which John pretends he has proved the point about Jesus' legs not 'being broken' on the cross (James' legs, it will be recalled, were 'broken' in the fall he took) because he had *already died* and, in any event, *it was improper that the Paschal lamb should be so defiled*.

Josephus, too, as already implied, raises this issue when comparing how the Idumaeans treated *the corpse* of the High Priest Ananus, by throwing it naked (perhaps this very *nakedness*, retribution for the stoning of James) outside the city without burial as food for jackals. In doing so, as will be recalled, he remarked the scrupulousness with which Jews usually took care of the dead, observing how they even 'broke the legs' of those being crucified so they would not remain on the cross past nightfall.[33] In the Talmudic passages we remarked above about crucifixion and stoning from *Tractate Sanhedrin*, the same point is made, quoting Deuteronomy 21:23 cited earlier, to the effect that:

> His body shall not *remain all night upon the tree*, but you shall surely bury him the same day, for he that *is hanged is a curse of God*.

Even this, John garbles, making it seem as if the point had something to do with 'the Sabbath' (not the 'night') – probably because he has heard or knows that the Jews begin the Sabbath at nightfall – that is, that 'the bodies should not remain on the cross *on the Sabbath*' (19:31). This he then links to 'preparing for the Passover', calling it 'the Sabbath'. This in itself has sent biblical scholars throughout the centuries to calendrical sources to determine when the Passover fell on a Sabbath, so they could then determine the true date of the crucifixion of Jesus.

Though, as just observed, this does recall the material in the Habakkuk *Pesher* about the Wicked Priest's attack on 'the Poor' partisans of the Righteous Teacher, 'causing them to stumble' or 'casting them down' on 'the Sabbath of their rest', the issue of breaking the bones in crucifixion probably has little or nothing to do with any 'Sabbath' or 'Feast Day', but is probably a garbling by John of a comment made by Josephus in connection with the treatment by 'the Zealots' along with their allies, 'the Idumaeans', of James' nemesis Ananus above.

The same is true for the point about the sun growing dark for three hours 'until the ninth hour' in the Synoptics (Matt. 27:46 and pars.) – again more fantasy, but this time based probably on Josephus' note at the end of the *Jewish War* of just the *opposite*. In giving the portents for the fall of the Temple, Josephus lists: a cow 'giving birth to a lamb in the midst of the Temple' at Passover time (*thus*), 'a star, which resembled a sword, and a comet standing over the city for a whole year', 'chariots and armoured battalions running through the clouds and surrounding cities', and one of the Temple gates, which was fixed in iron and bolted firmly to the ground, opening by itself in the middle of the night.

Among other such inanities, he also includes how, yet again, at Passover:

> At *the ninth hour* of the night [the repetition of the *actual* hour in the Synpotics just about proves literary interdependence on this point or, more

accurately, literary gamesmanship], *so great a light shone around the altar and the Temple, that it appeared to be the brightness of midday.* This light continued for half an hour . . . and was interpreted by the sacred Scribes as a portent of events that immediately followed upon it [meaning, God leaving the Temple and its destruction].[34]

Strictly speaking, John is correct in one sense, since a Feast Day was treated, legally speaking, systematically with the Sabbath, even if it did not fall on the Sabbath. But, as can be readily seen, the point he is exploiting here (about 'breaking the bones' of those crucified) has nothing whatever to do with either the 'Sabbath' *per se* or any Feast Day, but simply the scrupulousness the Jews showed in their care for the dead, described in Josephus, and how meticulously they carried out the commandment of Deuteronomy 21:23 about not leaving the bodies of 'hanged ones on a tree' past nightfall. That the point about a 'hanged one being a curse of God' occupied the attention of Christian exegetes to no small degree is made clear in both the presentation of Peter's attacks on 'the Jews' before the Sanhedrin and before Cornelius' household in Acts (5:30 and 10:39 – here Peter saying, 'God is not a respecter of persons') and Paul's theological exploitation of it in Galatians (3:12–13).

What is even more striking is that it can be seen that even here, as we just saw, we have an echo of the kinds of vocabulary being used in the Habakkuk *Pesher* from Qumran in its presentation of the death of the Righteous Teacher and several of his followers, called 'the Poor'. It will be recalled that in referring to difficulties over *Yom Kippur*, the very point being made here in John about a Feast Day being a Sabbath is also found there, when the point is made about *Yom Kippur* being a 'Fast Day, the Sabbath of their rest' (Lev. 16:31) – and this in regard to such crucial materials as well. Again, the parallels are startling.

For their part, for exegetes like those at Qumran, the 'Righteous Man', his 'soul', 'the Meek', and the 'no bones being broken' of Psalm 34 would have provided endless possibilities for exegesis where the death of James was concerned, and one can imagine what a *pesher* on this subject might have looked like. In fact, a *Pesher* on Psalm 37 does exist at Qumran – another '*Zaddik*' text – which is developed in a manner very much like this.[35] In it, 'the Violent Ones of the Gentiles' – as will be recalled – take vengeance on the Wicked Priest for what he had done to the Righteous Teacher, here referred to also as 'the [High] 'Priest', that is, 'the Opposition High Priest'.

In the Habakkuk *Pesher* this vengeance on the Wicked Priest is also described as involving 'the pollutions' or how they desecrated 'the flesh of his corpse' – a not unparallel subject where retribution is concerned.[36] Materials of this kind are the subject of intense exposition at Qumran and one can well imagine a similar *Pesher* on the themes found in Psalm 34 above. This has not yet come to light, but John certainly is heir to traditions of a not dissimilar kind, which in typical fashion he reverses.

In fact, one begins to see that basically the whole body of this Qumran-style literature *has been reversed*. Where would cynical ministrations of this kind have been carried out and who would have done it? Most probably in Greco-Hellenistic circles in hostile cities, such as Caesarea and Alexandria – even perhaps in Rome – where revolutionary literature of this genre would have been well known.

It is to the account of the attack on James by 'the Enemy' (Paul) in the Pseudoclementine *Recognitions* that we now must turn in order to make final sense of all this conflicting welter of data and these conflicting yet complementary details. Even without this tell-tale note of 'his legs broken' in Jerome's account of James' fall and his subsequent beating and stoning – which, for their part, New Testament exegetes have incorporated into their accounts of Jesus' death, albeit somewhat reversed – it would have been possible to sort out the various traditions which have been conflated to form a single unified story. But this note from Jerome simply clinches the presentation.

What early Church accounts are confusing – and this comparatively early, as early as Clement and Hegesippus in the mid-second century – is that there were *two* attacks on James, one in the mid-40s, for which Acts substitutes the attack on Stephen, itself paralleling the stoning of James in the 60s. The other attack on James, which results in his death, is the one in the 60s having to do with his *Sanhedrin* trial, which ends with his stoning.

These two attacks have been conflated in early Church accounts, like Jerome's, as they have come down to us, into *one single attack* that occurred in the 60s and resulted in his death, all of which contain the elements of James being 'cast down' or the 'fall' he takes, James' stoning, and his brains being beaten out with a laundryman's club. To the fall from the Pinnacle of the Temple, which James supposedly took according to all these accounts, Jerome – meticulous to a fault – now adds the specific element of 'his legs' being 'broken', which, along with the parallel note in the Pseudoclementine account of the earlier attack by Paul on

James, has gone into New Testament accounts of the death of Jesus.

We have already noted how this 'fall' or being 'cast down' or 'cast out' is incorporated into the accounts of Stephen's stoning and Judas *Iscariot*'s suicide, where it is Judas' stomach, not his brain, that 'bursts open'. The *real fall* James takes, however, is the one down the Temple stairs in the Pseudoclementine *Recognitions* in the 40s, after the attack on him by Paul, in which it is made crystal clear, James *broke either one* or *both of his legs*.[37] Otherwise, all the elements of *both* attacks on James are present in conflated form in these early Church accounts of the death of James. What Jerome has done is, inadvertently or otherwise, incorporated the element of James' legs 'being broken', which more properly belongs to the attack on James in the Pseudoclementine *Recognitions* in the 40s, into his picture of the stoning of James in the 60s, which is more or less what the others have done without being so forthcoming about it. All the elements are there: the 'headlong fall', the beating or clubbing, the bizarre stoning, and, finally in Jerome, 'his broken legs'.

If we now turn to this Pseudoclementine account of Paul's attack on James in the Temple, resulting in his fall from 'the Temple steps', *not* 'the Temple Pinnacle' as in later syntheses and *not* in his death, we are in a position finally to unlock all these puzzles. It is this that Luke's Acts, embarrassed as ever, is at such pains to cover up, turning it into its very oppposite, namely, *an attack by the Jews against the archetypal Gentile believer Stephen* – 'the Emperor Claudius' Servant' in Josephus; 'Achaia's first fruits' in Paul. All the same, Acts uses it as the springboard to introduce the 'Enemy' Paul, who then becomes the hero of its whole narrative.

Paul's Physical Assault on James in the Temple

Fortunate, indeed, are we to have the Pseudoclementines. Though these are generally held in contempt by scholars of an orthodox mindset, they contain traces of events that are of the most inestimable value for sorting out the history of early Christianity – if indeed we can call it this – in Palestine from the 40s to the 60s CE. For instance, there are letters from Clement to James, Peter to James, and James to Peter that introduce the *Homilies*, which contain material of the most interesting kind, particularly when it comes to linking early Christianity to the Dead Sea Scrolls. No wonder Jerome fell out with Rufinus, to whose translation we owe their survival in the West.

Mainly dealing with the confrontations between Peter and Simon

Magus in Caesarea – a key locale as we have seen – and elsewhere, the two more or less complementary versions that make up the whole are thought to incorporate material from a lost work about Peter, called the *Teaching of Peter* and another called the *Acts* or *Travels of Peter*, also referred to by Jerome.[38] They probably also have material, as we have seen as well, from that work referred to by Epiphanius as the *Anabathmoi Jacobou* or the *Ascents* or *Steps of James*.

There is no point in attempting a redaction history of the two versions, which, just as the Gospels and the Book of Acts, will probably never be known anyhow to everyone's satisfaction. Peter's positions are not entirely identifiable as first century, but neither are they orthodox in the sense of 'Pauline Christian' orthodoxy. There is, as we have seen, a version of James' instructions to overseas communities more accurate than anything found in Acts and absolute confirmation that Peter *never* kept 'table fellowship' with Gentiles – not to mention that he was a Hemerobaptist, 'greeted the sun every morning in prayer', and was a *vegetarian*. There are also ideas like 'the Primal Adam' and 'the True Prophet', a notation also found in the Qumran literature and echoed in the New Testament even as we have it, which move directly into Islam probably via the Elchasaites and Manichaeans.[39] Both are also identifiable with Ebionitism.

The former, as we have seen, is not unknown to the Koran, nor does it appear to be to Paul in his letters, and it has much in common with what later emerges in the *Shi'ite* version of Islam as the idea of the '*Imam*'. This incorporates a kind of incarnationism that is found in traditions associated with John the Baptist, which, not surprisingly, has much in common with the pre-existent '*Zaddik*' ideology found in the Qumran Hymns of the Dead Sea Scrolls.

The 'Hidden' tradition associated with this, also adhered, as will be recalled, to John. In Shi'ite Islam, the doctrine of the '*Imam*' – which, just as among Ebionites, Sabaeans, and Elchasaites, had something to do with the idea of a 'Standing One' – is also expressed in terms of being 'Hidden' or as 'the Hidden *Imam*'. In the Pseudoclementine *Recognitions*, this 'Hidden' tradition, as we saw, was expressed in terms of how: 'Christ, who was from the beginning and always, was ever present with the Pious, though secretly, through all their generations' (1.52).[40]

Not uninterestingly, directly following this and now evoking the 'hiding' of doctrines, we hear of how 'some of the Disciples of John':

separated themselves from the people, and proclaimed their own master [meaning John] as *the Christ* [1:54 – this would be a point followed by the Mandaeans in Iraq to this day].

We have already encountered this reference to 'separation' or 'being separated' or 'consecrated' above. If we now substitute in this description and ones like it the notation of 'the Primal Adam', or as Paul would have it, 'the Second Man' or 'Last Adam', for the words 'the Christ', a Greek idiom first demonstrably occurring, as suggested previously, in the Letters of Paul, we will not be far from the truth of this period.

For the purposes of this book, however, clearly by far the most important materials in the Pseudoclementines are to be found at the end of the First Book of the *Recognitions*. Though much in the *Recognitions* is paralleled in the *Homilies*, which has a slightly different arrangement and contains sometimes superior material, this material significantly is not.

This First Book tells the story of Clement, from an aristocratic family in Rome – possibly identifiable with that 'Flavius Clemens', executed like Epaphroditus (and possibly Josephus), by Domitian around 95 CE – who, after hearing Barnabas teaching in Rome, follows him to Caesarea in Palestine. There he is introduced to Peter, who is just in the midst of his debates with Simon *Magus* – identified definitively as a Samaritan here.[41]

In fact, it is cast in terms of a report to 'my Lord James' (1.14). This follows the scheme of the Letters from Peter to James and from Clement to James, which preface the *Homilies*, in which it is contended that periodic letters in the form of reports were to be *written to James*. At the end of this all-important Book One of the *Recognitions*, before James, who is 'limping on one foot' (note the original detail here), sends out Peter from the Jericho region to confront Simon *Magus* in Caesarea on the Palestine coast, James instructs Peter:

> Be sure you send me in writing every year an account of your sayings and doings, and especially at the end of every seven years.[42]

For his part, Clement addresses his Letter to James prefacing the *Homilies* as:

> The Bishop of Bishops, who rules Jerusalem . . . and the Churches everywhere.

Peter's Letter to James, which precedes this in the *Homilies*, begins with a similar salutation. In fact, if one wants almost a capsulization of Qumran doctrine, one could not do better than to read James' response to Peter at the beginning of the *Homilies*.

These documents certainly date from the third century or earlier.

Origen quotes a passage from the *Recognitions* in his Commentary on Genesis – which is where Rufinus, his admirer, may have learned of them – and Eusebius, who in the matter of the Agbarus correspondence (which we shall discuss below) had access to the archives in Edessa in Syria, certainly seems to know some facts from them. What is interesting, as the reader will by now realize, is that they do not evince any doubt that James was Bishop of Jerusalem or 'Bishop of Bishops' (meaning 'the Archbishop', as Clement himself refers to him) and the undisputed head of all Christianity in his time not Peter. However reticently or overwritten, this fact also emerges in chapters 12 and 15 of Acts, and onwards. It is also interesting to note that, as Acts grows more reliable after the introduction of the 'We Document' in chapter 16, it is, like the Pseudoclementines, also expressed in the first person plural or as a *first-person travel narrative* using the pronoun 'we'.

In the *Recognitions*, Peter, who is in the midst of his own debates with Simon *Magus* in Caesarea as explained, then tells Clement the story of the debates on the Temple steps between James and the High Priests or Temple Establishment, ending in the riot led by Paul – in which Paul picked up the 'faggot' mentioned above – that resulted in James being injured and left for dead. The fact of such interesting material delivered in such precise detail is not easily gainsaid, nor does it suffer from the often miraculous signs and wonders that mar parallel New Testament accounts. The opposite in fact – in the down-to-earth, often nitty-gritty detail we are in a world not so different from the disciplinary texts for things like 'masturbation' at Qumran, at least in this First Book of the Pseudoclementine *Recognitions* (deleted for obvious reasons in the Pseudoclementine *Homilies*).[43]

As Peter tells it to Clement, and Clement supposedly recounts it to James, the High Priest sent priests to ask the leaders of the Assembly in Jerusalem, led by James, if they would enter into debates on the Temple steps with the Orthodox Priesthood. They accept and preliminary debates between the Apostles, on the one hand, and Caiaphas and the other High Priests, on the other, ensue. As in parallel material in chapter 5 of Acts, leading up to the stoning of Stephen in chapter 7, the Pharisee Gamaliel speaks in support of the early Christians (1.65–1.67 and Acts 5:34–39).

In the midst of this, James 'the Bishop ['Bishop of Bishops' in 1:68] went up to the Temple . . . with the whole Church' (1:66). Though the subject of these speeches is not particularly enlightening and, like the Book of Acts, largely retrospective, including discourses on 'the True Prophet' and the nature of 'the Christ' – both identified with each other and then with 'the Primal Adam', John the Baptist's differences with Simon *Magus* (along with Dositheus, formerly among his Disciples), and the like; some of the historical detail is compelling. In fact, in the author's view, we have a truer picture of these clashes in the Temple and what really went on in the early Church in Jerusalem than in Acts.

For instance, when 'James the Bishop' went up to the Temple, there was 'a great multitude who had been waiting *since the middle of the night*' to see him. This kind of non-fantastic detail is startling. 'Therefore, standing on an elevation so that he might be seen by all the People' – this can be nothing other than the picture of James standing on the Pinnacle of the Temple in early Church accounts – James takes his stand, as the other Apostles had done 'on the steps of the Temple'. From here, James begins his discourse, which supposedly continues for seven days – shades of the *Anabathmoi Jacobou*.

One immediately recognizes that one is in the same milieu as that reflected via Hegesippus in Eusebius, of James being placed by the 'Scribes and Pharisees' on 'the Pinnacle of the Temple', so that he could be seen by all the People, however, the physical setting at least of the Pseudo-clementines is more convincing. Just as in the mix-ups in Jerome over James' 'legs being broken', the one account is in the 40s and the others are in the 60s CE. We are also in the world of Josephus' narrative of arguments between rival groups of Priests, the Establishment and those supported by 'the Poor', once again, even ending in riot or stone-throwing, and the accounts begin to converge.

At the point when James is about to win over 'all the People', including the Priests (compare this, with the notice in Acts about a large group of 'Priests' making their conversion – 6:7), an 'Enemy' entered the Temple with a few other men and started arguing with James (1:70). A marginal note in one manuscript states that this 'Enemy' was Saul. This is confirmed in the next section, because, after getting letters, as in Acts, from the Chief Priests, the Enemy pursues the Community – which has fled to Jericho – *all the way to Damascus.*

By his loud shouts, abuse, and vilification, this 'Enemy' raised such a clamour in the Temple that the people could no longer hear what James was saying. This 'Enemy'/Saul behaved 'like one insane, exciting everyone to murder' and 'setting an example himself, seized a strong stick from the altar', at which point there 'ensued a riot of beating and beaten on either side'.

One should note the intimate and precise detail here – often a sign of authenticity. According to the *Recognitions*, 'much blood was shed', followed by 'a confused flight, in the midst of which the Enemy attacked James, and threw him *headlong from the top of the steps*'. Again one should note the detail. This, of course, is James' 'headlong' fall from the Temple Pinnacle in Jerome, *et al.*

The version we have before us, here, is from Rufinus' Latin version. There is no Greek version, which is not surprising, but there is a Syriac version – again, not surprisingly. In it, this passage reads as follows:

> A certain man, who was an Enemy, with a few others came into the Temple near the altar. He cried out, saying: 'What are you doing, O Children of Israel? Are you so easily carried away by these miserable men, who stray after a magician [this, of course, a reference to Jesus]?'[44]

Argumentation then followed, and just at the point, when he was about to

> be overcome [in debate] by James the Bishop, he began to create a great commotion, so that matters that were being correctly and calmly explained could not be either properly examined, nor understood and believed. At that point, he raised an outcry over the weakness and foolishness of the Priests, reproaching them and crying out, 'Why do you delay? Why do you not immediately seize all those who are with him?' Then he rose and was first to seize a firebrand from the altar [that is, 'the faggot' in the Talmudic accounts of the young men among the Priests seizing clubs and beating someone – even a High Priest – serving at the altar in a state of uncleanness] and began beating [people] with it. The rest of the Priests, when they saw him, then followed his example. In the panic-stricken flight that ensued, some fell over others and others were beaten.

Here, then, is the parallel to the young men of 'the bolder sort' allied to the High Priests, beating the Poorer Priests on the threshing floors that immediately precedes Josephus' introduction of the Herodian he is calling 'Saulus' and the picture in Book Twenty of the *Antiquities* of the various brawls on the Temple Mount between 'Zealots' and the High Priests. Again, this is paralleled in early Church accounts, which always include the point of James being beaten – reflected too in parallel Gospel insistences on the 'beating' of Jesus.

One should also note in these Pseudoclementine accounts the allusion to a 'flight'. In both Latin and Syriac recensions, this 'flight' continues down to Jericho. This idea of a flight is in turn picked up in 'Flight' traditions of the early Church, specifically related to the Jerusalem Church of James the Just. This later 'Flight', which is supposed to have occurred some time prior to the fall of the Temple, is known among those conversant with early Church literature as the 'Pella Flight' tradition. The one in the Pseudoclementine *Recognitions* occurs in the early 40s. It is directly paralleled by the notice in the Book of Acts of a similar 'flight' after the stoning of Stephen and the riot Paul leads after that (8:1). In Acts' rather telescoped and somewhat inverted historical chronology, this 'flight' purportedly included everyone in the Church 'except the Apostles' and leads directly to the confrontation between Peter and Simon *Magus* in 'Samaria' (8:9–25).

The reason 'the Apostles' were not included in this flight is obvious. Immediately thereafter, according to the logic of Acts' rather topsy-turvy or collapsed narrative, they are, once again, in Jerusalem as if nothing had happened. The flight in the Pseudoclementines is also on the part of the whole Community, now estimated at some 'five thousand' souls, but this is to *the Jericho area*. This number for the members of the Community is paralleled in Acts 4:4 ('and the number of the men became about five thousand'), also amid confrontations between the Apostles and the rulers of the people in the Temple and probably on the Temple stairs!

To continue in the language of the Syriac:

> Much blood poured from those that had been killed. Now the Enemy *cast James down from the top of the stairs* [both Latin and Syriac use the word 'top' here], but since he fell as if he were dead, he did not [venture] to hit him a second time.

Here, of course, is the gore of the story of Judas *Iscariot*'s 'fall', not to mention its counterpart in early Church accounts of the smashing in of James' brains. Not only does 'the top of the stairs' metamorphose as these accounts are conflated with James' stoning, into 'the Pinnacle of the Temple', but the tell-tale allusion to 'casting down' is central to both groups of sources.

The account of this bloody mêlée is then followed by the picture of the Disciples going to '*James' house*' in Jerusalem with his seemingly 'lifeless body'. Here they 'spent the night *in prayer*'. This is, of course, paralleled by the notice in Acts about Peter going to 'Mary the mother of *John Mark's house*' to leave a message for 'James and the brothers', where in Acts' picture too, 'many are gathered *and praying*' (12:12–17). Anyone with intelligence should be able to appreciate, not only that both accounts are integrally related, but the kind of purposeful obfuscation that is going on in Acts both in kind and in substance.

> The Enemy, then, in front of the Priests, promised the High Priest Caiaphas that he would kill [the Latin uses the word 'arrest' here, as does Acts] all

those believing in Jesus. He set out for Damascus to go as one carrying letters from them, so that wherever he went, those that did not believe would help him destroy those who did. He wanted to go there first, because he thought that Peter had gone there.[45]

The Latin version of Jerome's erstwhile friend and later opponent Rufinus in the fourth- to fifth-century Church, as we have seen, expressed this as follows:

> The Enemy *attacked James* and *threw him headlong from the top of the stairs*, and thinking him dead, cared not to inflict further violence on him.

Where this application of the 'Enemy' terminology to Paul is concerned, one should remark that even in the sanitized version of these events in the *Homilies*, not only is Jesus described as 'the Man', that is, 'the Adam' or 'Primal Adam' – also identified with 'the True Prophet' – but in his prefatory Letter to James, Peter, called a 'most esteemed Disciple of *the Man*', describes how:

> Some from among the Gentiles have rejected my legal preaching and rather attached themselves to the lawless and trifling preaching of the man who is my Enemy.[46]

This note here in the *Recognitions* about James either being 'taken for dead' or being 'half dead' is picked up in Jerome's later account of the attack on James in the 60s, culminating in his *stoning*. It, as we have seen, combines Josephus and other early Church sources, but also includes the all-important notice about 'his legs being broken' based on the point in the Pseudoclementine *Recognitions* that follows – Peter speaking to Zacchaeus about a month later in Caesarea – that James was 'still lame on one foot' (1.73). That is, Jerome, obviously operating off additional interesting data, has conflated all three sources into a single whole.

This brings us back to the account in the Gospel of John above about how, after giving Jesus vinegar to drink, the soldiers 'when they saw he was already dead . . . did not *break his legs*'. Rather they '*broke the legs*' of the two that were crucified with him, after 'the Jews asked Pilate that *their legs might be broken*' (19:31–34). Not only is this repetition of the 'legs being broken' theme too insistent to believe that John does not know something more, but immediately preceding this, directly after the notice of the soldiers who crucify Jesus supposedly 'dividing up his clothes' to 'fulfil' Psalm 22:18 (19:24), John also refers to a 'house'. But this 'house' turns out to be the 'house' of 'the Disciple Jesus loved', in connection with which John now evokes Jesus' mother as well and, in another total absurdity which we shall address further below, '*his mother's sister* Mary the wife of Clopas' (19:25).

As we saw, in Matthew 27:56, this woman is called 'Mary the mother of James and Joses and the mother of the sons of Zebedee'; in Mark 15:40, 'Mary the Mother of James the Less and Joses, and Salome'. As John 19:25–27 pictures the exchange at this point, Jesus in some of his last words upon the cross, seeing 'the Disciple whom he loved *standing by*' (again, our 'standing' vocabulary), says to his *mother*, '"[This is] your son"', and to the Disciple, in words almost proverbial, '"[This is] your mother", and from that hour the Disciple took her into *his own home*'. This 'house' is clearly none other than 'the house of James', just encountered in the Pseudoclementine *Recognitions* account of the flight of those carrying James to his house above – refracted too in Acts 12:12's account of *Peter's flight* and going to leave a message for 'James and the brothers' at 'the house of Mary *the mother of John Mark*'!

Not only do we have the key motif in the first two of these notices of taking someone 'to' or 'into' a 'home' in Jerusalem, connected in some manner to personages belonging to *the family of Jesus*; but the Mary involved in the last of these has a son called 'John Mark'; in the first, she is instructed by 'the Disciple Jesus loved', usually taken to be another 'John', the so-called '*brother of James*', 'the son of Zebedee' and the alleged author of the Gospel. But most telling of all, in addition to the motif about a *house* he owns in Jerusalem, this Disciple is now *adopted as Mary's own son* and by extension, therefore, James' and Jesus' brother! All of this is just too incredible to be believed. Nor, we can be sure, are all these coincidences and overlaps accidental.

The Pseudoclementine account of a house owned by James in Jerusalem is the authentic or more straightforward one. All the others, including 'the upper room' where 'Mary the mother of Jesus and his brothers' 'steadfastly continued in one accord with prayer and supplication' and to which all the Apostles – including 'Judas [the brother] of James' – retreat in Acts 1:13–14, are either variations on this or obfuscations of it.

The Flight of James' Community to Jericho

To return to the language of Rufinus' Latin version of the Pseudoclementine *Recognitions*, not only is James not dead, but *only injured* or 'half dead', his associates carry him 'after evening came and the

Priests shut up the Temple . . . to *the house of James*'. Then 'before day-light', with some five thousand others – the number of the early Community in Acts and those called 'Essenes' in Josephus – they 'went down to Jericho'. There, *three days later*, they receive word

> that the Enemy had received a commission from Caiaphas, the Chief Priest, that he should arrest all who believed in Jesus, and should go to Damascus with his letters and that there also, employing the help of the unbelievers, he should raise havoc among the Faithful [this, paralleling the language of 'the Faith in the New Covenant in the Land of Damascus' in the Damascus Document above]. (1:71)

For the Book of Acts, Paul,

> having come to bring those bound to the Chief Priests, ever increasing in power, threw the Jews who were dwelling in Damascus into confusion [by the manner in which] he proved this is the Christ. (9:21–22)

As usual then, 'the Jews plotted to kill him'.

But for the Pseudoclementine *Recognitions*, when James is 'thrown down headlong' from the 'top of the Temple stairs' by the Enemy Paul and 'left for dead', he broke only one or both his legs. This is made clear, as we have just seen, in what subsequently follows in both recensions, because after 'thirty days', when the Enemy Paul 'passed through Jericho on the way to Damascus', James sends out Peter from somewhere outside Jericho – where the Community had gone – on his first missionary journey with orders to confront Simon *Magus* in Caesarea. This notice about the entire Community being in the neighbourhood of Jericho brings to mind, not only the site where the Qumran Scrolls were found, but the references in these to 'flights' or exoduses to 'the Land of Damascus'.

Again the precision of the geographical detail in the Pseudoclementine *Recognitions* is superior to Acts. In the *Recognitions*, as opposed to early Church tradition, we only have to wrestle with whether James fell from the top of the Temple stairs or the Pinnacle of the Temple – a minor difference – whereas in Acts we have to do with disembodied spirits, tablecloths from Heaven, individuals supposed to be on their way to Gaza, but ending up in Caesarea instead, 'Ethiopian' eunuchs, 'a prophet called Agabus', and similar flights of fancy.

As we saw, in Acts' picture of parallel events, after 'Saul agreed to Stephen's death',

> A great persecution broke out that day against the Church [*Ecclēsian*]

which was in Jerusalem and all were scattered throughout the countries of Judea and Samaria, *except the Apostles*. (8:1)

First then 'Philip went down to a city in Samaria [unnamed] and proclaimed the Christ to them' (8:5). This 'proclamation of the Christ to them' is similar to the proclamation of 'the True Prophet' and 'the Primal Adam', identified with 'the Christ', in parallel passages here in the Pseudoclementines.

There, he cast out evil spirits, healed the blind and the lame, and encountered Simon *Magus*, who, 'amazed at the signs and great works of Power [our Ebionite/Elchasaite *'Power'* language again] being done', was baptized (8:13). 'And when the Apostles in Jerusalem heard that Samaria had received the word of God, they sent Peter and John to them' (8:14). There follow confrontations over 'the laying on of the hands', pictured in the Letter of Clement to James, at the beginning of the Pseudoclementine *Homilies*, as the ceremony Peter used to make Clement his successor as Bishop of Rome (19) – following this in *Homilies* 1:6, Jesus is pictured as 'receiving *Power from God* . . . to make the deaf hear, the blind see . . . and to cast out every demon'.

Here in Acts, this 'laying on of the hands' is connected with the receipt of the Pauline 'Holy Spirit', for which Simon *Magus*, who is pictured as full of 'the gall of bitterness and the chains of Unrighteousness', first wishes to offer the Apostles 'Riches' (8:19–23). Then he 'repents' and the episode closes with them 'preaching the Gospel in many villages of the Samaritans' (8:18 and 8:25). It is interesting that in Acts, before Paul, 'still breathing out threats and manslaughter against the Lord's Disciples', gets his letters from the High Priest on his way to Damascus (9:1–30), there interposes the curious episode about Philip and the Treasurer of the Ethiopian Queen Kandakes, who agrees to 'go into the water' and be baptized (8:26–39).

We shall see in the next section how this episode relates to the conversion, described in Josephus, of Queen Helen of Adiabene in Northern Mesopotamia east of Edessa on the Persian border. A favourite character in the *Talmud* too because of her 'Riches', she sends her purchase agents – possibly including Paul – to Palestine and further afield, to buy grain because of *the Famine*, in connection with which Acts' method of historical obliteration and transformation will be totally revealed.[47]

Paralleling these events, for the *Recognitions*, James, 'still lame on one foot' from the injury he received in his fall from the Temple steps before being carried from the Temple by his supporters – notice once again the incredible, but not fantastic, detail – having missed Paul when he passed through Jericho on his way 'to Damascus', as described above, received word from someone called 'Zacchaeus' in Caesarea 'that one Simon, a Samaritan magician (from the village of Gitta) was leading many of our people astray and creating factional strife'. Again, it is worth repeating the description of him in the *Recognitions*:

> He claimed to be *the Standing One*, or in other words, *the Christ* and *the Great Power* [literally the meaning given the denotation *'Elchasai'* in Epiphanius] in Heaven, which is superior to the Creator of the world, while at the same time working many miracles [the Syriac adds, 'by magic']. (1:72)

James then sends out Peter on what amounts to the first missionary journey, adjuring him, as we have seen, to 'send me in writing every year an account of your sayings and doings, and especially at the end of every seven years'. Not only does this first missionary journey by Peter seem to arise somewhere in the neighbourhood of Jericho, that is, not far from presentday Qumran, but the Pseudoclementine *Recognitions*, yet again, evinces by this commission no doubt that James is the Supreme Ruler of the early Church even above Peter.

At this point in Acts, James hasn't even put in an appearance, unless, of course, he is the other 'James' – which is probably the case. Peter then goes to Caesarea and 'Zacchaeus' house', where he is to stay. It is when Zacchaeus asks after James, that Peter tells him he was 'still limping on one foot', because when he 'was called by the Priests and Caiaphas the High Priest to the Temple, James the Archbishop, stood on the top of the steps', when 'an Enemy did everything I have already mentioned and need not repeat' (1:73).

Curiously, so deeply has the author of the Pseudoclementines imbibed the fact and so deeply is it embedded in his narrative that James broke either one or both his legs in his fall, that he does not even say it *per se*, rather only giving us the effects of this fall thirty days later, when according to Peter James is 'still limping on one foot'. It is Jerome, also the heir of Palestinian tradition, who first tells us two or more centuries later that James' 'legs were broken' in the fall, now assimilated into the narrative of James' stoning and final demise. Nothing could better show us the authenticity and intimate detail of this First Book of the *Recognitions*, deleted from the *Homilies*, than this.

Curiously too, like the episode about 'James' house' in Jerusalem and

Jesus' mother both *adopting* and, in turn, *being adopted by* the 'Beloved' Apostle John, this episode has its counterpart in the Gospels as they have come down to us. This occurs, as will be recalled, in chapters 18–19 of the Gospel of Luke, the author also credited with Acts. In this episode, not James nor even Peter, but Jesus 'drew near to Jericho' (Luke 18:35), like Paul in Acts on his way to his fateful vision – unrecorded in the *Recognitions* – 'drew near to Damascus' (Acts 9:3). But like Paul in the Pseudoclementines Jesus, 'having entered, passed through Jericho', only the itinerary is just the reverse. Jesus is not on his way to Damascus or Caesarea, but to his fateful demise in Jerusalem (Luke 19:1).

In Luke, Jesus has just spoken in favour of the Righteousness of Roman 'tax collectors' over those 'trusting themselves to be Righteous', who observe the letter of the Law but 'despise others' who don't (18:9–14). He couldn't sound more like Paul here. From the language of the episode, Zacchaeus, also, seems to be a Gentile; at least, being a 'tax collector', he is classified as a 'Sinner' (19:7 – cf. Paul in Galatians 2:15 on Gentiles as 'Sinners').48

As with the identification of James' followers at the famous Jerusalem Conference in Acts as 'Pharisees' (15:5), all legal hair-splitters in the language of Jesus' preaching in this episode in Luke are referred to under the blanket heading of 'Pharisees'. To these, Jesus, speaking on behalf of the 'Unrighteous', 'rapacious', 'fornicators', and 'tax collectors', applies the favourite scriptural aphorism, 'everyone who exalts himself shall be humbled and he that humbles himself shall be exalted' (18:11–14). He has also just praised the 'Rich' Ruler, who 'keeps' all the Commandments and 'gives to the Poor'. Of course this is more like Queen Helen of Adiabene or her son Izates than any Palestinian Herodian Ruler, and here Jesus applies one additional beloved aphorism, that about 'the Rich Man entering the Kingdom of Heaven' and the camel, 'the eye of a needle' (18:18–25).49

This serves to introduce 'Zacchaeus' who is also one of these, 'a Chief Tax Collector' and 'Rich' (19:2). As the logic of the Gospel narrative continues, 'because he was small in height [this is serious], he climbed a sycamore tree in order to see [Jesus], for he was about to pass' (19:3–4). But Jesus rather calls him down, suddenly informing him – in the manner he does Paulinizing doctrine in general – 'Today I must stay in your house' (19:5). But of course, this is nothing but the house that Peter with more justification goes to in Caesarea in the Pseudoclementine narrative, 'Zacchaeus' being the leader of the nascent Messianic Community in Caesarea (Jewish or otherwise, it is impossible to say).

This is the same kind of 'house' manipulation one gets regarding 'James' house' in the *Recognitions*, 'the house of Mary *the mother of John Mark*', where James also is to be found, in Acts, and 'the house of the Disciple Jesus loved', whom Mary – 'his mother's sister' – adopts as a son and where she is about to go to live in the Gospel of John. Could anything be clearer than what is going on here and where the authentic tradition lies?

When the Jewish mob, which perhaps here and certainly elsewhere includes the Apostles, 'murmurs, saying, "He has gone in to stay with a Sinner,"' Zacchaeus responds that he has given half of what he owns 'to the Poor' and returned anything he 'has taken by fraud . . . four times' (19:8) – this from a 'Rich' Chief Tax Collector, in Roman practice in Palestine usually the Herodian King!

Just as Peter in his visit to the Roman Centurion's house in Caesarea in Acts (we already saw the relationship of this to King Herod Agrippa I), Jesus then spouts Pauline doctrine, observing, 'Salvation has come to this house today, because he is also a Son of Abraham'.⁵⁰ We have already alluded to the relationship of this phrase, 'Son of Abraham', to the genealogical situation of Herodians generally. In due course, we shall show the special significance it held for those in Northern Syria, Edessa, and Adiabene, Abraham's reputed birthplace.

Here for some reason Zacchaeus, making this speech, is suddenly described as 'standing' (before he was 'up in a sycamore tree' or 'hurrying' home), paralleling the reference to 'the Standing One' in James' instructions outside Jericho in the *Recognitions* to Peter, before the latter goes off to confront Simon *Magus* in Caesarea. Again, the relationship between this episode and Peter going to stay in 'Zacchaeus' house' in Caesarea, transformed and packed now with Gentile Christian motifs, should be unmistakable. Only, now it should be clear, that the same kind of retrospective absorption of materials we have already demonstrated to be transpiring in Acts is also occurring in the Gospels.

Peter's Visit to Cornelius and Simon's Visit to Agrippa

Paul's Letters from the High Priest and the Way to Damascus

It would now be well to look at how Acts introduces Paul and presents his behaviour after Stephen is 'cast out' of Jerusalem and 'stoned', and 'the witnesses laid *their clothes* at the feet of a young man called Saulus' (7:58). The Book of Acts follows the same sequence of events as the Pseudoclementines up to the point in the latter when Paul 'stopped on his way, while passing through Jericho going to Damascus' (1:71) – almost word for word, though reversed, the language of the 'Zacchaeus' episode, as we saw, involving Jesus in the Gospel of Luke.

At this point the Pseudoclementines branch off, depicting James – 'still limping on one foot' – sending off Peter to confront Simon *Magus* in Caesarea on his first missionary journey. In the meantime, James' Community has gone outside Jericho to visit the graves of some fellow brethren which miraculously 'whitened of themselves every year', thereby restraining the fury of their enemies, because they 'were held in remembrance before God' (1.71). For Acts, on the other hand, Paul now was 'drawing near Damascus' – as Jesus 'drew near Jericho' in the 'Zacchaeus' episode in Luke above – when suddenly he gets a vision and 'a light from Heaven shone all about him' (which is, of course, the counterpart of the 'whitening of the tombs' above).

The rest of Paul's 'Damascus-road' vision-drama ensues. The parallel between the 'light from Heaven that shone all around him' in Acts and the tombs of the two brothers that miraculously 'whitened of themselves every year' in the Pseudoclementine *Recognitions* should not be missed, nor should the additional possible parallel provided by the 'whitewashed wall' vocabulary Acts later depicts Paul as applying to the High Priest Ananias (23:3). Nor is Paul's Damascus-road vision paralleled in Galatians, which, it will be recalled, has Paul 'going directly away *into Arabia*' – whatever Paul means by this – and 'returning again to Damascus' only after this (1:18), and doesn't agree with Acts any more than the

Pseudoclementines do in the sequence of events or their substance. For Acts, after

> Pious Men buried Stephen and made great lamentations over him . . . Saul was ravaging the Assembly [*Ecclēsia*], entering house after house and dragging men and women [out], delivered [them] up to prison [8:3 – one should always compare the 'delivering up' language in Acts and the Gospels to that used in the Dead Sea Scrolls *vis-à-vis* Israel generally or backsliders and *Torah*-breakers in particular].

Here, interpose in Acts the two chapters we have described on Peter, Philip, and Simon *Magus* in Samaria, ending with Philip baptizing the Ethiopian Queen Kandakes' 'eunuch', who had power 'over all her Treasure' (8:27 – one might ask here, was there ever an '*Ethiopian* Queen', or is this not simply the 'Sheba' stories in the Bible, and why does she send her Treasurer to Palestine?), after which 'the Spirit of the Lord took Philip away, so the eunuch never saw him again' (9:39).

Then Philip, 'passed through all the cities, evangelizing them till he came to Caesarea'.

> But Saulus [Saul], still fuming threats and murder towards the Disciples of the Lord, went to the High Priest, asking for letters from him to the synagogues at Damascus. (9:1–2)

Note the plural usage 'synagogues' here – which also carries the sense of 'gathering together' or 'assemblies' in the Greek – which would support the idea of 'Damascus' as an area of some kind rather than simply a city. For the Qumran Damascus Document, 'Damascus' was the area outside 'the Land of Judah', where the wilderness 'camps' were located, which the priestly 'Penitents' and others went out to and to which, also, the Messianic 'Star' – also called 'the Interpreter of the *Torah*' – came. It is here that 'the Faith', 'Pact', or 'Covenant', called 'the New Covenant in the Land of Damascus', was raised – the New Covenant which 'the Liar together with the Men of War' deserted.[1]

The Greek phonetics of the word, 'Damascus', will have even more implications than this. However, it is hard to conceive of a 'Damascus', like the one specified here in Acts, as having numerous such 'synagogual centres'. Be this as it may, Acts continues:

> So that if he found any there [in Damascus] *of the Way*, whether men or women, he might bring them bound to Jerusalem. (9:1)

After 'the light shone about him' and the voice cried out from Heaven to him – like Peter on the rooftop in Jaffa – Paul is greeted at 'the house of Judas' on 'Straight' street in Damascus by one Ananias (9:11). Here, Ananias 'lays hands on' Paul, just as in the Pseudoclementines' Letter of Clement to James, Peter 'lays hands on' Clement, making him his successor as 'Bishop' (that is, of Rome).

Whatever one might think of these goings on at Acts' 'Damascus', those residing there repeat the same accusation we have already heard in Galatians 1:23:

> Is this not he, who in Jerusalem destroyed those who called on his Name and who has come here for this, to bring those bound to the Chief Priests. (9:21)

It should be noted that in whichever version – Establishment Acts or anti-Establishment *Recognitions* – Paul's relationship to the Chief Priests is never gainsaid. As already remarked, Acts uses this designation, 'of the Way', as a name for early Christianity in Palestine. It repeats this in several other contexts, once, as we saw, in describing why the Roman Governor Felix was so interested in Paul's teaching (24:22). This usage, directly related to the characterization of John the Baptist's activities in the wilderness – described in the Gospels as 'making a straight Way in the wilderness', itself reiterated in two places in the Qumran Community Rule – is also found across the board in Qumran usage generally.[2]

It is also instructive to contrast this theme of Paul getting letters from the High Priest to that of James (our Opposition High Priest, or, as Qumran would put it, 'the High Priest Commanding the Camps'), giving letters to and requiring periodic written reports from those, like Peter and Clement, commissioned as emissaries. In addition, the Letter of Peter to James and James' response in the Pseudoclementine *Homilies*, it will be recalled, are particularly firm on the point of not communicating doctrines to those found unworthy, in particular, not to *Gentiles*.

James even sets down a probationary period of six years before the postulant is allowed to enter the 'water where the regeneration of the Righteous takes place' (Ps. *Hom.* 4:1 – note the baptismal theme here). As opposed to this, the Gospels are fond of presenting Jesus as saying 'nothing is hidden which shall not be made manifest, nothing secret that shall not be known and come to light' (Luke 8:17) or, as Matthew puts this, 'I will utter things Hidden from the Foundation of the world' (13:35).[3]

Of course, too, in James' response to Peter, prefixing the *Homilies* –

which has all the hallmarks of authenticity, including the tremendous awe accorded James within the early Community – circumcision is a *sine qua non* for membership and, as Paul puts it in Galatians 3:29, being 'heirs according to the Promise'. For James in this response to Peter, 'keeping the Covenant' – the definition of 'the Sons of Zadok' at Qumran – entitles one to be 'a part with the Holy Ones' ('Saints' in English, which would include the Angels), as does 'living Piously'. But, pointing up this issue of secrecy and reversing Paul's 'cursing' language again, 'the Enemy' or 'Liar' – who clearly broke this oath of secrecy – 'shall be *accursed* living and dying and punished with Everlasting Perdition'.[4] At this, 'the Elders' are pictured to be 'in an agony of terror' – as well they might.

Acts and the Pseudoclementines: Common Elements and a Common Source

The conclusions it is now possible to draw should be fairly obvious. Whenever Acts comes to issues relating to James or Jesus' brothers and family members generally, it equivocates and dissimulates, trailing off finally into disinformation, sometimes even in the form of childish fantasy. Though sometimes humorous, especially when one is aware of what the parameters of the disputes in this period really were, this is almost always with uncharitable intent.

For instance, where the election of James as successor should have occurred, we are met only with stony silence and are not introduced to the 'Historical James' until chapter 12 after the removal of the other 'James'. Instead, we are presented with an obviously skewed election involving someone called 'Joseph Barsabas Justus', later 'Judas Barsabas', to replace someone called 'Judas *Iscariot*'. In turn, 'Judas *Iscariot*' has already been represented as someone who 'delivered up' or 'betrayed' the Messiah and both parts of his name relate, as we have seen, not only to members of Jesus' family itself, but to a revolutionary Movement founded by a third 'Judas', this time called 'the Galilean'. As it turns out, the latter, too, has at least two martyred children or grandchildren with names similar to those in Jesus' family in the Gospels.

When James *is* finally introduced in Acts, it is only after a whole series of events like the stoning of Stephen, Peter's encounter with Simon *Magus* in Samaria, Paul's vision on the road to Damascus, Peter's 'tablecloth' vision preceding his visit to the home of the 'Pious and God-Fearing' Roman Centurion Cornelius ('doing much charity – *Zedakah* in Hebrew –

and supplicating God continually'), 'Herod the King's' well-timed beheading of the other 'James', and Peter's arrest, seemingly by this same 'Herod'. After miraculously escaping from prison, Peter then goes to the house of 'Mary the mother of John Mark' to leave a message for the *real* James. Then he flees the country, never to be heard from really again – except to make a pro-forma and rather improbable appearance at the so-called 'Jerusalem Council' in chapter 15. With no explanation of why the death sentence on him has suddenly evaporated, there he is pictured as making a short speech supporting Paul and the Gentile Mission.[5]

Actually the circumstances surrounding Peter's arrest and miraculous escape are interesting, particularly as they contrast so markedly with Paul, who – four chapters later – declines to make such an escape. Instead, Paul ends up baptizing and saving his gaoler's soul and, for good measure, is even *invited to his house*, where he *shares his table*. (Acts 16:34). Where Peter is concerned, the emphasis on 'table fellowship' is paramount. The message is obvious. Paul, good Roman Citizen that he is, is careful of his gaoler's well-being, declining to escape even when he has the chance – this is in accord with his expressed philosophy in Romans 13 – whereas Peter, by escaping, ends up causing the death of not one, but *two* guards (no matter that Peter unlike Paul presumably had no Roman Citizenship).

When Acts does finally introduce James, it is, as we have repeatedly made plain, as if we were supposed to know who he was or had already met him. There is, as we saw, no introduction of him, no explanation of who he might be, no attempt to distinguish him from the other James, 'James the brother of John'. In fact, if it weren't for other early Church sources and Josephus we wouldn't even know he was Jesus' brother and Leader of the early Church in Palestine.

But, of course, in the manuscript available to the final redactor(s) of Acts, James *had* already *been introduced*, as we have explained, and, furthermore, the traces of this *are still present*. In the preface to his Gospel, addressed to someone only identified as 'Theophilus' ('God Lover'), Luke admits that he was compiling his data on the basis of other accounts and previous works (Acts 1:1–3). Rather, the author(s) of Acts – Luke or whoever – are at great pains to erase this fact, but they are unable to do so absolutely, because by chapter 12 James *must* come into the text, since he must be involved in the 'Jerusalem Council' that follows three chapters later, because the directives emanating from it are ascribed to his name and were presumably known.

In addition, it is James, by Paul's own testimony in Galatians 2:12, who has sent the messengers – the names of whom for the moment are immaterial – down to the Church in 'Antioch' (Acts 15:1). Acts has many names for these representatives, referring to this episode, as it were, in freeze frame, since it is so important – always coming back to it as one of the only really certain bits of information it can rely on until the 'We Document' intrudes into the text in the next chapter. And James must be present, too, for the climactic final confrontation with Paul five chapters later in chapter 21.

It is the position of this book that the authors of Acts and the authors of the Pseudoclementines are, in fact, working off the same source. Both are Hellenistic romances, but where points of contact can indisputedly be shown between the two narratives – as, for instance, in the First Book of the *Recognitions* – the Pseudoclementines are *more faithful* to their original source. Not only is there less fantasy, there is less obfuscation and out and out fabrication. This is particularly the case in the matter of the key attack on James in the *Recognitions*, where the 'Enemy' (Paul) is introduced, and we can see it paralleled in Acts by the attack on Stephen, introducing 'Saulus' (later known as Paul). But it is also true of the picture of Peter's conduct and teachings – the direct opposite of Acts.[6]

This is not the normal scholarly view, which holds the Pseudo-clementines as late. But on this point, scholars – many governed (as in the field of the Dead Sea Scrolls) by subconscious preconceptions or orientations they themselves may often be unaware of – are simply mistaken. There is no other response one can make. It is patent that the Pseudoclementines are superior, at least as narrative – and no doubt ideology and history as well – except where the 'We Document' begins to make its presence felt in the second part of Acts. Perhaps this was why Jerome was so angry at his erstwhile colleague Rufinus who published the Pseudoclementines in the West at the end of the fourth century, probably based on a Syriac original. It is also possibly the reason why no Greek version of the *Recognitions* has survived – the manuscript went directly from the Syriac into the Latin.

Granted, speeches in the Pseudoclementines cannot, perhaps, be relied on any more than those in Acts (there are exceptions), but neither can they in Josephus, to say nothing of the Gospels. It was the custom in Greco-Roman historical narrative from Thucydides onwards for the narrator to supply important speeches according to what he thought the speaker would or should have said. The same is true for Hebrew literature of the time – and earlier. Therefore, we refer to the vast body of this literature in whatever language as 'pseudepigraphic'. This approach has been raised to an art form in the Gospels, to the extent that little or nothing in them can be relied on as authentic representations of what Jesus did or might have said. The early chapters of the Book of Acts, too – though none the less creative – are on the whole even less convincing.

But where historical sequencing and actual physical actions go, the First Book of the Pseudoclementine *Recognitions* is very reliable indeed, as is the Book of Acts from chapter 16 onwards, where the 'We Document' first makes its appearance, thus giving Acts too the character of a travel narrative written by someone who actually accompanied its principal character, Paul, on his journeys. This is similar to the *modus operandi* of the Pseudoclementines, though, unlike these, Acts inexplicably shifts back and forth between first person plural and third person even in these later chapters.

In chapter 15, for instance, after the so-called 'Jerusalem Conference' and just prior to the eruption of the 'We Document', Acts asserts that 'the Apostles and Elders [Presbyters] with the whole Assembly [*Ecclēsia* again] decided to choose representatives to send down to Antioch with Paul and Barnabas' to deliver a letter containing James' directives to overseas communities. 'Judas surnamed Barsabas and Silas' were chosen (15:22) – here our amazing 'Barsabas' again, previously encountered in the 'election' to succeed Judas *Iscariot* as 'Joseph Barsabas surnamed Justus'.

Just to confuse things further, *Recognitions* 1:60, as we saw, says Barnabas was also 'called Matthias', the name of the victorious candidate in this election to fill Judas' 'Office' above. Complementary as ever, Acts 4:36, introducing 'Barnabas', calls him – like the Joseph Barsabas Justus above – 'Joses' and identifies him as 'a Levite of Cypriot origins'. But 'Joses' is also the name of Jesus' *fourth* brother in Scripture.

In 15:32 these representatives of James are called 'prophets' (like the 'Agabus' and the others who came down from Jerusalem earlier and supposedly predicted the Famine in 11:27), and immediately after the delivery of this letter (effect undescribed), Paul and Barnabas part company – where Acts is concerned, seemingly for good – because they have 'a violent quarrel' supposedly about John Mark, 'the man who *separated from* [them] in Pamphylia' (15:38–39)! To be sure, that these mysterious representatives, insisting on 'circumcision', were sent down from Jerusalem by James is covered quite emotionally by Paul in his attack on James and Peter as 'hypocrites' in Galatians 2:11–21, as is the real nature of the quarrel that broke out between Paul and Barnabas.

Interestingly enough, this first person plural voice makes itself felt in

Acts' narrative just at the point Paul crosses over with his *new companions* – the curious 'Silas' above and a new individual called 'Timothy', probably identical with 'Titus' in Galatians 2:1–3 above – into Europe or mainland Greece proper, where Paul presumably encounters 'Stephanos', his first convert in Achaia (1 Cor. 16:15). Paul has this Timothy, 'whose mother was a believing Jewess, but whose father was a Greek' – just the Herodian mix – circumcised, expressly for the purpose of these travels and, again, of course, 'because of *the Jews* who were in these places' (16:1–4)!

This is most revealing testimony and is paralleled by Paul's protestations in the same second chapter of Galatians above about 'those who come in to spy on the freedom we enjoy in Christ Jesus, so that they can reduce us to slavery', that is, 'slavery' to the Law, and how Titus, who was with him, 'being a Greek, was – according to him – not obliged to be circumcised' (Gal. 2:3–4).

Here, one should take note of additional overlaps and mix-ups, not only between Titus and Timothy, but also Silas and Silvanus, who are, as we have already remarked – despite attempts to portray them otherwise – probably the same person.7 The point is that they are Greeks or, in Silas' case, Hellenized Palestinians or Herodians, and join Paul after the row in Antioch as the only people now willing to travel with him, 'after the rest of the Jews', including Barnabas, 'jointly dissembled following' Peter in his 'hypocrisy' (Gal. 2:13). Paul is clearly talking, here, about Jews *within* the Movement, not outside it.

The Source of the Blunder about Abraham's Tomb in Stephen's Speech

After an interlude of two–three chapters, this 'We' material in Acts intrudes more insistently and more reliably in chapters 19–20, describing how Paul 'makes up his mind to go [back] to Jerusalem' for his last visit (19:21) and final confrontation with James the Just, who is ruling the Church there, in chapter 21. This ends with the description of how Paul is mobbed in the Temple at Pentecost. Actually, even material in the first half of Acts, despite thematic repetitions, can, where historical sequentiality goes if not tendentious ideology, be credited to some extent.

But where in Book One of the *Recognitions*, Clement, the first or second Gentile 'Pope', meets Barnabas in Rome and then Peter in Caesarea, there is no reason to doubt it – once again, the gist of doctrinal conversations aside. (In Book One of the *Homilies*, Clement meets Barnabas in Alexandria, where his ship was supposedly blown off course, and everything about James, except for the letters at the beginning and the notices about his leadership and instructions thereafter, has been deleted.

In the *Recognitions*, Peter tells Clement the story of the recent riot on the Temple Mount led by Paul, in which James was injured but not killed. When the narrative goes into such intimate detail about this attack by Paul on James, which is more extensively pictured and more pointedly focused than any other similar materials, it is especially convincing. This is particularly true when compared with the garbled nature of the narrative of the parallel attack on 'Stephen' in Acts, by which it appears to have been overwritten, which hardly makes any sense at all.

Briefly, to review Acts' sequencing here, once again: in Acts this stoning of Stephen in chapters 6–7 transpires against a backdrop 'of the Hellenists murmuring against the Hebrews' (6:1). The Apostles, most notably Peter and John, had been going to the Temple every day 'to pray' (Acts 3:1 – James 'his brother', whichever 'brother' intended, is notable for his absence). In these chapters, as in the Pseudoclementines, the 'Central Two' – the deletion of James saying everything – now discuss doctrinal matters with the crowds and argue with the Chief Priests. Even the words used to punctuate the action here, 'the Lord added those who were being saved to the Assembly daily' (Acts 2:47), are for all intents and purposes reproduced in the Pseudoclementine *Recognitions* narrative as follows:

> The Church of the Lord, which was constituted in Jerusalem, *was most plentifully multiplied* and *grew*, being governed with the most Righteous ordinances by James . . . (1:43)

As Acts would have it, the High Priests want to stop them from 'teaching in the Name Jesus' in the Temple (4:18 and 5:28). This parallels the debates in the Temple and the incident where the High Priests request James to speak to the crowds concerning the subject of Jesus in the early Church accounts we have presented and the *Recognitions*.

As already observed, after the riot led by Paul in the Temple, the *Recognitions* puts the number of James' followers, who flee to the unspecified locale outside of Jericho, at some 'five thousand' (1.71). Acts, too, clearly working off the same source, puts this:

> Many of those who had heard the word believed and the number of the men became *about five thousand*. (4:4)

Speeches by Paul's purported Rabbinic teacher, Gamaliel, now follow immediately in both accounts. In Acts 5:38, Gamaliel is someone who urges a more deliberate policy in dealing with 'these men', while in *Recognitions* 1.65, he is a secret supporter. Again, both narratives can be said to be using the same sequencing and, on the face of it, the same source, to which the *Recognitions* is not only more faithful, but also, seemingly, a more accurate and less tendentious presentation of it.

A case in point: Acts' version of Gamaliel's speech which, as already remarked, seems to be following Josephus, anachronistically places Judas the Galilean's 'Uprising in the days of the Census' *after* the beheading of Theudas (5:36–37). As we saw, the simple inclusion of the additional point about the crucifixion of *Judas the Galilean*'s two sons, which immediately follows *the beheading of Theudas* in Josephus' *Antiquities*, easily rectifies this defect.

Josephus' picture of the hostile arguments between the Syro-Hellenistic population and Jews in Caesarea in the 40s can also help put the arguments between 'Hellenists and Hebrews' that follow Gamaliel's speech in Acts into a more realistic historical setting. The *Recognitions* rather dispenses with these alleged arguments between 'Hellenists and Hebrews' over food distribution in the early Church entirely, moving directly into Paul's physical assault on James.

The Lukan author of Acts, however, now has 'Stephen' as part of the 'Hebrew' party, though this group is composed of people with entirely Greek names – 'Philip, Prochorus, Nicanor, Timon, Parmenas [notice the names from Plato's Dialogues] and Nicolaus, a convert from Antioch' (6:5). Herod's associate, 'Nicolaus of Damascus', who was intimately involved on Herod's behalf in politics in Rome and from whom Josephus lifted a good deal of data, would have been honoured.[8]

For their part the Pseudoclementines – both the *Homilies* and the *Recognitions* – probably more accurately (and certainly with less creative imagination), now list a plethora of people with both Hebrew- and Greek-sounding names as the members of 'Zacchaeus'' Community, which Peter enters in Caesarea. These include both Clement and Nicodemus (Ps. *Rec.* 2.1). As already signalled, the 'Stephen' in Acts, missing entirely from the Pseudoclementine narrative, has much in common with Paul's archetypal *Gentile* convert in Greece, whom Paul in 1 Corinthians calls his 'first fruit' in Achaia (mainland Greece).

Again, the reader should appreciate that 'Stephen' also is the name of the individual Josephus calls 'Caesar's Servant', who is on a mission of some kind *from Greece* (Corinth perhaps?). The time is around 50 CE, under the Roman Governor Cumanus, and 'the Innovators' or partisans, as we saw, beat this 'Stephen' up outside the walls of Jerusalem right after the stampede in the Temple, when the Roman soldier lifted his skirt and exposed his presumably uncircumcised privy parts to the Jewish crowd assembled in the Temple at Passover. In the aftermath of this episode, the reader will remember, the Roman soldiers tear up books of the Law outside Lydda and disturbances break out between Galileans and Samaritans in Samaria, incidents reflected, geographically speaking anyhow, in the curious confrontations and curings Philip and Peter make in these areas in Acts 8 and 9.

These two Stephens may have been the same individual in any case and, in this regard, one should remember that both Paul's and Josephus' 'Saulus' later on has contacts with people high up on the Imperial Staff or in 'the Emperor's household' in Corinth ('Achaia'), where Nero anyhow seems to have retreated. But in Acts, Luke has his 'Stephen', who for some reason appears to be presented as one of 'the Hebrews', arguing with a whole assortment of patently Hellenized groups in Jerusalem, called 'the Libertines, Cyrenians [Libyans – as, for instance, Luke probably himself], Alexandrians [the Egypt of Philo and his opponents], and those from Cilicia and Asia' (6:9), none of which makes any sense at all.

As Acts' picture continues, Stephen then is arrested on charges of 'blasphemy', literally 'because he *blasphemes this Holy Place and the Law*'. To be sure, the picture of such 'blasphemy' charges is very important where James' death is concerned, but, even more to the point regarding Stephen, they echo almost verbatim the charges against Paul, when, a decade or so later, around the time of the Temple Wall Affair – and with far more discernible cause – Paul is mobbed on the Temple Mount. As Acts, it will be recalled, expresses this:

> This is the man who teaches everyone everywhere, against the people and *the Law and this place*, and further he has brought Greeks [*Hellenas*] into the Temple and *defiled this Holy Place*. (21:28)

This is almost word for word the charge against Stephen, and just as Stephen in the earlier episode in Acts, Paul too is presented as giving a long speech at this point to the angry Jewish mob.

In the Stephen trial for 'blasphemy', the 'false witnesses' further contend that 'we have heard him saying that Jesus the Nazoraean would destroy this place and change the customs given to us by Moses' (6:14). But, of course, what we have here is nothing but the reverse and a -

reflection of James' arrest and trial for blasphemy two decades later, which, unlike the episode before us, really *did* happen and for exactly *opposite* reasons. Of course, here too, only Stephen is arrested, not Peter, nor John, not even James – still the *éminence grise* unmentioned in the narrative.

As the narrative continues, Stephen, with the 'face of an Angel', then goes on to give his long speech – some fifty-five lines – and, as Paul's later in Acts, purportedly in response to the High Priest and the *whole Jewish Sanhedrin* (6:12–15), though why a presumable *Greek* should be brought before a Jewish Sanhedrin is never explained, nor, clearly, does the author of Acts feel the need to explain it. Rather, Stephen tells them their entire history – on the face of it, a Gentile to Jews, patently absurd – typically ending with the most crucial of Gentile Christian accusations, already pre-saged in Paul (1 Thess. 2:15) and, needless to say, completely untrue:

> Which one of the Prophets did your fathers not persecute? And they killed the ones who announced the coming of the Just One, whose betrayers [the accusation against Judas *Iscariot*] and murderers you have now become. (Acts 7:52)

The reference to 'the Just One' is not only evocative of James' cognomen, but exactly parallels the point found in the Letter of James about killing 'the Just One' (Jas. 5:6). There, it will be recalled, not only did it precede the allusion to 'the coming of the Lord' and 'the Judge *standing* before the gate' (Jas. 5:8–5:9), but it was directed against 'the Rich', not against the Jews! In Acts too, it will be recalled, as in these accounts about James, the picture of Stephen, 'full of the Holy Spirit', is followed by his seeing the 'Glory of God' and 'the Heavens opening and the Son of Man *standing* at the right hand of God' (Acts 7:55–56).

But a glaring error in the speech Stephen makes as reproduced here by Luke actually allows one *to pinpoint the source of this speech*, as a result of which the entire episode unravels and its improvisation made plain. It is, as noted above, *Joshua's farewell speech* to the assembled tribes in Joshua 24:1–24, not unremarkably, at *Shechem in Samaria*. The play on the name 'Jesus' ('Yeshua' equalling 'Joshua') represented by this, too, would have pleased the Lukan author of Acts. The error occurs in line 7:14, when Stephen comes to telling how Joseph brought back the bodies of

> our ancestors . . . to Shechem and buried them in the tomb that Abraham had bought and paid for from the sons of Hamor the father of Shechem.

Unfortunately, as anyone versed in the Hebrew Bible would know, the ancestors were buried in a tomb called *Machpelah in Hebron which Abraham bought from Ephron the Hittite of the sons of Heth opposite Mamre* (Gen. 23)!⁹ It is Joseph, who is buried in the tomb mentioned by Stephen and it is *Jacob who buys it from Hamor the father of Schechem* (Gen. 34). This mistake, made in a speech supposedly delivered by a Gentile or archetypical Gentile convert to the whole Jewish Sanhedrin, would have given rise to the most incredible derision, as anyone familiar with the mindset of such an audience might attest.

Even if one granted that Stephen (whoever he was) never made such a foolish error, but only the authors of the Book of Acts did because of careless transcription; this will not do, because, first of all, the speech is lifted almost bodily from Joshua's speech. But, second of all, at the end of Joshua's speech, in fact, at the end of the Book of Joshua, after Joshua cautions against foreign gods, 'making a Covenant with the People . . . and wrote these things in the Book of the Law of God', the text concludes:

> *The bones of Joseph*, which the sons of Israel had brought from Egypt, *were buried at Shechem* in the portion of ground that *Jacob had bought for a hundred pieces of silver from the sons of Hamor the father of Shechem* (Josh. 24:32),

and we have almost word for word the source of Stephen's startling blunder, showing that this was where the author went to retrieve it, not to mention, its being practically the source of his whole speech in Acts! It becomes abundantly clear that someone was transcribing this information from Joshua either too quickly or too superficially – even perhaps from memory, though this is doubtful.¹⁰

Since we can now just about dismiss the whole Stephen episode, which one would have done on ideological and historical grounds anyhow – starting with the anachronism introducing it, regarding Theudas and Judas the Galilean drawn from a too superficial reproduction of Josephus' works – one can more or less present the background to this episode and, to a certain extent, material that will throw further light on the true circumstances surrounding the death of James. Once again, we are in the world of Josephus' *Antiquities*, where Theudas and his kind – people like James and Simon the two sons of Judas the Galilean, 'who drew away the people to revolt when Cyrenius came to take a census in Judea' – are mentioned.¹¹

Parallel Sequencing in Acts and Josephus: the Conflation Unravels

In Josephus too, as in Acts and the Pseudoclementines, it is always the sequence of the events – not necessarily the precise substance – that is important. Josephus moves from the 'impostor' or 'Magician' Theudas (Acts 5:36) to Tiberius Alexander (Acts 4:6), his crucifixion of James and Simon 'the two sons of Judas the Galilean' (Acts 5:37), to the riot after the Roman soldier exposed himself on the wing of the Temple at Passover, to the beating and robbing of 'Stephanos, Caesar's retainer', just outside Jerusalem by seditious 'Innovators' or 'Revolutionaries' (Acts 6–7).

This is followed, as we saw, by the problems between the Samaritans and Jews because of confrontations with 'the Galileans', who were travelling through their country (paralleled in Acts 8:1–25 by the confrontations of Philip and Peter with Simon *Magus* in 'Samaria'), and the crucifixion of the Jewish Messianic pretender 'Doetus' or 'Dortus' – 'Dorcas' in Acts (probably 'Dositheus' in the Pseudoclementines and other heresiologies) – and four of his colleagues at Lydda (paralleled in Acts 9:31–42). It is at this point that the High Priest Ananias and his Temple Captain, Ananus ben Ananus, are sent to Rome in bonds to give an account to Claudius of what they had done, and there make the acquaintance of Agrippa II.

An additional, but shorter, set of sequencing, with much in common with this one – in some respects overlapping it – goes from the stoning of James ('Stephen' in Acts), to the plundering of the tithes of the Poor Priests by the Richer ones (the theme of squabbling over the improper food distribution to the 'widows' in the background to the 'Stephen' episode in Acts 6:1–3),[12] to the riot led by Saulus, 'a kinsman of Agrippa', who with a bunch of bully-boys 'used Violence with the people', 'plundering those weaker than themselves', so that the 'city [Jerusalem] became greatly disordered and all things grew worse and worse among us'.[13] The riot led by Saulus in Acts (and the Pseudoclementines) is about as graphic.

These, not to mention three other matters overlapping material in Acts – the first is the visit by Simon the Head of 'an Assembly [*Ecclēsia*] in Jerusalem' to Caesarea to inspect the household of Agrippa I in the early 40s – to 'see what was being done there contrary to Law' – inverted in Acts' presentation of Peter visiting the Roman Centurion Cornelius' household in Caesarea (preceded by his vision of the Heavenly tablecloth giving him the Divine dispensation to do this).

Secondly, the problems between the Jewish and Greco-Syrian inhabitants of Caesarea. The latter, though inferior to the former in wealth, in Josephus' words, end up plundering them. This is paralleled, again in the background to the Stephen affair in Acts, by the squabbling between 'Hebrews and Hellenists' (6:1–15) – to say nothing of how, later in Acts, this same 'High Priest Ananias' goes down with 'the whole Sanhedrin' to Caesarea supposedly to complain about Paul (but apparently about no other 'Christians') for *introducing foreigners into the Temple* (Acts 24:1–25:12).

Finally, there is Acts 11:27–30's note of how one Agabus, 'a prophet', 'rose up' and 'via the Spirit' predicted the Famine, in relation to which Paul and Barnabas, commissioned by the Community in Antioch, visit Jerusalem to bring Famine-relief funds. This visit is not paralleled by Paul in Galatians. Rather he specifically denies any such visit there – this on the strength of an oath 'before God' that he 'does not lie' (Gal. 1:17–2:1). But it *is* paralleled by the note in Josephus about Queen Helen of Adiabene's grain-buying operations, in which she 'spent vast sums of money *in Egypt*', distributing it in Judea. This last is sandwiched in between Josephus' two notices about Theudas' beheading and the crucifixion of the two sons of Judas the Galilean, James and Simon, by Tiberius Alexander, who in Acts 4:6 actually does appear (somewhat anachronistically) as the enemy of *John* and *Peter*.

It is this grain-buying mission to Egypt on the part of Helen's Treasury agents, as we shall see, that will serve as the underpinning for Philip's encounter with the Treasurer of 'the Ethiopian Queen' Kandakes 'on the way . . . *to Gaza*' in Acts (8:26–38).[14] We have already alluded to the conversion of this Helen, Queen of Adiabene – East of Edessa, though perhaps connected to its domains – in connection with Paul and the mysterious 'Ananias' he meets, according to Acts, at Damascus (Acts 9:12–20). We shall have more to say about this Ananias and Helen in due course, when it comes to discussing the so-called 'prophet called Agabus', who, as Acts would have it, supposedly predicts the 'Great Famine' (11:28).

In Syriac sources, reliable or otherwise, Helen is always associated – as she is in Eusebius drawing on these – in some manner with the King of Edessa or the Osrhoeans ('Assyrians') called 'Abgarus' or 'Agbarus' – even contemporary commentators acknowledge the difficulty translating these names. Indeed, the legend concerning his conversion is very old and widely disseminated. Even Eusebius, referring to this king as 'the Great King of the Peoples [*Ethnōn*] beyond the Euphrates', reproduces it and there is a lively apocryphal tradition surrounding it.[15] All of this, not to mention 'the Egyptian' (very likely 'Simon *Magus*'), for whom Paul is mistaken in Acts 21:38 – also mentioned in Josephus.

It is curious that whereas Josephus, as we saw, appears to misplace the riot led by Saulus in the 40s, placing it after the stoning of James in the 60s; for its part Acts misplaces the stoning of James, replacing it with the stoning of Stephen in the 40s, following which, it too places – probably correctly – a riot led by Saulus. But Acts also uses the 'stoning' motif from the 60s to replace that of the physical assault on James by Paul in the 40s in the Pseudoclementines, transposing the latter with the former. There is very little one can do by way of explaining all these parallel inconsistencies, except remark them.

It is also clear from the *Antiquities*' sequencing of the assassination of Ananus' brother, the High Priest Jonathan, by 'Robbers' or '*Sicarii*' around 55 CE, leading to the Temple Wall Affair and the 'conspiracy' on the part of the High Priest Ananus and Agrippa II to remove James in 62 CE; that James is seen as being at the centre of these disturbances, at least in the eyes of an Establishment High Priest like Ananus and the Herodian King, Agrippa II – the King with whom Paul is portrayed as conversing *quite congenially* in Acts. If the relationship of Saulus – 'a kinsman of Agrippa' – with Paul can be confirmed, it is legitimate to ask, as we did earlier, just what Paul's repeated conversations during two years of protective custody in Caesarea with Agrippa II's brother-in-law, the Roman Governor Felix and with Festus and Agrippa II himself, were really about (Acts 24:24–26:32)?

If one places the *first* attack on James in the 40s, in which Paul leading a riot of angry priests in the Temple seems to have thrown James down the Temple steps and only injured him and, according to both the Pseudoclementines and Jerome, one or both his legs were broken, but he did not die; and the stoning of James, described in Josephus and in all early Church sources, in the 60s – then it is clear that there was not one but *two* attacks on James.

The first, in the 40s, was roughly as the *Recognitions* describes it. It was actually perpetrated by 'the Enemy' Paul. It is this Acts 9:1 tantalizingly refers to as Paul's 'threats and murders against the Disciples of the Lord' and, in 22:4, even quotes Paul as admitting, 'I persecuted this Way *unto death*'. But this attack did not result in James' death, only his 'headlong fall' from 'the top of the the Temple steps' (not 'the Temple Pinnacle' as in chronologically later early Church conflations).

The second attack is as described in Josephus and it, too, is refracted with additional fabulous accretions in the early Church accounts delineated above. This attack correctly came in the early 60s and really did involve a trial by a Pharisee/Sadducee Sanhedrin for 'blasphemy'. Unlike, however, Acts' descriptions of Stephen and Gospel representations of what took place at Jesus' trial, where James is concerned, a *full* Sanhedrin trial *really did take place* and really did involve 'blasphemy'. Both of these attacks have been compressed in all early Church accounts into a single whole and the single account of James' death in these in the early 60s. This process began with Hegesippus and Clement of Alexandria in the second century, ending with Jerome at the beginning of the fifth. The final result contains the elements from *both* attacks: *falling headlong down*, *being clubbed*, *praying on his knees*, and *being stoned*.

For its part Acts doesn't directly mention either attack, telling us only about the attack on Stephen (also conflated), while the *Recognitions* tells us only about *the attack on James in the 40s* which Acts replaces with the stoning of Stephen. Neither bothers to tell us about the stoning of James in the 60s – which is where an undoctored Acts probably should have ended. If one keeps one's eyes on the two elements of the fall from the Temple stairs and the stoning, one can sort these out. The keys to the conflation are the words, 'throwing' or 'casting down' (*kataballō* in Greek) and the 'headlong fall' James takes, at least in the first attack – in the New Testament, 'Judas *Iscariot*' and 'Stephen' along with him.

In the final early Church accounts, whether at Nag Hammadi or in the early Church fathers – even reflected in later Manichaean texts – these are also conflated with Rabbinic notices either about pushing someone down from a wall accidentally on purpose or making someone who is supposed to be stoned for infractions like 'blasphemy' accidentally fall into a hole, or actually having his head split open by 'Zealot' Priests in the Temple.

This language of 'casting down', expressing this in Greek in all these accounts of the attack on or death of James in early Church sources, not to mention that of Stephen in Acts, is but another reflection of the mysterious language circle at Qumran having to do in its Hebrew variation with *B–L–'*, 'swallowing' or 'consuming', and the associated nomenclature of 'Devilishness' connected to it in either language – which, in turn, is always applied in Qumran texts to *the destruction of the Righteous Teacher by a Wicked Establishment*.[16]

Parallels with the Gospels: James and Jesus on the Pinnacle –
Neither Ever Happened

To sum up: in the tradition known to the Pseudoclementines, but suppressed in Acts (though echoed three centuries later in Jerome's allusion to James' 'broken legs'), the attack by Paul on James in the 40s ends up with James only injuring one or both of his *legs*. It does not kill him. (Detail of this kind is quite astonishing.) Both attacks, the one ending in the fall from the Temple stairs and the other, stoning – with the curious addition (probably from Talmudic sources) about James' head being beaten in by a fuller's club, not to mention the note about his being 'cast down' – are conflated in early Church accounts into a single whole involving *both* a 'headlong fall' or 'being cast down' and a stoning resulting in James' death in the 60s.[17]

This last is also possibly reflected in notices in the Dead Sea Scrolls – depending on chronological problems in these – about the attack on or death of 'the Righteous One' or 'Righteous Teacher'. In fact, both attacks on James, the first by 'the Liar' Paul and the second by 'the Wicked Priest' Ananus, are reflected in the Scrolls, if the dating problems regarding these can be resolved to everyone's satisfaction – an unlikely prospect.

They are, however, very definitely reflected in other New Testament stories, like the ones about Judas *Iscariot* and Stephen above, but also even Jesus himself. In the Gospels, Jesus like John the Baptist is also 'led out into the wilderness by the Spirit, where he is tempted by the Devil' and, as we saw, in another one of those typical reversals based on motifs in the James story, to 'cast himself [*bale*] down from the Pinnacle of the Temple' (Matt. 4:1 and pars.). The key to the textual dependency here, of course, comes in the tell-tale use of the expression, 'the Pinnacle of the Temple', not to mention the allusion to 'casting down' accompanying it, which is verbatim the language of all the presentations of James' fall.

Even the note in these 'Temptation' stories about being 'in the wilderness' relates to the Damascus Document's presentation of the true 'Sons of Zadok' and 'the Priests', defined as 'Penitents', who go out 'from the Land of Judah to sojourn in the Land of Damascus'. Completing the circle of these allusions, this, in turn, again relates to the portrayal of John the Baptist in the Gospels as being out 'in the wilderness', language also applied in the Community Rule at Qumran to the activities of the Community it is describing – both of these being characterized as

'Temptation by the Devil' in this disparaging parody in the Synoptic Gospels.[18]

Actually, as one might have suspected from the beginning, there was no 'fall from the Pinnacle of the Temple' by James in the 60s, only the Sanhedrin trial for 'blasphemy' and the stoning – correctly recorded in Josephus. That this, too, in turn relates to the proclamation James made and the other activities he was involved in in the Temple, is confirmed in a rather bizarre manner in the Gospels themselves, where, as we saw, materials more appropriately relating to James are retrospectively absorbed into stories about Jesus.

In Matthew 9:2–8, Luke 5:17–26, and Mark 2:1–12, Jesus, who is portrayed as curing a man with palsy, 'forgives his sins'. In all of these, the locations in Galilee differ somewhat. In Matthew, Jesus has just crossed the Sea of Galilee in a boat 'to his own city'. In Mark and Luke he is in Capernaum. In all, however, the Scribes and/or Pharisees then cry out, 'blasphemy', and insist only God 'has the power to forgive sins'. Carefully considered, what is actually concretized in this exchange is the point in all the early Church accounts about James, that he *really did* go into the Holy of Holies on *Yom Kippur* to *ask forgiveness for the sins of the whole people* and *make atonement for them.*

Even in this obscure episode about Jesus' 'blasphemy' and his 'forgiving sins' in the Synoptics, the tell-tale allusions to 'the Son of Man', 'the Power' and 'glorying', present in all the above accounts of James' proclamation in the Temple, are incorporated, however tendentiously, into the context of Jesus curing this paralytic. Here Jesus is now made to say '*the Son of Man* has *Power* on earth to *forgive sins*', upon which the crowd then '*glorifies God*' – thus linking all these accounts together.

This is followed in all Synoptics by an episode where Jesus purposefully eats with 'Sinners' (in Gospel code, 'Gentiles') and 'tax collectors' (Herodians) – as opposed, for instance, to the barring of such classes from the Temple in the Temple Scroll alluding to the catchword '*balla*'' or '*Bela*''. Jesus even goes so far as to call one of his Apostles in Mark, 'Levi the son of Alphaeus' – this is supposed to be 'Matthew' – out of '*the tax office*' (Mark 2:14 and pars.)![19] The Scribes and Pharisees, echoing precisely the 'Zacchaeus' episode we just examined in Luke above, now 'murmur at his Disciples, saying, "Why do you *eat and drink with tax collectors and Sinners?*"' (Luke 5:30 and pars.). Jesus is then made to answer, rather pointedly, the now proverbial, '*I did not come to call the Righteous to repentance, but Sinners.*'

Aside from the clear attack on the way John the Baptist is portrayed in Josephus as well as in the Gospels, the whole reference to 'the Righteous' here, as with the parable relating to 'ninety-nine Righteous Ones in the wilderness' some ten chapters further along (also in the context of 'the tax collectors and Sinners' coming to hear him and the Scribes and Pharisees complaining about Jesus 'eating with them' – Luke 15:1–7 and Matt. 18:12–14), bears on the theme of James 'the Righteous One' and the 'Righteousness' in general of wilderness Communities like his and, for instance, Qumran.

To show that in all this symbolic and polemical repartee, we are still in the world of James' 'Righteous' *Yom Kippur* atonement, this is immediately followed in all Synoptic Gospels with an aspersion again, not surprisingly, on of all people, 'the Disciples of John', that is, John the Baptist. To compound this particular circle of *non sequiturs*, it is these *very classes* of 'Scribes and Pharisees' – just presented as 'murmuring against' Jesus and his Disciples 'eating and drinking with tax collectors and Sinners' – that John *fulminates against* and rejects, characterizing them as '*offspring of vipers*' (Matt. 3:7)!

Not only is this 'eating and drinking' theme basic, as we have seen, to differences between Paul and James, but here in the follow-up to these reverse 'blasphemy' and 'eating and drinking' charges in the Synoptics, 'John's Disciples', linked with 'the Pharisees', supposedly now complain:

> Why do we and the Pharisees *fast often*, but your Disciples *do not fast at all*? (Matt. 9:14 and pars.)

Luke 5:33 actually changes the 'fasting' here to 'eating and drinking', showing that in his mind all these matters are the same.

But, of course, as everyone knows, Jews 'fast' on *Yom Kippur*, and the direct evocation of the theme of 'fasting', immediately following the portrait of Jesus being accused of 'blasphemy' following his forgiving men their sins in the matter of *the curing of a paralytic*, ties this whole set of episodes and allusions to James' *Yom Kippur atonement in the Temple*. In addition, it is conveniently linked to an attack on 'the Disciples of John' – who, like those of the Qumran mindset and 'Nazirite' daily-bathers generally, obviously followed the Law in the most extreme manner conceivable – whom it compares to *the Pharisees*!

This linking of John's followers with 'the Pharisees' bears on the linking of James' representatives with 'the Pharisees' in Acts 15:5 (even though it was Paul who specifically claimed to be 'a Pharisee' in Phil. 3:5). These

'Pharisees', it will be recalled, complained at the 'Jerusalem Conference' over the issue of 'circumcision', and, according to the view of modern scholarship, represent the 'Judaization' of early Christianity at this point, a Judaization that never occurred. The opposite, of course, is the more likely scenario, that is, a progressively more all-encompassing Gentilization!

But this portraiture is patently tendentious and what we really have here in this language in these Gospel episodes is *symbolic skirmishing* between opposing polemical groups – 'Pharisee', at this point anyhow (if not elsewhere), representing a catchphrase for those following the Jamesian orientation on things like *circumcision, table fellowship* (that is, 'eating and drinking' or keeping dietary regulations), and the like.

Beelzebul, Belial, and *Satan Casting out Demons*

This same set of themes now recurs in another very significant episode that follows in Mark – some time later in Matthew and Luke – in regard to 'blasphemy', 'forgiveness for sins', allusion to 'the Son of Man', and Jesus' healing, this time of 'a blind and dumb man', as well as a demonic who is *leading him around*. Again 'the Pharisees' object, this time to the all-important formulation, 'casting out demons' (*ekballō*), supposedly being done with the help of '*Beelzebul*, Prince of Demons' – also now identified with 'Satan' (Mark 3:22–30, Matt. 12:22–37, and Luke 11:14–28).

This new terminology, 'Beelzebul', is obviously just another corruption of or variation on the 'Belial' one, but the lengthy speech that ensues, which is Jesus' response to the Pharisees and basically gibberish, turns on the confusion of the two terms, 'Beelzebul', that is, 'Belial', and 'Satan'. This, we have already encountered in Revelation above and identified as a peculiar characteristic of the literature of this period. But, not surprisingly, in relation to this too, the formulation 'casting out' (*ekballō*) is repeated approximately six times in just this one speech – a usage, it will be recalled, we have already encountered in Acts' picture of Stephen 'being *cast out* of the city and stoned' and which Josephus uses to describe what Essenes do to backsliders![20] For Matthew, not surprisingly, this episode ends with another evocation of the phrase 'offspring of vipers', this time attributed to Jesus *not John* (12:34).

For his part, Mark places this episode immediately following Jesus' appointment of the 'Twelve who would be with him', to whom he gives the authority on earth '*to cast out demons*' (*ekballein*). For Mark these include, 'Peter and James the son of Zebedee and John *the brother of James* . . . and James the son of Alphaeus and Thaddaeus and Simon the Canaanite and Judas *Iscariot*, who also betrayed him' (literally, 'delivered him up' – 3:16–19).

By contrast, in Luke 5:1–11, unlike the 'Beelzebul' and 'Satan casting out demons' material, this appointment episode is preceded – and in fact, it should be realized, paralleled – by Jesus' calling of Simon Peter and 'James and John the sons of Zebedee', Simon's fishing 'partners', all now presented as *fishermen on the Sea of Galilee*. Another long discussion then ensues, this time rather about their 'nets', which, of course, is simply another play on and adumbration of the 'Three Nets of Belial' theme. Whereas in the Markan scenario, it is Beelzebul 'casting out demons'; in Luke, Jesus' principal Apostles are pictured as 'washing' and 'letting down' their 'nets' (5:2–4). But later this will actually involve these being 'cast out' as well.²¹

In Mark, not only does this episode about Jesus appointing his Apostles follow an allusion to the crowds trying 'to touch' Jesus (3:10), paralleling Jerome, above, about the people in Jerusalem trying to touch James because of his superabundant 'Holiness'; but these episodes about Jesus 'blaspheming', John the Baptist 'fasting', and Beelzebul 'casting out demons', are followed, as in Matthew, with Jesus again evoking the twin issues of 'forgiving sins' and 'blaspheming' – this time directed to *'the Sons of Men'*. This is expressed in terms of 'whatsoever blasphemies they blasphemed' being forgiven, 'except the one who blasphemes against the Holy Spirit, who shall not be forgiven' (Mark 3:28–29 and Matt. 12:31–32) – while fascinating, in this context essentially meaningless except as polemics.

In both, this leads directly into a key attack by Jesus on *his mother and his brothers* (Mark 3:31–35 and Matt. 12:46–50). In Luke this attack does not come until 8:19–21, right before Jesus goes out on the boat, once again, with his Disciples to 'command' the wind and the raging sea, but *immediately after* the 'Jewish Christian' Parable of the Tares (in Matthew this comes in chapter 13). Not insignificantly, in the light of this tell-tale context, the mother and brothers of Jesus are described in all the Synoptics as 'standing outside' (again, the pivotal allusion to the Jewish Christian 'standing' ideology should be remarked), but unable to get into him 'because of the crowd'.

Jesus then responds, in a remark that has become proverbial, 'Who is my mother and who are my brothers?' Looking at his new Apostles sitting around him in a circle, he then pointedly adds, 'Behold, my mother and

my brothers.' All three Gospels now have him attach to this pronouncement a reference to that 'doing', so much connected to the name of James
and, as it turns out, the Teacher at Qumran – for Matthew and Mark,
'*doing the will* of my Father'; for Luke, '*doing the word* of God'.

A related episode in John now presents this 'blasphemy' as involving
Jesus making the twin claims of being 'the Christ' and 'the Son of God'
(also here in Mark 3:11 and as in the Synoptic trial scenes before the
Sanhedrin at the 'High Priest's house' above), for which 'the Jews' in this
picture now actually '*take up stones in order that they should stone him*'
(John 10:24–36). These are, of course, the two themes – together with the
third, the 'Son of Man' related to them – which we have already encountered with regard to the two attacks on James in the Pseudoclementines
and early Church sources above.

This conflation of the stoning of James for 'blasphemy' in the 60s, as
recorded in Josephus, with the account of the attack by Paul and James'
resultant 'headlong fall' from the Temple stairs in the 40s, gives some idea
of the lateness of these Gospel scenarios, late enough for these kinds of
conflations to have occurred and then been retrospectively absorbed,
albeit in something of a negative reversal, into the story of Jesus.
Conversely, this also means that the traditions about these attacks on
James and the transformations they underwent are fairly old and were, in
fact, widely disseminated very early, as early as these first Gospel portraits
incorporating aspects of them into the story of the life of their 'Jesus'.

These notices about Jesus' 'blasphemy' in the Gospels, not to mention
the charge against Stephen in Acts of 'speaking blasphemy' against Moses,
God, the Law, and the Temple, provide the best proof, however tendentious, that James was tried for 'blasphemy' as a result of the atonement he
made in the Holy of Holies on *Yom Kippur* on behalf of the whole people.
Once again, they show, however indirectly, the *modus operandi* of the
Gospel artificers. If one collates them, one finds that the signficant ones
are almost always connected to the motif of the 'Son of Man having
Power' to 'forgive sins on earth'. This, as already noted, was not blasphemous in itself – only the pronouncing of the Divine Name of God in
conjunction with an atonement of this kind. This is exactly what James
would have done in the Holy of Holies if these early Church reports have
any substance.

Outside Palestine, the significance of this, together with James' proclamation of 'the Son of Man coming on the clouds of Heaven with Power',
would easily have become garbled and confused with something relating

to his being able to, or in this instance the Messiah being able to, 'forgive men's sins' or 'forgive sins on earth', which in Palestine, of course, no one ever claimed, imagined, or thought to be an issue. What was thought in Palestine was that the atonement performed by the High Priest in the Temple on *Yom Kippur*, whether the Establishment one or the Opposition, was for *forgiveness of sins*. The association of words, like 'the Son of Man', 'Power', or 'glorified' with many of these passages in the Gospels, just further increases the points of contact with the proclamation James is also reported to have made in the Temple according to all accounts.

The motif of being 'in the wilderness', found in the Temptation of Jesus by *Satan* or *Belial*, also just tightens the connections with the similar allusions at Qumran about 'making a Way in the wilderness' or 'going out from the Land of Judah and dwelling in the Land of Damascus'. This last is connected to the definition of 'the Sons of Zadok' at Qumran or flights to the wilderness camps, again assimilated into all traditions about John the Baptist as well. The idea of a 'fall' or 'casting oneself down' in these materials, in any event, fits more logically and, it should be noted, more realistically into the story of James' lectures on the Temple stairs, reflected in another, no longer extant work reported by Epiphanius, the *Ascents of James*.

But the themes of James 'falling' or 'being cast down' from the 'top' of something – in the first instance, only injuring himself; in the second, being murdered – clings to James in all the traditions. There is, doubtlessly, an element of truth in it. It is also more credible than any parallel stories like those of Jesus' 'Temptation by the *Devil*' or Stephen's improbable execution. In the 60s, anyhow, if not the 40s, there was only a stoning not a fall. This stoning probably took place outside the city, as all sources and Acts' narrative about 'Stephen' suggest. Here James was buried on the spot, as both Eusebius' source and Jerome attest. Curiously enough, the story of James' Tomb together with its marker leaves off with the testimony of Jerome in the fourth–fifth centuries.

Three–four centuries later, the thread reappears, at least according to tradition, in the stories about bringing the bones or sarcophagus of someone also identified as 'James' – allegedly the *other* James – to a village outside Santiago de Compostela in Northern Spain, the pilgrimage to which continues to the present day.[22] Again, this is not long after the testimonies about the existence of James' burial marker leave off in Palestine. Since there probably really was no 'James the brother of John' and we know such a burial marker regarding James really *did exist*, wouldn't it be ironic, if, after all these years, what was being revered in this peculiar survival in Northern Spain were, in fact, the bones of 'James the brother of Jesus' not his fictional counterpart – not only ironic, but extremely fitting.

The idea of a fall from 'the Pinnacle of the Temple', reflected too in Jesus' Temptation by 'the Devil' or 'Satan', probably relates also to feats said to have been accomplished by Simon *Magus* who, once again, like Paul certainly went to Rome – probably with or following Felix and Drusilla, as Paul did. This idea of a fall, as already suggested – whether on the part of James or, by refraction, his alter ego Jesus – may have also developed via the over-active imagination of early pilgrims, who, as Jerome – nay even Hegesippus – suggest, were already visiting the place associated with his interment, popularly called 'the Tomb of St James' ever since, which from its location in the Kedron Valley looks directly up at 'the Pinnacle of the Temple' some hundred metres above. As we have suggested, the idea could have developed that James died from either being pushed or falling that distance.

The note in these traditions about a laundryman beating in James' brains with a club, however colourful, no doubt comes from all the various beatings we have reviewed above, in particular, Paul taking a faggot from the wood piled at the altar and calling on others to do the same, swinging it around wildly to begin the riot that ends in James being beaten, his fall, and his broken leg(s)! Vivid and realistic detail such as this is not to be dismissed lightly.

Nor is the vivid detail about a flight of the whole Community to the Jericho area thereafter, from where Peter is sent out by James on his first missionary journey to encounter Simon *Magus* in Caesarea. Nor that of James still 'limping' from his fall thirty days later. All these matters have been purposefully refashioned and systematically overwritten in the traditions that have gone into the Book of Acts in the manner we have seen – thus revealing the *modus operandi* behind these overwrites in a most patent manner.

The Talmudic material about the young priests taking a fellow priest outside the Temple and beating out his brains with clubs, if he served in a state of uncleanness – note how in the Pseudoclementine tradition, the 'Enemy', Paul calls to the *young priests* to help him – of course, relates to these traditions as well. So does the equally colourful one in the Second Apocalypse of James about James being forced to dig a pit and a heavy stone being placed upon his stomach, which comes directly from the *Mishnah Sanhedrin*'s descriptions of such stoning procedures.

What is even more interesting about this one in Nag Hammadi lore is that it also includes all the additional motifs of 'casting down', 'being thrown down from a great height', 'taking away the *Zaddik*', and James now 'standing' down in the hole! But in addition in this, the Pinnacle of the Temple is replaced by 'the great Cornerstone', thus linking it to traditions about Peter generally and allusions in the Qumran Scrolls to the Community Council being the Cornerstone, not to mention those in Scripture about Jesus being 'the Stone which the builders rejected'.

Peter's Visit to the Roman Centurion Cornelius in Caesarea

Finally, as we have seen, the encounter of Peter with the Roman Centurion Cornelius, 'the Righteous and Pious *God-Fearer*', as a result of which Peter learns he should not discriminate against Gentiles (as Paul, very definitely, pictures him as doing in Galatians 2:14), is simply an inversion of another episode in Josephus at the end of Book Nineteen of the *Antiquities*, leading into the all-important Book Twenty. Here, to recapitulate, 'a certain' Simon, the head of 'an Assembly' (*Ecclēsia*) of his own in Jerusalem, wishes to exclude Agrippa II's father, Agrippa I, *from the Temple as a foreigner*. As a result, Agrippa I invites this Simon *to visit his household in Caesarea* – the mirror reversal of Cornelius' invitation to Peter in Acts – to see what was done there 'contrary to Law'. The episode in Josephus ends somewhat indecisively with Agrippa merely dismissing the bothersome Simon with a gift and sending him on his way.

But it is this episode, correctly understood, that provides the key to unlocking what the real issue was between Simon *Magus* and Simon Peter in the confrontations that are made so much of by all traditions. This can be arrived at by a simple process of induction, abetted, as ever, by the *true*, consistently aggressive and always unbending traditions at Qumran. Whereas the demythologized and undoubtedly real 'Simon Peter' has an extremely aggressive and thoroughly uncompromising attitude towards the sexual misconduct of the Herodian family – most notably, the niece marriage, divorce, and marrying foreigners we have covered previously – just as the demythologized John the Baptist had preceding him (according to Josephus, only perhaps some seven or eight years before), the Simon in the New Testament learns to accept such foreigners, even as followers of 'Jesus' or the 'Saviour'.

Though Josephus' note about the visit of this 'Zealot' Simon to Caesarea is delivered only in an aside, it is most interesting. In it, Josephus portrays King Agrippa, whom he obviously felt some affection for, very sympathetically, claiming that:

> He was scrupulous in *keeping the Laws of his country*, neglecting no rite of purification, and doing all the appointed sacrifices daily.[23]

Agrippa, therefore, though parallel, is the very *opposite* of 'Cornelius' above. But, in contrasting him with his grandfather Herod the Great, whom he characterizes as 'malevolent, relentless in punishment, and showing no mercy on those he hated' and in fact 'more friendly to the Greeks than to the Jews', Josephus actually calls Agrippa '*chrēstos*', which means in Greek, gentle-tempered, generous, Righteous, or kindly.[24]

This is similar to the word Suetonius uses, in his *Lives of the Caesars*, to designate the Christian '*Christ*'. For Suetonius, the Jews were expelled from Rome in the time of Claudius – the time we have before us here, Agrippa being a friend of Claudius:

> Since the Jews constantly made disturbances at the instigation of *Chrestus*, he expelled them from Rome.

It is worth remarking that at this point – no date is given, but let us assume the mid-40s – the Romans did not distinguish at all for administrative purposes between Jews and so-called 'Christians', considering them all equally troublesome.

But Josephus, in distinguishing Agrippa I from his grandfather, the cruel Herod, describes him as:

> beneficent towards Gentiles [*Ethnē*] . . . mild-tempered and equally generous to all men. He was benevolent to foreigners, exhibiting his philanthropy to them too, but he was also gentle and even more compassionate to his own countrymen.

It is here Josephus employs the adjective in Greek, '*chrēstos*', to describe Agrippa I's character. One could remark, that these are precisely the parameters of the portrait of 'Christ' in the New Testament, who very much embodies such virtues (except where Jews are concerned).

This picture of Agrippa accords with Rabbinic portraiture as well. This is not surprising in view of the Pharisaic roots of Talmudic literature and Josephus' own Pharisaic preferences. The same is allegedly true of Paul. What all these quasi-Pharisees have in common, whatever their attitude towards Jewish Law, is that – as explained above – they were all prepared to live with Roman rule, and accommodate to it and, by extension, their appointeees in Palestine, such as the Herodians. '*Sicarii*', '*Zealots*', and other 'Messianists' evidently were not.

For instance, the *Mishnah* delineates an extremely revealing episode where Agrippa – whom 'the Sages praised' (probably Agrippa I) – was reading the Law in the Temple on *Succot* (Tabernacles), the obligation of the King on that Festival. (As we shall see, it is very likely that James was stoned on *Succot*, 62 CE, which, if true, would be extremely understandable if James were objecting to such kings being in the Temple and reading the Law at all.) When Agrippa came to the Deuteronomic King Law, 'You shall not put a foreigner over you, who is not your brother' (Deut. 17:15 – reiterated, not insignificantly, too in the Temple Scroll from Qumran), he begins to cry.²⁵ The Rabbis, who are gathered around him there, then cry out *three times*,

> 'You are our brother, you are our brother, you are our brother!'

In repetitions of this kind, one should always be mindful of how *Peter* in the Gospels denies the Messiah *three times* on the eve of his crucifixion, most notably in response to the question of 'the maids of the High Priest' (*thus*): 'Are you a Galilean?' – not to mention the peculiarity of their calling Jesus this and 'Nazoraean' (Matt. 26:69–75 and pars.). In the Book of Acts, the Heavenly Voice has to call out to Peter, again *three times*, before he realizes he should 'not make distinctions' between foreigners or call 'any man profane'.

Such points of contact aside, this episode in the *Talmud* is obviously the Pharisaic response to the episode in Josephus about that Simon 'with a very accurate knowledge of the Law', who convenes the above Assembly in order to exclude Agrippa I from the Temple as a foreigner – *following* the Deuteronomic King Law – 'since it belongs only to native Jews'.

The problem, here, is the problem in this period in microcosm and the issue behind a good deal of the unrest and dissatisfaction we have been witnessing, not only in relation to Herodians and Romans and their sacrifices and gifts in the Temple, but also between the Pharisaic/ Sadducean Establishment and their opponents, such as the 'Zealots', so-called 'Christians' – possibly identical to 'Galileans' and other 'Nazoraeans' – and other 'Messianist' groups like the Community reflected in the Qumran literature. Most people today – and this includes Jews – are simply unable to understand this, because they do not appreciate how 'the Herodians' were perceived at that time.

It is a popular impression that Herod was a *Jewish* King. This is simply untrue. This mistake has been encouraged as much by New Testament caricature, as it has by titles like 'the King of the Jews', superficially employed in that literature, the significance of which has been lost on most people. To be in Roman parlance, for instance, 'King of the Jews' at this time, one did not necessarily have to be Jewish!

For their part, Jews too have both encouraged and misunderstood this picture, partly out of ignorance and partly because their Rabbis under the Herodians – who determined the course of Judaism after the fall of the Temple – and writers like Josephus, for their own political reasons, went to great pains to legitimitize these same Herodians. This is the obsequious thrust of the above episode about Agrippa I, too, and sycophantish, unctuous behaviour of this kind generally in this period.

The opposite side of this coin is the rough treatment accorded this same Agrippa I – who supposedly so loved Judaism and Jewish causes – by the Simon above who convened an Assembly in Jerusalem to have him barred from the Temple as a foreigner, despite the fact his grandfather Herod built it – not to mention how Agrippa I was seen by a host of other Jewish Revolutionaries, 'Innovators', and 'Zealots', most of whom come to a bad end.

This attempt is followed up some twenty years later by the actual barring of his son, Agrippa II – so sympathetically portrayed in Acts – not only from the Temple, but all Jerusalem as well. His palace, too (which seems at one time to have sheltered, if not Paul, then certainly Josephus' 'Saulus'), along with those of other principal Herodians, was, as we saw, ultimately burned in the early days of the Uprising. These complaints on the part of Simon against Agrippa I are given short shrift by Josephus, one of the masters of obsequiousness in this period – he, Paul, and Rabbi Yohanan ben Zacchai can vie with each other on terms of relative equality where this 'crown' is concerned – and all three *survived*, or at least their legacy has.

But Herod, the progenitor of this family along with his father, the Idumaean Antipater, as we have shown, is not a Jew. He was a foreigner. As explained, his father seems to have been of Greco-Idumaean background – what today in this region would simply be called 'Arab' and, if Acts is any measure, probably was then as well (or 'Ethiopian') – and, as Josephus' testimony above reveals, he was hated by the people, because:

> He [Herod] was evil by nature, cruel in punishment, and merciless to those
> he hated, and everyone admitted that he was *more friendly to Greeks than
> to Jews*. For instance, he adorned foreign cities of foreigners with large gifts
> of money, building baths and theatres, erecting temples in some and
> porticoes in others, whereas there was not a single city of the Jews on which
> he deigned to bestow even minor restoration or any gift worth mentioning.

Aside from thumbing his nose at the Sanhedrin, executing Jewish
'Bandit' Leaders – the most notable being Hezekiah the father of that
Judas the Galilean so often mentioned above – and imposing his rule in
Palestine with Roman help, taking Jerusalem by storm in 37 BC by using
the troops provided him by Mark Anthony; Josephus also identifies him
as really the first 'Innovator'. In a very important section of the
Antiquities missing from the *War*, Josephus describes how Herod introduced into the practice of the people 'innovations that tended to the dis-
solution of their religion and the disuse of their own customs'.

In this section, too, Herod is portrayed as regarding 'Pollio the Pharisee
and Sameas and the greater part of their associates' with the highest
approbation.[26] In the very next lines, Josephus says almost the very same
things about Herod's attitude towards 'Essenes' (about whom, Josephus
says, 'he had a higher opinion than was consistent with their mortal
nature'), which provides a clue to the mix-up between these two groups in
Josephus. Whoever this second group was, it could not have been
'Essenes' of the type exemplified in the literature at Qumran – who, whatever else they were – are *never obsequious, never accommodating*.[27]

In describing Herod in the way he does, Josephus also details the dark
and utterly ruthless side of Herod's personality and the fawning nature of
parasitic Establishment groups like those Josephus calls 'Essenes' and
'Pharisees', exemplified by the obsequious behaviour of the two Rabbinic
teachers, Pollio and Sameas, who predicted Herod's 'future greatness'.
They were most likely the heads of a new Sanhedrin or governing body of
Jewish Elders that Herod constituted upon his destruction of the previous
Maccabean one. It is probable, as already remarked, that they are to be
identified with the proverbial 'Hillel and Shammai' of Jewish Talmudic
and Rabbinic lore.

In describing how Herod 'persecuted those who could not be persuaded
to acquiesce to his kind of government in all manner of ways', Josephus
also stresses his unpopularity. He puts this in the following manner, some
of which we have quoted previously:

The people talked against him everywhere. From those malcontents that were still more provoked and disturbed by his practices, he greatly guarded himself and took away the opportunities they might have to disturb him and made sure they were always at work [therefore his vast public works projects]. Nor did he permit the citizens either to meet together, nor to walk, nor eat together, but watched everything they did [Josephus has this from sources; otherwise it might not be so bold], and when they were caught, they were severely punished. And many were brought to the Citadel Hyrcania, both openly and in secret, and there put to death [just as John the Baptist was a half-century later at the Fortress Machaeros, directly across the Dead Sea from Hyrcania, by Herod's son, Antipas, and 'Jesus' – whoever he was – probably too].

But Josephus does not stop here. He goes on to describe Herod's almost paranoiac repressiveness, reminiscent of many more modern rulers of similar frame-of-mind:

> And there were spies set everywhere, both in the city and on the roads who watched those who gathered together. It is even reported that he himself did not neglect this kind of precaution, but that often he would personally dress like a private person and mix among the populace at night, to see what opinion they held of his government . . . and to be sure a great part of them, either to please him or out of fear of him, yielded to what he required of them. But as for those who were of a more open and generous disposition and indignant at the force he used among them [this, exactly the character of those more equitably minded men who, a century later according to Josephus, protested what was done to James the Just – not to mention the Simon above, the Head of 'an Assembly of his own in Jerusalem', who wanted to bar Agrippa I from the Temple as a foreigner], he [Herod] by one means or another did away with them.[28]

It is at this point Josephus comes to describe both Essenes and Pharisees, whom Herod 'held in such honour and thought higher of them than was consistent with their mortal natures', and, in particular, 'the reverence he [Herod] bore Pollio *the Pharisee*'. It is for this reason I have spoken of confusions between 'Essenes' and 'Pharisees' in Josephus' work.

This description cannot apply to those responsible for the literature at Qumran, which locale not far from *Jericho* seems to have been both repressed and destroyed during Herod's reign. Herod also had the last Maccabean claimant to the High Priesthood strangled in the swimming pool of his winter palace also just outside *Jericho*. If one were to judge only by the proximity of Qumran to this, its suppression would not be surprising. On the contrary, those responsible for the documents deposited there would have been rounded up among those 'taken to Hyrcania, both openly and in secret, and there put to death'. In this period, if one keeps one's eye on the attitude of groups towards Herod and others in the political Establishment, *pro* or *contra*, one will seldom go far astray.

The Ultimate Enemies: Herodians, High Priests, and Paul

This is the 'Great' Herod, the Herod, who according to Gospel inventiveness had all the Jewish children in the region of Bethlehem put to death (Matt. 2:16). He may not have done this, but he wanted to kill just about anyone who resisted him and quite often did. This story, as it stands, owes much to the Moses story in the Old Testament, but also to another event Josephus describes in detail, that of how, when close to death, Herod had many Jewish notables from the Jerusalem area arrested and held as hostage in a great stadium, with orders that, when he died, they should be put to death so that there would be much mourning and wailing surrounding his funeral. Of course, this never happened because, after his death, his successors, realizing what this would mean in political terms and the threat to public order, promptly released all those he had arrested.

But, in fact, Herod did kill the Jewish children, though, not perhaps as the Gospel of Matthew relates. Rather, he *killed his own children* by the last Maccabean Princess Mariamme. There were two of these, one of whom was the father of Agrippa I, Herodias, and Herod of Chalcis, whom we have been considering above. According to Rabbinic Law, Herod's children would have been Jewish if their mother was 'a Jewess', unlike Drusilla in the next generation – whom the author of the Book of Acts, somewhat facetiously, describes as 'a Jewess' – whose *mother was not*.

This is the situation, the ramifications of which we are dealing with in succeeding generations of Herod's heirs, the 'heirs', too, to his political and religious 'Innovations', Herod Antipas, Agrippas I and II, Bernice, Drusilla, Saulus, and others from the 30s to the 60s of the next century – not to mention the situation of John the Baptist, Theudas, Simon and James the two sons of Judas the Galilean, and the other 'Magicians', 'Innovators', and 'Revolutionaries', who opposed them and were destroyed in the same way that those who opposed Herod in the previous century were destroyed.

In particular, there is little doubt that the Simon who visited Agrippa I's household in Caesarea would eventually have been arrested, just as the 'Simon' who visits the house of the Roman Centurion in Acts was – though the reason for this arrest would have been somewhat different, in fact *the very opposite* of how Acts describes it. As we have noted, just such a repression is alluded to by Josephus, during the reign of Agrippa I's brother, Herod of Chalcis, the first husband of Bernice, who was also *his niece*. This Herod slays someone in prison, named 'Silas', formerly a faithful friend of Agrippa's, sharing all his earlier troubles, even his imprisonment in Rome.[29]

As we have reiterated, it is curious how many such 'Herodians' share the names of individuals Paul has to do with in Acts. For instance, Philip the son of Jacimus, as remarked, would also appear to have been the '*Strategos*' or Commander of both Agrippa I's and II's comparatively small army. In telling his story in his *Vita*, Josephus repeatedly has occasion to refer to the sending of the 'Twelve' and the 'Seventy', details that to a certain extent form the background of the introduction to the namesake of this Philip in Acts. But in the telling in Josephus, these are all groups Philip *sends out in order to rescue Agrippa II*.[30] For instance, Stephen in Acts, and to a certain extent Philip – if distinct from the 'Philip' reckoned among the Apostles – are often reckoned among 'the Seventy'. Elsewhere, of course, 'Philip' is also reckoned among 'the Twelve'. The confusion regarding these matters in early Church literature, which extends as well to both 'Barnabas' and 'Thaddaeus', is patent.[31]

It is individuals such as these, ranged around the family of Agrippa I and II, that we would identify with those called 'the Violent Ones' or 'the Violent Ones of the Gentiles' in two *Pesharim* at Qumran. It is individuals of this kind, too, who should be identified as the leaders of Josephus' 'Idumaeans'. As described, together with the Zealots, they wreak vengeance on the High Priests – particularly James' destroyer Ananus – as the Uprising moves into its most extreme phase.

In this regard, one should recall that Costobarus in the previous century – Paul's possible ancestor – was an 'Idumaean', perhaps the original 'Idumaean', whom Herod had executed for treason even though he had originally been married to his sister. Some of these 'Men of War', as Qumran would put it, or 'Violent Ones', support the Roman side; some the Jewish nationalist one. Often, like Queen Helen's kinsmen or descendants, whom we shall have a good deal more to say about in the next section, they simply change sides when the pendulum starts to swing.

Philip, for instance, was originally accused of fomenting the Uprising, until Agrippa II convinced the Romans otherwise.

One of the earliest leaders, for instance, of these Violent 'Idumaeans', as we saw, is 'Niger of Perea' – 'Perea' being the area across Jordan, where John the Baptist principally operated. His death right after Ananus' at the hands of these same 'Zealots', after he had been led 'through the middle of the city . . . crying out and showing the scars of his wounds', has many of the elements of that depicted of Jesus in Scripture. It is interesting that, after giving the gory details of deaths such as these and remarking how 'the Innovators' tried 'to turn the Poor against the Rich', Josephus, once again, reversing everything describes how 'the Zealots'

> trampled upon the laws of men and laughed at the Laws of God, ridiculing the oracles of the Prophets as the tricks of jugglers, yet did these same Prophets foretell many of the things concerning *Righteousness and Evil*, which, when these Zealots violated, they inadvertently brought about the fulfilment of those very same prophecies . . . [including one] that the city should be taken and the Temple burned, when sedition should take possession of the Jews and by their own hands, *pollute the Temple of God*. Now, while these Zealots *did not disbelieve these oracles, they made themselves the instruments of their accomplishment.*[32]

Not only should one remark the total reversal of the 'pollution of the Temple' charge, so integral to the 'Three Nets of Belial' at Qumran, now as in Paul turned against 'the Zealots' not vice versa; but this is a complete inversion of the way prophecy was actually used in the Qumran texts. In fact, it is almost totally in agreement with how it is being used in the New Testament, including 'the Little Apocalypse' attributed to Jesus.

In Acts' description of the 'prophets and teachers of the Church in Antioch', where Christians 'were first called Christians', there is also, as previously remarked, another unidentified Simeon 'who was also called Niger'. It is in this list, too, it will be recalled, that another individual – name otherwise obliterated – is identified as 'the foster brother of Herod the Tetrarch', the Herod Antipas, whose marriage to Agrippa I's sister Herodias ended with the execution of John the Baptist.

After Agrippa I's death in 44 CE, his brother Herod of Chalcis, married to Bernice, Agrippa's daughter, lived on for another five years. Bernice was for all intents and purposes one of the rulers of Caesarea during this time. One should note how the Roman soldiers of Caesarea, whom Josephus over and over castigates as having led to the violence between Jews and Hellenists there, out of hatred for Agrippa I, when he died, supposedly took his daughters' statues and carried them into the brothels, because the soldiers perceived him as trying to be a Jewish King.

Here Josephus tantalizingly remarked that 'they abused them to the utmost of their power and did such things to them as are too indecent to be related'.[33] Photius, one of the conservators of Josephus' writings, in a later note goes so far as to claim that these were *not the statues* of the young girls – Josephus makes a point of observing that Bernice was then sixteen, Mariamme ten, and Drusilla only six – but actually the girls themselves. In any event, as no one had the courage to check these troops for another twenty-five years, they continued on these rampages until Vespasian, in the aftermath of the Jewish War, finally had them disbanded. These are the troops to which the 'Pious and God-Fearing' Cornelius above is said to belong in Acts.[34]

Not only does Josephus admit that Bernice was a 'very Rich' woman indeed, but, in describing the arrangements made after Agrippa I's death for the marriages of her two younger sisters, Mariamme and Drusilla, he introduces the Simon we have mentioned above, another of these multitudinous 'magicians'. Mariamme, it will be recalled, after an initial marriage to Julius Archelaus, the son of the Temple Treasurer Helcias – a close associate of Herod of Chalcis and a descendant of a, probably Idumaean, crony of Herod by the same name – *divorced* him, another infraction subsumed under the heading of 'fornication' in the 'Three Nets of Belial' accusations in the Damascus Document from Qumran above. She ended up marrying the Alabarch of Alexandria, 'the principal man', as Josephus remarks, 'among the Alexandrian Jews for both family and wealth'.[35]

Josephus identifies Tiberius Alexander, whose father had also held this post and was therefore probably a cousin or brother of Mariamme's husband above, as, like Drusilla and ultimately Bernice herself, 'a back-slider from Judaism'. Portrayed as imprisoning 'Christian' leaders, such as Peter and John in Acts, he is also responsible, as we saw, for the mysterious crucifixion – missing from Acts – of Judas the Galilean's two sons, James and Simon, at the time of the Famine. He also resurfaces at the Roman siege of Jerusalem, when Vespasian leaves him in command before going to Rome to become Emperor. By this time, it would appear that the ever-present Bernice has already become Titus' mistress. As we have already noted several times above and Josephus too remarks, she also appears to have 'illicit connection with her brother' Agrippa II, upon whose arm she appears conversing intimately with Paul in Acts (25:23).

This would give Bernice the following series of consorts: *her uncle*, Herod of Chalcis, Polemo the King of Cilicia, who was persuaded *to circumcise* himself out of deference to the wishes of her father to marry her (nevertheless she divorced him), *her brother* Agrippa II, and Titus, the destroyer of Jerusalem and Emperor-to-be, a veritable who's who or rogues' gallery of the period. Not only was a marriage contracted for her next younger sister Mariamme with the putative relative of Tiberius Alexander (probably his brother) and the new Alabarch, while the latter was still Roman Procurator in Judea in the late 40s; her youngest sister, Drusilla, whom even Josephus opines, 'exceeded all other women in beauty', 'transgressed the Laws of her ancestors to marry Felix'.[36]

Drusilla had been promised by her father Agrippa I to the son of Antiochus, King of Commagene, another petty kingdom in Asia Minor bordering on Cilicia, Little Armenia, and Edessa ('the Land of the Osrhoeans'). As previously described, this individual, named Epiphanes, who later led a unit called 'the Macedonian Legion' in Titus' assault on the Temple, refused to circumcise himself and come over to the Jewish religion. Therefore, Drusilla was married instead to another foreign King, Azizus of Emesa (presentday Homs in Syria, north of Damascus), who *did agree to circumcise himself*. Felix, who came in 52 CE – two years before Claudius was poisoned by his own niece, Nero's mother Agrippina – now employs this Simon, the 'Cypriot Magician' (also called 'Atomus' – of course, here is a perfect example of our confusion of 'Cypriot' and 'Samaritan'), whom Josephus describes as Felix's 'friend' and clearly something of a Rasputin type, to 'persuade Drusilla to *divorce her present husband and marry him*'![37]

There is so much in these events that is against the stance at Qumran, that it would be impossible to detail it all, however, if we take this individual to be the demythologized Simon *Magus* and the other Simon, the Head of an Assembly or Church in Jerusalem, who wants to *bar Herodians from the Temple as foreigners* (an aspect of the 'pollution of the Temple' charge being made against the reigning Establishment in the Dead Sea Scrolls, so disingenuously *reversed* in Josephus above), the *demythologized Peter*; then, I think as noted above, we have the where-withal to determine what the nature of the dispute between the literarily obscured Simon Peter and Simon *Magus* in Caesarea really was.

As always in these instances and the case of John the Baptist's objections to Herodias' marriages and divorce in the previous generation, the issue is 'fornication', but fornication of a very special kind. The charges against this Establishment are best outlined in the Dead Sea Scrolls, providing, as we have explained, one of the best arguments for dating the Scrolls on the basis of internal, not external, parameters. Since the Scrolls are contemporary documents unaffected on the whole by retrospective or overseas doctrinal consenses, we can feel comfortable in being guided by their parameters, chronological fine points notwithstanding. These strictures are outlined in the Temple Scroll, the Letter(s) on Works Righteousness ('MMT'), and most clearly of all in the 'Three Nets of Belial' accusations in the Damascus Document.

'Fornication' is such an omnipresent obsession at Qumran that one could cite endless examples of the allusions to it, but even in terms of poetic imagery, the Scrolls are steeped in it. It is also a theme of the Letter of James and the Jerusalem Council directives, attributed to James in Acts and, by reflection, in Paul's letters. James' condemnation of it is also implied in early Church testimonies about his Nazirite life-style and life-long sexual continence – his (not probably Mary's) 'life-long virginity'. In the 'Three Nets of Belial' metaphor in the Damascus Document, 'fornication' is defined quite simply as taking a second wife while the first is still alive, that is, in terms of polygamy *and* divorce, both of which are condemned. Most striking of all, however, is the theme attached to it of *marriage with a niece*. As this last unfolds in the Damascus Document, it is connected to the charges of improper 'separation' and 'pollution of the Temple'.

Finally, as an over-arching aspect of all of these, the charge of 'sleeping with a woman during the blood of her period' is attached to the combination of all three: the charge of 'not separating according to *Torah*', 'pollution of the Temple', and 'fornication'.[38] This final charge is perhaps decisive where individuals like Drusilla and Bernice are concerned, who have connection with various gentile kings. Drusilla's final husband, Felix, brutally repressed 'impostors', 'Deceivers', and Opposition Leaders in Palestine generally and was the brother of Pallas, Nero's favourite courtier and *Treasurer*; Titus, Bernice's paramour – the destroyer of Jerusalem and future Emperor!

These charges are immediately followed in the next column of the Damascus Document by reference to having 'a Tongue full of insults' or 'blasphemies against the Laws of the Covenant of God' and the allusion to the 'nets' of the Establishment being those of 'spiders' and 'their off-spring, of vipers'. The first clearly parallels the use of 'Tongue' imagery in the Letter of James and the second again, as we have seen, the well-known attacks by John the Baptist on the Scribes and Pharisees in the New Testament (in some variations, also attributed to Jesus), which use the very same phraseology. The Damascus Document concludes at this point, delineating how the pollution of Herodians or foreigners generally could have been communicated to the Temple Establishment: 'Whoever approaches them cannot be cleansed. Like a thing accursed, his house is guilty, unless he was forced.'[39]

Certainly, no Jewish Priesthood, legitimate or otherwise, ever contemplated 'lying with women during their periods', as the Damascus Document so graphically expresses it, a ban with the power almost of a taboo in Judaism. But, coupled as it is with the twin complaints of improper 'separation of clean and unclean' and 'pollution of the Temple', one can well imagine this charge as applying to an establishment consorting with foreigners, such as the Herodians. Concretizing this further, this charge is then *directly* followed by the one banning niece marriage:

> Each man takes [to wife] the daughter of his brother and the daughter of his sister. But Moses said, 'You shall not approach your mother's sister [for sexual connection]. She is your mother's near kin.' (Lev. 18:13)

Almost modern in its use of analogy, the Damascus Document, as already remarked, then goes on to explain:

> But although the Law of incest was written for [the case] of men, it likewise extends to women. Therefore, when a brother's daughter uncovers the nakedness of her father's brother, she is [as his] near kin.

The Qumran position on these matters could not be clearer. One should also have regard for the allusion to 'incest' here. How the writers of the Scrolls would have condemned Agrippa II's reported incest with his sister Bernice.

There is a hint of this condemnation of incest, too, as the Damascus Document continues two columns later:

> The Princes of Judah are those who are Removers of the boundary marker [instead of 'Princes of Judah', read here 'Herodians'].

This quotation is from Hosea 5:10. It was already evoked in the description of the Law-breaking activities of the Liar in the First Column of the Document.

They are all apostates, for they have not turned aside from the Way of *Traitors* [language reversed in the New Testament]. Rather they have wallowed [or 'immersed themselves'] in *the ways of fornication* and *ill-gotten Riches* . . . every man of them has sinned against the flesh of his own flesh [meaning here, not only *nieces*, but possibly *sisters* as well], approaching them for fornication. And they have used their power for the sake of Riches and profit . . . 'Their wine is the venom of vipers and the cruel poison of asps.'[40]

The quotation being evoked here now is from Deuteronomy 32:33, and in it, we have a play on 'venom' and 'poison', which in Hebrew also have the synonyms and/or homonyms of 'anger' or 'Wrath'. The word 'wine' in Hebrew, too, also has a homonym in 'Greece', which will be played on in the *Pesher* to produce 'Greek-speaking Kings' (in our view *Herodians*). We have met this imagery before and will meet it again, in the context of 'the wine of the cup of God's Vengeance' in the Habakkuk *Pesher* and Revelation. In fact, in the manner of such a *'pesher'* or commentary, the Damascus Document now inteprets this:

The 'vipers' are *the Kings of the Peoples* and their 'wine' is *their ways*.

Here, not only is the 'wine' applied to what the Establishment does either to the people or its enemies, but the 'viper' language, which we have already encountered earlier in the Document and which the Gospels put into the mouths of either John the Baptist or Jesus, is *definitively applied to the Establishment*.

But this term, 'Kings of the Peoples', as already explained, is a well-known one in Roman jurisprudence in this period, where it is used to denote the petty kings, the Romans appointed as adminstrators and tax-farmers, in the East.[41] They were the 'Kings of the Peoples', the word '*Ethnē*' in this phraseology in Greek meaning 'Nations' or 'Gentiles'; in Latin, '*Gentes*'/'Gentiles'. This is also the way Paul uses it in expressing his own mission, directed to these same 'Peoples'. We could not, therefore, have a clearer dating tool, based on actual Roman administrative usage from this period, to confirm our interpretation of these allusions to refer to Herodians, who were 'Greek-speaking', Roman puppet Kings in the East, rather than to Maccabeans.

As the Damascus Document proceeds, these allusions are followed, once again, by recapitulation of the allusion to 'the Lying Spouter surely spouting' (Micah 2:6), all related to somone now referred to as something of a 'Windbag' – literally 'one who walks in the Spirit' or 'of confused

Spirit' ('wind' and 'Spirit' being the same word in Hebrew) and 'blows up storms' or 'spouted', 'prophesied', or 'rained down'/'poured out Lying upon them'. Not only do we have here a possible play on Paul's 'Holy Spirit' doctrines, but the use of 'rain' or 'storm' imagery, now inverted to relate not to the Teacher, but 'the Liar'/'Spouter'.[42]

This individual was referred to four columns before, following the evocation of 'the Three Nets of Belial', in terms of Ezekiel 13:7–16's 'Empty words and Lying visions', also having to do in Ezekiel and Micah with 'Lying prophets' prophesying 'Peace, when there is not peace', the whole of which activity being subsumed under the handy catchphrase of 'daubing upon the wall'.[43] Still earlier, at the beginning of the Damascus Document, in the midst of the 'removing the bound' and 'causing to wander astray in a trackless waste' metaphors – all denotive of teaching against the Law – this individual, it will be remembered, was referred to as 'pouring over Israel the waters of Lying', 'pouring' here deliberately expressed in terms of the Hebrew word 'spouting', an allusion, perhaps, to another of 'the Spouter of Lying's' favourite pastimes, baptism. We have already expressed the view that this person is Paul.

It should also be recalled that in the version of the 'Three Nets of Belial' found in Revelation, the 'net', which 'Balaam taught Balak to *cast [balein] down before the Sons of Israel*' was the twofold accusation of teaching them 'to commit fornication' and, the converse of the Jamesian position, 'to eat things sacrificed to idols'. This is not to mention the tell-tale interchange of the 'Satan' and 'Diabolos' vocabulary throughout this section – which Jesus struggles manfully to master in the 'Beelzebul' discourses above – and the whole 'Cup', 'wine', and 'Vengeance' symbolism one encounters generally in this book.

Paul's Contacts in the Household of Nero

Paul, of course, also knows this 'Belial' terminology, because he refers to it, however defectively, in 2 Corinthians 6:15. Not only, as we have seen, is the 'Belial' terminology relevant to Herodians, but the *'balla'*/'Bela''/ 'Balaam' circle of language, relating to this root in Hebrew, has to do with what the leaders of this Establishment did to those objecting to their behaviour, that is, 'swallowed' or 'consumed them' – 'Belial' in the Damascus Document becoming 'Balaam' in Revelation, 2 Peter, and Jude.

It is even possible, as we have suggested, that the circle relates to the 'Benjamin' appellation as well, a terminology that Paul applies to himself in Romans 11:1 (echoed in Acts 13:21). It is extremely unlikely that Jews were evoking their tribal affiliations by this time in their history – except for 'Priests' or 'Levites' – most other tribes having long since been absorbed into the principal group, Judah, the source of the appellation 'Jew' or 'Yehud'.[44] But in Paul's case, when he describes himself in Philippians 3:5 as 'of the race of Israel', 'a Hebrew of the Hebrews', he conspicuously avoids any reference to the appellative 'Jew'.

There is some indication that overseas Jews may have been using this 'Benjamin' appellation to apply to themselves too, though Paul might simply have been evoking his biblical namesake, the Benjaminite King Saul a thousand years before. Even more germane, as we have also suggested, it is possible that Herodians and others, because of their peculiar quasi-Jewish status, used the terminology – as Muhammad does 'Ishmael' in a later generation – to show that they too were originally 'heirs to the Promise and Children of Abraham', or, as Paul puts it, 'Israelites' and 'Hebrews' – but not 'Jews'.

It will be recalled that Edomites, too, were children of Abraham, but, in view of these very interesting overlaps between Edomites and Benjaminites in the matter of their eponymous ancestor, Bela' the son of Be'or (in biblical writ, both the first Edomite King and one of the principal Benjaminite clans – not to mention that Benjaminites in Judges 19–20 were referred to as 'sons of Belial'), the Herodians may have been turning the insults of their detractors around into testimony to their own legitimacy. If the Herodians were using this terminology and applying it to themselves, it would be further verification that Qumran's use of this cluster to imply everything negative – in fact, the epitome of Evil incarnate – and our identification of it as a leitmotif for Herodians is correct.

In Philippians also, Paul makes use of another allusion, as remarked, right out of the Community Rule from Qumran and applies it to Epaphroditus, whom he calls his 'brother and fellow worker', 'an odour, a sweet fragrance, an acceptable sacrifice, well pleasing to God' (2:25 and 4:18); whereas at Qumran it is applied to the members of the Community Council, who are described, as we saw, as 'a sweet fragrance', 'an acceptable sacrifice atoning for the land', and 'a tested Wall and Precious Corner-Stone . . . establishing the Holy Spirit according to Truth forever'. Also in the Community Rule, prayer rightly offered is described as 'a pleasing odour of Righteousness and Perfection of the Way, an acceptable free-will offering'.[45]

For his part in Philippians, after then referring to having '*Riches in the*

Glory of Christ', Paul sends his greetings 'to *every Holy One . . . especially those of the household of Caesar*' (4:19–22). This Epaphroditus would appear to be an interesting person. As we saw, his name, also, appears as the name of Josephus' editor and patron. Josephus refers to 'Epaphroditus' as the 'most excellent of men' and 'a lover of all kinds of learning . . . *principally the knowledge of History*,' who

> himself *had a part in great events* and *many turns of fortune* . . . showing the wonderful vigour of an excellent constitution and *an immovable virtuous resolution in them all*.[46]

Like Felix, a freedman of Nero, Epaphroditus was also involved in the latter's death, helping him commit suicide, though this may actually have been an assassination. As a reward, he would also appear afterwards to have been Domitian's secretary, until the latter turned on him and put him to death, supposedly for daring to *kill an Emperor*. As we saw, this was the time around 95 CE that Domitian was reputed to have put to death or banished two other 'Christians' in his household, Flavius Clemens (possibly Clement) and his wife or niece, Flavia Domitilla.

Paul also refers to Epaphroditus in Philippians 2:27 as at one point having been sick and near death. The reference to him in connection with 'the household of Caesar' in Philippians 4:22 makes it virtually certain we are speaking about the same person as the Epaphroditus just described above. One should note the parallel reference to 'those of [the household] of Aristobulus' in Romans 16:11 and 'the littlest Herod' in 16:13. Herod of Chalcis' son Aristobulus was certainly very close to Claudius, since the latter not only conferred upon him the Kingdom of Lower Armenia, but also the title of 'Friend'. Doubtlessly, he was on equally friendly terms with those in Nero's household as well and the Flavians after that.

It is a not incurious footnote to all these relationships that the offspring of the marriage of Drusilla and Felix perished in the 'conflagration of the mountain Vesuvius in the days of Titus Caesar', a thing Josephus promises to relate further, but never does.[47] Josephus, also, promises to tell more about the family of Philo and the Alabarch of Alexandria, but likewise never does.

Final Conclusions about Peter and Josephus' Simon

The situation should, therefore, be clear. What John the Baptist objected to on the part of Herodias and Herod Antipas was their 'fornication', to say nothing of their 'Riches'. The New Testament presentation of an arcane problem over levirate marriage may or may not have played a part. The issue of whether 'Philip' (actually Herod) did or did not have children is, in any event, moot. Herodias divorced 'Philip' (that is, Herod), which even Josephus notes was illegal. Nor did this 'Herod', who was the son of Herod's second wife called Mariamme, die at this point.

As the Gospel of Luke graphically expresses it, 'but Herod the Tetrarch was reproved by [John] concerning Herodias, the wife of his brother Philip' (3:19). The issue as Josephus graphically delineates it *vis-à-vis* Herodias was her marriage with, not one, but *two uncles* and her illegal *divorce* from the first of them, all things roundly condemned at Qumran and, no doubt, in John the Baptist's complaints against her as well, for which he loses his life.

Likewise, the confrontation between Peter and Simon *Magus*, so creatively enhanced in all our sources, had probably little to do with theological problems *per se*, though certainly these may have played a part – in particular, ideologies surrounding 'the True Prophet', 'the Primal Adam', and 'the Christ'. It is impossible to tell, but we do have it stated unequivocally by Josephus that there was a 'magician' called 'Simon' in Felix's employ.[48] Felix used this individual to convince Drusilla not only to 'break the Laws of her Ancestors' ('the First' in the Damascus Document), but to *divorce* a previous husband and marry another – all roundly condemned at Qumran – and, while the previous one had circumcised himself expressly to marry her, Felix, quite obviously, did not. Furthermore, in the Pseudoclementine *Recognitions*, which makes so much of Peter's confrontations with Simon *Magus* up and down the Palestine coast, we have it that James sent out Peter from somewhere outside of Jericho around this time *to confront Simon Magus in Caesarea*.

In all the materials about James, not insignificantly condemning 'fornication' as we saw, it is a most insistent theme, as it is in the literature centring around the Righteous Teacher at Qumran. In the latter, the issue is omnipresent. I think we can safely say that the same 'Simon', who wished *to bar Agrippa I from the Temple as a foreigner* despite the latter's obvious attempts at Piety, and inspected his household to see what was being done there contrary to Law, confronted Simon *Magus* in Caesarea as well and the issue between them was 'fornication' – the fornication of the Herodian family!

That the Felix, who employed a namesake of this Simon in the next decade was a foreigner, to say nothing of his repression of Opposition leaders and self-evident brutality, just compounded this same issue. Finally, one can take it as a given that Felix was neither circumcised nor scrupled to sleep with women during 'the blood' of their periods, not issues one can assume of very great moment in the Hellenistic world he functioned in.

This key allusion in the Damascus Document to this last practice relates, as we have seen, to *how foreigners were perceived in Palestine.* That is not to say that all foreigners did these things, only that this is how they would have been perceived in Palestine. These are the kinds of aspersions that would have circulated in everyday conversation – and everyone would have known what they meant. The calumny as it is present in the Damascus Document did not mean that *the High Priests* slept with women 'during *the blood* of their menstrual flow'. Rather, they most certainly did not.

But, as we have just shown, it meant they had commerce with people who did and, in the words of the Damascus Document, they incurred their 'pollution'. This meant primarily Herodians. In the case of the High Priests, they accepted their appointment from such Herodians, considered by extremist Zealots, utterly polluted, and worse still, from Roman Governors -- even sometimes for bribes. This is why 'the Zealots' and probably those represented by the literature at Qumran and early Christians, if they are not identical, were so intent on electing a High Priest of greater purity and Righteousness (Heb. 4:14 and 7:26).

This allusion to 'sleeping with women in their periods', which is directly connected in the Damascus Document to the one about 'each one (of them) marrying his brother's daughter', specifically has to do, therefore, with foreigners, and those perceived of as having *commerce or intercourse with foreigners.* This would include Herodian Kings and Princesses, all reckoned by extremists of the stripe of the Simon in Josephus above and those at Qumran, as 'foreigners'. In addition, such an aspersion would *include Paul* and his Gentile Mission. Peter, no doubt, confronted Simon *Magus* on issues such as these as well. Certainly the 'Peter' pictured in the Pseudoclementine *Homilies* would have. This is why Acts is at such pains to counter-indicate and reverse all such matters completely.

These are the parameters of 'Palestinian Christian' activity – these are the parameters of Qumran, not retrospective historical re-creation. These become transformed in what is perhaps one of the most cynical examples of overseas dissimulation or inversion into Peter learning that he should *not make distinctions* against 'foreigners' or 'uncircumcised men' (Acts 10:28 and 11:3). In effect, Peter is Paulinized, becoming the recipient of a Pauline-style Heavenly vision to confirm it, and on a rooftop in Jaffa no less! And this, when the Letter to the Galatians *specifically testifies* that he separated from Paul over this issue (2:12), despite being somewhat less stringent regarding it than James. This too is emphatically confirmed in the *Homilies*.

To add insult to injury, as we have seen, Peter is then portrayed as greeting a Roman Centurion from Caesarea and returning with him to visit his household there – a Roman Legionnaire who is portrayed as caring intensely about Judaism and all things Jewish, when over and over again Josephus makes it clear that it was these same legionnaires from Caesarea who exacerbated the problems in the country, no governor ever feeling confident enough over a twenty-year period to exercise control over them – finally goading the Jews to revolt against Rome!

That someone, overwriting this episode about the Jerusalem Simon's visit to Agrippa I's household in Caesarea and presenting it, rather, in terms of Peter visiting the house of the Roman Centurion Cornelius in Caesarea from 'the Italica Contingent', may or may not have intended to catch the attention of either Trajan or Hadrian to convince them of what a positive attitude their predecessors in the Italica Regiment had had to Christian leaders has to be considered. In this regard, not only did both Trajan and Hadrian come from the Roman garrison town of Italica in Spain but both were very active in putting down Messianic uprisings in Palestine and around the Mediterranean in succeeding years.[49]

In fact, Trajan's correspondence with the younger Pliny, who unlike the descendants of Drusilla and Felix survived the eruption of Vesuvius, raised issues not unrelated to these. It will be recalled that Trajan had requested Pliny in his capacity as Governor of Bithynia in Asia Minor to investigate 'Christians' there – obviously 'Gentile' ones. Eusebius, who preserves this from Tertullian (160–221 CE), has Pliny concluding:

> They did nothing evil or contrary to the laws [Roman Law] . . . beyond their *unwillingness to sacrifice to idols, he found nothing criminal in them.*

One should remark here – contrary to Paul – the observance of James' prohibition on 'eating things sacrificed to idols'. In addition, this is the verdict that basically reappears in the Roman Governor's mouth in Judea – if not Pliny's, certainly Pilate's – who in Luke, anyhow, after examining Jesus, concludes, 'I find no fault in this man' (23:4). John even more precisely echoes the words imputed to Pliny above, quoting Pilate as saying, 'I find no crime in him' (19:4). At this, Eusebius' version of Tertullian's testimony regarding this has Trajan ruling that 'Christians should not be inquired after further.' This is not precisely the outcome of the actual correspondence, which, as earlier remarked, has survived and records something of a less sanguine upshot.

As we saw too, Eusebius also records a similar episode that happened not long before, at least according to his understanding. This one, under Domitian (81–96), ends up in the arrest of 'the offspring of one of those considered *the brothers of the Lord, whose name was Judas*'. This is about the same time as the executions of Epaphroditus and Flavius Clemens and the exile of the latter's niece or wife, Flavia Domitilla. It is interesting that it is this Domitilla's servant – again curiously named 'Stephanos', who assassinates Domitian the same year.[50]

A third episode of this kind under Trajan (98–117), at the time seemingly of Messianic disturbances in Egypt and Cyrene (Libya), ends up in the torture and crucifixion of Simeon bar Cleophas, Jesus' 'cousin' or second brother, around 105–6 CE, who 'terminated his life with sufferings like those of our Lord'.[51] To confuse the matter still further, Eusebius, supposedly again following Hegesippus, supplies us with yet another note about a third such round-up under Vespasian even earlier. He explains:

> Vespasian gave an order that a search be made for *all descendants of David*, and this resulted in the infliction of another widespread persecution on the Jews.[52]

In all these notices, Eusebius basically uses the same words, 'A search was made for the Jews that were of the descendants of David.'[53]

One should note here again – if the notice is true – that the Roman administrative practice at the time treated so-called 'Christians', 'Messianists', and Jews virtually indistinguishably. 'Domitian had issued orders that the descendants of David should be slain', again showing, if true, that he knew the disturbances in Palestine in this period – which were apparently still going on – to be *Messianic*. Whereupon the descendants of Judas, as the brother of our Saviour according to the flesh, because they were of the family of David, and as such, also related to Christ . . . were brought to Domitian.[54]

Following Hegesippus now verbatim, Eusebius identifies these as 'the grandchildren of Judas, called the brother of our Lord according to the flesh.' Domitian examines them.

Here, again, the notice about 'the hardness of their bodies was evidence of their labour, and the calluses of their hands from their incessant work was evidence of their own labour', ever so slightly evokes how hard the calluses were on James' knees – this from all the 'incessant praying' he did in the Holy of Holies (note the repeat here of the word, 'incessant', as well). Like James, too, they are portrayed as answering the charges against them in terms of Jesus' *coming in Glory* to judge . . . every man *according to his works*. This is almost word for word a combination of the Letter of James and the account of James' proclamation in the Temple before the assembled Jewish crowds on Passover. Whereupon

> Domitian despising them . . . as simpletons, commanded them to be dis-
> missed and by Imperial order commanded that the persecution cease.

Domitian clearly treats them as simpletons, because politically they are no threat, their Kingdom being only other-worldly. Still, all of these descendants would appear to have been, once again, rounded up and executed under Trajan a decade later at the time Hegesippus describes the martyrdom of Simeon bar Cleophas, because, as he writes (paralleling Eusebius' earlier description of Stephen), these were the persons 'who took the lead of the whole Church as martyrs – in particular, the family of our Lord'.[55]

PART V

THE BROTHERS OF JESUS AS APOSTLES

The Apostleship of James, *Cephas*, and John

The Letters of Introduction from James

We should now look at the way the Gospels, Paul's Letters, and other materials present Jesus' brothers and family members generally. In the early Church accounts, as we saw, James is presented as an 'Apostle'. It is traditionally understood that the James, called 'the brother of the Lord,' is only a 'Bishop', not an 'Apostle', as if 'Apostle' were in some sense greater than 'Bishop'. Even this much is not widely appreciated and there is rarely any perception about who this second James was, nor is he ever spoken about to any extent.

In the first sixteen chapters of Acts before 'the We Document' begins to make its presence felt in the narrative, we have seen how the traces of real events lie just beneath the surface glittering like pebbles beneath the surface of a stream. Often these involve those who go by the designation, 'the Central Three' or 'the Twelve' – meaning 'the Twelve Apostles' – even 'the Seventy', meaning 'the Seventy Disciples'. Problems where these are concerned often have to do with the different enumerations of 'the Apostles' both in and outside of Scripture, which, in turn, are connected with problems regarding Jesus' brothers and family generally – and attempts either to diminish or to obliterate them. These, in their turn, are connected to the order of post-resurrection appearances by Jesus, which have been recognized as, in some manner, giving confirmation of one's status or place in the hierarchy of the early Church.

In the Pseudoclementines it becomes very clear that proper Apostles had to carry appointment letters of some kind from the 'Bishop of Bishops' James. At one point, this is expressed in words attributed to Peter (instructing Clement) as follows:

> Observe the greatest caution, that you *believe no teacher unless he brings the testimonial of James the Lord's brother from Jerusalem*, or whomever comes after him. *Under no circumstances*, receive anyone or consider him a

worthy and faithful teacher for preaching the word of Christ, unless he has gone up there, *been approved, and, as I say, brings a testimonial from there.* (Ps. *Rec.* 4.25)

The negation of this proposition is to be found in the Letters of Paul, who often shows his sensitivity to the issue of appointment letters or proper credentials, thereby indirectly verifying their existence.

This illustrates a point we have been emphasizing, about reading between the lines in our sources in order to discern what the accusations were that were circulating around different individuals or what the procedures were such individuals were reacting against or attempting to countermand. For instance, at the beginning of Galatians, in addition to his protesting that he 'does not lie' (1:20), Paul insists he is:

an Apostle, *not from men nor through man*, but through Jesus Christ and God the Father, who raised him from the dead [note again the 'man' or 'Adam' motif here]. (Gal. 1:1)

One should appreciate that what Paul is claiming here is that he has a direct appointment from *Jesus himself* – better still 'the Christ' – an individual whom in bodily form on earth he never seemingly encountered and the followers of whom he admits to 'persecuting', some even 'unto death' (Gal. 1:23).

This seemingly innocuous, formulary-style announcement of his Apostolic qualifications is, of course, a direct riposte to those who claim to have their appointment either directly from Jesus himself in his human form or who carry 'written' credentials from James – both of these physical manifestations – or both. These are the same genre of persons, who, as Paul expresses it again in the context of alluding to the brothers of Jesus in 1 Corinthians, would presume 'to examine' him (9:3). This should not be surprising, since what Paul is calling his work or mission depends on a direct 'revelation', as it were, via the mechanism of the Holy Spirit from the Supernatural Being, now residing in Heaven, he denotes as 'Christ Jesus' or 'Jesus Christ' (Gal. 2:2).

In 2 Corinthians 3:1, again employing the imagery of spiritualized 'Temple' and 'sacrifice' and the allegorizing approach he so loves, Paul pointedly picks up this issue of 'written' credentials – these obviously, as per Pseudoclementine tradition, from James. Referring in the manner of the Community Rule at Qumran to 'the odour of the Knowledge of him . . . the sweet fragrance of Christ',[1] Paul asks rhetorically, though none the less bitingly:

> Do we start again to recommend ourselves? Unlike some who need either letters to you or from you [*epistolōn*] to recommend [themselves], you are our letter, having been inscribed *in our hearts*, being known and read by all men, showing that you are *Christ's Letter* served by us, not being written with ink, not on *tablets of stone*, but with the Spirit of the Living God *on the fleshly tablets of the heart*.

Not only should one remark the clear play on and quasi-reversal of the 'uncircumcised heart' usage found in the Scrolls and based on the Prophet Ezekiel, but these ever-present 'some' – the catchphrase in Galatians and Acts for those from James who 'come down to Antioch'. Also the allusion to 'letters' (*epistolai*) here, not only refers back to the introductory letters in the Pseudoclementines, but indirectly also to the one containing James' Jerusalem Council decrees, which Acts pictures James as 'sending down' to Antioch with 'Judas *Barsabas*' and Silas (15:30).

In his riposte here, Paul achieves several things. First of all, he makes it clear that the people with whom he is arguing care about *written things*, particularly 'stone tablets', by which he clearly means the Ten Commandments. Plus these persons are *inside* not outside the Church. He is, in addition, both heaping scorn on those who require 'written' appointments and documentary 'recommendations' to serve as Apostles and using his favourite rhetorical device of 'teaching spiritual things by the Spirit' to do so (1 Cor. 2:13 and Rom. 2:29).

He then goes on in 2 Corinthians, continuing to use this kind of spiritualized imagery or allegorization to attack *the written letter of the Law*: 'for the letter kills, but the Spirit gives life' (3:6). Here is the 'Holy Spirit' language, upon which his own legitimacy and ministry so rest, but, in turn, as in the Letter to the Romans, now tied to the 'spiritualizing' process generally. The chasm, here, is that Paul is using *poetic* rhetorical devices to reply to interlocutors who are basically using *legal* concepts. It is an unbridgeable one.

Warming to this imagery, Paul now attacks both 'the Law' and 'Moses', the foundation pieces of the people opposing him, obviously meant to include James and the rest of the *Jewish* Apostles and 'Jerusalem Church' Leadership – and the standpoint of the Qumran literature as well – referring to all of these in one of the most biting aspersions conceivable, as '*the Service of death cut in letters into stone*' (2 Cor. 3:7). At the same time and always mindful of this issue of 'letters of recommendation', he evokes his idea of 'the New Covenant', which will now be 'not of the letter but of Spirit' (2 Cor. 3:6) – in other words not of the 'letter' of the proverbial Ten Commandments, but the 'spiritualization represented by 'the Holy Spirit'. Here the 'New Covenant' in the body and blood of Jesus Christ is presented as being opposed to *physical* letters – whether those sent out to certify its Apostles or those on stone – and totally allegorized.

Picking up, then, the imagery of 'Glory' and 'splendour' – in this instance, 'the splendour on Moses' face', which he says 'was bound to cease' – Paul now contrasts it with his own 'Service' or 'the Ministry of the Spirit in Glory' (2 Cor. 3:8). Not only are we playing once again on 'the Son of Man coming in Glory', already encountered with regard to James' proclamation in the Temple above; but one should compare the use here of this word 'serve' or 'Service', namely 'the Service of the Spirit', with how the Spouter of Lying's 'Service' is referred to in the Habakkuk *Pesher* at Qumran – that is, the 'Service of Vanity' or 'a Worthless Service'.[2]

Paul's use in this context too of phrases like 'the Servants of the New Covenant' and 'the Service of Righteousness in Glory' (2 Cor. 3:9), will be played on later in the 2 Corinthians by the use of the phrase 'the Servants of Righteousness', to attack those he will call 'Super Apostles' and even 'Pseudo-Apostles' (2 Cor. 11:13 and 11:15).

At this point, carried away by his enthusiasm for the spiritualizing imagery he is employing, Paul makes one of the most outrageous accusations ever made by one religion against another. Evoking an episode in Exodus in the Old Testament, when emerging from the Tent of Meeting, after speaking with God face to face, Moses veils himself so that the Children of Israel will not be irradiated from his brilliance or 'splendour' at having been in the Presence of God (Exod. 34:33); Paul rather asserts that Moses 'put a veil over his face, so that the Children of Israel would not notice the end of what had to fade' (3:13)! In other words, Moses was a deceiver and a charlatan, who veiled himself because he did not want the Children of Israel to see there was no 'splendour' associated with his relationship with God and the revelation of the Law consonant upon it. Regardless of the thrust of the various imageries being used or the rightness or wrongness of the polemics involved, no more scurrilous accusation has ever been recorded by the founder of one major world religion against that of another.

The relationship of these imageries to Jewish Mysticism of the Middle Ages makes it fair to ask whether this kind of thinking was actually already functioning in Paul's time? The very 'splendour' used to describe the brilliance on Moses' face as a result of his encounter with God becomes the title of the most representative and well-known document of this underground Jewish mystical religious tradition, popularly known as *Kabbalah*, 'The *Zohar*' or '*Book of Splendour*'.

Paul's Attacks on the 'Apostles of the Highest Degree'

Returning to the subject of these 'letters' of recommendation again at the end of 2 Corinthians, Paul responds to the charge that, though he writes strong and powerful 'letters' at a distance, in person his body is feeble, his speech even feebler. He does so by attacking these ever-recurring 'some' who, as he puts it,

> write their own recommendations, who, measuring themselves by themselves and comparing themselves to themselves, lack all understanding. (10:10–12)

Though unctuous and self-deprecating, yet biting in the extreme, Paul refers now to the 'Authority which *the Lord* gave' him – meaning *not* that which the Apostles or James gave him. He does so by using the language of 'building up and not tearing down' (2 Cor. 10:8), while at the same time starting to employ his language of 'boasting', which for him will serve as a substitute for *written credentials*. In 1 Corinthians 8:1–13, attacking those with 'weak consciences', who make 'stumbling blocks' over 'things sacrificed to idols', and evoking the Piety Commandment of 'loving God' – evoked to exactly opposite effect in the Letter of James 2:5–14 (also amid the language of 'stumbling') – it is rather 'Love' that 'builds up', as opposed to 'Knowledge' which 'puffs up'.

In fact, this same 'puffing up' language will be used at Qumran in the Habakkuk *Pesher*, in the prelude to its interpretation of the all-important Habakkuk 2:4 – 'the Righteous shall live by his Faith' (and is, in fact, based on Habakkuk 2:4), to attack those disagreeing with its interpretation of this fundamental scriptural passage (as well as that of Habakkuk 2:3 on 'the Delay of the *Parousia*' preceding it), who 'will not be pleased with their Judgement'. Not only is this 'puffed up' allusion based on the language of Habakkuk 2:4, the Habakkuk *Pesher* actually refers to the Righteous Teacher, as the person, 'in whose heart God put *the Knowledge* to interpret all of the words of His Servants the Prophets'.[3]

In both these passages, Paul is, again, using the same 'building' metaphor with which he began 1 Corinthians, where he referred to himself as the 'architect' of God's Community and the 'building' which was

Christ (1 Cor. 3:9–14). This, as we have already seen to some extent and will see further in Volume II, is important for determining the historical provenance of Qumran aspersions on 'the Spouter of Lying' in the Habakkuk *Pesher*, which as part of its attack on his 'Vain' or 'Worthless Service', refers to 'the Liar' as 'misleading Many to build' a Congregation ('Church') on 'Lying' and 'blood' 'for the sake of his Glory'.

Again, warming to his subject and the motifs of 'boasting' and his own 'foolishness' he has just evoked, Paul goes on – a second time protesting he 'does not lie' and again turning his opponents' accusations against themselves – to attack 'those people' he bitterly describes as 'Pseudo-Apostles, *Lying workmen disguising themselves as Apostles of Christ*' (2 Cor. 11:13). It should be appreciated that the assurance that he is 'not Lying', one encounters here, is repeated not only in Galatians, but throughout Romans, where he is also involved in 'spiritualizing' discussions of parallel doctrines.[4] In applying allusions such as 'Lying workmen disguising themselve as Apostles of Christ' and 'Pseudo-' or 'Counterfeit Apostles', one sees again the typical inversions of key themes both at Qumran and in the Letters of Paul which by now are becoming so familiar.

Playing on the comparison made earlier in 2 Corinthians 6:14–7:1 of 'Righteousness with lawlessness', 'Light with Darkness', 'Christ with Beliar', 'the Temple of God with idols', and 'being separate' and 'cleansing oneself of every defilement of flesh and Spirit to *Perfect Holiness*' (that is, being a *Nazirite*), Paul continues these various metaphors, asking rhetorically:

> And it is not wonderful that, if *even Satan disguises himself as an Angel of Light*, it is therefore, no great thing that his servants disguise themselves as *Servants of Righteousness*, whose *End shall be according to their works*. (2 Cor. 11:13–15)

Of course, not only does Paul identify the individuals he has in mind by the linguistic inversions he uses and the pun he makes on their principal doctrine – their 'End shall be according to' the 'works' they so extolled – but the allusion to 'the Servants of Righteousness', here, exactly parallels the kind of emphases one encounters at Qumran and in all traditions relating to James – including the Letter in his name.

Losing control of his 'Tongue' almost completely now – as even he acknowledges – Paul makes it unmistakably clear that his opponents in the Church actually are 'Hebrews' not others. In passing, one should also note the relation of this loss of control to the aspersion on 'the Tongue' being 'an uncontrollable Evil, full of death-bringing poison' in the Letter of James (3:5–12) and the derogations on 'the Pourer out of Lying'/ 'Spouter of Lying' or 'Comedian' at Qumran.[5]

> But if anyone wants brazenness – I am still talking as fool – then I can be just as brazen [alluding to the brazenness of those writing their own recommendations]. *Hebrews are they?* So am I. *Israelites are they?* So am I. *Of the seed of Abraham are they?* So am I. *Servants of Christ are they?* I must be insane to have to say this, but so am I, and *more than they, more because I have worked harder* [note Paul's allusion to 'working' here, in the sense of 'service' or 'labours', as opposed to Jamesian 'works', as we also have it in the Hebrew at Qumran, where the Liar's 'Service', 'Mission', or 'work' is at issue].[6] (2 Cor. 11:21–23)

It is also significant that when speaking of himself, as in Philippians above, Paul never calls himself 'a Jew' – a term that even the Dead Sea Scrolls attest was current in this period – only a 'Hebrew', an 'Israelite', and 'of the seed of Abraham'. Whether Paul means by these allusions simply his affiliation to 'Benjamin' – 'Benjamin' not being *Jewish per se* (meaning, of 'the Tribe' or 'House of Judah') only *Israelite* – or a further manipulation through the common ancestor, 'Bela'' or 'Belah', shared in the Bible by Benjaminites and Edomites (or 'Idumaeans') which would then include 'Herodians' as well, is impossible to say.

Given his emphasis on being of 'the seed of Abraham' and his theological concentration on the same individual, a claim, which, as we shall see, will have particular relevance for those in the area of Edessa (or Haran in Northern Syria, Abraham's city of origin) and probably Adiabene (and presaging the later one on behalf of all 'Arabs' by Muhammad in Islam and which Herodians as 'Edomites' also probably claimed), I would be disposed to respond in the affirmative – that Paul was alluding to wider, so-called 'Benjaminite' affiliations, whatever he meant by these.

Paul goes on to set forth this litany of boasting and suffering for some twenty-five more lines, the vehemence of which cannot fail to leave anyone who reads it speechless. It is in the midst of this that he again takes time out to aver that 'the God and Father our Lord Jesus Christ . . . *knows I do not lie*' (2 Cor. 11:31). Interestingly enough, this comes just before his reference to how

> In Damascus, *the Ethnarch of Aretas the King* was guarding the city of the Damascenes *wishing to arrest me*, but I escaped through a window and *was let down the wall in a basket.* (2 Cor 11:32–33)

As we saw, this is precisely the notice in Acts, when, after his conversion on the road to Damascus, 'he confounded the Jews living' there and, in turn, *the Jews 'plotted together to kill him'*:

> They were *watching the gates both day and night so as to kill him*, but the Disciples, taking him at night, *let him through the wall, lowering him in a basket* (Acts 9:22–25) –

unless there were two such escapes 'down the wall in a basket', which is very doubtful.

Once again, the Acts' historical method should be clear. Aside from covering up embarrassing facts about Paul's visit to Damascus, we have the typical and – in view of later history – completely slanderous transferral of the behaviour of the official of the *Arab King Aretas* to that of 'the Jews' and their 'plots to kill him'. If there were any 'plots' against Paul here, it would, in any event, only have been by *Zealots* and not *Jews per se*. A similar transferral takes place in the restrospective absorption of this 'plotting' theme into the story of Jesus in the Gospels. But here, if the 'Jesus' of Scripture can be proven to be historical, the 'plots' would rather have been on the part of Herodians and their underlings, again not 'Jews' *per se*.

Not only this, but this notice in 2 Corinthians, prior to which he swears by the name of 'the Father of Jesus Christ' he 'is not lying', clearly puts Paul on the side of 'Herod the Tetrarch', his putative relative as we have suggested, on behalf of whom he might even have been on a mission of some kind. Herod, it will be recalled, was quarrelling with Aretas over divorcing the latter's daughter to make way for his remarriage to Herodias. This resulted, as everyone knows, in John the Baptist, who obviously opposed this divorce, losing his head. The reason that Paul and Herod the Tetrarch can be seen as, at the very least, allied in some manner is that both are in a hostile relationship at this point to *the Arab King Aretas*.

Why else would Aretas' men be trying to arrest Paul, the date probably around 35–6 CE? But Josephus goes even further, observing that the Jews imputed Herod Antipas' defeat in battle at Aretas' hands at around this time to what he had done to John the Baptist. There is even the matter in these things of John's activities on the other side of the Jordan. Again, understood correctly, this notice in 2 Corinthians can be seen as extremely incriminating indeed and puts Paul on the side of *the enemies of John the Baptist* and possibly even his murderers. But this should not be surprising, for even Acts has Paul admitting to 'persecuting this Way unto death'.

Still, no one has ever imagined that this might mean John himself (Acts 22:4). But the suspicion that Paul had a hand in the destruction of John the Baptist – if this did occur, as Josephus seems to think, some time around 36 CE – must remain. If not, then not.

Again Paul goes on to make it very clear with whom he is arguing and who his opponents are in the matter of Apostleship and the necessary letters of recommendation accompanying it – high-minded and poetic assaults on the unnecessariness of such unspiritual letters notwithstanding – when he goes on to refer to 'danger from *pseudo-brothers*' (2 Cor. 11:26), which parallels the reference to 'Pseudo-Apostles as Lying workmen disguising themselves as Apostles of Christ' preceding it (2 Cor. 11:13). It is, therefore, 'brothers' of some kind, to whom he is replying.

Ending his response to his lack of credentials by 'boasting in' his own weaknesses and evoking 'the Power of the Christ', he twice admits that 'in this boasting I have become a fool' (12:6–11). But he then contends that he has been forced to do it, because instead of 'commending' him – again the play on letters of recommendation here – his communities have forced him to boast of his achievements and, as the Letter of James or the Qumran documents put it, *lose control over his Tongue.*

With this, he cannot refrain from making one final defiant, if obsequious, boast:

> For in nothing was I behind these *Apostles of the Highest Degree* as well, if *nothing I am.* (12:11)

In referring once more to these 'Super Apostles' in this manner he makes it unmistakably clear that they are the very same interlocutors to whom he referred earlier so venomously as being not only 'Hebrews', but 'Servants of Righteousness', 'Pseudo-Apostles', and 'Servants of Satan' – not to mention his aspersion on 'those reckoned as important' or the 'Pillars', whose 'importance *nothing* conferred', in Galatians 2:6–9. In regard to this last, one should note the repetition of the allusion 'nothing' here in 2 Corinthians too, now applied to 'the Apostles of the Highest Degree'.

Where Paul's use of this non-specific title 'Apostle' is concerned, it is noteworthy that he not only applies it 'to those that were Apostles before me' in Jerusalem in Galatians 1:17, but also to non-Jewish individuals he is on terms of intimate friendship with in Asia, Greece, and Rome. We already saw how in Philippians he calls Epaphroditus, 'his brother, fellow worker, and comrade in arms', an 'Apostle' as well (2:25). At the end of Philippians, as we saw, he even applies the above language of 'an odour of a sweet fragrance, an acceptable sacrifice, well pleasing to God', the Community Rule at Qumran applies to the members of its Community Council ('Twelve from Israel and Three Priests'), to Epaphroditus too. In 2 Corinthians 2:14–15, he applies even this Qumran 'sweet fragrance' and 'odour' language to himself.

In Philippians, this allusion to Epaphroditus is directly followed by the greeting 'to every Holy One ['Saint'] in Christ Jesus' and *especially those in the household of Caesar*' (4:18–22), a reference that would have made the inhabitants at Qumran blanch. As we saw, Epaphroditus was in all likelihood identical with Nero's secretary by the same name, ultimately involved in some peculiar way in the latter's murder or, at least, helping him commit suicide.

It will be recalled that Paul, also, uses this 'household' language in similar and related salutations at the end of Romans. In one of these, he refers to such persons as 'noted among the Apostles, who were in Christ before me' (16:7). This followed his greetings to his 'kinsman Herodion' – 'the *Littlest Herod*' – preceded by that to 'all those of the household of Aristobulus' (Rom. 16:10–11). Again it bears repeating, if Paul is the Herodian we take him for, this latter figure would be none other than Aristobulus, King of Lesser Armenia, the son of Herod of Chalcis, whose wife Salome, according to Gospel presentation, danced at Herod's 'birthday party' for the head of John the Baptist.

Among these '*noted Apostles* who were in Christ before' him, there is also a reference to one 'Junias', to whom Paul refers as well as his 'kinsman' – symbolic or real. This may well have been the 'nephew' Acts refers to, the son of Paul's sister with a house in Jerusalem, who saved Paul from the '*Sicarii*'-style assassins by informing the Roman Captain of the Citadel of the Nazirite-type oaths such cutthroats were taking, 'not to eat or drink till they had killed' Paul. There is no doubt that this individual, named Julius Archelaus, whose father was one Helcias, the Temple Treasurer and a descendant of a crony of Herod by the same name, like Josephus, also ended up *living in Rome*, where Josephus alludes to him as an avid reader of his works.7

There is also a greeting at the end of Romans to one 'Rufus', whom Paul also describes as 'the chosen of the Lord', and whose mother, in some kind of adoptionist manner – like Jesus on the cross to 'the beloved Disciple' – Paul calls his own (16:13). This recalls the individual the Gospel of Mark calls 'Simon of Cyrene', 'the father of Alexander and Rufus', who, 'coming from a field, carried the cross of Jesus' (15:21). The way Mark refers to 'Alexander and Rufus' they are known in some Gentile Christian Community – presumably Rome, from which Mark is often thought to originate.

In Josephus, coincidental or otherwise, there is another 'Rufus', a Roman soldier again, who at the end of the *War* does somewhat parallel things. What he does is make a daring foray, again across Jordan near Machaeros, where John the Baptist met his end, and 'carry off' one of the local Jewish partisans. This man is then crucified before his own town and because of his pitiful cries many surrendered, and those who did not were butchered and the women and children enslaved – this the 'carrying off' and 'cross' themes associated with one 'Rufus' in Josephus.[8]

A second 'Rufus', Josephus speaks of, is the Roman Commander, left in control of Jerusalem after Titus went to Rome for his victory celebrations, who, as Josephus himself opines, *turned Jerusalem into a ploughfield*. One hopes this was not what, using the phraseology of Paul's greeting here in Romans, he was 'chosen by God' to do. All these parallels may simply be coincidental, but they are nevertheless illustrative of the atmosphere of the times and what intercourse with individuals called 'Rufus' *in Rome*, where Mark is thought to have been written, might really have meant.

Coincidentally too, this last-named 'Rufus' is also associated with one 'Simon'. But this Simon, unlike the father of Rufus, 'Simon the Cyrene', who for Mark 'carries the cross for Jesus', is now 'Simon Bar Giora', a leader of the Revolutionaries. Josephus dwells on his capture in detail, revelling in telling us how through Rufus' determination, 'God brought this man to be punished'. As with Niger previously, after Jerusalem fell, Simon was apparently at first taken for dead by his partisans. But, like Niger too, staying 'three days' underground, to their amazement, he suddenly reappeared to his followers, who then 'took him for an apparition'. Again, all these common themes might be sheer coincidence, but Josephus concludes this episode with the pronouncement:

> His wicked actions did not escape the Divine Anger, nor is Justice too weak to punish offenders, but in time overtakes those that break its Laws and inflicts its punishments upon the Evil in a manner even much more severe, inasmuch as they expected to escape it on account of their not being punished immediately.[9]

This 'Simon' was kept by Titus to be featured in his victory parade in Rome, at the end of which he was beheaded.

Again for his part, Josephus follows his account of Simon's capture by Rufus with his descriptions of Titus celebrating his brother Domitian's 'birthday party' in Caesarea on his way to Rome, in which some *twenty-five hundred prisoners* were killed by burning, being eaten alive by animals, and in gladitorial contests. These were followed by similar festivities in continuation of these 'birthday celebrations' in Beirut, as we saw, where like numbers of prisoners were killed in even more impressive ceremonies.

The Testimony in Paul to James as Apostle and Brother of the Lord

Aside from referring to himself repeatedly as 'Apostle', Paul also makes it clear that James was *an Apostle*. All the other early Church accounts we have been considering present James as an Apostle as well. For example, to use the words Eusebius conserves from Hegesippus: 'this Apostle was Holy from his mother's womb'. It will be recalled that analogously, Paul also makes the same claim for himself, that God chose him from his 'mother's womb' and called him 'by His Grace to reveal his son in' him (Gal. 1:15–16).

Paul, of course, confirms James' Apostleship in his first reference to him in Galatians 1:19, which, paralleling Hegesippus above, reads: '*Of the other Apostles*, I saw none, except James the brother of the Lord.' This statement is in itself significant. Not only does he not even mention any other Apostle called 'James' at this point (who would have still been alive at this time), but Paul evinces no embarrassment whatsoever about James being 'the brother of the Lord'. He does not qualify it, as later - theologians do sometimes tortuously, nor try to explain it away by making excuses about it – for instance, that he was the son of a different mother or the son of a different father or the like. Nor does he treat it symbolically, which given his tendency to allegorize he might have done. He just states it as a known fact.

In the second place, as we saw, it contradicts Acts' presentation of events and their sequence. In Galatians, it will be recalled, Paul is answering the accusation that he 'seeks to please men' not God (1:10). This accusation echoes the charge found in the Letter of James, whoever makes himself a 'friend of the world, turns himself into an Enemy of God' (Jas. 4:3). This last, as we saw, in turn is the key epithet applied to Paul in all Judeo-Christian sources.

In Galatians, too, in describing how he 'ravaged the Assembly of God', Paul tells of how 'zealous [*zēlōtēs*] for the Traditions of his Fathers', beyond many of his contemporaries of his 'own race', he was – thereby effectively calling himself 'a Zealot' (1:14). In the process, as we saw as well, he assures everyone he 'does not lie' (1:20). This 'not Lying' contention is particularly relevant not only to the claim of having private 'revelations', but also to how, in undertaking to teach his version of the Good News 'among the Gentiles', he did not stop to discuss it with 'any flesh and blood, nor go up to Jerusalem (to consult) with those that *were Apostles before me*' (1:16). Notice here, again, he does not precisely specify the number of these 'Apostles'.

The import of this is obvious. One should also note his emphasis here on his idea of 'flesh-and-blood' Apostles, which emphasis for him is, of course, inferior to 'spiritual' ones. This accords with the fact that his appointment was 'not from men' and he was not interested in *written credentials* – neither letters written in ink or upon stone – from such persons either, which bring, as he so graphically puts it, only 'death' (2 Cor. 3:6–7).

This also relates to the accusation reflected here of 'trying to please men', thereby turning himself 'into the Enemy of God' – this, because he was not properly credentialled *by men*, either the Jerusalem Assembly, the Twelve, or the Inner Three. James, on the other hand, as per the Letter attributed to his name and in the manner of Abraham, because he (like Abraham) was perfectly 'Righteous', was the true 'Friend' or 'Beloved of God', as presumably all the 'Righteous Ones' were.

It is at this point, too, in Galatians that Paul claims he 'went away into Arabia and again returned to Damascus' – whatever might be meant by 'Arabia' and 'Damascus' here – and did not go up to Jerusalem for another *three years* (1:17–18). It is legitimate to inquire, in regard to this 'return to Damascus', whether it had anything to do with a first visit there at the time of the confrontation between Aretas and Herod Antipas, reflected in 2 Corinthians 11:32, also in conjunction with the affirmation about 'not Lying'.

The Letter of James at this point is attacking the 'Empty Man', who is teaching that Abraham 'was not justified by works' but Faith, which is, of course, what Paul is doing in Romans 4:2–5 and Galatians 3:5–10. Paul, on the other hand, likes to turn the epithet 'Empty' or 'Vain' – notations also found in the key Habakkuk *Pesher* passages describing the 'Mission' or 'Service' of the ideological adversary of the Righteous Teacher, 'the Liar' – against its ideological adversaries, by claiming that their endless nit-picking and debates over the Law of Moses are 'Empty' or 'Vain'.[10] In fact, he counsels his followers to stay apart from such things, which for

1 Corinthians 3:7 above would be 'the Service of death', or, as Revelation puts it, 'the Synagogue of Satan' (2:9).

For Acts, after Paul 'confounded *the Jews who dwelt in Damascus*' by the way he proved that Jesus was 'the Christ' – the same thing James is supposed to have been proving in early Church accounts of the events leading to the riot on the Temple Mount – '*the Jews* plotted to kill him' (9:22–23). Paul then escapes in the 'basket' episode – not from Aretas, as we saw, as in 2 Corinthians 11:32 above, but from 'the Jews', who were 'watching the gates night and day in order to kill him' (Acts 9:22–24). However preposterous, it should be recalled that this 2 Corinthians notice comes in the midst of Paul's attack on the 'Apostles of Surpassing Degree' as 'Pseudo-Apostles' and 'Servants of Satan', amid his bragging about his endless 'toil and service' and protestations about 'not Lying'.

When Paul gets to Jerusalem, he tries to 'join himself to the Disciples' – we have already seen the importance of this 'joining' language in the Dead Sea Scrolls earlier[11] – who are, not surprisingly, all afraid of him and 'don't believe he is a Disciple' (Acts 9:26). Barnabas then brings him 'to the Apostles', where he explains how Paul

> *saw the Lord in the Way,* speaking to him, and he had spoken boldly in Damascus in the Name of Jesus. (Acts 9:27)

Barnabas' description 'to the Apostles' of Paul's vision of the resurrected Jesus, which differs markedly from the way in which Acts earlier described it, is similar to the way Jesus appeared to one 'Cleopas' (Cleophas) and another unnamed person 'along the Way' in the Gospel of Luke and to James in the Gospel of the Hebrews, which we shall discuss in more detail below.

Be this as it may, Acts now records that Paul was with the Apostles 'in their comings and goings in Jerusalem, speaking boldly in the Name of the Lord Jesus'. This is paralleled in Galatians – or rather not paralleled – as follows (Paul speaking in the first person):

> Afterwards I came into the regions of Syria and Cilicia, but *I was not known by face to the Churches [Assemblies] in Christ in Judea,* who had only heard that he, who had formerly persecuted them, was now announcing the Gospel [and] the Faith he had once ravaged, and they were glorifying God in me [now, 'God' in him, not 'his Son' as earlier]. (Gal. 1:21–24)

In addition, leading into this, he also asserts as we have several times remarked,

> After three years I went up to Jerusalem to make Peter's acquaintance, and I remained with him for fifteen days, but *I did not see any of the other Apostles*, except James the brother of the Lord. (Gal. 1:18–20)

Of course, the two accounts here, Galatians and Acts, do not jibe at all. On the contrary, they contradict each other. Being earlier and on the surface anyhow not overwritten, Galatians is always to be preferred.

Acts finishes its version of this episode by having Paul now arguing with 'the Hellenists', blaming them – whoever they were and however illogical – for the problems he was having. It will be remembered that it was arguments between this same group and 'the Hebrews' that supposedly triggered Stephen's stoning two chapters before. It will also be recalled that in 2 Corinthians above, Paul's opponents, the 'Apostles of the Highest Rank' were described as 'Hebrews'. Acts recounts this now as follows:

> And he spoke and reasoned with *the Hellenists, but they took it in mind to put him to death*, but hearing of it, the brothers [whether symbolical or real] brought him down to Caesarea and sent him away to Tarsus. (9:29–30)

None of this, of course, makes any sense whatsoever and all is dissimulation or a garbled overwrite of other more embarrassing material, of which the underlying lines should be clear.

Paul also refers to both James and 'the brothers of the Lord' in 1 Corinthians, the latter in the context of a reference to 'those who would examine' him (9:5). It should immediately be clear that this usage 'brothers of the Lord' is a variation of the way Paul described James as 'the brother of the Lord' in Galatians 1:19. In 1 Corinthians, as we saw, Paul has just finished giving his answer to one of the key strictures of James' prohibitions to overseas communities as Acts presents them, 'things sacrificed to idols', accusing those who made an issue over such matters as 'weak' (1 Cor. 8:7–12).

This allusion to 'weakness', it will be recalled, is the same way he expressed himself with regard to those who 'eat nothing but vegetables' in Romans 14:2. There he used it, not only to apply to people who were vegetarians, but also in the more general sense to apply to those who made issues regarding dietary matters. In Romans, he had just evoked the Righteousness Commandment of 'loving your neighbour as yourself' (13:8–11), called in the Letter of James, 'the Royal Law according to the Scripture' (Jas. 2:8), and directed his followers 'to obey the governing

Authorities' and pay their taxes, since all governing officials are 'Servants of God' (Rom. 13:1–7).

Before going on to claim in the name of 'the Lord Jesus that nothing is unclean in itself' (Rom. 14:15) – this obviously meant to include unclean food as well as other things – Paul calls persons who eat only vegetables 'weak'. In the same vein in a grandiloquent flourish at the end of the 1 Corinthians' polemic against the 'weak consciences' of his opponents, who will not 'recline in an idol temple', nor 'eat things sacrificed to idols' (again, one should compare this with Peter's views in the *Homilies*), Paul states:

> Since *meat causes my brother to stumble* [strictly speaking, the language here is 'scandalize my brother', but Paul actually uses the language of 'stumbling' preceding this in 1 Cor. 8:9], *I will never eat flesh again for ever*, in order not to *cause my brother to stumble*. (8:13)[12]

This crucial language of 'scandalizing' or 'stumbling' is reiterated, following the citation of the all Righteousness Commandment, in the Letter of James in the famous allusion to '*stumbling* over one small point of the Law'.

At the conclusion to this Romans passage condemning vegetarianism and judging a brother's eating habits, Paul speaks, in a play on the whole Jewish Christian notion of 'adoptionist sonship', in terms of being 'received by' or 'adopted by God'. In the process, he repeatedly evokes the word 'standing', again implying he knows the 'Standing One' ideology as well:

> Do not let the one . . . who does not eat judge the one who eats, for God has *adopted him for Himself*. Can you judge another's servant? He *stands or falls* to his own master, and he shall be *made to stand*, for God is able to *make him stand*. (Rom. 14:3–4)

This recapitulates almost precisely the language introducing the 'Three Nets of Belial' in the Damascus Document, that:

> at the completion of the end of these years, there will be *no more joining to the House of Judah*, but each man *will stand on his own watchtower* [the Cairo version of this, which is probably wrong, has this as 'net'].[13]

Going back now to 1 Corinthians and continuing in this vein, as we saw, Paul concludes preparatory to launching into his monologue on 'Communion with the blood of Christ':

> All things are Lawful for me . . . eat everything that is sold in the market place. There is no need to raise questions of conscience [always a euphemism in Paul for the Law]. (1 Cor. 10:23–27)

At this point in 1 Corinthians, directly following his first reference to 'Communion with the blood of Christ' and imprecations to 'flee the worship of idols', to show that he is still talking about James' directives to overseas communities, Paul again raises the issue of 'things sacrificed to an idol', which he now discusses – somewhat disingenuously – in terms of his 'freedom being judged by another's conscience' (1 Cor. 10:28).

His meaning is, however, once again clear. Earlier, in raising this issue in terms of 'weakness', he had already used, as we saw, that same 'building' imagery so dear to the critics of the 'Spouter of Lying' at Qumran (1 Cor. 8:1–12).[14] He had also, it will be recalled, even repeated the very assertion, 'all things are Lawful to me' of 1 Corinthians 10:23, earlier in 6:12 in the midst of his 'food for the belly' and 'being joined to the flesh of a harlot' remarks, introducing the subject of 'fornication' in 1 Corinthians 6:9–6:20.

Now in chapter 9 of 1 Corinthians, preparatory to introducing his remark about 'the brothers of Jesus' travelling around with women – before delivering his excursus on 'being all things to all men' and 'running the race to win' – he asks defiantly, 'am I not free?' (1 Cor. 9:1). He asks this, starting with a direct reference to his own 'Apostleship in the Lord', as a prelude too to his remarks about 'making himself weak to gain those who were weak' or 'outside the Law to gain those outside the Law' (1 Cor. 9:20–22).

At the same time he reveals a defensiveness against charges of profiteering from his 'work' or 'mission' and using, as he puts it, 'the Authority' of his office to enjoy its fruits (by which he clearly means monetary ones) or even, as he so graphically puts it, 'to stop working'. In particular, he enjoys the opportunity to indulge in a little additional wordplay concerning his insistence on 'freedom from the Law', while, at the same time, teaching the Gospel for 'free' (9:18–19). All this, he puts somewhat rhetorically as follows:

> Am I not an Apostle? Am I not free [meaning 'free from the Law' and, by extension, free of Authority]? *Have I not seen Jesus Christ our Lord?* Are you not *my work in the Lord*? (1 Cor. 9:1)

Here, playing on the most well-known doctrine associated with James, 'Justification by works', he characterizes his Community as his 'works'.[15]

In referring to 'seeing Jesus' too here, Paul is not only comparing himself to the other principal Apostles, but seems to mean that whatever visionary experience this involved was in the course of things sufficient to make him an 'Apostle'. We shall see as we proceed that 'seeing Jesus' and the order in which this occurred were very important aspects to Apostleship generally.[16]

Paul now continues in this vein, thus proceeding to make his remark about 'the brothers of the Lord':

> Even if to others I am *not an Apostle* [here Paul certainly recognizes that there are those who do not accept his Apostolic credentials], without doubt I am to you. For you are the seal of my Apostleship in the Lord. (1 Cor. 9:2)

The reference to 'Apostleship in the Lord' parallels James as 'the brother of the Lord'.

As Paul continues, 'My answer to those who would examine me [here one should recall, again, that aside from questions as to his Apostleship, it was the task of 'the *Mebakker*' or 'Overseer' at Qumran to examine individuals accused of various infractions] is this. Do we not have authority to eat and drink?' (1 Cor. 9:3). Here the dietary matter again, now expressed in terms of Apostolic rewards.

> Do we not have authority to take a sister [or] wife around with us, as also the *other Apostles and the brothers of the Lord and Cephas do*? Or is it only Barnabas and I who do not have the authority not to work? Who serves as a soldier at any time at his own expense? (1 Cor. 9:4–6)

He also raises here the biblical injunction: 'You shall not muzzle an ox treading out corn' (Deut. 25:4), which 1 Timothy 5:18 repeats in almost exactly parallel context. Paul does this to again raise the issue of 'wages' or 'toil', as usual taking the opportunity to play yet again with his allegorizing language on 'sowing spiritual things' (1 Cor. 9:9–11).

His reference here to 'the brothers of the Lord' then repeats, as we saw, the ascription in Galatians 1:19, only now it is in the plural. In Galatians it was tied as an eponym to a single brother, James. Here it is meant to include all 'the brothers of Jesus', including James. That these are grouped systematically with and on the same level as 'Apostles' is clear from the context. In Galatians, this was even clearer, as James was actually considered part and parcel of what was meant by 'the other Apostles'.

There can be little doubt that Paul is dealing with the question of 'Authority' here – as he himself avers – his own and others' over him. He puts this in terms of 'the authority to eat and drink', a key component of his rupture with James, but a euphemism, too, in the Gospels and in Paul, used to attack a variety of individuals of the 'Jamesian' mindset generally –

the point being that James and his followers did *not freely eat* and certainly did *not drink*.

The additional motifs being evoked here, of profiteering from one's 'work' (in the sense of 'service' or 'mission') or even being exploited because of such 'work', also clearly bear on the outstanding differences between Paul and James, as leader opposed to foot soldier. In fact, as we saw, Paul enjoys using the language of military life – as he does sports and stadium athletics generally – so much so that one wonders if at some point he had not actually been a soldier himself.

The travelling around with women, as wife or in some other arrangement, would appear to relate to that brother of Jesus, known as 'Judas' or 'Jude' in other sources, sometimes referred to as 'Barnabas' and even, perhaps, 'Judas Barsabas'. But it clearly did not relate to either James or his and Jesus' alleged 'cousin', Simeon bar Cleophas, whom all our sources seem unanimous in identifying as *life-long* Nazirites (likewise, Peter).

No doubt James, anyhow, would have remained in Jerusalem and was never 'on the road', as it were, but, as we have seen, if Hegesippus, Epiphanius, and Jerome are accurate, he probably was a 'life-long virgin'. Epiphanius, it will be recalled, even puts forth a claim to the High Priesthood on his behalf based on his Naziritism and purity, which as far as he, anyhow, was concerned – and probably Jesus and Simeon as well – included absolute sexual continence. We have already seen the relationship of such claims both for the later 'Christian' doctrine of the 'Virgin' Mary, but also for Josephus' picture of the bathing '*Banus*' constantly did 'in cold water'.

This would not necessarily be the case for the other brothers, such as Judas, who, according to the several notices in Hegesippus and Eusebius, had children or grandchildren. The latter, as we just saw above, were examined in Domitian's time and again possibly in Trajan's. In this context, too, one must always keep 'Joseph' or 'Joses Barnabas' in mind. If he were one of these siblings, this would answer a lot of questions about the confusions regarding his prenom and eponym, how suddenly he materialized out of nowhere, and how Paul got into the Movement in the first place – but this is only a query.

The Tangle of Cephas, Clopas, and Simeon bar Cleophas
and Sequentiality in Acts Again

Paul's reference to 'Cephas' in the above citation is, as it is in Galatians 2:9, very interesting as well. Certainly, if Cephas is to be reckoned as an 'Apostle', then 'the brothers of the Lord' in this reference should be too. But here it is possible to entertain doubts as to precisely just who this mysterious 'Cephas', mentioned in conjunction with 'the other Apostles' and 'the brothers of the Lord' and in Galatians as one of the 'Pillars', might be?

Of course, a note about Peter travelling around with women of one kind or another – 'a sister, a wife' as Paul phrases it in 1 Corinthians 9:5 – would always be interesting, especially if, as Paul seems to feel, the accusations imply there was something improper about this, at least where he and Barnabas are concerned – if not others.

We have already explained that it is normally assumed that 'Cephas' is the Aramaic equivalent to 'Peter' or 'Rock' in Greek, and this might very well be the case. In fact, the author of John is very intent that we should understand this to be the case and specifically makes this identification, putting it in Jesus' mouth:

> Jesus said, 'You are Simon the son of Jonah. You shall be called *Cephas*, which means stone.' (1:43)

This is also very much the way John combines the two usages, '*Didymus*', meaning 'Twin' in Greek, and '*Thomas*', meaning 'Twin' in Aramaic, coming up with the name '*Didymus* Thomas' or 'Twin Twin' (11:16, etc.). As we shall see below, this Apostle – sometimes, confusingly, only called 'a Disciple' – was most likely called 'Judas Thomas', as he is in Nag Hammadi and Syriac texts and, as such, very likely identifiable with the third brother of Jesus by that name.

But although 1 Corinthians completely abjures the name 'Peter', using only the designation 'Cephas', as we saw, Galatians mixes the terminologies 'Cephas' and 'Peter' in one and the same context, so that it becomes unclear whether we are talking about the same or two different people. Before looking further at this very important single reference to 'Cephas' as part of the Central Three in Galatians – the rest are all to 'Peter' – it is important to note its linguistic relationship to several other names that appear from time to time.

These include 'Cleophas', in the references in the Gospels 'Cleopas' or 'Clopas', the so-called 'uncle' of Jesus and, according to Hegesippus, the 'brother' of Joseph; Simeon bar Cleophas, his son and James' and Jesus' so-called 'cousin'; and another individual who will also emerge in Gospel Apostle lists – once again, significantly, connected to James – 'James the son of Alphaeus'. In Greek, the difference in spelling between 'Cleophas' and 'Alphaeus' is really only the difference between a *kappa* and an *alpha* – often confused, in any event, in inscriptions on stone – a minuscule difference.

It should be appreciated that Simeon bar Cleophas, in addition to being the witness to the stoning of James in Epiphanius and, as we shall attempt to show, James' putative companion in Jesus' first post-resurrection appearance 'along the way' to Emmaus in the Gospel of Luke, was the successor to James 'in the Chair at Jerusalem', the second of the so-called '*Desposyni*', that is, those of the family of Jesus.[17] Simeon was reputed to have gone on functioning well into the 90s, if not into the next century under Trajan, when, according to Hegesippus via Eusebius, he was martyred in the same manner as Jesus.[18] But the important thing in all these reports is that Simeon bar Cleophas is the successor to James in Palestine, the second successor to Jesus, just as 'Simon Peter' or 'Cephas' – called 'Simeon' in Acts 15:14 – is considered to be the successor to Jesus in *Rome*.

Parallels such as this should not lightly be ignored, since they bear on Jesus' family members as 'Apostles'. It will emerge that the connections of Simeon bar Cleophas to Jesus are probably much closer than originally conceived. Additionally, if the Dead Sea Scrolls have any relationship to 'the Jerusalem Church' or 'Assembly' in Palestine, then the materials about the life and death of the Righteous Teacher, paralleling identifiable concepts and events in the life and person of James – particularly as regards his destruction or death – would have had to have been composed under the stewardship of a successor like Simeon bar Cleophas.

It is important also to note that, though Jerusalem would no longer have been the centre of activities of such a surviving Community as this, Simeon's 'Community' *had to exist somewhere*. Those areas denoted as the wilderness 'camps' at Qumran to a certain extent went on functioning – at least, this is the evidence provided by sites, such as Ein Feshka a little more than a kilometre south of the actual ruins of the fortress or settlement at Qumran (itself in the Jericho area) – certainly until the events culminating in the Bar Kochba Uprising (132–6 CE).[19] Bar Kochba's partisans were hiding out in areas like Qumran and places they designated in known correspondence from this period as 'the *Mezad ha-Hassidin*' – 'the Fortress of the Pious Ones' (some would identify '*Hassid*' with 'Essene', but this is not a provable point).[20]

Another linguistic variation of the name 'Cephas' is 'Caiaphas', famous for his role in Gospel pictures of the trial of Jesus. Recently a sarcophagus bearing either this name or 'Cephas' itself, written in cursive Hebrew – there is very little difference between the two in cursive writing – was found in the environs of Jerusalem.[21] Though both the survival of this linguistic relic from the past and the close relationship between the two names are remarkable, for our purposes, it is sufficient to consider Paul's reference to James in Galatians, also connected to Cephas, and his last reference to James in 1 Corinthians 15, again connected to Cephas.

Let us take the witness to James in Galatians first. This unequivocal reference to James' position as Leader of the early Church, also, includes the identification of him, as noted, as an 'Apostle' (Gal. 1:19). It is followed by Paul's note about his next visit to Jerusalem after an absence abroad of some 'fourteen years', taking Barnabas and Titus with him (Galatians 2:1-2 – this would be some time in the early 50s, depending on when one dates Paul's previous activities in Jerusalem and at Damascus); his protests over those 'spying on the freedom [he] enjoys in Christ Jesus' and circumcision, 'so that they might enslave' him, that is, subject him to Jewish Law (Gal. 2:4); and contemptuous reference to the Jerusalem Leadership as 'those esteemed as Pillars' and 'reputed to be something', not that their importance makes any difference as far as he is concerned. Nor did it 'confer anything', since 'God did not take note of' or 'make distinctions between the persons of men' (Gal. 2:6–9).

This reference to 'making no distinctions between men' is, as we saw, the mirror reversal of what is said in all these early Church accounts about James and, incredibly as it may seem, in Josephus about James' destroyer, the High Priest Ananus. To a certain extent it is also at the root of Peter's tablecloth vision in Acts, where he learns he can eat forbidden foods, to call no man and nothing unclean, and that 'in truth God makes no distinctions between men' (Acts 10:34). Peter, thus, becomes 'Paulinized' with a vengeance.

We have already shown how Peter's vision in Acts inadvertently demonstrates that Jesus never resolved the problem of 'table fellowship with Gentiles' during his lifetime, because if Jesus had, why would Peter, his purported closest associate, need a Pauline vision to confirm it? Still, it does have the force of demonstrating that whatever Jesus did teach, he did not teach this.

When compared with James' vision in the Temple on Passover of 'the Son of Man standing on the right hand of the Great Power about to come on the clouds' with the Heavenly Host, Peter's vision is even more instructive. As it will be recalled, for Peter, too, 'the Heavens opened', but rather than the Messiah coming with the Heavenly Host, what they reveal is 'a vessel being let down on the earth like a giant sheet, bound on its four corners' with all kinds of 'wild beasts and crawling things' upon it (10:11–12). The Heavenly Voice, rather than calling out 'this is My only begotten son', as in the Gospels – or some variation thereof – now tells Peter, 'Kill and eat!', then adding, 'What God has made clean, let no man call unclean' (Acts 10:13–15). Of course, on this Heavenly tablecloth are all kinds of animals forbidden Jews to eat – even carrion, the essence, it would appear, of the fourth category, 'strangled things' in James' prohibitions to overseas communities.

As we have seen, this permission is repeated *three times*, just as Peter in the Gospels is pictured as denying Jesus three times on the eve of his crucifixion and in the *Talmud*, the Rabbinic partisans of Herod Agrippa (I or II, it is immaterial) cry out to him three times in the Temple, when he comes to read the Deuteronomic King Law ('You shall not put a foreigner over you who is not your brother') on Tabernacles, 'You are our brother. You are our brother. You are our brother!'

The first incidence of these Heavenly voices out of the sky that I have been able to find, at least in Greek literature if not Hebrew, occurs in Sophocles' *Philoctetes*. There Odysseus and Achilles' son are attempting to convince Philoctetes – like Paul in Acts, also abandoned on a desert island and bitten by a snake – to desert his island cave and come to Troy, since the Trojans could be defeated only with the weapons he possesses. At first Philoctetes refuses, since he is so bitter at their earlier treatment of him. Only when a voice cries out from Heaven to him (in this case, Hercules'), telling him that, despite this, it is his destiny, does he agree. These kinds of Heavenly voices would, therefore, have been familiar to a literate, Greek-speaking audience.[22]

As Acts continues, instead of being part of the Heavenly Host coming in Glory with the Messiah to render Judgement on the Just and Unjust alike, as in the report of James' vision in Hegesippus and the War Scroll from Qumran; the 'Angel of God' or 'Holy Angel' now comes to the 'Righteous and God-Fearing' Roman Centurion Cornelius to fetch him and another 'pious' Roman soldier from Caesarea who attends him, and sends the latter to Peter's house (Acts 10:7 and 22). What fun all this must have been for those writing it!

Thereupon, Peter and 'some of the brothers from Jaffa' inform Cornelius and those of his household of the Heavenly vision Peter has just had, wherein God has just taught him, not only 'to consider no man profane or unclean'; but, repeating the now Paulinized injunction, 'God is not a respecter of persons, but in every Nation [Paul's *Ethnos* again] he that is a God-Fearer and works Righteousness is acceptable to Him' (Acts 10:34–35). Here is the point about God not 'deferring to' or 'taking note' of persons in Paul's Galatians above, with which we began this discussion.

These are, of course, as we have on several occasions pointed out, the very words used to describe James in all early Church sources. In these, they mean that James did not defer to persons of importance, particularly 'the Rich', treating Rich and Poor equally. But here they are used, in a further extension of Paul's attacks on the Leadership of the Jerusalem Assembly, to confirm his Gentile Mission as well. In a further play on James' praying and the 'works' associated with his name, it is now the 'prayer and charitable works' of the 'Pious' Roman Centurion that are characterized as 'being remembered before God' (Acts 10:31)!

While the sentiments are undeniably noble, they do not correspond to the socio-political situation in Palestine in this period at all. Here, they are directly followed by Peter now making the accusation *to the Roman Centurion and his household* that, 'in the country of the Jews and in Jerusalem', they put Jesus – now designated not as 'the Nazoraean' but as coming 'from Nazareth' – 'to death by hanging [him] on a tree' (10:39). 'Hanging upon a tree' and the 'curse' associated with it in Deuteronomy 21:22–23 is precisely the language Paul uses in Galatians 3:13 to reverse the arguments of his interlocutors against them – particularly those Leaders of the Jerusalem Church like James with whom he is arguing – who, using the Law, 'curse' him for breaking it.

For his part, as explained, Paul turns this allusion instead into the basis of his theological understanding of the significance of Christ's salvationary death for all mankind. As he puts it, 'Christ, having become a curse for us' by allowing himself 'to be hung upon a tree', 'redeemed us from the curse of the Law!'[23] The mastery of Platonic dialectic here is patent.

The focus of the narrator's interest in Acts is clearly revealed at this point. Those accompanying Peter here and ostensibly opposing the gist of his speech to Cornelius' household – who ultimately will turn out to be representative of all 'Gentiles' (*Ethnē*) – are, as in parallel passages in Galatians, specifically designated 'of the circumcision' (Acts 10:45). In Galatians, too, it will be recalled, these are identified with the omnipresent 'some' who 'came from James' (2:8 and 2:12).

It will also be recalled that in the episode of Paul circumcising Timothy, this was triggered by the 'Some, having come down from Judea, were teaching the brothers, "Unless you are circumcised according to the custom of Moses, you cannot be saved"' (Acts 15:1–2). Not only should the connections of this, we have pointed out, with the terminology '*Sicarii*' be appreciated, but this, in turn, provokes the so-called 'Jerusalem Council', as a result of which, Judas and Silas come down with Paul and Barnabas, with James' directives to overseas communities contained in a letter addressed to 'those in Antioch and Syria and Cilicia, brothers from among the Nations' (again '*Ethnē*' – Acts 15:23).

Since Antioch is in Syria, it is curious that it is mentioned separately. We have already suggested that this 'Antioch' is actually to be identified with the one further East, known also as 'Edessa', where an early 'Christian' Community was really known to have existed. Furthermore, we have already suggested as well that this 'letter' can be identified with that known in Qumran studies as '*MMT*' and what I have entitled in other contexts as a 'Letter(s) on Works Reckoned as Righteousness' or 'Some of our Words concerning the *Torah* of God'/'Some Works of the Law we Reckon as Justifying You'.[24] It is at this point, too, after the break with Barnabas, that Paul has Timothy – whose mother was a 'Jewess, but whose father was a Greek', the typical Herodian mix as we have seen – circumcised (Acts 16:1–3).

In the sequence represented by his vision, Peter is also pictured as proclaiming:

> To him, all the Prophets bear witness, that through his *Name* [meaning Jesus'] everyone that believes on him receives *remission of sins*. (10:43)

But earlier we saw that it is James' pronunciation of the forbidden 'Name' of God in the Holy of Holies, praying on behalf of the people for the *remission of their sins*, making what was in effect a *Yom Kippur*-style atonement on their behalf, that leads to his death by stoning. It is this which Hegesippus avers – applying the Isaiah 3:10 passage, 'Let us take away the Just One for he is abhorrent to us' to his death – that 'the Prophets foretold' concerning him.[25] Once again, we have themes from James' life reappearing in that of Jesus.

On the other hand, 'the Prophets' never did prophesy that the Messiah, or any other man for that matter, even a Supernatural One, would have the power to 'remit' or bring about the 'remission of sins'. This provides another good example of Acts' working method – and for that matter Paul's – such as it is.

For good measure, 'those of the circumcision', represented here as all the believers accompanying Peter,

> were amazed that *the gift of the Holy Spirit* [Paul's doctrine of 'Grace', as opposed to the 'Righteousness of works' or 'of the Law'] was being *poured out on the Gentiles as well.* (Acts 10:45)[26]

When Peter returns to report to 'the Apostles and brothers' in Jerusalem, Acts now portrays 'those of the circumcision arguing with him', just as, according to Paul in Galatians, they did with him. Both texts use 'those of the circumcision', only now Paul's 'Antioch' milieu is transformed into a Caesarean or Jerusalem one (Acts 10:45–11:2).

It is significant that this episode ends, as Acts puts it – after Peter's report that 'indeed God gave also repentance unto life to the Gentiles' – those in the Jerusalem Assembly now *'glorified God'* (Acts 11:18). Once again, this specifically echoes the episode about James' death in Hegesippus above, where those who heard his proclamation in the Temple of the Son of Man 'sitting on the right hand of the Great Power about to come on the clouds of Heaven', *'glorified in the testimony of James'*. Again the linguistic correspondences are precise. This is not to mention the 'Vainglory' mentioned in the Habakkuk *Pesher's* description of the 'Congregation' or 'Assembly' being erected by 'the Spouter of Lying'.

The whole matter of Peter's 'tablecloth' vision and its aftermath again ends in Acts with this tell-tale allusion to 'certain ones', now identified as 'Cypriots and Cyrenians', coming to Antioch to speak to the omnipresent 'Hellenists' again, though what such 'Hellenists' might have been doing at this point in 'Antioch' is never explained (11:20). There would clearly seem to be some inverse linguistic procedure operating around 'Hellenists', just as with 'Cananaean' or 'Cananite' and 'Zealot' in the Gospels. Again, here too, 'Hellenist' may be a replacement for 'Zealot' and/or 'Nazirite'. The same is true for 'Cypriot' and 'Cyrenian' – the former, anyhow, probably having to do with 'Samaritan'.

Not only does this episode again involve 'Barnabas being sent through to Antioch' (11:22–25), but these kinds of references to 'Cypriots or Cyrenians', as we have seen, are always worrisome. This is now followed up by *another episode*, where, following the note about Peter describing 'the Prophets' foretelling to Jesus and the parallel note in Hegesippus about 'the Prophets declaring' about James, 'prophets' are now said to 'come down from Jerusalem to Antioch' (11:27). This will give rise to the reference to Agabus *predicting the Famine* and the whole matter of Paul's Famine-relief activities again – contradicting Paul's claims about a *fourteen-year* absence in Galatians.

Still, it should be observed at this point that 'Barnabas' here parallels the notices in Syriac sources about 'Thaddaeus' – 'also called Lebbaeus' in some recensions of Matthew and 'Judas the son' or 'brother of James' in Luke – and 'Judas Thomas' being sent down to Agbarus' Kingdom, the capital of which was Edessa – as we shall see 'Antioch of the Osrhoeans'. Since in our view 'Antioch' in Acts is *Antioch of the Edessenes*, then the fact that this episode is used to describe this Community as the place where 'the Disciples were first called Christians' (11:26), is clearly of no mean import and, in fact, entirely credible.

The Central Three, the Poor, and Circumcision Again in Galatians

Where sequentiality is concerned, Acts moves from 'Agabus'' prediction of the Famine (46–8 CE) to Saul's and Barnabas' Famine-relief mission to Judea – about which it tells us nothing – on to the death of 'James *the brother of John*' (12:2), Peter's arrest and subsequent flight, and the introduction of James (12:17). As we have seen, its notice at this point about 'prophets coming down from Jerusalem to Antioch' parallels that in Galatians about the 'some coming from James', who were also 'of the circumcision'. These come down 'from Jerusalem to Antioch', triggering the confrontation there over the issue of table fellowship with Gentiles, which for Acts also involves circumcision and culminates in its presentation of the 'Jerusalem Conference'.

In Josephus the sequentiality is rather different. It goes from his lengthy description of the conversion of Queen Helen of Adiabene and her sons, Izates and Monobazus – the key issue again here being 'circumcision' – by one 'Ananias' (the name of the individual who met Paul in Damascus in Acts after his Damascus-road vision) and an unnamed other. The unnamed other (in our view Paul) teaches that circumcision is *unnecessary for Salvation*.

This is immediately followed by Queen Helen's dispatch of her representatives to buy grain in *Egypt and Cyprus* – in our view this is in part the root of all these 'Cypriot' and 'Cyrenian' denotations in Acts – also to relieve the Famine, followed by the beheading of Theudas and the crucifixion of James and Simon the two sons of Judas the Galilean. In fact, in another variation of these denotations – all part and parcel of Acts' basic dissembling – even Josephus' note at this point in his narrative about 'the Census of Cyrenius' here is precisely recapitulated in Luke's spelling of 'Cyrenians' in these various notices.[27]

For Paul, too, the key issue in the Galatians account, to some extent paralleling these things, is 'circumcision' – along with that of 'table fellowship' connected to it. In turn, 'circumcision' is very much tied to the matter of Apostleship, for directly after averring the Jamesian 'God does not accept the person of men' (Gal. 2:6) – again, the point with which we started this discussion – Paul sets out his understanding of Peter's 'Apostleship of the circumcision' in contrast to his own 'of the uncircumcision' or, as he also speaks about it, 'to the Gentiles' ('*Ethnē*' again). Curiously, in these several references in Galatians, Paul uses only the appellative 'Peter' not 'Cephas' (2:7–8). But immediately following these, he makes the reference to the Central Three or 'those reputed to be Pillars', identifying them as 'James and Cephas and John' in that order and by that nomenclature – for the first and only time in this letter introducing the name 'Cephas' (Gal. 2:9).

Whatever one might wish to make of this, Paul now goes on to aver that he shook hands with 'these Pillars' in agreement that he and Barnabas were to go 'to the Gentiles', while 'they to the circumcision' (2:9). It is for this reason that all these references to 'circumcision' in Acts, and their contrapositive in the matter of so-called 'Hellenists' – like 'Cananaeans' or 'Canaanites' elsewhere, as we have suggested, probably a substitute for '*Zealots*' and/or '*Sicarii*' – are so important, for they camouflage or, as it were, confuse the situation surrounding Apostleship generally – in particular the Apostleship of these 'Three' and Paul's own – and the central issue seemingly impinging on these things, *circumcision*.

For Paul, the only qualification he thinks he must observe with regard to his 'Mission' or 'Apostleship' is 'to be sure to remember *the Poor*', which, as he observes, was the very thing he 'was most intent on *doing*' (2:10). However, it is not clear here if his view of the conditions of his Apostleship was the point of view of the Central Three as well – it probably wasn't. The meaning of 'the Poor' here has been variously debated, but there can be little doubt that in some sense it refers to the pseudonym for James' Community in Jerusalem, from which the term 'Ebionites' has been derived. But this term, as we have been at pains to point out, also comprises one of the principal terms of self-designation in the literature at Qumran, particularly in the Habakkuk and Psalm 37 *Pesher*s, where it is specifically applied to the followers of the Righteous Teacher *in Jerusalem*.[28]

The matter and meaning of the allusion to 'the Poor' aside, in his testimony to James the Just being one of the Central Three – for this is obviously what he is saying – Paul again shows no embarrassment or reticence about James' exalted stature in the early Church, other than he is not impressed by it except when he finds it useful to be. Nor can there be any doubt that this is James the Leader of the early Church, 'the Bishop of Bishops', or, as Qumran would put it, 'the *Mebakker*' or 'Overseer'. Nor does Paul mention any other James. There is only James 'the brother of the Lord' or, if one prefers, 'the brother of Jesus', despite the fact that Gospels, downplaying him, refer to him rather derogatorily as James 'the Less' (Mark 15:40) or 'James the son of Alphaeus' (Mark 3:18 and pars.).

For Paul, James is patently either the equal of or superior to 'Cephas and John' – 'James' specifically designated as coming first in this triumverate – and if Cephas and John are to be reckoned among the Apostles, which most take as a given and as clearly implied by the application of the title 'Apostleship of the circumcision' to Peter (Gal. 2:8), then *so is James*. He was probably even greater than they. In other words, he was, as it were, the first among equals or 'the brother of the Lord', the principal 'Pillar', which indeed his other cognomen, 'the Just' or 'Righteous One', seems to imply.

As we have seen, Paul does not mention any 'James the *brother of John*' in other letters either – nor do the other New Testament letters, so apart from these testimonies in the Gospels and Acts we can have no idea who this other James was, if indeed he existed, which is doubtful. In the letters in the New Testament the only James ever mentioned is James 'the Just'. In Gospel lists and in the description of the witnesses to the crucifixion there is a 'James the Less' or 'the Littler James' – a designation clearly aimed at belittling him and contrasting him and contrast him with 'the Great James' – variously called 'James the brother of John', 'the son of Zebedee' (also known as '*Boanerges*' in the Gospel of Mark, 'the sons of Thunder' or 'Thunder Twins' – 3:17). This 'James the Less' is, also, to be identified with another James in Apostle lists called 'James the son of Alphaeus' (Matt. 10:3 and pars.), whom we shall show is identical to the James before us here. As should be clear, the *real Great James* is the one before us, the one Mark calls in an obvious attempt to reduce his status, *James the Less*.

But is *'Cephas'*, too, to be reckoned among the Apostles and is he the same as the individual usually called *'Peter'*? All other references in Galatians, as we have seen, are to 'Peter' not 'Cephas', but here Paul lists 'James, *Cephas*, and John' as the Central Triad of Pillar Apostles. The question cannot be answered on the basis of the data available to us, any more than the question of who Peter was, Gospel fantasizing about 'fishermen' on the Sea of Galilee notwithstanding. As we have seen, some early Church accounts definitely assume the two are separate or that there are two Cephases, listing 'Cephas' also among 'the Seventy'. But given what we have before us here in Galatians and the reference in the Gospel of John indicating that Simon was to be called 'Cephas' – even interpreted there to mean 'Stone' in Greek, thus, 'Peter' (1:42) – one can assume that for the purposes of discussion he is.

It is perhaps, also, proper to point out that, except for what we shall see to be the interpolation of 'the Twelve' in 1 Corinthians 15:5 – the point here being there were only 'Eleven' at the time – Paul *never* does number the Apostles. In fact, neither he nor anyone else at this juncture seems to have any idea of a limitation in the number of Apostles to a fixed number 'Twelve'. Acts, though, is very interested in this scenario in attempting to explain the problem of the election of a successor in early Church history – for it, as we have seen, a replacement for someone called 'Judas *Iscariot*' (most likely 'Judas the *Sicarios*') not for Jesus.

So are the Gospels, except for John. Though mentioning 'the Twelve', again in the context of negative allusion to Judas *Iscariot* – now called ('the son' or 'brother') 'of Simon *Iscariot* . . . one of the Twelve' (6:67–71) – and not unrelatedly, '*Didymus* Thomas one of the Twelve' (that is, 'Judas Thomas' – 20:24), John never actually enumerates them, probably because of problems over Jesus' brothers and family as well. Nor does John ever call these individuals 'Apostles' only 'Disciples'. For their part, the Synoptic Gospels both describe and enumerate the Twelve, enumerations we shall presently consider in attempting to develop more information about the person of James and the other 'brothers'.

James, *Cephas*, and John and Jesus' Transfiguration before the Central Three in the Gospels

Nor does Galatians speak about a core of 'Twelve' Central Apostles; rather only 'Apostles' in general. But it does, as we have just seen, enumerate the Central Three of 'James and *Cephas* and John', all persons Paul seems to know in some way or with whom he has had dealings. These are real people, not inventions or, as elsewhere, fantastic overlays.

For Acts, it will be recalled, someone called 'Apollos' (18:24) – also mentioned by Paul in 1 Corinthians 1:12–4:6 – is identified as preaching 'John's baptism' in Asia Minor. This, it implies, was a 'water baptism' only (compare with Paul in 1 Corinthians 3:6: 'I planted, Apollos *watered*, but God caused to grow'), the Ephesians never even having heard 'that there was such a thing as the Holy Spirit' (Acts 19:2).

The 'John' being referred to here is normally taken as 'John of Ephesus' and the 'John' in these various enumerations of the Central Three, whether 'the brother of James', 'the son of Zebedee', or some other. But, as we have argued, 'the baptism of repentance' attributed to Apollos here (Acts 19:4), as opposed to Paul's new 'Holy Spirit Baptism', would make more sense as a 'water baptism' if it had to do with the original John *the Baptist*, not another 'John'.

For his part, 'Cephas' – though not 'Peter' – is also mentioned, as we saw, twice more at the end of 1 Corinthians, both in connection in some way with James or 'the brothers of the Lord' (9:5 and 15:5). He is mentioned two additional times in the context of these references to Paul and Apollos at the beginning of 1 Corinthians as well, where baptism, 'the Holy Spirit', and 'building up' the 'building' are being discussed (1:12 and 3:22). It is worth remarking that in the context of these notices, too, Paul first mentions having 'baptized those of the household of Stephen' (1 Cor. 1:16). As already remarked, for the scheme of early Church history in Acts, the significance of this notice should be clear.

Further to the background of choosing the Central Three in the Synoptic Gospels, their 'appointment' is introduced by the presentation of Simon Peter as answering the question of Jesus as to 'Who do men say the Son of Man is?', with the familiar riposte, 'the Christ' or 'the Christ of God'. Matthew adds the tell-tale 'Son of the living God' we encountered in Jesus' trial scenarios above (Matt. 16:13–16 and pars.).

But when Peter then objects to Jesus' prediction of his own coming death and resurrection, Jesus is pictured as rebuking him. This rebuke Jesus frames in terms of worrying about 'the *things of men*, not the *things of God*', uttering the now famous 'Get thee behind me Satan' (Matt. 16:21–23 and pars.) – this, after he has just finished, in Matthew anyhow, designating Peter as 'the Rock' of his Church and giving him 'the keys to the Kingdom' (16:17–20)!

But Jesus' rebuke of Peter, here, again calls to mind the one in the Letter to James to its interlocutor Paul about the '*Friend of men* turning himself into *the Enemy of God*' and Paul's apparent response at the beginning of Galatians, that anyone preaching a Gospel different from his own should 'be cursed' (Gal 1:8–9). It will be recalled that for emphasis Paul repeats this twice and, seemingly satisfied with his own intolerant rhetoric, asks:

> So now, whom am I trying *to please, man or God*? Would you say it is *men's approval* I am looking for? If I still wanted that I should not be what I am, a *Servant of Christ* [note here, too, the possible play on 'Christ' as 'Man' or 'Primal Adam']. (Gal. 1:10)

Then bearing on his Apostleship and lack of either direct appointment or letters of appointment from James, he concludes:

> The fact is, brothers, and I want you to realize this, the Good News I preached is not a human message that I was *given by men*. (Gal. 1:11)

We had already suspected this, but here Paul makes it incontestably clear: 'It is something I learned only through *a revelation [apocalypseōs] of Jesus Christ*' (1:12).

So, for Paul, the Gospel he teaches is a direct revelation from the figure he calls 'Christ' or 'Christ Jesus', his Supernatural Redeemer figure or Guardian Angel, with whom, as it were, he is in direct communication in Heaven. This is a perfectly valid visionary experience for Paul, which should not be discounted. But it has nothing whatever to do with Jesus or his brother James, or any doctrines that can be attributed to them – and this, we submit, was also the attitude of Paul's detractors then.

In Matthew Jesus' rebuke of Peter also includes calling him 'a stumbling block' (16:23), language we have already seen to be charged with significance in the mutual polemics of the Letters of Paul and James. At this point too, leading directly into the introduction of 'the Central Three', the Synoptics hark back to Matthew's earlier allusion to 'the Son of Man', all then specifically evoking the vision attributed to James in all early Church sources of:

The Son of Man coming in the Glory of his Father with his Angels, and he shall then render unto every man according to his works (Matt. 16:27 and pars.),

but now rather attributing it to Jesus.

Over and over again we have encountered this vision, the essence of James' proclamation in the Temple when he was asked what was 'the Door to Jesus' or, in effect, who 'Jesus' was. We have also seen how this proclamation corresponds with the exegesis of the War Scroll at Qumran of the Messianic 'Star Prophecy' and its evocation of the Messiah coming with the Heavenly Host on the clouds 'to rain Judgement on all that grows' on earth – but here the correspondence is even closer, as 'the Holy Angels' of the War Scroll are being specifically evoked.

In 2 Corinthians 12:1–7, it will be recalled, Paul describes knowing a man 'fourteen years before' who had also been 'caught away to Paradise' – and known 'the magnificence of [Heavenly] revelations' (*apocalypseōn* again) and 'visions', 'hearing unutterable words'. Curiously the time frame here agrees with that in Galatians between his *two* visits to see James. In some sense, then, if this individual was James, it is possible to conceive that his visionary experience, which probably really did occur, made it more possible for Paul's more extended concept to find an even wider acceptance.

Of course, the Righteousness of 'works', Jesus is now pictured as speaking about in the Synoptics, runs directly counter to Pauline 'Faith' and 'Grace' doctrines, but it does *precisely reflect* the Qumran position on these matters, as it does the 'Jamesian' one generally (as it will Islam in succession to these).

The next statement Jesus is pictured as making in the Synoptics:

Verily, I say unto you, there are some of those *standing* here, who shall in no wise *taste of death* until they have *seen the Son of Man coming in his Kingdom* [Matthew 16:28; for Mark 9:1, which adds the words '*with Power*', this usage is '*standing by*']

is, once again, clearly emphasizing the 'Standing One' ideology of the early Christian Ebionites and Elchasaites (Mark even encompassing the idea of 'Power', that is, 'the Hidden' or 'Great Power'). It precisely parallels, too, the key definition of 'the Sons of Zadok' at Qumran. It will be recalled that 'the Sons of Zadok' were defined at a critical point in the Damascus Document, leading into the extended exposition of the 'Three Nets of Belial', as those 'who would *stand at the End of Time*' and 'justify the Righteous and condemn the Wicked'. Both 'the Son of Man coming with Power' above and 'the Sons of Zadok' here (not to mention the 'Standing One' ideology), are, of course, eschatological definitions involving the 'Last Times'/'Last Things'.

The idea, too, of '*seeing* the Son of Man', namely 'Jesus', also parallels that of '*seeing* His Salvation' (*Yeshu'ato*) at the end of the expository section of the Damascus Document we have noted above. Here in the Synoptics the allusion to such 'seeing' serves to introduce the appointment of 'Peter and James and John, *his brother*'. It will also include the imagery of miraculous 'whitening', already encountered in the Pseudoclementine *Recognitions* previously, in the account of how James' Community visited the tombs of two brothers outside Jericho, which miraculously 'whitened of themselves every year', thereby escaping the 'fury' of the Enemy Paul, who was passing through Jericho with letters from the High Priest in Jerusalem on his way to Damascus. James, it will be recalled, had been carried from Jerusalem to Jericho by the entire Community after the 'Enemy' Paul's assault on him in the Temple, in which he was injured, breaking one of or both his legs, but not killed.

As this miraculous 'whitening' imagery develops now in the Synoptics, it encompasses a usage that, just as in the instance of the 'little' Zacchaeus and Jesus passing through Jericho on his way to Jerusalem in the reverse manner of Paul passing through Jericho on his way to Damascus in the Pseudoclementine *Recognitions*, will tie it to both this same *Recognitions* and early Church accounts of the death of James, in the most forceful manner conceivable.

In this episode about the appointment of the Central Three in the Synoptics, Jesus takes 'Peter [not Cephas] and James and John his brother' (Jesus' or James'?) and, like Moses before him, 'went up on a high mountain to pray'. There, he 'was transfigured' before the Three 'and his face shone as the sun and his garments became effulgent white' (Matt. 17:1-3 and pars.). The Central Three also see him as conversing with Moses and Elijah, though how they can recognize these two individuals is never explained. For Luke, Jesus is 'in Glory', as are Moses and Elijah (9:31-32). But aside from this emphasis on the 'splendid effulgence' or 'miraculous whitening of the tombs', to be discussed further below (not to mention the 'clothes' theme once again); the main thrust of the episode is the revelation, by another of these omnipresent 'Heavenly voices', this time, not insignificantly, 'out of a cloud', that Jesus was God's Son.[29]

The familiar words of this revelation, quoted here in Matthew, 'This is my beloved son. In him I am well pleased' (17:5 – Mark and Luke vary this to 'hear you him'), are the same as those used at the beginning of the Synoptic Gospels to describe Jesus' baptism by John, when 'the Heavens were rent asunder and he saw the Spirit descending on him in the form of a dove' (Mark 1:10 and pars. – in the War Scroll from Qumran, it will be recalled, the Heavenly Host and 'the Spirits', coming on the clouds, descend like Judgemental 'rain').[30] In this picture of John baptizing Jesus, 'the voice out of Heaven' again is said to cry out, 'This is my beloved Son, in him I am well pleased' (Matt. 3:17 and pars.).

Whatever the significance of this reproduction, John the Baptist plays a role in the Transfiguration scene too (however indirect), since in all the Synoptics, he is identified with Elijah, a point Jesus himself is pictured as making to the Central Three immediately thereafter on the way down the mountain (Matt. 17:13 and Mark 9:13).[31] In this conversation with them, too, Jesus again picks up this motif of 'the Son of Man' and, by means of it, identifies himself as the Divine 'Son' – 'Man', it will be recalled, being identified with 'the First Man' or 'Primal Adam' (not to mention in Aramaic sources, that 'Enosh' or 'Man' is *John*) – and Jesus, even in Paul, being 'the Last Adam' or 'the Second Man, the Lord out of Heaven' (1 Cor. 15:45–47).

It should be clear that all these themes are being recapitulated here. If we now slightly transpose the way the Central Three are being described in this episode to not 'Peter and James and John *his brother*' but 'Peter and James *his brother* and John', as recorded by Paul in Galatians, we would, of course, achieve a more perfect fit, that is, James here being 'the brother of Jesus', not John being 'the brother of James'. Transpositions of this type, as already described, occur elsewhere in Acts or the Gospels, particularly in the presentation of James and John, 'the two sons of Zebedee', whoever such a 'Zebedee' might have been.

Discrepancies of this kind with how Paul enumerates the Central Three in Galatians, if taken at face value, become irreconcilable. But, we have already explained, in cases such as this Paul is to be taken as primary; the Gospels secondary. This would be the proper way out of the present conundrum as well, finally to take the Central Three as James the brother of Jesus, Cephas, and John and either to ignore or to discard Gospel refurbishments for the fictions they are.

John's Baptism in the Gospel of the Ebionites and Adoptionist Sonship

There are several other interesting aspects to this episode. In the first place, once more, we have imagery of 'cloud' or 'clouds' coupled with a voice or vision coming out of or related to them. On the face of it, the motif is evoked in order to compare Jesus with Moses, pictured in Exodus as going up the mountain into the clouds to receive his revelation too (Exod. 24:18). Yet again, however, what is basic here is that these revelations are all associated with allusion to the following motifs: 'the Heaven opening' or 'being torn asunder', 'voices from Heaven', 'the Son of Man', 'the Heavenly Host coming on the clouds of Heaven', and 'Glory' or 'glorying'.

In Jesus' Transfiguration before the Central Three here in the Synoptics, once again, there is the theme of 'the Son of Man' but he is not 'coming on the clouds of Heaven'. Rather, he is identified by 'a voice crying out from the cloud' as the '*Son*'. This directly connects up with the ideology preceding it, where Peter identifies Jesus as 'the Christ of God' or 'the Christ, *the Son of the living God*', which is itself followed by the promise to 'those *standing by*' that they will not die until they see '*the Son of Man* coming in his Kingdom' (Matthew 16:28 – in Mark, as we saw, this is '*seeing* the Kingdom of God'; in Luke, 'the Kingdom of God come with Power'). In all three, this promise, too, is preceded by yet another variation of these words, 'for *the Son of Man* will come in *the Glory of his Father with his Holy Angels*' (Matt. 16:27 and Mark 8:8). For Luke this is '*the Son of Man* will come in *his own Glory and the Glory of the Father and of the Holy Angels*' (Luke 9:26).

As should be clear, all these kinds of visions or revelations are typologically related to each other. In turn, they are typologically related to the proclamation attributed to James in early Church sources of 'the Son of Man sitting on the right hand of Power about to come on the clouds of Heaven' (again, note the 'Power' imagery), usually accompanied by the picture of the crowds 'glorying' in the Temple at Passover. In the Pseudoclementine *Recognitions*, anyhow, this episode takes place in the early 40s, at which point, the flight of James with the whole Community to the Jericho area ensues. Here James goes on functioning, sending out Peter on his first missionary journey.

The words that the 'voice out of Heaven' cries out in the John baptismal scene above anticipate, as we saw, Matthew's version of the words the 'voice out of the cloud' cries out to the Central Three on the mountain with Jesus, Moses, and Elijah. The two talking with Jesus on the mountain, whose 'clothing' is 'so white and dazzling', not only parallel the miraculous 'whitening of the tombs of the two brothers' in this Pseudoclementine account, but will anticipate the Angel(s) we shall encounter in the empty-tomb scenarios below, who likewise will be 'white and glowing'.

But for early commentators, such as Justin Martyr in the second century and the Ebionite Gospel reported by Epiphanius in the fourth, the words spoken by the Heavenly voice at Jesus' baptism are significantly different:

> This is my only begotten Son [as we shall see, the words Josephus applies to Queen Helen of Adiabene's favourite son, 'Izas' or 'Izates' – in Epiphanius' *Ebionite Gospel*, 'beloved Son']; *at this moment have I begotten you*.[32]

This brings the vision more in line with Jewish Christian and, for that matter, Qumran notions of Divine Sonship. These are normally referred to by scholars as 'adoptionist'. This means that at the moment one achieves Perfect 'Righteousness', completing this with the necessary purification of the body of uncleannesses by water – therefore the daily bathing – one becomes like unto a 'Son of God'. This notion of *plural* Divine Sonship, as we saw earlier, is widespread in the Gospels and the Qumran Scrolls, and in later Christian 'heresies'.[33]

These are the words used, as well, in the Letter to the Hebrews, which contains, not only the terminology of the 'New Covenant' (Heb. 8:8 and 9:15), but also that of a 'Righteous Priesthood', which then approaches the idea of 'Perfection' (Heb. 7:3–26 and 9:9–15). In describing this 'Priesthood', which it refers to as 'a Priesthood forever after the order of Melchizedek' and, in connection with which, it evokes this 'Perfection' ideology (6:20 and 7:10), it characterizes such 'a Priest' as being 'like a Son of God' (7:3). This, of course, is precisely how we have expounded the actual meaning of the terminology 'Son of Zadok' at Qumran.

But in the preface to its first allusion to this 'Priesthood' in 5:5 and the notions of 'Perfect Righteousness' associated with it, Hebrews also evokes the very same scriptural passage just encountered above in Justin Martyr's version of John's baptism of Jesus and likewise in the Gospel of the Ebionites: 'You are my Son; today I have begotten you.' As far as the author of the Letter to the Hebrews is concerned, this is a version of Psalm 2:7. But, like so many others in the New Testament, this is an extremely militant and nationalist psalm, full of Messianic imagery, including the 'Throne' of 'the Lord in Heaven' also evoked in Hebrews

1:8 and 8:1, 'the Sceptre', and even the Messiah himself, giving him 'the Nations for his inheritance' (Ps. 2:2–9). Hebrews again evokes 'the Throne' and 'the Sceptre of Righteousness' in its very first lines, adding 'the effulgence of His Glory' and repeating for the second time, the words 'You are my son; today I have begotten you' (Heb. 1:3–8)

As it well understands, its allusion to 'a Priest forever after the order of Melchizedek' is actually an allusion from another psalm, Psalm 110, in connection with which the important usages, 'being Holy from the womb', 'Strength', 'Power', and 'judging the Nations' are also evoked (110:2–5). But, of course, we have already seen how this imagery of 'being Holy from the womb' is used with regard to James – not to mention by the author of the Hymns at Qumran. Not only is this psalm, too, completely militant in the style of Qumran, but it begins with another allusion dear to Hebrews and obviously paraphrased in these proclamations attributed to James in the Temple above, 'Sit at My right hand and I will make your enemies your footstool' (Ps. 110:1).

This citation, too, is quoted word for word in these first lines of Hebrews (1:13). The first part of it, making one's 'enemies a footstool for his feet', is again repeated, in conjunction with allusion to 'being made Perfect in perpetual Holiness' and allusion to the John-like 'washing the body with pure water', in Hebrews 10:13–22. The implications of all these allusions should be obvious. The 'making one's enemies a footstool' imagery from this Psalm, together with the 'Sceptre' and 'Throne', are also favourites of Messianic symbolism at Qumran, most particularly, in the Damascus Document and the newly discovered expansion of Genesis Professor Wise and myself recently published, where they have a militant cast the equal of these original contexts in Psalms.[34]

In this last-mentioned 'Genesis Florilegium', they are combined with what is usually referred to as 'the *Shiloh* Prophecy' (Gen. 49:11), namely,

> The Sceptre shall not depart from Judah, nor the Staff [*Mehokkek*] from between his feet, until the *Shiloh* comes.

This 'Staff' imagery is also part and parcel of extensive Messianic exposition on Numbers 21:18 in the Damascus Document, where it is ultimately combined with interpretation of 'the Sceptre' that is 'to rule the world' of the 'Star Prophecy' from Numbers 24:17.[35] These various allusions to 'feet' and Psalm 110's related 'footstool' imagery are also played upon to some degree in Ebionite notions of the 'Standing One', 'ninety-six miles high'. Therefore, his 'shoes' or 'shoe-latchet', in effect, according to

Gospel variations of Jesus' baptism, John would be unworthy – to say nothing of being unable – 'to loose' or 'carry' (Matt. 3:11 and pars.)

The Brightness of Jesus' Clothes at the Transfiguration and Hegesippus' Reference to the 'Fuller's Club'

But even more important and crucial, in connecting the picture of these visions of Jesus' Transfiguration to the attack on James in the Temple, his proclamation there of 'the Son of Man coming on the clouds of Heaven', and his flight to the Jericho 'camps', is the imagery being used in the Synoptics to describe Jesus' resplendence at his Transfiguration. As already suggested, by using 'his face shone as the sun', Matthew 17:2 is drawing the correspondence with Moses talking to God on Mount Sinai, where there and later in the Tent of Meeting, his face also glowed after his encounter with God. As we saw, Paul scoffingly dismisses this imagery, in 2 Corinthians 3:7–18, asserting that Moses veiled himself because he didn't wish the Children of Israel to know the light – which he also repeatedly refers to as 'the Glory' – of the Law had expired.

Though this note about Jesus' shining 'face' is missing from Mark and Luke, all three insist that 'his clothing' became 'white as the light' (Matt. 17:2), 'white and effulgent' (Luke 9:29), or, as Mark, which is most complete, characterizes it,

> His *clothes* became *glistening*, exceedingly *white as snow*, so as *no fuller on earth can whiten them*. (9:3)

But here, once again, we have the all-important allusion to the 'fuller' or 'laundryman' of the early Church accounts – going back at least as far as Clement and Hegesippus – of the death of James, now totally transformed into an entirely new form where we would never have expected to find it.

The occurrence of this allusion here, where we have already encountered other allusions possibly related to materials such as the 'clothing' and the 'whitening' imagery, is, to say the least, surprising. This is the only allusion to 'laundryman' in the whole New Testament. Indirectly it ties all these imageries together in a most curious manner – namely, the 'laundryman' or 'fuller' motif in all early Church accounts of the death of James (which appears gratuitously to intrude here), along with the effulgence of Jesus' 'garments' or 'clothes' and the Pseudoclementines' miraculous 'whitening' of the brothers' tombs.

This motif of the 'clothes' or 'garments' will become even more insistent as we proceed. We have already seen it in the aftermath of *Stephen's stoning*, when those stoning him, for some unfathomable reason, 'deposit their clothes at the feet of a young man called 'Saul' (as already remarked, these should have been *Stephen's clothes*), or, in Jerome's 'Hebrew Gospel', when Jesus 'hands *his clothes* to the Servant of the High Priest'. This is not to mention the 'linen clothes' James wore, as did all 'Essene'/'Masbuthaean' daily bathers in these accounts of the special linen 'girdles' or bathing clothes they wore, which made such a big impression on all observers.[36] Now we see it here in the matter of Jesus' 'white and effulgent' clothing upon his Transfiguration. Presently we shall see it anew in the 'empty tomb' scenarios on the matter, again too, of the 'graveclothes'. White clothing would also have had a specific meaning to the audience of these accounts, namely that of being a member of the Community of all 'the Righteous' washed 'white' of their sins.

But these passages about Jesus' 'clothing', becoming 'white as light' and 'effulgent', are seemingly also incorporating the vocabulary of the 'miraculous whitening' of the adepts' tombs (here too the matter of the 'tomb' in the related stories of the faces 'like lightning' and 'the clothing as white as snow' of the 'Angel' or 'Angels' in Jesus' empty tomb), found in the Pseudoclementine *Recognitions* account of the flight by the injured James, together with the 'five thousand', to the Jericho area. These sepulchres, as we saw, also miraculously

> whitened of themselves every year, because of which miracle, the fury of many against us was restrained, because they perceived that our brothers were *remembered before God*. (1.71)

At Qumran, not only is this 'whitening' imagery, playing off the word 'Lebanon' in underlying biblical texts – 'Lebanon', as we saw, meaning 'white' in Hebrew – tied to the 'white clothes' worn by the Community Council and/or the Priests in the Temple; but this word 'fury' is the very one the Habakkuk *Pesher* used to describe the 'hot anger', with which, 'the Wicked Priest pursued the Righteous Teacher'. This language of 'Wrath' and 'Fury' is then played upon to produce various combinations and metaphorical reversals having to do with 'the Cup', Divine Vengeance, 'the Anger of God', and even the 'venom' of the Establishment and 'the wine' of its ways.

That the blessed dead should be 'remembered before God', as alluded to in connection with the 'miraculous whitening' of the brothers' tombs here in the *Recognitions*, is, in addition, also a fixture of Jewish *Yom*

Kippur observances even to this day. So too is the colour white – and, for instance, not wearing leather shoes – symbolizing such atoning purity. Problems surrounding such observances are alluded to in the passages surrounding the death of the Righteous Teacher in the Habakkuk *Pesher* and are, as we have seen, intrinsic in traditions about James' death as well, as they are in the accounts of his High Priestly atonement activities in the Holy of Holies on the Temple Mount also probably on *Yom Kippur*.

But these two episodes – firstly, the flight of James in the Pseudo-clementine *Recognitions*, culminating with 'miraculous whitening' of these tombs, the visit to which saves James and his followers from the Enemy Paul, and secondly, the story of the 'laundryman' or 'fuller beating in James' brains with a laundryman's club' – are now, not only connected, but seemingly combined in these rather more fantastic Gospel presentations of Jesus transfiguring himself before the core Apostles (Peter, James, and John 'his brother').

Such combinations, or variations on a theme, will be no more surprising than those we shall presently encounter surrounding Belial's 'nets' and the various adumbrations of the 'casting down' allusions related to it. In Mark, these 'whitening' and 'fuller' themes surrounding James' death, appear to become the single allusion, noted above, about how 'his clothes turned white as snow, so white that *no fuller on earth could have whitened them*'. But, in addition, these have been both preceded and followed by or even compounded with evocation of 'the Son of Man' and/or his 'coming' – the essence basically of James' proclamation in the Temple.

The result, then, of looking into these parallel testimonies about the Central Three in both Galatians and the Synoptics – the Gospel of John, dispensing with the problem altogether, never mentions any James at all, nor 'Apostles', only 'Disciples', in particular, 'the beloved Disciple' (taken to be John, but possibly even James himself) – leads us to a surprising result, which, if true, could not have been anticipated. If credible, it ties together our sources into a single whole and confirms, in the most round-about manner conceivable, that our hypothesis about the method of composition of these well-informed – if tendentious – Hellenistic romances, we call 'Gospels', is correct.

Pursuing the themes of the proclamation by James of the coming of the Son of Man, the attack on James in the Temple, and his death, has led us to results that we would not otherwise have imagined. In addition, however, as with the Gospel stories about Jesus being 'tempted by the Devil in the wilderness' or to 'throw himself down from the Pinnacle of the Temple', these stories about the flight of James, the 'miraculous whitening' of the 'brothers'' tombs, and the beating in of James' skull with a laundryman's club, must be older than or have preceded, at least, Mark's account of Jesus' 'Transfiguration' in its present form. The reason we say 'must' here is that these traditions about James and even their conflation must have preceded their reflection in the Gospels. This is, admittedly, a surprising conclusion, but the fair observer, upon reflection, will be forced, at least, to acknowledge its logic.

This means that either the Gospels are fairly late or the traditions about James, even in the conflated form in which we sometimes see them reflected in the Gospels, were actually circulating quite early. Either this or one has to take as historical Gospel narratives of a Temptation of Jesus by 'the Devil' or Jesus' Transfiguration before Moses, Elijah, and at least one 'Apostle' who probably never existed – at any rate not either as 'the brother of John' or 'the brother of James'. Stories such as these in the Gospels are patently even *more* mythological than traditions about James, which themselves have already undergone a certain amount of amalgamation and bowdlerization.

The 'white as snow' simile involved in these portraits of the Transfiguration of Jesus' 'clothes' brings us around too, however circuitously, to Daniel's original vision of 'the Ancient of Days, sitting upon the Throne, *whose raiment was white as snow*' (Dan. 7:9), not to mention the all-important proclamation directly following this of 'one like a Son of Man coming on the clouds of Heaven'. For Daniel, it was upon him that 'Sovereignty, Glory, and Kingship' would be conferred, 'whose Sovereignty would be an Eternal Sovereignty which would never pass away' (7:13–14). Again, the range and imagination of these ancient artificers and amalgamators are as breathtaking as they are impressive.

20

James the First to See Jesus

The Reversal of 'Hating the Men of the Pit' into 'Hating One's Family'

The reference to James at the end of 1 Corinthians is also connected to the twin topics of Apostleship and post-resurrection sightings of Jesus. Here we come directly to the matter of the existence or non-existence of 'the Twelve', at least from a Pauline perspective.

Before pursuing these issues, it should be pointed out that Paul, in the background to his first reference to the Central Three – the Historical Three of 'James the brother of the Lord, *Cephas*, and John' not the surreal one – even calls them 'the Apostleship of the circumcision'. Claiming that 'these Pillars' gave them (himself and Barnabas) 'their hand in agreement', he interprets this to mean that, just as he and Barnabas would go 'to the Gentiles', they (the Central Three and others) would go 'to the circumcision' (Gal. 2:7–8). The historical understanding of this was that there were or at least had been 'Twelve Tribes' of Israel and, therefore, the symbolical thrust of the idea of there being 'Twelve Apostles' in the first place was that, theoretically, they should go to the Twelve Tribes of Israel.

This is the thrust, too, of similar numerology at Qumran, for instance, that of the Community Rule, where the Community Council is distinctly enumerated as being composed of 'Twelve Men and Three Priests'.[1] The question of whether these 'Three Priests' – symbolical or real – were to be from among the 'Twelve' or in addition to them, as we saw, has never been fully resolved, though the implication of other documents leans towards the latter. For our purposes, however, it doesn't particularly matter, since most of these kinds of allusions are esoteric.

To turn momentarily to the Community Rule at Qumran, the same Column Eight, where this Inner Twelve and Inner Three are mentioned, also contains the first elucidation of the 'making a Straight Way in the wilderness' Prophecy from Isaiah 40:3, applied to John the Baptist's activities in the Gospels. In addition to interpreting this Prophecy in terms of 'separating from the habitation of the Men of Unrighteousness and going into the wilderness', this column also contains allusions to such Christian notions as making atonement by 'doing Righteousness [note the 'Jamesian' emphasis here] and suffering the sorrows of affliction' and, as we saw, 'Precious Cornerstone' imagery.

Using the kind of esoteric language that in Paul borders on allegorization, it describes the Community Council as the 'Holy Temple of Israel and the 'Assembly' or 'Church of the Holy of Holies for Aaron' and the 'Perfection of the Way' it embodies, in terms of 'a pleasing odour of Righteousness and an agreeable sacrifice', upon which 'to establish the Holy Spirit according to Eternal Truth'.[2] There are so many parallels of this kind in the Qumran corpus to early Christian notions, particularly in the Pauline corpus, that it would be impossible to catalogue them all. However, it is important to remark that the Qumran documents are less cosmopolitan and not antinomian at all, but rather always nationalist or xenophobic. They are also less prolix and more terse, but the themes and vocabulary are recognizably the same, albeit for the most part usually inverted.

Aside from these parallel imageries of spiritualized 'Temple', 'sacrifice', and 'atonement' in these all-important Columns Eight–Nine of the Community Rule, the orientation is always the opposite of Christianity as we know it, that is, Pauline or Overseas Christianity. For it, 'the Way', in the 'prepare in the wilderness the Way of the Lord' citation, is 'the study of the Law as commanded by the hand of Moses', not the Pauline descent of the Holy Spirit upon Jesus. According to this interpretation, 'the Penitents' in the wilderness are 'to separate from the Men of the Pit' – a play on our 'Nazirite' terminology again – for whom 'Everlasting hatred [not love] in a spirit of secrecy' is reserved.

They are instructed to '*do all* that is required' – again, it is important to remark the emphasis on 'doing' throughout these documents, an emphasis we call 'Jamesian' and the root of the word 'works' in Hebrew – to be as one '*zealous for the Law, whose time will be the Day of Vengeance*'. This is the second interpretation of the 'make a straight Way in the wilderness' prooftext from Isaiah 40:3 in the Community Rule at Qumran. That this is 'Zealot' needs no further elucidation. One can't get much more militant. But it is also combined with this esoteric, spiritualized imagery. For instance, one can even detect a basis for the atonement James is said to have made in early Church sources, in the description in this column of the Community Council as 'atoning for the guilt of sin and rebellious transgression and be a pleasing sacrifice for the land without the flesh of holocausts and the fat of sacrifice'.³

As we signalled, aside from being described as 'a pleasing sacrifice' and 'atoning for the Land', these members of the Community Council participate in some manner – just as Peter and to some extent 'John and James the sons of Zebedee' do in the Gospels – in an eschatological 'Judgement on Evil' or a type of Last Judgement.⁴ We just saw that in Matthew, after recognizing Jesus as 'the Christ and the Son of the Living God' and, in turn, being designated 'the Rock' upon which the Community will be built (imagery extant in this section of the Community Rule); Peter is given the keys to the Kingdom to 'bind on earth what will be bound in Heaven' and vice versa (Matt. 16:16–20) – and people still speak in terms of Peter being 'at the Gate' even today.

This notion of 'going to the circumcision', as described by Paul, is incorporated in the Gospel of Matthew as Jesus sending out 'his Twelve Disciples' with instructions not to go the 'way of the Gentiles, nor enter the cities of the Samaritans', but to go rather only to 'the House of Israel' (Matt. 10:1–5, 'House of Israel' here paralleling 'House of Judah' in the Dead Sea Scrolls above).⁵ Mark and Luke abjure the use of 'Disciples' – terminology also preferred in John – referring only to 'the Twelve' (Mark 6:7 and Luke 9:1). Matthew proceeds immediately to list 'the Twelve Apostles' (10:2–4). Jesus' instructions to the 'Apostles' here includes the 'casting out' language (*ekballō*), in this case, 'unclean spirits' or 'demons' – note the play on the Qumran language of 'uncleanness' here – so much a part of the presentation of the deaths of both Stephen and James, and this variation on the 'Belial'/'Balaam' language circle will even be used to characterize the activities of the Apostles in other ways.

These passages even contain veiled attacks on someone as important as Peter. In addition to details like those in the previous chapter in Matthew, that 'many tax collectors and Sinners came and *dined* with Jesus and his Disciples' (9:10), statements like 'Whosoever denies me before men, him also will I deny before my Father in Heaven' (10:33) have direct relevance to Peter, pictured in the Gospels, as we have already seen – among other such shortcomings – as having *denied Jesus three times* on his death night (Matt. 26:69–75). This, of course, is part and parcel of the retrospective polemics of these Paulinized and Hellenized, Gentile Christian Gospels as we have them.

They even contain explicit attacks on the secrecy of groups, such as those at Qumran and baptizing groups generally. We have just heard the stricture, 'Everlasting hatred for the Men of the Pit *in a Spirit of secrecy*', in the Community Rule's interpretation of the 'making a straight Way in the wilderness' citation – applied to John the Baptist in Christian Scripture. This is also the picture in the Pseudoclementines, which, as we saw, at the beginning of the *Homilies* present James, after receiving Peter's epistle, as requiring the Elders to swear 'not to communicate in any way, either by writing' or 'by giving them to a writer', to any unworthy person anything that they have learned or will be teaching.[6]

For Matthew, both this 'hatred for the Men of the Pit' and this 'secrecy' are reversed in the phraseology now taught by its 'Jesus', 'You shall be *hated by all* on account of *my Name*' and 'there is *nothing secret* that shall not be revealed, *nothing hidden* that shall not be made known' (10:22 and 26). This last even goes on to parody the 'Light' versus 'Dark' imagery, so prevalent in the Scrolls and elsewhere, proclaiming 'What I tell you in *the Dark*, speak in *the Light* and what is whispered in your ear, proclaim it *on the rooftops*' (Peter at Jaffa in Acts? – 10:27).

In the *Homilies*, the Epistle of Peter to James, giving rise to this response by James, even uses the Qumran language of 'the Pit', referring to how false teaching can drag people down 'into the Pit of Destruction' (1.3). As we saw, Peter is pictured as using the following language to characterize this:

> Some among the Gentiles have rejected my preaching about the Law, attaching themselves to a certain Lawless and trifling preaching of the Man who is *my Enemy* [this can either be thought of as applying to Paul or, as the case may be, Simon *Magus*]. (1.2)

In Matthew's charges by Jesus to *his Apostles*, however, this now becomes, instead of 'the man who is my Enemy': 'a man's Enemies shall be those of his own household' (10:36).

The polemical inversion here is patent. That this is an attack *on the brothers and family of Jesus* needs no further elucidation. The parallel to this in Luke now adds the Qumran language of 'a spirit of hatred against the Men of the Pit', also turning it against the family of Jesus instead:

> If a man comes to me and does not *hate his own father and mother and wife and children and brothers and sisters . . . he cannot be my Disciple.* (14:26)

This attack in Luke comes after the picture of Jesus having just attacked *dining with brothers, kinsmen, and the Rich*, rather than *the Poor, the blind, and the lame* (14:12–21), the last two, anyhow, it will be recalled, being some of the classes of persons forbidden to enter the Temple according to Temple Scroll parameters at Qumran. In turn, it is preceded by evocation of 'the Last being First and the First being Last' and aspersions on Jerusalem for 'killing the Prophets and *stoning them that are sent to her*', followed by allusion to 'the resurrection of the Righteous' (13:30–14:14)![7]

Nothing could better illustrate the manner in which the Gospels proceed than this, reversing themes found, for instance, in the Pseudo-clementines and at Qumran, turning them into but thinly disguised attacks on the family of Jesus and the Jerusalem Leadership (in the *Homilies*, 'the Elders' of 'the Jerusalem Church'). In Matthew these come directly after Jesus begins his charges to his 'Apostles', paralleling the opposite genre of imprecations James makes to 'the Elders' of the Community after receiving Peter's letter. So awe-inspiring was James in their sight that, as we saw, these Elders are pictured as 'being in an agony of terror' and calming down only after he speaks about how those 'keeping this Covenant' and 'living Piously' have 'a part with the Holy Ones' (1.4–5).

That versions of this material, along with documents with the vehemence of those at Qumran, were circulating in some manner among 'Opposition' Groups *before* the present documents we now call 'the Gospels' achieved their final form begins to emerge as the inevitable conclusion. Only the additional 'Truly, you shall not have gone through the cities of Israel till the Son of Man be come' in Matthew's version of Jesus' admonitions to *his* Apostles (with regard to which one should note the tell-tale motif of the 'coming of the Son of Man' again – 10:23), has an authentic 'Jamesian' ring to it.

Here, Matthew does appear, to some extent, to be picking up Galatians' delineation of the Apostles 'to the circumcision' and those to the 'uncircumcision', 'the Twelve' being but a further adumbration of this – perhaps reflecting Qumran usage as well. The reference to '*Cephas*' as one of the Central Three in Galatians is perhaps even more important than this delineation of 'the Twelve'. One should, as signalled, always keep open the possibility that this may be Simeon bar Cleophas, the claims of whom we shall delineate further below.

In regard to 'Simon' and 'Simeon' being slightly different names in Hebrew, one should note Luke's presentation of the 'Jerusalem Council' in Acts – ending in James sending out his rulings about 'Gentiles . . . keeping themselves from the pollutions of idols, fornication, strangled things, and blood' in the form of an Epistle again (15:20). Just before sending his emissaries, Judas and Silas, with this letter 'to Antioch' and right after Paul and Barnabas report about the 'miracles and wonders God had done by them among the Gentiles', James refers to how Peter, like himself, *opposes those who believed 'it was necessary to circumcise themselves and to keep the Law'* (Acts 15:5). This is, not only totally at odds with the picture in the Pseudoclementines, but also Paul's Letters – particularly Galatians.

At this point, as we have seen, James refers to Peter as 'Simeon', which may or may not be a redactional error (15:14). Coming at this juncture in the narrative, after Peter has already supposedly fled the country after escaping from prison and causing the death of his gaolers three chapters before, it is highly suspect. One should also, again, note that this language of 'keeping' is to be found in the Letter of James (2:8–10) and is the fundamental definition of the terminology 'the Sons of Zadok' at Qumran.

Here in the *Homilies'* picture of James' imprecations to the Elders of the Community, it comes amidst allusion as well to 'not Lying', 'being a part of the Holy Ones', not 'breaking' this oath to secrecy, and that *'doing anything contrary* to' this Covenant will 'make the universe hostile to' the supplicant (1:4). But this is the language we have just encountered in Matthew 15:22 as part of Jesus' instructions to his Disciples: 'and you shall be hated by all on account of my Name', albeit with inverted signification.

Turning back to Paul in 1 Corinthians: having just discussed the 'gift of languages' (12:30–14:39) – an ability Qumran also ascribes to 'the *Mebakker*'[8] – and the Church being both 'the members' of the body of Christ and the Temple (3:16–17 and 12:14–27); Paul now goes on to further explain his understanding of Apostleship in general, his place in the scheme of these Apostles (the number no longer being limited obviously to 'Twelve'), and inadvertently the post-resurrection sightings of Jesus, which have been rightly appreciated as having to do with one's rank or place in this early Church hierarchy (1 Cor. 15:1–20).

Notice, even here, how Paul ends all this not only with yet another reference to 'Adam' and 'Man' ('as all die in Adam, so shall all be made alive in Christ'), but also how Christ will 'put all his Enemies under his feet' – finally reversing and spiritualizing these again with the conclusion that the 'Last Enemy being nullified is Death' (1 Cor. 15:21–26).

The references to 'Tongues' or 'languages' – in Hebrew the two words are the same, a point Paul in 1 Corinthians 12:20–14:49 understands and plays on – are also important. Paul understands that this expression can also mean foreign languages and plays on this throughout these passages, wherein he also uses the language of 'building up', 'lips', 'zeal', and 'the secrets of his heart being made known' (14:21–39). This is exactly the language of the Damascus Document *vis-à-vis* the examination of postulants carried out by 'the *Mebakker*', as it is of the Qumran Hymns generally.[9]

Not only was this 'speaking in Tongues' one of the accoutrements of the Gentile Mission, that is, the mission by 'the Seventy' to what were considered by Jews to be 'the Seventy Nations' of mankind with their various 'Tongues', but it is also, as we have seen, played on in the Letter of James in the use of 'Tongue' imagery there – applied to the man who could not keep control over his 'Tongue', thereby 'turning himself into an Enemy of God'. These passages from James also use the imagery of 'members of the body' with inverted signification to the way Paul likes to use it here in 1 Corinthians and in Romans.[10]

Post-Resurrection Appearances to *Cephas* or *Peter* in 1 Corinthians or the Gospels

Having covered all these things including 'Communion with the blood of Christ', as Paul now explains it leading up to his last mention of James, the Gospel (in Greek, literally 'Glad Tidings'), which he announced to his communities, was more or less what he himself

> received, that Christ died for our sins according to the Scriptures and that he was buried, and that he was raised on the third day according to the Scriptures. (1 Cor. 15:4)

In connection with the proclamation of this 'Gospel', he uses the words, 'in which you also stand' and 'are being saved', and the phrase, 'unless you believed in vain'. As Paul put this:

> But, brothers, I reveal to you the Glad Tidings which I preached, which you also received, *in which you also stand*, by which also you are *being saved* – if you hold fast [the exact words encountered in parallel portions of the Damascus Document] to the Word which I preached to you (unless you *believed in vain*) – for I delivered to you in the first place what I also received . . . (1 Cor. 15:1–3).

All of these expressions exactly parallel vocabulary in use at Qumran, the 'standing' in particular, directly preceding the 'Three Nets of Belial' condemnations in the Damascus Document. Relating to the elaboration of 'the Sons of Zadok', this, it will be recalled, had to do with there being 'no more joining to the House of Judah, but each man *standing on* his own net' or 'watchtower'. Either of these would be equivalent to what Paul is intending by 'Word' or 'Gospel' here. This is not to mention the relationship of this word 'standing' generally to 'the *Standing One*' doctrine of the Ebionites and other Jamesian groups, we have already signalled above, and elaborations of the doctrine of Resurrection generally.

The last, 'believing in vain', Paul goes on to use repeatedly in this chapter, particularly as regards this same Resurrection and Christ having been 'raised from the dead' (15:14–17). Both this and the allusion to 'saved' parallels materials in the Habakkuk *Pesher*, in particular, the doctrines of the individual it designates as 'the Spouter of Lying'.[11] In describing these last, the Habakkuk *Pesher* uses the same set of words, 'Empty' and 'Vain' or 'Worthless', to describe what 'the Man of Lying' is 'building' and the 'vainglory' of his 'mission' or 'service'.

One should also appreciate that in the course of these references to 'speaking in Tongues', 'building up the Assembly', 'being zealous [*zēlōtai*] of Spirits', and 'being zealous to prophesy', Paul twice parodies the 'Zealot' terminology, reversing normal Palestinian recourse to this term and connecting it now instead to his idea of 'prophesying' and 'speaking in Tongues'. As he puts it, one should not forbid such things, as most 'Zealots for the Law', like James would undoubtedly have done, but 'be zealous' for them (1 Cor. 14:11 and 39).

In mentioning these two points about Christ 'being resurrected and dying for our sins', Paul is clearly signalling something of what must have been extremely early doctrine in Palestine. The *Resurrection* part of this is from Hosea 6:1–2, but there it occurs in the plural, in the sense of a *plural* restoration:

> After two days He will restore us to life, the third day will He raise us up to live before Him.

The interesting allusions that follow in Hosea to both 'Ephraim' and 'Judah' – widespread, as we have seen, in the usage at Qumran – the 'coming of rain', and the Prophets 'slaying them by the words' of their mouth (Hos. 6:3–5) are noteworthy as well. This last, for instance, as it becomes transformed in Gospel usage and transmitted, as it turns out, into the Koran, appears to develop into, the Jews 'killed all the Prophets'![12]

The notion of 'dying for our sins' harks back to Isaiah 53:10–12, a typical scriptural '*Zaddik*' passage, where it is applied to 'justifying the Many' or making them 'Righteous' and 'Justification' generally. Not only are these the basis of the presentation of the crucifixion of Jesus in

Christianity, they are also typical Qumran doctrines and very likely provide the basis for the organizational framework found there of the rank and file of the Community – called 'the Many' – being 'made Righteous' or 'Justified' by 'the Righteous Teacher'.[13]

To this, now, Paul finally attaches his list of post-resurrection appearances by Jesus. In modern times, this has always been thought of as containing an interpolation.[14] It probably does, since it is composed of two distinct parts, one differing from and more or less contradicting the other. The only real question has been which part contains the fabrication and which does not: the first, having to do with 'Cephas and the Twelve' or the second, referring to 'James then all the Apostles'. These are clearly parallel denotations and cannot really be seen as separate, but they do contradict one another.

The second, of course, is less doctrinaire and more general, but those of an orthodox and unquestioning mindset have always assumed the first to be authentic and the more accurate; and the second, the interpolation, representing a sinister attempt by the 'Jewish Christian' supporters of James not only to insinuate him into Apostle lists, but to gain equal status for him *with the Apostles*. It was impossible for persons of this outlook even to conceive of another scenario. We, of course, favour the second as the authentic history and consider the more orthodox to be the interpolation.

The passage in its interpolated form is already known at the end of the fourth century to Jerome, who in his usual meticulousness is anxious to cite materials from Jewish Christian sources giving support to this testimony of an appearance by Jesus – even a *first* appearance – to James, although not perhaps completely grasping the import of what he was reporting. The passage from 1 Corinthians 15:5–9, in which Paul seems to be claiming he was taught this in addition to the two doctrines mentioned above, reads as follows:

> and that he appeared to Cephas, then to the Twelve [the orthodox part]. Then he appeared to over five hundred brothers at once, most of whom now still remain, but *some have also fallen asleep*. Then he appeared to James, then to all the Apostles [indeterminate – the unorthodox part], and last of all, as if to one born out of term [literally, 'an abortion'] he appeared also to me. For I am *the least of the Apostles,* who is *not fit to be called an Apostle,* because I persecuted the Church ['Assembly'] of God [at Qumran, the very same usage occurs in the Second Column of the Community Rule, also in regard to one's rank within the Community].[15] But by the Grace of God, I am what I am, and His Grace towards me has not been Empty [or 'void'].

Not only do we have here terminology, 'the Last' or 'least of the Apostles', important for determining the historical provenance of polemical statements in the Gospels, attributed to Jesus, like 'the First shall be Last and the Last shall be First' – also reflecting Qumran 'Last' versus 'First' parameters – but also the 'Empty' or 'vain' language, which the Habakkuk *Pesher* uses when discussing the 'Worthless Service' of the Liar. Here, too, the number of 'Apostles' is indeterminate and simply plural again.

Paul goes on in this vein. Not only has he referred to this 'vanity' in connection with 'the Gospel he announces' above, but he repeats it a few lines later, saying,

> If Christ has not been raised, then our preaching is *worthless* [or 'void'] and your Faith, too, *also worthless*. (1 Cor. 15:14)

Note, too, the use of the word 'preaching' here, the very word Peter is pictured as using in his Letter to James, prefacing the Pseudoclementine *Homilies*, to describe '*the preaching* of the Man who is my Enemy' – not to mention similar 'Teaching' (*Kērygama*) attributed to him in early Church Apocrypha.[16]

First, one can say outright that it appears clear that the reference to 'Cephas and the Twelve' is just a superficial statement of what was perceived as orthodoxy by the time the interpolation was made, that is, if '*Cephas*' and 'Peter' are taken to be identical – which we should grant for the moment for the sake of the argument – then it is more likely that a statement of this sort is an interpolation than something that is patently schismatic and against the current of this orthodoxy.

The reference, too, to 'the Twelve' is the only reference of this kind in the Letters section of the New Testament, as opposed to in the Gospels and Acts. James does, distinctly and in line with Paul's references to 'those of the circumcision', address itself – seemingly with clear symbolical intent – 'to the Twelve Tribes of the Dispersion' (obviously meaning Israel – 1:1). This might simply relate, as we have seen, to the 'Twelve' members of the Community Council at Qumran, all of whom seem to be designated 'Men' of Israel and also figuratively compared to the actual *building of the Temple*, the 'Three Priests' ranged alongside them being compared to the 'Holy of Holies' or '*Inner Sanctum*' within it (one should also not ignore the whole 'Holiness' symbolism of these 'Nazirite'/'Rechabite'-style Priests, 'Holy to God' or 'Holy from their mother's womb').

But the point here is that even by Gospel parameters, the statement as it now appears in 1 Corinthians 15:6 is totally *impossible*, because there were supposedly only 'Eleven' Apostles at the time. Mark 16:14, though itself considered interpolated, nevertheless draws the correct inference from the data, and specifically states this: 'he appeared to *the Eleven*' – so do Acts 1:26, Matthew 28:16, and Luke 24:9 and 33.

This is another of those instances similar to Peter learning through his vision in Acts of the tablecloth, let down 'by its four corners' from Heaven, that he is permitted to *eat forbidden foods* and *keep table fellowship* or *associate with Gentiles*, which, if authentic, would totally gainsay the Gospel portrait of Jesus already having taught these things and indulging in, from a Palestinian point of view, behaviour that would seem even worse – namely, keeping the company of prostitutes, tax collectors, Rich officials, Roman soldiers, and the like. But for the Gospels 'Judas Iscariot', parodying 'Zealot' or '*Sicarii*' suicides, had already 'fallen' in 'the Field of Blood', or whatever he did that his entrails should 'burst open'; however the election of 'the Twelfth Apostle' – the beginning of Acts – has not yet occurred.

Interestingly enough, many of these post-resurrection scenes in the Gospels are often accompanied by the motif of sitting down to *eat*. For John, it is the Apostle called 'Thomas, one of the Twelve, called the Twin' ('*Didymus*' in Greek), missing from Jesus' first appearance to the Disciples in Jerusalem, who wishes to do more than just 'see Jesus'. In John, he wants to put his finger into the actual nail holes in Jesus' hands (John 20:24–25).

Whatever one might wish to say about this seeming 'first' appearance by Jesus to the Disciples in Jerusalem, *someone* is missing and we do not have Twelve even in John. We shall have more to say about this problem in due course, when discussing the relationship of Thomas to the 'Disciple' or 'Apostle' called 'Judas Thomas' and finally to Jesus' third brother, supposedly called 'Judas' as well, and, by extension, also the missing 'Judas *Iscariot*'. Later, along the shores of the Sea of Galilee, this 'Thomas' is among the Disciples, along with Peter and the so-called 'Disciple whom Jesus loved', to whom Jesus gives some 'bread' and 'fish' to eat (John 21:1–14).

For Luke, it is 'Cleopas' (*thus*) and another of these mysterious, unnamed others to whom Jesus first appears outside Jerusalem 'along the way' to Emmaus and 'breaks bread' with them. These then return and report this – also to 'the Eleven assembled' in Jerusalem (Luke 24:1–35). Where the ending of Mark is concerned, as we saw, in any event probably based on this material in Luke, after Jesus appeared 'to two of them as they walked on their way in the country', he simply 'appeared to the Eleven as they ate meat' (Mark 16:12–14). In Luke, too, Jesus also then 'stood among them' (that is 'the Eleven' gathered together in Jerusalem – note our 'standing' imagery again) and 'ate before them' (24:36–46).

Though Luke confines himself to appearances in and around Jerusalem only and does not move on to the Sea of Galilee, he also more or less repeats Paul's statement in 1 Corinthians 15:1 above about the Gospel he 'received' and on which his Disciples 'also should stand'. As Luke puts this, Jesus, like the Righteous Teacher in his scriptural exegesis sessions in the Habakkuk *Pesher* from Qumran,

> opened their understanding to understand the Scriptures, saying to them [that is, Jesus is here the scriptural exegete], 'Thus, it has been written, that the Christ should suffer and rise again from among the dead the third day and that repentance and remission of sins should be proclaimed in his Name to all the Nations, beginning at Jerusalem.' (Luke 24:45–47)

For Matthew 28:16, as in his presentation of Jesus' earlier Transfiguration on 'a high mountain' before the Three, 'the Eleven Disciples' go up 'to the mountain' in Galilee, where Jesus was supposed either to have first 'appointed them' or which he 'appointed for them'– the text is unclear here. The only problem is that there is no such 'mountain' where Jesus first 'appointed them' in Matthew, though there is in Mark and Luke (3:13 and 6:12). In Matthew, this 'mountain' is rather associated with things like the Sermon on the Mount, other miracles (5:1), or the Transfiguration above. Notwithstanding, as in the passage from Luke above, Jesus basically announces to them there what amount to the parameters of the Pauline Mission, including 'making Disciples of all the Nations' (*Ethnē*) and something resembling the 'Authority', Luke speaks of, to remit sins (28:18–19).

In the last line, however, there is also the quasi-'Rechabite' note of 'observing all the things' that they were 'commanded' and it is interesting that the phrase Matthew uses at the end, 'until the Completion of the Age' (28:20), is almost word for word what appears in particularly sensitive contexts at Qumran in the Habakkuk *Pesher* too, as well as the Damascus Document and Community Rule – 'the Last End' and also 'the Completion of the Age'.[17] Where Mark is concerned, these last sections are generally discounted anyhow, it being thought that the original ending of Mark – if it ever existed – somehow went missing.

However all of these fine points may be, it should be appreciated that there is no individual appearance to Peter on record in *any* of the Gospels. Therefore, there never could have been a *first* appearance to 'Peter' or 'Cephas', no matter what the listing, that is, unless we were to identify 'Cephas' with the 'Cleopas' to whom Jesus first appears in Luke 24:18. Strictly speaking, too, though Peter is pictured as charging into Jesus' tomb in two of the Gospels (Luke and John), even in these, he never actually *sees* the risen Christ only 'the linen clothes' lying there (Luke 24:12 and John 20:6).

John mentions these 'linen clothes' three times in three lines, though for him it is 'the Disciple whom Jesus loved' – one begins to suspect this is really a linguistic evasion for *James, not John* – who outruns Peter into the tomb which, except for these *clothes*, is empty (24:4–7). John also goes on to mention 'two Angels in white' who are then seen by Mary, now called 'Mary Magdalene' (20:12).

For the other Gospels, this matter of the Angel(s) and the various Marys occurs *before* either Peter and the other Apostle – whoever he was – charge into the empty tomb. In fact, the language they use to describe the 'clothing' of these Angels (in Matthew 28:2, it is a single 'Angel of the Lord' who rolled away the stone; in Mark 16:5, he is simply called 'a young man') basically recapitulates that already encountered above in Jesus' Transfiguration before Moses, Elijah, and his core Apostles in the three Synoptics, as we have seen, though without the comparison to the 'whiteness' of the laundryman's washing.

Matthew says that the face of this 'Angel of the Lord' was *as lightning* and his *clothing white as snow*' (28:3); in Mark, he is clothed, like our 'Essene' daily bathers 'in a *white* robe'; for Luke, the clothes of these Angels – there are, it should be recalled, two in Luke – were 'shining' (24:4). In fact, in the Synoptics, 'Mary Magdalene' and 'Mary *the mother of James*' – this is how Luke refers to her – never actually *see* Jesus but, rather, only these Angel(s).

For Mark, elaborating upon Matthew's laconic 'the other Mary', this Mary is 'Mary *the mother of James and Salome*' (16:1). Luke, to add to the confusion – and the obfuscation – even adds *a third woman* to these scenes, someone he now calls 'Joanna' (24:10). In Luke 8:3, where she is also a companion of Mary Magdalene, this Joanna, if it is the same individual, is also the wife of a *Herodian Official*! Whatever one wishes to make of this, she is, in all events, never heard from again.

John, whose focus is strictly on Mary Magdalene, allows this 'Mary' alone and no other, the *first* vision of the *resurrected Christ* (20:14–18), but this appearance, which is not part of the initial empty-tomb scenarios, is not paralleled in any of the other Gospels. For John, 'turning backwards', she 'saw Jesus *standing*' (note again the 'standing' motif in direct connection to Jesus' name)! Once again there is no 'first', individual appearance to Peter in Johannine tradition either.

As for the third point in Paul's testimony to the post-resurrection appearances of Jesus here in Corinthians – for us, the interpolated part – the appearance 'to five hundred brothers at once', there is no reference to an early appearance of such magnitude in any extant Gospel. Some might wish to see this as simply an extension of Jesus' appearance before 'the Eleven and those that were with them' after the Emmaus road episode in Luke (24:34 – in Mark 16:14, simply 'the Eleven as they reclined'). For John 19:20, this appearance is simply to 'the Disciples' plural – here again, Jesus, in the place they 'were assembled', 'the doors having been shut through *fear of the Jews*, came and *stood in their midst*'.

For perhaps the fourth time, we have the 'standing' attribute attached to Jesus' name (there will be more). For Matthew, there is no appearance at all in the Jerusalem area to 'the Eleven Disciples', but rather later 'on the mountain' in Galilee (Matt. 28:16).

It is, however, informative to compare the number 'five hundred' – 'of whom most remain until now, but some have also fallen asleep' – which Paul gives, to the figure 'five thousand' in the Pseudoclementine *Recognitions* (echoed too in the number of early converts in Acts) for the number of those *fleeing with James* to Jericho after the mêlée in the Temple, a few additional zeroes in ancient narratives like these meaning very little. Even the allusion in 1 Corinthians to 'some also fallen asleep' connected to these 'five hundred brothers' (note here, again, the 'brother' theme) carries with it some of the gist of the visit to the two sepulchres of the 'two brothers', 'remembered before God', which miraculously 'whitened of themselves every year' following this 'five-thousand'-man flight ('by which miracle the Fury of the Many against us was restrained, because they saw that our *brothers* were remembered before God').

In this allusion in the Pseudoclementines, as far-fetched as it may seem, there is, in addition to the common theme of 'brothers', the tell-tale reference to 'three days'. In 1 Corinthians 15:4, 'three days' are, of course, the amount of time, 'according to the Scripture', after Jesus' burial that he then 'appeared to Cephas, then to the Twelve, then to five hundred *brothers* at the same time'. In the *Recognitions*, it is the amount of time after the flight of the 'five thousand' to the Jericho area that it takes for information to be transmitted from 'Gamaliel' – in the Pseudoclementines, as we saw, considered a secret sympathizer; in Acts, someone who worries over Christians and Paul's alleged teacher (5:34 and 22:3) – that Paul had received his commission from the Chief Priest and was pursuing them, particularly Peter, 'to Damascus'.

The First Post-Resurrection Appearance to James and the Last to Paul

If we now look at the second part of this famous testimony by Paul in 1 Corinthians 15:7–8, which basically recapitulates and parallels the first part about 'Cephas, then the Twelve' (15:5–6),

> and after that [his death and resurrection 'according to the Scripture'], he appeared to James, then to all the Apostles, and last of all, as [if] to an abortion, he appeared also to me

and set aside the first part as not only inaccurate, but tendentious; one might at first glance assume that also here one has more dissembling or interpolation. But this is deceptive, as unlike the first part there is nothing inherently impossible or contradictory in the second part, except our preconceptions regarding it. If we discard these – which are rarely very well founded or thought out anyhow – we find ourselves on *very* firm ground indeed.

For example, we do not have 'Twelve Apostles', when there are supposed to be only 'Eleven'. Nor do we have an undocumented, *first appearance* to someone called 'Cephas' or the obviously inflated detail that 'then he appeared to over five hundred brothers the same time'. Rather, the notice about 'then to all the Apostles', which follows the note about this *first appearance to James*, is indeterminate and in line with all Paul's other references to 'the Apostles', which are always – except in this single instance of the interpolated first part – general and unqualified.

This would include the references in Galatians to 'the other Apostles' – James and Peter presumably among them – and in Philippians to Epaphroditus, whom Paul also calls an 'Apostle' (2:25), as well as the structure of 'Apostles and Prophets' in general he outlines in 1 Corinthians 12:28–29, reiterated, as well, in Ephesians 2:20 and 4:11. This is not to mention Paul's repeated allusions to himself as 'an Apostle of Jesus Christ' – in Romans 11:13 'the Apostle to the Gentiles' (a title also picked up in Islam for its 'True Prophet' or 'Apostle' Muhammad) –

and here in 1 Corinthians 15:9, 'the Least of the Apostles' and 'the Last', to whom Jesus appeared.

Of course there is no actual, physical appearance by Jesus to Paul on record, only the vision recorded in Acts of 'a light appearing out of Heaven' and a voice crying out to him as 'he drew near Damascus', identifying itself as 'Jesus' (9:3–5). But, given Paul's constant communication with the Supernatural-style Figure in Heaven, he usually refers to either as 'Christ Jesus' or 'Jesus Christ', one can assume that he took either one or all of these appearances as real.

In fact, as we have already suggested, his characterization of himself at the end of this testimony in 1 Corinthians 15:8–9 as being, not only the 'Last' but 'the Least of the Apostles', is very revealing, particularly as we saw, when one ranges it alongside favourite sayings attributed to Jesus in the Gospels, including 'the First shall be Last and the Last shall be First' (Luke 13:30 and pars.), 'suffer these Little Ones to come unto me' (Luke 18:16 and pars.), 'everyone that exalts himself shall be humbled, and he that humbles himself, shall be exalted' (Luke 9:48 and 14:11), and the like.

One has similar sets of allusions relating to the 'Little Ones that believe' (Matt. 18:1–6 and Mark 9:33–42, including 'the First shall be Last and the Last shall be First', here directed against *the Apostles themselves* – 'Belief' being the essence of the Pauline doctrine of 'Salvation by Faith'). In the Synoptics, this set of allusions ends with the encouragement that those 'leaving houses, brothers, sisters, father, mother, children, and lands for my sake and for the Gospel's sake, shall receive a hundredfold', punctuated again with the tell-tale 'Many that are First shall be Last, and the Last, First' (Mark 10:29–30 and pars. – note even the play on the terminology 'the Many', the rank and file at Qumran – also alluded to in the Pseudoclementine notice above).

These are the kinds of allusions, not to mention 'casting out demons' or 'devils', 'speaking in Tongues', miracles, and healings as 'mighty wonders and great works', which are the accoutrements of the Pauline Gentile Mission in Acts, as well as in the Gospels. Not only are they *not* paralleled at Qumran and *not* part of Apocalyptic Messianism in Palestine at this time, they constitute the exact opposite of Messsianism in Palestine at this time and the polemic *against* such a Messianism!

Also this 'Last' phraseology, Paul is using in 1 Corinthians 15:8, has a clear parallel at Qumran. As we saw, Qumran knows the language of 'the First' versus 'the Last', but there it has a completely different signification. In texts, such as the Damascus Document, 'the First' are 'the Ancestors', to whom God first *revealed the Law*, who set down 'the boundary markers' which 'the Lying Spouter' is described as 'removing'. 'The Last' are those in the present age or 'the Last Days' or 'the Last Generation', who in 'the Faith of the New Covenant in the Land of Damascus' rededicate themselves to the Old Covenant, namely, that of 'the First'. In this context, it is also helpful to keep in mind the conjunction of both 'the Last' and 'the Last Priests of Jerusalem' in the Habakkuk *Pesher* with 'the Last Days' or 'End Time'.[18]

Of course, Paul has changed this into a completely new signification having to do with his own appointment as Apostle (belittled by some), Jesus' revelations to him personally, and his new converts, who 'because he worked harder than any of the others' and 'by the Grace of God, became believers' (1 Cor. 15:10). In Galatians 2:15, as already remarked, Paul identified 'Sinners' with 'Gentiles', a 'Sinner' in such a context presumably being someone not born under the Covenant or the Law and, therefore, somehow born 'in Sin', as in Romans 5:12–6:23.

He alludes to this here in 1 Corinthians, too, observing 'death came into being through one Man, Adam, just as all men die in Adam', this as opposed to 'being made alive in Christ' (15:20–25). Not only do we have, as we have already noted, just the gentlest swipe at his opponents' 'Primal Adam' ideology, but Paul here, once again, displays his fertile mastery of allegory, wordplay, and repartee. One should also remark how this directly follows several allusions to 'worthless', preceding several to 'the End', when 'he will put all his enemies under his feet' – imagery from Psalm 110 already encountered above (1 Cor. 15:14 and 15:25).

At the end of 1 Corinthians, as we have on several occasions had cause to remark, Paul goes on to reveal what he calls another 'mystery' or 'secret', that all will not 'fall asleep' before the Kingdom comes, but that the living 'will be transformed instantaneously' into something 'incorruptible' and 'imperishable' (15:51–54). This is in line with doctrine in the Damascus Document above, about the Sons of Zadok being those 'who *will stand* at the End of Time'.

It should be recalled that in the Temple Scroll those forbidden not only to enter, but even to see the Sanctuary, are individuals like these prostitutes, fornicators, or 'Sinners', with whom Jesus so readily eats, or the blind, the lame, lepers, and others with bodily effusions of some kind. The War Scroll, pursuing what amounts to a kind of Holy War, also bans the same categories of persons from the wilderness 'camps', because, as it says, 'the Holy Angels' march with our legions or 'are in our camps'. The same idea of the 'Holy Angels being with us' is also reiterated in the Damascus Document. Being of the same imperishable and incorruptible substance, Paul is speaking about here at the end of 1 Corinthians, the Heavenly Host was considered to be unable to abide human pollution.[19]

To such notations, as already described, the Temple Scroll connected an allusion to *'balla''/*'swallowing' or 'Bela'', the name of the first Idumaean King and a son of someone with the same name as *Balaam*'s father; and, for that matter the 'skins' or 'things sacrificed to idols', alluded to by Paul in 1 Corinthians 6–9 and evoked, as well, in '*MMT*'. Both allusions, according to our exposition, have to do with Herodians and their polluted gifts in the Temple. Curiously enough, here in 1 Corinthians 15:54, Paul, too, now goes on to refer to this 'swallowing', but now in his most spiritualized transformation of all, 'death being *swallowed up* in Victory' – this, followed up by the even more famous query, 'death, where is your sting?' It will be recalled, he also made a similar such allusion to 'swallowing' in Galatians 5:15, in regard to what James called 'the Royal Law according to the Scripture' and internecine strife within the Community.

It is possible now to argue that we have in this notice about the order of these post-resurrection sightings in 1 Corinthians in Paul, the actual notice about a post-resurrection appearance by Jesus to James. If one deletes the first part of this notice about appearances to 'Cephas', 'the Twelve', and 'five hundred brothers at the same time', leaving only the second about first 'to James, then to all the Apostles, and last of all' to Paul, then this *is* a first appearance to James. Nor does the second half of this testimony, taken by itself, contradict previous notices in the letter about 'the brothers of the Lord', Barnabas, and Cephas travelling around with women, nor about James being reckoned 'among the Apostles' in Galatians – nor, for that matter, the other brothers of Jesus as Apostles, which we shall show to be the clear implication of Gospel Apostle lists and other sources.

In fact, the evidence of a first appearance to James *does* exist in apocryphal Gospels, early Church testimony, and can be ascertained to some extent in Gospel presentations even as we have them. This is, of course, just what we would expect in light of the contention in the Gospel of Thomas about Jesus' *direct* appointment of James: 'Jesus said to them ['the Disciples'], in the place where you are to go [paralleling John 20:19 above], go to James the Just, for whose sake Heaven and Earth came into existence', or, for that matter, in the same vein as we saw in the Pseudo-clementine *Recognitions*, that 'the Church of the Lord, which was constituted in Jerusalem, was most plentifully multiplied and grew, being governed with the most Righteous ordinances by James who was ordained Bishop in it *by the Lord*' (1.43).

In addition to these, both Apocalypses of James from Nag Hammadi contain numerous allusions that not only make this direct appointment implicit, but even a tradition of a first appearance to James 'on the mountain', called for some reason Golgotha ('Gaugelan'), but meaning, most probably, the Mount of Olives. Here Jesus is not only presented as naming James 'the Just One', but kissing him on the mouth (1 Apoc. Jas. 5.29–32), obviously a 'Disciple Jesus loved' if there ever was one. This is just what we would expect if James was, indeed, the *first successor* to his brother in Palestine, the Bishop of the Jerusalem Church – the parallel at Qumran being 'the *Mebakker*' delineated in the Damascus Document – and 'the Bishop of Bishops' or Leader of 'Christianity' worldwide, whatever might have been meant by this term at this point in its pre-Pauline embodiment. Actually, the Qumran documents would be a better approximation of what this was, at least in Palestine, than anything in the Pauline corpus, or the Gospels and the Book of Acts dependent on this corpus.

But in Jerome's testimony to James, given in his *Lives of Illustrious Men* above, he is sentient as ever in understanding the implications of Paul's testimony in Galatians 1:19, 'none of the other Apostles did I see, except James the brother of the Lord'. This he actually quotes. Jerome was the first to develop in any systematic manner that the brothers of Jesus *were* Apostles, which has become, because of him, more or less received doctrine in Catholicism, at least for those informed of Jerome's works. In doing this, he quotes a 'Gospel' which he claims to have translated both into Greek and Latin in its entirety and which he says Origen also used two centuries before. He calls this gospel, which is, of course, no longer extant, the 'Gospel according to the Hebrews'.

This Gospel, which Jerome also calls 'the Jewish Gospel', seems to have been called by other transmitters, the *Gospel of the Nazoraeans*, but it is unclear if the two are really distinct or just different versions of the same thing. The same can be said about the Gospel, which Jerome's contemporary and colleague, Epiphanius, identifies as being in use among 'the Ebionites'. Epiphanius also calls this 'the Gospel of the Hebrews', and we have already quoted the passage from it, which he preserved, on baptism and adoptionist sonship above.[20] Scholars generally refer to these as three distinct Gospels, but their relationship is impossible to determine on the basis of the data available to us, nor is it clear that they were ever really separate at all.

Jesus' First Appearance to James in the Gospel of the Hebrews

As Jerome reports it, this Gospel contained a slightly different picture of the baptismal scene than the one in Epiphanius above. It should be observed that despite the low opinion in which Epiphanius is usually held, in the matter of adoptionist baptism, the version he provides of these things preserves more original material and, given the doctrines of these groups, makes more sense than that which one finds in orthodox Scriptures. Where the first appearance to James is concerned, according to Jerome's testimony, 'after the account of the resurrection of the Saviour, it was recorded in the Gospel according to the Hebrews':

> But the Lord, after he had given his *linen clothes* to the Servant of the Priest ['the Priest' here and in Hebrew usage generally, particularly that at Qumran, almost always means the High Priest], went to James and appeared to him. For James had sworn that he would not *eat bread* from that hour in which he *drank the Cup of the Lord* until he should see him rising again from *those that sleep*.[21]

Not only do we have here our 'linen clothes' motif again, here making more sense than it does in other versions of such scenarios, but also the idea of 'those that sleep' already encountered in Paul's 1 Corinthians 15:6 testimony above.

In addition, there are several important symbolisms here. One is the 'Cup' symbolism, which we have already demonstrated to be in use at Qumran, particularly where the description of the death of the Righteous Teacher and the retribution visited on the Wicked Priest are concerned. This 'Cup' imagery is combined at Qumran with that of the 'Anger' or 'Wrath of God', so much so that playful wordplay develops between the two homophonic words in Hebrew, 'Cup' (*Chos*) and 'Anger' or 'Wrath' (*Cha'as*), which God will 'pour out' on those responsible for the destruction of the Righteous Teacher and 'the Poor' (*Ebionim*) with him.[22] This, in turn, is recapitulated in Revelation in terms of 'the wine of the Wrath of God which is *poured out full strength* into the Cup of His Anger' (15:10). The 'pouring' imagery, here, again inverts that being used relative to 'the Lying Spouter' at Qumran – 'Spouter', it will be recalled, being based on the Hebrew root for 'pouring'.

In this regard, one should recall, too, its use in Acts to denote the all-important 'pouring out upon them' of the Pauline 'Holy Spirit' at Pentecost (Acts 2:43 and 10:45). For Paul, too – and the Gospels – this language will also have implications for the 'pouring out' of the blood of Christ, now to be drunk in 'the Cup of the New Covenant in [his] blood', an allusion about which we shall have a good deal more to say in Volume II. 'Cup' imagery, as it is being used above to signal death, is also present, interestingly enough, in Gospel accounts of 'the Cup' which *John and James* – 'the two sons of Zebedee' – must drink to follow Jesus (Matt. 20:22–23 and Mark 10:38–39).

One should also remark the Nazirite oath-style procedures of 'swearing' not to eat or drink, present in the Gospel of the Hebrews account of James' behaviour after Jesus' death, which are similar to those of the would-be assassins of Paul in Acts, who 'put themselves under a curse *swearing not to eat or drink until they have killed Paul*' (Acts 23:12). These oaths 'not to eat or drink' are important. After the fall of the Temple, as signalled, many were taking such oaths in mourning for the Temple and putting themselves under a penance of some kind 'not to eat or drink', presumably, till they should see it rebuilt. So concerned were the Rabbis about such 'Nazirite'-style penances that, as we shall see, they attempted to discourage them in Judaism thereafter by designating those taking them 'Sinners'.

In doing so, they seem to be associating such oaths with the disaster that had befallen the people. Still, as remarked as well, a thousand years later, the Spanish–Jewish traveller, Benjamin of Tudela not only claims there were large numbers of *Jewish 'Rechabites'* in Arabia in 'Thema' or 'Tehama', north of Yemen ('Tayma'?), who were in a perennial state of fasting and wearing only black, 'mourning for Jerusalem and mourning for Zion'. As he describes it, these were taking oaths (in the *Jamesian* manner) 'to eat no meat and abstain from wine' and 'living in caves or makeshift houses'. This testimony is so unexpected and original, it is hard to believe he just made it up out of whole cloth.

The allusion to 'those that sleep' not only directly parallels the 'some fallen asleep' of Paul in 1 Corinthians 15:6 above, but also ties into the notice in the *Recognitions* about the sepulchres of the brothers miraculously 'whitening of themselves every year'. However, one cannot say if this connection is intrinsic or accidental. If real, then it is another in this long list of allusions connecting all these matters to the two separate attacks on James, the Jericho flight, and the death of James; and would bind the material attesting to a first appearance to James (whatever its validity) more closely to materials in the Pseudoclementines and early Church accounts, the allusion to 'falling asleep' relating to both Jesus' subsequent resurrection and the miraculous 'whitening' of 'the *two brothers'* tombs'.

Jerome continues:

> And again a little later ['later' meaning later in this narrative of a first appearance to James in the Gospel of the Hebrews], it says, '"Bring a table and bread," the Lord said.' And immediately it is added: 'He took the bread, blessed it, and breaking it, gave it to James the Just, saying to him, "My brother, eat your bread, for *the Son of Man is risen from among those that sleep."*'

Again one should remark the similarity of this to Last Supper narratives of Jesus announcing 'the New Covenant' (Matt. 26:26–29 and pars.) and the kind of vows reported of James in all early Church sources above – of lifelong abstinence from strong drink, animal flesh, and sexual activity. These themes, centring around abstention from food and drink or partaking of these with 'the Risen Christ', will proliferate in stories relating to post-resurrection appearances to Jesus' family members, particularly *his brothers*.

Jerome immediately follows this notice about Jesus 'breaking bread' and 'giving it to James the Just' to eat to commemorate his 'rising from among those that sleep', with his own details about how James 'was buried near the Temple, from which he had been 'cast down', his tomb-stone with its inscription being well known until the siege of Titus and the end of Hadrian's Reign'. Interestingly enough, in this context as we have seen, Jerome contends James 'ruled the Church in Jerusalem for thirty years until the Seventh Year of Nero', thereby dating James' rule from the early 30s and reinforcing, however circuitously, the impression that James was appointed by Jesus himself and that his succession was direct.

Most commentators, embracing the picture of Peter's intervening Leadership in Luke's Acts, would allow James only a twenty-year reign from the early 40s. All of this, however, is dependent on an accurate date for the crucifixion of Jesus, which cannot be determined with any precision on the basis of the available evidence. Josephus, as we saw, even seems to imply a date of about 35–6 for Herod Antipas' execution of John, which in the Gospels precedes the execution of Jesus!

Aside from this additional allusion to 'rising from among those that sleep', one should also remark the tell-tale use of the 'Son of Man' terminology again, allusion to which is always interesting in view of its connection to James' like-minded proclamation of this conceptuality in the Temple at Passover in early Church accounts of the run-up to his own death.

The Picture of the Orthodox Apostles as Fishermen in the Gospels

It is also useful to compare this account in the Gospel of the Hebrews of Jesus' *first* appearance to James with all the others in the Canonical Gospels incorporating this theme of 'breaking bread' and 'eating with' Jesus after his resurrection or his appearance to the Apostles while 'they were reclining' or 'eating', or, in fact 'eating' generally, which, as we discovered, is perhaps *the* crucial theme.

The most important of these occurs in the Gospel of John, following on the famous 'doubting Thomas' episode just cited above. In the latter, Thomas 'called *Didymus* [the Twin] one of the Twelve' (20:24) is *absent* from among 'the Disciples', just as Judas *Iscariot* is *absent* from the conclaves of 'the Eleven' following Jesus' death – but for completely different reasons. 'Judas' is absent because he supposedly 'betrayed' Jesus or 'delivered him up', subsequently committing suicide (John 13:2 and pars.).

These references to 'Judas' have clearly been understood historically as pejorative, just as those to 'Thomas' in the above sequence, who again pejoratively – illustrating just how these aspersions take hold – is popularly referred to as 'doubting'. The reason for this is because, as just seen, he 'will not *believe*' until he has actually *put his finger into the nail holes in Jesus' hands* (John 20:25) – again, though literarily effective, a *patently mythological* scenario. This is accompanied by the aspersion (Jesus responding to Thomas), again using the vocabulary of the Pauline Gentile Mission:

> You have [only] *believed* because you have *seen* me, Thomas, but blessed are they that have *not seen* and yet have *believed*. (John 20:29)

Not only should one note, here, the emphasis on the Pauline ideology of how *belief in Jesus saves one*, but it should be clear that this now retrospectively even confirms Paul's own belief itself, not to mention that of his communities. Again, it should be appreciated that Paul never actually *saw Jesus* or, if he did, *saw him* as Thomas is depicted as doing here, after his resurrection.

It should be kept in mind that, where these matters are concerned, both *Didymus Thomas* ('Twin Twin') and Judas *Iscariot* are probably connected in some manner with the members of Jesus' family itself and, where Thomas is concerned, tradition conserves the name of 'Judas' for him too. Where Judas is concerned, not only does John at one point even call him 'the *Iscariot*', making it clear that this has to be considered *a title* not a name (14:22); but, unlike the other Gospels, John four times also refers to him as 'of Simon *Iscariot*' (6:71, 12:4, 13:2 and 13:26). This has always been interpreted as 'Simon *Iscariot*'s *son*', but we shall presently see the relationship of this to another 'Apostle', around whose name confusion abounds, 'Simon the Zealot' or 'Simon the *Cananaean*' or 'Cananite', with regard to which one should keep in mind the interchangeability of these 'son' or 'brother' allusions in the Greek, all equally implied by the genitive construction 'of'. This individual, too, we shall ultimately identify as one of *Jesus' brothers*.

However this may be, following this appearance to the so-called 'doubting Thomas', Jesus next 'manifests himself again to the Disciples' at what John – but not the other Gospels – calls 'the Sea of Tiberias' (21:1). Named after the Roman Emperor Augustus' adopted son, Tiberias was built by Herod Antipas and is even today the biggest town on the Sea of Galilee. Here Thomas – again designated *Didymus*, 'the Twin' – is among the Disciples about to go fishing in the sea. These include Simon Peter, Nathanael (never mentioned in the Synoptic Gospels), the sons of Zebedee, and 'two others of his Disciples' (John 21:2). As we shall see, unnamed Disciples such as these will also be important in the Gospel of Luke's version of Jesus' first post-resurrection appearance to the two Disciples 'along the Way' to Emmaus.

Just as Jesus had just 'stood among them' in the room in the preceding 'Doubting Thomas' episode, 'Jesus *stood on the shore*' and asked the Disciples – whom he also now calls 'little children' – for food, instructing them to '*cast* [*balete*] *the net* to the right side of the boat' (our 'net' and 'casting' vocabulary once more – 21:4–6). Simon Peter, who

> was naked, *put on his upper garment* and *cast himself* [*ebalen*] into the sea. (21:7)

Here again, not only do we have our 'casting out'/'casting down' allusions, repeated *three times* in as many lines – once in Jesus' request to the Apostles and twice in descriptions of the actions they take; but now it is joined to the 'net' theme repeated *four times* in six lines (21:6–12). This is not to mention the references to the two 'sons of Zebedee' and the 'two' unnamed Disciples, who will be important for sorting out additional problems related to the 'brothers' presently, nor the curiousness of Peter *putting on his upper garment to cast himself into the sea*, again incorporating our 'clothing' theme and probably playing on 'Essene' *bathing attire* (to say nothing of the *Homilies*' picture of Peter's *daily bathing*).

It will be recalled that in the Damascus Document – not to mention its expansion in the 'Balaam'/'Balak' episode in Revelation – it is Belial who 'casts a net' before the Sons of Israel, catching them in the 'Three Nets' of 'fornication', 'Riches', and 'pollution of the Temple' mentioned above. For Revelation, 'Balaam teaches Balak' – all variations of this *ba–la–'a* language circle or symbolism, having to do with 'the Devil' (*'Diabolos'* in Greek) or 'Devilishness' – 'to cast [*balein*] a net before the sons of Israel *to eat the things sacrificed to idols* and *to commit fornication*' (Rev. 2:14). As previously remarked, both of these are immediately recognizable as the essence of James' instructions to overseas communities, not to mention forming, perhaps, the central focus of the Qumran Letter(s) called '*MMT*'. We could rest our case right here and would not have to proceed with a single additional argument, as, upon reflection, everything should be clear.

All this language having to do with 'Devilishness' and 'casting out'/'casting down', whether in Hebrew or Greek, has a strong pejorative flavour. We have already seen this in the 'swallowing' language at Qumran, the Hebrew root of both the names, 'Belial' and 'Balaam', and the 'casting down' language applied to James' death in all the Greek sources. But when the New Testament playfully applies this language and its variations either to Jesus' choosing his core Apostles or to his post-resurrection appearances to them, or both, the net result is to trivialize this language, reducing it to farce.

Hence the Apostles, inverting the depiction of 'Belial' in the Dead Sea Scrolls ('Beliar' in Paul), become peaceful 'fishermen' on the Sea of Galilee, 'casting down their nets'. In other appointment episodes, they are given the 'Authority', as we have seen, 'to *cast out* [*ekballō*] demons', like the Essenes do backsliders or 'the Zealots' do to James' destroyer, Ananus' *naked* body, when they 'cast it out' (again *ekballō*) from the walls of Jerusalem.

One should also note that it is 'the Disciple that Jesus loved', usually taken to be 'John' the reputed author of the Gospel, who characteristically first identifies the mysterious figure of Jesus 'standing on the shore' (whom the other Disciples do not recognize) as 'the Lord' (John 21:7). But as we have already remarked variously above, this Disciple, like the parallel narrator of the Protevangelium of James in the second century, is probably none other than James himself.[23]

But in the Synoptic Gospels, this episode depicting the principal Apostles as fishermen occurs *before* Jesus' resurrection not *after* it, when Jesus calls four of these – again two pairs of 'brothers' – along the Sea of Galilee, one of the most beloved episodes in Gospel narrative. These are now 'Simon who is called Peter' and 'his brother', now called 'Andrew' (but in Greek 'Andrew' means 'Man' – a variation of 'the First Man' or 'Primal Adam' ideology once again?) and 'the other two brothers, James the son of Zebedee and John *his brother*' (Matt. 4:18–22 and pars.).

In Mark 1:16, 'Simon and Andrew *the brother of Simon* are *casting* [*ballontas*] *a net* into the sea', while a little further along in Matthew 4:21, 'James the son of Zebedee and John *his brother*' are mending their 'nets'. Here, of course, not only do we have these various permutations and combinations of the 'brother' theme, but also of our 'casting down' and 'nets' themes with a vengeance. Mark adds the charming little detail, missing from Matthew, that Zebedee had 'hired servants' with him in his boat (Mark 1:20).

This episode, as it is retold in Luke 5:1–11, almost completely parallels the post-resurrection episodes in John. Meticulous as ever, Luke even gets the name of the Lake right. He calls it 'Gennesaret' (which he probably got from Josephus), not 'Tiberias' as in John – also probably the root of these various 'Nazareth' allusions. For Luke, it is 'the fishermen' who are now '*washing* their nets' at the start of the episode – not the two brothers, 'James the son of Zebedee and John his brother' – not 'mending' them (5:2), and he too repeats the word 'net' or 'nets' *four times* in five lines before he is done!

According to his version, Jesus now goes out in Simon's boat and is teaching the people from it,[24] when he tells Simon – again as in John above – this time, 'to let down' his 'net' (5:4). When it is all done – for they 'worked through the whole night'[25] – 'their net was breaking' and filled almost two boats to the sinking (5:7)! This note about the boats 'beginning to sink' makes it clear that his version cannot be divorced from Matthew 14:24–36 above, where, in trying to repeat Jesus' miracle of walking on the waters, Peter begins 'to sink' into the Sea of Galilee for lack of 'Faith'. For Luke, all then left their boats and followed him, Jesus uttering the now proverbial words that henceforth he (Peter) would be 'catching men' (5:10).

In Matthew and Mark, 'they left their nets and followed him' and Jesus, addressing all four, utters the even more famous, 'I shall make you *fishers of men*' (Matt. 4:18 and Mark 1:17). Both clearly play on and invert the above-mentioned allusions in the Damascus Document at Qumran about 'Belial' or 'the Devil' ('Balaam' and 'Balak' in Revelation) casting his 'net' to deceive Israel (in Revelation, this is literally 'cast a stumbling block before the Sons of Israel') or 'catch' men. The writers of these Hellenized New Testament parodies could not have been unaware of this.

For his part, Matthew again returns to this theme of 'casting a net into the sea and gathering together every kind' of fish in his famous series of 'Jewish Christian' parables in Matthew 13:1–53. These include the famous 'Parable of the Tares', condemning 'the Enemy', who, while all the men slept, 'came and sowed the tares among the wheat' (13:24–30). Once again, as in Luke above, Jesus is teaching *from a boat*, but now it is 'the crowd' which *stood on the shore* (Matt. 13:2). In Matthew, this comes right after the Gentile Christian episode about Jesus' curing a series of demonics (12:22–45) and his rejection of his 'mother and his brothers *standing outside* seeking to speak to him', in favour of his Disciples (12:46–50), providing a good example of Matthew's schizophrenia and rather representing the layering of various, contradictory sources (in Matthew, this is even preceded by a quotation from Isaiah 42:4 about 'the Gentiles [*Ethnē*] hoping in his Name').[26]

In the largely Jewish Christian parables that directly follow this, Jesus is ostensibly explaining what the Kingdom of Heaven is. In Jesus' final interpretation of this, 'the sower' once again is 'the Son of Man'; the good seed, 'the Sons of the Kingdom' (one might possibly even read here, 'the Sons of Zadok'); and 'the Enemy who sowed the tares', our old friend 'the Devil' or '*Diabolos*' – 'Belial' in the Scrolls (Matt. 13:36–42). Jesus then goes on to picture – in the spirit of the War Scroll at Qumran, the Letter of James, and James' proclamation in the Temple – how 'the Son of Man will send forth his Angels' to gather out of the Kingdom 'the tares sowed by *the Enemy*' and '*cast them* into the furnace of Fire' (*balousin*).

In doing so, he even employs language parallel to the 'stumbling block'/ 'scandal'[27] and 'Law-breaking' of the Letter of James – not to mention its reflection in Revelation's characterization of the teaching of 'Balaam' above – to describe these 'tares' (13:41). Then, after describing how 'the Righteous [here our identification of 'the Sons of Zadok' with 'the Sons of the Kingdom' is appropriate] shall shine forth as the sun in the Kingdom of their Father' (in Jesus' Transfiguration scene above, it is Jesus' face that 'shone as the sun'), he compares the Kingdom of Heaven to 'a large net cast [*blētheisē*] into the sea', *catching all different kinds of fish* – this, a clear Gentile Christian overlay, as in these various 'nets' and 'fishermen' episodes.

But the Parable ends on the same uncompromising, Palestinian Christian or 'Jamesian' note as the preceding one about 'the tares'. Here, instead of 'breaking bread' with Jesus and 'sitting down to eat', as in the majority of these episodes, the fishermen rather '*sit down* and gather the good into containers, and the bad they *cast away* [*ebalon*]'. This is now followed by the words:

> So shall it be at *the Completion of the Age*. The Angels will go out and *separate the Evil from among the midst of the Righteous* and *cast them [balousin] into the furnace of the Fire*. (Matt. 13:49–50)

This is an *authentic* Palestinian Christian tradition, because everything in it reflects what we know about these native Palestinian movements. Note, in particular, the allusions to 'separating the Righteous' and 'casting away the polluted' or 'Evil into the furnace of Fire at the Completion of the Age', typical of the vocabulary of Qumran. Not only are the usages 'Fire' and 'separation' strong there, but that of 'the Completion of the Age', as we have seen, is actually the phraseology encountered in Qumran vocabulary having to do with 'the Last Generation' or 'the End Time'.[28]

These 'casting's, of course, undergo even further transformation and refinement into the 'casting out spirits' or 'demons' (*ekballō*) in the New Testament, an 'Authority' or 'Power' given to the Apostles on their appointment by Jesus. We have already seen the opposite or reversal of this kind of usage in how Josephus portrays the Essenes as 'casting out' (again *ekballousi*) backsliders unwilling or unready to keep the practices of the Community or observe its secrets. It is also to be found, as we saw, in the usage Josephus applies to the 'casting' of James' nemesis, the High Priest Ananus' naked body, 'out' of the city without burial, as well as the 'casting down' of the body of the assassinated 'Rich' collaborator 'Zachariah' by the Zealots from the Pinnacle of the Temple into the Kedron Valley below![29]

The first of these is, of course, reversed in Acts' portrayal of the 'casting out' (*ekbalontes*) of its archetypical Gentile believer Stephen from the city, itself inverting the stoning of James. These are now further trivialized, as per the casting down of Belial's 'nets', in episodes relating to the 'Power' Jesus gives his Apostles 'to cast out demons' and the supernatural accoutrements attached to this – as, for instance, in Mark 3:15: 'and he appointed Twelve . . . to have authority to *cast out* demons' (*ekballein*) or Matthew 17:19's further elaboration of the same idea, following Jesus' Transfiguration on the mountain.

This directly precedes another episode about how Peter 'casts' (*bale*) his hook into the sea to get the money to pay the Roman tribute – an easy answer to the tax question. Here, 'the Disciples' (the Central Triad of Peter, James, and John 'his brother'), who are portrayed as being unable – unlike Jesus – even to cure a demonic boy, ask Jesus, 'why were we unable to cast out?' (*ekbalein* – meaning, the 'demon'). For perhaps the umpteenth time, Jesus gives the typical Pauline response, 'Because of your *unbelief*' (Matt. 17:20).

In another parallel reversal of this kind, using now the subject matter of Matthew's 'Parable of the Tares' above and again showing the various layers of inverted polemics going on here, Mark 4:26–32, also has Jesus teaching the people from *a boat*. Now the Parable is that of the Mustard Seed. Once again, a man is 'casting [*bale*] the seed on the ground', but now it grows into a quite gigantic tree, with 'great branches' (note the Messianic 'Branch' symbolism), 'larger than all the plants'. Though the meaning here should be clear even to the non-specialist, the fiercely apocalyptic, indigenous Palestinian attitude has now been completely pacified in a haze of Hellenizing intellectualization.

In another funny adumbration of the way this kind of 'casting out'/ 'casting down' language is used in the Gospels, directly after the 'Transfiguration' scene and the ensuing aspersion on the Central Three as being 'unable to cast out', as we just saw, Matthew 17:24–27 varies Jesus' position on the tax issue. At the same time Matthew employs the 'stumbling block'/'being scandalized' language, that is, so as 'not to offend' or 'scandalize them' ('them' being the *tax collectors*), and now has Peter 'casting [*bale*] a hook' into the sea to get a coin from a fish's mouth there in order to pay the Roman tax! This is supposed to be serious, the point presumably being, that he did this because he was unwilling to pay the tax himself or, Essene-style, did not carry coins on his person – or both. Notwithstanding, in typical Platonic repartee and not surprisingly following the ideology of Paul, Jesus is made laconically to conclude 'then the Sons are *truly free*.' Here, typically, *freedom from Rome* or *foreign oppression* is, now once more, ever so subtly transformed into Paul-style *freedom from the Law*.

The upshot is that, by looking into seemingly innocuous episodes about Jesus 'breaking bread' with his Apostles after his resurrection – relative to the first appearance to James hinted at by Paul in 1 Corinthians 15:7 – we are, once again, led to completely unexpected results about the whole 'Belial'/'Diabolos'/'casting out' circle of language, now turned into allusions about how the Apostles 'cast down their nets' or have the Authority 'to cast out demons', rather than how James was 'cast down' from the Temple steps or Temple Pinnacle.

Nor could we have foreseen where the investigation of such language and examples would lead us. In another transmogrification of this language circle, that of the 'tares' or the 'rotten fish' being 'cast into a furnace of Fire', we are led into a picture of the plight of 'Evil persons' generally at 'the Last Judgement', which does in fact parallel the Qumran response to how these same Evil persons 'swallowed' the Righteous Teacher and would themselves in turn 'be paid the Reward on Evil' or 'be swallowed' by 'the Cup of the Wrath of God' ('wherefore they shall *eat* the fruit of their doings' – Isaiah 3:10, applied to James' death in the second-century testimony of Hegesippus, preserved in Eusebius).[30]

John's 'Net Full of Fishes' Again and Luke's Emmaus Road Sighting

To return to the Gospel of John's testimony to Jesus' appearance to his 'Disciples' along the shore of the Sea of Galilee *after* his resurrection: after putting on his clothes 'to cast himself into the sea' ('for he was naked') Peter is *swimming to shore*. Nor does he this time appear to 'sink' for 'lack of Faith', as when he tries to walk on the waters in Matthew or as the parallel boats so 'full of fish' appear to be on the verge of doing in Luke's picture of Jesus' '*standing* by the Lake of Gennesaret' and calling his Apostles. Rather, he was,

> dragging the net full of one hundred and fifty-three large fishes to land, but though there were so many, *the net was not torn.* (John 21:11)

Again, this both parallels and inverts Luke's picture in the pre-resurrection episode about the calling of the Apostles of the 'great number of fishes that was breaking their net', so many that their boats were almost 'sinking' (Luke 5:6–7).

Meanwhile in John, the other Disciples, too, were dragging their 'net of fishes' to land, whether the same 'net' as Peter's or a different one is unclear (John 21:8–11):

> Jesus then said to them, 'Come and eat' . . . and took the bread and gave it to them. (21:12–13)

Here, of course, is the *pro forma* 'dining' and 'eating' scenario always part of these accounts and an integral element in the account of Jesus' *first appearance to James* in Jerome's 'Gospel according to the Hebrews'. Nor should the subtle play in Jesus' constant command to 'eat' and allusions in the Gospels, such as 'the Son of Man came eating and drinking' (Matt. 11:19 and Luke 7:34) on Paul's more over-arching and permissive understanding of the term 'eating' be missed. Nor, of course, the use of 'eating', we have just delineated above, to mean 'Vengeance' at Qumran; nor the allied usage in the Habakkuk *Pesher* – also in exposition of Habakkuk 1:14–16 on 'taking up with a fishhook, catching them in a net, and gathering them in a dragnet . . . and burning incense to his dragnet' – where 'eating' is interpreted to mean, 'tax collecting', whereby 'the *Kittim*' (or the Romans) 'gather their Riches together with all their booty like fish of the sea', 'parcelling out their yoke and their taxes, eating all the Peoples [that is, 'the *Ethnē*'] year by year'. Not only is this delineated in terms of their 'portion being fat' and their 'eating plenteous', but this is the same passage in which their burning incense to their 'dragnet' is interpreted in terms of their 'sacrificing to their standards and worshipping their weapons of war', as we shall demonstrate in Volume II, perhaps the key dating parameter where the Habakkuk *Pesher* is concerned.[31]

As far as this episode in the Gospel of John is concerned, the words attributed to Jesus here are, of course, basically the same ones that the mysterious voice cries out to Peter in the episode about the descent of the Heavenly tablecloth in Acts legitimatizing 'table fellowship' with Gentiles and more – thus demonstrating that all these episodes are playing their small but integrated part and being subjoined to Pauline theological arguments insisting on 'freedom from the Law'.

As John draws to a close, Jesus is not only presented as taking the bread and giving it to the Disciples, but – in light of its previous subject matter *about fishes* – he gives them '*some of the fish too*' (21:13). One is tempted to remark, yes and some big ones too – perhaps the biggest of all 'big fish' stories! For his part, John remarks, again prosaically, one might add, in view of the far-reaching implications of the subject matter:

> This was now *the third time* that Jesus was manifested to his Disciples, after having been *raised from among the dead*. (John 21:14)

The Gospel of John closes with the mini-episode about how Jesus asks Simon Peter whether he 'loves' him – again *three times*. We have already seen that, aside from purportedly being the number here of Jesus' post-resurrection appearances, 'three' is always associated with the subject of Peter's lack of Faith and poor stewardship in the other Gospels, where, for instance, Peter denies the Messiah *three times* on the eve of his crucifixion. In Acts too, as will be recalled, the voice from Heaven has to call out to Peter *three times* before he gets the message.

The theme of 'loving' is not only important *vis-à-vis* 'the Disciple Jesus loved', purportedly the author of this Gospel, it is important across a whole spectrum of ideas and related to the central ideology of these 'Opposition' groups of Abraham being 'the Friend of God' – in Hebrew, this is 'the Beloved of God' – found, of course, in the Letter of James, the Damascus Document, and later moving directly into the basic ideology of Islam. As we shall see, too, this theme will be of particular import to the propagation of these ideas into the Northern Syrian framework of 'Antioch', Edessa, or Haran, Abraham's place of origin – and, of course, the reason for their ultimate transmission into Islam.

It is also related to the theme of 'loving God', a motif to be encountered in all these documents, as for instance Paul in 1 Corinthians 8:3 and James 2:5, and the basic definition of 'Piety'. This, in turn, is the second part of the 'Righteousness'/'Piety' dichotomy of 'loving your fellow man' and 'loving God', as we have expounded it – also put in Jesus' mouth in the Gospels (Matt. 22:37–39 and pars.) and found in Paul's exposition of why *it is necessary to pay taxes to Rome* (Rom. 13:8–10).

Carrying on this 'love' motif, John concludes with Peter seeing 'the Disciple Jesus loved' and asking Jesus about him (21:20), and, in an aside, identifies him as the Disciple 'who had reclined on his breast at the [Last] Supper, asking "Lord, who is it who will deliver you up?"' and 'the Disciple who bears witness to these things and writing these things' (21:20–24).

This brings us back to the pretence, noted above, that James was the author of the second-century Infancy Gospel, known as the Protevangelium of James, in which the doctrine of Mary's 'perpetual virginity' was first announced and, in a kind of sardonic irony, *ascribed to James*. As we have already noted, the point, it seems, was, being Jesus' closest living relative, James should have known best about these things, even though it was *he* and patently *not Mary* who was the perpetual virgin – another incredible reversal. Again, these matters just serve to increase the overlaps between 'the Disciple Jesus loved' and James. For John, Jesus responds to Peter's query by, once again, lightly rebuking him, 'If I desire him to tarry until I come, what [is this] to you?' (John 21:22–23), again *repeated twice* for emphasis.

This allusion to 'tarrying till I come' is normally interpreted to mean the 'Second Coming' or what is often called 'the *Parousia* of Jesus', or, if one prefers, final eschatological Judgement or something like the proclamation attributed to James in interpretation of Daniel 7:13's 'Son of Man' of coming eschatological Judgement. In drawing connections to Qumran documents, it is important to note that in the run-up to the 'Jamesian'-style and seemingly eschatological exegesis in the Habakkuk *Pesher* of the all-important 'the Righteous shall live by his Faith' from Habakkuk 2:4, Habakkuk 2:3, 'if it tarries, wait for it', is also subjected to exegesis. In both the exposition is circumscribed by its application only to '*Torah*-Doers', the exegesis of Habakkuk 2:4 adding the additional qualification, '*Torah*-Doers in the House of Judah', meaning, it would appear, *only to native-born Jews*. The implication would appear to be, it does not apply to non-*Torah*-Doers *who are not Jews*.

The first part of Habakkuk 2:3, 'for there will be another vision about the time appointed for the Completion of the Age and it shall not Lie' contains significantly both the allusion to the 'Completion of the Age', paralleling Matthew above, and 'Lying' again. The commentary in the Habakkuk *Pesher* from Qumran reads as follows:

> Its interpretation is that the Last Age *will* be extended and shall exceed anything that the Prophets have foretold, for the Mysteries of God are astonishing. *If it tarries, wait for it, because it will surely come and not be delayed* [Hab 2:3]. Its interpretation concerns *the Men of Truth, the Doers of the Torah*, whose hand will not slacken from the Service of Truth, though the Last Age is extended around them, because all the Eras of God will come to their appointed End, as He determined them in the Mysteries of His Intelligence. *Behold, his [soul] is puffed up and not Upright within him* [Hab. 2:4]. Its interpretation is that their sins will be doubled upon them [playing on the allusion to 'puffed up' here] and they will not be pleased with their Judgement.[32]

'The Men of Truth', of course, may be contrasted to its opposite, 'the Men of Lying'; the same for 'the Service of Truth' and 'the Service of Lying', recalling Paul's similar contrasts in 2 Corinthians 9–11. There is also an inverse parallel in the stress on being 'puffed up' to Paul's attack on those 'measuring themselves by themselves and comparing themselves with themselves', 'the Highest Apostles', who, according to 2 Corinthians 10:12, write their own letters of recommendation (also 'those reputed to be important' in Galatians 2:6). In fact, as earlier remarked, Paul actually uses the very same allusion, 'puffed up', to criticize such persons five times in 1 Corinthians 4:6–19 and 1 Corinthians 8:1, comparing it significantly with 'love', which, he says, by comparison with the 'Knowledge' they pretend to have about 'things sacrificed to idols', does not 'puff' one 'up', but 'builds up' and 'is patient', 'not vainglorious' (1 Cor. 13:4)!

In this passage from the Habakkuk *Pesher*, there is absolutely no hint of any authority to 'remit sins'; nor can there be any doubt that we are speaking about a Final Judgement of some kind. The context too is clearly eschatological, concerning 'the Last Times'/'Last Things', and we are certainly in a framework of these New Testament allusions to 'the Completion of the Age' (Matt. 13:49). This is how this important allusion to 'waiting for' or 'tarrying' is defined in this preamble to the exegesis of Habakkuk 2:4, 'the Righteous shall live by his Faith', at Qumran, the exegetical foundation piece of Christianity as Paul understands it – this 'waiting' or 'tarrying' basically going by the name of 'the Delay of the *Parousia*' in modern Christian parlance.

This allusion to 'tarrying' or 'remaining' also occurs in the pivotal Emmaus road post-resurrection appearance in Luke and is transformed into something different again, this time that the Apostles should 'tarry' or 'wait in the city of Jerusalem' (24:47). Not paralleled in the other Gospels except for the one sentence, possibly spurious, we noted in Mark above: after Cleopas and an unnamed other Disciple encounter Jesus 'along the Way', Jesus, once again, 'reclines' and 'breaks bread' with them (Luke 24:30). The ethos of this episode, as well, despite its context, is basically 'Ebionite' or 'Jewish Christian'.

In it, Jesus is only 'a Man, a Prophet . . . mighty before God in work and word' and is 'delivered up', not specifically now by Judas *Iscariot* but by 'the Chief Priests' and 'Rulers' 'to Judgement of death' (Luke 24:19–20 – these words, 'a Prophet' and 'mighty before the Lord of the Throne', are also exactly those the Koran uses to describe its Messenger, Muhammad, in *Surah* 81:19–21).[33] Like the Teacher of Righteousness above, 'to whom God made known all the Mysteries of His Servants the Prophets' – also described as 'the Priest ['the High Priest'] in whose heart God placed insight to interpret all the words of His Servants the Prophets, through whom God foretold all that would happen to His people' – Jesus in this episode in Luke is essentially portrayed as an Interpreter of Scripture too (24:25–27 and 44–49).[34]

These two Disciples return to Jerusalem and report 'to the Eleven' and those with them 'the things in the Way and how he was known to them in the *breaking of the bread*' (Luke 24:35). At this point, Jesus '*stood among them*' again. What he now teaches this 'Assembly of the Eleven and those with them', in the manner of an Interpreter of Scripture again, is exactly what Paul says he received 'according to the Scriptures' in 1 Corinthians 15:3–4, right before his testimony about Jesus' post-resurrection appearance to James:

> It behoved the Christ to suffer and rise from among [the] dead on the third day, and repentance and remission of sins should be proclaimed in his Name to all Peoples [*Ethnē* again] beginning at Jerusalem. (Luke 24:46–47)

In 1 Corinthians, as we saw, Paul puts this:

> I transmitted to you in the first instance, what I also received, that Christ died for our sins, according to the Scriptures . . . and that he was raised from the third day, according to the Scriptures.

In Luke, one should also note the Pauline cast of the proclamation, 'to all Peoples', already presaged in Matthew 12:21 above.

In this appearance by Jesus in Jerusalem, as reported by Luke, the 'Doubting Thomas' material from John, where Jesus shows them the nail holes in his hands and feet, is once more combined in one and the same episode with the 'eating' theme; but instead of commanding the Disciples to 'eat' as in John – and by refraction, Peter's vision of the tablecloth in Acts, where the Heavenly voice commands him three times to 'eat' – Jesus asks, 'Have you anything that is eatable here?' (24:41). They then produce 'a broiled fish and part of a honeycomb'!

Not only is this immediately recognizable as the 'and some fish too' of the episode following Jesus' appearance by the Sea of Galilee in John, where Jesus tells the Disciples, to 'come and eat'; but to this is then added not only the note – again paralleling John above – about the Apostles in general 'being witnesses of these things', but the command 'to tarry' or 'remain' in Jerusalem until, as Luke puts it, 'you are clothed with Power from on High' (again our 'Great Power' vocabulary – 24:49). This is the third presentation of the 'tarrying' or 'remaining' theme, connected in John, anyhow, with 'the Disciple Jesus loved'.

Interestingly, this is also basically the implication of the saying in the newly discovered Gospel of Thomas above about Jesus' *direct appointment* of James as successor. In effect, Jesus is also telling his Disciples, in going to seek James, to return to Jerusalem and remain there. Like these others, too, the statement in Thomas is essentially eschatological, as it describes James as being of such importance that for his 'sake, Heaven and Earth came into existence'.

To conclude – instead of *coming down from Heaven*, as James is pictured as proclaiming it before the riot in the Temple that leads to his death; in Luke's denouement, as per these usual reversals and inversions, Jesus is 'carried up into Heaven' (Luke 24:51). As this is put in Mark's parallel text, which while considered spurious, still combines many of these themes from Messianic Prophecy now so familiar to us, he 'was received up into Heaven and *sat down at the right hand of God*' (Mark 16:19).

But in Luke, all the Apostles then 'returned to Jerusalem with great joy and were *continually in the Temple praising and blessing God*' (24:53). This return to Jerusalem is not paralleled in the other Gospels, which are more interested in their view of the Pauline 'going forth' and 'making Disciples of all the Peoples' (Matt. 28:19 and pars.). But it is paralleled by the sense of the notice from the Gospel of Thomas above, and even more importantly, in how James' Community is pictured as being in the Temple every day in early Church testimony and by refraction in Acts. This note about *being continually in the Temple* is not only striking, but once again 'Jamesian' in ethos and probably true.

This post-resurrection appearance, then, by Jesus to his most well-known Disciples along the shores of Lake Gennesaret – probably the origin of all these notices about 'Nazareth' as a city – in John lends further weight to the fact that all traditions, those of the early Church, Qumran, and New Testament raconteurs, are operating within the same *B–L–'/* 'Balaam'/'Belial' parameters. In addition, the New Testament writers, not to mention those of the early Church, appear to have had full knowledge of both the death scenario of James and the tradition of a first post-resurrection appearance to him, now altered and completely overwritten – though on the surface sometimes seemingly playfully, in the end always disparagingly – whether in the tradition of the Synoptic or the Johannine Gospels.

Last Supper Scenarios, the Emmaus Road, and the Cup of the Lord

Breaking Bread and *Eating* in Other Gospels

We should now return to other 'eating' and 'breaking-bread' scenarios in the Gospels. These not only incorporate the essence of this appearance by the Sea of Galilee in the Gospel of John in a more Jerusalem-oriented framework, but bear a direct relationship to Paul's theological formulation of 'Communion with the blood' of Christ, which Paul announces in 1 Corinthians 10:14–11:13 in the context of further allusions to 'eating and drinking' (11:29). In doing so, Paul addresses his discussion also to 'Beloved Ones' – this time his own (10:14).

Jesus' Jerusalem appearances are principally two in number. First, there is the one in John, preceding the appearance along the shore of the Sea of Galilee, *Didymus Judas Thomas* being absent and reproduced to some extent in Mark's documentation of an appearance by Jesus in Jerusalem 'to the Eleven as they were reclining' (Mark 16:14). The second of these manifestations in Jerusalem is Luke's Emmaus Road appearance – already analysed to some extent above – which also incorporates yet another allusion to 'reclining' (Luke 24:30), an allusion to some extent even echoed in John's evocation of 'the Disciple Jesus loved reclining on' his breast at 'the Last Supper' (13:23 and 21:20).

Circumscribed as it may be, Mark also alludes to this appearance in Luke to the two 'walking on their way into the country'. But, derogatory as ever, he emphasizes the lack of Pauline-style 'belief' connected to the report of this. For him, Jesus, even in these post-resurrection appearances, is once again censuring his core Apostles, namely the Jewish ones, or 'the Eleven' for 'their unbelief and hardness of heart, because *they did not believe those who had seen him risen*' (16:11–13). In these appearances, as remarked, Jesus also generally shows 'his hands and his feet' so, like Thomas, they can see the holes, or, as in Luke 24:41, when he asks for '*something eatable*', they give him 'a piece of broiled fish and a honeycomb'!

Luke's description of Jesus' appearance on the Emmaus Road, preceding his 'standing' in the midst of the Eleven as they were 'assembled' in Jerusalem, not only parallels Paul's vision along another road – this *to Damascus* – but actually ties all our themes together. It is that important and also almost completely paralleled by the description of the *first appearance* to James in the Gospel Jerome calls, 'according to the Hebrews'. This latter, it will be recalled, described how,

> after the Lord had given the linen clothes to the Servant of the Priest, he went to James and appeared to him. For James had sworn that he would not *eat bread* from that hour in which he drank the Cup of the Lord until he should see him risen again from among those that sleep.

Not only does this clearly play on James' seeming proclivity for Nazirite oath procedures (not to mention his Rechabitism), it appears to replace 'Last Supper' scenarios, where the Gospels picture Jesus announcing Paul's 'Holy Communion' doctrines. As already remarked, here too 'the Servant of the Priest' clearly means 'of the High Priest' bearing out Qumran usage to similar effect. Curiously enough, this 'Servant of the High Priest' reappears in the Gospels as the one whose ear Peter is also pictured as lopping off in the struggle when Jesus is arrested (Matt. 26:51 and pars.)! Finally, the excerpt from the Gospel of the Hebrews continues in Jerome as we saw:

> And again, a little later, it says, 'The Lord said, "Bring a table and bread!"' And immediately it adds, 'He took the bread, blessed it, broke it, and gave it to James the Just [there no longer being any doubt which James is intended here] and said to him, "My brother, eat your bread, for the Son of Man is risen from among those that sleep."'

Not only do we have here a parallel to both Jesus' breaking the bread and giving it to 'Cleopas' and the unnamed other along the Emmaus Road in the Gospel of Luke – here the words, 'he took the bread, blessed it, and, breaking it, gave it to them', are exactly the same as in Jerome's 'Hebrew' Gospel above – and to his principal 'Disciples' along the Sea of Galilee in the Gospel of John, which adds the words, 'and some fish too'; but something of the actual wording Paul uses in 1 Corinthians 11:24 in delineating his doctrine of 'Communion with' the body and blood of Jesus Christ, the basis too of these Gospel presentations of 'the Last Supper' – John's or the Synoptics', it makes little difference. Bringing all these allusions full circle, these Gospel 'Last Supper' scenarios also incorporate the references to 'Judas the *Iscariot*' or 'Judas [the son] of *Simon Iscariot*', which will be so telling when it comes to unravelling all the 'brother' allusions.

Before turning to this appearance to the two on the Road to Emmaus in Luke – one of whom unidentified – it would be well to look at these 'Last Supper' scenarios in the Gospels, the language of which is so paralleled, first in Paul's 1 Corinthians, but also in this excerpt about James from the lost Gospel of the Hebrews. In the Gospels, these 'Last Supper' scenarios are always introduced by references to 'Judas the *Iscariot*' in the Synoptics (Mark 14:10) and 'Judas [the son] of Simon *Iscariot*' in John 13:2. He, in turn, is almost always described as he 'who would deliver him up' or 'betray him' – language which, as we have seen, is actually repeatedly recapitulated in the Scrolls, but always with a completely differing signification – usually meaning God's Wrath on Israel for rebelliousness or Covenant-breaking.[1]

These descriptions of 'Judas *Iscariot*' also generally include a reference to 'Satan' (Luke 22:3) or 'the Devil/*Diabolos*' (John 13:2) – John, in a style typical, as we saw, of Qumran, the Book of Revelation, and the Koran, even interchanging both allusions in the same context (13:27). Characteristically, Luke also contains an attack on 'those who recline' and does so in the context of evocation of 'the Kings of the Peoples' (*Ethnōn*) – a term we identified in the Damascus Document as probably denoting *Herodian Kings* – which again introduces another of these seemingly completely unjustified attacks on 'Simon' (that is, 'Peter') as someone 'Satan has claimed for himself' (22:25–31).

Since this very phraseology, 'Kings of the Peoples', in addition to the Dead Sea Scrolls also appears in Roman legal practice where it is used to denote puppet kings in the East of the genre of these Herodians and others, this is yet another concrete philological link between the Gospels and the Scrolls. One cannot help but think of the parallel allusion in Josephus' picture of King Agrippa 'reclining' while eating and watching the Temple sacrifices from his balcony. In this connection, it should not be forgotten that it was the visit to the household of his father, Agrippa I, by a 'Simon' in Josephus, who wanted *to bar him* and *Herodians generally* from the Temple *as foreigners*, that we described as historical rather than some of the other visits and positions the New Testament pictures the individual it is calling 'Simon' as taking.

In Luke's picture of Jesus' repartee with and his aside to Simon at the Last Supper, contemptuously dismissing Simon's expressed willingness to be imprisoned and die with him, Jesus rather throws up to Simon his coming denial. This, according to Jesus as in the Gospels thereafter, will occur *three times* – or is it to be the cock that crows *three times*, another favourite piece of Gospel folklore (Luke 22:33–34 and 22:60)? Again, it is hard to conceive that in some esoteric manner all these citations are not connected. How ironic it would be if this favourite episode of Jesus at his Last Supper teaching his Disciples what amounts basically to the Greek Mystery Religion practice of consuming the body and blood of the living and dying god was connected in some manner to Agrippa II's eating habits and reclining while viewing the sacrifices in the Temple in a state of some kind of uncleanness in the Temple Wall Affair above (which we have already specified as leading directly to the elimination of James).

As Luke, however, continues this rebuke by Jesus, now playing also on this very 'table-fellowship' issue as it appears both in Paul's Letters, particularly Galatians, and earlier in the Gospels – but here Luke has Jesus swinging back to a more narrowly apocalyptic Jewish viewpoint:

> You may *eat and drink at my table* in my Kingdom and sit on Thrones judging the Twelve Tribes of Israel. (22:30–31)

Here, he not only returns to the Apostles participating in the Last Judgement, an activity which the Habakkuk *Pesher* ascribes to the 'Elect' of Israel, themselves synonymous, according to Damascus Document definition, with the *Sons of Zadok* '*called by Name* who would *stand* in the Last Days',[2] and the 'eating and drinking' theme now tied to the issue of table fellowship; but also to the Twelve Tribe scenario we have encountered regarding these things in Galatians above.

In the Gospels, Jesus is portrayed as 'reclining' with 'the Twelve' at the Passover meal at the Last Supper (John 13:1–30). Luke, for instance, has Jesus saying:

> I will not eat any more with you until it is fulfilled ['completed'] in the Kingdom of God, and [as in the Gospel of the Hebrews above] *taking his Cup*, he gave thanks saying, '. . . I will never again *drink of the fruit of the vine until the Kingdom of God has come*.' (22:16–18 and pars.)

Not only do we have here yet another play on the *Rechabite* or *Nazirite* theme of 'abstention from wine' – so relevant to being one of these 'Essene' or 'Nazoraean'-style Priests – but also James' oath in the Gospel of the Hebrews above, in which he 'swore that he would not eat bread from that hour in which he had drunk *the Cup of the Lord* until he should see him *risen from among those that sleep*'. Here, too, is another variation on

728

Paul's cry, basically attacking James' vegetarianism, 'So if meat ['bread' – 'bread' and 'meat' being interchangeable in these Hebrew–Greek translations] *causes my brother to stumble, I shall never eat flesh forever*' (1 Cor. 8:13).

Again one should have regard for the inversion here of the language of James 2:10's attack on he who 'stumbles on one point [of the Law], being guilty of [breaking] it all', and of 'scandals'/'stumbling blocks'/'Lawlessness' and 'offence' Matthew 13:41 pictures Jesus as using to describe 'the tares sown by the Enemy', which at the End of Time would be 'gathered up' and 'cast into a furnace of Fire'.

Not only do we have in this statement by Jesus at the Last Supper in the Synoptics a variation on the 'eating and drinking' theme again – so important in all early Church accounts of James' behaviour and interactions with Paul; but Jesus is portrayed, as well, as announcing almost a verbatim version of Paul's 'Communion with the blood of Christ' in 1 Corinthians 10–11, the letter with which we began our discussion of all these post-resurrection sightings of Jesus in the first place. Jesus' words here too, amount to a verbatim recapitulation of those the Gospel of the Hebrews attributes to James, also repeated to some degree in the sighting 'along the way' to Emmaus in the Gospel of Luke (24:30).

It is not even clear if this passage from the Gospel of the Hebrews about James – which obviously has nothing to do with any consumption, even symbolically, of 'the body' and 'blood' of Jesus by James, because James, according to all sources, neither *ate meat nor drank wine* and, in any event in Acts, *forbade the consumption of 'blood'* – is not the prototype or more primitive original of what Jesus was supposed to have said at 'the Last Supper' in the Gospels, wherein the Pauline symbolical consumption of 'the body' and 'blood' of Jesus is, perhaps, written over an originally more *Jamesian* core.

Communion with the Blood of Christ in Paul and at the Last Supper

Paul launches into this subject of 'Communion with the body' and 'blood of Christ' in 1 Corinthians 10:16 after first announcing that 'if food scandalizes [or 'offends'] my brother, I will never eat flesh forever' – this followed immediately by his reference to 'the brothers of the Lord and Cephas' (8:13–9:5) – and elaborating on his philosophy of 'winning' at all costs (9:18–27). When he does so, he addresses himself yet again to the 'Beloved Ones', admonishing them to 'flee from idolatry' (1 Cor. 10:14).

He says:

> The Cup of blessing which we bless, is it not Communion with the blood of
> Christ? The bread which we break, is it not Communion with the body of
> Christ? (1 Cor. 10:16),

and then goes on to allegorize on the Qumran language of 'the Many',
denoting himself and 'the Many' as the 'body', by which he means both
the body of the Church and the body of Christ (1 Cor. 10:17).[3] At the
same time he proceeds to invoke 'drinking the Cup of the Lord' and
'eating at the Lord's table' (1 Cor. 10:21), both encountered in Jerome's
account of Jesus' first appearance to James in the Gospel of the Hebrews.
It is at this point that he starts to contrast 'Communion with the blood of
Christ' and 'Communion with the body of Christ' with 'the sacrifices of
the other Israel' – the one 'according to the flesh' – which 'eats the
sacrifices *in Communion* with those at the altar' (1 Cor. 10:18).

In the peculiar manner in which his allegorizing logic works – and again
showing it is James with whom he is arguing – Paul actually alludes now to
these 'sacrifices in the Temple' in terms of the 'things sacrificed to idols' pro-
hibited in James' directives to overseas communities according to Acts' portrayal (15:29 and 21:25) – and, as we have now seen, '*MMT*' – yet again
reversing the original sense of this phrase. It becomes completely clear he is,
once more, talking about the more general theme of 'eating and drinking',
referring to it in terms of his characteristic language of 'causing offence'/
'stumbling', and 'all things being Lawful' to him (1 Cor. 10:23–32).

Just so there can be no mistaking what he means here, he now compares (albeit as obscurely as possible) these sacrifices in the Temple –
alluding to the tell-tale vocabulary of 'casting out demons' in the Gospels –
to 'the Cup of demons' and 'the table of demons' (1 Cor. 10:21). This
would have been totally shocking in a Palestinian milieu, though the idea
of the 'pollution of the Temple' sacrifices was, as we have seen, already
widespread in the Qumran documents, particularly in the 'Three Nets of
Belial' condemnations and '*MMT*', paralleling James' directives to overseas communities as we have shown above. We have already seen, too, in
the Pseudoclementine *Homilies* how Peter identifies this 'table of demons'
with eating 'food sacrificed to idols'. Still, it is another excellent example
of how Paul reverses the vocabulary of his interlocutors, using their ideological posture against themselves.

He ends this discussion, as we saw, by once again alluding to the theme
that characterizes his ideological position and with which he began the

discussion four chapters before: 'to me, all things are Lawful' (1 Cor. 10:23). There, in 1 Corinthians 6:13 it will be recalled, he went on to assert that 'meats are for the belly and the belly for meats' and used this and its relationship to 'flesh' and 'the body' generally, to move immediately to the theme of 'fornication', a second fundamental component of James' directives to overseas communities.

In his discussion of 'fornication', which does not differ markedly from parallel ones in the Letter of James or at Qumran, Paul raises the issues of marriage and divorce – both parts of the 'Three Nets of Belial' discussion of 'fornication' at Qumran – concluding, somewhat disingenuously, that '*circumcision* [another matter somewhat circuitously relating to 'fornication'] *is nothing*, but *keeping God's Commandments* is everything' (1 Cor. 7:19).

Now 'keeping the Covenant', it will be recollected, is the precise definition of the 'Sons of Zadok' at Qumran, who are defined in the Community Rule, as we saw, either as 'the Keepers of the Covenant' or 'the Priests who are the Keepers of the Covenant'. This kind of language is only slightly varied in the Letter of James which, amid the language of 'doing' and 'being a Doer' and 'keeping' but not 'breaking', sets forth the famous admonition, 'He who keeps the whole of the Law, but *stumbles* on one small point [recapitulating Paul above], is guilty of [breaking] it all' (Jas. 2:10).

It will also be recalled that this is exactly the language of the Rechabites, who were described as 'keeping the Commandments of their father Jonadab son of Rechab' – which they did faithfully – recapitulated at the end of Matthew in Jesus' final admonition on 'the Completion of the Age', 'to observe all things that I commanded you' (28:20). In Paul, typically, these are not 'their father's' but 'God's Commandments'; but he, anyhow, now seems to mean by this something quite different from the Covenant of 'Mount Sinai in Arabia', which 'corresponds to the present Jerusalem' and 'is Hagar', that is, 'slavery' (Gal. 4:24–25).

Exhibiting his usual defensiveness on issues of this kind – here specifically 'fornication' and 'circumcision' – Paul actually uses the 'throwing down'/'casting down' language and the 'net' symbolism of the 'Three Nets of Belial' section of the Damascus Document on 'fornication' above or those Balaam taught Balak 'to cast before' Israel in Revelation. He insists to his community that, in saying these things, he is not seeking '*to cast down [epibalō] a net before them*', but rather for their 'own good' that they '*may wait on* [or '*tarry*'] *for the Lord* without distraction' (1 Cor. 7:35). Here we have another absolutely incredible example of the kind of language parallels we have been following. In using this imagery, Paul makes it very clear that he knows the whole circle of language from Qumran relative to Belial 'casting down his nets' before Israel in the Damascus Document and, as well, probably that some, anyhow, were applying it to him!

Returning to Paul's second evocation of 'all things to me are Lawful' in 1 Corinthians 10:23, Paul uses this to move directly on to the two specific permissions, 'eat everything sold in the market place' and 'eat everything set before you', in connection with which he now cites a second time James' prohibition on eating things 'sacrificed to an idol' – with which, of course, he disagrees, alluding to it as 'a stumbling block' (1 Cor. 10:25–32).

This leads to Paul's further discussion in chapter 11 of the 'eating and drinking' theme, which, once again, he specifically relates to 'eating the Lord's supper'; and, both now – also a second time – to 'drinking the Cup of the Lord', as in the Gospel of the Hebrews' 'breaking bread' scene with James above, and the Cup of 'the New Covenant in [his] blood' (1 Cor. 11:20–29). Paul, for his part, puts this as follows:

> For *I received from the Lord,* that which I also delivered to you, the Lord Jesus, in the night in which he was delivered up, *took bread* and, after giving thanks, *he broke it and said, 'Take, eat . . .'* (1 Cor. 11:23–24)

Here again, we have the command, to 'eat', of the various post-resurrection scenarios already delineated above and in the scene about the command Peter receives in Acts on the rooftop of Jaffa before meeting the *Roman Centurion* Cornelius.

Paul purposefully juxtaposes his first use of the word 'delivered' with that of his second, 'delivered up' – in the New Testament normally associated with 'Judas *Iscariot*' (and, as we have now seen, widespread in the Dead Sea Scrolls, but to entirely different effect), but in Paul no 'Judas *Iscariot*' is mentioned.

> In the same manner also, [he took] the Cup after having eaten, saying, 'This Cup is the New Covenant in my blood . . . For as often as you *eat this bread* and *drink this Cup*, you announce the death of the Lord until he comes.' (1 Cor. 11:25–26)

We have already remarked how this 'New Covenant in my blood' relates to the 'New Covenant in the Land of Damascus' in the Dead Sea Scrolls – 'Cup of blood' in Hebrew and 'Damascus' in Greek being homophones.

21 Statue of Titus, the destroyer of Jerusalem and the Temple.   22 Statue of Josephus'
publisher Epaphroditus, who helped Nero commit suicide and was, seemingly, Paul's colleague
by the same name in Phil. 2:25 and 4:18.   23 Trajan (98–117 CE), who was reportedly
responsible for the deaths of Jesus' 'cousin' Simeon bar Cleophas and those of the descendants
of Jesus' third brother, Judas.   24 The Emperor Hadrian (117–138) – like Trajan from Italica
in Spain – who crushed the last Messianic Uprising, the Bar Kochba Revolt.

25 View of the Qumran cliffs from across the Wadi, showing Cave Four, where the bulk of the Scrolls were found – with the Dead Sea in the background.
26 View of Qumran graves showing North–South orientation. The Dead Sea is in the distance.

27 Ceremonial stairs leading to the Tomb of Queen Helen of Adiabene and her sons. Author and wife descending the steps.   28 Interior of the tomb of Helen's kinsmen, converts from Northern Syria and revolutionary heroes, mentioned variously in Josephus and Eusebius.   29 Balaam with the Messianic star from the catacombs in Rome, showing the Virgin with her 'only begotten' child. Josephus also refers to Helen's favourite son, Izates, as 'only begotten'.

30 View of the 'Land of Damascus' in the Syrian wilderness.
31 The Saleb of Syria, Beduin wanderers and tinkers, possibly descendants of
the Judeo-Christian Rechabites.

32 'The Pool of Abraham' at Edessa ('Antioch-by-Callirhoe') in Northern Syria –
'the Land of the Osrhoeans'.
33 Ruins at Pella in the Decapolis across the Jordan, to which 'the Pella Flight' of the
Jamesian Jerusalem Community allegedly occurred.

34 Arabian Petra, where Paul may have gone after 'Damascus' – although he may have gone further afield in 'Arabia'. 35 Ruins at Hellenistic Jerash across the Jordan in the Decapolis. 36 The Mandaeans, a Sabaean baptizing group in Southern Iraq, laying on of hands. 37 Legendary tomb of the Prophet 'Zechariah' next to the Tomb of James – probably connected to a Rich collaborator of that name whose body was 'cast down' without burial from the Temple Pinnacle into the Kedron Valley below by the Revolutionaries.

38 Columns 11–12 of the Habakkuk *Pesher* from Qumran, referring to 'the Cup of the Wrath of God' and 'the Day of Judgement'.

39 The Last Column of the Damascus Document at Qumran, referring to the reunion of the wilderness 'camps' at Pentecost, to curse all transgressing the Law.

40 Greek warning block in the Temple, forbidding Gentiles to enter the Sacred Precincts or Inner Court on pain of death.

41 Medallion supposedly depicting Paul and Peter.

42 Jewish coin from the Revolt against Rome showing 'the Cup', reading 'Year Three of the Redemption of Zion'. Others read 'Freedom of Zion'.

That Paul announces he 'received' this new insight 'from the Lord' – just as later in the prelude to his enumeration of Jesus' post-resurrection appearances he claims to be 'transferring' to his communities what he 'also received' about 'Christ dying for our sins according to the Scriptures' and being 'raised on the third day' – makes his claim at this point all the more decisive or important. This is also true where his first enunciation of this 'Cup of blessing' as 'Communion with the blood of Christ' is concerned, earlier in 1 Corinthians 10:14–23, preceded by his lengthy analyses of the two subjects from James' directives to overseas communities in Acts, 'fornication' and 'things sacrificed to idols'.

The implication of this claim preceding Jesus' post-resurrection appearances in 1 Corinthians 15 is that he 'received' these doctrines from the Apostles before him. In the case of Communion with the body and blood of Christ here in 1 Corinthians 11:23–27, the implication is clearly that he did 'not receive this from any man', but rather as a direct 'revelation from Jesus Christ' (Gal. 1:12). In fact, the implication of this, too, may be that no one else even knew of the doctrine. The Gospels, of course, make good this deficiency.

In fact, not only does Paul then proceed in 1 Corinthians 11:30 to cast aspersions on the 'weak' again, his favourite circumlocution for those in authority over him, who cause problems regarding 'eating and drinking', circumcision, and the like. Here he also calls them 'sickly' and repeats his 'Many are fallen asleep' allusion – he ties this to another allusion to the idea of being 'examined' (11:31). Previously being 'examined' for him had to do with his teaching credentials or lack of them, but here he asserts rather ominously:

> For he who *eats and drinks* unworthily, not seeing through to the body of the Lord, *eats and drinks Judgement to himself.* (1 Cor. 11:29)

Not only is the play on the language of 'eating and drinking' again self-evident, but now he is threatening those, who do not 'see' things in the manner he does, with 'Judgement'. This clearly has to do not with a reversal once again of the kinds of 'Judgement' his opponents would call down on him – as for instance that on 'Law-breakers' who 'do not keep the whole Law' and on those who claim their 'Faith will save them' in the Letter of James 2:10–14 – but *Divine* or *eschatological Judgement.*

Furthermore, in regard to this 'Judgement' he is using 'Cup' imagery, in particular, 'drinking the Cup of the Lord', imagery specifically employed at Qumran to describe the Vengeance God would take for the destruction of the Righteous Teacher and his partisans, called 'the Poor'. Just as importantly, this same Habakkuk *Pesher*, where this imagery so vividly occurs, and which described, as we saw, the ideological adversary it calls 'the Lying Spouter' as having:

> led *Many astray* to build a Worthless City upon blood and erect a Church ['Assembly'] on Lying, *for the sake of his Glory, tiring out Many with a Worthless Service* and *instructing them in works of Lying*, so that their works will be of Emptiness [or 'count for nothing'],

now calls down upon this 'Liar' and his associates the very same 'Fire with which they blasphemed and vilified the Elect of God' (in Qumran terminology, also 'the Sons of *Zadok*').[4] In both of these quotations, the one from Paul and the one from Qumran, one should note the repetition of the allusion to 'Many' and how Paul also uses the word 'Glory' – used here too in this passage in the Scrolls – as part of his allusion to 'eating and drinking' earlier in 1 Corinthians 10:31 and repeatedly through chapters 11 and 15. It should also be appreciated that throughout these passages about the destruction of 'the Righteous Teacher' from Qumran, the word '*drinking*' is being used to express this and the Divine Vengeance that will be taken for it.

In his prelude to his allusions to 'the other Apostles and Cephas and the brothers of the Lord' travelling around with women in chapter 9, it will be recalled, Paul protests (again playing on the language of 'eating and drinking'):

> Am I not an Apostle? Am I not free? Have I not seen Jesus Christ our Lord? Are you not my work in the Lord? If I am not an Apostle to others, at least I am to you . . . My defence to those who would *examine me* is, do we not have *authority to eat and drink*? (1 Cor. 9:1–4)

This, in turn, is preceded by the references to 'reclining in an idol-temple' and 'eating things sacrificed to idols', both of which Paul groups under the heading of 'loving God' (or 'Piety'), the first of the two 'Love' Commandments characterizing, it will be recalled, the doctrines of all Opposition Groups in this period – in particular, those of Josephus' 'Essenes' and the basis of Josephus' description of John the Baptist's teaching as well. Paul here studiedly concludes, 'food [literally, 'meat'] does not commend us to God', 'neither in not eating do we fall short' (1 Cor. 8:1–11), but his subtle plays on language and the way he turns the language his adversaries appear to be using *against him* back against them are canny.

Basically, what we have in Paul's reformulations in 1 Corinthians, ending in allusion to 'the Cup of the Lord', 'breaking bread', and 'Communion with the body' and 'blood of Christ', is none other than a variation of the scenario portrayed in the Gospel of the Hebrews, where James 'swore *not to eat bread* from the hour in which he *drank the Cup of the Lord* until he should see him risen again from among those that sleep', to which Jesus, 'breaking the bread' and 'giving it to James, reportedly responds, "My brother, eat your bread, for the Son of Man is risen from among those that sleep."' (Note, once again, the commonality with the 'Many falling asleep' language.)

This is especially true, since we already quoted Paul as quoting his 'Lord Jesus' to the effect that, 'This Cup is the New Covenant in my blood . . . For as often as you eat this bread and drink this Cup, you solemnly proclaim the death of the Lord until he comes'. The only real difference is that now Jesus' speech from the Gospel of the Hebrews is expanded to incorporate Paul's *new scenario* of 'Communion with the body and blood of Christ'.

The Negation of Paul's Mindset at Qumran

One can well imagine how, in particular, this would have infuriated those of a Qumran perspective, whose approach, as we have seen, would appear to be at the heart of what Paul is responding to. Paul's direct allusion to the fact that he is not 'throwing down a net before them' makes this about as clear as anything can. Paul knows full well what he is doing. Again, as we have pointed out *ad nauseam* – but it cannot be repeated too often – on almost all these issues Paul is systematically allegorizing and turning the Qumran positions back against them. He is doing the same to James, whose positions we know by refraction in Acts, the various early Church accounts we have encountered, and, to some extent, the Letter attributed to him in early Church usage.

That Paul groups his positions regarding 'dining in an idol-temple' and 'Communion with the blood of Christ' under the heading of 'loving God' or 'Piety' would have only infuriated groups like Qumran even more. One should note that in Josephus' descriptions of the 'Opposition' or 'Zealot' positions from the disturbances of 4 BC up to the events culminating in the Uprising against Rome, the constant demand on the part of the 'Opposition' forces is for a High Priest of 'greater purity' and 'higher Piety'. One also gets this demand reflected in the Letter to the Hebrews even as it has survived (4:15 and 7:26).

As we have also several times called attention to, the Letter of James refers to 'loving God' or 'Piety' in both the first and second chapters (1:12 and 2:5), the first with reference to 'the Crown [*Stephanon*] of Life promised' those loving God; the second, to the 'Beloved' or 'Poor' as 'Rich in Faith and heirs to the Kingdom promised to those that love Him'. In the background to both, the diatribe against 'the Religion' of 'the one who cannot control his Tongue, but has Lying in his heart' is said to be 'Worthless' (Jas. 1:26).

One should also note that in Josephus' picture of 'the Essenes', the Commandment of 'Piety towards God' is mentioned twice, once in connection with their daily bathing in cold water, eating habits, and wearing white linen garments, and a second time in connection with the oaths that such individuals take, 'not to tell Lies' and 'not to reveal any of their doctrines to others', nor communicate their doctrines, 'which they have received from their Forefathers' ('the First' at Qumran) in any manner different from how they 'have received them' themselves. Not only is this almost word for word the *Homilies*' picture of the fearsome impression made by James' imprecations to the Elders, when responding to Peter's Letter; but they are also precisely the words Paul repeatedly uses to describe the doctrines he 'has received'.[5]

It is important to realize that at Qumran the ban on the consumption of 'blood' is fundamental. The same pertains to James' directives to overseas communities, and one should see this equally where symbolic consumptions of 'blood' as in Paul are concerned as well. In the Damascus Document, the horror of 'blood' ranges from the attack on those who 'lie with women during the *blood of their menstrual flow*' to the charge of 'each man marrying the daughter of his brother or sister' (which focuses both of these as an attack on the Herodian family and those 'polluted' by their contacts with them), to the connection of the 'cutting off' of the Children of Israel in the wilderness to the assertion, 'because they ate the blood'.

This last, occurring at the beginning of Column Three in the Damascus Document, precedes these sections on the definition of 'the Sons of Zadok' and the exposition of the 'Three Nets of Belial' in Columns Four to Six. Just as we have had the allusion to 'keeping God's Commandments' in Paul's discussion of 'fornication' in 1 Corinthians 7:19; in Column Three of the Damascus Document, leading up to the evocation of the ban on 'blood', we have the references to Abraham being accounted 'Beloved' or 'Friend of God', because he 'kept the Commandments of God and did not choose the will of his own spirit' (one should compare this to Jas. 2:21–23 on Abraham), nor '*do* what seemed right in his own eyes and walk in stubbornness of heart'. As in the Letter of James, too, one should note the emphasis on both being a 'Keeper' and being a 'Doer'.⁶

Over and over in these passages about Abraham, Isaac, and Jacob being 'the Beloved' or 'Friends of God' in the Damascus Document, the text repeats the phrase 'keeping the Commandments of God' – note the parallel to Jeremiah's 'sons of Rechab', repeatedly being described as 'Keeping the commandments of their father', not to mention the description of these last in Islam as 'surrendering to God'. For the Damascus Document, it is as a result of 'not keeping' God's Commandment that the Heavenly Watchers fell – the allusion is to Genesis 6:2, where 'the sons of God have intercourse with the daughters of men'. Following this, the text evokes the Noahic Flood and then, finally, how the Children of Israel 'ate blood' in the wilderness and were, therefore, 'cut off'. It is because of these things that, in the world view of the Damascus Document, God's 'Wrath' is continually 'kindled against' the Children of Israel and they and 'their congregation' are continually being 'cut off' or 'delivered up'.⁷

From the very First Column, as we saw, which describes how the Lying Scoffer arose and 'poured over Israel [the same root as 'Spouting' in Hebrew] the waters of Lying . . . abolishing the Ways of Righteousness and removing the boundary which the First ['the Forefathers'] set down for their inheritance', the Damascus Document 'calls down on them the curses of His Covenant' and 'the avenging sword of the Covenant' – God's 'Wrath' and 'avenging sword' not Rome's.⁸ This is in line with 'curses' and 'cursing backsliders' and 'enemies' generally throughout the Qumran corpus, which is never gentle, forgiving, or accommodating.⁹

Paul, for instance, takes the opposite approach. A good example is in Romans 12:17, where he recommends 'not to return Evil for Evil', and follows this up with the quotation, once again addressed to the 'Beloved', 'Vengeance is mine. I will repay, saith the Lord' and, following this, 'overcome Evil with Good'. This includes the additional recommendations to feed your enemy 'when he is hungry and give him drink when thirsty' (Rom. 12:19–21). It will be immediately apparent that all of these are sayings attributed to Jesus in the Gospels, the only question being which – historically speaking – came first. The reason Paul gives, however, for such recommendations is often a touch more cynical than the Gospels, that, 'in so doing, you will heap coals on his [your enemy's] head' (Rom. 12:20).

This is almost exactly the kind of behaviour Josephus imputes to Paul's possible 'kinsman', Herod Agrippa I, who, as we saw, Josephus says 'was of a gentle and compassionate nature'. Particularly, in relation to the episode about Simon, the Head of a 'Church' or 'Assembly' of his own in Jerusalem, who wished to exclude this Agrippa from the Temple as a foreigner, Josephus emphasizes that King Agrippa 'esteemed mildness a better quality in a King than intemperance, knowing that moderation is more becoming in great men than passion'.[10] This is certainly very 'Christ'-like and Josephus, it will be recalled, does not hesitate to characterize Agrippa as '*chrēstos*'/'gracious'/'gentle'.

One should note in Romans, too, that when Paul discusses his doctrine of a 'Grace no longer of works', God 'thrusting aside' the Jews and how 'they killed' all the Prophets again, 'Salvation being granted to the Gentiles' and their now being 'zealous of' or 'jealous over' this; once again he employs the 'net', 'snare', and 'stumbling block'/'cause of offence'/'stumbling' language (Rom. 11:1–11). Not only does he also refer to 'Riches' here – the second of Belial's 'Nets' in the Damascus Document – now the Jews' 'stumbling' being 'the Riches of the world' and 'the Riches of the Gentiles' (Rom. 11:11–12) – but to his communities in the manner of the description of the Community Council at Qumran, as 'living sacrifices, Holy and well pleasing to God' (12:1), so that 'the offering up of the Gentiles might be pleasing, made Holy by the Holy Spirit' (15:16).[11]

In describing himself as being the 'Apostle of the Gentiles [*Ethnōn*]', Paul actually uses the words in the Habakkuk *Pesher* about the 'Worthlessness' of the Liar's 'Service' in erecting an 'Assembly' or 'Church upon Lying' and 'blood' 'for the sake of his Glory' – 'I *glorify my Service*' (Rom. 11:13). From here Paul moves immediately into evocation of the Messianic 'Root' and 'Branch' symbolism so dear to Qumran, but now applied to the new Gentile Christians as 'grafts' and the new 'Branches' upon the tree, the 'members' of Christ's body; while at the same time – in the manner of 1 Thessalonians 2:16 referring to 'killing the Lord Jesus and their own Prophets' – characterizing the Jews as 'Enemies for your sakes' (Rom. 11:16–28 and 12:4–5).

It is interesting that this eye-opening exhortation in the first three columns of the Damascus Document includes allusion to 'knowing Righteousness and understanding the works of God', 'breaking the Covenant', 'walking in Perfection', 'the Last Generation', and 'justifying the Wicked and condemning the Righteous'. This last is the direct opposite of the paradigmatic activity of 'the Sons of Zadok', who two columns later are rather described as 'standing in the Last Days' and 'justifying the Righteous and condemning the Wicked'.[12] This is the parallel of New Testament notions of 'Justification', but more in line with the Jamesian – not the Pauline – exposition of Habakkuk 2:4: 'the Righteous shall live by his Faith'. The Pauline riposte to this position, we have treated above, and it occupies a good part of Romans and Galatians.

These early passages of the Damascus Document contain allusion, as we have seen too, to 'men called by Name', as duly designated instruments of Salvation. This allusion is repeated two columns later as part of the definition of 'the Sons of Zadok' as 'the Elect of Israel', 'destined for Eternal life', in the course of which it is announced that 'all the Glory of Adam would be theirs'. In the Community Rule, the exact same language is repeated, but in the midst of baptismal imagery and 'pouring out' the Holy Spirit upon them.[13] This last is the glorified state of Heavenly or Eternal being, to which Paul himself makes repeated reference (1 Cor. 15:22 and 15:47) and which to some extent is also evoked in the Gospels.

As already observed, this phrase, 'called by Name', is transformed into 'called by this Name' or 'the Name of the Lord Jesus' in Acts and by Paul in 1 Corinthians (5:4 and 6:11).[14] As opposed to this, however, one should note the more Qumran-style way in which James 2:7 evokes 'the Good Name *by which you were called*', in conjunction significantly with allusion to 'not blaspheming' (that is to say, 'the Good Name') and evocation – as in these passages in the Damascus Document and Paul too – of 'the Royal Law according to the Scripture'.

It is interesting, that in the course of this allusion to 'being justified in the Name of the Lord Jesus and by the Spirit of our God' in 1 Corinthians 6:11, Paul also goes on to speak, it will be recalled, about 'being washed' and 'made Holy' (the 'consecration' or 'sanctification' in descriptions of James' 'Naziritism'), 'all things for me being Lawful', 'the body not being for fornication', and the members of Christ not 'being joined' to the flesh of a prostitute. The latter is contrasted, Qumran-style, with the more proper 'being joined to the Lord' (1 Cor. 6:11–20)

Regardless of the way 'prostitutes' are referred to in the Gospels (who generally are portrayed as being acceptable in Jesus' sight) and parallel plays on the language of 'fornication' at Qumran, this also evokes the Qumran language of 'join' and 'Joiners'. As we have earlier explained, this word most particularly occurs in Column Four of the Damascus Document in exposition of the crucial 'Zadokite Covenant' from Ezekiel 44:15, following these allusions in Columns Two–Three to 'God's Wrath' against those 'walking in the stubbornness of their own hearts' and 'Law-breakers' and being 'cut off in the wilderness' and/or 'being delivered up to the sword'.

Playing off the word 'Levites' – based on a Hebrew root meaning 'to be joined to' – and the apositive of 'the Sons of Zadok' in the underlying text; the exegesis that is developed had to do with 'and the Joiners with them' – meaning, it would appear, in 'the Land of Damascus' or the wilderness 'camps'.[15] It is also important to appreciate that in the course of the first allusion to 'Justification' in Column One, that is, the 'justifying the Wicked [possibly also 'Sinners'] and condemning the Righteous'; an attack on the Righteous One, literally on 'the soul of the Righteous One' (the *Zaddik*) is evoked, usually meaning one's mortal quick – in this case, possibly therefore a mortal attack. This reads as follows:

> They [the Covenant and Law-Breakers – in the Habakkuk *Pesher*, including 'the Traitors to the New Covenant'] banded together against the soul of the Righteous [One] and against all the walkers in Perfection [the 'Perfection' ideology so widespread at Qumran and in the New Testament],[16] execrating their soul [or 'being'], and they *pursued them with the sword, attempting to divide the People.*

One should note the use here of the idiom 'pursuing', also alluded to later in the Habakkuk *Pesher* in the attack on the Righteous Teacher by the Wicked Priest 'in the House of his Exile'. The ideology of sorts has recently been in the news and is developed in Rabbinic literature (perhaps even on the basis of usages here, since there is no mention of it in the Old Testament as such). In the matter of such 'pursuits', a death penalty could be pronounced, as 'the Zealots' no doubt would and did on those 'pursuing' one of their fellows *with intent to kill*.[17]

The use of the allusion 'soul' here is widespread at Qumran, particularly when evoking the suffering of 'the Poor' (always '*Ebionim*') or 'the Meek' in texts like the Qumran Hymns, but also new documents like the one Professor Wise and I recently entitled the 'Hymns of the Poor'.[18] One also finds such an allusion to the 'soul' in Paul, as, for instance, 'every soul of man' in Romans 2:9, used in the context of evocation of God's 'Wrath' and 'revelation of Righteous Judgement', echoing the language of these introductory exhortations in the Damascus Document, though here Paul is at his most circumspect. In these passages Paul again even alludes to the 'Jamesian' God 'not being a respecter of persons', but rather 'paying each according to his works' (2:5–2:11).

Paul also refers to 'soul' in 1 Corinthians 15:45 in relation to 'the First Man Adam becoming a living soul'. This, of course, is another aspect of how the 'Primal Adam' ideology was understood. One also finds it in the last line of the Letter of James, again having to do with 'saving a soul from death' (Jas. 5:20). This attack on 'the soul of the Righteous One' and his followers by 'the Liar' and his confederates in the Damascus Document probably best parallels the one by Paul on James – also called 'the *Zaddik*' – in the Pseudoclementines.

It is important to appreciate that, following the allusion to this attack at the end of Column One in the Damascus Document, the first allusion to 'raising up men called by Name' occurs – the second such allusion occurring two columns later in exegesis of 'the Sons of Zadok'. It is in this context that God in Column Two is referred to as 'revealing His Holy Spirit to them by the hand of His Messiah, and he or 'it is Truth', the ostensible reason given being 'that a remnant might be left to the land'.

One should realize that, as in the allusion to 'the sword of *no mere Adam*' in the exegesis of the 'Star Prophecy' in the War Scroll (referred to as well in Romans 11:26 above), the allusion to 'Messiah' is here singular not plural. One can see this by the singular verb and adjectival pronoun usages surrounding it, despite some scholarly attempts, purposeful or otherwise, to obscure it – one English translator even leaves out the next phrase, 'and in the explanation of His Name, their Names are (to be found)' – presumably because of this discrepancy. These allusions, which are always *singular* – however obscure their meaning may be – are extremely important, because, in the first place they reinforce the impression of the expectation of a *singular Messiah* at Qumran and, secondly, reference to him, as in Christianity, is accompanied by tell-tale allusion to the all-important 'Holy Spirit'.[19]

The Ban on the Consumption of Blood at Qumran and Eating and Drinking Judgement in Paul

To return to these allusions to the consumption of blood in the wilderness and Abraham as 'a Friend' or 'Beloved of God, because he kept the Commandments', in Column Three of the Damascus Document. In the Letter of James, too, a letter in which 'Law-breaking' and 'judging the Law' are condemned and 'Justification by works' and 'doing the Law' extolled, Abraham, as we saw, is also 'called Friend of God' in conjunction with 'being justified by works and not by Faith only' (Jas. 2:21–24).

We have already seen that in the Habakkuk *Pesher* above the interpretation of 'the Righteous shall live by his Faith' (Hab. 2:4) is circumscribed to 'the Doers of the *Torah* in the House of Judah', meaning, it would seem, '*Torah*-doing Jews'. Paul refers to these phraseologies, 'Doers of the Law being justified' and 'the Many being judged by the Law', in the passage where he refers to the 'soul of man' in Romans 2:9 above. But there he extends this to 'Greeks' and 'Gentiles', who can rather show 'the work of the Law written in their hearts' (2:15). The parallel here is to the dead letter of the Law written 'on stone tablets, not the fleshy tablets of the heart' in 2 Corinthians above, where it was also stated: 'for the letter kills, but the Spirit gives life' (3:6).

The Letter of James takes this point about Abraham being 'called a Friend of God' to insist, as we have seen – following evocation of 'the Tongue being but a little member' (note the play on Paul's 'members' imagery) – 'whosoever wishes to be a Friend of the world turns himself into an Enemy of God' (Jas. 4:4). It does this, also, following repeated allusion to 'boasting great things', 'kindling the Fire', and evocation of 'keeping the Royal Law according to the Scripture, "You shall love your neighbour as yourself"' (Jas. 2:8–3:6).

This last, as already explained, too, is the second of the two 'Love' Commandments, the 'Righteousness' Commandment, encompassing the sum total of Righteousness towards or one's obligations to one's fellow men – the first, 'loving God' or the 'Piety' Commandment having already been invoked in James 1:12 and 2:5. We also saw how Paul evokes this 'Righteousness' Commandment later in Romans in the aftermath of his analysis of 'the members' again or 'the Many being one body in Christ', 'not paying Evil for Evil', and one's obligation to the ruling Authorities, who, rather incredibly in view of their self-evident violence and brutality, according to him, 'are *no terror to good works*' (Rom. 12:4–13:3).

In this analysis in Romans 13, he applies the same language of 'receiving Judgement to themselves' to those 'who resist God's ordinance', as he did in 1 Corinthians 11:29 to those who, 'not seeing through to the body of the Lord' when they 'eat this bread and drink *the Cup of the Lord* unworthily'; not only 'shall be guilty of the body and blood of the Lord' (a variation on the blood-libel charge again), but in 'eating and drinking unworthily, eat and drink Judgement to themselves'. For Paul, as we saw, the Authorities (by which he clearly intends the *Imperial* ones) 'were appointed by God', a statement that, again, could not have failed to send his 'Zealot'/'Messianic' adversaries into paroxysms of rage. By the same token, since these derived their 'Authority . . . from God', one was obliged to obey them (Rom. 13:1).

These he calls 'Servants of God' (Rom. 13:6), reversing his allusion to 'the Apostles of the Highest Degree' as 'Servants of Satan' not Righteousness in 2 Corinthians 11:15. Put in another way, the Roman 'Authorities' not the Jerusalem 'Apostles' were 'Servants of God'. The last, whom he contemptuously dismissed as 'Pseudo-Apostles' and 'false work-men', only disguised themselves as 'Servants of Righteousness'! To these Authorities, 'taxes are due' (Rom. 13:7). This last clearly reappears in slightly variant form in the proverbial statement attributed to Jesus in the Gospels, in response to questioning from 'the Pharisees and Herodians' about the Lawfulness of paying the tax (the very parties that advocated paying the tax), 'render the things to Caesar that were Caesar's' (Matt. 22:17–21 and pars.) – all this in a prelude to the condemnation of the one who only 'eats vegetables' as opposed to 'the one who believes he may eat all things' in Romans 14:2.

Paul's characterization of such persons as 'weak' (15:1) or, in 14:1, 'weak in Faith', should be ranged alongside Jesus' rebuke to his principal Apostle Peter unable, as we saw, to walk on the waters and sinking into the sea, 'You of little Faith, why did you doubt?' (Matt. 14:31). For Paul, these 'ordinances' or 'Judgements' of God in Romans 13:2–3 are often little more than the laws and decrees of the Roman State and its Rulers. That he concludes his defence of paying tribute to the Roman Authorities by citing the Righteousness Commandment, 'loving one's neighbour', 'the Royal Law according to the Scripture' in James, would have just been the crowning blow to his opponents, for whom 'the Righteousness Commandment' was the be-all and end-all of all human conduct.

This leads up to his attack on vegetarianism and 'despising him who eats' (Rom. 14:3),[20] 'not destroying the work of God for the sake of food' – literally 'meat' (14:20). Here Paul concludes, putting paid to all these points, 'do not with your meat destroy him for whom Christ died' and 'I am persuaded that nothing is unclean in and of itself, *only to him who reckons things unclean is it unclean*' (14:14–15), concluding,

> For the Kingdom of God is not *eating and drinking*, but *Righteousness* and peace and joy *in the Holy Spirit*. For he who serves Christ in these things is *well pleasing to God and approved by men*. (14:17–18)

Once again, Paul combines the imagery of Qumran of the Community Council being a 'fragrance of Righteousness pleasing to God', with the repeated criticism of him of 'trying to please men' or 'being a Friend to the world', yet another example – if such were needed – of his striking control of rhetorical rejoinder.

He also inverts the 'stumbling over one small point of the Law' of the Letter of James, which itself followed evocation of the 'love your neighbour' Commandment, saying 'all things are clean, and Evil only to the man who, through *stumbling, eats*' (Rom. 14:20). Not only does this parallel his two-fold repetition of 'all things to me are Lawful' in 1 Corinthians, Paul now goes on to add, seemingly, even the 'Nazirite'/'Rechabite' scruple over 'drinking wine', characterizing such a scruple too as 'weak'.

This is quite incredible testimony because it shows Paul to be, at once, equally critical of people making a fetish of the Law, vegetarianism, and *Nazirite/Rechabite* abstention from wine – all things characteristic of James' behaviour and other 'Essene', 'Ebionite', 'Elchasaite' bathing types. As Paul puts this (he is on his best behaviour here, meaning, his most disingenuous):

> It is not right to *eat flesh* or *drink wine* or [to do] anything in what your brother *stumbles, is scandalized*, or *is weak* (Rom 14:21),

and concludes this attack on these 'weak stumblers', who do not eat flesh or are vegetarians or do not drink wine – that is, who make problems over 'eating and drinking' – by raising the twin issues so central to his concerns, 'lack of Faith' and 'doubting' – the two traits in the Gospels so characterizing core Apostles such as Peter, sinking into the Sea of Galilee for lack of 'Faith', or Thomas 'called *Didymus*', doubting his encounter with the risen Christ.

But Paul's attestation here to the whole theme of abstention from wine, which he puts on a par with 'eating only vegetables' and in his usual off-hand way dismisses as 'a stumbling block' or 'weak', in a roundabout manner indirectly confirms the early Church accounts of precisely such behaviour on the part of James and other like-minded 'life-long Nazirite' or 'Rechabite Priests'. Not only are these kinds of things the essence of the 'eating and drinking' aspersions (as in Matthew, 'the Son of Man came eating and drinking'), but they call into question the whole matter of Jesus' words at 'the Last Supper', as Paul represents them in 1 Corinthians 11:24 (refracted in orthodox Scripture as we have it).

Wounding Weak Consciences in Paul and
More Damascus Document Parallels

'Conscience', too, is the catchword Paul uses to express his contempt for those who, under the twin rubrics of 'loving God' and 'being weak', make problems over 'meat' or 'eating things sacrificed to idols' (or, in other words, 'reclining at an idol-Temple'). Here too, it will be recalled, Paul vowed – equally as disingenuously as the 'not drinking wine' he couples with it – 'never to eat flesh or meat again forever, so as not to cause the weak brother to stumble' or 'wound his weak conscience' (1 Cor. 8:3–13). Not only is Paul opposed to the wider aspect of the Jerusalem Church perspective, but he knows it so well that he can draw out and deride its every minute point. James and the rest of 'the Elders' in Jerusalem must have been at a complete loss as to how to deal with him.

In Romans 13, not only does he reverse the normal Palestinian thrust of 'loving your neighbour as yourself', but also another allusion to 'conscience', that is, 'fear' the Authorities (this, of course, the counterpart to the normal 'fearing God') and subject yourself to them, 'not only because of wrath [the Authorities' 'wrath'], but also for the sake of conscience' (Rom. 13:5). Instead of being a euphemism for meticulous observation of the Law, 'conscience' now becomes – along with the 'wrath' of and terror inspired by the Authorities (not to mention, 'loving your neighbour as yourself') – something that should impel the ordinary citizen to pay all the 'taxes' and 'tributes due' the State (13:6–10). The implied allusion here to 'Wrath of God', so much a part of Qumran vocabulary, now becomes, rather, the vengeance the State will take upon Evil-doers, for 'he' or 'it' – there is a *double entendre* here – 'does not wear the sword in vain' (13:4). Again, not only do we have here much of the vocabulary of Qumran reversed, but a more anti-'Zealot' and, in particular, anti-'*Sicarii*' point of view could not be imagined.

Not only is this contradicted, following Jesus' exposition of 'the Cup of the New Covenant' in his blood in Luke, by the picture of Jesus *instructing his Apostles* to 'purchase a sword' and their showing that they already have two! (22:36–38); but we encountered a version of this vocabulary in the First Column of the Damascus Document in the picture of those 'seeking to divide the People ['the Liar', 'Covenant-Breakers', and 'Traitors to the New Covenant'] *pursuing the Zaddik and all the Walkers in Perfection with the sword*'. Following allusion to the Children of Israel 'being cut off in the wilderness', because 'they ate blood', and 'cutting off' their kings, their land 'becoming desolate', in the Third Column; henceforth in the Damascus Document 'the sword', to which they 'are delivered up', becomes 'the avenging sword of the Covenant'![21]

Finally there is the evocation in these passages in Romans of the vocabulary of 'standing' again, so much a part of the Ebionite/Elchasaite 'Standing One' ideology, as we saw. Paul makes these allusions immediately after disparaging the person who 'being weak eats vegetables' and 'judges the one who eats' (Rom. 14:2–3), then going on to assert that God will 'receive' the one 'who eats' – the euphemism is for breaking dietary regulations and, no doubt, more (for instance, his version of Holy Communion or 'eating the body' and 'drinking the blood of Christ') – for Himself. Then he enlarges on this point as follows:

> He *stands or falls* to his own master, and he shall be *made to stand*, for God is able to *make him stand*. (14:4)

There can be little doubt that, once again, we have a version of the 'Jewish Christian' 'Standing One' ideology. In signalling the sense in Hebrew of 'standing' as resurrection, we have already shown the relationship of these words to the follow-up to the Damascus Document's exposition of the 'Sons of Zadok' – themselves defined as 'those who will stand in the *Last Days*':

> According to *the Covenant which God made with the First, to forgive their sins*, so too would God make atonement for [or 'through'] them –

Here the 'remission of sins' theme, but not by men – *by God*.

> And with the Completion of the Era of the number of these years, there will be no more *joining to the House of Judah* [meaning 'Jews'?], but rather each man shall stand on his own net [the word here is actually 'watchtower' in the manner in which it is used in the *Pesher* on Habakkuk 2:1]

in the sense of 'record' or 'works' – or, for that matter, Paul's 'falling to his own master' above – the mention of which triggers the 'Three Nets of Belial' expositions that follow.

In addition to the horror of 'consuming blood' preceding these allusions, the Damascus Document now goes on in Column Six, as we saw as well, to evoke in connection with 'the New Covenant in the Land of Damascus' and 'the Star Prophecy', what the Letter of James calls 'the Royal Law according to the Scripture', so disingenuously invoked by Paul in support of paying taxes to the Roman Authorities and submitting to foreign rule above: 'they shall each man love his brother as himself'.[22]

The allusions that follow this include: 'not to uncover the nakedness of near kin, but keeping away from fornication according to Law'. 'Keeping away' here is expressed in terms of the Hebrew verb *'lehinnazer'* – the root of the word 'Nazirite' in English. Two columns earlier this was the rationale for the ban on niece marriage, also part of the 'Three Nets of Belial' prohibition of 'fornication'. In fact, one begins to see that this usage, *'lehinnazer'* in Hebrew, is the root of the expression 'keep away' or 'abstain from' *in James' directives to overseas communities in Acts.*[23]

Preceding the evocation of the Righteousness Commandment at the end of Column Six of the Damascus Document was the admonition 'to separate between polluted and pure and to distinguish between Holy and profane', exactly the opposite, as explained, of what Acts says Peter learned on the rooftop in Jaffa.[24] This also included the commandment to 'separate from the Sons of the Pit' and, in Column Seven, 'from all pollutions according to Law, so that a man will *not defile his Holy Spirit, which God separated for them*'. This last is basically an allusion to either temporary or life-long Naziritism and being 'consecrated' or 'set aside as Perfectly Holy'.

This passage ends with another admonition *'to do* according to the exact sense of the Law' – again the tell-tale Jamesian note on 'doing' – 'everyone walking in these (Commandments) in Perfect Holiness relying on all they were transmitted of the Covenant of God, promising them [here, a variation of the word, 'Faithfulness'] to live for a thousand generations'.[25] As we saw, Paul uses this expression 'Perfect Holiness' in 2 Corinthians 7:1, addressing the 'Beloved Ones' again (in Hebrew, the 'Friends') and having just evoked the difference between Christ and Belial, intoning,

> So come out from among them and *be separated*, saith the Lord, and *the unclean touch* not and I will receive you, and I will be a Father to you, and you will be for me sons and daughters.[26]

'Having these promises [in the Damascus Document above, this is the promise 'to live for a thousand generations'] *cleanse [yourselves] from every pollution of flesh and spirit, Perfecting Holiness in fear of God*'.

In the Damascus Document, this section also includes the allusion to 'the offspring of vipers' (Isa. 59:5), applied to those

who defile their Holy Spirits, opening their mouth with a blaspheming

Tongue against the Laws of the Covenant of God saying, 'They are not sure.' They speak an Abomination [or 'a blasphemy'] concerning them.

This section of the Damascus Document draws to an end, following the allusion to 'separate from the Sons of the Pit', with the instruction 'to keep away from polluted or Evil Riches [this is expressed in terms of the Hebrew root N–Z–R or '*lehinnazer*' again, the root, as we have seen, of the English term 'Nazirite', meaning 'to be consecrated' or 'set aside'] [acquired by] vow or ban and [to keep away] from the Riches of the Temple [meaning the Temple Treasury] and robbing the Poor of His People'.²⁷

Towards the end, in the Eighth Column, it finally enjoins, 'standing before the Assembly of the Men of Perfect Holiness', where those who 'have spoken wrongly against the Laws of Righteousness and rejected the Covenant and Compact ['the Faith'] they raised in the Land of Damascus, the New Covenant' – including 'the Liar' – are condemned. Not only are such persons said to have 'put idols on their hearts' and 'walked in the stubbornness of their heart', but 'all the Holy Ones of the Most High' are described as having 'cursed him' and 'no one is to co-operate with him in regard to Riches [or 'purse'] or work [in the sense of 'Mission' or 'Service']'.²⁸ These, as the Document puts it, 'shall have no share in the House of the *Torah*', a spirit, as should be plain, that could not be more different from the Pauline. Not only does reference to 'the Man of Lying' directly follow, but in addition, so do two allusions to 'fearing God' and 'fearing His Name', coupled with the pronouncement that 'to those that love Him' (compare with James 2:5 above) and 'reckon His Name', God would reveal Salvation (*Yesha‘*) and Justification . . . for a thousand Generations.²⁹

The Damascus Document, as explained, was found in the 1890s in a collection of Hebrew manuscripts known as the Cairo *Genizah*. Representing documents from the Middle Ages, they were preserved in this probably Karaite – that is, anti-Rabbinic – ancient Jewish synagogue, but there was no context in which to place the two parallel versions of the document found there at the time. There were those in the early days of research concerning it who considered it to be a 'Jewish Christian' document of some sort, but were unable to go beyond that. We are now better able to place this all-important document in its proper context, aided by the complete corpus of the other documents from Qumran, the unrelenting and uncompromising ethos of which should be clear throughout.

That we have in the midst of these allusions by Paul to 'eating and drinking' and 'breaking the bread' in 1 Corinthians 10–11, evocation of 'taking the Cup' and 'the New Covenant in my blood' or 'Communion with the blood of Christ' (1 Cor. 10:16 and 11:25 – repeated in Matthew, Mark, and Luke in the context of the 'Last Supper'), is of the utmost importance. As Paul goes on to express it, 'for as often as you *eat this bread and drink this Cup*, you announce the death of the Lord until he comes' (11:26).

It should be appreciated further that the context in Paul is one of 'examining oneself' so as 'not to be judged' (1 Cor. 11:28–32), concepts that in the Letter of James come out in the context of subjecting yourself 'to God' (not the Roman State), and 'resisting the Devil' (*Diabolō* – Jas. 4:7–10), also seen as representing that State. The Letter of James puts it,

> He that speaks against a brother and judges his brother, *speaks against the Law* and judges the Law, but if you judge the Law, *you are not a Doer of the Law, but a judge.* (4:11)

This could not agree more with the passages from the Damascus Document just quoted above, which specifically include 'speaking erroneously against the Laws of Righteousness'. Even the expression, 'Doer of the Law', is to be found in two successive notices in the Habakkuk *Pesher*, fundamental both to the exposition of Habakkuk 2:3 on 'the Delay of the *Parousia*' and Habakkuk 2:4, 'the Righteous shall live by his Faith'.

For Paul the 'judging' in the Letter of James above is now applied to the man who 'eats and drinks unworthily', by which he means, 'not seeing through to the body of the Lord'. Such a man, as we just saw, is not only '*guilty of the body and blood of the Lord*', but moreover, '*eats and drinks Judgement to himself*' (11:27–29). Not only does this fly in the face of allusions like the one to 'putting idols on his heart' in the Damascus Document above and of the substance and spirit of the Letter attributed to James in the New Testament; '*abstention* [*'lehinnazer'*] *from things sacrificed to idols and from blood*' – just as at Qumran – form the centrepiece of the thrust of James' instructions to overseas communities, which in fact Paul appears to be answering in these passages from 1 Corinthians.

One should note that in 1 Corinthians 10:5, when discussing these things, Paul actually alludes to the Children of Israel 'being cut off in the wilderness' – found at this same point in the Damascus Document – but without telling why. In fact, he even uses these words 'cutting off', it will be recalled, to express what for him is one of the most biting remarks in the whole corpus, the hope in Galatians 5:12 that the circumcisers disturbing his communities, like the 'some sent by James' earlier in the same letter clearly from Jerusalem, would 'themselves cut off' – meaning, as we have previously explained, their own privy parts.

It is almost inconceivable that this could be accidental or that these things could have been misunderstood, though they have been for the better part of two millennia, particularly since Paul is combining all these allusions in 1 Corinthians. The only difference is that instead of 'abstaining from things sacrificed to idols and blood', Paul's communities are now being encouraged (or at least not discouraged) *to partake*, certainly *to partake of the blood of Christ*. This flies in the face of the James-like vegetarianism and Rechabite-style aversion to wine of all these Nazirite extremist groups, who neither consumed wine, nor ate meat at all. It also flies in the face of James' proscription on the consumption of blood in the Book of Acts, even as we have it, not to mention Jewish legal restrictions generally.

It cannot be that Paul misunderstood the true thrust of James' instructions to overseas communities (if these are the same or parallel to those enshrined in the document '*MMT*', all the more so). On the contrary, Paul reveals that he understands them very well. That these directives were *written down* in some manner is not only averred in Acts' account – such as it is – of an 'epistle' being sent down from James with two 'prophets', Judas (called by Acts) 'Barsabas', and Silas (15:22–23), but also by Paul in 1 Corinthians 10:11 (though, strictly speaking, this allusion more likely refers to these passages in the Damascus Document).

That in his delineation of these issues involving the 'Cup of blood', Paul is speaking figuratively and James literally is just the point. As we have repeatedly stressed, Paul allegorizes in the manner that Philo of Alexandria – his older contemporary – allegorized about the Old Testament. Only in Paul, everything emerging from a 'Jamesian' framework – and, as it were, the perspective of Qumran – is not only allegorized, but reversed.

It is no wonder that the world has for so long been confused about the true nature of what occurred at this crucial juncture in human history. But now that we have the Qumran documents to aid us (come down nineteen centuries after they were deposited as if to haunt us), it is no longer possible to be mistaken about the true nature of what occurred. Without these documents we could never have, using the words of Paul, 'seen through to it'.

The Cup of the Lord, Tombs that Whiten, and Linen Clothes Again

We can now return to this allusion in the Gospel of the Hebrews with a clearer understanding of this process and of what is at stake in considering all these parallel and interlocking testimonies about 'breaking the bread', 'eating', and 'the Cup of the Lord'. We can now see that the language of this short passage from the Gospel of the Hebrews, inadvertently preserved by Jerome, actually parallels Paul in 1 Corinthians 10–11 and, in turn, the Synoptic Gospels about 'eating and drinking' at the so-called 'Last Supper'.

But in the Gospel of the Hebrews, the episode, while including reference to 'the Cup of the Lord', is completely devoid of extrapolation into 'the Communion with' or 'the Cup of the New Covenant in' the blood of Jesus Christ, which nowhere did play or could have played a part in any *Palestinian* documents – only overseas or foreign ones. Whatever the redaction process involved, and however amazing it might at first seem, it is possible even to conclude that the Gospel of the Hebrews' version of the tradition about 'the Cup of the Lord', which James purportedly drank with Jesus, incorporating, as it does, a *first appearance* to James, represents an earlier version than orthodox Gospel ones – or even *the original* one. This was then inverted, in line with Paul's understanding of 'Communion' in 1 Corinthians 10:14–33 and 11:22–30, and retrospectively inserted into the history as it has come down to us.

In fact, this episode in this so-called 'Jewish Gospel' is not only paralleled in John's episode about Jesus' appearance along the Sea of Galilee, where in addition to 'giving them' some of the bread, *Jesus gives them* 'some of the fish too' (in Luke 24:42, this is turned around to '*they gave him* a piece of broiled fish and part of a honeycomb' and the locale is confined to Jerusalem); but even more completely in Luke's detailed story of a first appearance by Jesus to the 'two' outside Jerusalem on the Emmaus Road. If what we have just said is true, this would make the story about the first sighting by these two Disciples in Luke – one called 'Cleopas' – *later* than the one in the Gospel of the Hebrews – or at least the source on which it was based. To put this slightly differently, both are based on the same *Palestinian source about James*. This in our view is the proper conclusion to draw.

Though we have already described the basic outline of this episode above, it is worth considering it in more detail. This sighting is also noted in the Gospel of Mark, where characteristically (as in most other matters relating to the family of Jesus), it is for the most part erased (16:12–13). Whereas Luke only partially rubs out the identities of its principal protagonists, making it difficult to determine precisely what happened; Mark – whether editorially curtailed or otherwise – simply notes this initial appearance in the environs of Jerusalem and then moves on, following the approach of Matthew and John, to Galilee (for some reason the preferred focus of these other Gospels). Luke, it should be appreciated – in line with the saying attributed to Jesus in the Gospel of Thomas about 'going to James the Just', never does get to Galilee – but rather has every-one stay in Jerusalem, which is more sensible. Just as Mark also retains the traces of an appearance 'to the Eleven' as they reclined – like Agrippa II on his dining patio – again, Paul-like, Jesus chastises even his core Apostles for their lack of 'belief' or 'Faith' here.

Mark, as we just saw, also retains the traces of the appearance to the two on the Emmaus Road, which, like Luke, he places just before this additional appearance 'to the Eleven' in Jerusalem, noting that: 'After these things, he appeared in a different form' – this motif will also reappear in all three mistaken-identity episodes in John, where Jesus is either por-trayed as 'standing' in front of Mary Magdalene (20:14), 'standing among them' (20:26), and 'standing on the shore' (21:4), and be the reason no one recognizes him –

> to two of them as they walked in the country, and when they went and told it to the rest, they *did not believe them*. (Mark 16:12–13)

The 'things' Mark is referring to are for a start the report of a *first appearance* – not paralleled in the other Synoptics – 'to Mary Magdalene, from whom he *cast out* seven demons' (Mark 16:9)! Here, of course, is the language of 'casting out', 'casting down', and even sometimes 'casting into', an additional adumbration. Wherever the phraseology occurs, its basic relationship to the 'nets' Belial or Balaam 'cast before Israel' in the Damascus Document or Revelation and to the deaths of both the Righteous Teacher in the Dead Sea Scrolls and James in early Church sources, should always be appreciated.

The variations on this '*ballō*'/'casting' theme are so widespread and insistent in the Gospels, as we have seen, that these, in effect, begin to resemble divertimentos or excurses on this word. One particularly humorous example in Mark we did not cover above, which has to do, as in the Damascus Document above, with the 'Temple Treasury' again –

and, of course, by implication, its pollution – is Jesus' Parable about 'the Poor widow's two mites' (Mark 12:41–44 and Luke 21:1–4).

In Mark, Jesus tells the parable just after pronouncing the 'love your neighbour' Commandment in 12:31 and David, 'sitting at the right hand' of God and making his 'enemies his footstool' of Psalm 110:1, in 12:36 – just before the 'Little Apocalypse' (13:3–37). In Mark, the 'Poor widow' – note the play on the 'Poor' terminology again – 'casts into' the Treasury what appear to be her last 'two mites'. Here, the allusion, 'casting into' (*ebalen*), occurs *five times in just four lines*. The widow's contribution is not only favourably contrasted with what 'the Many' – the name, as we have seen, for the rank and file at Qumran – 'cast in' (*eballon*), but, significantly, also what 'the Rich cast in', a major theme of both the attack on the Establishment in the Letter of James and the parallel 'Three Nets of Belial' critique in the Damascus Document.

It should also be immediately apparent that this episode, partially paralleled in Luke, is but a further variation on Matthew's story of Judas *Iscariot* 'casting the thirty pieces of silver' he received for betraying Jesus 'into the Temple Treasury' (Matt. 27:3–10) – itself an adumbration of the Talmudic story about Jesus' recommendation, attributed to the James-like 'Jacob of Kfar Sechania' in the *Talmud*, to use not 'the *Poor* widow's', but *the Rich prostitute*'s gifts to the Temple Treasury to build a latrine for the High Priest and the whole 'Rechabite'/'Potter'/'blood' and 'poverty' circle of motifs encountered in our discussion of this.

Also part of 'these things', referred to in Mark before the appearance to 'the two as they walked along the Way', are the experiences of 'Mary the mother of James and Salome' – as we shall see below, obviously meant to be the mother of Jesus – who with Mary Magdalene witnesses the crucifixion and enters the empty tomb (Mark 15:40–16:8). Matthew simply calls her 'the other Mary', though five lines earlier, as a witness to the Crucifixion, he referred to her as 'Mary the mother of James and Joses and the mother of the sons of Zebedee' (Matt. 27:56–61). For Luke, who adds Joanna here (earlier in 8:3, the wife of a Herodian official!), Mary is simply and, perhaps most tellingly, '*Mary the mother of James*' (24:10).

In Luke and Matthew, these women are not, strictly speaking, recipients of a post-resurrection appearance by Jesus at all. Rather they are only the *witnesses to the empty tomb* and the *bearers of the rumour of his resurrection*. References to any unnamed or partially named 'two' in these accounts should also always be remarked; for instance in Luke, the two unnamed 'men in brilliant white clothing', who suddenly 'stood beside' Mary Magdalene, Joanna, and Mary *the mother of James* in the empty tomb (24:4 – note the allusion to 'standing' again here, as we will also encounter it repeatedly in John). In Matthew and Mark the two become one – in Matthew, an 'Angel of the Lord'; in Mark, 'a young man'.

There are also the 'two', chosen at the beginning of Acts 'to become a *witness of his resurrection*' to fill Judas *Iscariot*'s 'Office' – 'from which he fell away' – the first supposedly called Barsabas, also 'surnamed Justus' (Acts 1:21–26 – one should keep an eye, too, on the use of the word 'witness' here). We have repeatedly encountered another of these Barsabases, but there he was 'Judas Barsabas'. One should also always remark, as in all these Gospel portrayals, the castigation of these central figures for their lack of 'Belief' or of the key Pauline requirement of 'Faith'.

In Matthew and Mark, the appearance of the single individual sitting in the tomb or on a rock outside it – as in the scene of Jesus' Transfiguration before the Central Three 'on the mountain' – 'was as *lightning* and his clothing was *white as snow*' (Matt. 28:3). In Matthew's description of Jesus' Transfiguration before Moses and Elijah, it was Jesus' 'face, which *shone as the sun* and his clothing was *white as the light*' (17:2). We have already connected these kinds of miraculous 'whitening' notices to the description in the Pseudoclementine *Recognitions* of 'the tombs of the two brothers that *whitened of themselves* every year' following the escape of James' Community to Jericho.

One should remark the tell-tale number 'two' again in this seemingly innocuous sidelight, when the Community visits these tombs outside Jericho and thus escaped Paul pursuing Peter as far as Damascus. In the Pseudoclementine *Recognitions*, the '*tombs of the two brothers whitened of themselves every year*', paralleling Luke's version of the empty tomb, which had, it will be recalled, the three women and 'some [others]' surprised by the appearance in the tomb of '*two men standing beside them in brilliantly shining clothing*' (Luke 23:1–4).

To carry this line of thinking a little further, in the very next sentence in the *Recognitions*, where James sends out Peter on his first missionary journey to confront Simon in Caesarea (Ps. *Rec.* 1.71), Simon is identified as 'a *Samaritan* magician' – the accuracy of the Pseudoclementine description of Simon's geographical origins, as compared to the patent imprecision of Acts should always be remarked – who, to repeat:

led *Many* of our people *astray* [the typical language applied to the adversary

at Qumran, who 'rejected the Law', and false teachers generally], by asserting that he was 'the Standing One', that is in other words, 'the Christ' and
'the Great Power of the High God', which is superior to the Creator of the
world. (Ps. *Rec.* 1.72)

Not only do we have in these lines from the *Recognitions* an almost
perfect description of the relationship of the 'Primal Adam' ideology to
'the Christ' (as we have seen), but here the word 'standing' is applied in an
ideological manner to Jesus and not simply as a detail in narrative as in the
Gospels (for example, when Jesus' mother and brothers 'stood without',
unable to see him because of the crowd, or Jesus suddenly appeared
'standing' on the lake shore or in rooms or tombs among the Disciples or
'behind' Mary Magdalene in post-resurrection appearances – mostly in
John, mentioned above).[30] That this series of allusions to 'whitening', the
'two', and 'the Standing One' in the Pseudoclementine *Recognitions*
relates intrinsically and not just accidentally to these *empty tomb*
scenarios in the Gospels should be growing more and more apparent.

At this point in Mark, for instance, it is the 'young man, *sitting on the
right side clothed with a white robe*' (16:5) – in Matthew 28:2–3, it was
'an Angel of the Lord come down from Heaven', whose '*face was as lightning and his clothing white as snow*', *sitting on a stone*. Earlier in Mark
on the mountain when Jesus transfigured himself, Jesus' '*clothes became
brilliant, exceedingly white as snow, such as no fuller on earth would be
able to whiten*' (9:3).

We have already seen this last echoed in the language of the 'fuller'
beating out 'the Just One's' brains with 'the club that he used to beat out
clothes' in parallel early Church accounts based on second-century
sources, such as Clement and Hegesippus, of James' demise. But not only
was the 'fuller' language from these early accounts of the death of James
present in this description in Mark of Jesus' clothes on the Mount of
his Transfiguration, but incredibly, so too, as we also saw, was this
'whitening' language from the Pseudoclementine description of James'
Community's escape outside Jericho to view the tombs of the *two
brothers* after the attack on James by Paul!

Once again, however hard at first to conceptualize, in our view this
proves that the Gospel accounts are *later* than either of these, or at least
the sources upon which they are based. The Gospels are certainly every bit
as and even more fantastic. For its part, Acts 1:10, in its account of Jesus'
Ascension forty days after his resurrection, now has the 'two men standing

beside them in white clothes' – 'them' being now 'the Apostles'. Again there is the reprise of the 'standing' motif here – not to mention the number 'two' – followed in the very next line by the reference to the Apostles, now addressed as 'Men! Galileans!', also described as 'standing' once again and 'looking up at the Heavens' watching him go.

The picture of these 'two men' in white clothes in Acts repeats the Gospel of Luke's earlier picture of the 'two men standing *beside them*' – the 'them' now being the women and the ubiquitous 'some' again – and Gospel pictures generally of the 'resplendent white clothing' of these individuals, as it does the earlier words used in the Synoptics to describe Jesus' clothing, 'effulgent, exceedingly white as snow', on the mountain of his Transfiguration (Mark 9:3 and pars.).

For its part, the Gospel of John repeats Luke's scenario of 'two men' in 'star-like' clothing in the empty tomb, but these, incorporating a part of the motif in Matthew, are now simply 'two Angels in white'. Here, only Mary Magdalene sees them, no others, and this not till *after she* returns to the tomb a *second time* (John 20:12). Earlier in John, it was *she alone* who originally 'came to the tomb, while it was still dark and saw the stone taken away', but without any explanation of by whom or why (John 20:1).

At first she does not appear to enter the tomb. Rather she runs then to tell 'the Disciple Jesus loved' and Peter, who themselves run back and enter the tomb – first Peter, then the Disciple Jesus loved (John 20:2–6). For John, it is they who enter the tomb, not Mary Magdalene, Mary *the mother of James* and Joanna as in Luke. But instead of seeing the one or two men or Angels in the 'white' and 'brilliantly shining clothes standing there', as in Luke and the others, Peter and the Disciple Jesus loved only see 'the linen clothes lying there' – meaning, it would seem, *Jesus' grave-clothes* now – together with a 'napkin that had been about his head *neatly folded to one side*' (John 20:5–8)!

A separate episode then ensues in John after Peter and the Beloved Disciple go off, where Jesus then *actually* appears 'standing' behind Mary Magdalene alone (John 20:14), also reflected in the added material in Mark above. For John, this involves Mary Magdalene 'peeking into the tomb' *a second time* after Peter and the Disciple Jesus loved 'went on their way home again' (John 20:10–11). Several lines before, it had been 'the Disciple Jesus loved' who 'peeked' into the tomb, first seeing 'the *linen clothes lying there*, yet not going in' till Peter did (John 20:5).

It is during this second visit to the empty tomb in John, where it is now

Mary Magdalene '*standing* at the tomb weeping outside' (20:11), that she sees 'the two Angels in white' – now 'sitting one at the head and one at the feet of where the body of Jesus was laid' (20:12) – replicating the 'two men *standing* beside them in brilliant white clothes' that the three women had seen in their first visit to the empty tomb in Luke. It is at this moment, 'turning around, she saw Jesus *standing there*, but she did not know it was Jesus' (John 20:14). Here, of course, it is Mary Magdalene seeing Jesus as 'the Standing One'. No wonder she could not recognize him!

This point about 'not recognizing' Jesus is common to several of these accounts as we have explained, usually accompanied by the 'standing' language. This is always the case in John. Here, however, it is Jesus himself who is described as 'standing' before her when she turned around, not the 'two men in brilliant white clothes', twice described earlier in Luke and in Acts as 'standing beside them'. A few lines earlier, it will be recalled, it was Mary herself. All of these allusions, even in the orthodox Gospels as we have them, should be seen as reflections of the Ebionite/ Sabaean 'Standing One' ideology *par excellence*.

What the transmission mechanism could have been for combining these various concepts into a single narrative or narratives with slightly altered or trivialized signification is impossible to say. What is clear is that there were *earlier* traditions, which not only preceded the Gospels, as we presently have them, but read *quite differently* – perhaps even like those underlying the parallel materials about 'tomb', 'servants', 'clothing', and 'whitening' in the First Book of the Pseudoclementine *Recognitions* or the tradition about the first appearance to James preserved in Jerome's 'Gospel according to the Hebrews'.

The note about the 'linen clothes' in the Gospel of John – now meant to be the graveclothes of Jesus – is also very important. Now those who see 'the linen clothes lying there' in John – repeated three times in three lines, showing the emphasis the narrator is placing on them here – are not the two Marys and Luke's Joanna, or even Peter alone as in Luke, but now, first Peter and then 'the Disciple Jesus loved' (John 20:5–7). Even more to the point – and perhaps more accurately – they are the '*clothes*' *Jesus is pictured as giving to 'the Servant of the [High] Priest'* in Jerome's Gospel of the Hebrews.

If 'the Disciple Jesus loved' in John, who with Peter first sees these 'linen clothes lying' there, has any connection with James, then here again we have additional material bearing on post-resurrection appearances possibly involving family members of Jesus. These also must be seen as not unconnected with the theme of 'linen clothes' – bathing or otherwise – repeatedly encountered in descriptions about 'Essene'/'Sabaean' ritual bathing practices. These are the several permutations of the circle of materials we are dealing with here.

The theme of these 'linen clothes' also reappears, as we saw, in the note about 'the clothes the witnesses laid at' Paul's feet in Acts' account of the Jewish mob stoning Stephen. But here the material probably owes as much to the stoning of James in all early Church sources and Josephus, 'the clothes' – again probably 'white linen' – of course, having been *James'* clothes which, as we saw, as in all such stonings, were removed, *not the witnesses'*! In fact, here too, the stoning of James and the special 'linen clothes' he wore may have been the original core giving rise to these other variations.

Preceding his account of a *first* appearance to what appear to be members of Jesus' family on the Emmaus Road outside Jerusalem, Luke too – like John – also refers to these 'linen clothes lying by themselves'. This small addendum, not paralleled at all in Matthew and Mark, has Peter 'running to the tomb' *alone* – not as in John *with* 'the Disciple Jesus loved' – after the report by the three women 'to the Eleven and all the rest' (repeated in the next line as 'to the Apostles'[31] – Luke 24:9–10), which they took to be 'idle talk'. Then Peter, 'having risen up', ran to the tomb, because the other Apostles 'didn't believe them' (the 'not believing' theme in Mark 16:11 again). Now he, not Mary Magdalene, 'stoops down and seeing the *linen clothes lying alone*, went home wondering at what had happened' (Luke 24:11–12).

There is a certain parallel in the way Peter is the witness to these things, here, to the way Epiphanius in his version of Hegesippus has Simeon bar Cleophas as 'the witness' to the stoning of James. For his part, Eusebius, it will be recalled, rather describes this 'witness' as 'one of the Priests of the sons of Rechab, a son of the Rechabites spoken of by the Prophet Jeremiah'. Both allude to this in conjunction with the language of 'casting down' and the 'laundryman' and his 'club' allusion, we have been delineating above. For Eusebius, this is 'a club he used to beat out clothes'. For Jerome, describing this in slightly different language but nevertheless betraying the same source, 'such a club as laundrymen use to beat out clothes'.[32]

Acts' version of the stoning of Stephen above also has Stephen being 'cast out of the city'. We have already identified this as a substitution for Paul's attack on James in the Pseudoclementine *Recognitions*, where not only the language of 'casting' occurs – now 'casting down' – but also that of 'whitening'. At this point in Acts, as we just noted, 'the *witnesses lay their clothes* [completely incomprehensibly] *at the feet of a young man* named Saul', thus combining our 'witness', 'clothes', and 'feet' themes,[33] but now adding a new one, that of the 'young man' (Acts 7:58).

However convoluted it may seem, in Mark this 'young man' is now actually *in* the empty tomb, parallel to the 'two men' – plural in Luke – and the Angel, whose 'clothing was white as snow', 'sitting on' the stone in Matthew. Mark rather now describes him as '*sitting on* the right side, *clothed in a white robe*' (16:5). It is a not incurious coincidence that two lines before this reference to Saul as 'a young man' and Stephen being 'cast out of the city', Acts portrays Stephen as 'full of the Holy Spirit' and, like the witnesses to Jesus' Ascension earlier, 'looking into Heaven' and seeing 'Jesus *standing at the right hand* of God'.

Repeating this in the next line, but substituting the usage 'the Son of Man' for Jesus, Acts now has Stephen 'crying out' how he 'saw the Heavens opened and *the Son of Man* standing at the right hand of God' (7:55–56), a variation on what James is said to have proclaimed in the Temple in the early Church accounts before he 'was cast down' – even including the repetition of the words 'crying out', now attributed to Stephen.

Not only do we have here basically the language Mark combines to produce his version of the 'young man *sitting on the right*' side in the empty tomb (the 'clothing white as snow' in these pictures probably coming from Daniel 7:9's picture of 'the Ancient of Days', also evoked in these visions); but also that of our 'Primal Adam'/'Standing One' ideology again, now identified directly with Jesus. It should not be forgotten, too, that this language, 'the Son of Man *sitting on the right hand of Power* and coming on the clouds of Heaven', actually appears in Matthew 26:64 and Mark 14:62.

Our purpose in presenting the multiple variations on these repeating historical motifs is to demonstrate the fertile manner in which the Gospel artificers felt free to improvise or enlarge on their themes. These also provide vivid illustration of the endlessly creative manner with which they allowed their imaginations to rove across the real or historical events before them, creating a host of scriptural parodies.

Luke's Picture of the First Appearance to James along the Way to Emmaus

Again, it should be emphasized that Luke's account of what occurred in the empty tomb contains no mention of an actual physical appearance to Mary Magdalene, Mary *the mother of James*, or Joanna. The women only see the 'two men *standing* beside them in effulgent astral-like clothing'. Nor one to Peter, as per the implication of Paul's testimony in 1 Corinthians 15:5 – which we have already designated as an orthodox interpolation – who in Luke and John sees only 'the linen clothes lying by themselves'. Instead, Jesus appeared to 'two of them' – presumably either 'Apostles' or 'Disciples' – who 'were going the same day to a village called Emmaus, sixty furlongs [about seven and a half miles] from Jerusalem' (Luke 24:13).

It is interesting that the only mention of Emmaus in Josephus comes in the *Jewish War* following *the fall of the Temple*. Here, in the same breath that he tells us that the two drachmas' tax formerly paid by Jews to the Temple – the 'two mites' paid by the Poor widow in Gospel parody in Mark and Luke! – were *now to be paid directly to Rome* and that Titus was leasing *out the whole country*, Josephus tells us that Emmaus was only 'thirty furlongs from Jerusalem', not the 'sixty' as here in Acts. What is more, it was now to be settled by *eight hundred Roman army veterans at Titus' express order*.[34]

One should immediately remark the parallel represented by this appearance 'in the Way' – as the two put it to each other when discussing 'these things' afterwards, their 'heart burning within' them (Luke 24:32) – to presumable family members of Jesus and an appearance 'in the Way' that Paul was supposed to have experienced as he chased those 'of the Way' to Damascus, albeit in a somewhat more visionary (literally, 'apocalyptic') manner (Acts 9:2–8).[35] In Acts' picture of Ananias going to meet Paul in Damascus and 'laying hands on him', Ananias too for some reason – *not Paul* – announces that Jesus appeared to Paul 'in the Way in which' he came (Acts 9:17). Even here, there appears to be just a touch of parody of Jesus' words directly appointing James as successor, 'in the place where you are to go', in the Gospel of Thomas.

When Barnabas brings Paul to Jerusalem, telling the Apostles how Paul 'had spoken out boldly in Damascus in the Name of Jesus', Barnabas is now pictured as confirming once again how Paul 'saw the Lord in the Way' (Acts 9:27), which are, of course, the very words the two use here in Luke. In this sense, these are competitive, if antithetical, encounters with or visions of 'the Risen Christ'. In Luke's encounter, the two – one identified as 'Cleopas' – are conversing with each other along the way to Emmaus when 'Jesus draws near'; in Acts, Paul 'draws near to Damascus when suddenly a light from Heaven shone round about him' (9:3).

Again as is usual in these post-resurrection manifestations – in the Gospel of John and even Luke, usually associated with Jesus *'standing in their midst'* – they are unable to recognize him (Luke 24:15–18). This is a very important aspect of these encounters, usually signalling his other-worldly substantiality, but also his true nature as 'the Standing One' or 'Primal Adam'. The two then tell him all 'the things that had happened' (the language Mark later absorbs into his account), including the charge that 'the Chief Priests and our Rulers *delivered him up* to the death penalty and *crucified him*' (24:20).

However tendentious the author's intent in stating this last – the emphasis being on the word 'our' – it is still altogether more accurate than the repeated description of 'Judas *Iscariot*', the archetypical 'Zealot' or '*Sicarios*' of the kind of *Judas the Galilean* or *Judas Maccabee*, as 'delivering him up', or, for that matter, the equally misleading and malicious picture of the People crying out for Jesus' 'blood' and Pontius Pilate 'delivering Jesus up *to their will*' (Luke 23:24 and Matthew).

This formulation, 'their will', will reappear in the general 'delivered them up' formulae in Hebrew in the picture of the salvationary history of Israel in the Qumran Damascus Document. In it, 'delivering them up', as we saw, is a fixture of what God repeatedly did to 'those who walked in the *stubbornness of their heart*, deserting the Covenant', 'each choosing *his own will*' or 'doing what was right *in his own eyes*'. There, too, it is usually combined with the imagery of God's 'Visitation of the land' and, of course, as we saw as well, 'delivering up to the sword' – the real origin of the repeated use of such words like 'delivering up' and, for that matter, giving him over 'to their will'. We have already remarked the same kind of lateral transformation regarding the crucial words 'cutting off' used in these descriptions in the Damascus Document of God 'cutting off' His people in the wilderness because, for instance, 'they consumed blood', parodied with such devastating effect by Paul in Galatians.[36]

Here too, along the way to Emmaus, Jesus castigates the two for their lack of 'belief' and elucidates for them the scriptural meaning of his suffering and death (Luke 24:25). The same is true to some extent in the Gospel of the Hebrews of his lecturing James. But the words Jesus is

pictured here as using, 'slow of heart to believe', are also another variation of the words used in the above passages in the Damascus Document
about 'delivering up His people' or 'cutting off their males in the
wilderness' – 'stubbornness of their heart'. At Qumran, this is almost
always used in regard to 'the Liar' and implies 'rejecting', 'not doing', or
'breaking the Law', essentially the reverse of the more Pauline
signification here of 'not believing'.[37]

Jesus then goes on to 'expound to them the things about himself in all
the Scriptures', this a seeming follow-up to what Paul says he received
'according to the Scriptures' prior to his version of post-resurrection
appearances in 1 Corinthians 15:3–6. As we described, the Righteous
Teacher at Qumran, too, is always described as 'interpreting all the words
of His Servants the Prophets', God having put this 'Intelligence in his
heart' and 'revealed to him all the Mysteries of the words of His Servants
the Prophets'. Notice the parallel too in these kinds of notices to the
language Hegesippus uses in his account of the death of James, whose
cognomens, 'the Righteous One' and 'Protection of the People', 'the
Prophets' were said to have 'declared concerning him'.[38]

'Drawing near to the village where *they were going*', Jesus now
'reclined with them'. 'Taking the bread, he blessed it, and breaking it, he
gave [it] to them' (Luke 24:28–30). This is almost verbatim the language of
the Gospel of the Hebrews' account of the *first appearance to James* – not
to mention aspects of other accounts involving Jesus breaking bread and
eating with his principal Apostles or Disciples in Luke again and in John.
This is also the picture one gets in Paul in 1 Corinthians 11:23–27 about
how the Lord Jesus 'taking the bread, and having given thanks, broke it
and said, "Take and eat!"', as it is in the Gospel 'Last Supper' accounts
as they have come down to us, in particular, echoing this last almost
verbatim – the only difference being that in this appearance in Luke, as in
the Gospel of the Hebrews, there is nothing about 'Communion with the
blood of Christ' or 'the New Covenant in my blood'.

To put this in a somewhat different way, these two accounts, that of a
first appearance to at least one member of Jesus' family, his uncle Cleopas –
a point conveniently ignored in the Gospel of Luke – along the way to
Emmaus and that embodying a *first appearance to James* after 'the Lord
had given his linen clothes to the Servant of the [High] Priest' in the
Gospel of the Hebrews – this point as well doesn't appear in Gospel
accounts at all, but, as observed, may be the crux of the matter (note
again, the common element of 'the linen clothes') – are exactly the same.

The only difference is that, instead of breaking the bread and 'giving it to them' (Cleopas and the other) in the Gospel of Luke; in the Gospel of the Hebrews, Jesus 'breaks it and gives it *to James the Just*'.

It would be possible to conclude at this point that the unnamed other along with Cleopas in this account of a first appearance in Luke, to whom Jesus appears and with whom he breaks bread 'along the Way', erased for one reason or another or eliminated in the redaction process, is none other than *James the Just, the brother of Jesus*, himself, conveniently rubbed out in the Lukan redaction.

So here too – even in Luke's presentation then – we have the unmistakable traces, however obliterated, of the lost Palestinian tradition of *a first appearance to James* – confirmed for us by Paul in 1 Corinthians 15:7, when read in its uninterpolated form, that is, without the orthodox claim of 'Cephas', 'the Twelve', and the 'over five hundred brothers at once, the majority of whom remain till now, but some also *fallen asleep*'. This can now be read simply:

> For I delivered to you what in the first place I also received: that . . . [first] he appeared to James, then to all the Apostles [number indeterminate] and last of all he appeared also to me, as if to an abortion. For I am the least of the Apostles, who am not fit to be called an Apostle, because I persecuted *the Assembly of God* [this last expression appears so often in the Qumran corpus that it is pointless to count all the occurrences].

Of course, this is also supported by all sectarian traditions featuring James, as, for instance, that at Nag Hammadi. There, James is clearly 'the Beloved Disciple' and Jesus, who 'sits down on a stone' with him (like the Angel in Matthew 28:2), actually kisses him on the mouth, as we saw.[39]

At this point the account in the Gospel of Luke becomes rather confused, since now that 'they recognize him', Jesus vanishes (Luke 24:31)! Returning to Jerusalem, these two then 'relate the things in the Way' to the Eleven and those 'assembled' with them and how 'he was [made] known to them in the breaking of the bread' (24:35). Again, the difference is that in the Gospel of the Hebrews, it is James to whom 'these things' are made known, and it is he who learns, after Jesus breaks the bread and gives it to him, that 'the Son of Man is risen from among those *that sleep*'.

What Jesus says to James, 'My brother, eat your bread, for the Son of Man is risen from among those that sleep', also finds an echo in the Lukan story after the report of Mary Magdalene, Joanna, and Mary *the mother of James* about the empty tomb, preceding this episode of Peter, 'having risen up', running to the tomb only to find 'the linen clothes lying alone'.

We have also already remarked how this allusion to Jesus 'giving his *grave clothes* to the Servant of the [High] Priest', preceding this reference to James' Nazirite-style oath 'not to eat bread' (resembling nothing so much as the 'Nazirite'-style oath of the '*Sicarii*'-like Assassins 'not to eat or drink until they had killed Paul' in Acts 23:12), is refracted in Acts' account of the stoning of Stephen. Its presence here in the Gospel of the Hebrews, not only inextricably links this account to those in John and Luke of the linen clothes 'lying by themselves' or 'piled neatly to one side' in the empty tomb – but to all these various accounts involving *linen clothing* of one kind or another, indirectly implying that Jesus too wore such garb.

There is another parallel in this testimony in the Gospel of the Hebrews, which once again bears on the subject of 'not *eating or drinking*' and Christ 'being raised *the third day* according to the Scriptures' in 1 Corinthians 15:4. That is the point about 'James *swearing not to eat bread* from that hour in which he had *drunk the Cup of the Lord* [nothing here about any blood] until he should see him risen from among those that sleep' and Acts' competitive picture of Paul's vision 'along the Way' to Damascus. One should also keep in mind with regard to the former the Rabbinic attempts, we have already described, in the aftermath of the fall of the Temple, to discourage those taking like-minded oaths 'not to eat or drink' either mourning for Zion or till they should see the Temple rebuilt.[40]

In Acts, after 'hearing the voice but seeing no one', Paul's travelling companions – described as '*standing* speechless' – bring him to Damascus. Then Paul's eyes were 'opened', but it is now *he* who 'sees no one' (basically, the inability to recognize Jesus again, but also note the repetition of the word 'see') and 'he was *three days there not seeing* and *did not eat or drink*'. The language overlaps with what amounts, in effect, to James' swearing *not to eat or drink* for three days – not to mention some of these other groups and with much more historical veracity – should be clear.

For Paul in 1 Corinthians 11:25–27, it will be recalled, 'the Cup of blessing, which we bless, is Communion with the blood of Christ' or 'the Cup of the New Covenant in [his] blood'; and the bread, 'Communion with the body of Christ'. In the Gospel of the Hebrews, this 'Cup' is simply 'the Cup of the Lord', which Paul also refers to in 10:21 and 11:27. But, as per his wont, Paul turns somewhat aggressive on this point, linking '*eating and drinking* the Cup of the Lord unworthily', as we saw, to being 'guilty of the *body and blood of the Lord*' – notice the word 'Lord' here, as in the Gospel of the Hebrews, instead of the word 'Christ'.

He does the same two lines later, but in this instance he specifically defines 'eating and drinking unworthily', as '*not seeing through to the body of the Lord*' (11:29). For him, the person who does this then 'drinks Judgement unto himself'. Again, the implication of these two maledictions is that Paul is actually calling down the blood-libel accusation of being 'guilty of the blood' of Christ on his opponents, particularly, seemingly those within the Movement or 'Church' itself, even the very Leadership itself, including James, who do not interpret 'the Cup of the Lord' or 'see through to the body of the Lord' in the spiritualized manner he does. Again, note the repetition of the word 'seeing' occurs in all these accounts, even in the finale of the Damascus Document on 'seeing His *Yeshuʻa*' or 'His Salvation'.

In the light of such an attitude, the blood libel in the Gospels against a whole people, most of whom historically, as we have earlier explained, actually opposed the very same rulers and foreign powers Jesus and his followers seem to have done, is not surprising. These died in the hundreds of thousands seemingly for the very same reasons, but Paul's belligerence in these passages – for example, as regards 'circumcision' – fairly takes one's breath away, the command 'to love one's enemies', except perhaps Romans, for him seemingly having long since gone by the boards.

This is the point of view one encounters at Qumran, as well, which also employs the imagery of 'the Cup of the Lord' Paul alludes to here and part of the language of James' last encounter with Jesus on earth – however curtailed the account of it we get in Jerome's fragment from the Gospel of the Hebrews. Notwithstanding, at Qumran, Habakkuk 2:16: 'the Cup of the right hand of the Lord', is very definitely a 'Cup of Vengeance' or 'the Cup of the Wrath of God' – again inverted from the general presentation of Paul and the Gospels. In the Habakkuk *Pesher*, for instance, it is directed against 'Covenant-Breakers' and backsliders generally – in particular, 'the Wicked Priest' described as not 'circumcising the foreskin of his heart' – not in support of those setting aside the Law, as it would appear to be in the Gospels and here in Paul.

As the Habakkuk *Pesher* expresses this, the Wicked Priest, who himself 'swallowed' and acted murderously against 'God's Elect' – the Righteous Teacher and his followers, 'the *Ebionim*' or 'Poor' again – would himself be 'swallowed' or 'consumed' by 'the Cup of the Lord'ʼs Divine Vengeance, which 'he would drink to the dregs' or from which 'he would drink his fill'.

As he tendered them this 'cup', so too would God tender him 'the Cup' of His Divine Wrath and 'he would be *paid the reward he paid the Poor*'.[41]

This symbolism, which is basically that of 'the Cup of wine' or 'the wine Cup of God's Fury', is omnipresent at Qumran, as it is in Revelation. In both, it is not 'the body and blood of Christ' being consumed in some symbolical or esoteric manner, but rather 'the wine of the Cup of the Wrath of God' consuming God's enemies. This, too, may be something of the implied meaning of this 'Cup of the Lord', which James drinks in this last encounter with Jesus here in the Gospel of the Hebrews.

The belligerence we have just seen, with regard to 'drinking Judgement to oneself' and 'guilt for the blood of the Lord' in Paul, is also refracted to a certain degree in the Habakkuk *Pesher*'s fulsome condemnation of 'the Spouter of Lying' – characterized, it will be remembered, as 'building a Worthless City on blood and erecting an Assembly [or 'Church'] upon Lying'. This takes the form of expressing the wish that he would be 'subjected to the same Judgements of Fire, with which *he vilified and blasphemed the Elect of God*'.[42]

To return to the narrative in Luke: at this point either 'the Eleven and those assembled with them' or 'they' – it is not clear; presumably Cleopas and his other unspecified companion – say, '*the Lord has indeed risen and appeared to Simon*' (24:34), and, as we just saw, 'he was known to them in the breaking of the bread' (24:35). Here the text does not allow us to know if 'the Jerusalem Assembly' – this implied by those 'assembled with them' – is doing the speaking or Cleopas and the unnamed other Disciple. Even more to the point, it is not even clear if the reference is to 'Simon Peter' here or to some other 'Simon' – possibly even a 'Simeon'. Origen, as we saw, is so sure that the second unnamed person is 'Simon' that he even quotes this passage from Luke to this effect, but, even he does not tell us which 'Simon' this might be – Simeon bar Cleophas or Simon Peter. Again the words spoken, however, are a variation of the words Jesus is portrayed as speaking to James in the Hebrew Gospel, 'Eat your bread, my brother, for the Son of Man has indeed risen from among those that sleep.'

Of course, it has always been taken for granted in all orthodox circles without the slightest proof – the contrary as we have just seen – that the reference here in Luke to 'Simon', as the one to whom Jesus first appeared, is 'Simon Peter'. But at least in the logic of the narrative of Luke as we have just described it, it would make more sense if the reference here were to 'Simeon' or 'Simeon bar Cleophas'. At least, then, the garbled allusion to 'Cleopas' would be comprehensible.

The problem is that, as in the instance of the orthodox part of Paul's presentation of Jesus' post-resurrection appearances in 1 Corinthians 15:5–6 earlier and the reference there to an appearance to 'Cephas', there is no reported instance of an appearance to Peter alone at all, to say nothing of 'the Twelve', not even in the Lukan episode preceding this of Peter running back to the empty tomb but seeing 'only the linen clothes'.

Even this appearance in Luke to 'the Eleven and those assembled with them' – not 'to the Twelve' – when Jesus himself suddenly 'stands in their midst', does not occur until after 'the two' report his appearance to them on the Emmaus Road and the Community praising 'the Lord' for his having 'appeared to Simon'. The elements of this sudden appearance of Jesus *standing among* them at this assemblage of the Jerusalem Church, as we have seen, are basically those of the 'Doubting Thomas' episode in John – though here, as we observed, when Jesus asks for something to eat, they rather give him 'some broiled fish and a part of a honeycomb' (Luke 24:36–42), not just the 'and some fish too' as in John 21:13.

Therefore, a way out of the conundrum is to look at the report that follows the appearance to the two on the Road to Emmaus, of an 'appearance to Simon', in a different way. If we take the reference to 'Simon' rather to refer to the sighting which has just occurred 'in the Way' to 'Cleopas' and another, then this 'Cleopas' – certainly meant to represent Jesus' 'uncle' but, as usual, not so stated in Luke – can rather and with even more sense be seen as the son of this 'uncle', 'Simeon *bar Cleophas*', Jesus' 'cousin' and second successor in Palestine, and, according to Epiphanius, *the witness to the stoning of James*.

The second companion then, the unnamed other, who with 'Cleopas' *sits down and breaks bread with Jesus*, and then either *recognizes him* or *is recognized by him*, would or could be James, his 'cousin' and neatly rubbed out here in Luke. At the very least, it must be acknowledged that it is a *first appearance to family members*. Paul himself attests James was the recipient of a post-resurrection appearance by Jesus – perhaps even the *first to whom Jesus appeared*. Not only is such an appearance to James the Just also pictured here in Jerome's almost word-for-word copy of this appearance to 'the two along the Way' in this tiny fragment from the Gospel of the Hebrews; this episode would then, in effect, comprise the residue of *the native Palestinian appointment tradition*, confirming Jesus' two family members as his real successors in Palestine – not the clearly illusory overseas appointment episodes we get in the Gospels as we have them.

This is how we would interpret this curious *non sequitur* in the report of 'the two' to 'the assembled Eleven' in Jerusalem about an appearance to 'Simon' and the whole episode about Jesus' appearance to 'the two' – one of whom definitely his relation – 'along the Way' to Emmaus that precedes this in the Gospel of Luke. Interpreting these notices in this manner and linking them to the report in the Gospel of the Hebrews of a *first appearance to James* allows us, at least, to *begin* to approach convergence regarding many of these interlocking themes and the reality behind some of these very real Palestinian traditions.

Of course this proposition is not subject to any final proof, but the reference to 'Simon' here in the Gospel of Luke, and the variation of it one finds in Paul's 'Cephas' – itself possibly implying 'Simeon bar Cleophas' – is certainly most strange, especially since there is no single appearance to Peter on record in any Gospel, or any other source for that matter except this seeming interpolation in Paul's list of Jesus' post-resurrection appearances. We have already seen, as well, how the names 'Simon' and 'Simeon' are interchangeable in the version of James' speech at the so-called 'Jerusalem Council' in Acts, following the one allegedly given by Peter ('Cephas') in Acts 15:7–21.

Of course, for all three, Mark, Luke, and John, we do get Jesus' sudden appearance 'standing in the midst of them' – in Mark 16:14, 'while they were reclining'. For Matthew, this appearance to 'the Eleven Disciples' takes place in Galilee on 'the mountain Jesus had appointed them'. Then, too, one has the 'doubting' theme of the *Didymus* Thomas encounter in John, expressed here in Matthew as 'some doubted' (28:17).

Though Jesus basically proclaims a version of the Pauline 'Gentile Mission' here – 'Go, teach all Peoples [*Ethnē*], baptizing them *in the Name* of the Father, the Son and the Holy Spirit' (28:19); still the words he uses in conjunction with these having to do with 'Authority in Heaven and on Earth', yet again recall those in the Gospel of Thomas's picture of Jesus' *direct appointment of James* of 'go to James the Just, for whose sake Heaven and Earth came into existence'.

Even the words of Jesus' final Commandment, 'to observe all the things which I commanded you . . . until the Completion of the Age', again recall the words Jeremiah uses to describe the Commandments 'Jonadab son of Rechab' gave to his descendants. The only difference is that these were 'to drink no wine', 'plant no vineyards', and 'live only in tents' – if one adds the 'vegetarian' theme as well, all things dear to the totality of these 'Nazirite' or 'Rechabite' groups.

However this may be, something very peculiar is going on in these post-resurrection appearances by Jesus. Invariably, this would appear to relate to the downplaying or writing of James and the other brothers and family members of Jesus out of Scripture. This is not to mention the whole 'Cephas'/ 'Clopas'/'Cleophas' tangle, to which one should add the 'Alphaeus'/ 'Lebbaeus'/'Theudas'/'Thaddaeus'/'Judas Thomas'/'Addai' one below.

To sort out some of these manifold discrepancies, contradictions, and overlaps, we must turn to a consideration of 'the Brothers of Jesus as Apostles'. This will further illumine the downplaying and ultimate elimination of Jesus' brothers and family members from Scripture and the additional aspersions Jesus is pictured as 'casting upon' them (the pun is intentional), such as 'a Prophet is not without honour, except in his own country, among his own kin, and in his own house' – this directly following the first overt confirmation of the existence of these 'mother', 'brothers', and 'sisters' of Jesus as among his *most Faithful* followers in Mark 6:3–4 and Matthew 13:55–57.

Jesus' Brothers as Apostles

Cleopas, Cephas, and Clopas the Husband of Mary's Sister Mary

Who then is this mysterious 'Cleopas' who appears without introduction in this crucial Emmaus-road sighting episode in Luke? Not only do we have in Jesus' appearance to two seeming unknowns in the environs of Jerusalem the wherewithal to attach a tradition of this kind, even in the Gospels as we have them, to the person of James – thus, bearing out the second part of Paul's 1 Corinthians 15:6–7 enumeration of Jesus' post-resurrection appearances: 'he appeared to James, then to all the Apostles, and last of all, he also appeared to me' – but also, even perhaps, the wherewithal to attach it to the 'Cephas' who appears in the first part.

Admittedly, the appearances 'to the Twelve' and the 'over five hundred *brothers* at the same time', that follow this reference to a first appearance to someone called 'Cephas' – another variation of the flight of the 'five thousand' *brothers* to Jericho in the Pseudoclementine *Recognitions* after Paul's attack on James (note the common 'brother' theme again) – cannot be borne out. This is to say nothing of the contradiction represented by the mention of the two separate and successive appearances to the Apostles – the first, 'then to the Twelve', and the second, 'then to all the Apostles'.

True to some of these garbled parallels between the Gospels of Luke and John, there is a reference to this 'Clopas' (*thus*) in John – not in John's version of the post-resurrection appearances of Jesus, but his presentation of the witnesses to Jesus' crucifixion preceding these (John 19:25). For John all these are called 'Mary': 'his mother, and his mother's sister, Mary the wife of Clopas, and Mary Magdalene', so instead of one Mary, we now have three! Aside from this ephemeral 'Mary Magdalene' – out of whom Jesus cast 'seven demons' – probably another of these fictional overwrites over something – one can imagine the contortions indulged in by theologians and apologists over the millennia to reconcile Mary having as her sister *another Mary* – and this, even more germane, the wife of that Clopas clearly meant to be the same individual as that 'Cleopas' or 'Cleophas' again!

For some, 'Mary *the wife of Clopas*' is Mary's half-sister; for Jerome, *her niece*. But there is really no way out of the conundrum presented by such evasions. Mary patently *did not* have a 'sister Mary', regardless of the sanctity of the Gospels and that, as the word has evolved in English, they have become synonymous with the truth, namely, 'the Gospel Truth' or that some call them 'the word of God' (the 'God' perhaps of their persuasion, but not the historian's) – others, simply fiction. There is a difference between historical truth and literature. The Gospels, like the Pseudoclementines, are *literature*. There may be a kernel of truth lurking here and there like a pebble beneath the surface of a stream, which it is the task of the historian to discover and decipher.

Nowhere is this proposition more strikingly illustrated than in the absurdity of Mary being her *own sister* Mary. This confusion was probably based on either separate and conflicting descriptions of Mary before the redaction of these traditions or simply a grammatical error in the Greek, now encased in over eighteeen centuries of religious veneration. As text critics and historians, we should be able to decipher the reality behind this particular *non sequitur*. But to do so, we shall have to return again to the early Church historians and these stories about the 'witnesses' to the crucifixion and resurrection of Jesus, as well as the various Apostle lists in the Synoptic Gospels and the Book of Acts – there are none in John. In doing so, several other problems regarding the members of Jesus' family should become clarified.

For a start, let us reiterate that the initial stories about the brothers of Jesus in the Gospels – what Paul calls 'the brothers of the Lord' – show no embarrassment whatsoever about the reality of the 'brother' relationship, that is, whatever and whoever Jesus was *he had brothers*. That he also had a mother should be self-evident. He also seems to have had a 'sister' or 'sisters'. The Gospel of John, for instance, after the Prologue and the choosing of three of his 'Disciples' – 'two' of whom, at first unidentified, 'were *standing*' with John – from among the followers of John the Baptist, speaks about how 'his mother and his brothers' joined him along with other 'Disciples' (number indeterminate) at Capernaum very early in his Galilean career (2:12).

Matthew and Mark list Jesus' brothers quite straightforwardly as 'James and Joses and Simon and Judas' (13:55–56 and 6:3–5). The same goes for Jesus' mother Mary and 'his sisters', one of whom Mark

771

identifies in his version of the witnesses to the Crucifixion as 'Salome' (15:40). At the Crucifixion, she is explicitly identified as the sister of 'James the Less and Joses'; at the empty tomb, simply '(the sister) of James' (16:1). In this 'Less' sobriquet, as already observed, one can see the pejoration at work – it would perhaps be more appropriate to call him 'the More'.

In Matthew 13:55, for instance, when Jesus' mother, brothers and sisters are mentioned at the conclusion of the largely anti-Pauline series of Parables about 'the Tares' and 'the Drag Net' unique to it, Jesus' father is straightforwardly identified as 'the carpenter' – 'is this not the *son of the carpenter* [note the 'Rechabite' connotation of this]?' In Mark, the same statement turns into: 'is not this *the carpenter the son of Mary?*' (Mark 6:2), so that Jesus now becomes the proverbial 'Galilean' *carpenter* just as his principal 'Apostles' became 'Galilean' *fishermen*. Luke and John wisely simplify this into 'Joseph's son' (Luke 4:22). Interestingly, Mark's version already shows traces of doctrinal deformation and this has gone, via St Augustine, directly into the Koran, where Jesus is always designated as 'the Messiah *son of Mary*' and nothing else.[1]

In John, the depiction of Jesus as 'the son of Joseph' also occurs by the Sea of Galilee – called now, quite incisively, 'of Tiberias' – and even, more importantly, introduces his version of Jesus calling himself 'the living bread, which came from Heaven', and the concomitant conclusion, 'he *who eats my flesh and drinks my blood* shall have Eternal life' (John 6:42–58). This last bears on a point we just made relative to Jerome's parallel Gospel of the Hebrews, which has Jesus breaking bread and 'drinking the Lord's Cup' with James, an episode entirely *missing* from John's version of the 'Last Supper'. The rambling discourse John later pictures Jesus as giving there rather focuses on the 'Rechabite'-like phraseology encountered in the last line of Matthew, 'keeping my Commandments', as well as the unique reference to 'Judas [the son] of Simon *Iscariot delivering him up*', and long perorations on the Righteousness Commandment, basically expressed in terms of spirited wordplay on the commands to 'love me as I love you' and 'love one another' (John 13:1–15:17).

In fact, these references in John to 'eating my flesh and drinking my blood', which occur much earlier in the Gospels, begin with Jesus both crossing the Sea of Galilee and, at Passover, 'going up into the mountain' – as in the Transfiguration scenes in the Synoptic Gospels – and there sitting with his Disciples (6:1–3). Here he multiplies the fishes, as in the Synoptics again, but now it is before the men that 'recline . . . about five thousand in number' (John 6:1–10)! Though this is paralleled in Matthew 14:21 and Mark 6:44, later in Matthew 15:38–16:10 and Mark 8:9–20, this turns into 'four thousand'.

More significantly, John ends these early scenes moving back and forth across the Sea of Galilee, where Jesus multiplies the loaves and the fishes and they *actually* 'see him walking on the Sea', with the reference to 'Judas [the son] of Simon *Iscariot* . . . being one of the Twelve', 'about to *deliver him up*' (6:70–71). This parallels the note from his later 'Last Supper' scenario of Jesus 'dipping the morsel [as Jews at their Passover repast do] and giving it to Judas [the son] of Simon *Iscariot* (John 3:26). In the Gospel of the Hebrews, it will be recalled, this 'morsel', or, as the case may be, piece of 'bread', was given to *James*; only in this earlier discourse about 'being the Living Bread' and 'whoever eats my flesh and drinks my blood living in me' in the Gospel of John, Judas is actually identified with the 'Devil' (*Diabolos* – 'Belial' in Hebrew).

Even more to the point, in John, when Jesus makes the statement 'unless you have eaten the flesh of the Son of Man and drunk his blood, you shall not have life in yourselves' (6:53) – varying Paul's even more aggressive 'eating and drinking Judgement to himself, not seeing through to the body of the Lord' (1 Cor. 11:29) – this ends with the extremely prescient: 'from that time Many of his Disciples fell back and did not walk with him any more' (6:66).

Here the Qumran language of both 'walking with' and the 'Many' is patent. In the Damascus Document we even have, 'walking in these things in Perfect Holiness . . . according to the exact letter of the teaching of the *Torah*', as opposed to 'walking in the Way of the Wicked' and 'choosing their own will' and 'turning aside with the Men of Scoffing' and 'walking with the Man of Lying'![2] In fact, in relation to an allusion to 'Gehazi' and 'rejecting the Commandments of God and forsaking them to turn aside in stubbornness of heart', there is even a reference to 'all the men, who entered the New Covenant in the Land of Damascus, yet fell back and betrayed [it], *turning aside from the Fountain of Living Waters*'.[3]

Jesus is also pictured in this extremely pregnant passage here in John as wondering aloud – symbolically as ever – if 'the Twelve' would 'turn aside as well'. It is here that Simon Peter is quoted as applying the pivotal identification of Jesus, 'You are the Christ, the Son of the Living God' (John 6:67–69), also applied to him by the voice from the cloud 'on the mountain' at his Transfiguration or, even more significantly, by Peter just preceding this in all the Synoptics (Matt. 16:16–17:5 and pars. – in the former, significantly, the Disciples are described as 'falling on their face and being greatly terrified').

For his part in John, Jesus is described as 'knowing from the beginning who they were *who did not believe and who would deliver him up*' (6:64). Once again, as we have just elucidated, these constitute a variation of the words used in the Damascus Document: 'in the beginning God chose them not, and He knew their works before ever they were created', to describe the Evil Generations in the wilderness, 'whom He hated' and who were going to be 'cut off' for 'consuming blood' and be 'delivered up to the sword'!4

In the Synoptics, as we saw, all these enumerations are accompanied by attacks on Jesus' family and countrymen, aimed in the typical Pauline manner at distinguishing Jesus from both. These generally circulate about the formula, as noted, 'A Prophet is not without honour, except in his own country and in his own house' (Luke 4:25 and pars.). In case we didn't get the polemical thrust of its meaning, Mark adds: 'and *among his own kin*' (6:4). These are paralleled, as well, in the sayings in the episodes preceding these, when Jesus or his Disciples are 'casting out demons' – including doubtlessly even the 'seven demons he *cast* out' (*ekbeblēkei*) of Mary Magdalene (Luke 8:2 and Mark 16:9) – and his mother and brothers come to see him and are described as '*standing outside*' *calling to him* (Matt. 12:46–50 and Mark 3:31–35).

In Matthew 12:24–28 (paralleled in Mark 3:22–30), preceding this episode, this 'standing' language we have just highlighted in relation to it occurs *two* more times in two lines in the context of five more allusions in five lines to another weird circumlocution, 'Beelzebul Prince of the demons', 'casting out the demons' (*ekballei* again). This leads directly into the episode, basically disparaging Jesus' 'mother and his brothers', who were, as Luke puts it, 'unable to get to him *because of the crowd*' (Luke 8:19–21) – 'the crowd', patently symbolizing Paul's new Gentile Christian converts in the retrospective polemic this kind of invective represents.

When Jesus is told that his mother and brothers 'are standing outside', he responds in good Pauline style: 'Who is my mother and who are my brothers' (Matt. 12:48), this obviously being before the Mary cult gathered momentum in the second and third centuries. Jesus is then pictured as adding in all the Synoptics, gesturing towards his Disciples – in Luke he is speaking to the crowd – 'Behold *my mother and my brothers, for whoever shall do* the will of God *is my brother and sister and mother*' (Mark 3:35). The import of all this clear sectarian repartee, as we have implied, is to divorce Jesus from his family – and by extension his own people – and attach him to all the people of the world.

The Jamesian emphasis on 'doing' in these parallels is interesting too. Just so that we should make no mistake about its more cosmopolitan aspects and that the doctrine of Jesus as 'Son of God' should be attached to whatever is meant by this word 'doing', Matthew formulates the proposition as 'whosoever shall *do the will of my Father who is in Heaven*, he is my brother and sister and mother' (12:50). Luke, pointing to the crowd, makes the Jamesian thrust of all this – and one might add of Qumran – even clearer: 'My mother and my brothers are these which *hear* the word of God, and *do it*' (Luke 8:21).

It is also interesting that the context in the Synoptics here is one of 'doing mighty works and wonders', normally presented as including *raisings*, *healings*, *casting out demons*, and the like. In the War Scroll from Qumran, however, where these same 'mighty works and wonders' of God are referred to, these are the battles God has fought and the wonders He has done on behalf of his people as, for instance, overthrowing the chariots of the army of Pharaoh in the Red Sea and the like.[5] One is not making any value judgements here, as *healings*, *exorcisms*, *raisings*, and the like might be superior to military victories, depending on one's point of view, only showing how these terms were being used in Palestine in this period.

For instance, this particular sequence of largely 'Jewish Christian' Parables, ending with the formal introduction of Jesus' mother and brothers in Matthew 13:55–57, concludes with the laconic 'and he did not *do many mighty works* there because of their *unbelief*' (13:58). Mark adds, obviously a little embarrassed at all this invective, 'except he laid his hand on a few sick people and healed them' (6:6).

The Doctrine of the Perpetual Virginity of Mary (and James)

Chronologically, the embarrassment over the fact of Jesus' brothers, along with that about his paternity, develops later than these materials. For instance, in the Gospels we see little or no embarrassment over the matter of their actual *physical* relationship to Jesus – or to 'the Lord' as Paul would have it – only theological ones, in line with the aims and aspirations of the Pauline Mission to the Gentiles overseas, to downplay the perception of family members' proper doctrine – their 'Belief', as the Gospels succinctly term it – and the familial and national traditions upon which their status as successors was based.

But, as we have also seen, this is the case as well for attacks on Jesus' most intimate Apostles, particularly Peter, because of his role in the confrontation at 'Antioch' – as Paul presents it in Galatians. These, like Jesus' family members and by extrapolation Jews generally, are described as 'weak in Faith' – 'weak' being, as we saw, a favourite aspersion Paul uses to attack his antagonists within the Movement, who are supporting 'circumcision', 'the Law', and restrictive dietary practices and opposing 'table fellowship' with Gentiles, and those whose 'consciences are so weak', they eat only vegetables.

Paul, in 1 and 2 Corinthians, even goes so far in his histrionics, as we have seen, as to attack these 'Hebrew' Archapostles as 'disguising themselves as Servants of Righteousness' – a term widespread too at Qumran. Not only are these 'Super Apostles' for him – like 'Judas the son of Simon Iscariot' in John 6:71 above – really 'Servants of the Devil' (also, 'the Diabolos'), he ends by proclaiming in one and the same breath, 'eat everything sold in the market place' and that grandiloquently, he 'will never eat meat again forever' so as not to 'cause his brother to stumble' or 'scandalize' him (1 Cor. 8:13 and 10:25).

Even at the end of the second century, Tertullian (c. 160–221 CE) is still assuming that 'the brothers of the Lord' are his true brothers and their mother is Mary, who generated them through normal conjugal intercourse.[6] It is Origen (185–254 CE) in the next century, who is the first really to gainsay this in line with the growing reverence being accorded Mary, citing a book he and his predecessor, Clement of Alexandria – Tertullian's contemporary – both saw. He does so, not surprisingly, in commenting on the passages from Mark 6 and Matthew 13 we just have been discussing above.

Origen calls this book *'The Book of James'*, but we have been referring to it as the 'Protevangelium of James', and states, that though the Gospels imply his contemporaries considered Jesus to be *a man*, 'the son of Joseph and Mary', he 'was not a man, but something Divine'. Even more informative, he reveals the idea, 'the brothers of Jesus were the sons of Joseph by a former wife whom he married before Mary', was circulated by those 'who wish to preserve the honour of *Mary in virginity to the end'*.[7]

This idea of perpetual virginity – even after the birth of Jesus – was already circulating in two apocryphal works – one on the Old Testament, called the Ascension of Isaiah (11:9), and the other, as we have seen, called the Protevangelium of James. In the second, which seems to have been written to glorify Mary and which was ascribed to James – hence its title,

Joseph is an *elderly widower* (9.2)! The idea of such 'virginity' seems first to have been emphasized in the correspondence of Ignatius of Antioch at the end of the first century.[8] Also Justin Martyr, at the beginning of the second, was one of the first to accord Mary special prominence. He saw Mary as the good side of Eve; both of whom he considered virgins, giving rise to the idea that Mary brought life, but Eve, disobedience and death.[9]

The idea of Mary's perpetual virginity also gained momentum with the growing vogue virginity was beginning to enjoy in ascetic circles, not to mention its possible tie-in with James' paradigmatic *lifelong virginity*. Still Jesus' rebukes in the Synoptics not only of Mary, but the 'brothers' and all the *Jewish* Apostles troubled early commentators. These grappled with the idea of Mary's sinfulness and, in particular, whether she – unlike her son – was subject to the Pauline concept of 'original sin'.[10] Many cited the words Luke attributes to Mary, 'all generations will henceforth count me blessed' (1:48), not to mention the very ambiguous prophecy – attributed to one Simeon in the next chapter – about a 'sword piercing her soul too' (Luke 2:35 – here the Qumran 'soul' and 'sword' language again).

This 'prophecy' is attributed to 'the Righteous and Pious Simeon' in Luke's infancy narrative, to whom 'the Holy Spirit' revealed that 'he would not see death until he had seen *the Christ* of the Lord' (Luke 2:25–26). Again these words echo the traditions about James' 'seeing the Lord' and, very possibly, his kinsman and successor, Simeon bar Cleophas, too.

Here in Luke, this is expressed in terms of 'seeing Your Salvation' (Luke 2:30), the very words used at the end of the exhortative section of the Damascus Document just discussed above. Once again, just as this notice is accompanied in Luke by allusion to preparing for 'all Nations' a light 'of the Gentiles', the sense is completely the opposite of the concluding line of this section of the Damascus Document, which ends with the words: 'they will be victorious over all the Sons of the Earth . . . and see His Salvation, because they took refuge in His Holy Name'.[11]

Epiphanius in the late 300s is still resisting this cult and holding on to the idea that Jesus was born by natural means, that is, that Mary's virginity had been interrupted at least by a natural birth, if not natural generation. Having said this, however, he completely accepts Origen's idea that 'James was Joseph's son by his first wife', whoever this wife may have been. Still for him, it was James and the rest of 'Joseph's sons who *revered virginity and followed the Nazirite life-style*' – the very important reversal of Mary's alleged status.[12]

It is Jerome, prescient as ever and often responding to the true implications of the data before us, as even Epiphanius often does – albeit in a doctrinaire and tendentious manner – who, as we explained, sets the pattern for the modern, doctrinaire or at least 'Catholic', approach to the 'brothers': that Jesus' brothers were not 'brothers' at all, but rather 'cousins'. He is, of course, taking off in this, without perhaps realizing it, from the fact that Cleophas – as already reported above – was 'the brother of Joseph' and his son Simeon, therefore, the *cousin of Jesus*. However it never seems to have dawned on him that this would make 'Simeon' the *brother of James* and, as we shall presently see below, *Jesus* as well!

Jerome arrives at this conclusion by a comparison of the Apostle lists and correctly appreciating that 'James the son of Alphaeus' (Matt. 10:3 and pars.) – not to mention 'Judas [the brother] of James' (Luke 6:15–16) – had to be the son of that woman designated as Mary 'the sister of' her own sister Mary and 'the wife of Clopas' in John 19:25 ('Mary the mother of James and Joses and the mother of the two sons of Zebedee' in Matthew 27:56, 'Mary the mother of James the Less and Joses and Salome' in Mark 15:40, and 'Mary the mother of James' in Luke 24:10).[13]

This would make 'Alphaeus' and 'Clopas' the same person, as, of course, they most certainly were, the mix-up here simply being the difference between a Greek letter *kappa* and an *alpha*.[14] Interestingly enough the Levi later identified as Matthew and depicted as 'sitting at the tax office' (Matt. 9:9) is also designated as 'the son of Alphaeus' (Mark 2:14). This may provide the basis of Luke's later tie-in of 'Matthias' and the so-called 'Joseph Barsabas surnamed Justus' in the spurious election to replace Judas 'the *Iscariot*' (i.e., 'the *Sicarios*'), at the beginning of Acts.

It is left to Augustine, whose correspondence with Jerome on the worrisome conflict between Peter and Paul in Galatians we have discussed earlier – James, it would seem, totally ignored – to have the last word on the subject: 'The Lord was indeed born of woman, but he was conceived in her without man's co-operation':

> Begotten by the Father, He was not conceived by the Father. He was made *Man* in the mother, whom He himself had made, so that he might exist here for a while, sprung from her who could never and nowhere have existed except through His *Power* [note again, our Ebionite 'Primal Adam'/'Power' language even here – but then Augustine had originally been a Manichaean] . . . She in whose footsteps you are following had no human intercourse when she conceived. She remained a virgin when she brought forth her child. (Sermon 191)

While impressive for its rhetorical skill, this certainly is arcane. Augustine as well, while not denying that Mary was born subject to 'Original Sin', also championed the cause that she had been delivered of its effects 'by the Grace of rebirth'.[15]

As full of the most interesting intellectual contacts religious history proves to be, this is the position, as we have seen, that Muhammad also champions (thereby showing his very extensive training) a century and a half later and it has now become Islamic orthodoxy! For Muhammad, in the Koran, Jesus is, as we saw, always addressed as 'the son of Mary' never 'of Joseph', as in Luke and John, or 'the carpenter's son', as in Matthew. In addition, God was *not* his father, though God could have been if he wanted to be, since there is nothing beyond God's 'Power'. All God had to do is say to a thing, 'Be, and it is' (Koran 1.117). In his own inimitable way, Muhammad has got the point.

Trajan's Executions of Simeon bar Cleophas and the Descendants of Jesus' Brother Judas

This brings us back to the question of Simeon bar Cleophas and Cephas. In both Eusebius and Epiphanius, 'Cleophas' is identified as the father of Simeon bar Cleophas and the uncle of Jesus. Both are clearly, once again, dependent on Hegesippus. In two separate places Eusebius, in writing about Simeon bar Cleophas, the next to succeed among 'the Desposyni', that is, the family of Jesus, informs us that 'Hegesippus tells us that Cleophas was Joseph's brother'. This he tells us in the same breath as the fact that:

> After the martyrdom of James and the capture of Jerusalem *which immediately followed*, there is a *firm tradition* that those of the Apostles and Disciples of the Lord who were still alive, together with those that were related to the Lord according to the flesh, *assembled* from all parts [the 'Jerusalem Assembly' or 'Church' again] . . . to choose a fit person as *successor to James*. They *unanimously elected Simeon the son of Clopas, mentioned in the Gospel narratives*, to occupy the Episcopal Throne there, who was, so they say, *a cousin of the Saviour*.[16]

Not only does Eusebius in this testimony, taken from Hegesippus, display no embarrassment whatsoever at the actuality of the kinship of these 'Desposyni' to Jesus, once again we have another of these tell-tale 'elections'. Nor is it clear whether it is this 'Simeon' or his father, the so-called 'Clopas', the husband of Mary's sister Mary in the Gospel of

John, who is the one 'mentioned in the Gospel narratives'. If Simeon, then we have already described where.

Epiphanius, also dependent on Hegesippus, has little to add to this. He calls 'Simeon the son of his uncle, the son, that is, of *Joseph*'s brother Clopas'! But he also calls both of these 'the sons of Jacob called *Panther*', a story, curiously enough, that has also survived in a scurrilous Rabbinic tradition – Epiphanius' possible source – where Jesus is also called 'Jesus ben *Panthera*', the illegitimate son of a Roman Centurion! What all this might mean is impossible to tell, except that Epiphanius also identifies this Simeon 'his cousin, the son of Clopas', as 'standing at a distance' (again our 'standing' terminology intrudes, now with regard to Simeon) and the 'witness' to the stoning of 'the Just One'.[17]

In referring to these '*Desposyni*' – literally, 'of the Lord' – Eusebius records – also on the basis of Hegesippus – how first of all

> Vespasian, after the capture of Jerusalem, issued an order to ensure that no one who was of royal stock should be left among the Jews, that all descendants of David should be ferreted out and for this reason a further widespread persecution was again *inflicted upon the Jews* [note, this 'persecution' is not 'inflicted upon' the Christians].[18]

If this order can be confirmed, which, of course, has much in common with how Herod is pictured as attempting to round up the children in the region of Bethlehem in Matthew's infancy narrative some seventy years before – in fact, Eusebius himself draws this comparison – then it confirms that Vespasian properly appreciated that the root cause of the Uprising against Rome from 66 to 70 CE and the unrest continuing thereafter was Messianic. This is the writer's view and we have already shown it to be the implication of Josephus' data.

It is also the implication of the data in the Dead Sea Scrolls, which are thoroughly Messianic. It also gainsays the view of early Church fathers like Eusebius, who, encouraged by the picture in the Gospels, repeatedly averred that the Jews suffered all these things, because they *rejected the Messiah*.[19] On the contrary, the Jews suffered the things they suffered, because they *were so Messianic* – a point the authors of the Gospels are at great pains to disguise – and, as things transpired, rejected the view of the Messianism disseminated by people like Eusebius! In addition, it again demonstrates the root cause of the problems that continued to plague Palestine and most of the Eastern region of the Roman Empire as well – even as far as Rome itself.

Eusebius gives no further information on this point, instead going on to document the attempts by Domitian (81–96 CE), Vespasian's second son, to do the very same thing he pictures Vespasian as doing – as remarked above, in the questioning of the descendants of Jesus' third brother 'Judas' he supposedly and, no doubt, apocryphally indulged in. Eusebius, in describing this new 'persecution', again prefaces it by the notice that 'Domitian issued an order *for the execution of all those who were of David's line*' – this may have indeed been the case – while at the same time claiming Domitian's 'father Vespasian planned no Evil against us'.[20] It is hard to reconcile the two accounts, and either the order to execute all Messianic claimants of David's line originated under Domitian or he simply renewed an order his father made a decade or so before at the conclusion of the First Jewish Revolt against Rome.

Whatever the truth here, Eusebius goes on then to quote Hegesippus' account of the arrest and examination of Jesus' brother Jude's *two* descendants – some versions even claiming to know their names: 'Zoker' and 'James' – on a charge of being 'of the family of David'.[21] When Domitian discovered them to be common labourers and the Kingdom they professed, Heavenly and Angelic not temporal, he is pictured by Hegesippus, as we saw, as 'dismissing them as simpletons' and *rescinding* the decree – the reason being that an 'other-worldly' or spiritual Kingdom was clearly considered no threat to the power of Rome.

But the language used by Hegesippus here to describe this Kingdom 'at the End of the World, when he would come in Glory to judge the quick and the dead and *reward each according to his works*', recalls nothing so much as James' vision in the Temple of the Son of Man 'coming on the clouds of Heaven' with the Angelic Host, so vividly echoed as well in the picture in the War Scroll from Qumran of the 'multitude of Heavenly Holy Ones mighty in battle', not to mention, once again, the Letter of James' picture of the 'cries of the reapers reaching the ears of the Lord of Hosts' and the 'coming of the Lord' – and the 'Jamesian' emphasis generally on 'works'.

Regardless of the truth or falseness of these reports, after discussing 'the Ebionites' – whom we have identified as holding James' name in such high regard – Eusebius then goes on to recount the martyrdom of Simeon bar Cleophas, as he portrays it, in the reign of Trajan (98–117 CE).[22] As will be recalled, these 'Ebionites', who reject the notion of the Supernatural Christ, 'still cling tenaciously to the Law', notions that Eusebius, playing on the meaning of their name in Hebrew (which he understands), dismisses as '*poverty-stricken*'.

Once again, he gives us the same story about Simeon being accused of being a 'descendant of David and a Christian' – whatever might be meant by this term at this time – and a search being made for those 'of the family of David' we just encountered twice before under Vespasian and his son Domitian. Here, Eusebius claims, it will be recalled – echoing Josephus about the longevity of the Essenes and Epiphanius regarding James and other lifelong 'Nazirites' following the 'virginity life-style' – that Simeon was 'one hundred and twenty years old' when he died. For a third time, too, he notes that Simeon was 'the son of Mary the wife of Clopas', this time directly quoting Hegesippus to the effect that he was 'the son of the Lord's uncle'.[23] If nothing else, this demonstrates something very disconcerting to the Romans was going on in the Palestine region at this time.

It is this information Jerome also uses – this and the Gospel accounts of 'Mary the wife of Clopas' being 'the mother of James, Joses, and Salome' – to conclude that 'the brothers of Jesus' were actually his *cousins*. At the same time he neglects to point out, as just noted, that this would make Simeon bar Cleophas, the next in the line of these alleged *'Desposyni'*, Jesus' *second brother* ('Clopas' and 'Cleophas' being identical) – probably the one called 'Simon' in the Gospels. Of course, this would make what was developing in Palestine, as we have already suggested, something of a family 'Caliphate' – 'Caliph' meaning 'Successor' in Arabic.

Eusebius claims there were fifteen in the line of these so-called *'Desposyni'* down to the time of Simeon or Shim'on Bar Kochba and the Second Jewish Revolt from 132 to 136 CE. This sounds suspiciously similar to the number of the Community Council at Qumran, composed of – so it appears – 'Twelve Israelites' and 'three Priests', and not a list at all. Realistically speaking, fifteen 'Bishops' or 'Archbishops' – as the case may be – in some sixty–seventy years, sounds not a little hypothetical.

The Second Jewish Revolt, as indicated by the very nature of Simeon's cognomen *'Kochba'* ('the Star') was Messianic too. In fact, this 'Star', at which the Transjordanian 'Prophet' from Edom or Moab, 'Balaam' – to whom it is attributed in Numbers – points portentously in various scenes, is well represented on the frescos of the Christian Catacombs of Rome. Some of these even include Mary and the Christ child, making it crystal clear that among early Christians and in Rome, Balaam's 'Star Prophecy' was considered to be a prediction of *Jesus*.[24] This is also, of course, the implication of the birth narrative in Matthew, not to mention Paul's reference in Rom. 11:26.

The first successor to Simeon bar Cleophas in these fictionalized lists of

Desposyni is also someone Eusebius again portentously refers to as 'Justus', recalling the matter of the defeated candidate in the election to succeed 'Judas' depicted at the beginning of Acts. For his part, Epiphanius calls the individual, who succeeds Simeon, by the equally auspicious name of 'Judas'. Indeed, he may very well have been a descendant of Jesus' third brother 'Judas' or 'Judas of James' in Apostle lists and the Letter of Jude. For Eusebius, interestingly enough, 'Judas' is the name of the last or fifteenth on this list and we are back to where we started again.[25]

Regardless of the believability of Simeon bar Cleophas, 'the son of the Lord's uncle', being crucified at Moses' age of 'one hundred and twenty' – as in the case of Josephus' earlier description of those he is calling 'Essenes' at the time of the First Jewish Revolt – again 'the witnesses' marvel that 'he could bear such tortures'. On top of this, Eusebius then describes how at the same time 'the descendants of one of those considered *brothers of the Lord, named Judas*' were re-arrested under Trajan – it will be recalled they had previously so been arrested under Domitian – and *executed in similar fashion*.

As to the descendants of Jesus' *third brother Judas* generally – again quoting Hegesippus – Eusebius says 'they came forward and presided over every Church *as witnesses* and *members of the Lord's family*'. Again this point is totally missing from Acts. Also characterizing Simeon as being '*among the witnesses who bore testimony to what had both been heard and seen of the Lord*' (again, not even a word about this in the orthodox Gospels or Acts, unless we take the story of the 'two' witnesses on the road to Emmaus, so equivocally identified in Luke, to relate to either Simeon or James, or both – which we do) and 'dying a martyr's death', he concludes, still following Hegesippus:

> Until then, the Church remained as pure and uncorrupt as a virgin . . . but when the sacred band of Apostles and the generation of those who had been privileged to hear with their own ears the Divine wisdom, reached the ends of their lives and passed on, then impious error took shape through the *Lying and deceit of false teachers* [I think we can tell who a few of these might have been] who, seeing that none of the Apostles were left, shame-facedly preached, against the *proclamation of the Truth, their false Knowledge* [literally '*pseudo-Gnosis*'].[26]

Militant Messianism and Accommodating Messianism
in the Reign of Trajan

Directly after this, Eusebius goes on to give the account, already
remarked, of Pliny the Younger, Governor of Bithynia in Asia Minor,
who in response to Trajan's decree that Christians were to be investigated –
this must have been about 110–111 CE and connecting with our notices
above – wrote back that 'with the exception of their unwillingess *to
sacrifice to idols* [James' directive to overseas communities as we saw], he
found nothing criminal in them', basically the position the Gospels are
intent on attributing to Pontius Pilate regarding Jesus. Whereupon,
according to Eusebius, Trajan purportedly published his decree that
'Christians should not be sought after, but punished if they presented
themselves'.

This correspondence between Pliny and Trajan is still extant and, it
will be recalled, Pliny's evaluation of Christians is much harsher than
Eusebius portrays, though Trajan's response does seem to have been
unenthusiastic as far as 'searching for' Christians, recommending punishment only if 'accused and convicted'.[27] The problem is, therefore, just
what did happen in Trajan's reign, leading up to Bar Kochba's Revolt at
the end of Hadrian's reign (117–38 CE)? Unfortunately, with no Josephus
to document this period, our records are correspondingly meagre.

Other sources, such as important sections of Tacitus' works which
would have dealt with such matters, are infuriatingly missing, as is the
second section of Philo's *Mission to Gaius*, which doubtlessly would have
provided important information about the situation at the end of the 30s
both in Palestine and Rome, and even the calamitous outcome of this
mission. This is also true of the original of Hegesippus' work, from which
Eusebius and others quote so extensively and which seems still to have
been extant in the East up to Jerome's time.[28]

Trajan seems to have had to deal with a succession of Messianic upris-
ings in the Eastern Mediterranean, coincident with his campaigns against
the Parthians further East, including one by someone called 'Andreas'
('Andrew') – a name cropping up, with no substance whatsoever, in
Gospel enumerations of *Jesus' Disciples* – a Jewish Messianic leader in
Cyrene (presentday Libya), always an important hotbed of disaffection to
Rome. For Dio Cassius he skinned his victims, 'eating their flesh', and
anointed himself 'with their blood'. The Persian Parthians, as well, were

always fomenting trouble among Jewish Messianists in the Roman Empire. Though the situation in Palestine seems to have been more quiescent, owing to the recent cataclysmic events and their subsequent repressions, in Egypt, the entire Jewish population of some million or a million and a half persons seems to have been wiped out somewhere between 110 and 115 under Trajan, a devastation attested to only by poignant papyrological survivals in the trashheaps of Lower Egypt.[29]

These disturbances were, no doubt, the result of Messianic activity, but, once again, there was no Josephus to describe them. Still, this kind of Messianic activity was obviously more politically motivated than that described by Pliny in Asia Minor. But information of this kind does help us to surmise when a document like Acts might have reached the form we presently find it in. There can be little doubt that Acts incorporates material from Josephus' *Antiquities*, published in 93 CE – as do, seemingly, the Gospels. But the general atmosphere of obsequiousness to Rome, emphasis on an other-worldly Kingdom of Faith following the parameters of Paul, its insistence that Paul does not have problems with Roman officials – as, for instance, Peter did – *only with Jews*, and these both in and outside of Palestine, and finally, its transformation of the visit of Simon to the household of Agrippa I via the miracle of an artistic tablecloth into one where he now is prepared to visit the household of *a Roman Centurion* of the Italica Contingent in Caesarea, do type Acts as written perhaps later than Nerva (96–98 CE) – who by adopting Trajan as a son, paved the way for the latter to succeed him as Emperor.

Trajan's father, also called 'Trajan', as we saw, had been a hero of Palestine campaigning under Vespasian. Josephus refers to him extensively and he came from the Roman town of *Italica in Spain*. The episode of Simon's visit to Agrippa I's household in Caesarea could simply have been recast into one more fawning on Herodian Kings or Roman soldiers, as, for instance, the presentations of Jesus and John the Baptist are in the Gospels. It was not because Herodian Kings were no longer of moment in Palestine, but rather Roman Emperors *from Italica* – Hadrian's place of origin as well – were.

Actually we have two different streams of Messianism here, which had probably diverged since the time of Paul and others (Simon *Magus* for example, if he can be distinguished from Paul): firstly, one that is this-worldly, apocalyptic, nationalistic, and Law-oriented, anticipating a Messiah or Messianic return, which, with the help of the Heavenly Host in the Last Days, would be devastating, 'shedding Judgement like rain' –

as the War Scroll from Qumran luminously puts it – 'on all that grows on earth', and, as in Hegesippus' account of the descendants of 'Jesus' brother Judas', 'giving to everyone according to their works'. This is sometimes reflected in Paul, but not often.

The second is other-worldly, celestial, ethereal, and Hellenized – 'my Kingdom is not of this world' (John 18:36) – basically following the parameters that Paul usually outlines in his letters, who, by his own testimony, never saw the earthly Jesus and started his career by persecuting those of 'this Way even unto death' (Acts 22:4) and for whom 'the bearing of the sword' carries its own reward (Rom. 13:4). Paul is the Roman citizen *par excellence*, who wanted to found a community in which 'Greeks and Jews' could live harmoniously (Rom. 10:12 and pars.). He is also probably a Herodian.

It is very doubtful whether the Romans could always distinguish between these two streams of Messianism, which is the reason for some of the confusions in terminologies and happenstance in these testimonies. For instance, in the same breath that Eusebius tells us of Trajan's reply to Pliny recommending lighter surveillance of so-called 'Christians' in 'Asia', Eusebius tells us of the martyrdom of Ignatius, whom he identifies as 'the second after Peter to succeed to the Bishopric of Antioch' – another point we never heard before in Acts. This martyrdom, which seems to have occurred around the year 107, also under Trajan – though some would place it under Hadrian – therefore, more or less occurs around the year of the reported martyrdom of Simeon bar Cleophas, if Ignatius' dating can really be relied upon. For instance, Irenaeus and others, on the basis of a reference to 'beasts' in Ignatius' writings, infer he was executed by being thrown to animals! Such is the fuzziness of our sources.[30]

Several chapters later, as we noted, Eusebius tells how Papias (*c.* 60–135 CE) mentions a poison or snakebite story having to do with our same 'Justus surnamed Barsabas', the loser in the election to fill Judas Iscariot's 'Office' above, and other writings Papias received telling of 'a millennium after the Resurrection, when the Kingdom of Christ would set up in *material form on this earth*' – meaning not a spiritual Kingdom as in Paul. But, not only do Rabbinic sources, as we saw, contain a similar story about a snakebite cure performed by James' *alter ego*, Jacob of Kfar Sechania, on a curious individual called 'Ben Dama'; Eusebius condemns these notions as perverse, calling Papias a man 'of very little intelligence'[31] – yet Papias' description is exactly the presentation of the Damascus Document from Qumran, which twice refers to the 'Faith' or 'Compact'

God made 'with those that love Him' – in the context of reference to 'the New Covenant in the Land of Damascus' – 'to live for a thousand generations'.[32]

What then is the true situation under Trajan and did Simeon bar Cleophas' martyrdom by crucifixion occur at this point? It is impossible to say, only that the disturbances surrounding all of the agitation in this period and these executions, poorly documented as they are, give further evidence that Messianism – perceived of in a political as well as a religious manner – did not cease with the fall of the Temple and, no doubt, was still very active in Trajan's reign around the Eastern Mediterranean. This is the context in which we would place the martyrdom of Simeon bar Cleophas and the two sons or grandsons of Jesus' other brother 'Judas'.

Of course, it is always possible that Simeon was martyred under Domitian and the two descendants of Jesus' other brother Judas, who according to Hegesippus' testimony 'ruled the Churches everywhere', were the ones martyred under Trajan. This would make more sense chronologically, but it does not matter, because it still appears from all these notices that the Romans were actively hunting down individuals descended from or associated with the family of Jesus and that these executions, regardless of Eusebius' attempts to diminish or downplay them, did occur as part of the widespread Messianic agitation that was going on around the Mediterranean, particularly in the East.

As early as Claudius' reign in the 40s and 50s, as we saw, Suetonius tells us that the Jews were expelled from Rome for making agitation on behalf of one 'Chrestus' – obviously intended to mean 'Christ' (although we have already seen a similar usage, meaning 'benevolent', applied by Josephus to Agrippa I above) – the Romans not distinguishing between Jews and Christians at all at this point.[33] The effects of this expulsion do seem to be evidenced by Paul meeting people like Aquila and Priscilla in Asia Minor, converts to either Judaism or Christianity, it is difficult to say which (Acts 18:2). But this same Aquila or his namesake in the next century has been revered in Jewish tradition as the author of an Aramaic paraphrase of the Bible known to this day as the *Targum Onkelos*.[34]

To repeat, the Romans could not always distinguish between these two conflicting strains of Messianism, one virulent and nationalistic; the other more Hellenistic, benign, and other-worldly and, as it developed, more often than not, anti-Semitic, which would seem to be a contradiction in terms, though evidently it was not. It is this latter form of Messianism that has come down to us with its many emendations as the orthodox

'Christianity' we know; the former is really exemplified in the Dead Sea Scrolls and other movements, as, for instance, the one Josephus designates for lack of a better term 'Zealot' or even sometimes '*Sicarii*', which, as already suggested, may even be a quasi-anagram for 'Christian'. As such, too, it probably would also very definitely relate to 'the Party of the circumcision'.

In our view, James and his successors, such as Simeon bar Cleophas, still have to be seen as part of this more militant or virulent brand of Messianism. As such, they and persons like Judas, Jesus' third brother (about whom we shall have more to say presently) and his descendants – even the mysterious 'Elchasai', Simeon's seeming contemporary – really were responsible for the agitation that was occurring, certainly in Palestine and probably in Egypt, North Africa, and further east as well. Note the tell-tale name of the leader there, 'Andrew', possibly absorbed into Gospel accounts as 'the brother of Peter' and a harmless fisherman, 'casting' or 'mending his nets' on the Sea of Galilee. We would venture to suggest that even the martyrdoms, leading up to the Uprisings in 115 CE and the Second Uprising against Rome from 132 to 136 CE, were on account of this more virulent and militant form of Messianism.

Domitian and Trajan's attitudes, attested to by Eusebius and possibly also reflected in the Gospels as we have them, more or less governed the approach in the second century to this second, less threatening, more spiritualized form of Messianism (where this difference could be appreciated) – the Gospels, Acts, and the other documents of Paulinized 'Gentile Christianity' being most intent on *making this difference plain*.

For instance, the real persons thrown 'to the animals' in large numbers, at least in Caesarea and Beirut in the aftermath of the fall of the Temple, as Titus made his bloody way up the coastline and indulged in these several 'birthday celebrations' in honour of his equally bloodthirsty brother Domitian, *were captives from the Uprising against Rome*. No doubt thousands more perished as part of the sumptuous celebrations Titus and his father subsequently put on in Rome as well.

Epaphroditus and the Sequentiality of Events Leading
to the Martyrdom of James

In fact, as previously remarked, one can detect an interesting sequentiality in these events where James is concerned, which helps illumine some of the factors behind his removal. In the first place there is the confrontation between Simon and Agrippa I over barring foreigners – in this instance, including Herodians – from the Temple, which has as its counterpart in the next generation the erection of the Temple Wall, which triggered the stoning of James. The purpose of this wall, as we have explained, was not simply to bar Agrippa I's son Agrippa II from the Temple, but to bar his view of the sacrifices in the Temple as he reclined dining on the terrace of his palace. This is indicative of the real atmosphere in Palestine in this period – Gospel portraiture of the pastoral 'Galilean' countryside notwithstanding – and overseas it would have been perceived, no doubt, as the epitome of recalcitrant malevolence.

This kind of intolerant 'zeal' is reversed, for instance, in the Pauline Letter to the Ephesians, which not only contains the doctrine of 'Jesus as Temple' – enunciated by Paul as well in 1 Corinthians 3:10 and 12:27 – but also the opposite position, that there should 'no longer be strangers or foreign visitors' (Eph. 2:19). For it and for Paul, all are 'fellow citizens in the Household' or 'Temple of God', of which 'Jesus Christ is the Cornerstone' (2:20–22). This is also the picture in the Gospels. These are noble sentiments, to be sure, with wide appeal; but, in a Palestinian framework, they are historically inaccurate as the Dead Sea Scrolls now clearly testify – as did the Temple warning blocks, mentioned above, threatening death for strangers or foreigners entering the central area around the Temple even inadvertently.

After this confrontation in Caesarea and those that follow between Greeks and Jews throughout the next decade there, comes the assassination of the High Priest Jonathan, accompanied by Josephus' introduction of 'the *Sicarii*' responsible for it. Jonathan, it will be recalled, was the brother of that Ananus responsible for the death of James, and it is their father 'Annas' whom the Gospel of John pictures as interviewing Jesus before sending him bound to Caiaphas (18:13–24). It is at this point that John has Peter either '*standing* at the door' or '*standing*' by the fire outside Ananus' or Caiaphas' 'court' (the word 'standing' now appearing again five times in this episode). Here Peter denies the accusation of the 'kinsman' of 'the Servant of the High Priest', 'whose ear Peter *cut off*' (we have seen this vocabulary before), that he was one of Jesus' 'Disciples' (18:10 and 26). Of course, this same 'Servant of the High Priest' appears in Jerome's Gospel of the Hebrews, as the individual to whom Jesus gives his linen 'grave clothes'. Again, the thematic overlaps are startling, even if not immediately unravelled.

For the Synoptics, it will be recalled, this scene at 'the High Priest

Caiaphas' *House*' turns into a midnight sitting of the entire Sanhedrin of High Priests, Elders, and Scribes, and this supposedly at Passover, where the 'blasphemy' charge is made *against Jesus*, though it is impossible to say for what reason. In the Synoptics, not only is there no mention of a preliminary interview with Ananus, but Peter is now 'sitting' by the fire, not 'standing' (again our overlaps between 'sitting' and 'standing') – in fact, Luke never mentions the word 'standing' at all and the other two, only once. For them, what Peter is denying is rather the point that he either knows 'Jesus the Nazoraean' or that he is 'a Galilean' (Luke 22:54–62 and pars.).

The Gospel of John accurately portrays Caiaphas as the son-in-law of Ananus (18:13), which makes the Ananus responsible (along with Agrippa II) for James' death and the Jonathan slain by the '*Sicarii*' followers of 'Judas the *Galilean*', Caiaphas' brothers-in-law – Ananus the Younger being the son of Ananus the Elder.[35] Josephus rails against the assassination of this Jonathan, as we saw, and the bloodshed that followed as 'polluting' *both* city and Temple. In his discussion of these '*Sicarii*', whom he calls 'Robbers' (*Lēstai*), the 'clothes' theme reappears again too, but now associated with 'the daggers which these murderers carried under their *clothes*'!

As Josephus puts it – as we saw as well – once again reversing the 'Piety' language of 'loving God':

> This is the reason why, in my opinion, even God himself, out of *hatred for their Impiety, turned away from our city* and, because He deemed the Temple to be no longer a *clean dwelling place for Him*, brought the Romans upon us and *purified our city by fire*, while inflicting *slavery* upon us together with our wives and children, for He wished to *chasten us* by these calamities.[36]

The 'slavery' Josephus is speaking about here is different from the 'bondage' or 'slavery' Paul talks of at the end of Galatians, and this is a different kind of '*mea culpa*' confession from those one gets in the New Testament generally, which are, nevertheless, but a variation of it.

This is followed by the unlawful Sanhedrin trial, Ananus 'pursued' against James at his new 'House' of sitting (his '*Beit-Galuto*'), succeeded by James' stoning, which clearly indicate that James was identified as the centre of the agitation behind many of these things. That this 'blasphemy' trial was undoubtedly trumped up by the Herodian Authorities in conjunction with the Temple Establishment, and that both Agrippa II and

Ananus joined forces in it, further connects James to the source of both the Temple Wall Affair directed against Agrippa II and the assassination of Ananus' brother – Caiaphas' brother-in-law – Jonathan. This, in turn, leads to the fire in Rome, which Nero blamed on so-called 'Christians'. More sympathetic sources, however, perhaps prompted by some of these Christian 'friends' in high places we so often hear about – not the least of whom being the Pseudoclementines' 'Clement''s counterpart in Domitian's household, 'Flavius Clemens' – put the blame rather on Nero himself.[37]

Whatever the mechanism, Nero clearly seems to have decided to rid himself of Jews and Jewish agitation generally. He sends a Governor, Florus (64–66 CE), to Judea, who, by Josephus' own testimony, seems *intentionally* to goad the population into revolt.[38] At the same time Nero kicks his wife Poppea – for Josephus, 'a worshipper of God', in other words, 'a God-Fearer' – to death, presumably agitated by concerns over her interest in causes of this kind and other things, not to mention her pregnancy.

In the midst of the war in Judea, Nero is assassinated. Among those accused of having a hand in this would appear to be Paul's associate Epaphroditus, a man whom he called 'his brother, co-worker, and fellow soldier', an 'Apostle' (Phil. 2:25), and who, Josephus tells us, had 'participated in many important events'. Though some, as signalled earlier, will object to this three-fold identification; not only do Suetonius and others affirm that he was Nero's secretary – which would make Paul's intimations about 'Saints' in 'the household of Caesar' even more meaningful (Phil. 4:18) – but this same Epaphroditus re-emerges some years later – survivor as he appears to have been – as *Domitian's secretary* as well.

Not long before Domitian too was assassinated in 96 CE, Epaphroditus appears to have run afoul of him purportedly over his behaviour at the time of Nero's assassination, which Domitian used as a pretext, complaining that Epaphroditus dared to raise his hand against an Emperor, and had him executed. This is *very* peculiar indeed, coming from Domitian, and there would appear to be more behind these events than appears on the surface. Not only was this about the time that Domitian, as we have seen, was said to be rounding up all those of the family of David and possibly even the real year Simeon bar Cleophas was executed, 96 CE was also the year Flavia Domitilla, the wife or niece of Flavius Clemens, mentioned above, one of the consuls that year and Domitian's co-ruler, was, according to Eusebius, exiled for 'her testimony to Christ'.

In fact she was Domitian's niece and Flavius Clemens was his cousin.

Domitian, who was apparently childless, had designated their two sons his heirs – he had renamed them Vespasian and Flavia – that is, before he had Flavius Clemens executed *the same year* as Epaphroditus.[39] Many of these points we have made before, but it still bears repeating that Domitian was himself assassinated, an event Suetonius describes most vividly, by Domitilla's *own steward*, 'Stephanos' or 'Stephen' – an all too familiar name.

Suetonius, too, an individual who cannot be described as particularly philo-Semitic, describes Domitian's hatred, or at least cruelty towards Jews, attesting that he 'levied the tax against them' with the utmost vigour, even

> prosecuting those who, while not publicly acknowledging the Faith, yet lived as Jews, as well as *those who concealed their origins* and *did not pay the tribute levied against their people.*[40]

One such prosecution of a man 'ninety years old' – which may even have served as the model for the supposed prosecution of the *one hundred and twenty year-old* Simeon bar Cleophas – Suetonius himself acknowledges having witnessed as a boy, who 'was examined before the procurator to see whether he was circumcised' – not very different from more recent events in our purportedly modern world!

As we have already suggested, Epaphroditus would appear to be the same individual Josephus dedicates many of his works to, including the *Antiquities* and the *Vita*, and his words regarding him in the former – 'a lover of all kinds of learning, but principally delighted by the study of history' – are thoroughly modern, attesting to how little things have changed. Though the relationship to Domitian's Epaphroditus is contested – to say nothing of Paul's companion in touch with 'the Saints' in Nero's household – for Josephus, Epaphroditus, as we just saw, was a man who had experienced many important political events. Had Epaphroditus not encouraged him, Josephus would not have made the effort 'to overcome his sloth' and pour out the *Antiquities*.[41]

Much depends, of course, on how Josephus himself died and when, which is unclear, since no Josephus remained to chronicle it, but he too seems to have disappeared about the same time Epaphroditus did and possibly for similar reasons – maybe even because of information contained in the newly published *Antiquities* or *Vita* (both of which encouraged by Epaphroditus) that some may have found offensive. Some even try to explain these inconsistencies by proposing there were two Epaphrodituses working under both Domitian and Trajan, but the writer considers this highly unlikely, though there may have been a father and son. This is the same genre of problem surrounding the overlapping Messianic round-ups under Domitian and Trajan.

Whatever the conclusion, the Julio-Claudians, represented by the last Emperor of that line Nero, gave way to the Flavians who, abetted by a host of Jewish turncoats, such as Josephus and Tiberius Alexander, seem to have marketed their own version of Jewish Messianism, which, at the very least, was presented as submissive and deferential to the power of Rome and its emperors – this not to mention marketing a healthy dose of Greco-Alexandrian, Hellenistic anti-Semitism.

Epaphroditus and his Intellectual Circle

This brings us to another difficult subject: who could have written the original accounts, upon which so many of our Gospel episodes in the form we have them are based. This question, though puzzling scholars for generations, in the light of the above may not be as difficult to gain a measure of insight into as most may think. One must keep in mind the attitudes, the orientation, or, if one prefers, the *polemics*, which are in fact quite straightforward. With rare exceptions the point of view is almost always anti-Semitic, pro-Gentile, anti-national, and pro-Roman.

While employing the warp and woof of Jewish Messianism, this is exploited basically to produce a pro-Roman, spiritualized, Hellenistic-style mystery religion. Here, one must understand that, while all the Gospels exhibit differences, the Synoptics are basically variations on a theme – with more or less material added. John, while differing markedly as to specific historical points and development, still comes from the same Hellenistic, anti-Semitic mindset – even more extreme.

What we are speaking about here is the original core of materials and the mindset they evince, not the endless variations, addenda, or accretions, lesser or greater. The underlying mindset is on the whole consistent, while the variations, we have been witnessing, are so complex and creative that even the modern techniques of form, redaction, or text criticism have not succeeded in elucidating these in any generally acceptable manner, nor are they ever likely to do so to everyone's satisfaction. However, the central question must be, who might have had an interest in the *general thrust* of the presentation of Messianic events in Palestine all more or less have in common, to be sure, acquiring accretions as the original core went through manifold transformations and additions. Whose interests did the ideological thrust of this central core of material serve?

793

We have already given numerous examples of the orientation we have in mind, despite the variations, perhaps the most important aspect of which was to lighten and deflect the fundamental embarrassment over the Roman execution of Jesus as a subversive and anti-Roman agitator. This, anyhow, has to some extent come to be recognized by scholars. Out of it proceeds the positive portrayal, where possible (it almost always was), of Roman officials and Herodian puppets.

Two of the most obvious of these, we have highlighted, were the patent fraudulence of portraying Pontius Pilate's *high regard* for Jesus and 'his wife' – naturally unnamed and in a dream no less – as recognizing Jesus as 'a Righteous Man', the most revered concept in Judaism of the time, especially among 'Opposition groups'; and, secondly, the henpecked Herod the Tetrarch (it was hard to whitewash him), hesitating to execute John the Baptist, but rather, also, recognizing John as a 'Righteous Man' or '*Zaddik*', while the majority of Jews did not – yet being forced to execute John, because of the lascivious dance performed by a woman at his *birthday party*! Almost any fair-minded person would immediately recognize such portrayals as dissimulation.

We have also reviewed some of the other, more obvious *non sequitur*s in the core materials as we have them – all directed towards the same end – for instance, the impossibility of a Jewish Sanhedrin, composed of High Priests, Elders, and Scribes, meeting *in the middle of the night of Passover* at 'the High Priest's House' to hold a trial of someone for 'blasphemy'. Or the presentation of Peter as constantly misunderstanding the Master's teaching – Paul, of course, understands it – unable to walk on the waters of the Sea of Galilee because his 'Faith' was weak or denying the Master (this in all the Gospels) 'three times' on his death night, or the Messiah incarnate eating congenially with Roman tax collectors and other 'Sinners' (probably meant to include 'prostitutes'), while variously disparaging his own people and family. How delicious all this must have been for those who created it – and what good drama it made – but what poor history, as the Dead Sea Scrolls now amply demonstrate. Where the charge of 'blasphemy' is concerned, as we have explained, this should have been punished by *stoning* not *crucifixion* (anathema to Jews, whether turncoats or otherwise) and retrospectively assimilates the same charge made *against James* – in Establishment eyes with more cause, which does seem to have resulted in a stoning or, at least, a very intentional shove.

Who then would or could have produced the basic core of this kind of material before, like a snowball rolling down a hill, it grew into a massive accumulation of generally like-minded tradition? In the first place, the writers were extremely able craftsmen, who knew their material thoroughly. For instance, as we have been explaining, they had to know all the traditions associated with the death of James – even those represented by the later Pseudoclementine *Recognitions* and accounts in the early Church writers about James 'being cast down' from the Pinnacle of the Temple – and this at a very early time. They also probably knew the traditions about a first post-resurrection appearance to 'James, then to all the Apostles, and last of all, as if to an abortion, he also appeared to me', as Paul recounts it in 1 Corinthians 15:7–8. In fact, Paul says as much himself, implying there were already written documents or traditions relating to these things which he had 'received' (1 Cor. 15:3).

Paul did survive James, though by how many years must remain the subject of some debate. Still, after his final trip to 'see Nero' – either the earlier one in Acts, from 60 to 62 CE, when James was killed, or, depending on the point of view, the later one described in Josephus around 66 CE; one would have to observe, Paul or one or another of his associates, like Titus (Timothy?), Silas (Silvanus?), Luke ('Lucius of Cyrene'?) or even Epaphroditus himself would have had time to produce a rough version of some of the key events we are speaking about, incorporating the principles of good Roman citizenship, not Palestinian Messianism.

Epaphroditus, who must be seen as a prime candidate for the direction of this kind of activity, not only had a hand in the assassination of Nero, but was also Domitian's *Secretary for Letters*, before he too was executed by him on unspecified charges – probably, like his contemporary Flavius Clemens, for being a secret 'Christian'. One is not imagining these things. They *really* occurred, despite various attempts to obscure them.

The writers we are speaking about would also have known many of the works of Qumran, as we now have them revealed, particularly the Damascus Document, but also the Community Rule and War Scroll, which they systematically – sometimes even gleefully – reworked or subverted. In passage after passage, as we have signalled, they inverted fundamental Qumran imageries and orientations, turning them back upon their initial creators and reversing their import, capitalizing on their obvious weak points from a 'public relations' standpoint and ridiculing their inward-looking, intolerant, and idiosyncratic nationalism (sincere as it may have been) with devastating results.

This was a substantial intellectual feat, which could only have been effected by extremely able and well-informed minds – but without the discovery of the Dead Sea Scrolls as we now have them, we could never have understood this – suspected it, yes, but never *known* it – which is why their discovery is of such primary historical importance.

Even the Gospel of John, which differs so markedly from its Synoptic counterparts, exhibits a difference, as we noted, only in substance, not in kind. The orientation and playful inversion of Qumran themes are perhaps most glaringly and humorously illustrated by the almost total obfuscation of the report of a first appearance to James in the portrayal there of Jesus' post-resurrection appearance along the shore of the Sea of Galilee, and his principal Disciples as 'dragging their nets full of fishes'. Peter even had 'a hundred and fifty-three' 'large fishes' in his 'net', which 'though there were so many', yet 'was it not torn'.

This is particularly true when one is aware of what subsequently happened to the 'Galilean' fishermen around the shores of the Sea of Galilee under Titus and his colleague, Agrippa II, when, even as Josephus describes it, 'the whole sea ran red with their blood'. The old, the infirm, and the young were butchered and the rest given over to this same Agrippa to be sold as slaves. Titus, of course, kept back a few to cover his own expenses. Which returns us to our initial question, who could have written this kind of artful, yet nefarious material in its initial configuration, before it was elaborated upon and developed into a larger literature around the Hellenistic Mediterranean? Who would have had the knowledge to do so?

In the first place, there were quite a few well-educated and intelligent people, many of whom were very good writers, in the above circle of individuals. For instance, Josephus by his own testimony tells us that Agrippa II made over to him some ninety-nine of his letters to help him rewrite his earlier work, the *War*, in the *Antiquities*. In addition, he tells us that, not only did this same Epaphroditus – to whom the *Antiquities* was dedicated – sponsor his work, but it was read appreciatively by Julius Archelaus. He may well have been Paul's nephew, mentioned in Acts 23:16–23's account of Paul's marvellous rescue by Roman troops from the furious Jewish mob at the Festival of Pentecost – so critical to Acts' portrayal of the parameters of the new Pauline Gentile Mission – who wanted to kill him for introducing Gentiles into the Temple. In this regard, it should be observed that this *same* mob was not interested in killing James, though it had ample opportunity to do so. On the contrary, James seems to have been killed by the Establishment precisely *because* he was held in such high regard by the people, in particular, these same 'Zealots for the Law'.

Paul already refers in the Letter to the Romans, as we have also seen, to his 'kinsman the littlest Herod', who in all probability was Herod (4), the son of Aristobulus, King of Lesser Armenia, and the Salome who allegedly performed the lascivious dance ending up with the legendary portrait in Gospel tradition of John the Baptist's head upon the platter – which no one will ever forget. In addition to Josephus himself (who lived well into the 90s if not beyond), there were all of Philo of Alexandria's kinsmen and heirs, thoroughly compromised by contacts with Romans and Herodians, who certainly knew the allegorical approach to Scripture that Philo himself had pioneered.

It would not have been a very great step for any of these or even Paul, who is already doing so in his letters, to apply this approach to the literature and conceptualities found at Qumran. In particular, these kinsmen included, as we have seen, Tiberius Alexander, mentioned in Acts 4:6 along with Caiaphas and Ananus the High Priest in one of the few honest portrayals of a Roman official – but he was a Jewish turncoat, directly responsible for the execution of the Jewish revolutionary Leader Judas the Galilean's two sons in 48 CE, who, later, as Titus' adjutant, personally directed the siege of Jerusalem and final destruction of the Temple.

For good measure, the Romans even went on to destroy a sister temple that had been constructed in Heliopolis in Egypt in the Maccabean Period. Someone had to be giving them extremely good intelligence, to remove the root cause of so much of this anti-Roman agitation so decisively. These events in Egypt, as we have shown, were followed under Trajan around the time of or after the execution of Simeon bar Cleophas – as pictured in Christian sources – by the actual eradication of the entire Jewish population in Lower Egypt, perhaps numbering a million and a half souls. In addition, in Rome after the fall of Jerusalem were other individuals, retired there as hostages, all extremely well informed and cultivated, such as Antiochus of Commagene and his son, Epiphanes, who had led the 'Macedonian Legion' in the recent War.

Of course, where providing good intelligence was concerned, we have numerous candidates, Josephus himself being a self-admitted informant and interrogator of prisoners. Tiberius Alexander is identified by him as a Jewish backslider – the equivalent of the pot calling the kettle black. Then there are all the Herodians, including Bernice, the mistress of Titus the destroyer of the Temple and Tiberius Alexander's sister-in-law, from *two* marriages, not to mention the 'Saulus' who so mysteriously and ubiquitously keeps popping in and out of Josephus' picture of the last days of Jerusalem. There was also another 'Maccabean' Herodian resident in

Rome in these years, Tigranes, who was sent by Nero to be King of Armenia. His father, also Tigranes, had been King of Armenia before him and his son became King of Cilicia. All of these, too, 'deserted the Jewish Religion and went over to that of the Greeks'.[42]

Nor we do know what other clique might have been operating around the Roman Governor Felix – married to Bernice's other sister Drusilla – whose brother Pallas was Nero's favourite and who seems to have been involved in bringing Paul to Rome. Felix certainly seems to have been responsible for bringing Simon *Magus* to Rome (if there was a difference). There is also Gallio, the Roman Governor of Corinth and brother of Nero's adviser and major-domo, the famous Seneca. Acts revels in presenting this Gallio, a historical figure who can actually be identified as Governor of Corinth in 52 CE, as rescuing Paul from the anger of the Jewish mob and having the Head of the Synagogue there, it calls 'Sosthenes', flogged before 'the Judgement Seat' (18:17). To be sure, for Paul, significantly in 1 Corinthians 1:1, this same Sosthenes is one of his closest lieutenants 'and brother to the Church of God in Corinth'. This is to say nothing about Seneca himself, whose anti-Jewish feelings even Augustine feels constrained to remark and to whom a pseudepigraphic correspondence with Paul is attested.[43]

All of these were *very* literate men. Josephus even identifies his father, the priest 'Matthias' ('Matthew'), as a writer of great repute. Of course, one must always bear in mind that his father might have been the proto-type for the renowned 'Matthew', to whom the traditions incorporated in the First Gospel are attributed. In Mark 2:14, for some reason, it will be recalled, he is called 'Levi the son of Alphaeus', that is, 'Cleophas' and another of these alleged 'tax collectors'!

However this may be – as we saw – Josephus has very good contacts in Rome indeed. But with all his flaws, he could not have been responsible for the kind of materials upon which the Gospels as we have them were based – except tangentially – nor any other self-professing Jew, turncoat or otherwise. The rhetoric and drumbeat of anti-Semitic polemic are just too strong for that. Besides Josephus is too inordinately proud of his heritage, as he repeatedly demonstrates in the *Antiquities*, to have done this. But the information he possessed *could* certainly have been used by someone, as could that possessed by Agrippa II and his sister Bernice, both smarting over the loss of their palaces in Jerusalem – not to mention their sister Drusilla married to Felix, whose son, Antonius Agrippa, named after Agrippa II, was killed in the eruption of Vesuvius in 79 CE.

We have already seen Agrippa's anti-'Zealot' attitude in the Temple Wall Affair, where he insisted on watching the Temple sacrifices even while dining on his balcony. Not only did he make over his personal files for Josephus' use in writing the *Antiquities*, but it would not be surprising if the diary or travel document on which the latter part of Acts ('the We Document') is based containing such a flattering portrayal of him, his two sisters, and Felix, had somehow ultimately ended up in his possession. This would be all the more true, especially if Paul were, in fact, one of his 'kinsmen' – the direction in which our data more and more seems to be leading us. Bernice's nature we know from her connection with Titus, who functioned as Co-Emperor with his father in this period, and the Gospels do present an extremely benign portrait of 'Jesus' eating with 'tax collectors and Sinners', two particularly appropriate significations where Agrippa II and Bernice are concerned.

Julius Archelaus, too, who ended up in wealthy retirement in Rome reading Josephus' works in Rome (and 'could vouch for their accuracy'), had been a former brother-in-law of Bernice. He was the son of the Temple Treasurer, Helcias, whose father and grandfather (the genealogies are unclear here) had been Temple Treasurer before him and close associates of the earlier Herod. Another of his 'kinsmen', 'Antipas', had been a close associate of Josephus' 'Saulus' and also became Temple Treasurer before being executed by 'Zealots' in the midst of the Uprising as a 'Traitor'.

But the best candidate among this group for producing or sponsoring the production of materials of this kind – if indeed it is possible to trace such materials to a given source – turning what was basically an aggressively apocalyptic Messianism into a more benign and pacifistic one, would be someone of the experience and talents of an Epaphroditus – or even perhaps one or another of Paul's other travelling companions. The ascription of Acts to Luke basically says something of this kind and Luke himself – if, indeed, the author of the Gospel under his name and Acts – confirms this, telling us how knowledgeable he was in comparing sources. Epaphroditus was certainly very literate and probably more knowledgeable even than Luke. Plus he had all Josephus' works, which he had commissioned, to guide him. Then too, if he was a travelling companion of Paul, he probably knew Luke as well.

If he is, indeed, the same individual Paul mentions in Philippians (and elsewhere, possibly too, under the name of 'Erastus') as his *closest* associate (his 'Apostle') and 'fellow worker and fellow soldier' – and we can see no good reason for challenging this – then he knew Paul's mind

799

intimately, better probably than just about anyone else. He would also appear to have been extremely adventurous and personally brave, as Josephus attests as well. In fact, Epaphroditus' execution by Domitian – to say nothing of Domitian's own assassination by Flavia Domitilla's servant 'Stephen', obviously in vengeance for something – not to mention Epaphroditus' involvement in the death of Nero, does raise serious questions as to just what was going on beneath the surface of these events so close to the source of Imperial Power in Rome.

These are some of the things we shall never know, but the Gospels as we have them – whoever produced them – at their core are just too anti-Semitic to have been produced by anyone other than Gentiles. The animus against Jews – Jews of all stripes, even those representing the Leadership of the Jerusalem Church (called 'Pharisees' in Acts) – is just too intense and unremitting to be otherwise. It is no wonder that the effects of this continue to be felt today and grappled with by people who still argue over their cause.

It should not be forgotten, too, that both Philo and Josephus addressed works against Alexandrian anti-Semitic agitators, such as Apion, who himself led a 'Mission to Gaius' that apparently nullified the one led by Philo. An Apion-like character also makes an appearance in the Pseudo-clementines, where he was an associate of Simon *Magus*! Apion was actually a known historian at the Museum in Alexandria, who invented the ritual murder accusation against Jews. His successor as grammarian there, Chaeremon, like Seneca, was also a tutor of Nero.[44] Both had already completely falsified Jewish Old Testament history – falsifications that sent even Josephus into paroxysms of indignation.[45] Paul, too, as we have seen, was a master of such literary invective and allegorization.

This is, in fact, the circle of individuals (themselves having a very substantial knowledge of Josephus' works) to whom one might attribute the core of material that finally ends up – with numerous variations, expansions, and accretions – in what we call Gospels today, if, in fact, one can atttibute such a core to anyone known, as opposed to unknown trans-mitters. It is certainly the circle that produced Acts. Any of these individuals, or combinations thereof, could have been involved. Though the core of the Gospel materials had to go back to someone very close to or know-ledgeable about both the Qumran Community and 'the Jerusalem Community' of James, this could have been fleshed out and overwritten – as in Acts – some time after the momentous events of 95–6 CE, in the course of which so many individuals like Epaphroditus, Flavius Clemens, and possibly even Josephus himself, lost their lives. This is not to mention the martyrs in Palestine, reportedly under Trajan but perhaps before, such as Simeon bar Cleophas and the two descendants of Jesus' *third brother* Judas.

These are the problems and issues one must weigh in attempting to determine who might have been responsible for turning Palestinian Messianism on its ear and reversing its most precious and fundamental concepts and ethos into their mirror opposite.

The Martyrdom of Simeon bar Cleophas and the Traditions of the 'Pella Flight'

In the course of his discussion of the earlier 'calamities which at that time overwhelmed the whole nation in every part of the world' and estimating that by both famine and sword over 'one million one hundred thousand persons perished' in Judea alone as 'vengeance for *the guilt and Impiety of the Jews against the Christ of God*' (our tell-tale 'Piety' inversion again),[46] Eusebius makes one of his last references to James.

In doing so, he also delineates his sense of sequentiality in these matters, noting that:

> After the ascension of our Saviour, the Jews had followed up *their crimes against him* by devising *plot after plot* against his Disciples [the reversal of the 'plot' language, applied at Qumran to the death of the Righteous Teacher]. First *they stoned Stephen to death*, then *James the son of Zebedee and the brother of John* was beheaded, and *finally James*, the first after our Saviour's Ascension to be raised to the Bishop's Throne there [in Jerusalem], lost his life in the way described, while the remaining Apostles in constant danger from *murderous plots*, were driven out of Judea . . . to teach their message of *the Power of Christ* in every land.

Here, not only do we have the Primal Adam 'Great Power' language of the Ebionite Elchasaites of the period of Trajan that follows this, but the notice about the immediacy of James' ascendancy – the real 'election' behind the counterfeit one following Judas' death in Acts. Not only is James once again clearly being reckoned *among the Apostles*; but the stoning of 'Stephen', of course, is not exactly, as we have seen, what it seems to be, nor is the beheading of 'James the brother of John'. We have, therefore, aside from the Jesus scenario of the Gospels, *only the stoning of James* on which to base these perilous maledictions being pronounced here by Eusebius, the individual who assisted Christianity's rise to power in the Roman Empire.

His lurid description of 'the calamities' that then befell the Jews which follows is lifted almost bodily from Josephus' *Jewish War*, which describes how the Jews during the siege of Jerusalem even ended up *eating their own children*. All of this is foreseen, as far as Eusebius is concerned, by Jesus 'weeping over' Jerusalem in the Gospel of Luke and his prediction that it shall be 'levelled to the ground, both you and your children, not a stone upon a stone' (19:41–44).

Here, not only does Jesus 'draw near' Jerusalem, as Paul does Damascus in Acts and Jesus does to Jericho earlier in the Gospel, but the speech attributed to Jesus employs yet another variation of the 'casting' language to describe 'the rampart which your Enemies *will cast [peribalousin]* about you'. In Luke, in the very next line, Jesus goes on 'to *cast out* [here *ekballein*] those buying and selling in' the Temple (Luke 19:45). Jesus' malediction here includes the tell-tale 'Enemy' language, now appropriately applied to the Romans, but also that of the 'Visitation' ('and they shall not leave in you [Jerusalem] one stone upon another stone, because you did not know the Time of your Visitation') – widespread at Qumran, particularly in the Damascus Document – here either meaning his 'Visitation' or that which God brings 'by the hand of' the Romans. He is also using the 'Bulwark' or 'Rampart' language, whether accidentally or by design, which Eusebius will now go on to apply to James' role in Jerusalem as 'Protection of the People'.47

Eusebius now goes on to quote the Little Apocalypse, which in the Synoptics also directly follows this. This is where Jesus predicts that 'the anger against this People' will include even 'those with child and those giving suck in those days' and that 'Jerusalem would be trodden down by the Gentiles until the time of the Gentiles is completed' (Luke 21:20–24 and pars.). The former actually directly recapitulates the language the Habakkuk *Pesher* from Qumran uses to describe how the *Kittim* 'destroy with the sword young men, grown-ups, and old people, *women and children, and have no pity even on the fruit of the womb*'.48

Jesus is pictured here as calling these, 'the Days of Vengeance', language again completely replicated at Qumran or vice versa. At Qumran, it was applied in exegesis of the famous 'make a straight Way in the wilderness' passage from Isaiah 40:3 in the Community Rule – but, again with exactly opposite signification to here in the Little Apocalypse, on behalf of those 'zealous for the Law, whose time would be *the Day of Vengeance*'.49 This allusion is followed in all Synoptics by the constantly repeated proclamation, this time by Jesus, 'And then they shall see the Son of Man coming in a cloud with *great Power and Glory*' (Luke 21:27 and pars.).

Not only does the description of these persecutions under Domitian and Trajan in Eusebius begin with this reference to James and how Simeon bar Cleophas, Jesus' 'cousin', was unanimously elected to succeed him; the lengthy descriptions of Jerusalem's demise and her people's justified suffering – because of 'their crimes against the Christ of God' – end with the notice about James, 'called the brother of the Lord and the first Bishop'. This referred to how his presence and that of some of the other Apostles 'provided the city with a Strong Bulwark there', the imagery, coupled with the 'casting' language, we have just seen evoked in Luke to describe the Roman siegeworks preceding the destruction of the Temple 'stone by stone'.

Given early Church tradition connecting James' death to the fall of Jerusalem, excurses of this kind, ending with an allusion to James' role as 'Bulwark' or '*Oblias*', would be just what one would expect. Moreover, it is indeed interesting that Eusebius should attach the two executions related to James, that of 'Stephen' and the *other* 'James', to his view of the sequence of events leading up to James' death and the destruction of Jerusalem. This is also the sequence followed in Acts, but of course neglecting to mention anything about the death of James or the attack on him by Paul.

It is at the close of this sequence, too, that Eusebius makes his first reference to the famous 'Pella Flight'. Pella he describes as 'one of the cities of Perea' – the area beyond Jordan we have already specified as being where John the Baptist was executed – to which

> the people of the Jerusalem Church removed before the War began, on account of *an oracle given by revelation to men considered worthy* there.

We shall have more to say about this oracle later, but connected as it is to the fall of Jerusalem, at this point it cannot be totally divorced from the counter-oracle Jesus was just pictured as making with more or less detail about the destruction of Jerusalem, 'stone upon stone' by Roman armies and the suffering of its inhabitants.

As Eusebius pictures this oracle, here and hereafter, 'Those who believed in Christ removed from Jerusalem, and when these Holy Men [note the language of 'being Holy' or 'consecrated' again, as in James being 'Holy from his mother's womb'] had utterly abandoned the Royal metropolis of the Jews and the whole Land of Judea' (note, too, the parallel here with the language of the Damascus Document at Qumran, which twice uses these very words to command *the Sons of Zadok* and those with them to 'go out from the Land of Judah and sojourn in the Land of Damascus'),

> the *Judgement of God* finally overtook them for their *abominable crimes against the Christ and his Apostles*, entirely blotting out that Generation of Evil-Doers from among men.[50]

Eusebius appears almost gleeful here.

'Drinking the Cup' Imagery in the Gospels and at Qumran

Before leaving these materials about Simeon bar Cleophas, under whom the Pella Flight, if credible, must have occurred – some question it – it is well to look at a later statement Eusebius makes when enumerating the various Jewish and early Christian heresies, that 'James the Just suffered martyrdom for *the same reason* as the Lord'. In this, he is again dependent on Hegesippus and mentions the universal demand that Simeon bar Cleophas be elected Bishop and 'be second, because he was a *cousin of the Lord*'. But this parallels a statement he also made earlier, again dependent on Hegesippus, about how

> Simeon *the son of Clopas*, the second to have been appointed Bishop of the Church at Jerusalem . . . ended his life in martyrdom . . . suffering an end like that of the Lord . . . when Trajan was Emperor and Atticus Consul.[51]

Allied material in the Synoptics following allusion to 'the Son of Man sitting upon the Throne of his Glory' and allusion to his Apostles as 'sitting on Twelve Thrones, judging the Twelve Tribes of Israel' (Matt. 19:28), have James and John the sons of Zebedee come to Jesus and ask to sit on Jesus' right and left hand in 'Glory' (Mark 10:35–38). In Matthew 20:20, however, it is rather 'the mother of the sons of Zebedee' (later at the Crucifixion, she is 'Mary the mother of James and Joses and the mother of the sons of Zebedee' – 27:56) who makes this request. Interestingly, this request is also preceded by the pat anti-family instruction 'to the Disciples' to leave 'house or brothers or sisters or father or mother or children or lands for the sake of the Kingdom of God' (Luke 18:29 and pars.).

Luke places these notices right before Jesus, 'drawing near Jericho', visits the house of the Rich Chief Tax Collector and midget Zacchaeus and, directly thereafter, 'drawing near' Jerusalem, weeps over it, predicting its coming demolition stone by stone (18:13–19:44). Mark and

Matthew picture Jesus as quoting, in relation to his promise to those forsaking brothers, sisters, mothers, lands, etc., the clearly pro-Pauline, anti-Jerusalem Church, 'Many that are First shall be Last and the Last First' (Mark 10:31 and Matt. 19:30). Both 'the First' and 'the Many', as we have seen, are favourite usages at Qumran, the latter the preferred nomenclature for the rank and file; the former, the beneficiaries of 'the First Covenant'. Where 'the Last' is concerned, one should bear in mind Paul's similar characterization of himself at the end of his list of post-resurrection appearances by Jesus in 1 Corinthians 15:8 above, as well as the continual allusion at Qumran to 'Last Times'/'the Last Generation'.

In these two episodes about *two* brothers, asking 'to sit', as James else-where proclaims it, 'on the right hand' in 'Glory', Jesus responds: 'Are you able to drink the Cup which I drink?' When they answer in the affirmative, Jesus is then pictured as responding, 'My Cup indeed you shall drink' or 'the Cup I drink you shall drink', at which point, 'the ten' are pictured as being 'offended concerning the *two brothers*' (Matt. 20:20–24; Mark 10:35–41 adds their names, 'James and John').

But aside from the artificial designation 'sons of Zebedee', one must ask who these 'two brothers' really were. One should, also, note the same kind of imagery again reappears in John, when Peter strikes off the ear of 'the High Priest's Servant' – the same 'High Priest's Servant' that seems to be the recipient of the linen 'grave clothes' in the Gospel of the Hebrews episode cited above – and Jesus tells him to put away his sword (John 18:10). Here Jesus is pictured as saying, 'Should I not *drink the Cup* which the Father has given me?' (18:11), thus making it unmistakably clear that this kind of 'drinking the Cup' imagery is being applied to martyrdom and death – not to mention God's retribution for these things in the Book of Revelation and the Scrolls.

This 'Cup' imagery for death and God's Vengeance is crucial at Qumran in key passages in the Habakkuk *Pesher* dealing with the destruc-tion of the Righteous Teacher and 'the Cup of God's Wrath'. Here too it is expressed in terms, as already remarked, of 'the Cup of the right hand of the Lord' (Hab. 2:16), which the individual responsible for the 'destruction' or death of the Righteous Teacher and, as it were, 'the Poor' – would be forced to 'drink' or 'swallow' as well, and connected to the imagery of *ba–la–'a* or 'swallowing', which at Qumran is being employed to express both the ideas of being given this 'Cup to drink' and being 'destroyed'.

It should also be clear that it is inextricably tied up with 'the Cup of the Lord' allusion we have been discussing with regard to the Gospel of the

Hebrews above – uniquely reverberating too in Paul's version of what he reports Jesus said in his version of the 'Last Supper'. This shows that Paul, too, was well aware that this 'Cup of the Lord' symbolism was circulating among early Christian groups, but he was using it in a more esoteric way. It is this which is picked up in Gospel representations of this scenario, coupled with the betrayal by the archetypal 'Traitor', 'Judas *the Iscariot*' – only now minus the allusion 'of the Lord'.

This same imagery of 'the Cup of God's Vengeance' and 'the Cup of God's Anger' or 'Wrath' (partially based on Habakkuk 2:16 above, but also on that of 'the Cup of Trembling' in Isaiah 51:17–22) is present as well in Revelation, as we have seen. This is the same imagery we have just encountered in Luke's version of Jesus' speech, which refers to this 'Anger' or 'Wrath' and 'the days of Vengeance' (at Qumran the 'Zealot' 'Day of Vengeance' as noted above) in relation to Jerusalem being trodden underfoot and not even suckling mothers or babes being spared.

As Revelation expresses this, more in the style of Qumran than Jesus in the Gospels,

> He also shall *drink of the wine of the Fury of God*, which is *poured out full strength* ['undiluted' – the exact expression occurs in the Habakkuk *Pesher* and, of course, Isaiah 51:22] into *the Cup of His Wrath*. (15:10)[52]

Here, plainly, is the more militant variation of the words Luke uses to characterize Jesus' speech at the Last Supper, phrased in terms of the Pauline 'Cup of the New Covenant in my blood, which is *poured out* for you' (Luke 22:20) – but, of course, these do not mean the same thing at all.

One should also note in Revelation, the double use of the words 'Fury' and 'Wrath', which runs throughout Qumran as well – 'Fury' being sometimes played upon to produce the alternate sense of the Hebrew homonym 'venom', not to mention the *double entendre* embodied in the word 'wine' in the same Damascus Document above about 'the Kings of the Peoples being the vipers', their wine, 'the venom of vipers and the cruel poison of asps' from Deuteronomy 32:33 – this 'wine' being defined as *'the ways' of the Kings of the Peoples* (in our view Herodian ways).[53]

But 'John and James the two sons of Zebedee' in Matthew and Mark above *do not drink this 'Cup'*. Perhaps this 'James' does, but he is conveniently removed as Acts unfolds, as we saw, to make room for the introduction of the other and, in our view, the *real* James. On the basis of the data, John – whoever he was – *does not*. This is true whether he is identified with the John of Patmos, who purportedly wrote the Book of

Revelation, or John, the alleged author of the Fourth Gospel and 'Disciple Jesus loved', who in Eusebius was supposedly buried in Ephesus and, like James, *'wore the mitre' of the High Priest*.[54] So here we have a problem with the overt meaning of this episode.

But 'James his brother' – Jesus' brother not John's – and his 'cousin' Simeon bar Cleophas, or, as we shall presently demonstrate, his putative *second brother*, the successor to James in Jerusalem, do 'drink the Cup' that Jesus drank. Here, once again, our overlaps develop. Presumably too, a *third brother*, known variously as Judas, Judas of James, Judas *Thomas*, and, as we shall see below, even 'Judas the Zealot' and, perhaps, 'Judas *Iscariot*' 'the son' or 'brother of Simon *Iscariot*', does as well. He would also seem to have been known as 'Lebbaeus who was surnamed Thaddaeus' (Matt. 10:3), as we have seen.

So does the character Josephus calls 'Theudas', who may well also have been identical to this 'Thaddaeus' or 'Judas *the brother of James*', beheaded according to Josephus at about the same time as the so-called 'James *the brother of John*', who in Acts turns out to present such a problem where the true succession to Jesus is concerned. So do 'the grandsons' of this 'Judas' under Trajan according to Hegesippus, as we have seen above. So much for 'drinking the Cup of the Lord' and who drank it.

Eusebius reiterates these things several times in no uncertain terms, repeatedly quoting Hegesippus on all these round-ups and martyrdoms, which, as he puts it, occurred at a time when the Church was still 'a virgin, not yet been corrupted by vain discourse'![55] For his part, Paul cynically contrasts *'the Cup of the Lord'* with *'the Cup of demons'*, by which he, at first, seems to imply 'the cup' Gentiles drink in their religious rites, but finally identifying it, as it appears in another disparaging aside, as that which 'Israel according to the flesh partakes of at the altar' (1 Cor. 10:18). This also parallels 'the Lord's table'/'table of demons' turnabout in Paul (1 Cor. 10:14) – identified in the *Homilies* as James' 'food sacrificed to idols'.[56] As we saw, too, for him this 'Cup of the Lord' now becomes the Cup 'of the New Covenant in [Christ's] blood', language not surprisingly faithfully echoed in Luke's picture of the Last Supper (22:20).

The Apostle Lists in the Synoptic Gospels and Acts

In order finally to answer this question about Jesus' brothers as Apostles, we must look at the Apostle lists in the Gospels and Acts, and compare them with the descriptions of Mary's descendants at the Crucifixion and in post-resurrection appearances. To take Mark first, which in this instance actually does appear the most primitive, Jesus, as in Matthew's version of a post-resurrection appearance 'to the Eleven' in Galilee and scenes of his Transfiguration to the Central Three generally, 'went up into the mountain' and 'appointed Twelve that they might be with him' (Mark 3:13–14).

This trip up the mountain is basically the way Luke presents things too, only adding the additional point that Jesus also 'named' the Inner Twelve Disciples, 'Apostles', and 'went out into the mountain to pray' there (Luke 6:13). In Matthew, aside from a host of trips 'up into' and 'down the mountain' – for instance 'the very high mountain' where he was tempted by 'the Devil' (4:8)[57] or amid 'a great crowd', including 'calling the Disciples to him' to multiply the loaves and fishes (15:29–39) – Jesus does not 'go up' or 'out into' *any* mountain to appoint the 'Twelve' (as opposed seemingly to the implication of the notice about his post-resurrection instruction to 'the Eleven Disciples to go into Galilee to the mountain he had commanded' or 'appointed them' – meaning ambiguous here – Matt. 28:16) – the 'mountain' scene having already taken place earlier in the famous 'Sermon on the Mount' (Matt. 5:1–8:1).

For Mark these 'Twelve' are to be sent forth:

> to preach and to heal diseases and to have Authority to *cast out* demons [*ekballein* again]. And he added to Simon [the] name 'Peter', and James the [son] of Zebedee and John the brother of James [this, of course, is the exact same expression used in the Letter of Jude]. And he added to them [the] names *Boanerges*, which is 'Sons of Thunder' [the meaning of which is unclear, but whatever else, there is a certain militancy to this description, not to mention, again, perhaps dissimulation], and Andrew and Philip and Bartholomew and Matthew and Thomas and *James the [son] of Alphaeus and Thaddaeus and Simon the Cananite, and Judas Iscariot, who also delivered him up.* (3:14–19)

Despite the reversal of Acts' 'James *the brother of John*' into 'John *the brother of James*' and the militant 'rain' and 'cloud' imagery involved in the 'Sons of Thunder' definition for the mysterious '*Boanerges*',[58] the most striking thing about this enumeration of the Twelve Apostles in Mark is how few of them have any real substance. Except for Simon Peter, Thomas, Judas *Iscariot*, and, of course, James and John 'the sons' either of 'Zebedee' or 'Thunder' themselves – problems associated with the actuality of *their* existence aside – they are for the most part insubstantial.

Even core Apostles are insubstantial. True, there are a few traditions about Philip and Matthew – identified for some reason as 'Levi the son of Alphaeus' in Mark 2:14 – and a second 'Matthew' or 'Matthias' will be chosen, as per the picture in Acts 1:26 of the 'election' of the successor to replace Judas *Iscariot* which will confuse the situation still more.

But Bartholomew, Andrew, 'Simon the Cananite' (this is supposed to mean 'Canaanite', but, as we saw, obviously does not), 'James *the son of Alphaeus*' – in Markan attempts to identify Mary in later crucifixion-witness and post-resurrection scenarios, either called 'James the Less' or simply 'James' – have little or no substance. As we shall presently see, 'Thaddaeus', a key figure – in other reckonings 'Judas [the brother] of James' and even 'Judas the Zealot' – and Judas *Iscariot* (not to mention 'Simon the *Iscariot*') will overlap each other or other names on this list.

In Matthew, Jesus is rather portrayed as variously crossing back and forth across the Sea of Galilee or wandering around Galilee curing, raising dead persons, and 'casting out demons' generally (Matt. 9:1–13). The actual scene of his appointment of 'the Twelve' occurs in good dramatic style after his debarking from a boat. He then dines with 'tax collectors and Sinners', repeating the proverbial 'think not I have come to call the Righteous [this is precisely what the Dead Sea Scrolls would have thought] but the Sinners' and that he will replace 'old clothes . . . with new cloth' and 'put new wine in new wineskins' (Matt. 9:16–17 – we have been following these 'clothes', 'wine' and 'skin' themes extensively above).

In a prelude to his appointment of the Twelve Apostles, Jesus then alludes to the labourers, who supplicate 'the Lord of the Harvest' (Matt. 9:37–38). In the Letter ascribed to James and, of course, the series of Jewish Christian Parables of the Tares (Matt. 13:24–50), the harvest is more about 'harvesting the tares' and 'casting them into a furnace of Fire' – along with a lot of other things, baskets of 'rotten fish' for instance.

In the final apocalyptic Judgement section of James and the coming of 'early and late rain', these same 'harvest workers', who are being *cheated of their 'hire'* by the 'Rich' – much like another parable in Matthew 20:1–15 about 'hire', 'workers', and 'the Lord of the Vineyard', leading up to Jesus' pronouncement that 'the First shall be Last and the Last shall be First' (all with reverse signification again) and the mother of the sons of Zebedee's request on behalf of her sons 'to drink the Cup' Jesus will drink (Matt. 20:16–24) – are pictured as *'crying out to the Lord of Hosts'* for the imminent *'coming of the Lord'* and final apocalyptic 'Judgement' (that is, 'the Judge is *standing* before the Door' – Jas. 5:4–9).

In Matthew 10:1, Jesus 'calls his Twelve Disciples, and giving them *Authority over unclean spirits*, so as to *cast them out [ekballein]'* – not as 'the tares sown by the Enemy' and gathering the polluted fishes into baskets above, 'to separate the Wicked from the midst of the Righteous and cast them [*balousin*] into the furnace of Fire' – but rather, the 'Authority' is now 'to *heal every disease and bodily weakness'*, a distinctly more peaceful and less aggressive undertaking. Matthew now lists 'his Twelve Disciples' as follows:

> First Simon who is *called Peter* and Andrew *his brother*, James the [son] of Zebedee and John *his brother* [different from Mark above], Philip and Bartholomew, Thomas, and Matthew *the tax collector, James the [son] of Alphaeus*, and *Lebbaeus who was surnamed Thaddaeus, Simon the Cananite* [or 'Cananaean'], and *Judas Iscariot*, who also delivered him up. (Matt. 10:2–4)

The changes here are obvious. Now the 'brother' theme, attached to 'John the brother of James' in Mark above or vice versa in Acts, is attached to 'Andrew *his brother'* too. It will be recalled that in Greek, 'Andrew', besides being the name of a later Jewish Messianic leader (who led the Uprising in Egypt and Cyrene in 115–17 CE against Trajan and actually seems to have been called a 'King'),[59] also means 'Man' – in Hebrew or Aramaic, *'Adam'* or *'Enosh'*. This makes Peter – whether by coincidence or design – the *brother of 'Man'* as well. For his part, 'Andrew''s place in Matthew moves up accordingly, though we never hear *a single additional word about him* in Matthew again – and hardly anywhere else either, except in John.

As with Andrew, Mark's 'John the brother of James' is now also simply reduced to 'his brother' – whose, unspecified, though we are obviously to presume James', that is, 'James the son of Zebedee'. Now, however, a 'Lebbaeus' is included – never mentioned anywhere before and never to be mentioned again, except, for instance, in the *Recognitions*, where he takes the place not only of 'Thaddaeus' generally, but also the Apostle to be called 'Judas [the brother] of James' in Luke and Acts.

In Matthew's list, though missing from some recensions, 'Lebbaeus' is identified also with this mysterious Thaddaeus – now characterized, as we saw, as *Lebbaeus'* 'surname'! Matthew himself, as in 9:9 earlier and Mark 2:14 – where for some reason, as will be recalled, he was called 'Levi the [son] of Alphaeus' – is also, now, again called 'the tax collector' (Matt. 10:3). This is obviously totally tendentious and, in view of the history we have been delineating above, not a little slanderous as well.

Not only will 'Lebbaeus surnamed Thaddaeus' be replaced in Luke's listings by 'Judas [the brother] of James', another individual about whom we shall never hear another word in the Gospels again, but, with whom, by the end of the book, the reader will become very familiar. Since 'Alphaeus' in these lists, for some reason mixed up in Mark with both 'Matthew' and 'tax collecting', always has to do in some manner with *James* – probably, as we have suggested, a variation or deformation of 'Cleophas' – we again are verging in these things on matters related to individuals connected to Jesus' family.

It is true that in John's version of 'the Last Supper', this other 'Judas, *not the Iscariot*' (thus) does appear again – since the 'Judas [the son] of Simon *Iscariot*' has already received his 'morsel' ('dipped' by Jesus) and departed to 'deliver him up' – and, for some reason, it is he John represents as asking Jesus the question concerning why he is revealing himself (14:21–22). But these may simply be Johannine substitutions for Matthew 26:25's portrait of Judas asking Jesus, when all the Apostles 'dip with' him, 'is it I?', or Synoptic portrayals generally of Judas 'kissing' Jesus at his arrest – more shades of 'kissing' portraits, like those at Nag Hammadi of *Jesus kissing James*, or vice versa, or of 'the Disciple Jesus loved' generally.

Luke's Apostle list is probably the most edifying of all. He presents this in two places: the Gospel attributed to his name and the repetition of this in Acts, also ascribed to his authorship as explained. As one would expect, these two lists agree in almost every respect, differing only in the place accorded Andrew above – regarding which, Luke's Gospel follows Matthew and Acts follows Mark.

The enumeration in Acts takes place in 'the upper room' and follows the picture of Jesus himself 'commanding them' – as in the appointment logion about James in the Gospel of Thomas – 'not to leave Jerusalem' and ascending, '*hidden by a cloud*' (Acts 1:4–9). Curiously enough in the picture of the Apostles he had chosen looking up at Jesus as he 'ascends', the two men again, 'who *stood beside* them in *white clothing*' – presumably the same 'two men' who previously '*stood beside*' Mary Magdalene, 'Mary *the mother of James*', and Joanna 'in brilliantly shining clothes' (Luke 24:4), but now on the Mount of Olives – address all of them as 'Galileans!', asking 'Why *stand you* looking into the Heaven?'

Of course, *Judas Iscariot* is missing from the listing in 'the upper room'. This is because we are to assume Judas, in good *Sicarii* style, has already *committed suicide*, 'falling *headlong*' – this is the *exact adverb* used in the Pseudoclementine *Recognitions*' description of James' '*headlong*' fall down the Temple stairs after the attack on him by the Enemy Paul – and something, it is not clear just what, 'bursting open and all his entrails gushed out' (Acts 1:18)! With this caveat about the placement of Andrew, let us quote the list in the Gospel. Again Moses-like as in Mark, Jesus 'went out into the mountain', but this time ostensibly 'to pray'. It reads:

> Simon, whom he also named Peter, and Andrew *his brother* [so far so good], James and John [the appellatives 'sons of Zebedee', 'sons of Thunder' or 'his brother' are all, however, missing here in Luke, as they are in Acts], Philip and Bartholomew, Matthew and Thomas, *James the [son] of Alphaeus, Simon who was called Zealot, Judas [the brother] of James,* and *Judas Iscariot, who also became [the] Betrayer.* (Luke 6:12–16 and Acts 1:13)

The only difference between Luke's list in the Gospel and the one in Acts, as we have said, is that Andrew's place is changed and Judas *Iscariot* 'falls' away – literally.

But, there are two astonishing things about the list as Luke gives it. In the first place, there is no 'Thaddaeus' at all. Rather, as previously noted, he is called, both here and in Acts, 'Judas [the brother] of James'. But additionally, in actual order, his place is simply that accorded in Matthew and Mark to *Judas Iscariot.* This is particularly clear in Acts, when the second Judas – 'the *Iscariot*' or the '*son of Simon Iscariot*' in John – simply 'falls' away.

In addition, the 'Simon', who now follows *James the son of Alphaeus* in the listings, separating him from *Judas the brother of James* – in Matthew and Mark, it will be recalled, it was 'Lebbaeus surnamed Thaddaeus' or simply 'Thaddaeus', who separated *James the son of Alphaeus* from *Simon the Cananite* – is now quite straightforwardly and without embarrassment '*called Zealot*', not '*Cananite*', '*Canaanite*', or '*Cananaean*', or some other obfuscation or mistaken transliteration. In Acts, now minus the curious additional 'Judas' called 'the *Iscariot*', this is even more clearly rendered, because the *Simon the Zealot* – who again follows *James the son of Alphaeus,* preceding *Judas the brother of James* with no additional *Judas* to follow at all – is now really characterized as '*the Zealot*' and not the '*called Zēlōtēs*' of Luke 6:15 (Acts 1:13).

But in the Gospel of John, this Judas *Iscariot,* as we saw, is on four separate occasions designated 'the [son] of Simon *Iscariot*' (John 12:4, 13:26, etc.) – two of these last in conjunction with evoking the 'Devil' or '*Diabolos*' (John 6:70–71 and 13:2). The first of these conjunctions of both 'Simon *Iscariot*' and the 'Devil' occurs when Jesus is expounding his view of *eating his flesh* and *drinking his blood*, but this not at the 'Last Supper', but at Capernaum 'on the other side of the sea' (John 6:25–59).

The second of these does introduce 'the Last Supper', but this, it will be recalled, is now simply a Passover meal, completely divorced, it would appear, from anything to do with *eating and drinking Jesus' flesh and blood*. In this scene, which simply has Jesus identifying 'Judas the [son] of Simon *Iscariot*' (as we shall see this is more likely 'brother of Simon *Iscariot*') as the one who would 'deliver him up', Jesus 'dips the morsel and gives it to him' (John 13:26; in the Synoptics, Jesus is simply 'dipping in the dish' with all the Twelve – Matt. 26:23 and Mark 14:20). Otherwise the thrust is exactly the same as his 'breaking the bread' and 'giving it to James' in the Gospel of the Hebrews, the two of them going 'in the Way' in Luke – 'Cleopas' and a companion – or, later in John, to the Disciples by the Sea of Galilee.

In the next chapter, John also specifically refers to the 'Judas *not the Iscariot*', in the important context of Jesus expounding the two *Love* Commandments (14:22). The reason for this, as we saw, is quite simple. Aside from the complexities having to do with all these various 'Judas'es and 'Simon's, in John's narrative it is because 'Judas the [son] of Simon *Iscariot*' has already gone out to betray him after being fed the bread by Jesus in the previous chapter (13:26–30).

But here John has the loquacious Jesus holding forth at this dinner on a variety of topics in addition to the two *Love* Commandments for four more chapters – even including allusion to 'being *cast out as a dried-up Branch*' and '*cast into* a Fire' generally again, not to mention 'keeping my commandments' (John 15:6–10) – until 'Judas', now no longer referred to as 'Simon *Iscariot*'s son', finally arrives with soldiers 'from the Chief Priests and Pharisees'. 'Judas' is not only described as '*delivering him up and standing with them*', but it is at this point that Jesus tells Peter to sheath his sword – note the '*Sicarii*' motif again – and evokes the 'Cup' imagery we have treated above, that is, 'should I not *drink the Cup* which the Father has given me?' in relation to his own impending fate (John 18:2–11).

This reference to 'the *Iscariot*' side by side with 'the other Judas' – 'the brother of James' (elsewhere, as will become plain, 'Judas *Zēlōtēs*') – preceded by the definite article, is just what we have been attempting to point up. Whether accidental or otherwise, it does parallel the allusion to 'Simon *the Zealot*' or 'called *Zēlōtēs*' in Acts and Luke, with whose name we began this discussion. It will now be an open question whether the terminology '*Iscariot*' is a direct offshoot of the singular term in Greek '*Sicarios*' (plural, *Sicarioi*), as we have been signalling all along – the Greek *iota* and *sigma* simply being inverted – and its closest linguistic anagram.

The '*Sicarii*', as we have explained, are an earlier embodiment of the 'Zealot Movement' – if we can call it this. The terminology is pejorative, employed by Josephus and certainly their other enemies, and is clearly not something they themselves would have employed. 'Deceivers and impostors, feigning divine inspiration and fomenting revolutionary change', as Josephus puts it, it is also a term Acts 21:38 uses in relation to Paul's difficulties with the Jerusalem crowd, as we saw. But we have also seen its relationship throughout to 'those who circumcise', just as Origen attests and the Roman '*Lex Cornelia de Sicarius*' implies.

It is the *Sicarii* who are responsible for the assassination of the High Priest Jonathan, Caiaphas' brother-in-law and the brother of James' nemesis Ananus, the son of the Ananus in the Gospels, portrayed by John anyhow, as having a hand in events leading to the crucifixion of Jesus (18:13–24).[60] After this, Josephus introduces 'the Zealots' as being the group who are even more blood-thirsty than 'the *Sicarii*', '*polluting the hallowed ground* [the Temple], intoxicating themselves in the Temple and expending the spoils of their slaughtered victims on their *insatiable bellies*'. This characterization, laughable as it may be, once again, is simply the reverse of descriptions we get in the Dead Sea Scrolls – and, in its own way, the New Testament – of the Temple Establishment, the *deadly opponent* of both *Sicarii* and Zealots.[61]

It is these 'Zealots', it will be recalled, co-operating with the Idumaeans, whose 'fury' Josephus too now describes, who slaughter Ananus and Josephus' friend, Jesus the son of Gamala, 'casting out' their corpses 'naked to be devoured by dogs and beasts of prey' – here our 'casting out' and 'devouring' language used in the same context – probably the real basis for Stephen's 'being cast out of the city' in Acts: this, along with traditions surrounding the attacks on James and Josephus' characterization of how 'the Essenes' treated backsliders of the genus of a Paul or a 'Stephen'.[62]

To return to 'the *Sicarii*', for Josephus it is they who retreat from Jerusalem to the fortress Masada after one of their leaders, a son or grandson of Judas '*the Galilean*' named Menachem – who 'put on the royal purple' or, if one prefers, claimed the Throne of Israel – is stoned by collaborating High Priests in the early chaotic events of the Uprising – the only other stoning apart from James' that Josephus records in this period.

Under the leadership of another descendant of this 'Judas the *Galilean*', Eleazar ben Jair, they participate in the famous final suicide at Masada in 73 CE, parodied in the Gospel presentations of its 'Judas the *Iscariot*'. One should note that not only has Eleazar's name been found on an actual shard surviving on Masada, but both his names are paralleled in Scripture as we have it in the names 'Lazarus' and 'Jairus'.[63] With this connecting of Judas now with Simon and the use of the term 'the *Iscariot*' as a cognomen not a proper name, it now becomes an open question whether the two characters, Luke's 'Simon *the Zealot*' – also connected to 'Judas the brother of James' – and John's 'Simon *Iscariot*', are not to be equated. Both clearly show the revolutionary aspect of early 'Christians'.

In addition, one will now have seriously to consider whether the term 'Judas Zēlōtēs', found in a recently discovered Apocryphal Gospel, called the *Epistula Apostolorum*, which may date to the early second century, should not be taken more seriously.[64] This Gospel, generally following terminology found in John, lists the Apostles as: John, Thomas, Peter, Andrew, James, Philip, Bartholomew, Matthew, *Nathanael, Judas Zēlōtēs, and Cephas*.

The last three, as usual, are particularly interesting. 'Nathanael', who appeared in the early part of John with Philip in Galilee, was quoted there as saying, 'can anything good come out of Nazareth' – meaning undecipherable – and with '*Didymus* Thomas' and the others in the episode of Jesus' appearance at 'the Sea of Tiberias' at the end, is distinctly designated there as from '*Cana of Galilee*' (John 1:45–49 and 21:2). This last is not so different from the term 'Cananite' in Gospel Apostle lists, as we saw, nor the mysterious 'Kfar Sechania' (also 'Kfar Sama') in Rabbinic sources associated with James' curious stand-in 'Jacob'. In Synoptic reckonings, he is clearly taking the place of 'James the son of Alphaeus' (our James), which should surprise no one.

Even more to the point, 'Cephas' in this reckoning is now obviously distinct from Simon Peter, yet reckoned among the 'Apostles' not the 'Disciples' as in some other later Church listings. In this reckoning, he occupies the same position as and is clearly equivalent to the individual being called 'Simon Zēlōtēs' or 'Simon the Zealot' in Luke and Acts – 'Simon the Cananite' in Matthew and Mark (note the play on 'Cana' and 'Cananaean' again) – or, as we shall finally conclude below, Simeon bar Cleophas, the second *brother* – not 'cousin' – of Jesus. This individual called 'Cephas', and coming last in the list in the *Epistula Apostolorum*, also plainly occupies the same position as the 'Simon *Iscariot*' in John, called 'the father' – or 'brother' – 'of Judas *Iscariot*'.

'Judas Zēlōtēs' in the *Epistula Apostolorum* is clearly to be identified with that Apostle called 'Thaddaeus' in Mark or 'Lebbaeus surnamed Thaddaeus' in Matthew, the same individual that Luke calls, doubtlessly most accurately of all, 'Judas [the brother] of James'! Notice the same appellative in the first line of the Letter of Jude, now baldly calling himself 'Judas the brother of James' in clear expostulary prose. It is important that Luke in Acts 21:20, when talking about the greater part of James' followers in the Jerusalem Church, gives the actual basis for the derivation of this name, 'Zealots' or 'Zealots for the Law', also expressed as '*Zēlōtai*', about which we shall have more to say presently.

We shall have more to say presently about this Jude or Judas, who also appears to have had quite a few other names and whose grandchildren, according to Hegesippus, are so cruelly executed under Trajan. It is, however, also edifying to note that in Old Latin manuscripts of the Gospel of Matthew, the name of 'Lebbaeus surnamed Thaddaeus' is replaced by 'Judas the Zealot' as well. Where such perspicuity came from is impossible to say (possibly Syriac sources) – but these old medieval manuscript redactors certainly seemed to understand the gist of the traditions before them even better than many moderns do.

Much of the misinformation, circumlocution, and dissimulation turn on this 'Judas the brother of James' and on Simeon bar Cleophas/'Cephas'/ Simon the Zealot – including Mark and Matthew's garbled 'Simon the Cananaean' – as should be becoming clear. We shall also now find these same tell-tale allusions to 'Judas the Zealot' and 'Simon the Zealot' in the Syriac sources we shall treat further below.

23

Simeon bar Cleophas and Simon the Zealot

Simon the Cananite, Nathanael, and James

Actually the Simeon bar Cleophas/Simon *the Zealot*/Simon *Iscariot* complex is relatively easily untangled – or shall we say undeciphered. 'Cananaean' is an attempt in Greek, as many scholars now realize, to transliterate a Hebrew word, which then ends up either purposefully or out of ignorance as 'the Cananite', by which sobriquet most persons even today still call this second 'Simon'. But, as we have seen, the word is based on the Hebrew word for 'zeal', that is, *kin'at-Elohim* – *zeal for God* or *kin'at ha-Hoq* – *zeal for the Law*, so that, even as Matthew and Mark understand this cognomen as applied to Simon – or rather misunderstand it – it is based on the Hebrew phraseology 'zeal for the Law'.

We have already explained how this phraseology is based on the episode in the Book of Numbers from the Old Testament, in which the High Priest Phineas, the grandson of Aaron through Eleazar – a name of no mean import among persons involved in these movements and events – receives 'the Covenant of an Everlasting Priesthood . . . to *make atonement* over the Sons of Israel, because of his *zeal for God*' (Num. 25:12–13). This, in Numbers, is considered equivalent to the 'Covenant of Peace', simultaneously conferred upon Phineas for his 'exceedingly great zeal'.

Not only is this 'Covenant of Peace' – to be leader of the people and governor of the Sanctuary sealed with Phineas and his seed for ever – referred to as we saw in Ben Sira (45:24); it was generally considered identical with that Covenant accorded Noah, the man 'Righteous and Perfect in his generation, who walked with God', in Genesis. This is the view, anyhow, of Isaiah 54:9–10, where the phraseology, 'the days of Noah', is also used, an expression picked up, it should be recalled, in apocalyptic portions of the Gospels and applied in Matthew's version of the Little Apocalypse to the coming of 'the Son of Man on the clouds of Heaven with Power and great Glory' (24:30–37).[1]

It is also how 'the Covenant of Peace' sealed with Noah was expressed in books like the Medieval *Zohar* above. For this reason we have also termed it 'Noahic'. In addition, this 'Covenant of Peace' is also evoked on behalf of 'the Elect of the Holy People' (identified with 'the Poor' or '*Ebionim* of Your Deliverance') in the climactic section of the War Scroll from Qumran, where 'the Star Prophecy' is being expounded and the final apocalyptic war led by the Heavenly Holy Ones and the Messianic King set forth.[2] Phineas, then, also receives these two Covenants, really the same, on behalf of all his descendants 'forever', because of the 'exceeding great zeal' or 'burning zeal for God' he displayed in *killing backsliders*. These, it will be recalled, because they were *marrying foreigners* (note the relation of this to Herodian family practice), *introducing pollution into the camp of Israel in the wilderness* (Num. 25:6–11).

All of these themes, as should by now be apparent, are basic to the period before us and James' place in it. This theme of 'zeal' is also referred to in the Maccabean books, where Phineas' 'zeal for the Law' and 'keeping the Covenant' are now pictured as the rallying cry of Judas Maccabee's father Mattathias – the original Hebrew of the names 'Matthew' and 'Matthias' in the New Testament Greek – who kills the Seleucid Royal Commissioner and, with him, the collaborating Jew, willing to follow instructions forbidding the practice of Judaism, on the altar at Modein.

For 1 Maccabees 2:19–28, the latter's offence is described in terms of forsaking 'the Law' and 'customs of the Forefathers' and no longer 'keeping the Covenant of the First' – language pervasive at Qumran and echoed, as we have seen, sometimes polemically, in the New Testament. For 1 Maccabees 2:50, the implication is that Mattathias wins the High Priesthood in perpetuity for his descendants on account of his 'burning zeal for the Law' and willingness to sacrifice his life 'for the Covenant of the Forefathers'. This is, in fact, stated explicitly in 1 Maccabees 2:54, as we saw as well, where 'the Covenant of the Everlasting Priesthood' accorded Phineas, 'because he was exceedingly zealous for the Law', is once again evoked and obviously meant to be equivalent to the afore-mentioned 'Covenant of Peace'.

This is certainly the atmosphere in the time of Aristobulus II (*c.* 63 BC), who is unwilling to debase himself before Pompey and whose supporters go about the sacrifices, while the Romans – outpaced in this by their Pharisee confederates – slaughter these exceedingly Pious Priests in the Temple as they continue the sacrifices. It is also the atmosphere among the assembled crowd, who weep when they see Jonathan, the younger brother of Herod's *Maccabean* wife Mariamme, don the High Priestly vestments upon coming of age at thirteen (36 BC). Herod, thereupon, had him brutally murdered and, not long after that, his sister Mariamme too (29 BC).

Aside from the notice in the description of Paul's last visit to Jerusalem in the 'We Document' of Acts about *the majority* of James' followers in Jerusalem being 'Zealots for the Law' (21:20), one should also note the portrait in John's Gospel of Jesus' 'zeal' – in good Maccabean fashion – for his 'Father's House' and the purification of the same (John 2:17). Here John even paraphrases the words of Psalm 69:9, 'zeal for Your House consumes me', applying them to Jesus driving out the sellers and over-turning the tables of the money-changers *in the Temple at Passover time.*

John never does list all the Apostles, as we saw, though he does refer to Andrew as 'Simon Peter's brother', followed by Philip, who when Jesus 'wants to go into Galilee', finds Nathanael (1:40–45). The first of these two pairs appears among the Disciples of John the Baptist at the beginning of his ministry – this right after John, in response to the supposed question by 'those who had been sent from among the Pharisees': 'If you are not the Christ nor Elijah nor the Prophet [note the 'True Prophet' ideology alluded to here] why then do you baptize?', cryptically replies: 'In your midst *one stands* whom you do not know' (1:25–26 – the 'Standing One' ideology once again).

At first the Gospel of John – paralleling the 'two' along the Way to Emmaus later in Luke – only identifies this first pair (one of whom turns out to be 'Nathanael'), as 'two of his Disciples', with whom John 'was again *standing*' (1:35). Nathanael then goes and gets 'his *own* brother Simon' – the sobriquet 'Peter' is now missing from the denotation. It is right after this that Jesus is pictured as renaming Simon, '*Cephas*, which interpreted means "Stone"' (1:42). Clearly, there is some very peculiar textual rewriting going on here.

John does, however, refer to 'the Twelve', and whatever attempt there seems to be at a listing occurs in the post-resurrection sighting by the Sea of Galilee, containing the ubiquitous 'net' and 'casting down' motifs we have already described above. Simon Peter is now listed with 'Thomas called *Didymus*', whoever he is, instead of 'Andrew' and, once again, the omnipresent 'other two Disciples' appear this time alongside 'the sons of Zebedee' – both again unnamed.

Here, too, the mysterious 'Nathanael from Cana of Galilee' also appears. It is interesting that this 'Cana of Galilee' – mentioned four times in John, but in no *other* Gospel – is mentioned in only one other place in the literature of this period. This is by Josephus in his *Vita* who calls it 'a village of Galilee', at which he claims he made his headquarters (though usually he claims his headquarters was at 'Asochis').[3] In the one story John tells about Nathanael at the beginning of his Gospel, he is pictured as sitting 'under a fig tree' at or before the time Philip calls him. This, Jesus is supposed to have either 'seen' or 'foreseen' (John 1:48–50).

This motif of 'sitting under a carob tree' or 'fig tree' is to be encountered, as well, in Rabbinic stories about Honi the Circle Drawer or Onias the Righteous, whom we identified earlier as the putative ancestor or, at least, forerunner of John the Baptist and James. In Talmudic tradition, Honi falls asleep under this omnipresent carob or fig tree, before awakening in the generation of his grandson – that is, either Hanan the Hidden, John, one Abba Hilkiah (who like James supposedly also made rain), or James himself – seventy years later when the fruit is ripened. Then, because no one recognizes him – a familiar motif – he prays for death and, in the abrupt manner of Judas *Iscariot* in Gospel tradition, dies.[4]

In John's story, Jesus sees Nathanael – whom he supposedly greets with the words: 'Behold, in truth, an Israelite in whom there is no guile' (clearly the product of a non-Jewish author) – sitting 'under a fig tree', implying that this was somehow of great moment or a visionary or prophetical recognition of some kind. Not only does Nathanael now call Jesus 'Rabbi' – as in Nag Hammadi sources above about James and Jesus – but he immediately designates Jesus as 'the Son of God' and 'King of Israel' (1:47–49) and is the first to do so.

Thereupon Jesus predicts, because *he* has 'seen' Nathanael, that *Nathanael* will, in turn, '*see* greater things than this'. He predicts Nathanael 'will see the Heaven opened' – the very words used in Acts to describe *Stephen's* vision of 'the Son of Man standing at the right hand of God' – 'and the Angel of God ascending and descending on the Son of Man' (1:50–51). Whatever else it is supposed to mean, this last, of course, is just another variation of James' final apocalyptic vision of 'the Son of Man coming on the clouds of Heaven' with the Heavenly Host, in the Hegesippus tradition recorded in Eusebius, and one more element linking 'Nathanael' to James and, therefore, as will become plain, 'Cana' to 'Cananite' or 'Cananaean', not to mention the whole Honi 'Hidden' tradition attaching itself to members of this family.

In Rabbinic tradition, Honi, it will be recalled, 'was hidden' for seventy years because the terrain was so rocky, another link with the 'Hidden' traditions surrounding him and John and Jesus. Where the confusion or overlap of either 'fig' or 'carob' trees associated with these stories is concerned, both were considered by tradition to grow apart in rocky places and produce a kind of 'honey' that was eaten – usually as *poor man*'s food. In Rabbinic sources the passages 'honey out of a crag' (Deut. 32:13) and 'honey out of a rock' (Ps. 81:16) were applied to these genera of trees.[5] Again, we have the overlap with the food ascribed in Christian sources to John.

One final link-up in all these traditions: Simeon bar Yohai, the eponymous founder of *Zohar* tradition and a central figure of Jewish Kabbalistic lore, was said to have '*hidden*' himself with his son – also named Eleazar – in a cave for some twelve years at the time of the Bar Kochba Uprising (132–36 CE), again surviving on the honey or fruit of carobs or fig trees growing in these rocky areas.[6] It is interesting that when John mentions this 'Cana of Galilee', 'Jesus' mother' – again, as we have said, *always unnamed* in John –also suddenly materializes (as in the Synoptics, somewhat confrontationally – 2:1–2:4), as do 'his brothers' (2:12). Presumably she goes unnamed, because for John, '*Mary*' is 'the wife of Clopas'.

Aside from the final reference to 'Nathanael from Cana of Galilee' at the end of John, it is in the context of the other three references to 'Cana of Galilee', that Jesus is said to 'make water into wine' (mocking the 'Rechabite' or 'Nazirite' antipathy to wine?), 'manifesting his Glory, so that his Disciples believed on him' (John 2:11 and 4:46).

'Zeal for Your House Consumes Me'

Psalm 69, which John applies to Jesus' 'zeal' for *his* 'Father's House', is itself also a completely Messianic psalm. It is also '*Ebionite*', in the sense that it contains positive allusions to 'the Poor' (*Ebionim* – 69:33). It was obviously very important to the exegetes of early Christianity, because not only does it contain this allusion attributed to Jesus about *zeal* for his 'Father's House', but another familiar-sounding motif about being 'alienated from my brothers and estranged from my mother's other sons' (69:8), just encountered to some extent in this 'Cana of Galilee' episode in John above. It also contains the allusion to 'being given poison to eat and vinegar to drink' that is such a central element in Gospel Crucifixion narratives (69:21).

But the Psalm is also replete with Qumranisms like: 'let their table become a snare before them' – an important connotation for these various disputes (69:22) – 'swallowing' (69:15), 'the Righteous', 'the Meek', and 'the Pit' (69:29–32). It also contains reference to the Lord's 'Wrathful Anger' and his 'Fury being *poured out* upon them' – usually connected at Qumran to these 'drinking' and 'swallowing' motifs (69:24), but in a pro-Palestinian not a Hellenistic manner. In fact, it ends up on the thoroughly Zionistic note, despite the anti-Zionistic use made of several of these citations above in the Gospels:

> God will *save Zion* and *rebuild the towns of Judah*. They will be lived in, owned, inherited by His Servants' descendants, lived in by *those who love His Name*. (69:35–36)

It should be remarked that this episode in John evoking Jesus' 'zeal' for the Temple is slightly out of synch with the Synoptic Gospels, which place the Temple-cleansing and the clear note of violence it contains in the run-up to Jesus' last days in Jerusalem, thus making it appear that the Roman soldiers and Temple police had ample cause for arresting Jesus as a subversive disturbing the peace. This notion of 'zeal for the Law' and 'zeal for the Judgements of God', as we have seen, is also prevalent in the attitude of the documents at Qumran, making these last appear at once 'Zealot' as well as 'Messianic'.

Of course, Josephus shows that what popularly goes by the name of the 'Zealot' Movement also has its root motivation in the 'Messianic' or 'World Ruler Prophecy' found in these passages of Numbers leading up to this evocation of Phineas' *zeal* for the Law (24:17–25:15). At Qumran, 'zeal for the Judgements of Righteousness' is part of 'the Spirit of Truth' and 'the Way of Light' of 'the Sons of Righteousness' and the curses upon 'the men of the lot of Belial'.[7] The allusion to 'zeal for the Law' occurs in the crucial exegesis of the 'Way in the wilderness' Prophecy from Isaiah 40, utilized in the Gospels to characterize the activities of John the Baptist there. The Community Rule, as we saw, reads:

> He shall *separate* from every man who has not turned away from all *Unrighteousness*, and . . . *Everlasting hatred* for the Men of the Pit in a Spirit of secrecy . . . For he shall be like a man *zealous for the Law, whose time will be the Day of Vengeance!*[8]

One should also remark the use of this word 'zeal' throughout the Pauline corpus.[9] Since Paul actually seems to be playing on the language of his opponents – and these within the 'Movement' not outside it – its connotation is usually reversed. In 1 Corinthians, for example, Paul calls his communities 'zealous of spiritual things'. He uses the term there in connection with allusions to 'building up the Church' or 'Assembly' and, what would have infuriated Jerusalem more than anything, 'speaking in Tongues' (1 Cor. 14:12). In 2 Corinthians 7:11 he uses it, as here in the Community Rule, in connection with God's 'Anger' and 'Vengeance', but with exactly opposite signification.

He alludes twice to 'zeal' in Galatians, once in connection with the all-important allusion to 'being chosen' from his mother's womb, we have discussed above, even going so far as to imply that he himself had once been 'a Zealot' by pointing out how *exceedingly zealous for the traditions*' of his Fathers he had been (thus – Gal. 1:14). Even more tellingly, he uses it in Galatians 4:17–18 three times, this after attacking the Law as bringing death, attacking circumcision, and attacking the Jerusalem Leadership. Just following his own evocation of the 'Enemy' and 'Lying' epithets ('So your Enemy have I become by speaking Truth to you?' – 4:16), he proceeds to accuse his opponents – here clearly *within* the Movement and the very *ones* using these epithets against him – of being, '*zealous after you to exclude you*, so that you will be *zealous after them*', though not '*zealous for the right things*'! The play on their central concept of 'zeal' is hard to miss.

Perhaps his most characteristic use of the term comes in chapter 10 of Romans. This follows his insistence that the Gentiles attained 'a Righteousness of Faith', as opposed to Israel's failure to attain 'a Righteousness of the Law . . . because it was *not by Faith but by works of the Law*' (9:30–32 – note the play on the 'works' ideology normally associated with James). In turn the condemnation of the 'zeal for God' of the Jews in this passage, which we shall quote below, is followed in Romans 11:3 and 11:28 by variations of his accusations against the other Israel – 'the Israel according to the flesh' – of killing all the Prophets and being 'Enemies' of all men that we previously encountered in 1 Thessalonians 2:15.

In Romans 12:19, he plays off the emphasis in the Community Rule's interpretation of Isaiah 40:3 on zeal for 'the Day of Vengeance' – a term vividly used in Isaiah 63:4 amid the imagery of '*making the Peoples drunk with My Fury*' – by quoting Deuteronomy 32:35's 'Vengeance is mine . . . saith the Lord'. Finally, he completely attacks the Zealots in Romans 13:1–7, where he recommends, as we saw, 'paying taxes', because the Authorities 'have been appointed by God' and the tax collectors are, therefore, 'Servants of God'!

One should note, in addition, the admonition to 'feed your Enemy' in

Romans 12:20 and the 'Community as Temple'/'Community as sacrifice' imagery, 'the Many being one body in Christ' in Romans 12:1–5 – imagery also encountered in these passages in the Community Rule, above, expounding Isaiah 40:3's 'Way in the wilderness' in terms of 'zeal for the Law' and 'the Day of Vengeance'. Here, quoting Isaiah 8:14, which in the original Hebrew ends with the important 'net' and 'Pit' imagery, already discussed above – which he significantly omits – he reverses the 'Cornerstone' imagery from Isaiah 28:16 (also found in this section from the Community Rule about the Community Council being 'a House of Holiness for Israel' and 'an acceptable free-will offering'/'a sweet smell of Righteousness'), not to mention that language of 'stumbling' used in James 2:9 to emphasize the crucial point about 'keeping the whole Law'.

Now 'the Israel, following after a Law of Righteousness' and 'works of the Law', 'stumble over the Stone of Stumbling', 'a Stone of Stumbling in Zion and a Rock of offence' (in Greek, literally *'Petra'*, that is, *'Peter'*, here);[10] but instead of the words 'a net to the inhabitants of Jerusalem and a Pit' that follow in Isaiah 8:14, Paul goes back and substitutes the phrase 'and everyone that believes on him shall not be ashamed' that goes with the 'Cornerstone' and 'laying in Zion a sure Foundation Stone' imagery of Isaiah 28:16, with which he began, not Isaiah 8:14 (Rom. 9:32–33).

These too were the very words we just heard in the John 2:11 episode above about the miracles Jesus did in Cana of Galilee, 'revealing his Glory so that his Disciples *believed on him*' – not to mention the thrust of Psalm 69, which John goes on to quote in 2:17, about 'loving God' and 'loving His Name' generally. In fact, as we have repeatedly seen, Paul uses the Commandment to 'love your neighbour as yourself' to justify his whole panoply of anti-Zealot instructions, such as 'rendering tribute to all those due tribute' and obeying the ruling Authorities, 'who are no terror to good works', but are rather 'appointed by God'. The former possibly even plays on the Habakkuk *Pesher*'s verdict of Vengeance on the individual responsible for destroying the Righteous Teacher and the Poor: 'he shall be paid the reward with which he rewarded the Poor', also reflecting the Isaiah 3:10–11 passage applied to James' death in early Church literature, 'the reward of his hands shall be rewarded him'.[11]

These are all matters retrospectively inverted and superimposed in the Gospel portrait upon Jesus, so much so that it would be proper to call the individual who therein emerges, not Jesus, but Jesus/Paul. Is it any wonder that the Gospels portray their 'Jesus', not only as 'eating and drinking', but keeping 'table fellowship' with tax collectors? Wherever one finds allusions of this kind in Paul, retrospectively imposed on the portrait of 'Jesus' in the Gospels, the description 'Jesus/Paul' would be appropriate.

The complete passage, referred to above, from Romans 10:2-4 reads:

> For I bear witness to them [the Jews] that they have *zeal for God*, but *not according to Knowledge*, for *being ignorant of God's Righteousness* [Paul often means by 'Righteousness' of this kind, the Righteousness of the Law of the Roman State], but rather seeking to *establish their own Righteousness* [that is, 'the Righteousness of the Law', with which he began the whole passage – could anything better describe James?], they failed to submit to *the Righteousness of God*. Because for Righteousness, Christ is the end of the Law for anyone that believes.

Paul ends this particular discussion with the conclusion:

> For there is no difference between Jew and Greek, for that same Lord of all is *Rich* towards all who *call on Him* (10:12) –

here playing on Qumran allusions to 'Riches' and 'being called by Name' – both reversing and spiritualizing the outright attack one finds there and in James on 'the Rich' or 'Riches'.[12] Paul is at his allegorizing best here. It is small wonder that his opponents – again, those *within* the Movement not outside it – found him difficult to contend with.

All of these things are part and parcel of what it meant to have 'zeal for God' or, for that matter, to be a part of 'the Zealot Movement'. It is no wonder Mark and Matthew found these things confusing when it came to handling the cognomen of Jesus' possible cousin and putative *second brother*, 'Simeon' or 'Simon the Zealot', and, therefore, thought that in some manner we had to do with 'Cananite' or 'Canaanites'. The reader will probably feel the same bewilderment trying to make his or her way through these interlocking metaphors and terminologies.

The Essenes in Hippolytus of Rome

One work from Hippolytus of Rome (*c.* 160–235 CE), a contemporary of Clement of Alexandria (it is clearly authentic, though perhaps not from Hippolytus) was found in the last century at Mount Athos Monastery in Greece. Sometimes it is of the most astonishing clarity and perspicuity. Though basically reproducing Josephus' descriptions, as we have seen, according to this work there were *four* groups of Essenes.

The first are the more peace-loving kind many still associate with the term 'Essene'. These seek always 'to help the Righteous' and in addition to 'white garments' – our 'clothing' theme again – wear 'linen girdles' exactly in the manner all texts aver about James and, as we have seen, by implication, John the Baptist. Nor 'will they hate a person who injures them' – here the admonition in the New Testament attributed to Jesus, to 'love your enemies' (though at Qumran, it should be appreciated, the general position was 'hate the Sons of the Pit'). Paul-like, they seek to keep faith with Rulers, because their 'position of Authority cannot happen to anyone without God'. These may be early Essenes and are obviously the Essenes of Josephus, 'but after a lapse of time' – according to this work attributed to Hippolytus – 'they *split* into *four parties*'.[13]

There are those who will carry no coin, 'nor carry or look on any graven image', a position clearly reflected in the Gospels. These will not even enter a gate on which there are statues erected, considering it a violation of the Law – note the relationship of this to an incident, described by Josephus, where the two Rabbis encouraged their followers to pull down the eagle Herod had erected over one of the gates to the Temple 'contrary to the laws of their Forefathers' at the beginning of the disturbances leading to the establishment of the 'Zealot' Movement.[14]

But even more zealous than these, are those, who, on hearing anyone

discussing God and His Laws, if they suspect him to be an *uncircumcised person*, they will carefully observe him and when they meet a person of this description in any place alone [this will have relevance to the key conversion of Queen Helen of Adiabene's son Izates we shall describe below], they will *threaten to slay him if he refuses to undergo the rite of circumcision* [this clearly reflecting the situation at the beginning of the War with Rome, not the least of whom so treated was the Roman Commander in the Citadel – nor to mention those Origen is later designating '*Sicarii*'].[15] If he refuses to comply with this demand, they will not spare him, but rather execute him forthwith.

Not only are these extremely important passages – together with those about *four* groups of Essenes – significantly missing from Josephus' descriptions of his 'Essenes', but they also have great relevance to the difficulties Acts depicts Paul as having, including the accusations made against him – following the descriptions of the greater part of James' 'Jerusalem Church' followers as 'zealous for the Law' above – that (James speaking),

you teach *apostasy from Moses*, telling all the Jews among the Gentiles [*Ethnē*] *not to circumcise their children* nor walk in *our* Ways (Acts 21:21);

and the charge of 'the Jews from Asia', who recognize Paul in the Temple in Acts 21:28, of 'attempting to introduce Greeks or uncircumcised persons into the Temple', thereby 'polluting' it.

They also have great relevance to the kind of *Nazirite* oath the 'more than forty' *Jews* 'plotting' against Paul take thereafter, 'putting themselves under a *curse* [also expressed as 'with a curse we have cursed ourselves'] *not to eat or drink* until they had killed Paul' (Acts 23: 12–14); as they do to the comments he makes in Galatians about how Titus 'was *not compelled to be circumcised*' and 'the *false brothers* [his very words] who crept in secretly to spy on the freedom' he and his associates 'enjoy *in Christ Jesus* so that they might *reduce us to slavery*' (2:4).

There is no doubt what he means by 'freedom' and 'bondage' here. Aside from the play on the opposite side of the coin, those seeking *freedom from Rome* and willing to die for it; he means, *freedom from the Law* – in this instance, particularly the law governing circumcision – as opposed to the opposite party within 'the Church' or 'Assembly', that is, those 'Zealots' following James the Just, 'the brother of the Lord', called by Paul here in Galatians, 'of the circumcision', because *this is what they plainly insisted on.*

Hippolytus now makes it clear that it is because of this that this more extreme group of Essenes, who would slay *anyone daring to talk about the Law who was not circumcised*, 'were called *Zēlōtai* by some [that is 'Zealots'] and *Sicarii* by others'. Should we also not now, in view of the above 'oaths', call them 'Nazirites' (or even 'Priestly Rechabites')?

Taken at face value, this is absolutely devastating testimony, confirming the antiquity of the source, no matter to whom one wishes to attribute it (for ease of attribution we shall henceforth refer to it simply as 'Hippolytus'). Not only this, but it totally illuminates the situation in Palestine at this time and the real import of evoking Phineas' killing backsliders for introducing *pollution into the camp of Israel.*

'Hippolytus' now weaves this in with Josephus' account of 'Fourth Philosophy Zealots', by asserting, as Josephus does on two occasions, that they will

call no man Lord except the Deity, even though one should attempt to torture or even kill them.[16]

This is, of course, the 'freedom' and 'bondage' Paul reverses and allegorizes into freedom from the *very* Law these 'Zealot Essenes' are dying to protect. For his part, Josephus describes the bravery and 'immovable resolution' of this group, which he is now calling not 'the fourth group of Essenes', but 'the fourth school of Jewish Philosophy'!

These, he says,

> have an inviolable attachment to freedom [in Paul, freedom from the Law *and* circumcision] convinced that God alone is their only Ruler and Lord.

They did not mind suffering tortures or deaths of every kind, repeating the point made by Hippolytus above, nor 'could any such fear make them *call any man Lord*'. Their resolution 'was well known to a great many'. Josephus declines to say more for fear that, as he puts it, what he has described would 'be beneath the resolution they exhibit when undergoing pain'.[17]

This, clearly, is very similar to what goes by the name among early Christians of martyrdom. As a Roman interrogator of prisoners Josephus should certainly have known, 'for it was in the time of Gessius Florus' (also sent out by Nero at his wife Poppea's recommendation – this *after the fire in Rome*),

> who by his abusive and lawless actions caused the nation to grow wild with *this distemper,* provoking them *to revolt against the Romans.*

Thus Josephus' description of 'the *fourth* school of Jewish Philosophy' in his *Antiquities,* where he did deign to discuss the Movement begun by Judas the Galilean and his mysterious colleague '*Saddok*' at the time of the Census of Cyrenius some seventy years before – the same Census the Gospel of Luke equates with the birth of 'Jesus'.

In the *Jewish War,* as we have seen, Josephus does begin his well-known description of the '*three* philosophical schools among the Jews' at the point he mentions that 'a *certain Galilean,* whose name was Judas [in the *Antiquities,* it will be recalled, Judas does *not* come from Galilee, but rather Gaulonitis – today's Golan] incited his countrymen to revolt, upbraiding them as cowards if they *submitted to paying a tax to Rome* and would *after God, submit to mortal men as their Lords*', this the doctrine *parodied by Paul in Romans* and attributed by Hippolytus to his more militant group of 'Essenes' above.

But instead of now going on to describe Judas' sect – 'which was not at all like the rest' – Josephus at this point launches into his well-known description of the 'Essenes'. At the same time, he cuts the above piece from his description of the Movement founded by Judas and *Saddok* in the *Antiquities* and adds it to that of 'the Essenes' here in the *War.* He now says of these Essenes:

They are above pain . . . and as for death, *should it be for Glory* [we have encountered this 'Glory' in notices about Jesus and in the Scrolls above], they *esteem it better than living a long time*. And, indeed, *our War with the Romans gave abundant proofs what immovable resolutions they have in enduring sufferings* [that is, these 'Essenes' unlike some other groups – 'Pharisees' for instance – took part in the War against Rome] because, although they were *tortured and dismembered, burned and torn to bits, going through every kind of instrument of torture* [again, Josephus should know about this] to make them *blaspheme the Name of the Law-giver* or to *eat what was forbidden them* [our 'eating and drinking' theme again – in Hippolytus, it will be recalled, 'eating things sacrificed to idols'], yet could they not be made to do either of these, nor at the same time even to *flatter their torturers or shed a single tear*. Rather they smiled in their very pains and laughed scornfully at those inflicting these tortures on them, resigning their souls with great alacrity as *expecting to receive them back again*.

Not only do we have here, once again, the very essence of what is normally understood as 'Christian' martyrdom, but these are the very words ascribed to the literary prototypes of the Maccabean Movement in the Maccabee books two centuries before, where the doctrine of resurrection of the dead is first enunciated in a straightforward manner. This is in the 'Seven Brothers' episode in 2 Maccabees 7, caricatured in Gospel discussions of resurrection as we have already pointed out.[18] In the 'Seven Brothers' episode, the mother of the brothers urges each in turn to 'die for the Laws of his country', encouraged by the doctrine of resurrection from the dead.

As the martyred teacher of the Law, Eleazar, who 'preferring to *die gloriously* rather than live a *polluted life*', is made to express it in the episode just preceding this one, to teach the young an example of 'how to make a good death, zealously and nobly for the venerable and Holy Laws' (2 Macc. 6:28). The brothers are portrayed as disdaining life and limb 'for the sake of His Laws, hoping to receive them back again from Him', since 'it is for His Laws we die' (2 Macc. 7:9–12). For her part, the mother encourages the seventh brother to make a good death, averring that God,

in His Mercy will most surely *raise you up to both breath and life*, seeing you now despise your own life *for the sake of His Laws* . . . Fear not this brutal butcher, but prove yourself worthy of your brothers and *welcome death*, so that in His Mercy I shall *receive you back again in their company*. (2 Macc. 7:23–29)

This last is, surely, the explanation for the Masada suicide, to avoid pollution and to be reunited together again at the Resurrection – which is the reason that the 'bones' passage from Ezekiel has been found buried under the synagogue floor there.[19]

In the same book, Judas Maccabee, following these martyrdoms, after a particularly difficult battle, is portrayed as making a sacrifice on behalf of the fallen, in which

> he took full account of the Resurrection, for if he had not expected the fallen to rise again, it would have been altogether silly and superfluous to pray for the dead. But since he had in view the splendid recompense reserved for those who make a good death, the intention was completely *Holy and Pious*. (2 Macc. 12:45–46)

As the second and fourth brothers put this, after being *skinned alive* and otherwise tortured, because they would not *break the Law*,

> The King of the Universe will raise us up to new and everlasting life . . . whereas for you, there will be no Resurrection again to life. (2 Macc. 7:9–14)

In the parody of these things in the Synoptic Gospels, 'some of the Pharisees' – our ubiquitous 'some' again – '*with* the Herodians' (this is an important addition) 'send out spies to *ensnare*' (note the reverse signification here) Jesus about whether or not 'it was Lawful to pay tribute to Caesar' (Matt. 22:15–40 and pars.).

Here not only do we have the ubiquitous 'net' and 'snare' language – of course, with reverse signification – but also the 'tribute' question again. In addition, there is the theme of 'spying', also encountered in Paul's complaints against the Jerusalem Leadership of the Church, the 'some from James' or 'those of the circumcision' in Galatians 2:4–12, who 'come in by stealth *to spy out the freedom*' that Paul and his companions – Titus, for instance – 'enjoy in Christ Jesus, because they wish to *reduce us to bondage*', this a different kind of 'bondage' than that being referred to above where the tax question is concerned.

After this, a group identified as 'the Sadducees' comes, for whom 'there is no Resurrection' – the very words used in 2 Maccabees 7:14 above. Of course, the Sadducees are, also, the party Josephus identifies as denying the doctrine that the dead could enjoy immortal life, the knowledge of which Acts also portrays Paul as evincing (Acts 23:6–10). The situation being caricatured here in the Gospels also parodies the story of John the Baptist and the arcane Jewish legal custom of levirate marriage being alluded to there – in this episode relating to the 'Seven Brothers', each rather being portrayed as, in turn, 'leaving no seed behind' and, therefore, marrying the wife of the next (Matt. 22:23–33 and pars.).

Thus, instead of *noble* encouragement to martyrdom on the part of the mother to her seven sons – a thing few Jewish mothers would encourage even today – to die for the Holy Laws of their country, taking note of the doctrine of resurrection, as in 2 Maccabees, here each brother is basically portrayed as marrying the wife of the previous brother and the tragic pathos of the original story turned into something resembling comic farce. The 'Sadducees' – because of course it is known that they supposedly do not believe in the Resurrection (perhaps these 'Herodian Sadducees' did not, but the 'Qumran Sadducees' did) – then ask the nonsense question, which brother will get whose wife after the Resurrection (Matt. 22:28 and pars.).

Not only does this completely trivialize the basic Zealot Resurrection ideology, it shows clear knowledge of the direct connection of the 'Seven Brothers' story, as it was told here in 2 Maccabees, to the doctrine of resurrection – not to mention knowledge of Josephus' portrait of the 'Sadducees' generally. It also makes a mockery of the hope of resurrection being expressed in the willingness to undergo torture and the steadfast attachment to the Law described in Hippolytus' picture of his fourth group of 'Essenes' and Josephus' 'Fourth Philosophy' followers of Judas *the Galilean* and *Saddok* – that is, 'Zadok'.

Hippolytus' Naassenes, Ebionites, and Elchasaites

It is following this attestation of the longevity of these 'Essenes', 'many living over a century' – echoing Epiphanius' picture of James 'dying a virgin at the age of ninety-six' and Simeon bar Cleophas 'a hundred and twenty', both following 'the *Nazirite* life-style' – that Josephus gives the description about their willingness to undergo any kind of torture rather than 'blaspheme the Law-giver', 'eat what was forbidden them', or 'flatter their torturers', all clearly themes of this 'Seven Brothers' episode in 2 Maccabees above connected to its resurrection ideal.

These are hardly 'Essenes' as the appellation is normally understood and here Hippolytus' account a century later than Josephus is, as earlier remarked, in some respects manifestly superior. In any event, both are clearly using the *same* source – Hippolytus' source, which in some respects appears more complete or precise and adds key information that is either missing or has been discarded from his predecessor's, is even perhaps an *earlier* version of Josephus.

About this, the reader must make up his or her own mind, but in describing this last species of 'Essenes' *or* 'Zealots' – those he calls 'of the later period' – Hippolytus avers that they go so far even as to 'shun those who have digressed from their customs', a point totally in accord with Qumran practice, as we now have it revealed (not to mention, by Paul's own testimony in Galatians of his treatment by 'Peter' ['Cephas'?], Barnabas, and the others in 'Antioch' and the picture of Peter generally in the Pseudoclementine *Homilies*), and

> will *not even touch them* [nothing could be more un-'Christian']. If they happen to come in contact with them, they immediately *resort to bathing*, as if they had *touched a foreigner*.

Again, this point about 'bathing' and 'touching a foreigner' is completely missing from the present version of Josephus and totally in accord with the Pseudoclementine picture of Peter. Where did Hippolytus get it?

It is at this point that Hippolytus goes on to provide the information that *is* found in Josephus that 'many of them are long-lived, so as to live even *longer than a hundred years*'. But in Hippolytus' testimony, this point comes in connection with the extreme *bathing* practices and the *shunning of outsiders* of these *later-style, more uncompromising* 'Essenes' he calls either 'Zealots' or '*Sicarii*', not simply in connection with their willingness to undergo martyrdom as in Josephus' somewhat less ample testimony.

As Josephus puts this point about their longevity, this is 'because of the simplicity of their diet [by which he appears to be implying, like Hippolytus, that they *ate only vegetables*] and the regularity of the life-style they observe'. This culminates in his description of their willingness to undergo torture and martyrdom like the early Christians, but again of course for the absolutely opposite reasons – those reasons expressed by 2 Maccabees above not the Gospels and Acts.

Though Hippolytus is basically following Josephus' sequence again here, the language he uses is different. For the purposes of our identifications too this makes all the difference. He expresses this as follows:

> They assert, therefore, that the cause of this [their longevity] is their extreme devotion to Religion [this, of course, the very language James 1:26–27 is using] and condemnation of all excess in regard to *what they eat* and their *being temperate* and *incapable of anger*. And so it is that they despise death, rejoicing when they can *finish their course with a good conscience* [here Paul's 'running the course' and 'conscience' language in 1 Corinthians 8:7–10:25].

In this regard too, one should take note of Paul's continuous outbursts of anger in his letters and the rebukes the Letter of James gives to one who cannot 'control his Tongue' but rather 'deceives his heart' – 'the Religion' of such a one being either 'vain' or 'Worthless' (Jas. 1:26 and 3:10). These are also precisely the same kinds of rebukes one gets in the Community Rule and other documents at Qumran – including penances – particularly in the contrast of 'the two Spirits', 'the Spirit of Truth' and 'Light' with that of 'Evil', 'Lying', and 'of Belial'.[20]

Hippolytus continues:

> If, however, anyone would attempt to torture men of this description with the aim of inducing them *to eat, speak Evil of the Law* or *eat that which is sacrificed to an idol*, he will not effect his purpose, for these *submit to death and endure any torture rather than violate their consciences.*

Here not only is Hippolytus, once again, using the language of 'eating' and 'conscience' that Paul is using in 1 Corinthians 8:4–9:14 and 10:16–33 (in 8:12, referring to 'the *brothers*', '*weak* consciences', and eating only vegetables, Paul actually uses the *very* words, 'wounding their consciences'), Hippolytus is also employing the language of James' directives to overseas communities Paul also exploits, as we have seen, in his arguments with Community Leaders (principally James) who make problems over 'things sacrificed to idols' – 'a *stumbling block* to those that are *weak*' (1 Cor. 8:9).

That Hippolytus here actually evokes the very directive incontrovertibly (and probably uniquely) associated with *James'* name in the New Testament, which Paul so rails against in 1 Corinthians and which Peter quotes too in the Pseudoclementine *Homilies*,[21] makes it absolutely clear whom and what we are dealing with here. It would be impossible, I think, to achieve a more perfect match and better convergence of themes than this. These 'Zealot' Essenes are also *Jamesian*. Earlier in this section, as we saw, in the aftermath of alluding to 'loving God', 'love building up', not 'Knowledge puffing up' (1 Cor. 8:1–3) – all phraseologies encountered at Qumran – Paul even plays on all these conceptualities by ridiculing the 'Knowledge' of the 'some' (that is, those who 'came down from James'), who 'with conscience *of the idol* [the wordplay here works in the Greek only], eating as if of a thing *to* an idol', 'their "conscience", being weak, *is defiled*' (1 Cor. 8:7). Paul is at his allegorical and polemical best here, again reversing the ideology of his opponents against them with spellbinding rhetorical artistry.

His conclusion is a model of facetious dissimulation: 'Yet, if anyone sees you, having "Knowledge", eating in an idol Temple, will not the "conscience" of such a "weak being" be "built up" [meaning, in this context, 'strengthened'], causing him to eat "things sacrificed to idols"?' (1 Cor. 8:10). Therefore, 'through your "Knowledge", the "weak brother" will be destroyed . . . so if meat causes my brother *to stumble*, I will *never eat flesh forever* that I should not *cause my brother to stumble*' (1 Cor. 8:11–13).

He even goes on to use this word 'conscience' in Romans 13:5 to justify *paying taxes* to Rome – the same 'conscience' Hippolytus claims these 'Zealot' Essenes 'would submit to death and endure torture rather than defile' by 'eating things sacrificed to idols' (this reinforced, it will be recalled, by Pliny's testimony to the same 'unwillingness' on the part of early Christians in Bithynia and, as we have now seen, the 'Jamesian' letter or letters known as '*MMT*', in which the concern over 'things sacrificed to idols' where 'Gentiles' are concerned forms a central focus. We shall see the importance of this presently.) For his part, Paul, as we have also seen, couples this 'conscience' with the Authorities' justified 'wrath to him' who resists their carrying out God's 'Judgement' to recommend 'rendering tribute due to whom tribute was due' (Rom. 13:7).

We can say here that Paul and Hippolytus are basically talking about the same group. One even might go so far as to claim that Paul was among those 'cast out' (*ekballō*) of such a group, one reason perhaps for the New Testament's focus on this kind of language and its trivialization into that of 'casting out demons', the Authority for which Jesus accorded his principal Apostles.

In view of Josephus' notice about Nero sending Florus as Governor in Palestine with the express purpose, seemingly, of goading the Jews into revolt, it begins to look as if the circle of people around Nero we have described above – who were neither unsophisticated nor unintelligent (including people like Epaphroditus, Seneca, Felix's brother Pallas, and on its fringes someone even Josephus calls 'Saulus') – were willing even to wipe out a whole people. In the end, anyhow, their best general, Vespasian, was sent from Britain to rid the world of this pestilent Messianic agitation that was then disturbing the entire Mediterranean and inciting revolt against Roman Imperial Authority everywhere.

It is this then, which via the magic of literary re-creation, becomes converted in the traditions embodied by the Gospels and the Book of Acts into the picture of a pacifist, other-worldly Messianism, with harmless 'Disciples', such as 'Stephen' and Paul, who basically approve of foreign or Roman rule and do not oppose it. By the same token, their tormenters – as, for instance those 'Nazirite'-style oath-takers who 'vow not to eat or drink until they have killed Paul' – are essentially the very people obliterated *en masse* because of their propagation of this form of more militant Messianism, the more subversive 'disease-carriers' of the 'Nazoraean heresy', whom, as Acts 24:5 attests were abroad aroundthe Mediterranean, 'fomenting revolution among all the Jews in the inhabitable world'.

It is to this description of their continent life-style, their unwavering willingness to undergo death or torture rather than '*blaspheme their Law-giver* or *eat any forbidden things*' that Josephus attaches his picture of the 'resolution' these 'Essenes' showed in the *recent War with the Romans*, thereby tying Essenes of this kind to the Uprising against Rome in the manner of 'Zealots'. This, it will be recalled, is missing from Hippolytus' description. For Josephus the point, as we just saw, was simply 'eating *forbidden* things' or 'blaspheming the Law-giver', but the direct association here in Hippolytus of 'blaspheming' or 'speaking Evil against the Law' – the point is the same – with not eating 'things sacrificed to an idol' ties this description *absolutely* to the Community of James.

A final point, which becomes even more clear when inspecting the Greek of Josephus' description of the Essenes. At this point in his description of Essenes – interestingly enough, also, in regard to what he calls 'practising Piety towards the Deity', Josephus uses the 'casting out' language, discussed above in regard to Jesus 'casting out Evil demons' or Stephen being 'cast out'of Jerusalem by the Evil Jews, but this now in regard to those 'cast out from the group' or expelled (*ekballousi*). This language, as we saw, is rife in the Community Rule and Damascus Document from Qumran. Since the probationer had already sworn an oath only to eat the pure food of the Community – the 'eating and drinking' theme again – according to Josephus, he will, therefore, die unless he breaks his oath. This is exactly the same as at Qumran.[22]

The language Josephus uses to describe this, including 'not revealing secrets to others even if tortured to death', 'swearing to transmit these exactly as he received them himself', and always being 'a lover of Truth and an exposer of Liars', is almost word for word the language we encountered in the picture of the terrifying oath-taking required by James of the Elders of the Jerusalem Assembly, following Peter's Letter to him in the introduction to the Pseudoclementine *Homilies*. This is the kind of 'casting out', that is, 'casting' someone 'out' of the Community or 'expelling' him, that in the New Testament becomes, as we have now made clear, the Jews viciously 'casting Stephen out of the city' (*ekbalontes*) in Acts or the Apostles receiving 'the Authority to cast out Evil Demons' from Jesus in the Gospels (*ekballein*).

It also is interesting that in his description of the doctrines of the group Hippolytus calls 'the Naassenes' – a corruption seemingly of 'Nazoraeans' or 'Nazirites' and 'Essenes' – Hippolytus asserts that they received their ideas from numerous discourses which 'James the brother of the Lord handed down to *Mariamne*'. Whatever confusion may be involved here, the same idea appears, as we saw, in the Second Apocalypse of James from Nag Hammadi, where this individual is now called 'Mareim one of the Priests'. There, it will be remembered, he is associated with someone called 'Theuda, the father' or 'brother of the Just One *since he was a relative of his*',[23] and we are now on our way to solving the 'Thaddaeus'/ 'Theudas' problem as well.

One can assume that the discourses, which Hippolytus says James 'handed down', are basically the same as those which somehow re-appeared in the Pseudoclementine literature – or what other early Church writers refer to as the 'Travels' and/or the 'Preaching of Peter' – or, for instance, Epiphanius' 'Ascents of James'. Curiously enough, Hippolytus considers these 'Naassenes' to have been the first 'heresy' before even the Ebionites or Elchasaites, whatever Hippolytus might mean by 'heresy' at this point (the same word used to describe early Christianity in Acts 24:14, where it is also called 'the Way', and 28:22).

He says they believed 'the Christ' to be, in a kind of incarnationist (or '*Imam*'ate) doctrine, 'the Perfect Man' or 'the Primal Adam' – or simply 'Adam'. But, as we have seen above, these are just the ideas which in the Pseudoclementines come to be associated with Jewish Christianity or the Ebionites, as well – it will be recalled – as with 'the Standing One', not unrelated to all these allusions to 'standing' in the various Gospel accounts we have been looking at above. One can still find such teachings among groups called in Arabic 'the *Subba*' or 'the Sabaeans of the Marshes' – the 'Mandaeans' of Southern Iraq. Apparently 'Mandaean' was the name for the rank and file of such groups, the priestly élite being known as the *Nazoraeans*! '*Subba*', of course, meant to be baptized or immersed.[24]

For Hippolytus, this *Christ* or the *Perfect Man* – in Mandaean doctrine still the demiurge standing above the cosmos – descended on numerous individuals. This is a quasi-Gnostic doctrine. In the 'aeon' we have before us, the descent of this 'Christ' or 'Perfect Man' on Jesus occurred in the form of a dove – the picture, of course, disseminated in the Gospels and an idea not so different from Buddhism. Hippolytus also ascribes the same ideology to the 'Elchasaites', who seem to be a later adumbration of such groups, as well as to one 'Cerinthus', referred to by all these heresiologists, who was said to have taught 'the Ebionites'.

This doctrine of 'the Perfect Man' or 'Standing One' is also abroad among Shi'ites in Islam even today, albeit in a slightly different nexus, which seems to have developed out of the persistence of many of these groups and the central notions they all seemed to share in Northern Iraq. In Epiphanius, some two centuries after Hippolytus, these 'Naassenes' are called 'Nazareans' or 'Nazrenes' – the 'Nazoraeans' who go into the élite Priest Class of Mandaeans. For him, *they exist even before Christ* – as do our so-called 'Essenes' at Qumran – and are coincident with other similar groups he calls Daily Bathers/Hemerobaptists and 'Sebuaeans' (thus).

It is clear that the majority of these groups do not differ markedly from each other as to basics and we are really only witnessing overlapping designations and the transference of terminology from one language into another in this region. In Arabic and to Islam they are what – via the Aramaic and Syriac – come to be called 'Sabaeans', based on the word in those languages for baptism or immersion, *'masbuta'* – 'Masbuthaeans' according to some of Eusebius' reckonings. In Palestine, for example, one of the several names for them is 'Essenes'.

In the First Apocalypse of James from Nag Hammadi, where James is regarded as a kind of Supernatural Redeemer figure, James is encouraged to teach these things, firstly, to Addai and, secondly, to 'Salome and Mariam', and in the Second Apocalypse, to 'Mareim one of the Priests' above – this obviously the 'Mariamne' (also 'Mariamme' elsewhere at Nag Hammadi) in Hippolytus' descriptions of what he is calling 'Naassenes'. Like Matthew of Christian tradition – called in Mark, it will be recalled, 'Levi the son of Alphaeus' and, therefore, usually considered 'Priestly' or at least 'levitical' – he is described as doing the 'writing'.

We now can see where perhaps some of these criss-crosses between 'James the son of Alphaeus' and Matthew as 'Levi the son of Alphaeus' may have come from. Clearly we have a large measure of garbling and overlap here, but, whatever else these correspondences may imply, it is clear that as early as Hippolytus' time – second–third century CE – many of these doctrines, 'Gnostic' or otherwise, were being ascribed to 'James the brother of the Lord'.

One should also note that in addition to teaching that 'the Christ' descended on Jesus in the form of a dove above, Cerinthus, whom both

Hippolytus and Epiphanius list as preceding the Ebionites, is said to have taught that 'Jesus was *not born of a virgin*, but he sprang from Joseph and Mary similar to *the rest of men*', whom he only '*exceeded in Righteousness*, wisdom, and understanding'.[25] These are the doctrines, of course, that Eusebius, a century after Hippolytus, is ascribing to the 'Ebionites' not Cerinthus. According to Hippolytus, these Ebionites not only saw Christ in the manner of Cerinthus above, but 'live in all respects according to the Law of Moses, insisting that one could only be justified – that is, 'made Righteous' – in such a manner'.[26]

For Hippolytus, too, Cerinthus is already teaching the doctrine that 'Christ' did not suffer on the cross, but departed from Jesus at that moment. This reappears in slightly more developed form in the Gnostic texts at Nag Hammadi and, from thence, the Koran.[27] For some of these 'Gnostics', it was rather Simon of Cyrene, who carried the cross in Gospel accounts, who thus suffered (one should always watch this usage, 'Simon of Cyrene' because it may be that we have another mix-up with 'Simeon bar Cleophas', who actually *was crucified*). For Hippolytus, the Elchasaites, whom we have already met, have the same doctrine. For them 'the Christ', who is superior to the rest,

> is transfused into many bodies frequently and was now in Jesus . . . likewise this Jesus afterwards was continually being transfused into bodies and was manifested in many at different times.[28]

This doctrine is, of course, simply that of Shi'ite or *Imam*ate Islam, only now, instead of 'the Christ', the Supernatural figure is called 'the *Imam*' – again a term in Arabic bearing some relationship to 'the Standing One' or the 'One Standing before'; for other groups, 'the Primal' or 'Perfect Adam'. In Buddhism, of course, it is 'the *Buddha*'.

The Elchasaites follow a teacher called '*Elchasai*' – a name Hippolytus thinks translates as 'Righteous One'; for others, such as Epiphanius, as we saw, it is 'Great' or 'Hidden Power'. He is a contemporary in some respects to our Simeon bar Cleophas above – if the reports about Simeon's extreme longevity can be believed. These 'Elchasaites' are virtually indistinguishable from another group Epiphanius is later calling the 'Sampsaeans', another probable corruption or variation of the Syriac/Islamic 'Sabaeans' or 'Masbuthaeans', that is, Daily Bathers, below.

For Hippolytus, 'Elchasai' came in the third year of Trajan's reign (101 CE), the period of the latter's difficulties in the East with Parthia and the time both Eusebius and Epiphanius equate with Simeon bar Cleophas' martyrdom. It is also the time of Messianic unrest, as we have seen, in Egypt and North Africa under, of course, 'Andrew' or 'Andreas of Cyrene'. A book ascribed to '*Elchasai*' was apparently brought to Rome during the second year of Hadrian's reign (119 CE). This book included the important reference to 'the Standing One', already encountered above in the Pseudoclementines. There purportedly it was also a revelatory Angel 'standing' some 'ninety-six miles high' (in competing accounts this is the risen Christ), whose feet were approximately fourteen miles long![29]

The height of 'ninety-six' here, manifestly, is nothing but the number of years Epiphanius – two centuries later – considers to be *James' age* when he died. 'Elchasai', for Epiphanius, is 'a false prophet'. He joined the Ebionites, who it would appear – according to him – were already extant and no different from the 'Sampsaeans', 'Essenes' (Epiphanius also calls them 'Ossaeans'), and the 'Elchasaites', again tying all these groups together. (In fact, for Epiphanius, who amid all the confusion and fantasy sometimes has extremely good, factual material, the 'Elchasaites' and 'Sampsaeans' – at least in 'Arabia' and 'Perea' – are equivalent.) These all taught the doctrine that 'Christ' and 'Adam' ('Man' – '*Enosh*', as we saw, in Aramaic) were the same thing. As he puts it, 'the Spirit, which is Christ' put on 'Adam's body' or 'him who is called Jesus'.[30]

For Hippolytus, 'Elchasai' received this doctrine from a group in Northern Mesopotamia or Persia called 'the *Sobiai*', clearly once again, 'the Sabaeans' or 'Daily Bathers' we have already encountered in Islam above – but these now in *the first or second century* CE. Elsewhere in Hippolytus, it is clear this area is not far from 'the country of the *Adiabeni*', whom we shall now presently meet in the story of the conversion to Judaism or 'Christianity' of Queen Helen of Adiabene. It is also clear that these Mesopotamian '*Subba*' or 'Sabaeans' are no different really from Hippolytus' and Josephus' 'Essenes', the name simply being expressed in a different linguistic framework.

Conclusions as to James the son of Alphaeus, Simon the Zealot, and Judas the Brother of James

We are now getting to the point where we can draw some conclusions about these various overlaps, substitutions, and changes in Gospel lists where those called 'Apostles' are concerned. It is clear that the 'James the son of Alphaeus, Simon the Zealot, and Judas [the brother] of James' – also called in Greco-Syriac tradition 'Judas *Zēlōtēs*', that is, 'Judas the

Zealot' – are obviously those being reckoned in the picture of the Synoptic Gospels as 'the brothers of Jesus' and that, therefore also, 'Alphaeus' and 'Cleophas' (or 'Clopas') must be identical. The same as far as the term 'Lebbaeus' is concerned, which also may be a variation of another term we have already seen, above, applied to James, *Oblias*.

But one can go further. If one takes into account the witnesses to the execution and resurrection of Jesus – or, depending on the account, the empty tomb – it becomes quite clear that purposeful obfuscation or garbling of traditions is going on. Still, 'Mary the mother of James and Joses and the mother of the sons of Zebedee' in Matthew 27:56 and 'Mary the mother of James the less and of Joses and Salome' in Mark 15:40 and 'Mary the mother of James' in Luke 24:10 are all, simply, *Mary the mother of Jesus*. I think we can take this as a *first* conclusion.

In the Book of Acts, after 'James the brother of John' has conveniently been disposed of and the *real* James introduced – without any prior explanation or introduction, as if we should know who he was – the 'Mary the mother of John Mark', to whose house Peter goes after escaping from prison to leave a message for 'James and to the brothers' (12:12), is none other than this *same* 'Mary' – either 'Mary the mother of Jesus' or 'Mary the mother of James', despite obfuscations stemming from Mary being 'a life-long virgin' or James being *the son of Joseph by a previous wife* notwithstanding. In any event, this is precisely what she is called in Mark 16:1 and Luke 24:10.

'*James the Less*' is hardly James the less (Mark 15:40). Rather he is James *the Great* – James *the Just* – the victim of more obfuscation, in this instance aimed at 'belittling' him. The same for 'James the son of Alphaeus'. 'Mary the sister' of Jesus' mother 'and the wife of Clopas' in John 19:25 is, once again, simply James' or Jesus' mother Mary – if Jesus had a mother called Mary or if Mary had a son called Jesus (John doesn't know either point) – it being normally absurd for someone to have the same name as her own sister. Thus, the proliferation of all these Marys diminishes.

'Clopas', 'Cleopas', 'Cleophas', and 'Alphaeus' are simply Jesus' father Joseph or, as the case may be, Clopas or Cleophas – ideological attempts to dissociate Jesus from his forebears notwithstanding. Garblings or mix-ups such as these might strike the Western ear as surprising, until the nature of oral tradition is understood.

For instance, in the Middle East, the old Greek Constantinople has become, via the shortening 'Stanbul', today's 'Istanbul'. A city like Nablus on the West Bank of Palestine comes out of the Greek 'Neopolis', there being, for instance, no letter equivalent to 'p' in Western parlance in the Arabic alphabet. It is, in fact, the 'New City' which the Greeks built on the biblical city Shechem. Even the romantic and seemingly melodious name 'Andalusia' for Spain comes via the Arabic from the less pleasing one 'Vandals', that is, in Arabic, 'the Andals', who sacked Rome in the fourth century and came via Spain to Tunisia in North Africa – where the Arabs first encountered them.

There are many other such examples of the transference of names from one language to another in the literature – one being the *balla'*/Belial/ Balaam language circle we have already been discussing, which finds as its parallel in Greek the one ranging around *ballō*/'cast down' and 'the *Diabolos'*/the Devil, but this tangle has even deeper implications as we have been signalling.

This raises the question of whether Jesus' father was ever really called 'Joseph' at all except via literary re-creation. The Gospel of John, once again, implies something of this tangle, when Philip tells the Disciple it calls 'Nathanael' – either Bartholomew or our old friend, 'James the Less' again, in the Synoptics[31] and, in our view, James – at almost the first breath, that 'Andrew' and 'Peter'

> have found the one written of by Moses in the Law and the Prophets, 'Jesus the son of Joseph from Nazareth'. (1:46)

But if we take this statement at face value, there is, plainly, no 'Jesus the son of Joseph from Nazareth' written about in either the Mosaic Law (the five Books of Moses) or the Prophets.

At this point, too, John is anxious to mask the true thrust of the 'Nazoraean' terminology, which, as we have been discovering, means 'Keeper' – either 'Keeper of the Law' or 'Keeper of the Secrets' – transforming it into 'Nazareth'. Either this, or perhaps it relates to the 'Nazrene'/'Nazirite' usage, not to mention the 'Cana'/'Cananite'/ 'Cananaean' terminologies. There is, however, the biblical 'Joshua the son of Nun', of the Tribe of Ephraim, a 'son of Joseph'. It is passages of this kind in 'the Law of Moses' that John appears to be evoking. To put this in the shortest manner possible, the biblical 'Joshua', the individual upon whom Jesus is typed – Jesus being the closest Greek homophone to the name 'Joshua' or '*Yeshu'a*' in Hebrew, which literally does mean 'save' or 'Saviour' – really *was* a true 'son of Joseph'. This does not mean that the actual 'Jesus' of history *was*.

In addition, because of overlaps in the biblical text between the Books of Joshua and Judges, there is another twist to the relationship of this name 'Jesus' to 'Joshua'. Joshua, who is pictured as having died at the end of the Book of Joshua (24:29) and still dead at the beginning of Judges (1:1), is miraculously depicted as being alive again and giving his final instructions to the tribes in Judges 2:6. So here we have a scenario that some over-zealous biblical exegetes might have interpreted in terms of a dead-alive 'Joshua' or 'Jesus' in these two books too.

In addition, in Jewish tradition or folklore, two Messiahs are often pictured, a 'Messiah ben Judah' and a 'Messiah of Israel', matching the dual nature of the Southern and Northern Kingdoms. The Northern Kingdom was, in effect, the Kingdom of the descendants of Joseph, these being the most numerous and the principal tribe there. This was of course the tribe of Ephraim, Joshua's tribe. Therefore in Talmudic allusion, the latter is often dubbed the 'Messiah ben Joseph', that is, the 'Messiah the son of Joseph'.[32] The story of Jesus' birth parentage may, in fact, be no more complex than this.

These kinds of matters are perhaps also reflected to some extent in the Qumran notion of a dual or two Messiahs, if such a notion, in fact, exists at Qumran, which is questionable. The evidence is unclear and depends on the meaning of usages that may be idiomatic. All the same, the issue has to do with a priestly or a lay Messiah, as it does in Hebrews, or a combination of both, and has very little relevance to the question of Jesus' parentage, whether real or simply formulary.

The 'Papias' Fragment and Conclusions as to Jesus and Joses

However, there is a passage from the early Church father Papias (c. 60–135 CE) from Hierapolis in Asia Minor, a contemporary of the younger Pliny, that can help us tie all these passages together and resolve these difficulties. Papias is perhaps the oldest Church father, aside from Clement of Rome (c. 30–97) and Ignatius (c. 50–115), his older contemporary. Irenaeus (c. 130–200) calls Papias a friend of Polycarp (69–156) and a hearer of John, meaning the John of Ephesus to whom the Gospel is attributed.

Curiously Eusebius talks about Papias in the same breath he does the succession and martyrdom of Simeon bar Cleophas – whom he actually calls 'Simeon the son of Clopas' in the fragment he preserves from Hegesippus. He preserves the story from Papias, we have already mentioned above, about 'Justus surnamed Barsabas' surviving some dangerous poison – which so much resembles Rabbinic stories about the omnipresent Jacob of Kfar Sechania (Kfar Cana?) being able to cure snakebites – and whom we have already associated with the problem in Acts concerning leadership succession in Jerusalem.[33]

It is to Papias as well that Eusebius owes the information that Mark, who never saw the Lord, but who was called in 1 Peter 5:13 Peter's 'son', was Peter's associate and disciple overseas – probably in Rome – and that 'Matthew put together the oracles in the Hebrew language, and each interpreted them as best he could'.[34]

This last is very important information, because it gives us a certain insight into the manner in which the Scriptures were put together – in the first place, by culling biblical Scripture for the prophecies and passages relevant to Messianism. Some call these, 'Oracles of the Lord', but it should be clear they are Old Testament prophecies or proof-texts. Then there was the interpretation – that is, the various stories developed upon these proof-texts. This, too, completely accords with Qumran procedure in the *Pesharim*. However, in these last, the exegete usually confines himself to *one* text – though he is not above altering this to fit the interpretation he is intent upon – but sometimes he combines more than one text in one and the same context, as Paul does and in the Gospels.

But early as he is, even Papias came at a stage when information was already highly mythologized. It is interesting that Eusebius also associates him with mention of the Gospel of the Hebrews.[35] He attributes to him as well an ideology, well known in the Damascus Document from Qumran, but which Eusebius himself terms 'mythological', that 'after the Resurrection there will be *a period of a thousand years* when Christ's Kingdom will be set up *on this earth in material form*'. Eusebius finds this doctrine puzzling, guessing that Papias has 'misinterpreted Apostolic accounts perversely'.

No wonder Eusebius finds this doctrine puzzling, calling Papias 'of limited intelligence' and unable to understand the 'allegorical' nature of these things. Not only is this doctrine directly enunciated in the Damascus Document where the promise to 'those that *love* and *keep* My Commandments' of 'living for a thousand generations' is explicitly drawn,[36] it totally flies in the face of the description of the Kingdom and the Resurrection Paul gives, when talking about 'the First Man, *Adam*, becoming a living soul and *the Last Adam*, a life-giving Spirit' (1 Cor. 15:44–54), not to mention the kind of information that was obviously being communicated to Pliny the Younger about Christians in nearby Bithynia in Asia Minor.

A fragment from a medieval manuscript found at Oxford attributed to Papias has him saying that:

> Mary the wife of Cleophas or Alphaeus . . . was the mother of James the Bishop and Apostle, and of Simon, Thaddaeus, and one Joseph.[37]

This is very startling testimony. Not only does it unwaveringly confirm James' role as *both* Bishop and Apostle, but it also now affirms that one of these brothers, called 'Judas' in all other texts, is here simply and straightforwardly referred to as 'Thaddaeus', which was in any event the implication from Apostle lists where 'Thaddaeus' in Mark and 'Thaddaeus surnamed Lebbaeus' in some versions of Matthew give way to 'Judas [the brother] of James' in Luke.

Not only is this testimony startling, but, as we shall now go on to see, exactly in line with what we shall be discovering from other sources. Our conclusion is that, whoever wrote it, it is early, very early – and it *is* authentic. It also goes on to identify another 'Mary Salome the wife of Zebedee' as 'an aunt of the Lord' and the 'mother of John the Evangelist and James'. The fragment then goes on to note, ever so laconically, that she was probably 'the same as Mary [the wife] of Cleophas', all this obviously alluding to the infuriating notice in John about Mary being both 'the wife of Clopas' and 'the sister' of Jesus' mother (19:25).

The fragment (if it is genuine) already gives evidence that Jesus' brothers are slowly turning into 'cousins', finally made into a general doctrine by Jerome two centuries later. Mothers become aunts and finally even their *own* sisters! Fathers *turn into uncles*, all having to do with the growing doctrine of Jesus' divine birth and the concomitant 'perpetual virginity' of Mary, as concretized in the second century in the Protevangelium, ascribed to James as well. This Infancy Gospel also excludes all other births on Mary's part, thereby directly contradicting the Gospels even as we have them.

It may be that some of this reflects later emendation, but still the notice as we have it provides us with the key to sorting out all these confusing relationships and basically echoes what we have already been delineating and have come to suspect. In the first place it avers that Cleophas and Alphaeus are identical. We did not need this fragment to suspect this, but it confirms it. It also makes it very clear that this Cleophas or Alphaeus ('Clopas' in Hegesippus) was also the father of James and that, *of course*, James the son of Alphaeus in Apostle lists *is* our James.

Finally, it confirms that Cleophas cum Alphaeus was actually *the husband of Mary*. Whether he was also called 'Joseph' or not will never be known, but it is beside the point. It, also, ever so gently points to further garblings between 'Joses' and 'Joseph', which bear on those between 'Joseph Barsabas Justus' and 'Judas Barsabas' above. But 'Joses' really does appear to be the name of the *fourth brother*. All sources are more or less in agreement on this.

Mary and Cleophas (or Alphaeus) have *four sons* not five, to wit: James, Simon, Judas of James or Thaddaeus, and Joses. This Jude/Judas of James or Thaddaeus is also called Lebbaeus in some versions of Matthew, which possibly means '*Oblias*' or further garbles the name of the father of all these various children, Cleophas, Alphaeus, or 'Clopas'. This, of course, makes James and Simeon bar Cleophas *brothers* not 'cousins', as we have already come to suspect anyhow.

It is interesting that Tatian (*c.*115–185 CE), a student in Asia Minor of Justin Martyr (*c.*100–165), refers to James the son of Alphaeus also as 'James the *Lebbaean*' – again pointing to the basic overlap of this 'Lebbaeus' terminology with Eusebius' '*Oblias*' cognomen, also applied to James as we have seen. Once again, this confirms in the process that the latter is a type of surname or sobriquet applying not just to Judas, Judas Thomas, or Thaddaeus, but other members of the family as well – most notably *James*.

Eusebius, following Irenaeus, rails against this Tatian, who came from the border areas of the Persian Empire in Northern Mesopotamia near Adiabene, because he *followed the doctrine of vegetarianism*, rejected marriage as 'fornication', and, like James, *preferred celibacy*. Not only this, but according to Eusebius, he set aside Paul's works and the Acts of the Apostles completely and speculated concerning the sinfulness of Adam in contrast to the Salvation of 'the First Man' – that is, 'the Primal Adam'.[38]

The disputed notice from Papias, also, tries to clear up the supposed parentage of James and John and the notice in Matthew about Mary being 'the mother of James and Joses and the mother of the sons of Zebedee' (27:56). These last are now described as 'sons of another aunt of the Lord's' not 'Mary the mother of James the Less and Joseph, the wife of Alphaeus' (thus), but someone he calls 'Mary Salome' or just plain 'Salome'. In Mark, of course – it will be remembered – she is the sister 'of James the Less and Joses' (15:41) or, in 16:1, simply 'of James'. Clearly she is Jesus' sister, not his aunt or the mother of the so-called 'sons of Zebedee'.

It should be apparent by now that all these evasions circulating around the two 'sons of Zebedee' are really connected in some manner to the issue of James and his direct succession as Leader of the Jerusalem Community, which again we have suspected for a long time, and that 'Zebedee' is just another one of these nonsense names and one more stand-in for these 'Alphaeus'/'Lebbaeus' evasions. In fact the only real person by the name of John, other than John the Baptist and the individual Josephus designates as 'John the Essene', that ever really materializes in any of these sources is 'John the Evangelist', considered buried in Ephesus, though sometimes even he is confused with 'John the Presbyter' and ultimately even 'Presber John'.

'James the brother of John' has no substance whatsoever, except in Gospel enumerations of the Central Three, where he is simply a stand-in for the *real* James. In Acts, where he is executed, as we have seen, he is also a stand-in for Jesus' *third brother*, Jude or Judas. It is the 'brother' signification that has the real substance here – albeit again completely obscured and transformed – and if one keeps one's eyes on it, one will never go far wrong.

The Gospels just cannot present the real James as an Apostle, brother, and principal successor of Jesus – despite the fact that this is absolutely attested to without embarrassment by no less a witness than Paul himself – because of their anti-family, anti-national, and anti-Jewish or Palestinian Apostle orientation, the family of Jesus already having been presented as distinct from Jesus' true followers and real believers and, therefore, the need for this fictional James *the brother* of John and the fictional nomenclature 'Zebedee'.

This will be further borne out, and to our thinking, definitively so, when we treat the person of this *third brother* of Jesus – Judas, Judas Thomas, Judas the brother of James, or Thaddaeus below. In the meantime it can be averred without reservation that *all* the brothers of Jesus have very *real* substance, including James, Simon/Simon the Cananite/Simon the Zealot/Simeon bar Cleophas and very likely 'Simon *Iscariot* (the father or brother) of Judas', and Judas, also known as '*Zēlōtēs*' – however highly refracted or obscured these may have become in the literature as we have it.

But 'James the son of Zebedee' does not have any substance, nor seemingly does 'Joses', sometimes called in some manuscripts and here in the Papias fragment 'Joseph', the supposed fourth brother of Jesus. But the 'brother' theme connected to this 'James the brother of John' and the *beheading* do have real substance, and, as we have shown, simply relate to a *different brother of Jesus.*

Also 'Joses', when considered *very* carefully, has *real* substance, even though we never hear a single word about him and this is not apparent on the surface. Moreover, this is borne home by looking at the form of the two words in Greek, 'IOSES' and 'IESUS'. What becomes immediately apparent is that these are simply the *same name* and what Papias or his interpolator is telling us in their straightforward enumeration of the names of Cleophas' and Mary's sons is that there *were only four brothers*, all of whom *known*, all of whom *substantial*. The fourth brother is simply 'IESUS' or 'Jesus' himself! In fact, what has happened in these early transmissions is that Jesus has simply *turned into his own brother* (just as Mary has done her *own* sister).

But this should not be surprising. We cannot blame these early compilers or redactors, who may or may not have been aware of these transformations or substitutions, if they did not recognize these things, as almost all or most of them were foreigners. Nor do they seem to have recognized the conversion of Mary into her own sister Mary, nor the conversion of Jesus' father into his uncle. They do not even seem to be aware that Drusilla in Acts, the granddaughter of Herod, is not simply 'a Jewess' – or were they?

In other words, just as in Papias – as usual condemned by later theologians like Irenaeus or Eusebius – or the text attributed to Papias, one of the earliest traditions of the Church, there *were only four brothers* and *all* were sons of *Mary and Cleophas (Alphaeus).* Jesus (IESUS) is simply his own brother Joses (IOSES). This is the reason why nothing substantial is ever really said about this fourth brother 'Joses' – though he is mentioned in the Gospels (which may tell us something about their dating) – in any of the other early sources, as opposed to the other three brothers. Nor does he appear in the Apostle lists as these other three do, as we have shown. In fact, there is a lot said about this 'Joses', as all our Gospel traditions are about him, but our early transmitters don't know this or, at least, don't want to know it.

But how did this happen and why? When did Jesus become his own brother? When did fathers turn into uncles, brothers into cousins, and mothers into their own sisters? The answer is very simple and has been clear from the beginning. It is the growing concept of Jesus as the natural – or rather supernatural – 'Son of God', not, as at Qumran and in other 'Ebionite' materials, only a symbolical or 'adoptionist' one – in the sense that all these 'Perfectly Righteous' or 'Perfectly Holy Ones' *become* 'Sons of God'. Not only have we now found this notion at Qumran, it is widespread even in the New Testament as we have it – for instance in John 1:12, Matthew 5:45, Luke 20:36, Romans 8:14–17, and Galatians 3:26 – but, in particular, as we have seen above, 2 Corinthians 6:18.

In other words, as the doctrine of Christ as a Supernatural Being and the 'only begotten' Son of God gained momentum, all these shifts in genealogies became necessary too. It was necessary that 'Joseph' – or, as the case may be, Cleophas or another – no longer be the real father, but rather only the stepfather. Even the genealogies in the Synoptics show confusion on this issue, as does John.

Then Jesus' brothers could not have been his *real* brothers, but rather only half-brothers or brothers by a previous marriage of his father or even a different mother. By Jerome's time, they are simply his 'cousins'. Mary, as we have seen, could not be the mother of these brothers. Therefore in the Gospel of John she becomes the sister of another woman by the same name, whom Jerome anyhow – and this fragment attributed to Papias – properly recognizes as the *real* mother of the brothers – and all other absurdities and evasions follow accordingly.

Clearly, Jerome finds it impossible to admit for ideological reasons that this 'Mary the wife of Clopas' in John – in John, as we saw, 'Jesus' mother' is not even called *Mary* – could be *Jesus' real mother*. This leads him into a series of self-evident contradictions and evasions, most notably about the relationship of Simeon bar Cleophas and Jesus. Simeon, it should now be appreciated, had to have been Jesus' *second* brother, equivalent to 'Simon the Cananite' (*thus*) or 'Zealot', as well as being his second successor, at least in Palestine, if not perhaps worldwide as well, as some of our sources imply.

Of course, who the 'Peter' in the Gospels was, whether the same as 'Cephas' or different from him now takes on renewed significance. Are 'Cephas' and 'Cleophas' confused as well? Was Peter the same as this Simeon bar Cleophas or different from him? Was he the same as the 'Simon the Head of his own Church' or 'Assembly' in Jerusalem, who came to Caesarea, as described in Josephus, because he wanted to *bar* Herodians from the Temple as foreigners not admit them – and this, because they did *not* 'regularly observe the Law' – or different from him? These things will probably never be known, but the suspicion is strong that we have two 'Simon's or two 'Peter's, as the case may be – the traditions being somewhat crisscrossed.

How many of the traditions about the real Simeon bar Cleophas (in

Hegesippus, 'Clopas'), the putative second successor in the Church in Palestine, who Eusebius via Hegesippus tells us was an 'eye-witness and ear-witness of the Lord' and presided – together with the descendants of Jesus' *third brother Judas* – 'over the churches everywhere, being witnesses [or 'martyrs' as the case may be] and kinsmen of the Lord', have become confused with those surrounding Peter, 'the Rock of the Church' (Matthew 16:18: 'upon this *Rock* will I build my Church') in Rome?

Certainly the idea of 'Peter' being a direct successor to Jesus is not borne out by any *real Palestinian* traditions. These have obviously been refurbished in Acts, where, for instance, they portray Peter as *learning to accept Gentiles* and *eat forbidden foods with them.* Not only are these straightforwardly gainsaid in the Pseudoclementine *Homilies*, they are clearly refuted by Paul's account of his own experiences with 'Cephas' or 'Peter' in 'Antioch' – whichever 'Antioch' this will finally turn out to be. The idea, too, of Peter being 'Bishop of Bishops', the forerunner of the modern Popes and Leader of Christianity everywhere, owes much to the real position of this Simeon in Palestine – the putative second brother of Jesus. But the present state of our sources, overwritten and mythologized as they are, where Jesus' brothers and other family members are down-played and all but written out of the tradition, do not allow us to proceed further or achieve finality on this matter.

Suffice it to say that many of the traditions regarding Simeon – including that of a first sighting on the road to Emmaus, to 'Cleopas' and another, and which may or may not have involved 'Simeon' and not simply his father 'Cleophas' (Origen thinks it involved both, and says so explicitly) and most certainly has something to do with *the first appearance to James* reported in all sources – either overlap with or have been absorbed into traditions regarding 'Peter', the successor in Rome and linchpin of Western Christian claims to the mantle of Jesus, to whom no separate appearance ever occurred (at least not in the Gospels).

Eusebius and others, basing themselves again on Hegesippus, list fifteen 'Bishops of the Circumcision' in Jerusalem up to the time of the Bar Kochba War (132–36 CE). Though some of these names appear spurious, the third after 'James the brother of the Lord' and Simeon, significantly, is called 'Justus' – our 'Joseph surnamed Barsabas Justus', the defeated candidate in the election to succeed 'Judas' above, or just James again? – and the fourth, 'Zacchaeus', whom we met in the Pseudoclementine *Recognitions* in the course of Peter being sent out by James from some-where in the region of Jericho on his first missionary journey to

Caesarea.[39] For Epiphanius this third successor is simply 'Judas'.

These are the kinds of conclusions that can be arrived at by pursuing the question of what being a 'brother' meant and the Apostolic relationship of James the Just, 'the brother of the Lord', to Jesus. It is attention to detail and to the *real*, not spurious, *traditions about James* that led us to these insights. Before moving on to consider Jesus' equally interesting *third brother*, Jude or Judas, it would be well to say a few words about Eusebius' account of 'the *Ebionites*' – inserted in the midst of all these other notices above – who *held the name of James* in such reverence.

PART VI

JAMESIAN COMMUNITIES IN THE EAST

24

Judas the Brother of James and the Conversion of King Agbar

The Ebionites

The view that Jesus was simply 'a man, advanced above other men in Righteousness or virtue', and 'a Prophet', is the one normally associated in our sources with the Ebionites. We have already seen how this name is based even in Greek transliteration on the Hebrew word for 'the Poor'. This is also an important term of self-designation at Qumran, perhaps *the* most important one, and is even found combined with other important designations there, like 'the *Ebionei-Hesed*' – 'the Poor Ones of Piety'.[1]

It has several parallels in the Qumran literature, which are used more or less interchangeably with it, such as *"Ani'/"Anayyim'* – best translated as 'the Meek' – and *'Dallim'/*'the Downtrodden', though all can without distortion also be translated as 'the Poor'. In the literature at Qumran, it is quite clear that the leader – the Righteous Teacher/*'Zaddik'*, 'the *Moreh'* or *'Yoreh ha-Zedek'* – is 'the Teacher' or 'Fountain of Righteousness' and 'the Son of Zadok'/'Son of the *Zaddik' par excellence*. He is the leader of those even Qumran designates as 'the Poor' or *'Ebionim'* and in the all-important Habakkuk *Pesher*, which contains the key 'Jamesian' interpretation of Habakkuk 2:4 ('the Righteous shall live by his Faith'), his fate is connected with theirs.[2]

Jesus' famous Sermon on the Mount in Matthew is presented as addressed to 'the Poor' and 'the Meek', not to mention 'those that hunger or thirst after Righteousness' (5:3–6). This 'Righteousness should *exceed* that of the Scribes and the Pharisees' (5:20) and they 'should *be Perfect* even as [their] Father in Heaven is *Perfect*' (5:48). This passage also contains the allusion to *becoming* 'Sons [plural] of your Father in Heaven'. This is associated with James' 'Royal Law according to the Scripture', the *Righteousness* Commandment of 'love your neighbour and hate your enemy', now reinterpreted to mean 'loving your enemies' not hating them (5:43–44). Interestingly enough, this is accompanied by the

Jamesian and clearly anti-Pauline admonition, that not only would 'not one jot or tittle pass away from the Law', but

> whoever would *break one of these Commandments, even the least*, and teach to men to do so, would be called *least in the Kingdom of Heaven*. But whoever would *do and teach them*, he shall be called *great in the Kingdom of Heaven*. (Matt. 5:18–19)

These strictures are fairly famous and need no elucidation here, but what is interesting in the material addressed to 'the Poor' and 'the Meek' is its attachment to *Righteousness* and *Perfection*, two fundamental Qumran doctrines, as well as the stress on *doing*, another basic approach emphasized by both Qumran and in the Letter ascribed to James. The passage about 'not one jot or tittle passing away from the Law', however ambiguous the context may be, certainly doubles the passage in James 2:10 about 'keeping the whole of the Law, but stumbling on one small point, being guilty of [breaking it] all'. This passage, it will be remembered, comes amidst an attack on 'the Empty Man'/'the Tongue', who, in stressing how Abraham was 'justified by Faith', does not understand that Abraham was, rather, 'justified', or 'made Righteous by works' (James 2:20–24).

For Luke 6:20, these strictures are addressed simply to 'the Poor', while in Matthew 5:3 they are addressed, in what on the surface anyhow would appear to be a more Paulinized fashion, to '*the Poor in Spirit*', meaning, as in the case of Peter sinking into the sea for lack of Faith, those 'Poor' in the Pauline ingredient of the Holy Spirit. This is true, until one realizes that this allusion, 'Poor in Spirit', actually occurs in the critical column of the War Scroll from Qumran containing the allusion to the Messiah 'coming on the clouds' with the Heavenly Host and also seemingly addressed to 'the Poor' and 'the Meek'.[3] There, it will be recalled, it was used in exegesis of the Star Prophecy of Numbers 24:17 and as a synonym for 'those bent in the dust' to designate that group among whom the Messiah would place himself, to be as 'a flaming torch in the chaff . . . to consume Unrighteousness'.

One should also note in these passages from Matthew's Sermon on the Mount the interesting allusions that follow this discussion of the 'Love Commandment' to *eschatological rain*, also present in these War Scroll passages, or to 'the rain which will fall on the Righteous and Un-Righteous alike' (Matt. 5:46), not to mention the allusion to 'moth and rust eating up one's treasures on earth' (Matt. 6:19–20), paralleling what one finds in James 5:2–3's attack on the 'Rich', whose gold 'is all eaten away' and 'whose clothes [are] all eaten by moths' (albeit with somewhat diluted effect).

The attack on 'breaking one of the *least* of these Commandments' and teaching men 'not to *do* them' in Matthew 5:19 is, also, an obviously anti-Pauline assault and should be read in conjunction with Paul's protestestions about coming 'Last' and being 'the least of the Apostles' in 1 Corinthians 15:8 and Gospel inversions of these in its 'Last' versus 'First' transpositions. The Letter of James, too, employs 'the Poor' terminology – at one point, as we saw, in connection with alluding to the 'Piety Commandment' of 'loving God', and always in conjunction with condemning 'Law-breaking' and a stress on being 'a Doer' and 'doing', also found throughout the Scrolls.[4]

For Eusebius, the Ebionites are governed by 'an Evil Demon'. They were properly called Ebionites by those he calls 'the First', because of 'the Poor and mean opinions about Christ they cherished'. To put this in another way, their 'Christology' – the technical name for ideas about 'Christ' – was *poverty-stricken*. This is an incredible statement, and why? Because

> they considered him a *plain and ordinary man*, who *became Righteous* [or 'was justified'] through his advances in virtue, nothing more, and who had been born from the *natural intercourse of a man with Mary*.[5]

Of course, this statement would strike the modern ear as simple common sense, but for Eusebius, governed as he is by his notions of Divine Sonship and the perpetual virginity of Mary – as for generations of orthodox after him – this is *arch heresy*. It is also – in his view – patently ludicrous, which is what makes these 'Ebionites' such a laughing-stock and why their name, 'which in Hebrew means "Poor Man"' – clearly an honoured title coming directly out of the tradition of the Dead Sea Scrolls and the Community of James – 'attests to *the poverty of their intellect*'.

Eusebius goes on to tell us, what we already might have guessed, that

> They insisted on the *complete observance of the Law* and did not think that they could be *saved by Faith in Christ only*, but by a corresponding life.

This is the Jamesian position absolutely, both as reflected in the Letter ascribed to his name, which avers that 'Faith without works is dead' and where Abraham's 'Righteousness' or 'Justification' was concerned, that it is 'by Faith working with works and by his works his Faith was made

Perfect' (James 2:18–26). This is also the position of the Habakkuk *Pesher* from Qumran, addressed to 'the Doers of the *Torah* in the House of Judah' *not the non-Doers of the Torah outside it*. This, too, comes in exposition in the Habakkuk *Pesher* of the all-important Habakkuk 2:4, 'the Righteous shall live by his Faith', and is as well, importantly enough, attached to an allusion to being *'saved from the House of Judgement'*, in this context and, as it is so designated later in the *Pesher*, the 'Judgement that God would make' in 'the Last' or at 'the End of Days'.[6]

Eusebius also goes on to report that the group he is calling Ebionites 'evinced great *zeal in the precise observance of the Law*' and thought that Paul's Letters 'ought to be rejected, for they called him an *Apostate from the Law*'. Here, of course, is our 'Zealot' terminology once again, now directed where we would expect it to be. Where Paul is concerned, one cannot get much more specific than this. We shall hear more about opinions such as these, when it comes to considering some of Epiphanius' more specific and rather colourful – if not outright scandalous – contentions concerning Paul's origins (again, no doubt, based on Ebionite works). But regardless of what period one may think these comments of Eusebius refer to – a second-century CE sect or third-century CE sect tending towards Gnosticism – the relevance of these strictures to the first century and, in fact, the parallel positions of Qumran and the Jerusalem Community is hard to gainsay.

Finally Eusebius comments on how 'they observe the Sabbath and the rest of the ceremonial discipline of the Jews', by which he means the Law. Eusebius adds to this one a second group – probably representing a later stage – who, in addition to accepting the more orthodox virgin birth, also celebrate 'rites like ours in commemoration of the resurrection of the Saviour' – obviously meaning Easter. In any event, all seem to have 'used the Gospel of the Hebrews, esteeming the others as of but little value'. For this, in his view, they are to be considered 'Poor'.

Judas the Brother of James, Thaddaeus, and Judas the Zealot

We can now turn to more extensive data relating to Jesus' putative *third brother*, Judas ('Judas *Thomas*'/'Thaddaeus'). The extant notices about him are particularly interesting. I think we can grant that he is the individual called 'Judas the brother of James' in the New Testament Letter of Jude, not to mention the individual in Apostle lists following 'James the [son] of Alphaeus' and 'Simon the Cananaean' ('Simon who was called *Zēlōtēs*'), variously referred to as 'Thaddaeus' (Mark 3:18), 'Lebbaeus surnamed Thaddaeus' (Matt. 10:3), and, most realistically, 'Judas [the brother] of James' (Luke 6:16 and Acts 1:14).

It should also be noted, and this is important, that he is always followed by reference to another 'Judas' – this time, Judas *Iscariot*, called in the Gospel of John either 'the *Iscariot*' or 'the *son*' or 'brother of *Simon Iscariot*'. We have already noted this Judas' relationship to 'Simon the Cananite' or 'Zealot' in these lists and the one notice in the *Epistula Apostolorum* calling him 'Judas Zēlōtēs' or 'Judas the Zealot'. Interestingly enough, this too, it will be recalled, was immediately followed by reference to a 'Cephas' separate from 'Peter', who could be only either Simeon bar Cleophas or Simon the Zealot.

Now comes the rub. In an otherwise fairly conventional apocryphal text descending to us through the Syriac, the Apostolic Constitutions, which presents testamentary bequests from the various Apostles concerning Church organization; when it comes to discussing the bequest of 'Lebbaeus surnamed Thaddaeus' – this the clear nomenclature of the Gospel of Matthew only reversed – two variant manuscripts note he was also 'called *Judas the Zealot*'.[7]

The date of the Apostolic Constitutions is contended. Some have it as a typical second-century document – others earlier; according to some scholars (depending on how conventional its conventionalities are thought to be) later. Like the Pseudoclementines, also attested in Syriac, this text refers to James quite straightforwardly as 'the brother of Christ according to the flesh' – simply that, no attempt being made at equivocation or evasion. In addition, as in the *Recognitions*, the point is stressed that James was 'appointed Bishop of Jerusalem by *the Lord himself*'.[8]

In another interesting note in one of these variant manuscripts, following directly upon the one about 'Lebbaeus surnamed Thaddaeus' also being called 'Judas the Zealot', the claim is made that 'Simon the Cananaean', who directly follows 'James the son of Alphaeus' and 'Thaddaeus' in Matthew and Mark, was '*crowned with martyrdom in Judea in the reign of Domitian*'. This is very interesting, because it concurs with suggestions made above that the executions under Trajan of Simeon bar Cleophas and the grandsons of Jesus' brother Judas have been transposed in our sources – at least Simeon's has.

Since there were clearly Messianic troubles under Domitian – which were to be expected under such a Nero-like and seemingly demented Ruler – then the execution of Simeon bar Cleophas (under whose leadership the purported 'Flight' of the Jerusalem Community across Jordan to Pella would have occurred, if early Church traditions are to be credited – all the more so if Qumran materials can be taken into consideration, a question depending on chronology not content) could be put under Domitian's rule not Trajan's, when it more likely occurred.

This neatly fits in with the possibility of Josephus transposing traditions about the family of Judas the Galilean with those of the family of Jesus in the New Testament, or vice versa. Who, for instance, were these two 'Sons of Thunder' who purportedly 'drank the Cup' that Jesus drank (Mark 3:17 and 10:39)? The first pair of candidates that present themselves are (as we suggested), of course, James the Just 'the brother of Jesus' and this other brother, called, according to Luke, 'Simon the Zealot', but also possibly Simeon bar Cleophas.

The second and even more appropriate possibility would be 'James and Simon, the two sons of Judas the Galilean'. For some reason Josephus neglected to mention their crucifixon and Theudas' beheading preceding them in the *Jewish War*. Why? Nevertheless, in the *Antiquities* twenty years later, as we have seen, he *does* mention their execution, placing it under the Governorship of Tiberius Alexander, Philo's backsliding nephew, around 48 CE. In fact, he mentions it in the same breath he mentions 'the Famine' (*c.* 46–48 CE), directly following that of Theudas, whose beheading we have already remarked in connection with Jesus' *third brother* Judas and Acts' 'James the brother of John, with the sword' at about the same time.

As we already saw, too, the first pair of Jameses and Simons *did* 'drink the Cup' that Jesus drank, since they really *were crucified* in a preventive execution – also seemingly around Passover time. One can see how excitable the Jewish crowds became at festivals of this kind from Josephus' account of the riot that ensued after the Roman soldier on the wall or portico of the Temple exposed himself to the Jewish crowd at Passover, not long after under Cumanus, which resulted in a stampede in which, according to Josephus, 'thousands' were killed. Though undoubtedly exaggerated, it should be appreciated that recently a stampede occurred in a tunnel at a parallel festival, the Muslim Pilgrimage to Mecca, in which hundreds were similarly trampled to death.

It is not incurious, as previously observed, that it is the deletion of the mention of the execution of these two brothers in Acts that causes the anachronism regarding the note about Theudas coming *before* the Census of Cyrenius and the Revolt led by Judas the Galilean – all oddly put in the mouth of the *Pharisee* 'Gamaliel' as well (5:36–37 – should we rather read here the Pharisee 'Josephus' instead?). For Acts, the sequence, as will be recalled, was the deleted reference to the two brothers, 'James and Simon', and Theudas following the reference to Judas the Galilean. These proceed into the stoning of Stephen, Philip meeting the Treasurer of the Ethiopian Queen 'on the way to Gaza', Peter's visit to the Roman Legionnaire Cornelius in Caesarea, the 'prophet' called 'Agabus' coming down from Jerusalem to Antioch to predict the Famine 'that came to pass under Claudius', the beheading of 'James the brother of John', Peter's arrest, and finally the introduction of the *real* James.

For Josephus, as we have also seen, the order is: the visit of Simon the Head of his own Assembly in Jerusalem to Agrippa I's household in Caesarea, the beheading of Theudas, the Famine, followed by the mention of Queen Helen of Adiabene's Famine-relief efforts (which we shall now proceed to treat below), the preventive crucifixion of Judas the Galilean's *two sons* 'James and Simon', the attack on the Emperor's messenger Stephen in the midst of problems between Galileans and Samaritans and Greco-Syrian Legionnaires and Jews at Caesarea, and the stoning of James – itself followed by the riot led by one Saulus, a 'kinsman of Agrippa', leading up to the War against Rome.

That there are confusions, overlaps, and evasions going on here should be evident, but what precisely is at the root of them is more difficult to discern. Just as Josephus seems to have transposed the riot led by Saulus in the 40s – as reported in the Pseudoclementines and reflected even in Acts – to the 60s, so Acts has transposed the stoning of James in the 60s, *refurbishing it into the stoning of Stephen* in the 40s. It is possible (though not very probable) that Josephus somehow transposed the crucifixions of Jesus' brother Jude's two grandsons and that of Simeon bar Cleophas either under Domitian or Trajan to an earlier period. It is impossible to say. Simeon bar Cleophas *does seem to have been crucified*, however fabulously Christian tradition seems to have exaggerated his lifespan.

If executions of this kind did take place under Domitian and not Trajan, Josephus would have been alive to see and record them, albeit anachronistically, just as for some reason he omitted the executions of Judas the Galilean's two sons and of Theudas in his earlier *War*. How could he have failed to record these things then? Is it Agrippa II, residing in Rome, giving Josephus this new information, or is it Tiberius Alexander, Agrippa II's brother-in-law and, as Titus' deputy, the destroyer of Jerusalem? However these things may be, this notice about 'the martyrdom of Simon the Cananaean' taking place under *the reign of Domitian* from a variant manuscript of the Syriac Apostolic Constitutions has an accuracy and prescience about it that belies mere creative imagination or hearsay.

The execution of Theudas, immediately preceding these things, is, also no doubt, an important event to consider. The two variant notices about 'Lebbaeus surnamed Thaddaeus' in the Apostolic Constitutions, read:

> Thaddaeus, *also called Lebbaeus* and who was *surnamed Judas the Zealot,* *preached the truth to the Edessenes and the people of Mesopotamia,* when Abgarus ruled over Edessa.

One should first of all, as already remarked, note the reversal here of how this reference to 'Thaddeus' appears in Matthew and, in fact, the normative Apostolic Constitutions text. The variant text is more logical, since 'Thaddaeus' would appear to be a name, while 'Lebbaeus' a title of some kind – possibly, as previously observed, a garbling of 'Alphaeus', itself a garbling of 'Cleophas'. Directly following this, the notice also adds the interesting information that 'he was buried in *Berytus in Phoenicia*'.[9]

We have already remarked the kind of fun and games that went on in this Berytus or Beirut after the destruction of Jerusalem in 70 CE and Titus' celebration of his brother Domitian's birthday there, and Berytus does seem to have been a favourite possession of both Agrippa I and II. The information about 'Thaddaeus' or 'Judas the Zealot' being buried – after perhaps being executed – there is very precise and not found in any other sources. It is stated very matter-of-factly and, to the author's ears, while admittedly prejudiced, does have the ring of truth.

The point about this putative *third brother* of Jesus – since he is distinctly called 'Judas [the brother] of James' in Luke and Acts – like the second brother, 'Simon the Zealot', being 'a *Zealot*', is extremely interesting. Of course, it accords with the notice in the 'We Document' narrative in Acts – James speaking to Paul – about the majority of James' 'Jerusalem Church' supporters being 'Zealots for the Law' and we have already heard the same thing about this 'Judas' in the *Epistula Apostolorum* above. It is, in any event, something we would have expected from previous analyses, even if we had not encountered it so baldly and plainly presented in this variant manuscript of the Apostolic Constitutions here.

But what does it mean? Well, first of all it places all these individuals squarely in the 'Zealot' tradition. But secondly, it links up with a host of traditions – again mostly based on Syriac sources, but also summarized in Eusebius, writing in Greek and known throughout the Christian world –

about one 'Thomas' or, more accurately, 'Judas *Thomas*'. We have already encountered this Apostle in the Gospel attributed to his name from the so-called 'Gnostic' texts at Nag Hammadi. This Gospel begins quite matter-of-factly with the words:

> These are the *secret words*, which the Living Jesus spoke, and which *Didymus* Judas Thomas wrote down.

There are also Acts attributed to Thomas extant in Greek and Syriac, probably going back to a Syriac original, in which culture Thomas always bears the name of 'Judas' – 'Judas Thomas who is also called *Didymus*' – exactly as in the prologue to the Gospel of Thomas above (1.1).[10] In fact in these Acts, in which Thomas is always the custodian of the mysterious or esoteric words of Christ, he is not only identified with this brother of Jesus; but, as the Aramaic '*Thoma*' – echoed by the Greek '*Didymus*' – implies, his *twin* brother as well.[11]

We can dismiss doubling and overlaps with 'Thaddaeus', 'Lebbaeus', and 'Judas the brother of James' in the Synoptic Gospel lists. We can also dismiss dissembling, as in the Gospel of John's 'Twin Twin' equivocations, themselves accompanied by the themes of 'doubting' and 'eating' with Jesus which overlap Luke's account about Jesus' appearance to Cleopas and the unidentified other 'in the Way' to Emmaus and to James in the Gospel of the Hebrews.

In fact, the traditional Gospel Apostle lists, as we have seen, include few individuals of any real substance, and these lists with their variations have been transmitted into a plethora of other traditions, which occasionally provide additional bits of interesting information. For instance, in the Acts of Thomas, Thomas' burial scene contains elements of the empty-tomb scenario about Jesus in the Gospels, including the ever-present, tell-tale element of the 'linen clothes' again (Acts of Th. 12.168–70).

Of course, Thomas is not only important in Edessa and Mesopotamia in these variant manuscripts of the Apostolic Constitutions, but traditions about his activities go as far east as India, the place of his supposed burial in these apocryphal Acts, even though we have already seen this to have been Berytus in some manuscripts of the Apostolic Constitutions above. This is also the case for the Acts of Thaddaeus. But aside from this kind of cultural imperialism (Santiago de Compostela in Spain also honours traditions associated with its purported 'St James', themselves probably based on real materials about James the brother of Jesus' burial marker in the

Kedron Valley beneath the Pinnacle of the Temple in Jerusalem), Thomas is almost always presented in association with 'his *Disciple*' Thaddaeus (*thus*) in connection with traditions about the conversion of someone called King Abgarus or Agbarus (possibly a title having something to do with the allusion 'Great One' in Syriac or Aramaic) of the Edessenes or Osrhoeans – the last, a clear transliteration of *Assyrians*.

The 'Judas who Preached the Truth to the Edessenes'

This story is known as the conversion of King Agbarus. Actually in most sources he is called Abgarus, which is more correct, but in Latin the letters are often reversed, or replaced, as we saw, with letters like 'u', 'r', or 'c', and we prefer this other version of the name for reasons that will eventually become clear. This legend is, interestingly enough, first recorded in an actual written document by Eusebius himself, who for a change does not claim to have had it from other writers, but literally to have transcribed and translated it himself from an original Syriac chancellery office document in the Royal Archives of Edessa! At the end Eusebius actually provides a Syriac date to it, approximately 29–30 CE.[12]

Whatever the veracity of his claim, the materials do appear very old, that is, before the time of Eusebius, who hardly ranks as a creative writer. We shall, in fact, be able to detect their reflection just beneath the surface of Acts. Though some scholars – jaundiced as ever – take a dim view of them, trying to accord them a *later* rather than an *earlier* date, they are very widespread in the Syriac sources with so many multiple developments and divergences that it is hard to believe they could all be based on Eusebius' poor efforts.

In all these sources, Thomas, that is, Judas Thomas, sends out Thaddaeus – here our original conjunction of the two names again – after the Ascension of Jesus to evangelize the Edessenes (this is also the point about 'Judas the Zealot' in the Apostolic Constitutions above); and after this joins him there himself, ultimately travelling further into Mesopotamia and then on to India, as in the Acts of Thomas – the source of Indian legends circulating around his name.[13]

Edessa is an important centre of early Christianity, probably more important than the centre Acts attributes to Paul and his colleagues in nearby Antioch (11:20–26). Its cultural heritage is claimed by both Armenian and Syriac Christians, as are its kings. In fact, in the Greek, there were originally numerous 'Antioch's, as we have seen – 'Antiochus' being the name of the father of the first Seleucid King following Alexander the Great in this region, who apparently liked honouring the memory of his father. Edessa was one of these, being called Antiochia-by-Callirhoe or Edessa Orrhoe, the source of its present name in Turkey, 'Urfa'. So was another town at the southern tip of the Tigris and Euphrates, Antiochia Charax or Charax Spasini, which will figure prominently in our story.[14] This will make for very interesting mix-ups indeed – as it does in the Paul being at 'Antioch' story.

Aficionados of searches of this kind even trace the Holy Shroud of Turin back to this city, recent carbon-dating notwithstanding. Indeed, it is claimed in the literature associated with the Agbar/Abgar Legend that Jesus sent his image to the city.[15] Out of this also has sprung up a lively literature circulating around the individual 'Addai', a name clearly not unrelated to 'Thaddaeus' or vice versa, and even the name Edessa would appear to be based on a not unsimilar phonetic root, not to mention the name of Adiabene just a *little further east*. In fact, Adi is a religious name endemic to this region, revered even today by the quasi-pagans extant in the area called '*Yazidi*s'. We shall see below how it is also picked up in Muhammad's stories about ''Ād and Thamūd', and 'the Prophet' sent to the former, 'their brother Hūd' (in Hebrew, 'Yehudah' or 'Judas'), not to mention the one called in Arabic, 'Sāliḥ' or 'the Righteous One', sent to the latter.[16]

Eusebius himself is already referring to Thomas as Judas Thomas.[17] While acknowledging that Judas Thomas was an Apostle, he is confused about 'Thaddaeus', whom he appreciates appears with 'Barnabas' and 'Cephas' as members of 'the Seventy' in Clement of Alexandria's *Hypotyposes*. This is also something of the case in the Apostolic Constitutions above, 'the Seventy' being the Seventy Disciples or Elders stemming from Jewish ideas of the Seventy Nations or language-groups of mankind, as well as 'the Seventy' it took to make up a proper 'Assembly' or 'Sanhedrin'.[18]

In fact, Eusebius seems to be presenting the exchange of letters between Jesus and Agbarus, the King of the Osrhoeans, as an answer to some other materials that had recently appeared from Roman chancellery records, called the '*Acti Pilati*' that he considered scurrilous. The presently extant Acts of Pilate – so-called because of their attribution to Pilate – are rather pro-Christian documents attesting to Pilate's recognition of Jesus, but these other so-called 'Acts', which appear to have represented themselves as the *actual* administrative records of Pilate's Governorship, upset Eusebius so much because they claimed a different date for the Crucifixion of Jesus – around 21 CE.[19]

In truth the Romans did keep very careful administrative records, even in the provinces, and it would have been surprising if records such as these – called, in fact, 'acts' – had not once existed, but the 'Acti Pilati' Eusebius so rails against were obviously being circulated by enemies of Christianity. They claimed that Jesus was crucified in the seventh year of the reign of Tiberius, which commenced in the year 14 CE. Eusebius counters with the statement from Josephus that Pilate came to Palestine in 26 CE, thereby claiming these 'Acts' to be fraudulent, but there is no real proof of this proposition other than one remark about Pilate Josephus made.

Josephus himself might well have been mistaken about this and it would seem foolish purposefully to circulate something that could on the surface, anyhow, appear so patently fraudulent. If Pilate did come earlier, a 21 CE date for the Crucifixion of Jesus would help markedly in explaining why someone like Paul, who seems to have begun his career in the 30s, knows so little factually about him. It would also go a long way towards explaining the 'twenty-year' period of 'groping for the Way', referred to in the Damascus Document from the time of the death of the Messianic 'Root of Planting' to the rise of the Righteous Teacher.[20]

But however these things may be, for those who would dispute the age of traditions like that of the Agbarus legend, it should be appreciated that Hippolytus, a century before Eusebius, whose testimony about Josephus' so-called 'Essenes' we already found so full of startling precision and extra detail above, was already aware of the tradition concerning 'Judas the Zealot' and the Edessenes above, not to mention the one about 'Lebbaeus surnamed Thaddaeus' or 'Thaddaeus surnamed Lebbaeus' in the two variant editions of the Apostolic Constitutions being the same as 'Judas the Zealot'.

As another work attributed to Hippolytus puts this in a listing of the Twelve Apostles, it now combines both saying:

> Judas, also called Lebbaeus, preached to the people of Edessa and to all Mesopotamia, and fell asleep at Berytus and was buried there.[21]

On the face of it, this is absolutely startling testimony, because the Hippolytus work – if authentic, it would be from the second–third centuries – now combines the note about 'Judas the Zealot being buried in Berytus' from the variant manuscripts of the Apostolic Constitutions with the one about 'Lebbaeus being surnamed Thaddaeus' in the tradition represented by the Gospel of Matthew.

But in its listing of the Twelve Apostles this work (again ascribed to

Hippolytus) goes even further than this. Moving over to the matter of 'James the son of Alphaeus', obviously the first of our three brothers, it now by implication identifies him with James the Just, the brother of Jesus, saying:

> *James the son of Alphaeus*, when preaching in Jerusalem, *was stoned to death by the Jews and was buried there beside the Temple.*[22]

Nothing could be clearer than this, which is nothing but our tradition about James the brother of the Lord, called the Just One in all early Church sources. Whoever wrote this was unerringly prescient.

Clearly, by the end of the second century or the beginning of the third century, if this listing is authentic – and it certainly has the ring of authenticity – Hippolytus as far away as Rome already knew that 'James the son of Alphaeus' was *the same* as the James called 'the brother of the Lord' but, as he was not yet privy to Hegesippus' traditions about the latter's death (being transmitted at approximately the same time), he does not put them all together as relating to the same person. But this is certainly very important testimony for identifying 'James the son of Alphaeus' – 'James the Less' at a later point in Mark – with James the brother of the Lord, and, no doubt too, because of the garbling inherent in the name 'Alphaeus', 'James the son of Cleophas'.

In addition, in another fragment ascribed to him, found together with the previous list, purporting now to be a catalogue of 'the Seventy Apostles', by which is clearly meant 'the Seventy' – 'the Elders' or 'Disciples' of other reckonings – Hippolytus is presented as listing the first four of these – clearly meant to approximate the names of Jesus' brothers – as: 'James the Lord's brother, Bishop of Jerusalem', the second being 'Cleopas Bishop of Jerusalem'.[23] The spelling here is the spelling Luke uses in the matter of the first Emmaus Road appearance by Jesus to 'Cleopas', and there can be little doubt that what Hippolytus is presented as meaning or implying here – if not Luke – is that the recipient of this appearance *is* 'Simeon bar Cleophas', the second Bishop of the Jerusalem Church according to all sources.

Then he lists, regardless of contradictions as to who is or is not an 'Apostle', 'Matthias who filled the vacancy in the number of the Twelve Apostles' – it will be remembered, he supposedly filled the place of another 'Judas' and defeated a candidate called 'Joseph Barsabas Justus', nor should one forget the 'Alphaeus' cognomen tied to that Levi who surrogates for 'Matthew' in Mark 2:14 above – and fourth, 'Thaddaeus, who conveyed the epistle to Augarus [*thus*].'[24] In other words – if this recording is accurate –

Hippolytus has not yet put this 'Thaddaeus' together with 'Judas also called Lebbaeus' (whom he described 'as preaching to the people of Edessa and all Mesopotamia' in the listing of the Apostles attributed to him), even though the Gospels of Matthew and Luke (not to mention these variant manuscripts of the Apostolic Constitutions) have already done this for him – Luke quite straightforwardly calling him 'Judas the brother of James'.

But even more important than this, if we go back to the previous listing, this text attributed to Hippolytus now calls 'Simon the Cananaean' (or 'Zealot'),

> the son of Clopas, who is also [the brother of] Judas and became Bishop of Jerusalem after James the Just and fell asleep and was buried there at the age of 120 years.

Aside from again stressing the matter of Simeon bar Cleophas' apparent longevity, this important notice clearly identifies Simon the Cananite or Cananaean (that is, 'the Zealot') with Simeon bar Cleophas in a straightforward manner, as we have already done and the variant manuscript of the Apostolic Constitutions does as well. In addition, it affirms, as the fragment attributed to Papias quoted earlier, that 'Clopas' – regardless of what spelling one uses – was basically the father of these four children. It is hard to believe that all these fragments, whatever one makes of their origins, could be wrong on all these matters, especially since they make so much good sense!

The reference to 'Judas' too here – however garbled (we have added the phrase, 'the brother of', to clarify it) – again links Simon the Zealot, the son of Cleophas, *the second successor to Jesus in the Church at Jerusalem*, with Judas, not only in the matter of both being 'Zealots' or 'Cananaeans' – this being the basic implication of the notice as it stands – but also as far as both having the same father, once more our ever-present Cleopas, Clopas, or Alphaeus. It also relates – as over and over again in these notices – to the two *Iscariot*s, both, again also, called in the Johannine tradition if not the Synoptic, 'Judas' and 'Simon'.

The Conversion of King Agbar according to Eusebius

Equally important, if authentic – and in view of all the factors noted above, we think it is – this notice from Hippolytus on 'the Seventy Apostles' also provides vivid testimony that the Agbarus legend is a good deal older than Eusebius' recording of it and that the latter was not fantasizing or indulging in creative writing when he said he got it from the official archives of Edessa. Additionally, as in the case of Eusebius, it is already associating this tradition with the name of Thaddaeus (the 'Judas also called Lebbaeus') and our 'Judas *Thomas*' or 'Judas the brother of James', 'who preached the truth to the Edessenes and all Mesopotamia'.

Equally important too, as we have seen, Hippolytus or a copyist has already begun garbling or mixing up Abgarus' or Agbarus' name, calling him here 'Augarus'. We shall see why this becomes so important below. For Eusebius, the whole is based on Syriac sources and, as Hippolytus before him, Eusebius quotes these as calling Thaddaeus both an 'Apostle and one of the Seventy' and directly involves him, in addition, with an individual, 'Judas', he too now admits 'is also *Thomas*'. Interestingly enough, Eusebius' source presents the courier in this correspondence as someone called 'Ananias', the same name as the individual Acts introduces as Paul's associate when the latter comes to Damascus (9:12–17). It should not be forgotten too that at this point Paul was staying at the 'house' of someone called '*Judas*' on a 'street called Straight' (9:11)!

As we shall see, Josephus too mentions an individual he calls 'Ananias', who plays an important role in the parallel conversion of Queen Helen at approximately the same time – whether to Judaism or Christianity is not always clear in our sources.[25] Though for Josephus this is Judaism, for Armenian sources, which are also interested in the matter of Helen's conversion, it is, as the conversion of King Abgar, to Christianity. What is even more interesting is that these sources, which see Abgar as an *Armenian* King (which may simply mean he spoke Aramaic; he certainly was King of Edessa), claim that he had allied himself to Aretas, King of Petra in Arabia, thus increasing the pan-Arab ties among these 'Arab' Kings.

Therefore, when Herod Antipas – that is, 'Herod the Tetrarch' – repudiated Aretas' daughter to marry his niece Herodias, 'a circumstance in connection with which he had John the Baptist put to death' (this from Armenian historian Moses of Chorene in the fifth century – or perhaps later – echoing Josephus in the first), King Abgar gave Aretas military help in his defeat of Herod, by which Divine 'Vengeance was taken for the death of John the Baptist'.[26] However inflated such claims may at first appear, there may indeed be an element of truth in this idea of a link between these 'Arab' Kings, both as to history and in the light of the political axes developing here.

Later Herodian Kings, like Aristobulus, Herodias' nephew who was married to Herodias' daughter Salome, are put by the Romans in control of Lesser or Lower Armenia, as we saw. But, as opposed to them, the family developing around Helen of Adiabene just a little further east seems to have been highly esteemed in Palestine by resistance forces. Her son Izates, the convert to Judaism whom Josephus calls her 'only begotten', seems to have preferred circumcision. On the other hand, Helen, responding to the teaching of the Ananias just mentioned and another unnamed companion who has a lot in common with Paul, seems to have had a horror of the practice – and by extension, therefore, *actual* conversion to Judaism – which she appears to think will put Izates in ill repute with his subjects.[27]

This Izates will have an older brother named 'Monobazus' – Josephus also uses 'Bazeus' for this name, seemingly like 'Agbarus' (in some Latin manuscripts even 'Albarus'), a hereditary name or title within the family – and another, seemingly younger, son or 'kinsman' also named Monobazus, who is later one of the 'Jewish' Leaders in the Uprising against Rome. We shall have more to say about him and another of these 'kinsmen', his brother 'Kenedaeos' presently, but, for the moment, suffice it to record that they are among the first martyrs in this War.

These same Syriac sources even claim that Helen had originally been one of Agbarus' wives, another individual Josephus is calling 'Bazeus' or 'Monobazus', and also that he was *one of her brothers*, in consequence of which marriage, he allowed her the Kingdom further east we are calling 'Adiabene' (roughly equivalent to presentday Kurdistan). It should be appreciated, these kings had numerous wives, some merely formal arrangements for the purposes of child-bearing and other alliances, some even sisters or half-sisters. This is also an arrangement attested to in the Old Testament *vis-à-vis Abraham* (Gen. 20:12), who purportedly marries his half-sister, Sarah, and was said to have come from this area, Haran in Northern Syria and Edessa being contiguous and part of the same region – what Eusebius and others are calling at this point 'the Land of the Osrhoeans'.

The association of this area with Abraham – whether real or legend is immaterial – will also have great importance for Paul's constant evocation of Abraham in his writings, not to mention Muhammad in succession to him, whom as we shall see below is absorbing the traditions from this area six centuries later.

If Helen was, indeed, the wife of this 'Bazeus' or 'Monobazus' and Izates his son – and, it must be observed, Izates' parentage is very obscure even in Josephus – whether before putting her away or not putting her away, as the case may have been; this would draw the stories of these two conversions – his to 'Christianity' and hers to 'Judaism', depending on the eye of the beholder – even closer still. We shall see how materials in Acts by implication give credence to some of this in a completely unexpected and very powerful way.

Before moving on, one should note again how the name of her Kingdom too, 'Adiabene', which may simply have been a sub-province of this King – 'Bazeus' in Josephus; 'Abgarus' in Syriac and Armenian sources – incorporates a root, once again, phonetically parallel to the name, we have noted above, perennially associated with this region and this ominipresent Apostle *Addai*. As later Syriac documents would have it, quoting Eusebius:

> Thomas the Apostle, one of the Twelve, by a divine impulse, sent Thaddaeus, who was himself also numbered among the Seventy Disciples of Christ [this in accord with our other materials], to Edessa to be a preacher and Evangelist of the teaching of Christ.[28]

These documents also incorporate the correspondence Eusebius says he translated from the chancellery records of Edessa, to wit, how 'after the Ascension of Jesus, *Judas who is called Thomas*, sent him *Thaddaeus the Apostle, one of the Seventy*'. Note how the confusion between Thaddaeus 'as an Apostle' and 'one of the Seventy', already evident in the Hippolytus fragment and here in Eusebius (not to mention the Gospels), continues.

Eusebius returns to this affair again at the beginning of the Second Book of his *History* immediately after his discussion of how – now quoting Clement of Alexandria – there were 'two Jameses, one called *the Just*, who was thrown from a wing of the Temple and beaten to death with a fuller's club, and another, who was beheaded'. Eusebius now repeats what he has just said earlier, also quoted in the Syriac sources:

> But *Thomas*, under a divine impulse, sent *Thaddaeus* as preacher and Evangelist to proclaim the doctrine of Christ, as we have shown from the public documents found there.[29]

The sequencing of these events as Eusebius begins his Second Book, leading into Hegesippus' long presentation of the death of James is, as previously remarked, interesting. First he mentions the election to replace 'the *Traitor* Judas' and then the stoning of Stephen '*by the murderers of the Lord*'. But immediately after this, he introduces James as 'the brother of our Lord' and 'the son of Joseph' – no 'cousin' relationship here, though Mary is called 'the Virgin' – it is, therefore, the previous-wife theory. Here Eusebius immediately adds, as we saw earlier, that 'he was the first elected to the Episcopate of the Church at Jerusalem', only the point about being direct 'from Jesus' hand' is missing.

The implication, however, is that this event happened *directly* after Jesus' death, so if we discard the material from Acts about 'Judas *Iscariot*' and 'Stephen', then we do have roughly the proper sequence of events in the early Church. Eusebius, of course, does take the time to point out the translation of Stephen's name as 'Crown', associating it with his being 'the First' to 'carry off the martyrs' Crown', and we have already noted the relation of this to the *Nazirite* 'Crown' of the long hair worn by martyrs such as James. He then gives the notice from Clement about,

> The Lord imparting the gift of Knowledge to James the Just, to John, and to Peter after his resurrection. These delivered it to the rest of the Apostles, and they to the Seventy, of whom Barnabas was one.

Then the notice about Thomas sending Thaddaeus to 'the King of the Osrhoeans' – the Assyrians. The proximity of all these matters, bunched so soon after the death of 'the Lord', is interesting and, as we saw, after making the proper deletions, one does get a sense of the approximate history.

The Background of Agabus' Prediction of the Famine in Acts

Seven chapters further along, now following Acts as a source, Eusebius refers both to 'the Famine', because of which Paul and Barnabas were delegated by the brothers at the Church in Antioch to proceed to Jerusalem to bring Famine relief (Acts 11:28), and the martyrdom of James the son of Zebedee 'with the sword' (Acts 12:1).[30] At this point, Eusebius returns to Josephus as his source, quoting the passage about the 'impostor' or 'Deceiver called Theudas', who persuaded the multitude that 'he was *a prophet*' (it is from here that Acts takes its material about 'Agabus' being a 'prophet') and that he would take them to the other side of the Jordan – that is, Perea where John the Baptist had been executed – and repeat Joshua's miracle in the biblical Book under his name of 'dividing the Jordan at his command'. One should keep one's eyes on the parallels here with the miracles, he has already recited, done by 'Thaddaeus' – and in later Syriac sources, 'Judas *Thomas*' – in the Land of the Osrhoeans.

Eusebius, rather, immediately follows up these things with the story of

Queen Helen, referred to in most title epitomes of Eusebius' work as 'the Queen of the Osrhoeans'. This is triggered by his mention at the end of the preceding Chapter Eleven (giving the citation about the miracle Theudas – who called himself 'a prophet', but whom Josephus rather calls 'an impostor' – undertook to do) of the Famine again 'that took place under Claudius'. Eusebius does so, because his source, Josephus, also evoked this Famine directly following the story of Theudas' beheading and immediately preceding his mention of the crucifixion of James and Simon, the two sons of Judas the Galilean, 'who caused the people to revolt when Cyrenius came to make a census of the possessions of the Jews'.[31] As in Acts, where their deletion causes the anachronism of Theudas being described as coming *before* Judas the Galilean, Eusebius also declines to mention these two sons.

Of course, the reason Eusebius mentions Helen here is that Josephus did so as well at this point, describing how 'Queen Helen bought corn in Egypt at great cost and distributed it to those that were in need', because of 'the great Famine that happened in Judea'. The mention of this Famine at this point directly follows a brief aside about Tiberius Alexander, who succeeded Fadus (44–46), Theudas' executor, as Governor in 46 CE and whose 'Piety was not like that of his wealthy father [Philo of Alexandria's brother] the *Richest* among all his contemporaries'. Rather, as Josephus puts it, Tiberius Alexander 'did not continue in the Religion of his father'.[32]

Eusebius, following Acts once again, now turns to Barnabas and Paul and their Famine-relief mission 'to the Elders' (*Presbyters*) in Jerusalem taking the funds that were being sent up by 'the Disciples' at 'Antioch'. We are now patently in a contemporaneous situation. Eusebius had mentioned this mission and the Famine eight chapters before in Chapter Three in connection with 'Agabus' prophecy', the only problem being that Paul, in his corresponding description of these years in Galatians, *never* mentions such a journey or mission to Jerusalem. In fact, as we saw, he is quite emphatic to the contrary, saying in a statement leading up to his introduction of Peter and James that has over two millennia become almost proverbial:

> When it pleased God . . . by His Grace to reveal His Son in me that I should announce him as the Good News among the Nations, I *did not confer with people of flesh and blood*, nor did I go up to [confer – meaning Jerusalem] with *those who were Apostles before me*, but rather went away *into Arabia*

and [from thence] again *returned to Damascus*. Then after three years I went up to Jerusalem to make the acquaintance of Peter, though of the other Apostles, I saw none except *James the brother of the Lord*. (Gal. 1:15–19)

Here Paul assures his respondents in his own inimical style – as we have already seen as well – 'now the things that I write you, by God, I do not lie', continuing, 'then I came into the regions of Syria and Cilicia' – the regions of concern to us at this point in the discussion (Gal. 1:20–21).

To review, once again, the chronology: Paul points out that this was the reason he was 'unknown by sight among the Assemblies in Judea which were in Christ' ('they heard only that he who formerly persecuted us was now announcing the Good News'), before finally explaining, 'then after fourteen years I went up to Jerusalem again with Barnabas, taking Titus with me also' (Gal. 1:22–2:1). These 'fourteen years' put us somewhere into the early 50s, well past the time of 'the Famine' reported by Josephus.

Not only this, but in describing this *second* trip, Paul makes it clear it was not for Famine-relief activities, but rather he

> went up because of a revelation [*apocalypsin* – the same word he used earlier in Galatians 1:16 to describe God's 'revelation' of 'His Son' in him] to lay before them the Good News which I announce among the Nations .

Paul says he did this 'privately' (meaning, therefore, that he had not been summoned) to 'those reckoned as important' – the same persons he goes on to speak of as 'those reputed to be something' or 'reputed to be Pillars', whose importance 'nothing conferred' – so that 'I should not be running or have run in vain' (Gal. 2:2–9).

Paul uses this 'running' imagery again in 5:7 to encourage his communities who were 'running well', not to fall back to 'circumcision' and 'the Law'. Paul returns to it again, as we have seen, in the crucial section of 1 Corinthians 9:24–26, where he sets forth his philosophy of 'running the course to win', as opposed to the 'weak' people with 'their weak consciences' – including presumably James – who oppose him. Interestingly enough, even this imagery of 'running' reappears in the Habakkuk *Pesher* (Hab. 2:2), where it is applied to the Scriptural exegeses of the Righteous Teacher of Habakkuk 2:3 on 'the Delay of the *Parousia*' and Habakkuk 2:4.[33] In 1 Corinthians, Paul mixes it with 'winning the Crown [*Stephanon*]' of stadium athletics generally, including boxing. Calculated to infuriate his opponents within the Movement, this is the imagery he uses generally in this letter in support of his position on eating 'things sacrificed to idols' and responding to 'those who would judge him' on the Authority he claims 'to eat and drink'.

In Galatians, Paul follows up these assertions with the problem about whether 'Titus who was with me, being a Greek [*Hellēn*], was obliged to be circumcised'. He grows extremely heated over this, as we saw, virtually snarling at the 'some who came from James' and 'those of the circumcision' (2:12). This mounts to a crescendo, as he airs this problem in the next few chapters in his protestation 'so your Enemy I have become by *speaking the Truth* to you' (4:16) and his wish that 'those throwing you into confusion would *cut themselves off*' – having the dual meaning of throw themselves out of the Movement, but also 'cut' their own sexual members 'off' (5:12).

Not only is this a pun on circumcising – which will bear heavily on the Queen Helen episode and the malevolent refraction of it we shall presently identify in Acts, showing that this was the issue that was so infuriating Paul; but also, it will be recalled, on the language in the Damascus Document from Qumran about the Children of Israel being 'cut off in the wilderness', because 'they *ate blood*'.

In fact, in chapters 3–4 of Galatians, proceeding towards this climax, Paul, in delineating his new theology of how Jesus' death redeems us 'from the curse of the Law', as previously remarked as well, arrives at how 'keeping days and months and times and years' – so important to the Qumran ethos, that they are called there the 'monthly flags and festivals of Glory' – are 'weak and beggarly elements' that reduce one to 'bondage' (Gal. 4:9–10). Not only do we have the 'weakness' language again here, but also a play on that of 'the Poor'.

In Acts' version of parallel events, which are at times so confusing as to be almost unfathomable, Stephen is stoned because of problems with so-called 'Hellenists' (6:9). Paul gets his vision 'in the Way' to Damascus, where Ananias meets him at the house of 'Judas' – perhaps our 'Judas surnamed Thaddaeus' or 'Judas Thomas' or some other – Ananias then also abets him in 'confounding the Jews who dwelt in Damascus' (9:22 – this playing off Paul's language above of the circumcisers throwing his communities 'into confusion', as well, possibly, as the 'Rechabite'-style language of 'dwelling in the Land of Damascus' in the Damascus Document).

Then, because '*the Jews were conspiring together* to put him to death', Paul escapes 'down the walls of Damascus in a basket and flees to Jerusalem to join himself to the Disciples' (9:23–28), no mention of any intervening trip here 'into Arabia' as in Galatians 1:17. In Jerusalem, Paul is 'with them' in their comings and goings, that is, the Apostles and Barnabas, 'speaking boldly in the Name of the Lord Jesus' (9:28). Again this is totally opposed to the testimony in Galatians. The 'Hellenists', as in the case of Stephen previously – by now the code should be pretty clear (read 'Zealots') – now wish 'to put him [Paul] to death', but 'the brothers brought him down to Caesarea' and sent him away to Tarsus, meaning overseas (9:29–30). The text adds at this point, probably playing, as we saw, on the parallel difficulties in Josephus' description of the same period, 'Then, indeed, the Assemblies throughout all of Judea and Galilee and Samaria had peace' (9:31).

Now there intervene the episodes about Peter learning 'not to call any man [or 'thing'] unclean' and to accept Gentiles – to the chagrin of '*those of the circumcision*' (10:14–11:2). After this, '*certain ones of them*, men from Cyprus and Cyrene [the same as those Hellenists from 'Cyrene', 'Cilicia', and 'Asia', persecuting Stephen above?] came to Antioch to announce the Good News to the Hellenists'. Previously 'they had spoken the word to *no one except Jews*' (11:19–20). This is the beginning of Acts' picture of the Church 'in Antioch', where 'the Disciples were first called Christians' (11:26).

Two chapters later, Acts lists the founding members of this 'Church' or 'Assembly' as 'Barnabas', who had supposedly gone back to Tarsus to get Paul, 'bringing him to Antioch' (11:25), 'Simeon who was called Niger' (note the doubling here for names like Niger of Perea, the leader of the prorevolutionary Idumaeans who dies such a Jesus-like death at the hands of 'the Zealots', not to mention our old friend 'Simeon bar Cleophas'), 'Lucius the Cyrenian' (possibly Luke), and someone called 'Manaean, Herod the Tetrarch's foster brother, and Saul' (13:1).

As we have suggested, concerning names such as 'James the brother of John', we have a possible 'shell game' going on and the appellative, 'Herod the Tetrarch's' or 'Herod Antipas' foster brother' may really be descriptive of Paul, not the semi-nonsense name 'Manaen' (this is not to mention the relation of this name to the later name 'Mani' and the teacher who taught in the region of Mani's origins, Ananias again).

However this may be, at this point in its narrative Acts tells us that 'in these days prophets came down from Jerusalem to Antioch' (*thus*). Here we are allegedly still talking about 'Antioch' *in Syria*, not 'Antioch-by-Callirhoe' of the Edessenes, some two hundred miles to the north-east (11:27). One of these, one

Agabus, rose up and predicted *by the Spirit* a Great Famine, that was about to be over the whole habitable world, which came to pass under Claudius Caesar. (11:28)

This then triggers the notice about Barnabas' and Saul's Famine-relief mission to the Elders in Judea (11:29–30), which is immediately followed in 12:1 by the one about how 'at that time Herod the King stretched out [his] hands to mistreat some of the Assembly [the same word Josephus uses to describe the Simon who wanted to bar Agrippa I from the Temple as a foreigner], and he put James the brother of John to death with the sword'.

Seizing Peter, too, because he saw this 'was *pleasing to the Jews*' (again, the opposite is more likely) – it was the time of the Passover again – 'he imprisoned him'. This is the point at which Peter escapes and leaves the message for '*James and the brothers*' at 'the house of Mary the *mother of John Mark*', the first mention of James in Acts' narrative (12:3–17). Peter then leaves to 'go to another place'. Of course, all of this is completely anachronistic because 'the Great Famine' occurred between 46 and 48 CE and the events Acts appears to be describing occur before 44 CE and Agrippa I's death, which Acts, as we saw, then apparently goes on to describe (12:19–23).

But all this was introduced by the mention of Barnabas' and Saul's mission on behalf of the Antioch Christian Disciples 'to the brothers living in Judea', because of the Famine purportedly predicted by *the prophet Agabus* (11:29–30), but nothing about what Paul and Barnabas actually did on this mission or where they went *is ever described*. Instead we get all this other intervening information and the section ends with the completely uncommunicative:

Barnabas and Paul returned from Jerusalem, having completed their mission also bringing with them John Mark (12:25),

followed immediately at the beginning of the next chapter with the enumeration of the 'prophets and teachers of the Church at Antioch', which we have just described above.

Now Paul begins what are usually referred to as his 'missionary journeys', with a confrontation in Cyprus with a Jewish magician 'called *Bar-Jesus*', having much in common with Peter's confrontation with Simon *Magus* in Caesarea – in this regard, one should remember the confusion in our sources between 'Cyprus' and Simon's 'Cuthaean' origins in Samaria – and a sympathetic interview with the Roman proconsul there,

'Sergius Paulus' (13:6–12). It is at this point that 'John Mark' deserts them 'to return to Jerusalem' (13:13). After this, 'some Jews arrive from Antioch and Iconium', while Paul is teaching at Lystra 'and persuaded the crowds' – this still in Asia Minor – and Paul is stoned (14:19 – no 'We Document' yet present to verify any of this; it begins only in chapter 16 after 'the Jerusalem Council').

After this Paul and Barnabas return to Antioch. Then the ubiquitous 'certain ones came down from Judea' and taught the brothers: 'Unless you circumcise after the tradition of Moses you *cannot be saved*' (15:1 – note the word 'saved' here which will reappear in the Habakkuk *Pesher*'s crucial exegesis of Hab. 2:4). This triggers the famous 'Jerusalem Council', relating to 'the conversion of the Peoples' or 'the Nations', which is pictured as going to deal with the issue of whether it was 'necessary for them to circumcise and be charged with *keeping the Law of Moses*', but never really does so (15:3–5). This, of course, completely parallels Paul's obsession with these issues in Galatians, where he describes his return to Jerusalem after fourteen years, not because he was summoned, but as a result of 'a revelation', privately, to explain the Gospel as he 'proclaimed it among the Gentiles', lest somehow he should have '*run in vain*'.

At the end of this 'Conference', as Acts pictures it, James makes the famous rulings, already amply described, the gist of which are carried down to Antioch in a 'letter' delivered by 'Judas [now 'Barsabas'] and Silas', whom Acts describes as 'themselves prophets' (15:22–30). As far as Acts is concerned, everyone then 'rejoices at the consolation' and, supposedly, all 'go in peace' (15:31–33). Notwithstanding, 'after some days' Paul and Barnabas have a *violent quarrel*, ostensibly over 'John Mark', who had purportedly 'withdrawn from' their work in Pamphylia and 'would not co-operate with them' any more. It will be recalled, it was supposed to be *his* 'mother' Mary's house that Peter went to leave a message for 'James and the brothers' in Jerusalem. From 'John Mark', too, we never hear again. The language here is also significant, because of numerous parallels at Qumran.[34]

Paul now sets out for 'Syria and Cilicia' (at this point, allegedly with 'Silas'), never apparently to travel with Jewish companions again, while Barnabas parts company with him and 'sailed off to Cyprus' with John Mark (15:32–41). Finally – and, one might observe, blessedly – in chapter 16 the 'We Narrative' cuts in. Obviously very little of this jibes with Galatians, except the repeated motif and seeming core issue of whether new converts were going to be required to circumcise themselves or not.

Judging from Paul's anger in Galatians over this issue, it is clearly not resolved by the time he writes this letter either.

Nor do those who come from James either in Galatians or Acts seem to have the same view of the so-called 'Jerusalem Council' as Paul does. In fact, these various messengers, who repeatedly 'come down from James' and 'from Jerusalem to Antioch' – one even called 'Judas' in Acts (namely 'Judas *Barsabas*') – have much in common with 'Judas *Thomas* sending out Thaddaeus' to Edessa, as reported in Eusebius' Agbarus correspondence and its variations – whoever these two individuals really were.

However this may be, the whole issue of an intervening trip to Jerusalem by Paul for the purposes of Famine relief – supposedly triggered in Acts' account by the coming down from Jerusalem to Antioch of 'a prophet called Agabus' (paralleling the notice about 'Theudas claiming to be a prophet' in Josephus) – is just not covered in the Letter to the Galatians at all. On the other hand, Acts does not treat what Paul was doing in the intervening 'fourteen years', between the time he stayed with Peter 'for fifteen days' in Galatians and met 'James the brother of the Lord' – before going off 'to the regions of Syria and Cilicia' – and the time he returned (according to him, as a result of a *private* 'revelation') to put 'the Good News as he announced it among the Gentiles' before 'those reckoned as important'. The reference to 'Syria and Cilicia' *is*, however, mentioned at this point in Acts in conjunction with this new mission with this companion 'Silas' *after* the Jerusalem Council (Acts 15:41).

The 'prophet by the name of Agabus' does, of course, reappear – again fortuitously – in chapter 21 of Acts, just before Paul is about to go up on his last visit to Jerusalem to his final confrontation with James. Once more, the issue is Paul's teaching 'all Jews among the Nations [*Ethnē*] *not to circumcise their children nor walk in our ways*' – probably the truth of the matter. This comes right after the notice about the majority of James' followers being 'Zealots for the Law' (21:20–21). Even in the speech Acts now pictures James as giving, there is no doubt as to which national grouping he belongs. He is certainly *on the side of the Jews* – not those teaching them to *desert their ancestral customs* – but, of course, we are now in the 'We Document' in these events.

In the episode at Caesarea preceding this, Paul is pictured as staying at 'the house of Philip the Evangelist, one of the Seven', who 'has *four virgin daughters who prophesied*' (21:8–9). It will be recalled that later in Acts Paul is also pictured as staying in protective custody in Agrippa II's palace (23:35). The Philip in Josephus, who was the head of Agrippa II's army, likewise lived in Caesarea. As already remarked, Josephus specifically notes his 'two daughters', who miraculously escaped the mass suicide at Gamala in the early days of the War.

Interestingly enough, like the Saulus in Josephus, this Philip too is sent to Nero in Rome to give an account of his actions in surrendering Agrippa II's Palace to the insurgents in Jerusalem, an event in which Josephus' 'Saulus' seems to have been involved as well. Unlike Saulus, however, Philip seems to have returned safely to Palestine after this mission, Nero being too preoccupied with his own troubles by this time to see him.[35]

On the other hand, the 'prophet by the name of Agabus', once again described as 'a *somebody who came down from Judea*', now came to Paul at this house and 'taking hold of his girdle and tying his hands and feet up' in it (*thus*), cried out:

> Thus says the Holy Spirit: '*The Jews in Jerusalem* shall in this manner bind the man whose girdle this is and *deliver him up into the hands of the Nations*.' (21:10–12)

Not only do we have our tell-tale 'Gentile Christian' anti-Jewish animus again, but the same words, 'delivered up', used throughout the Gospels to describe Judas *Iscariot*'s treatment of Jesus and in the Scrolls to describe God's 'Judgement' or 'Visitation' for Vengeance on Jewish backsliders and Covenant-breakers. For Acts now, weaving in and out of the 'We Document', everyone present then begins to weep, begging Paul 'not to go up to Jerusalem', but he peremptorily dismisses these concerns, declaring he is 'ready to be bound and even die in Jerusalem for the Name of the Lord Jesus' (21:13).

Acts' Prophet Called Agabus and the Agbarus Legend

We are now in a position to sort out a good many of our threads and identify some further dissimulation in Acts – again at the expense of some favourite hagiographa in Christianity. At the same time, we shall be able to make clear just who this 'Thaddaeus' really was and, in the process, quite a few others. We shall return to the second prophecy that 'Agabus' is presented as making at the time of Paul's last visit to Jerusalem in Acts in Volume II, when discussing the mysterious oracle to leave Jerusalem given to *James' followers after his death* – presumably under the stewardship of Simeon bar Cleophas – which allegedly triggers 'the Pella Flight'.

This will also involve another mysterious oracle Josephus records *directly following James' death* about the fall of Jerusalem, given by 'one Jesus ben Ananias, a *simple field-worker*' (n.b. the 'field-working' theme again), who continued uttering it for seven and a half years until shortly before the fall of the Temple. The oracle 'Agabus' gives Paul here simply reverses that of the Pella Flight in the typical manner we have been observing, that is, instead of an oracle to *leave Jerusalem*, we have an oracle here that Paul should *not go up to Jerusalem*; the effect is the same.

But the first appearance of the prophet Agabus who 'came down from Jerusalem to Antioch' – this 'Agabus' certainly gets around quite a bit for 'a prophet' – was to foretell 'the Great Famine that was going to grip the whole earth' in the time of Claudius. I think we can identify it with the story of Queen Helen's erstwhile husband, 'Abgarus' or 'Agbarus', according to Syriac sources, or, at least, the Agbarus Legend as it no doubt appeared in these and in Eusebius (this is not to mention Paul's colleague 'Ananias', doubtlessly, one of 'the prophets and teachers' of the 'Antioch' Community). In Acts the episode about Agabus' prophecy, introducing Paul's Famine-relief mission, occurs right before *the beheading of James the brother of John*.

The notice in Syriac texts about Queen Helen's relationship with Agbarus is, of course, disputed; but Northern Syrian Kings of this kind did not just have single wives, but extended harems. Nor did they live with each of them; on the contrary, they parcelled out kingdoms or provinces to favourite wives and children in the manner hinted at in Josephus' account of Queen Helen's conversion – her husband is often suspiciously absent – and the place where her favourite son Izates, whose story we shall pick up below, lives will be quite different from that of her 'husband' (his supposed father) 'Bazeus' or 'Monobazus' (paralleling Abgarus or Agbarus in Aramaic/Syriac sources – 'Augarus' or 'Albarus' in Latin).

The key to all these matters is the notice in Acts about 'the Famine' and the reaction to it by 'the Antioch Community' of Paul and Barnabas and *Queen Helen's parallel Famine-relief activities in Josephus*, recapitulated in great detail in Eusebius' version of these matters. In fact Eusebius spends a considerable amount of time on these materials, as we saw, expounding them a second time in conjunction with his reproduction of Josephus' notice about the beheading of 'a certain impostor called Theudas'. He, as we saw and as Josephus asserts even in what Eusebius reproduces, also 'claimed to be *a prophet*' with perhaps more reason than this 'Agabus' in Acts.

This note in Josephus' *Antiquities* is inserted in between the two notices about the beheading of Theudas and the crucifixion of Judas the Galilean's two sons, James and Simon, at the time of *the Famine*, as we also saw – emasculated but still recognizable in Acts' anachronistic version in 5:36–37. Though ignoring, like Acts, this second event, what Eusebius reproduces from Josephus, who also refers to it twice – both in relation to *Helen's grain-buying* activities not *Paul's* – is worth quoting:

> And at that time, it came to pass that *the Great Famine* [the same words used in Acts] *took place in Judea*, in which the Queen, Helen, having purchased grain *in Egypt at great cost*, distributed it to the needy, as I have already related.[36]

In other words, there really was no 'prophet called Agabus', only our 'Agbarus Legend', the connection to which probably being that Queen Helen – even if only on a formal level for child-bearing purposes – was probably one of this so-called 'Abgarus'' wives, perhaps even his half-sister or sister, as in Old Testament versions of the Abraham story.

We have already shown the way towards eliminating the second prophecy attributed to this 'Agabus' as well – the one in Caesarea right before Paul's last trip to Jerusalem. In the latter case, it will not relate to any 'Agbarus' or 'Abgarus', but rather also an 'Ananias' – a name playing (as just noted above) an important part in all our stories, including Josephus' story of the conversion of Queen Helen and her son Izates, not to mention Acts' account of Paul's conversion in Damascus. This will be related to the 'Jesus ben Ananias', also just alluded to above and described in more detail at the beginning of this book.

Where the first prophecy ascribed to 'Agabus' is concerned, Acts has once again gone to great lengths to erase the connection of the Famine to Queen Helen's conversion – not to mention the execution of another pseudo-prophet, 'Theudas' – events fraught with significance where Jewish history and the Messianic Movement in Palestine are concerned. Instead, Acts overwrites these matters by what turns out to be childish nonsense. The writers of Acts certainly knew their audiences well.

The second prophecy ascribed to Agabus will also cover up another occurrence related to the life of James with, as we have already seen, equally childish storytelling. These incidents, in turn, also throw light on all the various goings up and down from Jerusalem, reflected in the 'Judas *Thomas*'/'Thaddaeus' materials in the Agbarus Legend and paralleled in the 'some who came from James', 'Agabus', and 'Judas Barsabas' episodes –

the last-named also sent 'with *an epistle from James*' (not from 'Thomas' or 'Jesus'), but always *from Jerusalem to 'Antioch'*. It should be observed that in the Syriac version of this correspondence and the headings of the Greek version of Eusebius, 'Ananias' plays a role as well, being the *courier between Agbarus and Jesus*.[37] It should be clear that the authors of Acts know all these materials and, in due course, we shall show the relationship of this correspondence with the 'letter(s)' known at Qumran as '*MMT*'.

In fact, all of these insights come from a consideration of the life of James and how it has been overwritten and transformed in biblical warrant as it has come down to us. To be sure, modern scholars will object that 'the Agbarus Legend' *is* late, only beginning with Eusebius. That is because they have chosen to regard it as late and because the sources – except Hippolytus – concerning it are relatively late. But Eusebius doesn't consider it late, and on such matters he is usually pretty reliable, if at times demented. Nor do Syriac and Armenian sources consider it late, but, of course, these are depreciated as well.

But the fact of the matter is that this notice in the Book of Acts connecting the Famine to 'a prophet Agabus', which in Josephus is connected to the real-life Queen Helen, *proves* as almost nothing else can – we shall see further proof below – how early all these materials are. The notice also raises questions as to just what Paul's and Barnabas' relation to Helen was and who this Barnabas really was?

In our view, at least Paul – if not Ananias – was among Queen Helen's *grain-buying agents in Egypt and Cyprus*. The gateway to Egypt has always been '*Gaza*', a fact that will loom large in Acts' later overwriting of these materials. Again, as amazing as it may at face value appear, we are in Acts in a narrative *later* than the original for these others, whether in Josephus or some of these Syriac sources. Helen, of course, is depicted in Josephus – and Eusebius following him, who calls both her and Abgarus, whom his Edessene chancellery document refers to as 'the Great King of the Peoples *beyond the Euphrates*', Rulers 'of the Osrhoeans' (it should be appreciated that Josephus also calls Helen's second son Monobazus, 'the King of Adiabene *beyond the Euphrates*') – as having sent her grain-buying agents out to conduct extensive Famine-relief activities, for which 'she won fame and widespread acclaim for herself and her family'.[38]

Aside from also identifying another town, Nisibis, very close to Edessa as 'Antioch' – this, along with other cities by this name, no doubt a contributing factor for so many of these confusions – Josephus also identifies Helen as having a relationship with a certain *Arab King*, he calls

'Abennerig' in Southern Iraq, who harbours Izates from his brothers' hostility. We should pay close attention to the usage 'Arab' or 'Arabia' in these accounts and, here too, the town where Izates is given sanctuary, Charax Spasini, is known as 'Antiochia' as well.

But the general locale of most of these events is Northern Syria and Iraq up to the border of the Kingdom of the Medes in Persia. It is also what has come sometimes to be called Armenia, since Josephus specifically refers to the area in which

> the remains of that ark wherein it is related that Noah escaped the Flood . . . are still shown to such that are desirous of seeing them,[39]

as part of it. This everyone knows to be Ararat in the part of North-Eastern Turkey formerly known as 'Armenia'. It is also the Kingdom Josephus says Izates later acquires from his father, though this is really further south in the region of *Abraham*'s Haran.

It should be noted, too, that just after considering the Elchasaites, whom he feels originated in this same area – at least in their incarnation as 'the *Sobiai*' or 'Sabaeans' – Hippolytus above makes exactly this point, that

> the dimensions and relics of this [ark] are, as we have explained, shown to this day in the mountains called Ararat, which are situated in the direction of *the country of the Adiabeni* [that is, *Adiabene*].[40]

In fact, the Jewish traveller, Benjamin of Tudela (c. 1159–73), even went to visit this mountain, which he said stood above an island in the Tigris River, on his journey from Haran through Nisibis to Arbela and Mosul. For him (as, clearly, for all these others), this is where Ararat was actually located – in the Land of Adiabene, just above the Tigris River, between Nisibis and Mosul – or *modernday Kurdistan*. Here, he claims, a large number of Jews in the tens of thousands were still living. In Mosul, for instance, there were three synagogues, one headed by 'Nahum *the Elchasaite*', whom Benjamin doesn't even see as non-Jewish. In this area, too, he describes the recent Messianic Uprising of one 'David Alroy', who, he claims, 'called for a war with all Gentiles', 'called himself Messiah', and 'made the conquest of Jerusalem his final goal'.[41]

The Conversion of Queen Helen
and the *Ethiopian Queen*'s Eunuch

Abraham's Homeland: Edessa to Adiabene

In order to understand these things, it is worth looking at the story of the conversion of Queen Helen as found in Josephus. The key issue which links this story to the other materials we have been attempting to delineate above is the one of 'circumcision'. This becomes, once again, the essence of the problem in the conversion of Queen Helen and her sons. Josephus presents the story at the beginning of the all-important Book Twenty, the last book of the *Antiquities*, which ends on the note of his account of James' death. The story is obviously important, because he goes into great detail and it takes up the whole first part of this book.

Helen is pictured as the Queen of a country called 'Adiabene'. We have already noted the connection of this name with both 'Addai' and 'Edessa' above. It is also important to note that for Muhammad in the Koran, "*Ād*' is the name of an ancient Arab Kingdom, and the name of the 'prophet' sent to them is '*Hūd*'.[1] The cities of this ancient kingdom are not very well documented. It is somewhere on the border with the Persians, at this point 'the Parthians', east of Asia Minor and Syria. The Rabbis speak of Helen in the same breath they do of Kurdistan, and, we have already seen that, as with Hippolytus and Benjamin of Tudela above, it is here too that they would locate Ararat.[2]

Josephus also speaks of Ararat in this context, but he calls the area in which it is found 'Carron' – whether the same as 'Carrhae' (Abraham's Haran) just south of Antioch Orrhoe or Edessa-by-Callirhoe is impossible to determine. This, he says, Helen's husband – whatever his original name, 'Bazeus' or 'Abgarus' – in the first instance, bestowed on Helen's younger son Izates, whom he seems hardly to know.[3] The area really is a buffer zone between the Romans in Syria and Armenia and the Parthians in Persia, and many armies have always passed back and forth through it. Therefore its importance.

As Josephus tells the story, Helen has two sons, Monobazus the older and Izates the younger – among a myriad other sons of this 'Great King'. These kings (like the Saud family in Arabia today) had a plethora of wives and sons. It was customary to kill all the latter when one or another of these sons gained ascendance, a point on which the story of Izates' (and for that matter Helen's) conversion to some extent turns, because Izates, our hero, declines to do this. The key issue, 'circumcision', or the lack thereof, where such 'conversions' are concerned, is also the key issue, as we have been discussing, between those in the 'Jerusalem Church' following James and the 'Gentile Mission' following Paul, as per Paul's own testimony in Galatians – indirectly refracted through the portrait in Acts. It is also the key issue, as we have now seen, surrounding the curious circumlocution '*Sicarii*' or, as Hippolytus terms them, '*Sicarii* Essenes', and their possible reformulation in the term, 'Christians'.

Not only is Izates' older brother called 'Monobazus' but, as we saw, Josephus also designates the father as being named 'Bazeus' or 'Monobazus' as well. So prevalent does this name appear to be that, like 'Herod' or 'Agbar', it is not clear whether it is a proper name or simply a title. In fact, another 'Monobazus', said to be a kinsman of Helen's son 'Monobazus King of Adiabene' turns up among the 'Zealot' Revolutionaries at the start of the War against Rome, along with another of these 'kinsmen' of either Helen or the King, 'Kenedaeos'. These two, along with Niger of Perea, already mentioned above, and Silas – formerly a member of King Agrippa II's army who 'deserted to the Jews' – are the really valiant fighters in the revolutionary army.[4]

Silas would appear to be the son of the previous Silas, who, as we saw, like Philip the son of Jacimus above, was commander of Agrippa I's army. Josephus calls 'Silas' a 'Babylonian' – whatever this means – as he does 'Philip', and they all seem to have been the descendants of a contingent of Babylonian horsemen the first Herod brought in from the plains region of Edessa and Adiabene, and settled in the 'Damascus' region to protect pilgrims coming from 'beyond the Euphrates' from local raiders.[5] Like Peter in Acts, Agrippa I, it will be recalled, had the elder Silas imprisoned, because, though his boon friend, Silas presumed to behave as an equal and would not sufficiently defer to him. After Agrippa's death, the Helcias ('Alexas') mentioned as the father of Paul's possible 'nephew', Julius Archelaus above (Acts 23:16), whose forebear had been another intimate of Herod and whose family Herod used for that reason to oversee the Temple Treasury, acting on behalf of Agrippa I's brother, Herod of Chalcis, *executed* the elder Silas. In turn, Julius Archelaus' other uncle and 'Saulus" cousin (also Temple Treasurer), Antipas, was assassinated by another 'Zealot' known as 'John *the son of Dorcas*' in 68 CE.[6]

However these things may be – these four, Helen's two kinsmen, Monobazus and Kenedaeos,[7] and Niger and Silas lead the *initial assault* on the Roman Army on its way up to Jerusalem at the Pass at Beit Horon in the first heady days of the Uprising, the success of which touched off the feeling that the longer war (66–70 CE), could be won. In this assault, this third Monobazus and his kinsman Kenedaeos were killed, but Niger, Silas (names familiar, as should be clear, to the early Christianity of Acts), and another individual, 'John the *Essene*', not previously mentioned in Josephus, led a follow-up assault on the Romans at the southern sea-coast town, Ashkelon, near Gaza.

If Josephus' testimony regarding the 'Essene' bravery and indifference to pain while undergoing torture were not sufficient, this is further proof of the active role so-called 'Essenes' took in the War against Rome. Here Silas and John were killed and Niger given up for dead in a subterranean cave. However, Jesus-like, he emerged alive again, much to the joy of his companions, who had been searching for him with lamentations on the battlefield for *three days* in order to *bury him*.[8] As we saw, this is not the only episode from Niger of Perea's life that appears retrospectively to have been absorbed into Jesus', as later he too is dragged through Jerusalem by the 'Zealots' – the reasons for which are unclear – 'showing the scars of his wounds' as he went. Once outside the city, he is executed (possibly even crucified), but not before he calls down on them, again as Jesus is portrayed as doing upon the Jews in the 'Little Apocalypse's of the New Testament, 'famine, pestilence, and internecine slaughter'.[9]

Josephus further clarifies who these two kinsmen of Helen are, martyred in the assault on the Roman army under Cestius at Beit-Horon – the traditional pass that had to be negotiated by invading armies on their way up to Jerusalem. Directly following the fall of Jerusalem, the sacrifice to their standards the Roman troops performed in the Temple facing eastwards, and their firing of the city, Josephus describes how, when the fire reached Queen Helen's palace in the middle of the city's acropolis area, Titus took the surrender of many of the 'sons and brothers of Izates the King', who were all obviously *still living in Jerusalem* in their grandmother's palace and those of her sons. These he took in bonds to Rome, having given them 'his right hand for [their] safety', and, while still angry at them, kept them as hostages, because of their political importance, 'as surety for their country's fealty to the Romans'.[10]

It is this group of individuals – namely, Idumaeans like Niger of Perea, pro-revolutionary Herodian Men-of-War such as Silas (Philip and Saulus would be examples of anti-revolutionary ones), and these descendants or brothers of Helen of Adiabene's son Izates – that we have suggested are alluded to at Qumran under the title of 'the Violent Ones of the Gentiles'. They may even be referred to as 'the Men of War', in the Damascus Document, 'who turned aside' and 'walked with the Man of Lying'.

Despite a certain tone of negativity in these references, 'the Violent Ones of the Gentiles', anyhow, are actually viewed with a certain amount of approbation, especially in the Psalm 37 *Pesher*, where they are credited with 'taking vengeance' for what had been done to 'the Righteous Teacher'/'the Priest', that is, 'the High Priest' or what we would consider to be 'the Opposition High Priest' of the sectarian alliance.[11]

In the Habakkuk *Pesher*, where they are simply referred to as 'the Violent Ones', they are also grouped with 'the Man of Lying', 'the Covenant-Breakers', and 'the Traitors to the New Covenant and the Last Days' ('who defiled His Holy Name'), with whom they actually seem to take part in the scriptural exegesis sessions of the Righteous Teacher. Therefore, depending on the dating of these documents, they may even have been part of 'the New Covenant in the Land of Damascus', referred to in the Damascus Document. In other work, I have identified them, along with people like 'John the Essene', as, if not the moving force, at least *the fighting arm of the Uprising against Rome*.

Helen's son Izates must have been dead for some time before this Uprising, because Josephus describes his funeral along with Helen's and the great funeral monuments erected for them by his older brother, the *second* Monobazus, outside the city. Eusebius, too, refers to these monuments, and they were actually found in the last century near the presentday American Colony Hotel and are still very splendid![12] For his part, Eusebius remarks that they were 'still being shown in the outskirts of Aelia' in his time. Aelia Capitolina was the name given Jerusalem by Hadrian after his brutal suppression of the Second Jewish Uprising under Bar Kochba from 132 to 136 CE – Aelius being Hadrian's given name – after which Jews were forbidden either to approach within eyesight of or live in the city.[13]

In Josephus' story about Izates' conversion, which he gives as a prelude to his presentation of the *beheading of Theudas* and *the crucifixion of Judas the Galilean's two sons*, Helen, as we saw, is just one of the King's many wives. She doesn't even appear to live with him. Rather, she is given this Kingdom further east on what would appear to be the outer edge of his dominions. Her son Izates, whom Josephus sometimes calls 'only begotten' – as the Gospel of John does Jesus – but sometimes as having an older brother, 'Monobazus' above, is by this time living in a town at the southern tip of the Tigris–Euphrates Delta called Charax-Spasini.[14]

This town would appear to be an important trading centre, which probably explains Izates' presence, not to mention the influences he encounters there. This would also appear to be true for the 'Jewish merchant Ananias', he meets there – much the same as Paul or the 'Ananias' Paul *also* met in 'Damascus' in Acts 9:10–17. Not only was Charax a centre for the Tigris River trade, but also areas further east. Two centuries later, Mani is said to have come from an 'Elchasaite' family there and 'the Mandaeans' ('the Sabaeans of the marshes') are still there to the present day. Izates is the guest of another King called, as we saw, 'Abennerig' – 'Abinergaos' according to his coins[15] – whose daughter he marries. Her name, 'Samachos'/'Amachos'/'Symachos', is suspiciously similar to the name of the wife of 'Abgar *Ukkama*' ('Abgar the Great') in Edessan chronicles – 'Abgar *Uchama*' in Eusebius' presentation of his conversion.[16]

What is not generally appreciated about all these individuals with their strange-sounding names is that all of them are considered to be 'Arabs' or 'Arabians' by people *outside their cultural framework*. Tacitus, for instance, calls Agbar or Abgar, 'Acbar King of the Arabs' and all the inhabitants around Edessa, 'Arabs'.[17] For Strabo, Mesopotamia, for the most part, was inhabited by 'Arab Chieftains' and the Osrhoeans, to whom both Helen and Agbar appertain according to Eusebius and who occupied the country from Edessa to the Land of Adiabene, are also '*Arabs*'.[18] All of these points are extremely significant in attempting to determine just where Paul had in mind, when he informs us in Galatians that, after his conversion, first he 'went away into *Arabia*' and only afterwards 'returned to Damascus', before 'going up to Jerusalem to make the acquaintance of Peter' and James the brother of the Lord (1:17–18).

For his part Eusebius, as we saw, calls Abgar, to whom Thaddaeus – both 'an Apostle and one of the Seventy' – and ultimately Judas Thomas are sent, 'the Great King of the Peoples [*Ethnōn*] beyond the Euphrates' – *exactly* the way Josephus describes *both Izates and his brother Monobazus*. These Kings would also appear to have had links to the 'Arabs' around Petra, somewhat confusingly called by modern scholars 'Nabataeans', meaning descendants of Ishmael's firstborn son Nabaioth in the Bible (Gen. 25:13).

By Paul's time, these 'Arabs' from Petra controlled Damascus, as he himself attests in 2 Corinthians 11:32 as we saw, again after noting, he 'does not lie'. This also makes his notice about his mysterious three-year sojourn in 'Arabia' and, afterwards, 'Damascus' – again in the context of protesting he 'does not lie' – so interesting (Gal. 1:17–20). Does Paul mean by 'Arabia' here only 'Petra' and possibly 'Damascus' – where in Acts he supposedly links up with Ananias – or has he been further afield, to Charax Spasini, for instance, Edessa, or even Adiabene? Aside from the 'Fertile Crescent' of cities extending from Damascus around to these Northern parts of Syria and Mesopotamia, and the legendary city of Palmyra on the direct caravan route to these areas – this trade being the source of the city's legendary wealth – these areas were mostly desert.

In fact, the fifth-century Armenian historian, Moses of Chorene – which some see as a pseudonym for a later ninth-century author – claims that Abgar helped his fellow 'Arab' King Aretas of Petra in his mini-war against Herod Antipas to avenge John the Baptist's murder – and John does, however indirectly, seem to be supporting Aretas' position on Herod's divorce of Aretas' daughter. In addition, this work attributed to Moses of Chorene makes it *very* clear that Helen was 'the first' of Abgar's wives, comparing her 'Piety' and her conversion to Abgar's. At the same time, by remarking her wheat distributions to 'the Poor' and her 'truly remarkable tomb, which was still to be seen before the Gate of Jerusalem', he makes it very clear she is Josephus' Helen![19]

To some extent Josephus turns this around, claiming that the Arab Kings from Petra were involved in some manner in the conflicts that broke out over Izates' succession *to his father*. For his part, Moses of Chorene records the defeat suffered by one of Herod's 'nephews' at Abgar's hands in Northern Syria. After this, he claims, Edessa was founded. The specificity of this information, in turn, does tally to some degree with material in Josephus about these same 'nephews' – the sons of Herod's brothers, Phasael, Joseph and Pheroras, and his sister Salome and their various marriages to his *own daughters*.[20]

While Paul does tell us in a notice that must date from around 35–37 CE, the year Aretas probably gained control of Damascus, that he (Paul) escaped from Aretas' Ethnarch by being 'let down from a window in the wall in a basket'; unfortunately, he does not tell us why the *Arab* King Aretas was chasing Paul, nor what he was doing in Damascus in the first place. Acts transforms this – much as the Gospels do the story of Jesus – as we have seen, into a plot *by 'the Jews'* in Damascus 'to kill Paul', none of which makes any sense, since he was supposedly sent there in the first place on a mission on behalf of the Jewish High Priest.

Of course, if Paul were a relative of Herod Antipas or his wife Herodias – who later sought the Kingdom for her new husband even over her brother Agrippa I – then there would have been reason enough for Paul's activity in this area, since Herod Antipas' Tetrarchy extended from Galilee across Jordan into Perea. In addition, *all* Herodians were related to the Arabian King of Petra, because Herod's mother seems to have been either a member of or related to that family.

Even more interesting, when considering Josephus' terminology of 'Idumaean', as we saw as well, Herod's sister had married one 'Costobarus', whom Josephus in turn identifies as an 'Idumaean' or 'Edomite'. This seems to be the line from which Paul's *Herodian* namesake 'Saulus' appears to have descended, since 'Saulus' is always linked in these notices in Josephus, two or three generations further along, with the two names 'Antipas' and 'Costobarus', the latter of whom Josephus identifies as Saulus' brother.[21]

Political motives aside, many of these so-called petty 'Kings of the Nations' or 'Peoples' (*Ethnōn*) – as the Romans referred to them – were little more than minor 'Arab Chieftains' as Strabo correctly points out. Pliny even refers to Charax Spasini, the town where Izates resided on the Persian Gulf, as 'a town of Arabia' and its inhabitants also, therefore, as simply 'Arabs'.[22] It should be remarked that even in the Koran some six centuries along, we have an echo of these matters in the stories of "ʿĀd and Thamūd' and the fact that Muhammad regards all these 'Tribes' or 'Peoples', and the messengers who were sent to them, as 'Arab' or 'Arabs'.

His ʿĀd and Thamūd, as suggested above, are clearly simply further garblings of the names 'Addai' and 'Judas Thomas' and his stories featuring them are little more than echoes of these events centring about both Edessa and Adiabene. In claiming they 'denied the *Messengers*', Muhammad identifies the first of these as the *Arabian* prophet Hūd 'the brother of ʿĀd'. 'Hūd' in Hebrew is nothing but 'Yehudah' or 'Judah' and, therefore, our old friend 'Judas the Zealot' or 'Judas the *brother* of *James*' (or even 'Judas *Barsabas*') again – 'sent to teach the Truth to the people of Edessa' – all this now in the Koran!

To 'Thamūd', which is always paired with "ʿĀd' in the Koran and basically replicates it, was sent 'their brother Sāliḥ', which simply means 'Righteous One' in Arabic; so, once again, we have both the themes of the 'Righteous One' and *his* '*brother*'! For Muhammad, 'Thamūd' is an area abounding in 'hills, springs, plains, and date palms' (Koran 7.75 and 26.148–9), which is a very good description of the area around Edessa and Haran, Abraham's homeland. It fits well the description Josephus gives of the Kingdom he calls 'Carron' (probably Edessa Carrhae – which he elsewhere identifies with Haran), that Izates' father gave him, wherein allegedly was found the ark constructed by Noah above. Though Muhammad confuses the area 'Thamūd' with the individual 'Hūd', that he is dealing with the story of the evangelization of these areas by the individuals, Judas *Thomas* and Addai (themselves confused in early Church sources), should be clear.

But Muhammad too repeatedly connects '"Ād' and 'Thamūd' with 'the People of Noah' and with Abraham (Koran 7.65–79 and 14.10 – this, the *Surah* entitled 'Abraham'). This is a very important conjunction, as both of these individuals were considered to be connected to these lands and the traditions about them. He also repeatedly mentions the ark (11.38–50, in the chapter dedicated to 'Hūd', not to mention 'Sāliḥ' and 26.106–20). The conjunction of 'Hūd' with 'Sāliḥ' is, of course, the conjunction of 'Judas' with 'his brother, the Righteous One' (probably James).

In Hippolytus' version of these things, as we saw above, Noah's ark is identified as landing 'in the Land of Adiabene' – in Josephus, these are the lands Izates' father gives him. A final note – in these stories, Abraham's city of origin, Haran, is usually connected in some manner with either the conversion of Helen or her sons, or that of 'King Agbar' correlating with it. This, as we have suggested, to some extent explains Paul's concentration on Abraham in his letters – not to mention Muhammad's similar emphasis succeeding to him – and, by extension, James 2:21's brusque response about the sacrifice of Isaac, an important matter in Hebrews 11:17–20 as well (also echoed in the Koran – 37.101–14).[23] This will also be seen to be the focus of both the admonitions and comparisons in the letter(s) known as '*MMT*'.

The Conversion of Queen Helen and Her Son Izates in Josephus

As Josephus then tells this story,

> a certain Jewish merchant, whose name was Ananias [we have already noted in this regard the Ananias in Acts' story of Paul's conversion 'in Damascus'], got among the women that belonged to the King and taught them to worship God according to the Jewish Religion.

Again one should remark the custom of multiple wives. The note here about Ananias being 'a merchant' is not surprising and adds to its authenticity, since certainly Charax Spasini, and Palmyra further north, were commercial centres. In this manner, Ananias 'was brought to the attention of Izates, whom he similarly won over through the *co-operation of the women*'.[24]

'At the same time another Jew' (unnamed), instructed Helen, who

> went over to them . . . and when he [Izates] perceived that his mother was very much pleased with Jewish customs, he hastened to convert and embraced them entirely.

It is hard to decipher where all this action is taking place, as even in Josephus there are two different versions of Izates' conversion. The first is at this Charax at the mouth of the Tigris on the Persian Gulf above, but in this second note, Josephus portrays Izates as hurrying north where his mother seems to be.

This is the legendary conversion of Queen Helen and, aside from the romantic elements, it must be opined that the two conversions – Paul's and Helen's – have much in common, particularly as Acts relates the former. For his part, Josephus is anxious to point out that Izates brought this 'Ananias' with him 'to Adiabene', when he was *summoned by his father to come into his Kingdom*. Who the 'other Jew' was, who converted Izates' mother Helen, is impossible to say, but the reader should be apprised that in Josephus, anyhow, we are in the same time frame as Ananias' purported conversion of Paul in Acts – at a time Paul by his own testimony had supposedly 'gone away into *Arabia*' (Gal. 1:17).

At this point in Josephus' narrative – as in Acts and Paul's letters above – the issue of 'circumcision' rears its ugly head. After Izates went back to Adiabene to take over from his brother Monobazus, whom Josephus portrays as holding his Kingdom for him after the death of his father 'Monobazus' (there would appear to be a few too many Monobazuses here), he finds the other sons of the King, 'his brethren', in bonds waiting to be executed as was the custom. Thinking this a barbarity and good politician that he is, Izates sends 'them and their children as hostages to Claudius Caesar in Rome' and the Persian King Artabanus 'for the same reason'. This is the same kind of situation that Josephus describes thirty years later, when Titus decides not to punish these 'sons and brothers of King Izates' for rebellion, but returns them rather to their previous state of being surety for fealty to Rome.[25]

However, it now turns out that, Talmudic sources notwithstanding, Helen's conversion is not quite what it appeared to be and she has, according to Josephus, been taught an imperfect form of Judaism by her teacher – *whoever* he was. Another teacher comes 'named Eleazar' ('Lazarus' in the New Testament), this now, the third teacher, who is specifically identified as 'coming from Galilee' – 'a Galilean', therefore, as the New Testament calls such types. Here we must be very insistent on reminding the reader about the name of those who followed Josephus' 'Fourth Philosophy' of Judas the Galilean and *Saddok*, who opposed paying the tax to Rome, have 'an inviolable attachment to liberty saying that God is their only Ruler and Lord' and, therefore, will 'not call any *man* Lord'.

Though at times Josephus is willing to apply the name of 'Zealot' to this group, particularly after the start of the Uprising against Rome and the destruction of the collaborating High Priests responsible for the death of James, and most particularly the group following one 'Eleazar' who take control of the Temple; others – such as those following the direct descendant of Judas above, 'Eleazar ben Jair', holed up on Masada – he also calls '*Sicarii*', because of the Arab-style curved dagger they carried under their garments. With this – according to Josephus – they *assassinated backsliders*, as, for instance, persons of Josephus' or Paul's ilk, not to mention the High Priest Ananus and his brother Jonathan or Herodians of the kind of Agrippa II and Bernice. (According to others, as we have seen, they used it *to circumcise*.)

Even people like Niger of Perea, a hero of the early stages of the War, fell afoul of such groups in some manner and was considered deficient. But not people like the 'kinsmen' or 'brothers' of Kings like Izates and Monobazus of Adiabene, who, just as obviously, met with their approval. As we saw, quoting Hegesippus, Eusebius applies the name 'Galileans' to this group when enumerating the various parties 'of the circumcision',[26] and even Josephus, when speaking of Izates' final decision to circumcise himself, mentions such 'zeal'.

This Eleazar, regardless of overlaps with others by this name,[27] is described by Josephus as very strict when it came to the ancestral Laws, and Izates, after encountering him, as

> feeling that he could not *thoroughly be a Jew unless he was circumcised* and ready to act accordingly.

Helen however is horrified, because she feels he will be rejected by his subjects if he is circumcised. With the help of 'Ananias', described now in Josephus' account as her son's 'tutor', she talks him out of it.

It will be recalled that in Eusebius' version of the conversion of King Agbarus (Moses of Chorene, as noted previously, calls this a title meaning 'Great One', which 'Westerners were unable to pronounce'), 'Ananias' was 'the courier' who delivered the King's letter to Jerusalem and returned with Jesus' response. In Josephus, 'Ananias' now argues that Izates

> might *worship God without being circumcised*, even though he did resolve
> to be a *zealous practitioner of Judaism, worship of God being superior to
> circumcision.*

Paul in Galatians, as we saw, describes himself similarly, as once 'progressing in Judaism beyond many contemporaries in my race, being more abundantly *zealous for the traditions of my fathers*' (1:14).

This too, of course, is the basic argument between Paul's position and the adherents of James, in regard to which, one should always keep in mind, the admonition in the Letter ascribed to James: 'whoever keeps the whole of the Law, but stumbles on one small point, is guilty of [breaking] it all' (2:10), which then goes on to attack the man whose position was that '*Abraham our father*' was 'justified by Faith', not by works.

These Edessenes of the country around Haran or those of Adiabene, the area to which some thought the ancient Israelites were exiled after the Assyrian conquest at the end of the 700s BC, probably did consider themselves 'Children of Abraham', as many in these areas still do today, as those following the later revelation of Muhammad did – also someone considered as once having been *a merchant* plying the caravan trade in these areas. We have already noted how Paul, while calling himself an 'Israelite of the Tribe of Benjamin' and even a 'Hebrew', never actually calls himself a 'Jew' and, as suggested, people of 'Herodian' or 'Idumaean' Arab extraction may well have considered themselves 'Children of Abraham', though not strictly speaking 'Jews' *per se.*

One should also keep in mind the problems over 'circumcision' centring around these kinds of royal families generally. Josephus describes the problems *Herodian* Princesses, such as Agrippa II's sisters (Herodias' nieces), Bernice and Drusilla, were having in contiguous areas of Asia Minor and Syria. Antiochus, the son of the King of Commagene, an area in between Paul's reputed homeland of Cilicia and Edessa and 'the Osrhoeans' of Adiabene (an area not a city), had been promised Drusilla by her father Agrippa I.

Josephus describes this son, like his father, also called Antiochus (Epiphanes), as a valiant warrior. Indeed later, it will be recalled, he did come to Jerusalem too with his 'Macedonian Legion' to aid Vespasian in his assault on Jerusalem. Despite this, both he and his father were themselves arrested after the Uprising on suspicion of harbouring seditious intentions against Rome. Now Josephus remarks his valour in fighting *against the Romans*. Again, like Queen Helen's relatives, both he and his father were forcibly brought to Rome and retired there, because of the friendship Vespasian had borne them previously.[28]

As we saw, in the end Drusilla's marriage to the younger Antiochus did not take place, because of his refusal *to be circumcised* – something Agrippa I, though not Agrippa II, seems to have insisted upon (therefore, Agrippa I's more 'Pious' reputation). Drusilla was then given to Azizus King of Emesa (presentday Homs, not far from Damascus) 'on his consent to be circumcised' at around the time Felix was sent to Palestine by Claudius. Claudius seems to have given Drusilla's brother, Agrippa II, Philip's Tetrarchy in Galilee and further territories of his around Damascus as a reward for this.[29]

It was at this point that Drusilla was convinced by a 'magician' called Simon or 'Atomus' (this last clearly reflecting 'the Primal Adam' ideology attributed to Simon *Magus* in the Pseudoclementines and other early Church heresiologies), 'by birth a Cypriot' – note Paul's confrontation with the parallel 'Elymus *Magus*' *on Cyprus* in Acts 13:8 – to divorce her husband and marry Felix, a thing that would have infuriated those like the 'Zealot'-style writers at Qumran and, no doubt, this 'Galilean' Eleazar in Josephus' story about King Izates' circumcision.

For her part, Bernice, Drusilla's sister, after she had been accused of incest with her brother Agrippa II, married Polemo, King of Cilicia (for Acts, anyhow, Paul's reputed place of origin), after he agreed 'to be circumcised'. She did this, as Josephus admits, 'to prove the libels, namely the one about her and her brother, false'. For his part, Polemo was prevailed upon to circumcise himself 'chiefly on account of her Riches'.[30] Bernice, it will be recalled, had previously been married to *her uncle*, Herod of Chalcis. Again one should note the links here with the 'Three Nets of Belial' charges in the Damascus Document, including Riches, fornication, niece marriage, and divorce.

Finally Bernice, as we have seen, 'giving up all pretences of Judaism, forsook Polemo too', that is, even after he had specifically *circumcised himself* to marry her – ultimately taking up with Titus who burned

Jerusalem and destroyed the Temple. It is doubtful if Agrippa II demanded circumcision on behalf of Bernice and Drusilla from their Roman consorts, Titus and Felix, which was, no doubt, the point of Simon *Magus*' intervention in the first place – at least where the latter was concerned if not the former.

In any event, Izates *does finally circumcise himself*, much to the chagrin of his mother, for Jews, the supposedly *heroic* Queen Helen. Josephus' description of this is informative in the extreme and, it appears, fairly factual. When the 'Galilean' teacher Eleazar

> entered into his [Izates'] palace to pay him his respects, and finding him *reading the Law of Moses*, he said: 'Shouldn't you consider, O King, that you unjustly break the principal of these Laws and bring offence to God himself. For you should not only read the Law, but all the more so *do what they command you to do*. How long will you remain uncircumcised? If you have not read *the Law about circumcision, and do not know the great Impiety you do by neglecting it, then read it now*.

This story, as we shall see below, will be fleshed out further in Rabbinic sources, which actually give the passage from Genesis in question (Gen. 17:9–14), importantly, once again, one of the chief commandments Abraham received from God.

In the Josephus version of these events, one should note the omnipresent theme of '*doing all that the Law commands*', so much a part of the Jamesian approach and so prevalent at Qumran. Moreover, it will appear in the final admonitions in the correspondence known among scholars as '*MMT*' – but which we call, 'Two Letters on the Works that will be Reckoned for you as Righteousness', which are also *addressed to a King* and end up by evoking *Abraham*. In fact, one should always note the theme of being 'commanded *to do*', so central to 'Rechabite' texts above, not to mention this constant thread of the theme of 'circumcision' running through all the episodes noted above. Obviously this was *the* problem, as it was for Hippolytus' second group of so-called 'Essenes', those he calls either 'Zealots' or '*Sicarii*', whom he even describes as *forcibly circumcising people* – a practice also carried out, as we have described, in the 'Zealot' War against Rome and probably during the Bar Kochba Uprising as well.

Queen Helen's Naziritism and the Suspected Adulteress
in Rabbinic Tradition

This episode has also not failed to leave its impression in Rabbinic sources as well, as it has in Acts' account of the conversion of the *Ethiopian eunuch*, 'the Treasurer of *the Ethiopian Queen Kandakes*' (*thus*). Let us look at the former first. In Rabbinic sources, of course, Helen's conversion is to Judaism and she is praised for her generosity. She is credited with giving a golden candelabra to the Temple, which stood above its entrance; and her son, Monobazus, the golden handles for the vessels used on the Day of Atonement – always an important ritual when discussing James' role as Opposition High Priest.[31]

These sources specifically recount that she donated a *golden tablet* to the Temple with the passage from Numbers 5:11–31 about 'the suspected adulteress' inscribed on it.[32] This is a startling point, because this passage is not only coupled with the one about the 'Nazirite' oath for both men or women, preceding it in Numbers (6:1–21), but Helen's own 'Naziritism' is also made much of in these same sources – that is, Helen was *very much* concerned about accusations such as adultery or fornication and, in addition, cared about *Naziritism* and *the Temple* generally. This is in marked contrast to the endless series of adulteries and like-minded legal infractions reported of Herodian Princesses above, who hardly seem to have evinced any embarrassment over these offences at all.

It is possible to conceive that Helen may have been accused of similar offences and, therefore, the penances imposed upon her described in Rabbinic sources under the heading of 'Naziritism'. But, in her case, the implication is that, aside from accepting these penances, she also challenged these accusations. It is a curious coincidence that 'Simon *Magus*', implicated in this matter of the fornication or adulteries of Herodian Princesses, as we have seen, also appears at this time with another 'Helen', whom he seems to have represented as a 'Queen' of some kind and with whom he ultimately seems to have appeared in Rome. As far as early Christian sources are concerned, he picked her up 'in a brothel in Sidon', meaning, she was no better than a prostitute.[33]

Where Helen is concerned, there may also have been some questions about her marriage, though if this marriage was to 'Agbarus', then there is also the additional issue of the nature of their relationship. For his part, Josephus represents it as being *between a brother and sister*. One should notice, as we have above, how Abraham from a similar venue is described as contracting the same kind of marriage with his sister – in this instance, Sarah. One should also take note of the name of Helen's supposed favourite son, Izates (also 'Izas' in Josephus – Isaac?). Here we start to approach the 'Christianity' of the kind exemplified in the description of James in early Church sources, his *life-long* 'Naziritism' and the clear interest shown in the sacrifice of Isaac in the Letter attributed to his name (2:21, not to mention Heb. 11:17) – and our sources start to converge.

According to Rabbinic sources, Helen took a 'temporary Nazirite oath', normally taken for periods of a month – as in the picture in Acts of the *penance* James requires of Paul in the Temple at Pentecost – but hers was for seven years! After this, she too went on pilgrimage to Jerusalem.[34] Rabbinic sources at this point claim that the hero of many of their accounts, Hillel, imposed another 'seven years' on her – even though by this time Hillel, who appears to have been Herod's 'Rabbi', was long since dead.

Rabbinic sources are quick to claim credit for Queen Helen, even though her sons *participated* in the War against Rome and may even have been among its instigators; while the archetypical founder of their Judaism, Yohanan ben Zacchai, did not. Rather, in an act of astonishing cynicism, he applied, as we have seen – as Josephus himself claims he did – the 'Messianic Prophecy', that a World Ruler would come out of Palestine, to the *Roman Emperor-to-be* Vespasian, who destroyed Jerusalem – thereby winning for himself and his followers, according to Talmudic sources, the Academy at Yavneh, where Rabbinic Judaism was born.

The reason given for the extraordinary back-to-back penances in these sources is supposed to be that 'Hillel' did not consider residence outside the land of Israel applicable, because where Nazirite-oath procedures were concerned, such residence rendered one *ritually unclean*. According to these sources, after the second penance a *third* seven-year period was prescribed for her, purportedly because she contracted some additional impurity by approaching a dead body – Izates' perhaps? But one can also imagine the existence of an additional financial motivation in extending these procedures having to do with her legendary philanthropy (and, in our view, if Helen was following the form of Judaism as that at Qumran, then this installation too benefited substantially from her largesse – not to mention that of her sons).

However, for our purposes, these claims are so extraordinary, because these are exactly the procedures that Acts in its climactic section pictures James as demanding from Paul – and *to pay the expenses of four others*, too, associated with Nazirite oath-type procedures in the Temple – also, supposedly, for *various infractions overseas*. In Paul's case, as we saw, these had to do with his laxness in 'regularly observing the Law' and, as it transpires in the riot in the Temple that follows, teaching '*Jews in Asia*' to break the Law and '*not to circumcise their children*', nor any longer 'to walk in the Ways' of their Ancestors, not to mention 'polluting the Temple' by introducing 'Greeks' into it (Acts 21:20–29).

Acts' account even emphasizes that James' followers were '*zealous for the Law*', as we have repeatedly noted, a word Josephus twice uses in explaining why Izates' subjects would not submit to a man 'who was zealous [*zēlōtēs*] for foreign practices' and which the teacher, Eleazar, he describes as being 'from Galilee', *who demanded Izates circumcise himself*, most certainly was.[35] As usual, Josephus is always a *little more precise* and well developed than the Rabbinic sources.

But it is also interesting that, according to these last, following the fall of the Temple, as we have already on several occasions remarked, the Rabbis try to discourage those taking such Nazirite oaths not to 'eat or drink' again. According to these, so distraught was the surviving population, that large numbers – this in a Rabbinic text – 'vowed not to eat meat or drink wine' and 'became ascetics' until they should see the Temple rebuilt'![36] We have already seen, too, that according to Benjamin of Tudela, 'Rechabite'-style ascetics, living in lean-tos and caves, were still taking such oaths a thousand years later in the Northern Arabian desert, out of 'mourning for Zion' and 'mourning for the Temple'.

In Acts, of course, these kinds of Nazirite-oath-taking individuals 'vow not to eat or drink till they have killed Paul' (23:12)! But, of course, not only are these the very characteristics we hear about in all the reports of James' life-style, but these are precisely the points we hear about, according to the Ebionite view of the post-resurrection appearance of Jesus to James, in the Gospel of the Hebrews above, who, according to our tradition, had 'vowed not to eat or drink' until he had 'seen *the Son of Man risen from the dead*'.

This theme of 'eating and drinking' has been, of course, omnipresent in the Letters of Paul we have considered above and this tradition associating *refusal* 'to eat and drink', not only with Nazirite-oath procedures, but also with grief over the destruction of the Temple by the Romans, just draws these parallels that much closer. Not only did the followers of James seem to have a particular predilection for this type of oath-taking and/or abstinence, but the 'eating and drinking' motifs, connected in most of our accounts to the post-resurrection appearances of Jesus, whether around Jerusalem or in Galilee, are transmogrified in other contexts, as we have seen, into more complex ideologies like Paul's '*eating this bread* and *drinking this cup*' and being in '*Communion with* the body and blood of Christ' (1 Cor. 11:27).

These, in turn, bring the complex of this imagery full circle, because, for the authors of the Gospels and for Paul in several places too – particularly in Ephesians attributed to him, insisting that there 'are no longer any foreign visitors in the House of God' (language similar to what one gets at Qumran), all being 'equal citizens' and 'members of the body' of Christ (Eph. 2:19–22 and 4:30–32) – Jesus' body is the Temple! Here the parallel with these post-fall of Jerusalem Zealots, who take Nazirite oaths 'not to eat or drink' until they should see it 'risen again', is complete.

To crystallize further the circularity of this point in our sources about Jesus or his body *being the Temple*, we saw that Josephus, in writing the *Jewish War*, tried to exculpate the Romans of blame for the burning and subsequent destruction of the Temple – particularly his patrons, the Flavians, to whom he owed his survival. Likewise, those responsible for writing the Gospels – in the spirit of Paul in 1 Thessalonians, characterizing the Jews as 'being contrary to' or 'the Enemies of all men', because they 'both killed the Lord Jesus and their own Prophets' – are anxious to relieve the Romans of any guilt in the crucifixion of Jesus.

These themes of 'the destruction of the Temple' and 'the destruction of Jesus' are parallel themes in our literature, literature, as Josephus himself observes, in large measure marred by its authors attempting – for obvious reasons – 'to flatter the Romans and vilify the Jews', to the extent that 'much falsehood' had been written in it, including obviously many of the materials before us here.

Though Rabbinic sources also connect Helen's Naziritism with an oath she took that she would become a Nazirite if her son returned safely from battle (a possibility that can be made sense of in Josephus as well), they connect such vows – which include the neither eating meat nor drinking wine early Church sources attest of James – with adultery too – therefore the connection of the two passages from Numbers about the adulterous wife and Naziritism we noted above with regard to Helen. At the conclusion of the vow one was obliged to make a sin offering, as Paul and the other four are pictured as doing in the Temple in Acts, in connection with which the head was shaved (21:24–26 – being the 'We Document', Acts is *very* accurate here).

Paul performs another of these peculiar head-shavings, normally done at the completion of a Nazirite oath – as Muslims even now do at the conclusion of their Pilgrimage to Mecca – as we saw, at Cenchrea in Greece (the Aegean sea port of Corinth) according to Acts 18:18. But head-shaving of this kind seems to have been recognized only *in the Temple* – as we have just noted above, the hair being consumed on the altar – and what Acts seems to be doing here is either confusing another trip to Jerusalem Paul made for the purposes of a Nazirite oath or misplacing the later one just discussed above.

But Helen's 'Naziritism', which in Rabbinic literature, anyhow, ultimately leads her to Jerusalem and to build a strategically located palace for herself and her kinsmen to live in,[37] Famine relief, and finally to be buried there in such magnificent funerary monuments that no commentator has failed to remark them, is also clearly connected to her son's decision *to circumcise himself* and his, if not her, outright conversion. None of these things was seemingly done for the purposes of monetary gain, which was generally the case with the tax-collecting Herodians, but for 'spiritual' reasons, as Paul himself would put it.

Izates' Circumcision and his Famine-Relief Expenditures

As Rabbinic sources describe this circumcision, both Izates *and* his brother Monobazus *are reading Genesis* – not Numbers as in the case of his mother's Naziritism and the gift of the plaque with the adulterous-wife passage above – and come upon the passage 'and you shall circumcise the flesh of your foreskin' (Gen. 17:11–12). God gives this command to Abraham not long after the passage about Abraham's 'Faith being reckoned for him as Righteousness' or 'justifying him', so important to the polemics of this period as we have shown (Gen. 15:6 – it should be noted that a variation of this passage even turns up in the conclusion of the 'Two Letters on Works Reckoned as Righteousness' – '*MMT*' from Qumran).[38] In Genesis, this Commandment to circumcise is considered to apply to all in his household, including '*any foreigner not one of your descendants*'.

Once again, as in the Letter of James involving the sacrifice of Izates' probable namesake, Isaac, and Paul's use of the example of Abraham's 'Faith counting for him as Righteousness' above, we have examples connected with the name of Abraham, being used for the benefit of persons living presumably in *the area of Haran*, considered *the homeland of the*

Abrahamic family. Just like the story of Agrippa I reading the *Torah* in the Temple on *Succot* and weeping over the matter of the Deuteronomic King Law, when they come to this passage, both Izates and his brother Monobazus begin to weep and immediately decide, unbeknown to their mother, *to circumcise themselves.*[39]

This is the story as Rabbinic literature would have it. It not only fleshes out Josephus' version further – for a change both agreeing on the essence of the contents – in addition, it adds Izates' brother Monobazus to the equation, actually insisting that both brothers knew about the necessity of these things, which from the perspective of later events in Palestine as they will unfold makes sense.

It is not only peculiar, but passing strange that the letter (or letters), called in the usually obscure jargon of scholars, '*MMT*', above – which became so controversial recently in disputes related to the Dead Sea Scrolls, appear, as just noted, to be *addressed to a King*. The first part of this 'letter(s)' actually focuses on the theme of the *uncleanness of Gentile sacrifices in the Temple*, particularly *grain offerings*, and does so – as already remarked – in the course of actually mentioning the very words 'things sacrificed to an idol' (1.3–1.9), so important to all our discussions of James so far!

To review: in the first part of this correspondence, too – which we call the 'First Letter'[40] – for the purposes of such sacrifices or offerings, Jerusalem is designated as 'the Holy Camp' and 'principal of the camps of Israel' (1.68–69). The second part (or 'Second Letter'), which actually mentions a previous letter having been sent, outlined:

> the works of the *Torah* that would be reckoned for your own welfare and that of your people, because we saw that you had the intelligence and the Knowledge of the *Torah* to understand all these things. (2.30–31)

These are the actual words used in the second part (or Second Letter) and follow the admonition: 'to remember David, for he was a *Man of Piety* [here the actual words used in Josephus' description of Eleazar's more 'zealous' conversion of Izates above] and he, too, was saved after many sufferings and forgiven' (2.28–29) – points Josephus also refers to in his descriptions of the trials and tribulations of Izates and his mother.

But even more importantly – and we have highlighted this point in all previous work, which is why we gave this letter(s) the name we gave it – it ends on the note, quoting Genesis from 15:6 on Abraham, as already remarked, and in direct contradiction to Paul, with the assurance 'that then at the Last Days, you will find some of our words to be true' and 'these are *the works*' that 'will be *reckoned as justifying you*' (1:2 and 2:33). One should compare this with Paul in Galatians 4:16, also *a letter*, who 'by speaking Truth to you', against 'those who were *zealous after you*', but improperly so, since they were '*zealous to exclude*', has become 'your Enemy'. All of what we have just quoted from the two parts of this '*MMT*' letter(s) above is also in *direct agreement* with the Letter of James, which in addition to citing this passage about Abraham above (2:23), evokes 'the Last Days' as well (5:3).

The constant reiteration of Abraham in all these contexts is important, too, as we have explained. Were it not for the technicality of the *two* letters – though, in fact, most see only one here (the Hebrew is Mishnaic, meaning from the time of Izates and thereafter) – one would almost assume that one has here the actual Qumran version of the correspondence, delivered by 'the courier Ananias', between 'Jesus' or, as the case may be, 'the Teacher of Righteousness' or James, and 'the Great King'.

In fact, in view of the evocation of these very Jamesian 'things sacrificed to idols', in the first part, the very basis of James' instructions to overseas communities as depicted in Acts, reproduced in the Pseudo-clementines and wrestled with so disingenuously by Paul in 1 Corinthians; and the second ending on the very note of the dispute between Paul and James of whether it was Abraham's 'works' or 'Faith' that 'were reckoned to him as Righteousness' and 'saving him', it does begin to make more and more sense – especially as one reads all the above-mentioned exchanges of 'correspondence'. Here at Qumran, we may have the actual record of the original correspondence, which was then changed by the magic of historical re-creation into the stories about the new 'Messiah' as we have them today.

If this is true, then the main lines of what has occurred take shape. Izates' and his mother's conversion to this more zealous form of Judaism in the end also contributed to the Uprising against Rome, in which Izates' brave 'sons' or 'kinsmen', Monobazus and Kenedaeos, sacrificed their lives in the first engagement, giving others 'a splendid example' of how to 'make a good death' and a 'Pious end'.[41] Not only did Helen and her two sons, Izates and Monobazus, have the finances to undertake their illustrious Famine-relief efforts and the splendid burial monuments accorded them in Jerusalem, they probably also had the finances to undertake far more.

So frightening was this form of Judaism, which was not only revolutionary, but also comprised this 'Sabaean' or daily-bathing type of

Nazirite extremism or asceticism (which still leaves its mark in Southern Iraq today and is to be seen in the remains of the bathing pools among the ruins at Qumran) that all has been transformed – even including the 'Ebionite'/'Sabaean' doctrine of 'the Standing One' – in the various stories we have, including the Gospels and the Book of Acts and those about 'King Agbarus' or 'the Great King of the Peoples beyond the Euphrates'.

We have already suggested that Paul and 'Barnabas', whose 'Antioch' Community is made so much of in Acts, were originally among Helen's grain-buying agents. So probably was the fabulous 'Ananias' in Acts, Josephus, and the 'Agbarus' stories. Those who undertook this transformation had the highest knowledge of texts and sources. They also knew the incendiary nature of the ideas that were involved and were intent on transforming them into something a little less inflammatory that could live under the aegis of Roman Authority and which Rome itself could live with. This was an important literary task, for which those who achieved it were eminently qualified.

As we have suggested, it was perhaps the most successful literary rewrite enterprise ever undertaken, *and accomplished*. By means of it, not only did Rome defeat its enemies militarily, which was the successful first step, but also then *literarily*. By it, we have new religious mythologization of a Hellenizing kind taking place on top of an originally native Palestinian core.

In his version of the story of Izates' conversion, as earlier remarked, Josephus also explains the reason behind all of these convolutions relating to circumcision very succinctly. Circumcision, in many of the areas under consideration here, put one into bad odour with one's subjects, who would consider – as Josephus pictures Helen herself putting it – that the individual involved

> *was zealous* for strange and foreign practices, which would produce disaffection, nor would they tolerate *the rule of a Jew* over them.[42]

This, in fact, does happen to Izates, who must actually go to war – the background for the *Talmud*'s portrayal of the original occasion of Helen's Nazirite vow – because of the endless disaffections of his people and nobles. These, in Josephus' words, hate him 'for abrogating the laws of their forefathers and being zealous for [*zēlōtēs*] foreign customs'.[43]

Obviously, because of all these trials, and 'God's Providence over' Izates, who 'committed himself to God the Protector . . . who was much more powerful than all men', Helen goes to Jerusalem to fulfil her vow –

here obviously the parallel to the notices about her 'Naziritism' in the *Talmud* – 'to worship at the Temple of God and offer her thank-offerings there'. Izates enthusiastically consents to her going and 'bestowed upon her a great deal of money'! This is in the year 45 or 46 CE around the time of the Theudas episode and the beginning of the Famine.

Izates dies around the year 55 CE, and if Josephus is correct in telling us he reigned for twenty-four years, this would mean he began his reign around the time Eusebius gives for his 'Agbarus' story in the Royal Archives at Edessa. Trajan finally put an end to the Kingdom of Adiabene – as he did much else – in the next century in the course of his wars with the Parthians in the East and Messianic disturbances around the Mediterranean generally. Josephus promised an additional account of the reign of Izates' brother Monobazus, but never in fact provided it.

In Rabbinic literature, in addition to the Monobazus above killed at the Pass at Beit Horon at the beginning of the Uprising, there are several references to a second-century *disciple of Rabbi Akiba* – the latter, perhaps the moving force behind the Bar Kochba Uprising and the most 'Zealot' of all Rabbis – called 'Monabaz', who must have been yet another descendant.[44] In fact, Akiba is married to one 'Ben Kalba Sabu'a''s daughter, probably another descendant as well, about whom we shall hear more below.[45]

As Josephus describes Helen's arrival, 'it was of very great advantage to the people of Jerusalem', who were at that time 'hard-pressed by Famine, so that many perished for want of money to purchase what they needed' (45–48 CE). It is not unlikely that Theudas' attempt – as a kind of Joshua (or 'Jesus') *redivivus* – at 'miracles' (to 'multiply the loaves'?) and to cross the Jordan in reverse, were connected with it, and there is material in Qumran sources about just such reverse exoduses across Jordan.

Helen then

> quickly sent a number of her attendants *to Alexandria* and *others to Cyprus* with large sums of money to buy grain and bring back large quantities of dried figs,

and when her son, too, 'was informed of this Famine, he sent a great sum of money to the principal men of Jerusalem'. The beneficence of this family is a constant theme of our sources. 'She thus left a most excellent memorial behind her by this benefaction which she bestowed on our whole nation.'

When Izates died around 55 CE, Helen appears to have returned to Adiabene from her extended residence in Jerusalem – possibly still observing her extended Nazirite vows, as Rabbinic sources would have it. Here she too died suddenly, apparently out of grief for her son. It is at this point Josephus tells of the splendid funerary monuments erected by Monobazus in Jerusalem for Helen, as well as for Izates, who also seems to have been buried there, monuments Josephus himself claims to have seen. These external monuments are nowhere extant today, but the underground tombs with their majestic staircase are, and these are indeed very impressive.[46]

It is this Famine, as we have seen, that Acts refers to exactly preceding its notice about 'Herod the King *beheading James the brother of John with the sword*'. As already suggested, this 'Herod' was probably Agrippa I's brother Herod of Chalcis (*d.* 49 CE) – probably also responsible for arresting Simon the head of an 'Assembly of his own in Jerusalem', who wanted to bar Herodians from the Temple – since he was was hardly as tolerant as his brother. In addition, at this point he was *married to his niece*, the hated Bernice, later Titus' mistress and probably involved with him – as we have suggested as well – in the decision to destroy the Temple.

Josephus attributes Theudas' death to Fadus (44–46 CE), but this 'Herod' ruled in conjunction with both him and Tiberius Alexander, who succeeded Fadus (46–49). Tiberius Alexander, it will be recalled, was Herod of Chalcis' brother-in-law as well, both through an earlier marriage of Bernice to his brother, Marcus Julius Alexander, and probably her sister, Mariamme, to one 'Demetrius', whom Josephus also calls 'Alabarch'[47] and 'the Richest' of the Jews in Alexandria. Helen's behaviour during this Famine is in marked contrast to people like the Roman Governor Fadus and Tiberius Alexander who, while himself doubtlessly 'fabulously Rich' and from Egypt, hardly appears to have gone to Alexandria to *buy grain for the people*. On the contrary, like Herod of Chalcis and Fadus, he executed the heroes of the people.

Tiberius Alexander was a Roman bureaucrat of the front rank, who – if his preventive execution of 'James and Simon' the two sons of Judas the Galilean also at the time of this Famine is any measure – seems to have been particularly brutal. He was later Governor of Egypt too, but when Vespasian went to Rome to become Emperor, he left Tiberius Alexander behind to assist his son Titus – or, more probably, oversee him – in the final assault on Jerusalem! Not only did he owe his ascent to power probably to Agrippa I (to whose family he was allied by marriage above), later in Rome he seems to have functioned with Titus as a kind of 'co-Consul' and was actually Prefect of the Praetorian Guard.[48]

Of course for Christians – in the event of famine – Jesus would simply have had to 'multiply the loaves', since he could do whatever he wanted by a command, and, unlike Theudas, he wouldn't need to part any waters (though he did 'walk on' them), and we have already noted above how he did this, for instance at the wedding feast in John in *'Cana of Galilee'*. In Matthew and Mark, Jesus performs the multiplication of the loaves twice, both 'apart in a desert place' – in Mark 7:31, the second time 'on the borders of the Decapolis'. Both put the number that are fed the second time, anyhow, at 'four thousand' (Matt. 15:38 and Mark 8:9).

For Acts, this is the number of 'the *Sicarii*', whom Josephus, too, has taken to mentioning at this point in his narrative, that 'the Egyptian' for whom Paul is mistaken *'led out into the desert'* (21:38) and earlier, it had Gamaliel – however anachronistically – put the number of Theudas' followers at 'about four hundred' (Acts 5:36). In John, the multiplication of the loaves is taken as a 'sign' that Jesus was 'the True Prophet' – as John charmingly puts this, 'this is *truly* the Prophet' (6:14). These are, of course, the same 'signs' Josephus repeatedly mentions these 'impostors', 'pseudo-prophets', or 'Deceivers' as attempting to do 'out in the wilderness' – 'there to show them the signs of their impending freedom', 'Salvation', or 'deliverance'.[49]

As will be recalled, Acts more or less couples this reference to 'Herod the King' putting 'James the brother of John to death with the sword' (12:2) with the prophecy by an unknown prophet called 'Agabus' – another of these persons who 'came down from Jerusalem' – of 'the Famine that would then overtake the civilized world' (11:28). This, in turn, paves the way for the introduction of James the Just, directly thereafter in the same chapter, whose sudden intrusion into the text seems, as we have seen, either to assume that he had already been introduced previously or that we should know who he is (Acts 12:17).

'Agabus', 'Agbarus', and Helen's and Paul's Parallel Grain-Buying Activities

We are now able to put all our sources together. What is Paul's relationship to Helen's grain-buying activities? Acts claims that he and Barnabas were sent by the Church in 'Antioch' – where Christians 'were first called Christians' – to bring funds to Jerusalem; but in Galatians Paul, as we have seen, nowhere refers to this mission, rather saying he 'went away into Arabia and then returned to Damascus' for three years. This is normally taken to mean the area around Petra but, as we have explained as well, it may have wider implications.

Then there is the second teacher in Josephus with the peculiarly Pauline approach, who teaches Queen Helen a form of Judaism in which '*the worship of God was more important than circumcision*' – but whom, for some reason, Josephus declines to name. This teacher seems to share this more easy-going approach to Jewish Law with the first teacher, 'Ananias', whom Josephus identifies as Izates' 'tutor' and *close associate*, who seems to follow Izates about wherever he goes. Of course in Eusebius and other Syriac versions of the King Abgar conversion, 'Ananias', as we saw, is the 'courier' to Jerusalem from 'the Great King of the Peoples beyond the Euphrates'.

It should also not be forgotten that this Edessa, to which according to Syriac/Armenian sources Helen also appertained, was also known as 'Antioch' – Antioch-by-Callirhoe or Edessa Orrhoe. It was, as we explained, only one of several of 'Antioch's – 'Antiochus' having been one of the most successful Seleucid Kings previously and 'Orrhoe' clearly reflecting the name for the inhabitants of this region in early Church accounts, 'the Osrhoeans'. 'Carrhae', too, is another town just south of this Antioch or Edessa, identified with Haran and associated, it will be recalled, with Izates in Josephus' version of these events.

But according to Acts' account, Paul, too, was associated in his conversion with someone named 'Ananias' – this time 'in Damascus'. Thereafter Ananias drops out of the Acts' version of these events, unless we can say that, like 'Agbarus', his name too is reflected in that of the so-called 'prophet Agabus', who came down from Jerusalem to Antioch in the days of the Great Famine under Claudius, or in the name of Paul's erstwhile associate, the unknown 'Manaen the foster brother of Herod the Tetrarch' in Acts, one of the original 'prophets and teachers of the Church' or 'Assembly in Antioch'.[50]

In Eusebius' account of the conversion of this 'Abgarus' and the missions of 'Judas Thomas' and/or 'Thaddaeus' to 'the Land of the Edessenes' or 'Osrhoeans' and further elaborations in Syriac and Armenian sources which, though denigrated by some, actually marshal a good many additional facts; Ananias is obviously meant to be the same person as in the Queen Helen story. Here, again, is something of the letter-carrying scenario of Acts' picture of James sending out 'Judas Barsabas' after the Jerusalem Conference or the 'courier' connection between the 'Agabus' story in Acts and these 'Ananias' scenarios, not to mention the 'letter(s)' we have just discussed above, known as '*MMT*' and probably the work of 'the Righteous Teacher' at Qumran.

For instance, in the fourth- or fifth-century Syriac work, known as the Doctrine of Addai – said to have been based on Eusebius, but much more extensive than anything he seems to have had access to – Ananias is Abgar's 'secretary' (in Josephus, as we saw, he was Izates' 'tutor'). Reference is distinctly made in the Doctrine of Addai to the story of the portrait Ananias had made of Jesus 'in choice paints', which he brought 'to his Lord King Abgar', the basis of presentday theories relating the fabulous Shroud of Turin to the city of Edessa, where Crusaders were thought to have come into possession of it.

Even more convincing, the collection of Syriac works, of which this one is a part, repeatedly refers to 'Simon Cephas', at one point even identifying him as 'Simon *the Galilean*'. He is said to have laid the foundation for the churches in Syria, Galatia, and Pontus, before going to Rome for further confrontations with Simon *Magus*.[51] Once again, here we have our two 'Simon's, Simon Peter and Simeon bar Cleophas, combined as in more orthodox works, such as Acts, into a single person. Nevertheless the identification of at least the second with 'Simon Zēlōtēs' or 'Simon the Cananite' (here now 'Simon the Galilean') stands. In fact, this second Simon may have been the person who really was involved in all these things – at least in eastern communities like Alexandria, 'Antioch', Edessa, and beyond in Adiabene.

What are we to make of all these sources? I think, first of all, we can say definitively, as we have above, that this mysterious 'prophet' called 'Agabus' is nothing more than a stand-in for 'Abgarus' or 'Agbarus' in the legends going under his name and their elaborations in works by Syriac authors and the overwriting going on here in Acts. Moses of Chorene, it will be remembered, even knows that Westerners have trouble pronouncing 'Abgarus" name, which he anyhow simply sees as *a title* meaning 'Great One'. This derivation of the name also reappears to some extent in Eusebius' original translation of the correspondence.

The overwriting of whatever was meant by 'the Agbarus Legend' at this time, and the courier named 'Ananias' involved in it, by the nonsense name of the pseudo-prophet 'Agabus' – who certainly *never* existed and later reappears at another crucial juncture of Acts' story of the further adventures of Paul and his 'loin-cloth' or 'girdle' – would be in line with Acts' working method, as we have been delineating it above with regard to quite a few other historically documentable events: that is, to distort, to dissimulate, to confuse, and to delete – sometimes even simply, to have fun, or, if one prefers, a more malevolent intent, to *make fun*!

This at least is the case for materials in the first sixteen chapters before the introduction of the 'We Document' and even, to some extent, after its introduction, where materials in this document, too, are sometimes transformed in a pro-Pauline manner, but always less fabulously. For instance, before Paul's final arrival in Rome, where the information in the 'We Document' once again grows rather shaky, Acts introduces the ritual shipwreck, probably based on Josephus' more believable account of his own experiences in this regard – also reappearing in the Pseudoclementine narratives. In Acts' recitation of this event, Paul survives a poisonous snakebite on an island (seemingly Malta – 28:1–6, only there are no poisonous snakes on the island of Malta).

There are the similar stories, it will be recalled, told according to Eusebius by Papias about 'Justus surnamed Barsabas' ('Barnabas who was also called Matthias' in the Pseudoclementine *Recognitions*) and about Jacob of Kfar Sechania ('Cana'/'Kfar *Sicarii*'?), the Rabbinic stand-in for James. In fact in one curious Talmudic story about another fabulous Messianic stand-in, 'Bar Daroma, who could jump a mile' – note the further 'Standing One' imagery and the parallel, too, with the individual Jacob cures, '*Ben Dama*' – '*Bar Daroma*' is, yet again, '*sitting in the outhouse*' (more parody of 'Essene' toilet practices), when he sees a poisonous snake, drops his bowels, and immediately dies (presumably *because he was so frightened*), thereby 'miraculously' saving the Roman Emperor from his powers! (*Git.* 57a, also mentioning 'Kfar Sechania').

There is only one problem with identifying 'Agabus' in Acts with this 'Agbarus' or 'Abgarus' in the legends going by his name. This would mean that Acts knows 'the Agbarus Legend', whereas many scholars, as remarked, think the first indication we have of this story is from Eusebius, that is, they give Eusebius credit for being a creative writer – a dubious proposition! Scholars are simply wrong on this point and it is the account we have before us here in Acts that *proves it* – in connection with which, Helen (and/or her son, 'the Great King' Izates) sends her representatives on her more real grain-buying expeditions *to Egypt and Cyprus* (the importance of which in Acts' narrative we shall also see momentarily) – its linking 'Agabus'' name with 'the Famine' being altogether *too coincidental* to be accidental.

In any event, as we have already seen, the fragments of the listings of 'the Twelve' and 'Seventy Apostles', attributed to Hippolytus in second-century

Rome, already knows the traditions connecting 'Judas called *Lebbaeus surnamed Thaddaeus*' (not '*Barsabas*') with the evangelization of 'the Edessenes *and all Mesopotamia*' and sending a letter to an individual called 'Augarus' – in the latter, it is 'Thaddaeus' who *conveys the letter*.[52] So do the two variant manuscripts of the Apostolic Constitutions, only now this individual is '*Thaddaeus called Lebbaeus . . . surnamed Judas the Zealot*, who preached the Truth to the Edessenes and the people of Mesopotamia when Abgarus ruled over Edessa'. Then there is also the relationship of all these matters to the contemporary beheadings of '*Theudas*', who claimed to be 'a prophet' but was really a 'Deceiver', and 'James *the brother of John*', which we shall unravel below.

But this really would make Helen a 'wife' of King Agbarus, as Syriac sources and Moses of Chorene claim. The matter of the sizeable harems these monarchs kept has already been pointed out and Helen's marital status even in Josephus' account is extremely vague. As well, 'Monobazus' or 'Bazeus' are – like 'Caesar', 'Herod', and even 'Abgarus' above – probably titles, reappearing as husband, son, grandson, and even *great-grandson*, if we are to take Rabbinic acounts seriously. Moreover, Helen is given territory within what seem to be her husband's domains (whoever he was) and seems to function in an independent manner as a kind of local grandee there, as her son Izates does elsewhere in his 'father's' domains – most notably the area around *Abraham's Haran*.

The whole area is referred to in all these sources as that of 'the Osrhoeans' – in Roman sources all considered 'Arabs', 'Acbar' being 'the King of the Arabs' – the relationship of Edessa to Adiabene further east being unclear, their being at least contiguous. What is clear, however, is that both areas have something to do with the archetypal prophetical figure 'Addai', who in our sources is associated either with 'Thomas' or 'Thaddaeus' (also related to this root 'Ad') or, in the Koran, the land called "Ād'. But the final confirmation of all these things, despite the doubts of many scholars, is the note that a future Edessene king, Abgar VII (109–116), probably the grandson of the Abgar or Agbar in our stories, was known as 'Abgar bar Ezad', that is, '*Abgar the son of Izates*' (not to mention the fact that in Josephus 'Izates' is sometimes 'Izas').[53] Here the relationship of Abgar to Izates is made concrete.

In fact, as we have already suggested above, in this fairly dubious relationship with her husband – and other perhaps even more scandalous rumours – may lie the source of Helen's documented interest in the 'suspected adulteress' passage from Numbers 5:11–31, which precedes the one about Nazirite oaths in that book – another of her evident passions. As previously noted, Helen's inscription of this passage on a gold plaque displayed in the Temple is in marked contrast to the attitude of adulterers in the Herodian family on this issue and, of course, in total conformity with what we hear in all sources about the concerns of John the Baptist, her apparent contemporary.

Since, as already observed, her attitude and that of her sons -- even her grandsons and great-grandsons – would appear to have been a competitive one to Herodians, it is possible that the plaque she contributed represented an attempt to embarrass the latter or rebuke them. Just as the Herodians were the Roman puppet kings in Palestine seemingly sponsored by and championing the Pharisees, so those in the Royal House of Adiabene seemed to have carried with them the hopes of Nazirite-style, more extreme Zealot and *Sicarii* groups. In fact, as we have suggested as well, the financing they provided Palestinian affairs probably did not just end with Famine-relief activities, though this is nowhere as clearly documented as their grain-buying. They may even have had something to do with the support of installations, as at Qumran – 'bathing' activity of this kind being quite popular among other 'Sabaeans' and 'Elchasaites' at the headwaters of the Euphrates continguous to their domains, as already remarked. Buffer state as they were, to some degree their interest in Palestinian affairs can be seen as a proxy for the even more formidable and inimitable enemies of the Romans, such as the Parthians further east.

This state of affairs can be seen under the Roman Emperor Trajan who, once more, began to make and unmake kings in this area and stamp out all Messianic disturbances, but whose career was probably cut short because of it. In 115–16, he actually put an end to the Kingdom of Adiabene, marching down the Tigris to take the Parthian capital Ctesiphon, and then to the head of the Persian Gulf at Charax Spasini. As if on signal, Messianic revolts broke out among the Jews in his rear around the Mediterranean at Cyrene, Egypt, Cyprus, and Crete, sparking other revolts in Armenia, Syria, and Northern Mesopotamia, suppressing which Trajan suddenly died in 117 CE.

This interest in 'harlots' and 'adulteresses' is also keen in Gospel accounts about Jesus, as it is at Qumran, providing yet another of these thematic circles. But in the Gospels Jesus is depicted, as we have on several occasions remarked, as keeping 'table fellowship' with 'Sinners' of this kind. Such behaviour, if it were true – *which it undoubtedly was not* – would have sent groups like those represented by the literature of Qumran into paroxysms of 'Righteous' indignation. Of course, according to Acts' distorted historiography, there were believers who were

> of the *sect of the Pharisees*, who rose up [at 'the Jerusalem Council'] and said, it was *necessary to circumcise* them [meaning, Gentiles] and that they *be obliged to keep the Law*. (Acts 15:5)

Of course, *real* 'Pharisees' at this time – like Paul and Jesus (as he is portrayed in Scripture) – had a very tolerant attitude on these matters.

But the use of the term 'Pharisees' in the New Testament, as in this instance here, is often a polemical code for attacks on Jerusalem Leaders like James, because of their nit-picking attitude over points of the Law – an attitude amply demonstrated in the document known as '*MMT*'. On the other hand, there are *real* Pharisees as well, of the kind, pictured in Scripture, politically anyhow, as harassing teachers like John the Baptist or Jesus. This picture is doubtlessly true, but these Pharisees were basically Herodian/Roman clients. To be sure, all this is very confusing for the newcomer, as it is for the veteran scholar, but attention to *political* attitudes towards Roman power and the Herodian Establishment, as pointed out in the Introduction, will soon put one on the right track in sorting out these conflicting codenames.

The 'suspected adulteress' in Numbers was supposed to drink some kind of horrific potion, that, if it destroyed her innards, would prove that she was guilty. If it did not, this would attest to her innocence. Such a fanciful procedure was hardly a *proof of adultery* at all in the normal sense of the word. In some respects was actually quite lenient, as someone with a strong constitution, as Helen undoubtedly had, probably would have survived it – if it were survivable – guilty or innocent.[54]

It is impossible to say what the intricacies of Helen's marital or sexual relations were and who was the father of which of her children. Even today, the institution of 'temporary marriage' is a recognized one in areas of Iran and Iraq, where Shi'ism has a hold and it seems to have been in widespread practice among 'Arabs' before the coming of Islam. There is also the issue of whether Helen's husband, 'Bazeus' or 'Monobazus', was her brother. Much as in the instance of her younger contemporary, the Herodian Bernice, that questions arose centring around the issue of 'fornication' concerning Helen's behaviour seems almost undeniable. Bernice, for her part, to combat these, adopted the strategy of marrying Polemo King of Emesa, another of these Hellenized Arab puppet-Kings in Syria north of Damascus – undoubtedly a paper marriage – *making him circumcise himself*, as we have seen, before she forsook him for Titus.

In addition, in Helen's case, there was the inordinate *love* she lavished upon her 'only begotten' Izates, as opposed to her other children – Izates' 'brother' Monobazus, for instance. For this love, she was apparently well requited by the stipend Izates bestowed upon her and the relative splendour in which she seems to have lived in Jerusalem, rivalling, if not surpassing in some respects, that of *Herodians*. Of course, that Izates supplanted his older brothers and other relatives would lend further credence to his having had a more important forebear, as does the fact of his descendant, Abgar VII, becoming the *Edessan King* from 109 to 116, the period, in which Trajan *put an end* to the separate 'Kingdom of Adiabene'.

Paul may have had a relationship with Royal circles of this kind, as he did with Herodians before his mysterious trip to Rome at the end of Acts. It should be noted that if Paul is connected in any way with the enigmatic 'Saulus, a relative of Agrippa', in Josephus, then the note the latter provides that this Herodian Saulus was sent to Nero in Achaia (Corinth) to brief him on the state of affairs in Palestine is extremely interesting.

This is the year 66 CE and the last one hears about Josephus' mysterious 'Saulus', who had earlier been the intermediary between 'the Peace Party' in Jerusalem – consisting of Herodians, Chief Priests, and principal Pharisees – and the Roman Army and that of Agrippa II outside it. This is the coalition of forces that finally calls in the Roman troops *to suppress* the Revolution (which certainly must be considered *popular*) then in progress. This notice about Saulus in Josephus also fits in very nicely with Paul's own claims of important contacts in 'the household of Caesar' ('Augustus' in Acts 25:21–25, that is, Augustus Caesar Nero), most notably Epaphroditus – also Josephus' putative publisher, and secretary to both Nero and Domitian and the former's accused assassin (Phil. 2:25 and 4:18).

As we have seen, Paul does not speak of any intervening trip to Jerusalem to deal with anything resembling Famine relief before the one resulting in the 'Jerusalem Council', where Acts pictures James as making his rulings on what was required of foreign proselytes, including: most notably, where '*MMT*' is concerned, abstention from 'things sacrificed to idols'; where Helen is concerned, abstention from 'fornication'; and where Paul is concerned, the ban on 'blood', implying presumably, too, 'Communion' with it. But Helen also sent representatives to Egypt and Cyprus 'to buy grain and figs', and Paul does seem to have been associated with a variety of people ostensibly from Cyprus as, for instance, the ubiquitous 'Joses Barnabas'.

The similarity of this name to 'Joseph Barsabas Justus', who doubled for James in the improbable election to replace 'the Twelfth Apostle' in Acts 1:22, should also be remarked. He, in turn, mysteriously transmogrifies into 'Judas Barsabas' in the story of the two messengers who carry James' 'letter' with his instructions to overseas communities down to 'Antioch' in Acts 15:22. In Acts 4:36 this 'Joses surnamed Barnabas' is 'a Levite of Cypriot origins', while in Mark 2:14 the individual the other Gospels are calling 'Matthew' is called 'Levi the son of Alphaeus'. But, as we have repeatedly seen, these 'Barnabas'/'Barsabas'/'Barabbas' names often have to do with writing over and the elimination of the members of Jesus' family from Scripture.

In Acts 21:16, before Paul goes up to Jerusalem to be mobbed by the Jewish crowd for allegedly bringing *Greeks* (*Hellēnas*) into the Temple (21:28), Paul has to do with another curious individual from Cyprus, this time named 'Mnason'. He is called 'an old Disciple' (meaning aged) and, once more, we are probably dealing with obfuscation. Like Paul's nephew, who ultimately rescues him from the 'Nazirite oath'-taking *Sicarii*, he too has lodgings in Jerusalem. The 'Manaen' we have already met, the 'foster brother of Herod the Tetrarch', it will be recalled, was grouped alongside 'those from Cyprus and Cyrene', including 'Lucius the Cyrenian' (Paul's putative travelling companion) as one of the five founding members of the 'Antioch' Community in Acts 11:20 and 13:1. These also include one 'Simeon', now mysteriously called 'Niger', a name we have previously, also, met under slightly different circumstance in Josephus above.

These 'men of Cyprus and Cyrene', who according to Acts' completely skewed narrative had scattered in the wake of the stoning of Stephen (that is, the attack by Paul on James in the Temple in the 40s), now speak to 'the Hellenists' (now '*Hellēnistas*') at Antioch – whoever these might have been in such a context – about 'the Gospel of the Lord Jesus', at which point 'the Assembly in Jerusalem' sends down Barnabas to Antioch to deal with this situation there (where 'the Disciples were first being called Christians' – Acts 11:22–26) – yet another reverberation of the story of Thomas sending down Thaddaeus, 'as an Apostle, one of the Seventy', to the Land of the Edessenes and Mesopotamia when Abgarus ruled in Edessa – not to mention James sending down 'Judas Barsabas' with the 'epistle' containing his directives.

One can say that here these inverted notices about 'Cyprus and Cyrene' are nothing other than the contrapositive of the notices in Josephus about Helen sending her grain-buying agents to 'Egypt and Cyprus'. In continuing mix-ups involving so-called 'Cypriots', 'Simeon' above, and Samaritans, Simon *Magus*, the double of Elymus *Magus* from Cyprus in Acts, is also in some texts – most notably Josephus – said to have come from *Cyprus* not Gitta in Samaria. Hippolytus, the Pseudoclementines, and Eusebius, quoting Justin Martyr, put this right.

Queen Helen and the Supposed *Ethiopian Queen* Kandakes in Acts

However, it is the material in Acts about Philip in Caesarea that clinches in an unequalled manner our identification of 'Agabus' as a stand-in for or rub-out of 'Agbarus', becoming the ultimate example of Acts' working method. The material about Philip is peculiar anyhow, and tradition is never quite sure whether he is *an Apostle* or only *one of the Seventy*. This is the same problem we have above with 'Thaddaeus' and 'Thomas'. The reason again should be obvious.

In Acts 6:2–5, Philip is grouped alongside 'Stephen', 'Nicanor', 'Nicolaus, a convert from Antioch', and other Greek-sounding names to create the 'Seven to serve tables' – note the play on the 'table fellowship' theme here – while the more 'Hebrew' Twelve 'served' the word of God. In Rabbinic tradition, doubtlessly not unrelated to this, 'Nicanor' is a *Rich Jew from Egypt* who, alongside Helen's gifts, gave the splendid Temple gates made of pure gold.

There seems to have been some competition among differing groups overseas to contribute to the Temple and we shall meet this 'Nicanor' again below. In Josephus, 'Nicolaus of Damascus' is the Herodian source of much of his writing – an actual diplomat in Rome.[55] 'Stephen' we have already met as the Emperor's Servant, 'despoiled of all his belongings' outside Jerusalem by marauding 'Bandits' (*Lēstai*) or 'Revolutionaries' after the deadly stampede in the Temple at Passover following the 'flashing' incident.

'Philip', not insignificantly, participates in John 6:5's version of the 'miracle of the loaves' above – like the first account of this miracle, before 'five thousand', but now at *Passover* – which leads up to Jesus' announcement of himself as 'the living bread' and instructing his Disciples 'to eat' his flesh and 'drink' his blood (6:50–58). Instead of the 'dates' added to the grain in Josephus' descriptions of Queen Helen's grain-buying activities in Egypt and Cyprus above, it is, of course, now the 'fish' of the various versions of Jesus' 'breaking bread' with his Disciples in his post-resurrection manifestations to them above, added to the 'loaves'.

In John, in answer to Jesus' question, 'where shall we buy loaves that these may eat?' (6:6), Philip is represented as responding in the language and manner of all these 'grain-buying' agent notices and the picture of Nicanor's fabulous wealth above: 'two hundred pieces of silver's worth of loaves is not sufficient for them even for a little to eat' (6:7). Other than these few points and the story of his confrontation with Simon *Magus* in Samaria, after which he makes his way, *via the road to Gaza in the South* to *Caesarea in the North*; the New Testament, again, knows next to nothing about 'Philip'.

Acts places the episode of Philip's circuitous trip – wherein he will finally meet *the Treasurer of the Ethiopian Queen Kandakes* – after the stoning of Stephen and Paul ravaging the Jerusalem Community, dragging people out of their houses and 'delivering them up', Judas *Iscariot*-like, to prison (8:1–3), but before his reported 'Damascus Road' vision and meeting with Ananias in Damascus in chapter 9. Acts presents Philip as something of a stand-in for Peter, who in any event comes to Samaria after him to rebuke Simon – that is, *Simon Magus* – for supposedly offering 'Riches' to Philip, himself, and John, the Samaria locale reflecting the 'Gitta' notices about Simon's origins in these other sources above.

One should note how, in all these episodes, the theme of money, 'Riches', or being someone's 'Treasury' or grain-buying agent, is played upon in various ways – usually negatively. This totally intrusive episode in Acts 8:4–40, in between the two episodes about Paul's activities in Jerusalem and 'Damascus', has Peter speaking James-like to Simon *Magus* – in the context, totally incomprehensibly:

> May *the money you have with you* be destroyed, because you thought the gift of God could be *acquired by Riches*. (Acts 8:18–20)

Peter's anger here is out of place and completely uncharacteristic, but it does echo the attacks on Paul for *profiteering by his ministry* that Paul responds to so emotionally in 1 Corinthians 9:3–12.

The words attributed to Peter, here too, are almost word for word those used by James in the attack on the 'Rich' in the conclusion of the Letter attributed to him:

> Come you Rich, weep, howl over the miseries that are coming on you. *Your Riches have rotted and your clothes have become moth-eaten.* Your gold and silver is mouldering away and their canker shall be a witness against you and shall eat your flesh. (James 5:1–3)

This comes right before the attack on these same 'Rich' for 'condemning and killing the Righteous One' and the evocation of the coming of the Lord and the Heavenly Host, presumably, as in Daniel and the War Scroll from Qumran, on the clouds of Heaven bringing Judgement like 'Spring rain' (5:4–10).

We have already paid considerable attention to the condemnation of 'Riches' in the *Three Nets of Belial* section of the Damascus Document from Qumran above. This will be developed further in the attack on the High Priest class for 'profiteering' and 'acquiring Riches' in the Habakkuk *Pesher*. Paul, too, couches his response to such 'profiteering' charges *against him* with an attack on those who would *'judge' him* for, among other things, 'eating and drinking', that is, that they should *'eat and drink Judgement* to' themselves (1 Cor. 9:3–11:29).

Acts' plot line then for some reason follows Philip, who is told by an 'Angel of the Lord' to go south, that is, *towards Gaza and Egypt*, even though his real destination seems to be north or west and *Caesarea on the Palestine coast* – where Paul, as we saw, later encounters him (8:26). 'On the way', he meets 'an Ethiopian man, a eunuch, one in power', as it turns out 'over all her Treasure' or *the Treasurer* of someone called 'Kandakes, the Queen of the Ethiopians' (8:27). Not only is the fact of this man being *the Keeper of the Treasure* noteworthy, but that he serves one *Kandakes, Queen of the Ethiopians*, even more so.

This is just our old friend, *Queen Helen of Adiabene*, again intruding into the text of Acts just where one would expect her to, but now concealed almost – but not quite – beyond all recognition. The masquerade has sufficed for almost two thousand years. Such is the power of mind-numbing devotion and dissimulation.

Of course, there were no *Ethiopian Queen*s at this time – except in pages of biblical archetype a thousand years earlier – and none certainly who *sent their agents* or *messengers to Jerusalem*. What, anyhow, would the 'Treasurers' of such 'Queens' be doing in Jerusalem in this period? But no matter; the point is that the name 'Kandakes' is but a thinly disguised variation on or overwrite of the name of Queen Helen's kinsman Kenedaeos – probably her *grandson*. We have already encountered this Kenedaeos, probably one of Izates' numerous sons, who, together with *his* brother – the third Monobazus – was killed in the forefront of the assault by Jewish freedom-fighters on the Roman troops coming up the Pass at Beit Horon in the opening days of the War against Rome, whose 'valour' even Josephus is forced to remark.[56] As with the confusion of *Iscariot* with *Sicarios*, or 'Alphaeus' and 'Cleophas', if we exchange an *iota* with a *kappa* here, we probably come very close to the truth. In this instance, *Ethiopian* has simply been substituted for *Arab*. What matter, for the Hellenistic Roman mindset all dark-skinned peoples were alike anyhow – and what fun!

This transformation, to which both the references to 'Treasure' and 'the *Queen of the Ethiopians*' (somebody had been reading his biblical story of Solomon and *the Queen of Sheba*) should have alerted us, is quite astonishing and of the same order as that about 'Agabus' which follows a few chapters later. 'Agabus', too, will appear later in Acts, in connection with Philip, in the story of Paul's staying at *Philip's house in Caesarea*.

In addition, this *substitution* or *overwrite* shows substantial knowledge, not only of texts and traditions – in this case, the story of the conversion of Queen Helen and her Famine-relief efforts (the 'Treasurer', here, being nothing but one of Queen Helen's grain-buying agents) and probably the main lines of the 'Agbarus' story (*the real one, not the legend*); but also of history and the fact that one of Helen's descendants or kinsmen, a *heroic one* at that who distinguished himself in the opening engagement of the War against Rome, was named 'Kenedaeos'. Of course, all of these are being rubbed out and overwritten, probably just because of this *heroism* and the relationship of this family with *Revolutionary Forces in Judea*!

There was almost certainly no 'Ethiopian Queen' in existence at this time. Certainly not one named 'Kandakes', nor anyone remotely resembling her; but here, in focusing on the story of this legendary 'Queen of Sheba', there is a *very real* play upon the kind of 'Sabaean' religious practices *Queen Helen* no doubt supported – 'Sheba' and 'Sabaean' being based on very close linguistic roots in Hebrew and other Semitic languages as well. In fact, the same confusion between 'Sabaean' meaning 'Daily Bather' and 'Sabaean' meaning 'South Arabian' or 'Ethiopian' has crept into the Koran and Islam as well.[57] Here someone is overwriting with *definite* knowledge. Such is the playfulness of the writers of Acts' *pseudo*-history. In these materials, too, as if we had not already suspected it, 'Philip' begins to take a giant nose-dive, historically speaking. But that these dissimulators have not scrupled to satirize the name of one of the holiest martyrs of the Jewish people – 'Kenedaeos' – a hero and a convert at that, who has, in the process, been forgotten even by the Jews themselves. Such are the power of successful rewriting and the consequences of widespread and almost congenital ignorance.

To take the name of this non-Jew and convert, who none the less was a *valiant freedom-fighter* and *real martyr* for his adopted people, and disembody and ridicule it in this way might not be upsetting for the general reader; but to anyone valuing that cultural heritage or tradition involved – particularly as these words have been taken by endless numbers of people, including even Muslims, as 'the Word of God' for the last almost twenty centuries – it will be seen as offensive in the extreme.

For the final and definitive proof, not only of the knowledgeability, but also the cynicism of those responsible for such transformations, one has only to continue the story as it is presented in Acts. Even though this Ethiopian 'eunuch' – the story, of course, is playing on 'circumcision', just as Paul is in Galatians 5:12 above – and 'the man over all the Queen's Treasure', is sitting in his chariot on the road returning from *Jerusalem to Gaza*, he is *reading the Bible* (as no doubt our author was) – in this case 'the Prophet Isaiah'. 'The Spirit' now counsels Philip to creep up on him and 'join himself' to his chariot (Acts 8:29).

Note the play here on the Qumran language of 'joining' again, which involves converts and the status of resident aliens or those attaching themselves to the Community in an associated status in the Nahum *Pesher* and Damascus Document above. There is also just the slightest hint of a play on the episode involving 'Jonadab the son of Rechab' too above – the prototype for the 'Rechabite'/'Zealot' Movement – who *jumped up on Jehu's chariot* to assist him in his God-ordained work and 'zeal for the Lord' (2 Kings 10:15–16).

At this point, of course, Philip hears the eunuch reading Isaiah, and then asks him, 'do you then know what you are reading?' (Acts 8:30). But this is nothing other than *the story from Josephus* about 'the Galilean' teacher Eleazar going into *Queen Helen's favourite son Izates* and finding him reading – not Isaiah – but the Law of Moses, namely the Genesis passage *commanding Abraham to circumcise all the males in his entourage 'and any stranger not of his seed' that was with him* (Gen. 17:10–27). In Josephus' story, Eleazar then asks *Izates whether he understood what he was reading* – these, it will be recalled, were the precise words – and informing him of his *Impiety in neglecting this Commandment*.[58]

The substitution of the Prophet Isaiah here for the Book of Genesis on God's command to Abraham to *circumcise himself and those travelling with him – even the stranger –* is significant, Isaiah being perhaps the fundamental Christian biblical proof-text. The maliciousness in substituting 'a *eunuch*' for Izates is equally clear. If there were any doubts about what we have been saying previously concerning Acts' working method, these can now utterly be laid to rest. As obscure and inconsequential as this episode may seem to be, all our observations about Acts' rewriting activity can now be thought of as confirmed. The reader will also begin to appreciate that what we have been saying about Acts' sources and its manner of treating them is true too – all too true – many much older than previously supposed, and, because of Acts' extremely successful if tendentious methodology, *older, in fact, than Acts itself.*

But this is no longer simply humorous rewriting or overwriting. The disparaging caricature of *Izates' circumcision* puts paid to this idea. We are now in the realm of outright forgery aimed at disinformation of a most insidious kind. Unfortunately, the methods of our other documents do not differ to any extent from what we are seeing here, and the whole foundational edifice of 'Gentile Christianity' must be seen as derivative and tendentious. This is not the case for 'Jamesian' *Nazirite* or *Nazoraean* 'Christianity', if we can call it this.

Of course in Luke's version of this story, now *the Ethiopian eunuch and Treasurer of Queen Kandakes* – not *Izates the son of Queen Helen* – is reading the key exegetical passage of Christian theology on the death of Jesus, Isaiah 53:7–8, the 'Suffering Servant', at which point Philip asks him if he understood 'to whom the Prophet was referring', and proceeds 'to evangelize him' – for which reason he is, no doubt, known as 'the Evangelist' when Paul encounters him some thirteen chapters further along in Acts, with his 'four virgin daughters *who prophesied*' (*thus*: 21:9) – or, 'beginning with *this Scripture*, preaches to him the Gospel of Jesus', as well he might have (Acts 8:34).

In our view this term, '*Evangelistēs*', is to be ranged alongside the terms, '*Stratēgos*', '*Stratopedarchēs*' or '*Stratarchēsantos*', General, Commander, or Commander-in-Chief, all terms Josephus applies to the *other* Philip in Caesarea at this time.[59] In fact, he uses the second of these specifically in linking *Saulus* and *Philip* together. They along with Saulus' brother Costobarus defected from Jerusalem, as we saw, and joined the Roman Commander Cestius' army outside the city at the beginning of the War. In fact, it is at this point that Josephus notes how:

> Cestius dispatched *Saul and his companions* [including, it would appear, Philip] at their request to Nero in Achaia [that is, Corinth], to inform him of the straits, they [the Roman army in Palestine] had been reduced to.

To return to Acts' 'Philip': coming to some water 'along the Way', he now baptizes the 'eunuch' when he agrees that 'Jesus Christ is the Son of

God' – all perfectly good Gentile Christian theology. The stand-in of this 'Ethiopian Queen's eunuch' for the Izates story should be patent, Philip now taking the place of Izates' 'Zealot' teacher Eleazar.

When they 'went down in the water', for both apparently then enter the water, 'the Spirit of the Lord' – instead of descending on the eunuch 'like a dove', as in the instance of Jesus in the Gospels baptized by John the Baptist – 'took Philip away' and *the eunuch never saw Philip again* (Acts 8:39). One might add, neither do we, because Philip is then miraculously transported to Azotus on his way to 'evangelize all the cities' on the way to Caesarea in the opposite direction to which he had previously been going (8:40) – in time presumably to meet Paul there a decade and a half later.

The narrative immediately returns, this interruption out of the way, to 'Saul breathing threat and slaughter against the Disciples of the Lord', getting letters from the High Priest *to the synagogues of Damascus* (Acts 9:1–2) – wherever these may have been – and we are on our way to his vision on the road to Damascus. But what is the point of all this? One point, anyhow, is that the reason Philip and the Ethiopian eunuch are on their way from Jerusalem to Gaza and not Caesarea is that Gaza is *the gateway to Egypt* and this is where Helen's Treasury agents were, doubtlessly, going to buy grain.

There is unquestionably a lot of truth in this episode lying just beneath the surface, including whatever relationship Paul, Barnabas, or Philip might have had to these grain-buying operations and, no doubt, to Helen's Treasury agents, but one cannot proceed further along this line – only to observe that, without a thorough grasp of the Queen Helen materials, one would never have suspected the resemblance of this episode to the conversion of Queen Helen's son Izates and Queen Helen sending her representatives on Famine relief to Egypt and Cyprus thereafter.[60]

The Lukan author of Acts obviously knows the Queen Helen materials thoroughly, including her relationship to 'Agabus'. That he sees fit to affix Paul and Barnabas to these matters relating to the Famine, when Paul himself does not even refer to it in his letters, is further proof that Paul was in some manner involved (with some of his 'Cypriot' and 'Cyrenian' colleagues) not only in Queen Helen's Famine-relief efforts, or those of her son, but also perhaps her conversion. Josephus opines that Izates also sent relief, this time in the form of 'money' or 'coin', much like the 'eunuch who had power over all the Treasure of the Ethiopian Queen' – read here, *'Arabian Queen'* or *'Sabaean Queen'*.

Though Josephus promises us a further account of 'the good works of this royal pair', he never provides it, but Talmudic materials also deal with this aspect of the activities of Helen's son – now called Monobazus. When his brother asks him why he has impoverished himself in such activities, he replies, how good it was to store up 'Riches' in Heaven in place of those on earth, which his ancestors stored up, favourite allusions in the New Testament as we have seen – not to mention the Damascus Document – and the gist of Peter's rebuke to Simon *Magus* in the first part of the Philip materials in Acts.[61]

As to the reference to this 'Treasury' official as a 'eunuch', this, of course, has *nothing whatever to do with 'Ethiopia'*, but rather the practices of the Parthian court and those within the Persian sphere of influence generally, as Adiabene most definitely was. Even more to the point, it relates to the perception of 'circumcision' – as in the Roman '*Lex Cornelia de Sicarius*' above – as a kind of sexual mutilation. In his full account of Izates' efforts to remain viable in a Persian buffer state, in addition to showing us how Izates' father originally gave him a Kingdom around Haran, where Noah's ark had landed; Josephus gives us a vivid picture of Izates' struggles, for which his mother no doubt took her famous 'Nazirite' oaths or promised to. This 'eunuch' status also suits the purposes of the authors of the Book of Acts in inverting Qumran materials such as they are, which would rather ban all classes of such persons – cripples, lepers, diseased persons, those with running sores or 'founts' (as it is expressed), and most certainly *eunuch*s – from the Temple, and, as a 'eunuch', he would hardly 'have come to Jerusalem to worship' in those days (8:27). Acts' authors knew this.

Those responsible for these materials had an uncanny control over them, as well as a highly developed – albeit derisive – sense of humour. This was much more developed than many of their medieval or modern heirs, who normally see nothing funny in these materials and *almost never laugh at them*, regardless of how preposterous, outrageous, or ribald what is being recounted really is. Rather they take everything extremely seriously, some even to the extent of swearing by their mortal souls on them. The authors of Acts would, doubtlessly also, have been very pleased by the success of their poor efforts, the materials having almost as much power today as they did two millennia ago. They would, however, not perhaps have been very surprised at the credulity of mankind or by its tendency towards self-hypnosis or even mass hysteria over such a long expanse of time, as they seem already to have understood this.

26

Judas Thomas and Theuda the Brother
of the Just One

Judas Thomas and *Thaddaeus* among the Edessenes

Let us return to our original – and on the whole more credible – Syriac sources and Eusebius about these and parallel events at Edessa. For these, 'Thomas' or 'Judas Thomas sends out Thaddaeus' (in Luke 'Judas the brother of James'; in Matthew, also 'Lebbaeus surnamed Thaddaeus') to evangelize the Edessenes. This is much the same picture Acts gives of *James sending Judas Barsabas and Silas* (as well as Paul and Barnabas at this time and previously) *down from Jerusalem to Antioch* to 'deliver the letter' containing his Jerusalem Council rulings – not to mention the other notices, already remarked above, about the 'some' who came down from Judea earlier, with which the 'Jerusalem Council' episode began, or 'Agabus' and the other 'prophets who came down from Jerusalem to Antioch' and 'predicted the Famine' even earlier than this.

In the List of the Seventy attributed to Hippolytus above, Thaddaeus is sent with 'the letter to Augarus'. As Eusebius puts this tradition, which he claims to have found in the Royal Archives of Edessa as we saw:

> After the Ascension of Jesus, *Judas, who is also called Thomas, sent Thaddaeus the Apostle, one of the Seventy*, to him.

'Him' is 'King Abgar the Great King of the Peoples beyond the Euphrates', 'the Seventy' clearly being a variation on the Jerusalem Assembly or Church (*Seventy* being the traditional number making up such Assemblies in Judaism heretofore).

In the list of the Twelve Apostles attributed to Hippolytus above, this 'Thaddaeus who carried the letter to Augarus', it will be recalled, is paralleled by and clearly the same as the

> Judas, also Lebbaeus, who preached the Truth to the Edessenes and to all Mesopotamia and fell asleep at Berytus and was buried there.

Not only do we have here the additional note about 'all Mesopotamia' –

923

which would presumably include Adiabene too – but the same overlaps we found in parallel Synoptic Gospel lists of the Twelve concerning 'Judas the brother of James' and 'Lebbaeus surnamed Thaddaeus' above.

In Eusebius and other Syriac sources, the story of the conversion of Queen Helen and her son to Judaism – albeit in Queen Helen's case seemingly a rather abbreviated form – found in Josephus and elaborated upon in Talmudic tradition, now becomes *the conversion of King Abgar to Christianity* (Abgar *Uchama* – 'Acbar, King of the Arabs' in Tacitus). This is not to say that the story, as Eusebius reproduces it, is either completely authentic or historical, nor that one can make any definitive identifications between Agbar and Izates or his father – or brother – 'Bazeus' or 'Monobazus'. On the contrary, one can't.

But it is to say that Acts is working off *very old* materials, older probably even than the version of this story Eusebius presents, and transforming or obliterating them accordingly, so embarrassing were they evidently already felt to have been. It is also to say that in these original materials, the Helen and Abgar conversions, were related, which, indeed, is already the gist of these other Syriac sources and Eusebius.

But, I think, we are also in a position to say that Queen Helen's form of Judaism, and that of her son Izates and those following him, like Monobazus in whichever generation – second, third, or fourth – and Kenedaeos, was not completely normative, despite Rabbinic claims and attempts to take it over; but more 'Zealot' or 'Jamesian'. This is implied by the note of extreme 'Naziritism' associated with it even in Rabbinic sources, which do not really understand it any more than orthodox Christian sources do, because it is so alien to them. In fact, both the former and the latter show extreme hostility to this form of Judaism, particularly after the fall of the Temple.

The Historicity of John, Simon, Jesus, and Paul

Before moving along to consider the traditions about a flight of the Jerusalem Community and others across Jordan just prior to the fall of the Temple, it would be well to summarize our conclusions concerning the relationship of 'Judas Thomas' to 'Thaddaeus surnamed Lebbaeus' – or vice versa in canonical Apostle lists – and this latter then to 'Judas [the brother] of James'. First of all, we must put aside all embarrassment or hesitation regarding lacunae, repetitions, overlaps, or flaws in canonical Apostle lists, realizing that those who compiled them didn't know much more about the Apostles than we do. If they did, they often wished to conceal it and, in any event, the so-called 'Twelve Apostle' scheme was largely retrospective and mythological.

Paul, for instance, only refers to 'the Twelve' in the disputed interpolated portion of 1 Corinthians 15:5–7, where he also lists the post-resurrection appearance to James. Elsewhere, as we saw, he speaks of 'Apostles' – plural – and aside from listing himself as one of these, even includes Titus/Timothy, Barnabas,[1] and even the mysterious Epaphroditus, whom Paul calls 'his Apostle' – and confusion and proliferation reigns. Therefore, if we find Thomas, Thaddaeus, Lebbaeus, Jude the brother of James, or even Judas *Iscariot* on the same Apostle list, it should not bother us at all. One might add to this mix Judas ('the son' or 'brother') of Simon *Iscariot* in the Gospel of John, which gives no actual list of 'the Twelve' at all.

The same can be said for the two 'Simon's in most lists – even more: Simon Peter, Simon Cephas, Simon the Zealot/Cananaean, Simon *Iscariot*, Simeon bar Cleophas, etc. As we have just seen above, early Syriac historical texts call the 'Simon *Cephas*', who went to Rome to preach, 'Simon the Galilean', and the variant manuscripts of the Apostolic Constitutions – originally a Syriac work – clearly imply that 'Simon the *Cananaean*' was the same as Jesus' 'cousin', Simeon bar Cleophas.

This is all the more true of all the Jameses: James the brother of John/ the son of Zebedee, James the son of Alphaeus (that is, Cleophas), James the Less, James the brother of Jesus, also surnamed the Just One, etc. Here, too, the list of the Twelve Apostles attributed to Hippolytus can help, for, as we have seen above,

> *James the son of Alphaeus*, when preaching in Jerusalem, was *stoned to death by the Jews* and *was buried beside the Temple.*

But of course, this is manifestly none other than 'James the Just', the only problem being that Hippolytus obviously doesn't know about or is unwilling to deal with *anything concerning a brother of Jesus*. Clearly he has not yet read Hegesippus, his younger contemporary in Palestine, but by the next century, Eusebius – being from Palestine – *has*.

This makes it incontestably clear that 'James the son of Alphaeus' in Apostle lists is *none other than James the brother of Jesus*, even according to someone *who has not read Hegesippus* – which we have already determined on the basis of other sources and simple common sense in any event. It also makes the identity of 'Cleophas' and 'Alphaeus' all but sure. 'Cleophas', too, therefore, becomes identical with the so-called

'Joseph' of Gospel narratives, the latter being perhaps a symbolical or allegoric appellation not a real one. It also makes Mary and Cleophas husband and wife and the mother and father of four brothers – which is the gist of the 'Papian' fragment above – 'James the Bishop and Apostle, Simon, Thaddaeus, and one Joseph. Here, of course, the interchangeability of 'Thaddaeus' with 'Judas of James' and 'Jude the brother of James' is made concrete.

We have already shown Joshua, the biblical prototype for 'Jesus', to have been a *descendant of Joseph* and, therefore, in some manner a 'Messiah ben Joseph' as Rabbinic vocabulary would express it. In like manner, Paul's Hebrew namesake 'Saul' is a member of 'the Tribe of Benjamin', as Paul then claims himself to be; Paul is a master of such allegorical reconstruction. In fact the very name 'Jesus' may be simply allegorical, as Eusebius himself suggests, derived from the Hebrew word meaning 'Saviour' (*'Yeshu'a'*), that is, not only is Joshua *cum* Jesus the one who will 'save his People', his very name *means* 'Saviour' in Hebrew.

The final question has to be – was there even a 'Jesus'? Given the creative-writing expertise of many of the people responsible for these materials, anything is possible. The rule of thumb must be, as we have seen, if he or she is not mentioned in a similar manner in external sources, then nothing is sacred and everything has to be questioned. These external sources may include early Church Fathers, when serious and not simply based on patently mythological story-telling or working up Messianic proof-texts. The same is true of the *Talmud*, which often preserves a kernel of truth – as these others do – however distorted or misunderstood it finally becomes.

In Jesus' case, however, the reply probably is in the affirmative, that he *did* exist, most of all because *Paul refers to him in his letters*, though this reticently. However tenuously or disingenuously, Paul is grappling with the facts of his life, particularly his crucifixion, though not with any precision or in the way this is presented in the Gospels. Nor do we even know that Paul has the right name for the character he is discussing and that, as discussed above, he is not using an esoteric or symbolical name meaning 'Salvation' for an unidentified agitator *crucified* some time before he (Paul) came on the scene.

This is not to say that Jesus was not, for instance, called 'Joses', the name of the fourth, but completely ephemeral, brother in Gospel enumerations – called 'Joseph' in the fragment attributed to Papias above, which has Cleophas and Mary as the parents of *four* brothers. For his part, Paul

926

knows nothing or next to nothing about the individual he almost always refers to as 'Christ Jesus' or 'Jesus Christ', except the fact of his crucifixion and purported resurrection. He rarely uses the name 'Jesus' alone, usually coupling it with this title, 'the Christ', making it seem to some degree as if Jesus is in some manner in Hebrew the equivalent of this word in Greek.

He also seems to know something, perhaps, about a 'Cup' or 'the Cup', which 'the Lord Jesus' blessed or drank with his principal associates before the events resulting in his death (1 Cor. 11:23), although this is not certain. Nothing else – no historical incidents, which is strange for someone who lived in such purported chronological proximity to Jesus – though, as we have suggested, maybe he did not and this individual, about whom he appears to know so little and calls 'Christ Jesus', was crucified earlier, as some Roman documents attested to by Eusebius suggest, say 21 CE, a period in which Josephus' data too are so very sketchy.

The Letter of James, for instance, also hardly mentions Jesus at all and, when it does, largely in a symbolical manner. Nor does Jude, the Letter attributed to 'the brother of James', though Jude does mention 'the Apostles of our Lord Jesus Christ', although he does not number them (1:17).

The story in the Scripture as we have it is probably drawn from a variety of sources, not the least of these being stories about 'the Egyptian', the revolutionary activities of whom and whose followers centred around 'the Mount of Olives'; the wilderness exoduses of several other 'impostors', 'false prophets', or revolutionary leaders; materials from the life and death of James retrospectively incorporated into the picture of Jesus' life and trial, as we have it; and an individual Josephus calls 'Jesus ben Ananias', killed by a Roman projectile several months before the fall of the Temple in 70 CE, whom we shall discuss in relation to the supposed *second prophecy* of 'Agabus' below – not to mention a good deal of creative writing.

This still leaves the situation regarding 'Simon *Cephas*' in abeyance, where it probably must remain, while at the same time remembering that traditions relating to the succession of the Church in Palestine, the real 'Mother Church', might have ultimately been transferred to or absorbed into traditions having to do with the Church in Rome – at the time no more than a minor appendage. This has certainly occurred to some extent where the story of James and the story of Jesus are concerned.

There is no reason why it could not have occurred with regard to the story of Simeon bar Cleophas being the 'second' in the Church after

James; and 'Simon Peter' or '*Cephas*', *the second* after Jesus in Rome. This is certainly the implication of Luke's curious Emmaus Road sighting, where a sighting to someone called 'Cleopas' with another – we have suggested 'James' – actually does occur, but where no appearance to any-one called 'Simon' ostensibly takes place. However, there may well have been and probably was a second, more Hellenistic-style 'Peter', as our sources also suggest, in Rome – though the Pseudoclementines' Peter is more 'Jamesian' even than James. This cannot be determined on the basis of the data before us. For Origen, in *Contra Celsus*, as we saw, the second individual on the Road to Emmaus, with whom 'Cleopas' is 'conversing' and to whom Jesus appeared, is very definitely called 'Simon' ('Simeon bar Cleophas'?) even in the Gospel of Luke.

The *orthodox* Peter was reportedly crucified 'upside-down' in Rome, this on the basis of a testimony recorded by Eusebius, allegedly from Origen's Commentary on Matthew, too, which has not been preserved.[2] This tradition has long been doubted by most scholars – sometimes many of these traditions look as if *they* have been turned *upside-down* – but no doubt Simeon bar Cleophas was crucified, probably under Domitian, as some Syriac documents do attest. Peter's crucifixion under Nero before or after Paul's beheading – most would prefer after – as reported by Eusebius on the basis of Tertullian,[3] is just *not verifiable*, though neither would be surprising in the wake of the general round-up of Jewish Revolutionaries and agitators that certainly occurred following the outbreak of the War against Rome.

In fact, such a round-up of Jewish Messianic agitators had already occurred in Rome prior to this, following the fire that broke out there soon after James' death *in Jerusalem*, which Nero anyhow blamed on 'Christians'. Later historians, as we have seen, blamed the fire on Nero himself to demonstrate his insanity. There is no easy way finally to get at the truth behind all these traditions.

However, no less an authority than Eusebius himself is sure that Paul *did* go free after his first imprisonment in Rome, which was hardly an imprisonment at all, but more like house arrest or protective custody. This was at almost exactly the time James was killed in Jerusalem. Though the authenticity of Pastorals like Timothy and Titus is disputed, 2 Timothy 4:16–17 does note how 'at my first trial nobody supported me'. This would not be surprising in view of the presentation we have developed here.

Paul also alludes, perhaps more authentically, in Romans 15:24 to a trip he intends to take to Spain, which many think he took. This would also appear to be the implication of Clement's Letter to the Corinthians 5. If he did, one wonders what contacts he used to get there. Seneca, the famous Stoic philosopher, who acted as Nero's prime minister before falling afoul of his changeable temper and being forced to commit suicide himself, was from Spain, as was his brother Gallio, pictured as warmly approving of Paul in Acts 18:12–17.

Paul, as we have seen, already knew persons 'in the household of Caesar', as did, indisputably, his 'fellow soldier and worker' Epaphroditus, whom we have identified with the same Epaphroditus later blamed by Domitian, whether justly or unjustly, as Nero's assassin. Epaphroditus had also been Domitian's secretary, by whom he seems to have been executed along with Flavius Clemens (Clement of Rome?) in 96. Some have conjectured that there was a second 'Epaphroditus', who was Trajan's secretary, perhaps a relative or his son, but this is probably based on confusions in Josephus' chronology.4 Emperors like Trajan (98–117) and Hadrian (117–138) also came from Spain, and Galba (68), who became Emperor for a year following Nero's assassination, had previously been governor there for a long time.

If that 'Saulus', Agrippa's 'kinsman', did somehow run afoul of Nero's unpredictable and volatile temperament, it would not have been surprising. The last trace of him in Josephus' work, after being the intermediary between 'the Peace Party' in Jerusalem, consisting of Pharisees, principal Sadducees, and Herodians, and the Roman Army outside Jerusalem, was being sent to Nero again *in Corinth* in Greece to report to him on the turmoil in Palestine. It is also around the time most think Paul was *beheaded in Rome* in 66 CE – if he was beheaded.

That someone like this Saulus or Paul might actually ultimately *have been beheaded* (as first reported by Tertullian – *c.*160–221 CE) in the political turmoil of this time – either before or in the aftermath of Nero's assassination – would not be surprising, though what the reason for such a beheading might have been is debatable and must remain an open question. Nor is there any reason to suppose that after Paul's initial quasi-house arrest in Rome in 60–62 CE (where the thread of Acts' narrative concludes), he might not have *gone back to Palestine.*

In fact, given the nature of his contacts in Palestine, both in Jerusalem and Caesarea, even as outlined in Acts, he may very well have. Acts' reticence on these matters, including the manner of his death, is unsatisfactory and leads one to suspect that perhaps he did go back. Luke, Acts' reputed author, certainly must have known more. In any event, as we have seen,

Acts is incomplete, also leaving James' and Peter's deaths untreated and just trailing off. One must ask why.

Of course, apart from the brothers of Jesus themselves and someone called 'Cephas' or 'Simon Peter' and someone else called 'John', neither the Gospels nor the Book of Acts knows very much about any of 'the Apostles' at all – this includes the erstwhile 'Philip' above. These sources really don't know very much about John or Peter either, as Luke in Acts makes perfectly plain.

Where 'John' is concerned, one should note the parallel with John the Baptist, with whom anyhow he is confused in Acts' portrait of confrontations at Ephesus over 'John's' *water baptism* or Paul's *baptism by the Holy Spirit* – matters Paul also alludes to in 1 Corinthians. This is not to mention Josephus' 'John the Essene' – another early 'Zealot' leader – who is killed along with Izates' two sons or kinsmen in the early days of the War against Rome.

Judas the Brother of James, *Thaddaeus*, and *Theuda*

This brings us to the third brother of Jesus, the individual denoted as 'Judas of James' or 'Thaddaeus'/'Lebbaeus surnamed Thaddaeus' in Gospel Apostle lists or the Papias fragment above – 'the brother of James' in the Letter attributed to this name in the New Testament. We have already seen that according to Eusebius (again following Hegesippus), the descendants of this brother were actually still alive in either Vespasian's, Domitian's, or Trajan's time – one can take one's pick here, as there appears to be some confusion. So was Simeon bar Cleophas who would, therefore, be their uncle or great-uncle as the case may be.

In this regard, one should not ignore the tradition recorded in a variant manuscript of the Apostolic Constitutions that Simon the Cananaean was martyred in Judea in the reign of Domitian as opposed to Eusebius' and Epiphanius' view, that he was crucified at the age of 'one hundred and twenty under Trajan'. These variant manuscripts of the Apostolic Constitutions, as we have been remarking, are fairly accurate on these matters and this tradition, in any event, makes more sense than the one in Eusebius and Epiphanius about 'Simeon' or the Apostle list attributed to Hippolytus about 'Simon the Zealot the son of Clopas, also [the brother of] Judas'.

One should look into the character called 'Simon of Cyrene' as well, who in Matthew 27:32 and Mark 15:21 supposedly *carries the cross for*

Jesus. In both, this is literally 'Simon the *Cyrenian*', and again – as in the case of Luke's 'Kandakes the Ethiopian Queen' – these designations often conceal real persons; in this case, again possibly Simeon bar Cleophas (in Hippolytus above, 'Simon the Cananaean'), *the witness*, according to Epiphanius, *to the stoning of James*.

Regardless of confusions of this 'Judas of James' or 'Thaddaeus' with 'Thomas', that is, 'Judas Thomas' – John goes further along the route of dissimulation with '*Didymus* Thomas' – we would also identify this individual with the *third* brother of Jesus, 'Judas' or 'Jude'. There are, in any event, plenty of confusions where he is concerned. As we have seen, the 'Lebbaeus surnamed Thaddaeus', in some manuscripts of Matthew and the originally Syriac, Apostolic Constitutions, most likely represents a further garbling of 'Alphaeus' (his father) and/or 'Cleophas', though one must always keep in mind the linguistic relationship of '*Lebbaeus*' to James' additional mysterious cognomen '*Oblias*'.

We have already noted how Syriac sources comment on the inability of Westerners to pronounce these names and in Arabic, anyhow, this kind of reversing of letters is common. One should appreciate that even today in Arabic – which often represents an older pronunciation than Hebrew – there is no '*p*' only a '*b*', so instead of 'Constantinople', for instance, one gets 'Istanbul', or instead of 'Neopolis' – Greek for 'New City', the 'New City' built on the old city of 'Shechem' – one gets 'Nablus'. Or, for instance, instead of 'Papa' or 'Pope', one gets 'Baba'!

There are similar confusions between the letters '*b*' and '*v*' in Hebrew (as there are in German), '*p*' and '*ph*' and '*z*', '*tz*', and '*s*', which accounts for some of the confusion when transliterating into the Greek about whether Jesus comes from 'Nazareth', is a 'Nazirite', or should be 'called a Nazrene', 'Nazoraean', or '*Nasrānī*' – the word for 'Christian' in Arabic. That 'Lebbaeus' contains approximations of two of the consonants of the names 'Alphaeus' and/or 'Cleophas', however garbled or distorted – not to mention '*Oblias*' – is still sufficient to establish a linguistic relationship. In any event, the Papias fragment knows that 'Alphaeus' and 'Cleophas' are equivalent too.

There can be little doubt that what Matthew and the Syriac sources paralleling him are trying to say (or not to say as the case may be) is that Thaddaeus is 'the son of Alphaeus' – or, if one prefers, 'Cleophas' – or 'the brother of James' too, or that he bore the same cognomen '*Oblias*' as James did (in the end it is the same). We should leave 'Joseph' as Jesus' father out of this equation as a total gloss, as Islam does. How puzzling it must have seemed to the author or redactor of some manuscripts of Matthew to have seen a tradition that 'Thaddaeus' – 'Judas of James' in Luke – who comes after 'James the son of Alphaeus' and before 'Simon the Cananaean'/'Zealot' in Matthew and Mark and after them in Luke, was also 'the son of Alphaeus'. Therefore he produced 'Lebbaeus who was surnamed Thaddaeus', whatever he thought this was supposed to mean.

This then also reappears in subsequent Syriac tradition as in the Apostolic Constitutions following Matthew, the two variant manuscripts of which, above, reproduced the note that 'Thaddaeus, also called Lebbaeus and surnamed Judas the Zealot, preached the truth to the Edessenes and the people of Mesopotamia when Agbarus ruled over Edessa and was buried in Berytus [Beirut] in Phoenicia'. The Apostle list attributed to Hippolytus, as we saw at the beginning of the chapter, basically says the same thing, though now he becomes 'Judas who is also Lebbaeus'. For the 'Papias' fragment above, 'Thaddaeus' is one of the four brothers of Jesus, whose mother was 'Mary the wife of Cleophas or Alphaeus'. Again the conjunction with 'Judas the Zealot' is made clear.

Berytus, it will be recalled, is the city where Titus continued his birth-day celebrations begun earlier in Caesarea in honour of his brother Domitian after the fall of Jerusalem in 70 CE, where upwards of 2,500 prisoners perished in games with animals and gladiatorial fights! At the time of the burial there of either this 'Thaddaeus' or 'Judas *Zēlōtēs*', this city was attached to the Kingdom of Herod of Chalcis in Syria, as it was at this point in 70 CE to his nephew King Agrippa II. But we have already implicated this Herod of Chalcis in the beheading, reported in Josephus around 45 CE, of *Theudas*!

Apart from the parallel tradition in Syriac sources about the burial of 'Addai'/'Thaddaeus' in Edessa, which cannot be verified, this is a startling piece of information, because it confirms what we have been thinking all along anyhow. Where Thomas is concerned, Eusebius following Origen would circumscribe his activities to Mesopotamia and Parthia (Persia). However, since the sphere of influence of the latter extended further east, traditions developed, as for instance those in the Greco-Syriac work known as the Acts of Thomas – purportedly composed in Edessa or its environs at the beginning of the third century – which (to some extent echo traditions about Mani) took his activities even as far as India – tradi-tions remaining to this day.[5]

As far as 'Thomas'' death was concerned, there is little information, though these Acts of Thomas echo to some extent the picture of

'Stephen's' death in Acts, but now it is 'outside the city' of some far-off *Indian Kingdom* not Jerusalem. Instead of being 'beheaded' or 'killed with the sword' – as in the instance of 'Theudas' or 'James the brother of John' – they have Thomas being run through by four spearmen! However, as with '*Addai*'/'Thaddaeus' in Syriac tradition, *his bones* are transferred to Edessa, though Indian traditions – like those about 'James *the brother of John*' in Spain – claiming him for their own, contest this.[6]

These Acts, plus newly found documents from Nag Hammadi in Egypt, such as the Book of Thomas the Contender, make no bones about the fact that Thomas was not only a 'brother' of Christ, but his 'twin' brother – therefore the appellation.[7] Regardless of the reliability of this 'twinning', once we draw the connection between Judas Thomas and Theudas, which we have been suggesting, then the individual signalled in these traditions by these various cognomens does function as *Jesus redivivus* or, if one prefers, a *Joshua redivivus*. As in the case of John the Baptist and Elijah, but with more cause, Theudas does attempt to part the River Jordan as Joshua did, though in the reverse direction, to leave not to enter.

We do not know what success he might have had in this, but before he could do so, Fadus the Roman Governor, ruling jointly with Herod of Chalcis above, slew many of his followers and, taking him prisoner, ultimately beheaded him (no doubt with Herod's consent). Theudas was not the only one of these 'impostors' to attempt to re-create the miracles of *Joshua* in the Old Testament in this period. Not long afterwards, as we saw, Josephus describes someone whom he calls only 'an Egyptian' in the governorship of Felix (52–59 CE), who also 'claimed to be a prophet', for whom Paul was mistaken in Acts 21:38.[8]

Josephus calls these kind of individuals 'impostors', 'Brigands', and 'Deceivers' as we have seen. These 'banded together, inciting large numbers to revolt, encouraging them to claim their freedom and threatening to *kill any who submitted to Roman Rule*' – the opposite of 'Jesus' in the Gospels. These, as we also saw, 'under the pretence of Divine inspiration, fostering Innovation and change in government, persuaded the masses to act like madmen and *led them out into the wilderness* in the belief that there God would show them *the signs of their impending Salvation*'.

We have seen the relation of these 'signs' to those Jesus was supposed to have done in the Gospels at '*Cana of Galilee*' or out 'in the wilderness', multiplying the loaves and the fishes 'so that his Disciples believed on him', or murmur, 'this is truly the Prophet who is coming into the world' (the 'True Prophet' ideology of the Ebionite Pseudoclementines). But for

Josephus, rather, as will be remembered, these *'plundered the houses of the Rich* . . . till all Judea was consumed with the effects of their frenzy, the flames of which were fanned ever more fiercely till it came to out-and-out warfare'.[9]

Both 'Theudas' and this 'Egyptian' are Joshua *redivivus*es or Joshua 'come-back-to-lifes'. Josephus even calls Theudas 'an impostor' or 'magician'.[10] For Acts 5:36, he just 'claimed to be somebody', which may be imbued with more significance than at first appears. The point is that this may be something of what was meant by this notion of 'twinning' in these various early Church sources so sympathetic to Thomas. None show any hesitation to identify 'Thomas' as 'Judas *Thomas*', that is 'Judas the Twin', alias '*Didymus* Thomas' or 'Twin Twin'. We get the point.

The final proof of all these propositions comes in the two Apocalypses of James from Nag Hammadi, texts we have looked at. These not only relate one 'Theuda' to James, but another individual, the 'Addai' one finds in Syriac texts (our 'Thaddaeus' again), in both Apocalypses playing parallel roles as *receiving information from* or *having it dictated to them by* James. In the Second Apocalypse of James, 'Theuda' is called, 'of the Just One and a relative of his', meaning again either 'his father' or, in this case, 'his brother' – since it is doubtful that Jesus' 'father' would still then have been alive. Here is *direct* testimony, which we did not have from any other source previously, linking the name 'Theuda' or 'Theudas' to Jesus, James, or 'the Just One' in a familial manner. It was already clear that 'Thaddaeus' alias 'Lebbaeus' alias 'Judas, the brother of James' was related in a *direct* family manner to James. Now we can see that probably 'Theudas' was too.

Where this 'Judas the brother of James' – known as 'Judas of James' and also 'Thaddaeus' – is concerned, we have already encountered the traditions from various sources that identify him, in the manner of his second brother Simon, as 'Judas the Zealot'. Again, this places him squarely in the 'Zealot'/'*Sicarii*' tradition, which should surprise no one. We have already had this title applied to the second brother in Scripture, 'Simon the Zealot', and, according to our other Syriac sources and Hippolytus, 'Simeon bar Cleophas' as well.

This accords nicely with our understanding of James' following in Jerusalem as primarily being made up – as Acts itself attests – of *'Zealots for the Law'*. Not only was James himself *exceedingly* 'zealous', but like 'the Righteous Teacher' pictured in the Qumran documents – with whom he has so much in common and, if '*MMT*' is any criterion, if not identical

934

to, at least contemporaneous – we see him as being the central spiritual force and the axis about which these Messianic and Revolutionary Movements turned in their desire to bring about *both religious and social change*, as pictured in Josephus above.

That this individual – call him Theudas, call him Thaddaeus, call him Judas of James or Judas the Zealot, or call him Judas *Thomas* – also at some point *went to Edessa*, concentres all our sources still further. In these, as well, traditions about one 'Addai' begin to assert themselves, both in fourth-century documents like the 'Doctrine of Addai' or in Syriac sources generally – not to mention, as we have now been able to see, the Koran. But all these individuals begin to coalesce, including the individual known as 'Thomas'/'Judas *Thomas*', who, in addition to sending out 'Addai' or 'Thaddaeus' to evangelize 'King Agbarus', seems to have gone down, not surprisingly, to Edessa himself at some point and, thereafter, Mesopotamia and Parthia – according to these Syriac traditions and Hippolytus – become the spheres of his activities. Since we can now place this 'Judas the brother of James' in 'Mesopotamia and Parthia', I think we can say he went to Adiabene as well – though probably not as far as India! This perhaps more appertains to Mani.

The Judas Who Taught the Truth to the Edessenes and James' Brother

If we now return to Acts' story about James sending down an individual called 'Judas Barsabas' with a letter 'to Antioch' (*cum* 'Edessa' or 'Adiabene') containing directives to overseas communities, particularly as related to *conversion of Gentiles*, while all the time keeping the 'brother' theme in mind and all the tricks and turns relating to it in all sources, a final synthesis of sorts begins to emerge.

One should also recall how in Acts at the time supposedly of filling 'Judas' *Office*' (*Episcopate*), Judas Barsabas had an *alter ego* 'Joseph called Barsabas who was surnamed Justus' (note the resemblance here to 'the Just One' in the Second Apocalypse of James), that is, James. If we now identify Judas Thomas/Thaddaeus/Jude the brother of James/Judas Barsabas with Theudas, our problems and redundancies begin to disappear. Not only are Theudas and Thaddaeus homophones, this brings us to a clearer understanding of just who was involved in this evangelization of the Edessenes and, by extension, Adiabene – and events implied by these stories as well.

Reversing the phraseology of *Judas Thomas* to *Thomas Judas* and contracting it more or less reduces to what we are seeing here as 'Thaddaeus' or 'Theudas', which in everyday speech would be even more pronounced. Not only does this help solve the problem of just what kind of imposture Theudas was allegedly involved in by wishing to part the Jordan river in reverse and effecting an egress to the lands on the other side of the Jordan not an ingress; but also just who the 'impostor' beheaded by 'Herod the King' at the beginning of chapter 12 in Acts really was. One really doesn't even have to go this far, as 'Theudas' is quite normally a stand-in for 'Yehuda' or 'Judas' anyhow.

Nor is the individual beheaded by 'Herod', 'James the brother of John' – more of our 'shellgame' again. Again, keeping our eye on the 'brother' theme really is critical. Nor is the individual sent down with the letter to 'Antioch' in the 'Agbarus' stories sent down by Judas *Thomas*; rather he is sent down by *James the brother of Jesus* – though he is James' brother. This is Thaddaeus, who is basically a double for Judas the brother of James, Theudas, and 'Judas the Zealot who preached the truth to the Edessenes'.

He is also a double for 'Judas *Barsabas*' in Acts. That is, James *sends down his own brother*, 'Judas the brother of James' – or, according to other vocabularies, 'Judas *Thomas*' or 'Theudas', the third brother of Jesus – for revolutionary/religious activity in Northern Syria and Mesopotamia (including Adiabene). Then the 'James the brother of John', who is also removed in the narrative of Acts at around the time of the Famine, as we saw, is simply 'Jude *the brother of Jesus*' or 'Jude *the brother of James*' too.

This is hardly very disconcerting, especially when one thinks of all the other pious overwrites we have encountered in this literature: for instance, in 'Agabus'' prediction of the Famine; the 'eunuch over Queen Kandakes' Treasure' on his way via Gaza presumably to Egypt (to buy grain?); or Peter going to 'the house of Mary the mother of John Mark' to leave a message 'for James and the brothers'. In fact, the inversion represented by the last, where the name 'John Mark' takes the place of 'James' or 'Jesus', is not much different from what we are encountering here, where 'James the brother of John' takes the place of '*Judas the brother of James*'.

Not only is it chronologically in synch, but it also makes the 'Zealot' nature of all these episodes abundantly clear, 'Theudas' obviously being another one of these 'Zealot'-type 'Deceivers' ('*Sicarii*' in Acts), about whom Josephus holds forth with such obvious ill-will. It also accords with the notices we have already discussed from Hegesippus about Jesus' *third brother* Judas having already been executed at the time his descendants are interviewed by Vespasian – and, again later, by either Domitian or Trajan – in the wake of the fall of the Temple and the collapse of the resistance against Rome after the *'Sicarii' suicide on Masada*.

There really is, therefore, a 'brother' killed around the time of the Famine, but it is not *James the brother of John*. It is 'Theudas', 'Thaddaeus', or 'Judas the brother of James'. 'Judas' is *the 'brother' killed*. Josephus is very meticulous in documenting these kinds of executions – plus, he enjoyed playing on the bloodthirsty imaginations of his audience, much as modern writers or script consultants do. He, therefore, misses very few of these – probably almost none – in documenting all the stonings and beheadings of significance in this period. What is interesting is the pattern and succession they follow.

Just as there was no 'Stephen' who was stoned 'by the Jews' – except 'the Emperor's Servant Stephen', who was beaten and robbed *outside the walls of Jerusalem* in this period by insurgents – there was no 'James *the son of Zebedee*'. All of this is patent dissimulation, but dissimulation towards a very clear goal, to downplay the role of and finally eliminate the *other James* – not James the Less but *James the Just* – from Scripture. But the traces of the originals of many of these reworkings are still there, lying just beneath the surface, and with a little enhancement they are restored with some ease.

There was no Central Leadership of James, John *his brother* (the shell-game continues), and Peter, as portrayed in the Gospels – this to displace the obvious Central Leadership as enumerated quite straightforwardly by Paul in Galatians of James the brother of the Lord, Cephas, and John. These, as Paul says, were 'the Pillars' of the early Christian Church in Jerusalem – 'the Jerusalem Assembly' (not, as he says, 'that their importance meant anything to' him). There may have been another 'John', possibly John the *Essene*, who along with Silas and Niger of Perea led the Zealot assault on Ashkelon near Gaza on the Palestinian seacoast. But there was no *second* James, just as there was no *second* Mary – not Mary 'the mother of the sons of Zebedee'; nor 'Mary the wife of Clopas', Jesus' mother's sister; nor, for that matter, was there an 'Agabus'.

There are many such substitutions too numerous to list. Had, for instance, there been a beheading of someone called 'James' at the time of Queen Helen's Famine-relief efforts, one can be quite sure that Josephus would have remarked it either in the *War* or in the *Antiquities* – as he does that of 'Theudas' and so many other blood-curdling cruelties. We can now transform all these stories about someone called 'Judas Thomas' sending someone called 'Thaddaeus' to 'Augarus' or 'Albarus' or 'Abgarus' (later even with a replica of Jesus' likeness – again we have just the slightest touch of the 'twinning' theme relating to 'Thomas' even in this) into James *sending his brother* 'Judas *the Zealot*' to Edessa and Adiabene to *evangelize the Edessenes and Osrhoeans*.

In this context, one should also keep in mind the third teacher who comes to Adiabene, whom Josephus says came from 'Galilee' and whose teaching about 'circumcision' so contrasted with the more accommodating teaching of Ananias, and his unnamed colleague (Paul?), who 'gets in among the King's women' but *does not insist on circumcision*.

This also puts the issue of the 'Naziritism' of Queen Helen, whom we have already identified as one of the numerous wives of this Ruler, into stark relief. He has, as we have suggested, perhaps given her a Kingdom of her own from among his possessions further east, just as in Syriac sources Abgarus *divides his Kingdom* between his two sons: one called 'Sannadroug' gets the area around Haran, Abraham's birthplace – this would clearly be 'Izates' in Josephus' version. In regard to the emphasis on Abraham in this area, it is worth reiterating one last time the theological interest in Abraham in both materials associated with James and his erst-while rival Paul (not to mention '*MMT*'), which has not failed to translate itself into Islam.

This Abgarus would appear to have died around the time that Theudas was beheaded in Palestine in 45–46 CE. One should also not forget that Armenian sources claim that he was in alliance with Aretas, King of Arabian Petra, and actually sent forces to aid him in his mini-war with the Herodian Tetrarch Herod Antipas, husband of Herodias, after John the Baptist's death.

In approximately the year 49 CE, the Romans appear to have carved up parts of this area and given them under the title of Lesser Armenia to Herod of Chalcis' son Aristobulus, the *second* husband of Herodias' in-famous daughter Salome: those who advertise themselves on their coinage as 'Great Lovers of Caesar' – and they were. This gave Herodians a foothold in these domains as well and was in exchange for Agrippa II succeeding to the Kingdom of his father Agrippa I, which his uncle Herod of Chalcis had been holding for him. It is this 'Herod' we consider to be alluded to in the execution of 'James the brother of John' in Acts and ultimately responsible for the beheading of '*Theudas*'.

Not only do the conditions of Izates' circumcision concur perfectly with the outlook of James, as expressed by refraction either in Paul's Letters or the Letter of James, the whole episode harmonizes very nicely with the theme of Helen's extreme Naziritism from Rabbinic sources. For the new 'Galilean' teacher, Izates 'was guilty of breaking the the Law and bringing offence to God himself'; and he is advised, 'not only to *read the Law*, but to *do what was commanded in it*'. For James, as at Qumran, the '*doing what was commanded*' theme is paramount and the point was, 'whoever shall keep the whole of the Law, but stumble on one (small point) is guilty of breaking it all'. It should be clear that, according to the parameters of the Letter of James, Izates' teacher is 'Jamesian'.

James' Naziritism and the Poor

Helen's 'Naziritism' is also exactly in conformity with this aspect of James' person and behaviour, as we have been observing it in early Church sources. For these sources, James is 'Holy' or 'consecrated from his mother's womb' – that is, he was a life-long Nazirite. The terms of such Naziritism are laid out in the chapter on Naziritism following that on the suspected adulteress in Numbers 5–6. This Naziritism is also expressed in the penance James imposes on Paul, before Paul is finally mobbed by the Jewish crowd in the Temple and rescued by Roman troops stationed there. These last were perhaps already on the alert to intervene in this manner following Paul's convenient stopover in Caesarea – the Roman administrative centre in Palestine – where Acts pictures the 'prophet Agabus' as supposedly warning him not to go up to Jerusalem.

In the case of Paul and the 'four others', whose expenses the 'We Document' in Acts informs us he must pay for, it is a temporary form of Naziritism. Here mythologization does seem finally to have gone by the boards, because Paul is obviously perceived of as being 'Rich' and capable of paying for these others. He himself avers the pains he went to in order to collect funds before going up to Jerusalem, presumably so that he could make a claim on the basis of such collections (1 Cor. 16:1–9 and 2 Cor. 8:1–9:15). In the case of Helen, too, her 'Naziritism' was supposed to have been temporary, though in Rabbinic sources, however exaggerated, it was to last for *twenty-one years*. So in their own queer way these claims do begin to verge on life-long Naziritism of a Jamesian kind.

So we are entitled to say that Jamesian Christianity and the approach reflected in the Dead Sea Scrolls, which put so much emphasis on the 'Perfection of Holiness' and the 'wilderness Way', involved a stress on

Naziritism. This included abstention from 'eating and drinking' – as Paul or Rabbinic literature would so euphemistically express it and, as both also appear to imply, abstention from 'eating' (meat). This last Paul himself angrily and contemptuously confirms in Romans 14:2 and 1 Corinthians 8:13, when talking about the 'weakness' of his opponents whom he declines to name, though they are obviously important because Paul calls them 'Hebrews', 'Servants of Righteousness', and 'Apostles of the Highest Rank'.

This stress on 'abstention from meat' was antithetical to Rabbinic Judaism as well, which after the fall of the Temple also tried to discourage such penances, obviously associating them, as we have seen, with revanchism connected with *the Temple* and that 'zeal' or Messianic 'fervour' Jesus himself is portrayed as displaying in John 2:17's picture of the cleansing of the Temple. Not only does the theme of this 'abstention from eating and drinking' get turned around in the Gospels into its mirror opposite, but finally this emphasis on Naziritism, too, becomes transmuted into something involving a *geographical location* – the same way that the 'Galilean' terminology does. In this case, the phrase, 'He shall *be called a Nazirite*', in this instance literally 'Nazoraean' – attributed to 'the Prophets' (Matt. 2:23), becomes Jesus came from 'Nazareth' or that Jesus is a 'Nazrene' – meaning unclear.

In both Judaism and Islam, Christians, as we have seen, are called either '*Nozrim*' or '*Nasrānī*'s, emanating of course from this '*Nazirite*' ideology or the related play on it in Hebrew, hinted at here, 'the Nazoraeans'. This, too, as explained, actually comes out of a Hebrew root, meaning 'keeping', namely, 'keeping the commands of their father' or 'keeping their secrets'. The Nazirite, of course, was just an extreme example of this, but even here the wordplay is homophonic, 'Nazirite' carrying the meaning of 'abstain' or 'keep away from' – the language, of course, of James' directives to overseas communities, as Acts reproduces them. In fact, in Hebrew, these would actually have been expressed in terms of the Hebrew verb, '*lehinnazer*' or '*lehazzir*' – as they are in the Damascus Document – the Hebrew root of the word 'Nazirite' in English.[11]

In addition to this usage 'keep away from', based on the Hebrew root N–Z–R, the terminology, '*linzor et ha-Brit*' ('to keep the Covenant'), also, actually exists among the Qumran documents and is, in fact, a synonym for a parallel usage found there, 'the Sons of Zadok'. The latter, as we have seen in the Community Rule, are defined as 'the Keepers of the Covenant' (the '*Shomrei ha-Brit*'); the former is found throughout the

Damascus Document.[12] It will also be recalled that the latter are defined in the Damascus Document as 'those who will *stand in the Last Days*' – note the play here on Ebionite/Elchasaite 'standing' terminology again. The 'keeping' aspect of this terminology is exactly the definition emphasized by modern-day offshoots of this orientation, 'the Sabaeans of the marshes' in Southern Iraq, who still hold the memory of John the Baptist dear and call their Priests, 'Nazoraeans'.[13]

This kind of wordplay, of course, moves into a further adumbration of the 'Sons of Zadok' terminology at Qumran, the '*Moreh ha-Zedek*' or the 'Teacher of Righteousness', and we have come full circle. This is *exactly* the role James played in all early Christian literature, evinced by his cognomen or title 'James the Just' or 'James the Righteous', so called because of the *extreme Righteousness* he practised, both in his uncompromising Naziritism and the *doctrine of Righteousness* he presumably taught. This both leads to and is evinced by another terminology, 'the Poor' (or 'the *Ebionim*'), so beloved at Qumran and a favourite self-designation there, as it is for early Christianity of the Jamesian cast or 'the Ebionites'.

The term, as we have seen, is an inevitable development out of following the 'Righteousness' Commandment, 'You shall love your neighbour as yourself', to its absolute limits, that is, that you cannot be completely Righteous towards your fellow man if there are economic distinctions between you and him or there is economic inequality. At Qumran, this is expressed in the Damascus Document as follows:

> [You shall] *separate between polluted and pure and distinguish between Holy and profane* . . . according to the Commandment of those entering *the New Covenant in the Land of Damascus* to set up the Holy Things according to their precise specifications, *to love each man his brother as himself, to strengthen the hand of the Meek, the Poor, and the Convert* . . . *to keep away from fornication* [*lehazzir* – this actually a phrase from James' directives to overseas communities] . . . *to separate from all pollutions according to Law* [here 'separate' and 'keep away from' are synonyms]. And no man shall *defile his Holy Spirit*, which God separated for them. Rather all should *walk in these things in Perfect Holiness* on the basis of all they were instructed in of the Covenant of God, Faithfully promising them that they *will live for a thousand Generations*.[14]

This is, also, exemplified in the Gospel picture of Jesus by favourite sayings like 'sooner would a camel go through the eye of a needle than a Rich Man to Heaven' (Matt. 19:24 and pars.) or, better still, in the denunciations of 'the Rich' found in the Letter of James.

Of course these denunciations of 'the Rich' and 'Riches' are also strong in the Qumran documents and run the gamut of almost all Josephus' notices about 'Deceivers' and 'impostors' leading the people astray by going out in the wilderness, there to show them 'the signs of their impending freedom' or 'Salvation'. In fact, as we have seen above, at the actual moment of burning the palaces of the most hated and 'Richest' of the High Priests, Ananias, and also the 'Rich' Herodians, Bernice and Agrippa II – it is noteworthy in this regard that Queen Helen's palace and those of her two sons, Izates and Monobazus, are spared throughout the Uprising, until the Romans put them to the torch at its conclusion[15] – Josephus says these partisans and extreme '*Sicarii*', whom he abominates as 'Robbers' (*Lēstai*), '*turn the Poor against the Rich*' and, in the process, *burn all the debt records*.

Hillel the proverbial leader of Pharisaic Judaism or Rabbinic Judaism-to-be – whose descendants became, after the destruction of the Temple, the Roman Patriarchs of Palestine, responsible among other things for collecting taxes – is, in fact, reputed to have made the continuation of these debts possible even past Sabbatical years, when in theory they were supposed to be forgiven, by a legal device known in Rabbinic literature as 'the *Prozbul*'.[16] James 5:1–5, on the other hand, railed – as we have seen – against 'the Rich' in the most apocalyptic and uncompromising way, threatening them with the coming Vengeance 'of the Lord of Hosts'. Consequent to this, James 5:6 blames 'the Rich' for 'putting the Righteous One to death' (presumably Jesus – but possibly even James himself) in contrast to Paul in 1 Thessalonians 2:14–15, who blames 'the Jews'.

Indeed, in all materials associated with James and the Righteous Teacher at Qumran, we inevitably hear about this antagonism to 'the Rich' and not making economic distinctions between men – therefore, the injunction given to Paul, not to forget to 'remember the Poor' in Galatians 2:10. This Paul claims he was 'most anxious to do', but whether he did or not is an open question. He certainly always made sure that, when he came to Jerusalem, he came with sufficient funds, which is why, no doubt, James says these things and, according to Acts, set him the penance of a Nazirite oath – usually thirty days, but in Acts 21:27, seven – and paying the expenses of four others under similar vow. At this point Paul is mobbed in the Temple, yet James, not surprisingly, is not!

Helen, of course – someone with whom Paul was possibly connected either directly or indirectly – did show, according to all sources, her anxiety to *remember the Poor*, as did her sons, Izates (also 'Izas' in Josephus) and

Monobazus. She did so at the sacrifice of a considerable amount of personal wealth, for which she won for herself and her sons, says the *Talmud*, a great name for ever more. Josephus says Izates too 'sent great sums of money to the Leaders in Jerusalem', which was 'distributed among the Poor' delivering Many, and one wonders just which 'Jerusalem Leadership' this could have been. It is also the kind of thing being played off, not a little disingenuously, in Acts' picture of the complaints brought by 'the Hellenists' against 'the Hebrews' regarding the 'daily distribution', leading up to the stoning of Stephen (6:1).

Helen and Izates' sons or kinsmen were clearly part of the 'Zealot' orientation, which, in our view, is indistinguishable at this point from the 'Messianic' one. They give themselves valiantly for their country's cause against Rome, even though they are only recent converts. This is mocked in Acts' presentation of the *Ethiopian* 'eunuch' (that is, someone who is *castrated*), who 'oversees the Treasure of the *Ethiopian Queen* Kandakes' and learns 'the Gospel of Jesus' from one 'Philip', thereafter wishing immediately to be *baptized* not *circumcised* – the 'Gospel', that is – among other things – clearly that of *peace with the Romans*.

Ben Kalba Sabu'a and the Nicodemus who Prepared the Body of Jesus

The *Talmud* also knows these problems of conversion either via baptism or circumcision and the issue still remains in Judaism today. For it, one Eliezer ben Hyrcanus – the Rabbi to whom Jacob of Kfar Sechania expounded Jesus the Nazorean's point about 'the High Priest's outhouse' – considers that 'circumcision is the *sine qua non* of conversion'. Another rabbi, called Rabbi Joshua, is generally presented as holding the view that only baptism was necessary, though in some versions of his discussion with R. Eliezer on the subject, he is rather quoted as having the view that, *in addition* to circumcision *also* baptism was required.[17] This is all very interesting in view of the problems surrounding the conversion of Helen's sons and the character called 'Eleazar' in Josephus.

In fact the *Talmud* knows another character, one 'Ben Kalba *Sabu'a*', who was also supposed to have been known for his generosity, fabulous wealth, and never turning away 'the Poor' from his home hungry. During the Roman siege of Jerusalem, he supposedly promised along with two other colleagues – one called '*the Treasurer*' – to supply Jerusalem with food for '*twenty-one years*'.[18] Not only are we getting here clear reflections of the details of the story of Queen Helen of Adiabene's conversion, Famine-relief mission, and other philanthropic activities; but this name 'Sabu'a' in Hebrew (sometimes transliterated 'Shebu'a') conserves a clear echo of the term 'Sabaean' – 'Sobiai' in the Greek of Hippolytus above – in other Semitic languages like Aramaic and Arabic. There is also just a hint of the word 'Sheba' here (though the root is slightly different) and, in this regard, one should note the confusion in Luke's Acts of 'Ethiopian' (in the Bible, also 'from Sheba') with 'Edessene' or 'Sabaean'.

The link-ups, too, with Luke's 'Treasury' agent story are obvious and one should remark that Josephus himself conserves a note about the fabulous palace of Queen Helen, not to mention those of her descendants, who stayed in Jerusalem during the War against Rome and did not leave it (which the Revolutionaries spared and did not burn).[19] In fact, *Ben Kalba Sabu'a*'s name is traditionally associated in Jewish sources with the tomb built by Queen Helen's son Monobazus for her and his brother Izates in Jerusalem (called in these sources, '*Kalba Sabua'a's cave*'). It can actually be translated – with a little creative ingenuity – to read, 'the son of the *Sabaean* Bitch', '*Kalbah*' bearing the meaning *'female dog'* in Hebrew (even if one does not allow this female sense for '*Kalba*' in Aramaic – it still translates as 'the son of the Sabaean dog' and where the confusion with 'Ethiopian' came from should be clear).

Not only did the daughter of this 'Ben Kalba Sabu'a' – who would on the above basis, then, be a caricature of Izates or Monobazus, or their relatives – supposedly marry the 'Zealot' Rabbi of the next generation, Akiba (also executed by Rome for sedition or Insurrection), one of whose most ardent students we have also heard was named 'Monabaz'; but Ben Kalba Sabu'a supposedly bequeathed to this 'Poor' Akiba half his wealth, when he finally came to marry his daughter with a huge following of twelve thousand Disciples![20] All of this is admittedly extremely abstruse, but Talmudic materials very often are.

Aside from an individual called in these sources '*Ben Zizit*' – like '*Ben Kalba Sabu'a*' surely another pseudonym of some kind – and often associated with him, Ben Kalba Sabu'a has another friend called 'Nakdimon ben Gurion'. He, too, is considered to be fabulously wealthy – though perhaps not as philanthropic as Ben Kalba Sabu'a and is also credited with the scheme to supply the city with grain for *twenty-one years*! It is these stores which the *Talmud* claims 'the Zealots' either burned or despoiled by *mixing them with mud*! A parallel burning of stores by 'the Zealots', which (as afterwards at Masada) 'might have sufficed them for many years of siege', in order to make the people fight harder, is confirmed in Josephus.[21]

One should note the curious conjunction of 'twenty-one years' with either the period of time between Theudas' revolutionary attempt at a reverse Exodus and the Famine in 45 to the outbreak of the Uprising in 66 and the 'twenty-one years' involved in Helen's repeated 'Nazirite' oaths. These notices also add to the suspicion of a role of these agents of Helen or Izates in encouraging this war. As the *Talmud* presents it, at one point this friend of 'Ben Kalba Sabu'a', 'Nakdimon ben Gurion', after promising to pay 'twelve talents of silver' to fill the water cisterns of the Temple – again the notice about these 'Rich' gifts to the Temple – *prays for rain* and performs a 'rain-making' miracle equivalent to James'.[22]

Whatever one may think of these stories, Nakdimon does seem to re-appear in the New Testament in the Gospel of John as 'Nicodemus', who *prepares the body of Jesus for burial* – again, in the tomb of the *'Rich' merchant* 'Joseph of Arimathaea'. The connection with the above tradition about 'Kalba Sabu'a' should be clear. He also would seem to appear in Josephus, who apparently reverses his name into 'Gurion the son of Nicomedes' (thus). In this episode, 'Nicomedes' is one of those attempting to save the Roman garrison in the Citadel, which wishes to surrender at the beginning of the Uprising and whose commander, it will be recalled, later *circumcised himself*. His associate in this attempt is, again, one *'Ananias* the son of Zadok'.[23]

We have already associated Saulus, Philip, and Antipas (whom Josephus not only identifies as the son of a Temple Treasurer and ultimately even, Treasurer himself), with this attempt to save the Roman garrison. In the later stages of the Uprising, when the 'Zealots' take control and slaughter High Priests like James' executioner Ananus, this namesake of Nicodemus is executed as a collaborator along with Niger – as is Saulus' apparent cousin Antipas above and another 'Rich' collaborator, 'Zachariah'. It is very likely this Zachariah's 'blood' that the Gospels of Matthew and Luke are accusing the Jews of shedding 'between the Temple and the altar', not the original Prophet Zechariah's.[24]

Not only does Josephus describe how 'the Zealots' trumped up a Sanhedrin trial, summoning 'the Seventy' to try this 'Zachariah the son of Bareis' or 'Bariscaeus' (in the New Testament this is 'Barachias') on a charge 'of betraying the state to the Romans and holding treasonable communications with Vespasian'; but also how they 'slew him in the midst of the Temple', 'casting him out of the Temple into the ravine below' (here our imagery of 'casting', now directed against a collaborator) which is the probable source of the legend about 'the Tomb of Zachariah' next to the 'Tomb of St James' in the Kedron Valley beneath the Temple Pinnacle. In this story, too, we probably have the contrapositive (and likely as not the source) of the story of James being 'cast down' from the Temple Pinnacle – reflected too in 'the tomb' attached to his name in this Valley.

In John 7:50, Nicodemus, like Hillel's grandson Gamaliel in the Pseudoclementine *Recognitions* and Acts, is a *secret believer* who comes to Jesus 'in the night' (John 3:1–21). Called a Pharisee and 'a ruler of the Jews' – which he was most certainly – it is he, as we just noted, who brings the ointments to anoint the body of Jesus in 'the tomb' provided by another of these 'Rich' merchants, called supposedly 'Joseph of Arimathaea' (19:38–42). Once again, we have come full circle and back to the stories about Queen Helen's wealth – to say nothing of her 'tomb'. Not only are these stories related to the activities of Helen's 'Treasury' agents in Palestine, but also possibly to James.

Queen Helen and her sons cannot really be conceived of as converts to Pharisaic or Rabbinic Judaism as such, the behaviour of whose progenitor R. Yohanan ben Zacchai we have already remarked. He, it will be recalled, had himself secretly smuggled out of Jerusalem in a coffin during the War – the only escape then possible. Not only did he basically 'hold treasonable communion with Vespasian', but (as Josephus also records of himself) proclaimed Vespasian as the Ruler who would come out of Palestine to rule the world, that is, the Messianic 'Star'. Rabbi Yohanan's behaviour – not to mention Josephus' – cannot be the behaviour one would predicate of either Helen or her sons. Nor can we really say that Helen and her sons were converted to Christianity as we know it – at least not the Pauline variety. More probably, and what seems to be emerging from our sources, they were converted to *Jamesian Christianity* or the kind of 'Zealotism' evinced in the Scrolls or the Judaism of extreme 'Naziritism'.

To show that the Messianic activity identified with her and her family continued down to the next century and the Bar Kochba affair, we have only to search through Talmudic records. As we have seen above, not only did the famous Rabbi Akiba – who would not preach *compromise with Rome* and for his pains was ultimately reputed to have been drawn and quartered by the Romans – have one of Helen's descendants called 'Monabaz' as his student, but he was also, as we saw, married to *the daughter of this same Ben Kalba Sabu'a*, half of whose wealth he supposedly inherited! I think this is sufficient to bring Rabbi Akiba into some sort of association with this family as well.

It is worth noting that, at first, Akiba supported the Second Jewish Uprising against Rome, that of Simeon bar Kosiba or Simon Bar Kochba, that is, 'the Son of the Star', in fact, designating him as Messiah, for which he was laughed at by his Rabbinic confrères.[25] This Uprising from 132 to 136 CE was every bit as fierce as the earlier one, but there was no Josephus to document it. It resulted in the Jews being finally barred from Jerusalem altogether, even from viewing it from a distance except once a year – the legendary '9th of the Month of Ab', the traditional date for the fall of the Temple in Jewish eyes. Not only is it easy to imagine the reasons behind such a ban, one can well imagine the bitterness of surviving Messianists towards those Rabbis choosing the safer road of the Academy at Yavneh, a feel for which comes through in Josephus' story of the surrender of Izates' 'brothers and kinsmen' to Titus at the end of the War.

These, in any event in our view, are the kinds of things that 'Judas *the Zealot*' or 'Judas the brother of James' *taught* the Edessenes. In Syriac sources as we saw, this *Judas* is connected to one 'Addai' – in the Koran ''Ād' – just as in the Gospels and Papias he is indistinguishable from 'Thaddaeus'. He is also, as we have shown, virtually indistinguishable from 'Judas *Thomas*'. Our identification of him with the 'Theudas' in Josephus, whose 'imposture' precedes the note about Helen's charitability, brings us full circle. It eliminates the problem of the beheading of another 'brother' *James*, as it does that of the competitive Leadership Triad of John and James the two sons of Zebedee and Peter. It is also finally verified in the Nag Hammadi literature and the two Apocalypses of James there.

It is also possibly verified elsewhere – in the Jewish catacombs of Rome. There, as we have seen, not only is 'Justus' a name being used in place of 'Zadok', which has important ramifications for tying James to the individual referred to in this manner at Qumran, but mix-ups and overlaps of various letters and misspellings are commonplace.

For instance, as already noted, *alpha* is confused with *lambda*, which may account for some of our Cleophas/Alphaeus/Lebbaeus mix-ups, and *chi* is regularly interchanged with *kappa* as in 'Sicarii', which again may bear on the transposition of 'Christian' with 'Sicarios'. Where 'Judas'/ 'Theudas' is concerned, the Y or I in 'Yehuda' or 'Judas' is often confused with T, which can move into Th as in 'Theodore' or, as it were, 'Theudas'.[26] The point is that these kinds of confusions in transliterations of phonemes, whether accidental or purposeful, are widespread.

Theuda and Addai in the Two Apocalypses of James from Nag Hammadi

The two Apocalypses of James from Nag Hammadi, like the more ortho-dox Protevangelium of James – which develops the notion of the 'perpetual virginity' of *Mary*, in effect, denying the possibility of any *actual* 'brother' relationship in a book ostensibly attributed to James – are to some degree also attributed to James. This 'James' is clearly intended to be 'James the brother of the Lord', because Jesus is presented as addressing him as 'James my brother' (24.15), but that is as far as both documents are willing to go in admitting any *actual* 'brother' relationship.

In fact, both try to deny it, the First adding, though 'not my brother materially'. The Second turns it around and has the 'James' character rather greet Jesus as 'my brother'. Then, somewhat in the manner of the Protevangelium above, Mary intervenes to deny the actuality of this, suggesting, like Jerome, that he is rather a *milk brother* or *step-brother* (50.19–20). Jesus then ultimately concludes, now to some extent echoing John 19:26 on 'the Disciple Jesus loved' adopting Jesus' mother above and the Qumran Scrolls on adoptionist sonship, 'Your father is not My Father, but My Father has become a Father to you' (51.20). It then goes on to evoke the word 'virgin' three times, but it is not clear which 'virgin' it means, James or 'Mary mother of God' (51.27–52.1).

This is evidently playing off some very old materials and obviously in the thick of some of the disputes on these issues as they were developing. Continuing in the context in which these greetings are exchanged, the First Apocalypse then goes on not only to announce that he (Jesus) will be 'seized the day after tomorrow', but also that James will be 'seized' (25.10–15), making it clear that the 'James' who, in the words of Matthew 20:22 and Mark 10:38, will 'drink the Cup' that Jesus has drunk will be *James the brother of the Lord* not some other 'James'. Interestingly, it then goes on to speak of Jerusalem giving 'the Cup of Bitterness to *the Sons of Light*' (25.17). This is clear Qumran phraseology, as it is the phraseology of Revelation, and carries with it the sense of martyrdom or Vengeance as we have seen (14:10, 16:19, and 18:6).

The First Apocalypse is framed in terms of a kind of dialogue between James, who is literally referred to as 'the Just One' (31.31–32.7), and someone he calls 'Rabbi', that is, 'my Master' or 'Teacher', clearly meant to be Jesus, told in the third person. The Second tells a parallel story, but this time largely, but not entirely, from James' own lips in the first person.

As we have said, both are clearly ascribed to James and as one would expect he plays the central role. Both, as described, clearly feature that 'kiss' that James gives or receives from his master Jesus (transformed into the 'kiss' that 'Judas *Iscariot*' supposedly *gives Jesus* in the Gospels?). In these Apocalypses, it is a kind of kiss of 'Knowledge' or of '*Sophia*'/ 'Wisdom', given with something of the affection Jesus is presented as showing to 'the Disciple [he] loved', who lies on his breast at the time of the 'breaking of bread' with 'Judas of Simon *Iscariot*' in John 13:23.

What is, however, important for our purposes regarding the connection of Addai/Thaddaeus/Theudas to James is that in the First Apocalypse the only other person of any substance who is mentioned, apart from Jesus the Rabbi and James his brother, is 'Addai'. This is the individual who is always presented as the Apostle or Evangelist sent out by 'Judas *Thomas*' to the Edessenes/Osrhoeans. He is called 'Thaddaeus', as we have seen, in the 'Abgarus' materials presented by Eusebius, and a lively apocrypha has developed about him in Syriac tradition. His name, too, as also remarked, is perhaps not totally unconnected with the name 'Edessa' and possibly that of 'Adiabene' as well. It is to him that James is instructed to reveal what he has learned from his master and putative brother Jesus (36.15–20).

Here, therefore, not only do we have James evidently being appointed successor by Jesus himself, but we have James (not 'Thomas') clearly involved with someone called 'Addai' or 'Thaddaeus'. James' death is just as clearly alluded to in the traditional manner of Origen, Eusebius and others (following either Hegesippus or Clement of Alexandria, or both),

> When you depart [or 'are killed'], immediately War will be made upon this land. [Weep] then for him who dwells in Jerusalem (36.20).

These words would, also, seem to embody something of the mysterious oracle to leave Jerusalem that the early Christian Community supposedly received following James' death, just prior to the appearance of Roman armies surrounding Jerusalem. It is also almost word for word from the prophecy of doom uttered by the mysterious 'Jesus ben Ananias', which he began to articulate immediately following James' death (the *Succot* following the *Yom Kippur* of 62 CE) and did not cease from proclaiming until his own death shortly before the fall of the Temple in 70 CE. We shall treat both these oracles further, when we examine the tradition of 'the Pella Flight' by the James' Community following his death and Acts' story about Agabus' *second prophecy* in Volume II.

The text continues, making it plain what it intended to say about Addai anyhow, though it is fragmentary:

> But let Addai take these things to heart. In the Tenth Year, let Addai sit and write them down, and when he writes them down . . . (36.21–25)

There is also an echo here of 'the epistle' James supposedly dictates or gives to 'Judas surnamed Barsabas' – Addai's or Thaddaeus' double – to take to Antioch at the conclusion of the Jerusalem Council in Acts, not to mention the one supposedly taken by 'Thaddaeus' on the part of 'Judas *Thomas*' to 'Abgarus' in other variations of this story. This we have already seen echoed in '*MMT*' or the two Letters on Works Righteousness, mysteriously found in so many copies at Qumran, the only letters of this kind extant there (this installation itself, with its multiple bathing pools, perhaps reconstructed after its destruction by Herod, owing to the munificence of 'the Ethiopian Queen' or the Nazirite-loving '*Sabaean* Bitch').

At the end of the First Apocalypse, James' death, as described in traditional early Church sources, is clearly referred to, including something of the gist of the '*Zaddik*' citation from Isaiah 3:10 associated with it in Eusebius via Hegesippus – not to mention Jesus' death in Scripture:

> They arose, saying, 'We have no part in this blood, for a Righteous Man will perish through Unrighteousness.' James departed . . . (46.17–22)

The text breaks off here. If nothing else, what is apparent in this text is that 'Addai' is being presented as James' Apostle or messenger in much the same way that 'Thaddaeus' is presented, in more orthodox treatments, as the Apostle or messenger of 'Judas *Thomas*' – whom we have already presented as that brother of James known as Jude, not to mention, being identical with 'Theudas'.

But this is exactly the sense of the Second Apocalypse, told in the form of a discourse of James, in which 'Addai''s place is basically taken by 'Theuda' – namely *Theudas*. This document over and over again focuses on James being called 'the Just One' and even, it would appear, 'the Beloved' or 'my Beloved' (49.9 and 56.17). It also mentions 'the fifth flight of steps' (45.25), though it is not always clear whether it is James being spoken of or Jesus, and quotes the verse from Isaiah 3:10 in the Septuagint version we have mentioned (61.12–20), associated with James' death via Hegesippus. Now it is put directly into the mouth of those who stone him:

> 'Come let us stone the Just One.' And they arose saying, 'Let us kill this man, that he may be taken from among us, for he is worthless to us.'[27]

950

This is, of course, exactly the paraphrase of Isaiah 3:10 in the Septuagint rendition. Not only does the narrative of the stoning of James then proceed at great length, including allusion to 'Standing' imagery and the 'Mighty Cornerstone' (61.22), but it also includes the words 'throwing down' and 'casting down' – 'from the height' – repeated twice (61.25). It also adds, as we have already remarked, additional gory details seemingly based on Rabbinic prescriptions for stoning and related, to some extent, to the matter of the 'laundryman's club' in traditional sources. These have them 'striking him as they dragged him along the ground'. Then,

> stretching him out and placing a stone on his abdomen, they all jumped on it, saying, 'You have erred!' Then, they raised him up, since he was still living, and made him dig a pit. They made him stand in it. After having covered him up to his stomach, they stoned him like this (62.1–14),

at which point James stretches out his hands and delivers a long prayer (here our 'praying' theme of Eusebius, Epiphanius, and Stephen in Acts), this time about 'being saved from death', and about 'Salvation' and 'Light'.

But the most important thing for the purposes of the story about Addai in the First Apocalypse, as we saw, is that in the Second Apocalypse, the individual to whom James dictates his discourse and who clearly takes the place of Addai in the First, is called 'Theuda [the 'father' or 'brother'] of the Just One, since he was a relative of his' (44.19) – this, and 'the steps', upon which either James or Jesus 'stands' or 'sits' in order to deliver his discourses (45.25). Here we are clearly in the milieu both of the Ascents of James – the *Anabathmoi Jacobou* evoked in Epiphanius – and the Pseudoclementine *Recognitions'* presentation of the debates on the Temple stairs with the High Priests, also refracted in various passages in the Book of Acts in connection with the other Apostles and *even at one point Paul* (Acts 21:40) – but not James!

I think that we can again state at this point that our case is proven. Here we have the corroboration necessary to show that this Theudas – also called 'Addai', also known as 'Thaddaeus' – who 'was a relative of his', was a *kinsman* or *brother of* Jesus or James, in fact, *his third brother* – 'the brother of the Just One' – known variously as 'Judas of James', 'Judas the brother of James', and 'Judas the Zealot'. It was the grandsons of this Judas, called by Hegesippus 'the brother according to the flesh of the Saviour', and by Eusebius, 'one of the reputed brothers of the Saviour', who are interviewed by Domitian because of their *Messianic lineage*. Finally they were martyred (again according to Hegesippus) along with another relative of Jesus, Simeon bar Cleophas – also variously 'Simon the Zealot'/'Simon the Cananite'/'*Cananaean*' – in the time of Trajan (in Simeon's/Simon's case, rather than Domitian's). It only remains to straighten out one or two last confusions centring about 'Judas *Iscariot*' or 'the *Iscariot*' and 'Judas [the 'son' or 'brother'] of Simon *Iscariot*'.

Judas *Iscariot* and Simon *Iscariot*

Not only are the traditions about Judas *Iscariot* malevolent on several counts – as a majority of mankind seems intuitively to have grasped – this is, no doubt, what the creative writers responsible for these materials intended. In addition, their presentations also play on the traditions about Jewish heroes from this period, namely Judas Maccabee so celebrated in the *Hanukkah* festivities associated with his name and that Judas the Galilean we have highlighted in this book, the founder of what Eusebius via Hegesippus, anyhow – if not Josephus – calls the '*Galilean*' Movement.

And this has to be what they are implying by this name, because Judas, as noted, did not come from Galilee, but rather the area adjacent to it known as Gaulonitis (today's 'Golan') – unless we are involved in confusions like those we have been encountering in the Gospels, where geographical names like 'Nazareth' (undocumented in 'Galilee' in Second Temple Times except in Scripture) is substituted for the very real concept of a 'Nazirite' or 'Nazoraean', that is, 'a Keeper'. A great deal of trouble is taken in these narratives to get Jesus *to Galilee*, even though the traditions they preserve rather have him *coming from Bethlehem*, the seat of the Davidic family of old.

Nathanael again (a seeming stand-in for James in the Gospel of John), for instance, asks 'Philip' above – when the latter announces that 'Andrew' and 'Peter' have found 'Jesus *the son of Joseph* who is from *Nazareth*' ('of whom Moses wrote in the Law and the Prophets'), 'Can any good thing *come out of Nazareth*'? (1:46). A few chapters later, as we saw, this question is then reprised after 'Many' in the crowd apply the Ebionite 'True Prophet' ideology to Jesus. Others in the crowd, then say, 'This is *the Christ*', to which still others, respond,

> Does the Christ then come out of Galilee? Did not the Scriptures say that the Christ comes from the seed of David and from Bethlehem, the city where David lived? (7:40–42)

This means that, firstly, Jesus does not come from Bethlehem, nor was he born there, and, secondly, 'Galilean' as a geographical placename – meaning 'to come from Galilee' – is preferred to 'Galilean' as an ideological designation – meaning to follow the Movement started by Judas and *Saddok* around the time of 'Jesus'' alleged birth. Interestingly enough, this episode ends with our 'Nicodemus' again, intervening and asking, whether the Law 'judges a man without first hearing from him and knowing what *he does*'. Whereupon the crowd responds, 'Are you also of Galilee? Search and see that no Prophet has arisen out of Galilee' (here again, obliquely, the 'True Prophet' ideology – 7:52).

This coincidence of the birth of 'Jesus' with that of 'the Fourth Philosophy' – which is either founded in the revolutionary events of 4 BC at the time of Herod's death or those coincident with the Tax Revolt of 6–7 CE (the same confusion exists between Matthew and Luke as to the date of the birth of Jesus, the former having him born around the time of Herod's death; the latter, at the time of the Census of Cyrenius in 6–7 CE) – is perhaps not simply accidental, as both are 'Zealots' in the *true* sense of the word.

But the animosity involved in these sleights of hand regarding the name 'Judas' is not simply related to these events. It is also related to the fact that *all Jews* – in fact, the very name 'Jew' itself – come from the designation 'House of Judah', as the Habakkuk *Pesher* at Qumran realizes, that is, 'Judas' or 'Jude' in Greek.[28] Therefore, a slur on the name of the one ends up, in fact, in a slur on the *whole people*. More importantly still, in some sense it is also related to the traditions surrounding Jesus' family members themselves. It is this we would like to focus on here, in order to part the cloud of unknowing and lift the fascination heightened by the allure of scandal hovering over the people as a whole.

In all orthodox Apostle lists, as we have seen, the individual known as 'Judas *Iscariot*' – in John, 'the *Iscariot*' – either follows the individual 'Simon the Cananaean'/'Cananite', as in Matthew and Mark, or 'Judas [the brother] of James', as in Luke. This title '*Iscariot*', plainly meant to be an approximation of some word in Hebrew, is, as already remarked, almost always further accompanied by the epithet in Greek, 'who *delivered him up*' – most often translated as 'who betrayed him'. For Luke, too, it will be recalled, 'Simon the *Cananite*' is 'Simon the *Zealot*', '*kana*'' in Hebrew translating into the word '*zēlos*' in Greek and from there on into English, another bit of Gospel sleight of hand. Luke also puts the name 'Judas of James' in between this 'Simon' and 'Judas *Iscariot*'.

That is, the name *Judas Iscariot* always follows the enumeration of these three others – namely, 'James the son of Alphaeus, Thaddaeus, and

Simon the Cananaean' – we have already identified through lengthy analysis above as Jesus' brothers. This, Jerome, by the end of the fourth century, had already come to realize, because he had intelligence, and used it – the only problem being the use he put it to. The names at the end then read (omitting 'James the son of Alphaeus'): 'Lebbaeus who was called Thaddaeus, Simon the Cananite, and Judas *Iscariot*' (Matt. 10:4), or simply, 'Thaddaeus and Simon the Cananite and Judas *Iscariot* (Mark 3:18), or 'Simon who was called *Zēlōtēs* and Judas of James and Judas *Iscariot*' (Luke 6:15–16). Acts 1:13 differs only in calling Simon simply 'Simon *Zēlōtēs*' or 'Simon the Zealot' as we have seen.

However the Gospel of John, which contains no Apostle list, simply calls Judas, in four different places, as we saw as well, 'of Simon *Iscariot*' or 'Simon *Iscariot*'s son' or 'brother' (6:71, 12:4, 13:3, and, most importantly of all, 13:26, where Jesus 'breaks the bread' and gives it to 'Judas of Simon *Iscariot*'. This is paralleled in the Gospel of the Hebrews above by Jesus 'breaking the bread and giving it to' *his brother James*.) At one point, as will be recalled, John is at pains to distinguish this 'Judas' from *another* Judas, 'not the *Iscariot*', among the Apostles, whom he has not mentioned before in the Gospel (14:22).

Here we are in the midst of his version of Jesus' speeches at the Last Supper. Not without significance, as we saw, Jesus is discussing important points about 'loving him' and 'being loved by God', amid repeated references to 'keeping' again, 'keeping the Commandments' and 'keeping my word' – Jesus', not, for instance, Jonadab the son of Rechab's. All this is given within the framework of repeated play on the first of the two 'Love' Commandments – a variation of the second having already been quoted in John 13:34, ending up with repeated reference to 'the Branch' – in Hebrew, *Nezer*, a further adumbration of the 'Nazoraean' symbolism (14:15–15:21).

John only notes that the *Judas* with whom Jesus is principally discussing these things, is 'not the *Iscariot*', because this first 'Judas' has already left the supper table in order 'to betray him'. This is probably an emendation by a later redactor who recognized the absurdity of still speaking to 'Judas' about 'love' and 'keeping the Commandments' when he had already gone out 'to betray him'. This also had the important side effect of playing on the 'love' one was supposed to exhibit towards one's fellow man, as opposed to the hatred embodied in the '*Sicarii*' ideal – a juxtaposition Paul too, in his letters, is never slow to exploit with regard to his enemies, whom he calls, as we saw, 'zealous to exclude' – not to mention the implied rebuke of Jesus' family members in this regard.

It would appear to be plain that this 'Judas *Iscariot*'/'the *Iscariot*'/'of Simon *Iscariot*' is not to be distinguished from Jesus' brother 'Judas of James', also called Thaddaeus, Lebbaeus (that is, 'Judas the son of *Alphaeus*' or '*Cleophas*'), Judas the Zealot, itself moving into Thomas/ Judas Thomas appellations. Nor is this so-called 'Simon *Iscariot*' in John to be distinguished from Simon the Zealot, Simon the Cananite, and probably also Simeon bar Cleophas, Jesus' purported *first* cousin – the multiplication of these Judases being not very different from the multiplication of Marys, Simons, and Jameses we have already encountered, but to even more deleterious effect.

This is because, historically speaking, the calumny involved in calling Judas 'the Traitor', with all its underlying resonances and implications – even where the family of Jesus itself was concerned – has echoed down the ages and hardly ameliorates even today. The placing of 'Judas of James' side by side with 'Judas *Iscariot*' in Lukan Apostle lists represents yet a further replication of this name and this theme. In fact, the theme of 'Traitors' and 'treachery' is another one familiar from the *Pesharim* or Commentaries at Qumran and, yet again – as always – we seem to have to do with the inversion or reversal of crucial Qumran themes. If James and the Righteous Teacher at Qumran can be equated, it also would represent yet another absorption of literary motifs having to do with James into the story of Jesus.

In these expositions of key biblical texts at Qumran, 'the Traitors' just about always have something to do with the individual we have identified as Paul's *alter ego*, 'the Liar and the men of his persuasion', including 'the Violent Ones'. Even in Scripture, it will be recalled, Paul is originally portrayed as using *violence with the people*. These 'Traitors' are portrayed as 'rejecting' both the Law and the scriptural exegesis of the Righteous Teacher and being 'Traitors to the New Covenant in the Land of Damascus'.[29] This is not to mention the total reversal of the 'delivering up' language – always associated with 'Judas *Iscariot*' – throughout the Damascus Document, in the sense of 'delivering up' backsliders or Covenant-Breakers to 'the Avenging Wrath of God' or 'the sword'.

Where the denigration of these close family members of Jesus in Scripture – in particular this 'Judas' – is concerned; in Johannine tradition as well, the 'missing Apostle' at the time of Jesus' purported post-resurrection appearance in Jerusalem to 'the Twelve' is 'Thomas surnamed *Didymus*' (John 20:24) – in other traditions, 'Judas *Thomas*' (more obfuscation). So here, just as in the Synoptics, the 'missing' Apostle is basically someone called 'Judas', again connected to traditions *associated with the family of Jesus*. In John, as we have seen, this Thomas will 'not believe' unless he can put his finger into the actual 'print of the nails' and 'his hand into his side' (*thus* – 20:25) – therefore, the pejorative appellation which is again, even today, still proverbial, 'Doubting Thomas'.

In the Gospel of the Hebrews, it will be recalled too, James 'will not eat' (and presumably 'not drink' either), until he has 'seen' Jesus or 'the Son of Man risen from among those that sleep' – more overlaps or transformations having to do basically with James and this other putative family member or brother, 'Judas'. Eight days later in John, 'Thomas' supposedly gets this additional appearance, which involves not 'eating' or 'breaking bread' this time, but 'putting his finger' *into Jesus' side*. The effect is essentially the same. Another appearance occurs by the Sea of Galilee with Nathanael and others above and, here, Jesus' 'taking the bread and giving it to them' does finally occur – and 'some of the fish too'. (In the story of Queen Helen and her son Izates' efforts, it will be recalled, it was 'grain [the bread] and dried figs'!)

The Synoptic accounts, of course, know nothing of all of this. Only Matthew and Mark have any real appearances along the Sea of Galilee. Though the 'breaking bread' and 'eating' are missing, the 'doubting' theme is present, at least in Matthew – Mark is questionable according to most scholars in any case. But in all of these, including Luke, the *missing Apostle* is now 'Judas *Iscariot*', not as in John, '*Thomas* called *Didymus*', that is, 'Judas' or 'Judas *Thomas*'. In the Lukan version of the appearance to 'the Eleven' in Jerusalem, as we saw, they give Jesus 'boiled fish' to eat and he shows them 'his hands and feet', this after having appeared to at least *one* family member on the Emmaus Road, with whom he 'broke bread' – as in the Gospel of the Hebrews.

It is difficult to avoid these confusions or overlaps in the traditions between Jesus' family members – particularly 'Jude' or 'Judas *Thomas*' – and 'Judas *Iscariot*'. In turn, these further overlap traditions having to do with James. The note about 'breaking bread' with Jesus in 'Last Supper' scenarios in the Synoptics, incorporating the Pauline overwrite about 'Communion with the body' and 'blood of Christ' – missing from the 'Last Supper' narrative in the Gospel of John – just reinforces these overlaps. John only has Jesus 'dipping the morsel and giving it to Judas [the son or brother] of Simon *Iscariot*' in a clear parody of Jewish Passover scenarios. No Communion. This comes much earlier in conjunction with the 'multiplication of the loaves and the fishes' after turning *water into wine* at 'Cana' in 'Galilee'.

The Synoptics, of course, do not have Jesus actually 'give the bread' to Judas *Iscariot*, as Jesus *does James* in the Gospel of the Hebrews above, though they do have Judas 'dipping his hand' with Jesus, as we saw (Matt. 26:23 and Mark 14:20), and put heavy stress on the 'eating and drinking' theme tying it to the theologically even more difficult, *Communion with the blood of Jesus Christ*. This last, even when taken symbolically, flies in the face of Jamesian prohibitions to overseas communities, forbidding the consumption of blood, not to mention those at Qumran, which found it abhorrent. We already noted the reversal in this regard of *Nazirite*-oath abstentions from 'eating and drinking', but even more telling, *Rechabite*/Jamesian abstention from 'drinking wine' altogether (also parodied in the 'Cana' miracle of 'turning water into wine' above).

But we have been watching overlaps and confusions of this kind with traditions relating to James the Just the *brother of Jesus* – always reproduced with a kind of negative or inverted effect – throughout the book. For instance, we have seen how Judas' 'kiss' of betrayal in the Synoptics (Matt. 26:49 and pars.) simply inverts the kiss that Jesus gives *his brother James* or vice versa in sectarian tradition about James in documents like the two Apocalypses of James at Nag Hammadi. This is not to mention the affection Jesus is pictured as feeling for *the Disciple he loved*, whom John portrays as lying on Jesus' bosom even as Judas is about to betray him (13:23). We have also seen how the election to replace Judas as the 'Twelfth Apostle' in Acts is probably little else than a substitution for the election of James as 'Overseer' of the early Church *in succession to his brother*, the 'Twelve Apostle' scheme being largely symbolic and this crucial and important election being totally missing from Acts' narrative as it has come down to us.

We have also seen how the bloody nature of Judas' suicide after betraying Jesus 'for money' not only parodies 'Zealot' suicides, in particular, the mass suicide of 'the *Sicarii*' on Masada at the end of the War; but, in fact, incorporates one or two elements from the classic scenarios for the *death of James*. These include 'throwing himself down', related to Belial 'casting his nets' generally before Israel – though for the Gospels it is 'Satan' that enters Judas when he is about to betray Jesus (Luke 22:3 and John 13:27). However, for John 13:2, it is once again, 'the Diabolos' who intrudes here. Whereas in the Damascus Document, 'Belial's Nets' are 'three kinds of Righteousness', for the Synoptic tradition Judas' 'headlong fall', or suicide, is his 'reward of Unrighteousness'.

Since the composition of the 'Twelve Man' Apostle scheme is so fraught with inconsistencies and uncertainties, it is hard to avoid the conclusion that the identification of the Apostle who 'betrayed' Jesus with Judas *Iscariot* – which has become such a set piece and one of the iconographies of Western Civilization – is, once again, just another of these malevolent addenda to tradition that has *no historical foundation whatsoever* – except further disparagement of the successors to and family of Jesus in Palestine. On the contrary, it is the product of some of the most successful historical rewriting ever accomplished. It is no wonder Plato wanted to bar the poets from his *Republic*. Familiar with the creation of stories about Deities in his own time, he knew whereof he spoke.

But the case before us has the additional aspect of being related to the subversion of the family of Jesus, particularly *James* – though sometimes Judas 'his brother', sometimes called 'Judas the Zealot' like his other brother 'Simon the Zealot'. Here, James *sometimes becomes* Judas, just as in the Book of Acts, Judas at one point *even becomes James*.

Even more revealing, though scholars have attempted to find the basis of the word '*Iscariot*' – obviously a Hebrew original transliterated bodily into the Greek – sometimes with ingenious results as we have seen: for instance, some have tried to call it the name of a village; others, an attempt at Hebrew double-think – none have succeeded in showing any origin for this word other than '*Sicarii*' (in actual Greek, '*Sicarioi*'), that is, the extreme wing of 'the Zealot Movement', which Josephus over and over again blames for assassinations and disturbances in Palestine, ending with the destruction of the Temple – note the additional play here on '*the Sicarii*' *causing the destruction of the Temple* and Judas *Iscariot, the destruction of Jesus.*

That, for John anyhow, Judas is also related to someone called 'Simon *Iscariot*' – missing from the Synoptics, though actually implied in the order of the names in the Apostle list in the Gospel of Luke – corroborates this still further. Nor should we forget that it is the last hold-outs among the followers of Judas the *Galilean* – the author along with '*Saddok*' of Josephus' 'Fourth Philosophy' or 'Zealot' Movement – under the leadership of another of this 'Judas'' descendants, 'Eleazar ben Jair', who commit suicide on Masada in pursuance of this creed. These are, in fact, the last remnants of these '*Sicarii*', against whom Josephus so rails. We have just mentioned the parody of this suicide implicit in 'Judas'' actions as portrayed in Matthew and Acts, not to mention the additional note of betrayal 'for money'. How delicious all this must have been for the authors of these accounts – and how diabolically successful.

Epilogue

A second volume, about half the length of the present one, has already been prepared. It will continue where this book leaves off on the subject of the Jamesian Communities in the East, the Pella Flight, Agabus' second prophecy, and the oracle of Jesus ben Ananias in the Temple from 62 to 70 CE – all connected with the death of James. It will also treat the true meaning of James' rain-making and the three to four direct confrontations between Paul and James in a more systematic manner – not to mention 'MMT' as a 'Jamesian' Letter to 'the Great King of the Peoples beyond the Euphrates'.

Finally it will treat the confrontations between the Righteous Teacher and the Liar in the Scrolls, going through the parallels between James and the Righteous Teacher at Qumran in meticulous detail. It will show the Habakkuk *Pesher* in any event – and by implication, all documents related by sense and nomenclature to it – to be first century. This will be a proof based on the clear sense of the internal data not the external. It will also treat the parallel 'Cup' imagery in both it and the New Testament, showing the intimate relationship between the Qumran 'New Covenant in the Land of Damascus' and the Pauline 'Cup of the New Covenant in (the) blood' of Christ.

In the present book, however, it was thought best to confine ourselves to arguments essentially delineating the parameters of James' existence, his importance for his time – if not for our own – and what he personally represented from the vantage point of New Testament and early Church sources, the Scrolls being used peripherally for purposes of external comparison and verification only. This was because, whereas the dating of early Christian documents is not the subject of inordinate differences of opinion, with the Scrolls it is different. Therefore, we have relegated such matters to the second volume, not wishing to impinge on the clear conclusions of the first based exclusively on New Testament documents, early Church sources, and Josephus.

In it, we have shown how materials in the Book of Acts were erased or overwritten where information relating to the life and death of James was concerned. In the process, the rather staggering loopholes in the New Testament, in the form we presently have it, were systematically and painstakingly set forth. This was true of the election of James and its parallel transformation in Acts into the election of the 'Twelfth Apostle' to replace 'the Traitor Judas *Iscariot*'. It is also true of the stoning of 'Stephen', murdered (according to Eusebius) by 'the murderers of the Lord'.

The attack by 'Jews' on Stephen – early identified by some scholars as a stand-in for the stoning of James (the stoning of Stephen actually occurring in Scripture where the assault on James by Paul should have occurred) – is paralleled in Josephus by the robbery and beating of the 'Emperor's Servant Stephen' by 'Zealot' Revolutionaries outside Jerusalem in 49 CE. It is also intimately related to the assassination by 'Stephen', Flavia Domitilla's servant, of the Emperor Domitian in 96 CE, itself probably in retaliation for Domitian's execution of *real* Christians like Flavius Clemens, her husband, and Epaphroditus, Josephus' putative publisher.

It is even more true of the relatively obscure passage having to do with Philip converting 'the eunuch of the *Ethiopian* Queen Kandakes', probably an overwrite of material relating to Queen Helen of Adiabene and her descendant 'Kenedaeos', who lost his life in the 'Zealot' assault on the Roman troops at the Pass at Beit Horon in the first days of the Uprising against Rome in 66 CE. The conversion of Queen Helen's two sons, Izates and Monobazus, is a pivotal event from all perspectives, political as well as financial. Its refurbishment had the additional benefit of heaping abuse on a favourite conversion episode of the Jews involving 'circumcision' – in the process vividly exemplifying the derisive invective involved.

Likewise, we have repeatedly shown how historical events were refurbished and changed in the history of early Christianity as represented in Acts. For instance, the visit of Peter to Caesarea to the 'Pious' Roman Centurion Cornelius – where Peter learns to accept Gentiles and not reject them – is a rewrite of the visit of Simon, the 'Zealot' Leader of 'a Church' of his own in Jerusalem (who wished to bar Herodians from the Temple as foreigners not admit them), to inspect the household of King Agrippa I in Caesarea in 44 CE in Josephus; and the beheading of 'James the brother of John' is a rewrite of the beheading of the Messianic Leader 'Theudas' – presumably 'Thaddaeus' alias 'Judas the brother of James' (also 'a relative of his' – Jesus').

The 'prophet' Agabus, who in Acts predicts the Famine that would grip the whole earth in Claudius' time (*c.*45 CE), was but a thinly disguised substitute for even more important events about the history of early Christianity overseas in this time, namely the conversion of 'King Abgarus' of Edessa (in Roman texts, 'Augarus', 'Albarus', or 'Acbarus'/ 'Agbarus') – 'the Great King of the Peoples beyond the Euphrates'. The episode is but another related to the conversion of Queen Helen of Adiabene – in Syriac/Armenian sources Abgarus' putative wife and probably one of his extensive harem – and her two sons.

We also suggested that the second 'prophecy', attributed to 'Agabus', warning Paul not to go up to Jerusalem (Acts 21:11), was a parallel over-write of the prophecy of one 'Jesus ben Ananias', documented in Josephus, who for seven and a half years, immediately following the death of James, prophesied the coming destruction of Jerusalem until he was killed by a Roman projectile shortly before its fall. At the same time, it parodied and inverted the early Christian oracle connected to it, also following the death of James, warning the Jerusalem Community followers of James to flee Jerusalem.

In the process, we showed how fulsome wordplay and parallel polemics were involved in these kinds of reformulations as well. For example, ideological notations, such as 'Nazirite', 'Nazoraean', 'Galilean', and '*Sicarios*', were turned into geographical locations. The 'casting down' language applied in all early Christian texts to James either being 'cast down headlong' from the Temple Pinnacle or Paul 'casting him down headlong' from its steps (not to mention in Stephen's being 'cast out of the city' or Judas *Iscariot*'s 'headlong fall') comes in for further expansion and variation in the 'casting down' metaphor employed in the New Testament's 'fishermen' and 'nets' allusions, relating to Jesus choosing his Apostles on the Sea of Galilee.

In the Habakkuk *Pesher* the 'casting' and 'dragnets full of fish' imagery from Habakkuk 1:14–16 is definitively interpreted in terms not only of taxation by the '*Kittim*' (in this context, the Romans), but also their *tax farming*, i.e., their 'parcelling out' their sovereignty and *tax collecting* among various petty rulers in the East (including, quite obviously, Herodians). This whole exercise is very pointedly characterized in the Habakkuk *Pesher* as 'their plenteous eating' – all developed in terms of the innumerable 'fish of the sea' they catch in 'their dragnets'.

Finally, the New Testament, once again, reverses this language, showing its awareness that it was being applied to Roman taxation, by having Jesus employ it to recommend 'casting a hook into the sea' of Galilee to get the money to pay such Roman taxes or tribute, or, reversing this again and returning to the original Jewish/Palestinian vengeful apocalyptic cast, 'casting the tares' or 'the polluted fish' into 'a furnace of Fire'.

In a further adumbration of this 'casting' language (sometimes even with comical or cartoon-like effect), and Belial or Balaam's 'nets' connected to it in the Scrolls and Revelation, the Gospels employ it to mean the 'Power' Jesus has or the 'Authority' he gives his Apostles 'to cast out Evil demons'. Not only can this be seen as parodying what 'Essenes' or groups like those responsible for the documents at Qumran do to backsliders – 'cast them out' (plays or caricatures of this kind are ingenious); but in Acts, 'the Jews'' casting out *James' double* Stephen to be stoned – not to mention Josephus' Zealots 'casting out' the naked body of James' nemesis, the High Priest Ananus, without burial from Jerusalem, thereby desecrating it.

Determinations of this kind were made solely on the basis of early Church sources, both in and outside the New Testament, and on the basis of Josephus – with peripheral verification and illustration only, where ethos was concerned, from the Dead Sea Scrolls. These, in turn, led to the question about how and why such incredible lacunae occurred and who could have been responsible for or benefited from them.

For instance, James and his 'Jerusalem Assembly' are able to go on functioning relatively without disturbance in the Jerusalem of the 40s to the 60s CE, while an individual like Paul can hardly set foot in the city without being mobbed – this because of fear of the Jewish populace as a whole, among whom individuals like James, John the Baptist, and presumably Jesus (if he was anything like them), appear to have been *very* popular.

Paul's escape from the representatives of the Arab King Aretas down the walls of Damascus in a basket, by his own testimony in 2 Corinthians 11:32–33, also bears this out (for Acts' picture of parallel events, it is *the Jews* from whom Paul is escaping). This is the same 'Arab King', whom, according to Josephus, the Jewish common people saw as taking vengeance on the Herodians for the death of John the Baptist in the mid-30s, the same period in which Paul admits to having 'persecuted' those of 'the Way' even 'unto death'.

All this rather is lumped together in Scripture, as it has come down to us, under the general heading of the perfidiousness of 'the Jews'. This becomes frozen in early Church theology by the time of the works of Clement of Alexandria ('Titus Flavius Clemens', clearly a descendant of previous 'Clement's), Tertullian, Irenaeus, Origen, and Eusebius in the third and fourth centuries as the 'guilt of the Jews for their crimes against the Christ of God'.

But this was hardly the case in the Palestine of the time. This is to mistake sectarian strife for strife with foreigners. Though John, Jesus, and James may have run afoul of sectarian strife, that is strife with other Jewish Establishment groups or Herodians, it was not the mass of Jews *per se* who were their enemies. Rather, the opposite is more likely the truth.

Finally, we have placed James at the centre of sectarian and popular agitation ending up in the fall of Jerusalem and we have identified the basic issues involved in such strife, particularly as these related to gifts from Gentiles and their admission into the Temple (considered 'pollution of the Temple' at Qumran) – reflected too in the Qumran document known as '*MMT*' and the hostility to 'things sacrificed to idols' it enunciates. We have been able to use these parameters to point out Paul's connections to the Herodian family and the kind of code that was being applied to such relationships – at Qumran and in Revelation, 2 Peter, and Jude involving 'Balaam', 'Belial', and 'Devilishness'.

It is these things that the Dead Sea Scrolls help put in sharp relief. Without the Scrolls we would only have suspected them, because of the mutually contradictory information in the New Testament and early Church documents. With the Scrolls for use as control, we get an entirely different picture of events in Palestine than either the New Testament or the documents of Rabbinic Judaism – now normative Judaism – provide. Whether James is to be identified with the Righteous Teacher at Qumran or simply a parallel successor is not the point – the Scrolls allow us to approach the Messianic Community of James with about as much precision as we are likely to have from any other source.

One hopes that the arguments put forth in this book will at least lift some of the purposeful misrepresentation and cloud of unknowing surrounding these issues. Once James has been rescued from the oblivion into which he was cast, abetted by one of the most successful rewrite enterprises ever accomplished – the Book of Acts (and one of the most fantastic) – it is necessary to deal with the new constellation of facts the reality of his being occasions. It will also no longer be possible to avoid, through endless scholarly debate and other evasion syndromes, the obvious solution to the problem of the Historical Jesus – the question of his actual physical existence as such aside - the answer to which is simple. Who and whatever James was, so was Jesus.

Chronological Charts

MACCABEAN PRIEST KINGS

Mattathias, 167–166 BC
Judas Maccabee, 166–160
Jonathan, 160–142
Simon, 142–134
John Hyrcanus, 134–104
Alexander Jannaeus, 103–76
Salome Alexandra, 76–67
Aristobulus II, 67–63
Hyrcanus II, 76–67 and 63–40
Antigonus, 40–37

HERODIAN KINGS, ETHNARCHS, OR TETRARCHS

Herod, Roman-supported King, 37–4 BC
Archelaus, Ethnarch of Judea, 4 BC – 7 CE
Herod Antipas, Tetrarch of Galilee and Perea, 4 BC – 39 CE
Philip, Tetrarch of Trachonitis, 4 BC – 34 CE
Agrippa I, Tetrarch and King, 37–44
Herod of Chalcis, 44–49
Agrippa II, 49–93

ROMAN GOVERNORS

Antipater (Herod's father), Procurator, 55–43 BC
Coponius, 6–9 CE
Ambivulus, 9–12
Rufus, 12–15
Valerius Gratus, 15–26 (perhaps 15–18)
Pontius Pilate, 26–37 (perhaps 18–37)
Fadus, 44–46
Tiberius Alexander, 46–48
Cumanus, 48–52
Felix, 52–60
Festus, 60–62
Albinus, 62–64
Florus, 64–66

ROMAN EMPERORS
FROM 60 BC TO 138 CE

Caesar, 60–44 BC
Mark Anthony and Octavius, 43–31 BC
Octavius (Augustus), 27 BC – 14 CE
Tiberius, 14–37
Caligula, 37–41
Claudius, 41–54
Nero, 54–68
Galba, 68–69
Otho, 69
Vitellius, 69
Vespasian, 69–79
Titus, 79–81
Domitian, 81–96
Nerva, 96–98
Trajan, 98–117
Hadrian, 117–138

EARLY CHURCH AND OTHER SOURCES

Philo of Alexandria, *c.* 30 BC – 45 CE
Clement of Rome, *c.* 30–97 CE
Josephus, 37–96
Ignatius, *c.* 50–115
Papias, *c.* 60–135
Pliny, 61–113
Polycarp, 69–156
Justin Martyr, *c.* 100–165
Hegesippus, *c.* 90–180
Tatian, *c.* 115–185
Lucian of Samosata, *c.* 125–180
Irenaeus, *c.* 130–200
Clement of Alexandria, *c.* 150–215
Tertullian, *c.* 160–221
Hippolytus, *c.* 160–235
Julius Africanus, *c.* 170–245
Origen, *c.* 185–254
Eusebius of Caesarea, *c.* 260–340
Epiphanius, 367–404
Jerome, 348–420
Rufinus of Aquileia, *c.* 350–410
Augustine, 354–430
St Cyril of Jerusalem, 375–444

The Maccabeans

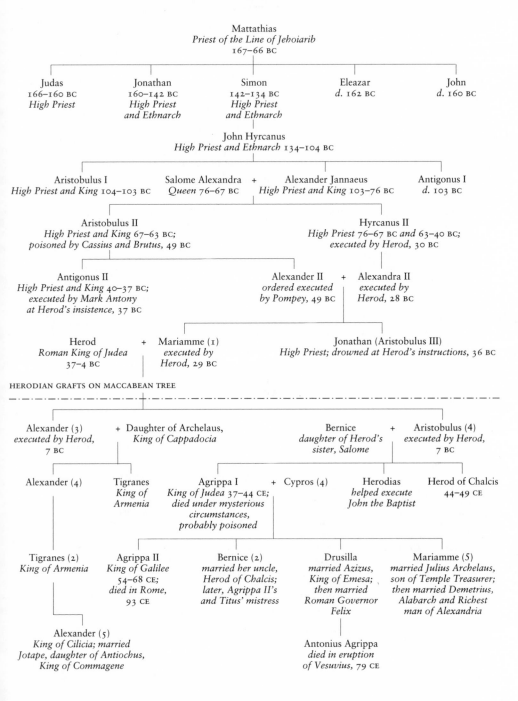

Mattathias
Priest of the Line of Jehoiarib
167–66 BC

Judas
166–160 BC
High Priest

Jonathan
160–142 BC
High Priest
and Ethnarch

Simon
142–134 BC
High Priest
and Ethnarch

Eleazar
d. 162 BC

John
d. 160 BC

John Hyrcanus
High Priest and Ethnarch 134–104 BC

Aristobulus I
High Priest and King 104–103 BC

Salome Alexandra
Queen 76–67 BC
+
Alexander Jannaeus
High Priest and King 103–76 BC

Antigonus I
d. 103 BC

Aristobulus II
High Priest and King 67–63 BC;
poisoned by Cassius and Brutus, 49 BC

Hyrcanus II
High Priest 76–67 BC and 63–40 BC;
executed by Herod, 30 BC

Antigonus II
High Priest and King 40–37 BC;
executed by Mark Antony
at Herod's insistence, 37 BC

Alexander II
ordered executed
by Pompey, 49 BC
+
Alexandra II
executed by
Herod, 28 BC

Herod
Roman King of Judea
37–4 BC
+
Mariamme (1)
executed by
Herod, 29 BC

Jonathan (Aristobulus III)
High Priest; drowned at Herod's instructions, 36 BC

HERODIAN GRAFTS ON MACCABEAN TREE

Alexander (3)
executed by Herod,
7 BC
+
Daughter of Archelaus,
King of Cappadocia

Bernice
daughter of Herod's
sister, Salome
+
Aristobulus (4)
executed by Herod,
7 BC

Alexander (4)

Tigranes
King of
Armenia

Agrippa I
King of Judea 37–44 CE;
died under mysterious
circumstances,
probably poisoned
+
Cypros (4)

Herodias
helped execute
John the Baptist

Herod of Chalcis
44–49 CE

Tigranes (2)
King of Armenia

Agrippa II
King of Galilee
54–68 CE;
died in Rome,
93 CE

Bernice (2)
married her uncle,
Herod of Chalcis;
later, Agrippa II's
and Titus' mistress

Drusilla
married Azizus,
King of Emesa;
then married
Roman Governor
Felix

Mariamme (5)
married Julius Archelaus,
son of Temple Treasurer;
then married Demetrius,
Alabarch and Richest
man of Alexandria

Alexander (5)
King of Cilicia; married
Jotape, daughter of Antiochus,
King of Commagene

Antonius Agrippa
died in eruption
of Vesuvius, 79 CE

The Herodians

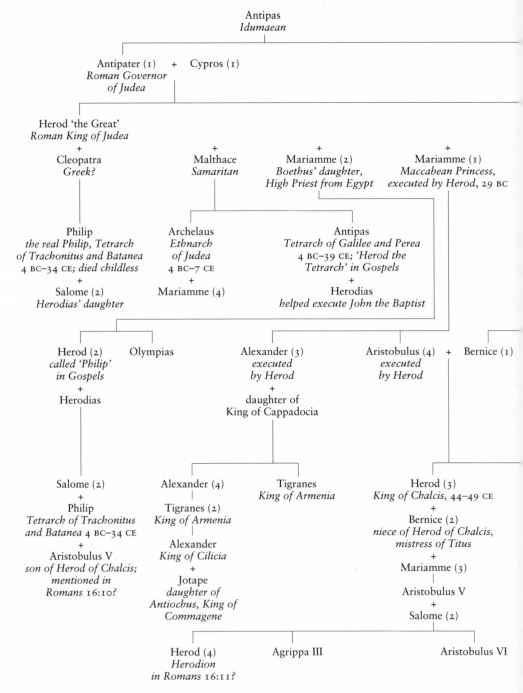

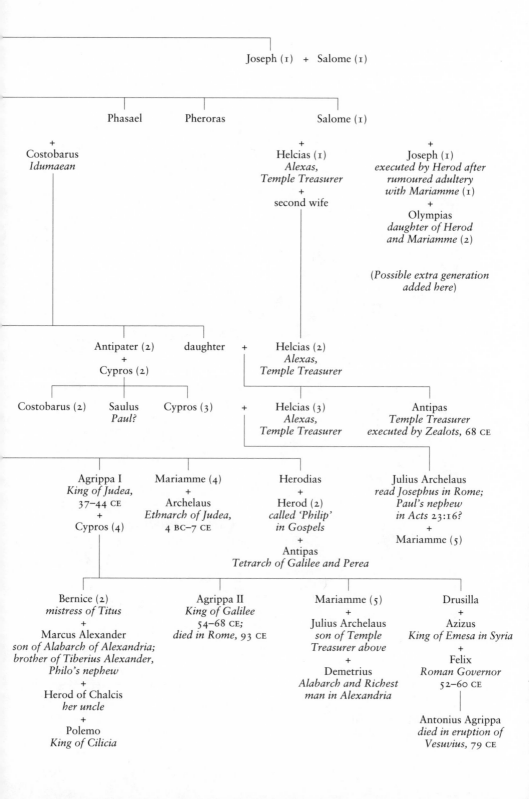

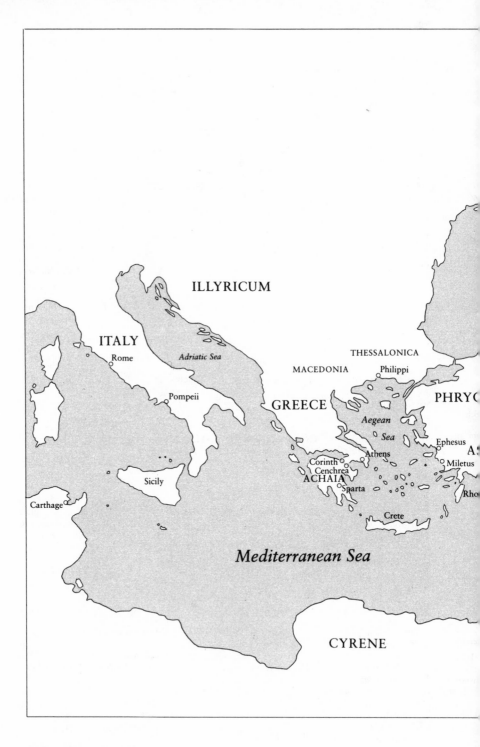

Caspian Sea

CAUCASUS MOUNTAINS

PARTHIA

k Sea

HYNIA

GALATIA

UPPER ARMENIA
MT ARARAT ▲
(Modern location)

LOWER ARMENIA

MT ARARAT (Classical location)

MEDIA

PERSIA

Ecbatana

CAPPADOCIA

Samosata   LAND OF THE EDESSENES
Nisibis
Arbela

ADIABENE

ioch of Pisidia

CILICIA

Edessa(Antiochia)
Haran(Carrhae)

COMMAGENE

Hierapolis

Tigris

um   Lystra   Tarsus

Antioch

Beroea (Aleppo)

Euphrates

BABYLONIA

Seleucia

Susa

Palmyra

Babylon

Charax Spasini
(Antiochia or Basrah)

CYPRUS

Orontes

Tripolis

COELE SYRIA

Persian
Gulf

Sidon

Damascus

Tyre

A   R   A   B   I   A

Jordan

Caesarea

Jerusalem

Ashkelon
Gaza

Qumran

IDUMAEA

Petra

N

Alexandria
Heliopolis

Memphis

EGYPT

500 miles

thynchus

Red Sea

Bernice

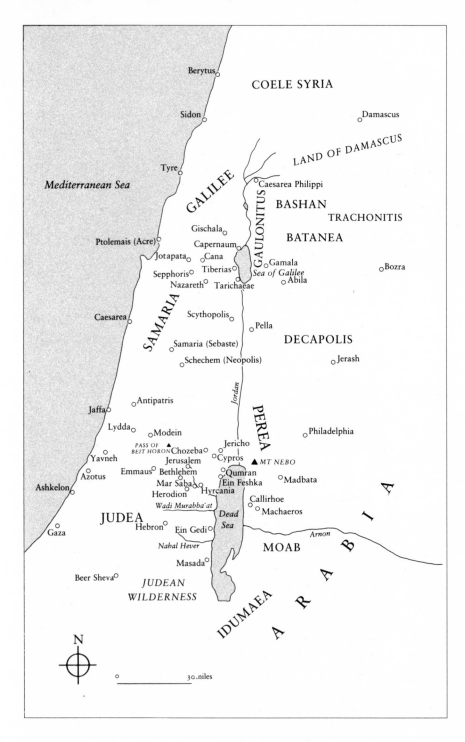

COELE SYRIA

Berytus

Damascus

Sidon

LAND OF DAMASCUS

Mediterranean Sea

Tyre

GALILEE

Caesarea Philippi

GAULONITUS

BASHAN

TRACHONITIS

Gischala

BATANEA

Capernaum

Ptolemais (Acre)

Jotapata

Cana

Gamala

Bozra

Sepphoris

Tiberias

Sea of Galilee

Nazareth

Tarichaeae

Abila

Caesarea

SAMARIA

Scythopolis

Pella

DECAPOLIS

Samaria (Sebaste)

Schechem (Neopolis)

Jerash

Jordan

Antipatris

PEREA

Jaffa

Lydda

Modein

Philadelphia

PASS OF
BEIT HORON

Chozeba

Jericho

Yavneh

Jerusalem

Cypros

MT NEBO

Azotus

Emmaus

Bethlehem

Qumran

Ashkelon

Mar Saba

Ein Feshka

Madbata

Herodion

Hyrcania

Wadi Murabba'at

Callirhoe

JUDEA

Hebron

Ein Gedi

Dead
Sea

Machaeros

Gaza

Nahal Hever

MOAB

Arnon

Masada

ARABIA

Beer Sheva

JUDEAN
WILDERNESS

IDUMAEA

N

0   30 miles

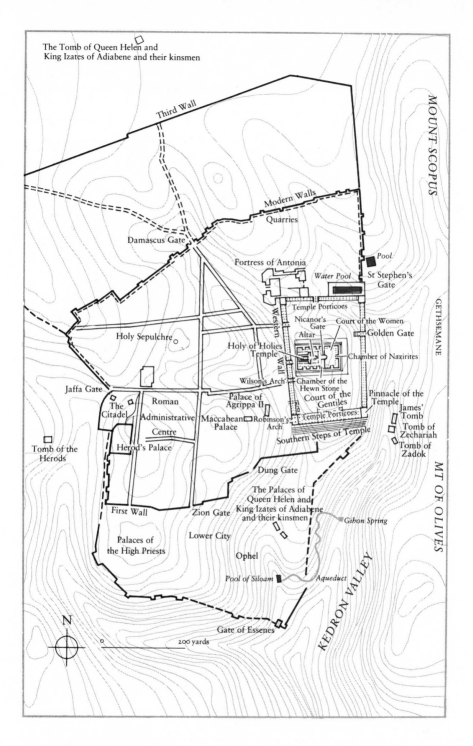

The Tomb of Queen Helen and
King Izates of Adiabene and their kinsmen

Third Wall

MOUNT SCOPUS

Modern Walls

Quarries

Damascus Gate

Fortress of Antonia

Pool

Water Pool

St Stephen's
Gate

GETHSEMANE

Temple Porticoes

Holy Sepulchre

Nicanor's
Gate
Altar

Court of the Women

Golden Gate

Holy of Holies
Temple

Chamber of Nazirites

Wilson's Arch

Chamber of the
Hewn Stone

Jaffa Gate

Palace of
Agrippa II

Court of the
Gentiles

Pinnacle of the
Temple

The
Citadel

Roman

Administrative

Maccabean
Palace

Robinson's
Arch

Temple Porticoes

James'
Tomb

Tomb of
Zechariah

Centre

Herod's Palace

Southern Steps of Temple

Tomb of
Zadok

Tomb of the
Herods

Dung Gate

MT OF OLIVES

The Palaces of
Queen Helen and
King Izates of Adiabene
and their kinsmen

First Wall

Zion Gate

Gihon Spring

Palaces of
the High Priests

Lower City

Ophel

Pool of Siloam

Aqueduct

KEDRON VALLEY

N

200 yards

Gate of Essenes

THE TEMPLE OF JERUSALEM   973

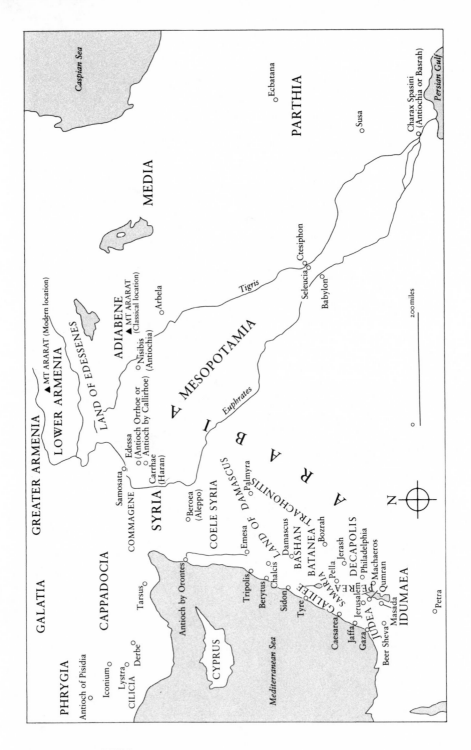

Caspian Sea

PARTHIA

Ecbatana

Susa

Charax Spasini
(Antiochia or Basrah)

Persian Gulf

MEDIA

ADIABENE

MT ARARAT (Modern location)

MT ARARAT (Classical location)

Arbela

Tigris

Ctesiphon

Seleucia

Babylon

MESOPOTAMIA

GREATER ARMENIA

LAND OF EDESSENES

LOWER ARMENIA

Nisibis
(Antiochia)

200 miles

Euphrates

Samosata

Edessa
(Antioch Orrhoe or
Antioch by Callirhoe)

Carrhae
(Haran)

SYRIA

COMMAGENE

Beroea
(Aleppo)

COELE SYRIA

DAMASCUS

Palmyra

A R A B I A

CAPPADOCIA

GALATIA

Tarsus

Emesa

Damascus

TRACHONITIS

LAND OF

Bozrah

N

PHRYGIA

Antioch of Pisidia

Iconium

Lystra

CILICIA

Derbe

Antioch by Orontes

CYPRUS

Tripolis

Berytus

Chalcis

Sidon

Tyre

BASHAN

BATANEA

Jerash

Pella

DECAPOLIS

Philadelphia

Machaeros

Qumran

SAMARIA

GALILEE

Caesarea

Jaffa

Jerusalem

Gaza

JUDEA

Masada

Beer Sheva

IDUMAEA

Petra

Mediterranean Sea

ARABIA AND SYRIA

974

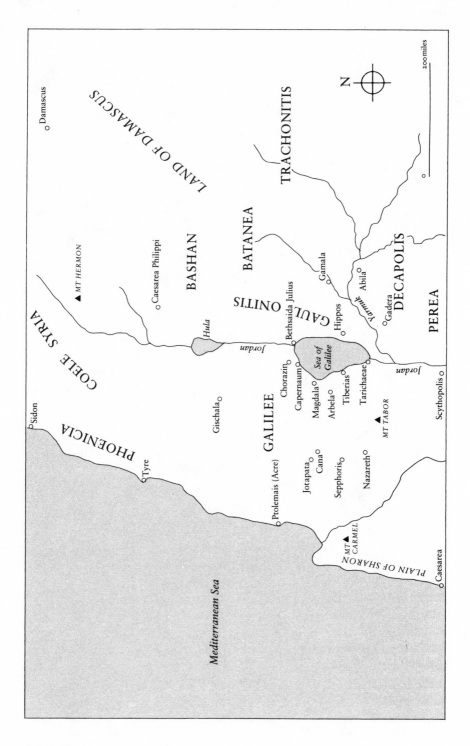

975

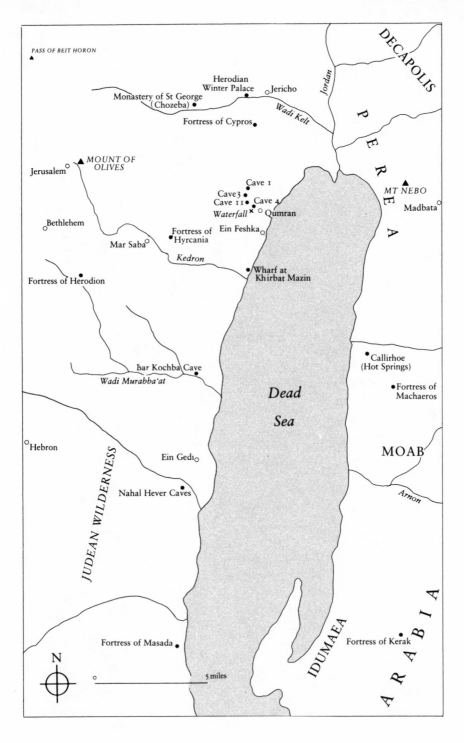

PASS OF BEIT HORON

DECAPOLIS

Herodian
Winter Palace   Jericho
Monastery of St George
(Chozeba)

Fortress of Cypros

Wadi Kelt

Jordan

P E R E A

Jerusalem   MOUNT OF
OLIVES

Cave 1

Cave 3
Cave 11   Cave 4
Waterfall   Qumran

MT NEBO

Madbata

Bethlehem

Fortress of
Hyrcania   Ein Feshka

Mar Saba

Kedron

Wharf at
Khirbat Mazin

Fortress of Herodion

Callirhoe
(Hot Springs)

Bar Kochba Cave

Wadi Murabba'at

Dead

Sea

Fortress of
Machaeros

Hebron

Ein Gedi

MOAB

Arnon

Nahal Hever Caves

JUDEAN WILDERNESS

I D U M A E A

Fortress of Masada

Fortress of Kerak

A R A B I A

N

5 miles

THE DEAD SEA   976

Note on Translations

This book tries to provide everything the reader will need in the text itself without going to secondary sources. Therefore, all important testimonies and sources should be at the reader's fingertips. Standard translations of Old or New Testament texts often sacrifice precision for readabibity or elegance. For instance, important words are not translated in a consistent manner and beauty or inspiration are often sought. Therefore, in all cases in both Old and New Testaments, we have followed the original Hebrew or Greek as closely and consistently as possible.

The same where the Dead Sea Scrolls are concerned. The available translations in English are often insufficient and misleading. Consistency and precision are neglected, fine points missed, and sometimes whole and important phrases deleted altogether.

The premier translation in English, for instance, often avoids using words like 'Holy Spirit', 'Justification', 'works', 'the Law', 'House of Judgement', 'Belial', 'the Messiah', etc., substituting words like 'spirit of holiness', 'deeds'/'acts', 'ordinances'/'precepts', 'condemned house', 'Satan', and 'anointed one'/'anointed ones' instead. In one such instance, the translation changes surrounding singular usages to plural and drops an important phrase without indicating it (seemingly because it either was expressed in the singular or could not otherwise be translated).

The same, for instance, is done in translations of the Letter of James in the New Testament, when it is stated, 'You [meaning 'the Rich'] killed the Righteous One. *He* offered you no resistance' (5:6). For various reasons, this is transformed into the plural, 'You killed the Righteous *Ones* [plural]. *They* offered you no resistance.' In this way, startling and important usages are marginalized or minimized.

More recent translations of the Dead Sea Scrolls are sometimes worse. Therefore we have preferred to make our own translations. The reader should be cautioned in this regard. There is no substitute for the original Greek or Hebrew as the case may be. As one translator cautions against another, so that translator will, in turn, caution against the first. The reader, dependent on translations, will simply have to compare and judge for him- or herself.

For example, one recent compendium, by F. García Martínez, has gone from the original Hebrew through Spanish into English. Though his volume is more complete than any preceding it (for which it is to be complimented); in it, language, terminological consistency, and precise English phraseology have been disregarded. One can see what was there – a plus, but that is all. One can get little impression of the ethos and splendour of the texts at all (this despite the fact that these translations are universally praised by the circle of academics to which Prof. Martínez belongs).

Where our own translations are concerned, we have preferred to err on the side of precision and accuracy rather than poetry or creative imagination (though we hope a modicum of splendour to be not altogether lacking). The same is true when it comes to both Old and New Testaments. For my recent translations of the Damascus Document, Community Rule, and Habakkuk *Pesher* from Qumran, the reader should consult *The Dead Sea Scrolls and the First Christians* (Rockport, 1996).

Where the early Church Fathers are concerned, for the most part we have followed the *Ante-Nicene Christian Library* (1867–71 edition) as the basis for translations. For Eusebius, we have generally preferred for greater precision to follow the original Greek. The same for Josephus, though in both cases we have consulted and sometimes had recourse to the Loeb Library and other translations. For instance, in the case of Josephus, we have also looked at the William Whiston translation from the eighteenth century and G. A. Williamson (1959). Where Eusebius is concerned, we also consulted the 1850 C. F. Cruse translation, G. A. Williamson (1966), and the 1890–92 *Nicene and Post-Nicene Christian Library*. The same for Jerome.

For the two Apocalypses of James from Nag Hammadi, we have for the most part followed the two sets of translations: *The Nag Hammadi Library in English* and Scott Kent Brown (1972), though sometimes we preferred to make our own. For Epiphanius, we consulted Philip R. Amidon's version (Oxford, 1990), Frank Williams (1987), Glenn Alan Koch (1976), and A. F. J. Klijn and G. J. Reinink (1973), before often also making our own.

The several passages from the Gospel of the Hebrews, the Protevangelium of James, and the *Epistula Apostolorum* are based on Jerome, the editions of E. Hennecke and W. Schneemelcher (1959), and M. R. James (1926). The lone passage from the Syriac version of the Pseudoclementine *Recognitions* was based on the presentation of my colleague, F. Stanley Jones, though here, too, sometimes we diverged.

All other passages from the Pseudoclementines were based on the *Ante-Nicene Christian Library*. All Arabic translations are my own. The point, as stated in the Introduction, is to make a consistent translation of a given term, such as 'Righteousness', 'Piety', 'the Poor', 'the Holy Spirit', 'Truth', 'Lying', 'works', 'House of Judgement'/'Day of Judgement', *'Belial'* (not 'Satan' – when a text wants to say 'Satan', it does so; when it wants to say 'Belial', it does so too), and 'swallow'/'cast down'.

Some translators take extreme liberties in these matters – some less. A study like this one depends on the precise vocabulary and absolute consistency across all texts, so that the reader will be able to recognize the same word, phrase, or term as it appears repeatedly in different contexts. In addition, all italics within quotations are my own to emphasize important ideas, words, or repetitions of same.

List of Abbreviations

Acts Th.	Acts of Thomas
Ad Cor.	Clement of Alexandria, Letter to the Corinthians
Ad Haer.	Irenaeus, *Against Heresies*
Ad Rom.	Ignatius, Letter to the Romans
Adv. Hel.	Jerome, *Against Helvidius*
Adv. Marcion	Tertullian, *Against Marcion*
ANCL	Anti-Nicene Christian Library (1867–71 edition)
Ant.	Josephus, *The Antiquities of the Jews*
Apion	Josephus, *Against Apion (Contra Apion)*
1 Apoc. Jas.	First Apocalypse of James
2 Apoc. Jas.	Second Apocalypse of James
Apoc. Pet.	Apocalypse of Peter
Apost. Const.	Apostolic Constitutions
APOT	*Apocrypha and Pseudepigrapha of the Old Testament* (ed. R. H. Charles)
ARN	*Abbot de Rabbi Nathan*
As. Moses	Assumption of Moses
b. San.	Babylonian *Talmud*, Tractate *Sanhedrin*
BAR	*Biblical Archaeology Review*
Baroccian.	Codice Barocciano
BASOR	*Bulletin of the American Scholls of Oriental Research*
CD	Cairo Damascus Document
Comm. on Gal.	Jerome, Commentary on Galatians
Comm. on John	Origen, Commentary of John
Comm. on Matt.	Origen, Commentary on Matthew
de Carne	Tertullian, *On the Body of Christ*
de Mens. et Pond.	Epiphanius, *De Mensuris et Ponderibus*
de Monog.	Tertullian, *On Monogamy*
de Verig. vel.	Tertullian, *On the Veiling of Virgins*
Dial.	Justin Martyr, *Dialogue with Trypho*

DSSU	*The Dead Sea Scrolls Uncovered* (ed. R. Eisenman and M. Wise)
EH	Eusebius, *Ecclesiastical History*
Enarr. in Ps. 34:3	Augustine, *Discourses on the Psalms*
Eph.	Ignatius, Letter to the Ephesians
Epist. Apost.	Epistle of the Apostles
Epist. B.	Epistle of Barnabas
Gen. R.	*Genesis Rabbah*
Gos. Th.	The Gospel of Thomas
Haeres.	Epiphanius, *Against Heresies* (*Panarion: The Medicine Box* in Latin)
H.N.	Pliny, *Natural History*
Haer.	Tertullian, *Against Heretics*
Hennecke	*The New Testament Apocrypha* (ed. E. Hennecke and W. Schneemelcher)
Hipp.	Hippolytus, *Refutation of all Heresies*
Hom. in Luc.	Origen, *Homilies on Luke*
HUCA	*Hebrew Union College Annual*
JJHP	*James the Just in the Habakkuk Pesher* (R. Eisenman)
j. Ta'an	Jerusalem *Talmud*, Tractate *Ta'anith*
Lam. R.	*Lamentations Rabbah*
M. San.	*Mishnah Sanhedrin*
Mur.	Wadi Murabba'at, Cave 1
MZCQ	*Maccabees, Zadokite, Christians and Qumran* (R. Eisenman)
Opus imperf. . C. Iul	Augustine, *Opus Imperfectum contra Secundum Juliani*
pars.	parallels
Protevang.	Protevangelium of James
Ps. *Hom.*	Pseudoclementine *Homilies*
Ps. Philo	Pseudo Philo
Ps. *Rec.*	Pseuclementine *Recognitions*
Quod Omnis	Philo, *On the Contemplative Life*
4QD	The Qumran Damascus Document (Cave 4)
1QH	The Qumran Hymns
1QM	The Qumran War Scroll
11QMelch	The Qumran Melchizedek Text

4QMMT	The Qumran Letter(s) on Works Reckoned as Righteousness from Qumran
1QpHab	The Qumran Habakkuk *Pesher*
4QpIs	The Qumran Isaiah *Pesher*
4QpNah	The Qumran Nahum *Pesher*
4QpPs 37	The Qumran Commentary on Psalm 37
1QS	The Qumran Community Rule
11QT	The Qumran Temple Scroll
4QTest	The Qumran Testimonia
Suet.	Suetonius, *The Twelve Caesars*
Tos. Kellim	*Tosefta Kellim*
Trall.	Ignatius, Letter to the Trallians
Vir. ill.	Jerome, *Lives of Illustrious Men*
Vita	Josephus, *Autobiography of Flavius Josephus*
War	*The Jewish War*

Notes

Introduction

1. Leiden, 1983 (henceforth *MZCQ*), p. XVII.
2. See Eusebius, *EH* 3.5.3; Epiphanius, *Haeres.* 29.7 and 30.2 and *de Mens. et Pond.* 15.
3. *War* 1.1.
4. The problem with dating the Crucifixion is that we have only Josephus to rely on for the year of Pontius Pilate's coming to Palestine, 26 CE (*Ant.* 18.35 and 89). But a document – the *Acta Pilati* purporting to be the acts of Pilate's procuratorship, appearing around 311 CE and reported by Eusebius (*EH* 1.9.2–4), which may or may not have been a forgery – dated this to 18–19 CE. Curiously, this accords with Tacitus' date (*Annals* 2.85) for the first expulsion of the Jews from Rome, which Josephus (*Ant.* 18.83) records (together with other salacious events) in the period of Pontius Pilate.
5. The horrifying record of the complete extermination of the Alexandria Community during the 115–17 CE revolt against Trajan has been dug out of the trash heaps of Lower Egypt; *vide* V. A. Tcherikover and A. Fuks, *Corpus Papyrorum Judaicarum*, Cambridge, Mass., 1957, pp. 85–8; and Josephus reports the complete extermination of the Caesarea community (he claims, 20,000 souls) 'in one hour'; *War* 2.457–8. In 2.495–8, he records that 50,000 Alexandrian Jews were butchered.
6. *War* 2.259 and 2.264/*Ant.* 20.168.
7. *War* 2.261–3/*Ant.* 20.169–71.
8. Cf. Koran 3.45, 4.156–7, and 19.20–21 with Augustine, Sermon 191.

Chapter 1

1. Koran 2.173, 5.3 (precisely reproducing Ps. *Hom.* 7.8, including the point of 'being suffocated'), 6.146, and 16.115. The reproduction here of this key formulation from Ps. *Hom.* 7.8 lends credence to the presumption of contact on Muhammad's part with an 'Edessene'/Northern Syrian cultural framework.
2. *EH* 2.23.25.
3. Augustine's Letters 28 (394 CE), 40 (397), and Jerome's response, Letter 72 (404).

Cf. Luther's 'Preface to the Epistles of St James and St Jude', *Works* 35.394–8.
4. *EH* 3.27.1.
5. Cf. Gal. 2:10 with 'the *Ebionim*'/'the Poor' as a term of self-designation throughout the Scrolls; e. g., 1QpHab 12.3–10, CD 6.21, 14.13, 1QH 2.32–3.25, 5.15–23, 1QM 11.7–13, 13.13–14, etc.
6. Matt. 5:20, Luke 6:20, and Jas. 2:2–6.
7. See 'Wall', 'Fortress'/'Bulwark' and 'Rock' symbolism in 1QH 3.35, 5.39, 6.25–9, 9.298, 1QS 8.7–8, and *EH* 3.7.8–9.
8. For 'Enemy', see Paul in Gal. 4:16, the Parable of the Tares in Matt. 13:25–39, Ps. *Rec.* 1.70–71, and Jas. 4:4.
9. Gal. 2:9; for James' followers as 'Zealots' – Acts 21:20.
10. In Gal. 2:7–8–11, whether erroneously or otherwise, Paul also uses the name 'Peter' side-by-side with 'Cephas' in the same context. Clement of Alexandria (*c.* 150–215) and others considered them two *different* persons, one an 'Apostle' and the other a 'Disciple' – *EH* 2.12.3.
11. *EH* 2.1.4.
12. This language of 'the First' versus 'the Last', important in the Gospels, is widespread at Qumran – cf. 'the First' for 'the Ancestors' or recipients of the First Covenant in CD 1.16, 3.10, 8.31–2 and 'the Last Times'/'Last Generation' in 1QpHab 2.5–7, 7.2–12, etc.
13. Gos. Th. 12 and Ps. *Rec.* 1.43.
14. John 11:16, 20:24, and 21:2.
15. See 4Q266, Eisenman and Wise, *Dead Sea Scrolls Uncovered* (henceforth *DSSU*), Penguin, 1992, pp. 218–19, 1QS 6.12–20, and CD 13.5–16.

Chapter 2

1. E.g., Heb. 2:17–3:1, 4:14, 6:20–8:1, etc.
2. Cf. Matt. 1:1–17 and Luke 3:23–38 with 1 Chr. 3:1–24.
3. *EH* 1.7.13–17.
4. 1 Chr. 5:28–41. Curiously enough, Ezra 7:1–2 gives Ezra the same genealogy as Jesus ben Yehozedek, a genealogy Neh. 11:10 – for its part – accords to 'Jedaiah'.
5. The spelling of these two related words is

virtually indistinguishable in Second Temple texts, in which doubling of letters is not indicated and *yod* and *waw* ('*i*' and '*o*') are not distinguished. In this book, we shall use capital letters to highlight important terms or concepts and italics, not only within quotations for emphasis, but also sometimes to indicate quoted words in the text.

6. His main function would appear to be to clean up the genealogies and embody 'Zealot' Priestly notions. In the same manner, the reference in Zech. 6:11–12 to Jesus b. Yehozedek as 'the Branch' seems to overwrite a reference to Zerubbabel as 'the Branch' and probably the original 'Suffering Servant'.

7. *Ant.* 20.247.

8. *Ps. Rec.* 1.53–4.

9. S. Luzki, *Orah Zaddikim*, Vienna, 1830, pp. 19ff.

10. *Ant.* 20.199 (relating to Ananus' condemnation of James).

11. For Rabbinic texts, see ARN 5.2. For Karaites, see 'al-Qirqisani's Account of the Jewish Sects of Christianity' in HUCA, v. 7, 1930, pp. 326 and 364–5.

12. Cf. *Ant.* 18.4–23 with *War* 2.118.

13. CD 8.37, 1QpHab 2.6–21, 8.11, 4QPs 37 2.17, and 4.10.

14. Cf. Matt. 22:17–21/Mark 12:14–17/Luke 20:22–5, for the portrait of Jesus – now proverbial (recapitulating Paul in Rom. 13:6–9, using James' 'Royal Law according to the Scripture' ('love your neighbour as yourself') in support of paying the tax) – recommending paying the Roman tribute.

15. 1 Macc. 2:1–70. Mattathias (in the manner of Ezra above, another possible 'Zealot' Priestly gloss) is mysteriously omitted from 2 Macc. 3:1–4:1's account in favour of 'Simeon the Zaddik's son, Onias (also probably 'the Righteous').

16. 1 Macc. 8:1–31, 12:7, and 14:16–24, possibly reflecting their mutual warlikeness – more likely, though, that the 'Philistines', who settled the Palestinian coast, were Mycenaean Greeks *related to the Spartans* or that Mount Ida in Crete had something to do with its Hebrew phoneme 'Yehud' or 'Jew'.

17. F. M. Cross, *The Ancient Library of Qumran*, New York, 1961, pp. 135–40; F. F. Bruce, *Second Thoughts on the Dead Sea Scrolls*, Exeter, 1956, p. 100; and G. Vermes, *The Dead Sea Scrolls in English*, London, 1962, pp. 62ff. This idea was first circulated in support of 'the Essene Hypothesis'. It is gainsaid by Ezra 2:59–63, admitting some Priests returning from Babylon could not prove their genealogies and were *converts* and 1 Macc. 2:1, claiming affiliation with the first and principal High Priestly Course of Jehoiarib (cf. 1 Chr. 24:6).

18. *Vita* 1.2–6.

19. Though in 1 Macc. 1:1, 'the *Kittim*' – clearly invading foreign armies from the West – appear to be from Macedonia; in 1QpHab 2.12–4.12 and 6.1–12, they have all characteristics of Romans: in particular, 'parcelling out their yoke and taxes' (this in interpretation of 'burning incense to his fishing net' and 'his eating being plenteous' from Hab. 1:16) and the *Imperial* Roman practice of 'sacrificing to their standards and worshipping their weapons of war' (when the deified Emperor's bust was on the standards – this in interpretation of '*taking with a fishhook, catching them in a net*, and *collecting them*' from Hab. 1:15).

20. *Ant.* 18.261–2/*War* 2.185–7 and Philo, *Mission to Gaius*, 186 and 207–8.

21. *War* 5.541–7.

22. *War* 6.310–15.

23. *War* 3.399–407. Cf. Suetonius, *The Twelve Caesars*, 10.4; Tacitus, *The Histories*, 2.78ff. and 5.13.

24. ARN 4.5, *b. Git.* 56a–b, *Lam. R.* 1.5.31 and *b. Yoma* 39b.

25. Cf. *Vita* 13–16 with *War* 3.346–9.

26. *Ant.* 20:189–90.

27. *Ant.* 20.197. The two had cemented their relationship in Rome following 'appeals to Caesar' in the wake of Messianic disturbances between Galileans, Samaritans, and Jews and the beating of 'the Emperor's Servant Stephen' in the late 40s and early 50s (*Ant.* 20.105–36). The 'conspiracy' is reflected in 1QpHab 12.6 on how 'the Wicked Priest conspired to destroy the Poor' (cf. too 1QH 4.10–13, etc.).

28. *War* 1.1–2. Italics in quotations are my own.

29. 1QpHab 6.2–12.

30. *War* 1.10–11.

31. Cf. *War* 1.12 with *EH* 2.6.3–8 (quoting Josephus and apparently, the lost Second Book of Philo's *Mission to Gaius*) and 3.5.6–7.

32. *War* 6.250–80 (also 1:10 above).

33. Cf. Matt. 26:68/Mark 14:58 with the 'Community as Temple' and its members, 'the members of Christ's body' in 1 Cor. 3:9–17, 6:14–17, 12:12–31, Rom. 12:4–5, etc.

Chapter 3

1. See, for instance, the picture of these 'camps' in 1QM 7.3–7, 12.6–7, 19.1, CD 12.22–14.8, and '*MMT*', Lines 2.66–70 in *DSSU*, p. 195.

2. 9.21; cf. Josephus in *War* 2.254–60 and *Ant.* 20.185–8. It should be appreciated that for Origen (185–254 CE) in *Contra Celsus* 2.13 (the same chapter in which he protests against Josephus' testimony that Jerusalem fell because of the death of James), 'the *Sicarii*' are those forcibly circumcising others in

violation of the Roman '*Lex Cornelia de Sicarius*' – though, if Jerome (Letter 84 to Pammachius and Oceanus) is correct, even Origen ('out of zeal for God, but not according to Knowledge' (*thus*) – Rom. 10:2) seems to have 'castrated himself with a knife'. Later we shall suggest '*Sicarios*' (cf. '*Iscariot*') as a quasi-anagram or pejorative homophone for 'Christian'.

3. *Haeres.* 19, 29.1.1–7.1, and 30.3.2. For him (20.3.2–4), the Ossaeans 'are no longer either Jews or Christians', but have become 'Ebionites' or 'Sampsaeans' (i.e., 'Sabaeans').

4. *On the Contemplative Life* 2.

5. See, for instance, *Ket.* 30b, where a man sentenced to stoning 'falls down from the roof' or *M. San.* 9.6 on 'the *Kanna'im*' killing a priest serving at the altar in a state of ritual uncleanness by splitting open his head with clubs and compare with *EH* 2.23.16–18 or 2 Apoc. Jas. 61–2.

6. The Hebrew verb '*kanna*'' has the root meaning of 'zeal'. Cf. Luke 6:15 with Matt. 10:4/Mark 3:18, but see also John 2:1–11 and 4:46 on '*Cana of Galilee*', the home village of 'Nathanael', whom elsewhere we shall show as essentially John's overwrite of James.

7. Hippolytus, 5.1–3 and 10.5. Like the Gospels, Epiphanius conserves both 'Nazarean' ('Nazrene') and 'Nazoraean', not to mention 'Nazirite' ('Naziraean'); 19.5.1–4 and 29.5.4–7. For Jerome, *Vir. ill.* 3, 'Nazarean' and 'Nazirite' are indistinguishable.

8. See 1QpHab 12.4–5; for 'the Simple Ones of Ephraim', see 4 QpNah 2.6 and 4.5. For 'the Way', see CD 1.11, 8.41, 1QS 4.22, 8.14–21 (in interpretation of Isa. 40:3), 9.2–8, etc.

9. Acts 9:2, 16:17 ('of Salvation'), 18:25–6 ('of the Lord'), 19:9, 19:23, 22:4, 24:14 (called 'a heresy'), and 24:22.

10. Cf. Phil. 2:25 and 4:18–22 with *Ant.* 1.8, *Vita* 430, and *Apion* 1.1, 2.1, and 2.296. Some would dispute this, but how many 'Epaphroditus's, 'involved in important events' and Nero's death or assassination, could there have been at this time?

11. Cf. *Ant.* 18.16–17/*War* 2.165 with Acts 23:8, Matt. 22:23–33, and pars.

12. See Cross, loc. cit., pp. 135–40, etc.

13. Cf. 1QpHab 2.6, CD 1.20–21, 4QD266 12–18 above, for instance, with Jas. 2:9–11.

14. CD 5.7–11, 7.1, and 8.5–7.

15. See Jas. 2:11 above and Acts 15:20, 15:29, and 21:25.

16. Josephus, *Ant.* 12.387, claims this Priest (Alcimus) was not of the high-priestly lineage, but he may be mistaken here.

17. 4QpNah 2.2–3 and *War* 1.92–4.

18. *War* 1.93–8/*Ant.* 13.372–83 and 2 Macc. 5:27.

19. 4QpNah 2.7–8. See also the reference to 'the Joiners (*Nilvim*) in the war of' in 4Q448,

'Paean to King Jonathan', *DSSU*, pp. 273–80.

20. *War* 1.127–32. As retold in *Ant.* 14.22–4, these events involve a 'rain-making' forerunner of James, whom Josephus calls 'Onias the Righteous', but known in Talmudic tradition as 'Honi the Circle-Drawer' (*b. Ta'an.* 19a and 23a–b).

21. *War* 1.148–51/*Ant.* 14.58–71.

22. *Ant.* 14.172–6 and 15.370.

23. *Ant.* 14.176 and 15.3–4.

24. John 19:19. Recently an inscription was found at Masada, 'Herod, King of Judea', even more accurate – for the Romans, in any event, one of 'the Kings of the Peoples' ('*Amim/Gentium*; cf. CD 8.10 and A. N. Sherwin-White, *The Roman Citizenship*, Oxford, 1939, pp. 272–5.

25. *Ant.* 15.368.

26. *Ant.* 18.10.

27. *War* 2.117–18/*Ant.* 18.23–5.

28. Matt. 22:15–22/Mark 12:13–17, etc. Again note Paul's position on 'paying taxes' in Rom. 13:6–10, followed, as in Matt. 22:39/Mark 12:33, by evocation of the Commandment 'to love your neighbour'. A more anti-'Zealot' position is unimaginable.

29. *War* 2.56/*Ant.* 17.271.

30. *Ant.* 18.6–10. One should compare this with Jesus' 'woes' against the 'Scribes and Pharisees' and 'the Little Apocalypse' (Matt. 23:1–24:31 and pars.). Josephus has detached a piece from his description of the steadfastness 'the Essenes' display in undergoing torture and their unwillingness to blaspheme the Law-Giver in *War* 2.151–3, and attached it to his description of Judas and *Saddok*'s 'Philosophy' in the *Antiquities*. Hippolytus (9.21) rather incorporates this imperviousness to torture and death into his description of both 'Zealot' and '*Sicarii* Essenes', but now rather apropos of their unwillingness to eat the '*things sacrificed to idols*' of James' directives to overseas communities in Acts – evoked (along with 'bathing') – as the essence of Peter's practice too in Ps. *Hom.* 7.8.

31. *War* 6.312–14.

32. *War* 2.425–9.

33. Cf. Jas. 5:1–7 with 1QpHab 12.3–10, 4QPs 37 2.9–3.10 ('the Church of the Poor'), and the new 'Hymns of the Poor' (4Q434–6) in *DSSU*, pp. 233–41 – but also the condemnation of 'polluted Evil Riches' in CD 4.17, 6.15–16, and 8.5–6.

34. *War* 1.10 and 2.418–19. This plural allusion to High Priestly clans is paralleled in 1 QpHab 9.4–5 by 'the Last Priests of Jerusalem' (i.e., 'the High Priests'), completely characteristic of the Herodian Establishment, not the Maccabean one previously, where there was only *one* life-long High Priest, is an excellent example of an 'internal' dating parameter. It is reinforced by the presence of 'the Star Prophecy', the first-century provenance of

which is attested to by Josephus (not to mention Matt. 2:2) and in 1QM 11.6–17, CD 7.18–8.3, and 4QTest 12–14.

35. *War* 2.450–56. Not only does this episode remind one of Hippolytus' '*Sicarii* Essenes', who threaten to slay any Gentile 'speaking about God and His Laws' who 'refuses to undergo circumcision' in 9.21; but also Origen's definition of '*Sicarii*', against whom the Roman '*Lex Cornelia de Sicarius*' seems to have been directed after Hadrian's suppression of the Bar Kochba Revolt if not before (nor in this regard should one forget the 'some from James' or 'the party of the circumcision', Paul so scathingly attacks in Gal. 2:12).

36. 1 Macc. 1:54, 2 Macc. 6:2, Dan. 11:31, and 12:11. Cf. Matt. 24:15 and Mark 13:14.

37. 1QS 1.15. and 4QD266 17–18 above.

38. *War* 1.535–7/*Ant.* 16.121–7 and 356.

39. Rom. 11:16–24. Note the language of 'casting out', 'net', 'stumbling block', 'Riches', and 'Salvation' by 'Grace no longer works' preceding this in 11:1–12.

40. *War* 1.437/*Ant.* 14.50–56.

41. See *Ant.* 20.247 above.

42. *Ant.* 20.6–16.

Chapter 4

1. *Ant.* 20.97–8. Acts 12:2 refers only to 'Herod the King', but in the New Testament all Herodians were known as 'Herod'. Herod of Chalcis is important because he was married to his *niece* Bernice and his son, Aristobulus, was married to the Salome, who according to legend danced for John the Baptist's head.

2. See Paul's defensiveness over this charge, Gal. 1:20, 2 Cor. 11:31, Rom. 9:1, etc. *Per contra*, see Jas. 3:5–14 attacking 'the Tongue'. For Ps. *Rec.* 1.70–71 Paul is the 'Enemy' alluded to in Gal. 4:16 and Jas. 4:4.

3. Gal. 2:2–9, 1 Cor. 8:1–13, 2 Cor. 3:1–9, 5:12, 10:12–16, 11:5–22, and 12:11.

4. Gos. Th. 12.

5. See, for instance, *Zohar* 1.59b on Noah and *b. San.* 97b on the 'thirty-six Righteous Ones' 'waiting for' the Messianic Era (preceding evocation of the *Shiloh* Prophecy [Gen. 49:10–11] in 98b). Importantly, this last is based on the same allusions to 'wait for *it*', from Hab. 2:3 preceding Hab. 2:4, expounded in terms of '*the Delay of the Parousia*' in 1QpHab 7.5–14.

6. Father Jose O'Callaghan's thesis ('New Testament Papyri in Qumran Cave 7?' in *Supplement to Journal of Biblical Literature*, 1972, pp. 1–14), has recently again been taken up in Germany. The attempt by M. D'Ancona and C. Thiede, *Eyewitness to Jesus*, London, 1995, to redate Matthew on the basis of the Oxford Magdalen Papyrus to

40 CE is based on the same superficial use of palaeographic data – ignoring the internal data – one encounters in Dead Sea Scroll studies.

7. Again reversing the 'Enemy' terminology of Ps. *Rec.* 1.70–71, Jas. 4:4 above. In turn, it also inverts the prototypical 'Friend of God' applied to Abraham in Jas. 2:23, CD 3.2–4, and Koran 4.126.

8. *EH* 2.6.3–8 and 3.5.1–3.7.7.

9. *War* 7.121–62. The Romans seem to have discovered the hiding places of the Temple Treasure by torturing one 'Phineas' (*War* 6.390–91, i.e., probably the same 'Phannius' mentioned in *War* 4.155).

10. Probably 'Lucius the Cyrenian' of Acts 13.1.

11. Ps. *Hom.* 2.51, 3.50, and 18.20; also Origen, *Comm. on John* 19.7.2.

12. The exception are the parables in Matt. 13:24–53 growing out of 'the Parable of the Tares', clearly Jewish Christian. One particularly good example of a pro-Pauline, anti-Jewish, parable is Matt. 22:1–14 (partially paralleled in Luke 14:7–24). Here a King (the Roman Emperor) makes a marriage feast, but the invitees (the Jews) refuse to come, *killing his servants* instead. He then 'sends his armies and destroyed these murderers and burned their city' (Jerusalem) and invites total strangers 'along the way' instead (in Luke 14:13 and 21, these are typically 'the Poor, the maimed, the blind, and the lame'). The meaning here is rarely very hard to grasp. Plus it is written *after the fall of the Temple* and layered with the anti-Pauline Parable of the Tares and philo-Jewish 'Sermon on the Mount' in the same Gospel.

13. Matt. 19:30 and 20:16/Mark 10:31/Luke 13:30.

14. Matt. 13:57/Mark 6:4/Luke 4:24.

15. Matt. 12:46–50/Mark 3:31–5/Luke 8:19–21.

16. Matt. 11:21/Luke 10:13.

17. See Paul in Gal. 1:15 identifying Gentiles as 'Sinners'.

18. Matt. 18:12–14/Luke 15:3–7. For Luke, the one lost sheep (or 'one Sinner repenting') is worth '*ninety-nine Righteous Ones in the wilderness*'.

19. In Hebrew 'Jesus', quite literally, means 'Saviour', a point Eusebius makes much of in *EH* 1.3.1–5.

20. Clement of Alexandria, *Strom.* 7.17.

21. *Ant.* 18.116–19. In the Gospels John's death occurs *before* Jesus' – whenever this was.

22. 20.100–104; cf. Acts 4:6, *War* 2.220, and 5.45–46.

23. *Vita* 48, 343, and 355. Though he is critical here, Josephus is usually obsequious and refers positively to Agrippa II. For Bernice's 'Riches' and the perception of her 'incest' with him, see *Ant.* 20.145–6 and *Vita* 119.

24. See Josephus' account of the conversion of

Queen Helen and her sons, *Ant.* 20.17–101.
Her kinsmen, Monobazus and Kenedaeos,
are among bravest Jewish revolutionary
commanders; *War* 2.520.

25. See Loeb *Josephus*, III., pp. 635–60 and
R. Eisler, *The Messiah Jesus and John the
Baptist*, London, 1931, for numerous passages
from this work.

26. *War* 6.288–315.

27. The 'Christ' ideology was an overseas, more
Hellenistic one. For Acts 11:26, Christians
were first called 'Christians' in Antioch – the
question will be, which 'Antioch'? But see
Hippolytus, 9.25, on 'the Christ' as 'a
war-like and powerful individual', who after
having 'gathered together the entire people of
the Jews', 'done battle with all Nations' (cf.
1QM at Qumran), and 'restored Jerusalem',
would fall by the edge of the sword' (cf. the
recent controversy over 4Q285, 'The
Messianic Leader' fragment, *DSSU*, pp. 24–9).
'Next would come the end and conflagration
of the universe', when 'each would be *rewarded according to his works*' – exactly the
scheme of Islam (Koran 74 and 82) to the present day, as well as James in *EH* 2.23.9 and
Jas. 4:11–5:10.

28. *Ant.* 18.63–4.

29. *Ant.* 18.81–4.

30. Tacitus, *Annals* 2.85 and *EH* 1.9.3–4 above.
Interesting too, this is the same year as the
suspicious death in Syria of Germanicus,
whom Augustus had forced Tiberius to adopt
as his successor. See also Suetonius 3.36 and
Dio Cassius 57.18.5.

31. The *Egesippus*, for instance, the Latin version
of Josephus' *War* (named after Eusebius' lost
source Hegesippus, which also interpolates
the 'Mundis and Paulina' episode from the
Antiquities), puts the crucifixion of Jesus
around 35–6 CE, the year before Pontius Pilate
was removed.

32. 5.26, picked up and co-ordinated in Acts 18:2
with Priscilla's and Aquilla's banishment from
Rome. For the *Talmud*, *A.Z.* 10b and *Git.*
56b above, 'Aquila' or 'Onkelos' is the son
of Kalonymus or Kolonikos (Clement?)
and *Titus' sister* and, therefore, like Flavius
Clemens below (and 'Clement' in the Pseudoclementines), *a relative of the Emperor*.

33. Tacitus, who had been Governor in Asia
Minor, uses this kind of language to describe
both Jews and Christians in *Annals* 2.85 and
15.44, as does his contemporary Pliny in
Letter 97 to Trajan. H. Idris Bell, *Jews and
Christians in Egypt*, London, 1934, pp. 25–7,
gives the text of the famous letter from
Claudius to the Jews of Egypt warning them
not to receive itinerant 'disease' carriers like
the Apostles and Acts 17:6–7 describes Paul in
exactly the same way, as does 24:5, calling
him 'a leader of the *Nazoraean Heresy*'.

34. *War* 2.258–9 and 264–5.

35. *Historia Sacra* 2.30–31.

36. 65.6.3.

Chapter 5

1. See Phil. 4:3, *EH* 3.4.8, and 3.15–16. Ps.
Rec. 7.8 identifies him as a close relative of
'Caesar'. Flavius Clemens and Domitilla, too,
were close relatives of Domitian (as their
names imply). The former was executed as
secret Christian in 95–6 CE (she appears only
to have been exiled – *EH* 3.18.4), also the
time individuals like Clement, Epaphroditus,
and Josephus disappear from the scene.

2. *EH* 2.15–16 and 3.39.14–16, quoting Papias.
Cf. 1 Pet. 5:13 and Col. 4:10.

3. The work was first published in the West, on
the basis of a now-lost Greek exemplar by
Rufinus of Aquileia (*c.* 350–410), originally a
close friend of Jerome. Later the two fell out
ostensibly over Origen, but possibly also this
work; cf. Jerome's *Preface to Ezekiel*, where
he celebrates that 'the scorpion lies beneath
the ground' and 'the many-headed hydra has
at last ceased to hiss at us'.

4. See Tertullian, *Apologeticus* 5 and 21 and
apocryphal Acts of Pilate; *per contra*, see
Philo, *Mission to Gaius* 302–3.

5. *Dial.* 23, 47, and 93.

6. Justin (100–165), for instance, knows a document he calls *The Memoirs of the Apostles*,
which reads, 'You are my son. On this day
have I begotten you,' instead of Matt. 3:17
and pars; *Dial.* 88 and 103.

7. See fragments in ANCL and *EH* 2.15.2 and
3.39.

8. Matt. 13:55/Mark 6:3.

9 *EH* quoting Justin Martyr, *Apology* 1.26,
who came from Samaria, and Ps. *Rec.* 2.7
and *Hom.* 6.7.

10. *Ant.* 19.332–4.

11. See, for instance, S. A. Birnbaum, *The Hebrew
Scripts*, Leiden, 1971, pp. 26–43 and 130–43;
F. M. Cross, 'The Development of Jewish
Scripts' in *The Bible and the Ancient Near
East*, ed. G. E. Wright, 1961, pp. 133–5 and
160–97; J. T. Milik, *Ten Years of Discovery
in the Wilderness of Judaea*, London, 1959,
pp. 57–8; and my detailed analyses in *MZCQ*,
pp. 28–31 and 78–89.

12. 4Q394–99, which Prof. Wise and I called
'Two Letters on Works Reckoned as
Righteousness' in *DSSU*, pp. 182–200.

13. See, for instance, Birnbaum, pp. 68–70 and
117–31.

14. 1QS 9.13–16 and 9.17–25.

15. 1QS 4.2–5.23 and 8.1–9.6.

16. G. Margoliouth, 'The Sadducean Christians
of Damascus', *The Expositor*, vols. 37–8,
London, 1911–12, pp. 499–517 and 213–35
and R. H. Charles, *Apocrypha and*

Pseudepigrapha of the Old Testament, II,
Oxford, 1913, pp. 794–7.

17. This was made by myself and Prof. Philip
Davies of Sheffield University, in a letter dated
16 March 1989 to J. Strugnell, then Head of
the International Team. It was followed up
by a second letter from me to him on 15 June
1989, responding to his to us of 15 May, and
two letters to Amir Drori, Head of the Israel
Antiquities Authority, of 2 May and 13 July.

18. For instance, the allusion to 'the Kings of the
Peoples' to describe the Ruling Elite (8.10),
their 'Riches' and 'niece marriage' (4.17–5.15
and 6.15–7.2), the application of the 'venom
of vipers' to the 'wine of their ways' (8.10–11),
the charge of 'polluting the Temple Treasury'
(6.15–16), the evocation of the 'Star Prophecy'
(7.18–21), etc.

19. These proposals were first set forth in the
letter of 2 May to the Head of the Antiquities
Authority above, in which the details of AMS
Carbon Testing were carefully explained and,
in lieu of achieving direct access, its application proposed. The Israeli Antiquities
Authority announced its decision to conduct
such tests (albeit in a selected manner) in
September 1989, four months after our initial
proposal, however the caveat we suggested,
that 'opposition scholars', who had originally
felt the need for them, be included in all
stages of the process was ignored. Instead,
'Consensus scholars' like John Strugnell, who
for thirty years had never felt the need to
conduct such tests, were included.

20. See the two reports, published in *Atiqot*,
the first in July 1991, pp. 27–32, G. Bonani,
M. Broshi, I Carmi, S. Ivy, J. Strugnell, and
W. Wolfi, 'Radiocarbon Dating of the Dead
Sea Scrolls' (also *Radiocarbon* 34, 1992,
pp. 843–9) and A. J. T. Jull, D. J. Donohue,
M. Broshi, and E. Tov, 'Radiocarbon Dating
of Scrolls and Linen Fragments from the
Judean Desert', in 1995, and evaluation of
these in *BAR*, July/August, 1995, p. 61. In
the first set of these, the Testament of Kohath
(*DSSU*, pp. 145–51), a Maccabean or
Herodian Era Document on internal grounds,
produced a date of 388–353 BC and dated
documents from the Wadi Murabba'at and
elsewhere either barely fell within or fell outside of dating parameters.

The second set of tests was totally skewed.
A sample of the Community Rule, a document
with precise parallels to known materials
about John the Baptist and which, on internal
grounds, clearly dates from the first century
CE, produced a date of *134–230 CE*, while a
second sample was dated to *346–317 BC*.
One papyrus contract, with an actual date of
135 CE, produced a date of *231–332 CE*, while
a document from the Nahal Hever, dated
128 CE, produced one of 86–314 CE. The

Habakkuk *Pesher*, also clearly a Roman Era
document – the first-century palaeographic
date of which has never really been contested –
on one run was give a date of *154–143* BC and
another 120–5 BC. But both it and the
Community Rule are documents that on the
basis of internal indicators were all written at
more or less the same time.

21. Resolution of the California State University,
Long Beach, *Conference on Scrolls, Caves,
and Hidden Manuscripts*, April 1990 (*BAR*,
September/October 1990, pp. 4–6).

22. See Malcolm W. Browne, 'Errors Feared in
Carbon Dating: Alternative Methods being
Used', *New York Times*, 4 June 1990. The
matter of pollutants (constantly referred to
in all reports) for documents such as the
Habakkuk *Pesher* – so often handled, treated,
and cleansed – is crucial.

23. See 'Radio Carbon Dating of the Dead Sea
Scrolls', p. 29 and diagrams, pp. 30–31.
Similar diagrams are provided in 'Radiocarbon
Dating of Scrolls', including comments like,
'with one exception, the dates of the documents determined by the C-14 tests are in
good agreement with the dates previously
suggested on the basis of palaeographical
analysis'. To be sure, when dating expectations such as these *did not calibrate*, additional
tests were done.

24. See 1QpHab 5.12–6.11 – where, in exposition
of Hab 1:14–16 on 'fish-hooks', 'catching in a
net'/'collecting them in a fisherman's net', and
'his eating being plenteous', the *Kittim* (i.e.,
the Romans) are also described as 'parcelling
out their yoke and their taxes, eating all the
Peoples' ('*Gentes*') – and 9.3–7, where the
'Riches with the booty' of 'the Last Priests of
Jerusalem' are described as 'being delivered up
to the hand of the Army of the *Kittim*'. But in
two places in *War* 1.153 and 354–7/*Ant.*
14.72 and 483–6, Josephus tells us that
Pompey in 63 BC and Herod in 37 BC both
specifically refrained from taking any booty.
In the Habakkuk *Pesher*, too, 'Lebanon'
imagery, usually applied in Rabbinic literature
to the 70 CE fall of the Temple, and the usage
'*abeit-Galuto*', describing the Wicked Priest's
discomfiture of the Righteous Teacher, will
be shown in Volume II to have a distinct first-
century ambience – as will the description of
'the *Kittim*' as 'sacrificing to their standards
and worshipping their weapons of war'.

Internal data of this kind makes a mockery
of external parameters like AMS C-14 data.
Since the same usages, vocabulary, and
dramatis personae move from Damascus
Document to Community Rule to Habakkuk
Pesher to Hymns, the idea that these documents could emanate from differing centuries –
according to recent C-14 tests, sometimes
three and four centuries apart – further

undercuts the reliability and credibility of this data. At the same time, one certainly would not want to use such results to rule out an otherwise convincing exposition that can make clear sense of the internal data.

25. See the multiple references to 'the Time of the End' or 'the Last Days'/'Last Era' in 1QpHab 2.7 and in the interpretation of Hab. 2:3–2:4 in 1QpHab 7.2–14. This is particularly true of the references to 'parcelling out their yoke and their taxes' and 'sacrificing to their standards' in 6.4–7 on Hab. 1:15–16 above.

26. These include Isa. 2–5, 10–11, 26–33, Hab. 1:4–2:4, Ps. 37:12–39, etc.

27. Ps. Rec. 1.71–2.

28. CD 9.17–22, 13.15–17, 14.8–12, 15.7–14, and 4QD266 1–16 above. Also 1QS 6.12–20.

29. See R. de Vaux, Archaeology and the Dead Sea Scrolls, Oxford, 1973, pp. 18–23, 33–45, and 64–71 and MZCQ, pp. 32–4, 55–6, and 91–4.

30. Cf. MZCQ, pp. 32–4 and 91–4 with note in Archaeology, May/June 1996, p. 21 and BAR, May/June 1996, p. 14.

31. See de Vaux, pp. 60–90 and P. Bar-Adon, 'Another Settlement of the Judean Desert', BASOR 227, 1977, pp. 1–25.

32. 1QpHab 9.3 above. For F. M. Cross, The Ancient Library of Qumran and Modern Biblical Studies, New York, 1961, p. 126, this is simply characterized – without explanation – as a reference to 'Pompey's conquest of Jerusalem'.

Chapter 6

1. Acts 6:2, Matt. 26:14–47 (and pars.) at 'Last Supper', and John 6:67 and 20:24. N.b. how in the Synoptics, it is 'Judas Iscariot' who is called 'one of the Twelve', whereas in John, it is 'Thomas' (i.e., 'Judas Thomas').

2. Eusebius does, reliable or otherwise; EH 2.25.5–8 and 3.1.2. The last contains an allusion to Peter being crucified 'upside down', first mentioned by Origen. Tertullian, who also refers to it, in De Praescrip. Haer. 36, was the first to claim Paul was beheaded in Rome under Nero, though Clement – immortalized in the Pseudoclementines – alludes to both martyrdoms in Ad. Cor. 1.5.

3. Clement in Ad. Cor. 1.5 speaks of Paul as having 'taught Righteousness to the whole world and come to the extreme limit of the West'. For my arguments concerning a possible return by Paul to Palestine between 62 and 66 CE, see 'Paul as Herodian' in The Dead Sea Scrolls and the First Christians (Element, 1996), pp. 241–5 (a paper, first presented to the Society of Biblical Literature in 1984).

4. Acts ends with Paul coming to Rome under Festus (60–62 CE) and 'preaching with all freedom' for 'two whole years in his own rented

house' (28:30–31). For Josephus, the death of James occurs directly following Festus' death (Ant. 20.197–203), so in both instances we are in 62 CE – a strange coincidence.

5. Two other 'Justus'es appear in Acts 18:7 and Col. 4:11 (called 'of the circumcision').

6. There are other possible glosses of this kind in Scripture, e.g. Ezra above. There are others in the Old Testament, such as Seth, a stand-in for Cain (Gen. 4:25–5:8). We shall meet many more in the New Testament.

7. This same 'Agabus' appears in Acts 11:27–8, as a 'prophet', who again 'came down from Jerusalem to Antioch' to predict the Famine which in Claudius' time 'was going to cover the whole habitable earth'. The Armenian Chronicler Moses of Chorene, 2.26, already notes the difficulty Greco-Syrians have pronouncing names of this kind and 'Abgar' comes into Latin as 'Agbar', 'Acbar', and even 'Albarus'. Eusebius calls him, 'Abgar the Great King of the Peoples beyond the Euphrates' or 'Abgar Uchama' (EH 1.13.2–6).

8. See the confusions even in John 6:71, 12:4, 13:3, and 13:26 with 'Simon Iscariot' (presumably 'Simon Zēlōtēs' in Luke 6:15 and Acts 1:13), but see John 14:22's 'the Iscariot'. i.e., probably 'the Sicarios'.

9. Cf. CD 5.6–7 (on 'the Three Nets of Belial'), 6.14–17, 7.3–4, 8.16, 9.14–23, 12.19–20, 1QS 5.1–10, 8.11–13 (in exposition of Isa. 40:3: 'make a Straight Way in the wilderness'), and 9.5–20 (likewise). This language, which has to do with 'separating pure from unclean, Holy from profane' (cf. Paul in 2 Cor. 6:17–7:1), has as its synonym that of 'lehinnazer' (CD 6.15), 'lehazzir' (7.1), and 'nazru' (8.8) – the 'Nazirite' language of 'keeping away'/'abstain from' – also the basis in Greek of James' directives to overseas communities in Acts 15:20–29 and 21:25 above.

10. Acts 13:1.

11. We shall discuss the relationship of this Antioch with Edessa, called 'Antioch Orrhoe' later.

12. The same for 'John his brother' (Matt. 4:21, etc.), Jesus 'the carpenter, the son of Mary' (Mark 6:3) or Jesus 'the carpenter's son' (Matt. 13:55), 'Judas the son (or 'brother') of Simon Iscariot', 'Zebedee', 'Agabus', 'Queen Kandakes', 'Dorcas', 'Zacchaeus', 'Arimathaea', and the like.

13. Cf. Heb. 3:1, 4:14–15, 5:5–6, 6:20–7:27, etc., with 'the Messiah from Aaron and Israel' in CD 1.7, 8.24, 12.23, 13.1, 14.19, 1QS 2.14, and 9.11.

14. 28 BC. Mariamme's sons were executed in 7–6 BC, two years before Herod's own death in 4 BC; Ant. 15.247–52/War 1.550–51. Clearly, much would have been different in Jewish history had they survived.

15. Paul actually calls himself the 'Apostle to the

Gentiles' (*Ethnōn*) in 11:13, a term
Muhammad later refined, and uses the phraseology, 'Greeks and Jews', again in 1 Cor. 1:24
and Gal. 3:28.

16. See, for instance, CD 1.7, 1QH 6.15–8.10,
    and 4Q 285 2–3 in *DSSU*, pp. 24–9 above.

17. Cf. Gal. 4:22–31. If Paul were, indeed, a
    Herodian, the wounded pride implicit in
    his allusion to 'Hagar' here would perhaps
    explain his reversal of the Jews' true genealogy.
    Note, as well, in introducing this in Rom. 9:3,
    Paul – again averring he 'does not lie' and his
    'great grief and pain' – alludes to making
    himself 'a curse from the Christ' meaning, it
    appears (as in Gal. 3:10–13) 'cursed' accord-
    ing to the Law.

18. For Islam, Abraham's sacrifice is that of
    Ishmael not Isaac, though this is nowhere
    specifically stated in Koran 37:101–14 – in
    fact, the specific mention of Isaac in 37:114
    rather makes it look as if the sacrifice he is
    referring to here is that of Isaac as well. This
    sacrifice of the 'only begotten Isaac' (Gen.
    22:2 and Heb. 11:17) is the key example Jas.
    2:21 uses against the 'Empty Man' in support
    of how and why 'Abraham was justified by
    works' and, therefore, the 'Friend of God'.
    Not only does Heb. 11:17 use it to support
    the Pauline counter-position – 'by Faith
    Abraham offered up' Isaac – but, as if in
    riposte to James too (2:25), Heb. 11:31 also
    says the same of 'Rahab the harlot'''s Faith.

19. *War* 2.218–19/*Ant.* 19.321–20.14.

20. The story of Agrippa I's intimacy with
    Caligula and Claudius is told in *War*
    2.179–218/*Ant.* 18.142–239, and reiterated in
    Roman sources.

21. Cf. Matt. 9:10–13, 11:19, 21:31–32, and pars.

22. *Ant.* 20.145. For the ban on 'niece' marriage
    and marriage with close family cousins, see
    CD 4:17–5.11, 7.1–2 (expressed in terms of
    '*lehazzir*'/'abstain' or 'keep away from'
    above), 8.6–7, and 11QT 66.11–17. For the
    tenth-century Karaite author al-Kirkisani too,
    'Zadok broke with Boethus' over the issue of
    'marriage with a niece', which, according to
    him, *Jesus taught as well*. 'He also forbade
    divorce just as the *Sadducees* did'; HUCA,
    pp. 363–5. But the 'Herodian Sadducees' *did
    not* forbid divorce; *Qumran Sadducees* did.

23. Suetonius 5.26, 39–45, and 6.28–34.

24. Deut. 25:5, the point 'the Sadducees' are pic-
    tured as making about 'the Seven Brothers'
    and the Resurrection in Matt. 22:23–33 and
    pars.

25. *War* 1.557–62/*Ant.* 18.109 and 136–7.

26. Cf. *Ant.* 18.136 and 20.143 with CD 5.1–2,
    11QT 57.17–18, and 66.11. The rest, no
    doubt, is probably only charming fiction. In
    this regard, one should note that Matt. 14:4
    attributes to John only the words: 'It is not
    lawful for you to have her' – nothing more.

Mark 6:18 adds 'your brother's wife'. Luke
3:18–20 doesn't identify either Herodias or
Salome – though he has 'Herod the Tetrarch'
right, but declines to name his 'brother'. John
omits the episode altogether.

27. 11QT 56.12–57.18 (cf. Deut. 17:15–17).

28. Deut. 21:23.

29. 4QpNah 2.8. *Per contra*, however, see *b. San.*
    45b–46b.

30. *War* 1.185 and 357/*Ant.* 14.125, 140, and
    20.245 (also see *War* 1.154, for Pompey earli-
    er in 63 BC after storming the Temple).

31. *Ant.* 20.101–2. We shall discuss this 'Famine'
    with regard to Paul's and Helen of Adiabene's
    parallel Famine-relief activities later.

32. *War* 1.657–60, directly following the Temple
    Eagle episode, which triggered the Uprising
    led by the two 'sophists' (rabbis), Judas
    Sepphoraeus and Matthias, which Herod
    survived to go bathing at Callirhoe near
    Machaeros. Wisely, Achelaus his successor
    does not carry out this command.

33. *War* 2.119–66/*Ant.* 18.11–25.

34. Cf. *Vita* 8–11 with Luke 2:43–52.

35. *Ant.* 18.10.

36. *Ant.* 20.97–9. 'The Many' (*Rabbim*), wide-
    spread in the Scrolls (CD, 1QS, 1QH, etc.).
    As even Cross realizes, p. 231, it is also
    widespread in the New Testament (see the
    examples he cites of Acts 6:2–5 (the Jerusalem
    Church), and 15:12 ('the Jerusalem Council'),
    and 15:30 (the Assembly at 'Antioch')).
    More than likely it is based on salvationary
    scheme of Isa. 53:11–12, 'My Servant, the
    Righteous One, will justify' or 'bear the sins
    of the Many' – a foundation piece of early
    Christian theology, as even Paul attests
    (1 Cor. 15:3).

37. Cf. *EH* 3.1–4 above. Also, '*Yesha*'/'*Yeshu'a*'
    (Salvation) is widespread in the Scrolls. Cf.
    4Q 416–18, 'The Children of Salvation',
    DSSU, pp. 241–9 and the last lines of CD
    8.42–57 (20.190–34): 'God will reveal
    Salvation (*Yesha'*) and Justification to those
    who fear His Name' ('the God-Fearers
    reckoning His Name') and 'they will *see His
    Salvation* (*Yeshu'a*), because they took refuge
    in His Holy Name'.

38. Mark 3:18; in Matt. 10:3 also 'Lebbaeus who
    was surnamed Thaddaeus'.

39. *EH* 3.19.1–20.7 and 3.32.1–8; cf. Hippolytus
    9.21's 'Zealot Essenes' (*War* 2.150–51).

40. *Ant.* 19.343–52. Josephus adores him (as the
    Talmud seems to do), and one should note his
    Jesus-like panegyric of him, even calling him
    '*chrēstos*'/'gentle' or 'noble' (19.328–31).

41. The actual language, 'withdrew from' and
    'would not co-operate in work', recapitulates
    the Community Rule's not 'co-operating with
    him in work or purse' and 'separating from'
    those who 'either overtly or covertly break
    one word of the *Torah* of Moses' (6.24–5,

7.22–5, and 8.21–4; cf. too, 4QD266 above, *DSSU*, p. 219).

42. 2.15.1–2, 3.39.15 (as do Clement and Papias), and 6.14.6–7 above. 1 Pet. 1.13 calls him 'my son' and Col. 4:10, 'the cousin of Barnabas'. Paul's bitterness resembles that in Gal. 2:11–14 towards Peter. In Acts 13:13, it is clear 'Mark' left Barnabas and Paul to report about the latter's teaching to Jerusalem.

43. *Ant.* 20.168–72. In Samaritan lore, a Messiah-like Redeemer figure, 'the *Taheb*', also a 'Joshua *redivivus*', was to rediscover the sacred objects on Mount Gerizim. Simon *Magus*, who along with one Dositheus – mentioned by heresiologists – were said to be Disciples of John the Baptist (e.g. Ps. *Rec.* 2.7–12/ *Hom.* 6.8), gives every indication of being one such 'magician' making claims of this kind, whose story in some respects overlaps with the 'Jesus' in Scripture. Again, the Roman *Lex Cornelia de Sicariis et Veneficis* seems to have been aimed precisely against such persons – '*veneficus*' meaning 'magicians'.

Chapter 7

1. In 1QpHab 11.3, the received version of Hab. 2:15's 'looking upon their privy parts' ('*me'oreihem*') has been transmuted into 'looking upon their *Mo'adeihem*' (Festivals) – but the sense re-emerges in 11.13, when 'the Wicked Priest' is characterized, using the parameters of Ezek. 44:7–9's description of foreigners, as 'not circumcising the foreskin of his heart'.

2. Cf. 1 Cor. 9:24–6's 'running the race to win' below. The 'running' vocabulary also appears in an important eschatological context in 1QpHab 6.16–17, leading up to another phrase, 'puffed up', in Hab. 2:4, introducing the famous: 'the Righteous shall live by his Faith'. Paul uses this allusion in his 1 Cor. 8:1ff. attack on the Jerusalem Leadership, its 'Piety', 'building up', and ban on 'eating things sacrificed to idols'. He also uses this word 'Revelation' (*Apocalypsis*) to speak of the Gospel he teaches in Gal. 1:12–16.

3. '*Ethnē*' in Greek; '*'Amim*'/'Peoples' or '*Go'im*'/'Nations' in Hebrew.

4. 1QpHab 10.9–12, His 'running in vain' here is also paralleled in the Habakkuk *Pesher*'s picture of the Lying Spouter's 'Worthless' or 'Vain Service' and 'Empty'/'vain works'.

5. CD 6.15, 7.1–2, and 8.8 above.

6. CD 3.1–9 (also see 8.49 and 1QS 2.15–17, applied to the 'curses of the Covenant' on all backsliders). This use of 'cutting off' at Qumran to some extent parallels the use there of 'delivered up' (usually 'to the avenging sword of the Covenant'), in turn, paralleled in the constant Gospel evocations of Judas *Iscariot* as 'delivering him up'. One should

also take note of the Qumran approach to 'running', evoked in the prelude to the exegesis of Hab. 2:3–4 in 1QpHab 6.16–8.3. This will also have – together with *b. San.* 97b below – a profound relationship to what goes in Christian theology under the title of 'the Delay of the *Parousia*', based on the Hebrew phraseology '*lo*' in 'Wait *for him*' or '*for it*' of Hab. 2:3.

7. 1QpHab 5.8–6:11 on 'swallowing' and 'plenteous eating' and 11.5–15 on being 'swallowed by the Cup of the Wrath of God'.

8. Nor is 'Silvanus', linked in Paul's letters to 'Timothy', mentioned in Acts. In Gal. 2:3, for example, Paul mentions 'Titus' in connection with circumcision and only in 2 Cor. 1:1 and 2 Tim. 4:10 do we get any possible overlap as regards Titus.

9. Cf. *EH* 2.23.10 on James being 'not a respecter of persons' or Jas. 4:4 comparing 'becoming a Friend of man' to being 'an Enemy of God'.

10. For Paul's defensivenss about 'not Lying', see Rom. 9:1, 2 Cor. 11:31, Gal. 1:20, etc., and *per contra*, Jas. 3:14. At Qumran, the ideological adversary of 'the Righteous Teacher' goes by the name of 'the Man' or 'Spouter of Lying'.

11. 1QH 6.25–9, 7.6–10, and 9.24–9.

12. Gal. 4:8–10 and 4Q286–87 ('The Chariots of Glory') in *DSSU*, pp. 222–30, a text which, in the manner of 1QS above, 'curses all the Sons of Belial' and with much in common with Kabbalistic imagery, especially the *Zohar*.

13. 2 Cor. 12:1–7; in Jewish *Hechalot* and/or Islamic Mysticism, 'the *Pardes*' or 'Garden'.

14. 1 Apoc. Jas. 31.5 and 2 Apoc. Jas. 56.15, paralleled in the 'kiss' the 'Traitor' Judas is pictured as giving Jesus in the Gospels (Matt. 26:49 and pars.).

15. 1QS 3.20–22 and 9.14. Cf. too 'the Messiah of Righteousness' in 4Q252, *DSSU*, pp. 85–9. Expressions like 'Sons of *Zedek*' and 'Sons of the *Zaddik*' are not scribal errors but, rather, interchangeable metaphor.

16. See, for instance, 4Q286–87 ('The Chariots of Glory') and 4Q 416–18, 'The Children of Salvation and Mystery of Existence', in *DSSU*, pp. 225–9 and 241–55, and compare with imagery in the works of the eleventh-century Jewish mystic poet, Solomon Ibn Gabirol, such as 'the Royal Crown' and 'the living waters'. 'The Fountain of Living Waters' is integral, too, to 'the New Covenant in the Land of Damascus' in CD 8.21–4.

17. See *Zohar* 3.218a–b on 'Phineas'. In 1.63a–68b Noah escapes the Adversary by 'hiding in the ark on the Day of the Lord's Anger'.

18. There is also a Phineas *redivivus* tradition, connected to the Elijah one and associated too with rain-making in the first-century

document known as Pseudo Philo (48.1).

19. We have already encountered this 'Standing One' ideology in the Pseudoclementines relating to Simon *Magus*' claims. It is very important to the Ebionites – in theory descending from James' 'Jerusalem Community'. Epiphanius, 19.4.1, on 'the Ossaeans' ('Essenes') also attributes it to '*Elchasai*' but, as we have seen – together with the associated 'Power' ideology – it is clearly reflected in the 'standing' vocabulary one finds in the Gospels and Qumran documents generally, as for example in the 'heights of (God's) Standing' in the 'Chariots of Glory' text and 'each man standing on his own watchtower' in CD 4.11 above.

20. See *b. San.* 97b. It is of the utmost importance that not only does this precede the citation of the *Shiloh* Prophecy in 98b from Gen. 49:10 (also found at Qumran in 4Q252 (*DSSU*, pp. 83–9), but the passage it is based on, the '*lo*' ('*lamed-waw*') of Hab. 2:3, is subjected to exegesis at Qumran too in 1QpHab 7.5–14, where it introduces the all-important 'Jamesian' exposition of Hab. 2:4. This is the material that goes in early Christianity under the title of 'the Delay of the *Parousia*'. But even in *Sanhedrin*, it is interpreted in terms of 'the Righteous Ones' who uphold the world and 'wait for' the Messianic Age (cf. John 21:22–3 on 'the Disciple Jesus loved'). Again, we have internal textual evidence placing the Habakkuk *Pesher in the first century!*

21. For the 'Righteousness' in the Scrolls, see CD 1.1 addressed to 'the Knowers of Righteousness' and CD 3.21–4.7 defining 'the Sons of Zadok' as those 'who would stand (up) in the Last Days' and 'justify ['make Righteous'] the Righteous and condemn the Wicked'. Also 1QS 2.24–5, 4.2–9, etc., CD 1.15–16, 8.34, and 8.55–6. Ben Sira begins its praise of 'the Men of Piety' with 'Noah the Righteous' (44:17). For 'Perfection', 'Perfection of Holiness' (sometimes combined with 'Righteousness'), and 'the Perfect of the Way', see 1QS 1.8, 1.28, 2.2, 3.9, 8.1–21, 9.2–8, 9.19, CD 1.19–21, 2.15–16, 8.24–30, etc.

22. *Haeres.* 78.14.1. Also see Volume II. Similar 'rain-making' will be ascribed to his possible forebear Honi ('Onias the Righteous') and Honi's descendant, 'Hanan the *Hidden*', probably John the Baptist.

23. See *BAR*, September/October, 1992, pp. 38–44. Two were found (testifying to the currency of this name-cluster in first-century Palestine), one inscribed simply with '*Kepha*'' (or *Kapha*') and another, also with '*Keipha*'' or '*Kaipha*'' (with a *yod*), possibly 'Caiaphas' – a name also related to '*Cephas*' in Aramo-Greek.

24. 1QS 8.1 – also the possible reference in 4Q251, the new *Halakhah* A text, 'A Pleasing Fragance', *DSSU*, pp. 200–205, to 'fif(teen men)' composing this Council, would solve this problem.

25. Paul proceeds with this 'teaching spiritual things spiritually' or 'in the words the Holy Spirit teaches' in 1 Cor. 3:9–17 and later in 1 Cor. 12:1–14:39 on 'the members of Christ's body' and 'speaking with Tongues'.

26. 1QS 8.3–10 and 9.3–6.

27. Cf. Gal. 2:9 with Matt. 17:1/Mark 9:2/Luke 9:28.

28. John 13:23, 19:26–7, and 21:20–24. This 'Disciple' – never specifically named – normally taken to be John, might, as in the parallel Protevangelium of James, just as likely be James; cf. note 20 above.

29. In 1 Cor. 1:12–16 and 3:6, Paul describes Apollos as 'watering'. This baptism, therefore, was probably a 'water baptism' and it would be reasonable to suppose simply John the Baptist's, not that of another John in Ephesus or Asia Minor.

30. This problem is followed up in early-Church accounts (e.g., *EH* 1.12.2 quoting Clement), where 'Cephas', like Thaddaeus and Philip, is listed as a 'Disciple' or 'one of the Seventy'.

31. See Origen, *Comm. in Matt.* 17 and Fragment 10, attributed to Papias in ANCL and listed as 'James the Bishop and Apostle, Simon, Thaddaeus, and one Joseph', the sons of 'Mary' and 'Cleophas or Alphaeus'.

32. The notice about an appearance to 'Cephas' (Cleophas?) in 1 Cor. 15:7 – if meant to designate Peter – has to be considered an orthodox interpolation.

33. Cf. Luke 9:28 (and pars.) in Jesus' 'Transfiguration' before his core Apostles. Allusion to such 'clothes' will be important to all traditions, especially regarding the white linen and bathing girdle worn by 'Essenes' (*War* 2.129, 137, Hippolytus, 9.16, and 18) and presumably James.

34. Luke 24:13. Stephen the Emperor's Servant in Josephus (*Ant.* 20.113), after riots over the Roman soldier who exposed himself in the Temple at Passover, is beaten 'about one hundred furlongs' from Jerusalem. Excavations have been going on in the region of Latrun – now the site of a Benedictine Monastery – for some time, but it is probably not this Emmaus.

35. These are paralleled in Luke 24:36–43 and John 21:10–13 about 'breaking bread' and eating 'fish' with Jesus. The idea of an appearance in Jerusalem 'to the Eleven as they sat at meat' in Mark 16:14 – considered defective – is paralleled in John 20:24 by one to all the Apostles, except 'Thomas one of the Twelve called *Didymus*'. In the Synoptics, 'Judas Iscariot' is the missing 'Apostle'. In Mark, this occurs following the appearance to the two

'on their way' (16:12–13), which, in addition to summarizing the Emmaus Road appearance to Cleopas and another in Luke, parallels the appearance to the *two Marys* in Matt. 28:9–10.

36. Origen, *Contra Celsus* 2.62, assumes the appearance on the Road to Emmaus was to 'Simon and Cleophas', meaning obviously, 'Simeon bar Cleophas'.

37. Cf. Ps. *Rec.* 1.70–71, Peter's Epistle to James, Ps. *Hom.* 2, and the Parable of the Tares in Matt. 13:19–50. The reflection of this terminology in Gal. 4:16, preceded by allusion to 'telling the Truth', vividly shows its currency even in the 50s.

38. Rom. 1:16–25 on Hab. 2:4, Rom. 3:1–8 on circumcision, Rom. 9:1, Gal. 1:20, 2 Cor. 11:31, Col. 3:9 (mentioning 'fornication' and 'blasphemy'). 2 Thess. 2:2–12, 1 Tim. 2:7, 4:2 (on vegetarianism), and Titus 1:1–11 (on empty-talkers and deceivers). But, as opposed to these, see 1 John 1:6–2:27 and 4:20–5:3 (on 'loving God' ['Piety'] and 'keeping His Commandments').

39. 1QS 8.13–16.

40. Gen. 25:13, 28:9, 36:3 and 1 Chr. 1:29. One should note that Basemath's son by Esau, Reul, was reputed in some accounts to be Moses' father-in-law. Josephus first uses the term in *War* 1.178, but more often he refers to them simply as 'Arabs'.

41. *War* 2.4–18, 556–8, and *Ant.* 20.14.

42. *War* 1.59/*Ant.* 14.80–81. Also see the condemnation of Scaurus in 4Q323–4, 'Priestly Courses III', *DSSU*, pp. 119–27. Named Antipater, he was the facilitator between Pompey and Hyrcanus II in the latter's struggle with his brother, Aristobulus II – whose granddaughter, Mariamme, Herod eventually married and duly executed.

43. CD 6.5–19, 7.18–20, 8.21, and 8.35. It is also the area, towards which Moses first led the people and Elijah too went into 'the wilderness of Damascus'; 1 Kings. 19:15.

44. Cf. 'dwelling in the Land of Damascus' in CD 6.3–5 and 8.21–3 above about digging the Fountain of living waters', 'erecting the New Covenant and the Compact ['Faith']', and also alluding to Elisha's rebuke of Gehazi there. One should also note, these are precisely the two points James is pictured as discussing on the steps of the Temple in Ps. *Rec.* 1.68–9.

45. Luke 24:32. The use of the allusion 'in the Way' is reprised in the appearance to the two 'as they walked going into the country' in Mark 16:12. Acts 9:27's description of Paul 'trying to *join himself* to the Disciples' is precisely that used in the Damascus Document (CD 4.3–11) to describe those 'joining' the 'Penitents of Israel' in the wilderness and presumably 'the New Covenant in the Land of Damascus'. Also note the vocabulary of

'naming' found too in the Damascus Document.

46. *Ant.* 18.134–41 and 20.145 describe Herodian marriages there and in Syria generally.

Chapter 8

1. Acts 15:20, 15:29, and 21:25 above.

2. The 'We Document' intervenes when Paul crosses the Hellespont. What can be said about previous 'missionary journeys' is unclear.

3. In Peter's Epistle to James introducing the *Homilies*, James is addressed as 'Lord and Bishop of the Holy Assembly' and in Clement's to James, 'the Lord and Bishop of Bishops, who rules Jerusalem, the Holy Assembly of the Hebrews and the Assemblies everywhere.' For Ps. *Rec.* 1.68 he is 'the Chief of the Bishops'.

4. For Jas. 2:6 this is literally 'the Kingdom promised to those who *love Him*' and preceding this in 1:12, 'the Crown ('*Stephanos*') the Lord promised to those who *love Him*'. Paul plays on this ideology – cf. his reference to 'loving God', amid references to 'joining', 'being puffed up', and his opponents' 'weak consciences,' in 1 Cor. 8:3–8 and, in conjunction with the 'Lying' terminology, in Rom. 8:28–9:1. 1 John above is also permeated with the phraseology and, for Josephus, *Ant.* 18.117 and *War* 2.128–35, 'Piety towards God' and 'Righteousness towards one's fellow man' are the foundations of both John the Baptist's teaching in the wilderness and 'Essene' ideology. Allusion to 'loving God' also permeates the Scrolls.

5. *EH* 3.27.2–6. In Eusebius' words (probably following Hegesippus), Paul 'they reject' as a heretic and 'an apostate from their Law' and 'they use the Gospel according to the Hebrews only'.

6. Michael Grant, *From Alexander to Cleopatra: The Hellenistic World*, New York, 1982, pp. 52–60. I am also indebted to my colleague Professor Stanley Jones for this suggestion. For Pliny too, Edessa is 'Antioch' and it was clearly a lively centre of early Christian evangelical activity; cf. J. B. Segal, *Edessa 'The Blessed City'*, Oxford, 1970, pp. 3–10, 62–109, and Ian Wilson, *The Shroud of Turin*, New York, 1977, pp. 106–28. As we shall see, the 'Agabus' in Acts 11:26, the 'some' who trigger the 'Jerusalem Council' (Acts 15:1 – 'from James' in Gal. 2:11), and Judas Barsabas (Acts 15:22–32 – like Judas, 'Agabus' is earlier also called 'a prophet') who delivers James' letter to 'Antioch', are, in effect, none other than 'Thaddaeus' (also 'Addai') and 'Judas Thomas' in all Syriac versions of the evangelization *of Edessa*. In

Koran 7.65–84, 11.50–75, etc., "Ãd",
'Thamūd', *Sāliḥ'* ('Just One'), 'Hūd' (Judas).

7. The use of the word 'judge' in Acts 15:19 to
describe James' rulings is significant in precisely reflecting the role accorded 'the *Mebakker'*
in Qumran documents (CD 14.5–12, 15.3–15,
etc.).

8. Cf. Letters 28 in 395 and 40 in 397 CE.
Jerome responds in 72 in 404 and 73 the
same year. What Augustine is worried about
(40.3.3) is that Paul accuses Peter and
Barnabas of 'not walking correctly according
to the Truth of the Gospel' (Gal. 2:14), while
in the same breath averring he 'does not lie'
(Gal. 1:20). But for Augustine, Paul *is* Lying
and is 'a Liar' here. In this exchange, both
manage to ignore James – mentioned in Gal.
1:19 and 2:12 – completely.

9. Cf. *EH* 2.23.18–19 for those associating
James' death with coming of armies and
Jerusalem's fall.

10. Cf. Jas. 2:8–10 on 'keeping the whole Law'.

11. 1QS 8.22–9.2 above. For additional 'expulsion'/'cursing' texts at Qumran, see 1QS
2.4–18, CD 15.1–16.1, 4QD266 above, and
4Q286 ('The Community Council curses
Belial') in *DSSU*, pp. 222–9). The language of
'work' ('service' or 'mission' – which is different from 'works') and 'separation' are widespread at Qumran.

12. 1QS 8.11–18, 9.6–11 (referring to 'the [True]
Prophet', 'the Men of Holiness the Walkers in
Perfection', and 'Judgement'), CD 5.7–11, and
6.17–7.9.

13. In exegesis of Isa. 40:3, quoted twice either in
whole or in part in 1QS 8.14 and 9.19–20.
Note here the language of 'dwelling', 'living'
or 'sojourning', just as in Acts 9:22, where
Paul confounds all those 'dwelling' at
Damascus. Cf. too Paul's allusions to 'Beliar'
(*thus*), the pollution of the idols, 'be separate',
'Perfecting Holiness' and 'being cleansed of
every pollution', in 2 Cor. 6:15–7:1.

14. 5.6–15.

15. *DSSU*, pp. 182–200, in particular, 1.1–10 of
the first part or First Letter, which alludes to
these in terms of the 'Jamesian' category of
'things sacrificed to idols', and 1.47–62 and
83–9, having to do with 'fornication', 'pollution', and marrying Gentiles generally. The
second part or the Second Letter picks up
these themes again in 2.5–9. Because it is
written to a 'Pious' King, aspiring towards
'discernment and Knowledge of the *Torah'*
and evokes the Jamesian position on
Abraham's 'works being reckoned to (him)
as Righteousness' (2.26–33), we shall in due
course identify it as a *Jamesian* letter to 'the
Great King of the Peoples beyond the
Euphrates' – or possibly even Queen Helen
of Adiabene's son, King Izates – or, in other
words, the *real* 'Agbarus' correspondence.

16. CD 5.7–11, recapitulated in 7.1–9, which
expresses these matters – like James' directives
in Acts – in terms of 'keeping away from' or
'abstaining from fornication' (*'lehinnazer'* or
'lehazzir' – the root of the word 'Nazirite'
again).

17. 'Walk' being a favourite expression in the
Qumran lexicon; cf. 1QS 8.18–9.19, CD
2.15–16, 3.2–18, 8.52, 12.21–13.23, etc.

18. Note how in Gal. 1:8–9, Paul begins by
'cursing' anyone preaching a Gospel different
from his own, even 'an Angel out of Heaven'.

19. See Ps. *Rec.* 1.39–47, *Hom.* 2.6–12, Matt.
21:11, Luke 1:76, John 6:14, and 7:40–41.
At Qumran, 1QS 9.11 – coupled with 'the
Messiah of Aaron and Israel' (singular).

20. 4QTest 5–8.

21. Koran 3.84, 7:157, 33:1–50, 81.19–23, etc.

22. Hippolytus 9.8–12, 10.25, *EH* 6.38, *Haeres.*
A53.1.1, 19.1–4–5, and 30.3.2.

23. *EH* 2.1.2 and cf. 'Forefathers' with 'the First'
in CD 1.4–2.6, 3.10, 8.16–17, etc. N.b. the
curious order, putting James' election 'at the
same time' as *the election to replace Judas
Iscariot* and *the stoning of Stephen*.

24. *EH* 1.12.1–3. Curiously here too he mentions
Matthias' election by lot, alluding to 'Justus
Barsabas' in the same breath he does James.

25. 1.13.1–22. This is an original story with
Eusebius. The sequence is important because
Thaddaeus and Thomas are involved.
Depending on the date we give Jesus, this
conversion might have taken place earlier.
Since 'Ananias' too is involved (and, therefore,
perhaps Paul), it also can be said, as we shall
see, to relate to the conversion of Queen
Helen and her son in *Ant.* 20.17–53.

26. *EH* 2.1.1. One should watch the use of the
word 'Crown' (*Stephanos*) associated with
Stephen's name here. We have already seen it
referred to in Jas. 1:12 and Josephus' description of the High Priest's 'Crown' (*Nezer*). As
such, it can also be thought of as evoking the
Nazirite's 'Crown' of hair.

27. 2.8.1–3.

28. 2.1.2. N.b. Eusebius introduces 'Virgin' in
place of 'she' in the normative Matt. 1:18 –
a theme too, not unconnected to James.

29. *EH* 1.12.3 and Acts 1:26. The theme of
'clothes' will always be important regarding
both James and Josephus' and Hippolytus'
descriptions of 'Essenes'.

30. *Ant.* 12.414, 419, and 434.

31. Matt. 21:8–10 (including reiteration of the
'True Prophet' ideology) and pars.

32. *War* 2.8/*Ant.* 17.207–8.

33. *War* 3.387–91.

34. *War* 4.154–7. Cf. *War* 6.390, mentioned
above, on 'Phineas the Temple Treasurer',
who surrenders the Temple Treasure.

35. Cf. Ps. Philo 48.1 with Matt. 11:14, 16:14
(and pars.), and 1 Kings 19:4–16. John

1:24–5, of course, specifically denies any connection of John to Elijah.

36. *B. Ta'an.* 22b–23b and *j. Ta'an.* 66d. In the latter, there are *two* 'Honi the Circle-Drawer's, one the grandson of the other.

37. Though not a Pauline letter *per se*, Ephesians refers to 'separation' and uses 'Foundation', 'Stone', 'Cornerstone', and 'building' imagery, asking its opponents to 'stop Lying' and 'speak Truth to one another' (2:12–4:25). Like the Community Rule and other Qumran documents, it uses 'offering' and 'sweet fragrance' imagery (5:2), speaks of 'Light', 'Dark', 'the Children of Light', and even, 'Let no one deceive you with Empty words, for the Wrath of God comes upon the Sons of Disobedience for these things' (5:6).

38. In fact, it should be noted that the priests in the Temple chose their daily duties and just about everything they did by lot; cf. *b. Yoma* 37a–41b and *Tam.* 26a–28b.

39. The imagery of 'Stone-Cutting' connected with this 'Phineas'' person, also, has some import *vis-à-vis* 'Rock' symbolism and 'Cornerstone of the Temple' imagery. Matt. 21:42 and pars. picture Jesus as employing the Stone which the builder's rejected has become the Cornerstone' of Ps. 118:22 to refer both to himself and the Gentile Mission overseas, and this 'Cornerstone' imagery is also present in 1QS 8.7–9 and 9.3–5's exposition of 'making a Way in the wilderness' and picture of the Community Council as both 'Temple' and 'sacrifice'.

40. *War* 7.395–7. Again, like priests, these people choose 'ten men' *to slay the others*. One should consider this suicide in relation to Jas. 2:21's evocation of Abraham's willingness to sacrifice his son Isaac as the epitome of 'Justification by works' or 'Faith Perfected by works' (*per contra*, see Heb. 11:17 noted earlier). Also see this 'testing' of Abraham, called 'of the Righteous' and referred to in Koran 37.100–112 above. Therefore, it is possible to imagine, where 'works Righteousness' theorizing goes, such behaviour being considered equivalent to that of the 'believing Abraham' the 'Friend of God' (Jas. 2:22–23). Acts 1:18, also operating within the same 'suicide'/ 'reward'/'*Sicarios*' framework, rather inverts this, turning it into 'the reward for Unrighteousness' 'Judas *Iscariot*' receives and the curious James-like 'fall' he takes.

41. *War* 7.260–63 on 'the *Sicarioi*'; *War* 7.268–74 on 'the Zealots'. Also *War* 4.161, 241, and 560–63 likewise. Cf. Jas. 1:12, 2:5 on 'loving God', and 2:8 on 'loving your neighbour as yourself' to the exact opposite sense. The same language is also completely reversed in the Dead Sea Scrolls; e.g., 1QpHab 12.10 on the Wicked Priest 'stealing the Riches of the Poor'; 8.11, 'gathering the Riches of the Men of Violence'; 9.4–5 on the profiteering of 'the Last Priests of Jerusalem' generally, and CD 6.16 and 8.5–8 to the opposite sense. In Josephus, the Revolutionaries sought 'to turn the Poor against the Rich' (*War* 2.437).

42. 1QpHab 2.1–6, CD 1.12, and 8.16–24.

43. N.b. Acts 1:26: 'They gave their lots and the lot fell on Matthias', to some extent echoing Josephus on the Masada suicide: 'the rule they made for casting their lots was that he whose lot it was should first kill the other nine and after all should kill himself' – this about the *Sicarii*. For Acts 1:18 and Matt. 27:6, 'Judas *Iscariot*', too, then appears to kill himself.

44. In 1QpHab 2.8–9 and 7.4–5, when 'the Righteous Teacher'/'(High) Priest' expounds a passage, this is characterized in terms of 'God putting in his heart the intelligence to interpret all the words of His Servants the Prophets, through whom God foretold all that was going to happen to His people' or 'making known to the Righteous Teacher all the Mysteries of the words of His servants the Prophets'. This also applied to Psalms, David being reckoned (as in the Koran) as a Prophet.

45. Cf., CD 4.2–3, 6.3–9, 7.13–21, and 1QM 1.2–3.

46. In Ps. 69:9, it is 'zeal for *Your* House has consumed me', but the whole Psalm is zealous. For 'the Poor' and 'the Meek' at Qumran, see 1QH 2.32–4, 3.25, 5.13–23, 7.10, CD 6.21, 14.13, 1QM 11.9–13, 13.13–14, and 4Q434–36 ('The Hymns of the Poor') in *DSSU*, pp. 233–41.

47. Ps. 69:14–15. Here too, not only is 'Salvation' (*Yesha'*) evoked – important in Qumran documents – but so is the word 'save' ('*hazzil*'/ '*yazzil*'), important in 1QpHab's interpretation of Hab. 2:4 on being 'saved from the House of Judgement' (8.2) and 'being saved on the Day of Judgement' (12.14).

48. For 'cursing' and 'Deceitfulness' ('*Remiyyah*') as applied to the Liar, see 1QS 2.4–18, 4.9–23 (including 'Tongue' imagery), and 8.22–9.8. Also see 4QpNah 2.8, in conjunction with 'Lying, a Tongue full of Lies', and 'deceiving Many'. For the 'blaspheming Tongue' in James, see 3:5–15.

49. CD 14.10–13.

50. CD 1.7, 5.15–16, 7.9, 7.21, 8.2–3, 8.25, 13.24, 1QS 3.14–18, and 4.12–26; for its use regarding 'the *Mebakker*' and 'the High Priest Commanding the Many', see CD 14.6–7, 15.8–10, and 1QS 5.22–4.

51. John 19:23–4 treats this episode somewhat differently. There the soldiers 'part the garments into four', one for each. After this, they 'cast lots', both related to Ps. 22:18, the Psalm – again, attributed to David – which also begins with the words, 'My God, my God, why have you forsaken me', and alludes to 'saving the

soul' of 'the Meek One' (22:20–26). If one fixes one's attention on things, such as 'clothes' or 'casting lots', one will never go far astray. For Mark 15:23, Jesus is given 'wine mixed with myrrh' to drink. Luke, wisely, ignores the episode.

52. See, too, 4Q434–36, 'The Hymns of the Poor', in *DSSU* above. A parallel, 'the soul of the *Zaddik*' – this from Ps. 94:21 in the same spirit as Ps. 109 – is used in CD 1.20–21 to describe an attack on the Righteous Teacher and his associates (called 'the Walkers in Perfection') by people 'pursuing them with the sword'.

53. 'Blood'/'*dam*' will always be important both at Qumran and here. At Qumran, see CD 3.6, 'City of Blood' in 4QpNah 2.1–2 (considered full of 'Lying'), and the Liar's 'worthless' Assembly, 'built upon blood', in 1QpHab 10.6–10 (Hab. 2:12). In 1QpHab 9.8 and 12.1–10, it rather has to do with 'the blood of Man ('*Adam*', possibly 'the Primal Adam') and the Violence done to the land' (Hab. 2:8/2:17).

54. Here 'Joseph called Barsabas surnamed Justus' is a write-in for James and carries either something of the meaning 'son of the father Joseph' or 'Saba' or 'Sabaean' ('bather'). We shall see the relevance of this last as we proceed. The 'Office', as we have seen, is that of 'Bishop' and the 'casting of lots' reappears in the story of the Roman soldiers 'casting lots' for Jesus' 'clothing' – 'clothes' always being an important theme.

55. Cf. *War* 2.253, 264, *Ant.* 20.124, 163, 167, etc. Jesus, too, is crucified between 'two thieves' ('*lēstai*', i.e., 'Bandits'; Matt. 27:38 and pars.).

56. *War* 7.410–47. N.b. in *War* 7.453, the probable basis for the description of Judas' death in Acts – this and *Vita* 424f. below.

57. *War* 7.253–5. Here the play of '*Christianoi*' on '*Sicarioi*' is perhaps sensible. We have already noted the relevance of all these matters to Hippolytus 9.21's description of '*Sicarii* Essenes', who also 'will call no man Lord even though one tortures or even kills them'.

58. *War* 7.437. Cf. Acts 16:20–21, 17:7, and 24:5 on Paul as a leader of 'the Nazoraean Heresy spreading insurrection among all the Jews in the habitable world' and claiming 'there is another King, Jesus'; and Claudius' letter to the Jews of Egypt, specifically cautioning them against receiving just such itinerant 'disease'-carriers; H. Idris Bell, loc. cit.

59. *Vita* 424f.: 'Jonathan . . . asserted that I had provided him with arms and money.' This is the accusation Justus of Tiberius revives in the 90s, possibly ending in the executions of Epaphroditus, Flavius Clemens ('Clement'?), and even Josephus himself. The former two are evidently secret 'Christians' within the

Imperial household. In any event, at this point Domitian is assassinated by Flavia Domitilla's servant 'Stephanos'.

60. *War* 7.452–3.
61. *Ant.* 18.27.
62. Cf. Tacitus, *Annals* 15.39 with Suetonius 6.38, and Dio Cassius 62.16–18.
63. As we shall see, this name 'Judas' may be a malicious play on the name of Jesus' *third* brother 'Jude'/'Judas of James'/'Judas the Zealot' or 'Judas (the brother) of Simon *Iscariot*' ('Simon the Zealot').
64. *Contra Celsus* 2.13 above.
65. 68.3–4. Certainly it was in effect after the Bar Kochba War, when we hear of a similar decree by Hadrian and when '*Sicarii*' property ('*Sicaricon*' in *b. Git.* 55b, *B.B.* 47b, etc. – more evasion) was being confiscated.
66. Letter 84 to Pammachius and Oceanus.

Chapter 9

1. 2.1.2.
2. 2.1.1.
3. 2.1.4. Compare this with Paul in 1 Cor. 15:3–9, which is already conflated.
4. 1.13.5.
5. See Moses of Chorene, 2.30–35, the Acts of Thomas, and the Doctrine of Addai the Apostle.
6. CD 8.9–11. The expression is known in Roman jurisprudence and applies to petty Kings in the East like the Herodians; see A. Sherwin-White, *The Roman Citizenship*, Oxford, 1939, pp. 270–75, the Romans being 'the Lord of the Peoples' ('*Princeps Gentium*'). See also how it is used in 1QpHab 6.7, 8.5–10.7, and 1QM 1.3 and Eusebius' description of the Arab King Agbar, 'the Great King of the Peoples (*Ethnōn*) beyond the Euphrates', not to mention Paul's 'Apostle to the Gentiles' (also *Ethnōn*).
7. Moses of Chorene, 2.35, calls her 'the first of Agbar's wives', to whom he gave the town of Haran. For Josephus, her son Izates receives this town from *his* father. Eusebius appears, also, to think Helen Agbar's 'Queen'.
8. *Ant.* 20.18. This goes back to stories about Abraham and Sarah being brother and sister, Edessa being considered their homeland. Interestingly enough, readings of Dio Cassius 68 refer to 'Agbarus' as 'Albarus'.
9. 20.39–41. Helen is worried that the people will never be content with being ruled by a Jew. Also in Acts 9:15, Ananias learns that Paul will bear God's Name 'before Peoples (*Ethnōn*) and Kings'.
10. Mark 3:17–19 and Luke 6:15–16. In some versions of Matt. 10:3, he is also identified with 'Lebbaeus' – another of these obvious garblings, probably meant to stand also for 'Alphaeus', i.e., 'Cleophas' below.

11. 20.49–53 and 101.
12. 2.12.1–3. Josephus also mentions these at the end of his story; 20.95. He says her son Izates also sent up relief, and Cyprus too is added to these stories – important for other notices in Acts.
13. 20.22–34. Then Antiochia Charax – modern-day Basra.
14. The second part of this correspondence is addressed to a king, who is urged to read 'the Book of Moses and the words of the Prophets' and 'to remember David', who was 'also saved from many sufferings and forgiven' (*DSSU*, pp. 199–200). It ends by evoking the words with which it began, about 'some of the works of the *Torah* we reckoned for your good and that of your People', which, to para-phrase God's words to Abraham in Gen. 15:6, 'would be reckoned to you as Righteousness' – words Paul (Gal. 3:6) and James 2:23 both evoke – the latter in the course of pointing out how, because of such 'reckoning', Abraham 'was called Friend of God'!
15. 2 variant mss. of the Apost. Const. 8.25, identifying him as 'Lebbaeus surnamed Thaddaeus', and Epist. Apost. 2. The Papias Fragment 10 above, also, makes it clear that 'Thaddaeus' is identical to the brother of Jesus called 'Judas'.
16. Luke 6:15, Acts 1:13. The List of the Twelve Apostles attributed to Hippolytus also calls him 'the son of Clopas . . . who became Bishop of Jerusalem after James the Just and fell asleep and was buried there at the age of 120 years'. For the Epist. Apost., he is simply 'Cephas'.
17. *Ant.* 20.41 (*zēloun*) and 20:47 (*Zēlōtēn*).
18. *EH* 2.13.4. This will have a parallel in Acts' description of Helen as 'the Ethiopian Queen'. Really this is Irenaeus' opinion, *Ad. Haer.* 1.23, also supported by Justin Martyr, First Apology 1.26. See too Hippolytus 6.15, Ps. *Rec.* 2.8–12 (where she is called 'Luna'), and Epiphanius, *Haeres.* 21.2.1–3.6 (based on Irenaeus and admitting Simon called himself 'the Great Power').
19. See *M. Naz.* 3:6 and below for repeated Nazirite periods said to be given her.
20. See Ps. *Rec.* 2.7–8 and below for 'Standing One' idea among Elchasaite and Ebionite groups. The 'Power' ideology will be impor-tant in all such notices and James' proclama-tion in the Temple of the coming of 'the Son of Man'.
21. Acts 2:3–6. Also note 'Tongues' used to exactly this effect and predicated of the *Mebakker* ('Bishop') in CD 14.9–10 and the Last Column (*DSSU*, p. 219), Line 10; and 'Tongue' imagery generally to attack 'the Liar' in James 1:26, 3:5–10, 1QS 4:11, CD 5.11–12, and 1QpNah 2.8.
22. *EH* 7.19; see also 3.7.8 below.

23. Apost. Const. 8.35
24. 2.23.3–4
25. *Vir. ill.* 2
26. Ibid.
27. See, for instance, Paul forcibly addressing the Jewish crowd from the 'steps' in Acts 21:40 and, of course, James 'cast down headlong' from the steps in Ps. *Rec.* 1.70.
28. See Paul about 'knowing a Man in Christ fourteen years ago' – perhaps James (the time frame agrees with Gal. 2:1; note too the 'Man' symbolism) – ascending 'to the Third Heaven' in 2 Cor. 12:2.
29. 78.1.7; also 66.19.6.
30. 78.7.7
31. 3.7.8.
32. For the Mysticism of Ascents and the Throne in the Koran, see 81:19–20; also 2.255, 84:19, (both coupled with the 'Jamesian' admonition, '*Believe and do good works*'), etc. – not to mention the whole tradition of the *Isrā* and *Mi'raj* (17:1 and 53:8–18), not unlike the one in the Gospel of the Hebrews – reported by Origen and Jerome – that the Holy Spirit took up Jesus by the hair and deposited him on Mount Tabor' (Hennecke, 1.164).
33. Acts 2:41, 2:47, 4:4, 5:14, 6:7, etc.
34. CD 13.7–13, 14:12, and 15.14. See also Cross, p. 232, who knows that the '*Mebakker*' and 'Bishop' are equivalent.
35. John 19:27 and Ps. *Rec.* 1.71.
36. See *DSSU*, p. 219 above, Lines 17–18. This is literally an expulsion text, as is the Chariots of Glory ('The Community Council curses Belial'), pp. 229–30 – as is its reversal in Peter's *condemnation of the Jews* for killing Christ in Acts 2:23 and 2:36 below.
37. See Acts 1:18 and 2:2–4.
38. CD 8.13 (Ms. B, 19.26); also 1.14–15 and 4.19–20.
39. 1 Cor. 11:27, 2 Cor. 3:6, Gal. 2:21, 3:10–21, and 6:13.
40. See CD 1.14–15, 4.19–20, 8.13, and 1QpHab 10.9.
41. CD 14.10. He then 'judges' and 'expels' people, and the like.
42. CD 1.14–15. Recently, in *Commentary* (January 1992), Robert Alter, a Professor in Comparative Literature at Berkeley ('How Important are the Scrolls?'), criticized me for pointing out the relationship of this 'spouting' imagery to that of 'pouring out'. Nevertheless it is unmistakable.
43. Joel 2:31 even contains an image of 'the sun turning to darkness', so much a part of the descriptions of the crucifixion of Jesus in the Gospels.
44. The imagery of Isa. 29–30, Ezek. 13 (includ-ing that of 'plastering on the wall'), and Mic. 2:11–16 is being used in CD 1.14, and 8:13 (19:26). This is a crucial set of metaphors at Qumran. Notice, in particular, Mic. 2:11,

which reads: 'If a man, walking in the Spirit and Lying, lies saying, "I will pour out [here the key '*attif*' of the Damascus Document] on you of wine and strong drink," he will be the Pourer Out [*Mattif*, i.e., 'the Spouter' at Qumran] of this people.' Note, too, that this allusion to 'wine' is played on in the crucial CD 8.9–12 material, introducing this from Deut. 32:33, about 'their wine is the venom of vipers', to produce 'Greek-speaking Kings' – 'Greece' and 'wine' being homonyms in Hebrew.

45. This is only in the Greek version quoted by Acts, not the Hebrew. Also Islam has inherited this view of David as a Prophet – signalled too in Line 10 of '*MMT*' above.

46. Acts 2:35, Matt. 22:44 (and pars.), and Heb. 1:13 and 10:13. At Qumran see, for instance, 1QM 12.11–15 and 19.3–7. See its reverse in Jas. 2:3.

47. As, for instance, Acts 2:17–18 and 10:45 on 'pouring out the gift of the Holy Spirit' or even 'the Cup of the New Covenant in my blood which is poured out for you' (introduced by allusion to 'never drinking' wine again' – Luke 22:18–20 and pars.)

48. Ps. *Rec.* 1.60.

49. Cf. Ps. *Rec.* 1.43: 'The Church of the Lord, which was constituted in Jerusalem, was most plentifully multiplied and grew, being governed with the most Righteous ordinances by James, who was ordained Bishop in it by the Lord.' In the Syriac, which like Rufinus' Latin also goes on to call James 'Archbishop', this reads: 'the Church in Jerusalem, which was established by our Lord, grew great while it was led justly and uprightly by James, whom our Lord appointed Bishop'.

50. Ps. *Rec.* 1.60. In this context, one should note Acts' own confusion between Judas Barsabas, Joseph Barsabas, and Joses Barnabas. We can add to this, 'Judas *Barsabas*', and 'Judas *Iscariot*'.

51. *EH* 2.23.7–11. At this point in the Letter of James too, following evocation of the imminent 'coming of the Lord', we also hear that the 'Judge *is standing* before the Gate' (Jas. 5.8–9 – note the 'standing' imagery).

52. Ps. *Rec.* 1.72 and 2.7.

53. *EH* 2.23.12–13.

54. *EH* 2.23; cf. Koran 2.25, 2,62 (evoking 'Sabaeans'), 2.82, 2.277, 3.113–15 (referring to 'People of the Book', called 'the Righteous', who keep all-night vigils), 4.25 (mentioning Abraham as the 'Friend' of God), 84.25, 113.3, etc.

55. 1QM 11.4–12:10, recapitulated in 18.13–19.3. The evocation of 'the King of Glory' and the Heavenly Host coming on the clouds of Heaven in exegesis of 'the Star Prophecy' is patent. Isa. 31:8 is also evoked to add the imagery of 'the sword of no mere

Adam'. Here, too, final apocalyptic Judgement will be executed 'by the hand of the Poor' (*Ebionim*) and 'those bent in the dust', who will be kindled 'like a burning torch in the straw to consume Unrighteousness and destroy all Evil and . . . justify the Judgement of Your Truth on all the sons of men'; cf. Matt. 3:12/Luke 3:17, quoting John the Baptist, to the effect that, 'the Fire, whose fan is in His hand will thoroughly cleanse His threshing floor and . . . burn the straw with unquenchable fire'.

56. Here Acts specifically uses the word 'standing' (not simply 'sitting'), after having alluded to the 'footstool' and the 'Throne' in 7:49. All these images will relate to the Ebionite/Elchasaite 'Standing One' vocabulary, the imagery of which – as we shall see – permeates the Gospels.

Chapter 10

1. *Tosefta Hul.* 2:22–3. Also see *b. A.Z.* 27b, *j. Shab.* 14:4, and *A.Z.* 2:2, 40d. Jacob wishes to cure in the name of Jesus b. Panthera, a favourite Talmudic way of referring to Jesus. The *Talmud* also knows another of these wonder-workers it cryptically refers to (also in the context of reference to 'Kfar Sechania') as '*Bar Daroma*, who could jump a mile'; but when he entered the privy and saw a snake – like Judas *Iscariot* in Acts – 'dropped his bowels and died' (*Git.* 57a).

2. *EH* 3.39.9.

3. See Acts 24:24–26:32; CD 4.17–7.4 and 8.3–11.

4. This 'going out to war' is the basis of the War Scroll's view of the desert 'camps', because 'the Holy Angels march with them' in the camps (1QM 7.3–8; cf. Deut. 23:10–14, also on the matter of the latrines, and CD 15.17 also on the Holy Angels in the camps). 4QMMT 1.47–70, the section on 'Jerusalem being the foremost of the *camps of Israel*', also treats the exclusion of Ammonites, Moabites, and presumably Edomites. The point is that no unclean thing should even be 'seen' in the camps. The Essenes, too, are described as following similar proscription in the matter of their latrines.

5. Mark 7:15 omits the 'casting out'/*ekballetai*, which is rather picked up in the next episode about the 'Greek woman of Syro-Phoenician origin' (in Matthew, another of these mysterious 'Cananaeans' or 'Cananites'!), who asks Jesus to cast an 'Evil Demon out of her daughter' (*ekballē* – 7:26). In both, the original passage about uncleanness and the privy is replete with 'mouth', 'lips', and 'heart' imagery, widespread in the Dead Sea Scrolls.

6. Following his notice about how the Essenes carry shovels everywhere to cover up their

excretion, Josephus also applies the '*ekballō*' language to how they 'cast out' backsliders (*ekbalousi*); *War* 2.137–44.

7. The allusion to dogs is important too in the Scrolls, as for instance, in 4QMMT 1.66–70 above, where it is literally applied to 'not bringing dogs into the Holy camp' – defined as Jerusalem, 'the foremost of the camps of Israel'. The reason, that 'they eat the bones with flesh still on them', relates to James' ban on 'carrion' in his directives to overseas communities as portrayed in Acts. Another variation, 'do not give what is Holy to dogs or cast down [again *balete*] pearls before swine', is to be found in Matt. 7:6's Sermon on the Mount.

8. This parable also includes allusion to 'the Completion of the Age', an expression intrinsic to Dead Sea Scrolls' scriptural exegesis.

9. 1QpHab 2.3–4, CD 6.19, and 8.35–45.

10. Gen. 9:4–7.

11. *Haeres.* 30.2.3 and 78.14.3.

12. This is the root of the Hebrew word, '*Nozrim*' for 'Christians', or 'Keepers', which now appears in the Rabbinic tradition and in Matt. 26:71, following these Last Supper events, before those surrounding 'the Field of Blood' and Pilate washing his hands of 'this innocent blood'.

13. 'Crown' in the sense of the prize won by athletes. Paul plays on this meaning in 1 Cor. 8:25. Also in Eusebius on Stephen's martyrdom (*EH* 2.1.1) – another link to the substitution of this character for James in the Book of Acts.

14. The Judas *Iscariot* episode, on the other hand, is missing from Mark and Luke. In Mark 12:41–4 and Luke 21:1–4, *balontōn*, repeated some six times in five lines.

15. This parable expresses the Kingdom of Heaven in terms of 'a net cast to the sea' and gathering the good, 'unpolluted' fish into 'vessels' or 'pots' (13:48).

16. The Greek Septuagint simply substitutes 'furnace' for 'Potter', i.e., 'cast them into the furnace in the House of the Lord'.

17. In this context, Paul's doctrine of Jesus' body as Temple should also be recalled. Not only is Paul, once again, using his general imagery of the spiritualized Temple and general concept of the Community or, as it were, Christ's body as the Temple, but also the members of the Community as 'the members of the body of Christ' (1 Cor. 12:2–27).

18. *War* 2.123.

19. '*Ger-nilveh*' in 4QpNah 2.9 and 3.5; '*Nilvim*' in CD 4.3 and 1QS 5.6.

20. CD 5.7–12. Here too, as in Paul, the 'joining' language is mixed with that of 'fornication' and 'blood'. Paul now moves directly into that of idolatry in the Temple and 'food sacrificed to idols' (1 Cor. 8:1–13).

21. Here, too, the Scrolls use the language of 'delivering up', but this not in the sense of betrayal, rather that of backsliders and Covenant-Breakers being 'delivered up to the sword' or 'the Vengeance of God'; cf. CD 1.6, 3.10–11, 7.13, and 8.1.

22. See *B.B.* 91b on 'Potters' and *Yalkut* Jeremiah 35:8ff., followed by the tradition in the *Yalkut* on Jer. 35:12, that the grandsons of the Rechabites served in the Temple and their daughters married the sons of the Priests. See even in Jer. 35:5, a play on these 'pots'. For Josephus, so scrupulous are the 'Essenes' that they carried a shovel with them and would not go outside of a circle even to defecate on the Sabbath. Not insignificantly, the so-called 'Dung Gate' in Jerusalem seems to have been called the 'Gate of the Essenes' in ancient times.

23. 1QS 5.2–9. Allusions to 'keeping' and 'doing' also proliferate in James 1:22–5, 2:8–13, and 4:11–17.

24. CD 4:3 and 6.5. See also Acts 9:2 and 9:22. Here, one assumes the 'living' or 'dwelling' was in tents.

25. Cf. 1QpHab 11.9–15, Rev. 14:10, 16:19, and 19:15.

26. John 6:48–58 puts this right after Jesus walks on the waters of the Sea of Galilee, in connection rather with his discussions on bread not wine, i.e., eating his flesh, the living bread, the manna which came down from Heaven but, once again, right before his reference to the coming treachery of 'Judas, Simon *Iscariot*'s son, one of the Twelve'. In due course, we shall show how 'Cup of Blood' in Hebrew ('*Chos Dam*') and 'Damascus' in Greek are homophones and linguistically related.

27. Note here the allusions to 'bread', as in Matt. 15:2 and 26:26, and 'loaves', as in 'the loaves and the fishes' above.

28. See, for instance, 1QS 6.1–92, CD 13.7–14.11, etc. For references to 'pouring out' at Qumran, see CD 1.14, 4.19–20, and 8.13, as well as 'the Spouter' or 'Pourer out of Lying' generally in 1QpHab 10.9.

29. CD 3.6–11. The passage also employs the 'cutting off' language Paul uses to different effect in Gal. 5:12.

30. 1QpHab 11.2–12.9. In Luke 22:31–8, this is immediately followed by the picture of Jesus rebuking 'Simon' Peter and the followers, then, arming themselves with not one but 'two' swords – John's 'Simon *Iscariot*' again.

31. 10:16 and 11:25–9. In the Scrolls, 'the Cup' is used to describe the death of the Righteous Teacher and the Vengeance God will take for this.

32. This is also mixed up with the portrait of him as drinking no wine. Not only do these flow into the 'eating the bread and drinking the cup' symbolisms of 11:23–30 and 'eating and drinking' generally as, for instance, with

regard to 'Cephas and the brothers of the
Lord' in 9:5; but even ultimately culminate in
repeated references to 'speaking in Tongues'
or 'the Tongues of men', ending in allusion to
'*being* zealous (*zēloute*) to prophesy' (1 Cor.
13:1–14:39).

33. *EH* 2.23.17.
34. See, for instance, Jerome's Letters 81, 82, 84
(comparing Origen to 'Judas the Zealot'!),
and his Preface to Ezekiel against Rufinus, his
erstwhile friend, and the publisher of both
Origen and, interestingly enough, the Pseudoclementine *Recognitions* in Latin. Also
Rufinus' response in Letter 80 and his two
Apologies attacking Jerome.
35. 1QS 3.20–22 and 9.14. Early scholars considered these scribal errors, but probably they
are not as they have since been found in newer
Qumran documents and are paralleled in the
New Testament (cf. Luke 20:36, 'Sons of the
Resurrection').
36. 2.23.20.
37. *Comm. in Matt.* 10.17. Also *Contra Celsum*
1.47 and 2.13 (here Origen identifies 'the
Sicarii' as those who circumcise themselves or
forcibly circumcise others). We shall discuss
this expression 'the Wrath of God' – which
also appears in 1QpHab 11.15's picture of
'the Cup' ('of the right hand of the Lord')
that would 'swallow' those who destoyed the
Righteous Teacher and the *Ebionim* – when
discussing 'the cup' Jesus gives James to drink
in his first post-resurrection appearance to
him below.
38. *Vir. ill.* 2.
39. The passages have to do with 'the Wicked
encompassing the Righteous' and 'the reward
of his hands will be paid him' – cf. 1QpHab
1.10, 5.8–9, 12.2, and 4QPs 37 4.19–21.
40. See, for instance, *Ant.* 18.117 on John and
War 2.128 and 139 on 'Essene' 'Piety towards
God'/'Righteousness towards men'. For James
see 2:5–8.
41. See CD 6.19–7.6, setting forth the parameters
of 'the New Covenant in the Land of
Damascus'.
42. See, for instance, CD 6.21 above and 1QM
11.9–13 and compare with Jas. 2:2–10 and
5:1–8.
43. Matt. 22:36–40 and pars.
44. *Dial.* 23, 47, and 93. Justin came from a
village in Samaria not far from Simon *Magus*'
place of origin.
45. *EH* 2.23.2–8.
46. Acts 3:14, 7:52, and 22:14 and see Jas. 5:6 –
also the 'Justification' theology based on it in
Rom. 2:13–5:5 and Gal. 2:16–3:26; *per contra*, Jas. 2:14–26. For Jesus as 'Nazoraean',
see Luke 18:37, 24:19 (and pars.), Acts 2:22,
4:10, 22:8, 26:9, etc.
47. Jas. 2:8 and CD 6.20. Paul also evokes this
Commandment, along with its companion,

'Loving God', in polemical juxtaposition with
James, as for instance, Rom. 13:9–10, Gal.
5:14, and 1 Cor. 8:3 – all the time playing
throughout on the 'love' theme.
48. 2.23.5.
49. 2.23.13 and Matt. 26:64/Mark 14:62 (also
16:19)/Luke 22:69. This language of 'Power'
is very important to Ebionite/Elchasaite
sectarianism.
50. Jerome, *Comm. on Gal.* 396 (1:19). For
fringes, see Num. 15:38–9.
51. Also see Mark 3:10 and Luke 6:19. As many
as touch it are cured. In Luke 7:38–9, another
woman, 'a Great Sinner' as compared to a
Syro-Phoenician, touches, kisses, and bathes
Jesus' feet and 'the Pharisees', who have *invited
him to eat*, grumble. In Matt. 8:3 and Mark
1:41, the scenario is reversed. Jesus now cures
a leper *by touching him*; in 8:15, after curing
the servant of a Centurion – whose Faith is
greater than all Israel! – he touches *Peter's
mother-in-law* (*thus*) and cures her! Elsewhere
he touches the eyes of two of the blind (Matt. 20:34 –
in Mark 8:22, he spits in them too). In Mark
10:13 and Luke 18:15, they bring little children to him to touch (in Luke 6:19 above,
whole multitudes). Typically, now it is rather
'the Disciples' (not 'the Pharisees') who object
and Jesus rebukes them.
52. It will be recalled that Simon *Magus*' 'Helen'
had been in brothels of Tyre, the sexual overtones of which are explicit. Here the issue is
'blood' – later it will be the eunuch of the
'Ethiopian' or 'Arab' Queen, the 'Syro-
Phoenician'/'Cananite' (also a code for
'Zealot') playing on 'Ethiopian' or 'Arab'.
53. *Haeres.* 29.4–1–2, even claiming that on that
basis he exercised the 'Ancient Priesthood',
implying 'the Order of Melchizedek'. This
whole section, 29.4.1–8.7, goes into these
various sorts of confusions between Nazirite/
Nazoraean/and Nazrene/Nazarean, the problem being that two different letters in Hebrew,
'tz' and 'z', go into Greek as a single letter –
generally 'z', but sometimes 's'.
54. 29.5.7.
55. 30.1.3 and 78.13.2–14.3.
56. Exod. 13:2, which uses the word 'Holy' in the
sense of 'sanctified' or 'consecrated'. Note the
prophecy that follows, attributed to a man
named 'Simeon' ('Simeon bar Cleophas'?),
who is called 'Righteous and Pious' and, just
before Jesus' family returns to 'Nazareth',
speaks about 'seeing your Salvation' – the very
words used in the last line of the narrative section of the Damascus Document (8.57), which
speaks about 'seeing His Salvation (*Yeshu'a*),
because they took refuge in His Holy Name'.
57. 29.5.6.
58. 19.2.1, 19.4.1–2, and 30.3.1–6.
59. In this scene, in which Peter denies Jesus three
times, Luke 22:56–62 only conserves Mark's

reference to being 'a Galilean', but twice adds an emphasis on 'Man'. Actually, originally there were probably two traditions, one using 'Jesus the Galilean'; and the other, 'Jesus the Nazoraean' – to say nothing of this Ebionite 'Primal Adam' or 'First Man' echo.

60. Here *tz* again, as in *Nezer* or 'Branch' – a further variation – but not *'z'* as in 'Nazirite'. Actually the Sea of Galilee, even in the Synoptics and as in Josephus, is known as 'Gennesaret' – 'Nazareth' nowhere appearing as such as a town in Galilee. It may have been, but there is no record of it either in the Bible or Josephus who fortified the towns of Galilee in this period.

61. 29.1.3–5.3, considering this term either to be based on David's father Jesse or Jesus himself. For Jesus' name as 'Oshea' or 'Hosea', see *Dial.* 113–16 and *EH* 1.2.2–3.4.

62. 1QH 9.24–36 (including allusions to 'Crown of Glory', 'Holy Spirit', and Divine Sonship) and 15.18–22 (including allusion to 'the *Zaddik*' and 'all the Glory of Adam'), but *per contra*, 4.29–32 (including allusions to 'Enosh' [Man], 'Son of Man' [Adam], and 'Power'). On consecration from the womb, see Isa. 49:1–5 and Jer. 1:5.

63. See, for instance, Ezek. 44:17–31's 'Sons of Zadok', wearing 'only linen', not 'shaving their heads', 'nor drinking wine' when serving in the Inner Court of the Temple – *nor eating carrion*. Ezek. 44:23 on 'teaching the difference between Holy and profane, clean and unclean' is also reproduced word for word in CD 6.17–18 on 'the New Covenant in the Land of Damascus' and James' 'Royal Law according to the Scripture'. Priests in the Temple also wore no sandals, which Epiphanius predicates of James as well. Epiphanius evokes the Samson story when speaking of both James' and *Peter's* Naziritism (29.5.7 and 30.15.2 – this referring to Clement's 'Travels of Peter' or the Pseudo-clementine *Homilies*, which also portrays Peter as a vegetarian and daily bather!). For Epiphanius, John the Baptist was a 'Nazirite' as well.

64. 29.6.1; for Hippolytus' 'Naassenes', see 5.1–3 and 10.5.

65. Luke 4:34 also uses 'Nazarene', but elsewhere and in Acts (2:22, 3:6, 4:10, etc.), 'Nazoraean'.

66. Num. 6:1–21, preceded by 'Suspected Adulteress', and *Nazir*.

67. This echoes 'eating and drinking' parodies in Gospel characterizations of John 'neither eating or drinking', while Jesus ('the Son of Man') 'came eating and drinking, a glutton and a wine-bibber' (Matt. 11:18–19 and Luke 7:33–4), further parodies in Paul's claim to 'eat and drink' and cursing his enemies as 'eating and drinking Judgement' to themselves (1 Cor. 8:7–10:31 and Cor. 11:20–29). On the

other hand, as we saw, large numbers vowed 'not to eat meat or drink wine' after the fall of the Temple, i.e., they became 'Jamesian' (*B.B.* 60b).

68. 1QS 8.13–14 and 9.9–24.

69. Cenchrea is the port on the Aegaean or Asiatic side of the Isthmus of Corinth, but there is real confusion as to Paul's chronology and itinerary here – the shaving probably representing another or later trip to Jerusalem he took.

70. Koran 2.173, 5.3, 6.146, and 16.115.

71. 1QS 9.19–20, referring to the 'Perfect Holiness' regime, 'walking Perfectly', and again hinting at James' 'Royal Law according to the Scripture', 'each with his neighbour'. At this point, Isa. 40:3 is evoked – quoted previously in its totality in 8.12–15. There 'the Way' was specifically defined as 'the study of the *Torah*'.

72. For Ps. *Rec.* 1.54, which dates the sects from the coming of John the Baptist, it is 'the Sadducees' who are described as having 'separated themselves', but these can hardly be the 'Sadducees' of more popular New Testament portraiture.

73. CD 4.4. This is the sense of Ezek. 37:10, Dan. 12:13, further expanded in *Lam. R.* 11.3.6, and *Zohar* 1.63a on Noah.

74. CD 5.7–11, 6.17–7.5, and 8.24–5.

75. Even more germane is the 'command' in 1QS 8.13–14 (interpreting Isa.40:3) to 'separate from the midst of the habitation of the Men of Unrighteousness to go into the wilderness "to prepare the Way of the Lord", as it is written: "Prepare in the wilderness the Way of the Lord. Make straight in the desert a Pathway for our God."'

76. 7.4–5 and 8.25. This is 'walking in Perfection' in 1QS 9.19 above.

77. 1QH 9.29–36 and 15.14–20.

78. For Gentile gifts, 'things sacrificed to idols', and 'pollution of the Temple', see 1.2–32; for 'fornication', 1.83–9; and evocation of Abraham's 'Justification', 1.2 and 2.33.

79. This is the same language used by the Emperor Claudius in his famous letter warning the Jews of Alexandria against receiving such itinerant 'disease-carriers', H. Idris Bell, *Jews and Christians in Egypt*, loc. cit., pp. 25ff.

80. 29.7.7, 30.2.7, and 18.1. For Epiphanius, Cochaba is in the Bashan. Even today, there is a village in Southern Lebanon called Kaukaba (i.e., Cochaba) and Eusebius records a tradition, via Julius Africanus (*c.* 170–245), that the *Desposyni* – the family and descendants of Jesus – came from 'the Jewish villages of Nazara and Cochaba' (*EH* 1.7.14).

81. See oaths to secrecy in *Homilies*' Epistle of Peter to James, 4.1, 1QS 9.17, and Josephus' 'Essenes', *War*, 2.141–2.

82. The usage is widespread in 1QH 6.15, 7.19, and 8.6–10 and based on the imagery in Isa. 11:1–4 and 60.21. It is paralleled by that of 'the Righteous Branch' in Jer. 23:5, 33:15, Zech. 3:8, and 6:12 and parodied by Paul in Rom. 11:16–24. Also see *DSSU*, pp. 24–9.

83. This 'life' and 'living' symbolism, strong in Paul, is strong in the documents at Qumran, as, for instance, CD 7:5–6, quoting Deut. 7:9, on keeping the Covenant. Here Paul is also playing on Hab. 2:4, 'the Righteous shall live by his Faith'.

84. Note Ebionite Pseudoclementine ideology here based on Deut. 18:15–19, which both Mani and Muhammad seem to have inherited.

85. The 'Imam' parallels Jewish Christian 'Standing One' ideologies and, of course, incarnationist 'Christ' conceptualities tied to it. The present leader of Syria is an Alawi or Nusayri and, as it turns out, many members of the army as well. What this tells us about 'Christian' history in Syria, i.e., 'the Land of Damascus', where so many of these sectarians groups emigrated, is difficult to say – only that echoes still persist.

86. 'Judas Sepphoraeus' was allegedly executed by Herod in 4 BC in the 'Temple Eagle' incident (*War* 1.648–55/*Ant.* 17.149–57), whereas Judas the Galilean broke into the armoury at Sepphoris at the start of the Tax Uprising in 6–7 CE (*War* 2.56).

87. *EH* 4.22.7. Josephus is always referring to 'Galileans' as, for instance, concerning conflicts with Samaritans around Lydda (*Ant.* 20.118–24) or the eradication of Jesus son of Sapphias around the 'Gennesaret'; see *Vita* 66, 102–3, and 197–206.

88. Except for Julius Africanus' reference to 'Nazara', there are no classical references to 'Nazareth' in Hebrew, the first incidence of which comes in the seventh-century liturgical poems of Eleazar Kallir of Caesarea, recapitulating material from a fourth-century inscription there. The first churches in Nazareth seem to be a product of the fifth century.

89. See *War* 2.56/*Ant.* 17.261 above.

90. *EH* 1.7.14, a word based on the same root as the English 'despot', meaning, 'Leaders'.

91. 30.2.7, and 30.18.1, that is, in the Bashan north of the Decapolis above. In Matthew, Jesus leaves 'Galilee' at this point. For Epiphanius, the whole area follows 'Ebion' or is 'Ebionite'.

92. Chozeba seems to have been a town in the Jericho area and is now the site of one of the most famous and earliest Christian monasteries, 'St George's' or 'Wadi Kelt' (1 Chr. 4:22–3 – already referred to with regard to 'Rechabites' above), whose inhabitants were 'Potters' dwelling in 'the King's plantations'. Bar Kochba signs his correspondence as 'Shim'on Ben Choseba' in this manner,

parodied in Talmudic literature as 'Bar Choziba'/'Son of the Liar'; see *Lam. R.* 11.4, where R. Akiba applies the Star Prophecy to him, which is mocked by the other Rabbis, and *j. Ta'an.* 68d, *b. San.* 97b, etc.

93. 1QM 11.6–17, CD 7.18–8.5, and 4QTest 9–13, preceded in 5–8 by Deut. 18:18–19 – 'the True Prophet'.

94. Note the important reference to 'Peoples' again. The *'Shiloh'* Prophecy' is to be found at Qumran (*DSSU*, pp. 83, 89) interpreted in terms of a singular 'Messiah of Righteousness, the Branch of David' and 'the Covenant of the Kingdom', 'the Staff' or 'Mehokkek'. This 'Mehokkek' is then further delineated in CD 6.3–11 on the basis of another prophecy from Num. 21:18 (which leads up to 'the Star Prophecy' in 24:16–17) in terms of 'the well', which 'the Penitents of Israel – who went out from the Land of Judah to sojourn in the Land of Damascus' – dug with the 'staves' ('the Laws'), which 'the Staff' ('the Interpreter of the *Torah*') decreed.

95. *B. San.* 105a–106b. Note Balaam pointing at the Star in two murals from the catacombs in Rome in picture sections. Much fun will be had with this name in word-play in this period and its relationship to terms such as the archetypical adversary 'Belial' – in Paul, the defective 'Beliar'. The 'eating' terminology, too, is strong at Qumran; cf., for instance, in 1QpHab 6.7 (interpreting Hab. 1:16–17), where the *Kittim* (here, *the Romans* and using 'fisherman' and 'nets' symbolism), parcel out their taxes, 'eating all the Peoples year by year . . . and have no pity even on the fruit of the womb'.

96. Or, at least, another of its archetypical 'Enemies', Gehazi. He too is referred to (along with Jannes and Jambres) in CD 8.20–21. 'Balaam' has more the character of Herod or Herodians generally; see R. T. Herford, *Christianity in Talmud and Midrash*, London, 1903, pp. 69–71, 99–109, and *JJHP*, pp. 90–94.

97. 1QM 11.7. Here the problem is always singular vs. plural Messiah(s). In this instance, the translation may be plural (though the 'no mere Adam' which follows is not), but elsewhere, as in 1QS 9.11 (where it is coupled with the Ebionite 'True Prophet' ideology), it is definitely singular. One decides it by surrounding adjectival and verbal allusions as the construct usage, '*Meshihei*', is idiomatic. In the Damascus Document, the corresponding expression ('the Messiah of' or 'from Aaron and Israel') is *always* singular.

98. Cf. our *Shiloh* analysis above. This '*Yoreh ha-Zedek*' parallels the '*Moreh ha-Zedek*' (Teacher of Righteousness) and the '*Mashiah ha-Zedek*' (Messiah of Righteousness – definitely Davidic and singular). 'Standing',

of course, can be 'arises' or 'be resurrected'.

99. 1QpHab 10.9–12 and CD 1.14–18.

100. See *Lam. R.* 11.4 above.

101. *War* 6.310–15.

102. CD 4.19–29 and 8.12–13 – the reference is to Ezek. 13:6–23 and Micah 2:6–11 on 'Lying' prophets 'crying peace when there is no peace'.

103. 2 Cor. 3:1–4:18 and 10:4–12:11.

Chapter 11

1. This turns out to be the subject of the first section of *'MMT'*,where Gentile gifts and sacrifices in the Temple are all considered 'things sacrificed to idols'; 4QMMT 1.9–10. Also note the language of 'idols', 'idolatry', and 'idol temples' generally in 1 Cor. 5:10–10:33.

2. Also see Rom. 11:9–11, quoting Ps 69: 22–23 about one's 'table being a snare, a trap, and a stumbling block and their reward', since 'Salvation is granted to the Peoples'; 1 Tim. 3:7, evoking 'the snare of the Devil' (*Diabolos*, i.e., 'Belial') amidst allusion to 'old wives' tales', 'blasphemy', 'Lying', 'being two-tongued', and who should be 'Bishop'; and 2 Tim. 2:26 again amidst reference to 'the Last Days', 'being Perfect in works', 'blasphemy', being 'puffed up', 'loving God', and the Damascus Document's tell-tale 'Jannes and Jambres'.

3. 1QpHab 10.9–12. For 'building' imagery in Paul, see 1 Cor. 3:9–14, referring to 'God's building' (cf. 1QS 2.22–23, 5.6, 8.8, etc.), 'laying the Foundations' (cf. 1QS 1.12–3.1, 8.7–10, 9.3–4, 1QM 1.16, 1QH 3.31, 17.13, etc.), and being the 'architect'; 8:1 about 'things sacrificed to idols', 'loving God, and playing on being 'puffed up' (cf. 1QpHab 7.14–16 on Hab. 2:4); 2 Cor. 5:1, Rom. 15:20 (again alluding to 'Foundations'), Gal. 2:18, and Eph. 2:20–22.

4. This is the same problem as in the characterization of John as 'not eating bread or drinking wine' (Luke 7:33). What is meant is 'meat' and that John was a vegetarian too!

5. Notice how Paul presents here what is, essentially, the basic formulation of Islam, *'lā ilāha illā Allah'*.

6. See 1QpHab 7.14–16 above, leading into the key exegesis on 'the Righteous shall live by his Faith'.

7. CD 6.17–7.7, evoking Ezek. 44:23 above. Here, not only is James' 'Royal Law according to the Scripture', 'to love each man his brother as himself', evoked; but also, 'strengthening the hand of the Meek, the Poor, and the Convert' and 'abstaining [expressed as *'lehazzir'*, based on the same Hebrew root, *N–Z–R*, as Nazirite] from

fornication', 'according to the Covenant of God ['the New Covenant in the Land of Damascus'] Faithfully promising them [those 'loving' God and 'keeping' the Commandments] that they would live for a thousand generations' (Deut. 7:9).

8. CD 8.42–3 also uses 'fear of God' language at this point.

9. 1.1–2. One should note this language of 'works', whether God's or man's, throughout the Qumran corpus.

10. See R. Eisler, *The Messiah Jesus and John the Baptist*, New York, 1931, pp. 236 and 614–15 points up confusions between the Hebrew/Aramaic word for 'locusts' and 'carobs'. Though Qumran permits eating locusts, they were to be boiled alive and not eaten raw (cf. CD 12.15 with Lev. 11:21–22 – nor should one eat the larvae of bees; Lev. 12:12). Nevertheless they were considered pests (Joel 1:7–2:15 and Nahum 3:17). In any event, there may be a parody here, as they only appeared in the region between April and June.

11. 30.13.4–5. He complains that they substitute 'honey cakes', which had 'the taste of manna', for 'locusts'. Originally, anyhow, though bees' honey was not strictly speaking forbidden, the 'honey' of Israel seems to have been a syrup made from either dates, carobs, or grapes, and, according to Exod. 16:31, 'manna' had the taste of 'cakes made with honey'.

12. In 1:35 and 2:23, Luke applies the same 'Holy from the womb' language to Jesus – more overlaps between traditions about Jesus and James. John 1:20–21 perhaps has it right when he pictures John the Baptist as denying being both the 'Christ' (essentially a translation into Greek of the incarnated 'Adam' ideology) and the Ebionite 'True Prophet' – but then, of course, the Synoptics portray John as the incarnated Elijah, which, according to John 1:21–5, he denies as well.

13. These were placed around the two Inner Courts of the Temple in both Hebrew and Greek, and read, 'Let no foreigner pass the railing and enter the platform around the Temple. Whoever is caught will have himself to blame for his ensuing death' or 'the responsibility for his ensuing death will be upon him'. Compare this with Matt. 27:25's picture of the cry of the Jewish crowd over Jesus' sentence to death: 'His blood (be) upon us and our children' (see Plate No. 40).

14. 6.11–15. This is the section about 'keeping away from fornication' and 'not defiling one's Holy Spirit,' but rather 'walking in Perfect Holiness' and strengthening 'the Poor' (6.21–7.5).

15. 1 Macc. 1:10–57 and 2 Macc. 6:1–9.

16. 1QM 7.3–6. As we showed in *DSSU*, pp. 269–73, these 'camps' are real and are

reflected in 4QMMT 1.35–6 and 66–70 above. One should also note the emphasis on 'volunteers' as in 1QS 5.1–6.13 and CD 6.3–9.

17. Last Column of CD 1–15. Cf. 'camps' in 17–19.

18. Ben Sira 52:9. The praise is for 'Simeon the *Zaddik*', another 'Righteous' precursor and High Priest in the Temple just preceding Judas Maccabee.

19. ARN 2.45 (referring to Gen. 6:9), though so too, it appears, were Adam, Joseph, Moses, and even 'the wicked Balaam'.

20. See Acts 3:14, 7:52, and 22:14.

21. CD 2.9–24.

22. Vermes turns the reference to a singular 'Messiah' here into a plural and omits the clause following it completely. Why?

23. 1QS 8.3–11. They also 'pay the Wicked their Reward'.

24. CD 2.11–13, 4.4–5, and see, in particular, 14.4.

25. Koran 2:31, and there are didactic passages, particularly in this *Surah* 2 of the Koran, that also parallel these exhortative ones in the Damascus Document.

26. See also Acts 4:7–5:41, 9:14–10:48, etc. and Ps. *Hom.* 3.21–39 on Adam as 'the True Prophet'.

27. Ben Sira 45:24. Cf. 50:24, *Zohar* 1.59b on Noah, and 1QM 12.3.

28. 4.218a–b on 'Phineas'.

29. This is paralleled word for word in the Community Rule 8.9 and 9.4–5.

30. *B. San.* 56a–60a.

31. CD 3.10 – note again the emphasis on 'doing'.

32. 4QpNah 2.1–2 and 1QpHab 10.9–12, including 'erecting an Assembly ['Church'] upon Lying for the sake of his Glory, tiring out Many with a Worthless Service, instructing them in works of Lying, so that their works would be of Emptiness'; cf. Jas. 2:20 on the 'Empty Man'.

33. CD 3.1–11 (including 'were cut off' and 'delivered up to the sword'); cf. also CD 2.8.

34. 15:20, 15:29, and 21:25.

35. Rom. 4:3, 4:22, and Gal. 3:3, but *per contra*, see Jas. 2:14–26 and 4QMMT 1.2 and 2.30–33.

36. The Damascus Document acutally uses the Hebrew, 'Beloved', in CD 3.2. Compare with Jas. 2:23 above and note how Paul uses this 'Beloved' terminology throughout his letters.

37. Ps. *Rec.* 1.70–71. There is also the telling use of it in the Parable of the Tares in Matt. 13:23–43 above.

38. It is interesting that here, too, Paul uses the 'casting out' language: 'cast out the slave woman and her son' (*ekbale*), not 'the one born according to the Promise to the free woman, which things are allegorized' (Gal. 4:24–31).

39. Cf. 2 Cor. 11:10–12:11.

40. 4QMMT 1.2 and 2.26–33 (note here, too, the tell-tale reference to 'fearing the *Torah*' as in 'fearing God' or 'God-Fearer').

41. 2 Cor. 6:14–18.

42. For example, CD 7.3–5, 1QH 9.29–30 above, and the use of 'Light' v. 'Dark' imagery throughout the Community Rule. The context of Paul's use of the phrase, 'be separated', in Isa. 52 would make an interesting *Pesher* of the Qumran kind. In 52:11 – as in the First Letter on Works Righteousness above – 'the vessels of the Lord' are referred to, culminating in the presentation of the 'suffering *Zaddik*' and 'Justification' in 53:11, the same 'justifying' activity predicated of 'the Sons of Zadok' (leading up to evocation of the 'Three Nets of Belial') in CD 4.7–15.

43. 2.412–14. Here Josephus uses the term '*Ethnōn*' as in Paul and 'the First' as at Qumran, claiming such an 'innovation into their religion' would lay the Jews open to 'the charge of Impiety', i.e., being the only people in the world, 'forbidding foreigners the right to sacrifice or worship . . . excluding even the Romans and Caesar', which could bring about similar retaliation. It did – nineteen centuries' worth.

44. 2.409–10.

45. See also Rom. 1:16, 10:12, and Col. 3:11.

46. In 1 Cor. 15:54 he even seems to be playing on (and reversing) the Qumran language of 'swallowing' – also implying death – in asserting his famous 'death was swallowed up in Victory' (itself parodying Hos. 13:14); and in Gal. 2:16–19, preceding 2:20, he revels in the word-play involved in 'dying to the Law to live to God' – asserting that, being a 'Breaker' himself and using both the language of 'throwing down' and 'building' again: 'no flesh [again, 'flesh' here implying circumcision] shall be *justified by works not the Law*', concluding 'for if Righteousness is through the Law, then Christ died for nothing'. But this, of course, is the exact opposite of 4QMMT 2.30–33 and Jas. 2:21 and 2:24 above.

47. *Ant.* 19.332–4.

48. *Ant.* 20.145.

49. One should note the 'eating and drinking' theme here again. This is expressed in the Gospels as the Son of Man – as opposed to John the Baptist and others like James – 'came eating and drinking' (Matt. 11:19 and Luke 7:34). Paul, too, labours over the theme, most notably when discussing Jesus' body and blood at 'the Last Supper' – where, it will be recalled, according to the Synoptics, Jesus vows never to 'drink wine again' until he drinks it 'new in the Kingdom'. Paul rather concludes on the note of his antagonists' 'eating and drinking Judgement to themselves'

(1 Cor. 11:29), having already asserted earlier (this regarding James' ban on 'food sacrificed to idols'), 'neither if we eat do we have an advantage, nor if we do not eat do we fall short' (1 Cor. 8:8). This is not to mention those of a 'Jamesian' frame of mind, condemned by the *Talmud*, who vow 'not to eat or drink' until they see the Temple restored (*B.B.* 60b above) and, as we shall see, James himself, in the Gospel of the Hebrews, who vows not to eat or drink until he should see Jesus 'risen from among those that sleep'.

50. Acts 23:17–32. We shall meet another such Captain commanding the Citadel, eight years later in Josephus below.

51. According to Josephus (*Ant.* 20.219–23), it was finished under Agrippa II in approximately 64 CE, though in *Ant.* 15.380–425, he states that Herod began the work in 23–22 BC (*War* 1.401 rather says in 26–25 BC) and finished it eight years later (the Temple itself being completed in a year and a half).

52. *Ant.* 20.189–200.

53. In Rev. 2:10, preceding this, it is reversed (as in the tares 'being cast into a furnace of Fire' in Matthew) into 'the *Diabolos casting some of you into prison*' (also *balein*), but it is clear that the New Testament knows that the meaning of '*Diabolos*' in Greek is based on this same 'casting' usage.

54. CD 4.15–16

55. Even in the Temple Scroll 47.13–14, the formulation, 'with skins sacrificed to idols' (*be'orot*), immediately following upon the material banning polluted individuals from the Temple, alluding to both *balla'* or Bela' and 'latrines' (46.10–18 – 'Bela'' like Balaam being the son of 'Be'or') appears to be playing in some manner on this language complex. Balak, it will be recalled, was King of Moab (Num. 22:7–24:25, ending in 'the Star Prophecy').

56. 2.427–8.

57. Not only is Rom. 13:3–7, on paying taxes to Rome, permeated with this language of 'fearing' (though now, repeatedly, it is 'fear' of the Roman Authorities) and 2 Cor. 7:1 on 'Perfecting Holiness'; but, most incongruous of all, so is Acts 10:2 and 10:22, describing the 'Pious' Roman Centurion Cornelius, 'known by the whole nation of the Jews as *doing* many compassionate works'. We can understand who wrote these documents on the basis of this statement alone. 'Cornelius' here might even incorporate a play on the Roman *Lex Cornelia de Sicarius et Veneficis*, named after the Roman magistrate forbidding bodily mutilation and sorcery – '*Sicarius*', in this context, referring to 'circumciser' not 'assassin'.

58. *Ant.* 20.216–18.

59. Note the Qumran term for the rank and file of

the Community is 'the Many' (*Rabbim*).

60. Here, too, a refraction of 'the Ten Just Men' or '*Zaddikim*' necessary to uphold the world, not to mention possible play on the 'Sons of Zadok' notation. In later usage, playing off the numerical value of '*lo*' in Hab. 2:3's 'wait *for him*', this becomes 'thirty-six'.

61. Koran 2.110, 2.139, 3.22, 3.115, 82.5, 84.6, etc. They are of the Righteous' (3.114). Nothing could better epitomize the Jamesian insistence on Abraham being saved by 'Faith and works working together' than this.

62. Koran 2.130–40, 3.67, etc. Here, Muhammad is using 'Muslim' ('he who surrenders to God's will') the way Jas. 2:23 is using 'Friend of God'.

63. They are also known among the Mandaeans even today ('the *Subba* of the Marshes', i.e., the Elchasaites or 'Sabaeans'), and to some extent, the Manichaean *Siddiqs* (*Fihrist* 9.1) – groups, among whom Muhammad appears to have spent time in his commercial travels into Southern Iraq.

64. The terminology 'Jew' is known at Qumran (4Q550 6.3 and 4Q324 *Mishmarot*), as is its more elegant synonym, 'House of Judah'. Though Paul implies as much Gal. 2.13–14 (notwithstanding that his testimony here sounds more that of *the convert*), only Acts unequivocally asserts it in 21.39 and 22.3.

65. See the Herodian family genealogy (pp. 968–9).

66. Looking at this episode in the context of the '*Lex Cornelia de Sicarius et Veneficis*', one must consider there is a touch of parody in it which bears on the mix-up between the quasi-anagrams 'Christian' and '*Iscariot*'. During and after the Bar Kochba War (132–36), the legislation enabling forcible confiscation of land and property seems to have been known as the '*Ius Sicaricon*' and, most particularly, included those defying Hadrian's decree forbidding circumcision – '*Sicarii*' now clearly considered to signify the party forcibly circumcising others. But this is exactly how Hippolytus describes the fourth and most extreme group of 'Essenes', whom he too calls '*Sicarii*' (9.21) in the portions missing from Josephus' descriptions and probably something of the real import of the term, '*Sicarius*'. Origen too (*c.* 185–254 – who, as we saw, seems to have mutilated or perhaps even circumcised himself) described the '*Sicarii*' of his own time 'as mutilating themselves contrary to the established laws and customs permitted the Jews alone'. As he describes it in *Contra Celsus* above (2.13 – the very section he provides the missing testimony from Josephus' *Jewish War* about Jerusalem falling *because of the death of James not Jesus*), such persons 'are put to death . . . the evidence of circumcision being sufficient to

ensure the death of him who had undergone it'. No wonder the New Testament is worried over the issue. From this perspective, those among 'Essenes' or so-called 'Zealots' dubbed 'Sicarii' has as much to do with demanding 'circumcision' (therefore, their 'curved knives'), as assassination. In fact, Paul is already showing his concern over such issues, calling James' followers, 'of the circumcision' (Rom. 4:9–12 and Gal. 2:7–12; cf. Col. 4:11). The issue is probably also central to Peter–Simon *Magus* confrontations in other milieux.

67. At Qumran, the terminology 'Simple Ones' also exists, but as ever with differing literary effect. There, not only are they described as 'doing the *Torah*', but they are basically the followers of the Righteous Teacher, identical with 'the Poor' and associated too with 'blood' – now *their blood*; 1QpHab 12.3–6. See also 4QpNah 1.6 and 3.3–5 (itself associated with 'City of Blood').

68. CD 8.42–44 and 11QT 46.11. The play in the latter on 'seeing the Temple' in 46.15 (homonyms in Hebrew) might be intentional.

69. CD 6.12–7.5, rife with the language of *N–Z–R*/'separation' or 'keeping away from' – the basis of Acts' picture of James' directives to overseas communities in Acts as well – and 'the New Covenant in the Land of Damascus'.

70. *EH* 2,23,4–5; *Haeres.* 78.14.1–2. The abstention from sexual activity, that Epiphanius adds, itself relates not to abstaining from bathing, but taking cold baths alluded to in our various traditions.

71. It should be noted that in Ezek. 44:20 on 'Sons of Zadok' in the Temple, this has to do with 'polling', which still involves 'a razor not touching one's head', but instead rather pulling the hair by hand. Nevertheless, 'the *Nezer*', normally thought of as the 'mitre' (headdress) or 'Crown' worn by the High Priest and bearing the plate with the motto 'Holy to God,' as we have seen, bears the secondary meaning of the unshorn hair or the Nazirites' 'Crown' – nor should one in this regard forget the name 'Stephenos' or the 'martyr's Crown' in Greek.

72. 78.14.5–6, deleted from *EH* 23 2.16–17. Important for the overlap between the stoning of Stephen and the stoning of James, the role of the witness – played in the latter by 'one of the Priests of the sons of Rechab, the Rechabim' – is played in Acts 7:58 by the angry and violent Saul in his days as 'Enemy' of the early Christian Community – 'zealous' above all others in persecuting it.

73. 'Rahab the Harlot' is often confused with this name 'Rechab' as well. Matt. 1:15, anyhow, considers Rahab not only a progenitor of David, but Jesus as well (for Matthew, Rahab is the mother of Boaz, but he spells 'Rachab'

like Rechab not 'Rahab'). For its part, Jas. 2:25 cites – along with Abraham's willingness to sacrifice his son Isaac – 'Rahab the harlot' as being 'justified by works', countering 'the Enemy' Paul's contention that 'Abraham was justified by Faith' (Rom. 4:3–5:1). In turn, James is countered in Heb. 11:17–31 on the importance of both Rahab's and Abraham's 'Faith'.

74. 1QS 5.9–11. Once again, the concept of 'separation' is attached to this definition as well. These are considered 'Men of Holiness' (5.13) and 'a Holy Assembly' (5.20), 'a Community of *Torah*' (5.2), and 'all the Glory of Adam will be theirs' (4.23).

75. 1QpHab 7.10–8.3.

76. Note, too, in Jas. 1:12 (together with allusion to 'the Crown of Life'), 2:5, and 2:13, the emphasis on 'doing Piety' and see CD 6.18–7.19 generally.

77. S. Goranson, 'Essenes': Etymology from '*Asah*' in *Revue de Qumran*, 1984, pp. 483–98. As he points out, Epiphanius actually calls these 'Ossaeans' or 'Ossenes'.

78. 29.1.3–5.5.

79. See Micah 5:2, Ruth 1:2, etc.

80. Judg. 1:16, 4:11, 1 Sam. 27:10, and 30:29. Note even the reference to Kenites in Balaam's Prophecy in Num. 24:21–2 above. 1 Chr. 2:25 literally states, the Kenites were 'the ancestors of the House of Rechab'. This is picked up in *San.* 104a–106a and *Sota* 11a, which makes the same connection, while at the same time insisting 'they were privileged to sit in the Chamber of Hewn Stone' in the Temple – seemingly as scribes.

81. Notice in 1 Chr. 4:21, the Potter clans among the Tribe of Judah are associated with the linen-makers – for whatever it's worth.

82. In Matt. 13:55 Jesus is 'the son of the carpenter'; in Mark 6:3, he is 'the carpenter the son of Mary' – which already shows substantial emendation. Therefore, also in the Gospels – including 'carpentry' in these 'tinker' trades – *Yozer*/'Potter' moves directly into '*Nozer*', Hebrew for Christian. This tangle is interesting, but one from which we shall probably not succeed in finding an exit.

83. See *Yalqut Shim'oni* on Jer. 35:12, *Siphre Num.* 78 on Num. 10:29, and *B.B.* 91b on 'Potters' above. Also see Eisler, pp. 234–45, for a full presentation of 'the *Saleb*'.

84. Benjamin of Tudela, *Travels*.

Chapter 12

1. 2.23.5–6.

2. 29.4.1–3 and 78.13.5–8.

3. 29.2.5–4.2. Psalm 110 is a very important one. It also includes the apocalyptic imagery of 'sitting at My right hand', the 'Sceptre', 'Strength', 'Power', and 'Wrath' we shall

repeatedly encounter (110:1–5). Needless to say, too, it is unabashedly Zionist. In this section from Epiphanius, which is often quite prescient, note the persistent 'Crown', mitre, and unshorn locks of the Nazirite imagery, all to similar effect.

4. 78,14.2–6. Epiphanius presents the cry of Simeon bar Cleophas with regard to the stoning as, 'Stop. Why are you stoning the Just One? See, he is uttering marvellous prayers for you'; in Eusebius this is simply, 'the Just One is praying for you' – in both the 'Just One' is used in place of James' name itself.

5. It is also interesting that Eusebius (3.31.3) presents the same information relating to John 'the Disciple Jesus loved' just preceding his description of Simeon bar Cleophas' death, quoting a letter from Polycrates (c.190 CE) to the effect that John, 'a martyr and a teacher, was a Priest who wore the mitre'. Again, these overlapping notices are interesting, especially since, for Epiphanius, it is rather James who is 'the Disciple Jesus loved'. Whatever the case, the plays on the 'Beloved' or 'Friend' theme should, once again, be remarked.

6. 11.2–8. Here, not only is the language of 'swallowing' used, but also that of 'the Poor' and 'causing them to stumble' or 'casting them down'.

7. Ant. 20.216–18. Note the opposite note of 'Law-breaking' in Jas. 2:9–11, 1QpHab 2:6, 8.16–17, and CD 1.20.

8. Ant. 20.160–61 and War 2.253. One should note here that the word 'Lēstēs' for 'Brigand' is the same as that of 'thief' in Matt. 27:38 and pars.

9. War 2.58–9.

10. War 2.264–6. At Qumran, we hear rather how the Rich Priests and their 'Violent' associates 'plunder the Poor' (1QpHab 8.11–9.6 and 12.7–10), the exact reversal of this. The antagonism towards 'Riches' there is patent, as it is in the Letter of James.

11. Ant. 20.173–8 and War 2.266–70.

12. CD 1.17–2.1. The only difference between this and early Christian theology – where, instead, it is Judas 'the Iscariot' who 'delivers up' Jesus – is that, whereas this is directed against one party of Jewish backsliders and collaborators in a situation of Jewish internecine and sectarian strife, there it is directed against the whole Jewish people by Hellenizing foreigners.

13. War 2.454–5. This situation of forced circumcision, as we have noted – later barred in Rome, a point vividly illustrated in attitudes expressed in the New Testament – is a characteristic of what both Hippolytus and Origen are calling 'Sicarii'. Note that according to Josephus, the two characters he is calling 'Saulus' and 'Philip' had been besieged at this time in Agrippa II's palace (War 2.556 and

Vita 46–61). This language of 'Judgement' and 'Visitation' is strong throughout the Dead Sea Scrolls; cf. CD 1.6–7, 2.6, 5.15–16, 7.9–8.3, 13.11 and 24, but also see Paul on 'drinking the Cup' improperly, thereby 'eating and drinking Judgement to oneself' (1 Cor. 11:28–29).

14. EH 3.3.5, the description of which continues to 3.8.2.

15. Ant. 20.180.

16. Ant. 20.181. Josephus repeats the same testimony in 20.206–7 after the death of James. Note here the point about 'Righteousness being overwhelmed'. At this point, one can picture Josephus as one of these 'Poorer Priests' – unless they represent a class of 'Rechabite' types – therefore his outrage. There are, as we have seen above, echoes of these events in the Habakkuk and Psalm 37 Peshers, including even the usage, 'the Wicked encompasses the Righteous'.

17. See 1QpHab 8.11–9.6 and 12.7–10 above on 'stealing Riches'.

18. Vita 11–12.

19. Those at Qumran at some point left Judea for the wilderness of Damascus; CD 4.3 and 6.5. From 1QM 1.1–4, it is clear that all the 'exiled Sons of Light' are in 'the wilderness of the Peoples', which can extend (as we shall show) as far north to 'Arabs' in Edessa and the Lands 'of the Peoples beyond the Euphrates'. Even the reference to 'Benjamin' in this passage as 'the Exile of the Desert' has something of the sense Paul gives it with regard to his genealogy. For CD 7.14–21, quoting Amos 5:26–7 and 9:11, 'the Tabernacle of David' will be exiled 'to the Land of the North' or 'Damascus'. John, too, was mostly active 'across Jordan' (in Moab and Perea – Luke 3:3, John 10:40, etc.). In this sense, the War Scroll provides us with a perfect blueprint for a final war led by people like the 'Zealot' sons of Acts' 'Ethiopian Queen' (as we shall show, Queen Helen of Adiabene) and other 'Essene'/'Sabaean' types.

20. War 2.155 and Hippolytus 9.21, in the same section that he alludes to them as forcible circumcisers or 'Sicarii' and how they refuse to eat 'things sacrificed to an idol', instead preferring martyrdom!

21. EH 3.31.1–4 and 4.22.4–5. Epiphanius in 66.19.7–9 and 78.14.6 also calls him 'the son of Clopas'. For Epiphanius in 78.14.5, James too ('the firstborn of Joseph's sons') lived to be ninety-six.

22. 29.15.1–4. According to him, the reason the Ebionites give for this is that animal fare is the product of sexual intercourse! Cf. Ps. Hom. 8.15, 10.1, 11.1 and Ps. Rec. 4.3, 8.1, etc. In particular, this agrees with the picture of Peter in Ps. Hom. 12.6, averring that Peter was a daily bather and a vegetarian (eating only

'bread and olives' – compare this with 'certain priestly friends' of Josephus imprisoned in Rome who ate only 'figs and nuts'; *Vita* 13). This, in turn, goes on to assert that Peter possessed only *a single cloak*, which he wore until it became threadbare, which precisely accords with Hippolytus 19.15's and Josephus' picture of 'Essenes' (*War* 2.126–7).

23. 78.14.1. Eusebius also uses the word 'virgin' after presenting the details of Simeon bar Cleophas' crucifixion – applying it rather to the Church being until then 'a pure and uncorrupted virgin' (3.32.7).

24. 78.1.3.

25. The Gospels and other sources in trying to protect Mary's 'virginity' or 'chasteness' then inflate this to *five* sons. In fact, Epiphanius, whether through inadvertence or not, actually calls Mary's third son 'Simeon' (i.e., Simeon bar Cleophas) not 'Simon' (78.8.1), the second brother age-wise being 'Joses', whom we shall later propose as being equivalent to 'Jesus'.

26. 1QS 8.15–9.23. For baptism in general and of 'the Holy Spirit' in particular, see 3.3–5 and 6–11.

27. 1QM 7.3–7.

28. There is also an oblique, if reverse, parallel in Paul's 'eating and drinking Judgement to oneself' (1 Cor. 11:29 above), 'shedding' being a synonym for 'pouring' in more Paulinized scriptural formulations.

29. 78.14.1. Cf. *War* 2.147–8. We shall treat this subject further in Volume II. Interestingly too, after the stoning of Honi – whom Josephus also calls 'Friend of God' ('Theophilus') – he depicts God as sending a whirlwind to punish those responsible for it; *Ant.* 14.25–8.

30. *EH* 3.18.5. Also *Vita* 336–67 and 424–30 addressed to the 'most excellent Epaphroditus'. Suet. 12.15–17, and Dio Cassius 47.14.2 make it clear that Flavius Clemens, anyhow, was executed by Domitian in 96. For Eusebius, Domitilla, whose name is associated with an early Christian catacomb in Rome the entrance to which was on her property, was only his niece, but for these others, his wife. Two sons, Vespasian II and Domitian II had been designated to succeed Domitian. In turn, Domitian was assassinated the same year by Domitilla's steward Stephen.

31. 4.22.4.

32. *DSSU*, pp. 230–33. Also the 'Sons of Dawn' cryptic text, pp. 160–65, has a note of this.

33. See E. S. Drower, *The Mandaeans of Iraq and Iran*, Oxford, 1937, pp. 1–19 and 100–124 and *The Secret Adam*, Oxford, 1960, pp. IX–XVII and 88–106. According to Mandaean tradition, the followers of John fled eastward in 37 CE, the approximate year Josephus, too, claims his execution took place.

34. 30.21.2. For *Haeres.* 30.18.1, such 'Ebionite'

groups have their roots in Moab, and Cochaba in the Bashan – Nabataea too. This 'Cochaba' in the Bashan is probably not too different from 'Chozeba' in Wadi Kelt.

35. Apost. Const. 6.6. We have already seen how Westerners cannot pronounce names like 'Abgarus', reversing them into 'Agbarus'. This 'Basmothaeans' is probably not completely unrelated to another Western linguistic confusion centring around the Medieval Templars, who, when declared heretical, were accused of worshipping one 'Baphomet'.

36. These marshes are being destroyed by Saddam Hussein in the wake of the recent Gulf War. The *Fihrist* 9.1 claims that the 'Sabaeans' originally came from Abraham's Haran, which would also seem to be the implication of the Mandaean *Haran Gawaita*. Even today baptism is called '*masbuta*' among Mandaeans and the term 'Sabaean' can be thought of as referring to nothing other than the Syriac 'Immersers' or 'Daily Bathers'.

37. 'Protected Peoples' or '*Dhimmis*'; Koran 2.62, 5.69, and 22.17. In traditional Islam, they are mistaken for a Southern Arabian people ('Sheba' in the Hebrew Bible). But the problem is the spelling. The spelling for Southern Arabia is different in Arabic.

38. 53.1.1–7. Epiphanius 8.9.1 and 11 also knows an earlier group called 'the Sebuaeans', whom along with Essenes, he groups as sects of the Samaritans. Their main feature was to have changed the calendar – a prominent fixture of the Qumran texts. Though he knows that 'Essenes' as such no longer exist, it is clear to him that 'Ossaeans' have been absorbed into the 'Sampsaeans', whom he says are neither Jews or Christians (20.3.4). It should, therefore, be clear that 'Sampsaeans' are equivalent to what go by the name of 'Masbuthaeans' in Syriac/'Sabaeans' in Islam.

39. *Natural History* 5.81.

40. *Menippus* 6–9. For these morning prayers of the 'Essenes', see *War* 2.128–9 and the 'Sons of the Dawn' text above. For Peter's morning prayers before bathing, see Ps. *Hom.* 10.1, 11.1, etc.

41. *War* 2.129 and 138; see also Hippolytus 9.16.

42. 9.9 and 10.25. Note that the chronology puts Elchasai in the Third Year of Trajan, contemporary therefore with Simeon bar Cleophas, who was purportedly martyred in the Ninth–Tenth Year of Trajan (*EH* 3.32.3).

43. 30.17.5, 19.4.1 (here the doctrine is originally 'Ossaean'), 30.3.1–6, and Abstract 30.2 in that order. In the latter two, he attributes the doctrine to all such groups, including 'Sampsaeans, Ossaeans, and Elchasaites'.

44. Hippolytus 5.1–3 and 10.5 claims James communicated this doctrine to 'Mariemme' or 'Mariem' – 'one of the Priests' in Second Apocalypse of James 44.11–22, which claims

he wrote it down together with 'Theuda the brother of the Just One, his relative'. Origen in *Contra Celsus* 5.62 also knows this 'Mariemme'. In the Koran 2.33–7, 3.36–59, 19.34, etc., Adam, being Heavenly, is above the Angels and a son of God; and 'the likeness of Jesus with Allah is the likeness of Adam'. Therefore Jesus is the Second Man born without a father, though unlike Adam he had a human mother. Hence, Jesus for Muhammad is 'son of Mary', the only man born of woman without a human father.

45. Ps. *Rec.* 2.7–8 and 1.72. Here too Epiphanius 21.2.3 agrees, as do all our sources, that Simon *Magus* also claimed to be 'the Great Power of God' and his consort, the 'whore' Helen, the Holy Spirit. Interestingly enough, like the 'Simon'/'Atomus' involved with Felix and Drusilla in Josephus, he 'taught people to perform unnatural sex acts and the defilement of fornication with women'; and like Acts' picture of the death of *Judas Iscariot*, one day 'the wretch fell down and died right in the middle of Rome' (21.5.1).

46. See, for instance, the allusions to 'all the Glory of Adam being theirs' in CD 3.20 (referring to 'building a House of Faith' and 'standing'), 1QS 4.23 (referring to 'Perfection of the Way' and 'Holy Spirit baptism'), and the 'sword of no mere Adam' in 1QM 11.11 (in exegesis of the Star Prophecy) – not to mention allusions to 'standing' throughout the Dead Sea Scrolls. Cf. too 1QH 4.30–32, alluding to 'Perfection of the Way', '*Enosh*', and 'Power'.

47. 9.21. Cf. Josephus' picture of the tortures such 'Essenes' were willing to undergo, rather than 'eat some forbidden thing' or 'blaspheme the Law-giver' (*War* 2.152) and, likewise, the followers of Judas the Galilean, who 'will not call *any man* Lord' (*Ant.* 18.23–4). But see Paul using 'conscience' as an argument to eat all forbidden things (1 Cor. 10:25–33) and compare this too with Ps. *Hom.* 7.8 (even using Paul's 'table of demons' language), where Peter preaches against 'food sacrificed to idols'. In addition, this provides the clue to 'strangled things' in Acts' pictures of James' instructions to overseas communities, that is, 'to abstain from dead beasts, from *animals which have been suffocated or caught by wild beasts*, and from blood'!

48. Al-Biruni, *Chronology of Ancient Nations*, 8.10–23. Elsewhere he contends 'the real Sabaeans' were remnants of captive Jews, such as 'Samaritans, who were transferred from Babylonia to Syria'. For Benjamin of Tudela, there was still a Jewish 'Elchasaite' Synagogue in Mosul (ancient Adiabene), when he visited there in 1164 CE.

49. For 'Sabi', see *Chronology* 8.23, 18.10, and 20.29. For 'Enosh', see *Ginza* 29, Drower, *Mandaeans*, pp. 4–18, quoting the *Haran*

Gawaita, and cf. Dan. 7:13's '*Bar Enosh*' – also 1QH 4.31 above. Curiously enough, Epiphanius 55.3.4 too thinks Daniel's father was someone called 'Sabaa'.

50. *Chronology* 8.23. For him these are scattered throughout Iraq, following an ancient Western religion different from the indigenous one at Haran; 18.10.

51. See R. de Vaux, *Archaeology and the Dead Sea Scrolls*, Oxford, 1973, pp. 52 and 88. G. R. Driver, *The Judaean Scrolls*, Oxford, 1965, pp. 45–8, observes that Karaite Jews also observe the custom.

52. *Fihrist* 9.1.

53. Al-Biruni, 8.24.

54. Actually they continue to drink a kind of non-alcoholic grape juice to this day; Drower, *Secret Adam*, pp. 84–7.

55. 9.1.

56. Drower, *Mandaeans*, pp. 7, 258, and 261–2.

57. For Elijah's rainmaking see 1 Kings 18:1–45. For Phineas as rainmaker, see Ps. Philo 48.1. Epiphanius 55.3.5 also gives Elijah's genealogy, as a 'son of Zadok', through Phineas.

58. Cf. 9.16 with *War* 2.129, 132, and 161.

59. *Haeres.* 30.13.4. It is the Rechabite 'wild' adjective that allows one to see through to the real data behind the popular conceptions of John.

60. *Vita* 11–12, i.e., he was in the words Epiphanius uses to describe James, 'a life-long virgin'. The description of John in Matt. 3:4 and Mark 1:6 as 'wearing a camel's hair coat and a leather girdle about his loins' is based on the description of Elijah in 2 Kings 1:8, denied in any event in John 1:21–5, which like Luke abjures describing John's clothing.

61. *Ant.* 18.116–19; Eisler, p. 223, following the Slavonic, suggests Josephus originally had '*wild*' man, thereby reflecting the Judas Maccabean/*Banus* '*wild*' plants' theme.

62. 1QS 3.3–12 and 20–23 above.

63. For Titus' *real* fun at such birthday anniversaries as in the Gospels, see *War* 7.37–9.

64. *Ant.* 18.106–37. Aretas and Herod Antipas came to blows over a border dispute relating, it appears, to an area near Damascus (one manuscript has 'Gamala'). Ultimately Antipas and Herodias are banished to Lyon (18.252, though *War* 2.183 says Spain), where Irenaeus surfaces in the next century.

65. Cf. 1QS 6.7–8 with Koran 3.113, 73.1–20, etc. But 'Elchasaite' bathing – as in Manichaeism – goes by the board in Islam.

66. *Ant.* 18.117: '*baptismos*' and '*baptisis*'.

67. Ps. *Rec.* 1.71.

68. *War* 2.120 and Hippolytus 9.13.

69. Cf. *EH* 2.23.5–6 with *Haeres.* 78.13.3 and *War* 2.123.

70. Cf. Hippolytus 9.21 with *War* 2.152. N.b., Hippolytus' 'Essenes' also appoint 'overseers' (cf. 9.14 with Acts 20:28).

71. His first usage of the term, 'zeal for the Law', actually occurs in *War* 1.655 at time of the Temple Eagle incident; but the term 'Zealot' really emerges only in *War* 4.160–61 concerning the malcontents opposing Ananus; and in 4.302–10, those surreptitiously opening the gates of Jerusalem to the Idumaeans to slaughter Ananus and his confrères.

72. *War* 7.270–74. When speaking of the 'Galilean' faction of them, in particular, in *War* 4.558–64; he even parodies their hatred of 'the Rich', 'plunder', and 'insatiable lust' for 'blood', by picturing them carousing in brothels, dressing and painting their faces like women. For more on their insatiable 'blood' lust, see 6.272.

73. 9.21. *War* 2.150–51 quickly brushes by this point. Cf. Acts 10:24; also Epiphanius' story (30.24.1–6) about how John the Evangelist, when meeting '*Ebion*' in a bathhouse in Asia, flees (though here and in 78.13.4, he admits John *never entered* any bathhouses and followed the virgin/vegetarian lifestyle of James absolutely!).

74. *Ant.* 15.373 and *War* 2.139–42; cf. the oaths James requires in Ps. *Hom.* 4–5 of the Epistle of Peter to James and 1QS 2.2–4.8.

75. Matt. 5:43–6, 19:19, 22:37–9 and pars. Jesus moves further into the Platonic/Socratic (but thoroughly un-Palestinian), 'love your enemies'. Also see Justin Martyr on the two ways, *Dial.* 23, 47, and 93, and *Ant.* 18.117 on John's *real* doctrines.

76. 1QS 9.21–2 and CD 8.332–3 (also 1QS 2.11–27). *Per contra*, see Paul, 1 Cor. 8:4–9, 10:19–32, and variously.

77. The 'cursing' here reverses the language of cursing in 1QS 2.4–18, which Paul admits in Gal. 3:10–13 was applied to him. Note, too, the play on Jamesian language of 'doing' again.

78. *War* 2.151–3, Hippolytus 9.21, *EH* 3.32.6, and Epiphanius 78.14.5 above. All these notices about the retrospective longevity of 'Essenes' – in particular their willingness to undergo torture or imperviousness to pain (in Josephus, 'in our recent War with the Romans') – are immediately followed by descriptions of martyrdom, crucifixion, stoning, burning, or being racked or torn to pieces.

79. *War* 2.148–9 and Hippolytus 9.20. Like the Gospels' Jesus, Josephus – though not Hippolytus – condemns this. He even remarks (2.138) the shovel all postulants are given, like a modern-day military recruit.

80. This is 'the New Covenant [and 'the Faith'] in the Land of Damascus'; CD 6.19–7.6 and 8.35–6.

81. 1QH 4.20–25, 9.29–36, 16.21–2, and 18.13–14. Hymns is virtually a paean on the Salvation of the Holy or separated ones. The 'standing' language is strong in it, as it is throughout the Scrolls, the Gospels, and in Paul. For CD 4.3–4, for instance (as we saw), 'the Sons of Zadok' are those who 'will stand in the Last Days'. In this passage in 1QH 9 9, which speaks of 'justifying God's Judgement', 'a Crown of Glory', and 'the Rock and Fortress of my Strength', there is total adoptionist sonship and 1QH 7.20 speaks of God being a 'Father to the Sons of *Hesed*'. In fact, this language of 'loving *Hesed*'/'Lovingkindness' is strong throughout the Scrolls, e.g., 1QS 2.24, 5.4, and 5.25. In this last (5.1–2), 'the Sons of Zadok' are those under whose Authority one 'volunteers' to be after 'separating from the Assembly ['Church'] of the Men of Unrighteousness'.

82. In it, one should also note the repeated condemnation of the 'Liar' and the final admonition, 'Little children, keep yourself from idols. Amen' (5:23). For this 'loving God,' too, see 1 Cor. 2:9, 8:3 above, 2 Thess. 3:5, and Rom. 8:28–39, employing CD 4's language of 'Foreknowledge', 'separation', and 'Justification'.

83. 1QS 5.20–23. Note too the 'Man' v. 'Son of Man' dichotomy.

84. No mention of Hegesippus – *Haeres.* 29.4.1.

85. M. *Mid.* 1:4, 5:3, *Par.* 3:7, b. *Tam.* 26b, and j. *Yoma* 40b; also *Ant.* 12.145 and *War* 4.205.

86. B. *Yoma* 30a–31a.

87. 78.14.2.

88. *War* 2.127 and Hippolytus 9.15. John's command is: 'let he who has two cloaks give to him who has none' (Luke 3:11). Ps. *Hom.* 12.6 confirms that Peter also wore 'only one coat and cloak' till it was threadbare and for *Haeres.* 78.13.3 James too 'wears no second coat, only a linen cloak'. To this day, religious Jews wear no leather footwear on *Yom Kippur* and Muslims wear no footwear in mosques.

89. Gen. 49:10. In 4Q252 5.2–4 , this reads: 'a Davidic descendant on the Throne shall not cease. For the Staff is the Covenant of the Kingdom. The Leaders of Israel, they are the feet [referred to in Gen 49:11], until the Messiah of Righteousness, the Branch of David comes.'

90. M. *Yoma* 8:1. The prohibition on 'eating and drinking' reflects Nazirite oath procedures even as recorded in Acts. The 'washing' here is assumed to be for pleasure, since the High Priest in *Yoma* 30a above certainly bathed.

91. There are good examples of these at Herodion, Jericho, and Masada.

92. 20.3.4 above.

93. In succession to his grandfather Herod; *Ant.* 20:15–16.

94. *Ant.* 19.353–5. See Herodian genealogy (pp. 968–9). This genealogy was suggested to me by Nikos Kokkinos of London University,

following my SBL 'Paul as Herodian' paper in 1984 (*The Dead Sea Scrolls and the First Christians*, Element, 1996, pp. 226–46). These are all persons connected in some way with the 'Idumaean' genealogy of Josephus' Saulus, his brother Costobarus, and their kinsman Antipas, like Helcias (3) also Temple Treasurer, assassinated by 'Brigands' (*Lēstai*) in 68 CE.

95. See CD 1, 4–5, and 8 and 1QpHab 2, 5, and 10.

96. *Haeres.* 30.21.1 and Ps. *Hom.* 13.4; cf. the reference to 'entering the water' with regard to touching 'the pure food of the Men of Holiness' in 1QS 5.13–14 – also the reference to 'Adam' in relation to immersion procedures and 'banishing Lying' in 3.4–4.23, i.e., these are 'Sabaeans' and 'Sampsaeans' with the 'Perfect Adam' ideology.

97. Cf. Matt. 10:2 and Mark 3:18 with Luke 6:16. Also compare 'Alphaeus' with 'Lebbaeus'.

98. See Apost. Const. 8.25, Epist. Apost. 1.2, and *EH* 1.13.4–22 and 2.1.6.

99. Ps. *Hom.* 7.8.

Chapter 13

1. 2.23.7.

2. See, for instance, Isa. 2–5, 10f., 14, 25–6, 29–33, 45, Zech. 10–11, Hab. 1–2, and Ps. 37, all subjected to exegesis in the form of *pesharim* at Qumran; also Isa. 53:11, 'the Suffering Servant' of early Christian exegesis, Ben Sira 44:17 on Noah, the 'Zaddik-the-Pillar-of-the-world' in Prov. 10:25, and Wisdom, a *Zaddik*-style book retelling biblical history in terms of it.

3. 78.7.5–9; see also 29.7.1–4.

4. 3.5.2–3; cf. *Haeres.* 29.7.7–8 and 30.2.7. One should compare this exit from 'the Land of Judea' to the parallel one of 'the Penitents of Israel to live in the Land of Damascus' in CD 4.3 and 6.5 and 'the Judgement of God' here to 1QpHab 12.12–13.4 to opposite effect (on 'the Day of Judgement' on all Gentile 'Servants of idols' and Jewish 'Evil Ones').

5. 3.7.8.

6. *War* 6.312–16; cf. *EH* 3.8.10–11.

7. *War* 6.302–4.

8. See S. G. F. Brandon, *Jesus and the Zealots*, New York, 1967, p. 263 and Slavonic Additions 12 in Loeb. In variant mss. of Matt. 27.16–17, Barabbas is called 'Jesus'. One should note, too, the 'casting' language in Luke 23:19's Barabbas being 'cast into prison'.

9. 3.5.4–7.2.

10. Both Acts and Josephus use this word 'a certain' or 'someone' (*tis*) to refer to Agabus and Jesus ben Ananias respectively (*War* 6.300). Note too, for Luke in Acts 13:1 the Antioch Community is composed of just such 'prophets and teachers'.

11. 1QH 2.32–4, 3.25, and 5.13–18. 'Soul', here, does not refer exactly to what it might mean in Greek, but something more like the 'quick of life' or 'being'.

12. CD 1.20–21.

13. 1QH 2.15–31, 5.22–4, etc.

14. 1.14–4.23 (including 'standing before You forever and walking in the Way of Your Heart, being established Victoriously'; cf. 1 Cor. 15:51–8).

15. 9.28–35.

16. 15.18–18.29.

17. 6.24–7.

18. 7.6–9.

19. Cf. '*Taxo*' in As. Moses 9.1.

20. 1QpHab 12.2ff. 4QpIs^c on 14:8ff. and on Zech. 11:11/Isa. 30:1ff., 4QpNah 1.7, and 4QpIs^a on 10:33f. It is clear from ARN 4.5, *Git.* 56a–b, *Yoma* 39b, and *Lam. R.* i.5.31 that such 'Lebanon' imagery is always applied to the fall of the Temple in 70 CE.

21. Cf. Dan. 7:13–14 with 1QM 11.17– 12.10, 19.1–2, Matt. 24:30/26:64 and Mark 13:26/14:62. This is varied in one usage in Ps. 77:12, where the 'mighty works' or 'mighty wonders' of God – also evoked in 1QM 10.8–9 – are evoked. Again the imagery is of war and battle, and 'the clouds which pour out water' and 'the Flood' are evoked (77:16–19). Here the imagery is varied to God showing His 'Strength among the Peoples' (77:14), imagery we shall encounter in the Habakkuk *Pesher* and War Scroll at Qumran, where even this allusion, 'Peoples', will have important connotations.

22. 8.5–14, 9.3–6, and 19–24, who are also described as an 'Everlasting Planting'. See Paul, in 1 Cor. 3:6–12 above, describing himself as doing the 'planting', planting 'God's Field', and 'the architect'; and cf. CD 8.33–5, describing the Qumran Community as a 'House of *Torah*'.

23. Ben Sira 50:24.

24. CD 7.13 and 8.3–24.

25. Not uncommon practice at the time. For instance, in the genealogy Josephus gives himself in *Vita* 1, the names 'Matthew' and 'Josephus' alternate.

26. *Ant.* 14.22–5.

27. *Ta'an.* 23b. Another funny Talmudic tradition, mentioned above and reminiscent of snake-bite traditions about 'Jacob of Kfar Sechania' and 'Justus Barsabas', has one 'Bar Daroma' drop 'his bowels and die' in the toilet – see p. 909.

28. 1.63a and 67b.

29. *Ta'an.* 23a – here both our 'carob' and '*redivivus*' themes again.

30. CD 4.19–20 and 8.12–13.

31. 78.14.1.

32. 1QM 7.6–7.

33. 78.13.3–5; see also 29.4.1.

34. 29.3.3–7 and 51.22.21.
35. 1QS 9.11. For 'the True Prophet', see Ps. *Rec.* 1.40–48, 5.10, 8.58–62, 10.51 and *Hom.* 2.6–13 and 3.49 (quoting Gen. 49:10 – the *Shiloh* Prophecy); cf. Deut. 18:18–19 in 4QTest 5–8 at Qumran.
36. CD 8.24, 12.23–13.1, and 14:19, all with singular verbs. Even in 1QS 9.11, the verb is singular, the usage being, therefore, idiomatic. See now too 'The Messiah of Heaven and Earth' text in *DSSU*, pp. 19–23 and CD 4.4 above on the Sons of Zadok 'standing up in the Last Days' as well.
37. See the exposition of the '*Shiloh*' Prophecy of Gen. 49:10 above and 11QMelch.
38. *War* 2.163–5 and *Ant.* 18.16–17. Cf. Acts 23:6–10 and 24:14–15, including the use of the word 'sect' (*heresis*) to describe 'the Way'. For the parody of this position in the Gospels, see the nonsense 'Seven Brothers' episode in Matt. 22:23–32 and pars. (itself based on the real 'Seven Brothers' story relating to Resurrection in 2 Macc. 7:1–41) – preceded by debates with the Herodians and Pharisees on the tribute question and followed by declaration of the Righteousness/Piety Commandments.
39. CD 6.17 above. For 'rebelling against God,' see 8.4 and 1QpHab 1.6 and 8.11–17.
40. Peter in Ps. *Hom.* 7.8 above adds 'suffocated', reflected in Acts 15:20–29 and 21:25 in James' prohibition on 'strangled things'.
41. 1 Apoc. 29.20, 35.5, 2 Apoc. 55.15–18, 56.16 (James even called 'Beloved' here), and 59.25.
42. See 1QH 9.29–35 and 11.9–14 above and the words from Heaven in Justin Martyr's *Dial.* 88 and 103's picture of Jesus' baptism, 'You are My son. Today I have begotten you' (Ps. 2:7 – reflected in Heb. 5:5–6 in connection with his 'being a Priest forever after the Order of Melchizedek' – Ps. 110:4). For Qumran these 'Sons of Zadok' enjoy a degree of pre-destination and/or pre-existence (linking up, to some extent, with the Prologue in the Gospel of John however Hellenized), are involved in the 'Righteousness' concept and eschatological 'condemnation' and 'Justification', and are to some extent supernatural, i.e., they participate in 'the Last Judgement'. This is the presentation of 1QpHab 4.14–5.5 as well.
43. Acts 4:1–5:17, *Ant.* 20.199 (on James' stoning), and Ps. *Rec.* 1.54.
44. 18:3–32. See also Ezek. 37:26 and Jer. 31:31.
45. 1QpHab 7.11–8.1. Cf. Jas. 1:22–6 and 2:12–13, introducing Hab. 2:4; also Epiphanius' 'Ossaeans' above.
46. CD 5.6–12, delineating 'fornication' and how 'they pollute the Temple, because they do not separate ['Holy from profane'] according to *Torah*'.
47. *EH* 3.27.1–4 and *Haeres.* 30.26.1–34.6
48. Ps. *Hom.* 2.15–17 and 42–53.

49. 3.16–4.12. Vermes translates the 'victoriously' here as 'forever', thereby missing the whole parallel with Paul in 1 Cor. 15:57.
50. *Ta'an.* 23a–b, *j. Ta'an.* 66b, and Ps. *Rec.* 1.44–55.
51. *War* 1.68–91/*Ant.* 13.300.
52. 4Q322–24, *DSSU*, pp. 119–27.
53. Probably Herod's Sanhedrin heads; *Pirke Abbot* 1.2–1.15 and ARN 4–13.
54. *Ant.* 14.28.
55. See *MZCQ*, p. 46 and Ezra 2:34–63 and Neh. 13:28.
56. *War* 1.95/*Ant.* 13.379.
57. 4QpNah 2.7–9.
58. See Aemilius Scaurus, Pompey's adjutant in 4Q322–24 ('Aemilius Kills').
59. *Ant.* 14.8.
60. *Ant.* 14.22–3.
61. 22.3–23.1. Cave-dwelling is important. Al-Kirkisani, HUCA, pp. 326f. and 363f., places 'the *Magharians*'/'Cave-Dwellers' after 'Zadok and Boethus' but before Jesus. In Rabbinic tradition, Simeon bar Yohai – the progenitor of *Zohar* tradition – and his son, also 'hide themselves in a cave' in the Trajan or Bar Kochba period; *Shab.* 33b.
62. Koran 19.22–3. In these Koranic stories, there is much overlap between Jesus and John; for instance in Koran 3:39, either Jesus or John (it is not clear which) – like James – is being described as 'chaste, a Prophet of the Righteous'. For John 1:45–51, Nathanael – whom we have already identified as a stand-in for James – who comes 'from Cana in Galilee', is 'sitting under a fig tree' when Jesus first sees him. Simeon bar Yohai and his son, above, miraculously survive by eating carobs, when after twelve years Elijah appears and 'stood before them' in the cave. Both carobs and figs were considered to exude 'honey'.
63. *War* 2.43–9; in *Vita* 21 Josephus reveals he is actually hiding in the Temple when all this occurred.
64. *Ta'an.* 23a. Such 'keys' resemble Peter's proverbial 'keys to the Kingdom'.
65. *Ant.* 18.25–8.
66. *War* 1.131–2. This passage actually mentions Scaurus, mentioned in 4Q322–4 above.
67. *War* 1.123–42. Josephus actually calls Antipater an 'Idumaean' here. As usual Hyrcanus' forces are for 'opening the gates to Pompey'; Aristobulus', resistance. The *Talmud* also actually gives Feast Day commemorations for the overthrow of the Sadducees and Aristobulus in Meg. *Ta'an.* 1, 4, 5, and 10, just the opposite of the commemorations recorded in 4Q322–4 above.
68. *War* 1.148. Aristobulus was sent to Rome in chains. His father-in-law and uncle were beheaded and, in due course, both his sons. During Caesar's war with Pompey, he was eventually poisoned. Antipater's connection

with Anthony served Herod very well, his
sons being brought up in Rome – Anthony's
heirs marrying Augustus'.

69. *Ant.* 14.176 and 15.3. Here Josephus confuses
'Sameas' (Shammai) with 'Pollio the Pharisee';
also see 15.368–72, where he appears to confuse Herod's affection for Hillel and Shammai
with his alleged regard for so-called 'Essenes' –
a matter that has confounded Qumran studies
as well.

70. *Ant.* 20.213–14. For Saulus as intermediary
between the Jerusalem 'Peace Party' and
Agrippa II and the Romans, see *War* 2.418
and 556–8. *War* 2.409–17 describing the
'Innovation' involved in the decision to stop
sacrificing on behalf of Romans leads directly
into this.

71. For discussions of similar kinds of such
'death-bringing poison', see CD 5.14–15 and
8.9–13. For the play on such 'poison' in
1QpHab 11.2–15, see Volume II.

72. CD 6.14–7.6.

73. CD 3.2–4.

74. *EH* 3.7.8.

75. 1QpHab 2.6, 8.16–17, and CD 1.8–20 above.
For Jas. 3:10, 'out of the same mouth issues
forth blessing and cursing'.

76. 4Q266 17–18. Cf. 1QS 3.10.

77. 3.11.1 (note the similar language in Islam in
the idea of a 'Caliph' or 'Successor').

78. 1QpHab 8.11–7. For 'the Kittim' generally,
see 2.11–6.11.

79. 1.47, 2.13, and *Comm. in Matt.* 10.17.

80. *Vir. ill.* 2. Note here, too, that Jerome claims
that the Apostles elected James (like Judas)
immediately after the Ascension and his attestation of James' 'Holiness' in his *Comm. on
Gal.* 1.19 above.

81. Luke 21:6, 20–24 and pars. (cf. also Luke
19:43–4 and Matt. 21:7).

82. 2.13 – the same section in which he attests
that *'Sicarii'* (by which he means non-Jews
practising circumcision) are immediately put
to death.

83. For Josephus, *Ant.* 18.117, John's baptism
was specifically *not* 'for remission of sins',
but 'bodily purification only, provided the
soul had already been purified by *doing*' or
'practising Righteousness' (note the Jamesian
emphasis here). Origen, on the other hand,
insists, following the Gospels, that 'John baptized for remission of sins', citing Josephus on
the 'promised purification to those who
underwent the rite' (implying purification
from sin), without any caveat concerning
'doing Righteousness'.

84. *Contra Celsus* 1.47.

85. Ibid.

86. 3.5.3 and 3.5.7.

87. 2.17.

88. *EH* 2.23.20.

89. *Vita* 363–4.

90. *Ant.* 18.80–84; cf. Suet. 3.36 and 5.25.

91. *Ant.* 18.85–7, considered to involve a Joshua
redivivus-style Redeemer figure known as 'the
Taheb' – possibly Simon *Magus.*

92. Slavonic Additions, Section 9.

93. Cf. *War* 2.651, and 4.314–25 with *Vita*
74–76, 189–261, 309–10.

94. *War* 4.319–20.

95. Cf. *War* 4.161–314 and 7.267–74 with
1QpHab 8.11–12.10, CD 4.13–5.17, 8.3–13,
etc.

96. Cf. *War* 4.227–325 with 1QpHab 2.6, 9.1–2,
4QpPs 37 2.14–20, and 4.5–10; and see
Volume II.

97. *War* 6.378–86. Josephus again takes the
opportunity to show Titus' magnanimity –
particularly towards non-Jews – though Titus
executes five leaders, two interestingly called
'John and James the sons of Sossius' and one
'Simon'.

98. *War* 4.324–5. Following this, Josephus tells
the story of 'Zachariah the son of Bariscaeus'
or 'Bareis', a 'Rich' Man, accused of betraying
the state to the Romans and holding treasonable communications with Vespasian
(4.335–44). Here too Josephus mentions how
'the Seventy' – meaning a rump Sanhedrin of
sorts – unanimously vote to acquit Zachariah
of these charges, but how 'the Zealots' then
slay him in the Temple and forthwith 'cast
him out of the Temple into the ravine below',
proceeding thereafter to beat the judges with
their swords. See also p. 945.

This episode is probably the real origin of
the so-called 'Tomb of Zachariah' below the
Temple Pinnacle in the Kedron Valley next to
James and the legend of James himself 'being
cast down' into the same valley. It is, more
than likely, also the origin of the reference to
'Zachariah son of Barachias' in Matt. 23:35,
whose blood like 'Abel the Righteous' is
'poured out upon the earth' (immediately followed by the gibe, 'O Jerusalem, Jerusalem,
who kill the Prophets and stone those who
have been sent to her'), 'Zechariah the son of
Berechiah' being the name of the Prophet of
the Restoration (Zech. 1:1). There is clearly
much overlap and confusion here.

99. *War* 4.323–4.

Chapter 14

1. 2.1.4–5.

2. 2.23.2–3.

3. *Vir. ill.* 2 above.

4. 4.22.1.

5. 4.20.7–8.

6. See 3.114, 84.25, etc., above.

7. 74.48, 78.40, 82.5–19, 84.6, etc.

8. Matt. 10:1, 24:30, 26:64, 28:18, etc. For
'Great Power', see Acts 4:33.

9. *War* 2.169–77/*Ant.* 18.55–65. Curiously

Tacitus, *Annals* 2.85 places the 'Paulina' (he calls her 'Vistilia') affair in 19 CE, lending further credence to Pontius Pilate coming to Palestine *before* 26 CE – possibly in 18–19.

10. *War* 2.175–6. In *Ant.* 18.62 (introducing the Jesus interpolations), Josephus changes his story completely. Strictly speaking, the actual resort to such bludgeoning occurred during the next 'tumult' when Pilate violated the Temple Treasure. Nevertheless, the first use of such '*Sicarii*'-style weapons for crowd control was Pontius Pilate's. This led to to Caius Caligula's attempt to have his *own* statue erected in the Temple in 41 CE, which was frustrated only by his assassination.

11. *Ta'an.* 23a–b.

12. *Ant.* 18.6–10 and *War* 6.310–15.

13. The real origin of this episode is probably to be found in *War* 1.312–13/*Ant.* 14.420–30, where the cave-dwelling father of seven children kills each in turn rather than surrender to Herod, before jumping to his own death, 'preferring death to slavery', a preview of Masada. Josephus calls all these cave-dwellers 'Brigands'.

14. See also James 2:3 and Psalm 110:1–4 above. See our analysis of parallel allusion to 'feet' in the 4Q252 *Shiloh* Prophecy exegesis in *DSSU*, pp. 83–9. This text insists that 'a Davidic descendant on the Throne shall not cease . . . until the Messiah of Righteousness comes', which brings us right back to these formulations in the Gospels of 'the Christ' as 'the son of David', not to mention those in the Letter to the Hebrews circulating around the play incorporated in the 'Melchizedek'/'King of Righteousness' terminology. Therefore, 'the Christ' in the New Testament is 'the Messiah of Righteousness' at Qumran.

15. 1QH Fragment 4.6. At Qumran 'Satan' is usually referred to as '*Mastemah*' or '*Mastemoth*', as in 1QM 13.4–16.5. See 'The Angels of *Mastemoth*', 'Pseudo-Ezekiel', 'The Demons of Death', 'The Community Council Curses Belial' in *DSSU*, 2 Cor. 11:14–12:7, 1 Tim. 1:20– 5:15, Rev. 2:9–22, 20:2–10, Koran 2.34–6, and 7.11–20.

16. Ps. *Rec.* 1.72, 2.7, Ps. *Hom.* 2.15–32, Hipp. 10.8, Apost. Const. 6.9, *EH* 2.1.10–11, 13–14, etc.

17. CD 3.18–4.7.

18. Note in Matt. 6:19–20 too the imagery of 'Your Riches ['Treasures'] being eaten up by moths and rust' of Jas. 5:2–3.

19. 5.1–3. See John 3:3–9, Gal. 4:28–31 ('cast out the slave woman and her son'), 1 Pet. 1:23, and 1 John. Note that Hippolytus' 'Naassenes' – equivalent to Epiphanius' 'Sebuaeans' (i.e., 'Sabaeans') – derive these doctrines from 'numerous discourses handed down by James the brother of the Lord to Mariamme' (again the parallel 'Mariamme'/

'Mareim' allusion of 2 Apoc. Jas. above).

20. 1QpHab 9.4–7 above. As previously, every instance of this usage 'delivered up' should be compared to constant Gospel allusion to 'Judas *Iscariot*' as 'delivering (Jesus) up'.

21. 12.14–13.4.

22. One should remark how many of these usages move directly into Islam, including the condemnation of idolators, the Day of Judgement, and even the idea of the 'Apostle to the Peoples' ('the Peoples' being those of the Eastern part of the Roman Empire and Northern Mesopotamia), Muhammad being that Apostle and Paul, because of the anti-Pauline Ebionite/Sabaean/Manichaean traditions Islam was heir to, long ago disappearing as a memorable figure. Paul, for instance, is never mentioned in the Koran, even though Muhammad basically co-opts his idea that Abraham *came before the Law* – for Muhammad, Abraham *comes before both Torah and Gospel* (Koran 2:124–35 and 3:65–9) and – as Christianity for Paul (Rom. 9:8, Gal. 3:7–9, etc.) – Islam is 'Abraham's Religion'.

23. 1QM 6.6 and 7.3–7 (as opposed to 'the uncircumcised in heart and body' of Ezek. 44:7).

24. 7.7–10 and 9.8–9.

25. 10.8–14 and 11.3–10.

26. 10.3–4.

27. 11.4–12, as is the exegesis in the Damascus Document. Translations often blur this. Regardless of whether the 'Messiah' references in CD 6.1 and 1QM 11.7 are singular or plural, 'the sword of no mere Adam' and 'the King of Glory' references following in 11.11–12.12 *are* singular. In CD 7.13–20, the citation is coupled with allusion to 'the fallen tent of David' (Amos 9:11) and the references there to 'King', 'Sceptre', and 'Staff' of Num. 21:18 (CD 6.1–11) are *always* singular. Interestingly, the famous interpolation in Josephus' *Ant.* 18.63, also, worries over whether it is legitimate to call Jesus a mere 'Man'.

28. In Acts 7:56, this is 'standing'.

29. *San.* 32b and 86b. 104a–106a and *Sota* 11a connect it with both Kenites and Rechabites above, considered 'privileged to sit in' it. In 41a, *Shab.* 15a, *R.H.* 31a–b, and *A.Z.* 8b, we hear that 'forty years before the destruction of the Temple, the Sanhedrin *was exiled* and took up residence in *Hanut*'. Some would identify this with 'the family of Hanan', i.e., Ananus; cf. the reference to 'the House of the High Priest' in Luke 22:53. However this may be, in Volume II we shall see how it relates to the 'House of Exile' in 1QpHab 11.4–6, in which the Wicked Priest 'pursued' and 'swallowed' the Righteous Teacher.

30. 1QM 11.9–13; see also *Zohar* 4.195a on 'Balak and Balaam', for how 'King David [i.e., the Messiah] placed himself among the Poor

and the Pious', i.e., 'those willing to sacrifice their lives for Sanctification of God's Name'.

31. It was the blood of these 'Seven Nations' that supposedly profaned the battle linen of the priests, 'who were Holy' in 9.8–9 above.

32. CD 7.19–20. See 4Q285 in *DSSU*, pp. 24–9. In both, he is clearly referred to as 'the *Nasi* ['Leader'] of the Assembly' or 'whole Assembly' – or 'Church' – and a kind of 'Bishop'. In turn, this links him to 'the *Mehokkek*'/'Staff', defined as 'the Interpreter of the *Torah*' in the exposition of Num. 21:8 in CD 6.3–11 above.

33. See Koran 73.12, 74.26 and 46, 82.8–19, etc. These 'Tares' Parables, referring to the 'Enemy' (13:28–39), also refer to 'opening one's mouth and uttering things hidden from the Foundation of the world' (13:35), based on Ps. 78:4. This Psalm, ending in evocation of the election of David as King, is replete with the language from the War Scroll of God's marvellous victories (78:9–14) and even that of 'raining' – God 'raining down manna ['Angel's food'] on them' in the wilderness (78:23–5) – even an allusion to consuming 'meat' or 'blood' in the wilderness, thereby kindling 'the Wrath of God' (78:26–34) of CD 3.5–9 above.

34. 1QM 11.11–14. The 'sword' referred to here (Isa. 31:8) sets the tone for the whole exegesis giving it its war-like, Messianic cast. It is the same uncompromising apocalyptic imagery as 'the Sceptre of his mouth' (Isa. 11:4), referred to in the *Pesher* on Isa. 10:25–11:15, which not only contains allusion to 'the Leader of the Assembly' and 'the shoot of Jesse and Branch (*Nezer*) from his roots' (Isa. 11:1) of 4Q285 above, but the 'felling of Lebanon by a Mighty One' (10:34) – imagery definitively tied in Rabbinic literature to *the fall of the Temple in 70 CE*. (ARN 4.5 and *Git.* 56a). In 12.12 below, this sword is 'to consume' or 'eat guilty flesh'.

35. 1QM 11.17–12.3.

36. 12.4–9. This language of 'command' gives way in the Damascus Document and Community Rule to that of 'Visitation', Divine or otherwise, based on the same root in Hebrew – sometimes for Vengeance, but sometimes for more Messianic purposes; e.g., CD 5.16, 7.9–8.5, 1QS 2.6, 3.14, and 4.11–14, but also CD 1.7, 13.24 and 1QS 3.18, 4.6–8 (perhaps most eloquently of all), and 4.26.

37. 18.12–19.4.

38. In Scripture, Jesus is the suffering 'Just One' (cf. Acts 3:14, 7:52, and 22:14 with Isa. 53:11).

39. Note the 'whitewashed tombs of the Righteous' allusions, preceding this in 23:27–9, followed by 'partaking of ['Communion'] the blood of' and 'murdering

the Prophets' – repeatedly reiterated in the Koran – and 'serpents, offspring of vipers' accusations of 23:30–37 – which include allusion to 'gathering her chicks under her wings' echoed in the Qumran 'Hymns of the Poor' (4Q436 1.8). Directly after these comes the 'stone by stone' allusions relating to the destruction of the Temple of 24:1–2.

40. 1QpHab 7.1–14. Interestingly enough, *Talmud Sanhedrin* 97b also interprets this phrase, 'wait for it', from Hab. 2:3 in terms of the Delay of the End Time, corroborating this point. But there, it also becomes the basis of the famous legend of 'the thirty-six Just Men' or 'the Righteous Ones' who uphold the world, 'lo' in Hebrew ('for him'/'for it') having the numerical value of 36.

41. On 'fortifying'/'strengthening', see CD 6.21, 8.41–57, and 14.14. The regulations in CD 14.21–2 and newly published 4QD267, Fragment 18.4, precisely overlap those in 1QS 7.4–18, showing the two documents to be contiguous. Particularly the one prohibiting 'spitting in the midst of a session of the Many' (1QS 7.13), exactly parallels Josephus' 'Essenes' in *War* 2.147 (the language equivalence is precise) – parodied in Jesus 'spitting' into the eyes of those he cures (Mark 8:23)!

42. CD 9.1, which, of course, applies very eloquently to the instance of Jesus. F. García Martínez (or his assistant) in his new translation seems deliberately to reverse this.

43. This is the same *'balló'* language Josephus uses to describe the 'casting out' of the body of Ananus without burial in *War* 4.324 (the 'Rich' Traitor Zachariah in 344) or the Essenes 'casting out' miscreants from the Community in 2.143.

44. *EH* 2.23.14–5.

45. 1QpHab 5.8–12.

46. 4QpNah 1.11f. The text breaks at this point, but the context is one of eschatological Judgement. 4QpNah 1.3–9 on 1:4 also evokes 'Lebanon', as does 4QpIsᵃ 3.2–8 above, both focusing on 'the Kittim'. So do Isa. 2–5, 14, 29–33 (Zech. 10–11), Hab. 2–3, all subjected to exegesis at Qumran. In Ps. 37:24, God 'upholds' the Poor/the Righteous 'with His hand; he shall not be cast down' (interpreted in terms of 'the Priest, the Teacher of Righteousness, whom [God] established to build an Assembly of His Elect'), just as in Hymns of the Poor (4Q436 1:8), 'He hid them in the shadow of His wings.'

47. Cf. ARN 4.5 and *Git.* 56a–b above. Also *Lam. R.* 1.5.31 and *Yoma* 39b. Both Isa. 10:34 (4QpIsᵃ) and Zech. 11:1 (4QpIsᶜ) are the classical allusions to the fall of the Temple in 70 CE. In 1QpHab 11.15–12.10, again because of the play on the 'white linen they wore' and the 'destruction of the Poor' – whose 'blood' is also evoked – by the Wicked

Priest, 'Lebanon' is identified as 'the Community Council'.

48. In both, the allusion is to 'robbing the Riches' or 'Property of the Poor' (*Ebionim*) – 1QpHab 12.10 and CD 6.16 (here the usage is 'robbing the Meek'/'*Ani*). Cf. too 1QpHab 1.7, 8.11, and 10.1.

49. Also note the resonance here between Pella and *Sela'im*/'Rocks'. We shall deal with the Pella Flight Oracle in early Christian tradition in more detail in Volume II. A *Pesher* on this whole first chapter of Nahum 1:2–8, containing reference to 'zeal', 'Vengeance', 'Wrath', 'Lebanon', 'Bulwark', 'whirlwind', 'Flood', and 'Fire', has now been found to exist. While fragmentary, it certainly relates to 'the *Kittim*' and eschatological themes generally.

50. 1QpHab 11.2–12.10.

51. For many years I had been attempting to gain access to the totality of the Qumran corpus to see if there was a *pesher* on Isa. 3:10–11 and, if there was, whether it was applied to the death of the Righteous Teacher. This was what partially drove my involvement in the struggle for freedom of access to the Dead Sea Scrolls. Ironically, the passage I was looking for was staring me in the face all along, but I had not seen it. It also forms the backbone of the *Pesher* on Ps. 37:32–3 (4QpPs 37 4.8–4.11).

52. 1QpHab 11.2–15. The allusion is based on Ezek. 44:7–9, but there is much wordplay here. This, also, will be treated fully in Volume II.

53. Ps. *Rec.* 1.70.

54. This picks up the theme of 'dwelling in the Land of Damascus' of CD 4.3, 6.5, and 6.21. It also picks up the theme of 'going out into the wilderness to prepare the Way of the Lord' in 1QS 8.13, not to mention that of 'the Sons of Benjamin, the *Diaspora* of the Desert' in 'the Desert of the Peoples' in 1QM 1.2–3 and the 'exile of the Tabernacle of Your King . . . to Damascus' (Amos 5:26–7), expounded in CD 7.15–19.

55. *War* 2.228/*Ant.* 20.113; cf. 1 Cor. 1:16 and 16:15–17.

56. Cf. Koran 2.10, 42, 79, 101, 111–13, 140, 174, 3.71, 3.75, 3.78, and 3.94–5.

57. *Vir. ill.* 2; cf. *EH* 2.23.18.

58. *Ant.* 15.320–32. See *Jerusalem Revealed*, ed. Y. Yadin, Jerusalem, 1975, p. 18.

59. Some see 'Josephus bar Matthew' (*Vita* 5) in the name – Josephus himself metamorphosing into this character.

60. CD 5.7, Matt. 26:28 and pars, and 1 Cor. 10:16 and 11:25. In Volume II we shall see more fully the linguistic connections of 'Damascus' with 'Cup of Blood'.

61. CD 5.13–15, 6.14–17, and 8.3–13.

62. 4QpNah 3.1 and 1QpHab 10.8–11.

63. 4QpNah 3.2–10 and 4.4–5. Here, amid the imagery of 'resident aliens' (*ger-nilveh*), con-demnation of crucifixion, 'leading Ephraim astray' and 'leading the Many astray [the opposite of the Righteous Teacher's proper 'Justifying' activity of 'justifying the Many'] through their false teaching, Lying Tongue, and Deceitful lips'; the *Pesher* ends by expressing the hope: 'When the Glory of Judah stands up [again our 'standing' imagery], the Simple of Ephraim [the counterpart of 'the Simple of Judah doing *Torah*' in 1QpHab 12.4–5] shall flee from their Assembly ['Church'], abandoning those who lead them astray, and join Israel.' The catchword 'Ephraim', paralleling 'Samaritan' in the Gospels and linking up with the earlier allusion, *ger-nilveh*/'resident alien' and '*Nilvim*' or 'Joiners' in CD 4.3, can be looked upon as Gentiles being taught a false doctrine of Salvation by a 'Lying' teacher.

64. For instance, Matt. 26:69 calls Jesus, 'Jesus the Galilean'.

65. Cf. Exod. 16:29. For CD 10.21 this is 1000 cubits.

66. Cf. *San.* 45a–b, 55b–57a, 81b–83b, etc.

67. Rom. 12:1–5, 1 Cor. 3.9–17, and 12:12–27.

68. *Dial.* 136–7; so does Hegesippus in Palestine, more or less contemporary with him, but rather *to James.* For 1QpHab 12.2–3 and 4QpPs 37 4.8–11, as we saw, its language is being applied to the death or destruction of *the Righteous Teacher.*

Chapter 15

1. *Haeres.* 78.13.2 and 14.5.

2. 78.14.6 (*EH* 2.23.17); cf. Jas. 5:16 on the efficacy of 'the fervent prayer of the Just One'.

3. *Haeres.* 30.3.1.

4. 1 Apoc. Jas. 25.14 (cf. 2 Apoc. Jas. 51.20).

5. *Contra Celsus* 5.62.

6. 1QpHab 11.10–15, following the 'building a worthless city upon blood' accusation of 10.6–10 and preceding those of 'the blood of Man' ('*Adam*' – Hab 2:17) in 12.1–10.

7. For Paul, of course, in 1 Cor. 10:21 and 11:27, 'the Cup of the Lord' is 'the blood of Christ', which for Luke 22:20 *is poured out for you*.' For the language of 'venom' and 'Wrath' at Qumran, see CD 1.21f., 2.21f. (also 'cutting off'), 8.9–12, etc.

8. 1QS 1.9, 2.16, 3.22ff., etc.

9. Cf. *War* 2.129 with Pliny's reply to Trajan on the Christians he knows in Asia Minor (10.96), who 'meet regularly before dawn to chant verses honouring Christ as God'; al-Biruni and the *Fihrist*, loc. cit.; and 4Q298 – 'The Sons of Dawn' (*DSSU*, pp. 160–65). Also see Peter, praying and bathing at dawn in Ps. *Hom.* 7.1, 10.1, 11.1, etc., and Lucian's *Menippus* above.

10. 1QS 8.5–9 and 9.4–5. Also 1QS 8.11–12 has something of the 'Hidden' ideology of John 12:36, 2 Apoc. Jas. 47.15, etc.

11. 1 Apoc. Jas. 25.15. Cf. 1QS 6.26–7.18 with CD 14.20–21 and new fragment 18.4 of 4QD266, vividly showing the overlap between these signalled earlier.

12. Cf. 1 Apoc. Jas. 34.15 with *EH* 3.5.3 and *Haeres.* 29.7.7–8.

13. For 'seizing' see, 25.10, 29.15, 30.5, 33.5, etc.; for 'casting', 27.5, 39.20, 40.15 (together with 'Cup' imagery), 40.20, 41.20, 42.20, 2 Apoc. Jas. 47.25, 59.25, 61.25, etc.

14. See also 44:15, 48:20, 49:10, 59:20, and 60:12–13.

15. Epist. B. 6. See, for instance, the allusion to 'the two Ways' ('the Way of Light' and 'the Way of Darkness' in 18–20) from 1QS 3.9–4.26; also 'the Day of Judgement' from 1QpHab 12.14–13.3 in 19–21.

16. *Dial.* 17 and 136–7; in both it and Barnabas, Emile Puech, of the Ecole Biblique in Jerusalem, claims to have found quotations from Qumran materials.

17. Epist. B. 6 (also alluding to the 'Primal Adam').

18. 63.15–30; cf. 1QpHab 8.2's exegesis of Hab. 2:4 ('the Righteous shall live by his Faith'), '*saved from* the House of Judgement', with 12.14's '*saved on* the Day of Judgement'. 61.20–62.15 also uses 'Stone' and 'Cornerstone' imagery.

19. 63.15 (Ps. *Rec.* 1.70–71).

20. *Vir. ill.* 2; also *Adv. Hel.* 21, in which, developing Epiphanius 78.14.3's theme of the 'sons of Joseph following the virgin life-style', he maintains *both* Mary *and* Joseph were 'virgins'.

21. *Vir. ill.* 2.

22. See 'the Priest', used to refer to the Righteous Teacher in 4QPs 37 3.13 and 1QpHab 2.8; *per contra*, 'the Wicked Priest' in 1QpHab 8.16 and 11.12.

23. *Ant.* 20.197–8.

24. *Ant.* 20.10–16; cf. Paul's possible greeting to this 'household' in Rom. 16:10–11.

25. Ps. *Rec.* 1.54. Note the similar language in the 'Beit Peleg' ('House of Separation') allusion in CD 8.45.

26. MZCQ, pp. 41–5.

27. Cf. CD 5.7–13, 6.14–17, 4QMMT 1.3–32, 56–76, and 2.6–33.

28. Cf. *Ant.* 13.372–404 with 4QpNah 2.5–8.

29. Acts 11:27 and 13:1.

30. *Ant.* 14.83–96 and 18.116–19. This string of fortresses, of which Qumran may be one, was originally built by the Maccabeans as outposts, as was Masada further south. Later they were taken over by Herodians. For instance, Herod used Hyrcania to store all his treasure. Finally they became resistance outposts.

31. Only on the point Josephus emphasizes regarding John Hyrcanus above, that 'the Pharisees have delivered to the people a great many observances in succession from their Elders not written in the *Torah* of Moses', while the Sadducees 'consider only those observances obligatory, which are in written Scripture, but do not observe those derived from the Traditions of the Forefathers', is there a resemblance between Sadducees of this kind and Qumran – these last, called '*Halakot*'/'Smooth Things' at Qumran, a pun on the Rabbinic usage '*Halachot*'/Traditions; *Ant.* 13.297–8.

32. ARN 5.2.

33. *Ant.* 20.180 and 205–8. At this point he is also using another synonym, '*Sicarioi*'.

34. *Ant.* 20.215 – *Lēstēs*. As it turns out, this Florus did more than anyone else to goad the people to revolt against Rome.

35. *Vita* 65.

36. *Ant.* 20.200–201; cf. 1QpHab 8.16–17 and Jas. 2:9–11.

37. *Ant.* 20.251.

38. Cf. 1QpHab 11.6–12.10 and CD 1.19–21, the latter employing the language of 'Law-breaking'. Even the wording attached to it, 'they rejoiced in strife among the People', is replicated in these accounts in Josephus.

39. *War* 2.243–47/*Ant.* 20.137.

40. Cf. 1QpHab 12.6 with 1QH 4.10.

41. *Vita* 343–4.

42. *Ant.* 204–7. Cf. *War* 2.253 earlier, mentioning the numbers of these Felix crucified; 2.254, identifying '*Sicarii*' as 'Bandits'; and Matt. 27:38–44 (and pars.) on those crucified with Jesus.

43. *War* 2.255–7. *Ant.* 20.204–7 first mentions the '*Sicarii*' immediately after James' death, telling us of their struggles with the High Priests and of Albinus' efforts to 'exterminate' them, a point – along with James' death – totally missing from the *War*.

44. *War* 4.323–4. N.b. this episode is immediately followed by the story of how 'the Zealots' now 'cast' the body of the Rich Traitor Zachariah out of the Temple into the ravine below (335–44).

45. *Ant.* 20.166. Here he only calls Jonathan's murderer's 'Brigands' (*Lēstēs*).

46. Cf. the 'Judea Capta' coins in this period.

47. *War* 6.312–15, ambiguous because Josephus and Rabbinic Judaism proper, then, go on to apply to Vespasian, their conqueror.

48. *War* 6.288–9.

49. *War* 7.407–53, following the description of the Masada suicide – in other words, just as the *Antiquities* appears to end with the aftermath of James' death; the *War* ends with the details of continued '*Sicarii*' disturbances in Egypt and North Africa.

50. *War* 2.411–14. In 2.407, those Josephus is calling 'Innovators' even pelt Agrippa II with stones and expel him from the city. See *War* 2.423, 2.455–6, and *Ant.* 20.166–7 for 'pollution of the Temple' charges against such persons.

51. *Ant.* 20.205–10. See Acts 23:2 for how he supposedly has Paul 'hit in the mouth'. In *War* 2.441–2, he too is killed by 'Brigands' (*Lēstēs*) and his palace burnt, as 'the *Sicarii*' (again identified as 'Brigands') 'turn the Poor against the Rich' (*War* 2.425–9).

52. *Ant.* 20.118–33. Here Acts seems aware that 'Dorcas' in Greek (Gazelle) means 'Tabitha' in Aramaic. Later, a son of someone Josephus calls 'Dorcas' in the *War*, will assassinate Saulus' colleague, the Temple Treasurer, Antipas.

53. Also Doetus, i.e., 'Dositheus'. The crucifixion of the Messiah in Lydda is important for Jews. In the first place, it probably relates to the slaying of the 'Messiah ben Joseph', supposed to precede the 'Messiah ben David' (*Suk.* 51a–52b) – 'Joseph', being the ancestor of the North, probably implies 'Samaritan', i.e., the 'Dorcas' or 'Doetus' here. It relates to the story of the crucifixion – also at Lydda – of one 'Ben Stada' (*San.* 67a; cf. 43a), censored in most *Talmud*s, but normally thought to be Jesus ('Ben Pandera' or 'Panthera'; cf. *Haeres.* 78.7.5). However, since in *Shab.* 104b, 'Ben Stada' is also said to have brought sorcery from Egypt, he is probably confused with another Samaritan claiming to be 'the Standing One' – Simon *Magus* again, the Rabbinic stories also giving some ribald stories about sexual paramours.

Here 'Ben Stada' is probably another corruption for 'Standing One', which in this instance brings us back to Simon *Magus*' Samaritan colleague or teacher – also a Disciple of John the Baptist – Dositheus (Ps. *Rec.* 2.7–12 and *Hom.* 2.17–32, including a similar tale about a sexual paramour, *Haeres.* 8.9.1–14.2.1, and Justin Martyr, 2 *Apology* 14–15, actually referring to 'Sotadists' regarding Simon). Interestingly, in Josephus (*War* 4.145–6), one 'John the son of Dorcas' (i.e., 'Doetus') is the 'Zealot' assassin who creeps into the Temple prison and kills Saulus' and Costobarus' kinsman, the Herodian Temple Treasurer, Antipas, who was awaiting trial on charges of being 'a Traitor' in the prelude to the killings of James' murderer Ananus and Zachariah above. If he was perchance the son of this Samaritan 'Dorcas'/'Doetus', his grudge would have been very powerful.

54. *Ant.* 20.167; also *War* 2.259 and 2.264–5 above.

55. *War* 2.261–3/*Ant.* 20.169–72.

56. Cf. 'Ben Stada''s Egyptian magic and Simon's in Ps. *Hom.* 2.22 above, as well as that 'Simon' or 'Atomus', the 'magician from Cyprus' in *Ant.* 20.142, who persuades Drusilla to divorce her husband and marry Felix; also the Simon-like 'Elymus *Magus*' in Acts 13:8, whom Paul also allegedly faces down in 'Cyprus' (In these accounts, as we

saw, 'Cyprus' is often confused with 'Samaria', i.e. , 'Gitta' with 'Kitta' or 'Kittim'. This, too, probably has something to do with the name for Samaritans, Josephus and other sources are using, 'Cuthaeans' (*Ant.* 9.288–90, 11.19–20 and 85–8, *War* 1.63, etc.), and Benjamin of Tudela is still using in his *Travels* a thousand years later.) Acts confuses all these things, but the Pseudoclementines, Justin Martyr (himself from Samaria), Eusebius, etc., have them more or less right.

57. *Ant.* 18.85–7. These are perhaps the *real* crucifixions during Pilate's tenure, paralleling the Messianic disturbances around Lydda some fifteen years later, which trigger the dispatch of Felix (52 CE; cf. *B.B.* 10b and *Pes.* 50a on the 'martyrs at Lydda'). Though a Samaritan, Josephus calls 'Doetus' 'a Leader of the Jews'; and his four colleagues, 'Innovators'. In New Testament materials, as we saw, there is much confusion between sectarian strife in Samaria and Jerusalem, events being *transferred to a Jerusalem milieu*. Mount Gerizim, too, is the 'Joshua'-of-old's centre of activities; cf. 'Stephen''s speech to his Jerusalem tormentors (Acts 7:1–50), lifted bodily from Joshua's farewell at Mount Gerizim (Josh. 24:2–32, including the error about *Joseph*'s bones; Acts 7:16).

58. *Haeres.* 20.3.4 and Ps. *Hom.* 2.23.

59. Cf. *War* 2.405–7, where Agrippa II – Jesus- and Paul-like – recommends paying taxes to Caesar. In response, 'the Innovators' pelt him with stones and ban him from Jerusalem, whereupon he withdraws and quits collecting taxes for the Romans, letting the Roman Governor do it for himself, and the Uprising begins!

60. *Ant.* 20.173–8.1

61. *Ant.* 20. 183–4. Josephus calls him 'Beryllus'. Some see this as meaning 'Burrus', the Head of Nero's Praetorian Guard, but this is not very convincing. Since Josephus also claims he was first 'Nero's tutor', he has most in common with Seneca, the legendary correspondence of Paul with whom is well known. In fact, Burrus and Seneca were basically partners, Burrus the military man; but Seneca being the 'intellectual' and 'Secretary', so this confusion would not be surprising – see *Annals* 14.52f., which claims Burrus' death in 62 CE 'broke Seneca's power'. For Seneca's own intense anti-Semitism, see Augustine, *City of God* 6.11, quoting him to the effect that 'the customs of that most accursed nation have gained such strength that they have now been received in all lands, so the conquered have given Laws to the conquerors'.

62. *Ant.* 20.178.

63. See *War* 3.289, for Trajan, the Commander of de Vaux's 'Tenth Legion', at Jotapata; 3.458–85 (67 CE), the massacre at Tarichaeae;

and 4.450, joining Vespasian at Jericho (68 CE), after subduing Perea across Jordan.

64. *Ant.* 20.14. This legislation, the origins of which are unclear, was named after a Roman magistrate called 'Cornelius' – possibly one of the Scipios or even Sulla – and, as explained, directed against *Sicarii* and Sorcerers.

65. *War* 2.253.

66. Cf. 1QS 8.4–9.21, 1QH 4.4–6.24, etc.

67. Cf. Josephus' language of 'disease' describing Judas and *Saddok*'s Fourth Philosophy; *Ant.* 18.6.

68. *Ant.* 20.131–6/*War* 2.242–6.

69. *Ant.* 20.181; cf. *Pes.* 57a about 'woes to the Sons of Boethus, who beat the people with staves', and the other High Priestly families. These 'Poor' among the Priests, who represent an 'Ancient' line, may be our 'Rechabite Priests'.

70. *Ant.* 20.206–7.

71. *Ant.* 20.188. Festus' Governorship is curiously abbreviated in the *War* and it is here that the missing passages about James' death – spoken of by Origen and Eusebius – probably were to be found.

72. *Ant.* 15.252–66/*War* 1.486–7.

73. *Ant.* 20.194–5; cf. 19.353–5.

74. *Ant.* 20.189–91.

75. *War* 2.407–27.

76. 11QT 46.9–18, referring to lepers; also see 4QMMT 1.47–62, referring to the blind and the deaf.

77. Cf. CD 7.18–20 and 1QM 11.6–12.18; also 'shooting stars' in 4Q246 2.1 – the 'Son of God' text.

78. *B. San.* 105a–106b. Jude 1:10–19, which also knows the '*Be'or*'-like language of 'animals' and 'the Lord coming with Myriads of His Holy Ones to execute Judgement against all' of the War Scroll above, continues in the Jamesian vein, 'to convict all the ungodly ones because of the *ungodly works* which they *did*'.

79. 1QpHab 12.5–6.

80. For Gehazi, Cain, and Korah, who 'was swallowed up' (Num. 16:30–34), see *b. San.* 90a and 115a–110a.

81. CD 8.20–22.

82. Cf. CD 1.12–18, 4.19–20, and 8.13 with 1QpHab 8.13.

83. Cf. 1QpHab 11.10–15 with CD 8.9–13.

84. CD 2.21–3.9.

85. See 1QpHab 5.8–12 on Hab. 1:13.

86. Rev. 2:9–28.

87. Where these are concerned and 'Benjamin', in particular, see 1QM 1.2–4, referring to 'Benjamin' as the '*Galut*' or 'Exile of the Desert', who are allied with 'the Sons of Levi' and 'the Sons of Judah' ('the Priests' and 'the Jews') and will fight with 'the Exiled Sons of Light' when they move from 'the Desert of the Peoples' (possibly as far north even as *Edessa*

and Adiabene) 'to the camp in the Desert of Jerusalem'. Additionally, see *San.* 99b, also preceding a reference to Gehazi's punishment and following one to the Messianic *Shiloh* Prophecy, on 'the family of Benjamin' as being somehow unclean.

88. 11QT 46.13–16 (cf. 4Q274 1.2).

89. 4QMMT 1.8–36 and 68–70.

90. 4QMMT 1.66–8. For the perfect description of this 'carrion', combined with 'things sacrificed to idols' of James' 'Jerusalem Council' directives and 'bathing', relative to *Peter*'s conduct, see Ps. *Hom.* 7.8 and cf. Koran 5.3. Also see Ps. *Hom.* 7.3–4.

91. 11QT 56.18–57.19 and 66.14–17.

92. 4QMMT 1.8–9 and 2.26–33.

93. *War* 1.401, 5.36–8, *Ant.* 15.380–425, 19.326, and 20.219–20.

94. Cf. See 4QD266 above, *DSSU*, pp. 217–19, and Acts 2:1–41 on the descent of the Holy Spirit on Pentecost.

95. *War* 2.225; cf. *Ant.* 20.105–12.

96. *War* 2.224.

97. 2.254–7.

98. For Poppea, see *Ant.* 20.195, regarding Helcias above, and *Vita* 16, and see the allusions to 'Joiners'/'joining' in CD 4.2 and 4QpNah 2.9 and 3.5, denoting 'resident aliens'. Also see CD 8.42–57 referring to just such 'God-Fearing'.

99. Phil. 4:18–22, also mentioning Epaphroditus. The Epistle of Clement 65 also mentions 'Claudius' and 'Valerius', names probably connected to the Neronian and Claudian families. Paul too has excellent relations with Seneca's brother Gallio (Acts 18:12–17). But not inconsequentially, the relationship is also probably true of Titus Flavius Clemens or 'Clement of Alexandria' later.

100. The observation is Josephus'; *Ant.* 20.252–7. Florus, too, it seems, obtained his post through Poppea's influence.

101. *Vita* 13.

102. *Vita* 360.

Chapter 16

1. Acts 23:2. Ananias was apparently the 'Richest' of the High Priests, but not always differentiable from Ananus (cf. *War* 2.243/ *Ant.* 20.204–13 with 197–203 on the death of James), which complicates the problem of 'Rich v. Poor' charges at Qumran and in the Letter of James.

2. *Ant.* 20.211–12.

3. Josephus even has one 'Jesus', the head of a band of Revolutionaries and the party 'of the Poor' on the Sea of Galilee, who takes to the boats to escape the Romans; another goes north with 500 'Galileans'; and a third, Jesus ben Ananias, is arrested by the High Priests

in collusion with the Roman Authorities and predicts the fall of Jerusalem, but this is *after the death of James* not Jesus.

4. *Ant.* 20.214; cf. *War* 2.418, 556–8, and 4.140–46 above. Antipas, it will be recalled, was assassinated as a Traitor by one 'John son of Dorcas' (or 'Doetus'?).

5. *Ant.* 19.354–5, 20.137–47, and *Contra Apion* 1.51.

6. *Ant.* 20.214.

7. 1QpHab 8.8–13. Interestingly enough, the allusion to 'puffed up' harks back to the exegesis of Hab. 2:4 from the previous column, which Paul too uses in 1 Cor. 8:1–13 to criticize the 'weak consciences' and 'vegetarianism' of the Jerusalem Church, particularly their insistence on '*keeping away from* food sacrificed to idols' – also Peter's position in Ps. *Hom.* 7.3–8.

8. 1QpHab 12.6–10.

9. For Antonia, which Herod built to honour Mark Antony, see *Ant.* 15.403–9. Saulus, Philip, Costobarus, and Antipas seem, rather, to have been in Agrippa II's Palace when the Citadel surrendered, after which they escaped from Jerusalem; cf. *War* 2.556–8 above. The intermediaries here are rather 'Ananias' and 'Nicodemus'' son; 2.449–56.

10. *Ant.* 18.138, suggested to me by Nikos Kokkinos of London in 1986.

11. *War* 2.449–56.

12. *War* 4.140–365.

13. *Ad Cor.* 5 (attributed to Clement of Rome), Tertullian, *Haer.* 36, *EH* 2.25.5, and 3.1.2, quoting Origen's *Commentary on Genesis*.

14. Jerome, *Vir. ill.* 11 considers them authentic; so does Augustine. But see M. R. James in *The Apocryphal New Testament*, Oxford, 1924, pp. 480–84, 'their composition is of the poorest kind'; however there is nothing preposterous in them and they resemble the excerpts Josephus provides in *Vita* 365–6 from Agrippa II's letters to him. For his part Gallio, too, may have been executed with another brother, Mela, and his son, Lucan, in the aftermath of the Piso Conspiracy in 65 CE. (*Annals* 15.65–16.17).

15. Paul calls Epaphroditus his 'fellow minister' and 'prisoner in Christ'. *Ad Cor.*, attributed to Clement, which does appear to think – if authentic – that Paul reached Spain (5), also testifies to these contacts (65); and there does appear to have been a clique of some kind operating within Imperial circles (particularly if Seneca was 'so often on our side', as persons as august as Tertullian [*De Anima* 20], Jerome, and Augustine seem to think) from Claudius' or Nero's time till Domitian, who eliminated it in 95–96 CE. For Ps. *Hom.* 12.8, its 'Clement' is also a very close 'kin of Caesar'.

16. *Ant.* 20.141–4.

17. *Ant.* 20.143.

18. Acts 13:1–12. It is in the aftermath of this that John Mark breaks with Paul and returns to Jerusalem (13:13).

19. *Ant.* 19.332–5.

20. *Ant.* 20.144 and Suet. 5.28.

21. *Ant.* 19.317–26.

22. *Ant.* 20.5.

23. *War* 4.359–63.

24. Helen's descendants fight the whole war on the revolutionary side, going over to the Romans only when all hope is lost at the end; cf. *War* 2.520 and 6.356–7. In fact, in 4.567, at a particularly difficult moment of internecine strife, many of those Josephus is actually calling 'Zealots' take refuge in the palace of one of her kinsmen called 'Grapte'.

25. *Ant.* 19.353. Helcias was probably not actually Temple Treasurer at this point, but *Strategos*, but his son, Saulus' kinsman Antipas, butchered by 'Zealots' in the next generation (i.e., by 'Dorcas'/'Doetus'/or 'Dositheus'' son John), was. This Silas, too, had a son – also called 'Silas' – who deserted from Agrippa II's army and joined the Revolutionaries. For Philip's *two* daughters, see *Vita* 36/ *War* 4.86–7.

26. *Ant.* 19.366.

27. Cf. *Ant.* 19.343–52 with Acts 12.21–3.

28. *Ant.* 20.139–43. For additional marital interactions in Syria and Asia, see 18.130–42.

29. 11.5.

30. *War* 7.38–9.

31. CD 4.19–21 (condemning divorce) and 8.13 (condemning 'Riches' and marriage with near relatives, including nieces).

32. CD 4.19–5.15

33. 11QT 66.14–17.

34. See Justin Martyr, 1.26, Hippolytus 6.15, *EH* 2.13, etc. Once again there is the parallel with Paul, who by his own testimony in 1 Cor. 9:5 is accused of travelling around with a Christian woman, as, according to him, do 'Cephas and the brothers of the Lord'.

35. *War* 4.319–20.

36. There was no Josephus to document them; one must go to the trash heaps of Lower Egypt to do so; but Dio Cassius, 68.32.1, says 220,000 persons perished in Cyrene after the Revolt of the Jewish leader there called 'Andreas'/'Man'. See, however, Josephus for the earlier massacres at Caesarea (2.457), Scythopolis (2.466–8), Alexandria (2.487–98), Damascus (2.559–60), Titus' 'games' at Caesarea Philippi (7.23–4), etc.

37. Cf. 1QS 8.21–4, CD 8.28–36, and 4QD266 14–16. Also see *War* 2.143–4 on those 'expelled [again '*ekballousi*'] from the ['Essene'] Community'.

38. Cf. confusions with 'Joseph called Barsabas surnamed Justus' in Acts 1:23 above (not to mention 'Joses surnamed Barnabas' in Acts

4:36, supposedly 'a Levite' from 'Cyprus').

39. Again, one encounters the Qumran 'separation' language – and additionally that of 'non-cooperation in purse or work'.
40. *War* 2.270/*Ant.* 20.182–4 and *Ant.* 20.193–6 – 'the Temple Wall Affair'.
41. For 'plot'/'conspiracy' language applied to the destruction of the Righteous Teacher's followers among 'the Poor' (*Ebionim*), see 1QpHab 12.5.
42. 1QpHab 5.8–12.

Chapter 17

1. *Vir. ill.* 2.
2. *B. San.* 45b–46b, 49b–50b, 53a–56b, etc., Lev. 24:14–16, and Deut. 17:2–5.
3. *ARN* 4.5; cf. *Git.* 56a–56b.
4. *EH* 3.33. Eusebius also notes 'their unwillingness to sacrifice to idols'. The extant Pliny, 10.96–7, doesn't say exactly this, though it does note the Christian habits of praying at dawn to Christ and that people were 'refusing to purchase *things to sacrifice to idols*'.
5. *EH* 3.20.1–4; cf. James' proclamation in *EH* 2.23.9 and 13 and Jas. 4:11–5:9 above. Here 'the calluses', that are mentioned, are on their hands from the hard work they performed, not on their 'knees'.
6. 2 Apoc. Jas. 62.10. Cf. how this element reappears in Talmudic descriptions of stoning in *b. San.* 45a–b.
7. Appianus, *Civil Wars* 1.120. For beheading in the *Talmud*, see *San.* 37b, 49b–56b, and *Ket.* 30b.
8. *Ant.* 18.119 and 20.98–9 (both the beheadings of 'Theudas' and 'James the brother of John' come in direct proximity to reference to the 'Great Famine').
9. *San.* 45a–b above and *Ket.* 30a–b.
10. *B. San.* 56a–56b and 60a.
11. 4Q246, *DSSU*, pp. 68–71. Cf. Wisd. 2:16, 'the Righteous One is God's son' with 1QH 9.30–36, Matt. 5:9-10, 5:45, Luke 20:36, etc.
12. Cf. Mark 11:15–18 and pars. with John 2:13–22.
13. Cf. Gen. 4:26 (Enoch), 12:8 and 14:4 (Abraham) with Exod. 3:14–15 (Moses).
14. T. Zahn in H.-J. Schoeps, *Paul: Theology of the Apostle in the Light of Jewish Religious History*, Philadelphia, 1961, p. 67.
15. *War* 2.7/*Ant.* 17.207–8
16. Cf. CD 4.3–7 with 1QS 5.2 and 5.9.
17. 1QpHab 4.14–5.5 (also 10.3–5 and 13).
18. CD 6.5; cf. the allusion to 'going out into the wilderness to prepare the Way of the Lord' in 1QS 8.13–14 and 9.19–24, not to mention that to 'the Sons of Benjamin, the *Galut* ['Dispersion'] of the Desert' and that to 'the Exiled Sons of Light in the Desert of the Peoples' (1QM 1.3). This will be very important when it comes to discussing the conver-

sion of the Kings of Adiabene further north.
19. CD 14.8–11, 15.8–15, 1QS 6.12, etc.; also Cross, p. 232.
20. For 'Oblias'/'Alphaeus'/'Lebbaeus' tangles, see *MZCQ*, p. 48.
21. Cf. 4QpPs 37 3.13–17 and 1QpHab 11.8 with Jas. 2:10, Rom. 13:13–23, and 1 Cor. 8:7–13 on 'things sacrificed to idols'.
22. In *Vita* 7–8, Josephus says he was of 'the highest repute in Jerusalem' and notes his 'pre-eminent Righteousness'.
23. Note the inverted play here on James' 'Friend of God' language.
24. *Ant* 20.202. As it turns out, the Rabbinic sources related to the 'Sanhedrin's Exile' from its normal place of sitting in the Stone Chamber on the Temple Mount, forty years prior to the fall of Jerusalem – which ultimately throw light on these mysterious notices in the Habakkuk *Pesher* about 'the Wicked Priest's House of Exile' and confrontations centring on *Yom Kippur* – claim that the Sanhedrin no longer had the power to impose the death penalty; *San.* 41a, *Shab.* 15a, *R.H.* 31a–b, *A.Z.* 8b, etc.
25. 1QpHab 11.4–8. As noted, some would equate this *'Hanut'* with 'the House of Hanan', i.e., 'Ananus'. For the Sanhedrin meeting at such a 'House' in the New Testament, see Luke 22:54 and Matt. 26:57.
26. 1QpHab 11.9–15. See also 4Q436 (Hymns of the Poor), Fragment 2:1–8, *DSSU*, pp. 236–41.
27. *Ket.* 30b. Also see 'casting down' into a pit generally as part of stoning in *San.* 45a.
28. *B. San.* 81b–82b; *Tos. Kelim* 1.6.
29. *B. Tam.* 29a–b and *Men.* 21b.
30. This psalm doesn't read this way in either the Masoretic or Septuagint, but rather, 'My strength is dried up and my tongue cleaves to the roof of my mouth' – transformed here to 'my mouth' or 'tongue being dried up'.
31. *B. San.* 44a–b, *Sota* 8a, and 23a.
32. Cf. *Ant.* 20.43–6 with Acts 15:1 (the 'some who came down from Jerusalem' to 'Antioch', triggering 'the Jerusalem Council').
33. *War* 4.317–18; cf. Deut. 21:23 and *b. San.* 46a–b.
34. *War* 6.288–301.
35. 4QpPs 37 2.12–20, 3.6–12, and 4.9–21, including allusion to 'cutting off', 'doing', God 'saving the Righteous One', and 'the Congregation' or 'Church of the Poor'.
36. 1QpHab 9.1–2 and 11.15–12.6.
37. Ps. *Rec.* 1.70–73.
38. *Vir. ill.* 1.
39. Ps. *Rec.* 1.16–48, 2.7, 5.10, *Hom.* 2.4–20, 22, 42–53 (including Deut. 18:15–19, reproduced in 4QTest 5–8 at Qumran).
40. It adds, 'especially with those who waited *for him*'. This theme is to be found in 1QpHab 7.9–14 on Hab. 2:3 ('the Delay of the

Parousia'), a passage also expounded, as we saw, in *San.* 97b above, where it is related to the 'times' of the Messianic Era and the 36 'Righteous Ones' that will sustain the world, based on the numerology of 'for him'. Cf. too, 'Hanan the Hidden' (John the Baptist?), the grandson of Honi the Circle-Drawer, *b. Ta'an.* 23b, and Luke 1.24 on Elizabeth (John's mother) 'hiding herself', paralleled in the Protevangelium of James (22.3–23.1), and Herod's alleged question, 'Where have you *hidden* your son?' For the *Talmud* – ribaldly parodying 'Essene' scrupulousness? – he is '*hidden in the toilet*'.

41. Ps. *Rec.* 1.7–12.

42. Ps. *Rec.* 1.72, 4.25, and Epistle of Clement to James 19–20.

43. For 4Q477, see *DSSU*, pp. 269–72.

44. Ps. *Rec.* 1.10.5.

45. I am indebted to my colleague S. Jones for the basis of this translation.

46. Epistle of Peter to James 2.

47. *Ant.* 20.51–3 and 101. For Helen as Nazirite, see *b. Naz.* 19b. In *Ket.* 7a, a ruling requiring her to be a Nazirite for seven years was said to have been made in 'Sidon'. Simon *Magus*, as we saw, was also reputed to travel with his 'Queen Helen' (Ps. *Hom.* 2.23–5 – *Rec.* 2.9–12 rather calls her 'Luna'). Early Church sources (*Ad. Haer.* 1.23.2 and *EH* 2.13.4) assert Simon picked her up in a brothel in Tyre! Whether she is the same as Helen of Adiabene, who, as we saw too, shows an extraordinary interest in the 'Suspected Adulteress' admonition (following reference to the pollution of the desert 'camp' (Num. 5:1–32) and preceding that on Naziritism generally (Num. 6:1–21); *Yoma* 37a/*Git.* 60a), is impossible to say.

48. Ps. *Rec.* 1.73–4. The 'Zacchaeus' referred to may be the father of the legendary Rabbi Yohanan ben Zacchai. That Yohanan has another relative that is 'Head of the *Sicarii* in Jerusalem' is made clear in *b. Git.* 56a.

49. For Helen and her son's 'Riches' and 'Piety', see *Ant.* 20.51–3 above, as well as *Yoma* 37a–b and *B.B.* 11a.

50. Cf. Paul's doctrine of the new Christians as the real 'Sons of Abraham' in Rom. 9:7–8 and Gal. 4:28). Herodians too were probably making the 'Sons of Abraham' claim (not to mention 'the Peoples' in the Edessa/Haran/Adiabene region) – just as 'Arabs' do today, though through Esau, not Ishmael (in any event related to Ishmael – Gen. 28:9). Muhammad, too, will inadvertently reflect some of the importance of Abraham and Noah to these Northern Syria/Kurdistan areas, when he begins to tell his stories of 'Ād and Thamūd, Hūd and Sāliḥ in *Surahs* 7, 11, 26, 27, etc.

Chapter 18

1. CD 8.21–38 (following evocation of 'Gehazi').

2. Cf. 1QS 8.13–9.21, etc.

3. Also see John 7:4–10 and Mark 4:22.

4. Epistle of Peter to James 4.1–4.

5. Acts 15:7–11, followed by a speech by James (15:14–18) *actually* containing materials from the Damascus Document at Qumran.

6. 'Saulus' too in Josephus. H.-J. Schoeps, *Theologie und Geschichte des Judenchristentums*, Tübingen, 1949, pp. 441ff. was the first to advance this theory, though he did not go as far in pointing up the language overlaps as we are doing between James' fall and the stoning of Stephen. In fact, the *Homilies* is often even more accurate, showing Peter as a daily bather, a vegetarian, and following James' directives to overseas communities, which include 'things sacrificed to idols' (which it identifies with 'the table of demons') and the precise identification of 'strangled things' with 'carrion' (7.8).

7. Only in 2 Tim. 1:2 and 4:10 – probably mistakenly – is there any overlap.

8. Cf. Josephus' long quotation from the Fourth Book of Nicolaus' *Histories* in *Ant.* 1.159 on Abraham's place of origin north of Babylon and how his name was 'still honoured in the region of Damascus'; also *Ant.* 17.315–17 on Nicolaus' defence of Herod against Jewish charges before Augustus, etc.

9. Of course, this may be a Samaritan source. We have already seen that Simon *Magus* and Dositheus (whom Josephus nevertheless calls 'a Jewish leader') were Samaritan 'Disciples' of John the Baptist; and the whole mix-up of 'the *Taheb*' – the Samaritan 'Joshua *redivivus*' – with traditions about 'Jesus' should always be kept in mind.

10. The 'dead-alive Joshua' or Jesus' 'resurrection' might even have been seen to be based on the confusing complex of Josh. 24:9, Judg. 1:1, and 2:6.

11. Cf. *Ant.* 20.97–102 with Acts 5:36–8; n.b. the reversal of 'drawing away'/'withdraw' ('apostacize') in the next sentence, but the parallel represented by the use of precisely *these same words*, 'drawing away to revolt' and 'the people' in *Ant.* 20.102. The literary dependence is, once again, plain.

12. Note in Acts 6:1–2, on the 'daily service', what is really being talked about is 'serving tables' – the author seemingly familiar with a quasi-monastic community such as at Qumran.

13. *Ant.* 20.214; cf. Acts 9:1 on 'Saulus'' riotous behaviour.

14. *Ant.* 20.101. The note about 'Egypt' in Josephus is important, 'Gaza' being the traditional gateway to Egypt, i.e., Queen

Kandakes' 'Treasurer' and Queen Helen's 'Treasury agents' were both *on their way to Egypt* (Helen's obviously with more cause).

15. *EH* 1.13.1–2.1.8 and 2.12.1. Cf. *Ant.* 20.17–96, 101 and Moses of Chorene 2.30–33.

16. E.g., 1QpHab 11.4–16 and 1QH 9.8–9, probably harking back to Hab. 1:13: 'the Wicked swallows one more Righteous than he'. Cf. Num. 16:30–34 above on Korah, who 'was swallowed up'.

17. Cf. the 'casting down' referred to in 1QpHab 11.8 above, as well as the 'casting down' in Talmudic accounts of stoning in *b. San.* 45a–b, certainly parodied in 2 Apoc. Jas. 61.20–62.15.

18. Matt. 4:1 and Luke 4:1 use 'Diabolos', but Mark 1:12, which curtails the episode, only 'Satan'.

19. In Luke 5:27, simply 'Levi'; Matt. 9:9, Matthew himself – but the whole confusion relates to the one about Barnabas above, 'called Joses a Levite from *Cyprus*', and the 'Joseph Barsabas *Justus*' tangle in the election of 'Matthias' (also Josephus' brother's name) to fill the place left by Judas. As we shall see, 'Alphaeus' will be simply another corruption of 'Cleophas' – Jesus' probable *real* father – and the reason behind these 'Cyprus' evasions begins to emerge.

20. *War* 2.143.

21. Matt. 13:47, John 21:6–8, etc.

22. It is interesting that the 'shell' symbolism associated with this is also a decorative motif of first-century BC–first century CE sarcophagi. The panel depicting the Temple façade over the niche in the synagogue at Dura-Europos (*c.*245 CE) depicts it as a motif above the entranceway to the Temple (because of which it becomes a feature of its *Torah* ark); for the synagogue at Capernaum, a decorative motif of one end of the original Ark. See E. R. Goodenough, *Jewish Symbols in the Greco-Roman Period*, New York, 1953, vol. III, plates 472, 498, and 499; and vol. XI, plates III, X, and 66; for an ossuary, vol. III, plate 161.

23. *Ant.* 19.331.

24. *Ant.* 19.329–31. This can even mean 'Upright' or 'Righteous'.

25. *M. Sota* 7:8; cf. *M. Bik.* 3–4.

26. *Ant.* 15.369–70.

27. *Ant.* 15.371–2. It should not be forgotten Josephus is working off sources – such as Nicolaus of Damascus – here, and may be reproducing their errors or conflating them.

28. *Ant.* 15.365–9.

29. *Ant.* 19.353; also 19.299 and 317–26.

30. *Vita* 46–61, particularly 56 (also 179–84).

31. *EH* 1.12.1–4, 2.1.5, and the two Lists of the Twelve Apostles and the Seventy attributed to Hippolytus in ANCL; cf. Luke 10:1 and Acts

6:2–5 and 21:8, reckoning Philip instead among 'the Seven'.

32. *War* 4.385–8. Therefore, instead of the Temple falling because of the death of James, whose followers Acts acknowledges were 'Zealots for the Law', the Temple falls because of such 'Zealots'.

33. *Ant.* 19.357.

34. Cf. Acts 10:1–6, 22, and 30–35 with *Ant.* 19.366. Surely the name 'Cornelius' is significant, particularly as 'the circumcision believers' are then mentioned in 10:45–11:3 and all of Peter's words here are directly contradicted in the Pseudoclementine *Homilies*.

35. *Ant.* 20.147.

36. *Ant.* 20.143.

37. Here for some reason the confusion of 'Cyprus' – as with 'Elymus *Magus*' in Acts 13:8 – with Simon *Magus*' real birthplace, 'Gitta in Samaria', which neither Josephus nor Acts seem to know.

38. CD 5.7–11.

39. CD 5.11–15.

40. CD 8.4–11.

41. See A. N. Sherwin-White, *The Roman Citizenship*, pp. 271–5 and cf. Paul 'speaking to the Gentiles' as 'the Apostle of *the Gentiles*' (*Ethnōn*) in Rom. 11:12–13; 1QpHab 5.12–6.11, applying Hab. 1:14–16 'fishing net' symbolism to the tax-farming of 'the *Kittim*', who 'sacrifice to their standards and worship their weapons of war . . . eating all the Peoples year by year'; and the use of 'the Peoples' (*ha-'Amim*) generally to refer to 'Herodians' at Qumran.

42. CD 8.12–13.

43. CD 4.19–5.2, attacking Rulers like the Herodians, who divorce and 'multiply wives unto themselves'. The sense is that 'the false prophets', encouraging them in these things, are the 'daubers upon the wall' of Ezek. 13:10 – also alluded to in CD 8.12 above.

44. See, for instance, the use of the word 'Jew' (*Yehudi*) in 4Q550, *DSSU*, pp. 99–103 and 4Q324 ('Aemilius Kills') on Priestly Courses, 119–26, as well as the more esoteric 'House of Judah' in the crucial CD 4.11–12 and 1QpHab (on Hab. 2:4) 8.1–3.

45. 1QS 8.5–10 and 9.4–6.

46. *Ant.* 1.8; cf. *Vita* 430, *Contra Apion* 1.1, 2.1, and 2.296.

47. *Ant.* 20.144 and 147.

48. As we saw, other versions call him 'Atomus', probably a variation on the 'Primal Adam' ideology which, all sources agree, Simon (like the 'Jesus' in Scripture with the descent of the 'dove') claimed to be.

49. Cf. Dio Cassius, 68.14.5–33.3 and 69.12.1–15 with *EH* 4.2.1–4.7.4 on the one led by 'Andreas'/'Man' or 'Adam' in Cyrene.

50. Suetonius, 12.15–17 and Dio Cassius, 67.14.1–18.2, while *EH* 3.18.4, probably

mistakenly, calls her his niece (he probably means 'relative'). Whatever the case, her estate (and probably 'Clement''s) becomes the site of the largest Christian catacomb in Rome.

51. 3.32.1–6. Eusebius (again quoting Hegesippus) seems to think, as we saw, that Simeon lived to be 'a hundred and twenty'. But, of course – aside from being the number of years ascribed to Moses in Scripture – this is simply an echo of Josephus' and Hippolytus' report of the longevity of these life-long, 'Essene'-like, Nazirite daily bathers. In James' case, according to Epiphanius, supposedly ninety-six years – others 'over a hundred'.

52. EH 3.12.1.

53. EH 3.19.1–20.9 (n.b. how, after telling us in 3.18.4 that Domitilla 'was banished' to an island; Eusebius picks up the thread of his narrative by telling us in 3.20.9 how 'the Apostle John' left an island).

54. EH 3.20.5.

55. EH 3.32.3–8. Here Eusebius, relying on Hegesippus, definitely calls 'Simon' (a moment earlier he was calling him 'Simeon') the son of 'Mary the wife of Clopas', which, of course, clearly makes him *the brother* of Jesus' other brothers. This is basically the same testimony given in the ANCL Papias Fragment 10.2, which simply calls her 'Mary the wife of Cleophas or Alphaeus'.

Chapter 19

1. Cf. 1QS 8.9 and 9.4–5 above on the Community Council as a 'pleasing odour and sweet fragrance', including 'spiritualized Temple' imagery and making an atonement through suffering; also Rom. 15:16, 'the offering up of the Peoples' as 'a pleasing sacrifice' and Phil. 4:18, Epaphroditus' efforts, the same.

2. 1QpHab 10.11–12 – even 'of Emptiness'; cf. Jas. 2:20's 'Empty Man', relating to Gen. 15:6 and Hab. 2:4.

3. 1QpHab 7.14–17, also on Hab. 2:4.

4. A theme also emphasized in Rom. 1:25, 3:7, 9:1, 2 Cor. 11:31, 2 Thess. 2:11, 1 Tim. 2:7 and Titus 1:2.

5. N.b. the imagery of 'the Holy Spirit' being 'poured out' here in Titus 3:6 as well; also the 'poison'/'wine' homonyms relate to the 'drinking the dregs'/'Cup of Wrath' in 1QpHab 11.14–15, CD 8.9–13, and the Hymns of the Poor (4Q436) 5–6 above.

6. 1QpHab 10.11–12 above.

7. *Contra Apion* 1.51. The 'Herod' Josephus also mentions here as one of his readers would seem to be the son of Aristobulus and Salome, possibly also mentioned in Rom. 16:11 ('the Littlest Herod'), where 'Aristobulus' household' is also mentioned. Julius was originally married to Mariamme the sister of Bernice

and Drusilla above, by whom he had a daughter, named Bernice too. Later Mariamme divorced him to contract a better marriage with Demetrius, the Alabarch of Alexandria, who was probably even 'Richer', by whom she had another son, Agrippinus (the Littlest Agrippa).

8. *War* 7.199–209. Josephus estimates some seventeen hundred men slain at Machaeros alone. EH 4.6.1 notes a third 'Rufus', as the Governor of Judea, who 'destroyed without mercy thousands upon thousands of men, women, and children, confiscating and subjecting their lands' at the time of the Bar Kochba Revolt.

9. *War* 7.32–4.

10. See, for instance, his attack on calendrical and festival observance as 'weak and beggarly elements' in Gal. 4:9. For 'Vain', see Gal. 2:2, 2:21, 4:56, etc.; for 'Vainglory' see Gal. 3:4, 4:11, 1 Cor. 15:2–58, Rom. 1:21, etc., and cf. the 'Glorying' the Liar does in his 'Lying Works' and 'Empty' and 'Worthless Service' in 1QpHab 10.11–12 above.

11. CD 4.3, 4QpNah 3.9, 4.5, etc.

12. Cf. the 'stumbling' language in Jas. 2:10, 1QpHab 11.8 above, 1QS 2.12–17, 3.24, 1QH 9.21–7, 16.23, 4Q525 (*DSSU*, pp. 170–76, referring to 'the stumbling block of the Tongue'), etc. For Peter in the Ps. *Hom.*, see 7.3–8.

13. 4.9–11. This is the same 'watchtower' referred to in Hab. 2:1, interpreted in 1QpHab 6.12–7.14 in terms of the Righteous Teacher's exposition of 'the Delay of the Last Era' (i.e., 'the *Parousia*').

14. 1QpHab 10.10 above.

15. Cf. Matt. 17:24–7 on the issue of paying the Temple tax (after the 70 CE War, forfeit to Roman coffers), 'the sons of man are free', however, to avoid 'causing them to stumble', one should 'cast a hook' into the sea and take the shekel from the mouth of a fish! In Hebrew, it should be recalled, there is a difference between 'works' and 'work' in the sense of 'labour' or 'mission'; therefore, at Qumran, when speaking about 'the Lying Spouter', we are speaking about his 'labour' or 'service' – not his 'works'. This does not come through in the Greek.

16. It will be recalled, in the very important passage at the end of the exhortative section of the Damascus Document (20.32–4), we hear about 'heeding the voice of the Righteous Teacher and not deserting the Laws of Righteousness', but rather 'prevailing' or 'being victorious over all the sons of earth' and 'seeing His Salvation [*Yeshu'a*], because they took refuge in His Holy Name'.

17. EH 1.7.14, 3.11.1, and 3.32.6. Here, Origen makes it clear the second person is 'Simon' – either 'Simon Cephas' or 'Simeon bar Cleophas'.

18. *EH* 3.32.1–6. As we saw, Eusebius' source here, Hegesippus, is calling him 'Simon the son of Clopas'. For the Papias Fragment 10.2 above, this is also the name of Jesus' third brother.

19. De Vaux, pp. 60–90 and P. Bar-Adon, loc. cit. Recently, as we have seen, among debris at Qumran, shards were found, which were receipts for supplies from '*Jericho*' and bearing the date formulae, 'Year 2' of the Uprising against Rome.

20. Mur. 45.6.

21. R. Reich, 'Caiaphas Name Inscribed on Bone Boxes', *BAR*, September/October, 1992, pp. 38–44. As we saw, one ossuary bore the name 'Kepha''; and the other, 'Keipha''.

22. The voice is speaking directly to Philoctetes 'from the High Seat of Heaven by the will of Zeus' (1420–46).

23. *B. San.* 45b–46b spends considerable time discussing it, the 'curse' allegedly being – as with archetypal 'Enemies' like Balaam, Do'eg, Korah, and Gehazi – because they 'cursed God'. But the hanging occurs only *after* stoning (i.e., because they were 'blasphemers'). Here the point seized upon in John 19:31–3 on 'breaking [Jesus'] legs' (not James), that the bodies 'were not to *remain all night upon the tree*' is reiterated (cf. too *War* 4.317–18 on Ananus' death). This John garbles into 'the Sabbath', 'a Feast Day' (cf. 1QpHab 11.4–8's description of 'the Wicked Priest swallowing' the Righteous Teacher in 'his House' ['of Exile'] and 'casting them down on the Fast Day, the Sabbath of their Rest' or 'at the completion of their Festival of Rest').

   But, as we saw, 4QpNah 1.7–9 makes it clear that, for it, the 'hanging a man up alive' is what is 'cursed' *not the man*. In any event, the New Testament makes its knowledge of these sources plain – including, for instance, 'rending the clothes' (*San.* 60a). In Paul's case (though *probably not* Jesus'), the 'curse', which he so deftly refashions, no doubt really was for 'blasphemy'. Also see Jas. 3:8–15 (on 'the Tongue'), 1QS 2.4–18, 4QD266 17, 4Q286 (*DSSU*, pp. 224–30: 'The Community Council Curses Belial'), where this kind of 'cursing' is tangible.

24. Both are clearly 'Epistle's, if not to 'Abgarus' ('the Great King of the Peoples beyond the Euphrates'; cf. Dio Cassius, 68.18.1–21.1, who, even in Trajan's time, calls him 'Augurus' – v. mss. 'Al-Barus', i.e., Josephus' 'Bazeus', Queen Helen's husband); then to King Izates, Helen's son (later in Josephus 'Izas'); cf. 4QMMT 2.9–33 addressed to a King who cares about 'the Book of Moses', 'Israel', and is to 'be justified' – like Abraham – 'by works'.

25. *EH* 2.23.7–8 and 15–16.

26. Again, note the typical language of 'pouring out', applied now, not just to Peter, but to 'Gentiles as well', language used at Qumran to describe the activities of the Liar, who 'poured out on Israel the waters of Lying' (CD 1.14–15) and 'spouted'/'poured out to them' (4.20/8.13).

27. Cf. *Ant.* 20.101–2 (spelling it 'Cyrinius'; for Luke 2:2, 'Cyrenius'), followed by the mention of Judas the Galilean and his two sons with Acts 6:9, 11:20, etc. – here, our 'Cypriots' and 'Cyrenians' again.

28. In 1QpHab 12.1–10, it is usually not appreciated that 'the Poor' (identified with 'the Simple of Judah doing *Torah*'), whose 'blood' (together, it would appear, with 'the blood of Man') is being spilled, are in Jerusalem. In 4QpPs 37 2.10 and 3.10, they are 'the Congregation' or 'Church of the Poor', who 'will be saved' (the 'saved' here is the same as that in the *Pesher* on Hab. 2:4 – 1QpHab 8.2 and 12.14) 'from all the nets of Belial'. These will 'inherit the whole world' (also 'the high mountain in Jerusalem'), 'while those cursed by [God] will be cut off' (Ps. 37:22; cf. Paul in Gal. 5:12, expressing the wish that the circumcisers – 'those throwing you into confusion' – '*Sicarii*' in Origen) 'would themselves cut off'!

29. Cf. both Moses in the cloud (Exod. 24:15–18 and 34:5) and 'the Son of Man coming on the clouds' (*EH* 2.23.13, Matt. 24:30, 26:64, and pars.). Luke adds, they 'appeared in Glory' and that they spoke about Jesus' coming death in Jerusalem, a subject not included in the others (9:28–31).

30. 1QM 12.8 and 19.1–2 (cf. Jas. 5:4–9). In the interplay of these imageries, 'rain' is, of course, not unrelated to baptism.

31. John 1.21–7 (including allusion to the 'Standing One'), however, as we saw, specifically denies this.

32. Cf. *Dial.* 88, 103, John 1:14–18, and 3:16–18 with *Ant.* 20.20. Also *Haeres.* 30.13.7, 'the Hebrew Gospel'.

33. Cf. Luke 6:35, 20.:36, Rom. 8:14–19, 2 Cor. 6:18, and Gal. 4:6 with 1QH 9.24–6.

34. Ps. 110:1, also evoking 'sitting at My right hand' and 'a Priest forever after the Order of Melchizedek'. For a new Qumran text, evoking this, see the Kabbalistic 4Q286 1.1–2 in *DSSU* pp. 222–30 ('The Chariots of Glory'), also uncompromisingly militant and probably alluding to 'the Standing One'.

35. CD 6.3–11 (also evoking the 'Standing One') and 7.14–21, again evoking his 'standing up', but also that 'the Tabernacle of the King' (Amos 5:26–7 – identified with 'the fallen Tabernacle of David'; Amos 9:11), would 'be exiled to Damascus' in 'the Land of the North' (interpretable as Edessa or Adiabene).

36. The point is that malefactors were stoned naked; cf. *b. San.* 44b–45a above. This has

been confused in Stephen's stoning with those involved in the stoning *being naked* (Acts 7:58). This relates to 'the linen clothes' in the empty tomb in John 20:5–7 (for the Synoptics, only 'a linen cloth'/burial shroud; Matt. 27:59, etc. –.a disputed notice from *San.* 43a claims Jesus too was first stoned). In turn, all become confused with the 'linen clothing' the Essenes wore and special 'white linen girdle' they wore out of modesty to bath (*War* 2.129–38, Hipp. 9.15–18, *EH* 2.23.6, etc.).

Chapter 20

1. 1QS 8.1.
2. 1QS 8.5–9.4.
3. 1QS 9.4–5 and 9.20–24.
4. Cf. Matt. 20:20–28/Mark 10:35–45 with 1QpHab 5.3.
5. CD 4.10–12 and 1QpHab 8.1–3 in exegesis of Hab. 2:4.
6. Epistle of Peter to James 4.1–3. Actually, the *Homilies* goes a good deal further than this, picturing Peter as insisting (at Tripoli): 'Above all, remember to shun any Apostle, teacher, or prophet who does not accurately compare his teaching with (that of) James, who was called the brother of my Lord and to whom was entrusted the Overseership of the Assembly of the Hebrews in Jerusalem – and this even if he comes to you with recommendations' (Ps. *Hom.* 11.35). Even more, it contends that '(the Evil One) promised He would send Apostles from among His subjects as Deceivers', having already 'disputed forty days with (our Lord and Prophet), but failed to prevail against him' (no word about 'in the wilderness') – a probable truer picture of the gist of this tradition than one gets in Gospel redaction.
7. Note the theme in Luke 13:23–8, preceding this, of 'entering by the narrow gate', 'shutting the door' (cf. CD 6.12–14 (Mal. 1:10), and 'standing outside' again (in Matt. 12:46–7, this language is used to describe '*his mother and his brothers*'), then turning into 'knocking at the door', and being 'cast out' (*ekballō*) of the Kingdom; following it, the use of the language of 'Glory' in the context of alluding to 'he that exalts himself being humbled and he that humbles himself being exalted' (Luke 14:10–11). In the process, Luke 14:5 specifically attacks the Qumran position (CD 11.13–14) on 'not taking an animal, that fell into a pit, out on the Sabbath.'
8. CD 14.9.
9. Ibid. and 1QH 2.15, 2.19, 5.12–16 (about 'the Poor'), 5.26–8 (alluding to 'Belial' and 'viper's venom'), 7.10–16, 12.14, 14.13, etc.
10. Cf. 1 Cor. 3:5–6 with 1 Cor. 12:14–31, Rom. 12:1–5 (including the 'living sacrifice, Holy and well-pleasing to God' language), etc.

11. 1QpHab 8.1–3 (on Hab. 2:4) and 10.10–12.
12. Koran 2.61, 3.21, 3.183, 4.155, etc.
13. CD 4.7 (reversing 1.19), 1QS 3.2–3, 1QH 13.16–17, 16.11, etc.
14. A. v. Harnack, 'Die Verklärungsgeschichte Jesu, der Gericht des Paulus (I. Kor. 15,3ff.) under die Beiden Christusvisionen des Petrus', *Sitzungsberichte der Preussischen Akademie*, 1922, pp. 62–80 – the first to point this out.
15. 1QS 2.22 (also 1:12); cf. 'House (of God)' and 'Community of Truth'/'His Truth' in 2.23–6, 'Holy Assembly' ('Church') in 2.16 and 5.20, 'Community of the Covenant' in 8.16, 'House of Faith' in CD 3.19, and 'House of the Torah' in CD 8.33 and 8.36.
16. Cf. Clement of Alexandria, 1.29, 2.15, *EH* 3.3.2, and Jerome, *Vir. ill.* 1.
17. 1QpHab 7.2–13, 1QS 4.13–25, CD 2.9–10, 4.8–11, etc.
18. 1QpHab 9.3–7; also see 2.7, 7.2–14 above, CD 1.4–16, 4.6–8, 6.2–11, and 8.16–32.
19. 1QM 7.6, 12.9, 19.1, and CD 15.17 (4Q267 Frag. 17).
20. *Haeres.* 30.13.7.
21. *Vir. ill.* 2.
22. 1QpHab 11.2–12.6. Also see Hymns of the Poor, 4Q436 1.5–6, above, with exactly the same imagery, paralleling it.
23. In this regard, one also should note John 21:2's allusion to 'Nathanael' – who replaces 'James the son of Alphaeus' in all of John's Apostolic reckonings and in the Epist. Apost. 2 – as being from the village of 'Cana in Galilee', a notation we shall connect (pp. 815–16) to both '*Kanna'im*' (Mark's and Matthew's 'Cananites' or 'Cananaeans' – Hebrew meaning, 'Zealots') and 'Galileans'. Not only will we have (pp. 819–21) the Honi the *Circle*-Drawer, *redivivus*-type episode in John 1:45–51 picturing Nathanael as 'sitting under a fig tree' when he first sees Jesus; this 'Cana of Galilee', where Jesus first 'made water into wine' (John 4:46), can perhaps be thought of as replacing the 'Kfar Sechania' (*A.Z.* 17a and *Git.* 57a)/'Sihnin' in Rabbinic traditions about its 'Jacob'.
24. Cf. Josephus' 'Jesus the son of Sapphias', whom he calls 'the Leader of the Party of the sailors and the Poor' (who fight the Romans to the last man in boats, 'until the whole Sea of Galilee ran red' with their blood in *Vita* 66–7 and *War* 3.498–531). In *Vita* 304–5 too, in the context of these struggles, Josephus himself takes to a boat to escape from Jesus' people across the Sea of Galilee.
25. Cf. the all-night vigils at Qumran (1QS 6.7) and later by Muhammad (Koran 93.3, etc.) and those from among the 'People of the Book' whom Muhammad calls 'of the Righteous', who also '*believe and do good works*' (Koran 3.113–15).
26. In Acts 15:14, at the 'Jerusalem Council', this

will now be James (recapitulating the 'Visitation' language in the Damascus Document) speaking about how 'Simeon' (Simon Peter) related 'how God *first visited the Peoples (Ethnōn)* to *take out a nation for His Name*' – in turn, echoing 'the Sons of Zadok' being 'called by Name' in CD 2.11–13 and 4.4–5 and 'taking refuge in His Holy Name' of CD 8.57. Also see Jas. 2:7 on 'the Good Name by which you are called', Paul in Rom. 10:13, 1 Cor. 1:2, etc.

27. Cf. Matt. 13:41–3 with Jas. 2:9–11; also Paul, Rom. 9:32–3, 14:13–21, 1 Cor. 8:9–13, Gal. 5.11, etc.

28. For 'Fire', see 1QS 2.8, CD 2.5, 5.13, 1QpHab 10.4–5, 12–13, etc.; for 'Completion of the Age', CD 4.8–10 and 1QpHab 7.2–7.

29. *War* 4.324 and 4.343.

30. Though this passage is applied to James' death in *EH* 2.23.15, its reflection is clearly seen in 1QpHab 12.2–3, in exposition of Hab. 2:17 on 'the blood of Man', on how the Wicked Priest 'would be paid the reward he paid the Poor'. It is also to be seen in 4QpPs 37 4.9–10 on the same subject.

31. 1QpHab 5.12–6.11..

32. 1QpHab 7.7–16. This passage is also subjected to exegesis in *b. San.* 97b, as we have seen. There, too, it is interpreted eschatologically in terms of 'the Delay of the *Parousia*' or 'the Last Age' and *'the thirty-six Righteous Ones'* who will uphold the world – once again, attesting to the First–Second century CE provenance of all these things.

33. This is, of course, the 'True Prophet' of Deut. 18:18–19, quoted in both 4QTest 5–8 and Ps. *Hom.* 3.53. But, most importantly, this is actually referred to in conjunction with 'the Messiah of Aaron and Israel' in 1QS 9.11.

34. 1QpHab 2.7–10, showing 'the Priest' (i.e., 'the High Priest') and 'the Teacher' are identical; cf. 1QpHab 7.4–14 – also beginning with the words, 'the Last Generation'.

Chapter 21

1. See CD 1.4, 'delivered them up to the sword'; 1.5-6, 'to be destroyed'; 1.17, 'to the avenging sword'; 3.10, 7.13, 8.1, 1QS 2.5, etc. – also connected to being 'cut off' in CD 3.1, 3.7–9, 1QS 2.6, 1QpHab 10.2, etc.

2. CD 4.3–7, 1QpHab 6.4–5, etc.

3. For 'the Many' at Qumran, see 1QS 6.1–21, 7.10–9.2, CD 13.7–14.11, etc.

4. 1QpHab 10.6; NB the purposeful contrast of the Liar's *''amal'*/'works' (Isa. 53:11 – 1QpHab 10.12) with the Righteous Teacher's (1QpHab 8.2).

5. Cf. *War* 2.128–9 and 141–2 with Epistle of Peter to James 4–5 and Paul in 1 Cor. 15:3.

6. Cf. CD 3.2–6 with Jas. 1:16–25, 2:5–13, and 4:11.

7. CD 2.8, 3.1–9, etc. above. The reference is to consuming the quail in Num. 11:31–4, though *per contra*, see Exod. 16:13/Ps .105:40.

8. CD 1.3–5, 1.14–2.1, 3.8–11, 5.13–21, 8.1, etc.

9. Cf. CD 8.14–36, 1QS 2.4–18, and 9.21–224, not 'loving' but 'Eternal hatred for the Sons of the Pit'.

10. *Ant.* 19.334, following his encounter with 'Simon'.

11. N.b. the 'Nazirite'-style 'Holiness' language (as at Qumran – CD 6.15, 7.3, and 8.8) being played upon here; a version of the Jews 'killing all the Prophets', this time ascribed to Elijah (1 Kgs. 19:10 and 14 – Rom. 11:3), but neglecting the allusion to a 'burning zeal for the Lord of Hosts' tied to these; and the 'net' and 'stumbling block' language, evoking David (Rom. 11:9), i.e., Ps. 69:22–3 – the same thoroughly 'Zionist' Psalm evoking 'zeal for Your House consumes me', 'let their camp be a ruin and no one inhabit their tents' (applied to Judas *Iscariot*'s death in Acts 1:20 – clearly, there was a Qumran-style *pesher* (not surprisingly) extant somewhere on this Psalm), God's 'burning Anger', 'being swallowed', 'given vinegar to drink', 'the Poor' (*Ebionim*), 'the Righteous' (*Zaddikim*), and God's 'Salvation' (*Yeshu'a*) – but all now related to how 'Salvation is granted to the Gentiles' (Rom. 11:11).

12. CD 1.1, 1.12, 1.19–21, 2.4, and 4.4–7.

13. CD 3.18–20, including allusion to 'forgiveness from sin' and 'building a House of Faith in Israel' (cf. Paul, 1 Cor. 3:9–12) and 1QS 4.20–23. Also see 4QpPs 37 3.1–2, promising (as in the Damascus Document) 'the Penitents in the wilderness' and 'the Congregation of the Poor' to 'live for a thousand generations'.

14. One should note these allusions to 'Name' and 'naming' not only throughout Acts, but also CD 2.13 (somehow deleted in Vermes' translation): 'and in the explanation of His Name [apparently the 'Messiah''s, which would make the reference in CD 2.12 singular] their names (are to be found?)'.

15. Literally, 'and the *Nilvim* with them' (CD 4.3). For the '*Nilvim*' as Gentiles, see Esther 9:27 and 4QpNah 2.9 and 3.5 above. Also see my article, 'A Cadre of Gentile God-Fearers at Qumran', *The Dead Sea Scrolls and the First Christians*, Rockport, 1996, pp. 313–31.

16. CD 1.20–21; cf. 2.15–15, 8.24–30, etc., Paul on 'the Perfection of Holiness (2 Cor. 7:1), and Matt. 5:48's Sermon on the Mount. This 'Perfection' ideology is really only a variation of the 'Primal Adam' one, *Adam having been born Perfect* (i.e., 'circumcised') according to Rabbinic lore.

17. 1QpHab 11.4–5. Cf. *b. San.* 72b–74a and 82a referring to Phineas' 'pursuit' of Zimri. The earliest example of 'pursuit' or 'pursuing' used

to refer to pursuing a legal proceeding I have been able to find, in fact, comes in the Greek in Plato's *Ethyphro* (3e–4a), which actually alludes to the 'pursuer' (*diōkō*) in such a context four times. See, too, even the modern evocation of this ideology, however tragically, in the recent assassination of the Israeli Prime Minister; *New York Times*, 12 November 1995, p. 6.

If this is a 'pursuer' ('*rodeph*') passage – which it and the parallel one in the Damascus Document (CD 1.21, also evoking '*pursuing them*' with the sword') – then what we have here is a blanket instigation to the 'Zealot' or '*Sicarii*' supporters or followers of the Righteous Teacher (or James, as the case may be) to kill the Wicked Priest because he was 'pursuing' the Righteous Teacher with the intent to put him to death.

18. *DSSU*, pp. 233–41 – 4Q436 2.1.

19. Cf. CD 2.12–13 above. The same puzzling reference to 'the Prophet and the Messiah(s) of Aaron and Israel' in 1QS 9.11, where once again the verb usage accompanying this compound subject is singular, should probably be considered idiomatic. For unequivocal references to a singular Messiah, see the Messiah of Heaven and Earth (4Q521) in *DSSU*, pp. 19–23, and CD 8.24, 12.23–13.1, and 14.19 (all, importantly, accompanied by allusion to the usage '*standing*').

20. Note, *per contra*, that at Qumran 'despising' or 'rejecting the *Torah*' is always the manner in which the Liar is referred to; cf. 1QpHab. 5.11–12, CD 3.17, 7.9, 8.19–31, 1QS 2.25–3.6, etc.

21. Cf. CD 1.20–21 with 1.17–18, 3.9–11, 7.81, and 8.49. Again, these allusions to 'cutting off' are very important *vis-à-vis* Paul's allusion to 'cutting off' the circumciser's sexual parts in Gal. 5:12, which will also bear on the characterization of 'Queen Kandakes' Treasury Agent' as a 'eunuch' in Acts 8:27 below.

22. 6.20 – this followed by the promise 'to live for a thousand generations' of Deut. 7:9 and 4QpPs 37 in 7.3–6 below.

23. The usage, found in CD 6.15, 7.3, and 8.8, is exactly the same as that in Acts 15:20, 29, and 21:25.

24. Cf. 6.17–18 with Acts 10.14–15, 10:28, and 11:9.

25. 7.6–7 and 8.43–5. Cf. 4QpPs 37 4.1–2.

26. Cf. 1QH 9.29–36 above.

27. CD 5.11–7.12; in 1QpHab 12.5–10, this is also '*Ebionim*'.

28. 8.18–36; cf. 1QS 8.19–24.

29. 8.31–6 and 42–5.

30. Matt. 12:46, Luke 24:36, John 20:14, 19, 26, 21:4, and Acts 1:10. For 'Standing One' and 'Great Power' language among the Sabaeans, see E. S. Drower, *The Secret Adam: A Study*

of *Nasoraean Gnosis*, Oxford, 1960, pp. IX–XVII, 21–33. and 88–98. 'Great Power', of course, in Aramaic relates to '*Elchasai*'.

31. 'The rest *with them*' now being *with* 'Mary Magdalene, Joanna, and Mary the mother of James' not the Apostles or 'the Eleven' of Luke 24:9.

32. *EH* 2.23.17–18, *Vir. ill.* 2, and *Haeres.* 78.15.5–6

33. Cf., for instance, John 20:12, where Mary Magdalene sees 'two Angels in white' sitting '*at the feet where the body of Jesus was laid*' (*thus*) or Matt. 28:9, when Mary Magdalene, now with 'the other Mary', run from the tomb 'to tell his Disciples' what 'the Angel of the Lord' had said, meet Jesus along the way and, '*taking hold of his feet*', worshipped him' – not to mention, Jesus '*standing among*' the Eleven and showing them his 'hands' and 'his 'feet' in Luke 24:40.

34. *War* 7.217–18.

35. Paul uses the exact words in Acts 9:17; Ananias, in 9:27. Again Paul says he 'saw the Lord in the Way' in Acts 26:13 and Acts says something the same about Philip in 8:36 and 39. In 22:4, it pictures Paul as admitting that he 'persecuted this Way unto death', calling it, as we saw, 'a sect' or 'heresy' in 24:14, opining Felix had 'a more accurate knowledge of the things concerning the Way' in 24:22.

36. 2.8 and 3.10–13.

37. For 'stubbornness of heart', see CD 2.17–3.5, 8.6–19, 30–36, 1QS 1.6, 2.14–26, and 9.9–11. For 'reject', see 1QpHab. 5.11–12, CD 3.10–17, 8.18–35, and 1QS 2.25–3.6 above.

38. Cf. 1QpHab 2.8–10 and 7.4–5 with *EH* 2.23.7.

39. 1 Apoc. Jas. 31.5–32.17 (now instead of Judas Iscariot kissing him) and 2 Apoc. Jas. 56.15. N.b. how in Matt. 28:2, the Angel sits upon a stone (in Mark 16:5, 'a young man sitting in the right side') or in Matt. 26:64, Mark 14:62, and James in *EH* 2.23.13, Jesus is 'sitting on the right hand of the Great Power'. In the Nag Hammadi Gospel of Philip, continuing these overlaps and confusions, he loves Mary Magdalene and 'kissed her often on the mouth' (59.5–10 and 63.35)!

The note about him (James or Jesus) being 'naked' in the context of judicial proceedings in 2 Apoc. 58.20 (46.15 is slightly different) also seemingly harks back to Rabbinic dictums about malefactors being stoned naked (*San.* 44b–45a). If this is true, then we have here the remnants of a very authentic account indeed, more authentic than its transmutation into 'the witnesses leaving *their* clothes' at *Saul's* 'feet' in the garbled version of the stoning of Stephen in Acts 7:58.

40. *B. B.B.* 60b. In fact, so seriously did the Rabbis regard Naziritism, that, not only did they discourage it (*Naz.* 19a and *Ned.* 77b),

but even considered Nazirites 'Sinners' (*Ta'an.*
11a and *Ned.* 10a). Still, a thousand years
later, as we have already seen, Benjamin of
Tudela reports that he has encountered cave-
dwelling, Jewish 'Rechabites' in the Arabian
Desert, who are taking precisely such oaths
'not to eat meat or drink wine' their whole
lives out of 'mourning for Jerusalem and
mourning for Zion'.

41. 1QpHab 12.2–3 – this, of course, clearly
incorporating the language of Isa. 3:9–11,
which *EH* 2.23.15–16 specifically applies to
the death of James. Cf. how in 4Q436 (Hymns
to the Poor) 1.4–6, the 'foreskin of the hearts'
of the Poor is also specifically said to be
'circumcised' and the same 'Wrath' and 'hot
Anger' language of the Habakkuk *Pesher* is
now reversed and directed against the enemies
of 'the Poor'.

42. 1QpHab 10.12–13.

Chapter 22

1. Cf. Sermon 191 with Koran 3.45, 4.157, and
19.19–23

2. CD 2.17–3.12, 7.4–8 (including the promise
to 'live for a thousand generations'), 8.19,
8.29–30, 8.34–8, 8.52, etc. There are many
more of similar genre in the Community Rule.

3. CD 8.20–31. For *San.* 100a (directly following allusion to 'the family of Benjamin' as
unclean and evocation of the *Shiloh* Prophecy
(Gen. 49:10) and Hab. 2:3 on 'the Delay of
the *Parousia*'), Gehazi was to be punished
because 'he called his master by Name'.

4. CD 2.6–3.12.

5. 1QM 6.6, 10.8–11.17, and 13.9–14.18 (again
including reference to 'the Poor').

6. *Adv. Marcion* 4.19 and *de Verig. vel.* 6; also
see *de Monog.* 8 on Jesus as Mary's first-born
son – but see how he attacks '*Ebion*''s idea
that Jesus too was born by natural generation
by evoking Paul's 'Primal Adam' and 'Second
Adam' ideas (*de Carne* 16–18; cf. Paul in
1 Cor. 15:45–7).

7. *Comm. in Matt.* 10.17; cf. too *Hom. in Luc.* 7.

8. *Ad Eph.* 18–19 (alluding to both Mary and
Jesus 'being Hidden' – as Protevang. 22.3–23.1/
Luke 1:24 – and the 'Power') and *Ad Trall.* 9.1.

9. *Dial.* 100; see also Irenaeus, *Ad. Haer.* 3.22.4,
4.33.1, 5.19.1 and Tertullian, *de Carne* 17
above.

10. Cf. Irenaeus, *Ad. Haer.* 3.16.7 and Tertullian,
de Carne 17 above.

11. CD 8.56–7/20.33–4, also including the idea
of 'their rejoicing', 'God making atonement'
either 'for' or 'through them', and 'their
heart(s) being Strengthened' – recalling Paul
on 'death, where is your sting' (1 Cor.
15:54–5).

12. *Haeres.* 29.4.1–7.1, 66.19.7–8, 78.8.2–9.6,
14.3, and 18.1–24.4.

13. *Vir. ill.* 2 and *Adv. Hel.* 12–21.

14. Cf. in H. J. Leon, 'The Names of the Jews of
Ancient Rome', *Transactions of the American
Philological Association*, 1928, p. 208, with
how the stonecutters frequently confused
alpha and *lambda* in inscriptions.

15. *Opus imperf. c. Iul.* 4.122; cf. *Enarr. in Ps.*
34:3.

16. *EH* 3.11.1.

17. *Haeres.* 78.14.6; cf. 66.19.7–8. This tradition
about Jesus being 'the son of Panthera' is
related to the 'Ben Stada' one (*b. San.* 67a and
Shab. 104b (uncensored versions). In these,
'*Stada*' is the mother; '*Panthera*' (more confusions with the male/female 'Standing One' traditions in Hippolytus 9.8, etc.) is the father.
But he is also called 'Pappos ben Judah', again
clearly intended to be identical with
'Cleophas' or 'Clopas'! The reader should
appreciate that one of the reasons for the
seeming lunacy of these Talmudic traditions
was the intended evasiveness – so effective
that sometimes they *even evaded their heirs*.
But in *Haeres.* 78.7.5, Epiphanius confirms
this identification of 'Panthera' with either
'Joseph' or 'Clopas' or both. He specifies in
no uncertain terms that *the father of Joseph*
and/or *Clopas* was called 'Jacob surnamed
Panthera', thereby not only verifying the basic
gist of this Talmudic tradition, but clarifying
it – in the process, verifying the identification
of 'Cleopas'/'Clopas' with 'Pappos ben
Judah'. 'Panthera' also possibly represents a
garbling of the Priestly clan of 'Kanthera' –
related to the Boethusians (whose tomb too
later becomes identified as that of 'St James') –
referred to in both Josephus and the *Talmud*
(cf. *Pes.* 57a and *MZCQ*, pp. 61–2).

18. *EH* 3.12 (cf. 3.20.1–4).

19. Cf. *EH* 2.6.8, 3.5.1–4, 3.5.6, etc.

20. *EH* 3.17

21. *EH* 3.19.1–20.7.

22. *EH* 3.32.1–6.

23. *EH* 3.32.3–6; cf. *Haeres.* 66.19.8 and 78.7.5.

24. See Plate no. 29. That Balaam is pointing to
the star may have further symbolism regarding the 'Bela''/'Belial'/'Balaam' language circle
not completely inapplicable to Paul; also see
b. Sota 36b, explaining in typically esoteric
fashion that 'Benjamin''s son was called
'Bela'', because 'he (Joseph) *was swallowed
up* (*nibla'*) among the Peoples'.

25. Cf. *EH* 3.35 with *Haeres.* 66.20.1.

26. 3.32.7–8. Here one should, once more, note
Origen's testimony, *Contra Celsus* 2.62,
straightforwardly designated the unnamed
other with 'Cleopas' to be 'Simon'; cf. *Haeres.*
78.8.1 above, identifying Jesus' third brother
as 'Simeon'.

27. Cf. *EH* 3.33 with Pliny the Younger, Letters
96–7. The year in question would appear to
be 110-11 CE.

28. The recent find of some forty-five burned manuscripts from the mid-500s from Petra may alter this situation.
29. Cf. *EH* 4.2.1–4 and Dio Cassius, 68.32.1–3.
30. *EH* 3.36.1–15; cf. Ignatius, *Ad Rom.* 5–6, Irenaeus, *Ad. Haer.* 5.28.4, etc.
31. Cf. *A.Z.* 17a and 27b with *EH* 3.39.6–13. Eusebius accuses him of 'misrepresenting Apostolic accounts' and 'not appreciating their mystic and allegorical nature'.
32. The promise is to those 'walking in Perfect Holiness' and 'keeping the Commandments' – CD 7.4–6. The same promise is made in CD 8.41–5, which adds 'God-Fearers' to this (i.e., 'the *Nilvim*' or attached Gentiles), and 4QpPs 37 4.2–4 in interpretation of Ps. 37:29's 'the Righteous Ones [*Zaddikim*] will inherit the earth'.
33. Suetonius 5.25. Curiously, as remarked, this seems to be confused with an earlier expulsion under Tiberius (18–19 CE), mentioned in Tacitus, *Annals* 2.85, which both Suetonius 3.36 and Dio Cassius 57.18.5 allude to.
34. Though probably confusing *two* Aquilas (the *Targum* being probably the work of a second one in the second century), one set of Talmudic allusions (*B.B.* 99a, *A.Z.* 10b, and *Git.* 56b) does call him 'a convert, the son of Kalonymos'/'Kolonikos, the son of Titus' sister', i.e., our Pseudoclementine 'Clement' (or 'Clemens') again; cf. too Paul's greetings in Rom. 16:6 and 1 Cor. 16:19. One should note, too, as we have above, that the real name of Clement of Alexandria was 'Titus Flavius Clemens', which would probably make him a distant kinsman of 'Clement of Rome' as well.
35. *War* 2.240–43, 54–60, and *Ant.* 20.162–5.
36. *Ant.* 20.166–7.
37. Tacitus, *Annals* 15.39–44, Suet. 6.38, and Dio Cassius 62.16–18.
38. *Ant.* 20.257.
39. *EH* 3.18.4. For Suet. 12.15 and Dio Cassius 67.14, as we saw, she is the wife (and cousin) of Flavius Clemens.
40. 12.2.
41. *Ant.* 1.8–9.
42. *Ant.* 18.140; also see Tacitus, *Annals* 14.26.
43. See Augustine, *City of God* 6.11 above and cf. Tertullian, *De Anima* 20 and 42, who calls him 'on our side'.
44. See E. G. Turner, 'Tiberius Iulias Alexander', *Journal of Roman Studies*, XIV, 1954, p. 55, who also notes that so important was Tiberius Alexander to the Flavian family, that aside from being Titus' military commander at the siege of Jerusalem; Tiberius Alexander also followed him to Rome, there to become Prefect of the Praetorian Guard! There, too, Tiberius Alexander appears to have been lampooned by Juvenal, *Satires* 1.131, who calls him the 'Egyptian Arabarch' (*thus*) and

recommends 'pissing against his triumphal statue like a dog against a lamp-post'. For his part, the second-century, Alexandrian Roman historian, Appianus, may even be a descendant of this 'Apion'.
45. *Apion* 2.8.
46. 3.5.3–7.9; n.b. the ghoulish use of Josephus' description of how they even ate their own children; 3.6.23–7.2.
47. *EH* 3.7.8–9. For 'Visitation' language at Qumran, see CD 1.7, 5.16, 7.9, 7.21, 13.24 and the new 4Q523 1.5 ('The Messiah of Heaven and Earth', *DSSU*, pp. 19–23).
48. 1QpHab 6.10–11.
49. 1QS 9.23. Also see 2.5–8, 4.11–13, 5.12–13, 10.20, 1QM 3.6–8 (on the battle standards), and 1QpHab 9.2.
50. *EH* 3.5.3.
51. Cf. 4.22.4 with 3.32.1–4 – date unclear, but elsewhere Eusebius implies it is 106–7 CE.
52. Cf. 1QpHab 11.2–15 on Hab. 2:15–16.
53. CD 8.9–13. Cf. the wordplay between 'privy parts'/'festivals'/'foreskin' and 'stagger' in 1QpHab 11.2–13; also 'foreskin' ('*arel*') and 'poison' (*ra'al*).
54. *EH* 3.31.2–3 and 5.24.3, quoting a letter from Polycrates (*c.* 190 CE).
55. *EH* 3.32.7 above.
56. These passages from Ps. *Hom.* 7.3–8 (also mentioning 'Appion' as a companion of Simon *Magus*), not only make it crystal clear that James' 'strangled things' in Acts 15:18–30 and 21:25 is 'carrion', both here and in the Koran; but that Paul's rhetorical gamesmanship ('Spouting' at Qumran) over 'eating in an idol temple'/'the table of demons' and James' 'things sacrificed to idols' in 1 Cor. 8:7–13 and 10:19–23 are just that – dissimulation. What is more, Paul knows the true position of the early Church on these things – here being enunciated quite unequivocally by Peter in the Pseudoclementine *Homilies*.
57. N.b. in 4:9 the ever-present allusion to 'falling down' – now *before the Devil to worship him*.
58. Cf. the 'Thunder' text (4Q318), edited in *DSSU*, pp. 258–63.
59. Dio Cassius 68.32; Eusebius 4.2.4–5 calls him 'Lucuas', so this 'Andrew'/'Andreas' does, in fact, seem to be a title.
60. In Luke 3:2 and Acts 4:6, he also persecutes the early Christian Community.
61. *War* 4.242–3. Cf. the reverse of this in 1QpHab 5.12–6.8's the Romans ('the *Kittim*') 'eating all Peoples' and 'devouring' their taxes 'year by year'.
62. *War* 4.314–25. In 4.342–4, as we saw, so is Zachariah's body. Here, it should be recalled that 'Stephen' means 'Crown', i.e., James' 'Crown' of Nazirite hair. For the rest of Josephus' encomium to Jesus ben Gamela, see 4.238–70. It is *he* who warns Josephus' father

of the plot recommended by Gamaliel's son Simon and Ananus to kill Josephus when he was Governor of Galilee (*Vita* 193–204).

63. Cf. Mark 5:21–43 with the shard bearing the name 'Ben Ya'ir' – i.e., 'Eleazar (Lazarus) ben Ya'ir' (Jairus), the '*Sicarii*' Commander (*War* 2.447 and 7.262–398 – Y. Yadin, *Masada*, London, 1966, p. 201). Both episodes, in fact, involve resurrection scenarios. Mark 5:25–34's is interrupted by the woman 'with a flow of blood' ('for twelve years'!) 'touching [Jesus'] clothes' – specifically forbidden at Qumran (CD 5.7). Note, here, the Central Three, 'Peter, James, and John *the brother of James*', are pictured as alone permitted to accompany Jesus in this magical adventure. Also, Jerome's more credible testimony in *Comm. on Gal.* 1:19 on how the people of Jerusalem used to touch the fringes of James' clothes as he passed, because he 'was so Holy'.

64. Epist. Apost. 2.

Chapter 23

1. Also see Luke 17:26 alluding to the 'coming of the Son of Man'.
2. 1QM 12.3.
3. *Vita* 86. However in 207, 233, and 384, he calls his headquarters, 'Asochis', which may be 'Sihnin' in the *Talmud* or Kfar Sechania above. Some would put 'Cana' on *the Plain of Asochis*.
4. B. Ta'an. 23a/j. Ta'an. 66b.
5. B. Sota 11b; cf. Ta'an. 23a for the rockiness of the locale in which Honi was 'hidden'.
6. B. Shab. 33b.
7. 1QS 2.15; in 4.10 among these latter, 'zeal for lustfulness'.
8. 1QS 9.20–23 (note the parallel to Luke 21:22's 'Days of Vengeance' above). This is a direct quote from Isa. 63:4, where it comes amid the 'Cup' imagery of 'making the Peoples drunk with My Fury'.
9. Rom. 10:2, the passage Jerome quotes to ridicule Origen's 'castrating himself with a knife'; 1 Cor. 14:12, here spiritualized; 2 Cor. 9:2, provoking the 'Many'; Gal. 4:17–18, repeated twice and directed against the circumcisers in the Church and evoking the 'Enemy' terminology; Phil. 3:6, his previous 'zeal in persecuting the Church'; Col. 4:13, Epaphr(oditus)'s 'zeal'; and Titus 2:14, 'zeal for good works'.
10. As we have seen this language of 'stumbling', 'scandal', and 'offence' throughout Paul, its meaning should by now be clear.
11. 1QpHab 12.2–3/EH 2.23.14–15.
12. Cf. 1QS 9.22–3 and CD 2.11 and 4.4. Here Paul concludes, as we saw, 'everyone who *calls on the Name of the Lord* shall be saved' (Rom. 10:13).
13. 9.16–28.

14. *War* 1.648–55/*Ant*. 17.149–57.
15. Cf. *War* 2.454 with *Contra Celsus* 2.13.
16. Cf. 9.21 with *War* 2.18 and *Ant*. 18.23.
17. *Ant*. 18.23–4.
18. Matt. 22:25–33 and pars.
19. Y. Yadin, *Masada*, pp. 184–9.
20. 1QS 2.5–17, 4.9–19, 8.21–9.2, etc.
21. Cf. Hipp. 9.21 with Ps. *Hom*. 7.3–4 and 8 above.
22. Cf. *War* 2.143–4 with 1QS 5.7–20, 7.17–25, etc.
23. Cf. Hipp. 5.2 and 10.5 with 2 Apoc. Jas. 44.15–20.
24. E. S. Drower, *The Secret Adam*, pp. XVI and 92–9.
25. Hipp. 7.21/10.17; also Irenaeus, 1.26. For *Haeres*. 28.1.2–5.3, 30.14.2, 30.26.1–2, 51.2.3, 3.6, 4.2, 10.4, etc. Cerinthus was a contemporary of Peter and *a colleague of Ebion*, who stressed circumcision and taught Christ was a mere man who appeared among the followers of John the Baptist. To Epiphanius, this seems most peculiar. Since he was also 'the seal of the Prophets', the succession into Islam is direct.
26. *EH* 3.27.
27. Cf. 7.21/10.17 above, Apoc. Pet. 81.4–24, 2 Seth 56.6–19, and Acts of John 88–101 (here, John 1:43–5's 'Philip and Nathanael' become John and 'James *my brother*' and the naked Jesus is the Standing One, with 'feet whiter than snow' and 'head touching Heaven') with Koran 3.56, 4.158–60, and 5.111 (n.b. for Koran 3.59 Jesus is also 'Adam' or the Primal Adam).
28. 10.25; cf. *Haeres*. 30.3.3–5 on the Ebionite/Sabaean/Ossaean/Elchasaite 'Adam'.
29. 9.8; cf. Luke 3:16 on John and Jesus' 'shoes'. In this context, too, one should also note '*Bar Daroma*' in Git. 57a, who, as we shall see later, '*could jump a mile*', and before whom even the (Roman) Emperor humbles himself – but who, when he sees a snake 'in the privy', is so frightened that 'he drops his bowels and (supposedly) dies'.
30. 30.3.1.
31. For parallels to 'Bartholomew', see *Ant*. 20.5 on the Jewish 'Arch-Bandit' leader 'Tholomaeus' in Perea.
32. He too was killed; cf. *Suk*. 52a–b above.
33. Cf. *EH* 3.39.9 with b. A.Z. 27b.
34. *EH* 2.15.1–2 and 3.39.15–16.
35. 3.39.16, which *Haeres*. 30.3.7 says Cerinthus and '*Ebion*' also used, calling it 'Matthew'.
36. Cf. *EH* 3.39.12 with CD 7.4–6, 8.40–45 and 4Qp Ps 37 3.1–2 above, evoking too 'the inheritance of Adam'.
37. ANCL Papias Frag. 10, already noted earlier.
38. 4.29.1–7; cf. Irenaeus 1.28 and 3.23. These are also the doctrines, it should be appreciated, Ps. *Hom*. attributes to *Peter*, as we saw.
39. 4.5.3 and Ps. *Rec*. 1.72–2.1. Also note the

Lukan recasting of this in Jesus' last journey to Jerusalem through Jericho (19:1–10) and the possible link of this to the Rabbinic hero, Johanan b. Zacchai above. Cf. too *Haeres.* 66.20.1.

Chapter 24

1. 1QH 5.23.
2. 1QpHab 7.17–8.3 and 11.4–12.10; cf. CD 6.11, 8.37, 1QS 9.14, etc.
3. 1QM 11.9–14; n.b. again the language of Isa. 3:9–11 here and cf. *Zohar* 4.195a above.
4. 1QpHab 7.11–8.1, 12.4–5, CD 1.1–10, 3.6–16, 8.29–44, etc.
5. *EH* 3.27.1–2.
6. Cf. 7.2–8.2 with 10.3–5 and 12.14–13.4.
7. See ANCL, note to Apost. Const. 8.25.
8. Apost. Const. 8.35.
9. Cf. Acts of Thaddaeus with same notice.
10. Acts of Thomas 1–11, but particularly, 139–70. Also see *EH* 1.13.11, Eusebius' own translation of the Abgar Legend, the Syriac Doctrine of the Apostles, and the Nag Hammadi Book of Thomas the Contender 138.2 and 142.7–8.
11. Acts of Thomas 11 and 39.
12. *EH* 1.13.5 and 22.
13. Cf. Acts of Thomas 16–170.
14. *Ant.* 1.145, 20.22, 20.34, and M. Grant, *From Alexander to Cleopatra*, New York, 1982, pp. 50–60.
15. Cf. *EH* 1.13.14–15 with Acts of Thaddaeus and Moses of Chorene 2.32.
16. Cf. Koran 29:39, 69:5–7, etc.
17. *EH* 1.13.11. Actually Eusebius only calls him 'Thomas'; it is the document he translates which refers to him as 'Judas, also called Thomas', thus reinforcing the impression of its greater reliability.
18. *EH* 1.12.1–3 and Apost. Const. 2.55. Here Eusebius is convinced his 'Apostle Peter' is different from Clement's 'Cephas'.
19. *EH* 1.9.2–4.
20. CD 1.9–11.
21. ANCL Appendix to Hippolytus: 'Hippolytus on the Twelve Apostles', also found in the two codices of the Coislinian or Seguierian Library.
22. Ibid.
23. ANCL: Codex Baroccian. 206.
24. The spelling here is the same as Dio Cassius 68.18–21.
25. *Ant.* 20.34–48; cf. *EH* 1.13.9.
26. 2.29. Some consider Moses is a ninth-century pseudograph – nevertheless the data often rings true.
27. *Ant.* 20.39–40; for 'only-begotten', 20.20.
28. Syriac manuscripts from the Nitrian Monastery in Lower Egypt in ANCL. This is the passage in *EH* 1.13.4, but 1.13.11 rather has Thaddaeus as an 'Apostle', which may be the source of these confusions. The Doctrine

of Addai too has him as an 'Apostle'. One should also recall the ANCL Papias Fragment 10, which has 'Thaddaeus' as the son of Mary and Cleophas/Alphaeus and the brother of 'James *the Bishop and Apostle*, Simon . . . and one Joseph' (thus). All mss., including the Koran, imply that his name – like Thomas – was 'Judas'.

29. *EH* 2.1.6.
30. *EH* 2.8–9. He first mentions this in 2.3.4 together with Acts' 'prophet Agabus'.
31. *Ant.* 20.101–2; cf. *EH* 2.11.1–12.1.
32. *Ant.* 20.100.
33. 1QpHab 7.1–14, interpreting 'reading and running' from Hab. 2:2 and Hab. 2:3, 'wait for it' (or 'him').
34. 1QS 8.16–9.21, CD 6.14–7.4, 8.25–36, etc.
35. *Vita* 407–9.
36. *EH* 2.11–12.1 (*Ant.* 20.101–2 above).
37. Cf. Acts of Thaddaeus, ANCL Syriac Eusebius, Moses of Chorene 2.32, and Acts of Addai.
38. *Ant.* 20.51–2. Cf. *b. Yoma* 37a and *Naz.* 19b–20a.
39. *Ant.* 20.25–6.
40. 9.8 and 10.26.
41. See Benjamin of Tudela, *Travels*, years 1163–65 CE.

Chapter 25

1. Koran 7.65–84, 11.50–89 (including the birth of *Isaac*), 26.124–55, 41.13–28, etc. In 9.70, 14.9, and 22.42 he links them to 'the Folk of Noah' and 'the People of Abraham'.
2. *Targum Onkelos* Gen. 8:4. *B.B.* 91a acknowledges it as Abraham's homeland, while *Yeb.* 16a agonizes over converts from there.
3. *Ant.* 20.24–6. Note *Ant.* 1.92–5, where Josephus, while acknowledging it to be in Armenia, also identifies it as 'the Mountain of the Kurds' and cites Nicolaus of Damascus calling it 'Baris'; cf. the variant reading in Dio Cassius 68.21, 'Al-Barus' for 'Augarus'/ 'Abgarus'. But Josephus' confusion over which of Helen's sons became king is patent. Moses of Chorene 2.35 below, considers her 'the first of Abgar's wives', who 'was sent to live in Charan [Haran] and given sovereignty over that part of Mesopotamia' by Abgar's 'sister's son'. Here Josephus (*Ant.* 20.18) concurs, calling Helen 'Bazeus' sister' (cf. Sarah as Abraham's sister – Gen. 12:13–19 and 20:2–12).
4. *War* 2.520; also 2.566 and 3.11–28.
5. *Ant.* 17.23–31.
6. *War* 4.14.
7. Cf. Ps. Philo 25.9–28.10 celebrating 'Kenaz' as a quasi-Messiah.
8. *War* 3.26–8.
9. *War* 4.359–64.
10. *War* 6.355–7. Josephus also mentions these

palaces in 4.567 and 5.253, the former in the context of reference to one 'Grapte a kinsman of King Izas of Adiabene', in whose palace 'the Zealots' took refuge.

11. 4QpPs 37 2.18–25 and 4.7–12; cf. 1QpHab 9.1–2.

12. *EH* 2.12.3, and *Ant.* 20.95–6 (where Josephus promises to tell us more about 'King Monobazus'' subsequent reign, but never does). In *War* 5.147, he also mentions these (together with something he calls '*the Fuller's Tomb*' along a rampart terminating in the Kedron Valley tombs), though here he seems to think Helen is 'the daughter of King Izat'. See also Moses of Chorene 2.35 below.

13. *EH* 2.12.3 and 4.6.4.

14. *Ant.* 20.17–23 and 34–7.

15. Cf. Segal, *Edessa the Blessed City*, p. 67.

16. Ibid., pp. 12 and 68–71, who calls her 'Shalmath' and dates Abgar Ukkama to 4 BC–50, also approximately 'Izates'' or 'Ezad''s dates. For ANCL, 'Abgar' dies in 45 CE.

17. *Annals* 6.44 and 12.12.

18. *Geography* 16.1.28. For Juvenal, it will be recalled, Tiberius Alexander is an 'Arabarch'.

19. 2.29–35.

20. Cf. Moses 2.29 with *Ant.* 17.12–18.

21. Cf. *Ant.* 15.252–66 with 20.214, *War* 2.418, and 2.556.

22. *H.N.* 6.31.136–9.

23. In Islam, this is taken to be the sacrifice of Ishmael, although Ishmael is never mentioned by name here, whereas Isaac is and called 'a Prophet of the Righteous' (37.113; cf. 100–101, 'of the Righteous', to designate Abraham's son). Also see 11.171–3 above on the birth of Isaac.

24. *Ant.* 20.34.

25. Cf. *Ant.* 20.36–7 with *War* 6.356.

26. *EH* 4.22.4.

27. Eleazar, it will be recalled, was the father of Phineas – the ancestor alike of Zadok and Elijah (Num. 25:7–11, 1 Chr. 6:3–4, etc.). Curiously, the *Talmud* (*Yeb.* 46a) records a controversy between R. Eliezer and R. Joshua, in which the former considers circumcision as the *sine qua non* for conversion; the latter, only baptism.

28. Where Josephus certainly knew them both; *War* 5.460–65 and 7.238–43. Antiochus the younger's assault on the walls of Jerusalem was repulsed by even more zealous Jews. Their capital Samosata near Edessa is on a triangle with Antioch and Tarsus.

29. *Ant.* 20.137–41. In 20.158, Sohemus becomes King of Emesa; and Aristobulus, Herod of Chalcis' son, Armenia. Emesa is on the way from Damascus to Edessa; and Chalcis, halfway between Damascus and Beirut. All of these people were simply provincial appointees (or 'Kings of the Peoples'), serving at the leave of Rome.

30. *Ant.* 20.145–6.

31. *B. Yoma* 37a and *Tosefta Pe'ah* 4:18.

32. *B. Git.* 60a and *Yoma* 37a.

33. Interestingly, a latterday Messiah of the Jews, Shabbatai Zevi, had a similar escapade with a supposed prostitute in the seventeenth century, but further we are unable to penetrate.

34. *Naz.* 19a–20b.; cf. Moses of Chorene 2.35 above.

35. *Ant.* 20:41 and 47.

36. *B.B.* 60b above. In *Ned.* 10a, as we saw, the Rabbis even designate such Nazirites abstaining from wine and all such 'ascetics', 'Sinners'.

37. *War* 4.567 (where Josephus calls him 'Izas'), 5.253, and 6.355 above.

38. 4QMMT 2.33 (*DSSU*, pp. 196–200).

39. Cf. *Gen. R.* 46.10 with *Ant.* 20.43–8.

40. *DSSU*, pp. 182–96.

41. Cf 2 Macc. 6:19–31, 12:44–5, and *War* 1.648–53.

42. *Ant.* 20.39–40.

43. *Ant.* 20.47; n.b. the reversal of 'Zealot' language here.

44. *B. Shab.* 68b.

45. *B. Ket.* 62b–63a.

46. See Plates nos. 27 and 28. Originally, the Kedron Valley tombs were mistaken for these monuments, but at least one of these seems to be of the family of Ananus; the other, Boethus, which for some reason was attributed by pilgrims to James.

47. *Ant.* 19.276–7 and 20.147. For Alexander the Alabarch (Philo's brother), see 18.159–60. E. G. Turner, in his article on 'Tiberius Iulius Alexander', p. 59, actually cites five receipts, dated between 37 and 43 CE, from the Red Sea trade in the name of 'Marcus Iulius Alexander'; and the firm of 'Nicanor' (whose fabulous gift of 'Golden Gates' to the Temple the *Talmud* never leaves off praising), many more. Where 'Tiberius Iulius Alexander' is concerned, Turner (pp. 55–7) also depicts him as an intimate participant in his uncle Philo's philosophical debates both as a respondent and subject in several dialogues.

48. E. G. Turner, pp. 58–61.

49. Josephus actually uses this word in *Ant.* 20.188 about an unnamed Deceiver or 'impostor', destroyed by Festus just preceding the Temple Wall Affair.

50. Acts 13:1. In this regard, too, one should not forget Clement of Alexandria 7.17's testimony that Paul was the student or teacher of 'Theudas'. Since he also says Valentinius was the latter's student, this would make 'Theudas' – if our 'Theudas' – equivalent to 'Ebion' or something of an 'Ebionite'.

51. ANCL: 'The Teaching of Simon *Cephas* in Rome', attached to 'The Doctrine of Addai' and 'The Teaching of the Apostles'.

52. Cf. ANCL: Hippolytus on the Twelve Apostles and Codex Baroccian. 206. Also

found in two codices of the Coislinian or Seguierian Library. In Acts 15:22–30, of course, it is 'Judas Barsabas' who conveys James' Letter to 'Antioch'. It will be but a short step from here to identify this letter as '*MMT*' – the only 'letter' found at Qumran – this in *multiple copies* and, therefore, its seeming importance.

53. J. B. Segal, *Edessa The Beloved City*, p. 15; cf. Josephus' designation of Helen's son as 'Izas' (*War* 4.567).

54. The same is the case for Muhammad's requirement of four witnesses for adultery in the Koran, which though at face value, seemingly harsh, was actually quite lenient, because four witnesses to adultery is almost an impossibility as Muhammad himself, quite clearly, demonstrates in the case when his favourite wife 'Ayesha was so accused (Koran 4.15 and 24:11–20).

55. *Ant.* 16.299–372, 17.219–316, etc.; for Nicanor, see *b. Yoma* 37a–b, etc.

56. *War* 2.520 above.

57. In the Koran, the spellings are different, 'Saba" meaning Sheba (27.22 and 34.15, including the title of the Surah) being spelled – as in the Bible – with an *alif* and 'Saba'' meaning 'Sabaean' (in Aramaic 'Masbuthaean' or 'Daily Bather' – 2.62, 5.69, 2217) being spelled – as in the Syriac – with an *ayin*.

58. *Ant.* 20.43–6. Also see *Gen. R.* 46.10, which actually knows the passage Izates was reading was Gen. 17:7–14, 'circumcise yourselves', and quotes it. This passage includes allusion to 'the uncircumcised' being 'cut off', parodied (as we have seen) by Paul in Gal. 5:12, and being called 'Covenant-Breakers' (Gen. 17:14), the actual vocabulary being used in 1QpHab 2.6, 8.17, and CD 1.20.

59. *War* 2.421, 2.556, 4.81, and *Vita* 407. Also note Phil. 2.25 and 2 Tim. 2:3–5 applying such military language to Apostles, etc.

60. *Ant.* 20.53.

61. *B.B.* 11a, quoting Isa. 3:10!

Chapter 26

1. Who in Ps. *Rec.* 1.60 is 'also called Matthias, who was substituted as an Apostle in the place of Judas [*Iscariot*]' in Acts; and elsewhere, as 'Joses surnamed Barnabas, a Levite of Cypriot origin' (Acts 4:36).

2. *EH* 3.1.2; cf. the ANCL Syriac 'Teaching of Simon *Cephas*' above and Clement, *Ad Cor.* 5. Tertullian in *Haer.* 36, not without a little hyperbole, only confirms the crucifixion part (which can also be said of Simeon bar Cleophas).

3. *EH* 2.25.5, this more credibly than Peter's. Cf. Teaching of Simon *Cephas* and Clement, *Ad Cor.* 5 above. For Tertullian, *Haer.* 36, 'Peter endures a passion like his Lord's' and 'Paul

wins his crown in a death like John's', meaning John the Baptist's!

4. The first seemingly, Grotius, in the seventeenth century (1583–1643). If there was, then he may have been a son, just as Trajan himself was the son of another Trajan, the Commander of Vespasian's Tenth Legion. Either this, or Domitian did not execute Epaphroditus in 96 (after accusing him of 'lifting his hand against an Emperor') or *Contra Apion* – where the disputed references occur and dated by some after 100 CE – must be dated before 95–6.

5. Cf. Mani Fragment M 4575 with Manichaean Psalm Book 194.13.

6. Acts of Thomas 163–70, including the same 'empty tomb'/'resurrection' scenarios as in the Gospels.

7. Acts of Thomas 39, Thomas the Contender 138.10–13, etc.

8. *Ant.* 20.167–72/*War* 2.258–63. Interestingly enough, this is the only one of such 'impostor' episodes which appears *both* in the *War* and *Antiquities*, most others being passed over in silence in the *War*.

9. *War* 2.264–5.

10. *Ant.* 20.97. The word is '*goēs*'; cf. 2 Tim. 3:13 '*goētes*'/'wizards' or 'Deceivers'.

11. Cf. CD 6.15, 7.1, and 8.8.

12. Cf. 4QTest 17 (Deut. 33:9), '*britcha yinzor*'/ 'he kept Your Covenant'.

13. E. S. Drower, *The Secret Adam*, IX, XIV, and *The Mandaeans of Iraq and Iran*, pp. 1–17.

14. CD 6.17–7.3; cf. 4QpPs 37 3.1–2 and 4.2–3, which adds, 'all the inheritance of Adam will be theirs'.

15. *War* 6.354–63.

16. M. *Sheb.* 10:3–7, M. *Git.* 4:3, *b. Arak.* 31b–32a, etc.

17. *B. Yeb.* 46a above.

18. Cf. ARN 6.3 with *Git.* 56a. In the latter, too, the theme of the 'twenty-one years' of Helen's Nazirite oath period is reproduced in the years of grain these three were able to provide because of their 'Riches'. In ARN, the 'twenty-one years' of grain storage are said to be Ben Kalba Sabu'a's alone, the bread 'baked and kneaded' from this supply 'enough to provide every inhabitant of Jerusalem'!

19. *War* 6.355–8. On the other hand, they specifically burned the Herodian palaces (2.427).

20. B. *Ket.* 62b–63a and *Ned.* 50a. The connection to R. Akiba, the spiritual leader of the Second Jewish Revolt (132–6 CE – who designated Bar Kochba, 'Messiah'), called in *Ket.* 62b, '*Ben Kalba Sabu'a*'s shepherd', is pivotal. Both *Git.* 56a and ARN 6.3 interpret '*Sabu'a*' – playing on the Aramaic '*sabbi'a*'/'satiated' (in Syriac related to 'immersion' or 'bathing') and '*kalba*' (masculine 'dog') – 'whoever entered his house hungry as a dog came out absolutely full'. Though humorous, this must be seen as

Rabbinic hyperbole and cannot be considered the real explanation. The dissimulation going on probably has to do with the family's connections to R. Akiba, not to mention its earlier ones to the First Jewish Revolt and – in our view – probable support of the *bathing facility* at Qumran.

In this regard, the association of Ben Kalba Sabu'a's name with 'twenty-one years' of grain-storage and distribution (the period of Queen Helen's alleged Nazirite oaths in *Naz.* 19b–20a) is fundamental; that is, not only was Akiba's wife (for whom he ultimately assembled '24,000 Disciples') the daughter of this revolutionary and probable daily-bathing 'Sabaean' family from Adiabene, but so was Akiba's disciple 'Monabaz' (*Shab.* 68b–69b). The story is a touching one. Not only did the daughter of 'Ben Kalba Sabu'a' choose R. Akiba when he was only one of her father's poor 'shepherds', she encouraged and financed his *24 years of studies* (*Ket.* 63a). Then (like Helen's series of Nazirite oaths), after twice returning to her with '12,000 Disciples', as most representatives of this tradition, he too was finally martyred.

21. *War* 5.24–5. For Nakdimon's wealth, that of his daughter (another of these 'Mary's or 'Miriam's – in *Lam. R.* 1.16.47, confused with 'Boethus' daughter', i.e. probably the Rich High Priest Ananias) – for the Rabbis, 'Nakdimon''s used to 'spend 500 gold dinars daily on perfume'! – and the 'woollen clothes' supposedly spread beneath Nakdimon's feet for him to walk on, which '*the Poor* rolled up' (more dissimulation – explained in terms of 'a camel's burden'); see *Ket.* 65a–67a and *Lam. R.* 1.16.48.

22. Cf. ARN 6.3 and *Ta'an.* 19b–20a with *Haeres.* 78.14.1. Epiphanius who, as we saw, knows Rabbinic tradition, echoes *Ket.* 67a's 'woollen clothes' theme in immediately going on to evoke James' not wearing 'woollen clothes' – not to mention 'his *knees being hard as a camel's*'! In both ARN and *Ta'an.* – now involving a *foreign 'Lord' who goes to 'bath-house*'s or '*bathes*' – the twelve wells of water Nakdimon borrows and the twelve talents of

gold he receives for them before filling twelve more (again like the 'twenty-one years' and the periods of Helen's 'Nazirite' oaths) replace the double penance of 'twelve years' Rabbi Akiba works for Ben Kalba Sabu'a's daughter.

The miracle attributed to Nakdimon (including 'wrapping himself in a cloak') of making the sun shine as well as making it rain is Elijah's in Jas. 5:16–18 and 1 Kings 17–18. As we shall see in Volume 11, *Ta'an.* 20a finally admits that 'Nakdimon''s real name was 'Boni', now, of course, evoking James' putative forerunner 'Honi' and the same genre of stories about him. Even Simeon b. Shetah's words in these traditions about Honi (*Ta'an.* 23a) now become the words as making the foreign 'Lord' speaks to him. Of course, Nakdimon never did make rain, nor wrap his cloak around himself and pray for it, only Honi and his heirs. One could also remark to some benefit the re-emergence of this note in Muhammad's Koran, Surahs 73.1–6 and 74.1–26.

23. *War* 2.451, 628, and *Vita* 197–332, possibly related to earlier merchants named 'Ananias'.

24. *War* 4.335–44. Even the theme of blood shed 'between the Temple and the altar' is lifted directly from Josephus' picture of sectarian strife in the Temple, leading up to the burning of the stores, and the many 'who fell among their own sacrifices, sprinkling their blood upon the altar', which 'pollutions', turncoat that he is, Josephus obsequiously pictures the Romans – the instruments of God's will! – 'purging by fire.' (5.17–20).

25. *Lam. R.* 2.2.4.

26. H. J. Leon, 'The Names of the Jews of Ancient Rome', pp. 207–12.

27. 2 Apoc. Jas. 61.10–20.

28. 1Qp Hab 8.1–2 (on Hab. 2:4) and CD 4.10–11 (on 'the Completion of the Age').

29. 1QpHab 2.2–6, 5.8–12, and CD 8.4–36. Not only are such 'Covenant-Breakers' directly referred to in 1QpHab 2.6 and CD 1.20 (alluding to the Lying Spouter) above, but such 'Covenant-breaking' is the essence of the passage from Gen. 17:14 requiring 'circumcision' Izates is pictured as reading from the *Torah* above.

Index